THE ROUTLEDGE ENCYCLOPEDIA OF TAOISM

CHOICE Outstanding Academic Title 2008

"With a focus on the history and traditions of Taoism, this work effectively challenges romanticized views that reduce the richness of these traditions to the *Daode jing* (*Tao Te Ching*) and the *Zhuangzi* (*Chuang Tzu*). The encyclopedia includes a 196-page overview that could serve as a superb intermediate textbook on Taoism."

G. J. Reece (American University), *Choice*

"The depth of the entries and variety of subjects covered are impressive, creating a must-have reference for anyone interested in Taoism."

Christine Pesch (Yale University), *Theological Librarianship*

The Routledge Encyclopedia of Taoism provides comprehensive coverage of Taoist religion, thought, and history, reflecting the current state of Taoist scholarship. It contains hundreds of entries authored by an international body of experts which cover areas such as schools and traditions, texts, persons, and sacred sites. Terms are given in their original characters, transliterated and translated. The encyclopedia is thoroughly cross-referenced and indexed, and also includes a chronology and bibliography. It is invaluable for students and scholars in the fields of religious studies, philosophy and religion, and Asian history and culture.

Fabrizio Pregadio has taught at the University of Venice (1996–97), the Technical University of Berlin (1998–2001), Stanford University (2001–08), and McGill University in Montreal (2009–10).

THE ROUTLEDGE ENCYCLOPEDIA OF TAOISM

Volume II: M–Z

Edited by

Fabrizio Pregadio

Routledge
Taylor & Francis Group

LONDON AND NEW YORK

First published 2008
by Routledge
First published in paperback 2011
by Routledge
2 Park Square, Milton Park, Abingdon, Oxon, OX14 4RN

Simultaneously published in the USA and Canada
by Routledge
711 Third Avenue, New York, NY 10017

Routledge is an imprint of the Taylor & Francis Group, an informa business

British Library Cataloguing in Publication Data
A catalogue record for this book is available from the British Library

Library of Congress Cataloging in Publication Data
A catalog record for this book has been requested

ISBN: 978–0–7007–1200–7 (hbk 2 volume set)
ISBN: 978–0–415–67815–5 (pbk 2 volume set)
ISBN: 978–0–415–69548–7 (ebk 2 volume set)

Typeset in Dante
by Birdtrack Press

Table of Contents

Volume I

Volume II

Encyclopedia of Taoism
Volume II

Ma Yu

馬鈺

1123–84; original *ming*: Congyi 從義; *zi*: Yifu 宜甫, Xuanbao 玄寶;
hao: Danyang zi 丹陽子 (Master of Cinnabar Yang)

The *Quanzhen master Ma Yu (Ma Danyang) was the heir of an affluent family living at the tip of the Shandong peninsula. So rich as to be nicknamed "he who owns half the prefecture" (*banzhou* 半州), he seems to have led an idle life and to have had a keen interest in Taoist pursuits, becoming a friend of an ascetic called Li Wumeng 李無夢 but not establishing formal links with any Taoist institution.

In 1167, *Wang Zhe arrived in Ma's hometown as a hermit from Shaanxi and met Ma at a gathering of the local gentry. Ma was impressed by Wang and invited him to stay at his home. Wang built a hut, the Quanzhen an 全真菴 (Hermitage for Completing Authenticity), where he began to receive disciples. In the winter of 1167–68, he enclosed himself in the hut for one hundred days (from the first of the tenth lunar month to the tenth of the first lunar month), a practice that later became the paradigm of the *huandu* retreat. During that time, Wang regularly sent poems and sliced pears (*fenli* 分梨) to Ma and his wife, *Sun Bu'er, to convince them to separate (*fenli* 分離) from each other and live as celibate ascetics. These poetic exchanges were later edited in the *Fenli shihua ji* 分梨十化集 (Anthology of the Ten Stages of Pear-Slicing; CT 1155). In the spring of 1168, Ma finally assented to his master's injunctions and became a renouncer. From then on, he followed Wang on his mountain retreats and tours of the Quanzhen association halls. Wang repeatedly tested Ma by sending him to beg in places where he had formerly been the local rich man. By the time he died in Kaifeng (Henan) in early 1170, Wang deemed Ma to have achieved spiritual transformation and anointed him as his spiritual heir.

From 1170 to 1172, Ma visited the sites of Wang's earlier ascetic life together with three other intimate disciples, *Tan Chuduan, *Liu Chuxuan, and *Qiu Chuji. They carried Wang's coffin back from Kaifeng, buried him in the Zuting 祖庭 (Ancestral Court, his former hermitage), and observed the mourning rites for the prescribed period of over two years. In 1174 his three fellow disciples left, but Ma stayed at the Zuting enclosed in a *huandu* for three years. Many young adepts from Shaanxi, Shanxi, and Henan began to gather around him and build an active community primarily devoted to the teaching of *neidan*. After 1178, Ma became more active and toured the area, preaching in official foundations (*guan* 觀), private chapels (*an* 庵 or 菴), and private houses, directing various rituals, and enclosing himself in *huandu* built for him for periods of one hundred days, where he received his most devoted adepts.

In 1182, Ma returned to his native Shandong, possibly forced to do so by a local government suspicious of itinerant preachers. He revived the lay associations (*hui* 會) founded by Wang and performed miracles; the most famous was the apparition of a city floating on the sea, which resulted in the local fishermen ceasing the killing of living beings and burning their fishing nets. Finally, Ma learned of his former wife's death and died himself shortly thereafter.

Ma Yu and Sun Bu'er. The story of Ma Yu and his wife Sun Bu'er, one of the most fascinating in the vast Taoist lore, was elaborated in several "romances of the Seven Real Men" written in the *zhanghui xiaoshuo* 章回小說 novelistic style during the Ming and Qing periods (Endres 1985). Ma and Sun loved each other but had to separate to achieve their spiritual aims. They did so gradually, with much hesitancy. Ma's fame in popular fiction must be related to his role as someone who successfully sublimates his normal marital life. Several Quanzhen masters, beginning with Wang Zhe himself, did so in a cruder way by repudiating wife and children, never to see them again. One of the thirty or so extant Yuan texts of *zaju* 雜劇 (variety plays), called *Ma Danyang sandu Ren fengzi* 馬丹陽三度壬風子 (Ma Danyang Converts Three Times Crazy Ren), compounds the sexual issue with the question of killing living beings as a profession. Ren is a butcher whom Ma convinces to leave his trade as well as his family. His wife and children are thus abandoned and resourceless, which they remonstrate against with reason, but in vain. Ma also figures prominently in several other *zaju* plays extant only in late Ming editions, and is often included in later anthologies of popular hagiography. Whereas Qiu Chuji came to play the most prominent role within the later Quanzhen tradition, Ma became the best known in popular lore.

Ma Yu is also remembered as a great poet. His abundant literary productions were anthologized separately by various groups of disciples and are consequently dispersed in several texts, a process similar to the editing of Wang Zhe's poetry. The Taoist Canon includes the *Jinyu ji* 金玉集 (Anthology of Gold and Jade; CT 1149), the *Jianwu ji* 漸悟集 (Anthology of Gradual Awakening; CT 1142), and the *Shenguang can* 神光燦 (Luster of Divine Radiance; CT 1150). Many of Ma's poems also appear in Wang's own anthologies. In addition, a long speech and a collection of recorded sayings attributed to him are also extant (see under **yulu*).

Vincent GOOSSAERT

📖 Boltz J. M. 1987a, 149–55; Endres 1985; Hachiya Kunio 1987; Hachiya Kunio 1992a; Hawkes 1981; Marsone 2001a, 103

※ Sun Bu'er; Quanzhen

Magu

麻姑

Magu first appears in the historical record in the *Shenxian zhuan* (Biographies of Divine Immortals), compiled in the fourth century. In some modern versions of that collection—those that appear to be reconstitutions based on the *Taiping guangji* 太平廣記 (Extensive Records of the Taiping Xingguo Reign Period)—she receives an independent biography but it is not cited by the middle of the Tang so cannot reliably be regarded as early. She does, however, feature strongly in the *Shenxian zhuan* biographies of *Wang Yuan and Cai Jing 蔡經 which form one continuous narrative.

In that story, the immortal Wang Yuan summons Magu while he is at the Cai family home in Wu 吳 (Jiangsu and part of Zhejiang). She appears to the sounds of drums and bells and accompanied by horsemen, a beautiful young woman of 18 or 19. By the Song period, at the latest, Magu is sometimes thought to be Wang Yuan's sister. After Magu arrives, she, Wang, Cai and his family perform the ritual of the "traveling cuisines" (*xingchu* 行廚; see *chu) which is described as a banquet, the centerpiece being a roasted, mystical *lin* 麟 beast (sometimes identified as a unicorn). Magu also scatters rice on the ground, transforming it into cinnabar for Cai's sister-in-law's ten-day-old baby, a performance Wang Yuan laughingly dismisses as a "transformation trick" and a "game of youth." Magu's most idiosyncratic feature is that her fingernails look like birds' talons. At one point, Cai thinks to himself that such nails would be very convenient for an itchy back. Wang, of course, can read Cai's thoughts and upbraids him for this insubordination, whipping him with an invisible whip.

Magu's age—and the question of the scale of time in which immortals exist—has been a topic of interest to later generations of Taoists and literati. Although she appears young, at one point Magu says to Wang Yuan, "I have not been seen for an instant in more than five hundred years." Later she says that "since last I was received I have seen the Eastern Sea become mulberry groves and fields three times." The latter statement is typically taken to refer to the periodic drying out and refilling of the Eastern Sea (on what we would call geological time scales) over which Magu travels on her way from the magical island of *Penglai to the mainland.

The later history of Magu is rather confused. There are records of two Magu mountains (Magu shan 麻姑山): one in present-day Jiangxi near the town of Nancheng 南城 close to the border with Fujian and one in present-day Anhui near Xuancheng 宣成. The former is listed as the twenty-eighth of the thirty-six lesser Grotto-Heavens (see *dongtian and fudi). In the story that is found in the *Shenxian zhuan*, Magu is not presented as having any specifically non-immortal existence, though the standard Taoist understanding of immortals would demand that she had one. Thus, the existence of traditions claiming that she came from Jianchang 建昌 (the present-day Nancheng, near this Magu shan), refined the elixir there and attained immortality should not occasion surprise. This was also the mountain that the famous Tang calligrapher and Taoist Yan Zhenqing 顏真卿 (709–85) visited and described in his well-known *Magu xiantan ji* 麻姑仙壇記 (Record of the Platform from which Magu Ascended to Immortality). That inscription is now most commonly found as a calligraphy copytext. She was also the subject of poems by the Tang Taoist poet Cao Tang 曹唐 (fl. 847–83), beautifully studied by Edward Schafer (1985).

Magu is also regarded as having cultivated the Dao on Mount Guxu (Guxu shan 姑徐山) in the south east of Mouzhou 牟州 district (eastern Shandong). In some senses this tradition accords best with the original story which, with its references to Penglai and the Eastern Sea, would seem to indicate that Magu had a much more northern affiliation than the site of her eponymous mountains.

Wolfram Eberhard (1968, 123–25) gives various scattered references to her appearances in local traditions.

Benjamin PENNY

📖 Campany 2002, 259–70; Despeux 1990, 61–66; Eberhard 1968, 123–25; Kohn 1993b, 355–58; Little 2000b, 334; Liu Ts'un-yan 1997, 412–20; Schafer 1985, 90–102

※ HAGIOGRAPHY

Maming sheng

馬鳴生 (or: 馬明生)

Maming sheng is an immortal who is said to have lived during the Han dynasty although, since he is credited with a presence on earth of over 500 years, he must also have lived during other periods as well. He is known primarily from two biographies of the *Shenxian zhuan* (Biographies of Divine Immortals): one under his own name and the biography of *Yin Changsheng (trans. Campany 2002, 274–77). The latter biography is reliably early but the former is not cited by the mid-Tang so must be regarded as of questionable provenance.

In the Yin Changsheng biography, Yin sought Maming out as he had heard that Maming had attained the Dao of "transcending the generations" (*dushi* 度世). In conventional style Maming tested Yin's seriousness, in this case having his prospective student serve him as a slave for more than ten years. Of the twelve followers Maming had, Yin alone remained. At that point Maming sheng said, "Truly you are able to attain the Dao." They then proceeded to Mount Qingcheng (*Qingcheng shan, Sichuan) where Maming bestowed the *Taiqing jing* (Scripture of Great Clarity) on him.

From his own biography we find that Ma's original name was He Junxian 和君賢 and that he came from Linzi 臨淄 (Shandong). When Maming died young, a spirit gave him medicine and he came back to life. Later, Maming obtained the *Taiyang shendan jing* 太陽神丹經 (Scripture of the Divine Elixirs of Great Yang) in three chapters. On refining this elixir he only took a half measure and became an earthly immortal. He was seen around the empire for more than 550 years before eventually rising bodily into heaven.

Both Yin and Ma, under the names Ma Ming and Yin Sheng, are listed in the *Housheng daojun lieji* (Chronicle of the Lord of the Dao, Saint of the Latter Age) as among those ordered to descend to earth and give instruction.

Benjamin PENNY

📖 Campany 2002, 325–26

※ HAGIOGRAPHY

Maojun

茅君

Lord Mao

Mao Ying 茅盈, better known as Maojun, is one of the founding divinities of the *Shangqing school of Taoism. According to traditional accounts, he lived during the Later Han dynasty and was the eldest of three brothers (the other two are Mao Gu 茅固 and Mao Zhong 茅衷) who moved from Xianyang 咸陽 (Shaanxi) to Mount Gouqu (Gouqu shan 句曲山, Jiangsu) to practice the Dao. As their renown grew, the name of the mountain was changed to Mount Mao (*Maoshan) and its three main peaks were called Higher Mao (Damao 大茅), Middle Mao (Zhongmao 中茅), and Lesser Mao (Xiaomao 小茅).

With the development of Shangqing, Lord Mao was endowed with new godly attributes. The biography of the Queen Mother of the West (*Xiwang mu) in *Du Guangting's *Yongcheng jixian lu* (1.9a–20b) describes how, in I BCE,

Lord Mao received a visit from the goddess, who bestowed titles and secret teachings upon him, and assigned him a divine spouse, *Wei Huacun. The biography describes the divine encounter between the Queen Mother and Lord Mao in lavish detail: Lord Mao is given various life-extending plants and "numinous mushrooms" (*zhi), and he and his brothers are granted talismans (*FU), seals, and sacred scriptures. Then the Queen Mother prepares Lady Wei to meet her future husband, who will become her disciple in the Shangqing mysteries. The core of the Shangqing revelations is believed to be the result of this encounter.

Du Guangting's account of Lord Mao and his brothers is based on a fourth- or fifth-century text partly preserved as "Sanshen ji" 三神紀 (Chronicle of the Three Divinities) in *Maoshan zhi 5. The latter is the most complete of three extant biographies of Maojun; the other two are in the *Shenxian zhuan and the *Yunji qiqian (104.10b–20a), respectively. As noted by Susan Cahill (1993, 186), the meeting between Maojun and the Queen Mother is set so early in Taoist history as an expedient to place the beginning of the Shangqing tradition before the origin of the Way of the Celestial Masters (*Tianshi dao).

Elena VALUSSI

📖 Cahill 1993, 183–89; Campany 2002, 326–28; Chen Guofu 1963, 9–11; Robinet 1984, 2: 389–98; Strickmann 1979, passim

※ Maoshan; Shangqing; HAGIOGRAPHY

Maoshan

茅山

Mount Mao (Jiangsu)

Initially named Mount Gouqu (Gouqu shan 句曲山), Mount Mao is located south of Nanjing (Jiangsu). The highest peak rises to a height of about 600 m. Within Taoist sacred geography, the mountain was considered the site of the eighth Grotto-Heaven (*dongtian), called Huayang 華陽 (Flourishing Yang), which was perceived to be connected via subterranean conduits to Mount Emei (*Emei shan, Sichuan), Mount Tai (*Taishan, Shandong), the Luofu Mountains (*Luofu shan, Guangdong), and the Linwu grotto (Linwu dong 林屋洞) under Mount Dongting (Dongting shan 洞庭山) in Lake Taihu 太湖 (Jiangsu). Mount Mao was also the site of one of the seventy-two Blissful Lands (*fudi). Filled with caverns, it was famous for its diverse pharmacopoeia, elixir ingredients, and "numinous mushrooms" (*zhi).

The mountain received its name due to its association with the three Mao brothers (Mao Ying 茅盈, Mao Zhong 茅衷, and Mao Gu 茅固; see under *Maojun), who alighted on its three peaks during the Han dynasty, practiced there, ascended from its peaks as transcendents, and were later venerated within the *Shangqing tradition. Indeed, the mountain has almost became synonymous with the Shangqing school, which originated there between the fourth and fifth centuries. Xu Hui 許翽 (341–ca. 370), the son of Xu Mi 許謐 (303–76), was among the first to retire to Mount Mao to study the newly revealed scriptures (for details, see under *Yang Xi). Later, in 492, *Tao Hongjing (456–536) retired to Mount Mao to study those texts and found the hallowed site to be particularly efficacious for compounding elixirs. In Tao's wake, Mount Mao became an important Taoist religious center for both male and female practitioners (who shared the site with Buddhists), and a favorite destination for pilgrims. During the Tang dynasty it was home to a number of influential Shangqing patriarchs, including *Wang Yuanzhi (528–635) and *Li Hanguang (683–769). However, for several reasons it is a misnomer to refer to the Shangqing tradition, as is still sometimes done, by the name "Maoshan Taoism." The mountain was also related to other Taoist lineages, and much of the history of the Shangqing tradition took place away from it. The activities of Shangqing patriarchs such as *Pan Shizheng (585–682) and *Sima Chengzhen (647–735), for instance, are allied more closely with Mount Song (*Songshan, Henan) than with Mount Mao, where significant gaps in the lineage's transmission occurred (Sakauchi Shigeo 1988).

During the Song dynasty, Mount Mao was home to a new set of revelations which, while rooted to some extent in the Shangqing tradition, are characterized by their emphasis on exorcism. In 1120, in particular, a disciple of Zhang Daoling was said to have appeared to *Lu Shizhong (fl. 1120–30) at Mount Mao and revealed to him the location of the founding text of the Yutang 玉堂 (Jade Hall) ritual tradition. While Mount Mao remained an important Taoist center throughout the Ming and Qing dynasties, its proximity to the urban center of Nanjing led to the destruction of many abbeys during periods of political turmoil and war in the nineteenth and twentieth centuries. Mount Mao recovered from those recent setbacks, however, and remains an important Taoist site today.

The Taoist Canon preserves a rather abundant textual record for Mount Mao. The *Maoshan zhi (Monograph of Mount Mao), compiled by the forty-fifth Shangqing patriarch Liu Dabin 劉大彬 (fl. 1317–28), is a massive text dedicated to the history of the mountain. Chapters 11–14 of the *Zhengao (Declarations of the Perfected) also contain much information about the site.

James ROBSON

📖 Bertuccioli 1974; Bumbacher 2000a; Miyakawa Hisayuki 1964, 176–87; Nara Yukihiro 1998, 118–21; Schafer 1989; Strickmann 1981, 28–57; Sun Kekuan 1968, 82–92

※ Maojun; *Maoshan zhi*; Shangqing; TAOIST SACRED SITES

Maoshan zhi

茅山志

Monograph of Mount Mao

The *Maoshan zhi* (CT 304), a gazetteer on *Maoshan (Jiangsu), the mountains that served as the first center of the *Shangqing order, was compiled by Liu Dabin 劉大彬 (fl. 1317–28), the forty-fifth Shangqing patriarch. Although Liu's preface is dated January 2 of 1329, he completed the text sometime before 1326. The work originally had fifteen chapters, but the present version has thirty-three. Since the materials in the gazetteer do not seem to date after Liu finished the work, some later editor apparently restructured the *Maoshan zhi*. Liu had in his possession a previous text in four chapters on Mount Mao that was compiled in 1150. It was, however, unsatisfactory since it contained only titles and brief descriptions.

Liu divided his work into twelve parts. Part one (j. 1–4) is a collection of documents issued by the throne dated from 1 CE to 1319. These documents concern the conferral of titles, the bestowal of gifts, the establishment of abbeys, bans on cutting down trees in the mountains, the rites of Casting Dragon Tablets (*tou longjian), correspondence between emperors and patriarchs with replies from the prelates, and other matters.

Part two (j. 5) is a chronicle of the three Mao 茅 brothers (see *Maojun) who purportedly flourished in the Former Han dynasty and after whom the mountains were named. They became the gods who administered the subterranean world beneath Mount Mao where the spirits of the dead resided.

Part three (j. 6–7) is partly a guide to geographical features: mountains as well as peaks and grottoes; waters including springs, streams and pools; and rocks. Liu recounts the mythology and history associated with those places. The section also describes bridges, altars, pavilions, and terraces located in the mountains.

Part four (j. 8) is really an appendix to the previous section. However, in this section Liu treats particular geographical features or edifices that had more historical significance than the others.

Part five (*j.* 9) is a catalogue of 226 scriptures, biographies and other matter that consists of four lists from various sources. The provenance of the first two is unknown. The third was compiled in the Song dynasty probably in the early twelfth century. The fourth consists of extracts from the bibliographical section of Zheng Qiao's 鄭樵 (1104–62) *Tongzhi* 通志 (Comprehensive Monographs) completed around 1161.

Part six (*j.* 10–12) consists of two parts. The first is a short enumeration of the deities venerated by the Shangqing order. The second is a collection of brief biographies of the forty-five patriarchs beginning with *Wei Huacun and concluding with Liu Dabin himself.

Part seven (*j.* 13–14) is a description of the palaces and bureaus of the Grotto-Heaven (see *dongtian* and *fudi*) that lies beneath Mount Mao. Women who have achieved the Dao occupy two of the three palaces while male Perfected occupy the last as well as one of the bureaus. Each year the Lord Azure Lad of the Eastern Sea (*Qingtong) conducts a tour of inspection of the palaces. The three Mao brothers govern the three remaining bureaus that constitute effectively the administration of the underworld, mostly concerned with fixing the destiny of the dead in the afterlife. Liu then goes on to provide the titles of the officials working in the three bureaus and names of the immortals who serve there. Then he supplies the names of the occupants of the palaces.

Part eight (*j.* 15–16) covers eminent persons—abbots, abbesses, priests, priestesses, scholars, officials, hermits, and others—who in one way or another had some affiliation with the monastic complex on Mount Mao. This includes ten descendants of the Celestial Master *Zhang Daoling, two of them female.

Part nine (*j.* 17–18) is a guide to the religious edifices on Mount Mao—temples, abbeys, cloisters, halls, hermitages, and the like. Whenever possible, Liu provides the dates of their establishment, the name of the patron who sponsored them, and the circumstances under which they were erected. Often, however, he simply supplies their titles and locations.

Part ten (*j.* 19) is a description of "numinous mushrooms" (*zhi) and famous trees that existed on the mountains at various times.

Part eleven (*j.* 20–27) is a collection of inscriptions for stele. They concern abbeys, altars, patriarchs, springs, "cinnabar wells" (*danjing* 丹井), conferral of registers (*LU), and other subjects.

Part twelve (*j.* 28–33) is a collection of poetry dating from the sixth century to the thirteenth century. The last chapter, however, contains miscellaneous writings such as prefaces, letters and inscriptions.

Although much of the material in the *Maoshan zhi* can be found in other works of the Taoist Canon and secular works, the text is one of the most useful reference works for the study of the Shangqing order. Its value lies in the fact that Liu Dabin classified his materials so that a researcher can pursue a line of study without the distraction of extraneous matter. Furthermore, whenever possible, Liu ordered the contents of the treatise according to their dates.

Charles D. BENN

📖 Boltz J. M. 1987a, 103–5; Chen Guofu 1963, 247–50; Qing Xitai 1994, 2: 210–12; Schafer 1989; Sun Kekuan 1968, 75–82

※ Maoshan; Shangqing

Mawangdui manuscripts

In December 1973, archaeologists clearing tomb no. 3 at Mawangdui 馬王堆, Changsha 長沙 (Hunan), discovered a cache of texts written mostly on silk folded in a lacquer box. They were placed there to accompany Li Cang 利蒼, Lord of Dai 軑侯, who died in 168 BCE, into the afterlife. This was the main discovery of ancient texts since the opening of the hidden library at *Dunhuang in the early twentieth century. Although in some cases badly damaged, and even fragmented into small pieces as a result of the fraying of the silk at the edges of the folds, and although some of the texts still remain unpublished after thirty years, this discovery has been of major significance for the understanding of the early history of Taoism.

Among the manuscripts were two copies of the *Daode jing*; the earliest version of the *Yijing* with the earliest version of the *Xici* 繫辭 (Appended Statements) and four previously unknown commentaries; manuscripts associated with *Huang-Lao Taoism (Yates 1997); texts on medicine and Nourishing Life (*yangsheng) earlier than the *Huangdi neijing (Inner Scripture of the Yellow Emperor), that reveal the use of exorcism, magic, talismans (*FU), abstention from cereals (*bigu), and other techniques of macrobiotic hygiene, together with drug and other therapies in the period leading up to the creation of the medicine of systematic correspondence (Harper 1998; Lo Vivienne 2001); philosophical texts from the Confucian tradition (Wei Qipeng 1991; Pang Pu 1980); Five Phase (*wuxing) texts and three texts and two Nine Palace (*jiugong) charts concerned with divination according to the *xingde* 刑德 (Punishment and Virtue) method (Kalinowski 1998–99; Chen Songchang 2001); a drawing of the deity *Taiyi (Li Ling 1995–96; see fig. 71); historical texts; and several maps.

The Mawangdui Yijing. The manuscript of the *Yijing* is significant in many ways (Shaughnessy 1994; Shaughnessy 1996a; Deng Qiubo 1996; Xing Wen 1997). The order of the sixty-four hexagrams is different from the received version.

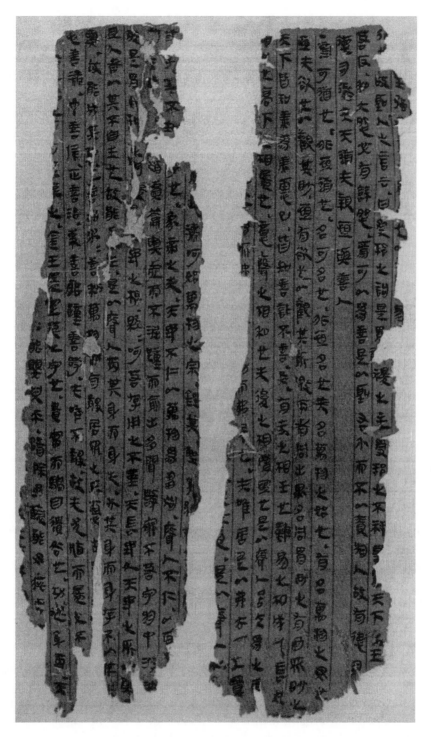

Fig. 57. Fragments of the Mawangdui manuscript of the *Daode jing* (*jia* 甲 version).
Reproduced from Guojia wenwuju Guwenxian yanjiushi 1980–85, vol. 1.

Thirty-three of the names of the hexagrams are different from those in the received version, the most important being "Key" (*jian* 鍵) for *qian* 乾 ䷀ and "Flow" (*chuan* 川) for *kun* 坤 ䷁. There are also a great number of variant graphs in the body of the text that could well have significant philosophical implications. Edward Shaughnessy (1996b) suggests that the original referents of "Key" and "Flow" were the male and female genitalia respectively, rather than the abstract notions of Heaven and Earth. The four lost commentaries have been titled *Ersanzi wen* 二三子問 (The Several Disciples Asked), *Yi zhi yi* 易之義 (The Properties of the *Changes*), *Yao* 要 (Essentials), and *Mu He* 繆和 and *Zhao Li* 昭力, the names of students who pose questions to their teachers on the interpretation of the *Yijing*. Some scholars argue that the manuscript version of the *Xici*, which is shorter than the received version, was originally Taoist in orientation and that it was later conflated with the later part of *Yi zhi yi*, which is Confucian in philosophical orientation and discusses the names of the hexagrams. The received version of the *Xici* can now be seen to derive from multiple sources, including the *Yi zhi yi* and the *Yao*.

The Mawangdui Laozi. There are two versions of the *Daode jing* preserved at Mawangdui (Boltz W. G. 1984). Text A (*jia* 甲) was copied in small seal script graphs (*xiaozhuan* 小篆) probably before the reign of Liu Bang 劉邦 (Gaozu, r. 202–195 BCE), the founder of the Han dynasty. Text B (*yi* 乙) was copied in clerical script (*lishu* 隸書) during his reign. These are the earliest surviving complete texts of the *Daode jing*, very similar in philosophical content to the received text (the *Guodian tomb in the state of Chu, dating approximately 300 BCE, only preserves a limited number of passages). The differences between the manuscripts and the received text have generated much academic debate (Lau 1982; Henricks 1989; Gao Ming 1996). The texts are not divided into individual chapters, as is the eighty-one chapter version of the received text. The division in the received text was made later in the Han dynasty in such a way that the coherence and flow of the argument is at some points obscured, and some passages have been misplaced. In addition, the order of the text in the Mawangdui manuscripts is reversed so that what is now known as the *De* 德 section (chapters 38–81) precedes the *Dao* 道 section (chapters 1–37), the same order that is found in the "Explicating the *Laozi*" ("Jie Lao" 解老) chapter of the *Han Feizi* 韓非子 (Liao 1939–59, 1: 169–206). This suggests that there were two traditions of ordering the text. But whether the manuscript versions should be interpreted as stressing political and military policies for ordering the world, while the reverse order in the received text stresses metaphysics—the former being used by scholars of the law (*fa* 法) and the latter by the Taoists—is still under discussion. Finally, the manuscripts include many more grammatical particles than the received version, reducing the text's opacity.

Robin D. S. YATES

📖 Harper 1998; Fu Juyou and Chen Songchang 1992; Guojia wenwuju Guwenxian yanjiushi 1980–85; Henricks 1986b; Jan Yün-hua 1977; Loewe 1977; Riegel 1975; Wu Hung 1992; Yamada Keiji 1985

Mazu

媽祖

Centuries of lore surround the goddess popularly called Mazu or Tianshang shengmu 天上聖母 (Holy Mother in Heaven). Present-day circles of her devotees generally concur that she was born in 960 to the Lin 林 family of Putian 莆田 (Fujian), was given the name Mo(niang) 默(娘), and died at the age of twenty-eight in the year 987. Initially revered for her skills in prophecy, she came to be regarded foremost as the guardian angel of seafarers. Imperial entitlements from the twelfth to nineteenth century signify her sustained acceptance within the canon of deities sanctioned by state authority. Numerous shrines emerged on Mazu's behalf in coastal and inland communities alike. Many temples bear the designation Tianfei 天妃 (Celestial Consort) or Tianhou 天后 (Cantonese: Tin Hau, Celestial Empress), from titles granted by imperial decree in 1281 and 1683, respectively. Over five hundred temples are dedicated to Mazu in Taiwan alone. The vast majority are registered as Taoist institutions, but a small minority claim Buddhist affiliation. Shrines in Mazu's memory also exist in Chinese settlements from Singapore and Nagasaki to São Paulo and San Francisco. Festivals at the temple traditionally mark her date of birth on the twenty-third day of the third lunar month and her demise on the ninth day of the ninth lunar month. Mazu's endurance as a guardian figure of Chinese communities easily reflects the degree to which devotees have adapted their perceptions of her authority to the ever-changing demands on their lives.

Contemporary views of Mazu are shaped by hagiographic and scriptural accounts from the Ming and Qing periods. The concise entry on Tianfei in the *Soushen ji* (In Search of the Sacred) of 1593 identifies her father as Chief Military Inspector Lin Yuan 林愿 of Pu(tian). His daughter is said to have been blessed with the skill of foretelling the destiny of others. Upon her demise, villagers honored her memory by constructing a shrine on the isle of Meizhou 湄洲. The single episode recorded in this account demonstrating her divine power tells the story behind the first instance of imperial entitlement. The ambassador to Koryŏ 高麗 Lu Yundi 路允迪 (fl. 1122–29) reportedly found himself aboard the only ship to survive a typhoon, guided to safety by the descent of the goddess on the masthead. His testimony

Fig. 58. Entrance to Mazu temple (Tianhou gong 天后宮, Palace of the Celestial Empress) in Lukang 鹿港, Taiwan. Photograph by Julian Pas.

led Song Huizong (r. 1100–1125) to reward her shrine with offerings in 1123, authorizing as well a plaque bearing the inscription Shunji 順濟 (Compliant Salvation).

An eclectic late Ming hagiographic anthology published in 1909 by Ye Dehui 葉德輝 (1864–1927) as the *Sanjiao yuanliu soushen daquan* 三教源流搜神大全 (Great Compendium on the Origins and Development of the Three Teachings and Search for the Sacred) dates Tianfei's birth to 742. This event reportedly transpired through the divine intervention of the bodhisattva Guanyin of the South Sea (Nanhai Guanyin 南海觀音), to whom Mazu herself is often compared. The story that has become the mainstay of her legacy concerns a state of trance that her parents mistook for a seizure. When they managed to arouse their daughter, she cried out in despair over her inability to save all of her brothers at sea. Confirmation of her vision came when the surviving sons returned home and described how they witnessed the drowning of the eldest as they saw their own boats secured by a young girl, apparently none other than the projected spirit of their own sister. Distraught at the loss of her eldest brother, Lin Mo vowed to remain single and took her last breath seated in meditation. Thereafter, she gained the reputation for being able to answer the prayers of all women seeking to be with child. The establishment

of a shrine at Meizhou is linked to the imperial title of Linghui furen 靈慧
夫人 (Lady of Numinous Wisdom) dating to 1156. Her alleged protection of
the renowned navy commander Zheng He 鄭和 (1371–1435; DMB 194–200) is
cited as the source of inspiration in 1409 for the imperial title Huguo bimin
miaoling zhaoying hongren puji tianfei 護國庇民妙靈昭應弘仁普濟天妃
(Celestial Consort of Universal Salvation, Wondrous Numen, Brilliant Resonance, and Magnanimous Benevolence, Protecting the State and Sheltering
the People).

Putative descendants of Mazu, Lin Yaoyu 林堯俞 (fl. 1589) and Lin Linchang
林麟焻 (fl. 1670), are responsible for transmitting a long episodic narrative
entitled *Tianfei xiansheng lu* 天妃顯聖錄 (Account of the Blessings Revealed
by the Celestial Consort). An old Taoist Master named Xuantong 玄通 is said
to have recognized her Buddha-nature (*foxing* 佛性 or *buddhatā*) conducive to
her messianic mission. She reportedly mastered the *Xuanwei bifa* 玄微祕法
(Secret Rites of Mysterious Tenuity) that he bestowed upon her at the age of
thirteen. Three years later, the recovery of a talisman from a well purportedly
led to a remarkable enhancement of her miraculous faculties. The episode
concerning her state of trance differs in naming her father as the one she
had failed to rescue at sea. Later popular accounts commonly claim instead
that Tianfei lost her own life saving her father, reinforcing the ideal of a filial
daughter.

The Taoist Canon contains a scriptural counterpart to hagiographic legend
entitled *Taishang Laojun shuo Tianfei jiuku lingyan jing* 太上老君說天妃救苦
靈驗經 (Scripture Spoken by the Most High Lord Lao on the Numinous Efficacy of the Celestial Consort in Relieving Suffering; CT 649). It tells the story
of how *Laojun became aware of countless victims of drowning on various
waterways. To show his compassion, he ordered the descent of Miaoxing
yunü 妙行玉女 (Jade Woman of Wondrous Deeds) so that she might fulfill
her pledge to ease the burdens of all humankind. A variant form of the 1409
title is recorded here, amplified by the epithet Fudou 輔斗 (Sustaining the
Dipper) designating Tianfei's origins as a star within the constellation of the
Northern Dipper (*beidou). The astral deity incarnated as the filial daughter
of Meizhou not only vows protection of anyone travelling by boat but also
promises to oversee all aspects of life and death, from warding off thieves
and tyrants to assuring success in childbirth and scholastic pursuits. Anyone
facing hardship is promised relief by devoutly calling her name and reciting
the scripture.

A manuscript copy of a cognate scripture collected in Tainan 臺南 (Taiwan)
by Kristofer Schipper matches the 1420 printing within the Tenri Library
collection in Nara, published in the *Zangwai daoshu* (3: 781–86). The latter
compilation (20: 357–87) also reprints the richly detailed 1881 account of the

renowned Hangzhou (Zhejiang) shrine, entitled *Chengbei Tianhou gong zhi* 城北天后宮志 (Monograph of the Palace of the Celestial Empress North of the City Walls).

Judith M. BOLTZ

📖 Boltz J. M. 1986a; Cai Xianghui 1989; Li Lulu 1994; Li Xianzhang 1979; Maspero 1981, 145–47; Ruitenbeek 1999; Wädow 1992

※ HAGIOGRAPHY; TAOISM AND POPULAR RELIGION

menshen

門神

door gods

As the principal point where good and evil influences enter a Chinese house, the main door has long received special ritual attention. Considerable care is devoted to its proper geomantic location and orientation, and various apotropaic instruments are installed to defend it against the intrusion of malevolent spirits, including talismans (*FU), mirrors (see under *jing and *jian*), the *taiji* 太極 symbol (see *Taiji tu), and most importantly the door gods as supernatural guardians. In modern times, these gods are usually represented by the printed pictures, renewed each lunar New Year festival, of two fierce-looking warriors pasted on the main door.

Sacrifices to a door spirit are already recorded in the *Liji* 禮記 (Records of Rites; trans. Legge 1885, 2: 207), and by the time of the Han dynasty we find frequent references to two door gods named Shen Shu 神荼 and Yu Lü 鬱壘, whose names and/or images were painted on peachwood tablets and attached to the door. In late medieval China, these two ancient deities began to be replaced by the effigies of various apotheosized military heroes, most importantly the Tang dynasty generals Qin Shubao 秦叔寶 (?–638) and Yuchi Gong 尉遲恭 (alias Hu Jingde 胡敬德, 585–658), who today still dominate the iconography of the door gods. Besides these "martial door gods" (*wu menshen* 武門神), there are several "civil door gods" (*wen menshen* 文門神), images of scholarly or otherwise auspicious figures that are usually pasted on interior doors of the household to attract blessings.

The door gods are part of popular religious practice and belief and do not play a significant role in Taoist ritual. However, Taoist temples and monasteries frequently provide their main entrances with other supernatural guardians, such as a green dragon (*qinglong* 青龍) and a white tiger (*baihu* 白虎).

Philip CLART

📖 Bodde 1975, 127–38; Fong 1989; Ma Shutian 1997, 235–47; Maspero 1981, 115–17

※ TAOISM AND POPULAR RELIGION

Miao Shanshi

苗善時

fl. 1288–1324; *zi*: Taisu 太素; *hao*: Shi'an 實庵 (Hermitage of Verity),
Jinlian daoshi 金蓮道士 (Taoist Master of the Golden Lotus),
Xuanyi gaoshi 玄一高士 (Eminent Master of Mysterious Unity)

A native of Jinling 金陵 (near Nanjing, Jiangsu), Miao Shanshi was a master of the Southern Lineage (*Nanzong) of *neidan*. He was a disciple of *Li Daochun, whose Retreat of Central Harmony (Zhonghe jingshi 中和靖室) in Jinling was a flourishing center of the Gate of Mystery (Xuanmen 玄門) movement. Its masters emphasized the study of the *Daode jing*, the *Zhuangzi*, the *Yijing*, and major Buddhist *sūtras*, along with the inner alchemical practice in *Zhang Boduan's tradition and the observance of *Quanzhen precepts. Miao seems to have enjoyed a high rank among Li's disciples, as he refers to himself as Prior (*zhitang* 知堂).

Besides the third chapter of the *Qing'an Yingchan zi yulu* 清庵瑩蟾子語錄 (Recorded Sayings of [Li] Qing'an, Master of the Shining Toad; 1288; CT 1060), containing materials related to Li Daochun, three texts are attributed to Miao Shanshi. The first is the *Chunyang dijun shenhua miaotong ji* 純陽帝君神化妙通紀 (Chronicle of the Divine Transformations and Wondrous Powers of the Imperial Lord of Pure Yang; CT 305; Mori Yuria 1992a; trans. Ang 1993), dating from after 1310. This collection of 108 pious anecdotes depicts *Lü Dongbin as a savior of the deserving and the needy. Most of the tales circulated widely during the Song period, but Miao adds moral and religious overtones to them. Two-thirds of the texts accompanying the murals in the hall dedicated to Lü in the *Yongle gong (Palace of Eternal Joy) derive from this work.

The second text is the *Xuanjiao da gong'an* 玄教大公案 (Great Enigmatic Sayings of the Mysterious Teaching; 1324; CT 1065), consisting of sixty-four lectures—corresponding to the sixty-four hexagrams of the *Yijing*—on passages of the *Daode jing*, the *Zhuangzi*, and the *Yijing*. Miao's adoption of Chan methods is especially notable here. The third text, the *Sanyuan miaoben fushou zhenjing* 三元妙本福壽真經 (Authentic Scripture on Happiness and Longevity and the Wondrous Origin of the Three Primes; CT 651), is a short liturgical work with a postface by Miao dated 1324.

Farzeen BALDRIAN-HUSSEIN

📖 Boltz J. M. 1987a, 67, 182–83; Chen Yuan 1988, 729–31; Mori Yuria 1992a

※ Li Daochun; *neidan*; Nanzong

mijue

密訣 (or: 祕訣)

Secret Instructions

In present-day Taoism, *mijue* is used as the generic term for the manuals of a practitioner, which contain the methods that are somehow considered most crucial, and that are therefore most restricted in their circulation. In the current forms of the classical *Zhengyi liturgy, the term refers to the "secret manuals" that are possessed exclusively by the Taoist ritual master (*daozhang*), and which contain instructions mostly concerning those inner, "esoteric" parts of ritual that are the domain of the high priest (*gaogong* 高功) alone. More than any other manuscript, the secret manual owned by such a priest represents the family heirloom that he will transmit in full only to his son, his successor. A classical Zhengyi priest copies his *mijue* at his ordination, and it typically has the format of a small square volume, which he may carry with him in his pocket during services.

The material included in the present-day *mijue* is derived mostly from the new, exorcistic traditions of the Song dynasty, such as the *Tianxin zhengfa and *Qingwei traditions, and in some cases it occurs in almost identical form in the early compilations of the methods of these traditions found in the *Daozang*. But while it seems possible that personal secret manuals used by practicing priests during the Song dynasty may have served as sources for these large-scale and systematic compilations, the precise category of text that corresponds to the form of *mijue* used in present-day classical Zhengyi Taoism is very scarcely represented in the Canon. A notable exception is chapter 31 of the *Daofa huiyuan*, the fourteenth-century compendium of methods of "thunder magic" (see *leifa*). It is the companion volume to the preceding

chapter 30, which contains the text of a ritual of Announcement (*zougao* 奏
告; see **fabiao*) of the Qingwei tradition. Chapter 31 is entitled *Xuanshu yujue
bizhi* 玄樞玉訣祕旨 (Jade Instructions and Secret Purport of the Mysterious
Pivot), and gives descriptions of the methods of preparing the holy water
that accompany the ritual of Announcement, a method of making an inner
journey to heaven in order to deliver a petition, and a variety of divination
techniques.

The structure and contents of this text are quite similar to the *mijue* transmitted by the classical Zhengyi priests of southern Taiwan. Their manuals
carry titles such as *Xuanke miaojue* 玄科妙訣, "Wondrous Instructions for
the Mysterious Liturgy," or *Bichuan yujue* 祕傳玉訣, "Secretly Transmitted
Jade Instructions," sometimes preceded by an attribution to the first Celestial
Master, **Zhang Daoling, and a phrase indicating that they originate from
Mount Longhu (**Longhu shan, Jiangxi). The contents of the manuals pertain exclusively to the "pure liturgy" of **jiao* ceremonies, not to the funerary
liturgy, and they mainly focus on the "inner" aspects of the performance of
the high priest, that is, on visualization practices and the incantations that are
pronounced inwardly, or just inaudibly, by the high priest during the performance.

Poul ANDERSEN

📖 Mitamura Keiko 1998; Saso 1978a

※ *jiao*; ORDINATION AND PRIESTHOOD

Min Yide

閔一得

1748–1836; original *ming*: Tiaofu 苕甫; *zi*: Buzhi 補之, Xiaogen
小艮; *hao*: Lanyun zi 懶雲子 (Master of the Lazy Clouds)

Min Yide, who came from a family of Wuxing 吳興 (Zhejiang), was the eleventh
patriarch of the **Longmen school and is also regarded as the founder of its
Shanghai branch called Fangbian pai 方便派 (Branch of the Skillful Methods).
In his childhood, as he was of a feeble constitution, his father, Min Genfu 閔
艮甫, who was a Provincial Graduate (*juren* 舉人) in Henan, took him to the
**Tongbo guan (Abbey of the Paulownias and Cypresses) on Mount Tiantai
(**Tiantai shan, Zhejiang). Here the tenth Longmen patriarch, Gao Dongli 高東
籬 (?–1768), healed him with the help of physiological techniques. As Gao was
already at an advanced age, Min studied with Shen Yibing 沈一炳 (1708–86),

a disciple of Gao's who first taught Min the basic Longmen principles and then became his main master. As his father had wished, after his recovery Min completed his studies, and became a Department Vice Magistrate (*zhou sima* 州司馬) in Yunnan.

It was probably at that time that he met several Taoist masters linked to a Longmen Taoist-Tantric branch called Xizhu xinzong 西竺心宗 (Heart Lineage of Western India). The founding of this branch is ascribed to Jizu daozhe 雞足道者 (Man of the Dao from Chicken Claw Mountain; fl. 1790), a legendary figure who played an important role in Min's spiritual development and was himself a recipient of the Longmen ordination. Min states that this master gave him the *Chishi tuoluoni jing* 持世陀羅尼經 (*Vasu[n]dhārā-dhāraṇī*; T. 1162), which is included in Min's *Gu Shuyinlou cangshu* 古書隱樓藏書 (Collection of the Ancient Hidden Pavilion of Books; Qing Xitai 1994, 2: 184–86). Other biographies say that Min also received a meditation method related to *Doumu (Mother of the Dipper) and compiled the *Dafan xiantian fanyi doufa* 大梵先天梵音斗法 (Dipper Method of the Precelestial Sanskrit Sounds of the Great Brahmā), a collection of mantras based on their Sanskrit pronunciation.

Min Yide thus was not only initiated into the Longmen school by his master Shen Yibing, but also allegedly received the teachings of its Xizhu xinzong branch from Jizu daozhe. He then decided to withdraw to Mount Jingai (Jingai shan 金蓋山, Zhejiang), where he devoted himself to writing the history of the patriarchs and various branches of the Longmen school. The title of his ten-*juan* work, the *Jingai xindeng* 金蓋心燈 (Transmission of the Heart-Lamp from Mount Jingai), shows that Min paid special attention to the Longmen tradition based on that mountain. Meanwhile, he also gathered several Longmen texts on *neidan in his *Gu Shuyinlou cangshu*, a collection that later served as the basis for his *Daozang xubian* (Sequel to the Taoist Canon; 1834).

Monica ESPOSITO

📖 Esposito 1992; Esposito 1997, 80–84; Esposito 2001; Mori Yuria 1994; Qing Xitai 1988–95, 4: 116–27

※ *Daozang xubian*; *neidan*; Longmen

Minghe yuyin

鳴鶴餘音

Echoes of Cranes' Songs

The *Minghe yuyin* is the most famous collection of Song-Jin and Yuan Taoist poetry, and an excellent example of how such poetry circulated within society at large. The anthology has a rather complex history. The celebrated Yuan scholar Yu Ji 虞集 (1272–1348) was invited to write poems in reply to a set of twenty *ci* 詞 (lyrics) written by a Taoist master named Feng 馮, and made famous by a courtesan who sang them to large audiences. Yu wrote his own twelve poems to the same melody, and both sets appear under the title *Minghe yuyin*, together with a preface explaining their origin, in Yu Ji's anthology. In 1347, a southern *Quanzhen Taoist, Peng Zhizhong 彭致中, collected these and many other Taoist poems of various origins and edited a much larger anthology under the same title. The master Feng whose lyrical work initiated the whole undertaking was actually also a Quanzhen master, only known by his *zi*, Changquan 長筌. His collected works, *Dongyuan ji* 洞淵集 (Anthology of the Cavernous Abyss; CT 1064), include the poems that inspired Yu Ji along with many others.

Although Yu Ji was mainly affiliated with the *Zhengyi order, he appears to have willingly associated his name with an editorial venture that popularized Quanzhen poetry in the south. This was a favorite method of propagation for Quanzhen Taoism; anthologies of poetry and collected sayings were circulated in areas where the tradition was not well established. The *Minghe yuyin*, however, is not a sectarian book, as it includes—to varying extents—all major trends of mystical Taoist poetry of this period, *neidan* being by far the main element. Of the 508 texts, largely consisting of *ci* along with a few *shi* 詩 (regulated poems) and prose texts, 248 are by Quanzhen masters (most notably *Qiu Chuji, *Ma Yu, Feng Changquan and *Song Defang). *Lü Dongbin alone has 114 works included in the collection, and his immortal companions have eighteen. Eminent Song Taoists have thirty-three (with sixteen for *Bai Yuchan), Yu Ji has twelve, and the remaining eighty-three are either by late Yuan Taoists or by unidentified authors. Many poems are known from other anthologies, but quite a few are unique, like Song Defang's sixty-three *ci*.

Despite its large number of sources, the *Minghe yuyin* has a kind of cohesiveness. Poems are usually lyrical, extol the bliss of immortality, and urge readers or listeners to strive for aloofness from this world. Many are in the *daoqing* 道情 style (Ono Shihei 1964), and most must have been a popular corpus of songs to be used during festivals at temples and in theatrical productions. Therefore, it is quite logical that the more speculative trend of *Nanzong poetry is not much represented. On the other hand, a major characteristic of *neidan* poetry, direct revelation by an immortal through spirit writing (see *fuji*), is evident in these works.

An early Ming edition of the *Minghe yuyin*, alternatively titled *Quanzhen zongyan fangwai xuanyan* 全真宗眼方外玄言 (Mysterious Words of the Spiritual World from the Ancestral Eye of the Quanzhen), is kept at the National Library in Taiwan. Although this version is shorter than the standard *Daozang* edition (CT 1100), it also includes otherwise unknown texts on communal Taoist practice, especially the *zuobo, and therefore shows an even stronger Quanzhen influence.

Vincent GOOSSAERT

📖 Boltz J. M. 1987a, 188–90

※ Quanzhen

mingmen

命門

Gate of the Vital Force

In the Chinese medical literature, the term *mingmen* (also rendered as Gate of Life) denotes the right kidney in its function of procreation. The *mingmen* is therefore related to the Original Pneuma (*yuanqi) or Yang Pneuma (*yangqi* 陽氣), also called Real Fire (*zhenhuo* 真火). The same term also refers to an acupoint located along the Control Channel between the second and third lumbar vertebrae (see *dumai and *renmai*).

Neidan texts often designate *mingmen* as a synonym for the lower Cinnabar Field (*dantian). Although the *mingmen* can be physically located in the umbilical region or be related to the kidneys, spleen, nose, and so on, it shares the ambivalent meaning of other key alchemical terms. In fact, the *mingmen* is the center beyond all spatial and temporal categories. It has no shape, but all polarities can be resumed in it and all transformations can take place within it. As the point where breath ascends and descends, and where thought can be perceived in its perpetual fluctuations between movement and quiescence (*dong and *jing*), it is a symbol of the "mechanism of Life and Death" (*shengsi zhi ji* 生死之機).

Monica ESPOSITO

📖 Robinet 1993, 79–80

※ TAOIST VIEWS OF THE HUMAN BODY

mingtang

明堂

Hall of Light; Bright Hall

In ancient China, the Hall of Light or Bright Hall was a sacred building used for imperial ceremonies (Major 1993, 221–24). Its round roof and square foundation symbolized Heaven and Earth, respectively. The inner space was divided into five or nine sections or rooms, which represented the spatial structure of the world according to the *wuxing and the "magic square" based on the number 9, respectively (see the entries *Taiyi and *Hetu and Luoshu). The Hall of Light was also the house of the calendar, where emperors ritually inaugurated the seasons. Emperors supported and secured the cosmic order of space and time by pacing the hall in a circle.

In Taoism, however, mingtang indicates a space within the human body that is important in longevity and transmutation practices. Although the location of the Hall of Light varies according to different texts, most Taoist traditions understand mingtang as an area situated within the head. In this view, the center of the brain contains several chambers or palaces; they are usually nine, resembling the structure of cosmic space. The three main palaces are called Hall of Light, Muddy Pellet (*niwan), and Cavern Chamber (dongfang 洞房). Names and descriptions of the other palaces vary. (On these palaces see the entry *dantian.)

The Hall of Light is already mentioned in *Ge Hong's (283–343) *Baopu zi (j. 18), where it is situated one inch behind the area between the eyebrows and is one of the loci in the body where the One (*yi; see under *Taiyi) manifests itself. The topology of the nine palaces is developed in the *Suling jing and the *Ciyi jing, two of the main *Shangqing scriptures. Other Shangqing texts give different descriptions of the brain, but they all consider the Hall of Light to be one of its main palaces. Many later Taoist traditions adopted this notion, and the mingtang also appears in charts of the human body (in particular, the *Neijing tu and Xiuzhen tu).

The Hall of Light and other palaces are dwelling places for the gods within the body. According to the Suling jing, the gods residing in the Hall of Light look like newborn infants. They exhale a red fire that quenches the adept's thirst and illuminates his way when he travels at night. The gods' task is to protect adepts from harmful influences and demons. During meditation, adepts absorb the red breath of the gods, which helps them to purify their bodies.

Martina DARGA

📖 Despeux 1994, 71, 79; Granet 1934, 102–3, 178–82; Maspero 1951; Maspero 1981, 455–59 and passim; Robinet 1984, 1: 125–26; Robinet 1993, 127–31; Wang Shiren 1987

※ *dantian*; *niwan*; TAOIST VIEWS OF THE HUMAN BODY

Mo Qiyan

莫起炎

1226–94; *hao*: Yueding zhenren 月鼎真人
(Perfected of the Moon Tripod)

Hagiographies relate that this native of Huzhou 湖州 (Zhejiang) failed to pass the civil service exams three times before he abandon this route to pursue success as a dedicated Taoist priest. One of the most important *Shenxiao (Divine Empyrean) adepts, Mo learned the Thunder Rites (*leifa*) and received associated writings from divine beings. When he established his ritual practice in Zhejiang during the 1250s, he saw his tradition as rooted in the great Shenxiao systematizer, *Wang Wenqing (1093–1153). Mo regarded the most powerful part of his ritual repertoire to have been the Thunderclap Rites (*leiting* 雷霆; see *leifa*), which he believed had emerged, in part, as a reaction to the Taoist ritual forms that relied too heavily on the use of talismans (*FU). Mo later built up his clientele in the Nanfeng 南豐 area of Jiangxi and became the source of *Wang Weiyi's (fl. 1264–1304) teachings. The *Daofa huiyuan* (Corpus of Taoist Ritual, *j.* 77 and *j.* 95) also contains some short texts with Mo's name that are worthy of further study.

Lowell SKAR

📖 Boltz J. M. 1987a, 188–90; Qing Xitai 1994, 1: 346

※ *leifa*; Shenxiao

muyu

沐浴

Bathing; ablutions

1. Ritual

In Taoist ritual, "bathing" is the name of one of the rites performed as part of the Yellow Register Retreat (*huanglu zhai*) and the ritual of Merit (*gongde*) for the salvation of the deceased, during which the spirit of the deceased is summoned and bathed in a ceremony of purification. According to the *Wushang huanglu dazhai licheng yi* (Standard Liturgies of the Supreme Great Yellow Register Retreat; 1.7a–12a), the night before the Orthodox Offering (*zhengjiao*), the spirit of the deceased is summoned, bathed, taken in audience before the gods, and fed (id., *j.* 26). On the night of the second day, i.e., the day of the Orthodox Offering, a bathing rite is held for orphan spirits (id., *j.* 29).

In the ritual of Merit performed in present-day Taiwan, Bathing generally follows the rite of the Destruction of Hell (*poyu*). After the deceased has been released from the underworld, he is bathed, purified, and given a change of clothing. A low chair is placed in one corner of the Spirit Hall (*lingtang* 靈堂), where the deceased is enshrined, and a basin filled with water is placed on it. Surrounded by a screen, this is considered to be the ritual bath. A towel is placed in the basin, and miniature clothes for the spirit to change into are also prepared. The priest, standing to one side, calls the spirit by waving the Banner for Summoning the Celestial Soul (*zhaohun fan* 召魂旛; see *kaitong minglu*) and conducts the deceased to the bath. When this is done, he burns the miniature clothes and silver paper, signifying that the deceased has been given new clothing.

ASANO Haruji

📖 Lagerwey 1981b, 174–75; Lagerwey 1987c,183–84; Ōfuchi Ninji 1983, 537–40

※ *gongde*; *huanglu zhai*

2. Neidan

In *neidan*, the so-called ablutions are a stage of fire phasing (*huohou*). As their name suggests, they represent a time of purification or decontamination in which Fire and Water neither rise nor descend. *Qi* (pneuma) takes twice this time of rest for each cycle of refining: first during its advancement or expansion along the Control Channel, when it reaches the cyclical character *mao* 卯 (the autumn equinox), i.e., the moment of balance between Yang and Yin before

Yang becomes more powerful; and then during its retraction or contraction along the Function Channel, when it reaches the cyclical character *you* 酉 (spring equinox), i.e., the moment of equality between Yin and Yang before Yin becomes more powerful. (On these two channels, see the entry *dumai and *renmai*.) With reference to the two cyclical characters, the ablutions are often simply called *maoyou* 卯酉.

As the ablutions allow one temporarily to reside at the core of vacuity, they are indispensable "intermediary moments" in fire phasing. Their role is to prevent an adept from becoming attached to external features in the practice of activity (Yang) or inactivity (Yin). Thanks to these pauses, one can both retain and transcend Yin-Yang dualism during the cycles of purification that mark the alchemical transformation. These pauses, therefore, play the role of the Center-Heart of the alchemical Work; they are an ideal space within which one can reiterate and make visible the union of Yin and Yang in order to harvest the fruit that is progressively refined through the practice.

Monica ESPOSITO

📖 Esposito 1997, 46–50; Robinet 1989a, 314–21; Robinet 1995a, 232–33

※ *dumai* and *renmai*; *huohou*; *neidan*

Nanyue

南嶽

Southern Peak

As the name Nanyue indicates, this mountain is the southernmost of the Five Peaks, or Five Marchmounts (*wuyue). Nanyue thus was initially an important site within the imperial cult as a destination on the emperor's ritual progress around the imperium. In occupying the southern position, this mountain has been filled with all the symbolic associations afforded by the *wuxing system of correspondences (red, fire, and so forth). From the fourth and fifth centuries onward, however, Nanyue has been a mountain steeped in both Taoist and Buddhist religious history. While Taoism was officially instituted at the southern peak as part of Tang Xuanzong's (r. 712–56) decree in 726, which stated that the Five Peaks were henceforth to be understood to be under the control of the deities of the *Shangqing Taoist pantheon and that Taoist monasteries were to be built at each of the Five Peaks, Mount Nanyue's Taoist history is much older.

In many sources, Mount Nanyue's connection to Taoism gets mapped back into remote antiquity. Mythical connections were established, for example, in the *Nanyue xiaolu (Short Record of the Southern Peak) between *Chisong zi and Nanyue. The *Yunji qiqian often refers to both as a figure named Nanyue Chisong zi 南嶽赤松子 (e.g., 9.2b and 74.18b). It is unclear when Chisong zi was definitively associated with Nanyue, but the connection is already found in *Tao Hongjing's (456–536) *Zhengao (14.19a). In later centuries, Nanyue's landscape was literally filled with Taoist toponyms: Immortal Peak (Xianfeng 仙峰), Immortal Gathering Peak (Huixian feng 會仙峰), Numinous Mushroom Peak (Lingzhi feng 靈芝峰), Cavern of the Nine Perfected (Jiuzhen dong 九真洞), and Flying Talisman Peak (Feifu feng 飛符峰). Places on the mountain were also included in the expanding network of Taoist sacred sites, as Nanyue was considered to be the home of one Grotto-Heaven and four Blissful Lands (*dongtian and fudi; see *Du Guangting's Dongtian fudi yuedu mingshan ji 洞天福地嶽瀆名山記, CT 599). Significant Taoist abbeys were constructed at Mount Nanyue, and in 738 a Taoist on the mountain was entrusted with the rite of Casting Dragon Tablets (*tou longjian; see the Tang-dynasty inscription "Nanyue toulong gaowen" 南嶽投龍告文 in Chen Yuan 1988, 122, and Chavannes 1919, 56–57). Through the Tang and Song dynasties, Nanyue remained an important site for Taoists, and was associated with a group of nine Taoists who were said to have ascended as transcendents from sites on the mountain (see list under entry for *Nanyue jiu zhenren zhuan*). Mount Nanyue was also the location of a female Taoist cult dedicated to the memory of *Wei Huacun (Despeux 1990, 56–60), and received much imperial patronage during the reign of Song Huizong (r. 1100–1125). In recent years there have been projects to restore Taoist abbeys (*guan* 觀) and Buddhist monasteries (*si* 寺) on Mount Nanyue.

The Southern Peak is now generally understood to refer to Mount Heng, in present-day Hunan province, but this has not always been the case. Through-out history there has been much confusion about the different sites associated with the designation "Nanyue." In addition to Mount Heng (Hunan), other sites that Taoists have considered to be the location of the Southern Peak include: Mount Tianzhu (Tianzhu shan 天柱山, Anhui; see *Hengshan 衡山 and *Huoshan), Mount Tiantai (*Tiantai shan, Zhejiang; see *Huoshan), and Da Huoshan 大霍山 (Fujian; see *Huoshan). During the reign of Han Wudi (r. 141–87 BCE) the designation "Southern Peak" was shifted from Mount Heng (*Hengshan 衡山, Hunan) to Mount Tianzhu (also called Huoshan, Anhui), where rituals directed to the Southern Peak were performed. During the reign of Sui Yangdi (r. 604–17), Mount Heng was restored as the Southern Peak.

The main textual source for Mount Nanyue is the thorough monograph on the site titled *Nanyue zongsheng ji* (Anthology of Highlights of the Southern Peak), which is found in both the Taoist Canon (CT 606) and the Buddhist Canon (T. 2097). Other significant Taoist sources include the *Nanyue xiaolu* and the *Nanyue jiu zhenren zhuan* (Biographies of the Nine Perfected of the Southern Peak; CT 452).

James ROBSON

📖 Boltz J. M. 1987a, 109–10; Robson 1995; Sunayama Minoru 1990, 411–13

※ Hengshan [Hunan]; Huoshan; *wuyue*; *Nanyue jiu zhenren zhuan*; *Nanyue xiaolu*; *Nanyue zongsheng ji*; TAOIST SACRED SITES

Nanyue jiu zhenren zhuan

南嶽九真人傳

Biographies of the Nine Perfected of the Southern Peak

This undated text (CT 452) is attributed to Liao Shen 廖侁 (mid-eleventh century). Based on internal evidence, it appears that Liao compiled his work during the Northern Song dynasty (960–1127). In his preface, he mentions that the contemporary Military Affairs Commissioner (*shumi shi* 樞密使) was Sun

Mian 孫沔, who historical records indicate obtained the *jinshi* degree during the Tianxi reign period (1017–21) of the Song emperor Zhenzong (r. 997–1022). Since the *Nanyue jiu zhenren zhuan* is listed in Zheng Qiao's 鄭樵 (1104–62) *Tongzhi* 通志 (Comprehensive Monographs; van der Loon 1984, 121), it must have been in circulation prior to 1162.

The *Nanyue jiu zhenren zhuan* contains a collection of biographies that detail the practices that led to the attainment of transcendence by nine eminent Taoists associated with Mount *Nanyue (*Hengshan 衡山, Hunan) during the Six Dynasties. The Nine Perfected of Nanyue include: Chen Xingming 陳興明 (?–265), Shi Cun 施存 (?–300), Yin Daoquan 尹道全 (?–315), Xu Lingqi 徐靈期 (?–473 or 474), Chen Huidu 陳慧度 (?–484), Zhang Tanyao 張曇要 (?–494), Zhang Shizhen 張始珍 (?–504), Wang Lingyu 王靈輿 (?–512), and Deng Yuzhi 鄧郁之 (fl. 483–493). These are the same names that were already listed in the Tang dynasty (902) *Nanyue xiaolu (Short Record of the Southern Peak) as having ascended as Perfected from the Southern Peak. Some of the practices connected with these figures are associated with the *Shangqing tradition (Ren Jiyu 1990, 183 and Robinet 1984, 1: 224), and one of them, Xu Lingqi, is mentioned in relation to the dissemination of the *Lingbao scriptures (Bokenkamp 1983, 441). The *Nanyue jiu zhenren zhuan* stresses that the Southern Peak was a particularly efficacious site for undertaking religious practices necessary to ascend as a transcendent.

James ROBSON

※ Nanyue

Nanyue xiaolu

南嶽小錄

Short Record of the Southern Peak

The *Nanyue xiaolu* (CT 453) is a Tang-dynasty record of the sacred sites and Taoist figures at Mount *Nanyue (*Hengshan 衡山, Hunan). Its preface, dated 902, indicates that it was written by a Taoist practitioner at Mount Nanyue named Li Chongzhao 李沖昭 (ninth century; also known as Li Zhongzhao 李仲昭). After the Huang Chao 黃巢 rebellion (874–84), writings concerning Nanyue were becoming dispersed, so Li collected as much information as he could about the site from inscriptions and other scattered documents and recorded them in the *Nanyue xiaolu*.

Following the preface is a section that consists of a narrative of the main highlights of Mount Nanyue. Citing references in the *Zhouli* 周禮 (Rites of the Zhou), and other classical sources, the author emphasizes that Mount Nanyue's status was on par with that of an imperial office holder and that it is a formidable guardian of the South. The text also emphasizes that Mount Nanyue is a sacred realm replete with numinous *qi and with a Grotto-Heaven and Blissful Lands (*dongtian and *fudi*), and that it is an efficacious place to live and practice in order to ascend as a transcendent. The middle portion of the text comprises several sections divided into short detailed entries on each of the five main peaks (*wufeng* 五峰), three streams (*sanjian* 三澗), abbeys, palaces, pavilions, platforms, cloisters, altars, and an entry on the Zhuling 朱陵 Grotto-Heaven. The final section consists of two lists. The first is a list of the "Nine Perfected of the previous generation" (*qiandai jiu zhenren* 前代九真人), whose names agree with those in the *Nanyue jiu zhenren zhuan* (Biographies of the Nine Perfected of the Southern Peak), and the dates and locations on the mountain that they ascended as Perfected. The second is a list of fourteen Taoists at Mount Nanyue who "attained the Dao during the Tang dynasty." Some of the material in the *Nanyue xiaolu* was later incorporated into subsequent monographs on Mount Nanyue, such as the *Nanyue zongsheng ji* (Anthology of Highlights of the Southern Peak). In addition to valuable detailed information on specific Taoist sites at Mount Nanyue, the *Nanyue xiaolu* also contains information on the veneration of *Wei Huacun on the mountain (Schafer 1979, 33).

James ROBSON

📖 Boltz J. M. 1987a, 110

※ Nanyue

Nanyue zongsheng ji

南嶽總勝集

Anthology of Highlights of the Southern Peak

The *Nanyue zongsheng ji* is an extensive record of Mount *Nanyue (*Hengshan 衡山, Hunan) that was compiled by the Song dynasty writer Chen Tianfu 陳田夫 (twelfth century), who wrote a preface to the text dated 1163. Internal evidence indicates, however, that the text was later emended (Boltz J. M. 1987a, 110).

Texts with the title *Nanyue zongsheng ji* are included in both the Taoist and Buddhist canons. The "long" version of the text that is contained in the Taishō canon (T. 2097) is divided into three *juan*. The first contains Chen's "Preface," a brief note on the sources consulted in his compilation, and a short history of the mountain, followed by entries on the main peaks, the locations of the Grotto-Heavens and Blissful Lands (*dongtian* and *fudi*), lists of geographical features (rivers, creeks, springs, and cliffs), cultural relics (altars and *stūpas*), and textual references to Nanyue found in other historical materials (many of which are no longer extant). The second *juan* contains passages on Taoist abbeys (*guan* 觀), cloisters (*yuan* 院), and palaces (*gong* 宮), and on Buddhist monasteries (*si* 寺). There are entries for fourteen abbeys, five cloisters, seven palaces and sixty-three monasteries. This *juan* also contains a short section on botanical information (lists of trees, plants, flowers, herbs, and pharmacological information). The final *juan* contains biographical entries on approximately forty-five eminent Nanyue hermits, including Taoists, Buddhists, and popular local figures.

The "short" version of the *Nanyue zongsheng ji* contained in the *Daozang* (CT 606) is an abridgment of the Taishō edition. The *Daozang* text merely contains twenty-eight entries on Taoist abbeys, courts, and palaces, and all of the Buddhist material has been edited out.

James ROBSON

📖 Boltz J. M. 1987a, 109–10; Robinet 1984, 1: 199, 224, and 233; Robson 1995, 226–27

※ Nanyue

Nanzong

南宗

Southern Lineage

The division of the *neidan* tradition into formal lineages began in the late twelfth century. In the north, then under the Jurchen Jin dynasty, *Wang Zhe (1113–70) and his disciples formed the *Quanzhen order, which emphasized monastic discipline, ascetic practices, and celibacy, and also incorporated some *neidan* practices. The formation of a southern lineage, subsequently known as Nanzong, took place almost a century later. Its putative founder, *Zhang Boduan (987?–1082), is attributed with the main scripture of the lineage, the *Wuzhen pian (Folios on Awakening to Perfection). Zhang reportedly attained enlightenment after he received teachings from a Perfected in Chengdu (Sichuan), identified by the twelfth century as *Liu Haichan. Thus

Zhang's teachings were directly linked to Liu's masters, *Zhongli Quan and
*Lü Dongbin. This triad is also the source of the Quanzhen teachings.

The main representatives of Nanzong after Zhang Boduan are related to
each other through master-disciple transmission of texts and oral teachings.
They are *Shi Tai (?–1158), *Xue Daoguang (1078?–1191), and *Chen Nan (?–1213).
Only toward the end of the Song and the beginning of the Yuan dynasty did
*Bai Yuchan (1194–1229?, a disciple of Chen Nan) and his followers first give
Nanzong the semblance of an organized school. Bai and his disciple, *Peng
Si (fl. 1217–51), founded retreats in renowned religious centers and acquired
a large number of disciples. Some scholars, indeed, suggest that Bai—an
ordained Taoist who combined Zhang Boduan's teachings with the Thunder
Rites (*leifa)—is the actual founder of Nanzong.

The identity of Nanzong. The date at which the term Nanzong was first used
is unclear. The designation Five Patriarchs of the Southern Lineage (*nanzong
wuzu* 南宗五祖) apparently was inspired by the legacy of the Five Patriarchs
(*wuzu* 五祖) and the Seven Perfected (*qizhen* 七真; see table 17) of Quanzhen.
Significantly, when the Yuan rulers bestowed honors on members of the
Quanzhen, *Taiyi, *Zhengyi, and other orders in 1269, no representative of
Nanzong was included: the Five Patriarchs of Quanzhen were given the title
of Perfected Lords (*zhenjun* 真君), while *Qiu Chuji and others received the
title of Perfected (*zhenren*). On the other hand, a thirteenth-century work
compiled by disciples of Bai Yuchan formulates a similar classification, which
possibly was a pious invention of Bai himself (Qing Xitai 1994, 1: 155). It lists
three Perfected Lords, namely, Zhongli Quan, Lü Dongbin, and Liu Haichan,
and five Perfected: Zhang Boduan, Shi Tai, Xue Daoguang, Chen Nan, and
Bai Yuchan (*Haiqiong chuandao ji* 海瓊傳道集; CT 1309, preface, 1b). As the
latter list does not mention the Quanzhen patriarchs, the Nanzong masters
at that time apparently accepted a common origin with Quanzhen but considered themselves different from the latter school. Later, however, a second-
generation disciple of Bai Yuchan, *Li Daochun (fl. 1288–92), gave Nanzong
and Quanzhen the same status by stating that they had a common source
and belonged to the same family. Around 1330, *Chen Zhixu (1290-after 1335)
completed the integration process by subordinating the Five Patriarchs of
Nanzong to the Five Patriarchs and the Seven Perfected of Quanzhen. Thus
Nanzong disappeared as an independent movement and was subsequently
referred to as a part of Quanzhen.

As a whole, the references to a Northern and Southern Lineage (Beizong
北宗) appear to reflect an arbitrary distinction within Quanzhen created in
imitation of the similar division within Chan Buddhism. In fact, although
Nanzong and Quanzhen are frequently mentioned together, the Nanzong
masters were actually linked to or assimilated by other orders as well. For

instance, Bai Yuchan himself, with his Thunder Rites, was associated with both the *Shenxiao and Zhengyi traditions.

Lines of transmission. The disappearance of Nanzong as a separate entity did not lessen the influence of its doctrinal and textual tradition. Two main branches developed from the original lineage. The first is the Pure Cultivation (Qingxiu 清修) branch, which takes Zhang Boduan, Shi Tai, and Xue Daoguang as its earliest representatives. The form of cultivation employed by this branch entailed individual practices to join the complementary principles within the human being and transmute them into the inner elixir. The final goal was to become a "celestial immortal" (*tianxian* 天仙) and transcend all realms of existence. With Chen Nan, Xue Daoguang's disciple, the situation changed: Chen is known to have combined the *neidan* tradition with the Thunder Rites and with healing procedures. His disciple, Bai Yuchan, carried on his teachings.

The second line of transmission within Nanzong is the so-called Joint Cultivation (Shuangxiu 雙修) or Yin-Yang 陰陽 branch, represented by Zhang Boduan, Liu Yongnian 劉永年 (fl. 1138–68), and *Weng Baoguang (fl. 1173). This line is linked to a Tantric interpretation of the *Wuzhen pian*, especially the practice of the joint cultivation (*shuangxiu*) of inner nature and vital force (*xing* and *ming*), Yin and Yang, or male and female. While the goal is the same as that of the Pure Cultivation branch, the initial stage of the practice—the union of Yin and Yang—requires a partner. Although for Zhang Boduan "joint cultivation" originally meant the joint practice of Buddhism (*xing*) and Taoism (*ming*), later commentators of the *Wuzhen pian* interpreted this notion in diverse ways.

The influence of Nanzong can also be seen in the writings of such later masters of *neidan* as *Li Xiyue (1806–56), founder of the Western Branch (Xipai 西派); *Lu Xixing (1520–1601 or 1606), founder of the Eastern Branch (Dongpai 東派); *Liu Yiming (1734–1821), of the *Longmen (Gate of the Dragon) school; *Wu Shouyang (1574–1644) and *Liu Huayang (1735–99), founders of the *Wu-Liu school; and *Zhao Bichen (1860-after 1933), who also belonged to the Wu-Liu school.

Practices. The Nanzong doctrines can be summed up in the phrase *xianming houxing* 先命後性 ("first the vital force, then the inner nature"). Emphasis lies first on the practice of increasing the vital force through methods of self-cultivation, and then on meditation to achieve enlightenment. This is the same system found in the *Zhong-Lü texts, which the *neidan* practices of Nanzong follow to some extent, although their sequence differs according to individual branches and masters. On the other hand, Quanzhen begins with meditation and claims that the life-force will be reinforced naturally. These theoretical distinctions, however, are not always followed by individual masters or schools.

Farzeen BALDRIAN-HUSSEIN

📖 Boltz J. M. 1987a, 173–86; Chen Bing 1985; Chen Guofu 1963, 439–44; Qing Xitai 1988–95, 3: 143–80 and 365–84; Qing Xitai 1994, 1: 155–57; Ren Jiyu 1990, 504–11; Robinet 1997b, 224–25

※ *neidan*; for other related entries see the Synoptic Table of Contents, sec. IV.3 ("Alchemy: Nanzong and Later Related Authors and Texts")

neidan

內丹

inner elixir; inner alchemy

The form of doctrine and practice conventionally known as *neidan* involves a synthesis of theories derived from the cosmological trends of *waidan (external alchemy), metaphysical speculations expressed through the emblems of the *Yijing* and other cosmological patterns, and techniques originally belonging to *yangsheng (Nourishing Life) traditions such as *MEDITATION, breathing (*xingqi), gymnastics (*daoyin), and sexual hygiene (*fangzhong shu). The aim of *neidan* is described as achieving immortality or a state of union with the Dao; this is variously imagined as attaining the rank of a celestial immortal (*tianxian* 天仙), becoming a "celestial official" (*tianguan* 天官) in the otherworldly bureaucracy, joining one's spirit with the Dao (*yu shen he dao* 與神合道), or obtaining "release from the corpse" (*shijie). In all these instances, a *neidan* master is thought not to die, but to undergo a voluntary metamorphosis.

As a general term, *neidan*—usually called in the sources *jindan dao* 金丹道 or Way of the Golden Elixir—is considered to be complementary to *waidan*. However, while *waidan* traditions are attested in China since at least the second century BCE, *neidan* as we know it today is a relatively late development. Some techniques used in *neidan* go back to preimperial times, but its heyday seems to be linked with that of the *Zhouyi cantong qi* and its interpretations during the Tang and the Song dynasties. The increase in popularity of *neidan* largely coincided with the decline of *waidan*.

Schools and texts. The term *neidan* is often believed to have first occurred in the biographies of Deng Yuzhi 鄧郁之 (fl. 483–493) and *Su Yuanming (fl. ca.

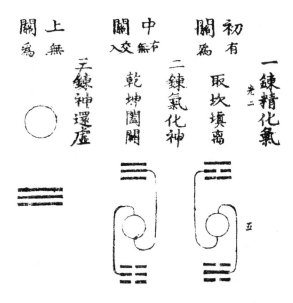

Fig. 59. The *neidan* process represented by trigrams of the
Book of Changes (*Yijing). Right to left: Exchanging the inner
lines of *li* 離 ☲ and *kan* 坎 ☵; joining *qian* 乾 ☰ and *kun* 坤
☷; restoring Oneness, represented by *qian* 乾 ☰. The accompanying text relates these three diagrams to the three stages
of the alchemical process: "refining essence into pneuma,"
"refining pneuma into spirit," and "refining spirit and reverting to Emptiness." *Zhonghe ji (Anthology of Central
Harmony; CT 249), 2.6a-b.

600). It is also found in the vow pronounced in 559 by the Tiantai Buddhist
master Huisi 慧思 (515–77). The authenticity of the relevant passages is doubtful, however (Baldrian-Hussein 1989–90, 164–71). The term was seldom used
throughout the late Tang and Five Dynasties period, which nevertheless saw
the appearance of several individual *neidan* writings in prose, such as those by
*Liu Zhigu (before 663-after 756), Tao Zhi 陶埴 (?–825), and *Peng Xiao (?–955),
and the formation of the two earliest known bodies of *neidan* teachings and
texts, those of the *Zhenyuan and *Zhong-Lü schools.

Use of the term *neidan* became widespread only toward the beginning of
the Song period, when *neidan* evolved into a highly complex system in both its
theoretical and practical aspects. Traditional Chinese ideas on the interdepen-
dence of macrocosm and microcosm, as well as medical theories based on the
*Huangdi neijing (Inner Scripture of the Yellow Emperor), were incorporated
in various forms and with different emphases to form new systems of theory
and practice. The notions of Yin and Yang, *wuxing, essence, pneuma, and

spirit (*jing, qi, shen*) were at the basis of the alchemical discourse, together with the use of the *Yijing* trigrams and hexagrams and with speculations concerning the *Taiji tu* (Diagram of the Great Ultimate). Buddhist (especially Chan) and Confucian doctrines were also often integrated within the system. *Neidan* adepts could thus claim to represent the Three Teachings (Confucianism, Taoism, and Buddhism) since their systems borrowed from a wide gamut of Chinese conceptions.

This new doctrinal background was paralleled by a change in the form of teaching. Originally, the *neidan* adepts did not belong to any particular group of Taoists; they were mostly individuals who practiced the art with the help of a master or followed the instructions of certain texts. With the establishment of the *Quanzhen order, this individual tradition changed. New groups and schools emerged all over China—especially the *Nanzong lineage—offering new interpretations of the most important texts.

While the Tang *neidan* writings were mostly *lun* 論 (discourses or discussions on a topic), Song authors often preferred to present their material as dialogues between master and disciple or in the form of *yulu (recorded sayings). Charts (*tu* 圖) illustrating the macrocosmic/microcosmic processes were also widely used during this period. Another form often employed by *neidan* authors, especially during the Northern Song dynasty, was poetry, the best-known examples of which are the *Ruyao jing, the *Qinyuan chun, and *Zhang Boduan's (987?–1082) *Wuzhen pian.

During the Ming-Qing period, five main *neidan* schools existed:

1. Northern Lineage (Beizong 北宗) or Quanzhen (Complete Perfection), founded by *Wang Zhe (1113–70)

2. Southern Lineage (*Nanzong 南宗), which follows in the footsteps of Zhang Boduan

3. Central Branch (Zhongpai 中派), whose main proponent was *Li Daochun (fl. 1288–92)

4. Western Branch (Xipai 西派), founded by *Li Xiyue (1806–56)

5. Eastern Branch (Dongpai 東派), founded by *Lu Xixing (1520–1601 or 1606)

Several other schools, however, also emerged during the Ming and Qing dynasties, such as the *Wu-Liu and *Longmen schools.

Doctrines and practices. The *neidan* literature uses a metaphorical language addressed to readers on different planes. The texts go into great detail in describing the alchemical process, its ingredients—for instance, red cinnabar and black lead, or lead and mercury, or Dragon and Tiger (*longhu)—and their hierogamies and phases of transmutation; they establish correspondences between the organs and their functions in the human body, the eight trigrams (*bagua*), the *wuxing*, and so forth, in various categorical groups (see fig. 10).

The notion that every human being is at a certain level in the search of enlightenment is expressed by the concept of *yinyuan* 因緣 (causality). *Wu Shouyang writes that the simple fact that one even hears of his text is because one was predestined to encounter it, whereas Zhang Boduan claims that, upon reading his work, anyone at the right level will be immediately enlightened. The preface to the *Lingbao bifa* (Complete Methods of the Numinous Treasure) states that the Dao cannot be expressed in words, and then proceeds to elaborate a whole system of alchemical methods in three levels to be put into practice. At the end of the book, however, a commentator states that the true teaching is not expressed at all in the written word.

Most texts explain the alchemical practice in three levels, sometimes called Three Accomplishments (*sancheng* 三成) or Three Vehicles (*sansheng* 三乘). All agree that the ultimate objective is returning or reverting (*fan, huan* 還) to the Dao and to the Origin. This objective can only be achieved in a state of perfection. Procedures are only needed to help adepts to overcome their own particular deficiencies; as a Zhong-Lü text explains, they are like nets used for fishing that one discards after the fish has been caught.

The basic methods employed in *neidan* do not vary much among the different schools: most authors follow the division into three stages, which in turn correspond to the transformation of the three basic endowments that constitute a human being, namely, essence (*lianjing huaqi* 鍊精化氣, "refining essence into pneuma"), pneuma (*lianqi huashen* 鍊氣化神, "refining pneuma into spirit") and spirit (*lianshen huanxu* 鍊神還虛, "refining spirit and reverting to Emptiness"). The successful practice results in the formation of the inner elixir (*neidan*), or Embryo of Sainthood (*shengtai*), and the realization of the Dao. This is described as a "reversion to the origin" (*huanyuan* 還元) by which adepts transcend all modes of space and time. The ultimate transfiguration occurs when the adept discards his human body.

In more detail, the process can be described as consisting of the following steps: 1. installation of the metaphoric inner "laboratory" ("laying the foundations," *zhuji* 築基); 2. union of Yin and Yang; 3. gathering of the ingredients for the alchemical medicine (*caiyao* 採藥); 4. nourishment of the Embryo of Sainthood through fire phasing (*huohou*); and 5. birth of the new self. This process involves first a cosmic homology that includes various psycho-physiological techniques to homologize the adept with cosmic rhythms and cycles, and to generate a new cosmos out of Chaos. This is followed by an inversion and regression that is expressed as "reversing" (*diandao* 顛倒) the cyclical order or "going against the current" (*niliu* 逆流). This stage is marked by a total withdrawal toward one's center, whereby one reverses the process of decline and gradually reverts back to the Dao. The process is concluded by the dissolution of the cosmos and its reintegration into the Dao and the state of non-differentiation.

Farzeen BALDRIAN-HUSSEIN

📖 Baldrian-Hussein 1989–90; Despeux 1994; Esposito 1997; Katō Chie 2002; Little 2000b, 337–55; Needham 1983; Pregadio 1996; Pregadio 2006a; Pregadio and Skar 2000; Qing Xitai 1994, 1: 330–36; Robinet 1989a; Robinet 1989–90; Robinet 1991; Robinet 1992; Robinet 1995a; Robinet 1997b, 212–56; Sakade Yoshinobu 1988b; Seidel 1989–90, 264–65

※ *jindan*; for other related entries see the Synoptic Table of Contents, sec. IV.3 ("Alchemy")

neiguan

內觀

inner observation; inner contemplation; inner vision

Neiguan is a practice of turning one's eyes inward and seeing the interior state of one's body and mind. The term can indicate seeing colors in the inner organs, visualization of deities, observation of the movements of vital energy, detached analysis of mental activities, and the development of a non-judgmental attitude toward all things. It becomes central in Taoist literature in the Tang dynasty, when it is connected with the Buddhist concept of insight, also expressed with the word *guan* 觀 and indicating the development of wisdom along the lines of the Buddhist teaching, i.e., impermanence, no-self, and suffering.

Unlike Buddhists, however, Taoists continue to emphasize the presence of gods within the body and the importance of physical energy in the practice of *neiguan*. They see the more concrete forms of inner vision as leading gradually to the appreciation of subtler forces and eventually opening up the "observation of emptiness" (*kongguan* 空觀), or the joining of one's conscious vision with the Dao.

Livia KOHN

📖 Kohn 1989b; Robinet 1997b, 202–11; Sakade Yoshinobu 1983b; Sakade Yoshinobu 1988b

※ MEDITATION AND VISUALIZATION

Neijing tu and Xiuzhen tu

內經圖 or 內景圖 · 修真圖

Chart of the Inner Warp (or: Chart of the Inner Landscape); Chart for the Cultivation of Perfection

The *Neijing tu* and the *Xiuzhen tu* are two charts of the human body. They are first mentioned in the Qing period and are probably late, but their origins are unclear. Both charts are cognate to Yanluo zi's 煙蘿子 (tenth century?) diagrams of the body found in the *Xiuzhen shishu* (18.2a–3a; see fig. 12), which include anatomical details but add elements of *neidan* symbolism. A synthesis of Yanluo zi's charts was later drawn on a lateral representation of the body in the *Huangdi bashiyi nanjing zuantu jujie* 黃帝八十一難經纂圖句解 (Charts and Explications on the Scripture of the Eighty-One Difficult Points [in the Inner Scripture] of the Yellow Emperor; preface dated 1269; CT 1024, preface, 4a–b) and in the 1478 edition of the Song-dynasty *Shilin guangji* 事林廣記 (Extensive Records of the Forest of Affairs; see Needham 1983, 110–11). Moreover, some alchemical elements of the body are foreshadowed in two charts that represent the body as a mountain, contained in *Xiao Yingsou's *Duren shangpin miaojing neiyi* 度人上品妙經內義 (Inner Meaning of the Wondrous Scripture of the Upper Chapters on Salvation; CT 90, 8a–b; see fig. 13) and in *Chen Zhixu's *Jindan dayao* (*Tu* 圖; CT 1068, 3a–b). These alchemical elements reappear in the *Neijing tu*.

Inner Landscape. The *Neijing tu* represents a side view of the body. The head is Mount *Kunlun and the spinal cord is a meandering watercourse flowing out from it. The pole star and the Northern Dipper (*beidou*) represent the heart, and the buffalo ploughing and planting the elixir of life represents the intestines. The accompanying text contains the names of the gods of the five viscera (*wuzang*) and the gallbladder according to the *Huangting jing* (Scripture of the Yellow Court) and the symbolism of *neidan*. The chart was engraved in 1886 on a stele in Beijing's *Baiyun guan (Abbey of the White Clouds) on Liu Chengyin's 劉誠印 (or Liu Suyun 劉素雲) initiative, based on an old silk scroll found on Mount Song (*Songshan, Henan). A colored scroll, kept in the Museum of the History of Chinese Traditional Medicine in Beijing, was painted at the Palace of Fulfilled Wishes (Ruyi guan 如意館) of the Imperial Palace during the Qing period.

Cultivation of Perfection. Similar in form to the *Neijing tu*, but representing a front

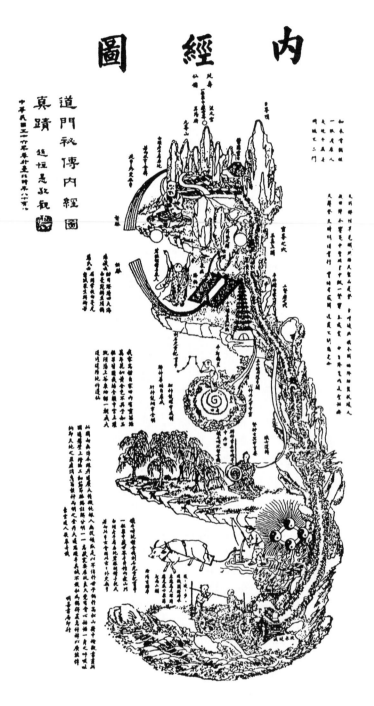

Fig. 60. *Neijing tu* (Chart of the Inner Warp).
*Baiyun guan (Abbey of the White Clouds), Beijing (1886).

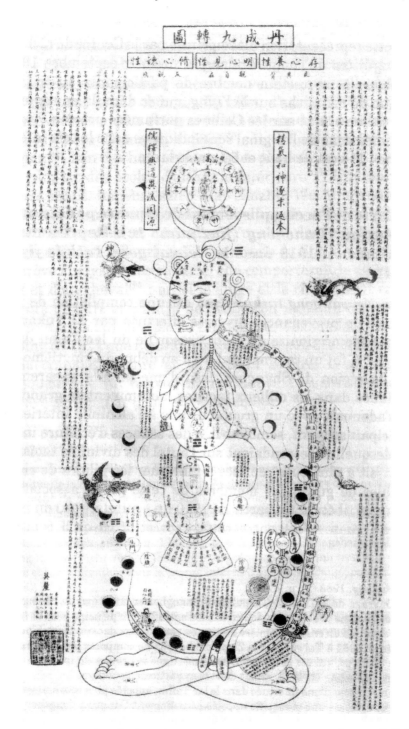

Fig. 61. *Xiuzhen tu* (Chart for the Cultivation of Perfection). *Neiwai gong tushuo jiyao* 內外功圖說輯要 (Essentials of Illustrated Explanations for Inner and Outer Practices; 1920).

view of the body, the *Xiuzhen tu* is richer and includes a longer text. Several versions with different titles are known to have existed in both northern and southern China. At present, the following five versions are known:

1. A stele in the Sanyuan gong 三元宮 (Palace of the Three Primes) in Guangzhou (Canton), engraved in 1812 by Qiu Fengshan 邱鳳山 (also known as Xingzhou 行舟) when the temple abbot was Ning Liyong 寧黎永.

2. A version from Mount Wudang (*Wudang shan, Hubei), printed in 1924 and entitled *Xiuzhen quantu* 修真全圖 (Complete Chart for the Cultivation of Perfection). An earlier version seems to have circulated on Mount Wudang, engraved on wood in 1888 by Wu Mingxuan 吳明玄 of the *Longmen school.

3. The *Dancheng jiuzhuan tu* 丹成九轉圖 (Chart of the Nine Cycles for Achieving the Elixir), printed in the *Neiwai gong tushuo jiyao* 內外功圖說輯要 (Essentials of Illustrated Explanations for Inner and Outer Practices) in 1920. The author of this work, Xi Yukang 席裕康, was a trader active in the Shanghai area.

4. Another *Xiuzhen quantu*, printed by Duan Fu 段甫 in Chengdu in 1922. A copy of this chart was given to Joseph Needham in 1943.

5. The undated *Xiuzhen tu* in Beijing's Baiyun guan. Its inscription reads: "Representation obtained from a friend in the Dao, Guo Yicheng 郭一澄, at the Erxian an 二仙庵 (Hermitage of the Two Immortals), *Qingyang gong (Palace of the Black Ram), Chengdu. Guo took it to Weiyang 維陽 (Yangzhou 揚州, Jiangsu) where I could contemplate it. I had it engraved on wood to circulate it widely."

The various versions of the *Xiuzhen tu* are all associated with the Longmen tradition. The elements that distinguish this chart from the *Neijing tu* are mainly related to the Thunder Rites (*leifa)—in particular, the spiral at the level of the kidneys, the nine "orifices of hell" at the base of the spine, and the three curls at the top of the head that represent the three primordial breaths according to the *Tianxin zhengfa tradition. The chart also represents the main parts of the body, including the Cinnabar Fields (*dantian), the Three Passes (*sanguan, represented by the three chariots) of the back, the throat, the paradisiac and infernal worlds, and the body's divinities according to the *Huangting jing*, and also shows the firing process (*huohou). The whole is reminiscent of a talisman illustrating a divine body that connects to the sacred world.

Catherine DESPEUX

📖 Despeux 1994; Lagerwey 1991, 128–35; Little 2000b, 350–51; Needham 1983,

110–18; Rousselle 1933; Sakade Yoshinobu 1991; Wang D. T. 1991–92; Yamada Toshiaki 1995a

※ *neidan*; *yangsheng*; TAOIST VIEWS OF THE HUMAN BODY

Neiye

內業

Inner Cultivation

A long-overlooked text of classical times, the *Neiye* ("Inner Cultivation" or "Inner Development") is a text of some 1,600 characters, written in rhymed prose, a form close to that of the *Daode jing*. It sometimes echoes that text and the *Zhuangzi*, but it lacks many of the concerns found in those works. Generally dated to 350–300 BCE, it is preserved in the *Guanzi* 管子 (j. 49), along with two later, apparently derivative texts, *Xinshu* 心術 (Arts of the Heart), *shang* 上 and *xia* 下 (j. 36–37).

The *Neiye* had extremely profound effects on Taoism and Chinese culture. It seems to have influenced the form, and certain contents, of the *Daode jing*; the self-cultivation beliefs and practices of many later Taoists (from the *Huainan zi* and *Taiping jing* to the twentieth-century); and certain fundamental concepts of traditional Chinese medicine. It may also have influenced Neo-Confucian ideals of self-cultivation, by way of Mencius' (Mengzi 孟子, ca. 370–ca. 290 BCE) teachings on cultivating the *xin* (heart-mind) and building up *qi* (*Mengzi* 2A.2; trans. Legge 1895, 185–96).

The *Neiye* seems to be the earliest extant text that explains and encourages self-cultivation through daily, practiced regulation of the forces of life. Those forces include *qi* ("life-energy," the universal force that gives life to all things); and *jing* ("vital essence," one's innate reservoir of *qi*). (There is no trace here of the much later Chinese concept that *jing* referred to reproductive fluids.) Like Mencius, the *Neiye* suggests that the *xin* was originally as it should be, but now needs rectification (*zheng*). The *xin* becomes agitated by excessive activity, which leads to dissipation of one's *jing*, resulting in confusion, sickness, and death. To preserve one's health and vitality, one must quieten (*jing*) one's *xin*. Then one can attract and retain *qi*, and other vaguely interrelated forces, such as *shen* ("spirit" or "spiritual consciousness"), and *dao* 道 (a vague term, apparently interchangeable with *shen* and *qi*). (Such concepts are explained more intelligibly in passages of the *Huainan zi*: see Roth 1991a). In the *Neiye*, *shen* and *dao* are external realities, which one must learn to draw into oneself by purifying the body/mind/heart. Since such forces come and go, one must work daily to keep the body well-regulated (e.g., by dietary moderation and proper breathing). But, again like Mencius (and *Daode jing* 55), the *Neiye* warns against forceful efforts to control the *qi*: one cannot make it arrive or stay by an act of will, but only by purifying and realigning oneself. One's ability to achieve those ends is a matter of one's *de* 德, "inner power" (cognate with homonym *de* 得, "get/getting"). If one's *de* is sufficient, one will attract and retain *qi/shen/dao*. Here, *de* retains its general archaic sense of "a proper disposition toward the unseen forces of life," so it also carries moral overtones. (Mencius, for his part, taught building up one's *qi* by acts of "correctness," *yi*.) A person who does these things well is called a "sage" or a "saint" (*shengren*)—the term for the human ideal shared by the *Daode jing* and by Neo-Confucians like Zhu Xi 朱熹 (1130–1200). One finds nothing gender-specific about any of the *Neiye's* concepts, and it is quite conceivable that women as well as men may have engaged in such practices.

To understand the place of the *Neiye's* teachings among the currents of classical China, certain points warrant notice. First, the *Neiye* displays no interest in political matters: unlike the *Daode jing*, which offers lessons for rulers, the *Neiye* gives no such advice. The sage is apparently not assumed either to have or to aspire to political authority. The text does argue that the "gentleman" (*junzi* 君子) who has a well-governed *xin* will transform all around him (suggesting influence by a disciple of Confucius). But there is no mention of such Confucian ideals as *li* 禮 (proper ritual/social behavior) or *ren* 仁 (benevolence). Yet, nowhere does the *Neiye* ridicule Confucian ideals, as the *Daode jing* and *Zhuangzi* do. There is in fact little evidence that the contributors/redactors of the *Neiye* were even acquainted with the concerns of other now-well-known classical "schools." There is no evidence of awareness of the teachings of the Mohists, the Legalists, or the Yin-Yang theorists. The *Neiye* does not share Confucius' and Mozi's belief in *tian* 天 (Heaven) as an agency that had instituted the world's processes, wished certain courses to be followed, and sometimes acted in life's events. In addition, there is no trace in the *Neiye* of certain concerns of others whom we commonly class as "Taoist." For instance, there is no idealization of a simple society or a simple life (as in *Daode jing* 80 and other "Primitivist" passages of that text and *Zhuangzi*). There is also no trace of other ideas found in *Zhuangzi*: there is no critique of language (e.g., as engendering misconceptions of reality); no questioning the capacity of the human mind to comprehend reality; no attack on "conventional" views; and no argument that life is an unrelenting process of change.

There is no trace of the assumption, found in both *Zhuangzi* and the *Daode jing*, that in antiquity people had lived in an ideal manner, and that later generations had somehow "lost the way." And there is no trace in the *Neiye* of several key themes of the *Daode jing*: there is no advice for warriors, no exhortation to engage in "feminine" behaviors; no exhortation to practice non-action (*wuwei); no altruistic moral teachings (e.g., that enlightened self-restraint ultimately benefits self and others alike); no concept of "the Dao" as mother, and no ruminations on "Being" or "Non-being." And there is no teaching that the ideal person is someone radically different from other members of society, someone with a truer knowledge of reality.

Like the *Daode jing*, the *Neiye* is devoid of proper names (personal or geographical, real or fictive), and refers to no specific events (legendary or historic). It was clearly composed to encourage the practice of a fairly specific model of bio-spiritual self-cultivation, which would bring the practitioner into accord with the full realities of life. The continuities of such practices in later Taoism (and segments of Confucianism) need more extensive study.

Russell KIRKLAND

☍ Graham 1989, 100–105; Kirkland 1997b; Rickett 1985–98, 1: 151–79 (trans.); Rickett 1993; Roth 1996, 123–34 (part. trans.); Roth 1999a (trans.)

※ *yangsheng*; MEDITATION AND VISUALIZATION

Nie Shidao

聶師道

844–911; *zi*: Zongwei 宗微; *hao*: Wenzheng xiansheng 問政先生
(Elder of Mount Wenzheng)

Nie Shidao, who came from Shezhou 歙州 (Anhui), belonged to a *Shangqing Taoist lineage based on Mount Tiantai (*Tiantai shan, Zhejiang). From an early age, he devoted himself to the cultivation of the Dao and to dietary practices, and was admired for his virtue and filiality. He became a *daoshi in 857, at the age of thirteen, and received ritual registers (*LU) in 859. Anxious to visit eminent sages, he made pilgrimages to several mountains including Mount Wenzheng (Wenzheng shan 問政山, Anhui) and the Southern Peak (*Nanyue), where he spent some time at the Zhaoxian guan 招仙觀 (Abbey of Summoning the Immortals). He was a disciple of *Lüqiu Fangyuan (?–902), a Taoist recluse associated with the Taoist Canon edition of the *Taiping jing (Scripture of Great Peace).

Yang Xingmi 楊行密 (?–907), who became Prince of Wu 吳 in 902, built for Nie the Xuanyuan gong 玄元宮 (Palace of Mysterious Origin) in Guangling 廣陵 (Jiangsu), and conferred on him the honorific title Xiaoyao dashi 逍遙 大師 (The Great Master of Free and Easy Wandering). Among the over five hundred disciples reportedly gathered by Nie was Wang Qixia 王棲霞 (882–943), who later became the nineteenth patriarch of the Shangqing lineage, thanks to Nie's support (Sakauchi Shigeo 1988).

Grégoire ESPESSET

📖 Qing Xitai 1994, 1: 294

※ Lüqiu Fangyuan; Shangqing

Ning Benli

寧本立

1101–81; *zi*: Daoli 道立; *hao*: Zanhua xiansheng 贊化先生 (Elder Who Assists Transformation); also known as Ning Quanzhen 寧全真

Ning Benli, the first codifier of the *Lingbao dafa (Great Rites of the Numinous Treasure) tradition of Taoist ritual, was from Kaifeng (Henan), the capital of the Northern Song dynasty. He reportedly studied the writings of various ancient schools of thought, medicine, pharmacology, prognostication arts, and other esoteric and technical disciplines, and was a disciple of Tian Sizhen 田思真, a Taoist master of Mount Tiantai (*Tiantai shan, Zhejiang). According to Hong Mai's 洪邁 (1123–1202) *Yijian zhi* 夷堅志 (Heard and Written by Yijian), Ning's ritual and exorcistic activities in the Tiantai area had already won him a reputation by 1154. Song Gaozong (r. 1127–62) granted him the honorific title Dongwei gaoshi 洞微高士 (Eminent Master Pervading the Subtlety), and his disciples called him Kaiguang jiuku zhenren 開光救苦真人 (The Perfected Who Spreads Radiance and Relieves Suffering).

Ning is deemed to have received codifications and liturgical material traditionally traced to *Lu Xiujing (406–77), the major codifier of the early Lingbao tradition. Two compendiums in the Taoist Canon describe his ritual practices. The first is the *Shangqing lingbao dafa (Great Rites of the Numinous Treasure of Highest Clarity; CT 1221), compiled by Wang Qizhen 王契真 (fl. ca. 1250), where Ning's teachings appear in *juan* 66. The second work is the *Lingbao lingjiao jidu jinshu (Golden Writings for Deliverance by the Sect Leader of the Numinous Treasure Tradition) in 320 *juan*, edited by Lin Weifu 林偉夫 (1239–1302). The preface to this work—the largest ritual collection in the Taoist Canon—contains an account of its transmission, in which Ning seems to have played a major role.

Grégoire ESPESSET

📖 Boltz J. M. 1987a, 43–45; Qing Xitai 1994, 1: 326–27

※ *Lingbao lingjiao jidu jinshu*; *Shangqing lingbao dafa*; Lingbao dafa

Nippon dōkyō gakkai

日本道教學會

Japanese Association of Taoist Studies

The Nippon dōkyō gakkai was founded in October 1950 by a group of fourteen scholars, including Fukui Kōjun 福井康順 (chairman), Kimura Eiichi 木村英一, Kubo Noritada 窪德忠, Murakami Yoshimi 村上嘉實, Sakai Tadao 酒井忠夫, Tsukamoto Zenryū 塚本善隆, and Yoshioka Yoshitoyo 吉岡義豊, with the purpose of "promoting wide-ranging research on Taoism and the popular religion and culture of East Asia." The Association's journal, *Tōhō shūkyō* 東方宗教 (Journal of Eastern Religions), was inaugurated in December 1951 and has been published biannually since then.

The Association has greatly contributed to the study of Taoism in Japan and abroad. Its annual conference attracts reports which are then published in *Tōhō shūkyō*. Since 1989, moreover, the Japan Association of Taoist Research Prize has been offered to young scholars whose articles, submitted to *Tōhō shūkyō*, have been judged the best. In 1985, the Association celebrated its thirty-fifth anniversary with a symposium on "The State of Taoist Studies and Its Issues." In November 1999, the fiftieth anniversary was celebrated with a lecture series on "Taoism and Popular Cults in East Asia."

In 2003, the Association's membership had reached around 600, including some fifty non-Japanese scholars. The current chairman (2004) is Horiike Nobuo 堀池信夫 of the University of Tsukuba.

SAKADE Yoshinobu

niwan

泥丸

Muddy Pellet

The *niwan* or Muddy Pellet is one of the Nine Palaces (*jiugong) in the head (see fig. 62). Starting from (1) the Hall of Light (*mingtang gong* 明堂宮; see *mingtang) located one inch (*cun* 寸) behind the point between the eyes, and

Fig. 62. The Nine Palaces of the Mud Pellet (*niwan*).
(a) *Shangqing lingbao dafa* (Great Rites of the Numinous Treasure of Highest Clarity; CT 1221), 3.23a. (b) *Jiugong zifang tu* 九宮紫房圖 (Charts of the Purple Rooms of the Nine Palaces; CT 156), 1b. (c) Diagram showing the arrangement of the nine palaces or "rooms." The leftmost palace in the lower row is located between the eyebrows. The upper Cinnabar Field (*dantian*) proper is the third palace in the lower row. Reproduced from Noguchi Tetsurō et al. 1994, 422.

(2) the Cavern Chamber (*dongfang gong* 洞房宮) two inches behind that point, one finds (3) the Muddy Pellet (*niwan gong* 泥丸宮) three inches further inside. The other Palaces are (4) the Palace of the Flowing Pearl (*liuzhu gong* 流珠宮) and (5) the Palace of the Jade Emperor (*Yudi gong* 玉帝宮), respectively located four and five inches inside; (6) the Celestial Court (*tianting gong* 天庭宮), one inch above the Hall of Light; (7) the Palace of Ultimate Reality (*jizhen gong* 極真宮), one inch above the Palace of the Jade Emperor; (8) the Palace of Mysterious Cinnabar (*xuandan gong* 玄丹宮), one inch above the *niwan*; and (9) the Palace of the Great Sovereign (*Taihuang gong* 太皇宮), one inch above the Palace of the Flowing Pearl.

Since the *niwan* occupies the central position in the head, it is also regarded as the sum total of the Nine Palaces. This may be the origin of its name: contrary to the interpretation of Henri Maspero (1981, 457), who deemed *niwan* to derive from the Sanskrit term *nirvāṇa*, Ishida Hidemi (1987a, 219) has suggested that it may allude to the round form (*wan* 丸 or "pellet") of the brain and to the central agent Soil (*ni* 泥 or "mud"). Other names of the *niwan* allude to its centrality. For example, *Bai Yuchan states in his *Ziqing zhixuan ji* 紫清指玄集 (Anthology on Pointing to the Origin by the Master of Purple Clarity; *Daozang jinhua lu* ed., 4b): "In the head there are Nine Palaces that communicate with the Nine Heavens (*jiutian) above. In the center there is the Palace called *niwan*, Yellow Court (*huangting* 黃庭), *Kunlun, or Tiangu 天谷 or Celestial Valley." As an image of Heaven within the body, the *niwan* is called the Yellow Court because it embodies the qualities of center, where all transformations take place. Since the center is located on the vertical axis that connects Heaven to Earth and Humanity, the *niwan* is also called "Kunlun," a term that usually denotes the *axis mundi*. Hence the *niwan* is the Upper Cinnabar Field (Heaven), related to the Lower (Earth) and Middle (Humanity) Cinnabar Fields (see *dantian*). It is "the One that connects the Three" (*yi guan santian* 一貫三田).

Under the name *baihui* 百會 (lit., "one hundred gatherings"), the *niwan* is the starting and arrival point of the circuit established by the Control Channel and the Function Channel (*dumai and renmai*; fig. 31). Incorporating the Control Channel at its uppermost point at the crown of the head, it is the sanctuary in which the Yang Spirit (*yangshen* 陽神) is stored before its return to emptiness (see *chushen*).

Monica ESPOSITO

📖 Despeux 1994, 130–33; Kakiuchi Tomoyuki 1998; Maspero 1981, 455–57; Robinet 1984, 1: 125–26; Yamada Toshiaki 1988a

※ *dantian*; *mingtang*; TAOIST VIEWS OF THE HUMAN BODY

nüdan

女丹

inner alchemy for women

One of the earliest references to *neidan* practices for women is found in *Xue Daoguang's (1078?–1191) commentary to the *Wuzhen pian* (in *Wuzhen pian sanzhu* 悟真篇三注; CT 142, 2.4a), but the sources for women's alchemical practices can be traced to the texts on sexual techniques (*fangzhong shu*). A description of how women have to practice in different ways than men is included, for instance, in the biography of Peijun 裴君 (Lord Pei; YJQQ 105.3b) as part of the transmission of longevity practices for men and women (*nannü keyi changsheng zhi dao* 男女可以長生之道). A *neidan* literature specifically devoted to women, however, developed only between the end of the Ming and the beginning of the Qing dynasties. While the general principles of *nüdan* are the same as those of *neidan* for men, there are differences reflecting the female nature and physical constitution.

Since a woman's congenital energy is based on blood, the first stage of the alchemical practice for her consists of the sublimation of blood into *qi* (pneuma). This sublimation, known as the Beheading of the Red Dragon (*zhan chilong*), is meant to stop the physiological hemorrhage that harms a woman each month by causing her to lose creative energy. The sublimation of blood into *qi* is the counterpart of the sublimation of the seminal essence (*jing*) into *qi* by a male adept: the "essential blood" (*jingxue* 精血) or Red Dragon (*chilong* 赤龍) in a woman is the opposite and complementary aspect of the "spiritual vitality" (*shenqi* 神氣) or White Tiger (*baihu* 白虎) in a man.

Moreover, while the White Tiger, as a male or igneous Water, resides in a man's testicles, the Red Dragon, as a feminine or aqueous Fire, resides in a woman's breasts. This explains why a man and a woman begin their practices from exactly opposite Cinnabar Fields (*dantian*). A woman first must concentrate on the Brook of Milk (*ruxi* 乳溪) in the center of her chest (also known as *qixue* 氣穴 or Cavity of Pneuma), and gently massage her breasts to activate the circulation of blood and *qi*. The breasts are regarded as the receptacle of pure secretions that can enrich her natural endowment of *qi*. Once purified, blood descends to the lower Cinnabar Field (at the level of the navel) and is transformed into *qi*. By contrast, since a man's constitutional energy is associated with his seminal essence and his genital organs (which are in turn related to the kidneys), the process for him begins with concentration on the lower Cinnabar Field (also called *qixue*). After having gradually accumulated and purified his essence, he can sublimate it into *qi* and lead it to the upper Cinnabar Field (at the level of the brain).

This different placement is related to the traditional theories of sexual reproduction. While menstrual blood and seminal essence are the basic ingredients of human procreation, in the inverted world of the alchemical work they are used to generate the immortal embryo (*shengtai, Embryo of Sainthood). For that purpose, the two ingredients must invert their natures and go against the laws that govern the ordinary world, to return to their state "before Heaven" (*xiantian). A woman therefore should work on her blood before it is transformed into menses, and a man on his essence before it becomes sperm. These pure ingredients thus represent the reservoirs of power, the *materia prima* for the alchemical work, while in their impure form they are simply synonyms of sterility, death, and the incapacity of generating. This explains why a woman should concentrate on the premenstrual phase of her cycle—some texts specify two and half days before—and stop practicing during menstruation. The premenstrual phase represents for her the moment to catch the Pure Yin (*chunyin* 純陰), just as the preejaculation moment is for a man the time to catch the Pure Yang (*chunyang* 純陽).

One can thus understand the meaning of practices such as the Beheading of the Red Dragon, which for women consists of "stopping the menstrual blood." Its counterpart for men is called Taming the White Tiger (*jiang baihu* 降白虎) and consists of "stopping the spermatic flow." This "stopping" marks the distinction between the ordinary procreation of those who follow the normal course of events and generate another human being (*shun* 順, lit., "continuation"), and the transcendent procreation of those who, by mastering this course and by reversing it, are capable of re-generating themselves (*ni* 逆, lit., "inversion"). The stage of the Beheading of the Red Dragon in inner alchemy for women provides therefore full control over time and body—as does the control of seminal essence in masculine alchemy—since it is the emblem of the mastery of passions and of all "emotional and discursive outflows."

After this stage, a woman follows the same three-stage process as in *neidan* for men. She thus gains access to the stage of convergence of all contraries, in which there is no longer any distinction between practices for men and women. The *nüdan* texts describe a woman deprived of sexual attributes and endowed with an androgynous body; the retraction of breasts corresponds the retraction of testicles in a man. The Beheading of the Red Dragon, however, corresponds only to the Lesser Celestial Circuit (*xiao zhoutian* 小周天; see *zhoutian) if a woman limits herself exclusively to the physiological results of the practice. According to *neidan* principles, a woman must also realize the Greater Celestial Circuit (*da zhoutian* 大周天) in order to produce the Embryo of Immortality.

Monica ESPOSITO

📖 Despeux 1990; Esposito 1998a; Esposito 2004a; Wile 1992, 192–219

※ *jindan*; *neidan*; WOMEN IN TAOISM

Nüqing guilü

女青鬼律

Demon Statutes of Nüqing

The *Nüqing guilü*, in six *juan* (CT 790), is a text of the Way of the Celestial Masters (*Tianshi dao) that probably dates to the fourth century. The date is suggested by its eschatological vision, which seems to be inspired by Buddhism, and by the use of the term "seed-people" (*zhongmin). Neither of these themes appears in Taoist literature before 360 CE. At the same time, the *Nüqing guilü* does not mention the doctrine of the Three Heavens (see *santian and *liutian*), central to the Celestial Masters tradition of the Liu Song dynasty, thus suggesting a pre-fifth-century date.

The text begins with a description of the decline the world is entering, with harmful energies in all five directions, as well as innumerable predators and reptiles. Demons are said to be flying about everywhere, people are dying, and the good order of the world has disintegrated. In fact, demons number in the billions and no one is safe from them any longer.

In response to this situation, the text provides detailed instructions on how to keep demons at bay. It lists the names, appearances, and exact locations of demons, describing, for example, the third elder demon of Southvillage (Nanfang 南方), with his name Che Ni 車匿, his location in the northwest and his activity as manager of the records of the dead (1.1b–2a). Similarly, the demon of Great Harmony (Taihe 太和) has a head but no body and a frightening appearance; his name is Zibei 子碑 (2.6a). Calling out the names of the demons at a moment of crisis will keep them away or force them to appear in their true shapes. Reciting lists of names in a formal liturgy over a period of time will ensure good fortune and freedom from their nasty effects.

As the world approaches its end, those who do not know the names of the demons and do not practice Taoism will be exterminated through war, starvation, and disease. Eventually the world will be cleansed so that the new era of the Dao can begin. Then, Great Peace (*taiping*) will rule everywhere and the faithful will return to their country of origin.

Livia KOHN

📖 Kobayashi Masayoshi 1990, 376–78, 415–20; Lai Chi-tim 2002; Strickmann 2002, 79–88

※ APOCALYPTIC ESCHATOLOGY; DEMONS AND SPIRITS

Pan Shizheng

潘師正

585–682; *zi*: Zizhen 子真

Pan Shizheng, the eleventh *Shangqing patriarch or Grand Master (*zongshi* 宗師), was the spiritual heir of *Wang Yuanzhi, and the transmitter of Wang's authority to *Sima Chengzhen, the greatest of all Tang Taoists.

Pan's life is known from biographies in the Standard Histories (*Jiu Tangshu*, 192.5126; *Xin Tangshu*, 196.5605) and in Taoist sources (e.g., *Lishi zhenxian tidao tongjian*, 25.4b–7b; *Maoshan zhi*, 11.1a–2a). The standard biographies report that during the reign of Sui Yangdi (r. 604–17), Pan took ordination as a *daoshi* and studied under Wang, then lived for many years as a recluse on Mount Song (*Songshan, Henan), the "Central Peak" near Luoyang. From 676 to 683, he received several visits from Tang Gaozong (r. 649–83) and Empress Wu (r. 690–705). Gaozong apparently sought to glorify himself by associating with an "honored recluse" (Kirkland 1992–93, 153–56), but as in certain other cases, the association seems to have been less substantial than the ruler wished.

The Taoist biographies report that in 676 Gaozong requested "talismans and texts" (*fushu* 符書), but that Pan refused. The Standard Histories do not mention this event, though we know that Tang Xuanzong (r. 712–56) later received such a transmission from Sima Chengzhen. Scholars have speculated as to why Pan would have denied Gaozong's request (e.g., Benn 1977, 49–50). On one level, the issue seems to be one of great political significance, since the conveyance of such materials had for centuries signified religious sanction of a worthy ruler (Seidel 1983a; Kirkland 1997a). If Pan did refuse Gaozong such materials, the implication would have been that Gaozong's reign was spiritually deficient. Some have suggested (Benn 1977, 50) that Pan declined because the Empress Wu was already exercising more power than was acceptable in a sanctified reign. But more innocent explanations are possible. For instance, the talismans of the Shangqing order consisted primarily of diplomas that certified a certain degree of spiritual attainment on the recipient's part. Perhaps Pan merely judged Gaozong insufficiently advanced in spiritual matters to receive such certification. Or perhaps Pan was just reluctant to involve himself in politics, like Sima's successor, *Li Hanguang (see Kirkland 1986b). It is also conceivable that the Taoist reports of the incident were merely reflections of events concerning Sima, Li or similar figures of the period.

Though no writings are attributed to Pan, the *Daozang* preserves a purported colloquy between him and Gaozong, the *Daomen jingfa xiangcheng cixu* 道門 經法相承次序 (The Scriptures and Methods of Taoism in Orderly Sequence; CT 1128). Barrett (1996, 38–39) notes that the opening section summarizes basic elements of Taoist belief and practice; the conclusion constitutes a glossary of Taoist terms; and the body of the work reports Pan's answers to Gaozong's questions about the number and organization of the Taoist heavenly beings. The actual provenance of the text remains uncertain.

The standard biographies report that when Pan died in 682, both Gaozong and Empress Wu "brooded over it endlessly." They granted Pan a noble rank, and canonized him as the Elder Who Embodies the Mystery (Tixuan xian-sheng 體玄先生). But it remains unclear whether he ever welcomed imperial attentions. The data suggest that he may have been little more than a coveted worthy, whose true importance derived from his associations with Wang Yuanzhi and Sima Chengzhen.

Russell KIRKLAND

📖 Barrett 1996, 38–39; Benn 1977, 49–50; Chen Guofu 1963, 50–52; Kirkland 1986b, 44; Qing Xitai 1988–95, 2: 128–32

※ Shangqing

Pantao gong

蟠桃宮

Palace of the Peaches of Immortality (Beijing)

The Pantao gong was a famous Taoist temple in Beijing that is no longer extant today. Its full name, Huguo taiping Pantao gong 護國太平蟠桃宮 (Palace of the Peaches of Immortality for Protecting the State and Great Peace), reveals its association with the Queen Mother of the West (*Xiwang mu), in whose garden grew the peaches of immortality. The temple was located on the eastern end of the Great East Avenue (Dong dajie 東大街) in Beijing's Chongwen 崇文 district, i.e., inside Dongbian Gate (Dongbian men 東便門), south of the bridge across the city moat. Construction was begun during the Ming dynasty, but the temple was rebuilt in 1662.

In the front and rear pavilions inside the temple compound, ceremonies were offered to the Queen Mother of the West and the Mother of the Dipper (*Doumu), respectively. In front of the temple gate there were flagpoles and stone lions; on the side walls of the compound were inlays of glazed yellow tiles with green edges on which the four characters *pantao shenghui* 蟠桃盛會, "Great Assembly of the Peaches of Immortality," were written. At the temple gate, ceremonies were offered to *Wang lingguan. Inside the two halls, all kinds of divinities and immortals were revered.

During the Ming, Qing, and Republican periods, from the first to the third days of the third lunar month, a great festival at the Pantao gong celebrated the birthday of the Queen Mother of the West. According to the records, seventy to eighty percent of Beijing's citizens visited the festival, which indicates that the temple attracted an extremely large number of worshippers. The festival drew a variety of entertainment and amusements, and the stalls of street peddlers offering all sorts of goods stretched over a length of three *li* (about 1.5 km). In 1987, the Pantao gong was destroyed to make way for a construction project by the city government.

CHEN Yaoting

※ TEMPLES AND SHRINES

Peng Dingqiu

彭定求

1645–1719; *zi*: Qinzhi 勤止, Nanyun 南畇; *hao*: Shougang daoren 守綱道人 (The Taoist Who Guards The Guideline), Yongzhen shanren 詠真山人 (The Mountain Man Who Chants The Truth)

Peng Dingqiu was born in Changzhou 長洲 (Jiangsu) to a family of military descent. After he obtained his *jinshi* degree in 1676 or 1686 (*Qingshi gao* 304 and 480, respectively), he served as a Senior Compiler (*xiuzhuan* 修撰) at the Hanlin Academy in Beijing. In 1689 he returned to Changzhou to visit his ailing father, who died before he arrived there. Peng joined the Hanlin Academy again in 1693, but soon decided to retire to Changzhou and devote himself to self-cultivation. One of the first activities he organized in his hometown was a vegetarian society, modeled after the Doufu hui 豆腐會 (Association of Bean Curd Eaters) founded by Gao Panlong 高攀龍 (1562–1626; DMB 701–10).

Peng's main contribution to Taoist studies is the original edition of the *Daozang jiyao*. His role in the compilation of this collection has been questioned by several scholars, but was recently reasserted (Qing Xitai 1988–95, 4: 455–61). Apparently Peng began to work on the *Daozang jiyao* soon after he retired from his official post in 1693. At the same time he produced various types of works that yield an image of him as both a Confucian scholar and a Taoist devotee. These include the *Gaowang yin* 高望吟 (Chant of High Aspirations), the *Yinyang shihui lu* 陰陽釋毀錄 (Account of the Defamation of Buddhism according to Yin and Yang), and the *Rumen fayu* 儒門法語 (Exemplary Sayings of the Confucian School). Peng's interest in Taoism is also witnessed by his edition of the *Zhenquan* 真詮 (Veritable Truth), a text by the Ming author Yang Daosheng 陽道生, completed in 1710.

Elena VALUSSI

📖 Qing Xitai 1988–95, 4: 455–61; Suter 1943–44; Yoshioka Yoshitoyo 1955, 175–76; Zhu Yueli 1992, 327–38

※ *Daozang jiyao*

Peng Haogu

彭好古

fl. 1597–1600; *zi*: Bojian 伯籛; *hao*: Yihe jushi 一壑居士
(Retired Gentleman of the One Ocean)

Not much is known about Peng Haogu, a native of Xiling 西陵 (Hubei). According to the prefaces in his *Daoyan neiwai bijue quanshu* 道言內外祕訣全書 (Complete Writings of Secret Instruction on Inner and Outer Taoist Teachings), he was a follower of the Pure Cultivation (*qingxiu* 清修) branch of *Nanzong. In the preface to this compendium, which was completed between 1597 and 1600, Peng Haogu states: "When Confucius speaks of *xing* and *ming* (inner nature and life), he explains only the shadow (*ying* 影) but not the form (*xing*); when the Buddha explains *xing* and *ming*, *xing* is the form, *ming* is the shadow; when Laozi explains *xing* and *ming*, he explains shadow and form together." Peng's collection thus emulates the way of Laozi conceived of as a complete illustration of Taoist teachings.

The *Daoyan*—as the collection is often known for short—is divided into Inner and Outer Teachings (*neiyan* 內言 and *waiyan* 外言). The Inner Teachings include texts in prose and verse, in turn arranged into two sets. The first set contains such texts as the *Daode jing*, the *Yinfu jing*, the *Qingjing jing*, the *Dingguan jing*, the *Duren jing*, the *Wuchu jing*, the *Xinyin jing*, and the *Taixi jing*. The second set contains *neidan works such as the *Ruyao jing*, the *Zhong-Lü chuandao ji*, the *Lingbao bifa*, and the *Jindan sibai zi*. The Outer Teachings, on the other hand, contain among others the *Longhu jing*, the *Guwen Zhouyi cantong qi*, and the *Wuzhen pian*, as well as works attributed to *Xu Xun and

*Bai Yuchan. Several of these texts include Peng Haogu's own commentaries. The entire collection is reprinted in the *Zangwai daoshu* (vol. 6).

Farzeen BALDRIAN-HUSSEIN

※ *neidan*

Peng Si

彭耜

fl. 1217–51; *zi*: Jiyi 季益; *hao*: Helin 鶴林 (Crane Forest)

This heir to an important Fuzhou (Fujian) clan based in Sanshan 三山, Changle 長樂, was, together with the equally well-bred Liu Yuanchang 留元長 (fl. 1217–37) from Jinjiang 晉江 (Fujian), part of the core pair of *Bai Yuchan's (1194–1229?) disciples who did the most to promote his teachings in elite circles during the last half-century of Song rule. Growing up in a literati family, Peng only realized his true calling—studying inner alchemy (*neidan*), Thunder Rites (*leifa*), and the Divine Empyrean (*Shenxiao*) tradition—after meeting master Bai Yuchan around 1215. Peng and his closest disciple, Pan Changji 盤常吉 (like Liu and his main follower, Zhou Xiqing 周希清) seem to have entered the religious life after their initiation (with several others) by Bai Yuchan late in 1218. Bai also presided over a funerary ceremony for Peng's father, Peng Yan 彭演, in 1222. After his initiation, Peng set up a retreat he called the Helin jing 鶴林靖 (Quiet of the Crane Forest), where he continued his studies in the teachings of Confucius and Laozi, and also successfully treated the afflicted in his area with talismans (*FU) and ritual.

Peng and Liu had assembled forty *juan* of their master's works for publication by 1237 and had enlisted the scholar-official Pan Fang 盤枋 to write a preface. Finally, in 1251, Peng added a colophon to the collected correspondence he and his fellow disciples had exchanged with their master over the years (*Haiqiong Bai zhenren yulu* 海瓊白真人語錄; CT 1307, 4.21b). Peng also compiled the *Chongbi danjing* (Scripture of the Elixir for Piercing the Jasper Heaven) on behalf of his master Bai and a Sichuan patron interested in alchemy named Meng Xu 孟煦, who approached him several times in the early 1220s.

Besides loyally following and promoting Bai Yuchan and his teachings, Peng was also an important scholar of the *Daode jing*. He produced a series of texts on this scripture that continue where the Northern Song scholar *Chen Jingyuan's efforts left off. The main text, which gathers parts of twenty different commentaries from the eleventh and twelfth centuries, is the eighteen-*juan*

Daode zhenjing jizhu 道德真經集注 (Collected Commentaries to the Authentic Scripture of the Dao and Its Virtue; CT 707). Peng's 1229 preface refers to a twelve-*juan* version of the work. Two supplementary works, the *Daode zhenjing jizhu shiwen* 道德真經集注釋文 (Exegesis to Collected Commentaries to the Authentic Scripture of the Dao and Its Virtue; CT 708) and the *Daode zhenjing jizhu zashuo* 道德真經集注雜說 (Miscellaneous Discussions to Collected Commentaries to the Authentic Scripture of the Dao and Its Virtue; CT 709), provide clues on the sources and approach employed by Peng, and show how Laozi has both been revered by the state and provided a textual model for sagely governance.

Lowell SKAR

📖 Boltz J. M. 1987a, 219–21

※ *neidan*

Peng Xiao

彭曉

?–955; *zi*: Xiuchuan 秀川; *hao*: Zhenyi zi 真一子
(Master of the Authentic One)

A native of Yongkang 永康 (Sichuan), Peng Xiao changed his original surname, Cheng 程, to Peng out of reverence for *Pengzu (*Lishi zhenxian tidao tongjian*; 43.7b–8a). He served the Shu dynasty first as Magistrate of the Jintang 金堂 district, and later as Vice Director of the Ministry of Rites and as Military Supervisor. His works include the *Zhouyi cantong qi fenzhang tong zhenyi* 周易參同契分章通真義 (Real Meaning of the *Zhouyi cantong qi*, with a Division into Sections; CT 1002), the *Huandan neixiang jin yaoshi* 還丹內象金鑰匙 (Golden Key to the Inner Images of the Reverted Elixir; YJQQ 70.1a–14a), and a lost commentary to the *Yinfu jing (Scripture of the Hidden Accordance).

Peng Xiao's exegesis of the *Zhouyi cantong qi*, completed in 947, is remarkable not only for his commentary but also for the version of the *Cantong qi* that he edited, which represents a watershed between the text found in the two earlier Tang commentaries (see under *Zhouyi cantong qi*) and most later versions. Peng submitted the text of the *Cantong qi* to a substantial rearrangement, dividing it into ninety sections, placing the "Song of the Tripod" ("Dingqi ge" 鼎器歌) in a separate *pian*, relocating several lines, and changing many individual words. His work, moreover, contains an appendix entitled "Chart of the Bright Mirror" ("Mingjing tu" 明鏡圖), a diagram complete with explanatory notes that illustrates several cosmological devices used in the *Cantong qi* (see Needham 1983, 55–59). In the Taoist Canon, the chart is printed with the final sections of the *Cantong qi* as a separate work entitled *Zhouyi cantong qi dingqi ge mingjing tu* 周易參同契鼎器歌明鏡圖 (The "Song of the Tripod" and the "Chart of the Bright Mirror" of the *Zhouyi cantong qi*; CT 1003), but both Peng Xiao's preface and the other extant editions of his commentary show that the two texts originally formed a single work.

The extent of the variations that Peng Xiao brought to the text of the *Cantong qi*, however, is difficult to ascertain. In 1208, the astronomer Bao Huanzhi 鮑澣之 (fl. 1207–1210) reedited Peng's work based on Zhu Xi's 朱熹 (1130–1200) recension for the text of the *Cantong qi* (**Zhouyi cantong qi kaoyi*), and on Zheng Huan's 鄭煥 (fl. 1142?) lost edition for Peng's own notes. He followed, however, other editions when they agreed with each other against those of Zhu Xi and Zheng Huan. Judging from the examples that Bao provides of his alterations (CT 1003, 6b–8a), Peng's original text appears to have been closer to the Tang text of the *Cantong qi* than it is now. Further evidence of alterations is provided by a quotation from the lost commentary by Zhang Sui 張隨, who lived one century after Peng Xiao (CT 1003, 1a).

The *Fenzhang tong zhenyi* is the first extant *neidan commentary to the *Cantong qi*, and a major source for the study of the *neidan* traditions before the rise of the Southern Lineage (*Nanzong). It was held in high esteem by the Southern Lineage, as shown, for instance, by quotations in the commentary to the *Wuzhen pian (Folios on Awakening to Reality) found in *j.* 26–30 of the *Xiuzhen shishu, and in the *Wuzhen pian zhushu* 悟真篇注疏 (Commentary and Subcommentary to the *Wuzhen pian*; CT 141). Moreover, the three-*juan* anonymous *neidan* commentary in the Taoist Canon (*Zhouyi cantong qi zhu* 周易參同契注; CT 1000) follows Peng Xiao's recension so faithfully that it may serve to verify the accuracy of the various editions of Peng's work.

Fabrizio PREGADIO

📖 Li Dahua 1996; Meng Naichang 1993a, 41–44; Qing Xitai 1988–95, 2: 521–33; Qing Xitai 1994, 1: 288–89; Robinet 1995a, 36–39

※ *neidan*

Penglai

蓬萊

Belief in the existence of the paradisiacal isles Penglai, Fangzhang 方丈, and Yingzhou 瀛洲 in the seas off China's eastern coast originated in the coastal populations of the ancient states of Yan 燕 and Qi 齊 (modern Shandong).

Finding these mountain isles became a special preoccupation of rulers like Kings Wei (Weiwang 威王, r. 334–320 BCE) and Xuan (Xuanwang 宣王, r. 319–301 BCE) of Qi, King Zhao (Zhaowang 昭王, r. 311–279 BCE) of Yan, Qin Shi huangdi (r. 221–210 BCE; see *Xu Fu), and Han Wudi (r. 141–87 BCE), who believed they could attain immortality by consuming the isles' herbs. When Wudi had the artificial lake Taiye 太液 (Great Fluid) dredged near the Jianzhang 建章 Palace, its four islands were named after the ancient three, plus Huliang 壺梁 which probably represented the turtle or fish believed to bear the isles through the ocean (*Shiji*, 28.1402; trans. Watson 1961, 66). An alternative name for Fangzhang, Fanghu 方壺 (Square Pot), may have been a combined name for Fanghu and Huliang that persisted through the association with folklore about worlds concealed in gourds. Yet another alternative name for Fangzhang, Fangzhu 方諸 (Square Speculum), appears later in *Shangqing scriptures; the "speculum" was a mirror used for dew-collection (Schafer 1985, 109–10; Kroll 1985, 79).

The *Liezi* describes a larger set of five isles that also included Daiyu 岱輿 (Great Carriage) and Yuanqiao 員嶠 (Rounded Ridge). They originally drifted about in the ocean, then were carried on the raised heads of giant turtles. Later a giant caught some of the turtles, so that Yuanqiao and Daiyu drifted north and sank (5.52–53; trans. Graham 1960, 97–98). The name Penglai suggests the meaning of "coming [like a windblown] tumbleweed or pond nuphar" (Schafer 1985, 56), the name Fangzhang may connote the large square feast table filled with rare delicacies mentioned by Mencius (*Mengzi* 孟子, 7B.34; trans. Legge 1895, 496), while Yingzhou simply means "Ocean Isle." More fanciful descriptions of the five isles and various mountains may be found in Wang Jia's 王嘉 (?–ca. 324) *Shiyi ji* 拾遺記 (Uncollected Records; Foster 1974, 295–302; Campany 1996, 64–67 and 306–18).

Further east lay Fusang 扶桑 (Supporting Mulberry), described in early sources like the *Chuci* 楚辭 (Songs of Chu; trans. Hawkes 1985, 73, 113, and 300), the *Shanhai jing* 山海經 (Scripture of Mountains and Seas; trans. Mathieu 1983, 438 and 539), and others as the vast tree of sunrise, where the ten suns perched birdlike on its branches. Ancient artistic depictions show a tree with nine orbs among its branches, the tenth sun of legend probably being in transit across the skies of the mundane world (Allan 1991, 19–56).

Another set of ten immense isles or continents, including Yingzhou, arrayed in distant seas around the known world were initially described in Later Han omenological literature (Li Fengmao 1986, 128–29). These were later brought into Shangqing cosmology, as described in the *Waiguo fangpin Qingtong neiwen* 外國放品青童內文 (Inner Script of the Azure Lad on the Distribution of the Outer Realms; CT 1373), which probably dates to the Eastern Jin period (Robinet 1984, 2: 97–100), and one later, highly influential apocryphon, the *Shizhou ji* (Record of the Ten Continents).

To the ten continents, the *Shizhou ji* adds four island paradises, including one Canghai dao 藏海島 (Watchet Sea Isle) in the north, and two mountain paradises, *Kunlun and Zhongshan 種山. In one version of the text, the pure freshwater seas around Yingzhou and Fusang are separated from common oceans by a ribbon-shaped land called Daizhou 帶洲. Fusang is described as an isle covered with giant mulberry trees that grow in mutually supporting pairs. The paradises are homes of earthly transcendents (*dixian* 地仙) and ruled by various perfected officials of Shangqing Taoism.

In the *Waiguo fangpin Qingtong neiwen*, the four seas of *Shizhou ji* become continents with Sanskrit names, and nine of the ten continents become countries. Kunlun is shifted from the northwest to the world's center, and the *Shizhou ji*'s descriptions of exotic flora and fauna are abridged or eliminated entirely as the emphasis shifts toward mineral elixirs, the immortal residences and bureaucracy, and the correct recital of spells. In addition, heavens and hells are distinguished, revealing a strong Buddhist influence, whereas the *Shizhou ji* retains more of the simple terrestrial geography of its Han sources (see *sanshiliu tian*). The extensive descriptions of such far-off lands in Shangqing literature are intended to prepare the adept for his or her eventual translation there.

Thomas E. SMITH

📖 Foster 1974; Kamitsuka Yoshiko 1990; Kroll 1985; Li Fengmao 1986, 123–85; Little 2000b, 370–71 and 377; Schafer 1985, 51–60; Smith Th. E. 1990; Smith Th. E. 1992

※ TAOISM AND CHINESE MYTHOLOGY

Pengzu

彭祖

Ancestor Peng

According to the *Liexian zhuan* (Biographies of Exemplary Immortals; trans. Kaltenmark 1953, 82–84), Pengzu was a high officer of the Yin 殷 kingdom (in present-day Henan). His surname was Qian 籛 and his given name was Keng 鏗. By the end of the Yin dynasty he had reached the age of about eight hundred years old thanks to his practice of gymnastics (*daoyin) and circulation of breath (*xingqi). Mentions of his longevity are also found in the *Xunzi* 荀子 and the *Zhuangzi, suggesting that this view of Pengzu had become current by the Warring States period.

Pengzu's biography in a later work, the *Shenxian zhuan (Biographies of Divine Immortals), however, states that he achieved an extremely long life through sexual techniques (*fangzhong shu). Similarly, the *Baopu zi (trans. Ware 1966, 217–18), quoting the anonymous Pengzu jing 彭祖經 (Scripture of Pengzu), describes him as a high government officer who lived throughout the Xia dynasty until the Yin. He taught the sexual techniques to the king of Yin, who employed them effectively. When Pengzu realized that the king wanted to obtain sole control of those techniques, he left Yin. At that time he was some seven or eight hundred years old. This account indicates that by the early fourth century Pengzu was regarded as having obtained longevity through sexual practices.

The link between these apparently conflicting views is provided by the manuscript entitled Shiwen 十問 (Ten Questions; trans. Harper 1998, 385–411), excavated from a Han tomb at *Mawangdui. This text records an answer that Pengzu gave to the immortal *Wangzi Qiao concerning the *qi of human beings, namely that one should perfect one's sexual energy through gymnastics and breathing. In a similar way, the Yinshu 引書 (Book on Pulling; see Harper 1998, 30–33 and 110–19), another manuscript excavated from a tomb at Zhangjiashan 張家山 (Hubei), speaks of perfecting one's sexual energy, specifically identifying this as the "Way of Pengzu." These references suggest that Pengzu was seen from early times as a practitioner of sexual techniques, which were closely related to gymnastics and breathing and performed in order to obtain longevity.

The Pengzu jing thus appears to have been a manual that described a variety of longevity techniques with a focus on sexual practices. While this work was lost at an early date in China, several quotations from it are found in chapter 28 of the *Ishinpō (Methods from the Heart of Medicine; 984).

SAKADE Yoshinobu

📖 Campany 2002, 172–86; Harper 1998, 110–11; Kaltenmark 1953, 82–84; Sakade Yoshinobu 1985; Yoshikawa Tadao 1995a; Zhu Haoxi 1995

※ daoyin; fangzhong shu; HAGIOGRAPHY

po

魄

Yin soul(s); earthly soul(s)

See *hun and po 魂 · 魄.

poyu

破獄

Destruction of Hell

The Destruction of Hell, also known as Attack on the Fortress (*dacheng* 打城), is a rite performed during the ritual of Merit (*gongde*). Its purpose is to break open the gates of hell and obtain the release of the souls of the dead who are trapped there. The origins of this rite, which was performed as part of the *Lingbao *zhai* (Retreat) rituals in the Six Dynasties period, can be partly traced to the idea of illuminating the nine realms of the underworld (*jiuyou* 九幽), with the purpose of the enlightenment and salvation of the dead. As used in Song and later times, the term *poyu* exhibits the influence of esoteric Buddhist ideas and rites seen in such works as the *Sanzhong xidi po diyu zhuan yezhang chu sanjie bimi tuoluoni fa* 三種悉地破地獄轉業障出三界祕密陀羅尼法 (Method of the Secret Dhāraṇī of the Three Types of Siddhi for Destroying Hell, Transforming the Barriers of *Karma*, and Leaving the Three Realms; T. 905), written around 830.

MARUYAMA Hiroshi

📖 Lagerwey 1987c, 216–37

※ *gongde*

pudu

普度

universal salvation

1. The term

The term *pudu* refers to the salvation of all human beings. Similar ideas of universal love, concern for the immortality of all beings, and the link between one's own salvation and the sins of one's ancestors are found in early religious Taoist and alchemical traditions. Under Buddhist influence, the notion of rebirth appeared in the *Lingbao scriptures, leading to a wider soteriological goal: Taoist practitioners not only aimed for their own transcendence but also sought to save others through ritual means. The *Duren jing (Scripture on Salvation) mentions the term *pudu* several times, referring to "illimitable, universal salvation without end." Other terms indicating the salvation of all appear throughout the Lingbao corpus.

Along with several other concepts and imagery, the Lingbao school derived the idea of universal salvation from Mahāyāna (Great Vehicle) Buddhist scriptures. One such Buddhist text was the *Amitābha Sūtra* (*Sukhāvatīvyūha-sūtra*; *Amituo sanye sanfo salou fotan guodu rendao jing* 啊彌陀三耶三佛薩樓佛檀過度人道經; T. 362), translated into Chinese by Zhi Qian 支謙 (third century) whose many writings had a direct influence on the Lingbao corpus. According to Mahāyāna texts, the pejoratively termed Hīnayāna (Lesser Vehicle) Buddhist tradition aimed at individual salvation only whereas Mahāyāna worked for the salvation of all beings. Similarly, Lingbao Taoism presented itself as saving all in contrast to the individual practices of the *Shangqing and other schools of Taoism.

Amy Lynn MILLER

📖 Boltz J. M. 1983; Robinet 1997b, 152–55

※ Lingbao; REBIRTH; TAOISM AND CHINESE BUDDHISM

2. The ritual

Just as the concept of *pudu* (universal salvation) lies at the heart of the *Lingbao codification, so, too, did the *pudu* ritual emerge as a central feature of Lingbao liturgy. It is the Taoist counterpart to the so-called *yulanpen* 盂蘭盆 (*avalambana*?) ritual of salvation popularized in Tantric teachings conveyed by Amoghavajra (Bukong 不空, 705–74). Like its Buddhist analogue, the *pudu* ritual came to be closely identified with the tradition of commemorating the dead on the fifteenth day of the seventh lunar month, known as *zhongyuan* 中元.

The origins of contemporary *pudu* practice are conventionally traced to the Lingbao patriarch *Ge Xuan (trad. 164–244). Accounts of how Ge was rewarded for his deliverance of ghosts by performing a ritual of *jilian* 祭鍊 (oblatory refinement) are recorded in hagiographic lore dating to the Yuan and Ming. His service on the fifteenth day of the tenth lunar month (*xiayuan* 下元) of 214 reportedly led to his compilation of a penitential guide for the lay community. One text ascribed to Ge in the Taoist Canon, the *Jiuyou chan* 九幽懺 (Penance of the Nine Shades; CT 543), is presumed to be the work of *Li Hanguang (683–769), whose name is attached to the preface. The fact that this preeminent *Shangqing patriarch was a contemporary of Amoghavajra invites speculation as to the nature of the symbiotic relationship between Tantric and Lingbao rituals of salvation emerging during the Tang period.

Contemporary *pudu* ritual practice is still firmly anchored in the legacy of the early Lingbao canon codified by *Lu Xiujing (406–77). Its foundations are perhaps most readily apparent in the *Mingzhen ke* 明真科 (Code of the Luminous Perfected; CT 1411). The *zhai* ritual of purification prescribed in this text is to be conducted within a family courtyard for the benefit of all the *hun*-souls of the deceased (*sihun* 死魂; see *hun* and *po*) suffering incarceration in the netherworld. But it is the redemption of the celebrant's own ancestors that appears to be of foremost concern.

Derivative *pudu* ritual codes are primarily directed toward the salvation of *guhun* 孤魂, orphaned or desolate souls. Such was the designation of the spirits of those whose demise had not been properly commemorated. Taken before their time by tragic circumstances, *guhun* were perceived to be an innately threatening presence to the living and thus in need of pacification. Those who engage in a *pudu* service thus seek reconciliation with these masses of unknown dead. Details may differ from one region to the next, but if there is any single identifying feature linking diverse *pudu* practices it is the weight of kinship ties that seems to persist above all.

Fieldwork and textual studies of the *pudu* service to date largely reflect the practices in Fujian, Taiwan, Hong Kong, as well as Honolulu. The service is typically scheduled on the closing evening of a *jiao (Offering) ritual staged on temple grounds. Such events are communal affairs sponsored by civic leaders who themselves have specific roles to play in the ritual itself. The crowds these events attract are usually drawn more by the spectacle of the feast and operatic presentations honoring the deceased than by the ritual performance undertaken on their behalf.

Significant narrative and dramatic features of contemporary *pudu* ritual can be traced to the *huanglu* 黃籙 (Yellow Register) protocols codified by *Du Guangting (850–933; see *huanglu zhai*) and ritual formularies on *liandu (Salvation through Refinement) compiled from the Song to Ming. Many songs and incantations also find their echo in Buddhist ritual formularies. The *pudu* service is by and large a hybrid form of ritual, the merit (*gongde*) of which is dependent upon the cooperative efforts of a host of divine forces representing the spirit realms of diverse Taoist, Buddhist, and local traditions. The image of the bodhisattva Guanyin 觀音 at Mount Putuo (Putuo shan 普陀山) is often evoked together with tutelary deities in support of the *sanqing trinity.

The Taoist Master who serves as celebrant (the high priest, or *gaogong* 高功; see *daozhang*) typically takes on the identity of *Jiuku tianzun (Celestial Worthy Who Relieves Suffering) in presiding over the deliverance of *guhun*. Assisted by the chief cantor, or *dujiang*, and an ensemble of musicians, the celebrant guides the *guhun* on their path to redemption through a combination of song, chant, and recitation. The fundamental role he assumes in this vividly choreographed mission is that of a father, expressing time and again a profound sense of grief and compassion for all lost souls. What the *pudu* service thus serves to endorse overall is the perception that all of humanity finds its brethren in the community of the dead as well as the living.

Judith M. BOLTZ

📖 Bokenkamp 1996c; Boltz J. M. 1983; Boltz J. M. 1996; Lagerwey 1987c, 20–21, 58–59, 199–200, and 230–35; Lü and Lagerwey 1992, 29–34; Ōfuchi Ninji 1983, 391–404, 752–72, 786–814, and 883–900; Orzech 2002; Pang D. 1977

※ *jiao*; *zhai*; REBIRTH

Puhua tianzun

普化天尊

Celestial Worthy of Universal Transformation

Puhua tianzun, also known as Leisheng Puhua tianzun 雷聲普化天尊 (Celestial Worthy of the Sound of Thunder of Universal Transformation), is the deity said to have revealed the *Yushu jing* (Scripture of the Jade Pivot), a text that originated among the followers of *Bai Yuchan (1194–1229?) during the Southern Song period. The god is the personification of the creative power of the universe as symbolized by thunder. As such, he is the highest deity of the exorcistic Thunder Rites (*leifa*).

In the *Shenxiao pantheon, Puhua tianzun is one of the Nine Monarchs (*jiuchen* 九宸; see under *Changsheng dadi) and is flanked by *Jiuku tianzun (Celestial Worthy Who Relieves Suffering). In Taoist iconography, he is portrayed with the attributes of Samantabhadra (Puxian 普賢), the bodhisattva who rides an elephant.

Caroline GYSS

※ *Yushu jing*; *leifa*; DEITIES: THE PANTHEON

Q

qi

氣

pneuma (breath, energy, vital force)

See *jing, qi, shen* 精 · 氣 · 神.

qigong

氣功

"practice of *qi*"; "efficiency of *qi*"

Qigong is a product of the twentieth century, but is rooted in the earlier tradition. The term is mentioned in the Tang period to designate the "practice of *qi*," and in the Song period the "efficiency of *qi*." In modern times, it has taken on a new meaning and refers not only to Nourishing Life (*yangsheng*) but also to martial and therapeutic techniques. As the term *qigong* signifies both "practice" and "efficiency" of *qi*, it can embrace all types of techniques, both traditional and modern.

Depending on the doctrinal and social context of these practices, historians currently divide *qigong* into six branches: a Taoist *qigong*, a Buddhist *qigong*, a Confucian *qigong*, a medical *qigong*, a martial *qigong*, and a popular *qigong* (including the methods of rural exorcists and sorcerers). According to the features of the practice, they also distinguish between a "strong *qigong*" (*ying qigong* 硬氣功), incorporating martial techniques, and a "soft *qigong*" (*ruan qigong* 軟氣功). The latter is further divided into two groups:

1. *Jinggong* 靜功, or the practice of *qi* in rest, which traditionally was called "sitting in oblivion" (*zuowang*) by Taoists, "sitting in *dhyāna*" (*chanzuo* 禪坐) by Buddhists, and "quiet sitting" (*jingzuo* 靜坐) by Neo-Confucians. These sitting practices can be accompanied by breathing, visualization, and mental concentration.

2. *Donggong* 動功, or the practice of *qi* in movement, which includes the gymnastic traditions (*daoyin*) of medical doctors, Taoists, and Buddhists. The induction of spontaneous movements (*zifa donggong* 自發動功) is derived from traditional trance techniques (Despeux 1997).

New practices essentially created in the 1980s were much debated and criticized by traditional religious personalities, *qigong* followers, and authorities. Certain practices, such as the "Soaring Crane form" (*hexiang zhuang* 鶴翔庄), lead to spontaneous movements that were said to cause illness, probably because of their close connection with trance states. Some techniques that emphasize collective practices and promote the establishment of a so-called "area of *qi*" (*qichang* 氣場) to increase efficiency were also strongly criticized; for instance, the method taught by Yan Xin 嚴新, a master who organized collective *qigong* sessions in stadiums with a capacity of up to about ten thousand, was very popular but aroused suspicion among the authorities. As for the therapeutic technique of the *qigong* master who heals people at a distance through his energy or his hands—a method that actually revives the traditional Taoist practice of "spreading breath" (**buqi*)—the possible existence of an "outer energy" (*waiqi* 外氣) and its efficacy have been debated at length.

Official *qigong* institutions appeared in the 1950s and 1960s and were at first exclusively concerned with therapeutics. One of the main *qigong* promoters at the time was Liu Guizhen 劉貴珍 (1920–83). A friend of Mao Zedong, he returned to his village after developing a stomach ulcer and practiced breathing and meditation exercises under a Taoist master. Later he created a new method called "practice of inner nourishment" (*neiyang gong* 內養功) and founded *qigong* therapy institutes in Tangshan 唐山 (Hebei) in 1954 and in Beidaihe 北戴河 (Hebei) in 1956. These institutes were destroyed during the Cultural Revolution, and then partly reconstructed after 1980 when *qigong* flourished again.

From that time, *qigong* began to invade the town parks where masters and followers practice in the morning. Some religious personalities who described themselves as "*qigong* masters" felt encouraged to revive forgotten or little-known practices, or to create new techniques based on the traditional ones. *Qigong* had both enthusiasts and critics among the authorities. Although its therapeutic function was always essential, certain officials wanted to move *qigong* beyond the realm of individual practice and propound it to the masses and to society, even to the state, because they saw in it economic advantages and the possibility of asserting the specific identity of China, its power and its modernity. *Qigong* was taught in schools and universities and became the object of international congresses and scientific research, and numerous specialized journals and books were published on the subject. Other officials viewed it as charlatanism and superstition, and mistrusted the subversive potential of certain movements. An example is the Falun gong 法輪功 (Practices of the Wheel of the Law), a form of *qigong* allegedly rooted in the Buddhist tradition, which in 1999 organized demonstrations in Beijing and other Chinese cities and was outlawed shortly afterward.

Catherine DESPEUX

📖 Chen Bing 1989; Despeux 1997; Esposito 1995; Micollier 1996; Miura Kunio 1989; Penny 1993; Wang Buxiong and Zhou Shirong 1989; Xu Jian 1999

※ yangsheng

Qingcheng shan

青城山

Mount Qingcheng (Sichuan)

Mount Qingcheng (lit., "Green Citadel") is one peak (about 1600 m high) in a larger chain of mountains overlooking a rich irrigated plain, with the famous Guanxian 灌縣 irrigation works that feed the entire Chengdu basin located just at its base (Chengdu, the capital of Sichuan, is some 60 km to the southeast). The mountain must have been a sacred site already during the time of the Shu 蜀 kingdom before unification with China in the third century BCE. It was closely associated with the nascent Way of the Celestial Masters (*Tianshi dao) during the second century CE. The founding moment of that church, Laozi's appearance to *Zhang Daoling in 142, took place on Mount Heming (*Heming shan), near Mount Qingcheng. Zhang Daoling's lore on Mount Qingcheng is attested as early as the fourth century, as shown by his biography in the *Shenxian zhuan (Biographies of Divine Immortals; trans. Campany 2002, 349–54). *Fan Changsheng, a Taoist leader of one Celestial Masters branch, built an autarchic community on Mount Qingcheng around 300, and later supported a messianic general who founded a short-lived dynasty (see under *Dacheng).

The later history of Mount Qingcheng is known thanks to the great Taoist scholar *Du Guangting, who lived there during the late eighth and early ninth centuries and left records pertaining both to the institutions on the mountain and to popular cults associated with it. The major temples, then as now, are the Jianfu gong 建福宮 (Palace for the Establishment of Blessings) at the foot of the mountain, dedicated to Ningfeng zi 甯封子 (an immortal of antiquity considered to be the god of the mountain, and honored as such in Tang official cults), and, on the mountain itself, the Shangqing gong 上清宮 (Palace of Highest Clarity) and the Changdao guan 常道觀 (Abbey of the Constant Dao). The latter is also known as Tianshi dong 天師洞 (Cavern of the Celestial Master) because it is built around a cave where Zhang Daoling is said to have meditated. The Zhangs of Mount Longhu (*Longhu shan) maintained a strong relationship with that temple. All three temples were founded in the late Six Dynasties or early Tang.

The circumstances of the advent of the *Quanzhen order at Mount Qingcheng are not known. There must have been a Quanzhen presence on the mountain during the Yuan, but sources are scarce, as in the whole of Sichuan which was hit particularly hard by war and depopulation during the thirteenth century. The mountain, as well as closely related monasteries in Chengdu, namely the *Qingyang gong (Palace of the Black Ram) and Erxian an 二仙 庵 (Hermitage of the Two Immortals), have been managed since the late seventeenth century by Quanzhen Taoists of a local *Longmen sub-lineage called Dantai bidong 丹臺碧洞 (Jasper Cavern of the Cinnabar Terrace). Mount Qingcheng was one of the first Taoist sites to operate anew after 1978, and a Quanzhen ordination took place there in 1995. Ever since the nineteenth century, moreover, Sichuan Quanzhen bas been famous for its alchemical traditions for women (*nüdan), and there is now once again a community of nuns on Mount Qingcheng devoted to its practice.

Vincent GOOSSAERT

📖 Hachiya Kunio 1990, 1: 124–77, 294–96, 2: 133–74, 286–87; Peterson T. H. 1995; Wang Chunwu 1994

※ TAOIST SACRED SITES

qingjing

清靜

clarity and quiescence

The term *qingjing* and the ideas surrounding it made their first appearance in *Daode jing* 45: "Clear and quiescent, this is the correct mode of all under heaven." Later the expression was linked to *Huang-Lao thought and used to refer to a way of government that assured a peaceful life for the people by not burdening them with excessive demands.

Taoism has consistently attached importance to *qingjing* as the ideal state of body and mind. The *Xiang'er* commentary to the *Daode jing* says: "Taoists should value their essence and spirit. Clarity and quiescence are the basis" (see Bokenkamp 1997, 121). In the mid-Tang period, the idea of *qingjing* became the central theme of the *Qingjing jing* (Scripture of Clarity and Quiescence), which states that when the mind is constantly calm and quiet, it becomes clear, desires are eliminated, and one attains the Dao. The *Qingjing jing* was widely read in later times and more than ten commentaries were written on it, including those by *Du Guangting (850–933) and *Li Daochun (fl. 1288–92). It was also prized as a basic text by the *Quanzhen school. Attesting to the importance of the concept of *qingjing* within Quanzhen, one of its branches was called Qingjing, and *Sun Bu'er (1119–83) took the sobriquet Vagabond of Clarity and Quiescence (Qingjing sanren 清靜散人). Little, however, is known about the Qingjing branch of Quanzhen except that its practices included *neidan.

In ancient times, the characters *jing* 靜 and *jing* 淨 (whose meanings were later differentiated into "quiescence" and "purity") were interchangeable and *qingjing* 清靜 could also be written *qingjing* 清淨. For instance, in the *Shiji* (Records of the Historian; j. 130) Laozi is described as "transforming himself through non-action (*wuwei) and establishing himself as correct through clarity and purity (*qingjing* 清淨)." This compound cannot but call to mind Buddhist terminology. The idea of *qingjing* already existed in early Buddhism, since terms equivalent to the Chinese compound *qingjing* 清淨 can be found in both Sanskrit and Pāli (*pariśuddhi, viśuddhi*; "clear and pure," free from defilement), and was later developed within Mahāyāna (Great Vehicle) Buddhism into the idea of the "innately pure mind" (meaning that the mind of sentient beings is inherently pure and free from defilement). Whereas Chinese Buddhism always uses the compound *qingjing* 清淨 (clarity and purity) rather than *qingjing* 清靜 (clarity and quiescence), Taoism uses both interchangeably. When *qingjing* 清淨 (clarity and purity) is used, however, there is ample room for considering a Buddhist influence.

MIURA Kunio

📖 Hosokawa Kazutoshi 1987; Qing Xitai 1994, 2: 273–77; see also bibliography for the entry *Qingjing jing

※ *Qingjing jing*; MEDITATION AND VISUALIZATION

Qingjing jing

清靜經

Scripture of Clarity and Quiescence

The *Qingjing jing*, dating from the mid-Tang period, appears variously in the Taoist Canon, both alone (CT 620) and with commentary (CT 755 to CT 760, and CT 974), as well as in a slightly longer—and possibly earlier—version known as the *Qingjing xinjing* 清靜心經 (Heart Scripture of Clarity and Quiescence; CT 1169). Spoken by *Laojun himself and written in verses of four characters, the text combines the thought and phrasing of the *Daode jing* with the practice of Taoist observation (*guan*) and the structure of the Buddhist *Banruo xinjing* 般若心經 (Heart Sūtra of Perfect Wisdom). Following the latter's model, the *Qingjing jing*, as much as the earlier *Xiaozai huming miaojing* 消災護命妙經 (Wondrous Scripture on Dispelling Disasters and Protecting Life; CT 19), is a collection of essential or "heart" passages that is used less for inspiration and doctrinal teaching than for ritual recitation (*songjing*).

The text first describes the nature of the Dao as divided into Yin and Yang, clear and turbid (*qing* 清 and *zhuo* 濁), moving and quiescent (*dong* and *jing*), and stresses the importance of the mind in the creation of desires and worldly entanglements. It recommends the practice of observation to counteract this, i.e., the observation of other beings, the self, and the mind, which results in the realization that none of these really exist. The practitioner has reached the observation of emptiness (*kongguan* 空觀). The latter part of the work reverses direction and outlines the decline from pure spirit to falling into hell: spirit (*shen*) develops consciousness or mind (*xin*), and mind develops greed and attachment toward the myriad beings. Greed then leads to involvement, illusory imagining, and erroneous ways, which trap beings in the chain of rebirth and, as they sink deeper into the quagmire of desire, causes them to fall into hell.

The earliest extant commentary to the *Qingjing jing* is by *Du Guangting (850–933; CT 759). The text rose to great prominence in the Song dynasty, when it was used in the Southern Lineage (*Nanzong) by such masters as *Bai Yuchan (1194–1229?), *Li Daochun (fl. 1288–92), and *Wang Jie (?–ca. 1380), all of whom interpreted it in a *neidan* context (CT 757, 755, and 760, respectively). Later the *Qingjing jing* became a central scripture of the *Quanzhen school, in whose monasteries it is recited to the present day as part of the regular morning and evening devotions.

Livia KOHN

📖 Balfour 1884, 70–73 (trans.); Fukui Fumimasa 1987, 280–85; Ishida Hidemi 1987b (crit. ed. and trans.); Kohn 1993b, 24–29 (trans.); Mitamura Keiko 1994; Wong Eva 1992 (trans. of comm. by Shuijing zi 水精子)

※ *qingjing*; MEDITATION AND VISUALIZATION

qingtan

清談

Pure Conversation

Pure Conversation was a style of discourse that developed during the Wei (220–65) and Jin (265–420) dynasties. It has its roots in the metaphysical and political discussions of the Later Han dynasty (25–220), particularly character evaluations known as "pure critiques" (*qingyi* 清議). Pure Conversation eventually developed into a sophisticated intellectual game, consisting of rounds of debate during which the "host" would propose a principle, and the "guest" would present his objection. Debaters often accentuated their arguments with dramatic gestures employing fly-whisks or the sleeves of their robes.

The Zhengshi reign period (240–48) of the Wei dynasty is generally considered the golden age of Pure Conversation. The brightest stars of this period were *Wang Bi (226–49) and He Yan 何晏 (190–249), leaders of a school of metaphysical thought drawing on the *Daode jing*, the *Zhuangzi*, and the *Yijing* known as Arcane Learning (*Xuanxue). The political turbulence of the following generation led its greatest Pure Conversationalists, including *Xi Kang (223–62) and the poet Ruan Ji 阮籍 (210–63; Holzman 1976), to pursue a life of reclusion and spontaneity as an alternative to engagement in the world.

During the Jin dynasty, Pure Conversation became increasingly formalized, with debaters specializing in particular topics. With the rising popularity of Buddhist texts such as the *Vimalakīrti-nirdeśa-sūtra* (Teaching of Vimalakīrti) and the *Prajñāpāramitā* (Perfection of Wisdom) literature, the monk Zhi Dun 支盾 (314–66, also known as Zhi Daolin 支道林) became one of the most celebrated Pure Conversationalists of the fourth century. Liu Yiqing 劉義慶 (403–43) compiled anecdotes and sayings attributed to the great Pure Conversationalists in his *Shishuo xinyu* 世說新語 (New Account of Tales of the World; trans. Mather 1976).

Theodore A. COOK

📖 Balázs 1948; Chan A. K. L. 1991b, 25–28; Henricks 1983; Tang Changru 1955, 289–350; Yü Ying-shih 1985; Zhou Shaoxian 1966

Qingtong

青童

Azure Lad

Azure Lad, despite his unassuming name, is one of the main deities in *Shang-qing Taoism. He is also commonly referred to in Taoist texts as Shangxiang Qingtong jun 上相青童君 (Lord Azure Lad, Supreme Minister) or Fangzhu Qingtong jun 方諸青童君 (Lord Azure Lad of Fangzhu). As Supreme Minister, his position in the celestial hierarchy is just below that of Lijun 李君 (Lord Li), and as the lord of the paradise isle of Fangzhu 方諸 in the east, he is strongly associated with spring, dawn, and the regenerative forces of Yang. References to a Haitong 海童 (Sea Lad) or Donghai jun 東海君 (Lord of the Eastern Sea) may already be found in Eastern Jin poetry and *zhiguai* 志怪 fiction ("records of the strange"), and his identity seems to have developed in eastern China from the earlier, more shadowy figure Dongwang gong 東王公 (King Lord of the East). As such, he becomes to some extent a male counterpart of *Xiwang mu (Queen Mother of the West), and Fangzhu becomes the counterpart of Mount *Kunlun, Xiwang mu's abode.

Azure Lad more specifically manages the affairs of earthly transcendents (*dixian* 地仙); he functions as the Great Director of Destinies (Da siming 大司命; see *Siming) over the other Directors of Destinies in the Five Peaks (*wuyue*) and the various Grotto-Heavens (*dongtian*; see *Zhengao, 4.9b, 9.22a). The master name lists of those destined for immortality or death are kept in his palace at Fangzhu. After visiting other Grotto-Heavens and examining the earthly transcendents' progress, he returns to Fangzhu every *dingmao* 丁卯 day (the fourth of the sexagesimal cycle; *Zhengao* 9.15b). Thus he is often recorded in Shangqing texts as revealing scriptures to worthy adepts.

Thomas E. SMITH

📖 Kamitsuka Yoshiko 1990; Kroll 1985; Kroll 1986b; Schafer 1985, 108–21

※ Shangqing

Qingwei

清微

Pure Tenuity

The Qingwei ritual system took shape in late thirteenth-century Fujian. Its main extant texts were first codified by *Huang Shunshen (1224-after 1286), who claimed to have received them from Nan Bidao 南畢道 (1196-?). As "the synthesis of all traditions," these texts and their associated rituals wed the Thunderclap rites (leiting 雷霆; see *leifa) used by the *Shenxiao (Divine Empyrean) and *Lingbao dafa (Great Rites of the Numinous Treasure) legacies to the heritage of Tantric Buddhism. Although early sources claim to be grounded in teachings that passed through a line of five Guangxi spiritual matriarchs purported to have lived in Tang times, the first codifications of this system boast a patriarchal line that leads to Fujian literati in the mid-thirteenth century. By the end of the thirteenth century, the Qingwei teachings had spread to many areas of south China, including major centers on Mount Wudang (*Wudang shan, Hubei) and in Jiangxi, and by Ming times, Taoist priests saw the Qingwei and Shenxiao systems as the main Taoist ritual programs available.

Chapters 1–55 of the *Daofa huiyuan (Corpus of Taoist Ritual; CT 1220) contain a collection of Qingwei manuals. Besides these works, six other texts form the core of the Qingwei legacy in the Taoist Canon:

1. Qingwei xuanshu zougao yi 清微玄樞奏告儀 (Protocols for Announcements to the Mysterious Pivot of the Pure Tenuity; CT 218) by Yang Xizhen 楊希真 (1101–24), a disciple of Huang Shunshen from Mount Wudang, which consists of a manual on submitting petitions.

2. *Qingwei xianpu (Register of Pure Tenuity Transcendents; CT 171), compiled by Chen Cai 陳采 in 1293, which may also derive from Huang Shunshen's teachings, but asserts that the Qingwei tradition was created by the matriarch Zu Shu 祖舒 (fl. 889–904) who first blended Thunderclap rituals and Tantric Buddhist maṇḍalas.

3. Qingwei yuanjiang dafa 清微元降大法 (Great Rites Based on the Original Revelations of the Pure Tenuity; CT 223), probably from the fourteenth century, which offers the most comprehensive treatment of Qingwei ritual and focuses on rites for saving dead ancestors.

4. Qingwei zhaifa 清微齋法 (Rituals for the Pure Tenuity Retreat; CT 224), also from the fourteenth century, which shows how Qingwei adapted the Lingbao Retreat (*zhai) into its ritual system.

5. *Qingwei danjue* 清微丹訣 (Elixir Instructions for the Pure Tenuity; CT 278), also from the fourteenth century, which emphasizes the complementarity of *neidan and Qingwei ritual.

6. *Qingwei shenlie bifa* 清微神烈祕法 (Secret Rites of the Divine Candescence of the Pure Tenuity; CT 222), dating from the late Yuan, with diagrams for conquering demons in the Qingwei Thunder Rites tradition.

This substantial textual material, which has scarcely been studied, provides the basis for one of the last major traditions to be included in the Ming Taoist Canon.

Lowell SKAR

📖 Boltz J. M. 1987a, 38–41, 68–70; Davis E. 2001, 29–30; Despeux 2000a; Qing Xitai 1988–95, 3: 137–41 and 340–43; Qing Xitai 1994, 1: 141–48; Reiter 1988a, 40–52; Schipper 1987

※ Huang Shunshen; *Qingwei xianpu*

Qingwei xianpu

清微仙譜

Register of Pure Tenuity Transcendents

Consisting of cosmological-cum-hagiographic accounts of how the *Qingwei tradition was passed down from exalted deities to its late Southern Song synthesizer, *Huang Shunshen (1224-after 1286), this work's worldly existence can be credited to Huang's disciple, Chen Cai 陳采, who wrote a preface dated 1293. The text (CT 171) includes sections on the early transmission of Qingwei teachings, and charts of the transmissions of the *Shangqing, *Lingbao, Daode 道德 (i.e., *Laozi*), and *Zhengyi traditions, which the Qingwei "Synthetic Way" (*huidao* 會道) claimed to blend. These charts, which serve as rosters of deities to be summoned during the performance of rituals, include the lineage that ends with the eleventh patriarch, Huang Shunshen, who appears to have synthesized the tradition for his many followers.

Lowell SKAR

📖 Boltz J. M. 1987a, 39, 68-70

※ Huang Shunshen; Qingwei

Qingyang gong

青羊宮

Palace of the Black Ram (Chengdu, Sichuan)

The Qingyang gong is the major Taoist sanctuary in Chengdu (Sichuan), built at the site where Laozi allegedly met *Yin Xi for the second time, identified him as a fully realized Taoist, and empowered him to join him on his western journey as a full partner. The legend tells how Yin Xi was to recognize Laozi through the sign of a black ewe (although the sheep at the temple today have prominent horns and are definitely rams), which was to be sold, bought, or otherwise present when he appeared.

The story is first recorded in the Tang collection *Sandong zhunang* (The Pearl Satchel of the Three Caverns) and is given prominent status in a Tang inscription at the temple—at this time still called Zhongxuan guan 中玄觀 (Abbey of Central Mystery) and located at Black Ram Market. The text, by the scholar-official Yue Penggui 樂朋龜, is contained in the *Xichuan Qingyang gong beiming* 西川青羊宮碑銘 (Stele Inscription at the Palace of the Black Ram in Sichuan; CT 964), dated 884. It begins with an outline of Laozi's life and then describes how, in October 883, a *jiao* (Offering) ceremony was held in the temple. Suddenly a red glow illuminated the area, coalescing into a purple hue near a plum tree. Bowing, the officiating priest advanced and had the indicated spot excavated to uncover a solid square brick. It bore six characters in ancient seal script that read: "The Most High Lord brings peace to the upheaval of [the reign period] Central Harmony." Not only was this wondrous text written in a "seal script" that had not been in use for a millennium, but the brick itself was like an ancient lithophone, making marvelous sounds when struck and appearing luminous like jade when examined closely.

After an exchange of several memorials and formal orders, all faithfully recorded in the inscription, the temple was formally renamed Qingyang gong, granted several new halls and a large piece of land, and honored with gifts of cash and valuables. The officiating priest was promoted in rank and given high emoluments. In addition, great festivals were held at Taoist institutions throughout the empire, and Yue Penggui was entrusted with writing the inscription. The Qingyang gong thereby became the major Taoist center it still is today.

Livia KOHN

📖 Hachiya Kunio 1990, 1: 113–22 and 293, 2: 122–31 and 285; Kusuyama Haruki 1978; Qing Xitai 1994, 4: 265–66; Yūsa Noboru 1986

※ TEMPLES AND SHRINES

Qinyuan chun

沁園春

Spring in the Garden by the Qin River

This short alchemical lyric (*ci* 詞), ascribed to *Lü Dongbin, is one of the most famous texts of the *Zhong-Lü tradition. The date of the work is uncertain. Its transmission is recounted in an anecdote found in Liu Fu's 劉斧 (1040–after 1113) *Qingsuo gaoyi* 青瑣高議 (Notes and Opinions Deserving the Highest Consideration; Shanghai guji chubanshe ed., *Qianji* 前集, 8.82). This source states that the poem was revealed by a cobbler to a scholar named Cui Zhong 崔中 in Yueyang 嶽陽 (Hunan), a cultic center associated with Lü Dongbin. Since the cobbler was illiterate, he asked Cui to write down the words for him. Asked who he was, the cobbler answered with an anagram. Cui reported the strange encounter to the governor of Yueyang, who immediately recognized the cobbler as Lü Dongbin.

The poem is reproduced in several collections, and differing interpretations abound. The main commentaries in the Taoist Canon are those by a Li zhenren 李真人 (Perfected Li) in the *Longhu huandan jue* 龍虎還丹訣 (Instructions on the Reverted Elixir of the Dragon and Tiger; Northern Song; CT 1084, 8b–16a); Li Jianyi 李簡易 (fl. 1264–66) in the *Yuqi zi danjing zhiyao* 玉谿子丹經指要 (Essential Directions on the Scriptures of the Elixirs by the Master of the Jade Gorge; 1264; CT 245, 3.11b–16b); Xiao Tingzhi 蕭廷芝 (fl. 1260–64) in the *Jindan dacheng ji* (*Xiuzhen shishu*; CT 263, 13.9b–17b); and *Yu Yan in the *Qinyuan chun danci zhujie* 沁園春丹詞注解 (Commentary and Explication of the Alchemical Lyric *Qinyuan chun*; CT 136). The commentary by Yu Yan is of special interest because of the texts and authors quoted therein.

The *neidan process described in the poem consists of the collection of Real Yang (*zhenyang* 真陽) at the *zi hour, its union with Real Yin (*zhenyin* 真陰) to obtain the elixir seed, the purification by fire phasing (*huohou), and the gestation and birth of the immortal. To achieve transfiguration and return to the Dao, the adept should first accomplish 3,000 meritorious deeds.

Farzeen BALDRIAN-HUSSEIN

📖 Baldrian-Hussein 1985

※ Lü Dongbin; *neidan*; Zhong-Lü

Qiu Chuji

丘處機

1148–1227; *zi*: Tongmi 通密;
hao: Changchun 長春 (Perpetual Spring)

Qiu Chuji (Qiu Changchun) is the youngest of the Seven Real Men (*qizhen* 七真; see table 17), the paradigmatic group of *Wang Zhe's disciples that formed the first generation of *Quanzhen masters. While some of these figures, such as *Tan Chuduan or *Ma Yu, had been already experienced in Taoist and other teachings when they became Wang's disciples, Qiu came as a twenty year-old orphan keen on self-cultivation but unable to find proper guidance. Some accounts even suggest that he learned to read with Wang, which seems unlikely. Another later legend has him begging an old woman who lives as an ascetic in the mountains to instruct him in immortality techniques. The lady then directs him to Wang, describing the master as the only person able to unravel the secrets of Taoism for the benefit of all.

When Qiu found in Wang the master he was looking for, he placed himself entirely at his service and became one of his four core disciples. He accompanied his master on his last journey, and then helped carry his coffin to the Zhongnan mountains (Zhongnan shan 終南山, Shaanxi). After the three-year mourning period, while Ma Yu stayed near Wang's tomb, the other three went their ways to complete their ascetic training. Qiu spent six years in Panxi 磻溪 (Shaanxi), and seven more years in Longmen 龍門 (on the Shaanxi-Gansu border), practicing typical Quanzhen austerities such as standing on one foot for days, going without sleep for weeks, roaming half-naked in the midst of winter, staying by the fireside during the scorching heat of summer, not eating, and fraternizing with mountain beasts. Worst of all, according to his disciples' recorded sayings, were the mental states of fright and demonic hallucinations experienced under such conditions, which Qiu had to overcome to gain complete control of his mind.

Now a mature Taoist, Qiu must have begun to teach during this period, for he emerges then as a famous religious figure. Between 1186 and 1191, he stayed at the Zuting 祖庭 (Ancestral Court), the temple and conventual buildings erected around Wang's grave, which later became the Chongyang gong 重陽宮 (Palace of Double Yang). Ma Yu had directed this community until his departure in 1182, and since then it had been quite active on its own. Qiu was also summoned to the Jin court in 1188. In 1191, he went back to his native Shandong, where he began to gather disciples and built several new abbeys,

Fig. 63. Qiu Chuji. Reproduced from Zhongguo daojiao xiehui 1983.

which he organized as a network so that he could obtain funds to buy new abbey licenses. In 1195 the Zuting was closed down, an event that brought to a peak the tension between the Quanzhen order and the Jin state, which had been rising since 1190. In this predicament, the Shaanxi Quanzhen leaders turned to Qiu, who managed to save the Zuting. This suggests that—although the later Quanzhen hagiographies have the four disciples Ma Yu, Tan Chuduan, *Liu Chuxuan, and Qiu Chuji become successive patriarchs, which would have made Liu the patriarch at that time—it was Qiu who actually mastered a corporate leadership of the order.

In the following years, large areas of northern China and especially Shandong were plunged into chaos as a result of the 1194 Yellow River defluviation, Mongol invasions, war between the Song and Jin, and various rebellions. The Quanzhen's autonomous organization grew under Qiu's leadership and proved increasingly efficient, enabling him to run relief operations and gain a political position. Qiu was already an old man when he was summoned by the Mongol emperor, Chinggis khan (Taizu, r. 1206–27), in 1219. Accompanied by eighteen of his most eminent disciples, Qiu made the long and arduous journey to central Asia to finally meet the khan in 1222. This event, the most famous of his life, is told in detail in the *Changchun zhenren xiyou ji (Records of a Journey to the West by the Real Man Changchun). Qiu's influence on the khan is difficult to estimate, but the subsequent privileges enjoyed by the Quanzhen order were put to good use for the civilian population. Qiu was therefore granted a biography in the official history (Yuanshi, j. 202), a rare feat for a religious leader, and has been since then considered to be a savior whose actions helped to spare thousands of Chinese lives.

Back in Beijing in 1224, Qiu took control of the largest Taoist monastery there, the Tianchang guan 天長觀 (Abbey of Celestial Perpetuity), which was soon renamed Changchun gong 長春宮 (Palace of Perpetual Spring) in his honor. From this base, he began to organize a nationwide autonomous hierarchical structure for the Quanzhen order, which, after the fall of the remaining Jin territory in 1234, extended to the whole of northern China. When he died in 1227, he was buried next to the Changchun gong, and a subordinate monastery, the *Baiyun guan (Abbey of the White Clouds), was built around it. Subsequent Quanzhen patriarchs continued to be based there.

Qiu's life is known from a variety of sources, including several hagiographic accounts and a host of inscriptions that are either devoted to him or mention his actions. A more familiar picture of the man and his teachings emerges from the anecdotes told by his disciples *Wang Zhijin and *Yin Zhiping in their recorded sayings. Moreover, an extended biography, the Xuanfeng qinghui tu 玄風慶會圖 (Felicitous Meetings with the Mysterious School, with Illustrations; Katz P. R. 2001), was published on several occasions, including a very fine 1305 Hangzhou edition, the first juan of which is still extant but not widely available: in it Qiu's life is divided into accounts of independent events each embellished by an illustration. This genre was also used to recount in both book and mural form the lives of *Lü Dongbin and Wang Zhe (the text is lost but surely inspired the murals in the Pavilion of Pure Yang, or Chunyang dian 純陽殿, of the *Yongle gong), as well as the life of Laozi and his eighty-one transformations (see *Laojun bashiyi hua tu). This is no mere coincidence: Qiu's travels to the west to convert the "barbarians" (i.e., the Mongols) were likened to Laozi's similar venture, and Qiu's successor to Quanzhen patriarchy, Yin Zhiping, was considered to be a new *Yin Xi.

Only a portion of Qiu's own writings is extant. Some poems are included in the *Panxi ji* 磻溪集 (Anthology of the Master from Panxi; CT 1159), dating from 1208 (Wong Shiu Hon 1988b; Qing Xitai 1994, 2: 215–16). Other poems by Qiu are found in the *Changchun zhenren xiyou ji* and the *Minghe yuyin (Echoes of Cranes' Songs; CT 1100). Biographical data provide more titles of his lost books, some of which may actually have overlapped with the extant works. A *Mingdao ji* 鳴道集 (Anthology of Songs to the Dao) seems to have been extant until the mid-Ming, as it is quoted in the *Zhenquan* 真詮 (Veritable Truth; *Daozang jiyao, vol. 15). A *neidan treatise, the *Dadan zhizhi* 大丹直指 (Straightforward Directions on the Great Elixir; CT 244), is attributed to him, but this is very likely a later attribution because the text is not mentioned in any biographical source, and also because Qiu does not seem to have been fond of theoretical writing.

Vincent GOOSSAERT

📖 Boltz J. M. 1987a, 66–67, 157–60; de Rachewiltz and Russell 1984; Endres 1985; Eskildsen 2001; Marsone 2001a, 105; Qing Xitai 1988–95, 3: 183–207; Qing Xitai 1994, 1: 333–34; Yao Tao-chung 1986; Zhao Yi 1999; Zhou Shaoxian 1982

※ *Changchun zhenren xiyou ji*; *Minghe yuyin*; Quanzhen

Qiu Zhao'ao

仇兆鰲

1638–1713; *zi*: Cangzhu 滄柱; *hao*: Zhiji zi 知幾子
(Master Who Knows the Subtle Beginnings)

Born in the Yin 鄞 district of Zhejiang, Qiu Zhao was a disciple of Huang Zongxi 黃宗羲 (1610–95; ECCP 351–54) and obtained his *jinshi* degree in 1685. He entered the Hanlin Academy in Beijing but later retired to devote himself to the practice of *neidan. He studied with Tao Susi 陶素耜 (fl. 1676) and received the *Zhouyi cantong qi (Token for the Agreement of the Three According to the Book of Changes) from a master of Mount Wuyi (*Wuyi shan, Fujian).

Besides commentaries to Confucian classics and to Du Fu's 杜甫 (712–70) poems, Qiu wrote two valuable compilations of notes on the *Wuzhen pian (Folios on Awakening to Reality) and the Cantong qi. The former, entitled Wuzhen pian jizhu 悟真篇集注 (Collected Commentaries to the Wuzhen pian; 1703, printed in 1713), contains selections from nine commentaries, including those of *Weng Baoguang, *Chen Zhixu, *Lu Xixing, and *Peng Haogu. The second, entitled Guben Zhouyi cantong qi jizhu 古本周易參同契 (Collected Commentaries to the Ancient Version of the Zhouyi cantong qi; 1704, printed in 1710), contains selections from sixteen commentaries, including those of *Peng Xiao, Zhu Xi 朱熹 (see *Zhouyi cantong qi kaoyi), *Chen Xianwei, and *Yu Yan. It also includes passages of Du Yicheng's 杜一誠 (fl. 1517) lost commentary, the first known work to be based on the "ancient text" (guwen 古文) version of the Cantong qi. Both compilations also include Qiu's own notes and diagrams.

Fabrizio PREGADIO

※ neidan

qixue

氣血

"breath and blood"

Qixue refers to "breath" (*qi) and "blood" (xue), which are viewed as flowing constantly through the body, being mutually transformed into one another. Qixue permeates the entire body, but it is thought to be particularly prone to flow within the conduits (*jingluo). In Chinese medicine, acupuncture and moxibustion treatment is directed at regulating its flow and balancing any form of excess. Qi is generally attributed with Yang aspects and xue with Yin aspects, though the terms are sometimes used interchangeably, depending on the context in which they are mentioned. In those cases qi and xue do not designate different entities, but different aspects of the same entity. This view is however not univocally given in the *Huangdi neijing. In Lingshu 靈樞 30 (Numinous Pivot; see Huangdi neijing), for instance, *jing (essence) is opposed to qi, and xue to mai 脈 (conduits or channels); but jing, qi, xue, and mai are all said to be aspects of qi. Here qi is used in two different senses: once it is mentioned in a narrow sense as an opposite of jing, and once in a wider sense as a superordinate term that embraces many different aspects of the phenomenal world. Blood is defined in this chapter as the qi that the "middle burner" (*zhongjiao* 中焦, the stomach system) receives and transforms into a red liquid.

Elisabeth HSU

📖 Larre 1982, 183–86; Porkert 1974, 166–86; Sivin 1987, 46–53, 147–71

※ *jing, qi, shen*

Qizhen nianpu

七真年譜

Chronology of the Seven Real Men

The *Qizhen nianpu* (CT 175), compiled in 1271, is one of the three extant historiographical works written by the *Quanzhen master *Li Daoqian. The author uses all major historiographical formats to recount the history of Quanzhen; the present text is akin to the antique style of the chronology as it provides in a serious tone, year after year, the whereabouts and major deeds of *Wang Zhe and his disciples, the Seven Real Men (*qizhen* 七真; see table 17). The sources are varied, including biographies (notably the *Qizhen xianzhuan* 七真仙傳; see *Jinlian zhengzong ji*), inscriptions, and the literary anthologies of the Seven Real Men. In his postface, Li explains that he has found the latter especially reliable.

The *Qizhen nianpu* spans 116 years, from Wang Zhe's birth (in lunar year 1112, corresponding to January 1113) to *Qiu Chuji's death in 1227. Each year's entry first mentions the age either of Wang Zhe (until 1170) or of one of his four favorite disciples in this sequence: *Ma Yu, *Tan Chuduan, *Liu Chuxuan, and finally Qiu Chuji. The text thus implies that each of the four in turn headed the Quanzhen order, a theory with no historical basis. Related events focus on the social activities of the masters, especially their ascetic prowess in public, their ritual performances, and their relationship to the state. Unpleasant events, however, such as the Quanzhen proscription in 1190–97, are omitted, and controversial ones (like the story of a Buddhist monk breaking two of Tan Chuduan's teeth) are written anew (here the culprit is a beggar). The *Qizhen nianpu* was therefore contrived to present a consensual version of Quanzhen's history when its political role was being questioned at the imperial court.

Vincent GOOSSAERT

📖 Boltz J. M. 1987a, 68; Chen Guofu 1963, 243; Qing Xitai 1994, 2: 199–200

※ Li Daoqian; Quanzhen

Quanzhen

全真

Completion of Authenticity; Complete Reality; Complete Perfection

Quanzhen is today the main official branch of Taoism in continental China. This status is not primarily due to its doctrines, for Quanzhen tenets do not radically differ from those of other Taoist schools, but rather to its celibate and communal mode of life. At least since the Tang, the Chinese state wanted Taoists to conform to Buddhist standards, but although Buddhist-style monasteries had existed since the fifth century, regulations imposing celibacy on Taoists had largely remained unheeded. The appearance around 1170 of Quanzhen, the first Taoist monastic order, whose members could more easily be registered and wore distinctive garments, apparently fit the state's religious policy of segregation between the lay and religious. Although its fortunes were not as good under the Ming dynasty as they were in the Yuan and Qing periods, Quanzhen has consistently enjoyed official protection since 1197. In this position, Quanzhen has played a major role in transmitting Taoist texts and practices, especially through the persecutions of the twentieth century.

Early history: 1170 to 1368. Quanzhen was founded by a charismatic preacher, *Wang Zhe, a *neidan* practitioner who lived as a hermit in the Zhongnan mountains (Zhongnan shan 終南山, Shaanxi) and reportedly was guided by the popular immortals *Zhongli Quan, *Lü Dongbin, and *Liu Haichan. In 1167, Wang moved to Shandong and converted adepts, seven of whom were selected by later hagiography as the first generation of Quanzhen masters, the Seven Real Men (*qizhen* 七真): *Ma Yu, *Sun Bu'er, *Tan Chuduan, *Liu Chuxuan, *Qiu Chuji, *Wang Chuyi, and *Hao Datong (see table 17). Although Wang had already started to teach and attract disciples in Shaanxi, the formal foundation of Quanzhen is traditionally associated with the setting up of five lay associations (*hui* 會) that were later to support the movement. Wang then took his four favorite disciples (Ma, Tan, Liu, and Qiu) back to the west, and died on the way. The four disciples carried his coffin back to the Zhongnan mountains, where they founded a community and then dispersed to practice asceticism and proselytize in various areas of northern China. Later Quanzhen hagiography relates that the four main disciples became patriarchs (*zongshi* 宗師) in turn after the death of the founder. Actually, the patriarchy was not created before the 1220s.

Table 17

FIRST VERSION	SECOND VERSION
Five Patriarchs	
1 Donghua dijun 東華帝君	1 Laozi 老子
2 Zhongli Quan 鍾離權	2 Donghua dijun
3 Lü Dongbin 呂洞賓	3 Zhongli Quan
4 Liu Haichan 劉海蟾	4 Lü Dongbin
5 Wang Zhe 王嚞 (1113–70)	5 Liu Haichan
Seven Real Men	
1 Ma Yu 馬鈺 (1123–84)	1 Wang Zhe
2 Tan Chuduan 譚處端 (1123–85)	2 Ma Yu
3 Liu Chuxuan 劉處玄 (1147–1203)	3 Tan Chuduan
4 Qiu Chuji 邱處機 (1148–1227)	4 Liu Chuxuan
5 Wang Chuyi 王處一 (1142–1217)	5 Qiu Chuji
6 Hao Datong 郝大通 (1140–1213)	6 Wang Chuyi
7 Sun Bu'er 孫不二 (1119–83)	7 Hao Datong

The Five Patriarchs (*wuzu* 五祖) and the Seven Real Men
(or Seven Perfected, *qizhen* 七真) of Quanzhen.

During its first decades, Quanzhen had no official existence. The teachings halls (*tang* 堂) and hermitages (*an* 庵 or 菴) founded then were not recognized by the state and many masters were not ordained Taoists. As the Quanzhen teachings quickly became popular, adepts were often invited into *guan* 觀, the usually family-run official headquarters for Taoist communities. Quanzhen adepts, however, seem to have felt that they did not really belong to such hereditary institutions, and usually founded new institutions as open teaching centers supported by lay groups. The situation deteriorated when these foundations were forbidden by the state. Quanzhen was banned in 1190 and its main center, the community built around Wang Zhe's grave in Shaanxi, was closed in 1195.

Under the management of Qiu Chuji, however, Quanzhen had built its own network and in 1197 managed to buy official recognition on favorable terms from an already depleted Jin state. Quanzhen's autonomy grew even more during the troubled times of the early thirteenth century, and when the Mongol emperor Chinggis khan (Taizu, r. 1206–27) summoned Qiu, it was in his capacity as a leader of a movement exercising influence over the whole country. In the most famous episode of Quanzhen's history, Qiu travelled to see the khan in 1222 and came back with decrees conferring on him a host of fiscal and political privileges (see under *Changchun zhenren xiyou ji*).

Historians have long debated the precise extent of those privileges and whether the order abused them. What seems clear is that Quanzhen became the official form of Taoism, and that most of the independent *guan* converted to it. When the Mongols conquered the remnants of the Jin empire in 1234, Quanzhen leaders, who were on good terms with the local Chinese and foreign chiefs, secured the conversion of the important centers in Shanxi, Shaanxi and Henan. This rapid development was backed by an autonomous organization, at the head of which was the powerful patriarch who nominated a religious administration answering only to him. This autonomy allowed Quanzhen to thrive during a time of chaos, and to raise funds on a nation-wide scale for projects of both a social nature (famine relief, ransoms, and so forth) and a religious nature, the most spectacular of which is the compilation of the largest-ever Taoist Canon between 1237 and 1244 (see *Xuandu baozang).

Controversy arose quickly, however, and some influential Buddhist hierarchs accused Quanzhen of appropriating Buddhist temples. What probably happened is that Quanzhen masters repaired and managed many abandoned religious sites, usually with the approval of local leaders. Even the Confucian school in Beijing was run by Quanzhen masters for several decades. This disruption of the religious status quo was considered dangerous, and when a doctrinal controversy arose around the old huahu 化胡 ("conversions of the barbarians"; see *Huahu jing) theme, the Buddhists secured in 1255, and again in 1258, a formal disavowal in court of the Quanzhen leaders. In a largely unrelated event, the ageing emperor Khubilai (Shizu, r. 1260–1294) reacted angrily to some religious brawls in Beijing, as well as to several military defeats, and condemned the Quanzhen-compiled Taoist Canon to be burned in 1281. Quanzhen activities also were curtailed for a time.

The debates did not have the devastating effects on Quanzhen that some historians have assumed. The best measure of the order's vitality, a chart of the numbers of Quanzhen stelae erected per year (with a total of over 500 for the 1170–1368 period), shows that its peak was indeed reached in the 1260s and slightly declined after that but remained at a high level until the 1340s. The rapid development of the order was limited when most of the earlier Taoist centers had already been converted to it, and when the pace of establishing new centers had naturally slowed. The Buddhist reaction was probably no more than one of several limiting factors. It is estimated that around the year 1300, Quanzhen had some 4,000 monasteries in northern China. Its inroads into southern China after 1276 were quantitatively more modest, probably because the social conditions were different and the southern religious scene had been already transformed by other renewal movements.

In the fourteenth century, many Taoist schools—including the newly introduced *Xuanjiao—were competing for support at court, although they also collaborated with each other. Favors went to each of them in turn, and Quanzhen had another a glorious day in 1310, when a new canonization bestowed titles on its ancestors and past patriarchs even grander than those granted in an earlier 1269 decree. These court politics, however, meant little for the vigorous Quanzhen institutions in the provinces. The earlier independence and power of the patriarchs had mostly gone, but at the local level, Quanzhen monasteries continued until 1368 to enjoy the legal and administrative independence characteristic of the Yuan religious policy.

Six centuries of Quanzhen presence. During the Ming period, Quanzhen exerted far less influence than it had under the Mongols, chiefly due to the end of its state-declared autonomy. The Quanzhen clergy and institutions were integrated into the religious bureaucracy whose head was the Celestial Master (*tianshi*) of the *Zhengyi order. Some of its main formation centers, such as the *Baiyun guan (Abbey of the White Clouds) in Beijing, were also directed by Zhengyi dignitaries. At the same time, Quanzhen ascetic training drew admiration from Taoists of all obediences: its status was acknowledged in such Zhengyi texts as the *Daomen shigui and the *Tianhuang zhidao Taiqing yuce. These methods were taught in the small Quanzhen communities (*daoyuan*) that were attached to most major Taoist centers, regardless of their affiliation.

This lack of institutional control, however, impeded Quanzhen's vitality, and the centralizing brotherhood of the Yuan dynasty (when almost all monks and nuns, whatever their generation, had shared a few common characters in their religious names) gave way during the Ming to more and more branches or lineages (*pai* 派). At the very end of the Ming, the *Longmen lineage (the most prestigious, although apparently not a very ancient one) began to restore Quanzhen's former independence. Its actual founder, *Wang Changyue (?–1680), benefited from Manchu's support and changed the monastic ordination system, which since then was controlled by Longmen masters. In the wake of this renewal movement, coupled with political change, Longmen gained control of many monasteries and convents throughout the country. During the late Qing, most eminent Quanzhen writers came from southern China, such as *Min Yide (1748–1836) and *Chen Minggui (1824–81), and some gazetteers of Quanzhen institutions were compiled in the Jiangnan 江南 area. Archival data, however, suggest that in the mid-eighteenth century most of the 25,000 or so officially recognized Quanzhen Taoists (according to the Taoist Association, there were 20,000 in 2002) lived in northern China, and that therefore their geographical distribution had not changed much since the Yuan.

The historical significance of Quanzhen can be assessed from several points of view. Its role in the political and social history of the Yuan period can hardly be overestimated. Quanzhen is not a transitory phenomenon linked to the Mongol invasion, however, but needs to be explained on the basis of long-term trends. One of these is the closure of Taoist institutions that had become hereditary, each cleric adopting a disciple from his kin. The need to open Taoism to all with true vocations prompted the appearance during the twelfth century of several movements, including the *Taiyi and the *Zhen dadao, which expanded quickly by offering instruction to all. These movements rejected or modified the traditional ordination procedures, which usually limited the number of disciples of each master to one. Quanzhen amplified this renewal with the founding of lay associations for the practice of *neidan*, and by admitting novices of all ages and social classes. One should also mention the important role played by women, who accounted for about one third of the Quanzhen clergy during the Yuan dynasty. In later times, Quanzhen did not play as large a role in channelling religious vocations, but managed to remain open to outsiders. Entry into the novitiate was limited to small "private" temples (*zisun* 子孫), while ordination was monopolized by the large "public" monasteries (*shifang* 十方). In both instances, all applicants were considered, and the selection—necessitated by the economic limitations of Quanzhen institutions—was based not on financial contributions but on individual will and endurance. This entailed very harsh trials. In addition, lay Quanzhen groups developed in the early nineteenth century in the Jiangnan and Guangdong areas. These groups ran spirit-writing shrines devoted to Lü Dongbin, who received lay disciples as Quanzhen practitioners (see under *fuji*).

Original institutions for a Taoist renewal. Most of Quanzhen's institutions can be explained as an opening of the Taoist tradition to society at large. The early urge to proselytism gave way to a more restrained style of predication. Yet Quanzhen's literary production of all periods is characterized by both its conservative nature (it does not attempt to reinterpret or add to previous revelations) and its self-avowed function to spread Taoist values and practices to the laity (Quanzhen texts are pedagogical rather that doctrinal). It seems, moreover, that only a small number of Quanzhen texts were added to the edition of the Canon published in 1244. The present Canon contains a large number of Quanzhen texts only because its editors compensated for the irretrievable losses suffered in 1281 with newer Song, Jin and Yuan works. It is important to consider that these texts are not canonical at all. With the possible exception of a few forged "scriptures"—especially the *Taigu jing* 太古經 (Scripture of Great Antiquity) and the *Chiwen donggu jing* 赤文洞古經 (Scripture of Cavernous Antiquity in Red Script)—Quanzhen did not avail itself of any written revelation. The Canon contains sixty Quanzhen works, not including those by Taoists claiming a Quanzhen descent but mainly belonging to the Southern Lineage (*Nanzong) of *neidan*. Besides these, one can retrieve from various sources eighty-one titles of lost Quanzhen works of the Yuan period, apparently confirming a similar pattern: mainly poetry, gathered either in individual or collective anthologies (the *Minghe yuyin* being the most famous), as well as hagiographies, commentaries and didactic works (such as rules and methods).

All these texts were in general circulation and entirely exoteric. Moreover, Quanzhen produced neither ritual nor *neidan* works during the Yuan period. Modern Quanzhen ritual, with the exception of the daily morning and evening services in temples, and the monastic ordination, does not differ much from non-Quanzhen ritual. The major departure is the Quanzhen musical style, which emphasizes Buddhist-influenced choral recitations (see *songjing*). This does not mean that Quanzhen masters were not interested in such topics: they were actually very active in ritual activities, and their liturgical titles show that they recited all major liturgies current during the Yuan. The same holds for *neidan*: the masters read and commented on the classical works in this genre and did not deem it necessary to create new texts. They rather chose to condense their message and make it available to all, with no changes, through their poetry. Its prevalent themes are conversion and the wonders of inner transmutation through *neidan*.

Whereas most believers simply took part in the rituals, the cult to the immortals, and perhaps meditation classes, others chose to join the order. An adept who converted to Quanzhen took up celibate life. After a novitiate (fixed at three years in late imperial times, but probably of variable length in the Yuan period), he or she was ordained and took the monastic precepts (*chuzhen jie* 初 真戒 or "initial precepts for perfection"). A Quanzhen ordination certificate dating from 1244 found at the *Yongle gong shows that Quanzhen actually used the Tang text of these precepts without substantial changes. Only the Longmen school later slightly modified it. If one stayed in a monastery, one also had to abide by the rules (see *MONASTIC CODE), but these changed from place to place and in general were not different from those of other Taoists. Quanzhen education was standard in some respects, although emphasis on practical skills (medicine, carpentry, management, and so forth) seems to have been important, especially in Yuan times. Liturgical skills were acquired on an individual basis.

The most prestigious part of Quanzhen pedagogy, and the main reason that many Taoists of other schools came to spend time in Quanzhen communities, is self-cultivation. Quanzhen disciples were given alchemical poems to meditate on, rather in the fashion of a question to be mulled over (*niantou* 念 頭) until enlightenment arose. The reading and discussion of *neidan* treatises does not seem to have played an important role during the Yuan, but it did so from the Ming onward, when the scriptures of the more speculative Southern Lineage were adopted within Quanzhen as the ultimate reference. Quanzhen education also developed specific techniques to help its adepts concentrate on self-cultivation. One was the *huandu, which involved enclosed meditation in a cell for a long period of time, helping adepts to sever links with the mundane world. Quanzhen also developed a communal practice of alchemical meditation (see under *zuobo*).

Vincent GOOSSAERT

📖 Boltz J. M. 1987a, 64–68 and 123–28; Chen Yuan 1962, 1–80; Goossaert 1997; Goossaert 2001; Goossaert 2004; Hachiya Kunio 1998; Kohn 2003c; Kubo Noritada 1967; Marsone 2001a; Marsone 2001b; Qing Xitai 1988–95, 3: passim and 4: 280–329; Qing Xitai 1994, 1: 170–82; Yao Tao-chung 1980; Yao Tad 2000

※ *yulu*; Longmen; MONASTIC CODE; MONASTICISM; TAOIST LAY ASSOCIATIONS; for other related entries see the Synoptic Table of Contents, sec. III.8 ("Quanzhen")

Rao Dongtian

饒洞天

fl. 994

Rao Dongtian was one of the two original founders of the *Tianxin zhengfa tradition, second in this capacity only to *Tan Zixiao, from whom he is said to have learned the practical methods of priesthood. According to the preface to the *Shangqing tianxin zhengfa* 上清天心正法 (Correct Method of the Celestial Heart of the Highest Clarity; CT 566) by *Deng Yougong, Rao was a scholar in retirement (*chushi* 處士), living on Mount Huagai (Huagai shan 華蓋山) in central Jiangxi. Deng Yougong reports that one night in 994 Rao saw a multicolored light shining all the way up to heaven from one of the summits, and the following morning when he dug into the ground at the spot from which the light had emitted, he found an encasement of books containing a set of "the secret formulas of the Celestial Heart" (*Tianxin bishi* 天心祕式). Still not knowing how to put the "rubrical instructions" (*juemu* 訣目) and the "precious models" (*yuge* 玉格) into practice, he met a divine person who advised him to become a disciple of Tan Zixiao. Tan transmitted his teaching to Rao and further referred him to the Benevolent and Holy Emperor of Mount Tai, Equal to Heaven (Taishan tianqi rensheng di 泰山天齊仁聖帝), from whom Rao obtained the soldiers of his "army of spirits" (*yinbing* 陰兵). Thus equipped with a complete tradition, he became the "first patriarch of the Tianxin tradition" (CT 566, preface, 1a–b).

The tradition established by Rao Dongtian was transmitted on Mount Huagai, where it reached Deng Yougong through the successive transmissions of four masters. Deng appears to have been active in the late eleventh and the early twelfth centuries and was the editor of the *Shangqing tianxin zhengfa*, one of the main early compilations of the methods of the Tianxin tradition. He also edited the *Shangqing gusui lingwen guilü* 上清骨髓靈文鬼律 (Devil's Code of the Spinal Numinous Script of the Highest Clarity; CT 461), the so-called "devil's code" (i.e., the religious code) of the tradition. In the preface to this work Deng attributes the creation of the code to Rao, the "founding immortal" (*zuxian* 祖仙), identifying its method with the "secret text" (*biwen* 祕文) unearthed by Rao on Mount Huagai. He states that Rao elaborated the code on the basis of a comparison with the laws and regulations of the worldly administration (see *Shangqing lingbao dafa*, CT 1223, 43.17a, where Jin Yunzhong 金允中 advances a similar view). It appears that the text was widely diffused among the Taoists of northern Jiangxi, because Deng relates that he searched for copies in monasteries in Hongzhou 洪州 (Jiangxi), Nankang 南康 (Jiangxi), on Mount Lu (*Lushan, Jiangxi), and in Shuzhou 舒州 (south-western corner of Anhui). He says that in this way he obtained "five versions of the Highest Clarity code," and that he edited the present version on the basis of a collation of these five versions, arranging the entries in accordance with the original form (CT 461, preface 3a). It would stand to reason, in light of these accounts, that Rao's main contribution to the Tianxin tradition consisted of the religious code, and that furthermore his codification of the institutional forms of the Tianxin tradition was widely influential in the whole region.

Poul ANDERSEN

📖 Andersen 1991, 14–17 and 81–96; Andersen 1996; Boltz J. M. 1987a, 33; Drexler 1994, 24; Hymes 2002, 26–48 and 271–80; Qing Xitai 1999

※ Tan Zixiao; Tianxin zhengfa

Rong Cheng

容成

Rong Cheng is an ancient master of esoteric techniques, especially known for sexual practices (*fangzhong shu*). His hagiography in the *Liexian zhuan*; trans. Kaltenmark 1953, 55–60) refers to him as the teacher of the Yellow Emperor (*Huangdi), King Mu of Zhou (Muwang, r. 956–918 BCE), and Laozi. These references are elaborated in other early texts such as the *Zhuangzi* (trans. Watson 1968, 112 and 283). Several sources identify him with *Guangcheng zi; a comparison of the latter's teachings and terminology in *Zhuangzi* 4 to *Daode jing* 6, suggests that—as long as the identification between them is cor-rect—Rong Cheng's teachings may indeed be an early source for Laozi (Rao Zongyi 1998).

The fourth of the ten interviews between mythical rulers and sages con-tained in the *Mawangdui manuscript, the *Shiwen* 十問 (Ten Questions; trans. Harper 1998, 385–411), is between the Yellow Emperor and Rong Cheng who expounds on breathing techniques and preservation of pneuma (*qi*). An-other mythical cluster identifies Rong Cheng as an ancient ruler (*Zhuangzi* 4), lording over a paradisiacal era when men and animals lived in harmony (*Huainan zi* 8).

At least five Han *fangshi* are said to have practiced Rong Cheng's methods of sexual cultivation: *Zuo Ci, Gan Shi 甘始, Dongguo Yannian 東郭延年, Feng Junda 封君達, and Ling Shouguang 泠壽光 (*Hou Hanshu*, 82B.2740 and 2750; *Bowu zhi* 博物志 7). These practices were specifically condemned by the early Celestial Masters in the *Xiang'er commentary to the *Daode jing* (Bokenkamp 1997, 43–44).

Gil RAZ

📖 Bokenkamp 1997, 43, 87, and 125; Campany 2002, 358–59; Kaltenmark 1953, 55–60; Li Ling 2000b, 350–93; Ngo 1976, 126–27; Rao Zongyi 1956, 12, 38, and 74–75; Rao Zongyi 1998

※ *fangzhong shu*; HAGIOGRAPHY

Ruyao jing

入藥鏡

Mirror for Compounding the Medicine

Attributed to the Sichuan master Cui Xifan 崔希范 (ca. 880–940), this dense ancient-style poem of 246 characters, divided into eighty-two three-character lines, lays out the basic elements of *neidan. The title refers to mixing healing medicines, here meant as a metaphor for compounding the inner elixir. In the millennium or so since it began circulating in the world, the text has produced much controversy and commentary, usually focused on whether it advocates sexual practices. Zeng Zao 曾慥 strongly criticized sexual interpretations of the text (*Daoshu*, j. 3.4b–7b, j. 37). An annotated poetic version included in Xiao Tingzhi's 蕭廷芝 (fl. 1260–64) *Jindan dacheng ji (Anthology on the Great Achievement of the Golden Elixir), which is now in the *Xiuzhen shishu (Ten Books on the Cultivation of Perfection, 13.1a–9b) together with a different prose edition (21.6b–9b), is also critical of these interpretations. The poetic version annotated by *Wang Jie (?– ca. 1380) found in the *Cui gong ruyao jing zhujie* 崔公入藥鏡注解 (Commentary and Explications to the *Ruyao jing* by Sir Cui; CT 135) was later combined with the commentaries of the Ming scholars Li Panlong 李攀龍 (1514–70; DMB 845–47 and IC 545–47) and *Peng Haogu (fl. 1597–1600) as the *Ruyao jing hejie* 入藥鏡合解 (Collected Explications of the *Ruyao jing*; *Daozang jiyao*, vol. 11).

This is one of the earliest texts to clearly distinguish the vital energies said to exist before the phenomenal unfolding of the cosmos (*xiantian) from the vital energies circulating in the phenomenal world (*houtian). A thorough study of the text's versions, commentaries, and uses would be most welcome.

Lowell SKAR

📖 Boltz J. M. 1987a, 234, 236

※ *neidan*

ruyi

入意

Reading the Document of Intention

The Document of Intention (*yiwen* 意文) is read during individual rites within a Taoist ritual. It states who is performing the ritual and for what purpose, based on the notion that if this were omitted, the deities would not know whom to help or how, and the ritual would be ineffective.

Memorials and other documents sent to the deities are burned during individual rites. The Taoist priest (*daoshi) uses the Document of Intention throughout the entire ritual, however, and it is read out by the assistant cantor (*fujiang* 副講) whenever the liturgical manuals say it is necessary, for example during the rite for Lighting the Incense Burner (*falu). Essential information in the Document of Intention includes the Taoist name and rank of the priest performing the ritual, the names of the sponsors and their functions in the ritual, the type of ritual being performed, and its time, place, and program. For those who have commissioned the ritual, it is important that their names and those of their relatives are spelled and pronounced correctly. Sometimes the list of names grows to remarkable proportions, and it may take several priests a long time to recite them all. For scholars, the analysis of the Document of Intention is valuable for the sociological study of Taoist ritual.

MARUYAMA Hiroshi

📖 Ōfuchi Ninji 1983, 213–14

※ *gongde; jiao; shu; zhai*

Sa Shoujian

薩守堅

fl. 1141–78?; *hao*: Fenyang Sa ke 汾陽薩客
(Stranger Sa of Fenyang); also known as Sa Jian 薩堅

The provenance of Sa Shoujian remains uncertain. Yuan and Ming *zaju* 雜劇 (variety plays) feature a protagonist by this name, as does a long episodic narrative compiled in 1603 by Deng Zhimo 鄧志謨. The roots of Deng's work, *Sa zhenren zhouzao ji* 薩真人咒棗記 (Record of Spellbinding Jujubes and the Perfected Sa), rest in well-established hagiographic lore.

Two anthologies in the Taoist Canon contain the story of Sa Shoujian. The shorter version in the *Soushen ji (In Search of the Sacred) of 1593 is clearly derivative of the account in the *Lishi zhenxian tidao tongjian (Xubian 續編), compiled by Zhao Daoyi 趙道一 (fl. 1294–1307). Sa's place of origin is given as either Nanhua 南華 (Shandong) or Xihe 西河 (Shanxi). The *Soushen ji* and later hagiographies locate the latter site in Shu 蜀 (Sichuan) but Sa's *hao* establishes an association with Fenyang 汾陽 (Shanxi). He apparently served as a physician in Shu because he is said to have left that region when one of his patients died after taking medicine he had prescribed. This loss led Sa to abandon medical practice and set out in search of celebrated experts in Taoist ritual. He was not aware that the three men he encountered en route to Xinzhou 信州 (Jiangxi) were avatars of precisely those with whom he sought to study, the thirtieth Celestial Master *Zhang Jixian (1092–1126), and *Shenxiao specialists *Lin Lingsu (1076–1120) and *Wang Wenqing (1093–1153). One gave him a letter of introduction to the Celestial Master headquarters at Mount Longhu (*Longhu shan, Jiangxi) and magical jujubes that with the proper incantation would produce cash sufficient for daily needs. From his companions Sa received gifts of *leifa (Thunder Rites) and a fan guaranteed to cure illness. After presenting the letter, Sa realized that he had already succeeded in his quest and thereafter made great use of the instruction he had received.

The second episode common to hagiographic accounts testifies to the exalted level of ritual practice for which Sa became known. It is the story of how he overcame a wayward city god who eventually submitted to Sa's superior authority and then came to be recognized as *Wang lingguan, paramount guardian of Taoist abbeys. Sa himself is said to have expired seated in meditation in Zhangzhou 漳州 (Fujian).

Writings on Thunder Rites ascribed to Sa are recorded in the *Daofa huiyuan

(Corpus of Taoist Ritual). Zhou Side 周思得 (1359–1451), a renowned Taoist Master from Qiantang 錢塘 (Zhejiang), was so successful in his application of rituals in the name of Wang lingguan that the Yongle Emperor (r. 1403–24) established a shrine just outside the imperial compound. The Xuande Emperor (r. 1426–35) elevated this shrine to the status of an abbey and authorized entitlements for both Wang and Sa, designating the latter as Chong'en zhenjun 崇恩 真君 (Perfected Lord of Lofty Compassion). The popularity of Sa in theatrical and narrative works is presumably due in part to continued imperial sanction of his enshrinement during the Ming. Adherents of the Xihe pai 西河派, a branch of the Shenxiao school of ritual practice, have also kept his memory alive.

Judith M. BOLTZ

     Boltz J. M. 1987a, 47–48, 187; Boltz J. M. 1993a, 284–85; Ono Shihei 1982

※ *leifa*

sanchao

三朝

Three Audiences

The "three audiences" are the Morning Audience (*zaochao* 早朝), the Noon Audience (*wuchao* 午朝), and the Evening Audience (*wanchao* 晚朝). In the classical Taoist *jiao liturgy, transmitted for instance by *Zhengyi priests in major cities of continental China, such as Shanghai and Quanzhou 泉州 (Fujian), as well as in many parts of Taiwan, the audiences are the core rituals performed on the central day (or days) of the ceremony, through which the main goal of communication with the supreme celestial deities is achieved. They are referred to as rituals of *xingdao ("walking [or: practicing] the Way"), both in references within the ritual texts themselves, and in classifications found in ritual compendia from as early as the Six Dynasties. The tradition of holding three audiences in one day is attested in the writings of *Du Guangting (850–933), who further describes the more complete programs of nine rituals of *xingdao*, performed on three consecutive days (see *Huanglu zhaiyi* 黃籙齋 儀, CT 507, j. 1–9).

The audiences always include the presentation of offerings to the supreme deities, and in some regional traditions in modern times this aspect is given special emphasis. Thus, for instance, in the *jiao* ceremonies of Changzhou 長州, Hong Kong, a regular daily rhythm is set by the "three audiences and three repentances" (*sanchao sanchan* 三朝三懺; see *chanhui), which focus on displays of vegetarian offerings on outdoor tables, as well as on expressions of repentance for sins committed, and on praying for forgiveness on behalf of the people of the community (see Choi Chi-Cheung 1995, and Tanaka Issei 1989b). In the classical form of the audiences, the presentations of offerings are central elements of the ritual performed inside the closed sacred area, and they consist of triple presentations of incense and tea to the Three Clarities (*sanqing), followed by hymns and dancing. The ritual also focuses on the transmission of a document, which in the Morning Audience is termed Transmitting the Declaration (*chengci* 呈詞), and differently in the other audiences, depending on the specific designation of the document used. On especially important occasions the transmission of the document comprises the complex meditational or "ecstatic" practices of the high priest (*gaogong* 高功; see *daozhang), referred to as *fuzhang* 伏章, "submitting the petition," through which he performs a journey to heaven in order to deliver the document to the Most High. The audiences thus not only define the central parts of the program, but also in a sense—that is, from the perspective of the priests—represent the high point of the liturgy, in terms of the inner realization of the encounter with the gods, and the effective delivery of the supplication that describes the overall purpose of the service.

Poul ANDERSEN

📖 Andersen 1990; Andersen 1995; Lagerwey 1987c, 106–9 and passim; Lü and Lagerwey 1992, 39–44; Matsumoto Kōichi 1983; Ōfuchi Ninji 1983, 297–332; Saso 1975, 1481–1628, 2223–2354, and 3191–3322; Saso 1978b, 208–14 and passim; Schipper 1975c, 8–11; Schipper 1993, 91–99; Zhang Enpu 1954

※ *xingdao*; *jiao*

sandong

三洞

Three Caverns

See entry in "Taoism: An Overview," p. oo.

Sandong jingshu mulu

三洞經書目錄

Index of Scriptures and Writings of the Three Caverns

This listing of Taoist scriptures, the earliest comprehensive canonical list known to modern scholarship, was presented to the throne on imperial command by the Taoist *Lu Xiujing in 471. While Lu's work does not survive, its listing of the *Lingbao scriptures is cited in the *Tongmen lun* 通門論 (Comprehensive Treatise on the Doctrine) of Song Wenming 宋文明 (fl. 549–51; see *Lingbao jingmu*). From later Taoist works and Buddhist polemical treatises, we can gain some idea of the structure of the catalogue.

Lu's catalogue originally comprised 1,228 *juan* of texts, of which 138 had not yet been revealed on earth. The texts were divided into three "caverns" or "comprehensive collections": *Dongzhen* 洞真 (Cavern of Perfection), *Dongxuan* 洞玄 (Cavern of Mystery), and *Dongshen* 洞神 (Cavern of Spirit). All subsequent Taoist Canons were organized into these Three Caverns (*SANDONG).

The Three Caverns contained, respectively, the *Shangqing, Lingbao, and the *Sanhuang wen* scriptural collections. The Caverns were also associated with specific heavens, deities, and the successive revelation of their contents in previous *kalpa*-cycles. The Caverns are listed in descending order, from the highest and most exalted, Shangqing, to the lowest, Sanhuang. This grading of deities, heavens, and practices seems to accord with the dispositions of the original Lingbao scriptures, which held that while the doctrines of the Shangqing scriptures were the most exalted, they were correspondingly difficult and perhaps should not have been revealed in the human realm and that the *Sanhuang wen* contained lesser practices.

Buddhist polemics state that the catalogue listed 186 *juan* of Shangqing scriptures, of which sixty-nine were unrevealed, and thirty-six *juan* of Lingbao scriptures, of which fifteen were unrevealed. They go on to point out that these "unrevealed" texts were later supplied by writers of the fifth and sixth centuries. They further complain that subsequent Taoist Canons contained the works of philosophers such as *Zhuangzi and *Liezi, *zhiguai* 志怪 literature ("records of the strange"), such as the *Liexian zhuan* and *Shenxian zhuan*, as well as technical works on hygiene, geomancy, medicine, dietetics, fortune telling and the like—none of which were listed in Lu's catalogue.

Given that we have no information on five-sixths of the catalog's contents—Did it contain, for instance Celestial Master writings? If so, where were these placed?—scholars have devoted the majority of their efforts to exploring the history of the Three Caverns concept itself. The most influential opinion is that the tripartite division of Lu's catalogue was influenced by the Three Vehicles (*sansheng* 三乘, Skt. *triyāna*) of Buddhism. These are, in descending order, those of the bodhisattvas, the pratyekabuddhas, and the auditors. As presented, for instance, in the *Lotus Sūtra* (*Saddharmapuṇḍarīka-sūtra*), invocation of three vehicles was always intended to highlight the superiority of the Mahāyāna (Great Vehicle) bodhisattva path. In that the Three Caverns are a ranking of practice, the Three Vehicles may have played some role in their formulation, though specific Taoist comparisons of their Three Caverns with the Three Vehicles appear only in the Tang. The early Lingbao scriptures, on which Lu based his catalogue, on the other hand, claim that all three Caverns are the "greater vehicle," while comparing the three to the "three mounds" (*sanfen* 三墳), an expression used in Han and later Confucian writings to designate the writings attributed to the three ancient sage-kings, the Yellow Emperor (*Huangdi), the Divine Husbandman (Shennong 神農), and Fu Xi 伏羲. As the Three Caverns can be traced to the Shangqing and Lingbao scriptures, it is more accurate to see the origin of Lu's organization of his "canon" as growing naturally from indigenous concepts such as the three ages of antiquity, together with early Taoist cosmological notions of the Three Heavens.

Stephen R. BOKENKAMP

📖 Bokenkamp 2001; Chen Guofu 1963, 1–2 and 106–7; Kohn 1995a, 130–38 and 218–19; Ōfuchi Ninji 1974; Ōfuchi Ninji 1979; Ozaki Masaharu 1983b, 75–88; Qing Xitai 1988–95, 1: 543–46

※ Lu Xiujing; DAOZANG AND SUBSIDIARY COMPILATIONS; SANDONG

Sandong qionggang

三洞瓊綱

Exquisite Compendium of the Three Caverns

Writings on the history of the Taoist Canon commonly apply this title to the canon compiled during the Kaiyuan reign period (713–41). Most primary sources, however, give *Sandong qionggang* as the title of the catalogue for what later generations referred to as the *Kaiyuan daozang* 開元道藏 (Taoist Canon of the Kaiyuan Reign Period). The first component of this title alludes to the conventional threefold division of the Taoist Canon into Three Caverns (*SANDONG). Some accounts refer to this compilation by the alternative title of *Qionggang jingmu* 瓊綱經目 (Catalogue of the Scriptures of the Exquisite

Compendium). Like the catalogue *Yin Wencao (622–88) compiled in connection with the first Tang canon of 675, the Kaiyuan catalogue is no longer
extant. The text of a *Dunhuang ms. of 718 (P. 2861) traced to the *Sandong
qionggang* (Maspero 1981, 314–15) is actually a fragment of a sixth-century anthology (Ōfuchi Ninji 1978–79, 1: 337).

Sources not only differ on the title but also on the size of both the text and
canon it accompanied. *Du Guangting wrote in 891 that Tang Xuanzong (r.
712–56) author[iz]ed a *Qionggang jingmu* accounting for altogether 7,300 *juan*. This
imperial enterprise allegedly arose in response to a proliferation of scriptures
and teachings during the Kaiyuan reign period. A somewhat larger perspective
is conveyed in an extant postface from a bibliographic unit of the lost *Sanchao
guoshi* 三朝國史 (State History of Three Reigns) of 1030, documenting the
years 960–1022 of Song Taizu, Taizong, and Zhenzong. As preserved in the
Wenxian tongkao 文獻通考 (General Study of Literary Submissions) by Ma
Duanlin 馬端臨 (1254–1325), this postface claims that a canon resulted during
the Kaiyuan reign period from sorting through a range of Taoist teachings that
started coming into prominence after the Later Han. Here the catalogue is titled
Sandong qionggang and is said to have accounted for a collection totalling 3,744
juan. The same title given by Du Guangting but a different tally of the canon
is recorded in a historical outline appended to the *Daozang quejing mulu* (Index
of Scriptures Missing from the Taoist Canon). This outline, dated 1275, credits
Xuanzong with authorizing the compilation of a *Qionggang jingmu* accounting
for 5,700 *juan* rather than 7,300 *juan*. The preceding statement in the outline
gives the latter sum as the size of the canon catalogued by Yin Wencao.

The *Daozang quejing mulu* itself lists a *Sandong qionggang* in 5 *juan* as miss-
ing. Three Song bibliographies make note of a *Sandong qionggang* in 3 *juan*. It
is already marked as a missing text in the 1144 list reconstructed from the lost
Song imperial library catalogue, the *Chongwen zongmu* 崇文總目 (Complete
Catalogue [of the Institute] for the Veneration of Literature). The entry in the
bibliography of the *Xin Tangshu* (New History of the Tang) compiled under
Ouyang Xiu 歐陽修 (1007–72) ascribes a *Sandong qionggang* in 3 *juan* to "Taoist
Master Zhang Xianting" 道士張仙庭 (van der Loon 1984, 74). This attribution may very well have been drawn from the original *Chongwen zongmu* that
Ouyang helped see to completion in 1042. An identical entry is incongruently
recorded in the subdivision on talismanic registers in the inventory of Taoist
texts within the *Tongzhi* 通志 (Comprehensive Monographs) by Zheng Qiao
鄭樵 (1104–62; SB 146–56). Largely derived from earlier bibliographies, this
inventory includes within the subdivision on catalogues an entry for a *Kaiyuan
daojing mu* 開元道經目 (Catalogue of Taoist Scriptures of the Kaiyuan Reign
Period) in 1 *juan*. The provenance of this apparent counterpart to Zhang
Xianting's compilation is unclear.

The significance of the *Sandong qionggang* and *Kaiyuan daozang* it served cannot be overestimated. In 749 Xuanzong established a precedent by assigning the Institute for the Veneration of the Mystery (Chongxuan guan 崇玄館) the task of making copies of the canon for dispersal throughout the empire. Just how many copies were actually completed and distributed is not known. There is evidence to suggest that copies held in the major temple compounds did survive subsequent uprisings and the fall of the Tang. In any case, later generations working on recompilations of the canon seem to have had recourse to at least some vestige of the canon and its catalogue.

Judith M. BOLTZ

📖 Chen Guofu 1963, 1.114–27; Chen Jinhong 1992; van der Loon 1984, 4–10, 15–17, 37, and 74; Maspero 1981, 314–15

※ DAOZANG AND SUBSIDIARY COMPILATIONS

Sandong qunxian lu

三洞群仙錄

Accounts of the Gathered Immortals from the Three Caverns

The *Sandong qunxian lu* (CT 1248) is an anthology of selections from biographies of immortals, compiled by 1154 by Chen Baoguang 陳葆光, with a preface written by Lin Jizhong 林季仲 (fl. 1121–57) dating from that year. Chen was a *Zhengyi Taoist from present day Jiangsu, and the preface claims that he compiled this anthology to argue that immortality was a state that could be attained by any person, given sufficient study, and did not require that someone be fated to attain it. Like the *Xianyuan bianzhu (Paired Pearls from the Garden of Immortals) it is an important source for lost biographies or portions of biographies and it follows the pattern established in that anthology for citing a pair of biographies in each entry. At twenty chapters it is, however, much longer and its range of source texts is broader, encompassing texts composed as late as the Song. This very breadth presents its own difficulties as the attributions sometimes lack credibility with the biographies of some figures cited from works complete before they were born, or with the same entry cited from different source texts. In addition, some selections are cited from texts that are themselves anthologies.

Benjamin PENNY

📖 Boltz J. M. 1987a, 59; Chen Guofu 1963, 241–42; Qing Xitai 1994, 2: 194

※ HAGIOGRAPHY

Sandong zhunang

三洞珠囊

The Pearl Satchel of the Three Caverns

The *Sandong zhunang* (CT 1139) is a ten-*juan* collection of excerpts from scriptures, biographies, and other texts dating from the second through the sixth centuries. All that is known of the author, Wang Xuanhe 王懸和, is that he was the calligrapher for two inscriptions of imperial texts carved on stelae in Sichuan in 664 and 684. This suggests that he may have served the Tang court in some capacity during the reign of Emperor Gaozong (649–83) and could have compiled this work at the behest of the throne.

Wang organized the materials of his compendium under thirty-three rubrics that covered roughly nine subjects:

1. Salvation, including not only the attainment of immortality, but also the healing of the ill (*juan* 1).

2. Priestly vocation: asceticism (2.1a–4a); eremitism (2.4a–5a); and service to the state (imperial summons, 2.5a–8a).

3. Longevity and immortality: diet (*juan* 3); abstention from eating cereals (4.1a–5b); elixirs (4.5b–9a); and alchemical furnaces and incense braziers (4.9a–11a).

4. Meditation (5.1a–5a) and long fasts (5.5a–11b).

5. Rituals: Retreat assemblies (*zhaihui* 齋會, 6.1a–2a); casting dragon tablets (*tou longjian) in rivers and off mountains (2.8a–12a); rules governing the transmission of scriptures, registers, precepts, etc. (6.3a–4b); penalties for forsaking or losing the same (6.2a–3a); the rites for transmitting and maintaining the eight precepts (6.13b–14a); taboos concerning the performance of rites for establishing merit (6.4b–13a); and clacking teeth and swallowing saliva (*juan* 10).

6. Cosmology: the twenty-four parishes (*zhi, 7.1a–15a); the twenty-four pneumas (*qi, 7.15a–16b); the twenty-four hells (7.16b–17b); the twenty-four parish offices (*zhi* 職, 7.17b–19b); the twenty-four signs of divine grace (green dragons, white tigers, phoenixes, etc., 7.19b–21b); the twenty-four authentic charts (*zhentu* 真圖, 7.21b–22a); the twenty-eight lunar lodges (7.25a–26a); the thirty-two heavens (*sanshi'er tian*) as well as their gods and corresponding hells (7.26a–35a); and the division and conversion of paradises (8.32a–34a).

7. Divinities: the twenty-seven ranks of saints, perfected, immortals, etc. (7.22a–24b); and the physical appearance of the gods and immortals (8.1a–24a).

8. Time: celestial era titles and important dates (8.24a–32a); figures for *kalpas* (*jie*, 9.1a–5b) and sacred hours and holy days (9.20b–22a).

9. The hagiography of Laozi: his role as a preceptor to emperors (9.5b–8a) and his "conversion of the barbarians" (*huahu* 化胡, 9.8b–20b).

The *Sandong zhunang* is one of the most important works in the *Daozang* for several reasons. First, it preserves passages from works that are no longer extant. For example, it contains some ninety-five citations from the lost *Daoxue zhuan* (Biographies of Those who Studied the Dao, originally twenty scrolls) compiled by Ma Shu 馬樞 (522–81) in the second half of the sixth century; it was these materials that enabled Chen Guofu (1963, 454–504) to partially reconstruct Ma's collection. Second, in cases where Taoist texts have survived more or less intact, passages in Wang's collection serve as a basis for authenticating them. Finally, the compendium serves as a measure of what scriptures and liturgies were available to Taoists of the seventh century.

Charles D. BENN

📖 Boltz J. M. 1987a, 228; Chen Guofu 1963, 240; Ōfuchi Ninji and Ishii Masako 1988, 118–35 (list of texts cited); Reiter 1990a

sanguan

三官

Three Offices

The Three Offices of Heaven, Earth, and Water are recorded in the earliest historical accounts of the Celestial Master movement (*Tianshi dao). There we read that sinners and criminals would seek absolution from the Three Offices by writing our three confessions and sending them off by placing the petition to the Heaven Office high on a mountain, burying the petition to the Earth Office in the ground, and throwing the petition to the Water Office into a body of water.

The early Celestial Master scripture *Chisong zi zhangli* (Master Red-Pine's Almanac of Petitions) records that it is the Three Offices who will choose the "seed-people" (*zhongmin*) destined to survive the apocalypse and repopulate the world of Great Peace. Later Taoist scriptures like the *Taishang sanyuan cifu* *shezui jie'e xiaozai yansheng baoming miaojing* 太上三元賜福赦罪解厄消災延生保命妙經 (Wondrous Scripture of the Most High Three Primes that Confers Happiness, Liberates from Faults, Eliminates Dangers, Dispels Disasters, Extends One's Life, and Preserves One's Destiny; CT 1442) associate the Three Offices with the festivals of the Three Primes (held on the fifteenth day of the first, seventh, and tenth lunar month for Heaven, Earth, and Water, respectively; see under *sanhui), and associate the offices with different functions: the Office of Heaven is said to be in charge of distributing blessings, whereas the Earth Office pardoned those guilty of transgressions and the Water Office eliminated any disasters or misfortunes that might have become associated with the individual.

Despite this positive interpretation, Taoist scriptures often identity the Three Offices as a place of posthumous torture and interrogation and some sources associate the Three Offices with the Taoist hell of *Fengdu. It is clear that officials in the Three Offices have as their primary duty the maintenance on a registers recording both good and evil acts and the correlation of these records with the actual fates of both the living and the dead. They employ torture to ascertain relevant facts and as a form of punishment, and on that basis assign punishments that can affect not only the individual in question but his or her ancestors in the other world and his descendents yet to be born. Conversely, positive notations in their records can result in similar good fortune for the individual and his or her entire family. It does not seem that officials of the Three Offices are directly responsible for observing and record human actions; one passage mentions that the gods of the body perform this function and we might assume that the Stove God (*Zaoshen) worshipped in every household and local Gods of Soil and Grain (Sheji 社稷) fulfilled this function as well.

Within Taoism, the Three Offices seem to have been displaced by the system of hells centering on Fengdu and by the popular system of Ten Kings of Hell, but they are still the object of popular veneration and their temples are found throughout China. There are various popular traditions concerning the identity of the heads of the Three Offices, including one that identifies them as the sage kings Yao 堯 (Heaven), Shun 舜 (Earth), and Yu 禹 (Water) and one that identifies them as villainous officials who served evil King You ("Benighted") of Zhou (Youwang 幽王, r. 781–771 BCE).

Terry KLEEMAN

📖 Little 2000b, 233–36; Qing Xitai 1994, 3: 35–36

※ Tianshi dao; DEITIES: THE PANTHEON

sanguan

三關

Three Passes

The three stages of *neidan* practice are often represented as an initiatory path symbolized by the crossing over of three Passes. These Passes represent barriers along the Control Channel in the phase of yangization, and along the Function Channel in the phase of yinization (see *dumai* and *renmai*; on "yangization" and "yinization," see *huohou*.) Located along the spinal column, they mark the ascension of pneuma (*qi*) or the progression of Yang Fire (*yanghuo* 陽 火), also known as Martial Fire (*wuhuo* 武火), to the upper Cinnabar Field (*dantian*) in the summit of the head, followed by the descent of the Yin Fire (*yinfu* 陰符), also known as Civil Fire (*wenhuo* 文火), to the lower Cinnabar Field at the level of the navel.

The first pass, at the level of the coccyx, is called *weilü* 尾閭 (Caudal Funnel). This term refers to a mythical place mentioned in *Zhuangzi* 17, an orifice in the ocean where water endlessly leaks away without ever being exhausted. In the human body, this place is located in the "aquatic region" of the hip basin that forms the base of the trunk. It represents the pivot of energy presided over by the kidneys, which are the sanctuary of the essence (*jing*) and organs of water. According to some texts, the *weilü* is located at the level of the third vertebra above the coccyx and is called by various names such as *changqiang* 長強 (Long and Powerful), or *sancha lu* 三岔路 (Three-Forked Road), *heche lu* 河車路 (Path of the River Chariot).

The second pass, located in the middle of the spinal column where it joins the ribs at chest level (at the shoulder blades), is called *jiaji* 夾脊 (Spinal Handle). The two characters *jia* and *ji* are also found in *Zhuangzi* 30, where they are separately employed to describe the sword of the Son of Heaven that "pierces the floating clouds above and penetrates the weft of the earth below." Expanding on the image of the celestial sword, this Pass is qualified as "dual" (*shuangguan* 雙關) as it is not only physically inserted between the heart and the vertebrae but also represents the interstice between Earth (Yin, Lead) and Heaven (Yang, Mercury). Some texts therefore emphasize that it is located exactly in the middle of the twenty-four vertebrae. From this center, the pneuma can ascend or descend, climbing to Heaven or plunging again into the abysses.

The third pass is at the level of the occipital bone and is called *yuzhen* 玉枕 (Jade Pillow). It is also referred to as *tiebi* 鐵壁 (Iron Wall), as it is regarded as the most difficult barrier to overcome.

Within the three-stage process of *neidan*, the first Pass is the locus of the sublimation of essence into pneuma, and is connected to the lower Cinnabar Field. The second Pass is the place where pneuma is sublimated into spirit (*shen*); it plays the role of the Center, and is the middle Cinnabar Field linked to the heart. This Pass is also related to the lower Cinnabar Field, however, as it represents the moment of transition from the lower to upper Fields. The third Pass is the place where the final sublimation of *shen* takes place with its return to Emptiness. In a general way, this designates the part of the upper Cinnabar Field where the spiritual embryo (*shengtai*) is realized at the end of the alchemical work.

Monica ESPOSITO

📖 Despeux 1994, 80–87; Esposito 1993, 65–73; Esposito 1997, 51–63; Robinet 1993, 80–82

※ *dumai* and *renmai*; *huohou*; *xuanguan*; *neidan*

sanhuang

三皇

Three Sovereigns

While the Three Sovereigns are generally considered to be mythical emperors of ancient times, there is no consensus among different sources as to their identity. In the *Shujing* 書經 (Book of Documents) they are Fu Xi 伏羲, Shennong 神農, and *Huangdi (the Yellow Emperor). In the *Shiji* (Records of the Historian; j. 6), they are given variously as the Sovereign of Heaven (Tianhuang 天皇), the Sovereign of Earth (Dihuang 地皇), and the Great Sovereign (Taihuang 泰皇), or as the Sovereigns of Heaven, Earth, and Humanity. In the *Baihu tongyi* 白虎通義 (Comprehensive Accounts from the White Tiger [Hall]) they are Fu Xi, Shennong, and Zhu Rong 祝融 (the fire god). In an apocryphon on the *Liji* 禮記 (Records of Rites) they are Suiren 燧人, Fu Xi, and Shennong, and in an apocryphon on the *Chunqiu* 春秋 (Spring and Autumn Annals) they are Fu Xi, Shennong, and Nü Gua 女媧.

In Taoist sources, the Three Sovereigns are usually regarded as the Sovereigns of Heaven, Earth, and Humanity. Fragments of the now-lost *Sanhuang jing* 三皇經 (Scripture of the Three Sovereigns; see *Sanhuang wen*) preserve this tradition. According to a quotation from this text in the *Wushang biyao* (Supreme Secret Essentials; 6.5b), "the Sovereign of Heaven rules over pneuma (*qi*), the Sovereign of Earth rules over spirit (*shen*), and the Sovereign of Humanity rules over life (*sheng* 生). Together, these three give rise to virtue (**de*) and transform the ten thousand things." The same text states that "the Three Sovereigns are the Venerable Gods of the Three Caverns (*sandong zhi zunshen* 三洞之尊神) and the Ancestral Pneuma of Great Being (*dayou zhi zuqi* 大有 之祖氣)" (6.5a). One can see here an attempt by followers of the *Sanhuang jing* to contest the low rank assigned to the Cavern of Spirit (*dongshen* 洞神, to which belong the Sanhuang texts) among the Three Caverns (**SANDONG*), by assigning the *Sanhuang jing* a higher status with authority over the other two Caverns. A related source, the *Taishang dongshen sanhuang yi* 太上洞神三 皇儀 (Highest Liturgy for the Three Sovereigns of the Cavern of Spirit; CT 803), states that "the Highest Emperor Sovereign of Heaven governs life, the Highest Emperor Sovereign of Earth deletes [your name from] the registers of death (*siji* 死籍), and the Highest Emperor Sovereign of Humanity abolishes misfortune due to sin."

Rituals addressed to the Three Sovereigns are found in *Wushang biyao* 49 (Lagerwey 1981b, 152–56) and in **Lu Xiujing's (406–77) Wugan wen* 五感文 (Text on the Five Commemorations; CT 1278). While in Lu's work the Retreat of the Three Sovereigns (*sanhuang zhai* 三皇齋) is performed to obtain immortality, the early-eighth-century **Daojiao yishu* (Pivot of Meaning of the Taoist Teaching, 2.21a) places the same ritual at the head of a list of seven *zhai*, stating that its purpose is also to "protect the nation."

YAMADA Toshiaki

📖 Andersen 1994; Chen Guofu 1963, 71–78; Robinet 1984, 1: 27–29

※ *Sanhuang wen*; DEITIES: THE PANTHEON

Sanhuang wen

三皇文

Script of the Three Sovereigns

The *Sanhuang wen*, also known as *Sanhuang neiwen* 三皇內文 (Inner Script of the Three Sovereigns) and *Sanhuang jing* 三皇經 (Scripture of the Three Sovereigns), is the main scripture of the Cavern of Spirit (Dongshen 洞神) division of the Taoist Canon. The original text, which is not extant, appears to have contained talismans (**FU*) and explanatory texts. It was so named because it was revealed by the Sovereigns of Heaven, Earth, and Humanity (see **sanhuang*).

While there is no reliable evidence to tell us exactly when the scripture first appeared, the earliest record of its existence is in chapter 19 of the *Baopu zi* (Book of the Master Who Embraces Simplicity). Here *Ge Hong (283–343) emphasizes its value, writing: "I heard my master *Zheng Yin say that among the important writings on the Dao none surpasses the *Sanhuang neiwen* and the *Wuyue zhenxing tu* (Charts of the Real Forms of the Five Peaks)." In Ge's time, the *Sanhuang wen* was in three scrolls and was believed to be related to the writings revealed to Bo He 帛和. It could not be transmitted even by a master, and only those who entered a mountain with sincere intentions could see it. Moreover, the scripture was deemed to have the power to quell demons and banish misfortune: "If a household possesses this scripture, one can keep away evil and noxious demons, quell unhealthy pneumas (*qi), intercept calamities, and neutralize misfortunes." In the same chapter of his work, Ge Hong also writes: "If a master of the Dao wishes to search for long life and enters a mountain holding this text, he will ward off tigers, wolves, and mountain sprites. The five poisons (*wudu* 五毒) and the hundred evils (*baixie* 百邪) will not dare to come near him." After a period of purification and fasting lasting a hundred days, one could command the celestial deities, the Director of Destinies (*Siming), and various other major and minor gods. In Ge Hong's time, therefore, the *Sanhuang wen* was primarily seen as a protective talisman.

History of the text. Both the *Erjiao lun* 二教論 (Essay on the Two Teachings), by the Northern Zhou Buddhist priest Dao'an 道安 (312–85; Lagerwey 1981b, 21–28), and the *Xiaodao lun* (Essays to Ridicule the Dao), by Zhen Luan 甄鸞 (fl. 535–81), report that the *Sanhuang wen* had been created by *Bao Jing (?–ca. 330, Ge Hong's father-in-law), and that when this was discovered he was sentenced to death. Later, the "Sanhuang jingshuo" 三皇經說 (Explanation of the *Scripture of the Three Sovereigns*; YJQQ 1) states that when Bao was fasting and meditating in a cavern, the scripture appeared spontaneously on its walls. This version of the *Sanhuang wen* is the one that was later transmitted to Ge Hong, and is known as the "Ancient Script of the Three Sovereigns" ("Gu Sanhuang wen" 古三皇文).

Not long after these alleged events, the "Tianwen dazi" 天文大字 (Celestial Script in Great Characters) was added to the text, and according to the *Xuanmen dayi (Great Meaning of the School of Mysteries), when *Lu Xiujing (406–77) transmitted it to his student *Sun Youyue (399–489), it consisted of four scrolls. By the mid-sixth century it was expanded to ten scrolls and then to eleven scrolls. This version of the text appears to be the one known as the *Dongshen jing* 洞神經 (Scripture of the Cavern of Spirit), consisting of the three-scroll *Sanhuang wen* and the eight-scroll *Badi jing* 八帝經 (Scripture of the Eight Emperors).

Three other liturgical and ritual texts were later added to make a fourteen-scroll *Dongshen jing*. Its content is described in the *Taishang dongshen sanhuang yi* 太上洞神三皇儀 (Highest Liturgy for the Three Sovereigns of the Cavern of Spirit; CT 803). The first three scrolls contain the *Sanhuang wen* and the talismans and charts relating to them, organized as one scroll for each Sovereign. The following eight scrolls are the *Badi jing*. The final three scrolls give liturgies for the Retreat (*zhai) and the Audience (*chao* 朝) of the Three Sovereigns and details of the transmission of the scripture. This appears to represent the form in which the *Dongshen jing* was incorporated into the Taoist Canon as the lowest of its Three Caverns (*SANDONG).

This work was, however, an expansion of the original *Sanhuang wen*. Already in the *Zhengao (Authentic Declarations), *Tao Hongjing (456–536) remarks that "although the *Script* is said to be in the world, this is not its true form" (5.4a). It is clear therefore that the *Sanhuang wen* to which Tao refers is not the same *Sanhuang wen* that existed in olden times. The connection between the two is unclear, but what had come to be called *Sanhuang wen* must have incorporated other, different talismans and scriptures. In this form, the *Sanhuang wen* was popular during the Tang dynasty, and Taoist priests were required to know it well. In 646, however, the *Sanhuang wen* was proscribed as deceptive, and its importance declined thereafter.

YAMADA Toshiaki

📖 Andersen 1994; Chen Guofu 1963, 71–78; Fukui Kōjun 1958, 170–204; Liu Zhongyu 1993; Ōfuchi Ninji 1997, 219–96 (= 1964, 277–343); Ren Jiyu 1990, 124–27; Schipper 1965, 28–29; Seidel 1983a, 325–27

※ *sanhuang*

sanhui

三會

Three Assemblies

The *sanhui* are gatherings of the Taoist community, priests and laymen, in the first, seventh, and tenth lunar months. Early sources give the dates as the seventh (one source gives the fifth) day of the first lunar month, the seventh day of the seventh lunar month, and the fifth day of the tenth lunar month, but later observances were held on the fifteenth day of each of these lunar months and referred to as the Three Primes (*sanyuan). On these occasions, believers assembled at their local parish (*zhi) to report any births, deaths and marriages to the local priest or libationer (*jijiu), so that the population registers could be corrected. It was believed that divine representatives of the Three

Offices (*sanguan*, of Heaven, Earth, and Water) also attended and emended their sacred registers on the basis of the updated profane counterparts held by the libationers, thus assuring that fates would be dispensed accurately. Parishioners would offer contributions to the church, including pledges of faith (*xin* 信) and the annual tithe in grain. Those who had reason to celebrate on these occasions would host a feast or "cuisine" (*chu) for other members of the community in proportion to the significance of their auspicious event and their means.

Accounts of these "cuisines" emphasize both the sharing of food and the affirmation of the unique, religious merit-based social order of the Taoist community. The Three Assemblies thus took the place of the biannual community festivals to the Gods of Soil and Grain (Sheji 社稷) in promoting cohesion within the community and reproducing the local social structure, but they also permitted the church to keep track of its members and to reinforce its moral strictures with public readings of its codes of conduct and the public confession of sins. Once the primary festivals had been moved to the fifteenth, the day of the full moon, the two sets of dates were sometimes explained by claiming that the Three Officers update their records on the dates of the Three Assemblies but submit them to Heaven on the Three Primes. A late popular interpretation identifies the Three Primes as the birthdays of the Three Officers.

Terry KLEEMAN

📖 Ōfuchi Ninji 1991, 334–42 and 367–76; Stein R. A. 1979, 69–72

※ *chu*; Tianshi dao

sanqing

三清

Three Clarities; Three Purities; Three Pure Ones

The *sanqing* are originally three superior heavens, called Yuqing 玉清 (Jade Clarity), Shangqing 上清 (Highest Clarity), and Taiqing 太清 (Great Clarity; see table 18), located immediately below the *Daluo tian (Great Canopy Heaven). Divine beings and immortals reside in each of the three heavens, guarding scriptures and sacred instructions that they reveal on occasion for the sake of suffering humanity. The most famous texts associated with one of the heavens are the materials of the *Shangqing revelations, transmitted to earth in 364–70. But materials from Taiqing, too, made it to the planet and appear in a tradition of alchemical works and instructions known by this name (see under *Taiqing).

Table 18

THREE CLARITIES (*sanqing* 三清)	Jade Clarity (Yuqing 玉清)	Highest Clarity (Shangqing 上清)	Great Clarity (Taiqing 太清)
THREE ORIGINS (*sanyuan* 三元)	Chaotic Cavern (hundong 混洞)	Red Chaos (chihun 赤混)	Dark and Silent (mingji 冥寂)
THREE TREASURE LORDS (san baojun 三寶君)	Celestial Treasure (Tianbao jun 天寶君)	Numinous Treasure (Lingbao jun 靈寶君)	Divine Treasure (Shenbao jun 神寶君)
THREE HEAVENS (santian 三天)	Pure Tenuity (Qingwei tian 清微天)	Leftovers of Yu's Food (Yuyu tian 禹餘天)	Great Scarlet (Dachi tian 大赤天)
THREE PNEUMAS (sanqi 三氣)	Inaugural (Green) (shiqing 始青)	Original (Yellow) (yuanhuang 元黃)	Mysterious (White) (xuanbai 玄白)
THREE CAVERNS (*sandong* 三洞)	Reality (Dongzhen 洞真)	Mystery (Dongxuan 洞玄)	Spirit (Dongshen 洞神)
THREE CELESTIAL WORTHIES (san tianzun 三天尊)	Original Commencement (Yuanshi 元始)	Numinous Treasure (Lingbao 靈寶)	Way and Virtue (Daode 道德)

The Three Clarities (*sanqing*) and their associations with heavens, deities, pneumas, etc. Based on *Daojiao sandong zongyuan* 道教三洞宗元 (Lineal Origins of the Three Caverns of the Taoist Teaching), in YJQQ 3.4b–5a. For the full names of the Three Origins, see the entry *sanyuan*.

Heavens and deities. The three heavens are further associated with the three highest deities of the Taoist pantheon, and with specific sets of scriptures classified as the Three Caverns (*SANDONG). The identification of heavens, gods, and scriptures is first apparent in the *Shengshen jing* (Scripture of the Life-Giving Spirits), a mixture of Celestial Masters (*Tianshi dao) and *Lingbao materials dated to the early fifth century. According to this text, when the cosmos was first created the three basic energies—Mysterious (*xuan* 玄), Original (*yuan* 元), and Inaugural (*shi* 始)—combined to form a heavenly sound. The sound coagulated into the numinous writings of the heavens, which took shape as the Three Elders (Sanlao 三老) who in turn brought forth the three superior lords and three major heavens of Taoism.

Once established in this combination, the Three Clarities became predominantly known as the gods associated with the three major Caverns or schools of the medieval religion. They were identified as the Celestial Worthy of Original Commencement (Yuanshi tianzun 元始天尊) who represents Jade Clarity, the Celestial Worthy of Numinous Treasure (Lingbao tianzun 靈寶天尊) of Highest Clarity, and the Celestial Worthy of the Way and Its Virtue (Daode tianzun 道德天尊), the highest god of Great Clarity (see fig. 64).

a

b

c

Fig. 64. The Three Clarities (*sanqing*). (a) Lingbao tianzun 靈寶天尊 (Celestial Worthy of Numinous Treasure). (b) Yuanshi tianzun 元始天尊 (Celestial Worthy of Original Commencement). (c) Daode tianzun 道德天尊 (Celestial Worthy of the Way and its Virtue). *Baiyun guan (Abbey of the White Clouds), Beijing. See Little 2000b, 228, 229, and 230.

The three different gods were yet understood to be ultimately one in their symbolization of the Dao. They are therefore correctly described as a trinity and not merely a triad of gods.

The three major gods. The first among the three gods, the Celestial Worthy of Original Commencement, represents the cosmic and creative aspect of the Dao and is usually presented in full divine regalia in the center of the group. He first appears with his full title around the year 485 in Yan Dong's 嚴東 commentary to the *Duren jing (Scripture on Salvation; CT 87). The expression *yuanshi* 元始 can be traced back to a term for cosmic origination found in the *Huainan zi*; the title *tianzun* 天尊 is an adaptation of an epithet of the Buddha, known as the "Worldly Worthy" or World-Honored One (*shizun* 世尊).

The second god of the group, the Celestial Worthy of Numinous Treasure, is also known as the Most High Lord of the Dao (Taishang daojun 太上道君) or simply as the Most High (Taishang 太上). Seated to the left of the Celestial Worthy, he functions as his mouthpiece and serves as the revealer of sacred scriptures. He appears most prominently, and with an extensive biography, in the Lingbao scriptures, where he is characterized as the disciple and messenger of the Celestial Worthy. The relationship between the two deities is patterned on Mahāyāna (Great Vehicle) Buddhism, with the Celestial Worthy residing above the known universe and the Lord of the Dao, his disciple and follower, begging for instruction to help suffering humanity.

The third god, seated to the right of the central deity, is the Celestial Worthy of the Way and Its Virtue, who is Lord Lao (*Laojun). He is described as the disciple of the Lord of the Dao, with whose help he becomes a Perfected. His main function is to maintain close contact with humanity; as such, for instance, he serves as the ancestor of the Tang dynasty and appears in various visions and miracles. Again, this echoes Buddhist models, in which the third divinity is the savior bodhisattva concerned most closely with human fate.

The first scriptural description of the three gods is found in the *Fengdao kejie (Codes and Precepts for Worshipping the Dao) of the early Tang. It lists the gods with their formal titles (2.1a):

1. Celestial Worthy of Original Commencement, Supreme King of the Law (Wushang fawang Yuanshi tianzun 無上法王元始天尊)

2. Great Dao of Jade Dawn, Highest Sovereign of Emptiness (Taishang xuhuang Yuchen dadao 太上虛皇玉晨大道)

3. Celestial Worthy of the Great One, Most Exalted Laozi (Gaoshang Laozi Taiyi tianzun 高上老子太一天尊)

Even earlier, however, are several stelae depicting three deities described as the Three Worthies (*sanzun* 三尊), the first of which dates from 508 and was found at the Shihong si 石泓寺 (Monastery of the Stone Pool) in Fuzhou (Fujian), with further works following in 515, 521, 567, and 572, and many more produced under the Tang (Kamitsuka Yoshiko 1998, 68–69). These records suggest an active effort at Taoist integration throughout the sixth century, which eventually resulted in the establishment of the standard trinity of three gods who are ultimately one.

Livia KOHN

📖 Kamitsuka Yoshiko 1993; Kohn 1998b, 121–27; Lagerwey 1981b, 33–38 and passim; Little 2000b, 228–32; Pontynen 1980; Qing Xitai 1988–95, 1: 523–30; Pregadio 2006b, 152–55; Robinet 1984, 1: 130–33; see also bibliography for the entry *SANDONG

※ DEITIES: THE PANTHEON; SANDONG

sanshi and *jiuchong*

三尸 · 九蟲

three corpses and nine worms

The three corpses and the nine worms (see fig. 65) are two sets of parasites said to live inside the human body. The three corpses, also known as the three worms (*sanchong* 三蟲), attack their host in several ways. They cause disease, invite other disease-causing agents into the body, and report their host's transgressions to heaven so as to shorten his life span. The nine worms, some of which may correspond to parasites such as roundworms or tapeworms, weaken the host's body and cause a variety of physical symptoms. These parasites were expelled by means of drugs, visualization techniques, or cutting off consumption of the grains that provide their sustenance (see under *bigu).

In his *Lunheng* 論衡 (Balanced Discussions; trans. Forke 1907–11, 2: 363), Wang Chong 王充 (27–ca. 100 CE) compares the three worms to leeches that attack the body from the inside. According to the *Liexian zhuan (Biographies of Exemplary Immortals; trans. Kaltenmark 1953, 177–78), the Taoist master Ruan Qiu 阮丘 rid his disciple Zhu Huang 朱璜 of the three corpses by means of a combination of seven drugs administered over a period of a hundred days. According to the *Baopu zi (trans. Ware 1966, 115–16), the three corpses report a person's transgressions on the *gengshen day (the fifty-seventh of the sixty-day cycle) to the Director of Destinies (*Siming), who deducts a certain number of days from the person's life for each misdeed. One way of stopping this report is to stay awake for the entire *gengshen* day, thus preventing the corpses from leaving one's body.

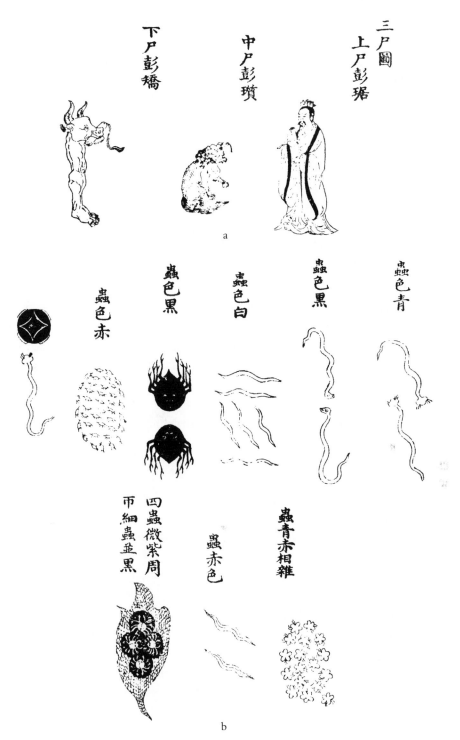

三尸圖

上尸彭琚　中尸彭瓚　下尸彭矯

蟲色青　蟲色黑　蟲色白　蟲色黑　蟲色赤

蟲青赤相雜　蟲赤色　四蟲微紫周币細蟲並黑

a

b

Fig. 65. (a) The "three corpses" (*sanshi*). (b) The "nine worms" (*jiuchong*). *Chu sanshi jiuchong baosheng jing* 除三尸九蟲保生經 (Scripture on Expelling the Three Corpses and Nine Worms to Protect Life; CT 871), 7a–8b and 9b–13a.

The *Chu sanshi jiuchong baosheng jing* 除三尸九蟲保生經 (Scripture on Expelling the Three Corpses and Nine Worms to Protect Life; CT 871), probably dating to the ninth century, gives the names of the corpses and the worms, and describes the symptoms they cause. The three corpses are:

1. The upper corpse, Peng Ju 彭琚, lives in the head. Symptoms of its attack include a feeling of heaviness in the head, blurred vision, deafness, and excessive flow of tears and mucus.

2. The middle corpse, Peng Zhi 彭瓆, dwells in the heart and stomach. It attacks the heart, and makes its host crave sensual pleasures.

3. The lower corpse, Peng Jiao 彭矯, resides in the stomach and legs. It causes the Ocean of Pneuma (*qihai* 氣海, an area corresponding to the lower *dantian) to leak, and makes its host lust after women.

The nine worms are:

1. The "ambush worm" (*fuchong* 伏蟲) saps people's strength by feeding off their essence and blood.

2. The "coiling worm" (*huichong* 蚘蟲) infests the body in pairs of male and female that live above and below the heart, consuming their host's blood.

3. The "inch-long white worm" (*cun baichong* 寸白蟲) chews into the stomach, weakening the inner organs and damaging the digestive tract.

4. The "flesh worm" (*rouchong* 肉蟲) causes itching and weakens the sinews and back.

5. The "lung worm" (*feichong* 肺蟲) causes coughing, phlegm buildup, and difficulty in breathing.

6. The "stomach worm" (*weichong* 胃蟲) consumes food from its host's stomach, causing hunger.

7. The "obstructing worm" (*gechong* 膈蟲) dulls the senses, induces drowsiness, and causes nightmares.

8. The "red worm" (*chichong* 赤蟲) causes stagnation of the blood and pneuma, heaviness in the waist, and ringing in the ears.

9. The "wriggling worm" (*qiaochong* 蹺蟲) causes itching sores on the skin and tooth decay.

The text contains illustrations and descriptions of the three corpses and the nine worms, and methods for expelling them from the body.

Theodore A. COOK

📖 Benn 2002, 216–17, 222–24; Kohn 1993–95; Lévi 1983; Maspero 1981, 331–39; Robinet 1993, 139; Strickmann 2002, 77–78; Yamada Toshiaki 1989b, 107–8 and 109–12

※ TAOIST VIEWS OF THE HUMAN BODY

sanshi'er tian

三十二天

Thirty-two Heavens

The system of thirty-two heavens, along with those of eight, ten, and thirty-six heavens (*sanshiliu tian*), appears throughout the *Lingbao scriptures. Formed at the beginning of the cosmos from the Three Pneumas (*sanqi* 三氣; see *santian* and *liutian*), the Thirty-two Heavens are visualized in Lingbao meditation and ritual. While the Thirty-six Heavens of the *Shangqing tradition are situated vertically in space, the Thirty-two Heavens of Lingbao are located horizontally in the four directions, encircling the Jade Capitol Mountain (Yujing shan 玉京山) in the Great Canopy Heaven (*Daluo tian). (For the names of these heavens, see table 19.)

The system of thirty-two heavens reveals Indian Buddhist influence. In such texts as the *Duren jing (Scripture on Salvation) and the *Miedu wulian shengshi miaojing* 滅度五鍊生尸妙經 (Wondrous Scripture on Salvation through Extinction and the Fivefold Refinement of the Corpse; CT 369), the Thirty-two Heavens often appear along with the Great Canopy Heaven, recalling at least in numerical terms the thirty-three heavens (*trāyastriṃśa*) of Indian Buddhist cosmology, which are the second lowest set of heavens situated at the summit of Mount Sumeru.

Like the heavens of Indian Buddhism, the Thirty-two Heavens of Lingbao are divided among the Three Realms (*sanjie* 三界) of desire (*yu* 欲, six heavens), form (*se* 色, twelve heavens) and formlessness (*wuse* 無色, ten heavens). (For another subdivision of the Three Realms into six, eighteen, and four heavens, respectively, see table 20.) Four heavens beyond the world of formlessness are added to reach the number thirty-two. Several Lingbao scriptures also use a pseudo-Sanskrit language in *dhāraṇī*-like phrases attached to the various heavens and the names of their rulers (see *dafan yinyu).

Amy Lynn MILLER

📖 Bokenkamp 1983, 462–65; Bokenkamp 1997, 383–84; Lagerwey 1981b, 34–38; Robinet 1984, 1: 131–33; Sunayama Minoru 1990, 283–301; Qing Xitai 1994, 4: 119–22; Zürcher 1980, 121–29

※ *sanshiliu tian*; *jiutian*; Lingbao

Table 19

HEAVENS	SECRET NAMES OF RULERS
East	
1　Taihuang huangzeng 太黃皇曾	Yujian yuming 鬱鑑玉明
2　Taiming yuwan 太明玉完	Xu'a natian 須阿那田
3　Qingming hetong 清明何童	Yuanyu qijing 元育齊京
4　Xuantai pingyu 玄胎平育	Liudu neixian 劉度內鮮
5　Yuanming wenju 元明文舉	Chou falun 醜法輪
6　Shangming qiyao moyi 上明七曜摩夷	Tianhui yan 恬憶延
7　Xuwu yueheng 虛無越衡	Zheng dingguang 正定光
8　Taiji mengyi 太極濛翳	Quyu jiuchang 曲育九昌
South	
1　Chiming heyang 赤明和陽	Lijin shangzhen 理禁上真
2　Xuanming gonghua 玄明恭華	Kongyao chouyin 空謠醜音
3　Yaoming zongpiao 耀明宗飄	Chong guangming 重光明
4　Zhuluo huangjia 竺落皇笳	Moyi miaobian 摩夷妙辯
5　Xuming tangyao 虛明堂曜	Ajia lousheng 阿Λ婁生
6　Guanming duanjing 觀明端靜	Yumi luoqian 鬱密羅千
7　Xuanming gongqing 玄明恭慶	Longluo puti 龍羅菩提
8　Taihuan jiyao 太煥極瑤	Wanli wuyan 宛離無延
West	
1　Yuanzai kongsheng 元載孔昇	Kaizhen dingguang 開真定光
2　Tai'an huangya 太安皇崖	Polou a'tan 婆婁阿貪
3　Xianding jifeng 顯定極風	Zhaozhen tong 招真童
4　Shihuang xiaomang 始黃孝芒	Saluo louwang 薩羅婁王
5　Taihuang wengzhong furong 太黃翁重浮容	Minba kuang 閔巴狂
6　Wusi jiangyou 無思江由	Ming fanguang 明梵光
7　Shangye ruanle 上楪阮樂	Bobo lan 勃勃藍
8　Wuji tanshi 無極曇誓	Piaonu qionglong 飄弩穹隆
North	
1　Haoting xiaodu 皓庭宵度	Huijue hun 慧覺昏
2　Yuantong yuandong 淵通元洞	Fanxing guansheng 梵行觀生
3　Taiwen hanchong miaocheng 太文翰寵妙成	Nayu chouying 那育醜瑛
4　Taisu xiule jinshang 太素秀樂禁上	Longluo juechang 龍羅覺長
5　Taixu wushang changrong 太虛無上常融	Zongjian guishen 總監鬼神
6　Taishi yulong tengsheng 太釋玉隆騰勝	Miaomiao xingyuan 眇眇行元
7　Longbian fandu 龍變梵度	Yunshang xuanxuan 運上玄玄
8　Taiji pingyu jiayi 太極平育賈奕	Daze famen 大擇法門

The Thirty-two Heavens (*sanshi'er tian*). Source: *Duren shangpin miaojing sizhu* 度人上品妙經 四注 (Four Commentaries to the Wondrous Scripture of Highest Rank on Salvation; CT 87), 2.43a–54b.

Sanshiliu shuifa

三十六水法

Methods of the Thirty-Six Aqueous Solutions

The *Sanshiliu shuifa* describes methods for preparations often used in *waidan practices at intermediate stages during the compounding of elixirs. These methods are frequently referred to in the early *Taiqing texts and in their commentaries. Traditionally attributed to the Eight Sirs (Bagong 八公, a group of *fangshi who are also said to have taken part in the compilation of the *Huainan zi), the text was known to *Ge Hong, who cites a *Sanshiliu shuijing* 三十六水 經 (Scripture of the Thirty-Six Aqueous Solutions) in his *Baopu zi.

The present version (CT 930) contains fifty-nine methods for the solution of forty-two minerals. Internal evidence shows that the methods for the last seven minerals were appended to an earlier version containing those for the first thirty-six (one of which is missing in the present version). Quotations from both the original and appended portions in the commentary to the *Jiudan jing (*Huangdi jiuding shendan jingjue* 黃帝九鼎神丹經訣; CT 885, 19.2a) indicate that the text had assumed its present form by the mid-seventh century. A short final section (11b–12b) describes ritual rules and lists days on which the compounding of the elixir should not take place.

Fabrizio PREGADIO

📖 Meng Naichang 1993a, 91–96; Needham 1980, 167–210; Ts'ao, Ho, and Needham 1959 (trans., omits the section on ritual)

※ *waidan*

sanshiliu tian

三十六天

Thirty-six Heavens

The Thirty-six Heavens belong, in one of their enumerations, to the *Shangqing tradition of Taoism. The locus classicus for their enumeration is the *Waiguo fangpin Qingtong neiwen* 外國放品青童內文 (Inner Script of the Azure Lad on the Distribution of the Outer Realms; CT 1373), a later Shangqing text

Table 20

1 *Daluo tian 大羅天	

*Three Clarities (*sanqing 三清, 3 heavens)*

2 Yuqing 玉清	4 Taiqing 太清
3 Shangqing 上清	

*Seed-people (*zhongmin 種民, 4 heavens)*

5 Pingyu jiayi 平育賈奕	7 Yulong tengsheng 玉隆騰勝
6 Longbian fandu 龍變梵度	8 Wushang changrong 無上常融

Realm of Formlessness (wuse jie 無色界, 4 heavens)

9 Xiule jinshang 秀樂禁上	11 Yuantong yuandong 淵通元洞
10 Hanchong miaocheng 翰寵妙成	12 Haoting xiaodu 皓庭霄度

Realm of Form (sejie 色界, 18 heavens)

13 Wuji tanshi 無極曇誓	22 Xuanming gongqing 玄明恭慶
14 Shangdie ruanle 上揲阮樂	23 Guanming duanjing 觀明端靜
15 Wusi jiangyou 無思江由	24 Xuming tangyao 虛明堂曜
16 Taihuang wengzhong 太黃翁重	25 Zhuluo huangjia 竺落皇笳
17 Shihuang xiaomang 始黃孝芒	26 Yaoming zongpiao 曜明宗飄
18 Xianding jifeng 顯定極風	27 Xuanming gonghua 玄明恭華
19 Tai'an huangya 太安皇崖	28 Chiming heyang 赤明和陽
20 Yuanzai kongsheng 元載孔昇	29 Taiji mengyi 太極濛翳
21 Taihuan jiyao 太煥極瑤	30 Xuwu yueheng 虛無越衡

Realm of Desire (yujie 欲界, 6 heavens)

31 Qiyao moyi 七曜摩夷	34 Qingming hetong 清明何童
32 Yuanming wenju 元明文舉	35 Taiming yuwan 太明玉完
33 Xuantai pingyu 玄胎平育	36 Taihuang huangzeng 太皇黃曾

The Thirty-six Heavens (*sanshiliu tian*). Source: YJQQ 21.

influenced by *Lingbao Taoism and Buddhist cosmology (Robinet 1984, 2: 97–100). In this scripture, cosmology is based on the Nine Heavens (*jiutian), each of which contains three additional heavens for a total of thirty-six. Although the Nine Heavens have Buddhist names, this system is derived from earlier Chinese notions.

In contrast to the Thirty-two Heavens (*sanshi'er tian*) of Lingbao, which are located horizontally in the four directions, the Thirty-six Heavens are situated in a pyramid shape and correspond to thirty-six subterranean countries, the latter of which are divided among the six directions. On the eight nodal days of the year (*bajie* 八節, namely, equinoxes, solstices, and the first day of each season), the kings of the Thirty-six Heavens tour the universe.

Later Taoist texts attempted to create a synthesis of these different cosmological representations. During the Tang dynasty, in particular, the *Daojiao yishu (Pivot of Meaning of the Taoist Teaching, 7.5b) links the systems of the Three Heavens and the Nine Heavens to arrive at thirty-six heavens. Other later texts tried to reconcile the Thirty-two Heavens of Lingbao with the Thirty-six Heavens of Shangqing, and to link the Three Realms (sanjie 三界, i.e., desire, form, formlessness) of Buddhism with the Heavens of the Three Clarities of Taoism. The main codification (see table 20) enumerates: 1. the supreme Great Canopy Heaven (*Daluo tian); 2. the Heavens of the Three Clarities (*sanqing); 3. the Four Heavens of the Seed-People (si zhongmin tian 四種民天); 4. the heavens of the Three Realms (sanjie 三界) of desire (yu 欲, six heavens), form (se 色, eighteen heavens), and formlessness (wuse 無色, four heavens).

Amy Lynn MILLER

📖 Lagerwey 1981b, 34–38; Qing Xitai 1988–95, 2: 426–28; Qing Xitai 1994, 2: 342–45 and 4: 119–22; Robinet 1984, 1: 131–33; Sunayama Minoru 1990, 283–301; Zürcher 1980, 121–29

※ sanshi'er tian; jiutian; Shangqing

santian and liutian

三天 · 六天

Three Heavens and Six Heavens

The term santian or Three Heavens first appears in the *Lingbao wufu xu (Prolegomena to the Five Talismans of the Numinous Treasure), a fourth-century text based on ideas and practices of Han dynasty *fangshi. Here the Three Heavens are mentioned most commonly in the names of specific talismans (*FU), and may refer to the highest of the Nine Heavens (*jiutian), frequently mentioned in early literature (see Maspero 1924).

In organized Taoism, the notion of Three Heavens becomes central in the doctrine of the southern Celestial Masters (*Tianshi dao) of the fifth century, in which they designate the original realms of the Dao generated from the Three Pneumas (sanqi 三氣): Mysterious (xuan 玄), Original (yuan 元), and Inaugural (shi 始). Texts of this period, notably the *Santian neijie jing (Scripture of the Inner Explication of the Three Heavens), claim that *Zhang Daoling in the second century established the benevolent and pure Three Heavens after abolishing the demonic and evil Six Heavens, which people had supposedly worshipped until then.

The idea of the Six Heavens first arises in the Western Jin period (265–316), when the realm of the dead is associated with a mountain called *Fengdu (or Luofeng 羅酆). Since in the scheme of the *wuxing death is associated with the north and the north in turn with the number six, the idea developed of Six Palaces (liugong 六宮) of the dead situated in the north. Found first in *Ge Hong's *Baopu zi, the concept is then employed in *Shangqing cosmology where, as described in the Tianguan santu jing 天關三圖經 (Scripture of the Three Heavenly Passes; CT 1366), each pavilion is given a name, an overseeing divine official, and a specific administrative role (Robinet 1984, 2: 163–69; Kohn 1993b, 257–67; Mollier 1997, 359–61). Only after the Six Heavens have been integrated into the *Lingbao scriptures at the end of the fourth century do they become part of the cosmology of the Celestial Masters, who until then had located the realm of the dead at Mount Tai (*Taishan, Shandong) in the east.

The contrast between the Three Heavens and the Six Heavens in Taoism stands for the distinction between the pure gods of the Dao, who emanate directly from the original energy of creation and are representative of the pure powers of life, and the impure demons and spirits of popular religion who, according to Taoists, represent the vengeful powers of the dead.

Livia KOHN

📖 Bokenkamp 1997, 188–94; Kobayashi Masayoshi 1990, 482–510; Wang Zongyu 1999

※ *Santian neijie jing*

Santian neijie jing

三天內解經

Scripture of the Inner Explication of the Three Heavens

The *Santian neijie jing*, in two *juan* (CT 1205), is a text of the southern Way of the Celestial Masters (*Tianshi dao) that can be dated to around the beginning of the Liu Song dynasty (mid-fifth century). Its first *juan* expounds the basic worldview of the group, outlining the creation of the universe by the Dao and Lord Lao (*Laojun), the unfolding of the three major world religions—Taoism (east), Buddhism (west), and Yin-Yang practice (south)—and the development of the organization of the Celestial Masters. In terms of the latter, it emphasizes the replacement of the corrupt and despicable Six Heavens (the cosmology of the Confucian ritual system) with the pure and eminent Three Heavens of the Dao (see under *santian and *liutian*), made up of the Three Pneumas (*sanqi* 三氣): Mysterious (*xuan* 玄), Original (*yuan* 元), and Inaugural (*shi* 始). The three pneumas also give rise to Lord Lao, who then creates his own mother, the Jade Woman of Mysterious Wonder (Xuanmiao yunü 玄妙玉女), from cosmic energies, and then orchestrates his own birth and life. At the end of the latter, he moreover orders *Yin Xi to become the Buddha and thereby deliver the pure Dao to the western "barbarians." The text provides an integrated worldview and represents a justification of Celestial Masters' beliefs for the benefit of the Liu Song court.

The second *juan* deals more specifically with moral rules and theoretical doctrines, associates the Dao with non-action (*wuwei*) and outlines details of *zhai* or Retreats. It also presents a discussion of Taoism versus Buddhism in terms of greater and lesser vehicles, again contrasting the purity and eminence of the Dao with the more primitive and simple practices of Buddhists.

Livia KOHN

📖 Bokenkamp 1997, 186–229 (trans. of *j.* 1); Lai Chi-tim 1998b; Robinet 1997b, 67–69; Schipper 1999b (part. trans.); Seidel 1969, 82–84; Wang Zongyu 1999

※ *santian* and *liutian*; Tianshi dao

sanwu

三五

Three and Five; "Three Fives"

The expression *sanwu* is deemed to sum up the whole world and the connections between its multiple levels. The number 3 (*san*) refers, for instance, to the three celestial bodies (sun, moon, and stars), the three minerals (pearl, jade, and gold), and the three corporeal organs (ears, nose, and mouth); the number 5 (*wu*) refers to the Five Agents (*wuxing*) and various related sets of entities, such as the five planets (*wuxing* 五星), the five peaks (*wuyue*), and the five viscera (*wuzang*). Most often, however, these two numbers refer to the vertical and horizontal dimensions of the cosmos: Heaven, Earth and Humanity, or Yin, Yang and their harmony, on one hand, and the four cardinal points plus the center, on the other. In physiology, they correspond to the three vertical parts of the body (head, chest, and abdomen) and the five viscera. They also stand in hierarchical relationship with each other: Three is celestial while Five is terrestrial, and many texts accordingly number the heavens by three or multiples of three, while five or multiples of five is the number are associated with the earth.

In cosmogony, the Three comes before the Five. The Three refers to the Three Pneumas (*sanqi* 三氣; see *santian* and *liutian*), the Three Primes (*sanyuan*), the Three Sovereigns (*sanhuang*), or the Three Heavens (*santian*; see *santian* and *liutian*). The Five refers to the Five Agents, the five directions (*wufang* 五方), or the five virtues (*wude* 五德). Similarly, the Three Pneumas precede the five precosmic geneses called Five Greats (*wutai* 五太; see *cosmogony*). Three and Five are often related to Eight: for instance, the three kinds of precosmic Chaos plus five gives the eight luminous spirits (the "eight effulgences," *bajing*).

As it is used in the *Zhouyi cantong qi*, the expression *sanwu* is especially important in *neidan*. Here the number 5 is seen as the addition of the numbers assigned to Wood-East (3) and Fire-South (2) on one hand, and to Metal-West (4) and Water-North (1) on the other (see table 25). With Soil, the Center (5), these three sets form the "Three Fives" that must be merged into the One. In particular, these emblems are equated with inner nature (*xing* 性) and spirit (*shen*) with regard to the mind, and with emotions (*qing* 情) and essence (*jing*) with regard to the body. Together with intention (*yi*), these are the three entities that *neidan* adepts join with each other to return (*fan*) to the One.

Isabelle ROBINET

📖 Robinet 1994a, 100–101

※ NUMEROLOGY; COSMOGONY; COSMOLOGY

sanyi

三一

Three Ones; Three-in-One

The Three Ones, or Three-in-One, emerge when the original Oneness (*yi*) of the cosmos first divides into Yin and Yang, and then rejoins these forces in a new harmony. In this way a set of three is created that recovers a renewed original Oneness. The notion of the Three Ones also applies to the three fundamental powers (*sancai* 三才) of the universe—Heaven, Earth, and Humanity—and to the basic factors of human life—essence, pneuma, and spirit (*jing, qi, shen*).

In *Shangqing Taoism, the Three Ones are deities who reside in the Cinnabar Fields (*dantian), the main energy centers of the body. They are the Emperor One (Diyi 帝一), the Feminine One (Ciyi 雌一), and the Masculine One (Xiongyi 雄一), also known as the Upper, Middle, and Lower Ones. Each is further linked with a specific sacred text, the *Dadong zhenjing, the *Ciyi jing (or the *Taidan yinshu), and the *Suling jing, respectively. Born originally through the fusion of primordial energy, they arise first in the Northern Dipper (*beidou), the central constellation in the sky, from which they manifest on all levels in the cosmos.

According to a method transmitted by Xuanzi 玄子 (the Mysterious Master, also known as Juanzi 涓子) and recorded in the Suling jing (CT 1314, 27a–38b), an adept who wants to visualize the Three Ones should first select the proper time, prepare the meditation chamber (*jingshi), and purify himself through bathing and fasting. Once in the holy room, he burns incense (see *jinxiang), grinds his teeth, and sits down facing east. Closing his eyes, he begins with the Upper One, first imagining a red energy in the Palace of the Muddy Pellet (niwan gong 泥丸宮) in the head, the upper Cinnabar Field (see *niwan). Within this ball of energy, he then sees a red sun, about 9 cm in diameter, whose radiance makes him fall into oblivion. When this is achieved, the ruler of this Palace, known as the Red Infant (chizi 赤子), appears in his head. The Red Infant holds the Talisman of the Divine Tiger (shenhu fu 神虎符) in his hand and is accompanied by an attendant who holds the Dadong zhenjing and is the deity of the teeth, the tongue, and the skull.

The Middle One resides in the Crimson Palace (jianggong 絳宮) of the heart, the middle Cinnabar Field. His energy is also red but measures only 7 cm in diameter. He also appears once the adept has entered a state of deep absorption. Known as the Sovereign Lord of Original Cinnabar (Yuandan huangjun 元丹皇君), he holds the Most Exalted Talisman of the Feminine One (Ciyi gaoshang fu 雌一高上符) in his right hand and the planet Mars in his left hand. His attendant holds the Ciyi jing and is the deity of the essences of the five inner organs.

The Lower One is the master of the Gate of the Vital Force (*mingmen), the lower Cinnabar Field. To make him appear, adepts visualize a white sun 5 cm in diameter, then see him as the god Ying'er 嬰兒 (Infant), the Original King of the Yellow Court (Huangting yuanwang 黃庭元王) in the lower center of the body. He holds a copy of the Suling jing and the planet Venus in his hands. His attendant, master over the subtle essences of the body, is the deity of the extremities, senses, blood, and intestines.

The Three Ones with their attendants thus control the entire body. They are present in all human beings but seldom display their immortal powers because ordinary people are likely to ignore or even harm them. As one neglects this power of cosmic purity within, one's body becomes weaker and sicker and eventually dies.

Livia KOHN

📖 Andersen 1979; Kohn 1989a; Kohn 1993b, 204–14; Li Ling 2000b, 239–52; Maspero 1981, 364–72; Robinet 1984, 1: 30–32 and 80–82; Robinet 1993, 124–31; Robinet 1994a; Robinet 1995c

※ Taiyi; *yi* [oneness]; INNER DEITIES; MEDITATION AND VISUALIZATION

sanyuan

三元

Three Primes; Three Origins

1. The term

The term Three Primes refers to the original, precosmic pneumas of the world that prefigure its tripartition and also exist on the theological and human levels. In their most fundamental role, they represent three modes of emptiness, called Chaotic Cavern, Great Emptiness Origin (*hundong taiwu yuan* 混洞太無元), Red Chaos, Great Emptiness Origin (*chihun taiwu yuan* 赤混太無元), and Dark and Silent, Mysterious Pervasive Origin (*mingji xuantong yuan* 冥寂玄通元). These are transformed into three divinities (also called *sanyuan*) that rule over the Three Caverns (*SANDONG). In a related meaning, *sanyuan* also denotes the Three Pneumas (*sanqi* 三氣), namely, Mysterious (*xuan* 玄), Original (*yuan* 元), and Inaugural (*shi* 始), and the Three Original Pure Ladies (Sansu yuanjun 三素元君) who are mothers of the Five Gods (*wushen* 五神) of the registers of life (*shengji* 生籍; see under *Taidan yinshu*).

On the physiological level, *sanyuan* has various meanings. It refers to the three Cinnabar Fields (*dantian*) and their guardian divinities; to head, heart, and kidneys; or to head, abdomen, and feet. In *neidan* texts, *sanyuan* alludes to the three components of the human being, namely, essence, pneuma, and spirit (*jing, qi, shen*), in their original (*yuan*) or precosmic state. Finally, in ritual *sanyuan* designates three Retreats (*zhai*) addressed to Heaven, Earth, and Water, held on the fifteenth day of the first, seventh, and tenth lunar months.

Isabelle ROBINET

2. The pneumas

According to early Taoist cosmogony, the fundamental One Pneuma (*yiqi* 一氣) divides into three: Mysterious (*xuan* 玄), Original (*yuan* 元), and Inaugural (*shi* 始). From these Three Pneumas, the Three Heavens (*santian* 三天) and the Three Caverns (*SANDONG) of the Taoist Canon are formed (*Yebao yinyuan jing*, sec. 26). The relations among the Three Pneumas, the Three Heavens, the realms of the Three Clarities (*sanqing jing* 三清竟; see *sanqing), and the Three Treasure Lords (*san baojun* 三寶君) are shown in table 18.

In the *Shengshen jing*, the Three Pneumas are referred to as the Three Primes. The "Daojiao sandong zongyuan" 道教三洞宗元 (Lineal Origins of the Three Caverns of the Taoist Teaching; YJQQ 3.4a–7b), however, distinguishes them by outlining a sequence that leads from Non-being (*wu) to Wondrous Oneness (*miaoyi* 妙一), then to the Three Primes, the Three Pneumas, and finally the Three Powers (*sancai* 三才, i.e., Heaven, Earth, and Humanity). This text says that the three Treasure Lords are "generated by transformation" (*huasheng* 化生) from each of the Three Primes, and associates the Three Pneumas with the colors green, yellow, and white, respectively.

MIURA Kunio

3. The days

Three great feast days came to be associated with the Three Primes: the fifteenth days of the first lunar month (*shangyuan* 上元), seventh lunar month (*zhongyuan* 中元), and tenth lunar month (*xiayuan* 下元), respectively the birthdays of the Officer of Heaven, the Officer of Earth, and the Officer of Water (see *sanguan). The Lantern Festival was held on the fifteenth of the first lunar month, while the fifteenth of the seventh lunar month coincided with the highly popular Buddhist *yulanpen* 盂蘭盆 (*avalambana*) festival.

Opinion varies concerning which rituals in the *zhongyuan* and *yulanpen* observances originated first, but certainly there was a considerable amount of mutual influence between Buddhism and Taoism; furthermore, the fifteenth of the seventh lunar month was of great importance as the day when offerings were made to the ancestral spirits and sins were remitted. Both religious traditions conducted rituals to destroy sin, observed almsgiving, and performed the rites of Universal Salvation (*pudu, Taoist) and Oblation to the Hungry Spirits (*shi egui* 施餓鬼, Buddhist) for the repose of the souls of the dead, and to ensure that harmful forces did not interfere with the world of the living.

YAMADA Toshiaki

📖 Akizuki Kan'ei 1961; Akizuki Kan'ei 1965; Maspero 1981, 158–59; Lagerwey

1987c, 20–22; Ōfuchi Ninji 1991, 407–36; Qing Xitai 1994, 2: 316–19; Yoshioka Yoshitoyo 1959–76, 1: 369–77; Yoshioka Yoshitoyo 1970a

※ *dantian*; *sanhui*; *sanyi*; COSMOGONY; SANDONG; SEASONAL OBSERVANCES

Shangqing

上清

Highest Clarity

The term Shangqing initially denoted a corpus of scriptures revealed to *Yang Xi (330–86) between 364 and 370 (see table 21). With later "apocryphal" texts, these scriptures were adopted by the southern Chinese aristocracy in the fifth and sixth centuries and were assigned the highest rank within the Three Caverns (*SANDONG) of the Taoist Canon. Later, the same term also designated a religious movement, whose actual founder was *Tao Hongjing (456–536), with its own patriarchs (see table 22), holy places, liturgy, and a large number of other texts.

As a body of doctrines and practices, Shangqing developed in southeastern China after the imperial court and the upper classes fled from the north, which had been invaded by non-Chinese peoples, and settled in the Jiangnan 江南 region. Here they were confronted by a local Chinese aristocracy of long standing that sought to reaffirm its own traditions over those imported from the north. Shangqing thus marked a revival of the religious legacy of southern China. Claiming to be on a higher level than its forerunners, it consists of a synthesis of the native ecstatic tradition, the late-Zhou and Han traditions of immortality seekers, and the religion of the Celestial Masters (*Tianshi dao) imported from the north. Besides a few local cults, Shangqing also incorporated—in a superficial way, but for the first time in Taoism—some features borrowed from Buddhism, and its sources show traces of the debates on *wu and *you* (Non-being and Being) that had engaged the *Xuanxue (Arcane Learning) thinkers. All these elements were blended into a coherent whole, imbued with reminiscences of old Chinese myths and of the literary tradition represented by the *Chuci* 楚辭 (Songs of Chu; trans. Hawkes 1985) and by Sima Xiangru 司馬相如 (ca. 179–117 BCE; Hervouet 1972). This gave the Shangqing texts a remarkable poetic and literary quality, and secured them success among the Chinese intelligentsia.

History. The revelations received by Yang Xi were addressed to the Xu family, especially Xu Mi 許謐 (303–76) and his son Xu Hui 許翽 (341–ca. 370), of whom

Table 21

NO.	RECEIVED TEXT	TITLE
1	CT 5, 6, 7, 103	*Dadong zhenjing 大洞真經 (Authentic Scripture of the Great Cavern)
2	CT 1378	Jinzhen yuguang bajing feijing 金真玉光八景飛經 (Winged Scripture of the Jade Radiance of Golden Truth and of the Eight Effulgences)
3	CT 426, 1323	*Basu jing 八素經 (Scripture of the Eight Pure Ladies)
4	CT 1316	Bu tiangang niexing qiyuan jing 步天綱躡星七元經 (Scripture of the Seven Primes on Pacing the Celestial Guideline and Treading the Stars)
5	CT 1376, 1377	*Jiuzhen zhongjing 九真中經 (Central Scripture of the Nine Real Men)
6	[lost]	Bianhua qishisi fang jing 變化七十四方經 (Scripture on the Methods of the Seventy-four Transformations)
7	[lost]	Santian zhengfa jing 三天正法經 (Scripture of the Orthodox Law of the Three Heavens)
8	CT 33	Huangqi yangjing sandao shunxing jing 黃氣陽精三道順行經 (Scripture on Following the Course of the Three Paths of the Yellow Pneuma [=Moon] and the Yang Essence [=Sun])
9	CT 1373	Waiguo fangpin Qingtong neiwen 外國放品青童內文 (Inner Script of the Azure Lad on the Distribution of the Outer Realms)
10	CT 179, 255, 442, 639	*Lingshu ziwen 靈書紫文 (Numinous Writings in Purple Script)
11	CT 1332	Zidu yanguang shenyuan bian jing 紫度炎光神元變經 (Scripture on the Transformation of the Fiery Radiant Divine Origin, Written on Purple [Tablets])
12	CT 1315	Qingyao zishu jingen zhongjing 青要紫書金根眾經 (Collected Scriptures of the [Lord of?] Qingyao on the Golden Root, Written on Purple [Tablets])
13	CT 1327	Sanjiu suyu yujing zhenjue 三九素語玉經真訣 (Authentic Instructions on the Jade Scripture of the Pure Words of the Three [Primes] and the Nine [Old Lords])
14	CT 354	Sanyuan yujian sanyuan bujing 三元玉檢三元布經 (Scripture on the Distribution of the Three Primes, Jade Seal of the Three Primes)
15	[lost]	Shijing jinguang cangjing lu [recte: lian?] xing jing 石精金光藏精 (錄) [鍊?] 形經 (Scripture on the Essence of Stone and the Radiance of Metal for Hiding One's Shape and Refining [?] One's Form)
16	CT 1359	Danjing daojing yindi bashu jing 丹景道精隱地八術經 (Scripture on the Effulgence of Cinnabar and the Essence of the Dao and on the Eight Arts to Conceal Onself within the Earth)
17	CT 1331	Shenzhou qizhuan qibian wutian jing 神州七轉七變舞天經 (Scripture of the Divine Continent on the Dance in Heaven in Seven Revolutions and Seven Transformations)
18	CT 1330	*Taidan yinshu 太丹隱書 (Concealed Writ of the Great Cinnabar [Palace])
19	CT 1317	Kaitian santu qixing yidu jing 開天三圖七星移度經 (Scripture on Crossing through the Three [Celestial] Passes and the Seven Stars to the Opening of Heaven)

Table 21 (*cont.*)

NO.	RECEIVED TEXT	TITLE
20	CT 1382	*Jiudan shanghua taijing zhongji* 九丹上化胎精中記 (Central Records of the Essence of the Embryo and the Upper Transformation of the Ninefold Elixir)
21	CT 1329	*Jiuchi banfu wudi nei zhenjing* 九赤班符五帝內真經 (Scripture of the Nine Red Bundled Talismans and the Inner Authenticity of the Five Emperors)
22	CT 1334 (?)	*Shenhu shangfu xiaomo zhihui jing* 神虎上符消魔智慧經 (Scripture of Wisdom on the Superior Talismans of the Divine Tigers and on [the Drugs for] Subduing the Minor Demons)
23	CT 1372	*Gaoshang yuchen fengtai qusu shangjing* 高上玉晨鳳臺曲素上經 (Superior Scripture of the Most Exalted Jade Dawn and the [Eight] Pure [Ladies] of the Palace of the Phoenix Terrace)
24	CT 83, 1351	*Baihu heihe feixing yujing* 白羽黑翮飛行羽經 (Winged Scripture on Flying with the White-Winged and the Black-Feathered [Phoenixes])
25	CT 84, 1391	*Qionggong lingfei liujia zuoyou shangfu* 瓊宮靈飛六甲左右上符 (Superior Talismans of the Left and the Right of the Six *Jia* for the Numinous Flight to Exquisite Palace)
26	CT 56	*Yupei jindang Taiji jinshu shangjing* 玉佩金璫太極金書上經 (Superior Scripture of the Jade Pendant and the Golden Ring Written on Golden [Tablets] in the Great Ultimate)
27	CT 1393	*Jiuling taimiao Guishan xuanlu* 九靈太妙龜山玄籙 (Mysterious Register of the Turtle Mountain from the Great Wonder of [the Palace of] the Nine Numina)
28	CT 1361, 1369	*Qisheng xuanji huitian jiuxiao jing* 七聖玄紀迴天九霄經 (Scripture of the Mysterious Records of the Seven Saints for the Return to the Nine Celestial Empyreans)
29	CT 1380	*Taishang huangsu sishisi fang jing* 太上黃素四十四方經 (Most High Scripure of the Fourty-four Methods Written on Yellow Silk)
30	CT 55	**Taixiao langshu qiongwen dizhang* 太霄琅書瓊文帝章 (Precious Writ of the Great Empyrean on the Exquisite Text of the Imperial Statement)
31	CT 1357	*Gaoshang miemo dongjing jinxuan yuqing yinshu* 高上滅魔洞景金玄玉清隱書 (Most Exalted Concealed Writ of the Jade Clarity of Cavernous Effulgence and Golden Mystery for the Extermination of Demons)
32	CT 1336, 1337	*Taiwei tian dijun jinhu zhenfu* 太微天帝君金虎真符 (Authentic Talismans of the Golden Tigers of the Imperial Lord of the Heaven of Great Tenuity)
33	CT 1333	*Taiwei tian dijun shenhu yujing zhenfu* 太微天帝君神虎玉經真符 (Authentic Talismans of the Jade Scripture of the Divine Tigers of the Imperial Lord of the Heaven of Great Tenuity)
34	—	*Taishang huangting neijing yujing Taidi neishu* 太上黃庭內景玉經太帝內書 (Most High Jade Scripture of the Inner Effulgences of the Yellow Court, Inner Writ of the Great Emperor) [see **Huangting jing*]

The Shangqing textual corpus. See Robinet 1984, 2: 15–22 and passim. Some titles are given in abbreviated form, and some translations are tentative. The received *Santian zhengfa jing* (CT 1203; cf. no. 7 above) is not a Shangqing text.

Table 22

1 *Wei Huacun (251–334) 魏華存	24 Mao Fengrou 毛奉柔
2 *Yang Xi (330–86) 楊羲	25 *Liu Hunkang (1035–1108) 劉混康
3 Xu Mi (303–76) 許謐	26 Da Jingzhi (1068–1113) 笪淨之
4 Xu Hui (341–ca. 370) 許翽	27 Xu Xihe (?–1127) 徐希和
5 Ma Lang 馬朗	28 Jiang Jingche (?–1146) 蔣景徹
6 Ma Han 馬罕	29 Li Jinghe (?–1150) 李景合
7 *Lu Xiujing (406–77) 陸修靜	30 Li Jingying (?–1164) 李景暎
8 *Sun Youyue (399–489) 孫游嶽	31 Xu Shoujing (?–1195) 徐守經
9 *Tao Hongjing (456–536) 陶弘景	32 Qin Ruda (?–1195) 秦汝達
10 *Wang Yuanzhi (528–635) 王遠知	33 Xing Rujia (?–1209) 邢汝嘉
11 *Pan Shizheng (585–682) 潘師正	34 Xue Ruji (?–1214) 薛汝積
12 *Sima Chengzhen (647–735) 司馬承禎	35 Ren Yuanfu (1176–1239) 任元阜
13 *Li Hanguang (683–769) 李含光	36 Bao Zhizhen (?–1251) 鮑志真
14 Wei Jingzhao (694–785) 韋景昭	37 Tang Zhidao (?–1258) 湯志道
15 Huang Dongyuan (698–792) 黃洞元	38 Jiang Zongying (?–1281) 蔣宗瑛
16 Sun Zhiqing 孫智清	39 Jing Yuanfan 景元範
17 Wu Fatong (825–907) 吳法通	40 Liu Zongchang 劉宗昶
18 Liu Dechang 劉得常	41 Wang Zhixin (?–1273) 王志心
19 Wang Qixia (882–943) 王棲霞	42 Zhai Zhiying (?–1276) 翟志穎
20 Cheng Yanzhao (912–90) 成延昭	43 Xu Daoqi (1236–1291) 許道杞
21 Jiang Yuanji (?–998) 蔣元吉	44 Wang Daomeng (1242–1314) 王道孟
22 Wan Baochong 萬保沖	45 Liu Dabin (fl. 1317–28) 劉大彬
23 *Zhu Ziying (976–1029) 朱自英	

The forty-five Shangqing patriarchs. Source: *Maoshan zhi
(Monograph of Mount Mao; CT 304), j. 11–12.

Yang Xi was a client. The Xus, who had been related for many generations
to *Ge Hong's family, were based in Jurong 句容 (near Nanjing, Jiangsu). Xu
Mi's grandson, Xu Huangmin 許黃民 (361–429), disseminated the Shangqing
manuscripts when he moved further south to Zhejiang, and upon his death
bequeathed them to the Ma 馬 and Du 杜 families. These events marked the
first dispersion of the original manuscripts, which was to be followed by several
others. In the early fifth century, Wang Lingqi 王靈期 and Xu Huangmin's
son, Xu Rongdi 許榮弟 (fl. 431–32), produced many forgeries.

Before Tao Hongjing, several medieval Taoists—notably *Lu Xiujing
(406–77) and *Gu Huan (420/428–483/491)—tried to reassemble the original
texts, but Tao's effort was by far the most successful. Also thanks to his work,
the school became the foremost Taoist tradition between the sixth and tenth
centuries. Emperors interested in the Shangqing scriptures bestowed their
favors upon the patriarchs of the school, including *Sun Youyue (399–489), Tao
Hongjing, *Wang Yuanzhi (528–635), *Pan Shizheng (585–682), *Sima Chengzhen (646–735), and *Li Hanguang (683–769). Shangqing texts were the main

sources of Taoist encyclopedias of that time (especially the *Wushang biyao
and the *Sandong zhunang), and served as inspiration to *Wu Yun (?–778), Li
Bai 李白 (Li Bo, 701–62), and many other poets. In Song times, patriarchs like
*Zhu Ziying (976–1029) and *Liu Hunkang (1035–1108) initiated emperors and
their families into the Shangqing mysteries. The Taoist section of the *Taiping
yulan* 太平御覽 (Imperial Readings of the Taiping Xingguo Reign Period), a
major encyclopedia published in 983, and the ritual collections compiled in
that period, such as the *Wushang xuanyuan santian Yutang dafa* 無上玄元三
天玉堂大法 (Great Rites of the Jade Hall of the Three Heavens, of the Supreme Mysterious Origin; CT 220), contain significant portions of Shangqing
materials. From the thirteenth century, the Shangqing school lost much of its
authority as the Celestial Masters gained ascendancy. The Shangqing registers
(*LU), however, still ranked above all others.

Salvation and immortality. As a religion, Shangqing reconciles different ideas
about salvation based on a threefold conception of the human being:

1. A human being is a complex individual: immortality implies the unification of the spirits and entities that compose and animate the person.

2. A human being is linked to his ancestors whose sins and merits fall on
   him, and his salvation cannot be separated from theirs.

3. Salvation involves a cosmicization and is thus universal, in the sense that
   the adept inwardly becomes one with the universe.

In Shangqing, immortality is a private pursuit, without the intervention of
human intermediaries. The ultimate goal of the adept's quest is illustrated by
the image of the cosmic saint (*shengren), which is rooted in the *Zhuangzi,
the *Liezi, and the *Huainan zi, and integrates features drawn from popular
imagery. Once an adept has obtained immortality, he will dwell in Emptiness
and his body will emanate a supernatural radiance. He will enjoy eternal
youth, have supernatural powers, and become one with the great forces of
the universe. The terms used to describe this state indicate a transcendence
of the dualism of life and death; for instance, the adept asks to "take his pleasure far away, where there is no round or square, deeply beyond phenomena,
where Non-being and Being blend in Darkness," and to be born and die with
the Void.

Immortality is no longer as evidently physical as it was in Ge Hong's tradition; if it is a bodily immortality, it involves the achievement of a spiritual
body through meditation. Shangqing adepts aim at having their names written
in the registers of life (*shengji* 生籍) held by divinities, or at unraveling the
mortal knots that human beings are born with (Robinet 1993, 139–43). Salvation can also be obtained after death: an adept can ascend from the state of

an "underworld governor" (*dixia zhu* 地下主, an immortal of inferior rank) to that of a celestial immortal. The Shangqing idea of rebirth as a way of salvation is very different from the Buddhist notion of reincarnation, and is an innovation that heralds *neidan*.

Human beings have three main possibilities for rebirth. One of them is based on a new view of *shijie* (release from the corpse) as a stage of Taoist ascesis: when purification during life has remained incomplete, the body awaits purification in an intermediary realm such as the Great Yin (Taiyin 太陰). The adept may also be reborn in paradises where he undergoes purification by fire and is revived as an immortal. Finally, rebirth can also occur during one's lifetime, through experiencing again one's embryonic development. The latter method is called "nine transmutations" (*jiuzhuan* 九轉) or "ninefold elixir" (*jiudan* 九丹), two terms that relate rebirth to alchemy but on a purely spiritual level.

Gods and spirits. In their relationships with divine beings, adepts strive to become one with them, sometimes with a touch of chaste love. Divinities are intercessors who appear to the believer and help him on his way to salvation, giving him the keys to celestial palaces, revealing their names and toponymy to him, and nourishing him with cosmic or celestial effluvia. The gods descend into the adept and guide him to the celestial kingdoms, hand in hand, where they share their pastimes with him. This relationship is remarkably different from the one described in the scriptures of the Celestial Masters. It is expressed in numerous hymns blending bliss, exaltation, and mystical joy that appear for the first time in a Taoist movement.

The various gods are all different forms of the Primordial Beginning, and can take many appearances. Among the highest are the Celestial King of Original Commencement (Yuanshi tianwang 元始天王, see *sanqing*); the Most High Lord of the Dao (Taishang daojun 太上道君); the Imperial Lord (Dijun 帝君); the Imperial Lord of the Golden Portal (*Jinque dijun*), who is also known as the Saint of the Latter Age (*housheng*) and is identified with *Li Hong (Laozi's appellation as the messiah); the Queen Mother of the West (*Xiwang mu); and her companion *Qingtong (Azure Lad). Their primary role is to serve as mediators, and they are at the source of major revealed texts.

Shangqing inherits the Taoist vision of humanity as embodying many spirits, which is first found in the Han "weft texts" or *weishu* 緯書 (see *TAOISM AND THE APOCRYPHA; the names of several spirits are the same or similar in both corpora). Cosmic deities, including the gods of the stars, the planets, and the five sectors of space, play a fundamental role in visualizations. They descend into the believer's body to make it luminous. Many live simultaneously in the heavens and within the human being, regularly inspecting the lives of adepts and updating the registers of life and death. Shangqing also maintains the earlier notions of the three Cinnabar Fields (*dantian*) and the Three Corpses (*sanshi*; see *sanshi* and *jiuchong*). In contrast to the Three Palaces of earlier times, however, Shangqing texts imagine that the brain is divided into Nine Palaces (*jiugong*), which became a standard feature of Taoist subtle physiology. In addition, twenty-four effulgent gods dwell in the body, divided into three groups of eight known as the *bajing* (Eight Effulgences), each of which is governed by one of the Three Pure Ladies (Sansu 三素). These spirits play a key role in unraveling the mortal knots of the body. The Five Gods (*wushen* 五 神) of the registers of life, who live in the brain, lungs, liver, heart, and lower abdomen, are directed by the Great One (*Taiyi*) in the brain (see *Taidan yinshu*).

Cosmology and cosmography. Shangqing cosmology follows the traditional Chinese pattern based on the numbers 3 and 5 (see *sanwu*): a vertical three-fold division into Heaven, Earth, and Humanity corresponds to a horizontal fivefold division into the *wuxing*. There are Nine Great Primordial Heavens created from pure cosmic pneuma, each of which in turn gives rise to three heavens for a total of thirty-six heavens (*sanshiliu tian*). Another series is formed by eight heavens arranged horizontally. The Heavens of the Three Clarities (*sanqing*) are superior stages in the adept's progress. Other paradises are the stations of the sun, moon, and other astral bodies (planets, constellations, and the Northern Dipper or *beidou*), as well as the far ends of the earth, sometimes designated after ancient myths. The Southern Paradise is a place of purification and rebirth.

Besides the traditional Five Peaks (*wuyue*), Shangqing cosmography includes other sacred mountains corresponding to the Grotto-Heavens and the Blissful Lands (*dongtian* and *fudi*). The axis of the world is Mount *Kunlun, also called Xigui shan 西龜山 (Turtle Mountain of the West) or Longshan 龍 山 (Dragon Mountain). Other mountains, such as the Renniao shan 人鳥山 (Mountain of the Bird-Men), play an analogous role.

The underworld is a counterpart of the Dipper. Located in the mountain-city of *Fengdu, its administration is governed by the Northern Emperor (*Beidi) and is organized into six courts that judge the dead (six is a Yin number, related to obscurity and death). The end of the world, often evoked in Shangqing scriptures, is described in the *Santian zhengfa jing* 三天正法經 (Scripture of the Orthodox Law of the Three Heavens; CT 1203; Ozaki Masaharu 1974), in a way reminiscent of ideas already found in the *Hanshu* (History of the Former Han). The end of a cosmic cycle comes when the Yin and Yang pneumas reach their point of exhaustion. A lesser cycle ends after 3,600 celestial Yang or 3,300 terrestrial Yin revolutions, while a greater cycle ends after 9,900 celestial Yang or 9,300 terrestrial Yin revolutions. The Mother of

Water (Shuimu 水母), a "celestial horse" (*tianma* 天馬), a "great bird" (*daniao* 大鳥), and Li Hong are the judges who, at that time, descend to earth to judge humanity.

Practices. Unlike the communal rites of the Celestial Masters, the Shangqing practices are individual and emphasize *MEDITATION AND VISUALIZATION. The bureaucratic and theurgic aspects of the Celestial Masters' relationship to their gods are ignored: the celestial beings are not summoned with petitions but are invoked with prayers or chants, and there are no warlike struggles with demonic spirits. Physiological techniques and the ingestion of drugs and herbs are considered as minor; sexual practices are condemned or are interiorized and sublimated. The ritual aspect of the practices is flexible, and one is not impelled to observe the formal rules if it is impossible to do so.

The great variety of Shangqing practices can be categorized as follows:

1. Charms, recitations (*songjing*), and hymns, usually accompanied by visualizations (*cun*), whose purpose is to exterminate demons, summon spirits, or obtain salvation.

2. Visualization of spirits, some celestial and some corporeal (often both), who come to animate and spiritualize the body (see *Huangting jing* and *Dadong zhenjing*). The adept blends them all into one, and unites himself with them. Often at the end of these visualizations everything in the world and outside of it becomes effulgent. This group also includes the method of the Three Ones (*sanyi*) described in the *Ciyi jing*, the *Suling jing*, and the *Jiuzhen zhongjing*.

3. Ecstatic metamorphoses (see *bianhua*).

4. Methods aiming at having one's name inscribed in the "registers of life" (*Ciyi jing*, *Basu jing*, and *Taidan yinshu*).

5. Methods for loosening the mortal knots of the embryo (*Basu jing*, *Jiuzhen zhongjing*, and *Taidan yinshu*).

6. Ecstatic excursions (*yuanyou*) and absorption of astral efflorescences (*Basu jing* and *Jiuzhen zhongjing*).

Interiorization is the major innovative feature of Shangqing, and its main legacy for Taoism. It consists of actualizing (*cun*), i.e., giving existence to entities pertaining to an imaginative and mystical world that lies between spiritual and physical existence (see *xiang*). The adept has direct access to the sacred: the role of intermediary is not played by priests or other ritual officiants but by the scriptures themselves, which organize and codify relations between humanity and the gods, and between ordinary and sacred life. The importance of the written texts is emphasized to such a degree that the master's role consists only in certifying their legitimate transmission. The Shangqing scriptures are divine and precosmic, a token bestowed by the deities that promises salvation.

Isabelle ROBINET

📖 Chen Guofu 1963, 7–62; Esposito 2004b; Ishii Masako 1980; Kamitsuka Yoshiko 1999, 15–297; Kohn 1992a, 108–16; Ozaki Masaharu 1983d; Qing Xitai 1988–95, 1: 336–77 and 2: 125–41; Ren Jiyu 1990, 133–42; Robinet 1984; Robinet 1993; Robinet 1997b, 114–48; Robinet 2000; Strickmann 1977; Strickmann 1981; Sun Kekuan 1968, 75–155

※ For related entries see the Synoptic Table of Contents, sec. III.4 ("Shang-qing")

Shangqing dao leishi xiang

上清道類事相

Classified Survey of Shangqing Taoism

Wang Xuanhe 王懸和 (fl. 664–84) compiled the *Shangqing dao leishi xiang* (CT 1132) in four *juan*. The text consists entirely of citations from works that date to the Six Dynasties and has six divisions: "Immortal Observatories" ("Xianguan 仙觀"); "Lofts and Pavilions" ("Louge 樓閣"); "Immortal Chambers" ("Xianfang 仙房"); "Jeweled Terraces" ("Baotai 寶臺"); "Elegant Chambers" ("Qiongshi 瓊室"); and "Dwellings and Spirit Shrines" ("Zhaiyu lingmiao 宅宇靈廟"). As its rubrics indicate, the compendium concerns Taoist edifices—celestial, terrestrial and subterranean.

There are citations from over one hundred texts in this compendium. Despite the title they concern not only *Shangqing works, but also sources of other categories, including *Zhengyi* 正一 (*Tianshi dao scriptures), *Taixuan* 太玄 (the *Daode jing* and related texts), *Dongshen* 洞神 (*Sanhuang wen*), and *Dongxuan* 洞玄 (*Lingbao scriptures), as well as hagiographies and other unaffiliated writings. Some of the quotations derive from texts now lost or passages missing from extant works in the present-day Taoist Canon. Others supply variant readings to surviving scriptures. The title of Wang's anthology is not suggestive of its contents and there is no preface. This may indicate that the surviving chapters are a fragment of a larger work, like Wang's *Sandong zhunang*, that covered a greater range of topics than it now does.

For the most part, the contents of the *Shangqing dao leishi xiang* is devoted to the edifices of the otherworld: the palaces of celestial rulers, the archives where scriptures are stored waiting for an auspicious moment when they can be revealed to an anointed saint, heavenly sites where the immortals and perfected cultivated the Dao, and the like. As such it provides a handy guide for reconstructing the cosmography of medieval Taoism. Perhaps more importantly, Wang cites a number of passages, mainly from the *Daoxue zhuan* in the first section, on the establishment of mundane abbeys during the fifth and sixth centuries. This is probably the only survey of that sort of activity and an invaluable source for the growth of Taoism and imperial patronage for it. On the whole, however, the text is far less important than Wang's *Sandong zhunang*.

Charles D. BENN

📖 Boltz J. M. 1987a, 228; Ōfuchi Ninji and Ishii Masako 1988, 136–49 (list of texts cited); Reiter 1992

※ Shangqing

Shangqing gong

上清宮

Palace of Highest Clarity (Mount Longhu)

The Shangqing gong is the central temple on Mount Longhu (*Longhu shan, Jiangxi), the seat of the Celestial Masters' *Zhengyi institution since about the ninth century. Mount Longhu became covered with temples during the Song and Yuan periods; they are described in a partly extant Yuan gazetteer, the *Longhu shanzhi* 龍虎山志 (Monograph of Mount Longhu), and in a more detailed 1740 edition of the same work, authored by one of the most prestigious *faguan* 法官 (lit., "officers of the [exorcistic] ritual") ever, *Lou Jinyuan (1689–1776). Some of these temples had disappeared by Ming and Qing times, but the regular income of the institution (landed property, ordination fees, donations) and occasional liberalities of the court for large-scale restorations ensured that the major temples were kept in excellent condition until the destruction of many by the various revolutionary armies during the 1930s. Longhu shan is now operating again, on a more modest scale.

Ever since the Song, the central temple on the mountain has been the Shangqing gong (a title granted in 1113 to a temple that was probably founded a few centuries earlier). All major rituals, including ordinations, were held there. Also noteworthy is the Zhengyi guan 正一觀 (Abbey of Orthodox Unity), devoted to *Zhang Daoling. Equally important was the Celestial Master's residence, the Zhenren fu 真人府 (Bureau of the Real Man; Tianshi fu 天

師府 or Bureau of the Celestial Master before the Ming), located about one kilometer from the Shangqing gong. These were the offices where the Celestial Master and his *faguan* attended to the bureaucratic work of ordaining priests and canonizing local gods, and corresponded with Taoists and officials all over China. Twenty-four residences or **daoyuan* around the Shangqing gong housed both the permanent Taoist staff and visiting priests from all over China, some coming just for ordination, others spending several years on the mountains for comprehensive training. It would seem that these *daoyuan* were divided according to lineage, and perhaps also by geographical origin of the resident priests. Longhu shan was quite ecumenical and even had a small **Quanzhen community.

Vincent GOOSSAERT

📖 Hachiya Kunio 1990, 1: 278–79, 2: 265–66; Qing Xitai 1994, 4: 248–250; Zhang Jintao 1994

※ Longhu shan; Zhengyi; TEMPLES AND SHRINES

Shangqing huangshu guodu yi

上清黃書過度儀

Liturgy of Passage of the Yellow Writ of Highest Clarity

The *Shangqing huangshu guodu yi* (CT 1294) contains ritual prescriptions for "passing and crossing" (*guodu*) difficulties in the context of a detailed ritual involving the union of Yin and Yang **qi*, and of male and female participants. This text may date from the second through the fifth centuries CE, and reflects the integration of ritualized visualization, invocation, and sexual techniques.

The title of the text reflects the diverse influences on its origin. The term *huangshu* 黃書 (Yellow Writ) indicates its connection to the *fangzhong* 房中 (arts of the bedchamber) tradition (see **fangzhong shu*). The term *guodu* 過度 suggests a connection with the correlative prescriptions for daily activities ubiquitous in the Warring States and early imperial periods. The fourth-century composite **Dongyuan shenzhou jing* (Scripture of the Divine Spells of the Cavernous Abyss) notes that if people use the *huangshu* without *guodu*, they will have many illnesses, agricultural and sericultural failures, and ultimately fail to live out their full life span (see Mollier 1990, 150). In alchemical contexts, *guodu* refers to the correlation of the measurement of reagents to the periods of the day. Thus, while the form of the text is indicated by the term *yi* 儀 (ceremony, or liturgy), indicating it is part of the genre of **keyi* (ritual codes), the references to the twelve Earthly Branches (*dizhi* 地支; see **ganzhi*), five directions, and the spirits of the sexagesimal cycle show its sources in the genre of correlative prescriptions, and its instructions on the union of Yin and Yang show its sources in sexual cultivation literature.

The *Shangqing huangshu guodu yi* details a ritual wherein a couple moves through different activities, or "passes" (*guo* 過), guided by a master. In the first stage, *rujing* 入靖 (entering the purification chamber), the couple stand and take part in a scripted dialogue with the master. They then proceed through passes involving the visualization of different spirits and kinds of *qi*, recitations, breathing exercises, touching and massaging, invocations and apotropaic spells, and at one point penetration with the *yuyue* 玉籥 ("jade flute," i.e., penis). These different activities are interspersed with each other, and the position, direction and movement of the participants is all carefully choreographed. The correlation of the parts of the body and the ritual space with the spirits of the Nine Palaces (**jiugong*), the sexagesimal cycle, their combination in the Three Primes (**sanyuan*), and the five viscera (**wuzang*), implies that an important goal of the ritual was the visualization and the invocation of the spirits as a way of bringing the bodies of the participants in line with the cosmic order.

In the *Daozang*, rites based on the union of *qi* are represented in the *Shangqing huangshu guodu yi* and the more theoretical *Dongzhen huangshu* 洞真黃書 (Yellow Writ of the Cavern of Perfection; CT 1343). Differences in the way that male and female participants are referred to, and other factors, indicate that the rites incorporate elements from different sources. According to the *Dongzhen huangshu*, the *huangshu* were presented by Laozi to the first Celestial Master **Zhang Daoling in 142 CE. Parts of the text probably date back to that time, while other parts date to the Wei-Jin period. It was likely that it was this ritual, or rituals like it, that were the object of condemnation by Eastern Jin reformers of the **Tianshi dao tradition like **Kou Qianzhi (365?–448).

Mark CSIKSZENTMIHALYI

📖 Ge Zhaoguang 1999; Kalinowski 1985; Kobayashi Masayoshi 1990, 357–66; Maspero 1981, 533–41

※ *fangzhong shu; heqi; zhongmin*

Shangqing lingbao dafa

上清靈寶大法

Great Rites of the Numinous Treasure of Highest Clarity

The Taoist Canon contains two thirteenth-century texts with this title that present two very different views of the *Lingbao dafa tradition. Both rely on the *Lingbao wuliang duren shangjing dafa* (Great Rites of the Superior Scripture of the Numinous Treasure on Limitless Salvation) or a close cognate text. While both show signs of additions and changes over the years, the earlier of the two (CT 1223, with table of contents in CT 1222) was likely compiled by the strident liturgical purist and critic of the innovations in Southern Song Taoist ritual, Jin Yunzhong 金允中 (fl. 1224–25). In this work he stresses the continued centrality of canonical *Lingbao rituals whose simple liturgies and scriptures derive from the Highest Clarity (*shangqing* 上清) Heaven. Codified by such figures as *Lu Xiujing (406–77), *Zhang Wanfu (fl. 710–13), and *Du Guangting (850–933) and passed down without interruption since Tang times to his masters, these ancient Taoist ritual writings from the Central Plains also include the newer *Tongchu (Youthful Incipience) rituals. From this classicist perspective, he strongly criticizes more recent ritual innovations, elaborate practices, and inner excesses that proponents claim come from heaven, in particular the Lingbao dafa tradition that *Ning Benli (1101–81) had earlier codified in the *Tiantai region.

Wang Qizhen's 王契真 (fl. ca. 1250) compendium (CT 1221), by contrast, may be seen as a substantial response to Jin's criticisms. Although often seeming to present the Lingbao dafa as a powerful ritual system apart from the people and places most strongly associated with its origins and evolution, Wang clearly identifies himself as continuing the work of Ning Benli, its earliest codifier. In generalizing the tradition beyond its local sources, the ritual programs of salvation appearing in the chapters of this text seem even more abstract. Wang saw the Yellow Register Retreat (*huanglu zhai) as the most flexible of all ritual programs, one that was appropriate for the living and the dead, for elite and ordinary people, and for both women and men. The compilation's twenty-four rubrics include a systematic introduction (*j.* 1) and account of basic Lingbao dafa practices (*j.* 2–4), followed by a description of recitation and inner practices (*j.* 5), and exorcistic practices of talismanic healing (*j.* 6–7). Longer sections deal with exorcistic practices for accumulating merit, based on the *Duren jing (*j.* 12–26), rites of transmission and various Retreat rites for the dead, including those for the Yellow Register (*j.* 39–48), Salvation through Refinement (**liandu, j.* 49–53), and traditional Retreat (**zhai*) ceremonies. Wang Qizhen's text was expanded in early Ming times (Boltz J. M. 1994, 27).

Lowell SKAR

📖 Boltz J. M. 1987a, 43–44, 45–46; Davis E. 2001, 173–76; Maruyama Hiroshi 1994a

※ Lingbao dafa

Shangsheng xiuzhen sanyao

上乘修真三要

The Three Principles of the Cultivation of Perfection
According to the Higher Vehicle

The author of this text (CT 267), indicated as Yuanming laoren 圓明老人 (Old Man of Full Enlightenment), is probably the *Quanzhen master Gao Daokuan 高道寬 (1195–1277). The "three principles" mentioned in the title are inner nature and vital force (*xing and ming) and mind (*xin).

The first section deals with inner nature. It is inspired by the Chan allegory of training the ox as found in the ten pictures by Puming 普明 (late eleventh century), which were popular during the Yuan period. Each picture is followed by a poem and a short commentary, also in verse. The commentaries describe the progressive whitening of the horse, which represents the process of purification. The first ten pictures represent the horse training, the eleventh shows a circle containing a man, and the twelfth a circle containing an infant. This part of the text ends with the picture of a circle surrounding the Purple Gold Immortal (Zijin xian 紫金仙), i.e., Laozi. The second section focuses on vital force, and describes the *neidan practice in the tradition of the *Zhouyi cantong qi with several illustrations.

The horse symbolizes creative thought (or Intention, *yi), as opposed to the ox which represents the mind. The metaphor of the horse's training was not unknown in Taoist literature and had been used at an early date in *Huainan zi 14: "Settle your mind and fix your thoughts (pingxin dingyi 平心定意), . . . ride the mind and attune yourself to the horse (yuxin tiao hu ma 御心調乎馬)." However, its appearance in the present text should be seen in the context of the controversies between Buddhism and Taoism in the mid-thirteenth century. In the Shuogua 說卦 (Explanation of the Trigrams) appendix to the *Yijing, the horse corresponds to qian 乾 ☰ (Pure Yang) and the ox corresponds to *kun* 坤 ☷ (Pure Yin). The use of the horse thus alludes to the superiority of the Taoist adept, who is able to create an immortal body of Pure Yang, while the Buddhist follower reaches liberation without having entirely eliminated the Yin.

Catherine DESPEUX

📖 Despeux 1981a

※ *neidan*; TAOISM AND CHINESE BUDDHISM

shanshu

善書

morality books

The term *shanshu* has been used in China since the Song dynasty to refer to a variety of works (also known as *quanshi wen* 勸世文 or "books to exhort the age") with the pronounced didactic intent to exhort people to practice virtue and eschew evil. Taoist sources were particularly important to some of the oldest and most imitated examples of *shanshu*, and Taoist teachings have been an important component of the variously weighted mix of Taoist, Buddhist, Confucian, and regional ideas used in these works to reach as broad an audience as possible. Generally, *shanshu* share some form of belief in the law of cause and effect, that is, the cosmic process of retribution by which good and bad actions have consequences for this life, subsequent lives, and even the lives of one's descendants. These consequences might include the realization of Taoist immortality, punishment in the hells of the underworld (*diyu* 地獄, the "earth prisons"), or the attainment of this-worldly tangibles such as long life, social position, wealth, and male progeny. Typically, contributions to the dissemination of *shanshu* were also thought to earn merit and became a conventional form of religious piety and social morality.

Genres and definition. The term *shanshu* does not designate a formal genre and many types of texts have been labelled *shanshu*. Based on recent scholarship alone, *shanshu* can include revealed sectarian scriptures such as precious scrolls (*baojuan), ledgers of merit and demerit (*gongguo ge* 功過格), family instructions (*zhijia geyan* 治家格言), collections of miracle tales (*lingyan ji* 靈驗記 and *yingyan ji* 應驗記), stories of virtuous behavior (such as the *Ershisi xiao de gushi* 二十四孝的故事 or *Twenty-Four Stories of Filiality*), daily-use encyclopedias, almanacs, children's primers, community contracts, the imperially-issued Sacred Edicts (*shengyu* 聖語), popular operas, spirit-writing texts (see *fuji), revealed tales of "cause and effect across three incarnations" (*sanshi yinguo* 三世因果), guides to self-examination, and twentieth-century moralistic self-help books. While some of these texts were imperially sponsored and widely used in educational settings, others were apt to be confiscated due to their association with illegal sectarian groups. Many *shanshu* in the past, and in Taiwan today, appear to be the products of small cult groups that gather to receive spirit-writing revelations from a particular deity, who may descend into a medium or a writing device. Others are beheld in dreams or are records of visionary journeys. Transcriptions are written up, sometimes given commentary to explain their essential meaning, and donations are solicited to fund the printing of copies to distribute freely at temples, bookstores, and religious restaurants.

The current tendency is to use the term *shanshu* to designate those works not associated with doctrinal, sectarian followings, although continued investigation seems destined to emphasize the fluidity of moral and religious concerns. In this regard, some scholars look to morality books for evidence of a pan-Chinese "popular" religion; others see *shanshu* as a major vehicle by which fundamental Taoist ideas diffused throughout Chinese culture. Technically, traditional use of the term *shanshu* would evoke associations with more educated social circles, but such associations were part of the wider appeal of this literature. In fact, *shanshu* were usually written in either the vernacular or very accessible classical Chinese. While commentary and citations from the classics might be provided by editors from the scholar-official class, the frequent inclusion of entertaining stories, illustrations, lists of merit-earning sponsors, and instructions to disseminate freely all suggest that such works were idealistically intended to go beyond any one religious or social group.

History. Historically, morality books were particularly widespread in the late Ming and early Qing, but evidence for their popularity goes back to the Song dynasty and extends down to the present day. Key conceptual and linguistic elements can be found in the *Yijing, Han dynasty cosmological texts, the *Taiping jing (Scripture of Great Peace), as well as later Taoist and Buddhist works. While the basic idea of cosmic retribution for one's actions has been described as the fundamental belief of Chinese religion since the beginning of its recorded history, the more narrowly-defined Taoist contributions were also significant, especially the orchestration of merit accumulation from good deeds, self-examination, practices for nourishing life (*yangsheng) and cultivating perfection (*xiuzhen* 修真) with a vast otherworldly bureaucracy of spirits—residing both in the heavens and the body—who watch over human activity. While these ideas can be found in the *Huang-Lao, Great Peace (Taiping dao 太平道; see *Yellow Turbans) and Celestial Masters (*Tianshi dao) teachings of the Later Han dynasty, notably the *Xiang'er* commentary to the *Daode jing*, they are most developed by *Ge Hong (283–343), whose *Baopu zi* specifies how much accumulated merit is needed to become a celestial immortal as opposed to an earthly immortal (trans. Ware 1966, 66–67, 115–19). Buddhist concepts of *karma*, transmigration, universal salvation (*pudu*), and the imagery of the hells of the underworld were increasingly joined to Taoist ideas of retribution for virtue and vice, forming the context for such early *shanshu* as the famous *Taishang ganying pian* (Folios of the Most High on Retribution). The influence of local cults of the Tang and Song dynasties also led to *shanshu* in which deities like the *Wenchang, the Stove God (*Zaoshen) and Guandi 關帝 (*Guan Yu) assumed more Taoist features to become identified with overseeing human behavior and dispensing revelations about retribution, morality, and fated life span. Alongside the *Taishang ganying pian*, the (*Wenchang dijun*) *Yinzhi wen* 文昌帝君陰騭文 (Essay [of Imperial Lord Wenchang] on Secret Virtue; trans. Suzuki and Carus 1906b, and Kleeman 1996, 70–71) and the (*Guansheng dijun*) *Jueshi zhenjing* 關聖帝君覺世真經 (Authentic Scripture [of Imperial Lord Guan] to Awaken the World) are the most frequently cited examples of traditional *shanshu*. Sponsors often proclaimed a desire to spread the message of these tracts even to the illiterate, and these texts appear to have spanned many social levels but may not have had the visual impact of yet another ubiquitous tract, the *Yuli chaozhuan* 玉曆鈔傳 (Transcribed Annals of the Jade Calendar; eleventh century), which described the ten courts of the underworld where retribution was exacted for human misdeeds.

While early morality books were a vehicle for the dissemination of Taoist internal and external cosmological ideas, there is also evidence that popular concern with moral retribution influenced in turn the shape of Taoist institutions and teachings in the late Song and after. For example, the *Quanzhen order, founded in the twelfth century, focused as much on moral exhortations and disciplines as inner alchemical (*neidan*) and meditational techniques for immortality. The legendary immortal and *neidan* adept *Lü Dongbin, worshipped in Quanzhen Taoism, was associated with a number of *shanshu*. Similarly, a ledger of merits and demerits that originated in the twelfth-century Taoist sect of *Xu Xun became particularly popular among many members of the educated class in the late Ming and early Qing. Their emphasis on the individual's responsibility to assume the task of scrutinizing and recording merits and demerits may have helped to bring Neo-Confucian concerns with determining one's own fate to bear on older Taoist *neidan* traditions.

Besides those noted above, the Ming-dynasty Taoist Canon includes the *Taiwei xianjun gongguo ge* 太微仙君功過格 (Ledger of Merit and Demerit of the Immortal Lord of Great Tenuity; CT 186) and several Stove God texts (CT 69, 208, and 364). The *Daozang jiyao* contains commentaries on the *Taishang ganying pian* (vol. 6), other ledgers (vol. 23), and several texts associated with Wenchang and Lü Dongbin that many would call *shanshu*. In 1936, the Leshan she 樂善社 (Love of Virtue Society) published a large number of *shanshu* in a collection entitled *Fushou baozang* 福壽寶藏 (Precious Treasury of Happiness and Longevity; Shanghai: Daozhong shuju), also known as *Zhenben shanshu* 珍本善書 (Precious Morality Books). *Shanshu* are still being written, printed and distributed today in China and quite prolifically in Taiwan.

Catherine BELL

📖 Bell 1996a; Brokaw 1991, 3–64; Cai Maotang 1974–76; Chen Xia 1999; Eberhard 1967; Kubo Noritada 1977, 361–68; Qing Xitai and Li Gang 1985; Sakai Tadao 1960; Yoshioka Yoshitoyo 1952, 70–192; You Zi'an 1999; Zheng Zhiming 1988b

※ *baojuan*; ETHICS AND MORALS; TAOISM AND CHINESE BUDDHISM

Shao Yizheng

邵以正

?–1462; *hao*: Chengkang zi 承康子 (Master Who Bears Well-being),
Zhizhi daoren 止止道人 (The Taoist Who Stills Stillness)

For reasons that remain unclear, Shao Yizheng's parents left their ancestral home in Gusu 姑蘇 (Jiangsu) and relocated in Kunming 昆明 (Yunnan) during the Hongwu reign period (1368–98). It was there that Shao's birth is said to have followed in response to a prophetic dream of a jade peach. When he reached adulthood, Shao became the preeminent disciple of *Liu Yuanran (1351–1432), patriarch of the *Jingming dao (Pure and Bright Way). In 1425 Liu was summoned to take charge of the Taoist affairs of state and Shao accompanied him to the capital where he served as Taoist Registrar and ultimately inherited Liu's post. He is best known for being the person given the authority to oversee the completion and printing of the *Da Ming daozang jing* 大明道藏經 (Scriptures of the Taoist Canon of the Great Ming), popularly known as the *Zhengtong daozang* (Taoist Canon of the Zhengtong Reign Period). A collection of his master's teachings that Shao compiled, the *Changchun Liu zhenren yulu* 長春劉真人語錄 (Recorded Sayings of the Perfected Liu Changchun), may be found in the *Gezhi congshu* 格致叢書 (Collectanea of Commensurate Exempla) of 1603. A variant version of the *Jingming zhongxiao quanshu* (Complete Writings of the Pure and Bright [Way of] Loyalty and Filiality) edited by Shao is in the library of Naikaku bunko in Tokyo.

The restoration of a hall in the main temple compound at Mount Mao (*Maoshan, Jiangsu), undertaken from 1449 to 1453, is among the building projects for which Shao was able to secure funding. He was himself personally responsible for establishing a shrine honoring Liu at the Longquan guan 龍泉觀 (Abbey of the Dragon Springs) in Kunming. In 1476, Shao's most renowned disciple Yu Daochun 喻道純 in turn oversaw the erection of a stele at his master's own shrine in the same temple compound, engraved with a tribute composed by the literatus Shang Lu 商輅 (1414–86; DMB 1161–63).

Judith M. BOLTZ

📖 Chen Yuan 1988, 1253–66 passim; Oyanagi Shigeta 1934, 22–23

※ Liu Yuanran; *Zhengtong daozang*; Jingming dao

Shao Yong

邵雍

1012–77; zi: Yaofu 堯夫

Shao Yong was a famous Song philosopher and poet who was later called one of the Five Masters of the Northern Song dynasty (*Bei Song wuzi* 北宋五子). A native of Fanyang 範陽 (Hebei), in his youth he followed his father to Gongcheng 共成 (Henan), where he studied the doctrines related to the *Yijing under Li Zhicai 李之才. In his thirties, he relocated to Luoyang, where he styled his home the Den of Peace and Bliss (Anle wo 安樂窩) and maintained close contacts with Sima Guang 司馬光 (1019–86) and other scholars. During the Jiayou reign period (1056–63), Shao was repeatedly recommended to Song Renzong (r. 1022–63) but declined any official appointment on the grounds of his poor health. In his later years he lived as a recluse at Hundred Springs (Baiyuan 百源) on Mount Sumen (Sumen shan 蘇門山, Henan), and was therefore posthumously called the Elder from Hundred Springs (Baiyuan xiansheng 百源先生).

As attested by his *Huangji jingshi* 皇極經世 (Supreme Principles that Rule the World), which is included in the *Daozang* (CT 1040), Shao was an expert in the cosmology of the *Yijing* and the teaching of "images and numbers" (*xiangshu* 象數). In this and other writings he proposes to explain natural phenomena and human affairs by drawing on the changes and transformations, the waning and waxing of the images and numbers themselves in the eight trigrams (*bagua). Shao Yong's knowledge of the *xiantian ("prior to heaven") interpretation and the images and numbers was based on the teachings of *Chen Tuan, the eminent Taoist of the Northern Song. According to Zhu Zhen's 朱震 biography in the *Songshi* (History of the Song; 349.12907–8), "Chen Tuan transmitted the *Xiantian tu* 先天圖 (Diagram of the Noumenal World; see *Taiji tu) to Zhong Fang 種放, Zhong Fang transmitted it to Mu Xiu 穆修, Mu Xiu transmitted it to Li Zhicai, and Li Zhicai transmitted it to Shao Yong." Shao Yong held Chen Tuan in high esteem, and in one poem he writes:

> I read Chen Tuan's writings
> And then I saw his portrait
> Now I know the present and the past
> Man's long presence on earth.

The *Daozang* also includes the *Yichuan jirang ji* 伊川擊壤集 (Anthology of Beating on the Ground at Yichuan; CT 1042), which contains more than 1,400 poems and songs by Shao (on the title of this text see Birdwhistell 1989, 259 n. 25). His poetry, based on reasoning and refined with rhetorical skill, initiated the practice of philosophical poetry that was to become fashionable among Song literati. Shao also secretly practiced *neidan. In a poem dedicated to his home in Luoyang, the Den of Peace and Bliss, he writes:

> I half remember that I do not remember my dream after I wake
> I feel like grieving without feeling sadness in times of leisure
> Wrapped up, I lie on my side and try to recall—no desire to get up
> Outside the window-screens, flowers are falling—disorder begins.

These lines were greatly praised by Sima Guang and other literati.

Shao Yong's thoughts on the *Yijing* are different from those of Zhu Xi 朱熹 (1130–1200; SB 282–90) and other Song literati. Nevertheless, according to the *Song Yuan xue'an* 宋元學案 (Documents on Scholarship in the Song and Yuan), "it was none other than Zhu Xi who held Shao Yong's arrangement of the eight trigrams according to the *xiantian* interpretation in highest esteem." In his "Liu xiansheng huaxiang zan" 六先生畫像贊 ("Eulogy on the Portraits of Six Elders"), Zhu Xi praises Shao Yong with the following words: "Heaven makes brave men, and the brave ones overshadow the age."

CHEN Yaoting

📖 Birdwhistell 1989; Fung Yu-lan 1952–53, 2: 451–76; Sattler 1976; Wyatt 1996; Smith K. et al. 1990, 100–135; Yu Dunkang 1997

※ TAOISM AND NEO-CONFUCIANISM

Shao Yuanjie

邵元節

1459–1539; *zi*: Zhongkang 仲康; *hao*: Xueya 雪崖 (Snowy Cliff)

Shao Yuanjie was a Taoist priest trained in the *Zhengyi tradition on Mount Longhu (*Longhu shan, Jiangxi). After he entered the mountain at the age of fourteen *sui*, his understanding of the Way became so superb that it was thought to exceed that of the Celestial Masters themselves. He was eventually summoned to court in 1524 by the Jiajing Emperor (r. 1522–66). Much to the latter's appreciation, Shao presented Taoism as supplementary to the models provided by the rulers of antiquity. In 1539, the emperor planned a journey to the south, but Shao was too ill to accompany him and instead recommended his confidant *Tao Zhongwen. Shao died shortly thereafter in the same year.

Both Shao Yuanjie and his successor Tao Zhongwen served the emperor as specialists in rites to produce rain and snow, imperial progeny, cosmic harmony, and so forth. Shao's elaborate rituals to procure a male heir to the throne were successful, a significant achievement when we consider that the Jiajing Emperor himself was not the natural son of his predecessor. This matter was also at the root of fierce discussions within the bureaucracy throughout the Jiajing reign about appropriate forms of imperial ancestor worship. These debates further inspired the emperor's trust in figures such as Shao and Tao Zhongwen, rather than in overly critical bureaucrats. After this feat, Shao was charged with overseeing the bureaucracy of Taoist monasteries and the proper ordination of monks and priests. He received the highest honors, including the title of Perfected (*zhenren*) and the official degree of First Rank usually reserved for the Celestial Master (*tianshi*) and the foremost imperial bureaucrats. As further rewards for his services he was given valuable items attesting to his ritual legitimacy, as well as land and administrative posts for his descendants.

When we compare the biographies of Shao Yuanjie and Tao Zhongwen that were written shortly after their deaths (rather than the later critical writings), we find significant differences between them. Shao's biographers emphasize his intellectual and ritual abilities, and show that his efforts to procure male imperial progeny consisted of extensive classical rituals for establishing cosmic harmony (*jiao). Tao's biographers instead stress his ability to deal with the emperor's specific life crises through a (probably more vernacular) type of ritual using "talismanic water" (*fushui* 符水).

Most of the personal post-mortem honors bestowed upon Shao Yuanjie were recalled immediately after the enthronement of the Jiajing Emperor's successor, the Longqing Emperor (r. 1567–72). This reversal was part of a radical, Confucian-inspired overturning of Jiajing ritual policies, not limited to those supported by Taoist specialists but also including state rituals. Shao's practices at court are an example of the close relation between these two sets of religious practices. First of all, his activities as recorded in the *Shilu* 實錄 (Veritable Records) and in his posthumous biographies were ordinary Taoist rites; second, many state rituals based themselves on notions of the ritual management of cosmic processes very similar to those underlying classical Taoist ritual.

Barend ter HAAR

📖 Berling 1998, 966–70; Fisher 1990; Liu Ts'un-yan 1976c; Lü Xichen 1991, 361–83; Shi Yanfeng 1992; Zhuang Hongyi 1986, passim

※ Tao Zhongwen; Zhengyi; TAOISM AND THE STATE

shen

神

spirit

See *jing, qi, shen* 精 · 氣 · 神.

shengren

聖人

saint; saintly man; sage

Although Taoist texts distinguish the *shengren* or saint from the *xianren* or immortal, the two figures are close to each other. Both the *Daode jing* and the *Xici* 繫辭 (Appended Statements, a portion of the *Yijing*) often allude to the saint only by the term *shengren*. In the *Zhuangzi*, the first source to describe the saint in detail, he is called *shengren*, *zhenren* (Real Man), *shenren* (Divine Man), or *zhiren* 至人 (Accomplished Man). These descriptions, which combine metaphysical and fantastic features, are one of the main links between the *Zhuangzi* and the later Taoist tradition. The saint plays a positive role in them, complementary to his negative or apophatic aspect; he is the answer to all the questions that Zhuangzi asks and leaves unanswered.

In the second century BCE, the basic features of the Taoist saint are outlined in the *Huainan zi. Despite some differences, the image drawn in this text and those mentioned above, as well as in the Guanzi 管子 (Rickett 1993), the *Baopu zi, the *Shangqing scriptures, and the Taoist hagiographies, is similar. Moreover, the saint is close to the Great Man (daren 大人) praised by poets influenced by Taoist thought, such as Sima Xiangru 司馬相如 (ca. 179–117 BCE; Hervouet 1972) or Ruan Ji 阮籍 (210–63 CE; Holzman 1976). The saint is one and anonymous and cannot be manifold, which is the main distinction between him and the immortal.

The Taoist saint also shares some skills with the magicians, and yet is different from them. Although his image is tricked out with details springing from popular imagery, he is a metaphysical and cosmological character, the human incarnation of the Dao, similar to a limiting line between the Dao and humanity, or between the universe and humanity. Unlike the Confucian sage, moreover, the Taoist saint is not characterized by moral qualities but by an active and mystical participation in the natural workings of life and the world. Usually he is not involved in the government of the state, with the exception of the saint of the Daode jing and the Huainan zi who reconciles the spiritual and metaphysical spheres with the function of cosmic ruler and guide for humans. In the Shangqing texts, where the saint is constantly present, he represents the goal of the adept's practices and hence the most powerful motivator of the Taoist quest, as his divine powers are said to be a result of his Taoist practices. Paradoxically, therefore, the saint justifies these practices by transcending them.

The saint is evanescent, unpredictable, dynamic, flexible, and ubiquitous. He is forever unchanged and centered in the Dao, but is as elusive as the Dao and emptiness itself. He can die and be reborn. He flies through the air and goes beyond the world. He is master of the elements and of space and time, and commands demons and spirits. He hides himself at a distance from the world or lives in the very midst of it, for example in the marketplace. *Ge Hong says that "he is so high than no one can reach him, so deep that no one can penetrate to his depth" (Baopu zi 1). The saint accommodates himself so well to his environment as to pass unnoticed: ordinary people cannot see him. Alone and unique, "he remains in Unity and knows no dualism" (Huainan zi 7), yet can be both here and there and multiply himself. His sight and hearing are sharp and penetrating; knowing the secrets of time, he can predict the future. He is "dark and obscure, and as brilliant as the sun and the moon" (Huainan zi 2), and is "a mirror of Heaven and Earth" (Zhuangzi 13). He can make himself invisible because he knows how to recover the subtle, ethereal state. Returning to the Original Pneuma (*yuanqi*) and the original darkness, he can become no longer perceptible.

As a mediator, the saint measures and discloses the distance that divides Heaven and Earth and gives rise to the world. He dominates Yin and Yang, and stands above, below, and beyond the world, yet is in its center. He animates the universe, whose vivid signification he embodies, organizes, and harmonizes, and whose unity he bears witness to and guarantees. He joins the visible and the invisible and all other polarities. His magical powers are symbolic of the animating creativity of the Dao; as all symbols do, he simultaneously hides and unveils the secret of life and the world.

For those who reject the devotional and religious aspect of Taoism, the saint plays the same mediating role that a god does in religion. He is the model of perfect and complete humanity and its inspired guide, a cosmic figure who embodies emptiness or the Dao in an abstract, anonymous, yet vivid way. He transcends the opposition of life and death and embraces all immortals and gods.

Isabelle ROBINET

📖 Kohn 1993b, 281–90; Larre 1982, 145–53; Robinet 1993, 42–48; Robinet 1996a, 48–51 and 137–53; Robinet 1997b, passim

※ *shenren*; *xianren*; *zhenren*; TRANSCENDENCE AND IMMORTALITY

Shengshen jing

生神經

Scripture of the Life-Giving Spirits

The nine hymns that form the core of this early fifth-century *Lingbao scripture (found in the Taoist Canon as the *Ziran jiutian shengshen zhangjing* 自然九天生神章經; CT 318) are those which the spirits of the body chant during the critical ninth month of foetal development, after the fetus has been nurtured with the pneumas (*qi*) of the Nine Heavens (*jiutian*). Containing the hidden names of the body's spirits, these stanzas might be recited by the living to reverse the dissolution of the body's spirits and thereby achieve salvation.

The text describes the pneumas of the Nine Heavens as deriving from the three primal pneumas that emanate from the Dao at the beginning of each new *kalpa*-cycle. In the *kalpa*-cycles of the distant past, the three crystallized to govern in the form of the lords Tianbao 天寶 (Celestial Treasure), Lingbao 靈寶 (Numinous Treasure), and Shenbao 神寶 (Divine Treasure), the revered spirits of the Great Cavern (Dadong 大洞), Cavern of Mystery (Dongxuan 洞玄), and Cavern of Spirit (Dongshen 洞神), respectively (see *SANDONG). During their impossibly long tenures, each of these deities (in fact but different names of a single spirit) promulgated "writings" (*shu* 書), primeval forms of the Lingbao scriptures. The text also includes stanzas for each of these three original heavens and a concluding pair of encomia composed by the Perfected of the Great Ultimate, Xu Laile 徐來勒.

In that this early account of the Three Caverns, which appears to be an elaboration of an account first found in the *Sanhuang wen (at least as recorded in the *Wushang biyao; Lagerwey 1981b, 104), seems to directly prefigure *Lu Xiujing's tripartite division of Taoist texts, this aspect of the scripture has attracted the most scholarly attention. In addition to its possible connections with the *Sanhuang wen*, this scripture also represents a reworking of the early Celestial Master concept of the Three Pneumas (*sanqi* 三氣), *Shangqing ideas concerning cosmology and the form of the human body, and Buddhist doctrine regarding *kalpa*-cycles and the Buddhas of successive ages. While Buddhist-sounding names are here given to each of the Nine Heavens, descriptions of Nine Heavens, sometimes with esoteric names, are found in such early works as the *Huainan zi*.

The practice proposed in this text is arduous, but simple. Adepts are to recite the text in their chambers nine times a day over a period of 1,000 days, during which they observe the laws of ritual purity and do not involve themselves with mundane affairs. Those who complete this practice are promised the hope of joining the 1,112,000 "seed-people" (*zhongmin) who will avoid the coming disasters of the *jiashen* 甲申 year (the twenty-first of the sexagesimal cycle; see table 10) and fill the depleted ranks of celestial officials. As part of rituals for the dead, this scripture remained current in later Taoist practice, as attested in Hong Mai's 洪邁 (1123–1202) *Yijian zhi* 夷堅志 (Heard and Written by Yijian). Commentaries found in the Taoist Canon include those of Wang Xichao 土希巢 (fl. 1205; CT 397), *Dong Sijing (fl. 1246–60; CT 396), and Zhang Shouqing 張守清 (fl. 1332; CT 398).

Stephen R. BOKENKAMP

📖 Bokenkamp 1983, 480; Boltz J. M. 1987a, 211–14; Fukui Kōjun 1958, 187–204; Kobayashi Masayoshi 1990, 217–40; Ōfuchi Ninji 1978–79, 1: 19 (crit. notes on the Dunhuang ms.) and 2: 8–9 (reprod. of the Dunhuang ms.); Robinet 1984, 1: 131 and 2: 173–74; Zürcher 1980, 125–26

※ Lingbao

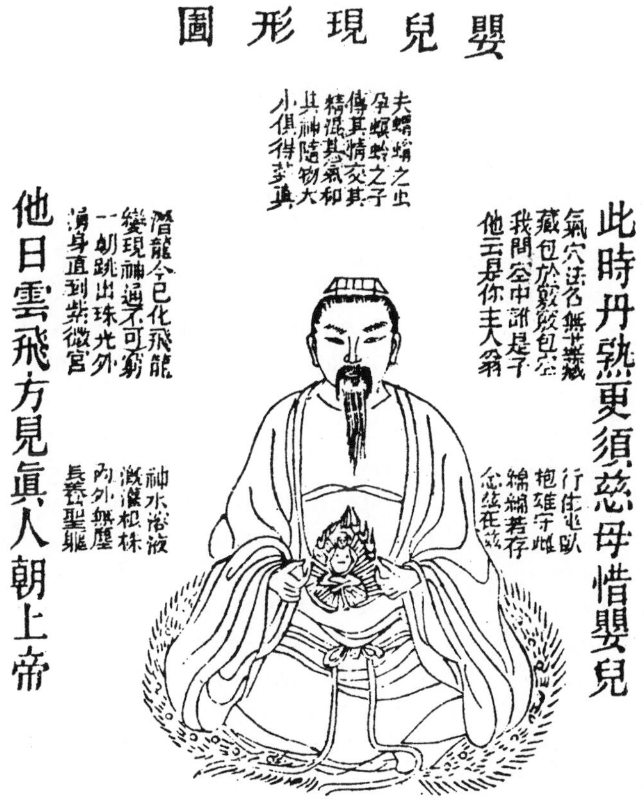

嬰兒現形圖

他日雲飛方見真人朝上帝

潛龍令已化飛龍
變現神過不可窮
一朝跳出珠光外
潚身直到紫微宮

神水瓊液
激濯根株
內外無塵
長養聖軀

夫蜾蠃之正
孕螟蛉之子
傳其情交其氣
精混其物
其神隨物大和
小俱得象物真

此時丹熟更須慈母惜嬰兒

氣穴法名無苓藏
藏包於毅發包盈
我閒公中部是子
他云身你圭人翁

行住坐卧
抱雄守雌
綿綿若存
念茲在茲

Fig. 66. Generation of the inner Infant (*ying'er* 嬰兒). **Xingming guizhi* 性命圭旨 (Principles of Balanced Cultivation of Inner Nature and Vital Force).

shengtai

聖胎

Embryo of Sainthood; Sacred Embryo

In **neidan*, the term *shengtai* denotes the achievement of the elixir of immortality. Among its synonyms are Mysterious Pearl (*xuanzhu* 玄珠), Spiritual Pearl (*shenzhu* 神珠), Infant (*ying'er* 嬰兒), and Embryo of the Dao (*daotai* 道胎). This embryo represents a new life, true and eternal in its quality, generated by the inner alchemical practice. The **Zhouyi cantong qi* (Token for the Agreement of the Three According to the *Book of Changes*) and many later texts compare its formation to the growth of a fetus inside the mother's womb;

the birth of the spiritual embryo is usually connected with its transcendence of the mortal body.

In the practices aimed at transforming the body's energies, the formation of the embryo is closely related to the purification and merging of essence, energy, and spirit (*jing, qi, shen). Beyond this, texts of different dates define the embryo and explain its formation in various ways. The embryo as the perfected elixir can denote the real energy (zhenqi 真氣) or original energy (*yuanqi) which, according to *Zhong-Lü sources, achieves fullness after three hundred days of transformation. The *Wuzhen pian (Folios on Awakening to Perfection) defines the embryo as the energy of the One. In this text, the embryo also represents the female within the male, i.e., the Yin of the human being that is enclosed and transformed by the Yang.

Comparing the development of the embryo to the revelation of Buddhahood is typical of neidan texts of the Ming period. For instance, the *Xingming guizhi (Principles of Balanced Cultivation of Inner Nature and Vital Force) uses Body of the Law (fashen 法身, dharmakāya) as a synonym for shengtai. The birth of the embryo represents the appearance of the original spirit (yuanshen 元神) or Buddhahood and is understood as enlightenment. The process leading to the birth of the embryo consists of the purification of inner nature and vital force (*xing and ming). Thus the true inner nature and vital force come into being, which in turn is equated to the return to emptiness. The embryo also indicates the unity of body (shen 身), heart (*xin), and intention (*yi) in a state of quiescence without motion.

Finally, the embryo is related to the practice of "embryonic breathing" or "breathing of the embryo" (*taixi), which denotes breathing like a child in the womb. References to this technique date from the fourth century onward. Various methods of embryonic breathing have been developed but all of them share the fundamental idea that breath nourishes the body by circulating through its vital centers.

Martina DARGA

📖 Baldrian-Hussein 1984, 233–34; Darga 1999, 141, 159, 184; Despeux 1979, 68–71; Despeux 1994, 75; Engelhardt 1987, 109–10; Homann 1976, 9; Katō Chie 2000; Katō Chie 2002; Robinet 1995a, 217 and 236

※ jindan; neidan

shenren

神人

divine man; spirit man

Midway between man and deity, the *shenren* transcends human existence. The clearest picture of him is found in the first chapter of the *Zhuangzi.

> There is a divine man living in the distant Gushe 姑射 mountains. His skin and flesh are like ice and snow and his body is as supple as a girl's. He does not eat the five grains, but sucks the wind and drinks the dew. He rides the pneuma of the clouds and has the dragon as his steed, roaming beyond the Four Seas (*sihai* 四海, i.e., the bounds of the universe). With his spirit coagulated (*ning* 凝, i.e., concentrated and unmoving), he protects all things from injury and every year he causes the five grains to ripen. (See also trans. Watson 1968, 33)

The *Zhuangzi* adds that the *shenren* does not drown if a flood comes, nor is he burned by heat that melts metal and stone, and that even the dust and grime of his body could produce saintly rulers such as Yao 堯 and Shun 舜 (Watson 1968, 34).

Elsewhere the *Zhuangzi* mentions the *shenren*, though in less detail: "The accomplished man (*zhiren* 至人) is selfless; the divine man takes no credit for his deeds; the saint (*shengren) is nameless" (chapter 1; see Watson 1968, 32). "The celestial man (*tianren* 天人) does not depart from the source (*zong* 宗); the divine man does not depart from the essence (*jing); the accomplished man does not depart from reality (*zhen* 真). The saint makes Heaven his source, virtue (*de) his root, and the Dao his gate, and he is able to see through change" (chapter 33; see Watson 1968, 362).

The concept of *shenren* in Taoism is mediated by the views of the *Zhuangzi*. The term is often used in the sense of "divine immortal" (*shenxian* 神仙) and also constitutes a category within the hierarchy of celestial beings. While in the *Zhuangzi* terms like "divine man," "accomplished man," "saint," and "real man" (*zhenren) may not imply ranking, in the *Taiping jing (Scripture of Great Peace; j. 71), for instance, the Real Man rules on earth and the Divine Man in heaven, and there is a clear hierarchy with the *shenren* ranked first, the *zhenren* second, and the *xianren (immortal) third. The *Taiping jing* (j. 40) also describes the ascent from *xianren* through *zhenren* to *shenren*. In the *Dingguan jing* (Scripture on Concentration and Observation; Kohn 1987a, 141), those who have attained the Way are ranked in seven stages. After one obtains concentration, health, and longevity, the spiritual states of *xianren*, *zhenren*, and *shengren* appear as the fourth to the sixth stages, with the *Zhuangzi*'s "accomplished man" (*zhiren*) graded as the highest ranking.

MIURA Kunio

📖 Robinet 1993, 42–48; Yamada Toshiaki 1983b, 338–40

※ *shengren*; *xianren*; *zhenren*; TRANSCENDENCE AND IMMORTALITY

Shenxian kexue lun

神仙可學論

An Essay on How One May Become a Divine Immortal Through Training

This essay is now to be found only in the literary anthology of its author, *Wu Yun (?–778), the *Zongxuan xiansheng wenji* 宗玄先生文集 (Collected Works of the Elder Who Takes Mystery as His Ancestor; CT 1051, 2.9b–16a), and in YJQQ 93, or in later compilations drawing on these sources. Until the Southern Song dynasty, however, it circulated independently, to judge by its appearance in bibliographies of that period. Although some of Wu's other short pieces are also listed independently, the *Shenxian kexue lun* stands out for its clear invitation to a form of Taoism trenchantly distinguished from rival systems yet acceptable to cultured persons like Wu Yun himself. The essay explicitly challenges *Xi Kang's (223–62) notion that immortals are always differently constituted from us, and outlines seven steps that take us further away from the goal of immortality, plus seven steps whereby we may approach it. The former cover wrong conceptions of religion, tacitly including not only Buddhism and Confucianism but also some pharmacological and alchemical approaches to Taoism as well. The positive steps embody mental self-cultivation of a type that is reconcilable, for example, with official duties. In the final part of the essay it is conceded that some familiarity with the technical literature of Taoism and its physiological exercises will be required, but Wu Yun does not go into details: the essay is a call to a way of life, not a complete description.

T. H. BARRETT

📖 Qing Xitai 1988–95, 2: 249–53

※ Wu Yun

Shenxian zhuan

神仙傳

Biographies of Divine Immortals

The *Shenxian zhuan* is generally regarded as the second collection of immortals' biographies to have survived after the *Liexian zhuan (Biographies of Exemplary Immortals), although it is much longer and the biographies it contains are more detailed in terms of the stages in the immortals' life and transcendence. Its biographies also present more rounded narratives of their subjects' lives. There is no complete version of it in the Taoist Canon. Early references to the *Shenxian zhuan* generally refer to it being divided into ten chapters, a structure followed by surviving editions—which all postdate the destruction of the Song Canon. Liang Su 梁蕭 (753–93; IC 562–63), a Buddhist scholar of the Tang, reports in his *Shenxian zhuan lun* 神仙傳論 (On the *Shenxian zhuan*; *Quan Tang wen*, Zhonghua shuju repr. of the 1814 edition, 519.10a–11a) that the *Shenxian zhuan* had 190 biographies but modern versions have only ninety or so.

The *Shenxian zhuan* is traditionally ascribed to *Ge Hong (283–343). Ge himself claims credit for compiling a text by this name in his autobiographical essay which has become attached to the *Baopu zi (trans. Ware 1966, 17), as well as in a preface to the *Shenxian zhuan*, although the attribution of this preface to Ge is dubious. However, both Pei Songzhi 裴松之 in his commentary to the *Sanguo zhi* (History of the Three Kingdoms, completed before 429) and biographies of *Tao Hongjing (456–536) also note Ge as responsible for *Shenxian zhuan*. Thus, within one hundred years after Ge's death there is credible external evidence linking his name to the *Shenxian zhuan*.

From the point of view of the modern student of Taoism, the difficulty that remains is that there is no sound method of reconstructing the original *Shenxian zhuan*. All we can do is to determine, at any particular date, which biographies had been in circulation by that time. For instance, in the early to mid-Tang (736 to be precise) some sixty-nine biographies had been cited. Interestingly, of these sixty-nine, there are already some that no longer appear in modern versions such as those of Gaoqiu gong 高丘公 and Kangfeng zi 康風子 and there are some famous biographies such as those of Mozi 墨子 and Wei Boyang 魏伯陽 that do not appear. Thus, we should bear in mind that the modern versions of the text leave out some of the biographies of the original and quite possibly also contain whole biographies that may date from as late as the Song.

On the other hand, when we compare the texts that have come down to us with early quotations from them, they appear to be remarkably well-preserved. There is some evidence of miscopying or minor textual emendation, and in a few cases parts of biographies have disappeared, but by and large the texts themselves appear to have been granted editorial respect.

The *Shenxian zhuan* has many of the first biographies of important figures found in the Taoist tradition: *Zhang Daoling, the founder of the Celestial Masters (*Tianshi dao), receives his first biography here as do *Ge Xuan and *Maojun, pivotal in the *Lingbao and *Shangqing schools, respectively. Laozi and *Pengzu, who are both in *Liexian zhuan*, also receive biographies in the *Shenxian zhuan* but of much greater length than in the earlier collection. Wei Boyang, the foundational figure in the alchemical tradition is recorded (although as noted above his biography may be a late insertion). Hugong 壺公, the classic "gourd immortal," receives a biography as does Liu An 劉安, the author of the *Huainan zi*—the latter is important as a statement from within the Taoist tradition that counterbalances the Confucian propaganda of his *Shiji* (Records of the Historian) biography. Within each biography the concentration is on the main subject with little or no attention to his or her forebears or followers. This may be simply a characteristic of the biographical genre represented here or, equally, it may be that the particular sectarian importance of these figures was a creation of later times.

The biographies provide a wealth of information about how immortality was viewed in early medieval China, detailing important features of how immortals, and those who sought immortality, lived, their extraordinary abilities, their relationship to other people and society at large, including government at all levels, the way they interacted with other spiritual beings, the drugs they concocted, and how they transformed their environments and themselves.

There exists no complete edition of the *Shenxian zhuan* in the Taoist Canon. Most scholars refer to the *Longwei bishu* 龍威祕書 edition (1794, reconstructed almost entirely from *Taiping guangji* 太平廣記 texts) or to the Ming version included in the *Siku quanshu* 四庫全書 (1782). Neither of these is entirely satisfactory.

Benjamin PENNY

📖 Bumbacher 2000b; Campany 2002 (trans.); Durrant 1986; Fukui Kōjun 1951; Fukui Kōjun 1983 (trans.); Güntsch 1988 (trans.); Kominami Ichirō 1974; Kominami Ichirō 1978; Penny 1996b; Sawada Mizuho 1988

※ Ge Hong; HAGIOGRAPHY

Shenxiao

神霄

Divine Empyrean

The term Shenxiao refers to both an exalted celestial region and a religious movement named after that region which arose during the Song dynasty (960–1279) and proceeded to make a major impact on the development of Taoist beliefs and practices. The factors underlying the appearance and growth of this movement have yet to be fully determined, but appear to have involved patronage by the part of the Northern Song emperor Huizong (r. 1100–1125), as well as the ability of Shenxiao leaders like *Lin Lingsu (1076–1120). to combine their new revelations with elements of popular religion as well as *Shangqing and *Lingbao Taoism. For example, the opening mythic sequence of the Shenxiao scripture *Gaoshang Shenxiao zongshi shoujing shi* (An Exemplar on the Scriptures Received by the Lineal Master of the Most Exalted Divine Empyrean) appears to have been inspired by these two venerable Taoist traditions. Another important factor was the impact of Tantric Buddhism, which spread throughout much of China during the Tang-Song era (Xiao Dengfu 1993; Mitamura Keiko 1998; Strickmann 1996). Although most histories of Taoism emphasize the Shenxiao movement's presence at the court of Emperor Huizong, its most lasting impact on Chinese culture may be found in the rites that Taoist priests (*daoshi*) and ritual masters (*fashi*) have performed in southern China and Taiwan for at least the past eight centuries and up to the present day.

History. The origins of the Shenxiao movement are unclear, but its development reflects the ongoing interaction between the state, organized Taoism, and religious traditions indigenous to south China, including both Han and non-Han rites distinguished by the worship of popular local deities and the performance of so-called Thunder Rites (*leifa*). The Shenxiao movement made a sudden and dramatic appearance in the historical record beginning in 1116 with the presentation of Lin Lingsu at the court of Emperor Huizong. Lin, a native of Wenzhou 溫州 (Zhejiang), gained great influence at court by convincing the emperor that he (Huizong) was the terrestrial incarnation of a major Shenxiao deity, the Great Emperor of Long Life (*Changsheng dadi). Lin and his allies at court also made a significant contribution to the publication of the Song-dynasty edition of the Taoist Canon (*Zhenghe Wanshou daozang*), including the scripture which heads the Ming-dynasty edition of the Canon still extant today, the *Lingbao wuliang duren shangpin miaojing* 靈寶無量度人

上品妙經 (Wondrous Scripture of the Upper Chapters of the Numinous Treasure on Limitless Salvation; CT 1). This text, at sixty-one *juan* one of the longest works in the Canon, represents a ritual reworking of the Lingbao movement's *Duren jing (Scripture on Salvation), which Michel Strickmann has convincingly shown was intended to assert the scriptural supremacy of the Shenxiao movement while also propagating a message of salvation for the Song dynasty and paeans of praise for its rulers (Strickmann 1978b, 339, 350–51). Huizong's devotion to the Shenxiao movement prompted him to issue an imperial decree stating that all Taoist (and many Buddhist) temples and monasteries be placed under the control of Shenxiao practitioners, although the extent to which this was enforced remains unclear (Qing Xitai 1988–95, 2: 605–11; Ren Jiyu 1990, 472–82; Sun Kekuan 1965, 93–122).

Rituals and cults. Although Lin Lingsu's influence at court proved to be short-lived (by 1119 he had disappeared under mysterious circumstances), other Shenxiao masters such as Lin's disciple *Wang Wenqing (1093–1153) and later leaders such as *Mo Qiyan (1226–94) actively spread its teachings, enabling it to become one of the most influential ritual movements of the Southern Song dynasty. These and other individuals gained particular renown for the exorcistic rituals they practiced, especially Thunder Rites. Such rituals also shaped the careers of non-Shenxiao practitioners, including the famed Southern Taoist *Bai Yuchan (1194–1229?), who is said to have authored a number of Thunder Rites manuals in the *Daofa huiyuan, and referred to himself as a "Vagrant Official of the Divine Empyrean" (Shenxiao sanli 神霄散吏; Berling 1993). The popularity of Thunder Rites was not restricted to ritual specialists, for, as Judith M. Boltz has convincingly shown, Southern Song local officials struggling to counter the influence of local cults they considered "heterodox" (*xie* 邪) or "illicit/licentious" (*yin* 淫; see *yinsi*) did not hesitate to call on Shenxiao masters, or even study under them as disciples (see the entries *TAOISM AND LOCAL COMMUNITIES; *TAOISM AND LOCAL CULTS).

Apart from Thunder Rites, the Shenxiao movement shaped the development of Taoism and local cults in other ways as well. Many Shenxiao masters incorporated popular local deities into their ritual traditions, and also helped found or restore temples to these spirits. One example is the plague-quelling deity *Wen Qiong, also known as Marshal Wen (Wen Yuanshuai 溫元帥), whose earliest known hagiography was composed by the Shenxiao Taoist master Huang Gongjin 黃公瑾 (fl. 1274). Shenxiao masters appear to have played key roles in the construction of some of Wen's oldest temples (Katz P. R. 1995a), and helped popularize his cult through rituals featuring the expulsion of plague boats (often referred to as Plague Offerings or *wenjiao), including one text preserved in *j.* 220 of the *Daofa huiyuan* entitled *Shenxiao qianwen song-chuan yi* 神霄遣瘟送船儀 (Divine Empyrean Liturgy for Expelling Epidemics and Sending off the Boats). Wen's cult eventually spread throughout much of south China, and became highly popular in Fujian and Taiwan, where he is worshipped as a Royal Lord (*wangye*) known as Lord Chi (Chi Wangye 池王爺). (For more details see the entries *Wen Qiong, *wangye, and *wenjiao.)

Shenxiao in the history of Taoism. The Shenxiao movement was eventually absorbed into Celestial Master Taoism (*Tianshi dao), most likely after Khubilai khan granted the Celestial Masters control over all "Taoist" movements in south China in 1273 prior to his final conquest of the region. However, the Shenxiao movement's influence on Taoism and popular religion persists to the present day. Cults to deities such as Marshal Wen continue to exist and even thrive in south China and Taiwan, and ethnographers have documented the ongoing popularity in these regions of boat expulsion rituals currently performed by local ritual masters or Celestial Master Taoist priests yet clearly linked to the Shenxiao rites mentioned above (for bibliographic references see the entry *wenjiao). The publication of collections of liturgical texts in works such as the *Zangwai daoshu* (Taoist Texts Outside the Canon), as well as the field reports of scholars who continue to study Taoism today (especially the 80-volume *Minsu quyi congshu* 民俗曲藝叢書) promise to shed even further light on the significance of the Shenxiao movement in Chinese religions.

Should the Shenxiao movement as it existed during the Song dynasty be considered "Taoist" or as a part of a "Taoist renaissance" occurring during the Song dynasty? In attempting to answer this question, it might be useful to recall that the Shenxiao movement was not originally a part of institutionalized Taoism but represented one of many local ritual traditions (including *Qingwei, *Tianxin zhengfa, *Tongchu, etc.) which interacted with established Taoist movements during the Song and Yuan dynasties. Song-dynasty Shenxiao masters do not appear to have been ordained as Taoist priests, nor did they worship the First Celestial Master *Zhang Daoling as their movement's patriarch. Moreover, many of the rites performed by Shenxiao ritual masters utilized possession techniques adopted from the practices of local mediums (Boltz J. M. 1993a; Katz P. R. 1995a, 32). It is true that leading Shenxiao masters like Lin Lingsu were not simply religious innovators but also drew on established Taoist traditions, but this appears to have been an attempt to establish the movement's prestige and legitimacy in the eyes of the state and perhaps other religious movements as well. Therefore, one may prefer to treat the Shenxiao movement as a local ritual tradition that should only be considered to be Taoist after its absorption into Celestial Master Taoism at the end of the thirteenth century.

Paul R. KATZ

📖 Berling 1993; Boltz J. M. 1987a, 26–33; Boltz J. M. 1993a; Chen Bing 1986;

Katz P. R. 1995a, 32–38; Kang Bao 1997; Lagerwey 1987c, 253–64; Matsumoto Kōichi 1982; Qing Xitai 1988–95, 2: 594–670 passim; Ren Jiyu 1990, 472–82 and 560–65; Skar 1996–97; Skar 2000, passim; Strickmann 1975; Strickmann 1978b; Sun Kekuan 1965, 93–122; Xiao Dengfu 1993

※ For related entries see the Synoptic Table of Contents, sec. III.7 ("Song, Jin, and Yuan: Shenxiao")

Sheyang zhenzhong fang

攝養枕中方

Pillow Book of Methods for Preserving and Nourishing Life

The *Sheyang zhenzhong fang*, commonly attributed to the eminent physician *Sun Simiao (fl. 673), is an important text on *yangsheng (Nourishing Life), stressing moral cultivation and mental discipline as fundamental to the quest for longevity and eventually immortality. Except for the last section, consisting of the *Cunshen lianqi ming (Inscription on the Visualization of Spirit and Refinement of Pneuma) which either was incorporated into the text by the compilers of the *Yunji qiqian (j. 33) or originally existed as an appendix, the *Sheyang zhenzhong fang* concentrates on five main subjects: prudence and attention, prohibitions (*jinji), gymnastics (*daoyin), circulating breath (*xingqi), and guarding the One (*shouyi).

The text has come down to us in fragments and with numerous interpolations and distortions. However, comparing the *Sheyang zhenzhong fang* with the anonymous *Zhenzhong ji* 枕中記 (Notes Kept Inside the Pillow; CT 837), and taking other Tang sources and bibliographic records into account, it seems clear that Sun Simiao did write a work called *Zhenzhong ji* or *Zhenzhong fang*, fragments of which are included in the *Sheyang zhenzhong fang* as well as in the present *Zhenzhong ji*.

The five sections of the text are as follows:

1. "Prudence and Attention" ("Zishen" 自慎), explaining that prudence is important for those who nourish their inner nature and that "the basis of prudence is awe."

2. "Proscriptions and Prohibitions" ("Jinji" 禁忌), including taboos on certain days of the months, dietary prohibitions, advice for daily life, and a clear rejection of sexual practices (*fangzhong shu).

3. "Daoyin" ("Daoyin" 導引), mainly concerned with techniques of self-massage, but also describing how to practice a *daoyin* exercise for the neck and head.

4. "Circulating Breath" ("Xingqi" 行氣), emphasizing embryonic breathing (*taixi*) as the most significant practice: "In the practice of embryonic breathing, neither the nose nor the mouth are used. Instead, one breathes in the manner of an embryo inside the womb: when you have achieved this you have truly attained the Dao" (YJQQ 33.9b).

5. "Guarding the One" ("Shouyi" 守一), describing methods of visualization in the three Cinnabar Fields (*dantian*) of the head, chest, and abdomen.

Ute ENGELHARDT

📖 Engelhardt 1989, 277–90

※ Sun Simiao; *yangsheng*; MEDITATION AND VISUALIZATION

Shi Jianwu

施肩吾

fl. 820–35; *zi*: Xisheng 希聖; *hao*: Dongzhai 東齋 (Eastern Retreat),
Huayang zhenren 華陽真人 (Perfected of Flourishing Yang)

This noteworthy Tang poet and long-time resident of the Western Hills (*Xishan, Jiangxi) was known as an heir to the teachings of the immortal *Xu Xun, whose cult center was located there. Born to an official family in the Fenshui 分水 district of Muzhou 睦州 (Zhejiang), Shi also had a keen interest in the divine transcendents and ways to attain immortality. Around a decade after becoming a Presented Scholar (*jinshi*) in 820, Shi went into retreat in the Western Hills, where he first met Xu Xun, who passed on "five works of instructions on the Inner Elixir (*neidan*) and divine prescriptions on the Outer Elixir (*waidan*)." After receiving additional teachings in the "Great Way of inner refinement with the Reverted Elixir of the Golden Liquor (*jinye huandan* 金液還丹)" from *Lü Dongbin—who reputedly received them from *Zhongli Quan—in the Western Hills, Shi remained in retreat there, devoting himself to poetry and contemplation, and earning the name of the Perfected of Flourishing Yang (Huayang zhenren).

Five texts found in the Ming Taoist Canon are tied to Shi Jianwu's name:

1. *Xishan qunxian huizhen ji* (Records of the Gathered Immortals and Assembled Perfected of the Western Hills; CT 246), supposedly compiled by Shi.

2. *Taibai jing* 太白經 (Book of the Great White; CT 934), an older text (whose title refers to Original Pneuma, *yuanqi*), to which Shi added a summarizing verse.

3. *Yangsheng bianyi jue* 養生辯疑訣 (Instructions on Resolving Doubts in Nourishing Life; CT 853), a short work drafted by Shi.

4. *Yinfu jing jijie* 陰符經集解 (Collected Explications of the *Yinfu jing*; CT III), to which Shi added his annotations.

5. *Zhong-Lü chuandao ji (Anthology of Zhongli Quan's Transmission of the Dao to Lü Dongbin; CT 1017, j. 39–41, and CT 263, j. 14–16), transmitted by Shi.

Few of the above works, however, show clear evidence of having been actually written by Shi Jianwu. Parts of the *Daoshu (Pivot of the Dao) also bear his name. Further study of these materials, together with the more than 200 poems included in literary works of the Tang dynasty, will provide a fuller portrait of this important late Tang figure.

Shi's hagiography and associated writings helped establish deeper southern roots for the new *neidan* traditions that became popular among literati from the tenth century on. Intimate ties to both a venerable southern religious center and elements of the new contemplative alchemy now classed as the *Zhong-Lü tradition made Shi's teachings important to later figures in the *neidan* traditions, such as *Bai Yuchan (1194–1229?) and those in his circle. Although legends praise Shi for his learning, calligraphy, and expertise in laboratory alchemy, he is best known today for his mastery of the cluster of practices and traditions meant to produce the inner elixir and his ties to Zhongli Quan and Lü Dongbin.

Lowell SKAR

📖 Boltz J. M. 1987a, 139–40; Qing Xitai 1994, 1: 301–3

※ *Xishan qunxian huizhen ji*; *Zhong-Lü chuandao ji*; *neidan*; Zhong-Lü

Shi Tai

石泰

?–1158; *zi*: Dezhi 得之; *hao*: Xinglin 杏林 (Forest of Apricots),
Cuixuan zi 翠玄子 (Master of Emerald Mystery)

Shi Tai (Shi Xinglin), a native of Changzhou 常州 (Shaanxi), is the second patriarch of the Southern Lineage (*Nanzong) of *neidan*. His dates are difficult to ascertain; Chinese scholars often suggest the years 1022 to 1158 based on the assumption that Shi lived 136 years, as stated in his biography in the *Lishi zhenxian tidao tongjian (49.12b–13b).

The account given in that biography mostly derives from the tale of *Xue Daoguang's encounter with Shi Tai as told in the "Xue Zixian shiji" 薛紫賢 事蹟 (Traces of Xue Zixian; in *Wuzhen zhizhi xiangshuo sansheng biyao* 悟真直 指詳說三乘祕要, CT 143, 16b–24b). Here Shi Tai relates how he met *Zhang Boduan in Shaanxi. Zhang had been falsely accused of having committed an error in his secretarial duties, and was being taken away in shackles. Shi Tai was acquainted with the local prefect and managed to have Zhang released. Zhang then explained that he had disregarded his master's warning by trans- mitting his teaching thrice to someone unfit to receive it, and had been struck by adversities each time. His master, however, had also said that he should reveal the doctrine to anyone who helped him in time of need. Thus Shi Tai received teachings from Zhang Boduan as a token of gratitude. He practiced those teachings and attained the Dao, after which he wrote the *Huanyuan pian* 還源篇 (Folios on Reverting to the Source; CT 1091). This tale, based on a passage of Zhang's postface to the *Wuzhen pian*, clearly was intended to legitimize the lineage of the Nanzong teachings.

Similar in format to the *Wuzhen pian*, the *Huanyuan pian* contains eighty-one pentasyllabic poems on *neidan*, written one year after Shi Tai's alleged encounter with Zhang Boduan. Both the preface and the poems are duplicated in *j.* 2 of the *Xiuzhen shishu*. The *Xiuzhen shishu* (7.9b–10b) also includes a postface writ- ten by Shi Tai to a poem by Xue Daoguang. While Zhang Boduan advocates the practice of Taoist techniques followed by Chan meditation, Shi Tai only mentions the Golden Elixir (*jindan*), and in doing so criticizes the *Zhong-Lü teachings as being merely composed of "mercury and lead" (*Huanyuan pian*, 8b–9a). He also diverges from the idea of the unity of the Three Teachings by discounting both Confucianism and Buddhism, although his acceptance of Chan Buddhism emerges in his description of sudden enlightenment (*dunfa* 頓法 or "subitist methods").

Farzeen BALDRIAN-HUSSEIN

📖 Boltz J. M. 1987a, 175; Chen Bing 1985, 36

※ *neidan*; Nanzong

shijie

尸 解

"release by means of a corpse"; mortuary liberation

Taoist explanations of death were diverse and conflicting. Overall, Taoism seems to have held that death cannot be avoided, and yet death can be transcended. There was no clear or comprehensive explanation of such matters. Yet, beginning with the *Liexian zhuan* (Biographies of Exemplary Immortals) of Han times, accounts of superlative Taoists often tell the reader, directly or indirectly, that the person involved did not really die. Some great figures simply ascended to heaven, in plain view, like the Yellow Emperor (*Huangdi; Kohn 1993b, 351–52). Others ascended under less clear circumstances, and such figures were commonly said to have undergone *shijie*, "release from the corpse" or "mortuary liberation."

Shijie was thus a form of "ascension" or "transformation" (Kohn 1993b, 303–4). Since many traditions suggest that bodily death need not entail death of the spirit, especially for the most saintly, it would not surprise us to read of Taoists who ascended to heaven and left behind a body. But accounts of *shijie* are notable for *denying* that the person had left behind a real corpse. The *Shiji* (Records of the Historian; 28.1368–69) mentions people who "shed their mortal forms and melted away" (*xingjie xiaohua* 形解銷化). The meaning of that phrase is unclear. But ancient and medieval accounts of extraordinary Taoistic characters often depict a death that was not a real death. One example is the Tang thaumaturge *Ye Fashan. Accounts of his non-death (e.g., *Tang Ye zhenren zhuan* 唐葉真人傳; CT 779) report that at the age of 106, Ye "secretly ingested a divine elixir. . . . At the hour of noon, [Ye] transformed his corpse into a sword. A nebulous chariot called at his door. . . . All the people of the city saw a column of azure smoke rising . . . directly up to touch the heavens. . . . A year after the funeral, the inner and outer coffins opened by themselves. But when the clothing, cap, sword and shoes were seen, it was only then realized that [Ye] had not died, but had really only 'arisen lightly.'" Such accounts are deliberately unclear about what, precisely, had occurred, and the various elements cannot be intelligibly reconciled. In *Huang Lingwei's coffin, only a shroud and a screed appeared; in *Sima Chengzhen's, a staff and pair of shoes.

Such phenomena indicated that the subject had ascended to heaven at the time of apparent death, and that the body had either been transformed into the objects in question, or had somehow been translated away. In all such cases, there was a set of events that corresponded outwardly to a conventional human death and burial, but the details revealed that the subject had not died a *real* death at all. The concept of *shijie* was thus a product of the religious imagination, designed to suggest a method of transcending mortality that could not otherwise be conveyed. Hence, translating the term is very difficult. The term *shi* denotes "corpse," so the term *shijie* is commonly translated "liberation by means of a corpse." But in actuality, most accounts of *shijie* make clear that the subject did not *actually* die, and though all the appearances of death were involved, no corpse was really left behind.

Russell KIRKLAND

📖　Campany 1996, 251 and 298–99; Campany 2002, 52–60; Lagerwey 1981b, 185–87; Pregadio 2004, 117–27; Robinet 1979b; Robinet 1993, 167–69; Robinet 1997b, 100–103; Strickmann 1979, 130–31; Yoshikawa Tadao 1992b

※　DEATH AND AFTERLIFE; TRANSCENDENCE AND IMMORTALITY

Shiyao erya

石藥爾雅

Synonymic Dictionary of Mineral Materia Medica

The *Shiyao erya* (CT 901), compiled by Mei Biao 梅彪 in 806, is the only extant *waidan lexicon. The preface says that the work aims not only to make the understanding of alchemy easier, but also to supplement the *Erya* 爾雅 (Literary Lexicon), a classical dictionary probably dating from the third century BCE that does not contain entries on minerals. Consequently, some Chinese bibliographers of the Qing dynasty classified the text among the Confucian classics.

The work consists of two chapters. The first, which includes the lexicon proper, lists 526 synonyms under 164 headings (or 167, also counting sub-entries). The second contains three lists of names and synonyms of elixirs, a list of alchemical methods, and a bibliography of about one hundred works. Mei Biao does not mention his sources, but many secret names of elixirs are the same as those listed in the *Taiqing shibi ji (2.9a–b and 2.9b–10a). In a valuable study, Chen Guofu (1983, 383–442) has collected references to other possible sources, along with supplementary secret terms of substances, names of elixirs and methods, and titles of lost and extant *waidan* texts.

The lexicon provides a noteworthy overview of the alchemical language, showing that its secret nomenclature largely draws on allusions to the Yin and Yang value of the substances, their relation to the *wuxing, their physical features, and their alchemical or chemical properties.

Fabrizio PREGADIO

📖   Chen Guofu 1983, 383–442; Needham 1976; Pregadio 1986; Wong Shiu Hon 1989

※ waidan

Shizhou ji

十洲記

Record of the Ten Continents

The Shizhou ji, a text of the Six Dynasties, describes a set of terrestrial paradises in the immense seas that surround the known world. Its putative author, *Dongfang Shuo, appears in the introduction and conclusion describing these paradises to Han Wudi (r. 141–87 BCE), after that ruler concludes his famous meeting with the Queen Mother of the West (*Xiwang mu) as described in the *Han Wudi neizhuan (Inner Biography of Emperor Wu of the Han). Besides the Ten Continents of the title (which include Yingzhou 瀛洲, one of the three sea isles mentioned in the Shiji or Records of the Historian), he also describes four island paradises (Canghai dao 藏海島, Fangzhang 方丈, Fusang 扶桑, and *Penglai) and two mountain paradises (mounts *Kunlun and Zhong 種山). Anecdotal passages are added after three of the paradises.

For its anecdotes and descriptions of far-off lands, the Shizhou ji is often discussed as a work of zhiguai 志怪 or "records of the strange" fiction (Li Jianguo 1984, 167–71; Wang Guoliang 1984, 309–11). However, the core of the text, which describes the positions, vast dimensions, flora, and fauna of the Ten Continents, is formed from omenological literature of the Han dynasty. The rest appears to have been added around the fifth century, with the purpose of making it an integral part of the *Shangqing-based apocryphal vision of the Han Wudi neizhuan and the Han Wudi waizhuan 漢武帝外傳 (Outer Biography of Emperor Wu of the Han). The descriptions function as background to the "Charts of the Real Forms of the Ten Continents of the Divine Transcendents" (shenxian shizhou zhenxing tu 神仙十洲真形圖), which complement the more famous *Wuyue zhenxing tu (Charts of the Real Forms of the Five Peaks).

Besides the independent version in the Taoist Canon (CT 598), which is the best preserved, there are three other versions of the text: in the *Yunji qiqian (j. 26); in the Song anthology *Xu tanzhu* 續談助 (Sequel to an Aid to Conversation; twelfth century); and the version found in numerous Ming and Qing anthologies. The last few pages of the *Yunji qiqian* version are unfortunately jumbled. The version in the Ming and Qing anthologies differs only slightly from the version in the Canon, which presents the Ten Continents in the same order they are listed in the *Han Wudi neizhuan*. The *Xu tanzhu* version, though abridged, preserves what is probably the pre-*neizhuan* sequence of the ten continents, and it also preserves the description of Daizhou 帶洲, a ribbon-shaped piece of land that separates the pure, freshwater seas around Yingzhou and Fusang from ordinary seas.

Thomas E. SMITH

📖 Campany 1996, 53–54 and 318–21; Kohn 1993b, 48–55; Li Fengmao 1986, 123–85; Smith Th. E. 1990 (trans.); Smith Th. E. 1992, 196–226 and 536–62 (trans.); Wang Guoliang 1993

※ Dongfang Shuo

shoujue

手訣

"instructions (for practices) in the hand"

Shoujue is the overall term for a number of different hand gestures and techniques executed with one or both hands, used by Taoist practitioners during the performance of ritual, or as ad hoc methods of protection against evil influences. They may be divided into two main categories that, in practice, overlap considerably, namely: 1. "seals," *yin* 印, or *shouyin* 手印 (that is, mudrās); 2. "instructions concerning points in the palm of the hand," *zhangmu jue* 掌目訣, more commonly referred to simply as *juemu* 訣目, "points (ruled by) instructions."

The first category is obviously influenced by, and in some cases directly borrowed from, Tantric Buddhism, and in fact in Taoist liturgy this type of hand-gesturing is particularly important in those rituals that were originally taken over from Buddhism. Thus for instance in the classical *Zhengyi liturgy of southern Taiwan, "Tantric" mudrās are used first and foremost in the ritual of Universal Salvation (*pudu), and they include, notably, the important Heart Seal for the Transformation of Food (*bianshi xinyin* 變食心印), which takes

Fig. 67. Taoist Master He Canghai of Taichung, Taiwan, performs a mudrā during a ritual of
exorcism in Taichung (January
1978). Photograph by Julian Pas.

the form of a complicated intertwining of the fingers of both hands, whose
function is to multiply the already huge quantities of offerings displayed in
this ritual, so they will be sufficient to feed all of the "orphaned souls" (*guhun*
孤魂) invited to the feast. The second category likewise appears to be inspired
by Tantric ritual, though in this case the techniques clearly were reinterpreted
within the framework of Chinese cosmological schemata, and further developed in combination with indigenous systems of divination.

The earliest Taoist references to ritual "practices in the hand(s)" are found
in texts of the late Tang dynasty, for instance in the **Jinsuo liuzhu yin* (Guide
to the Golden Lock and the Flowing Pearls). The section with illustrations of
"practices in the palm of the hand" (*zhangjue* 掌訣, i.e., *juemu*) that originally
formed part of this work has not been preserved, though a fragment that
seems to be derived from it is included in the **Taishang zhuguo jiumin zongzhen
biyao* (8.13b–14b; by Yuan Miaozong 元妙宗, preface dated 1116), in a chapter
devoted to forms of **bugang* ("walking along the guideline"). The association

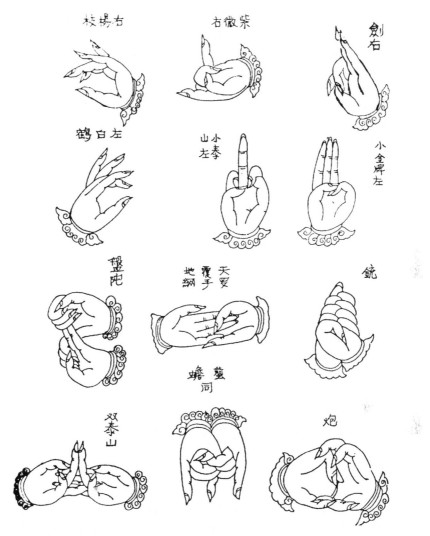

Fig. 68. Mudrās or "instructions (for practices in) the hand" (*shoujue*).
Reproduced from Li Yuanguo 1988.

of *juemu* with forms of *bugang* in these texts is far from coincidental, as one
of the most characteristic functions of this category of practices in the hand
in Taoist ritual is to execute a "walk" with the thumb in the palm of the left
hand, by lightly "tapping" or "pinching" (the term is usually *qia* 掐 or *nian* 捻)
a sequence of points in the hand. The walk in the hand is typically required to
be synchronized with a parallel walk with the feet on the ground that follows
the same patterns, which constitutes the practice of *bugang* proper, as well as
with visualizations of a flight through the corresponding sections of heaven;

thus the overall result is a unified movement on the three cosmic planes: in heaven, on earth, and in the human realm.

The practice of touching points in the hand is viewed as a way of activating (or sometimes suppressing) the divine forces in the corresponding segments of the universe, within the body, or through the body of the high priest (*gaogong* 高功; see **daozhang*). In *bugang*, as well as in the Lighting of the Incense Burner (**falu*), which is the opening rite of most major rituals in the classical liturgy, the practice contributes to the "transformation of the body" (**bianshen*) of the high priest, while in the latter case it also serves the purpose of effecting the externalization of the energies and the subordinate spirits residing within his body (**chushen*). It seems clear that from the beginning, practices in the hand were viewed as in some sense "magically" efficacious, particularly in commanding spirits and demons, and it is probably for this reason that they are sometimes referred to as "instructions for transformations" (*huajue* 化訣).

Poul ANDERSEN

📖 Andersen 1989–90b; Hu Tiancheng, He Dejun, and Duan Ming 1999; Mitamura Keiko 2002; Saso 1978a

※ *bianshen*; *bugang*

shouyi

守一

guarding the One; maintaining Oneness

The term *shouyi*, which appears in Taoist literature from an early period, indicates a form of concentrative meditation that focuses all attention upon one point or god in the body. The purpose of this practice is to attain total absorption in the object and thus perceive the oneness of being.

The first form of guarding the One is the concentration on different colored lights in the various inner organs of the body, with the goal of retaining the vital energy within them and thereby extending one's life span. This practice is mentioned in an offshoot of the **Taiping jing* (Scripture of Great Peace), the *Taiping jing shengjun bizhi* 太平經聖君祕旨 (Secret Directions of the Holy Lord on the Scripture of Great Peace; CT 1102; trans. Kohn 1993b, 193–97). The next mention is in **Ge Hong's **Baopu zi* (trans. Ware 1966, 303–4), where the practice consists of visualizing the One (**yi*) located both in the stars above and in the center of the body below. The result of the practice is not only long life, but control over all bodily functions and appearances, along with the utter freedom of immortality. *Shangqing Taoism expands the practice to include visualization (*cun) and constant maintenance of the Three Ones (*sanyi), the gods in the three Cinnabar Fields (*dantian) located in abdomen, heart, and head. Described in the *Suling jing (Scripture [of the Celestial Palace] of the Immaculate Numen; CT 1314), this form of the technique leads to long life, perfect health, and attainment of the powers of the immortals.

As Buddhist methods of meditation gain a stronger influence on the Chinese religious scene, "guarding the One" too becomes less concerned with forms of visualization and more with emotional control and techniques of mental one-pointedness. Later texts, such as the Yannian yisuan fa 延年益算 法 (Method of Extending the Number of One's Years; CT 1271), describe the practice in combination with physical stretches and massages, and point to the attainment of inner calm and serenity. Gods here play a lesser role than emotions and to attain peace within one should think of one's own death and the transitoriness of all. The same tendency is also observed in the Tang work Sandong zhongjie wen 三洞眾戒文 (All Precepts of the Three Caverns; CT 178; Benn 1991, 138–41), which emphasizes the need for moral integrity and obedience of the precepts (*jie), and then defines its goal as the attainment of mental calm that will allow spirit (*shen) and energy (*qi) to be at peace and thus confer longevity.

This shift from visualization to mental tranquillity continues in the Song dynasty, where shouyi appears as a basic exercise in the texts of inner alchemy (*neidan), whose purpose is to protect the center of life within and thus allow the transformation of bodily energies into pure spirit and the Dao. In all cases, however, the term indicates one-pointedness of mind, which focuses on a single object of meditation.

Livia KOHN

📖 Andersen 1979; Bokenkamp 1993; Kohn 1989a; Kamitsuka Yoshiko 1999, 252–63 and 348–53; Maspero 1981, 364–72; Robinet 1984, 1: 30–32 and 41–43; Robinet 1993, 120–38; Schipper 1993, 130–59; Yoshioka Yoshitoyo 1976a

※ yi [oneness]; INNER DEITIES; MEDITATION AND VISUALIZATION

shu

疏

Statement

The Statement is a document sent to the deities outlining the purpose of a particular Taoist ritual. The word *shu* means to send information in the form of an itemized statement and indicates the forwarding of a petition to the secular government. It is used also in Taoist ritual, where the task of the priest is to communicate with the deities through such documents. Written documents are sent to deities and Buddhas in Buddhism and popular cults as well, but Taoism offers the earliest examples of their use in ritual.

The first instance within Taoism of sending documents to the deities occurred in the early Way of the Celestial Masters (*Tianshi dao), in the form of sending petitions (*shangzhang* 上章) to celestial officials. From the Six Dynasties period to the Tang, various kinds of documents were used, such as the *ci* 詞 (declaration) and the *biao* 表 (memorial; see *baibiao). By the Song dynasty, the type of document sent depended on the rank of the deity. For example, the *zou* 奏 (a word that denotes a presentation submitted to an emperor) was sent to the highest-ranking deities, such as the Three Clarities (*sanqing) and the Four Sovereigns (*siyu* 四御, namely *Yuhuang, Taihuang 太皇, Tianhuang 天皇, and Tuhuang 土皇); the *shen* 申 (notification to a superior) to the Five Masters of the Numinous Treasure (Lingbao wushi 靈寶五師), the Celestial Ministry (*tiansheng* 天省), the Northern Dipper (*beidou), the Three Offices (*sanguan, of Heaven, Earth, and Water), and the deities of the Eastern Peak (Dongyue 東嶽) and of the underworld (*Fengdu); and the *die* 牒 (mandate) to the Gods of Walls and Moats (*Chenghuang) and the local gods, as well as the various celestial officials, generals, and soldiers who take part in rituals.

A model of a typical Statement appears in the *Shangqing lingbao dafa* (Great Rites of the Numinous Treasure of Highest Clarity; CT 1223, *j.* 29) by the Song-dynasty codifier Jin Yunzhong 金允中 (fl. 1224–25). It opens with a description of the Taoist priest's religious ranking and then continues, "Your humble servant (*name*), fearful and trembling, pays obeisance and makes repeated prostrations as he addresses himself to Heaven." Next the priest records in detail the names and addresses of those who are sponsoring the ritual, as well as the name of the ritual itself, its purpose, how long it will take, and the program of rites that will be performed. The priest presents the Statement with the words, "Respectfully he memorializes before the Jade Throne of such-

Fig. 69. Taoist Master Chen Rongsheng 陳榮盛 recites a Statement (*shu*) during a **jiao* celebration at the Yuhuang gong 玉皇宮 (Palace of the Jade Sovereign) in Tainan, Taiwan (October 1994). Photograph by Julian Pas.

and-such a Celestial Worthy, humbly seeking Heaven's compassion." He prays that the Statement be approved, that orders and instructions will be given to the deities concerned, and that all may proceed according to the Statement's request. This sequence forms the central part of the document. At the end, the priest states his fear that the Statement may in some way have offended the majesty of Heaven and records the date, and his rank and name.

The Statement is placed into an envelope and deposited in a rectangular box. After the rite of dispatch, it is burned. To ensure that it will be sent safely and quickly, auxiliary documents called *guan* 關 ("passport") are dispatched to deities of the Prime Marshals (*yuanshuai* 元帥) class who are in charge of dispatch and security. The Statement does not go directly to the deity to whom it is addressed, but must pass through a celestial bureau called Tianshu yuan 天樞院 (Department of the Pivot of Heaven) where it is checked for mistakes and omissions. Also, through meditation, the high priest (*gaogong* 高功; see **daozhang*) is deemed to be able to ascend to the place where the deity dwells, to present the Statement and to see the deity officially endorse it. As a result of these procedures, the agreement of the deities is obtained.

A large number of documents are used in Taoist ritual. Their preparation is time-consuming, as they must be all written out by the high priest before the performance of a ritual. Their content is based on models contained in collections called *wenjian* 文檢 ("writing models"). A basic distinction between high-ranking and ordinary Taoist priests is whether or not they are trained to prepare the necessary documents. In present-day Taiwan, a large number of sample documents are available in collections such as the *Jiaoshi da wenjian* 醮事大文檢 (Great Writing Models for the Offering Ritual), the *Gongde da wenjian* 功德大文檢 (Great Writing Models for the Ritual of Merit), and the *Shuyi zaji* 疏意雜記 (Miscellaneous Notes on the Statement).

MARUYAMA Hiroshi

📖 Ōfuchi Ninji 1983, 213–16, 404–22; Qing Xitai 1994, 3: 246–51; Schipper 1974; see also bibliography for the entry **baibiao*

※ *baibiao*

shuangxiu

雙修

joint cultivation

The term *shuangxiu* denotes the joint cultivation of **xing* and *ming* (inner nature and vital force), which is the objective of the **neidan* schools. The relevant practices differ according to the priority accorded to *xing* or *ming*. The practices focused on **shen* or spiritual activity (e.g., the contemplation of the pure mind and the understanding of its nature) belong to the domain of *xing*, while those focused on **qi* or pneuma (e.g., breath-circulation exercises and methods of controlling the psycho-physiological functions) belong to the domain of *ming*. An essential implied feature is that *xing* and *ming* refer to the eternal duality between Yin and Yang which must be realized as a "nondualistic-duality." Non-duality subsumes "the duality of twoness and non-twoness," since only thus can duality be overcome. In the alchemical process, the transcended duality is symbolized by such binary terms as Dragon and Tiger (**longhu*), Lead and Mercury, and so forth, which are summed up by the notions of *xing* and *ming* on which the adept works. Each binary term can change into Yin or Yang by exchanging its feminine or masculine attributes, in order to remove attachment both to itself and to the other. With a different outlook, the sexual schools use the term *shuangxiu* to refer to the union of Yin and Yang through intercourse.

For the alchemical schools, the Yin-Yang duality must be incorporated and overcome in one's own experience. This may be done in various ways according to the adept's individuality and qualifications. Joint cultivation may consist of gradual methods that depend on the field of *ming* or "action" (*youwei* 有為). Their aim is progressively to distinguish and separate Yin from Yang, what belongs to the ordinary body from what belongs to the subtle body (*ming* practices), and what belongs to the ordinary mind from what is related to the pure mind (*xing* practices). This brings about a progressive transformation of the constituents of body and mind from a coarse to a subtle state, which corresponds to a complete modification of bodily and mental habits. Conversely, joint cultivation may also begin with a realization of inherent non-duality by realizing the true nature of mind, through contemplative practices belonging to the field of *xing* or "non-action" (*wuwei*). As the term *shuangxiu* indicates, however, the *xing* practices cannot be separated from the *ming* practices, and vice versa; it is only for maieutic purposes that they are taught in a separate and progressive way. From the perspective of the fruit of practice, they are fully interdependent and simultaneous.

Ultimately, the goal of joint cultivation, which the alchemical texts express as "the encompassing marvel of Form and Spirit" (*xingshen jumiao* 形神俱 妙), consists in overcoming all dualities and contradictions by realizing that they originally issue from a single source. For the discursive mind, because of the mixture with temporal conditioning, they are separated and conceived as "dual." Once reality is contemplated from the point of view of the Absolute, a view is achieved in which duality is transcended, and *xing* and *ming* return to the One (*yi*) or the Dao.

Monica ESPOSITO

📖 App 1994, 41–45; Cleary 1987, 14–16; Robinet 1986a; Robinet 1995a, 44–46, 67–70, 164–95

※ *xing* and *ming*; *neidan*

Siji mingke jing

四極明科經

Scripture of the Illustrious Code of the Four Poles

This work (CT 184), the first and standard collection of rules of the *Shangqing school, was compiled in the late fifth century, after *Lu Xiujing and before *Tao Hongjing. It contains 120 rules in five *juan*. The text begins with a general introduction (1.1a–9a), then presents the rules of the Five Emperors (*wudi* 五 帝) of the five directions—East/green, West/white, South/red, North/black, and Center/yellow. In each case, the emperor is given a formal title and linked with one of the Five Peaks (*wuyue*). Next appear the rules, listing the appropriate celestial positions and titles to be awarded, and the relevant sacred scriptures to be transmitted to the immortals-to-be. Instructions on recitation, meditation and visualization follow, joined by warnings never in any way to add to or subtract from the scriptures and to observe the proper purifications before handling them.

The text claims to be revealed by the Lord of the Dao (Daojun 道君) to the Imperial Lord of the Golden Portal (*Jinque dijun*), also known as the Saint of the Latter Age (*housheng*). The introduction outlines the overall structure of the otherworldly bureaucracy. Officers of the left preside over Yang transgressions, such as killing, theft of celestial treasures, unwarranted leakage of numinous texts, cursing and swearing; officers of the right govern Yin transgressions, which include harboring schemes, disobedience, planning to harm others, and never remembering the Dao; and officers of the center rule over doubts and duplicity, lack of reverence and faith, desecration of divine objects, and various unholy wishes. Each officer, moreover, is in charge of a large staff, including not only lesser guards and bailiffs but also the Five Emperors themselves.

In addition, the system extends to the earth: from the various grottoes in the Five Peaks, it administers the sins of people of the Nine Prefectures (*jiufu* 九府). Each mountain has 120 officials, 1,200 bailiffs, and 50,000 troops, and rules over the souls of the dead for 10,000 *kalpas* (1.5b).

The 120 rules of the *Siji mingke* are recited and worshipped like a talisman or sacred scripture, in themselves containing the power of ascension to the Dao. Unless observed properly, and with the right purifications and rituals, all efforts to attain the Dao will come to naught.

Livia KOHN

📖 Ozaki Masaharu 1977; Robinet 1984, 1: 209–10 and 2: 428–30

※ *jie* [precepts]; Shangqing

siling

四靈

Four Numina

The Four Numina are spirits that are represented as animals, and in later Taoism take on the role of guardians of the four points of the compass. Comprising the Green Dragon (*qinglong* 青龍), White Tiger (*baihu* 白虎), Red Sparrow (*zhuque* 朱雀) and Dark Warrior (*xuanwu* 玄武), the Four Numina are also identified by the names Meng Zhang 孟章, Jian Bing 監兵, Ling Guang 靈光, and Gui Ming 軌明, respectively. Because of their association with the four directions they play an important part in later Taoist ritual practices, such as in exorcism, penance, and purification rituals. Images of all Four Numina, especially Dark Warrior, may be found in many Taoist temples.

The locus classicus for the Four Numina as guardians of the four directions is a passage in a detailed description of the Former Han capital Chang'an in the *Sanfu huangtu* 三輔黃圖 (Yellow Chart of the Three Districts), a work that itself probably dates from the Six Dynasties or the Tang period. The "Palace of Eternity" ("Weiyang gong" 未央宮) chapter of the text explains the construction of the capital: "Green Dragon, White Tiger, Red Sparrow, and Dark Warrior are Heaven's Four Numina and it uses them to keep the four directions in order. The ruler draws on this model in constructing his palaces and chambers." While the late date of the text might mean that this description is apocryphal, the profusion of references to the Four Numina in the Han makes it conceivable that they did indeed play a part in Chang'an palace architecture.

Origins. The earliest references to the Four Numina are to an entirely different set of animals. The term "four numina" is used in the "Liyun" 禮運 (Cycles of Ritual) chapter of the Han dynasty *Liji* 禮記 (Records of Rites; trans. Legge 1885, 1: 384) to refer to the unicorn, phoenix, tortoise, and dragon. Early references to this set of numina indicate that they were not associated with the four directions but considered the epitomes of the four classes of animal: those with fur (unicorn), feathers (phoenix), scales (dragon), and shell (tortoise). They were likened to the sage, the epitome of the human being (Zhang Mengwen 1986, 528). An apocryphal text associated with the *Liji*, the *Jiming zheng* 稽命徵 (Proof of the Ultimate Mandate), labels the combination of the same four animals with the White Tiger as the "five numina" and perhaps signifies an intermediate stage between the early Han conception and the Taoist Four Numina. The latter set is found on a number of Han-dynasty grave goods, the earliest known being an early Former Han wine warming vessel that depicts a tiger, dragon, bird, and tortoise—the tortoise being Dark Warrior (Ni Run'an 1999, 83).

The Four Numina are probably a hybrid of Zhou dynasty guardian spirits associated with the four directions and Han dynasty astronomical totems associated with the same directions. The colors of the Four Numina probably originated with deities that defended against attacks from the four directions. Their colors correspond to those of the spirits to be sacrificed to when being attacked by enemies in the Zhou text *Mozi* 墨子 (Book of Master Mo), with red and black spirits defending one from attacks from the south and north, and green and white defending one from east and west, respectively. The same association of colors with sacrifices at directional altars is found in the description of the first emperor of Han's sacrifices to the "emperors of the four directions" in the *Shiji*'s (Records of the Historian; ca. 100 BCE) monograph on *feng* 封 and *shan* 禪 sacrifices ("Fengshan shu" 封禪書, 28.1378). The animals of the Four Numina are associated with the four quadrants of the night sky (Ni Run'an 1999, 85), each comprising seven of the twenty-eight lunar lodges (*xiu*). This association is seen as early as the astronomical chapter of the *Huainan zi* (Book of the Master of Huainan; ca. 139 BCE) where the Green Dragon (*canglong* 蒼龍) is in the east, the White Tiger in the west, the Red Sparrow in the south, and the Dark Warrior in the west (Major 1993, 70–72). The various factors that had earlier appeared separately are combined in the "Quli" 曲禮 (Details of Ritual) chapter of the *Liji*, which refers to four positions of carriages in this order: "Red Bird in front and Dark Warrior in the rear, Green Dragon on the left and White Tiger on the right" (see Legge 1885, 1: 91–92).

The Four Numina in Taoism. The earliest mentions in texts associated with institutional Taoism mirror the military context of the *Liji*. The Six Dynasties *Baopu zi* (Book of the Master Who Embraces Simplicity) depicts the Most High Lord Lao flanked by twelve Green Dragons on his right, twenty-six White Tigers on his left, twenty-four Red Sparrows in front, and seventy-two Dark Warriors to the rear (Ware 1966, 256–57). A similar array appears in the *Beiji qiyuan ting bijue* 北極七元庭祕訣 (Secret Instructions of the Hall of the Seven Primordials of the Northern Pole; YJQQ 25) and incorporates the names Meng Zhang, Jian Bing, Ling Guang, and Gui Ming.

In the Tang and Song, the Four Numina were incorporated into the Taoist liturgy, where they were summoned to the altar to protect it from demons. An early reference is made in part 52 of *Du Guangting's (850–933) *Huanglu zhaiyi* 黃籙齋儀 (Liturgies for the Yellow Register Retreat; 891; CT 507). Other texts record the talismans (*FU) of the Four Numina and the invocations used in such ritual contexts, as well as in liturgy devoted to Presenting the Memorial (*jinbiao* 進表; see *baibiao*) in which the Four Numina played a central role (Ding Changyun 1997, 118–20).

In later imperial Taoism, Dark Warrior became the most important of the Four Numina, based on the perception of his power over demons. Originally represented as tortoise, or a snake fighting with a tortoise (Ni Run'an 1999, 83), Dark Warrior came to be depicted as a fierce warrior with both animals at his feet (Ding Changyun 1997, 116). He also came to be identified as the eighty-second transformation of the Dark Emperor (Xuandi 玄帝), the eighty-first having been Laozi. When the graph *xuan* 玄 became taboo following the death of the Song Emperor Zhenzong in 1022, Dark Warrior was referred to as Perfected Warrior (*Zhenwu). He is the object of numerous rituals in the Taoist Canon. An example is the rituals of penance in two Northern Song dynasty texts named after him, the *Zhenwu lingying hushi xiaozai miezui baochan* 真武靈應護世消災滅罪寶懺 (Precious Penances for the Numinous Response of the Perfected Warrior to Protect the Age, Dispel Disasters, and Eliminate Guilt; ca. 1100; CT 814) and the *Beiji Zhenwu puci dushi fachan* 北極真武普慈 度世法懺 (Orthodox Penance for Universal Compassion and Salvation of the Perfected Warrior of the Northern Pole; ca. 1100; CT 815). In the Ming, many of the particular methods associated with Dark Warrior were incorporated by Zhou Side 周思得 (1359–1451) into his *Shangqing lingbao jidu dacheng jinshu* 上清靈寶濟度大成金書 (Golden Writings on the Great Achievement of Deliverance of the Numinous Treasure of Highest Clarity).

Mark CSIKSZENTMIHALYI

📖 Ding Changyun 1997; Little 2000b, 129; Major 1985–86; Ni Run'an 1999; Zhang Mengwen 1982

※ Zhenwu; COSMOLOGY

Sima Chengzhen

司馬承禎

647–735; *zi*: Ziwei 子微; *hao*: Daoyin 道隱 (Recluse of the Dao), Baiyun zi 白雲子 (Master of the White Cloud), Zhenyi xiansheng 貞一先生 (Elder of Pure Unity)

Sima Chengzhen was perhaps the most important Taoist of Tang times. Author of notable works on meditation and self-cultivation, he also inherited *Pan Shizheng's mantle as *Shangqing patriarch or Grand Master (*zongshi* 宗師), and was the acknowledged leader of Taoism in his day. An accomplished poet, painter and calligrapher, he associated with many of the period's leading lit-terateurs, including Li Bai 李白 (701–62). Yet he was probably most significant in a political context. In a period when rulers routinely patronized numerous Taoistic characters, Sima was regarded by Tang emperors and literati alike as a perfect political exemplar, a sagely counselor who legitimized the rulers. Beyond playing that role, as other Taoists of the period did, Sima brought the Shangqing heritage into the state cult. In 731, after Tang Xuanzong (r. 712–56) performed the *feng* 封 ritual to Heaven on Mount Tai (*Taishan, Shandong), he accepted Sima's advice to establish temples to the "transcendent officials" at the Five Peaks (*wuyue). At that point in history, Taoism enjoyed a social, political, and cultural eminence that, like the Tang imperium itself, would diminish greatly after the An Lushan 安祿山 and Shi Siming 史思明 uprisings (755–63), and never be fully regained.

Sima's life is extremely well-documented: over three dozen biographies survive, including two near-contemporary memorial inscriptions by government functionaries. (A third such text, composed in the name of Xuanzong himself, is now lost.) Sima is also the subject of four other biographies of Tang date, and later accounts preserve valuable data. According to the inscriptions and earliest documentary texts (e.g., Zhenxi 真系, in YJQQ 5.14b–16a), Sima was descended from a collateral branch of the clan that had ruled China as the Jin dynasty (265–420). His father and grandfather had each held government posts, but Chengzhen's inclinations were more religious. Nothing is known of his early life. At the age of twenty-one, he became a disciple of Pan Shizheng on Mount Song (*Songshan, Henan), and sometime later received Pan's transmission of the Shangqing registers and scriptures. After wandering among the land's sacred mountains, he was summoned to the capital by Empress Wu (r. 690–705). A ninth-century text preserved in the Buddhist canon (Tiantai shan ji 天臺山記; T. 2096) provides some details of his activities in that period. In 711 Sima was summoned to court by Tang Ruizong (r. 684–90, 710–12), and provided advice on government. Afterward, court poets dedicated more than a hundred poems to Sima, many of which survive (Kroll 1978). In 721/722 or 724/725 (the biographies disagree), he was summoned to Xuanzong's court, and reportedly bestowed Shangqing "scriptures and methods" (jingfa 經法) or "methods and registers" (falu 法錄) upon the emperor. He then assumed residence at an abbey on Mount Wangwu (*Wangwu shan, Henan), which the emperor had established for him. (Though counted as a prelate of the Shangqing lineage, which originated on Mount Mao or *Maoshan, Sima never visited that mountain; it was his successor, *Li Hanguang, who reestablished the Shangqing tradition there.) While on Mount Wangwu, Sima copied and collated Taoist texts, and reedited the *Dengzhen yinjue (Concealed Instructions for the Ascent to Perfection), a collection of materials on ritual and spiritual perfection by *Tao Hongjing. To supplement it, he composed the Xiuzhen bizhi 修真祕旨 (Secret Directions for Cultivating Perfection), now lost. Sima was renowned for his calligraphy, and created a style called "Golden Shears" for which he was celebrated in later ages. Apparently by imperial order, he wrote out the Daode jing in three styles of script for engraving as the "correct text."

After more trips to Xuanzong's court came the 731 institution of ritual observances to the Shangqing Perfected Ones at the land's Five Peaks. An account by *Du Guangting (Tiantan Wangwu shan shengji ji; CT 969, 4a–5a) states that Ruizong's daughter, the Taoist priestess known as Yuzhen 玉真

(Jade Perfected), was fond of Sima; the Standard Histories report that in 735 she was ordered to perform the *jinlu zhai (Golden Register Retreat) with him at his abbey on Mount Wangwu (Benn 1991, 14–15). Du reports Sima's death date as 727, and the official historians (*Jiu Tangshu*, 192.5127–29; *Xin Tangshu*, 196.5605–6) seem to follow him. All other texts, however, agree that he died 12 July 735, at the age of eighty-nine, which accords with the rest of the record. One of the inscription texts reports that Sima underwent *shijie (mortuary liberation) after having announced, "I have already received official duties in the Arcane Metropolis (Xuandu 玄都)." Xuanzong composed a memorial inscription, canonized Sima as Zhenyi xiansheng, and conferred noble rank upon him. One of the early accounts reports that though Sima had many disciples, "only Li Hanguang and Jiao Jingzhen 焦靜真 received his Dao" (*Zhenxi*; YJQQ 5.15b–16a) Jiao, a little-known "refined mistress" (*lianshi* 錬士), was also widely extolled by poets of the period (Kroll 1981, 22–30).

Sima edited or composed some fifteen works; besides those mentioned above were several on Shangqing biography and sacred geography (Kohn 1987a, 21–23). Of dubious authorship is the *Daoti lun* 道體論 (Essay on the Embodiment of the Dao; CT 1035; part. trans. Kohn 1993b, 19–24). A writing that apparently had little influence until the twelfth century was Sima's *Fuqi jingyi lun (Essay on the Essential Meaning of the Ingestion of Breath); it concerns the more physiological aspects of maintaining personal well-being (Engelhardt 1987; Engelhardt 1989). From Sima's own day into the tenth century, his most influential work seems to have been his *Zuowang lun (Essay on Sitting in Oblivion; CT 1036), a text on meditation (Kohn 1987a; Kohn 1993b, 235–41). Here, Sima seems to have been influenced by the *Xisheng jing, the *Dingguan jing, and *Sun Simiao's *Cunshen lianqi ming. Yet Sima names as his chief inspiration "The Master of Heavenly Seclusion," the unknown author of the *Tianyin zi, which Sima edited (Kohn 1993b, 80–86). In his preface to it, Sima argues that the path of spiritual transcendence (*shenxian* 神仙) goes beyond mere study, and requires practice of "various techniques to cultivate and refine body and energy, to nourish and harmonize mind and emptiness" (Kohn 1993b, 80). In the *Zuowang lun*, Sima describes the path as consisting of seven stages, of which the last is "Realizing the Dao." It shows occasional traces of Buddhist ideas (like "cutting off *karma*"), presumably owing to his association with the Buddhists of Mount Tiantai (*Tiantai shan, Zhejiang), where Sima lived until 723/724. The concept of the Taoist life suggested in these texts seems to have influenced Sima's younger contemporary, the poet *Wu Yun, and may have helped shape the ideals of Taoists of later ages, such as *Wang Zhe.

Russell KIRKLAND

📖 Chen Guofu 1963, 52–58; Engelhardt 1987 (trans. of *Fuqi jingyi lun*); Kirkland

1986a, 43–71, 220–97; Kirkland 1997a; Kohn 1987a (trans. of *Zuowang lun*); Kohn 1993b, 19–24 (part. trans. of *Daoti lun*), 80–86 (trans. of *Tianyin zi*), and 235–41 (part. trans. of *Zuowang lun*); Kroll 1978; Qing Xitai 1988–95, 2: 225–38; Robinet 1987e

※ *Fuqi jingyi lun; Tianyin zi; Zuowang lun;* Shangqing

Siming

司命

Director of Destinies

The Director of Destinies is the deity that controls the life span of human beings. His name is first mentioned in an inscription on a bronze utensil dating from the sixth century BCE. Two poems in the *Chuci* 楚辭 (Songs of Chu; trans. Hawkes 1985, 109–12) are entitled "The Greater Director of Destinies" and "The Lesser Director of Destinies" ("Da siming" 大司命 and "Shao siming" 少司命), but nothing is known in detail about beliefs surrounding these gods at that time (third to second centuries BCE). Siming also appears as the name of a celestial body in the astronomical chapter of the *Shiji* (Records of the Historian; trans. Chavannes 1895–1905, 3: 342). The *Fengsu tongyi* 風俗通義 (Comprehensive Accounts of Popular Customs; *j.* 8), compiled by Ying Shao 應邵 (ca. 140–ca. 206), relates that the imperial court had for generations venerated Siming on the first day that was marked by the cyclical character *hai* 亥 after the winter solstice, while commoners made offerings to wooden effigies of him in spring and autumn.

The fourth star of the six-star constellation known as Literary Glory (*wenchang* 文昌), located above the Northern Dipper (*beidou), is called Siming. A parallel notion developed that the Northern Dipper itself is the Director of Destinies. The Northern Dipper is deemed to control human birth and death, which may be at the origin of the belief that three worms or "corpses" (*sanshi*; see *sanshi and *jiuchong*) influence the life span of each individual by ascending to Heaven and reporting his or her misdeeds. As stated in *j.* 6 of the *Baopu zi (Book of the Master Who Embraces Simplicity), the three worms "ascend to heaven every fifty-seventh day (*gengshen; see table 10) of the sexagesimal cycle and report transgressions and faults to the Director of Destinies. . . . For major misdeeds, the life span is reduced by 300 days, and for minor ones, by three days" (see Ware 1966, 115).

In a related popular belief, the Stove God (*Zaoshen) ascends to heaven at the end of each year (in most cases, the twenty-third day of the twelfth lunar month) and reports to the Director of Destinies about the good and bad behavior of the members of the household. In other cases, it was believed that the Director of Destinies himself, or a representative, appears in the world below in human form to observe the good and bad behavior of the people. From the Tang dynasty onward, the Stove God himself was identified as the Director of Destinies, an association that has continued to the present day.

YAMADA Toshiaki

📖 Inahata Kōichirō 1979; Sawada Mizuho 1968, 54–59; Yūsa Noboru 1983, 343–45

※ Zaoshen; TAOISM AND POPULAR RELIGION

Song Defang

宋德方

1183–1247; *zi*: Guangdao 廣道; *hao*: Piyun 披雲 (Clad in Clouds)

Song Defang is mainly known as the compiler of the *Xuandu baozang*, the next to last compilation of the Taoist Canon. Available sources (mainly epigraphic) draw a picture of a man who excelled in several different endeavors, however, and whose ideal was the restoration of Taoism as the great national Chinese religion under the aegis of the *Quanzhen order.

Song came from the tip of the Shandong peninsula, where Quanzhen was formally founded. His mother, probably a member of a Quanzhen lay association, made him a novice at the age of eleven. He was ordained by *Wang Chuyi, and became a disciple first of *Liu Chuxuan, the most distinguished writer among the Seven Real Men (*qizhen* 七真; see table 17), then of *Qiu Chuji, who made Song one of his most trusted lieutenants. Accordingly, Song was one of the eighteen disciples who accompanied Qiu on his western travels.

From his return in 1223 until the early 1230s, Song Defang lived in Beijing, participating in the Quanzhen autonomous administration that was taking shape around the seat of the patriarch at the Changchun gong 長春宮 (Palace of Perpetual Spring, today's *Baiyun guan) while cultivating scholarly interests. When the plain of the Yellow River finally fell to the Mongol armies, Song went south and, with other charismatic masters such as *Yin Zhiping and *Wang Zhijin, took upon himself the task of managing large-scale Quanzhen development in these areas. Song especially took charge of Shanxi, where he visited many sites and started many foundations. At Mount Long (Longshan 龍山), near Taiyuan 太原, he expanded an earlier cave temple and had many statues carved from the cliffs, a major achievement of Taoist monumental art. Further south, he took control of the prestigious Mount Wangwu (*Wangwu shan, Henan) and of a temple located at the supposed birthplace of *Lü Dong-bin, which he turned into one of the main Quanzhen monastic centers, the *Yongle gong. Song was particularly esteemed by the Mongol court, which, besides regular functional and honorific titles, bestowed upon him the title of Celestial Master (*tianshi* 天師) in 1251, a unique case among the northern Taoists of the Yuan period.

It was from his base in southern Shanxi—a traditionally important printing area where a Buddhist Canon had been published some decades earlier—that Song organized the compilation of a Taoist Canon. He set up dozens of local offices that retrieved the earlier *Da Jin Xuandu baozang*, cut the blocks, and printed the collection without substantial public support. The whole task was completed between 1237 and 1244, a credit to Song's leadership and to Quan-zhen's efficient organization on a national level. This Canon had a dramatic destiny, as it was burned in 1281 to satisfy one of Emperor Khubilai's fits of rage. Song's own works, entitled *Lequan ji* 樂全集 (Anthology of Complete Bliss), were also lost, but a fair number of his poems are extant in the *Minghe yuyin* (Echoes of Cranes' Songs).

Vincent GOOSSAERT

📖 van der Loon 1984, 50–56

※ Yongle gong; *Xuandu baozang*; Quanzhen

songjing

誦經

recitation; chanting

The term *songjing*, which is first mentioned in the *Xunzi* 荀子 (third century BCE), originally refers to a method of acquiring thorough knowledge of a text by memorizing it. This meaning is retained in Taoism, where the term also ac-quires another meaning. Since several Taoist scriptures were deemed to record the words of deities, possessing and reciting them made them comparable to talismans (*FU) and spells (*zhou* 咒). For instance, the *Dongyuan shenzhou jing* (Scripture of the Divine Spells of the Cavernous Abyss), the earliest por-tions of which date from the latter half of the fourth century, mentions two efficacious uses of the scripture: one could possess it as a talisman, as well as recite and chant it.

Examples of the virtues of reciting texts are found throughout Taoist literature. The central *Lingbao scripture, the *Duren jing (Scripture on Salvation),
emphasizes the specific merits of chanting its lines. In his *Lingbao zhai shuo
guangzhu jiefa dengzhu yuanyi* 洞玄靈寶齋說光燭戒罰燈祝願儀 (Explana-
tion of Candle-Illumination, Precepts and Penalties, Lamps, Invocations, and
Vows for Lingbao Retreats; CT 524), *Lu Xiujing (406–77) uses recitation and
chanting to purify the residual *karma* derived from speech (*kouye* 口業). From
a *Shangqing perspective, *Tao Hongjing (456–536) records in his *Zhengao
(Declarations of the Perfected) the effectiveness of reciting the *Dadong zhenjing
(Authentic Scripture of the Great Cavern) and other Shangqing texts, saying
that this will result in the attainment of longevity.

These examples show that recitation and chanting of Taoist scriptures
became widespread from around the middle of the fifth century. While
Buddhism may have influenced this custom, the *Sanguo zhi* (History of the
Three Kingdoms) records that *Zhang Daoling had a follower who "practiced
over and over again" (*duxi* 都習) the *Daode jing*. Memorization was the chief
learning method of the time, and this account shows that recitation of scriptures was performed within Taoism from the earliest period.

YAMADA Toshiaki

📖 Lagerwey 1981b, 141–43; Qing Xitai 1994, 3: 194–97; Yamada Toshiaki 1999,
229–62

Songshan

嵩山

Mount Song (Henan)

Mount Song is a large chain of mountains rising to 1500 m and located in
Dengfeng 登封 district (Henan), not far from Luoyang. It is ranked as one of
the Grotto-Heavens (*dongtian*) and is usually divided between the Taishi 太
室 and Shaoshi 少室 ranges. It has been considered as the Central of the Five
Peaks (*wuyue*) since the late Zhou period.

The Zhongyue miao 中嶽廟 (Shrine of the Central Peak), located on a
plain not far from the mountains, was the site for official sacrifices to the
Central Peak but also accommodated popular cults. The large temple complex
is still standing and now houses the local Taoist Association and a number of
*Quanzhen clerics. The mountain itself is dotted with numerous monasteries
and hermitages. But although there have been Taoists living on Mount Song

throughout two millennia (including *Kou Qianzhi and *Pan Shizheng), with several hermitages built for them, the mountain has always been predominantly Buddhist. Its most famous site and today its major attraction, the Shaolin si 少林寺 (Monastery of the Small Forest), is a major Chan monastery and also the training center for a distinctive martial arts tradition that appeared during the fifteenth century.

Vincent GOOSSAERT

📖 Geil 1926, 165–215

※ *wuyue*; TAOIST SACRED SITES

Soushen ji

搜神記

In Search of the Sacred

There are two texts called *Soushen ji* that are of relevance to the study of Taoism. The first is from the fourth century and is attributed to Gan Bao 干寶 (ca. 340). Gan was an official of middle rank under the Eastern Jin and his work is a compilation of the strange and marvellous in twenty chapters. Usually considered under the rubric of *zhiguai* 志怪 or "records of the strange," this *Soushen ji* is not specifically concerned with Taoist subjects but some of its anecdotes and stories concern Taoist figures or Taoist topics. Indeed its first chapter is almost entirely given over to records of people regarded, in Taoist texts, as immortals.

The other *Soushen ji* has a preface by Luo Maodeng 羅懋登 (fl. 1593–98). This work (CT 1476) is a collection of biographies of deities in six chapters ranging from famous figures of past who were granted an otherworldly existence, to the gods honored in local cults and officially recognized. It begins with short essays devoted to Confucius, Śākyamuni and Lord Lao and its contents, as a whole, display a certain non-exclusive view of the inhabitants of the divine realms. Nonetheless, the preponderance of figures from the Taoist tradition is noticeable.

Benjamin PENNY

📖 Boltz J. M. 1987a, 59, 61–62, and 274–75; Campany 1996, 55–62, 69–75, and 146–50; DeWoskin and Crump 1996; Kohn 1993b, 296–99; Mathieu 2000

※ HAGIOGRAPHY

Su Lin

素林

third century; *zi*: Zixuan 子玄

Su Lin is a saint of the *Shangqing tradition. His hagiography, entitled *Xuanzhou shangqing Sujun zhuan* 玄洲上卿素君傳 (Biography of Lord Su, Senior Minister of the Mysterious Continent), was revealed by his disciple, *Ziyang zhenren. The extant version in the *Yunji qiqian* (104.1a–4b) is shorter than the original and the instructions that were appended to it are now found in the *Suling jing*. These instructions concern two practices for Guarding the One (*shouyi): the method of the Nine Palaces (*jiugong; Robinet 1984, 2: 293–93) and the method of the Five Dippers and the Three Ones (*wudou sanyi* 五斗三一; Robinet 1984, 2: 300–301).

Su, who was from Qushui 曲水 (Jiangsu), is also known as Real Man of the Central Peak (Zhongyue zhenren 中嶽真人) and Real Man of the Five Peaks (Wuyue zhenren 五嶽真人). His masters were Qin Gao 琴高, Qiusheng 仇生, and Juanzi 涓子, all of whom have biographies in the *Liexian zhuan* (trans. Kaltenmark 1953, 104–7, 81–82, 68–71). The first two masters taught him minor practices, including a technique to expel the Three Corpses (*sanshi*; see *sanshi and jiuchong) and alchemical and breathing techniques that confer immortality but do not grant ascension to heaven. Later, Juanzi gave him the method of the Five Dippers and the Three Ones. After practicing this method, Su told his disciple Ziyang zhenren that he had received the title of Senior Minister of the Mysterious Continent (Xuanzhou shangqing 玄洲上卿), and ascended to heaven in broad daylight on a chariot of clouds.

Isabelle ROBINET

📖 Andersen 1979, 8–10; Chen Guofu 1963, 11; Robinet 1984, 2: 365–68

※ *Suling jing*; Shangqing; HAGIOGRAPHY

Su Yuanming

蘇元明

hao: Qingxia zi 青霞子 (Master of Azure Mist); also known as
Su Yuanlang 蘇元郎

According to traditional accounts, Su Yuanming retired to the Valley of Azure
Mist (Qingxia gu 青霞谷) in the Luofu Mountains (*Luofu shan, Guangdong)
during the Sui period. Already 300 years old at the time, he had previously
studied the Dao with *Maojun on Mount Mao (*Maoshan, Jiangsu). Upon his
arrival at the Luofu Mountains, his disciples questioned him about the ingestion of certain "numinous mushrooms" (*zhi) that granted immortality. Su
answered that those mushrooms should not be sought in the mountains, but
within the Eight Effulgences (*bajing) of one's inner body. His reply is often
believed to be the earliest evidence of the shift to a type of inner cultivation
practice that would eventually give rise to *neidan. However, the account
reported above is based on the *Zhidao pian* 旨道篇 (Folios Pointing to the
Dao), a work now lost that is first mentioned in the bibliographic treatise
of the *Songshi* (History of the Song; van der Loon 1984, 102), dating from no
earlier than 1345.

Other sources mention a hermit, also known as Master of Azure Mist, who
used to refine cinnabar on the Luofu Mountains at the end of the Han. Both
Michel Soymié (1956, 28, 120 and 122) and Chen Guofu (1983, 314–18) have suggested that these traditions conflate accounts of two semilegendary characters
who shared the same sobriquet. Chen also points out that the Sui-dynasty Su
Yuanlang was credited with knowledge of both *waidan and *neidan*. In fact,
the bibliographic treatise of the *Xin Tangshu* (New History of the Tang; van
der Loon 1984, 91) attributes to Su the original version of an extant *waidan*
work, the *Taiqing shibi ji (Records of the Stone Wall of Great Clarity); and
the bibliography of alchemical texts in the *Shiyao erya (Synonymic Dictionary
of Mineral Materia Medica, 2.3a), mostly devoted to *waidan* works, mentions
a lost *Qingxia zi jue* 青霞子訣 (Instructions of the Master of Azure Mist).

Su was believed to be still alive in 789, when he reportedly received the
Longhu yuanzhi 龍虎元旨 (The Original Purport of the Dragon and Tiger;
CT 1083) from the immortal Dong Shiyuan 董師元. This *neidan* text is the
only work in the current Taoist Canon to bear Su's name as its author.

Elena VALUSSI

📖 Baldrian-Hussein 1989–90, 165–67; Chen Guofu 1983, 314–18; Needham 1976, 130–31; Qing Xitai 1988–95, 2: 516–19; Soymié 1956, 28, 120, and 122

※ HAGIOGRAPHY

Suling jing

素靈經

Scripture [of the Celestial Palace] of the Immaculate Numen

The *Suling jing* was revealed to *Su Lin, a *Shangqing saint. It consists of a collection of texts of various origins dating from the Han to the late fifth century, some of which antedate the Shangqing revelations but were adopted by this school. The text is mainly concerned with the Three Ones (*sanyi) and describes methods also outlined in the *Dengzhen yinjue* (Concealed Instructions for the Ascent to Reality), the *Shangqing wozhong jue* 上清握中訣 (Shangqing Handbook of Instructions; CT 140; Robinet 1984, 2: 353–58), and the biography of Peijun 裴君 (Lord Pei; YJQQ 105; Robinet 1984, 2: 375–84), a Shangqing saint who appeared to *Yang Xi. It can be divided into five sections, the last of which documents an early stage of the division of Taoist scriptures into three hierarchical classes, anticipating the scheme of the Three Caverns (*SANDONG). The present version, entitled *Suling Dayou miaojing* 素靈大有妙經 (Scripture [of the Celestial Palaces] of the Immaculate Numen and Great Existence; CT 1314), is incomplete and has undergone interpolations. In its title, Suling and Dayou are the names of celestial palaces where the original version of the text is kept.

The first part (1a–12a) of this work focuses the Three Ones who represent, on the cosmic level, Heaven, Earth, and Water (see *sanguan; this tripartition demonstrates a relation with the *Tianshi dao and its cosmology). Each of the Three Ones rules on a palace in the Suling heaven and in one of the three Cinnabar Fields (*dantian), and is associated with one of three Shangqing sacred scriptures: the *Dadong zhenjing*, the *Ciyi jing*, and the *Suling jing*. The adept meditates on the Three Ones by visualizing colored pneumas; then the officers of the Three Caverns descend from their celestial palaces to the adept's Cinnabar Fields.

The second part (12b–24b), which in the received version is rather in disorder, describes the male and female divinities who reside in the Nine Palaces (*jiugong) of the brain and form the Masculine One (Xiongyi 雄一) and the Feminine One (Ciyi 雌一). Among the Nine Palaces, the one called Mysterious Cinnabar (Xuandan 玄丹) is connected with the Northern Dipper (*beidou) and the Great One (*Taiyi).

The third part (24b–41a) contains a version of the method of the Three Primes and the Authentic One (*sanyuan zhenyi* 三元真一), originally appended to Su Lin's biography. It describes the Three Ones, who are associated with the Three Primes (*sanyuan), the three scriptures mentioned above, and the three basic components of human beings: essence, pneuma, and spirit (*jing, qi, shen). This section also contains the first part of an important meditation technique named after the Five Dippers and the Three Ones (*wudou sanyi* 五斗三一), which is described in other texts and is also related to Su Lin's biography. It is one of the variants of the method of Guarding the One (*shouyi) and consists of ascending to the Dipper with the gods of the Three Ones of the Cinnabar Fields. (For more details on this section see *sanyi.)

The fourth part (41a–44a) contains invocations to major Shangqing gods. This section may have been part of the biography of Peijun.

The fifth and final part (44a–68b) contains the *Jiuzhen mingke* 九真明科 (Illustrious Code of the Nine Real Men). This code details rules related to the transmission of sacred texts. The scriptures are divided into three categories, referred to as the Three Caverns (consisting only of Shangqing texts), followed by a fourth containing the so-called "three extraordinary texts" (*sanqi* 三奇) mentioned above. The *Jiuzhen mingke* collects, systematizes, and completes rules of transmission scattered throughout various other Shangqing texts, and is a precursor of the *Siji mingke jing (Scripture of the Illustrious Code of the Four Poles).

Isabelle ROBINET

📖 Andersen 1979; Robinet 1984, 1: 76–85 and 2: 285–301; Robinet 1993, 124–31

※ Su Lin; Shangqing

Sun Bu'er

孫不二

1119–83; original *ming*: Fuchun 富春; *hao*: Qingjing sanren 清靜
散人 (Vagabond of Clarity and Quiescence), Xiangu 仙姑 (Transcendent Maiden)

Sun Bu'er is the only female to be counted among the so-called Seven Perfected (*qizhen* 七真; see table 17), the designation commonly applied to the circle of followers established by the founder of the *Quanzhen school *Wang Zhe (1113–70) in Ninghai 寧海 (Shandong). Her family gave her the name

Fuchun, whereas Wang honored Sun with the names Bu'er (Non-Dual) and
Qingjing sanren when she became his disciple. The Qingjing branch of the
Quanzhen school is dedicated to a legacy of *neidan teachings conveyed in her
name.

Hagiographies dating from the mid-thirteenth to early fourteenth century
tell variant stories concerning Sun Bu'er. All generally agree on the dates of
major events in her life as recorded in the *Qizhen nianpu, compiled in 1271
by the Quanzhen archivist *Li Daoqian (1219–96). She was born on the fifth
day of the first lunar month (16 February) of 1119 to a well-established family
of Ninghai. Her father is identified as Sun Zhongyi 孫忠翊 in the *Jinlian
zhengzong ji, compiled in 1241 by the eminent Qin Zhi'an 秦志安 (1188–1244).
A derivative hagiography of 1316 alternatively registers his name as Sun Zhongxian 孫忠顯. As a child, Fuchun was regarded as highly gifted, with a natural
talent for both letters and arts. She was given in marriage to Ma Yifu 馬宜甫
(1123–84), the son of a wealthy family in Ninghai. Their three sons Tingzhen
庭珍, Tingrui 庭瑞, and Tinggui 庭珪 were said to have received the benefit
of her instruction from infancy to matrimony.

When Wang Zhe arrived at Ninghai from Mount Zhongnan (Zhongnan
shan 終南山, Shaanxi) in the summer of 1167, Ma and Sun welcomed him to
their home. After spending over three months locked up in a retreat on their
property, Wang emerged early in 1168. A month later Ma Yifu left home to
pursue his studies with Wang and thereafter was known as *Ma Yu or Ma
Danyang 馬丹陽. The next year Sun presented herself at the Jinlian tang 金
蓮堂 (Golden Lotus Hall) on the Ninghai estate of Zhou Botong 周伯通,
where Wang and his disciples resided. According to the account in the Qizhen
nianpu, Wang at that time provided her not only with new names but also
with the Tianfu yunzhuan bijue 天符雲篆祕訣 (Secret Instructions on the
Nebular Seal-Script of Celestial Talismans). He taught her how to beg for alms
out on the streets and also told her to settle into a retreat of her own. Sun
remained under Wang's tutelage until he left in late 1170 for Bianliang 汴梁
(Henan). Wang passed away shortly thereafter and his disciples accompanied
his remains back to Mount Zhongnan for burial. In the harshness of winter,
Sun embarked on a pilgrimage to his grave. When she encountered Ma, he
inscribed a verse denying their relation as husband and wife, yet anticipating
their reunion once each had independently achieved a state of perfection.

Sun headed east and by 1175 had settled in Luoyang (Henan), where she
attracted a large following. She pursued a life of austerity until her demise on
the twenty-ninth day of the twelfth lunar month of 1182 (24 January 1183). The
verse to the tune "Bu suanzi" 卜算子 (Casting lots) recorded in hagiographies
as Sun's farewell to her disciples is among the ci 詞 lyrics ascribed to her in
the *Minghe yuyin (Echoes of Cranes' Songs) compiled ca. 1347. The collection

of regulated verse attributed to Sun Bu'er in the *Daozang jiyao* (vol. 15) and other late anthologies remains unattested prior to the Qing.

Judith M. BOLTZ

📖 Boltz J. M. 1987a, 145–46, 155–56; Despeux 1990, 111–26; Endres 1985

※ Ma Yu; *nüdan*; Quanzhen; WOMEN IN TAOISM

Sun En

孫恩

?–402; *zi*: Lingxiu 靈秀

Sun En, a descendant of the imperial family of the Wu dynasty, came from Langya 瑯琊 (Shandong). In 398, he joined his paternal uncle Sun Tai 孫泰, an influential political and religious leader in the southeastern coastal regions of present-day Zhejiang, and planned with him a major uprising. While Sun Tai was accused of conspiracy and executed with his six sons, Sun En managed to escape and probably took refuge in the islands off the coast.

In 399, having succeeded his uncle as the head of the rebellion, Sun took advantage of the political tensions in the Eastern Jin empire and captured Guiji 會稽 (Zhejiang), which became his operational base. Sun proclaimed himself "General Subduing the East" (Zhengdong jiangjun 征東將軍) and called his soldiers "Long-living" (*changsheng* 長生). He gained several victories in eight neighboring districts, capturing cities and ordering large-scale executions. According to some sources, the rebels numbered one hundred thousand men, and between seventy and eighty percent of the population in the area controlled by Sun was killed. A pro-Sun-En faction may even have risen at the capital.

Andi (r. 396–418), the ruler of the Eastern Jin, entrusted Liu Yu 劉裕 (356–422, the future founder of the Liu Song dynasty) with a major counterattack campaign. Sun's chief officers were captured and executed. Sun himself escaped from Guiji and fled back to the islands with a large number of fighters, followers, and prisoners. In the summer of the year 400, Sun led coastal piracy raids and captured cities near Guiji, but then withdrew to Nanshan 南山. In the winter of the same year, he gained victory at Yuyao 餘姚, but his troops fled before Liu Yu's army. In the following year, Sun's attempts in the Hangzhou and Shanghai areas to establish himself upon the continent failed. He thus decided to sail up the Yangzi River to attack the capital Jiankang 建康 (Jiangsu) but was rebuffed by imperial troops and withdrew to Yuzhou 郁洲. In 402, after a final short-lived victory in Linhai 臨海 (Zhejiang), Sun committed suicide by throwing himself into the sea. About one hundred of Sun's followers and concubines believed him to have turned into an "Immortal of Water" (*shuixian* 水仙) and imitated him. The insurrection was continued by Lu Xun 盧循 (?–411?), the husband of Sun's younger sister, who finally was defeated by Liu Yu.

From the religious point of view, the evocation of Sun En's rebellion in the sources is rather laconic. The Sun family is said to have been of *Tianshi dao obedience, but Liu Yu also reportedly resorted to Tianshi dao practices in setting out magical defences during the imperial campaign. Sun En's movement, which may have practiced collective sexual rites (see *heqi*), probably took advantage of preexistent local cults and borrowed from various religious currents, including the *Yellow Turbans movement and traditions of immortality-seeking, as suggested by the "Long-living" designation and the interpretation given to Sun's suicide.

Grégoire ESPESSET

📖 Eichhorn 1954a; Eichhorn 1954b; Miyakawa Hisayuki 1971; Miyakawa Hisayuki 1972; Miyakawa Hisayuki 1979; Qing Xitai 1994, 1: 239–40

※ TAOISM AND LOCAL CULTS

Sun Simiao

孫思邈

fl. 673 (traditional dates 581–682)

1. Life

Sun Simiao (whose name is also pronounced Sun Simo) was one of the greatest Chinese physicians and one of the best-known alchemists. He figures in both Taoist and Buddhist writings and is celebrated in temples dedicated to him as the King of Medicine (*yaowang). His biography in both histories of the Tang (trans. Sivin 1968, 81–144) is veiled in legend and there is controversy over his traditional dates, 581–682. It seems that at a fairly early age he retired to Mount Taibai (Taibai shan 太白山, Shaanxi), about 150 km from his ancestral home Huayuan 華原 (near Chang'an). He was in Emperor Gaozong's retinue in 673 but retired from the court, on account of illness, apparently in 674. From autobiographical notes (in contrast to the official accounts), it becomes apparent also that he travelled widely throughout his life, most notably to Sichuan.

There is no doubt that Sun was deeply involved with Taoist thought and practice, although it remains a matter of debate whether or not he was a

Taoist initiate. Since he quotes spells that the Celestial Masters used in exorcistic ritual in his *Qianjin yifang* (*j.* 29–30; on this work see below), he must have had substantial knowledge of the Way of the Celestial Masters (*Tianshi dao). His writings also address the topic of Nourishing Life (*yangsheng) and Nourishing Inner Nature (*yangxing* 養性). Moreover, *j.* 26 of his *Qianjin fang*, which can be regarded as the first extant Chinese text on dietetics (Engelhardt 2001, 176–84), takes account of Taoist writings (on this work see below).

Sun was also knowledgeable about Buddhist writings and practices. Thus, in his medical writings he refers to Indian massage techniques, mentions methods for treating conditions comparable to beriberi as described in works edited by Buddhist monks, reproduces Sanskrit incantations, and includes Buddhist meditation practices. He seems primarily to have been interested in the doctrines of the Tiantai 天臺 and Huayan 華嚴 schools, and in light of this some of his writings—particularly those on medical ethics, for which he is well known—acquire a new meaning.

Elisabeth HSU

2. Sun Simiao and Chinese medicine

Sun Simiao composed two great medical treatises, each of which comprises thirty *juan*: the *Qianjin fang* 千金方 (Prescriptions Worth a Thousand), compiled before 659, and the *Qianjin yifang* 千金翼方 (Revised Prescriptions Worth a Thousand), compiled after 659. Their dates are given with respect to the *Xinxiu bencao* 新修本草 (Newly Revised Pharmacopoeia), published in 659, which contains citations of the former, while large sections are quoted by the latter (in its *j.* 1–4). The *Qianjin fang* is also known as *Beiji qianjin yaofang* 備急千金要方 (Essential Prescriptions Worth a Thousand, for Urgent Need).

The introduction to the *Qianjin fang*, frequently quoted by later authors, discusses medical ethics, diagnostics, and principles of treatment (*j.* 1), while the bulk of the book is concerned with various disorders (in *j.* 2–23); it contains prescriptions still highly valued today partly because Sun is thought to have tested them in medical practice himself. Thus, Sun discusses women's (*j.* 2–4) and children's (*j.* 5) disorders, disorders of the seven orifices (*j.* 6), disorders of winds and poisons and the *qi in the feet (or "gout," *j.* 7), disorders of winds in general (*j.* 8), "cold damage disorders" (*shanghan* 傷寒, *j.* 9–10), disorders attributed to the five viscera (*wuzang) and the "six receptacles" (*liufu* 六腑; *j.* 11–20), "wasting thirst" (*xiaohe* 消渴, often equated with diabetes; *j.* 21), swellings and boils (*j.* 22), and hemorrhoids and leakages (*j.* 23). He devotes the last few chapters to detoxification recipes (*j.* 24), the treatment of acute conditions (*j.* 25), dietetics (*j.* 26), Nourishing Life (*j.* 27; on this chapter see below), pulse diagnostics (*j.* 28), and acupuncture and moxibustion (*j.* 29–30; trans. Despeux 1987).

The book belongs among the main Chinese medical works. It is in large part cited in the *Waitai biyao* 外臺祕要 (Secret Essentials from the Outer Platform) and the *Ishinpō (Methods from the Heart of Medicine). It was reedited in the Northern Song by Lin Yi 林億 and his team. This version is now lost and modern editions are based on a similar recension, which certainly survived from 1315 onward in Japan.

Elisabeth HSU

3. Sun Simiao and *yangsheng* (Nourishing Life)

The *yangsheng (Nourishing Life) methods described in Sun Simiao's writings are essentially based on the now-lost *Yangsheng yaoji (Essentials of Nourishing Life; early fourth century). They include gymnastics (*daoyin), breathing, and sexual techniques (*fangzhong shu), as well as rules and advice for daily life. These methods, influenced by Buddhist notions, emphasize the benefits of concentration and tranquillity of mind.

The main *yangsheng* document that was certainly written by Sun Simiao is chapter 27 of the *Qianjin fang*. Entitled "Yangxing" 養性 (Nourishing Inner Nature), this chapter is divided into eight parts: 1. "Preface to Nourishing Inner Nature" ("Yangxing xu" 養性序); 2. "Nourishing Inner Nature according to Daolin" (i.e., Zhi Dun 支盾, 314–66; "Daolin yangxing" 道林養性); 3. "Methods for Everyday Life" ("Juchu fa" 居處法); 4. "Methods for Massage" ("Anmo fa" 按摩法); 5. "Methods for the Regulation of the Breath" ("Tiaoqi fa" 調氣法); 6. "Ingestion [of Breath]" ("Fushi" 服食); 7. "Miscellaneous Prohibitions of the Yellow Emperor" ("Huangdi zaji" 黃帝雜忌); 8. "Restoring [Energy] through the Arts of the Bedchamber" ("Fangzhong buyi" 房中補益). Some sections of this chapter are similar to those of the *Yangxing yanming lu (On Nourishing Inner Nature and Extending Life), a work sometimes attributed to *Tao Hongjing or to Sun Simiao and also based for the most part on the *Yangsheng yaoji*.

Five other *yangsheng* texts are attributed to Sun Simiao in the Taoist Canon:

1. *Cunshen lianqi ming (Inscription on the Visualization of Spirit and Refinement of Pneuma; CT 834).

2. *Baosheng ming* 保生銘 (Inscription on Protecting Life; CT 835), containing advice and interdictions for daily life, with an emphasis on the benefits of tranquillity of mind.

3. *Sheyang zhenzhong fang (Pillow Book of Methods for Preserving and Nourishing Life), similar to the anonymous *Zhenzhong ji* 枕中記 (Notes Kept Inside the Pillow; CT 837) except for the last part on plants and the practice of abstention from cereals.

4. *Sheyang lun* 攝養論 (Essay on Preserving and Nourishing Life; CT 841), giving advice for each month of the year on food, sleeping and waking, and auspicious and inauspicious actions.

5. *Fushou lun* 福壽論 (Essay on Happiness and Longevity; CT 1426), a four-page treatise concerned with precepts for daily life, massage and gymnastics, respect for calendrical interdictions, and tranquillity of mind.

Catherine DESPEUX

4. Sun Simiao and alchemy

The main source testifying to Sun Simiao's interest in **waidan* is the **Taiqing danjing yaojue* (Essential Instructions from the Scripture of the Elixirs of Great Clarity), an anthology containing about thirty methods that Sun chose from those he had tested. The *Qianjin fang* also gives methods for making the crucible and the Mud of the Six-and-One (**liuyi ni*; Sivin 1968, 262–64) and contains other passages that reflect firsthand knowledge of the alchemical arts. Sun's alchemical experiments are also documented in the record of his medical disorders, which include poisoning due to ingestion of mineral substances (Sivin 1968, 249–51).

Among Sun Simiao's disciples was Meng Shen 孟詵 (621–718), best known as the author of the original version of the *Shiliao bencao* 食療本草 (Pharmacopoeia for Healing through Nutrition; Unschuld 1986, 208–12) but also famous for detecting that some gold presented to Empress Wu (r. 690–705) had been obtained through an alchemical process.

Fabrizio PREGADIO

📖 Despeux 1987; Engelhardt 1989; Needham 1976, 132–38 and 140; Qing Xitai 1988–95, 2: 311–37; Sakade Yoshinobu 1989b; Sakade Yoshinobu 1992b; Sivin 1968; Unschuld 1985, 42–45; Unschuld 1994

※ *Cunshen lianqi ming*; *Sheyang zhenzhong fang*; *Taiqing danjing yaojue*; *waidan*; *yangsheng*

Sun Youyue

孫遊嶽

399–489; *zi*: Xuanda 玄達 (*or*: Yingda 穎達)

Sun Youyue, a Taoist master during the Liu Song and Qi dynasties (420–79; 479–502), came from Yongkang 永康 (Sichuan), and is said to have descended from the family of the former rulers of the state of Wu 吳 (229–80). After studying under various teachers, he eventually took *Lu Xiujing (406–77) as his master at Mount Jinyun (Jinyun shan 縉雲山, Zhejiang). He practiced abstention from cereals (*bigu) with the help of a drug called Pellet of the Valley Immortal (guxian wan 谷仙丸) and reportedly spent forty-seven years on Mount Jinyun without contact to the outside world. In 468, when Lu Xiujing was invited to the capital Jiankang, Sun went with him, returning to Mount Jinyun upon Lu's death in 477. There he maintained a close friendship with Zhu Boyu 褚伯玉, Zhang Lingmin 章靈民, Zhu Sengbiao 朱僧標, and others.

In 484, Sun was summoned to the capital and became the head of the Xingshi guan 興世館 (Abbey for the Prosperity of the World). His fame grew among the intellectuals there as the true successor of *Yang Xi (330–86), and of Xu Mi 許謐 (303–76) and his son Xu Hui 許翽 (341–ca. 370). As a result, many sought his acquaintance, including Kong Dezhang 孔德璋 and Liu Xiaobiao 劉孝標, while others studied under him, such as Shen Yue 沈約 (441–513; IC 680–82), Lu Jingzhen 陸景真, and Chen Baoshi 陳寶識. The young *Tao Hongjing was also among his disciples; he received talismans, charts, scriptures and ritual methods from Sun, thereby taking his first steps in Taoist practice. Eventually Sun fell ill and, having been refused permission to return to Mount Jinyun, died in the capital in 489. The scriptures he had inherited from Lu Xiujing and the transmission lineage of Yang Xi he passed on to his sole close disciple, Tao Hongjing. These events contributed to the formation of *Shangqing Taoism.

There are virtually no historical sources that allow us to know the thought and teachings of Sun Youyue, and therefore it is not easy to clarify his position within the history of Taoism. Nevertheless, when Li Bo 李渤 produced the Zhenxi [zhuan] 真系[傳] ([Biographies of the] True Lineage; YJQQ 5) in 805, he placed Sun firmly within the Shangqing lineage as the eighth patriarch, between Lu Xiujing and Tao Hongjing. Sun's role in transmitting to Tao the many scriptures and materials bequeathed to him by Liu must have been highly regarded. Whether this estimation is correct or not would require a reappraisal not based on a Shangqing viewpoint.

MUGITANI Kunio

📖 Chen Guofu 1963, 44–46

※ Shangqing

suqi

宿啟

Nocturnal Invocation

The Nocturnal Invocation is a preparatory rite carried out on the evening of the first or second day of a three-day Offering (*jiao). Through it the construction of the altar is accomplished. The ancient version of the ritual is described by *Lu Xiujing (406–77) in his *Lingbao zhai shuo guangzhu jiefa dengzhu yuanyi* 靈寶齋說光燭戒罰燈祝願儀 (Explanation of Candle-Illumination, Precepts and Penalties, Lamps, Invocations, and Vows for Lingbao Retreats; CT 524) and in *j*. 48 of the *Wushang biyao* (Supreme Secret Essentials; Lagerwey 1981b, 150–52). The formalized version of the Tang and Song dynasties may be found in *j*. 16 of Jiang Shuyu's 蔣叔輿 (1162–1223) *Wushang huanglu dazhai licheng yi* (Standard Liturgies of the Supreme Great Yellow Register Retreat).

The Nocturnal Invocation comprises the ritual series Lighting the Incense Burner (*falu), Invocation of Masters and Saints (*qi shisheng* 啟師聖), Homage to the (Ten) Directions (*lifang* 禮方), Repentance (*chanhui), Three Invocations (*sanqi* 三啟), and Three Homages (*sanli* 三禮). After the five Authentic Scripts (*zhenwen* 真文) are placed in the five directions on the altar, the rite continues with the recitation of the ten precepts (*shijie* 十戒) and the formal assignment of tasks to each of the six priests or assistants: the high priest (*gaogong* 高功; see *daozhang), the chief cantor (*dujiang), the inspector of the Retreat (*jianzhai* 監齋), the keeper of scriptures (*shijing* 侍經), the keeper of incense (*shixiang* 侍香), and the keeper of lamps (*shideng* 侍燈).

As practiced in present-day Taiwan, the Nocturnal Invocation is characterized by the rite of Sealing the Altar (*jintan) and placing the five Authentic Scripts in the five directions. As the rite includes the presentation of a written memorial to the Celestial Worthy of Universal Transformation (*Puhua tianzun), a post-Song deity, it may be considered a new form that developed in early modern times.

MARUYAMA Hiroshi

📖 Lagerwey 1987c, 90–105; Matsumoto Kōichi 1983, 220; Ōfuchi Ninji 1983, 279–97

※ *jiao*

Taidan yinshu

太丹隱書

Concealed Writ of the Great Cinnabar [Palace]

The received version of the *Taidan yinshu*, one of the revealed *Shangqing texts, is found in the *Taiyi dijun taidan yinshu xuanjing* 太一帝君太丹隱書玄經 (Mysterious Scripture of the Concealed Writ of the Great Cinnabar [Palace] of the Great One and the Imperial Lord; CT 1330). Although the text has been reedited and is not in a good shape, it contains important materials often quoted in other Shangqing sources. Closely related to the *Ciyi jing*, it focuses on the Imperial Lord (Dijun 帝君) as the highest god, and deals with the regeneration of the adept with the help of the Great One (*Taiyi).

After an introduction on its own revelation, the *Taidan yinshu* describes the spiritual components of the human being, whose life is owed to the Original Father (Yuanfu 元父) and the Mysterious Mother (Xuanmu 玄母). The main gods mentioned in the text are the Imperial Lord, the Great One, the Emperors of the Nine Heavens (*jiutian), the Three Primes (*sanyuan) who live in the Cinnabar Fields (*dantian), the nine *hun* souls (see *hun and *po*) of the August Heaven (Huangtian 皇天) in the brain, the Five Gods (*wushen* 五神) of the registers of life (*shengji* 生籍), and the twenty-four corporeal spirits (see *bajing). Next the *Taidan yinshu* gives details on several meditation methods, such as those for visualizing the sun and the moon in various parts of the body, and those whose purpose is to have one's name inscribed in the registers of life. Some of the latter methods are performed under the aegis of the Imperial Lord, but they all require the mediation of the Five Gods of the registers: Taiyi 太一, the "master of the embryo," who dwells in the brain; Wuying 無英 who rules over the essence, in the liver; Baiyuan 白元 who presides over the *hun* and *po* souls, in the lungs; *Siming 司命, the Director of Destinies, who dwells in the sexual organs; and Taokang 桃康, the spirit of the Gate of the Vital Force (*mingmen) and the sexual energies, who lives in the lower Cinnabar Field during the day and in the brain, to the right of Taiyi, at night. These gods are responsible for one's destiny and length of life.

Then the text continues with descriptions of other meditation practices. One of them is the method of the Threefold Union (*sanhe* 三合), which is a variant of the meditation on the Three Ones (*sanyi; see *Suling jing). It consists of uniting with the gods of the three Cinnabar Fields, namely, Taiyi (in the brain), the god of the Crimson Palace (*jianggong* 絳宮, in the heart), and the god of the Yellow Court (*huangting* 黃庭, here in the lower Cinnabar Field). There follows an invocation to have one's faults forgiven by the Imperial Lord, and a method to expel the Three Corpses (*sanshi*; see **sanshi* and *jiuchong*) with the help of the Imperial Lord and the main divinities who preside over human life.

Finally, the *Taidan yinshu* contains an important method for untying the mortal knots of the embryo, which is often referred to in other texts and is also found in the *Taidan yinshu jie bao shi'er jiejie tujue* 太丹隱書解胞十二結節圖訣 (Illustrated Instructions for Untying the Twelve Embryonic Knots according to the Concealed Writ of the Great Cinnabar [Palace]; CT 1384). It explains that during the period of embryonic life the human being generates twelve mortal knots, four for each of the three main parts of the body. These knots must be untied to achieve liberation (Robinet 1993, 139–43).

Isabelle ROBINET

📖 Robinet 1984, 2: 151–62; Robinet 1993, 138–51

※ Shangqing

taiji

太極

Great Ultimate

See **wuji* and *taiji* 無極 · 太極.

taiji quan

太極拳

"boxing of the Great Ultimate"

The basic practice of *taiji quan* consists in performing a series of movements in an upright position; its particularity lies in the fact that the starting point is theoretically the same as the finishing point. *Taiji quan* shares this feature with the Taoist cosmic dances and step movements in rituals (see **bugang*). The number of movements varies according to the schools: only 36 in the more modern schools and 72, 105, 108, 172 or even 200 for the traditional ones. Each movement carries a name that evokes its martial application, the imitation of an animal posture, a mythological symbolism, or simply its description.

The movement series are completed by exercises with a partner using fixed steps (*tuishou* 推手) or free steps (*sanshou* 散手) meant to develop concentration, psychological and energetic qualities, and the martial application of the movement series. This technique is classified in the schools as "inner boxing" (*neijia quan* 內家拳) as opposed to "outer boxing" (*waijia quan* 外家拳). The martial force used is not muscular force (*li* 力), but an inner force (*jing* 勁) that comes from the flexibility of the body and the unobstructed circulation of the real pneuma (*zhenqi* 真氣) inside the body. *Taiji quan* shares this feature with the *neidan* practices: the adept's body is one with the *taiji (Great Ultimate) of the universe and functions according to the same principles.

The legendary origins of *taiji quan* can be traced back to *Zhang Sanfeng, an immortal said to have lived between the late Yuan and early Ming period. As far as the rare documents allow us to reconstruct its history, this martial technique developed from the seventeenth century onward within the Chen 陳 family of Chenjia gou 陳家溝 (Henan), whose first known member associated with *taiji quan* was Chen Wangting 陳王庭 (1600–1680). Chen was famous in Shandong province for his military arts; in 1641 he was the commander of the militia who defended the Wen 溫 district, but he retired in 1644, disillusioned by the collapse of the Ming dynasty. The technique was exported from the Chen family circle by a certain Yang Luchan 楊露禪 (1799–1872), who came from Yongnian 永年 (Hebei) and served the Chens. Yang spied every night on the practice of the Chen family and brought *taiji quan* to Beijing, where he was recommended to the Qing court to teach it. He created the Yang style of *taiji quan*, which became famous thanks to his three sons and his grandson, Yang Chengfu 楊澄甫, and which later spread throughout China, considered more as a gymnastic practice for health than a martial art. One of Yang Luchan's sons, Yang Fenghou 楊鳳候, handed this style down to Wu Quanyou 吳全佑 (1834–1902), whose son Wu Jianquan 吳鑒泉 (1870–1942) created the Wu style. Wu Yuxiang 武禹襄 (1812?–1880?), who had learned under Yang Luchan and Chen Qingping 陳青萍 (1795–1868), in turn handed it down to his nephew Li Yiyu 李亦畬 (1832–92), who transmitted it to Hao Weizhen 郝為真 (1849–1920) before it was finally passed on to Sun Lutang 孫祿堂 (1861–1932). Thus *taiji quan* includes not only the Yang style but also the Li, Hao, and Sun styles.

Catherine DESPEUX

📖 Despeux 1981b; Dufresne and Nguyen 1994; Engelhardt 1981; Vercammen 1991; Wile 1983; Wile 1996

※ *yangsheng*

Taiji tu

太極圖

Diagram of the Great Ultimate

Neo-Confucians adopted the *Taiji tu* after Zhou Dunyi's 周敦頤 (1017–73; SB 277–81) *Taiji tu shuo* 太極圖說 (Explanation of the Diagram of the Great Ultimate) was placed at the head of the Neo-Confucian system by Zhu Xi 朱熹 (1130–1200; SB 282–90). There is evidence, however, that this diagram originated in a Taoist milieu together with the *Xiantian tu* 先天圖 (Diagram of the Noumenal World) and the term **wuji* (Ultimateless, Infinite). Several sources in particular report that the *Taiji tu* derives from the *Wuji tu* 無極圖 (Diagram of the Ultimateless), which according to the *Fozu tongji* 佛祖統紀 (Comprehensive Chronicle of the Buddhas and Patriarchs; T. 2035) was transmitted by *Chen Tuan (ca. 920–89) in 971. Taoist sources mention a line of transmission that begins with Chen Tuan and his master Mayi daozhe 麻衣道者 (The Hemp-Clad Man of the Dao) and then divides in two branches, the first leading to Neo-Confucians, and the second either to numerologists or to **neidan* authors.

In Taoist texts, the *Taiji tu* appears in several variant forms but usually has a circular shape. It can be a blank white circle, a white circle with a dot in the center, two concentric circles (black or Yin outside, white or Yang inside), or four concentric circles (the three external ones half black and half white, and the inner one white). In some instances the *taiji* is also represented by alternating black and white dots arranged in an almond shape. The most common drawings, however, depict Yin containing Yang and vice versa; this image can mean that in the precosmic state Yin and Yang are joined together, but also hints at the mixing of Yin and Yang in the cosmos where everything encompasses its contrary, and the endless cycles of Yin and Yang or movement and quiescence (**dong* and *jing*) that engender each other. In some Thunder Rites (**leifa*), the *Taiji tu* represents thunder and lightning joined together. As for the well-known spiral form of the *taiji*, called the "fishlike form," it is not found in the *Daozang*; it seems to have first appeared in early Ming times and is common in **taiji quan* milieux. An intriguing issue is the occurrence of the *taiji* figure, especially the fishlike one, in Roman emblems dating from the late fourth or early fifth century CE (Monastra 1998).

As found in Taoist texts, the *taiji* diagrams often have titles indicating that the Great Ultimate is the origin of the world; *taiji* in fact is also the name of the last of the precosmic geneses called Five Greats (*wutai* 五太), just before

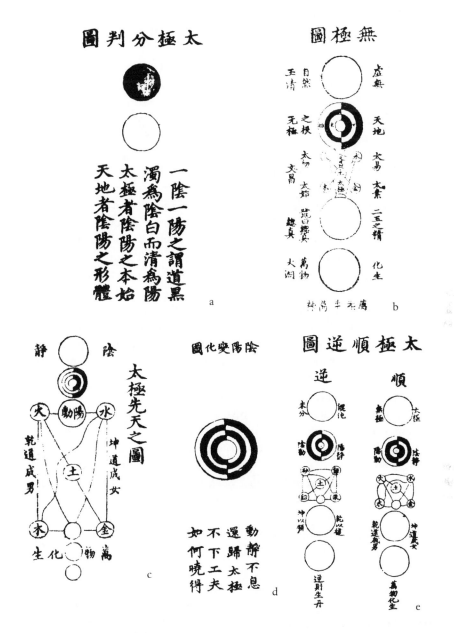

Fig. 70. Representations of the *Taiji tu* (Diagram of the Great Ultimate) and the *Wuji tu* 無極 圖 (Diagram of the Ultimateless). (a) "Division of the Great Ultimate" ("Taiji fenpan tu"), in *Jindan dayao tu* 金丹大要圖 (Great Essentials of the Golden Elixir: Diagrams; CT 1068), 1a. (b) "Diagram of the Ultimateless" ("Wuji tu"), in *Wenchang dadong xianjing zhu* 文昌大洞仙經注 (Commentary to the Immortal Scripture of the Great Cavern by Wenchang; CT 103), 1.9a. (c) "Diagram of the Great Ultimate Before Heaven" ("Taiji xiantian zhi tu"), in *Zhenyuan miaojing tu* 真元妙經圖 (Wondrous Scripture and Diagrams of Zhenyuan; CT 437), 3b. (d) "Diagram of the Transformations of Yin and Yang" ("Yinyang bianhua tu"), in *Daofa xinchuan* 道法心傳 (Heart-to-Heart Transmission of Taoist Rites; CT 1253), 31b. (e) "Diagram of the Continuation and Inversion of the Great Ultimate" ("Taiji shunni tu"), in *Jindan dayao tu*, 3a.

the One divides into the Two (see *COSMOGONY). These diagrams are variously called "The Great Ultimate Encompasses the Three in One" ("Taiji hansan wei yi" 太極函三為一), "The Great Ultimate Generates the Two Principles" ("Taiji sheng liangyi" 太極生兩儀), "The Transformation of the Great Ultimate" ("Taiji bianhua" 太極變化), or "The Division of the Great Ultimate" ("Taiji fenpan tu" 太極分判圖; see fig. 70(a)). Other titles allude to the unity expressed by the notion of Great Ultimate, e.g., "The Great Ultimate Pervades the One" ("Taiji guanyi" 太極貫一). The representations with alternating black and white circles are called "Diagram of the Ultimateless" ("Wuji tu"; fig. 70(b)), "Diagram of the Great Ultimate Before Heaven" ("Taiji xiantian zhi tu" 太極先天之圖; fig. 70(c)), "Diagram of the Transformations of Yin and Yang" ("Yinyang bianhua tu" 陰陽變化圖; fig. 70(d)), or "Diagram of the Reciprocal Operation of Thunder and Lightning" ("Leiting huyong tu" 雷霆互用圖).

The Taoist commentaries and interpretations of the *Taiji tu* differ from the one given by Zhou Dunyi. Those based on *neidan* doctrines distinguish between the "Great Ultimate Before Heaven" and the "Great Ultimate After Heaven," and refer to the normal cosmogonic sequence and its inversion through the alchemical process. The normal sequence (called *shun* 順 or "continuation") goes from top to bottom and represents the generation of the world, while the inverted sequence (*ni* 逆 or "inversion") goes from bottom to top and represents the generation of the inner elixir. In a diagram found in the *Jindan dayao* (*Tu* 圖; CT 1068, 3a; fig. 70(e)), in particular, the top blank circle represents the *wuji* and *taiji* in the diagram of the normal cosmogonic order, but stands for "Chaos still undivided" (*hundun wei fen* 混沌未分) in the diagram of the inverted sequence. In this diagram, moreover, Yang is placed on the right and is linked to quiescence, while Yin is on the left and is related to movement, a reversal of their positions in the diagram of the normal cosmogonic order.

Isabelle ROBINET

📖 Fung Yu-lan 1952–53, 2: 434–76; Li Shen 1991; Li Yuanguo 1987, 95–105; Li Yuanguo 1990; Needham 1956, 460–72; Robinet 1990b; Rong Zhaozu 1994; Tu Wei-ming 1987b; Yang Guanghui and Chen Hanming 1995, 211–22

※ Chen Tuan; *wuji* and *taiji*; *xiantian* and *houtian*; COSMOLOGY; COSMOGONY

taiping

太平

Great Peace; Great Equality

The notion of *taiping* refers to the stability of social life. Few pre-Han sources mention this term besides the *Zhuangzi* (*j.* 13), where it denotes the condition of training the self and relying on the spontaneous workings of Heaven. From the Han period onward, the notion of *taiping* became widespread. It was adopted by *Huang-Lao thought and was formalized by Dong Zhongshu 董仲舒 (ca. 195–115 BCE) into the theory of the mutual relationship between Heaven and humanity. Examples of the use of the term *taiping* are also found in the Han "weft" texts (*weishu* 緯書; see *TAOISM AND THE APOCRYPHA).

The main Han source on the notion of *taiping* is the *Taiping jing* (Scripture of Great Peace). This work teaches that while the Central Harmony (*zhonghe* 中和) of Yin and Yang nourishes all beings and brings contentment to the people, the emperor is responsible for realizing this condition within society. In the golden times of high antiquity, the Original Pneuma (*yuanqi*) that nourishes all beings in Heaven and on Earth circulated within people and supported life. This state of things was lost when the Original Pneuma became sullied, because of faults committed by people in claiming exclusive possession of Dao and *de (virtue) and in accumulating riches. People of later ages inherit responsibility for these faults, and their accumulation leads to natural disasters, wars, and epidemics at a social level, and to misfortune for individuals and their households. This is known as "inherited burden" (*chengfu). If the emperor reestablishes the "society of Great Peace," however, the chains of "inherited burden" will be broken, wise men will receive appointment in the government, and moral reform and welfare will be encouraged.

Some literati of the first two centuries CE, such as Wang Fu 王符 (78–163 CE), regarded the politics of their time as having reached the preliminary stage of "advancing to peace" (*shengping* 升平) rather than Great Peace itself, and saw moral reform, welfare, and the promotion of the wise as the best ways to realize Great Peace. He Xiu 何休 (129–82 CE) emphasized an evolutionary process based on the harmony of Yin and Yang, moving from "decline and disorder" (*shuailuan* 衰亂) through "advancing to peace" and finally to Great Peace, and to this end sought to reestablish the rites (*li* 禮) and other institutions as they were supposed to have been practiced during the Spring and Autumn period (770–476 BCE).

These and related notions were incorporated into Taoism. The *Xiang'er commentary to the *Daode jing*, a work produced by the Way of the Celestial Masters (*Tianshi dao), emphasizes the need for meditating on the Dao in order to manifest the Great Peace. During the Six Dynasties, with the growth of eschatological thought, some saw the Great Peace as an ideal condition beyond the human world, while others believed that Great Peace would be brought into human society by the Imperial Lord of the Golden Portal (*Jinque dijun). In the early sixth century, there was a belief that the Moon-Bright Lad (Yueguang tongzi 月光童子) had appeared and would bring about the state of Great Peace among the people (see Zürcher 1982). Similar ideas have continued to influence political ideologies in China until recent times. *Taiping*, in particular, was a central notion used in the revival of Gongyang Learning (*Gongyang xue* 公羊學) at the end of the Qing period, and in the Taiping rebellion of the nineteenth century.

YAMADA Toshiaki

   Eichhorn 1957; Hendrischke 1992; Pokora 1961; Qing Xitai 1994, 2: 320–23; Seidel 1969, passim; Seidel 1987d

※ TAOISM AND THE STATE

Taiping jing

太平經

Scripture of Great Peace

The *Taiping jing* is one of the earliest Taoist scriptures, parts of which probably derive from the Later Han dynasty, and possibly even earlier. However, as yet unresolved textual problems have prevented the dating of the *Taiping jing* being established with certainty. Equally, although there is consensus that the text does not derive from one hand, there is, as yet, no agreement on precisely which parts of the *Taiping jing* belong with which other parts. The original appears to have had 170 chapters and was also subdivided, in parallel, into 366 sections.

   The *Taiping jing* survives in two forms in the *Daozang*. First, fifty-seven chapters from the original 170 are found under the title *Taiping jing* (CT 1101). Secondly, excerpts from the whole make up the *Taiping jingchao* 太平經鈔 (Excerpts from the Scripture of Great Peace; CT 1101, j. 1), although not every chapter is represented in this selection. This *Taiping jingchao* comes from the hand of *Lüqiu Fangyuan, a Taoist priest who received the registers on

Mount Tiantai (*Tiantai shan, Zhejiang) and underwent transformation in 902. These two works, with the addition of a few citations from the text not found in either, form the basis for the modern collated version of the *Taiping jing* edited by Wang Ming and published under the title *Taiping jing hejiao* 太 平經合校 (Wang Ming 1960). It is also fortunate that a table of contents for the *Taiping jing* survives in a *Dunhuang manuscript (S. 4226) which indicates that the chapter titles of the modern text differ in only minor ways from those current at the end of the sixth century.

It has long been noted that two texts presented to the throne at the end of the first century BCE and in the mid-second century CE may be related to the *Taiping jing*. The first text was called *Tianguan li baoyuan taiping jing* 天官歷 包元太平經 (Scripture of Great Peace that Protects the Mandate According to the Calendar of Heaven's Official, although this may in fact be the names of two texts). It was presented by a Gan Zhongke 甘忠可 from Qi 齊 (Shandong), an area long associated with magical and religious innovation, in the reign of Han Chengdi (r. 33–7 BCE). The second was called *Taiping qingling shu* 太平青領書 (Book of Great Peace with Headings Written in Blue) which was presented to Han Shundi (r. 125–144 CE) by Gong Song 宮嵩 who had received it from his teacher *Gan Ji; it was re-presented to Han Huandi (r. 146–168 CE) in 166 by Xiang Kai 襄楷.

The *Taiping jing* that we know today, incomplete as it certainly is, remains one of the longest Taoist scriptures. It is also one of the most varied in terms of the form that the writing takes. Much of the book is written as dialogue with the largest stratum of text relating conversations between a Heavenly or Celestial Master (*tianshi* 天師) and six Realized Men (*zhenren* 真人). In this part, the language of the text is not concise and rather repetitive, giving the impression that the Realized Men are not particularly competent students. Within this first stratum, a short but important text, under the title "Declaration of the [Celestial] Master" ("Shice wen" 師策文; Wang Ming 1960, 62) is found. It is notable for the obvious importance the authors of *Taiping jing* gave it, because they provide instructions on how it should be interpreted. It may, therefore, predate the rest of the text. In a second much smaller stratum the position of the Celestial Master is taken by a Celestial Lord (Tianjun 天君) and the mode of expression is somewhat more terse. Chapters in the form of charts, diagrams and *fuwen* 複文, an unintelligible script that appears to be based on the repetition of various component parts of standard characters, are also present.

The doctrine of the *Taiping jing* is based on the idea, already present in Warring States texts, that an era of Great Peace (*taiping*) will descend on the empire if its governance is based on returning to the Dao. Such a state existed in High Antiquity (*shanggu* 上古) but was lost as government meddled and society declined into decadence. To regain Great Peace the ruler should follow the dictates of a Celestial Book (*tianshu* 天書) possessed by the Celestial Master and which he instructs the Realized Men to pass on to a ruler of high virtue. The scripture teaches that the ruler should make sure all beings are in their proper place and that there is harmony between the parallel tripartite divisions of the cosmos: Yin, Yang, and the Central Harmony (*zhonghe* 中和); Heaven, Earth, and Humanity; the ruler, his ministers, and the people; and so forth. The *Taiping jing* thus promised salvation for the society.

However, one of the most characteristic features of the *Taiping jing* is the prevalence of an idea that focused directly on the individual: *chengfu* or "inherited burden." *Chengfu* refers to a system whereby the effects of transgressions are passed from one generation to the next—neatly explaining the phenomenon, troublesome for religions in many cultures, of good people suffering, and evil prospering. At the same time the text warns that individual behavior must be rectified if calamities are not to be visited on future generations by the same mechanism. In other words, the *Taiping jing* proclaims for itself the powerful and central role of breaking the nexus between the transgressions of past generations and fate of future generations, asserting its own program of reform as the key to a proper society. If this reform is realized, the government and the people will not act or think in ways that generate *chengfu*. In addition, the text—in some parts—stresses the importance of individual meditational practice in the form of *shouyi* (guarding the One), as a way of getting rid of *chengfu*. Clearly related to *baoyi* 抱一 (embracing the One) meditation, *shouyi* also leads to the lengthening of life. The distinction here between social and meditational mechanisms for the eradication of *chengfu* has been interpreted by at least one scholar as indicating different strata of text.

One of the characteristic ways in which the effects of *chengfu* are manifest is in the form of disease, and the *Taiping jing* is very concerned with healing. In addition to the use of *shouyi* to rid the body of diseases, it also discusses medicinal plants, the use of talismans (*FU), acupuncture and related therapies, breathing practices, and music as healing methods.

Benjamin PENNY

📖 Espesset 2002; Fukui Kōjun 1958, 214–55; Hachiya Kunio 1983; Harada Jirō 1984; Kaltenmark 1979b; Kamitsuka Yoshiko 1999, 301–60; Kandel 1979; Kusuyama Haruki 1983c; Mansvelt Beck 1980; Ōfuchi Ninji 1978–79, 1: 327–29 (crit. notes on the Dunhuang ms.) and 2: 703–12 (reprod. of the Dunhuang ms.); Ōfuchi Ninji 1991, 79–136; Ōfuchi Ninji 1997, 507–56; Penny 1990; Peterson J. O. 1989–90; Seidel 1983a, 335–40; Takahashi Tadahiko 1984; Takahashi Tadahiko 1986; Takahashi Tadahiko 1988; Wang Ming 1960 (crit. ed.); Wang Ming 1984c; Wang Ming 1984d; Yoshioka Yoshitoyo 1970b; Yoshioka Yoshitoyo 1976a, 315–51

※ *taiping*; Yellow Turbans

Taiqing

太清

Great Clarity

As shown by passages of the *Zhuangzi (Watson 1968, 356), the *Huainan zi (Robinet 1993, 42), and other early texts, the term *taiqing* originally denoted the inner spiritual state of the Taoist adept. From the third or fourth century on, it also came to designate the Heaven that grants revelation of alchemical doctrines and scriptures, and by extension the main tradition of early *waidan*. When, at the beginning of the sixth century, the Taoist Canon was expanded with the addition of the Four Supplements (*sifu* 四輔; see *DAOZANG AND SUBSIDIARY COMPILATIONS), one of them was entitled "Taiqing" and devoted to *waidan* and related texts.

In chapter 4 of his *Baopu zi (ca. 317; trans. Ware 1966, 69–70, 75–82, and 89–91), *Ge Hong quotes from, or summarizes, three scriptures that formed the core of the Taiqing tradition: the *Taiqing jing (Scripture of Great Clarity), the *Jiudan jing (Scripture of the Nine Elixirs), and the *Jinye jing (Scripture of the Golden Liquor). These writings are entirely or partially preserved in the present Taoist Canon (see under the respective entries). Another extant early text, the *Sanshiliu shuifa (Methods of the Thirty-Six Aqueous Solutions), is quoted both by Ge Hong and in the received versions of the three main Taiqing writings.

According to Ge Hong and other sources, the Taiqing corpus originated at the end of the second century with revelations obtained by *Zuo Ci. Ge Hong's work shows how the alchemical disciplines interacted with the local practices of Jiangnan, especially those involving the use of talismans and the ingestion of herbal drugs for exorcistic and therapeutic purposes. The Taiqing elixirs shared with them the power of keeping away the demons and harmful spirits that cause illnesses. Other purposes of ingesting the elixirs in the Taiqing tradition include achieving immortality, receiving protection from major and minor deities, and acquiring magical powers. Consistent with this background, the alchemical process is described in the Taiqing sources as a sequence of ritual actions marked by invocations and offerings to divine beings. Its main stages are the transmission from master to disciple, the establishment of the ritual area, the choice of an auspicious time, the compounding of the elixir, its offering to the gods, and its ingestion.

No Taiqing source, on the other hand, describes the alchemical process using the patterns, imagery, and language of Chinese cosmology and its system of correspondences. The few instances of methods related to simple cosmological configurations—e.g., those based on five ingredients, related to the *wuxing*—are not typical of the tradition as a whole, whose main methods are characterized by the use of a large number of ingredients with no clear relation to cosmological principles. Indeed, the cosmological system at the basis of Taiqing alchemy is not explicitly described in its sources; we only get glimpses of it through the prominence assigned to the Mud of the Six-and-One (*liuyi ni*), a compound used to lute the crucible. Its seven ingredients represent to the seven stages of cosmogony described in some pre-Han and Han sources.

The Taiqing tradition progressively declined from the Tang period, paralleling the rise in importance of the *Zhouyi cantong qi*. No original Taiqing text appears to have been written after the Six Dynasties. The two main Tang works associated with this tradition—the *Taiqing danjing yaojue* (Essential Instructions from the Scripture of the Elixirs of Great Clarity) and the *Taiqing shibi ji* (Records of the Stone Wall of Great Clarity)—consist of selections from expanded versions of the original *Taiqing qing* compiled during the Six Dynasties and Tang periods.

Fabrizio PREGADIO

📖 Campany 2002, 31–47; Chen Guofu 1963, 89–98; Pregadio 1991; Pregadio 2006b

※ *waidan*; for other related entries see the Synoptic Table of Contents, sec. IV.3 ("Alchemy: Taiqing")

Taiqing danjing yaojue

太清丹經要訣

Essential Instructions from the Scripture of the
Elixirs of Great Clarity

Along with the *Taiqing shibi ji* (Records of the Stone Wall of Great Clarity), the *Taiqing danjing yaojue* (YJQQ 71) is one of two extant Tang anthologies of the *Taiqing tradition. Both works were compiled by drawing on the expanded versions of the *Taiqing jing* (Scripture of Great Clarity) that circulated during the Six Dynasties. The text was compiled by *Sun Simiao (fl. 673), who states in a preface that he selected recipes that gave clear directions and that he had personally tested.

Using the terse language typical of the Taiqing texts, the *Danjing yaojue* describes about thirty methods. They are introduced by three lists of synonyms of names of elixirs that are closely related to those found in the *Taiqing shibi ji* and the *Shiyao erya* (Synonymic Dictionary of Mineral Materia Medica). Among the recipes is a method for making the Mud of the Six-and-One (*liuyi ni*) similar to the one given in another extant Taiqing text, the *Jiudan jing* (Scripture of the Nine Elixirs), but also including details on each of the seven ingredients (3b–7b). The *Taiqing danjing yaojue*, moreover, is one of three Taiqing sources that describe the preparation of a pellet used to keep away demons during the compounding of the elixirs (27a). The other two methods are in the *Taiqing jing tianshi koujue* 太清經天師口訣 (CT 883, 14a–b) and the *Huangdi jiuding shendan jingjue* 黃帝九鼎神丹經訣 (CT 885, 5.9a–10a, containing the reproduction of an identically-named talisman; see fig. 5(d)).

Fabrizio PREGADIO

📖 Meng Naichang 1993a, 48–49; Needham 1976, 132–38; Pregadio 2006b, 59–61; Sivin 1968 (trans.)

※ Sun Simiao; *Taiqing jing*; *waidan*; Taiqing

Taiqing gong

太清宮

Palace of Great Clarity (1. Bozhou, Henan; 2. Chang'an)

Besides several others, there were two compounds called Taiqing gong that were especially important in Tang China. The older was an abbey at Bozhou 亳州 (present-day Luyi 鹿邑, Henan) that purportedly rested on the site of Laozi's birthplace and had been a place of veneration for the deity since the second century. Xuanzong (r. 712–56) bestowed the title Taiqing gong on it in 742. Taiqing 太清 or Great Clarity was the lowest of three celestial regions beneath the *Daluo tian* (Great Canopy Heaven) where Taoist deities resided and Laozi presided (see *sanqing*). The emperor gave it the status of Palace (*gong* 宮) because Laozi was a celestial ruler and had revealed the location of a statue of himself to the emperor. The complex at Bozhou was the recipient of great patronage from the throne throughout the Tang dynasty. By the late ninth century it encompassed seven hundred *jian* 間 (an architectural unit of measure defined as the space between four pillars) and one thousand trees.

The second Taiqing gong was an abbey established by Xuanzong in Chang'an, the capital of the Tang dynasty. The emperor originally founded it by converting his former mansion into an ancestral shrine (*miao* 廟) in 740 because the reigning family claimed Laozi as an ancestor. He had ancestral rites performed there, not only to Laozi, but also to deceased Tang emperors whose spirit tablets were installed in the shrine. Xuanzong had statues of Laozi, four leading Taoist philosophers of the pre-Han epoch—including *Zhuangzi and *Liezi—as well as Confucius, apparently because tradition had it that Confucius visited Laozi to learn about rites (the temple at Bozhou must also have served as a site for imperial ancestral rites since in contained statues or images of previous Tang emperors). In 743 the emperor changed the name of the Chang'an's sanctuary to Taiqing gong.

Both abbeys became part of an empire-wide system of abbeys dedicated to Laozi when Xuanzong ordered the establishment of abbeys for the god in all 320 prefectures of the empire during 742. The primary reason for that enactment was to promote the Tang's Taoist ideology. By fostering Laozi's cult as a state religion the emperor was propagating the notion that peace and prosperity of the dynasty, state, and its citizens depended on the spiritual protection and blessing of the deity. According to ancient Chinese belief, ancestors in the afterlife always ensured the welfare of their living descendants as long as the latter maintained sacrifices and worshipped their forbears.

The political-religious significance of the Taiqing gong in Chang'an was manifest first in its iconography. Xuanzong had statues of himself as well as of his most important ministers installed there. His successors, Suzong (r. 756–62) and Dezong (r. 779–805), followed suit and had images of themselves erected in the abbey, but apparently not for their eminent officials. Second, Xuanzong appointed one of his highest ranking ministers to the post of Commissioner for the Taiqing gong, and it became the habit of later Tang emperors to confer the title on their most important officials. The Taiqing gong in Chang'an was no doubt demolished or dismantled in 904 along with the rest of the city on the orders of a warlord, but that in Bozhou survived into the Song dynasty along with a copy of the Taoist Canon.

Charles D. BENN

📖 Benn 1977, 185–237; Ding Huang 1979–80; Qing Xitai 1994, 4: 255–57; Schafer 1987

❋ TEMPLES AND SHRINES

Taiqing jing

太清經

Scripture of Great Clarity

The now-lost *Taiqing jing* was the central scripture of the early *Taiqing tradi-tion of *waidan*. The text was based on the method for making the Elixir of Great Clarity (*taiqing dan* 太清丹), which according to *Ge Hong's summary in his *Baopu zi* (trans. Ware 1966, 82–83) was obtained in nine cycles of heat-ing; the final addition of cinnabar transmuted it into a powerful Reverted Elixir (*huandan*). Ge Hong also provides details on the revelation of the text and on a rite performed after the compounding to offer the elixir to several gods.

The scripture gave life to a vast textual tradition: not only was it progres-sively expanded into the sixty-two chapter version included in the Song Taoist Canon (see *Daozang quejing mulu*, 2.1b), but around 500 CE it also gave its name to one of the Four Supplements (*sifu* 四輔) of the Taoist Canon (see *DAOZANG AND SUBSIDIARY COMPILATIONS). The *Taiqing jing tianshi koujue* 太清經天師口訣 (Oral Instructions of the Celestial Master on the Scripture of Great Clarity; CT 883) is the text closest to the original scripture among the works once included in this sizeable body of literature. After an introduction on the ceremony of transmission, this work contains two texts unrelated to each other. The first, entitled "Taiqing shendan jingjue" 太清神丹經訣 (In-structions on the Scripture of the Divine Elixir of Great Clarity, 1b–4b), quotes and comments on several passages of the original *Taiqing jing*. The second, entitled "Chisong zi zhouhou yaojue" 赤松子肘後藥訣 (Instructions on Medicines to Keep at Hand by Master Red-Pine, 4b–15b), is cast as a dialogue during which *Chisong zi transmits the methods of the Three Powders and the Five Salves (*sansan wugao* 三散五膏) to Yunyang zi 雲陽子. Parts of both texts are reproduced in the seventh-century commentary to the *Jiudan jing* with the title of the present version, showing that they were already part of a single work by the end of the Six Dynasties or the first decades of the Tang (see *Huangdi jiuding shendan jingjue* 黃帝九鼎神丹經訣; CT 885, 5.10a and 17.4b–5a).

The "Taiqing shendan jingjue" does not make it possible to fully recon-struct the method of the Elixir of Great Clarity, which appears to have been based on mercury. The only parts of the process described in detail are those concerned with the ceremony of transmission (1a–b) and the preparation of the crucible (3a–b; see under *fu). The section on transmission mentions the gages offered by the disciple to his master—gold, silver, cotton, and silk—and describes the penalties facing those who carelessly disclose the practices: failure in any undertaking, decrease of life span, and punishment of their ancestors in the Mysterious Metropolis (Xuandu 玄都). The section on the crucible states that the vessel should be used to compound the Elixir of the Great Clarity, the Nine Elixirs (jiudan 九丹), the Golden Liquor (*jinye), and the *Langgan, i.e., all the main elixirs of the early Taiqing tradition.

Fabrizio PREGADIO

📖 Pregadio 1991, 571–74; Pregadio 2006b, 54–55, 108–10

※ waidan; Taiqing

Taiqing shibi ji

太清石壁記

Records of the Stone Wall of Great Clarity

The *Taiqing shibi ji* is a collection of *waidan methods followed by sections dealing with the ingestion of elixirs. It was edited in three chapters during the Qianyuan period (758–59) of the Tang by an anonymous officer of Jianzhou 劍州 (Sichuan) on the basis of an earlier version ascribed to *Su Yuanming (or Su Yuanlang 蘇元郎; Xin Tangshu, 59.5a). The present version (CT 881) is attributed to a Chuze xiansheng 楚澤先生 (Elder of the Moorlands of Chu).

The text derives from the corpus of writings that developed around the *Taiqing jing (Scripture of Great Clarity) during the Six Dynasties. It contains more than sixty recipes, often followed by details of their medical properties. The third juan is mainly concerned with rules for the ingestion of the elixirs and descriptions of their effects. Other sections of particular interest contain lists of auspicious and inauspicious days for compounding the elixir (1.4a–b), directions for making the furnace and the crucible (1.14a–b), and the method for an "Inner Elixir" (neidan 內丹) composed of mineral substances (2.7b–8a). Many alternative names for the elixirs, usually listed together with their recipes, are the same as those given in a closely related text belonging to the Taiqing corpus, *Sun Simiao's *Taiqing danjing yaojue. The same synonyms are also found in the *Shiyao erya (2.3b and 2.7a), which mentions both a Shibi ji and a Chuze jing 楚澤經 (Scripture of the Moorlands of Chu).

Fabrizio PREGADIO

📖 Meng Naichang 1993a, 46–48; Needham 1974, 282–94 passim; Pregadio 2006b, 59–61; Sivin 1968, 76–79 and 258–59

※ *waidan*; *Taiqing jing*; Taiqing

Taishan

泰山

Mount Tai (Shandong)

As the most revered of the Five Peaks (*wuyue*), Mount Tai or the Eastern Peak is one of the centers of Chinese sacred geography. In contrast to other sacred mountains, which are actually whole ranges with many summits and valleys, Mount Tai is really one impressive peak (1545 m high) visible from the surrounding plains. For the most part, the pilgrimage trail consists of a single staircase. Mount Tai is mentioned in the earliest Chinese written records and has ever since been included in countless classical and vernacular proverbs and locutions; together with the Yellow River, it is a crucial anchor of Chinese cultural identity. Like all mountains, Mount Tai is revered for stabilizing or maintaining (*zhen* 鎮) the country, and small stones named after it (the *Taishan shigandang* 泰山石敢當) are placed in small roadside shrines throughout China.

Mount Tai also enjoyed a privileged relationship with the imperial court. Emperors with exceptional accomplishments were required to climb the mountain and proclaim their merit to Heaven in the *feng* 封 ritual. This was followed by another ritual, the *shan* 禪, which took place on a small hill nearby. These illustrious but rarely performed rituals claimed the greatest antiquity but were actually foreshadowed by the visit of Qin Shi huangdi (219 BCE) and created by Han Wudi (110 BCE). The *feng* and *shan* rituals reasserted the imperial monopoly on the cult to the mountain god. Yet the popular cult to the god of Mount Tai and the pilgrimage to the mountain are equally ancient. During the Han, and probably before, it was believed that the souls of the dead would rest under Mount Tai, and sick people would come to the mountain to beg for a longer life span.

The beliefs connecting Mount Tai with the realm of the dead, and therefore with the possibility of being removed, temporarily or eternally, from the registers of death (*siji* 死籍), developed in many directions. Buddhism and Taoism both charged *Dongyue dadi, the god of Mount Tai, with the judgement of souls, and temples of his cult multiplied after the tenth century. The same beliefs inspired a pilgrimage that became China's grandest.

Starting from the official temple, the Daimiao 岱廟 (Shrine of Mount Tai, which like all hermitages on the mountain, has been managed by *Quanzhen clerics since the 1240s) in the city of Tai'an 泰安, the pilgrimage trail leads up the mountain in a few hours' arduous climb. Pilgrims often climbed at night to see the sun rise on the summit. Unlike many other mountains, pilgrims visited Mount Tai all year round, but since the Ming period such activity has been particularly intense in the fourth lunar month for the birthday of *Bixia yuanjun (Original Princess of the Jasper Mist), the daughter of the mountain god. Pilgrims, mostly organized in associations, arrived by the hundreds of thousands every year in Ming and Qing times, and continue to do so to this day. The incense tax levied on all pilgrims was then a major revenue for the governor of Shandong province. Pilgrims with all sorts of intentions were moved to visit the Eastern Peak, from merry women-only religious associations to the desperate who came to the holy mountain ready to commit ritual sacrifice or suicide.

Vincent GOOSSAERT

📖 Boltz J. M. 1987a, 105–7; Chavannes 1910b; Geil 1926, 1–116; Idema 1997; Kroll 1983; Liu Hui 1994

※ Dongyue dadi; *wuyue*; TAOIST SACRED SITES

Taishang ganying pian

太上感應篇

Folios of the Most High on Retribution

The *Taishang ganying pian* is a short anonymous tract (about 1,275 characters), probably composed in the second half of the Northern Song dynasty and traditionally regarded as the first and most paradigmatic morality book (*shanshu*). While closely associated with Taoism—it has been generally interpreted as the words of Laozi and included in several Taoist Canons—the *Ganying pian* also draws on sources beyond Taoism to present a message geared to a broad audience. It became a staple of moral education and popular religion by virtue of its pithy depiction of the cosmic laws of retribution by which the good and evil that people do generate positive or negative consequences for their well-being, length of life, spiritual attainments, and future generations. The opening lines, the first of which is taken from the *Zuozhuan* 左傳 (Commentary of Zuo; third century BCE), became a familiar proverb in traditional

Chinese culture: "Calamity and fortune have no gates (not fixed or fated), rather people themselves summon them; retribution for good and evil is like the shadow that follows the form."

The *Ganying pian* was endlessly reprinted in cheap mass-produced pamphlets as well as lavishly illustrated multivolume editions with commentary. The oldest extant copies, printed one- and eight-*juan* Yuan dynasty editions (one dated 1296), are housed in the Beijing National Library. The text is first listed in the *Bishu sheng xubian dao siku queshu mu* 祕書省續編到四庫書目 (Imperial Library's Supplementary Catalogue of Books Missing from the Four Repositories; 1145), and then in the bibliographic treatise of the *Songshi* (History of the Song; van der Loon 1984, 89). Scholars associate the emergence of the *Ganying pian* and texts like it with two historical developments, namely, the maturing relationship of Taoism and local cults seen in the Tang dynasty, which led to revelations from a variety of deities recasting older teachings, and Taoist sectarian developments during the political upheavals of the Song, which emphasized internal forms of self-cultivation linked to inner alchemy (*neidan) and personal morality by using more universal formulations that left room for Buddhist and Confucian elements.

The notion of retribution. The *Ganying pian* composed a fresh understanding of moral retribution by combining several ideas, most basic of which was the ancient conviction that heaven responds (*ganying* 感應) to the morality of human action. Indebted to a discussion in *Ge Hong's *Baopu zi (trans. Ware 1966, 66–67, 115–19), the *Ganying pian* asserted the importance of renouncing evil and accumulating virtue to attain immortality, with 300 good deeds needed to become an earthly transcendent (*dixian* 地仙) and 1,200 to become a celestial transcendent (*tianxian* 天仙). Yet it also made clear that moral action brings divine protection and good fortune in this life too, while a notion of repentance borrowed from the Buddhist *Dhammapada* enabled it to argue that evil can always be redressed by good. The text describes the spiritual overseers of human deeds: in the heavens the constellation of the Three Terraces (*santai* 三台, three pairs of stars in *Ursa Major*; see fig. 23), including the Star Lords of the Northern Dipper (*Beidou xingjun) and the Director of Destinies (*Siming); on a social plane, the domestically-positioned Stove God (*Zaoshen) who reports each month; and within the individual, the Three Corpses (*sanshi*; see *sanshi and *jiuchong*) who are eager to report misdeeds that hasten their own liberation from the body at death. Echoing the *Baopu zi* system, the heavenly overseers can reduce one's life span by one hundred-day units (*suan* 算) or twelve-year units (*ji* 紀). Lists of good and evil deeds make clear that scale and intentionality make a difference, while traditional taboos against acts of disrespect to the gods are as problematic as wickedness to other living beings.

Editions, commentaries, and translations. The earliest known edition of the *Ganying pian* was transmitted with commentary by one Li Changling 李昌齡 about 1165. There is some scholarly consensus that Li Changling was Li Shi 李 石 (?–ca. 1182) of Sichuan, a *jinshi* degree-holder, who gives an autobiographical account in another work, *Leshan lu* 樂善錄 (Records of a Love of Virtue), of how he published the *Ganying pian*. Most scholars disregard the traditional attribution to a prominent Aid to the Censor-in-chief under the Northern Song with the same name (938–1008). Early editions of the *Ganying pian* also include hymns by the Celestial Master of Empty Quiescence (Xujing tianshi 虛靖天師), a title conferred on the *Zhengyi Celestial Master, *Zhang Jixian (1092–1126), by Song Huizong (r. 1100–1125) in 1105. A century later, the *Ganying pian* was specially published and distributed by order of Song Lizong (r. 1224–64), probably the edition in which Zheng Qingzhi's 鄭清之 (1176–1251; SB 156–63) praise poems were added to Li's commentary to form the eight-*juan* edition, still extant, which was later subdivided into thirty *juan* in the Ming dynasty Taoist Canon (CT 1167). The Canon edition is accompanied by numerous prefaces dating from 1231 to 1349, and a section entitled "Jishu lingyan" 紀述靈驗 (Chronicle of Numinous Efficacy; elsewhere "Lingyan ji" 靈驗記) where, in a style ultimately derived from Buddhist treatments of the *Lotus* and *Diamond sūtras* among others, stories give proof of the efficacy of devotion to the tract.

To accumulate merit, fulfill vows, or perform a recognizably moral service, various eminent figures republished the *Ganying pian* with commentaries. While Li Changling stressed the spirit of the Three Teachings (Confucianism, Taoism, and Buddhism), scholar-officials like Zhen Dexiu 真德秀 (1178–1235), Hui Dong 惠棟 (1697–1758; ECCP 357–58) and Yu Yue 俞樾 (1821–1906; ECCP 944–45), among others, emphasized its Confucian morality for the masses. It was often accompanied by the *Taiwei xianjun gongguo ge* 太微仙君功過格 (Ledger of Merit and Demerit of the Immortal Lord of Great Tenuity; CT 186), which was written about 1171 by a Taoist master of *Xu Xun's sect and became a model for other ledgers in Taoist, Buddhist, and Neo-Confucian circles. The *Ganying pian* was also closely associated with the *Yinzhi wen* 陰騭文 (Essay on Secret Virtue; trans. Suzuki and Carus 1906b, and Kleeman 1996, 70–71), a rather similar tract ascribed to the deity *Wenchang. As distribution of the *Ganying pian*, like all morality books, was thought to be a virtue that earned one merit, large and small donations toward its printing were conventional ways of doing good. It is still distributed free in many temples.

There are many translations of the *Ganying pian* into Western languages, especially English, and some include the illustrated stories that often dressed it up. An abridged edition of Huang Zhengyuan's 黃正元 *Taishang ganying pian tushuo* 太上感應篇圖說 (Illustrated Explanations on the Folios of the Most

High on Retribution; 1755; see Bell 1996b), perhaps the most elaborate of its kind, was recently reprinted in Beijing (Zhang Zhaoyu 1995). Early Western missionaries and Sinologists (Julien 1835; Legge 1891, 2: 235–46; Suzuki and Carus 1906a) were as taken with the *Ganying pian*'s popularity as its moral seriousness; now missionary efforts outside China also include the *Ganying pian* (Wong Eva 1994) in a highly interpreted translation with an unreliable historical description.

Catherine BELL

Bell 1996a; Bell 1996b; Brokaw 1991, 28–60; Legge 1891, 2: 235–46 (trans.); Sakai Tadao 1960, 359–68, 404–32; Yoshioka Yoshitoyo 1952, 70–122; Zheng Zhiming 1988b, 41–98; Zhu Yueli 1983b

※ *baojuan*; *shanshu*; ETHICS AND MORALS

Taishang zhuguo jiumin zongzhen biyao

太上助國救民總真祕要

Secret Essentials of the Totality of Perfected, of the Most High, for Assisting the Country and Saving the People

The *Zongzhen biyao* (CT 1227) is the earliest surviving comprehensive compilation of the methods of the *Tianxin zhengfa tradition. It was compiled in ten *juan* by Yuan Miaozong 元妙宗 (fl. 1086–1116), who contributed it to the Taoist Canon of Song Huizong (the *Zhenghe Wanshou daozang*). In his preface, dated the first of March 1116, the author relates that for more than thirty years he traveled all over the empire, asking Taoist masters about their methods and in this way obtaining a complete repertoire. For several years he lived in Nanyang 南陽 (Henan), healing people by means of talismanic water (*fushui* 符水). Finally he was summoned to the capital and in 1115 set to work on the collation of the texts of the new Canon. He thus had a chance to go through the entire collection and found that it was deficient in the talismanic methods of exorcism and curing. To compensate for this lack, he drew up this compilation of what he had received as "oral instructions of secret practices [connected with] the writing of talismans" (*fufa biyong koujue* 符法祕用口訣).

The main contents of the book are as follows:

1. *Quxie yuan qingzhi xingyong ge* 驅邪院請治行用格 (Models for the Practices of Appealing for Restoration, of the Department of Exorcism; 1.2a–8b): programs for large services of exorcism, including services for curing illness,

for saving dead ancestors (who cause trouble to the living), for obtaining succession, and for the destruction of temples for unorthodox deities.

2. *Douxia lingwen fuzhou* 斗下靈文符咒 (Numinous Script and Talismanic Spells of the Jurisdiction of the Dipper): basic instructions for the writing of talismans (2.10a–13a, 18b–21a), and descriptions of the three fundamental talismans and the two main seals of the Tianxin tradition (2.13a–18b).

3. A series of talismanic methods for curing consumption and other kinds of illness (3.1a–15a), followed by a section entitled *Tianpeng jiuzhi fa* 天蓬救治法 (Method of Tianpeng for Saving People and Restoring Order; 3.15a–28b). It is a method of exorcism related to the group of thirty-six generals headed by Tianpeng 天蓬 (the spirit of the ninth star of the Northern Dipper, *beidou) and based on the recitation of the ancient Tianpeng spell (*Tianpeng zhou; see *Zhengao, 10.10b–11a).

4–6. A separate corpus entitled *Shangqing yinshu gusui lingwen* 上清隱書骨髓靈文 (Spinal Numinous Script of the Concealed Writ of Highest Clarity). *Juan* 4 contains the nine ancient *Gusui lingwen* talismans, found also in the *Shangqing tianxin zhengfa* 上清天心正法 (CT 566, 3.9b–21a). They constitute the basic text (*benwen* 本文) of the *Gusui lingwen* and are followed in the present book by an additional set of ten talismans (*j.* 5). The final part of the *Gusui lingwen* is the "devil's code" (*guilü* 鬼律; *j.* 6), which appears to be derived from the separate version *Shangqing gusui lingwen guilü* 上清骨髓靈文鬼律 (Devil's Code of the Spinal Numinous Script of the Highest Clarity; CT 461), established by *Deng Yougong.

7. *Kaozhao fa* 考召法 (Method of Inspecting [Devils] and Summoning [Spirits]), an ancient *Zhengyi method, related particularly to the Generals of the Three Primes (Sanyuan jiangjun 三元將軍) and relying on a Register of the Three and the Five for Inspecting and Summoning (*sanwu kaozhao zhi lu* 三五考召之錄).

8. Practices of "walking along the guideline" (*bugang).

9–10. Models for ritual documents and descriptions of some characteristic individual rites of the Tianxin zhengfa.

Poul ANDERSEN

📖 Andersen 1991, 92–96; Andersen 1996; Boltz J. M. 1987a, 34–35; Drexler 1994, 25–74; Qing Xitai 1999

※ Deng Yougong; Tianxin zhengfa

taixi

胎息

embryonic breathing

In one of its two meanings, *taixi* designates a way of breathing similar to that of the embryo. Breathing through the nose appears to stop and is replaced by breathing through the navel and the pores of the skin. In the second meaning, *taixi* is performed by **neidan* adepts in the abdomen. The latter meaning has been influenced by Buddhist notions and practices such as the concept of *tathāgatagarbha* ("embryo of the *tathāgata*," sometimes translated in Chinese as **shengtai* or Embryo of Sainthood) and the refinement and cessation of breathing, mentioned in *dhyāna* breathing techniques, according to which inner breathing ceases when concentration of the mind increases.

One of the first mentions of *taixi* occurs in the fifth-century biography of Wang Zhen 王真 (Later Han), which states that he and others "were able to practice embryonic breathing and feed themselves like an embryo (*taishi* 胎食)" (*Hou Hanshu*, 82.2751). In the Tang period, the *Yanling xiansheng ji xinjiu fuqi jing* 延陵先生集新舊服氣經 (Scripture on New and Old Methods for the Ingestion of Breath Collected by the Elder of Yanling; CT 825, 17a) defines the technique as follows: "One must carefully pull the breath while inspiring and expiring so that the Original Breath (**yuanqi*) does not exit the body. Thus the outer and inner breaths do not mix and one achieves embryonic breathing." According to the **Taixi jing* (Scripture of Embryonic Breathing, 1a) "the embryo is formed within the stored breath, and breathing occurs from within the embryo."

The literature concerning embryonic breathing developed during the Tang and the early Song periods. The main texts dealing with this technique are:

1. *Taixi jing* 胎息經 (Scripture of Embryonic Breathing; CT 14)

2. *Taixi jing zhu* 胎息經注 (Commentary to the Scripture of Embryonic Breathing; CT 130; trans. Huang Jane 1987–90, 1: 43–47)

3. *Taixi biyao gejue* 胎息祕要歌訣 (Songs and Instructions on the Secret Essentials of Embryonic Breathing; CT 131; trans. Huang Jane 1987–90, 1: 49–54)

4. *Yangsheng taixi qijing* 養生胎息氣經 (Scripture of Embryonic Breathing and Nourishing Life; CT 819)

5. *Taixi baoyi ge* 胎息抱一歌 (Song of Embryonic Breathing and Embracing the One; CT 827)

6. *Taixi jingwei lun* 胎息精微論 (Essay on the Subtlety of Embryonic Breathing; CT 829)

7. *Zhuzhen shengtai shenyong jue* 諸真聖胎神用訣 (Instructions of the Real Men on the Divine Operation of the Embryo of Sainthood; CT 826)

8. The "Taixi pian" 胎息篇 chapter of the *Daoshu (Pivot of the Dao; CT 1017, 14.8b–13a)

In *neidan*, embryonic breathing occurs at the second of the three stages of the practice, when breath is refined and transmuted into spirit (*lianqi huashen* 鍊氣化神). This breathing feeds the embryo (i.e., the *shen*, spirit) that rises to the *niwan (the upper *dantian or Cinnabar Field) when it reaches maturity.

The above-mentioned *Zhuzhen shengtai shenyong jue* attributes embryonic breathing methods to divinities like Laozi, the Yellow Old Lord of the Center (Zhongyang Huanglao jun 中央黃老君), and the Venerable Mother of Mount Li (Lishan laomu 驪山老母); to semilegendary characters such as *Zhang Guolao, *Guigu zi, and *Liu Haichan; to historical characters like *Ge Hong, *Chen Tuan, Yanluo zi 煙蘿子, and Langran zi 郎然子; to Bodhidharma (the patriarch of Chan Buddhism); and to female adepts like Immortal Maiden He (He xiangu 何仙姑), Immortal Maiden Li (Li xiangu 李仙姑), and Cao Wenyi 曹文逸 (fl. 1119–25).

Catherine DESPEUX

📖 Esposito 1998b; Katō Chie 2002, 114–26; Maspero 1981, 459–505

※ *Taixi jing; yangsheng*

Taixi jing

胎息經

Scripture of Embryonic Breathing

The *Taixi jing* is a text consisting of only 88 characters that states the general principles of "embryonic breathing" (*taixi). A work with this title is listed in *Baopu zi 19 but is not mentioned in the bibliographic chapter of the *Suishu* (History of the Sui).

Besides an unannotated edition (CT 14), the Taoist Canon includes a single commentary on this text, the *Taixi jing zhu* 胎息經注 (Commentary to the Scripture of Embryonic Breathing; CT 130, and YJQQ 60.27a–28b), attributed to *Huanzhen xiansheng. The commentary dates to the Tang period and is the first of several commentaries that later appeared during the Song and Ming periods. Huanzhen locates the embryo three inches below the navel, a place that he describes as the lower Cinnabar Field (see *dantian), the Mysterious Female (*xuanpin), and the Ocean of Pneuma (qihai 氣海).

Catherine DESPEUX

📖 Balfour 1884, 63–65 (trans.); Huang Jane 1987–90, 1: 43–47 (trans. of Taixi jing zhu)

※ taixi; yangsheng

Taixiao langshu

太霄琅書

Precious Writ of the Great Empyrean

The Taoist Canon contains three *Shangqing texts entitled Taixiao langshu. The first is the Taixiao langshu qiongwen dizhang jing 太霄琅書瓊文帝章經 (Precious Writ of the Great Empyrean, Scripture of the Exquisite Text of the Imperial Statement; CT 55). The second is the Taishang taixiao langshu 太上太霄琅書 (Precious Writ of the Highest Great Empyrean; CT 1352), whose first juan corresponds to CT 55. The third is the Taixiao langshu qiongwen dizhang jue 太霄琅書瓊文帝章訣 (Precious Writ of the Great Empyrean, Instructions on the Exquisite Text of the Imperial Statement; CT 129), which corresponds to j. 5 of CT 1352.

The first text (CT 55) is related to the huifeng 迴風 (whirlwind) method (see *Dadong zhenjing) and to methods of the Feminine One (Ciyi 雌一), which pertain to the apocryphal practices associated with the Dadong zhenjing. It contains short descriptions of the Nine Heavens (*jiutian) and mentions the dates on which their messengers descend to earth to inspect its inhabitants. At that time, adepts should sing the stanzas related to these heavens in order to have their names inscribed in the celestial registers of life (shengji 生籍). There follow a list of the names of the kings of the Nine Heavens, hymns addressed to them, and "seals" (or talismanic characters, yin 印) formed by their essences. If one carries these seals on one's body, one can summon the officers of the Five Peaks (*wuyue) and expel malevolent forces.

The second text (CT 1352) is a composite ten-juan work containing layers of different dates. Some portions also appear in the *Wushang biyao, which shows that they date from before the sixth century. Many are certainly later; some are Shangqing songs, and some display evident *Lingbao features. This work attests to the evolution of a form of institutionalized Taoism seen as the inner complement of Confucianism. Except for *j*. 1, the Shangqing vocabulary, images and saints are absent from this text, most of which emphasizes the observance of religious prescriptions, ritual rules, and moral virtues. *Juan* 3 and part of *j*. 5 consist of codes for the transmission of sacred texts analogous to those in the *Siji mingke jing* (Scripture of the Illustrious Code of the Four Poles). Most of *j*. 4 is dedicated to Taoist vestments, and *j*. 6 describes a ritual. The tenth *juan* is datable to the Six Dynasties and is close in content and style to the Shangqing texts; part of it (10.2b–5b) is incorporated in a later ritual found in the *Badao mingji jing* 八道命籍經 (Scripture of the Register of Destiny of the Eight Ways; CT 1328, 2.21a–23b).

Isabelle ROBINET

📖 Ōfuchi Ninji 1991, 281–86; Robinet 1984, 1: 201, 216, and 2: 233–35

※ Shangqing

Taiyi

太一, 太乙, 泰一

The Great One

The term Taiyi has been variously translated as the Great (or Supreme) One, the Great Monad, Great Unity, or Great Oneness. It stands for the cosmic Oneness, or Unity (*yi*), at the base of the universe, as well as for the experience of this "oneness." It also refers to the personification of this abstract principle or experience in the form of a supreme stellar deity, namely the god Taiyi, who resides in the large reddish star Kochab (ß Ursae Minoris), and who has been viewed as a supreme god of heaven since the late Warring States period.

The god Taiyi retained this status in the Taoist traditions of the Six Dynasties, though with a clear emphasis on his special role as a supreme administrator of human destinies, that is, as the Celestial Emperor (Tiandi 天帝), who on special days of the year receives reports on the moral conduct of individual human beings from his Eight Envoys (*ba shizhe* 八使者) and adjusts the celestial records of the destiny of each individual in accordance with these reports (see for instance *Wushang biyao*, 9.4a–11b; Lagerwey 1981b, 88–89). As a corresponding supreme god of the inner pantheon of the human body, addressed in Taoist physiological and meditative practices and documented since the late Han or the early Six Dynasties, Taiyi has been viewed, furthermore, as representing the immortal identity, or "true self" (*zhenwu* 真吾, *zhenwo* 真我), of a person.

Fig. 71. Early representation of the Great One (Taiyi), shown on top of the
Mawangdui manuscript *Bibing tu* 避兵圖 (Chart for Averting Weapons).
Sketch reproduced from Li Ling 2000b, 234. See also Li Ling 1995–96.

The earliest discussion of Taiyi as a cosmogonic principle is found in the
*Guodian manuscripts of the second half of the fourth century BCE, in a sepa-
rate text which begins: *Taiyi sheng shui* 太一生水, "The Great One generated
Water." In the speculative cosmologies of the Former Han *weishu* 緯書 ("weft
texts"; see *TAOISM AND THE APOCRYPHA), as well as in most subsequent cosmological thought, the role of water as the medium of the activity of Taiyi
was replaced by the similar role of "breath" (*qi*), and indeed in the *weishu*,
Taiyi is commonly identified with the "primordial breath" (*yuanqi*). It should
be noted, however, that even in this context, the aquatic qualities of this breath
are greatly emphasized, and the star that is the residence of Taiyi is viewed as
the "source" of the breath, which is "scooped out" into the universe by means
of the Northern Dipper (*beidou*), and which "flows" through the universe and
thereby animates the world. The concept of this movement of the primordial
breath—translated into the vision of the procession of the high god Taiyi
through nine celestial palaces (*jiugong*)—constitutes a fundamental model

of the structure of space-time, which to this day is used in a large variety of Chinese techniques of divination. During the early Han dynasty it provided one of several templates for the construction of the Hall of Light (*mingtang, in which the emperor personified the god as he performed his annual ritual circumambulations), and it has continued to be used as a fundamental pattern for the structure of the Taoist ritual area, in which the priests likewise identify with Taiyi as they perform, for instance, the practice of *bugang, "walking along the guideline" (often in accordance with the same patterns as those used in the divinatory practices).

The definition of the term Taiyi as referring to the "true self" or "primordial spirit" (yuanshen 元神) of the practitioner of Taoist methods is clearly related to some earlier uses of the term in philosophical texts of the late Warring States, where it appears to refer to a kind of mystical experience of "oneness," accessible for instance in ritual (Eno 1990, 174–79). In the Lüshi chunqiu 呂氏春秋 (Springs and Autumns of Mr. Lü; 239 BCE; trans. Knoblock and Riegel 2000, 136), the root of music is said to be in Taiyi, and in the Liji 禮記 (Records of Rites, compiled during the early Han; trans. Legge 1885, 1: 386–88) we are told that ritual is based on "Great Oneness" (Dayi 大一). In his commentary on the *Huainan zi (139 BCE), Gao You 高誘 (fl. 205–212 CE) in one place defines the concept by saying that "Taiyi is the primordial spirit that embraces all things" (14.462), and the Huainan zi itself concludes a discussion of practices of concentrating the *hun and po souls inside one's body by stating that "in this way one may communicate with the Great One (or: Great Oneness) above. The essence of Great Oneness communicates with the Way of Heaven" (9.270). Indeed, the cult of Taiyi adopted at court in 134 BCE by Han Wudi appears to have had a good deal in common with popular shamanic practices, and also for this reason was apparently abhorred by some Confucian officials. In a way new to imperial worship, the high god was expected to descend into the ritual area, as prescribed for instance in some weishu, which refer to the constellation of the Three Terraces (santai 三台, three pairs of stars in Ursa Major; see fig. 23) as representing "the road along which Taiyi descends and ascends," and which state that: "When the drums sound in the eastern suburb the ancestral souls arrive, and the god Taiyi descends" (Andersen 1989–90b, 29–30).

While the position of Taiyi in imperial ritual declined around the beginning of the Common Era, the god retained his position at a more popular level of society, and he once again came to the fore in the early Taoist movements of the latter half of the second century. The god was important in the movement of the *Yellow Turbans, and he is frequently mentioned in the grave writs that document the mortuary liturgy of the *Zhengyi tradition of the Six Dynasties. We know, furthermore, from the account of Taoist liturgy found in the Suishu (History of the Sui; completed 644), that in the capacity of a supreme ruler of the firmament—and a supreme regulator of human destinies—Taiyi was placed as the highest among the array of stellar gods to whom offerings were presented in the nightly *jiao ceremonies, which had attained paramount importance by this time (35.1092–93).

A reminder of this role is found also in the ancient Zhengyi practice of Presenting the Memorial (*baibiao), that is, the Taoist priest's meditative journey to heaven in order to deliver a written prayer to the supreme gods, which was transmitted during the Song dynasty in the texts of the *Tianxin zhengfa, and which has survived in many present-day liturgies. In the texts prescribing the form of the audience in heaven, the highest level of deity is referred to as the Most High (Taishang 太上). The Most High is accompanied by a deputy ruler of the universe, who executes his will concerning the petition, and who is none other than Taiyi.

Poul ANDERSEN

📖 Andersen 1989–90b; Cammann 1961, 60–76; Ding Peiren 1984; Kalinowski 1985; Kaltenmark 1961; Kohn 1989a, 134–37; Li Ling 1991; Li Ling 1994; Li Ling 1995–96; Little 2000b, 242–43; Loewe 1974, 169–92; Maspero 1951; Robinet 1993, 119–51; Robinet 1995c; Wang Shiren 1987; Zhou Shirong 1990

※ *sanyi*; *yi* [oneness]; DEITIES: THE PANTHEON

Taiyi jiao

太一教

Teaching of the Great One

The Taiyi jiao is one of the new religious schools that appeared in the mid-twelfth century in northern China, then under the rule of the Jin (Jurchen) dynasty. Like similar contemporary movements, including the *Quanzhen, *Zhen dadao and Buddhist Dhūta 頭陀 schools, the Taiyi jiao developed its own organization and initiation structures and spread rapidly thanks to the participation and support of a large number of lay adepts. After the medieval peasant Taoist communities—in which all members received a formal religious education—disappeared around the end of the first millennium, the Taiyi jiao can be seen to have arisen as a reaction to the sclerosis of Taoist institutions, where access to priesthood was monopolized by hereditary families protected by the state. In fact, the Taiyi jiao and other contemporary movements played an important role in the diffusion and renewal of Taoist ritual and practice in society at large.

The Taiyi predication began around 1138 with Xiao Baozhen 蕭抱珍 (?–1166; Qing Xitai 1994, 1: 331), who was active in present-day northern Henan. As early as 1148, Xiao was recognized by the Jin court and set up an independent organization conceived along familial lines. He later chose one of his children as his successor, and all subsequent patriarchs had to change their family names to Xiao. The functions of patriarch and other important positions were usually held by persons whose ancestors had been influential patrons or members of the school. While control of the order was limited to a few families, however, access to initiation seems to have been largely open, and ordinations were apparently conducted on a large scale.

Such proselytizing, as well as the probably illegal public initiations given by Taiyi masters, caused the order to run into conflict with the Jin rulers in 1190. At that time, however, the Jin were rapidly weakening, and the confrontation was short-lived and devoid of any fundamental ideological contradiction. A few decades later, the Mongols acknowledged the positive role played by the Taiyi jiao in Chinese society, recognized its independent institutions, and granted it almost complete autonomy. Khubilai khan (Shizu, r. 1260–1294) also bestowed special favors on the fourth patriarch, *Xiao Fudao (fl. 1214–52), whom he greatly esteemed. Taiyi shrines were built in the new capital, Beijing, and its leaders were regularly invited to perform state rituals well into the mid-fourteenth century. The Taiyi jiao is not heard of anymore after this period, and does not seem to have survived the demise of the Yuan.

Like the contemporary Zhen dadao, the Taiyi jiao has not left written sources either in the *Daozang* or elsewhere. Therefore, we have only the faintest idea of the contents of Taiyi scriptures. The little we know suggests that individual practices such as *neidan* did not acquire the importance they had in the Quanzhen or Zhen dadao orders. The history of the Taiyi jiao is mainly documented by stele inscriptions, many of which are preserved in the collected works of Wang Yun 王惲 (1227–1304), an eminent scholar at the court of Khubilai who was a native of Jixian 汲縣 (Henan), the cradle of Taiyi, and maintained close contacts with the Taiyi hierarchy. The scope of Taiyi's influence, however, can be gauged from the tomb inscriptions of some wealthy community leaders of this period who, although mainly active as farmers or merchants, also benefited from initiation into Taiyi and acted as religious leaders.

Vincent GOOSSAERT

📖 Chen Yuan 1962, 110–49; Hu Qide 1996; Qing Xitai 1988–95, 3: 2–20 and 267–84; Qing Xitai 1994, 1: 158–63; Yao Tao-chung 1980, 27–33

※ Xiao Fudao

Taiyi jinhua zongzhi

太一金華宗旨

The Ultimate Purport of the Golden Flower of the Great One

Better known as the *Secret of the Golden Flower*, this is a famous **neidan* text that the Western world came to know through Richard Wilhelm's 1929 translation. The Chinese text used by Wilhelm was edited by Zhanran Huizhen zi 湛然慧真子 in 1921. Besides this, at least five more versions are available, all of which date to the late Qing dynasty and are ascribed to **Lü Dongbin, who revealed them through spirit writing (see **fuji*):

1. *Xiantian xuwu Taiyi jinhua zongzhi* 先天虛無太一金華宗旨 (The Ultimate Purport of the Golden Flower of the Great One of the Emptiness before Heaven), in *j.* 49 of Shao Zhilin's 邵志琳 (1748–1810) **Lüzu quanshu* (Complete Writings of Ancestor Lü; 1775).

2. *Fuyou shangdi tianxian jinhua zongzhi* 孚佑上帝天仙金華宗旨 (The Ultimate Purport of the Golden Flower of Celestial Immortality by the Highest Emperor, Savior of the Needy), in *j.* 2 of Jiang Yuanting's 蔣元庭 (1755–1819) *Quanshu zhengzong* 全書正宗 (The Orthodox Tradition of the Complete Writings; 1803). This version is associated with the Tianxian 天仙 (Celestial Immortal) school, a lineage related by spirit writing to Lü Dongbin under the guide of Liu Shouyuan 柳守元 and Jiang Yuanting.

3. *Xiantian xuwu Taiyi jinhua zongzhi*, in *j.* 10 of the *Lüzu quanshu zongzheng* 呂祖全書宗正 (The Orthodoxy of the Tradition of the Complete Writings by Ancestor Lü; 1852), edited by Chen Mou 陳謀.

4. *Jinhua zongzhi*, in the **Daozang jiyao* (vol. 12). This version is identical to no. 2 above and was probably already included in the edition of the *Daozang jiyao* published by Jiang Yuanting between 1796 and 1819.

5. *Lü zushi xiantian xuwu Taiyi jinhua zongzhi* 呂祖師先天虛無太一金華宗旨 (The Ultimate Purport of the Golden Flower of the Great One of the Emptiness before Heaven by the Ancestral Master Lü), first published in **Min Yide's (1748–1836) *Gu Shuyinlou cangshu* 古書隱樓藏書 (Collection of the Ancient Hidden Pavilion of Books; Qing Xitai 1994, 2: 184–86) and in his **Daozang xubian* (Sequel to the Taoist Canon; 1834). The text is presented as having been transmitted in 1688 by Lü Dongbin to **Longmen masters at the Longqiao 龍嶠 (Dragon's Ridge) hermitage of Mount Jingai. The Longmen school recognized this as its fundamental doctrinal text.

6. *Changsheng shu* 長生術 (The Art of Long Life), in Huizhen zi's *Changsheng shu Xuming fang hekan* 長生術續命方合刊 (Joint Publication of *The Art of Long Life* and *Methods for Increasing the Vital Force*; 1921).

In all the above editions, the text is divided into thirteen sections. The first section presents important variants in the fifth edition, which gives much more information on the method of opening the Heart of Heaven (**tianxin*) than in other versions. Moreover, in the fifth and sixth edition each section is followed by a commentary. Except for these differences, the texts of the six editions are virtually identical.

The *Taiyi jinhua zongzhi* symbolizes the achievement of the alchemical work as the generation of the Golden Flower, here meant as a synonym for the Golden Elixir (**jindan*) and a metaphor for the transmutation of spiritual light, or the return of the Spirit to the Dao. The main practice of this text is the "reversion of the light" (*huiguang* 回光), inspired by the contemplative method of *zhiguan* 止觀 (*śamatha-vipaśyanā*; "cessation and insight") as practiced within the Tiantai 天臺 school of Buddhism (see **guan*), but also explained in terms of the Confucian *zhizhi* 止知 (cessation of knowledge) as the means for stopping the discursive flow of thinking and contemplating the real nature of the mind.

Monica ESPOSITO

📖 Cleary 1991b (trans.); Esposito 1996; Esposito 1998c; Miyuki Mokusen 1967; Mori Yuria 1998; Mori Yuria 2002; Wilhelm R. 1929 (trans.)

※ Lü Dongbin; *neidan*; Longmen

Tan Chuduan

譚處端

1123–85; original *ming*: Yu 玉; *zi*: Boyu 伯玉, Zhengtong 正通; *hao*: Changzhen 長真 (Perpetual Reality)

Tan Chuduan, the oldest of **Wang Zhe's disciples, converted to Taoism at the ripe age of forty-four. The son of an artisan's family, he came to Wang Zhe as a sick man looking for a cure. Wang healed him just by touching him and having Tan share a bath with him. Tan then left his wife and children and followed Wang until the latter's death. He subsequently headed for Luoyang (Henan) where he led a life of urban asceticism (*dayin* 大隱 or "great reclusion"), living in the midst of the city and taking part in all sorts of social activities while practicing non-attachment to worldly affairs. He was given a hermitage near an abbey famous for its association with an eleventh-century *neidan* master. From this humble position, he began to teach and attracted a wide audience. He also effected miracles by invoking the deity *Zhenwu.

Tan's poetry is anthologized in the *Shuiyun ji* 水雲集 (Anthology of Water and Clouds; 1187; CT 1160). One of his most famous poems, the "Baigu shi" 白骨詩 (Verses on the Bones of the Dead), is an excellent example of *Quanzhen predication: as the human body is bound to decay faster than we think, we should generate something immortal inside of us before it is too late. The same theme is found in the poetry of Wang Zhe and other Quanzhen masters, and was depicted in the murals of the *Yongle gong. The poem was carved on stone in Luoyang in 1183, with an illustration.

Vincent GOOSSAERT

📖 Boltz J. M. 1987a, 160–62; Endres 1985; Hachiya Kunio 1989; Idema 1993; Marsone 2001a, 103–4; Reiter 1996

※ Quanzhen

Tan Zixiao

譚紫霄

fl. 935-after 963

Tan Zixiao, a *daoshi* from Quanzhou 泉州 (Fujian), is referred to in early historical sources as the original founder of the *Tianxin zhengfa tradition. He served the fourth ruler of the Kingdom of Min 閩, Wang Chang 王昶 (r. 935–39), from whom he received the title Zhengyi xiansheng 正一先生 (Elder of Orthodox Unity); and he collaborated with the medium Chen Shouyuan 陳守元, who at the court of Wang Chang was elevated to the status of Celestial Master (see *Xin Wudai shi*, 68.851). According to the biography of Tan in the *Nan Tangshu* 南唐書 (History of the Southern Tang; 17.2b–3a) by Lu You 陸游 (1125–1210), Chen had found "the talismans of *Zhang Daoling of the Han, written in red and black as fresh as new," on several tens of wooden slips buried in the ground in a bronze bowl. Not knowing how to use them he passed them on to Tan, who penetrated their mysteries and thereafter declared that he had obtained the Tianxin zhengfa of Zhang Daoling.

The sources agree that after the fall of Min, Tan went into hiding on Mount Lu (*Lushan) in northern Jiangxi, where he acquired a following of more than a hundred students, and where, according to the *Lushan ji* 廬山記 (Records of

Mount Lu; 2.1033–34), by Chen Shunyu 陳舜俞 (eleventh century), he established the Qiyin guan 棲隱觀 (Abbey of Dwelling in Concealment). Lu You ends his account by stating that those today who declare themselves to be of the Tianxin tradition "refer to [Tan] Zixiao as their patriarch." This assessment is confirmed both by the earliest compilation of the methods of the Tianxin tradition, the *Taishang zhuguo jiumin zongzhen biyao* (2.6b), which in its list of patriarchs refers to Tan Zixiao and his alleged student, *Rao Dongtian, as the two "transmitters of the teaching" (*chuanjiao* 傳教), and by the account of the history of the tradition given by Jin Yunzhong 金允中 (fl. 1224–25) in the *Shangqing lingbao dafa* (CT 1223, 43.16b–17a). According to Jin, the core elements of the Tianxin tradition originally derived from the tradition of the first Celestial Master of the Han dynasty. Having fallen into oblivion during the period of disunity, he continues, they were restored only after the Five Dynasties, by Tan Zixiao and Rao Dongtian.

The teachings and practices of Tan Zixiao are described both by Lu You and in Ma Ling's 馬令 *Nan Tangshu* (24.2b–3a; 1105), in terms that are closely similar to the methods described in the texts of the Tianxin tradition. Both authors emphasize his use of talismans in order to control demonic forces and cure illness, and Ma Ling adds a number of details that are in fact typical of the tradition, such as the methods of *bugang, the "method of lighting lamps" (*randeng fa* 燃燈法), as well as the specific worship of the Black Killer (*Heisha).

Poul ANDERSEN

📖 Andersen 1991, 14–18 and 81–96; Andersen 1996, 145–47; Davis E. 2001, 21–24; Lin Shengli 1989; Qing Xitai 1999; Schafer 1954, 96–100

※ Tianxin zhengfa

tâng-ki (or *jitong*)

童乩 (*or:* 乩童)

spirit-medium

Tâng-ki and *jitong* are the Hokkien and Mandarin versions respectively of a term used in Taiwanese popular religion for spirit-mediums, i.e., for religious specialists subject to possession by spirits who speak and act through them. While different terms are used in other dialect areas, corresponding forms of spirit-mediumship can be found *mutatis mutandis* throughout China and among overseas Chinese communities. *Tâng-ki* can be of either gender, but male mediums are more common than female ones.

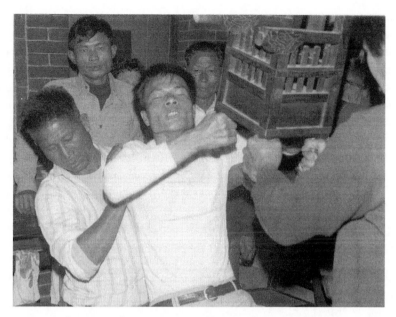

Fig. 72. A medium in Taichung, Taiwan, wields a wooden divination chair as the deity descends into his body (December 1977). Photograph by Julian Pas. See also fig. 17.

The literal meaning of *tâng-ki* is "divining youth," which points on the one hand to the fact that this role is often—though by no means exclusively—filled by young rather than older men. On the other hand, it refers to the widely held belief that the medium has been given a short life span and his service to the gods is a way to improve his fate and prolong his life. At a still deeper level, the entranced medium is believed to temporarily abandon his own destiny (*yun* 運) and become similar to a young child whose destiny is not yet determined at the time of birth, but only commences in later childhood (at any point between the ages of four months and ten years). Viewed in this way, the medium's powers are derived from a combination of the child's liminality with the authority of the possessing deity.

The relationship between a god and his prospective medium is usually initiated by the former, not by the latter. Mediumship does not carry high social prestige, in fact quite to the contrary is stigmatized to a certain extent, and many prospective mediums are therefore at first reluctant to heed the deity's call expressed in dreams, messages by other mediums, illnesses, and spontaneous trances. If he finally succumbs to the god's demand, the candidate undergoes a period of training under the direction of a ritual specialist, often a Red-head Taoist (i.e., a *hoat-su* / *fashi*; see *hongtou* and *wutou*), who may later become his assistant, interpreter, and manager (*toh-thâu* / *zhuotou* 桌頭). Once this training is concluded, the new medium will serve as his patron deity's mouthpiece whenever that god's advice is needed. While in villages séances are generally held on an as-needed basis, urban spirit-shrines (*shentan* 神壇) may run a regular schedule of séances when clients may come to see the deity about any problems they are experiencing. Health problems are topmost on the list of issues brought before the gods and the dispensation of medical advice, herbal prescriptions, and efficacious talismans is an important part of a *tâng-ki*'s ordinary practice. In addition, *tâng-ki* are a common sight at temple festivals and processions where they represent the gods' active participation in the event.

The authenticity of the medium's trance is proven by feats of self-mortification such as drilling metal skewers through his skin, flagellating his back with a ball of sharp nails, and walking on a bed of burning coals. To the onlookers these feats are proof of the imperviousness to pain and serious injury produced by the presence of a divine spirit. Further evidence of authentic possession is provided by the behavioral changes in the medium that accompany the onset of trance, such as stylized body movements, altered voice, and unusual speech patterns.

Tâng-ki are religious specialists proper to popular religion and are in fact one of its most important channels of communication with the gods. Since its inception, Taoism has tended to demarcate itself from popular religion in general, and has rejected the mediums as spokespersons of its "demons" in particular. Taoist disdain for the popular mediums continues to be expressed today in their almost complete exclusion from "orthodox" rituals conducted by Black-head Taoist priests (i.e., the **daoshi*). Red-head Taoists on the other hand maintain a much closer relationship with popular religion and its *tâng-ki*. As we have seen, they often serve as mediums' managers, and mediums are frequently employed in the "minor rites" (*xiaofa* 小法) which are en important part of the Red-head ritual repertoire. This close cooperation of *fashi* and medium constitutes part of an extensive grey area of contact and overlap, where popular religion is pressed into the service of Taoism and Taoist ritual in turn is popularized.

Philip CLART

📖 Berthier 1987; Cheu Hock Tong 1988, Davis E. 2001, 87–114 and passim; Elliott 1955; Jordan 1972, 67–86; Kagan and Wasescha 1982; Schipper 1993, 45–55

※ *hongtou* and *wutou*; TAOISM AND MEDIUM CULTS; TAOISM AND POPULAR RELIGION

Tanluan

曇鸞

488–554

Tanluan is regarded retrospectively by Pure Land Buddhists in Japan as first of the founding fathers of their religious tradition. In China, by contrast, he seems chiefly to have been remembered, from the time of his first biography in the *Xu gaoseng zhuan* 續高僧傳 (Sequel to the Biographies of Eminent Monks) of Daoxuan 道宣 (596–667), for his interest in Taoist macrobiotic techniques: a text on breathing exercises named there would appear to have survived in the *Daozang* as the *Yanling xiansheng ji xinjiu fuqi jing* 延陵先生集新舊服氣 經 (Scripture on New and Old Methods for the Ingestion of Breath Collected by the Elder of Yanling; CT 825, and YJQQ 59). This interest is explained in his biography as having arisen as a result of the interruption by illness of his studies in the voluminous Buddhist literature of his day; he is even said to have left the Northern Wei regime under which he was born to consult *Tao Hongjing in South China. Only a meeting with Bodhiruci, who is said to have recommended Pure Land literature as of infinitely greater efficacy than any Taoist work, set him forth on his Pure Land studies, now chiefly represented by his commentary, the *Wangsheng lun zhu* 往生論注 (Commentary to the Treatise on Rebirth; T. 1819; trans. Inagaki Hisao 1998), on a work ascribed to Vasubandhu.

The latter work does, indeed, show a familiarity with Taoism, and betrays some literary influence and one overt quotation from the *Baopu zi*. Yet doctrinally Tanluan quite clearly insists on the superiority of the Pure Land of the Buddha Amitābha as outside our world system: orthodox Buddhism would assert that Taoist heavens, were they to exist, could only belong to the defiled level of our own triple world system, albeit to its upper reaches. His ethical thought, too, assigns value only to the good actions of bodhisattvas, those dedicated to future Buddhahood, rather than to the actions of ordinary men or even gods. Evidently any form of syncretism is far from Tanluan's mind, and the sense of priorities dramatically conveyed by his biography (whatever its literal truth) is indeed confirmed.

But Tanluan's awareness of Taoism—perhaps even the choice of a Taoist name, Xuanzhong si 玄中寺 (Monastery of the Mysterious Center), for the monastery in which he resided—can certainly be understood against the evidence from epigraphy and manuscripts retrieved from *Dunhuang for a tendency toward religious syncretism in Northern Wei society. The theoretical means put forward by Tanluan for asserting the superiority of Buddhism, for their part, seem of a piece with southern (primarily Liang dynasty) efforts toward distinguishing between native, "secular" Chinese culture (including religious culture) and the higher world of Buddhism, which allowed a place for both, thus in effect challenging any syncretic tendencies. Thus Tanluan, like many Buddhists after him, might take a legitimate interest in Taoist macrobiotic techniques on the understanding that they were of limited, "this-worldly" value. Salvation from the cycle of birth and death, however, lay for him with Buddhism alone. Though Tanluan's efforts undoubtedly helped to legitimate the rise of a popular Pure Land Buddhism, a retrospective view of him that does not see his syncretic environment cannot do justice to his thought. Unfortunately, most writings on him do not grasp this point.

T. H. BARRETT

📖 Corless 1987; Michihata Ryōshū 1961; Michihata Ryōshū 1969

※ TAOISM AND CHINESE BUDDHISM

Tao Hongjing

陶弘景

456–536; *zi*: Tongming 通明; *hao*: Huayang yinju 華陽隱居
(Hermit of Flourishing Yang)

An eminent scholar and calligrapher, an expert in pharmacopoeia and alchemy, and a highly productive author, Tao Hongjing was the actual founder of *Shang-qing Taoism and one of the brightest intellectual figures of the Six Dynasties. He was born in Danyang 丹陽 (near Nanjing, Jiangsu) from a southern family of landowners and scholars. His father and paternal grandfather were experts in medicinal drugs and accomplished calligraphers, while his mother and maternal grandfather seem to have been Buddhist devotees.

When he was barely aged ten, Tao studied the *Shenxian zhuan (Biographies of Divine Immortals) and the practices of Nourishing Life (*yangsheng). When he was about twenty-five, Gaodi (r. 479–82), the ruler of the Southern Qi dynasty, appointed him tutor to the imperial princes. Gaodi's successor, Wudi (r. 482–93), designated him General of the Left Guard of the Palace in 483, but the following year Tao had to leave office to mourn his mother's death. In 490, he travelled eastward to visit eminent Taoist masters, and possibly commissioned by the emperor to search for valuable relics. He renounced his official career in 492 and retired on Mount Mao (*Maoshan, Jiangsu), where he founded the Huayang guan 華陽館 (Abbey of Flourishing Yang).

When the Liang dynasty came to power in 502, Tao wisely remained on Mount Mao and was not affected by the anti-Taoist decrees of 504 and 517. In 514, Liang Wudi (r. 502–49) ordered the Zhuyang guan 朱陽館 (Abbey of Vermilion Yang) to be built on Mount Mao. Tao retired there the following year, but was often visited by the emperor as a private counselor and thus gained the appellation Grand Councilor amid Mountains (Shanzhong zaixiang 山中宰相). Very little is known of the last two decades of his life. He received the posthumous titles of Zhenbai xiansheng 貞白先生 (Upright Elder) and Huayang zhenren 華陽真人 (Perfected of Flourishing Yang), and in Tang times was posthumously made the ninth patriarch of the Shangqing lineage.

The Taoist. Tao Hongjing inherited the traditions of the *Daode jing* and the *Zhuangzi* along with *Ge Hong's tradition of immortality seeking. Around the age of thirty, he received initiation into *Lingbao Taoism from *Sun Youyue. Tao also studied Buddhism and is even reported to have been the master of *Tanluan (488–554). Some architectural elements from Tao's tomb, discovered on Mount Mao during the Cultural Revolution and matching a description given in the *Maoshan zhi (Monograph of Mount Mao, 8.6a–b), bear an inscription calling him "a disciple of the Buddha and of the Most High Lord Lao."

From 497, Tao experimented with sword foundry, sponsored by the emperor who lent him Huang Wenqing 黃文慶 (a blacksmith from the imperial workshops who also become a Taoist initiate in 505) as an assistant. Around 504, he turned to *waidan with Wudi's support, and studied several methods that he successively discarded because of unavailable ingredients. Eventually, in 505, he decided to compound the Reverted Elixir in Nine Cycles (jiuzhuan huandan 九轉還丹). In spite of long research and preparatory work, the compounding failed twice, on New Year's day 506 and 507.

Disappointed, Tao decided to leave Mount Mao and engaged in a five-year journey to the southeast, from 508 to 512. Another attempt to produce the elixir failed during those years. In 512, he reached the "Greater Mount Huo" (Da Huoshan 大霍山; Strickmann 1979, 152), the heavenly dwelling of two Perfected of Shangqing, *Wei Huacun and Mao Ying 茅盈 (see *Maojun). Tao may have been interested in computations that prognosticated the advent of a Sage in that renchen 壬辰 year (the twenty-ninth of the sexagesimal cycle; see table 10 and the entry *APOCALYPTIC ESCHATOLOGY), but he soon left the mountain and sailed to Muliu 木溜 island, off the Zhejiang coast. Here his journey abruptly ended when an imperial messenger ordered him to return to the capital. Some accounts report that Tao eventually managed to compound either the Elixir of Nine Cycles or a white powder called Sublimated Elixir (feidan 飛丹).

Tao gathered several disciples, the best known of whom are Zhou Ziliang 周子良 (497–516), whom he met during his journey of 508–12, and Sun Wentao 孫文韜, an accomplished calligrapher.

The author and bibliographer. Tao Hongjing's literary career began early with the *Xunshan zhi* 尋山志 (Monograph of Mount Xun). This short text, written at the age of fifteen, is found in his collected writings, the *Huayang Tao yinju ji* 華陽陶隱居集 (Anthology of Tao, the Hermit of Flourishing Yang; CT 1050, 1.1b–3b). In his youth, he also wrote essays, commentaries, and a large unfinished encyclopedia, the *Xueyuan* 學苑 (Garden of Learning), which he asked his nephew Tao Yi 陶翊 to complete when he retired on Mount Mao.

From 483, Tao became interested in the Shangqing revelations granted to *Yang Xi more than a century earlier and decided to collect the original autograph manuscripts, using calligraphy as one of the criteria to establish their authenticity. He began to gather the manuscripts in 488 and his major acquisitions date from that year to 490. When he retired to Mount Mao in 492 he intended to edit the manuscripts, drawing inspiration from *Gu Huan's now-lost *Zhenji jing* 真迹經 (Scripture of the Traces of the Perfected), an earlier but in Tao's view unsatisfying account of Yang Xi's revelations. In 498–99, supported by the emperor, Tao compiled and fully annotated the manuscripts. His enterprise resulted in two major works, the *Zhengao (Declarations of the Perfected; CT 1016) and the *Dengzhen yinjue (Concealed Instructions for the Ascent to Perfection; CT 421).

Tao also drew a table of Shangqing divinities and immortals, the *Zhenling weiye tu (Chart of the Ranks and Functions of the Perfected Numinous Beings; CT 167), now extant in a later edition by *Lüqiu Fangyuan (?–902), and compiled a complete catalogue of Shangqing texts, originally found in the *Dengzhen yinjue* but no longer preserved. Moreover, the Shangqing revelations inspired Tao to compose a commentary to one of the texts received by Yang Xi, the *Jianjing* 劍經 (Scripture of the Sword), which is now found in the *Taiping yulan* 太平御覽 (Imperial Readings of the Taiping Xingguo Reign Period; 983; j. 665). Later, in 517, Tao edited the *Zhoushi mingtong ji* 周氏冥通記 (Records of Mr. Zhou's Communications with the Unseen; CT 302; trans. Mugitani Kunio and Yoshikawa Tadao 2003, part. trans. Bokenkamp 1996a), based on the autograph manuscripts from the revelations bestowed upon his disciple Zhou Ziliang, who had committed suicide in 516 after receiving successive visions of the Perfected.

Tao was also interested in pharmacopoeia and medicine. Shortly after completing the *Zhengao*, he compiled the *Bencao jing jizhu* 本草經集注 (Collected Commentaries to the Canonical Pharmacopoeia), a reedition of a Han treatise ascribed to Shennong, the legendary inventor of agriculture and pharmacology. Tao appended a critical commentary including references to alchemical texts and information drawn from other early pharmacological sources.

An incomplete collection of fragments of Shangqing texts, the *Shangqing wozhong jue* 上清握中訣 (Shangqing Handbook of Instructions; CT 140), is ascribed to Tao Hongjing but is probably apocryphal. It is also unlikely that the commentary in the *Mingtang yuanzhen jingjue* 明堂元真經訣 (Instructions on the Scripture of the Original Perfected of the Hall of Light; CT 424; see Schafer 1978a), attributed to Tao, was actually written by him.

During the last two decades of his life, Tao appears to have reduced his literary production. Only two stele inscriptions date from this period, one devoted to Xu Mai 許邁 (300–348; see *Yang Xi), dating from 518, and one to *Ge Xuan, dating from 522. Both inscriptions are found in the *Huayang Tao yinju ji* (CT 1050, 2.1a–8b).

Grégoire ESPESSET

📖 Bell 1987b; Chen Guofu 1963, 46–47; Giles L. 1948, 106–9; Ishii Masako 1971; Little 2000b, 180–81; Mugitani Kunio 1976; Qing Xitai 1988–95, 1: 501–23; Qing Xitai 1994, 1: 251–53; Strickmann 1979; Sunayama Minoru 1990, 93–122; Wang Ming 1984e

※ *Dengzhen yinjue*; *Zhengao*; *Zhenling weiye tu*; Shangqing

Tao Zhongwen

陶仲文

ca. 1481–1560; original *ming*: Tao Dianzhen 陶典真

Tao Zhongwen was from Huanggang 黃岡 (Hubei). He started his career as a minor official, rising from the post of clerk to district official. In his youth, he learned the healing practice of "spells with talismanic water" (*fushui jue* 符水訣), which consisted of mixing the ashes of burned talismans into water and pronouncing spells over it. By ingesting or spitting this empowered water, one could exorcize demonic beings from a person's body or from a specific place. *Shao Yuanjie regularly visited the residence of Tao's father when Tao was still a boy, which suggests that Tao's father was also interested in Taoist ritual practices. There is no evidence, however, that either Tao or his father were initiated Taoist priests.

Early in the reign of the Jiajing Emperor (r. 1522–66), Tao Zhongwen was in the capital waiting for an appointment in Shandong province. By then, Shao Yuanjie had already grown old and was looking for a successor. Since he could not exorcize the Black Disasters (*heisheng* 黑眚) from the imperial palace, he asked his old acquaintance Tao to do this for him. These demons caused recurrent mass panics during the Ming period and were feared by people of all social levels. Tao successfully expelled them with an exorcistic sword onto which he had spit some talismanic water. Later, his prayers healed the crown prince from pocks. On an imperial tour to the south, he predicted a fire in the imperial encampment and said he would be able to protect only the emperor. Things happened precisely as he had foretold.

In the middle of 1551, the threat of the Mongol king Altan khaghan became especially severe. One of the leaders of a large Chinese colony in his territory claimed to possess a spell that enabled him to kill people and make city walls collapse. The official sources claim that this man was an adherent of the White Lotus Teachings (Bailian jiao 白蓮教), a common label for disapproved religious teachings and ritual (magical) practices (ter Haar 1991). Tao Zhongwen established a "ritual altar to quell the barbarians by setting up amulets" (*lifu zhenlu fatan* 立符鎮虜法壇), which was discarded after relations with the Mongols were again normalized.

Thanks to his ritual skills, Tao became an advisor to the Jiajing Emperor, and received honorific titles and a higher salary as well as expensive gifts. Shortly before he died, however, he asked to be dismissed on the grounds of his age and returned a whole range of gifts, which were used to restore the Lugou Bridge 盧溝橋 (better known as the Marco Polo Bridge) near Beijing. Meanwhile, considerable resentment had built up among Confucian ideologues against the imperial ritual politics, undoubtedly strengthened by the emperor's favoring of Shao Yuanjie, Tao Zhongwen, and other ritual specialists. Tao particularly was seen as the cause of the Jiajing Emperor's increased interest in the practices of Nourishing Life (*yangsheng). Although much of the criticism does not seem to be based on fact, both Shao and Tao have received a rather negative historiographical judgement, which culminated in the posthumous removal of their personal honors under Jiajing's son and successor, the short-lived Longqing Emperor (r. 1567–72).

Barend ter HAAR

📖 Berling 1998, 966–70; Fisher 1990; ter Haar 1991, 151–52, 155–66, 174–76, and passim; Liu Ts'un-yan 1976d; Lü Xichen 1991, 361–83; Shi Yanfeng 1992

※ Shao Yuanjie; TAOISM AND THE STATE

ti

體

substance

See *ti and yong 體 · 用.

ti and yong

體 · 用

substance and function

The terms ti and yong are variously rendered as "substance" or "essence," and "function" or "application" or "activity," respectively. Together they constitute a paradigm that has played an important role in Chinese thought at least since the *Xuanxue (Arcane Learning) speculations, when *Wang Bi gave ti a metaphysical import by equating it with Non-being (*wu) or emptiness (xu 虛). The ti-yong polarity also provided a basic conceptual framework for Buddhist thought, which in turn was adopted by Taoism.

In Western terms, the relation between ti and yong parallels that between being and becoming, potentiality and actuality, subject and predicate, or language and discourse (although the terms do not have the same meaning, the relation itself is comparable). Language, for instance, is a potential tool for discourse, "that by which" (suoyi 所以) discourse is possible, and has no significance or efficacy if it is not practiced. Similarly, substance without function has no reality and remains what Taoists call "vain emptiness" (wankong 頑空). Moreover, the existence of ti and yong is reciprocal in the same way that a subject exists only if it has an attribute or does something. For example, "walking" as a substantive is the ti of "walking" as a verb. Without the act of walking, and without a subject who is walking, no walk is possible, but at the same time one cannot separate the walking person from his or her act of walking. Ti and yong, therefore, are two aspects of the same reality, different but inseparable. Ti is said to be the "ancestor" (zu 祖) or the "ruler" (zhu 主), but an ancestor does not exist without descendants and a ruler does not exist without subjects.

The distinction between ti and yong pertains to the domain "subsequent to form" (or: "below the form," xing er xia 形而下), i.e., the phenomenal world of thought and language; only within the phenomenal world can there be a distinction between noumenon and phenomenon, which are one and the same. The *ti* of the Dao is primordial Chaos (**hundun*), and its *yong* is the Great Ultimate (**taiji*), but the Great Ultimate is the *ti* of the Five Agents (**wuxing*). From the point of view of the phenomenal world, *ti* is the noumenal world (**xiantian*) and permanence (*chang* 常) or emptiness (*xu*); *yong* is the phenomenal world (**houtian*) and change (*bian* 變) or fullness (*shi* 實, in the sense of "reality"). *Yong* is expansion, the movement to the outside and multiplicity (*shun* 順 or "continuation"), and *ti* is the return to the source, the movement of reversal (*ni* 逆 or "inversion"). *Yong* is the specific nature of each being, *ti* is their unity. In terms of movement and quiescence (**dong* and *jing*), quiescence is *yong* in relation to the Dao or Emptiness (it is its functioning), but is *ti* in relation to movement, in the sense that it is the root of spontaneous functioning in accord with the circumstances. In alchemical terms, *ti* is Mercury and the inner nature, and *yong* is Lead and the vital force (see **xing* and *ming*).

The dialectic relation between *ti* and *yong* is the same as that between Non-being and Being (**wu* and *you*). In his commentary to the *Daode jing* (*Daode zhenjing guangsheng yi* 道德真經廣聖義; CT 725), *Du Guangting applies the *ti-yong* dialectic in relation to Non-being and Being in the Buddhist sense, using a didactic dialectical procedure to analyze *li* 理 (the Absolute) and *shi* 事 (the phenomena). For instance, if one takes the Dao as fundamental Non-being and *ti*, then its name and workings are Being and *yong*, respectively, and everything is subsumed by Non-being. But one can take Being as *ti* and Non-being as *yong* to make Non-being operate.

Isabelle ROBINET

📖 Chan A. K. L. 1991b, 65–68

※ *dong* and *jing*; *wu* and *you*

Tianhuang zhidao Taiqing yuce

天皇至道太清玉冊

Jade Fascicles of Great Clarity on the Ultimate Way of the Celestial Sovereign

*Zhu Quan (1378–1448), son of the Hongwu Emperor (r. 1368–98), compiled this encyclopedic anthology on Taoist lore. A copy of the text in eight *juan* is recorded in the 1607 **Wanli xu daozang* (Supplementary Taoist Canon of the Wanli Reign Period). This manual (CT 1483) opens with a preface dated to the ninth day of the first lunar month of 1444, bearing Zhu's *nom de plume* Nanji xialing laoren quxian 南極遐齡老人臞仙 (Gaunt Transcendent, Long-lived Old Man of the Southern Pole). Elsewhere in the text the compiler's name is given as Nanji chongxu miaodao zhenjun xialing laoren quxian 南極冲虛妙道真君 遐齡老人臞仙 (Gaunt Transcendent, Long-lived Old Man, Perfected Lord of the Wondrous Way of the Unfathomable Emptiness of the Southern Pole).

Zhu explains in his preface (1.1a–3a) that he sought to fill a gap by providing a comprehensive reference work on everything of importance to the history of Taoism. An introductory essay (1.3b–8b) entitled "Yuandao" 原道 (Original Way) traces the foundation of the Tiandao 天道 (Celestial Way), or Zhengdao 正道 (Orthodox Way), to *Huangdi, Laozi, and *Zhuangzi. In his eagerness to promote the superiority of indigenous over non-Chinese teachings, Zhu encouraged his readers to view the Orthodox Way and the legacy of Confucius as a unified heritage.

The table of contents (1.8b–9a) reveals that the copy of the text incorporated into the Taoist Canon originally consisted of two *juan*, with nine headings listed in the first and ten in the second chapter. The nineteen headings and representative subject matter of each are listed below, as recorded in the eight-*juan* text in the Taoist Canon:

1. "Cleaving Open Heaven and Earth" ("Kaipi tiandi" 開闢天地, 1.9a–21b): cosmology, astronomy, meteorology.

2. "Origins and Development of the Taoist Teaching" ("Daojiao yuanliu" 道 教源流, 1.22a–33a): Laozi, Tianshi 天師, Nanpai 南派 (Southern branch), i.e., *Nanzong, Beipai 北派 (Northern branch), i.e., *Quanzhen.

3. "Draconic Script of the Celestial Sovereign" ("Tianhuang longwen" 天皇 龍文, 2.1a–25b): Taoist Canon, lost titles, anti-Taoist writings, *Zhengyi registers and scriptures, ritual post titles.

4. "Orbiting Creation" ("Ganyun zaohua" 幹運造化, 3.1a–17b): Jade Hall choreography, manipulations, and directives.

5. "Protocols for Offering Rituals" ("Jiaoshi yifan" 醮事儀範, 3.17b–25a): memorials, talismans, participants.

6. "Mysterious Secrets of the Heart of Heaven" ("Tianxin xuanbi" 天心玄 祕, 3.25a–31b): classified categories of ritual.

7. "Order of Offices for Taoist Schools" ("Daomen guanzhi" 道門官制, 3.31b–34b): historical context for clerical titles.

8. "Celestial Statutes in Red Script" ("Chiwen tianlü" 赤文天律, 3.34b–47a): regulations for clergy and laity.

9. "Rules of Purity and Protocols" ("Qinggui yifan" 清規儀範, 4.1a–29b): *jiao posts and malpractice penalties, monastic posts and etiquette.

10. "Abbeys and Altars" ("Gongdian tanshan" 宮殿壇墠, 5.1a–10a): architectural terminology.

11. "Protocols for Honoring Sanctity" ("Fengsheng yizhi" 奉聖儀制, 5.10a–15b): deities, images, shrines, decor, and offerings.

12. "Celestial Music and Transcendent Accoutrements" ("Tianyue xianzhang" 天樂仙仗, 5.15b–30a): musical selections and instruments, banners, pennants, and lantern arrangements.

13. "Protocols of Complete Perfection" ("Quanzhen yishi" 全真儀式, 5.30a–36a): meditation by clepsydra.

14. "Cap and Gown System" ("Guanfu zhidu" 冠服制度, 6.1a–6a): headgear, garments, and footwear.

15. "Implements for Cultivating Perfection" ("Xiuzhen qiyong" 修真器用, 6.6a–13a; two sheets of twenty-five columns each from the 1607 printing, corresponding to 6.12a6–13a10 and 6.13a11–14b5, are printed in reverse order in modern editions of the Taoist Canon): furnishings, utensils.

16. "Numinous Script of the Jade Bookbag" ("Yuji lingwen" 玉笈靈文, 6.13a–36b): Xiandao 仙道 (Way of Transcendence), conversion of non-Chinese kingdoms, guidelines for cultivating perfection.

17. "Auspicious Days for Cultivation of Reverence" ("Chaoxiu jichen" 朝修吉辰, 7.1a–28b): calendar of holy days, lists of festival days and calendrical taboos.

18. "Numerically Categorized Memorabilia" ("Shumu jishi" 數目紀事, 8.1a–32b): lists of terms, proper names and places by numerological association.

19. "Offerings for jiao Rituals" ("Jiaoxian jipin" 醮獻祭品, 8.32b–35b): foodstuffs and drinks.

Zhu draws on a diverse body of material in compiling this vade mecum, ranging from his own exegeses to hagiographic, narrative, and historical accounts. Corresponding passages to sources he fails to identify may often be found in other texts of the Taoist Canon. Excerpts of unit 4 in chapter 3, for example, find their match in the *Wushang xuanyuan santian Yutang dafa* 無上玄元三天玉堂大法 (Great Rites of the Jade Hall of the Three Heavens, of the Supreme Mysterious Origin; CT 220), ascribed to *Lu Shizhong (fl. 1120–30).

Judith M. BOLTZ

📖 Boltz J. M. 1987a, 237–42; Boltz J. M. 1994, 10–11

※ Zhu Quan

tianku

填庫

Filling the Treasury

Filling the Treasury is a rite performed on behalf of the deceased by his family, with the purpose of returning the money that was borrowed when he was born to the Celestial Treasury. If this rite is not performed, it is thought that the unpaid debt will negatively influence the fate of the deceased and his descendants. The amount of money to be returned is determined by the year of birth according to the Chinese zodiac; a handling charge is also taken into account.

The money to be returned to the Treasury is called "birth money" (*shousheng qian* 受生錢) or "natal-destiny money" (*benming qian* 本命錢), and consists of dozens of bundles of rectangular white paper (see *zhiqian). At the beginning of the rite, the priest performs the mudrās of the Three Treasures (*sanbao* 三寶, i.e., the Dao, the Scriptures, and the Masters). A record (*die* 牒) is issued in two copies (in the form of a divided talisman) as an auxiliary document for the deceased to take with him to deliver to the Treasury official. Besides the amount stipulated for the Treasury, money is also necessary for use in the underworld; a vast amount of Treasury money is accordingly burned to be sent to the soul of the deceased person.

The idea of "filling the treasury" is shared by both Taoism and Buddhism. The documents in two copies used in this rite had not yet taken a fixed form in the *Lingbao rites of the Song dynasty, and their use was only formalized in the Yellow Register Retreat (*huanglu zhai) that developed from the Ming period onward.

MARUYAMA Hiroshi

📖 Hou Ching-lang 1975; Lagerwey 1987c, 188–89; Ōfuchi Ninji 1983, 546–54; Seidel 1978a

※ *gongde; zhiqian*

tianmen and *dihu*

天門 · 地戶

Gate of Heaven and Door of Earth

While an early use of the term *tianmen* appears in *Daode jing* 10 ("the Gate of Heaven opens and shuts"), no mention is made of *dihu* until the Han dynasty. A comparatively early example of both expressions used in conjunction is in the *Wu Yue chunqiu* 吳越春秋 (Spring and Autumn Annals of the States of Wu and Yue), a work probably dating from the Han period but containing later additions (Lagerwey 1993b). When the King of Wu, Helü (r. 514–496 BCE), was building the city walls of Suzhou (Jiangsu) according to the plans of Wu Zixu 伍子胥, he made a gate in the northwest to represent the Gate of Heaven, and a gate in the southeast to represent the Door of Earth.

The placement of the Gate of Heaven in the northwest and the Door of Earth in the southeast is explained by the principle of Chinese cosmography and topography that there is an "insufficiency" or a "gap" (*buzu* 不足) of Heaven in the northwest and of Earth in the southeast. The same directional axis is also used in Taoist rituals and ceremonies. As shown in *Du Guangting's (850–933) *Jinlu zhai qitan yi* 金錄齋啟壇儀 (Liturgies for Inaugurating the Altar of the Golden Register Retreat; CT 483), four gateways are to be arranged around the altar: the Gate of Heaven to the northwest, the Door of Earth to the southeast, the Gate of the Sun (*rimen* 日門) to the northeast, and the Gate of the Moon (*yuemen* 月門) to the southwest.

In the context of self-cultivation practices, the Gate of Heaven is the nose and the Door of Earth is the mouth. The nose breathes in and out the pneuma (*qi*) of Heaven, and the mouth absorbs the pneuma of the Earth through its intake of food.

MIURA Kunio

📖 Lagerwey 1987c, 11–17, 31–36, and passim; Matsumura Takumi 1992; Stein R. A. 1990, 209–22

※ COSMOLOGY

Tianpeng zhou

天蓬咒

Tianpeng spell

Tianpeng ("Heavenly Mugwort") is the name of an exorcistic deity related to the Northern Emperor (*Beidi). *Tao Hongjing's *Zhengao (10.10b) describes a meditation practice called "Northern Emperor's Method of Killing Demons" (*Beidi shagui zhi fa* 北帝殺鬼之法), which includes a powerful spell to repel demons. This is the Tianpeng spell, whose effectiveness is often mentioned in Tang and Song Taoist texts such as *Du Guangting's *Daojiao lingyan ji* (10.7b). The spell (trans. Mollier 1997, 358) begins with the invocation "O Tianpeng! O Tianpeng!" and is structured in four-character verses, with twenty-four verses in total.

Tianpeng is depicted as an old man with a blue tongue, green teeth, and four eyes. Riding upon a dragon, he holds an imperial bell in one hand, and brandishes a sword or a large axe in the other hand with which he cuts down demons. Around the fourth century he came to be worshipped as a popular god, and the Tianpeng spell has existed since that time. By the Song period, he was called Tianpeng Yuanshuai 天蓬元帥 (Marshal Tianpeng).

YAMADA Toshiaki

📖 Liu Zhiwan 1987; Mollier 1997, 355–59; Strickmann 2002, 100–101

※ Beidi; Heisha

tianshi

天師

Celestial Master

Scholars generally apply the term *tianshi* both to the institutions characteristic of the early *Tianshi dao (Way of the Celestial Masters) and to a lineage that claims to connect modern *Zhengyi leaders back to *Zhang Daoling (see table 23). Some have also begun referring to certain loosely defined traditions of the Six Dynasty period as "the Southern Celestial Masters" (Nickerson 2000) and "the Northern Celestial Masters" (Kohn 2000c).

In earliest usage, *tianshi* was simply a term for an especially insightful teacher. In *Zhuangzi* 24 (trans. Watson 1968, 266), an unnamed young boy takes a moment away from herding horses to give advice about how to govern the empire; the Yellow Emperor (*Huangdi) kowtows and calls him *tianshi*. Later, *tianshi* is the term for an unnamed teacher in the *Taiping jing* (Scripture of Great Peace), which depicts "conferences between a 'celestial master' and his disciples, a group of 'Perfected'" (Hendrischke 2000, 143; Hendrischke 1985).

Based on modern Zhengyi tradition, twentieth-century scholars generally accepted that the first historical person to claim the mantle of *tianshi* was Zhang Daoling. But the historical facts of the Tianshi dao and related movements remain unclear. Various texts attribute various titles to Zhang Daoling, *Zhang Heng, *Zhang Lu, and Taiping 太平 leader Zhang Jue 張角. But it is uncertain which of them, if any, actually used the title *tianshi*; or to which of them, if any, it might first have been applied (see Kleeman 1998, 84).

In the Six Dynasties and Tang, the term *tianshi* was claimed by, or applied to, a wide variety of individuals in a wide variety of contexts. Few were named Zhang 張, and few had any direct connection to the early Tianshi dao leaders. For instance, the fourth-century *Huayang guozhi* 華陽國志 (Monograph of the Land South of Mount Hua) reports that in 277 one Chen Rui 陳瑞, who "styled himself Celestial Master," was executed. In 424, *Kou Qianzhi was declared Celestial Master by the Toba emperor Taiwu (r. 424–52). Zhang descendants occasionally appear in Six Dynasty materials, but it does not seem that they claimed, or were recognized as entitled to claim, the title *tianshi*.

During the reign of Tang Xuanzong (712–56), a "Celestial Master Chen" (Chen tianshi 陳天師) is said to have been among those who taught "ingestion of breath" (*fuqi). But the title *tianshi* may have been retroactively applied to him, for he does not appear in biographical texts until Song times. The same is true of Zhang Gao 張高, the only person surnamed Zhang to be mentioned as a *tianshi* in regard to Tang times (Kirkland 1984). The *Lishi zhenxian tidao tongjian* (19.7a–b) of Zhao Daoyi 趙道一 (fl. 1294–1307) says that Xuanzong conferred upon Zhang Gao the title of "Celestial Master in the Han Lineage" (Hanzu tianshi 漢祖天師). But no such event is attested in Tang sources; no such title appears in Tang sources, in reference to Zhang Gao or anyone else; and Zhang Gao himself appears nowhere in the abundant Taoist literature of the period, or even in the voluminous writings of *Du Guangting. Even if we credit Zhao's report, it represents Zhang as someone who "embraced the formulas of the Perfected Ones" and "would drink up to a gallon of liquor without becoming intoxicated," suggesting that any such title was honorific, not confirmation that Zhang led a community that kept alive old Tianshi dao traditions.

Meanwhile, Tang sources do accord the title of *tianshi* to various men (apparently no women) who were likewise not in any lineage traceable to Tianshi dao leaders. One was a theurgist named Hu Huichao 胡惠超 (?–703), who was called "Celestial Master Hu" in an inscription text by Yan Zhenqing 顏真卿, ca. 775. By the early tenth century, *any* memorable Taoist was called a *tianshi*. The second Shu ruler denominated Du Guangting "the Celestial Master Who Transmits Truth" (Chuanzhen tianshi 傳真天師), and Du himself accorded the title "Celestial Master" not only to *Sima Chengzhen but even to *Ye Fashan. In the *Xu xianzhuan* (Sequel to Biographies of Immortals), Sima's successor *Li Hanguang has *tianshi* in his title; and elsewhere two of Sima's other disciples are called *tianshi*. In the *Sandong qunxian lu* (Accounts of the Gathered Immortals from the Three Caverns) of 1154, even the poet *Wu Yun is entitled a *tianshi*. However, no source firmly datable to Tang times mentions any *tianshi* surnamed Zhang.

Tenth-century writings by Du and others mention members of the Zhang clan who lived at Mount Longhu (*Longhu shan, Jiangxi) and purported to be descendants of Zhang Daoling. Their "propagandistic activity" (Barrett 1994b, 96–97) included concocting historical events and persons designed to portray themselves as heirs to an unbroken lineage of "Celestial Masters," just as their contemporaries at Mount Mao (*Maoshan, Jiangsu) were fabricating a lineage of *Shangqing "Grand Masters" (*zongshi* 宗師) to compete with the model that Chan Buddhists of that period had devised (Kirkland 2004). Much later, in Ming times, *Zhang Zhengchang (1335–78) codified such claims in the *Han tianshi shijia* (Lineage of the Han Celestial Master), but Henri Maspero shows that its compilers "had no document covering the period which goes from the Han to the T'ang, and that their imagination alone attempted to establish relationships" between such figures as Zhang Lu, Zhang Gao, and the twelfth-century figure *Zhang Jixian (Maspero 1981, 398).

Russell KIRKLAND

📖 Barrett 1994b; Hendrischke 1985; Hendrischke 2000; Kleeman 1998, 66–80; Maspero 1981, 373–400

※ Tianshi dao; Zhengyi

Tianshi dao

天師道

Way of the Celestial Masters

The founding of the Way of the Celestial Masters or Tianshi dao in modern Sichuan province during the second century CE marks the formal establishment of the Taoist religion. The movement traces its origins to a dramatic revelation to *Zhang Daoling in 142 CE, when Laozi descended to him atop Mount Heming (*Heming shan) in order to establish a new covenant between the true gods of Taoism and the people. The central feature of its teaching was a rejection of the blood sacrifice offered to the traditional gods of the community and the state in favor of a new relationship between humankind and a newly revealed transcendent pantheon of Taoist deities. The movement was originally theocratic in concept, seeking to create a utopian state that would replace the Chinese imperial institution and looking forward to a world of Great Peace (*taiping) that would take shape after a series of apocalyptic disasters and travails (see *APOCALYPTIC ESCHATOLOGY). Although these millenarian beliefs faded, the Taoist community structure that had been developed by this time survived in local communities across China for centuries and the community libationers (*jijiu) evolved into a sacerdotal lineage of priests that have married, lived in the community, and passed on their office hereditarily for nearly two millennia (see table 23). Today, there is still a Celestial Master who claims direct descent from Zhang Daoling, and the overwhelming majority of non-monastic Taoist priests both within China and in the Chinese diaspora have identified themselves as part of this tradition.

Origins and early history. The term Celestial Master (*tianshi) occurs first in *Zhuangzi 24 (trans. Watson 1968, 266), where the Yellow Emperor (*Huangdi) uses the term to praise a sagacious young boy herding horses whom he meets while on a journey in search of the "great clod" (*dakuai* 大塊). There is also a Celestial Master in the *Taiping jing (Scripture of Great Peace, parts of which may date to the Han), but there he is a wholly divine figure who instructs the Perfected (*zhenren) and responds to their questions. The Celestial Master who founded the Taoist religion is a mortal, Zhang Daoling, who is selected by the divine Laozi (*Laojun) to create a new covenant between humanity and the awesome powers of the true Taoist heavens. He transmitted leadership of the group to his son *Zhang Heng, known as the "inheriting master" (*sishi* 嗣師), who passed it on to his son, *Zhang Lu, known as the "continuing master" (*xishi* 系師). Zhang Lu should be considered the substantive organizer, if not the actual founder of the group, and he is the likely author of the only work we can associate with the early Celestial Master movement, the *Xiang'er commentary to the Daode jing, so his importance is not solely organizational.

The origins of the Way of the Celestial Masters are to be found in a variety of beliefs and practices of the Warring States and Han periods. The most significant of these were:

1. The Han Confucian understanding of an active Heaven and Earth that respond to human action (*ganying* 感應) through natural occurrences that reflect their approbation or condemnation.

Table 23

1	*Zhang Daoling (second c.) 張道陵	33	Zhang Jingyuan 張景淵
2	*Zhang Heng (?–179) 張衡	34	Zhang Qingxian 張慶先
3	*Zhang Lu (?–215 or 216) 張魯	35	*Zhang Keda (1218–63) 張可大
4	Zhang Sheng 張盛	36	*Zhang Zongyan (1244–91) 張宗演
5	Zhang Zhaocheng 張昭成	37	Zhang Yudi (?–1294) 張與棣
6	Zhang Jiao 張椒	38	Zhang Yucai (?–1316) 張與材
7	Zhang Hui 張回	39	*Zhang Sicheng (?–1344?) 張嗣成
8	Zhang Jiong 張迥	40	Zhang Side (?–1353) 張嗣德
9	Zhang Fu 張符	41	Zhang Zhengyan (?–1359) 張正言
10	*Zhang Zixiang (fl. ca. 600?) 張子祥	42	*Zhang Zhengchang (1335–78) 張正常
11	Zhang Tongxuan 張通玄	43	*Zhang Yuchu (1361–1410) 張宇初
12	Zhang Heng 張恆	44	Zhang Yuqing (1364–1427) 張宇清
13	Zhang Guang 張光	45	Zhang Maocheng 張懋丞
14	Zhang Cizheng 張慈正	46	Zhang Yuanji 張元吉
15	Zhang Gao (fl. ca. 735?) 張高	47	Zhang Xuanqing 張玄慶
16	Zhang Yingshao 張應韶	48	Zhang Yanpian (1480–1550) 張彥頨
17	Zhang Yi 張頤	49	Zhang Yongxu (?–1566) 張永緒
18	Zhang Shiyuan 張士元	50	*Zhang Guoxiang (?–1611) 張國祥
19	Zhang Xiu 張修	51	Zhang Xianyong 張顯庸
20	Zhang Chen 張諶	52	Zhang Yingjing 張應京
21	Zhang Bingyi 張秉一	53	Zhang Hongren 張洪任
22	Zhang Shan 張善	54	Zhang Jizong (?–1716) 張繼宗
23	Zhang Jiwen 張季文	55	Zhang Xilin (?–1727) 張錫麟
24	Zhang Zhengsui (fl. 1015) 張正隨	56	Zhang Yulong (?–1752) 張遇隆
25	Zhang Qianyao 張乾曜	57	Zhang Cunyi (?–1779) 張存義
26	Zhang Sizong 張嗣宗	58	Zhang Qilong (?–1798) 張起隆
27	Zhang Xiangzhong 張象中	59	Zhang Yu 張鈺
28	Zhang Dunfu (fl. 1077) 張敦復	60	Zhang Peiyuan (?–1859) 張培源
29	Zhang Jingduan (1049?–1100?) 張景端	61	Zhang Renzheng (1841–1903) 張仁晸
30	*Zhang Jixian (1092–1126) 張繼先	62	*Zhang Yuanxu (1862–1924) 張元旭
31	Zhang Shixiu 張時修	63	*Zhang Enpu (1904–69) 張恩溥
32	Zhang Shouzhen (?–1176) 張守真	64	Zhang Yuanxian 張源先

The sixty-four Celestial Masters (*liushisi dai tianshi* 六十四代天師).

2. The prophecies and apocryphal texts (*chenwei* 讖緯; see *TAOISM AND THE APOCRYPHA) that, appearing near the end of the Former Han, fed beliefs in esoteric meanings to traditional texts and encouraged the linking of signs or portents with dramatic political changes.

3. A widespread faith, evident first in Mozi 墨子 (ca. 470–ca. 400 BCE), that Heaven has impartial, unwavering moral standards for humanity and that its representatives will reward and punish individuals for their adherence to or transgression of these precepts.

4. The growing popular belief that divine teachers like Laozi have played a significant, recurring role in Chinese political history, appearing age after

age under different names and guises to act as advisors to emperors, and that these sacred sages continue to appear today in human form to guide the people and the government onto the right path.

5. A conviction among many that current natural and human disasters reflected divine disapproval of an increasingly evil world, that conditions would only worsen as disorder and civil war left commoners unprotected against both human and demonic malefactors, and that supernatural aid was essential for survival against the increasing threat.

6. A belief among some that this situation would worsen until a crisis was reached, when many would die, after which a realm of Great Peace would be established, where all members of society would be cared for and their basic needs met.

The central teaching of the early movement, the Covenant with the Powers of Orthodox Unity (*zhengyi mengwei* 正一盟威), was encapsulated in the Pure Bond (*qingyue* 清約): "The gods do not eat or drink, the master does not accept money." This stricture demanded the rejection of blood sacrifice, central to popular and state cult, and the traditional gods that accepted it, in favor of transcendent Taoist deities who did not rely upon, and hence could not be swayed by, their worshippers, and Taoist priests who offered their services as appropriate, without the prompting of material payment. Some scholars attribute the "Outer" version of the **Huangting jing* (Scripture of the Yellow Court) to the early Celestial Masters on the basis of two references in the "Dadao jia lingjie" 大道家令戒 (Commands and Admonitions for the Families of the Great Dao; trans. Bokenkamp 1997, 172 and 175); they argue that meditation on gods of the body was an important part of Celestial Master practice (Ōfuchi Ninji 1991, 263–272). We also know that they chanted the text of the *Daode jing* chorally, interpreting it according to the *Xiang'er* commentary. The histories record a great concern with sin, which was observed and recorded by the Three Offices (**sanguan*, of Heaven, Earth, and Water), and could only be expiated through written confessions submitted to each office. These may be related to early codes like the **Xiang'er jie* (*Xiang'er* Precepts) and the **Laojun shuo yibai bashi jie* (The Hundred and Eighty Precepts Spoken by Lord Lao). The characterization of the movement's teachings in historical sources as focusing on the *guidao* 鬼道 or "demonic way" probably reflects the widespread concern about demonic attacks and the specific ritual methods promoted by the Celestial Masters to counter them. The *Xiang'er* commentary makes clear that members of the early movement saw themselves threatened not only by demons but also by demonically-inspired heretical movements.

The earliest hard evidence for the movement is a stele dated to 173 CE, which records the initiation of a group of new libationers or Taoist priests.

The stele clearly names the group as the Way of the Celestial Master (Tianshi daofa 天師道法) and confirms that there were already rituals of initiation and a body of sacred, esoteric texts conferred on initiates. Historical accounts of the movement in the official histories of Later Han and Three Kingdoms periods were written by outsiders, but probably based on near contemporary documents. They record numerous aspects of the administration of the early movement. They note that the territory under the Celestial Master sway was divided into twenty-four parishes (*zhi), each headed by a Parish-heading Great Libationer, that there were "charity lodges" (yishe 義舍) where the indigent and hungry could always find food, and that the parishes organized communal works projects to repair roads and bridges. The best known feature of the group was an annual tithe of five pecks (dou 斗, approximately 9 liters) of rice, which presumably supported the charitable operations and high officers of the movement. The institution of three annual Assemblies (*sanhui), held initially on seventh day of the first lunar month, the seventh day of the seventh lunar month, and the fifth day of the tenth lunar month, then moving to the fifteenth of each lunar month, seems to date back to this early stage of the movement, as do the "cuisines" (*chu) or non-sacrificial feasts hosted by the faithful on these occasions.

Zhang Lu was able to establish an independent base of power in Hanzhong 漢中 and northern Sichuan region during the 180s and although he never formally declared independence from the central government, he ruled over a theocratic state where church functionaries replaced government officials and the Celestial Master church assumed all the local functions traditionally filled by the government until 215. Historical sources record the defeat of another local Sichuanese religious leader, Zhang Xiu 張脩, during this period, but Xiu is sometimes identified as a *Yellow Turban and sometimes as a follower of the Celestial Masters, and fragmentary surviving sources do not permit us to resolve the question. In any case, the nascent state fell before the armies of Cao Cao 曹操 in 215, but Zhang Lu was treated well and his offspring intermarried with the Caos. The followers of the religion were subject to a massive relocation that moved some of them northwest into the Gansu corridor and other east to the capital region in central North China. Around 300 a large group of those Taoists transported to the northwest, many of them non-Chinese minorities, came back to the Sichuan region and established the state of Great Perfection (*Dacheng, 306–47), with a Taoist master, *Fan Changsheng, as Preceptor of State.

Six Dynasties and Tang. It would seem that Cao Cao's resettlements transmitted Celestial Master Taoism together with its distinctive community structure across North China, and that the mass migrations following the fall of North China in 317 carried this movement to South China. In the fifth-century *Daomen *kelüe* (Abridged Codes for the Taoist Community), *Lu Xiujing laments that in his day institutions like the Assemblies were not being observed according to proper rules and libationer positions were becoming hereditary. Similar complaints were first voiced by Zhang Lu through a spirit medium in 255, as recorded in the "Dadao jia lingjie" 大道家令戒 (Commands and Admonitions for the Families of the Great Dao; trans. Bokenkamp 1997, 148–85), and were the subject of *Kou Qianzhi's reform in North China as well. We should perhaps understand these as reflecting conflicts inherent in the Taoist community structure rather than a serious transformation in Taoist practice. The date at which these Celestial Master communities disappeared remains one of the great mysteries of Chinese social history.

Celestial Master priests do not figure prominently in late medieval sources and the term Celestial Master had by the Tang been debased to the point that it could be used for any prominent Taoist, but this does not mean that the Celestial Master lineage and its scriptural heritage were insignificant. On the contrary, by the Tang, the Celestial Master scriptural corpus was ensconced at the base of the ordination hierarchy. The graded series of ordinations by which children grew into full members of the church were Celestial Master ordinations and the foundational set of precepts that linked all Taoists in a common ethical stance were Celestial Master precepts. Their scriptural legacy centered on a large number of model petitions (*zhang* 章) that working Taoists might use in responding to the varied supernatural threats their parishioners might face. The more exalted ordinations and their elegant revealed texts might have been more effective in garnering imperial favor and attracting clients, but it is doubtful anyone ever went long without recourse to the basic petitions or considered their own conduct without reference to the precepts that they learned as a Celestial Master Taoist. (For the later history of the Way of the Celestial Masters, see the entry *Zhengyi.)

Terry KLEEMAN

📖 Barrett 1994b; Bokenkamp 1997; Chen Guofu 1963, 98–101, 260–61, 275–76, and 308–69; Fukui Kōjun 1958, 2–61; Guo Shusen 1990; Hendrischke 2000; Kleeman 1998; Kobayashi Masayoshi 1995; Kohn 2000c; Maeda Shigeki 1995; Nickerson 2000; Ōfuchi Ninji 1991, 136–59, 309–406; Qing Xitai 1988–95, 1: 146–92 and 2: passim; Qing Xitai 1994, 1: 84–91; Ren Jiyu 1990, 42–57; Robinet 1997b, 53–77; Stein R. A. 1963; Zhang Jiyu 1990

※ Wudoumi dao; Zhengyi; for other related entries see the Synoptic Table of Contents, sec. III.2 ("Tianshi dao")

Tiantai shan

天臺山 (or: 天台山)

Mount Tiantai (Zhejiang)

Mount Tiantai, also referred to in Taoist sources by the names of its subsidiary peaks such as Mount Tongbo (Tongbo shan 桐柏山) and Mount Chicheng (Chicheng shan 赤城山), is part of a larger mountain range located in Zhejiang. Within Buddhism, Tiantai is synonymous with the lineage founded by Zhiyi 智顗 (530–98; Hurvitz 1962) that was named after that mountain. Although it is less commonly known, the mountain also had a long Taoist history, dating at least from the early fourth century when *Ge Hong (283–343) mentioned it in his *Baopu zi as a site perfect for training to become a transcendent and for compounding elixirs. More importantly, Mount Tiantai is remembered in Taoist history as a site associated with the revelation of *Lingbao texts to *Ge Xuan (trad. 164–244) and with the formation of the *Lingbao dafa (Great Rites of the Numinous Treasure) during the Song dynasty.

In the Tang period, *Sima Chengzhen (647–735) lived at Mount Tiantai at the Abbey of the Paulownias and Cypresses (*Tongbo guan), which later came to house a large Taoist library. Tiantai was also where *Du Guangting initially trained under Ying Yijie 應夷節 (810–94). In the late Tang (ninth century) there was a movement away from Mount Heng (*Hengshan 衡山, Hunan) to Tiantai by Taoists in the lineage descending from Sima Chengzhen and leading to Du Guangting (Verellen 1989, 19–27).

Monographs on Mount Tiantai survive in both the Buddhist and Taoist canons. The Tiantai shan ji 天臺山記 (Records of Mount Tiantai), compiled by Xu Lingfu 徐靈府 (ca. 760–841), is in the Taishō Buddhist Canon (T. 2096). The Tiantai shanzhi 天臺山志 (Monograph of Mount Tiantai), compiled anonymously in 1367, is in the Taoist Canon (CT 603). Mount Tiantai also became well known throughout China following Sun Chuo's 孫綽 (314–71) You Tiantai shan fu 遊天臺山賦 (Rhapsody on Wandering on Mount Tiantai), a description of a mystical ascent of the mountain that was later included in the Wenxuan 文選 (Literary Anthology; trans. Knechtges 1982–96, 2: 243–53).

James ROBSON

📖 Boltz J. M. 1987a, 43–46, 111; Inoue Ichii 1931; Maspero 1914, 54–67; Mather 1961

※ Tongbo guan; TAOIST SACRED SITES

tianxin

天心

Heart of Heaven; Celestial Heart

The term *tianxin* first appears in the expression "Heart of Heaven and Earth" (*tiandi zhi xin* 天地之心), found in the "Commentary to the Judgements" (*Tuanzhuan* 彖傳) on the hexagram *fu* 復 ䷗ (Return, no. 24) of the *Yijing*. Immobile in its essence, it is the central space, the interstice between movement and quiescence (*dong* and *jing*). From the point of view of Heaven, it represents the pole star; from the point of view of human beings, it is the True Intention (*zhenyi* 真意; see *yi*).

Indiscernible if one tries to seize it, the Heart of Heaven is symbolized by the winter solstice (*zi*), which in turn represents the moment when the One is about to divide itself into the Two and to manifest itself. In *neidan* practice it is located in different parts of the body, including the lower, middle, and upper Cinnabar Fields (*dantian*), corresponding to the levels of the navel, heart, and top of the head. However, in its ultimate sense as the Mysterious Pass (*xuanguan*), the Heart of Heaven is beyond space and time. To experience its opening, one can temporarily identify it with the lower Cinnabar Field, the locus of transformation where one perceives the appearance of the initial sparkle of Pure Yang (*chunyang* 純陽). This is therefore only a place of momentary emergence, a temporary support that helps an adept to understand that the Heart of Heaven is ultimately the same cavity as the cosmos in which beings are born and die. The interstice that separates enlightenment from discursive thought can only be experienced through pure thinking—the True Intention—when the Center is established in the simultaneous and threefold experience of the three Cinnabar Fields.

Monica ESPOSITO

📖 Cleary 1986a, 76–77; Kamitsuka Yoshiko 1999, 338–40; Robinet 1995c

※ *xuanguan*; *yi* [intention]; *neidan*

Tianxin zhengfa

天心正法

Correct Method (*or:* Rectifying Rites) of the Celestial Heart

The Tianxin tradition is the earliest, and one of the most influential, of the new Taoist exorcistic and therapeutic traditions that became important during the Song dynasty. It had already appeared in southeastern China by the tenth century, but the central corpus of texts, which represents its earliest documented form, was compiled only in the beginning of the twelfth century. They are, notably, the *Taishang zhuguo jiumin zongzhen biyao* (Secret Essentials of the Totality of Perfected, of the Most High, for Assisting the Country and Saving the People), contributed to the Taoist Canon of emperor Song Huizong by Yuan Miaozong 元妙宗 in 1116; and the works by *Deng Yougong, who appears to have been active prior to this date, but whose main work, the *Shangqing tianxin zhengfa* 上清天心正法 (Correct Method of the Celestial Heart of the Highest Clarity; CT 566), has survived only in an edition that seems to have been reworked around the middle of the twelfth century.

Affiliation of the tradition. It is clear from these texts that the term *tianxin, used to name the tradition, refers to the constellation of the Northern Dipper (*beidou) as a whole, not only to the sixth star (which in some early divination texts goes by the same name). The texts likewise are unambiguous concerning the affiliation of the Tianxin tradition, in terms of its historical transmission in the world. Thus the *Zongzhen biyao* states that the Tianxin methods "issue from the lineage of Orthodox Unity (*Zhengyi zhi zong* 正一之宗). They constitute the central authority for impeaching and controlling [demonic forces]" (1.1a).

In subsequent Taoist history, this understanding of the affiliation and origin of the tradition gained acceptance not only among the practitioners of its methods, but also among writers and liturgists representing other traditions. Thus, for instance, the early-thirteenth-century exegete and codifier of the *Lingbao dafa (Great Rites of the Numinous Treasure) tradition, Jin Yunzhong 金允中 (fl. 1224–25), opens his account of the history of the Tianxin tradition by stating that its core elements (i.e., the three fundamental talismans and the two basic seals) originally derived from the tradition of the (first) Celestial Master of the Han dynasty. Having fallen into oblivion during the period of disunity, they were restored only after the period of the Five Dynasties by *Tan Zixiao and *Rao Dongtian, who according to Jin placed them in a new,

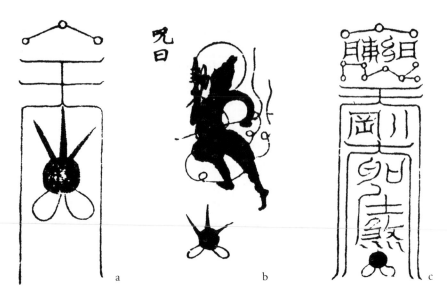

Fig. 73. The three main Tianxin zhengfa talismans: (a) *Sanguang fu* 三光符 (Talisman of the Three Radiances); (b) *Heisha fu* 黑煞符 (Talisman of the Black Killer; see *Heisha); (c) *Tiangang fu* 天罡符 (Talisman of the Celestial Guideline). *Shangqing tianxin zhengfa* 上清天心正法 (Correct Method of the Celestial Heart of the Highest Clarity; CT 566), 3.4a, 6b, and 7a.

contemporary framework of codes and regulations (*Shangqing lingbao dafa*; CT 1223, 43.16b–17a).

Some scholars have suggested that the tradition is nonetheless best understood as a development of the local cultic traditions on Mount Huagai (Huagai shan 華蓋山) in central Jiangxi, where Rao Dongtian had unearthed "the secret formulas of the Celestial Heart" in 994, and where the tradition was transmitted throughout the eleventh century. They have argued that the many indications found in Tianxin texts of an affiliation with the *Zhengyi tradition are due to a later process of editing that reflects the growing influence of the organization of the Celestial Masters toward the end of the Song dynasty. It is true that we know very little about the form of the Tianxin tradition as it was transmitted during the eleventh century; however, some of the key elements of the tradition, such as the methods of *bugang*, and the all-important method of "submitting the petition" (that is, the meditational journey to heaven in order to present a written prayer to the supreme deities; see *baibiao*), are clearly cognate with, or in some cases descend directly from, earlier Zhengyi forms. The same is true for the quintessential "method of inspecting and summoning" (*kaozhao fa* 考召法, i.e., the method of capturing and expelling the evil spirits causing illness by entering people's bodies), which in the *Zongzhen biyao* is based on the sections of the *Jinsuo liuzhu yin* (Guide to the Golden

Lock and the Flowing Pearls) that contain materials of the Zhengyi tradition. It is treated there as an ancient Zhengyi method and referred to the *Zhengyi kaozhao yi* 正一考召儀, and the tradition practiced is defined as the "method of the Celestial Heart of the tradition of Orthodox Unity" (*Tianxin zhengyi zhi fa* 天心正一之法), a phrase that may conceivably be the earliest preserved use of the name of the Tianxin tradition, and which in any case clearly defines the tradition as a form of Zhengyi (*Jinsuo liuzhu yin*, 4.5a–7b; *Zongzhen biyao*, 7.3a–5a).

The notion of an original connection between the Tianxin and the Zhengyi traditions is supported, furthermore, by external historical accounts of the life of its purported first patriarch, Tan Zixiao, who was, to be sure, a *daoshi from Quanzhou 泉州 (Fujian), and not associated with Mount Huagai. According to the *Nan Tang shu* 南唐書 (History of the Southern Tang; *j.* 17) by Lu You 陸游 (1125–1210), Tan was active in the 930s in the Kingdom of Min 閩, where he received the title Zhengyi xiansheng 正一先生 (Elder of Orthodox Unity) from the ruler, Wang Chang 王昶 (r. 935–39), and where he transmitted "the talismans of *Zhang Daoling" that he had received from the medium Chen Shouyuan 陳守元, who at the court of Wang Chang had been elevated to the status of Celestial Master. After the fall of Min, Tan went into hiding on Mount Lu (*Lushan) in northern Jiangxi, where he appeared in a nightly session "with disheveled hair and brandishing a sword," to perform the "interrogating and controlling" (*kaozhi* 考治) of a female ghost who had afflicted the Military Commissioner of Wuchang 武昌 (Hubei), He Jingzhu 何敬洙, with illness. The obvious model for this appearance is the spirit-mediums (*shentong* 神童) that are known to have played a major role in Tianxin practices during the Song dynasty. It seems highly likely that the phenomenon of spirit-possession, and the writing of talismans by mediums in trance, contributed substantially to the creation of the talismanic core of the Tianxin tradition. In any case, the overall image of the origin of the Tianxin tradition that emerges from the material reviewed above clearly points to a renewal of Taoism, not simply from within, but as the result of a syncretism between popular mediumistic practices and the ancient forms of ritual transmitted by Zhengyi priests.

Pantheon and practices. As a deified patriarch of the Tianxin tradition, Zhang Daoling is referred to in the texts as the Envoy of the Department of Exorcism (Quxie yuan shi 驅邪院使). The Department of Exorcism is the celestial bureau to which Tianxin priests were assigned, and from which the army of generals and soldiers assisting them were called forth. It is presided over by the Northern Emperor (*Beidi), who is also referred to as the "ancestral master" (*zushi* 祖師), and who seems to be identical with the supreme god of the central heavens, the Great Emperor of Purple Tenuity (Ziwei dadi 紫微大帝). He is assisted by the "great generals" of the Department of Exorcism, notably the group of thirty-six generals headed by Tianpeng 天蓬, the deity corresponding to the ninth star of the Northern Dipper (see under *Tianpeng zhou*). Further down in the hierarchy there are the generals of the Eastern Peak (Dongyue 東嶽), who lead the ranks of spirit-soldiers assisting the priest.

Aided by this army, the Tianxin priest may perform services of exorcism on behalf of the living. He typically begins by assuming the persona of the deity presiding over the specific method applied, through the rite of "transformation of the spirit" (*bianshen*), in which he visualizes himself in the shape and appearance of the deity in question, in order to take command of the army of spirits to be sent into battle against evil influences. A central role in commanding the presence of the spirits and using their powers against the forces of evil is played by the many talismans of the tradition, and in particular by the three fundamental talismans: *Sanguang fu* 三光符, *Heisha fu* 黑煞符, and *Tiangang fu* 天罡符 (fig. 73; see for instance *Shangqing tianxin zhengfa*, 3.1a–9a). As is clear from Hong Mai's 洪邁 (1123–1202) *Yijian zhi* 夷堅志 (Heard and Written by Yijian), practitioners of the Tianxin tradition during the Southern Song commonly performed large-scale liturgies, typically referred to as "Offerings of the Yellow Register" (see *huanglu zhai*), and sometimes also funerary services.

Social context and legacy. It is quite clear from several anecdotes in the *Yijian zhi* that during the twelfth century the Tianxin tradition achieved a certain popularity among members of the scholar-official class, especially as a means of combating "illicit cults" (*yinsi*) and destroying "heterodox" temples in the territories that they administered. However, the notion that essentially the tradition should be viewed as a reflection of the fundamental mentality of this social class, and as a set of ritual tools designed specifically to meet the needs of its members, surely is somewhat exaggerated. The emphasis on the so-called "bureaucratic metaphor," and on the judicial approach to ritual practice—as exemplified by the crucial method of "interrogating and summoning"—is by no means unique to the Tianxin tradition, but has been a staple of Taoist liturgy ever since its origin in the latter part of the second century CE. Moreover, a review of the social background of the many "ritual masters" of the tradition, referred to in the *Yijian zhi*, shows that the vast majority were either commoners or *daoshi*, while those who came from elite families, and who achieved fame for their talents, typically are shown to have studied with a master in order to be ordained as a Taoist priest, and thus to have become full-time clerics.

In any case, the passing interest among the class of scholar-officials in the cultivation of the methods of the Tianxin tradition, along with those of the new systems of Thunder Rites (*leifa*), does not appear to have survived long after the end of the Song dynasty. The forms of the Tianxin tradition that have survived to the present day are, on the one hand, the elements found in current versions of Zhengyi liturgy in southern China and Taiwan and, on the other hand, the remarkable preservation of Taoism as a communal religion among the Yao living in South China, Laos, and Thailand (see *TAOISM AND THE YAO PEOPLE). The Yao themselves in some contexts refer to this religion as a form of Tianxin zhengfa, and they appear to have been converted to it already during the Song dynasty.

Poul ANDERSEN

📖 Andersen 1991, 14–18 and 79–131; Andersen 1996; Boltz J. M. 1985, 64–172; Boltz J. M. 1987a, 33–38; Boltz J. M. 1993a; Davis E. 2001, 21–24; Drexler 1994; Hymes 1996, 37–39 and 56–65; Hymes 2002, 26–46 and passim; Maruyama Hiroshi 1995; Qing Xitai 1994, 1: 129–33; Qing Xitai 1999; Strickmann 1996, 231–41

※ For related entries see the Synoptic Table of Contents, sec. III.7 ("Song, Jin, and Yuan: Tianxin zhengfa")

Tianyin zi

天隱子

Book of the Master of Heavenly Seclusion

Since its inception in the mid-Tang, the *Tianyin zi* has been one of the most popular works of Taoist meditation and is still widely read among *qigong practitioners today. Besides its edition as an independent text in the Taoist Canon (CT 1026), a variant version is found in the Song anthology *Daoshu (2.4a–6b). The received text is attributed to *Sima Chengzhen (647–735); it is not clear whether he wrote it himself, however, or whether he received the teaching from the rather mysterious Master of Heavenly Seclusion (Tianyin zi) and only edited it. The text is very short and presents a tight summary of the essentials of Taoist practice in eight sections: 1. "Spirit Immortality" ("Shenxian" 神仙); 2. "Simplicity" ("Yijian" 易簡); 3. "Gradual Progress toward the Gate [of the Dao]" ("Jianmen"); 4. "Fasting and Abstention" ("Zhaijie" 齋戒); 5. "Seclusion" ("Anchu" 安處); 6. "Visualization and Imagination" ("Cunxiang" 存想); 7. "Sitting in Oblivion" ("Zuowang"); 8. "Spirit Liberation" ("Shenjie" 神解).

The first three of these serve as an introduction, first defining the goal of the practice as "settling the spirit within" and liberating oneself from all emotions, thus attaining immortality; then emphasizing the essential simplicity and directness of the teaching and its practice; and finally giving an outline and basic definition of the five key types of practices.

The sections on the five practices, then, begin with physical purification through keeping one's body and environment clean and abstaining from all defiling contacts and impure foods. They continue with the proper living arrangements in a small secluded hut that is neither too light nor too dark, neither too hot nor too cold, allowing the perfect balance of Yin and Yang. Meditation begins with visualization of the gods within the body, establishing concentration of mind and insight into the divine. It proceeds through a deep trance state of total absorption or oblivion, with the mind unmoving and the body solid and firm. Finally the spirit emerges from its physical shell and is liberated through moving along freely with the changes of the cosmos.

The general outline of practices in the main body of the text is further supplemented by a postface that bears Sima Chengzhen's name and specifies details of practice, including preparatory measures, such as swallowing the saliva, how to perform breathing exercises, and the best hours for food intake. It further describes how to circulate energy through the body and make it penetrate the *niwan cavern in the head, in each case giving optimal times and duration for the practice.

Livia KOHN

📖 Kohn 1987a, 145–55 (trans.); Kohn 1987b (trans.)

※ Sima Chengzhen; MEDITATION AND VISUALIZATION

tiaoqi

調氣

regulating breath

Tiaoqi usually refers to methods for regulating the outer breathing. These exercises are often performed before breath control and retention, and allow one to concentrate the mind and reach a state of quiet. Inspiration always occurs through the nose, called Gate of Heaven, and expiration through the mouth, called Door of Earth (*tianmen and dihu). Breathing should be subtle and inaudible.

Several methods originally found in the lost *Yangsheng yaoji (Essentials of Nourishing Life; early fourth century) are quoted in the *Ishinpō (Methods from the Heart of Medicine) and in Tang sources on breathing techniques. These include *Sun Simiao's Qianjin fang 千金方 (Prescriptions Worth a

Thousand; *j.* 27); the *Daolin shesheng lun* 道林攝生論 ([Zhi] Daolin's Essay on Preserving Life; CT 1427); the *Songshan Taiwu xiansheng qijing* 嵩山太無先生 氣經 (Scripture on Breath by the Elder of Great Non-Being from Mount Song; CT 824; 1.4a; trans. Huang Jane 1987–90, 1: 16); the *Huanzhen xiansheng fu nei yuanqi jue* 幻真先生服內元氣訣 (Instructions on the Ingestion of the Inner Original Breath According to the Elder of Illusory Perfection; CT 828, 2b, and YJQQ 60.16a; trans. Despeux 1988, 69, from the version in the **Chifeng sui*); the *Tiaoqi jing* 調氣經 (Scripture on the Regulation of Breath; CT 820, 5a and 16a–17a; trans. Huang Jane 1987–90, 1: 73–74 and 88–89); and the *Qifa yao miaozhi jue* 氣法要妙至訣 (Wondrous Ultimate Instructions on the Essentials of the Breathing Methods; CT 831, 3b–4a; trans. Huang Jane 1987–90, 2: 205–7).

Strictly speaking, the *tiaoqi* method consists of inhaling and exhaling until breathing becomes regular, and of ingesting the regulated breath. However, *tiaoqi* sometimes refers to regulating and harmonizing inner breath. Examples of this practice are found in the *Qianjin fang* and in *Taiqing tiaoqi jing*.

Catherine DESPEUX

※ *yangsheng*

Tongbo guan

桐柏觀

Abbey of the Paulownias and Cypresses (Mount Tongbo)

This important Taoist religious center is located on Mount Tongbo (Tongbo shan 桐柏山) in the **Tiantai* range (Zhejiang). The mid-Tang official Cui Shang 崔尚 claims that Tongbo and Tiantai refer to the same hills in south Zhejiang, but Tongbo was the original name. Its namesake was the sobriquet of immortal **Wangzi Qiao*, Tongbo zhenren 桐柏真人 (Perfected of the Paulownia and Cypress Grove). Legends recount **Ge Xuan* (trad. 164–244) building an alchemical retreat in 239, and Tang Ruizong (r. 684–90, 710–12) sponsored an abbey for the Taoist Master **Sima Chengzhen* (647–735) in 711. This abbey drew many Buddhists from nearby sanctuaries and became the site of a collection of Taoist writings, and the area took on Sima's name as one of the seventy-two Blissful Lands (**fudi*). The official Xia Song 夏竦 praises the temple's fine Taoist manuscript collection, which was delivered to the Song capital by imperial order in 985.

Later accounts claim that **Zhang Boduan* (987?–1082) resided there around the time it was elevated from the status of Abbey (*guan* 觀) to that Palace (*gong* 宮). The local official Cao Xun 曹勛 finished building a bigger complex in

1168, which burned down in 1367 but was rebuilt in Ming times, although Xu Xiake 徐霞客 (1587–1641) found it in disrepair during his visit in 1613. A major expansion and refurbishing in the Yongzheng reign period (1723–35) was followed by another Republican-era rebuilding.

Lowell SKAR

📖 Boltz J. M. 1987a, 111

※ Tiantai shan; TEMPLES AND SHRINES

Tongchu

童初

Youthful Incipience

This important ritual tradition, known as the Great Rites of Youthful Incipience (*Tongchu dafa* 童初大法), was a twelfth-century revival of the *Shangqing tradition that integrated into it much from the widely circulated *Tianxin zhengfa (Correct Method of the Celestial Heart) and Celestial Masters' *Zhengyi (Orthodox Unity) tradition. It continued to influence many traditions in Southern Song times. The system originated in the Mount Mao (*Maoshan, Jiangsu) area during the reign of Song Huizong (r. 1100–1125). More particularly, it stems from the spiritual discoveries in the Tongchu Grotto-Heaven (Tongchu dongtian 童初洞天) by Yang Xizhen 楊希真 (1101–24), a rice merchant's son from Yizhen 儀真 (Jiangsu). Feigning madness, Yang entered the Huayang cavern (Huayang dong 華陽洞) in 1120, and returned the following year to teach the ritual system he had mastered while in the divine realm (*Maoshan zhi, 16.4b–5a).

The textual sources of the Tongchu tradition are found in four collections within the *Daofa huiyuan (Corpus of Taoist Ritual; CT 1220):

1. *Shangqing Tianpeng fumo dafa* 上清天蓬伏魔大法 (Great Rites of Tianpeng for Suppressing Demons According to the Highest Clarity Tradition), in *j.* 156–68, which was compiled by Yang Xizhen and deals with rites of the Tianpeng 天蓬 spirit (see *Tianpeng zhou).

2. *Sisheng fumo dafa* 四聖伏魔大法 (Great Rites for Suppressing Demons by the Four Saints), in *j.* 169–70, which describes methods dating from the Northern Song period.

3. *Shangqing Tongchu wuyuan sufu yuce* 上清童初五元素府玉冊 (Jade Fascicles from the Immaculate Bureaus of the Five Primordials, in the Highest Clarity Tongchu Tradition), in *j.* 171–78, which represents the extant core

of the tradition. It names Yang Xizhen as the founder of the Tongchu tradition, but concludes with a postface dated 1225 by Jin Yunzhong 金允中 (fl. 1224–25), the ritual classicist of the Southern Song.

4. *Shangqing wuyuan yuce jiuling feibu zhangzou bifa* 上清五元玉冊九靈飛步章奏祕法 (Secret Rites for Submitting Petitions and the Soaring Pace of the Nine Numina, from the Jade Fascicles of the Five Primordials in the Highest Clarity Tradition), in *j.* 179–87, which claims to derive from the *Shenxiao (Divine Empyrean) master *Wang Wenqing (1093–1153), and contains methods of presenting petitions that originate from the Celestial Master's tradition.

The Tongchu ritual codes link the Four Saints (*sisheng* 四聖) of the Tianxin system with *Zhang Daoling. They also include conspicuous references to the Fire-bell talisman (*huoling fu* 火鈴符; see *huoling*) and the Tianpeng spell (*Tianpeng zhou*), both derived from Shangqing sources.

Lowell SKAR

📖 Boltz J. M. 1987a, 30–33

Tongdao guan

通道觀

Abbey of the Pervasive Way (1. Chang'an; 2. Mount Zhongnan)

Two temples called Tongdao guan existed during the Northern Zhou period (557–81). The first, which was actually closer to an institute for religious studies than a temple, was established in Chang'an by Zhou Wudi (r. 560–78). Pursuing a policy to build a rich country and a strong army, Zhou Wudi issued a decree against both Taoism and Buddhism in the fifth lunar month of 574 and determined to close down any shrines not mentioned in the literature on the Confucian rites. A few weeks later, however, he set up the Tongdao guan, which had as its basis the unity of the Three Teachings, centering on Confucianism. Of the 120 "Tongdao guan scholars" who worked there, the names of only five are known: *Fu Yi (554–639), Zhang Songzhi 張嵩之, Changsun Zhi 長孫熾, and the Buddhists Pu Kuang 普曠 and Yan Cong 彥琮. In 582, was Sui Wendi (r. 581–604) merged the Tongdao guan with the largest Taoist temple in Chang'an, the *Xuandu guan (Abbey of the Mysterious Metropolis). The reconstituted Xuandu guan continued to exist in Chang'an until the time of Tang Xuanzong (r. 712–56).

The second Tongdao guan was a Taoist temple established at Tiangu 天谷 (Shaanxi) at the foot of Mount Zhongnan (Zhongnan shan 終南山), southwest of Xi'an, at around the same time the other Tongdao guan was founded in Chang'an. Ten well-known Taoists who resided there, including Yan Da 嚴達 (514–609), Wang Yan 王延 (520–604), and Yu Changwen 于長文, were collectively known as the "Ten Elders of Tiangu" (Lagerwey 1981b, 15) and edited and revised Taoist texts. There are no clear records of this temple after the Northern Zhou period.

YAMADA Toshiaki

📖 Kubo Noritada 1980; Lagerwey 1981b, 4–21; Sunayama Minoru 1990, 135–39; Yamazaki Hiroshi 1979

※ Xuandu guan; TEMPLES AND SHRINES

tou longjian

投龍簡

Casting Dragon Tablets

The ritual of Casting Dragon Tablets evolved from the "handwritten documents of the Three Offices" (*sanguan shoushu* 三官手書; see *sanguan) of the early Celestial Master movement (*Tianshi dao). To heal their sick parishioners, priests of that order made three copies of a confessional in which the ill declared their desire to repent. Then the clerics dispatched the first copy to the Office of Waters by sinking it in a river, the second to the Office of Earth by burying it underground, and the last to the Office of Heaven by depositing it on a mountain (Nickerson 1997, 232–34).

The oldest protocols for performing the Casting of Dragon Tablets appear in the *Chishu yujue miaojing* 赤書玉訣妙經 (Wondrous Scripture of Jade Instructions in Red Script; CT 352, 1.5a–7b), a *Lingbao text of the fifth century. Those conventions called for inscribing writs in vermilion ink on three tablets of ginkgo wood 34 cm long and 6 cm wide. The texts of those documents supply particulars about ordinands, priests, or patrons, including their names, ages, and months of birth. The writs were petitions or prayers addressed to the rulers of the waters, holy mountains, and soil. In them supplicants implored the gods to excise records of their sins in divine registers (*LU) so that they could attain immortality. The tablets were then wrapped in azure paper, bound with azure thread and tossed into rivers, thrown into mountain caves, and buried in the ground at the petitioner's residence along with nine gold knobs and a gold dragon.

Salvation of this sort was strictly a bureaucratic affair in which the remission of sins was a matter of altering records. The rite did not require the supplicant to enumerate any specific sins or to express any contrition for them.

Charles D. BENN

📖 Benn 1991, 69–71; Chavannes 1919

Tudi gong

土地公

Earth God

Shrines to the Earth God (also known as Fude zhengshen 福德正神, Orthodox Deity of Blessings and Virtue) are the most common religious buildings in the Chinese countryside, each village or neighborhood possessing at least one such shrine. Often compared to a local official, the Earth God is a low ranking member of the celestial bureaucracy, charged with supervising humans and spirits in the territory under his jurisdiction. An Earth God's authority is confined strictly to his own locality, adjacent areas having their own Earth Gods, whose positions are usually believed to be filled by the souls of meritorious local men, who were posthumously rewarded with divine office. In addition to his daily sacrifices, the Earth God receives a birthday celebration on the second day of the second lunar month, and in some areas another celebration on the fifteenth day of the eighth lunar month. In return for the sacrificial attention bestowed upon him, the Earth God is expected to keep the locality free of evil spirits, to provide good harvests, and in general to ensure the community's well-being.

The roots of the Earth God cult are ancient, going back to the cult of the Gods of Soil and Grain (Sheji 社稷) of the classical period; to this day, Shegong 社公 occurs as an alternate appellation of the Earth God. Another classical term, Sovereign Earth (Houtu 后土), is still in use nowadays for the Earth God images set up to guard tombs. While Taoist "merit" (*gongde*) rites stress the special responsibility of the Earth God for the spirits of the departed, the Earth God also features frequently in the rites for the living (*jiao*), where he (and thus the local community he represents) is integrated into the Taoist ritual order. This is most conspicuous in the "Divine Spell for the Pacification of the Earth [God]" (*An tudi shenzhou* 安土地神咒), a standard prefatory part of Taoist ritual scriptures, which calls upon the Earth God to fulfill his duties conscientiously and to "return toward the Orthodox Way" (*hui xiang zhengdao* 回向正道).

Philip CLART

📖 Chamberlayne 1966; Chavannes 1910a; Lagerwey 1987c, passim; Ma Shutian 1996, 47–49; Müller 1980; Schipper 1977a

※ TAOISM AND LOCAL COMMUNITIES; TAOISM AND LOCAL CULTS; TAOISM AND POPULAR RELIGION

tuna

吐 納

exhaling and inhaling

Tuna is an abbreviation of the phrase *tugu naxin* 吐故納新, "exhaling the old and inhaling the new (breath)." This term is first found in chapter 15 of the *Zhuangzi*, which states: "Breathing in and out [while emitting] the sounds *chui* 吹 or *xu* 噓, exhaling the old and inhaling the new [breath], hanging like the bear and stretching like the bird, these are only methods for longevity" (see trans. Watson 1968, 167–68).

Tuna and *tugu naxin* are generic terms for breathing practices meant to expel the impure and pathogenic *qi from the body. Liu Gen 劉根, a third-century *fangshi, is attributed with this description: "Feeding the body with the living breath (*shengqi* 生氣) and exhaling the dead breath (*siqi* 死氣) allows you to subsist for a long time. When you inhale through the nose, you actually inhale the life breath. When you exhale through the mouth, you exhale the death breath" (*Yangxing yanming lu, 2.2a).

Catherine DESPEUX

※ *yangsheng*

tutan zhai

塗炭齋

Mud and Soot Retreat

The Mud and Soot Retreat is a ritual of the Way of the Celestial Masters
(*Tianshi dao) that was performed from the Six Dynasties to the early Tang
period. Some scholars have suggested that it was already practiced at the end
of the Later Han period, but there is no definite evidence for this. Like other
early Retreat rituals (*zhai), the Mud and Soot Retreat was meant to eliminate
defilements through repentance for past sins. Its benefits could reach a person's
deceased parents and ancestors, who would be freed from the netherworld if
the descendant had a Taoist priest (*daoshi) perform it on their behalf.

In his *Wugan wen* 五感文 (Text on the Five Commemorations; CT 1278),
*Lu Xiujing (406–77) records two types of Mud and Soot Retreats. One of
them, called the Three Primes Mud and Soot Retreat (*sanyuan tutan zhai* 三
元塗炭齋), was deemed to be especially meritorious as it included the Five
Commemorations (*wugan* 五感), through which a believer expressed his
gratitude to his parents, the deities, and the masters (Verellen 1999). In the
ritual, the priest smeared his face with mud, disheveled his hair, and bound
himself within the perimeter of the altar—or bound his hands—to represent
the sufferings of the netherworld. Then he lay on the ground and confessed his
sins. He did this three times during the day and three times during the night.
This ordeal was said to be particularly beneficial during the winter, with the
priest standing in snow and ice.

YAMADA Toshiaki

📖 Kohn 1993b, 107–12; Lagerwey 1981b, 156–58; Maspero 1981, 384–86

※ *zhai*

W

waidan

外 丹

external elixir; external alchemy

The term *waidan* conventionally denotes a broad and diverse range of doctrines and practices focused on the compounding of elixirs whose ingredients are minerals, metals, and—less frequently—plants. This designation is often contrasted to *neidan* or "inner alchemy," but the two terms originated within the context of *neidan* itself, where they initially referred to facets or stages of the inner alchemical process (Robinet 1991).

Waidan has a history of about fifteen centuries, from its origins in the Han period to its culmination in the Tang, followed by its decline in the Song and Yuan and its virtual disappearance in Ming times. Its extant literature consists of about one hundred sources preserved in the Taoist Canon. These texts show that while early *waidan* was mainly concerned with the world of gods and demons and with the performance of ceremonies and other ritual actions addressed to deities, the later tradition used alchemical symbolism to represent the origins and functioning of the cosmos, and the return to the original state of being. This shift took place between the end of the Six Dynasties and the beginning of the Tang, and played a crucial role in the development of *neidan*.

History. The first mention of alchemy in China is associated with *Li Shaojun, a *fangshi* who, around 133 BCE, suggested that Han Wudi (r. 141–87) should perform an alchemical method in preparation for the *feng* 封 and *shan* 禪 rituals to Heaven and Earth. The ingestion of elixirs is first mentioned in the *Yantie lun* 鹽鐵論 (Discourses on Salt and Iron), dating from ca. 60 BCE. Around the same time, Liu Xiang 劉向 (77–8 or 6 BCE) also tried to compound alchemical gold based on a text entitled *Hongbao yuanbi shu* 鴻寶苑祕術 (Arts from the Garden of Secrets of the Vast Treasure). Bibliographic sources confirm that this and other works compiled under the patronage of Liu An 劉安 (179?–122; see *Huainan zi) contained materials on alchemy.

After these fragmentary and often unclear details, the earliest known corpus of texts related to *waidan* is the one belonging to the *Taiqing (Great Clarity) tradition, which developed from the early third century CE. Its main scriptures were the *Taiqing jing (Scripture of Great Clarity), the *Jiudan jing (Scripture of the Nine Elixirs), and the *Jinye jing (Scripture of the Golden Liquor), three works that, according to *Ge Hong and other sources, were revealed to *Zuo Ci at the end of the Han. Both Ge Hong's *Baopu zi* and the received versions of these scriptures in the Taoist Canon show that the Taiqing tradition developed in Jiangnan in close relation to local exorcistic and ritual practices. Fifty years after Ge Hong, the *Shangqing school of Taoism accepted some earlier *waidan* works into its revealed scriptures (see under *langgan*). Although Shangqing used the *waidan* process mainly as a support for meditation practices, the language, techniques, and rites in these works are largely the same as those of the Taiqing scriptures.

Around the time the Shangqing doctrines were taking shape, the *Zhouyi cantong qi* (Token for the Agreement of the Three According to the *Book of Changes*) also circulated in Jiangnan. Its original version, related to the Han "studies on the Changes" (*yixue* 易學), was augmented during the Six Dynasties and became, from the Tang period onward, the main scripture of both *waidan* and *neidan*. Unlike the earlier Taiqing tradition, which focuses on ritual, the *Cantong qi* is based on correlative cosmology and uses cosmological, astronomical, and alchemical emblems to describe the relation of the Dao to the cosmos. The two main emblems at the basis of its discourse are Real Mercury (*zhenhong* 真汞) and Real Lead (*zhenqian* 真鉛), corresponding to Original Yin and Original Yang, respectively. This new view of the alchemical process not only influenced the later development of *waidan*, but also paved the way for the rise of *neidan*.

During the Tang dynasty, which is often called "the golden age of Chinese alchemy," the tradition based on the *Cantong qi* acquired importance and methods based on mercury and lead became typical of the tradition. This development is reflected in several works related to the *Cantong qi*, which explain their preference for processes based on lead and mercury instead of cinnabar, saying that Yang (cinnabar) alone cannot produce the elixir. Although the majority of Tang *waidan* texts are related to the *Cantong qi*, an important example of methods based on the refining of cinnabar is found in the works of *Chen Shaowei. Also in the Tang, imperial patronage of *waidan* intensified, but elixir poisoning caused the death of Wuzong (r. 840–46), Xuanzong (r. 846–59), and possibly also Xianzong (r. 805–20).

Waidan progressively declined from the late Tang onward, and sources dating from the Song and later periods mostly consist of anthologies of earlier writings and methods. By that time, the soteriological import of alchemy had already been transferred to *neidan*.

Doctrines. The two main *waidan* subtraditions outlined above present different views of the alchemical process. The Taiqing sources have virtually no concern for the abstract notions of cosmology; in these texts, the compounding of the elixir is part of a sequence of actions marked by the performance of rites and ceremonies for the transmission from master to disciple, the protection of the laboratory, the kindling of the fire, and the ingestion of the elixir. The alchemical medicines are valued not only for their property of conferring longevity and immortality, but also for enabling adepts to communicate with divinities and keep away dangerous spirits, especially those that cause illnesses.

In the tradition based on the *Cantong qi*, however, the system of correlative cosmology has primary importance. Substances, instruments, and processes have an emblematic meaning, and the purpose of making the elixir is to trace in a reverse order the stages of cosmogony, which are in the first place ontologic states. Accordingly, each stage of the alchemical process is related to a stage of the cosmogonic process, and is designed to move the adept back through the corresponding cosmological configurations: from Yin and Yang as they appear in the conditioned cosmos (native lead and native cinnabar, respectively), to the recovery of authentic Yin and Yang (refined mercury and refined lead, respectively), ending with their merging into Oneness, represented by the elixir itself.

The *Cantong qi* and its related texts also introduced a new view of time into the alchemical doctrines. While the Taiqing sources do not explicate the cosmological basis of their heating methods, several later texts describe the system of fire phasing (*huohou*), which patterns the heating of the elixir on the major time cycles of the cosmos. The correspondences between the compounding of the elixir and the larger cosmological cycles allow alchemists to perform in a short time the same task that nature would achieve in thousands of years. The definition of the elixir as a "time-controlling substance" (Sivin 1980, 243) aptly describes this facet of the alchemical work in the tradition based on the *Cantong qi*.

Instruments and methods. The alchemical process takes place in a laboratory, called Chamber of the Elixirs (*danshi* 丹室, *danwu* 丹屋, or *danfang* 丹房). The furnace (*lu* 爐; see *dinglu*) or stove (*zao* 竈) is typically placed on a three-stage platform or "altar" (*tan* 壇). The crucible (*fu*) or tripod (*ding* 鼎) is arranged over the stove or sometimes inside it.

The main methods of the *waidan* tradition are those for the preparation of the Reverted Elixir (*huandan*), a designation that refers to several different processes. Prominent among them are those for refining mercury from cinnabar and for joining lead and mercury. Several sources describe the preparation of the Golden Liquor (*jinye*), another term applied to different elixirs. Typical processes also include aqueous solutions, used as intermediary stages in the compounding of elixirs (see *Sanshiliu shuifa*), and the Flowery Pond (*huachi* 華池), an acetic bath often used to soak the ingredients before they are placed in the crucible.

Fabrizio PREGADIO

📖 Chen Guofu 1963, 370–437; Chen Guofu 1983; Eliade 1978, 109–26; Ho Peng Yoke 1979; Meng Naichang 1993a; Murakami Yoshimi 1983; Needham 1976; Needham 1980; Pregadio 1996; Pregadio 2000; Pregadio 2006b; Seidel 1989–90, 262–64; Sivin 1968; Sivin 1976; Sivin 1980; Zhao Kuanghua 1989; Zhao Kuanghua and Zhou Xihua 1998

※ *jindan*; for other related entries see the Synoptic Table of Contents, sec. IV.3 ("Alchemy")

Wang Bi

王弼

226–49; *zi*: Fusi 輔嗣

Wang Bi, the author of commentaries to the *Daode jing*, the *Yijing, and the *Lunyu* 論語 (Analects) of Confucius, played an important role in the "pure conversations" (*qingtan*) that were in vogue within the *Xuanxue (Arcane Learning) milieu. He devised new arrangements of the *Daode jing* and the *Yijing*, and established standard editions of both works. A short note on his life is appended to Zhong Hui's 鍾會 (225–64) biography in the *Sanguo zhi* (History of the Three Kingdoms; trans. Fung Yu-lan 1952–53, 2: 179–80).

In contrast to the exegesis of Han times, Wang Bi's works show no concern for longevity techniques or for cosmological patterns based on numerical symbolism. Wang views the world as a whole, pervaded by a single Principle. He deemphasizes the naturalistic, numerological, and polemical approaches to the *Yijing*, simplifying its interpretation and offering a new exegetical model widely accepted by later scholars. Focusing on the ontological level, he highlights the constant order and "reason" (*li* 理) that underlie the fluctuations of the world. For Wang, this "reason" is knowable; one can take it as a guide in one's life and behave according to the cosmic and temporal situation and the position a thing occupies within it.

This perspective lays the foundations of a society ordered according to the hierarchical and moral principles of Confucianism. As Howard L. Goodman (1985) has convincingly shown, however, this influence is more apparent in Wang's commentary to the *Yijing* (completed by Han Kangbo 韓康伯, ?–ca. 385) than in his exegesis of the *Daode jing*. In the latter work, Wang gives the word *dao* 道 a metaphysical meaning close to the one it has in the *Zhuangzi* and the *Huainan zi*. The Dao is *wu* or Non-being, an absence of substance or entity, even conceptual. It is indescribable, unique, and cannot be matched to anything. It is the source of the world not in the temporal sense but in the sense of an atemporal priority: as shown by the *Zhuangzi*, the notion of "beginning" can only lead to a *regressus ad infinitum* and to the absence of any temporal beginning.

In Wang Bi's apophatic thought, *wu* or Non-being is the Absolute that cannot and should not endure determination by name, qualification or form. *Wu* is a synonym of the Ultimate (*ji* 極; see *wuji* and *taiji*), the Beginning (*shi* 始), and the permanent (*chang* 常). It is "that by which" (*suoyi* 所以) things are, their true existence to which they are bound to return (*fan*). This can be accomplished through a "decrease" (*sun* 損) similar to the work of a gardener who clears away the weeds. Paradoxically, those who do so become complete because they are redirected to *wu*, which is equivalent to the One.

Although the notion of the Dao as absence of anything implies its transcendence, this does not mean there is no connection between Non-being and Being (*you*), the phenomenal world. Quiescence, says Wang Bi, is not the opposite of movement, nor is silence the opposite of speech. *Wu* must be mediated by *you* because "it cannot be made manifest by *wu*." Being, therefore, is the manifestation of Non-being. However, Wang Bi emphasizes the importance of Non-being much more than that of Being.

In Wang Bi's view, the sage is one who does not "name" things; he is not, therefore, the Confucian sage who applies "correct names" (*zhengming* 正名) to things. Wang's ideas in this respect draw both from the *Yijing* and from the notion of the Taoist saint (*shengren*). As in the *Xici* 繫辭 (Appended Statements, a portion of the *Yijing*), the sage pays attention to change, discerns the moment in which an event takes shape, and relies on the underlying order of the world, which he illuminates; as in the *Daode jing*, he is intuitively in harmony with the Way and "hides his light," which reaches into the dark. As in both of them, he is compliant and modest.

Isabelle ROBINET

📖 Chan A. K. L. 1991b; Chan A. K. L. 1998; Fung Yu-lan 1952–53, 2: 179–89; Lou Yulie 1980 (crit. ed.); Lynn 1994 (trans. of *Yijing* comm.); Lynn 1999 (trans. of *Daode jing* comm.); Mou Zongsan 1974, 100–168; Robinet 1977, 56–77; Robinet 1987f; Rump 1979; Wagner 1986; Wagner 1989; Wagner 2000

※ *qingtan*; Xuanxue

Wang Bing

王冰

fl. 762; *hao*: Qixuan zi 啟玄子 (Master Who Inaugurates the Mystery) *or* Qiyuan zi 啟元子 (Master Who Inaugurates the Origin)

Wang Bing is known as the editor and commentator of the *Suwen* 素問 (Plain Questions; see **Huangdi neijing*), presented to the throne in 762. Apparently, he held the post of Director of the Imperial Stud (*taipu ling* 太樸令) in that year, but apart from this hardly any biographical details are known. His commentary to the *Suwen* as well as his *hao* would suggest that he moved in Taoist circles. Furthermore, he states in his preface to the *Suwen* that from early on he practiced the arts of Nourishing Life (**yangsheng*). In that preface he also names two persons with surnames Guo 郭 and Zhang 張 as his masters, and in the preface to another work attributed to him, the *Xuanzhu miyu* 玄珠密語 (Secret Sayings of [Master] Mysterious Pearl), which unlike the *Suwen* commentary is written in a rather rustic style, he mentions yet another master called Xuanzhu 玄珠 (Mysterious Pearl), a name that can be traced to the **Zhuangzi* and may reveal a Taoist commitment.

This Taoist orientation is evident in several other works attributed to Wang Bing, all of which deal with the doctrine of the "five circulatory phases and six seasonal influences" (*wuyun liuqi* 五運六氣). These include most notably the *Suwen liuqi Xuanzhu miyu* 素問六氣玄珠密語 (Secret Sayings of [Master] Mysterious Pearl on the Six Seasonal Influences of the Plain Questions; also known as the above *Xuanzhu miyu*) in ten or seventeen *juan*, the *Tianyuan yuce* 天元玉冊 (Jade Fascicles of Celestial Primordiality) in twenty-eight or thirty *juan*, the *Zhaoming yinzhi* 昭明隱旨 (Concealed Directions on the Bright Light) in three *juan*, and the *Yuanhe jiyong jing* 元和紀用經 (Scripture on the Use of the Calendar of Original Harmony) in one *juan*. Seven chapters in the *Suwen* are entirely written in terms of this doctrine, namely *juan* 66–71 and 74, and received opinion has it that these chapters were interpolated by Wang Bing; they constitute about one third of the *Suwen*.

Elisabeth HSU

📖 Despeux 2001; Ma Jixing 1990, 101; Yang Shizhe et al. 1998, 174–76

Wang Changyue

王常月

?–1680; original *ming*: Ping 平; *hao*: Kunyang zi 崑陽子
(Master of Yang of Mount Kunlun)

Wang Changyue is a key figure credited with the promotion of the *Quanzhen "renaissance," which allegedly took place in the late Ming and early Qing periods under the name of the *Longmen branch (Esposito 2000, 627–32). In 1656, as the abbot of the *Baiyun guan (Abbey of the White Clouds) in Beijing, Wang was said to have revived the ancient tradition of *Qiu Chuji (1148–1227) and to have restored Taoist discipline. More precisely, Wang may be regarded as the state-approved founder of the Longmen lineage. Under his guidance, Longmen became a genuine school with an "orthodox" lineage and organized temples. In this lineage, Wang figures as the seventh patriarch and marks the beginning of new era. The compilation of a putative work called *Bojian* 鉢鑑 (Examination of the Bowl) is also attributed to him. It is regarded as the fundamental source of Longmen history and lineage to which *Min Yide's *Jingai xindeng* 金蓋心燈 (Transmission of the Mind-Lamp from Mount Jingai) refers.

According to some biographers, Wang was born in 1521, but others give a date of 1594. He came from a Taoist family of the prefecture of Lu'an 潞安 (Shanxi). When he was still an adolescent, he left his family and travelled to famous mountains to search for enlightened masters. In 1628, he is said to have finally met the sixth Longmen patriarch Zhao Fuyang 趙復陽 on Mount Wangwu (*Wangwu shan, Henan). Zhao gave him the lineage name of Changyue (Everlasting Moons, which alludes to the several months Wang had to wait before receiving teachings from Zhao) along with teachings on Taoist discipline. After practicing them and having progressed in his study of the Three Teachings (Confucianism, Taoism and Buddhism), he met master Zhao again in the Jiugong mountains (Jiugong shan 九宮山, Hubei). This last meeting served to confirm Wang's spiritual progress and to proclaim him as the seventh Longmen patriarch of the Vinaya Line (*lüshi* 律師), entitled to transmit the Longmen discipline. Zhao is also said to have foretold Wang's future role as abbot of the Baiyun guan, a prophecy confirmed in 1655. In 1656, Wang built an ordination platform (*jietan* 戒壇; see fig. 75) at the Baiyun guan to perform public ordinations for Taoist novices.

The content of these ordinations was established by Wang in his work entitled *Chuzhen jielü (Initial Precepts and Observances for Perfection) as well

Fig. 74. Wang Changyue. Reproduced from Zhongguo daojiao xiehui 1983.

as in a later compilation by Wang's disciples known as *Biyuan tanjing* 碧苑壇經 (Platform Sūtra of the Jasper Garden). This text (whose title alludes to the famous *Platform Sūtra* of the sixth Chan patriarch, Huineng 慧能) is found in the first volume of the *Gu Shuyinlou cangshu* 古書隱樓藏書 (Collection of the Ancient Hidden Pavilion of Books; Qing Xitai 1994, 2: 184–86) and in the *Zangwai daoshu* (vol. 12). Another version known under the title *Longmen xinfa* 龍門心法 (Core Teachings of Longmen) is also included in the *Zangwai daoshu*. It consists of discourses given during an ordination held by Wang in 1663 at the Biyuan guan 碧苑觀 (Abbey of the Jasper Garden) in Nanjing.

Wang Changyue's teachings focus on the progressive path of the "three-stage great ordination" (*santan dajie* 三壇大戒, lit., "ordination of the threefold

Fig. 75. Ordination platform (Jietan 戒壇). *Baiyun guan (Abbey of the White Clouds), Beijing.
Reproduced from Zhongguo daojiao xiehui 1983.

altar"): Initial Precepts for Perfection (*chuzhen jie* 初真戒), Intermediate Precepts (*zhongji jie* 中極戒), and Precepts for Celestial Immortality (*tianxian jie*
天仙戒). This system represented the sine qua non for realizing an "orthodox
enlightenment" and was said to be attainable only under the guidance of a
Longmen Vinaya master (*lüshi*).

From Wang Changyue onward, an official Longmen lineage was established
at the Baiyun guan. Its abbot was chosen from among Longmen Vinaya masters
and was responsible for public ordinations. In this way, Longmen became the
main school in charge of public ordinations for all Taoist priests in north and
south China. Wang Changyue is said to have ordained thousand of disciples
in Beijing, Nanjing, Hangzhou, Wudang and elsewhere, and thanks to him
the Longmen has remained the dominant lineage to this day.

Monica ESPOSITO

📖 Despeux 1990, 147–55; Esposito 2001; Esposito 2004c; Mori Yuria 1994; Qing
Xitai 1988–95, 4: 77–100; Qing Xitai 1994, 1: 392–93

※ *Chuzhen jielü*; *jie* [precepts]; Longmen; MONASTIC CODE

Wang Chuyi

王處一

1142–1217; *zi*: Yuyang 玉陽; *hao*: Yuyang zi 玉陽子 (Master
of Jade Yang), Tixuan zhenren 體玄真人 (Real Man Who
Embodies the Mystery)

Wang Chuyi is one of the Seven Real Men (*qizhen* 七真; see table 17) who
epitomize the first generation of *Quanzhen masters. His religious life began
before his encounter with *Wang Zhe: as a child he had revelations, and from
then on he lived as an eccentric hermit with his mother. Wang Zhe converted
him to *neidan* ascetic training at the age of twenty-six, but their association
lasted only for a year. Wang Chuyi probably continued his Taoist education
under other masters, and eventually became famous enough to be summoned
to the Jin court in 1188 and again in 1198. His standing seems to have greatly
helped the Quanzhen's negotiations with the state in 1190–97, when a conflict
erupted over the order's reluctance to abide by the directive to register monasteries and clergy. From 1197 until his death, he directed a sizable monastic
community in Shandong.

Wang stands apart in the group of the Seven Real Men for several reasons.
He was graced with an individual hagiographic work, the *Tixuan zhenren xianyi
lu* 體玄真人顯異錄 (Account of the Miraculous Manifestations of the Real
Man Who Embodies the Mystery; CT 594). This work sheds more light on
his liturgical activities than do the collective Quanzhen hagiographies—for
example, the *Jinlian zhengzong ji*—which insist on ascetic training. Although
Wang Chuyi is not a member of Wang Zhe's inner circle of four favorite
disciples, who receive the best of the later hagiographers' attention, his role
in fashioning Quanzhen self-identity is larger than it may at first appear. First,
his political influence in the 1190s helped in the development of the order's
institutional independence. Moreover, when Quanzhen, around the 1230s, had
fully absorbed all the major liturgical lineages of traditional Taoism (including
those of the *Lingbao grand ritual and the various newer *leifa* or Thunder
Rites), the importance of Wang Chuyi's contribution to this process of integration became clear. Several second-generation Quanzhen masters reportedly
learned their ritual skills from him. With *Qiu Chuji, he is also one of the
two early Quanzhen masters known to have performed large scale official
ordinations as early as 1201, and therefore to have adapted the older monastic
ordination procedures to the nascent Quanzhen institutions. Furthermore,
Wang seems to have played a major role in fashioning the Quanzhen's sacred

history, especially regarding the advent of the cult addressed to Donghua dijun 東華帝君 (Imperial Lord of Eastern Florescence).

Like all the Seven Real Men except *Sun Bu'er, Wang has left a poetical anthology, the *Yunguang ji* 雲光集 (Anthology of Cloudy Radiance; CT 1152), entitled after the grotto where Wang attained enlightenment. This work actually documents spiritual teachings largely homogeneous with those of his fellow-disciples. Of special note are Wang's exchanges with the five lay associations (*hui* 會) founded by Wang Zhe in Shandong, which proves how deeply Wang Chuyi was involved in Quanzhen's institutional development and its popularization of *neidan* meditation practices.

Vincent GOOSSAERT

📖 Boltz J. M. 1987a, 66 and 163–65; Endres 1985; Marsone 2001a, 105–6; Mori Yuria 1992b

※ Quanzhen

Wang Jie

王玠

?–ca. 1380; *zi*: Daoyuan 道淵; *hao*: Hunran zi 混然子
(Master of Chaotic Origin)

A native of Nanchang (Jiangxi), Wang benefited from the teachings of *Li Daochun (fl. 1288–92), and devoted himself to interpreting contemplative treatises, or to interpreting texts as contemplative treatises. Besides arranging for the publication of Master Li's *Qing'an Yingchan zi yulu* 清庵應蟬子語錄 (Recorded Sayings of the Master Who Responds to the Cicadas in the Pure Retreat; CT 1060), edited by Chai Yuangao 柴元皋 in 1288, Wang also collated Li's essays on salvation called the *Santian yisui* 三天易髓 (The Mutable Marrow of the Three Heavens; CT 250).

The first chapter of Wang's own compilation, the *Huanzhen ji* 還真集 (Anthology of Reverting to Perfection; CT 1074), includes diagrams, followed by instructions for imagining the creation of the inner elixir (*neidan) within the body. The second chapter amplifies the next stages of the contemplative process and discusses some of its potential results, including the route to becoming long-lived and a transcendent. Praise for the unity of the Three Teachings (Confucianism, Taoism, and Buddhism) is also an important theme in this text, which boasts a preface dated to 1392 by the forty-third Celestial

Master, *Zhang Yuchu (1361–1410). While remarking on the practical usefulness of Wang's text, which he first acquired in 1392 from his disciple Yuan Wenyi 袁文逸, Zhang also emphasizes that Li Daochun is heir to *Zhang Boduan's (987?–1082) approach to compounding the inner elixir. In the annotations Wang gives to two scriptures, the *Xiaozai huming miaojing zhu* 消災護命妙經注 (Commentary to the Wondrous Scripture on Dispelling Disasters and Protecting Life; CT 100) and the *Qingjing miaojing zuantu jiezhu* 清靜妙經纂圖解注 (Compilation of Illustrations and Explications on the Wondrous Scripture of Clarity and Quiescence; CT 760), he uses inner alchemy and cosmological language to explicate each text.

Lowell SKAR

📖 Boltz J. M. 1987a, 183–84

※ Li Daochun; *neidan*

Wang lingguan

王靈官

Numinous Officer Wang

Numinous Officer Wang, also referred to as Marshal Wang (Wang Yuanshuai 王元帥), is best known as the guardian deity of Taoist temples. His image is often housed in a Hall of the Numinous Officer (Lingguan dian 靈官殿) at the entrance to a Taoist temple or monastery, one vivid example being at the Abbey of the White Clouds (*Baiyun guan) in Beijing (Yoshioka Yoshitoyo 1979, 250–51). Numinous Officer Wang is also mentioned in novels like the *Xiyou ji* 西遊記 (Journey to the West) as a guardian of the palace of the Jade Sovereign (*Yuhuang).

Some hagiographic accounts of the Numinous Officer claim that his name was Wang Shan 王善, and that he had been a disciple of *Sa Shoujian (fl. 1141–78?), a renowned practitioner of Thunder Rites (*leifa). His cult appears to have been popular in southwest China, where he was worshipped as a thunder god or a fire god, although some stories mentioning child sacrifice hint at perhaps more sinister origins of his cult. A Taoist from Hangzhou (Zhejiang) named Zhou Side 周思得 (1359–1451) is said to have practiced rituals to Wang in Beijing during the reign of the Yongle Emperor (1403–24), which may have contributed to his cult's legitimacy and historical development.

Above all, Wang is worshipped as an exorcistic deity who can ward off or expel demons, as can be seen in rituals invoking him preserved in the *Daofa huiyuan* (j. 241–43). He also takes the stage during performances of ritual operas in order to exorcise demons.

Paul R. KATZ

📖 van der Loon 1977; Lü Zongli and Luan Baoqun 1991, 881–86

※ TEMPLES AND SHRINES

Wang Qinruo

王欽若

962–1025

Wang Qinruo was one of the most successful and influential officials of his day, enjoying the attentive ear of Song Zhenzong (r. 997–1022) from 997 until his forced retirement from the office of Chancellor in 1019. He made a comeback in 1022 under Song Renzong (r. 1022–63) and died in office in 1025. He was an able administrator who thoroughly enjoyed, and sometimes abused, the exercise of power. His ultimate place in history, however, rests on his leading role in state ritual affairs throughout the Zhenzong reign.

In 1005, the Song had concluded the Shanyuan Treaty with the Khitan, widely perceived as dishonorable because they were forced to accept of their enemy on equal ritual terms, and because of the inclusion of indemnities. The treaty initiated a period of relative internal and external peace, in which Zhenzong and his advisors placed Song imperial authority on a stronger footing through the public, large-scale enactment of the emperor's function as ritual center of All-under-Heaven (which included the Khitan and other non-Chinese groups). Wang Qinruo played an important role in these activities. In 1005, he took part in a court debate on the southern suburban rituals (*jiaosi* 郊祀). He was also active in the compilation of the *Cefu yuangui* 冊府元龜 (Outstanding Models from the Storehouse of Literature; 1013), a compendium of administrative documents from past dynasties to serve as an aid in government. He was, moreover, in charge of compiling the imperially ordered Canon of 1016, the *Da Song Tiangong baozang*, and engaged himself in matters of content as well. Nonetheless, he was not a Taoist priest, nor did he advise his emperor from an exclusively Taoist point of view.

The central ritual event in Zhenzong's reign was the performance of the *feng* 封 and *shan* 禪 ceremonies to Heaven and Earth at Mount Tai (*Taishan, Shandong) in 1008, preceded by the well-orchestrated receipt of "letters from Heaven" (*tianshu* 天書), auspicious omens, and repeated requests by local people from the Mount Tai region to carry out these sacrifices. As it had been with the earlier Chinese emperors who had considered performing the *feng* and *shan* ceremonies, and often proceeded at great length with the preparations before desisting, deliberations at the Song court were extremely circumspect. Wang Qinruo was the decisive influence in carrying out the rituals, with Zhenzong in the appropriate role of an emperor worried about overburdening his people.

In essence, Wang Qinruo and Zhenzong merely brought to its logical conclusion a ritual program for building dynastic legitimacy that had been started by the dynastic founders Taizu (r. 960–76) and Taizong (r. 976–97). Taoist rituals were an important—but by no means exclusive—part of this program. The increasingly negative historiography in the following decades reflects the subsequent victory of a different view on legitimation, which de-emphasized the direct intervention of Heaven in the bestowal of its mandate to rule and stressed the moral nature of imperial rule, which quasi-automatically bestowed the Heavenly Mandate (*tianming* 天命). From this point of view, Wang Qinruo was a manipulator of heavenly signs and imperial rituals, or even a Taoist in Confucian disguise, whereas he and other early Song ritual specialists were merely continuing Tang and older traditions of imperial ritual practice supported by large segments of the political-scholarly elite of their day. Since in those days Taoist and state ritual traditions were still very close to each other, early Song legitimation activities naturally showed similarities with Taoist ritual in general and involved the performance of specific Taoist rituals and the support of Taoist institutions. Ultimately, the ritual specialist was the emperor, not a Taoist priest, and his advisors were secular officials, not Taoist priests. The common qualification of these activities as Taoist results from a biased historiography, which prefers to associate such rituals with superstition or a supposedly marginal religious tradition, rather than mainstream Confucianism or state ritual.

Although Wang Qinruo wrote extensively, only one of his works is entirely preserved, the **Yisheng baode zhuan* (Biography of [the Perfected Lord] Assisting Sanctity and Protecting Virtue). Otherwise, only shorter pieces of his are extant, of which the prose texts (in complete or summary form) have been gathered in the *Song quanwen* 宋全文 (Complete Prose of the Song).

Barend ter HAAR

📖 Boltz J. M. 1987a, 83–86; Cahill 1980; Chen Guofu 1963, 131–33; Eichhorn 1964; van der Loon 1984, 29–37; Qing Xitai 1988–95, 2: 534–93; Schmidt-Glintzer 1981; Wechsler 1985, 107–22 and 170–94; Yamauchi M. 1976

※ *Da Song Tiangong baozang*; *Yisheng baode zhuan*; TAOISM AND THE STATE

Wang Weiyi

王惟一

fl. 1264–1304; *zi*: Jingyang 景陽; *hao*: Leiting sanli 雷霆散吏
(Vagrant Official of the Thunderclap)

This major disciple of *Mo Qiyan (1226–94), hailing from Songjiang 松江 (near Shanghai, Jiangsu), practiced and promoted both the Thunder Rites (*leifa*) and inner alchemy (*neidan*) during Yuan times. Although he received a classical education in his youth, Wang later used his understanding of matters of life and death based on the *Daode jing* as a point of entry for studying modes of longevity and transcendence. This led him to seek out teachings on inner alchemy, and may have brought him into contact with someone in the circle of *Li Daochun (fl. 1288–92).

His eventual enlightenment led him to compose one of his works that is still extant in the Ming Taoist Canon, the *Mingdao pian* 明道篇 (Folios on Elucidating the Way; CT 273), which structurally resembles the *Wuzhen pian* (Folios on Awakening to Perfection) by *Zhang Boduan (987?–1082). The second work bearing Wang's name, the *Daofa xinchuan* 道法心傳 (Heart-to-Heart Transmission of Taoist Rites; CT 1253), has an author's preface dated 1294. A collection of mnemonic instructional verses, it is grounded in the traditions Wang learned from Mo Qiyan, who practiced the Thunderclap Rites (*leiting* 雷霆; see *leifa*). Wang explains that these rites are superior to the various ritual practices that make heavy use of talismans (*FU) because they depend solely on concentrating one's inner vital powers for ritual purposes. In both of these texts, Wang uses the quatrain form to praise the values of internally creating the powers of thunder to subdue the demonic agents troubling the world.

Lowell SKAR

📖 Boltz J. M. 1987a, 16–88

※ Mo Qiyan; *leifa*; *neidan*

Wang Wenqing

王文卿

1093–1153; *zi*: Shudao 述道; *hao*: Chonghe zi 冲和子 (Master of
the Unfathomable Harmony), Yuyi ren 遇異人 (The One Who
Encounters The Marvellous); also known as Wang Jun 王俊

Wang Wenqing, who came from Jianchang 建昌 (Jiangxi), was a Thunder
Rites (*leifa*) specialist of the *Shenxiao legacy. Shenxiao enjoyed a high status
during most of Song Huizong's reign (1100–1125), but his imperial favor was
terminated in 1119. After *Lin Lingsu's disappearance from the capital in that
year, Wang became the main Shenxiao representative at court. In 1122, Huizong,
seemingly reconciled with the Taoists, offered Wang residence in the Jiuyang
zongzhen gong 九陽總真宮 (Palace of the Complete Perfection of the Ninefold Yang) and granted him the honorific title of Elder of the Unfathomable
Emptiness and the Wondrous Dao (Chongxu miaodao xiansheng 冲虛妙道先
生). Huizong's ephemeral successor, Song Qinzong (r. 1125–27), also conferred
a title on Wang and posthumous titles on his parents. However, Wang soon
decided to renounce the world and live in retirement. In 1143, Song Gaozong
(r. 1127–62) invited him to court, but he declined the summons. He died ten
years later at the Qingdu guan 清都觀 (Abbey of the Clear Metropolis) in
Nanfeng 南豐 (Guangdong).

Wang Wenqing is attributed with several sections of the ritual compendium *Daofa huiyuan (Corpus of Taoist Ritual) dealing with the Thunder
Rites, including the "Xuanzhu ge" 玄珠歌 (Song of the Mysterious Pearl; *j.*
70), Thunderclap (Leiting 雷霆) writings (67.11a–29a, and the whole of *j.* 76),
and prefaces to the Five Thunder Rites of Yushu 玉樞 (Jade Pivot; *j.* 56) and
the Five Thunder Rites of Shenxiao (Divine Empyrean; *j.* 61). An illustrated
supplement to the *Duren jing, entitled *Duren shangpin miaojing futu* 度人上品
妙經符圖 (Talismans and Diagrams of the Wondrous Scripture of the Upper
Chapters on Salvation; CT 147), is also ascribed to him. Another work, the
Chongxu tongmiao shichen Wang xiansheng jiahua 冲虛通妙侍宸王先生家話
(Teachings of Elder Wang of the Unfathomable Emptiness and the Pervading
Marvel, Servant of the Emperor; CT 1250), reports conversations between
Wang and his disciple Yuan Tingzhi 袁庭植.

Grégoire ESPESSET

📖 Boltz J. M. 1987a, 26–30; Hymes 2002, 147–70; Qing Xitai 1994, 1: 321–22

※ *leifa*; Shenxiao

Wang Xuanfu

王玄甫

1. ?–345 or 365; *hao*: Zhongyue zhenren 中嶽真人 (Perfected of
the Central Peak) 2. *hao*: Donghua dijun 東華帝君 (Imperial Lord
of Eastern Florescence), Donghua zi 東華子 (Master of Eastern
Florescence), Zifu Shaoyang jun 紫府少陽君 (Minor Yang Lord of
the Purple Bureau [Grotto-Heaven]), Huayang zhenren 華陽真人
(Perfected of Flourishing Yang)

There are two transcendents named Wang Xuanfu. The first is a minor figure
first mentioned in the *Zhengao* (14.7b–8a), and the second is an important
figure in *Quanzhen Taoism.

The first Wang Xuanfu was one of many persons who attained immortality
in 365, while the *Shangqing deities were appearing before *Yang Xi. Some
versions of his biography in the Taoist Canon, however, report his ascension
occurring in 345. Wang was a man from Pei 沛 (Jiangsu) who, by a combination
of techniques, including meditating for thirty-four years, ascended to heaven
in broad daylight on a cloud-carriage drawn by dragons. He was appointed
Perfected of the Central Peak with his friend Deng Boyuan 鄧伯元 at the
Northern Terrace of the Mysterious Garden (Bei Xuanpu tai 北玄圃臺).

The second Wang Xuanfu, better known as Donghua dijun, was the first
of the Five Patriarchs (*wuzu* 五祖) of Quanzhen Taoism (see table 17). The
obscurity of his origins and even the dynasty when he lived on earth seems to
indicate that his name was selected to bring the origins of Quanzhen teachings
further back into hoary antiquity. The only points of agreement among his
biographies is that he had a distinctive appearance at birth, that he received
a set of scriptures from the Supreme Perfected of the White Clouds (Baiyun
shangzhen 白雲上真), and that he passed his teachings to *Zhongli Quan
(*Jinlian zhengzong ji*, 1.1a–b; *Jinlian zhengzong xianyuan xiangzhuan* 金蓮正宗
仙源像傳, CT 174, 13b–14a; *Lishi zhenxian tidao tongjian*, 20.5a). His ascent
to heaven is celebrated on the sixteenth day of the tenth lunar month. As the
Divine Lord of Eastern Florescence, he is associated with the paradisiacal isle
of Fangzhu 方諸 (*Soushen ji*, 1.6b–8b).

Thomas E. SMITH

📖 Reiter 1985

※ Quanzhen; Shangqing; HAGIOGRAPHY

Wang Yuan

王遠

fl. 146–95; *zi*: Fangping 方平

Wang Yuan, who was a native of Donghai 東海 (Shandong), is primarily known from his biography in the *Shenxian zhuan* in which he is associated with the immortal *Magu. In this biography Wang is described as having a reasonably standard official career, despite an interest in esoteric texts and an ability to foretell the future, before resigning to cultivate the Dao. In typical fashion, he refuses to serve Han Huandi (r. 146–168 CE) and, instead, lives in the house of the official Chen Dan 陳耽. After some thirty years, Wang announces his imminent transformation and attains release from the corpse (*shijie) in 185 (this date is ascertained by cross-checking with the details of Chen Dan's career as it is revealed in the *Hou Hanshu* or *History of the Later Han*).

After transformation, Wang departs for Mount Guacang (Guacang shan 括蒼山, Zhejiang). On the way, he visits the house of one Cai Jing 蔡經, a commoner who Wang instructs as he is fated for transcendence. Cai, in turn, transforms. Ten years later Cai Jing returns home to announce that Wang Yuan will soon arrive. Wang arrives in glory and, in turn, summons Magu. When the three of them are present, they perform the cuisine ritual (see *chu) along with Cai Jing's family. Then the whole party gets drunk on Heavenly wine. Later, in conversation, it is revealed that Wang "normally rules over Mount *Kunlun and comes and goes to the Luofu Mountains (*Luofu shan) and Mount Guacang" and that he "sets in order the affairs of the Heavenly departments." (For other details on the story of Wang Yuan, Cai Jing, and Magu, see under *Magu.)

Wang Yuan's identity is, however, somewhat more complex. The *Laozi bianhua jing* (Scripture of the Transformations of Laozi) lists Wang Fangping as a transformation of Laozi, placing him in the Han, immediately preceding Laozi's manifestations near Chengdu in the Yangjia reign period (132–36 CE). This Wang Fangping is clearly too early to be the same as the Wang Yuan of the *Shenxian zhuan*. On the other hand, texts related to the twenty-four parishes (*zhi) of the early Celestial Masters (preserved in the *Yunji qiqian* as well as in *Du Guangting's *Dongtian fudi yuedu mingshan ji* 洞天福地嶽瀆名山記, CT 599) have Wang Fangping receiving a revelation from Laozi.

In addition to this confusion, Wang Yuan has also been identified as Lord Wang of the Western Citadel (Xicheng Wangjun 西城王君). An equivalence between Wang Yuan and Lord Wang of the Western Citadel is of significant interest as Lord Wang of the Western Citadel plays a major role in the transmission of certain texts and techniques that are central to *Shangqing Taoism and was, notably, the teacher of Mao Ying 茅盈 (see *Maojun). In his *Zhenling weiye tu (Chart of the Ranks and Functions of the Perfected Numinous Beings), *Tao Hongjing lists Lord Wang (under his extended title), with the commentary (by *Lüqiu Fangyuan, transformed 902) claiming that he is "Wang Yuan, zi Fangping." Lord Wang's biography in the *Maoshan zhi (early fourteenth century), a treatise dealing with the spiritual home of Shangqing Taoism, is unambiguous in making this identification. The same identification is made in the *Qingwei xianpu (Register of Pure Tenuity Transcendents) of 1293, which is related to the *Qingwei scriptural tradition.

Unfortunately, Lord Wang of the Western Citadel appears to have been active in the first century BCE (as in the *Santian neijie jing) and in the early years CE, at least a century and a half before Wang Yuan attained transcendence.

Benjamin PENNY

📖 Bokenkamp 1997, 213 and 351–52; Campany 2002, 259–70; Chen Guofu 1963, 12; Seidel 1969, 68

※ Wangwu shan; HAGIOGRAPHY

Wang Yuanzhi

王遠知 (*or*: 王遠智)

528–635; *zi*: Deguang 德廣

Wang Yuanzhi was the leader who stimulated the Tang rulers' allegiance to Taoism. He was the successor to the spiritual authority of the preeminent Taoist of the late Six Dynasties period, *Tao Hongjing. In the annals of the *Shangqing order, Wang is designated as the tradition's tenth patriarch or Grand Master (*zongshi* 宗師). Beyond his involvement in drawing rulers toward Taoism, relatively little is known of Wang's life. No writings are attributed to him, and we know virtually nothing of his beliefs or practice. His importance thus lies in his establishment of the political eminence of Taoism at the outset of the Tang, and in his transmission of that eminence to *Pan Shizheng and ultimately to *Sima Chengzhen.

Wang has biographies both in the dynastic histories (*Jiu Tangshu*, 192.5125–26; *Xin Tangshu*, 204.5803–4) and in the *Daozang* (e.g., Zhenxi 真系, in YJQQ 5.11a–13a; *Maoshan zhi, 22.1a–11a). Wang's parents had both been members of the elite of south China, but Wang turned to the religious life, studying under a little-known disciple of Tao named Zang Jin 臧矜. In time, Wang became sufficiently well known to be summoned both to the court of the short-lived Chen dynasty of south China (557–89) and to that of Sui Yangdi (r. 604–17). Though known as a supporter of Buddhism, Yangdi formally summoned Wang to court and "personally performed the ceremonies of a disciple," thereby recognizing the centuries-old paradigm of the Taoist master as the teacher of sovereigns (*diwang shi* 帝王師). When Yangdi proposed moving the capital to the south, Wang warned against the move, but Yangdi ignored his advice. That act apparently persuaded Wang that Yangdi was no longer the legitimate Son of Heaven, a position that had needed Taoist confirmation for hundreds of years. Wang therefore turned his attention to Li Yuan 李淵 (Gaozu, r. 618–26), the future founder of the Tang dynasty: Wang reportedly told Li that he would become the next emperor, and "secretly transmitted to him the [Taoist] sacred registers and the [Heavenly] Mandate."

Some scholars have argued that Wang initiated the prophecies that identified Li's ancestor as the Taoist sage Laozi, an identification that became a crucial element of Tang legitimatory doctrine and justified the extensive Tang promotion of Taoism. There is little evidence to support the argument that it was Wang who initiated such ideas. But in 621 he did recognize Gaozu's successor, Taizong (r. 626–49), as "the Son of Heaven of Great Peace" (*Taiping tianzi* 太平天子). Taizong reportedly offered Wang a government position, but Wang naturally declined, whereupon the emperor built an abbey for him at Mount Mao (*Maoshan, Jiangsu). Just before Wang's death in 635, Taizong issued a rescript expressing gratitude for Wang's gracious and conscientious attentions. In 680 Tang Gaozong (r. 649–83) canonized and ennobled Wang, and in 684 Empress Wu lauded Wang in an edict. The Standard Histories suggest that Wang lived some 126 years, but the Taoist biographies establish that he died 1 November 635, at the age of 107.

Russell KIRKLAND

📖 Barrett 1996, 28; Benn 1977, 31–43; Chen Guofu 1963, 47; Kirkland 1986b, 43–44; Reiter 1998, 20–28; Wechsler 1985, 69–73; Yoshikawa Tadao 1990

※ Shangqing

Wang Zhe

王嚞

1113–70; original *ming*: Zhongfu 中孚; *zi*: Yunqing 允卿, Zhiming
知明; *hao*: Chongyang 重陽 (Double Yang)

Wang Zhe (Wang Chongyang), the founder of the *Quanzhen order, was born
into a wealthy family near Xianyang 咸陽, west of Xi'an (Shaanxi). When he
was a teenager, the area became engulfed in the war between the Jin and the
Song, and was not at peace until the 1160s. This situation curtailed Wang's
ambitions, and he seems to have eventually renounced efforts to become a
scholar and then to build a military career. He moved to the area just north
of the Zhongnan mountains (Zhongnan shan 終南山), where apparently he
turned into a drunkard and a local bully. In 1159 he reportedly met two "extraordinary persons," later identified by the Quanzhen tradition as *Lü Dongbin
and *Zhongli Quan, who made a profound impression on him. He met them
again one year later and began to devote himself to self-cultivation.

From 1160 to 1163, he lived in a self-made grave called "tomb of the living
dead" (*huosi ren mu* 活死人墓), then moved to a hermitage shared with two
other ascetics. In 1167, he burned the hermitage down and headed for faraway
Shandong, where his predication met with great success. In each of the five
districts at the tip of the Shandong peninsula, he founded a lay association (*hui*
會) with a name beginning with "Three Teachings" and a specific denomina-
tion. Each association had a meeting hall (*tang* 堂) where devotees convened
for prayer and meditation. Wang visited these groups regularly and wrote for
them prose and poetic texts conveying his ethical and *neidan* pedagogy. Later
tradition isolates among his disciples a paradigmatic group of seven, known
as the Seven Real Men (*qizhen* 七真): *Ma Yu, *Tan Chuduan, *Liu Chuxuan,
*Qiu Chuji, *Wang Chuyi, *Hao Datong and *Sun Bu'er (see table 17). Wang
wanted to take them back to Shaanxi to convert his native area, but he died
on the way, in Kaifeng (Henan).

Wang belongs to the hagiographic category of people who create new
religions. The construction of his legend includes the portrait of a sinner converted fairly late—at the age of forty-six—to religious life, and of a forceful and
independent man more akin to a soldier than an official. Whereas Quanzhen's
later history is well charted by a host of sources (mainly inscriptions), Wang's
life stands apart since no contemporary records except his own works are
extant. The first comprehensive accounts of his life are an inscription dated

1232 and several later hagiographic documents. These, on the other hand, are very rich and cover a vast array of genres, including a pictorial representation of his life among the murals of the *Yongle gong. A comparison of this hagiography with Wang's extant poetry, which we have no reason to consider spurious, reveals that the broad outlines of his life's events are reliable, but the real character behind them is rather difficult to apprehend.

One of the most fascinating accounts of Wang's life is an autobiographical poem, the "Wuzhen ge" 悟真歌 or "Song on Awakening to Reality" (in *Chongyang Quanzhen ji, 9.11b–12b). Many themes in this text later became standard elements of the Quanzhen self-image and were repeatedly employed in inscriptions and hagiographies. For instance, when Wang decides to devote himself to the pursuit of immortality, he breaks off his relationship with his wife and children in an abrupt way, telling them that their plight is not anymore of his concern. This violent scene was included in many later Quanzhen Taoists' biographies, and was represented in excruciating detail in a theatre play (see under *Ma Yu).

Wang Zhe wrote a considerable amount of poetry that circulated as isolated pieces: there has never been a unique authoritative collection. Much of what we have was collected by Ma Yu and his disciples in the 1180s, and so emphasizes Wang's privileged relation with Ma. These works consist of a large collection of poems in various genres entitled *Chongyang Quanzhen ji (Anthology on the Completion of Authenticity, by [Wang] Chongyang; CT 1153), and of two compilations of his poetic exchanges with Ma, the Jiaohua ji 教化集 (Anthology of Religious Conversions; CT 1154) and the Fenli shihua ji 分梨十化集 (Anthology of the Ten Stages of Pear-Slicing; CT 1155). Many poems are found in two of these three works, which suggests an intricate compilation process. On the other hand, the Chongyang zhenren shou Danyang ershisi jue 重陽真人授丹陽二十四訣 (The Twenty-Four Instructions Given to [Ma] Danyang by the Real Man [Wang] Chongyang; CT 1158) seems to be apocryphal. Other works in the Daozang attributed to Wang are also of highly doubtful authenticity. These include a short exposition of the Taoist lifestyle, entitled *Chongyang lijiao shiwu lun (Fifteen Essays by [Wang] Chongyang to Establish His Teaching; CT 1233), and an original *neidan treatise, the Jinguan yusuo jue 金關玉鎖訣 (Instructions on the Golden Chain and the Jade Lock; CT 1156).

Vincent GOOSSAERT

📖 Boltz J. M. 1987a, 143–48; Eskildsen 2001; Hachiya Kunio 1992a; Kubo Noritada 1987b; Marsone 2001a, 97–101; Marsone 2001b; Qing Xitai 1994, 1: 328–29; Reiter 1994; Wong Shiu Hon 1981

※ *Chongyang lijiao shiwu lun*; *Chongyang Quanzhen ji*; Quanzhen

Wang Zhijin

王志謹

1178–1263; *hao*: Qiyun zi 棲雲子
(Master Dwelling among the Clouds)

Wang Zhijin is one of the most famous *Quanzhen masters of the third generation. He became an adept at the age of twenty under the tutelage of *Hao
Datong. After Hao's death in 1213, he led an ascetic vagrant life before settling
on Mount Pan (Panshan 盤山), a small mountain with a long Buddhist tradition located between today's Beijing and Tianjin. When *Qiu Chuji returned
to Beijing from his famous journey to Chinggis khan's camp, Wang formally
became one of his disciples. When Qiu died in 1227, Wang left Mount Pan to
set up new communities and, after the final demise of the Jin rule, was one
of the first Quanzhen masters under Mongol authority to go on missionary
tours in the valley of the Yellow River. His lifetime task was to build a large
monastery in Kaifeng, on the spot where *Wang Zhe had died; this was to
become the Chaoyuan gong 朝元宮 (Palace of the Audience with the [Three]
Primes), of which one tower is still standing. Although Wang's teaching and
ritual activities extended throughout the whole of northern China, where he
travelled tirelessly, most of his branch communities, often named Qiyun guan
棲雲觀 (Abbey of Dwelling among the Clouds) after his *hao*, were located near
Kaifeng, in the northern part of present-day Henan. His national prestige was
recognized in 1263 when, while still alive, he was awarded with a six-character
title of *zhenren*.

Wang's major legacy is surely his recorded sayings, the *Panshan Qiyun Wang
zhenren yulu* 盤山棲雲王真人語錄 (Recorded Sayings of the Real Man Wang
Qiyun from Mount Pan; 1247; CT 1059). This was the most famous Quanzhen
yulu, as attested by its inclusion in the *Xiuzhen shishu* (j. 53) and by numerous
later quotations and prefaces, including one by the famous late-Ming philosopher Jiao Hong 焦竑 (1541–1620). The received text is well established: the
Daozang and a Yuan edition kept at the Beijing National Library are identical,
while the *Xiuzhen shishu* edition is almost the same, except for the entirely different order of the 101 anecdotes. This is remarkable for a collection of random
jottings, compiled without a preconceived plan during the author's lifetime and
written in colloquial language. Throughout this lively work, Wang appears as
a passionate preacher, not averse to using Chan-like tricks, jokes or riddles to
elicit enlightenment in his audience, but especially prone to tell the stories of

immortals and Quanzhen patriarchs inflicting trials upon their followers to test their control over body and mind. Qiu Chuji figures prominently in many anecdotes, and appears as a paragon of the search for immortality whom all adepts should emulate. Although the *Panshan yulu* does not display theoretical peculiarities, it has a voice of its own in the larger corpus of Quanzhen literature. The pervasive theme of death, and the preference of absolute fluidity of mind over the use of mental symbols in meditation techniques, show that Wang's teachings as well as his person were all about directly coming to grasp the "great affair of life and death" (*shengsi dashi* 生死大事).

Vincent GOOSSAERT

📖 Boltz J. M. 1987a, 170–72 and 236

※ Hao Datong; Quanzhen

Wangwu shan

王屋山

Mount Wangwu (Henan)

Mount Wangwu, on the Henan-Shanxi border about 50 km north of Luoyang, gained special prominence within *Shangqing Taoism, which made it the domain of Lord Wang of the Western Citadel (Xicheng Wangjun 西城王君; see under *Wang Yuan). Numerous Shangqing scriptures and methods are said to have been revealed or secreted on Mount Wangwu. Accordingly, the mountain was listed as the foremost of the ten great Grotto-Heavens (*da dongtian* 大洞天) in the systematized sacred geography by *Du Guangting, the *Dongtian fudi yuedu mingshan ji* 洞天福地嶽瀆名山記 (Records of Grotto-Heavens, Blissful Lands, Peaks, Rivers, and Famous Mountains; CT 599). The *Wangwu shanzhi* 王屋山志 (Monograph of Mount Wangwu) by Li Guiyi 李歸一, originally compiled in 877, also provides much topographic and biographical information.

Due to its proximity to the capital and the prominence of the Shangqing lineage, Mount Wangwu became a focus of imperial attention during the Tang dynasty. It was a site for imperial rites of "casting the dragons" (see *tou longjian) as well imperially sponsored Taoist establishments. The local god of Mount Wangwu aided in quelling the An Lushan 安祿山 and Shi Siming 史思明 uprisings (755–63) and was ennobled by Tang Xuanzong (r. 712–56) as Celestial King of the Numina and Spirits (Zongling mingshen tianwang 總靈明神天王).

Among the important establishments on the mountain was the Yangtai guan 陽臺觀 (Abbey of the Yang Platform), the residence of *Sima Cheng-zhen (646–735). Repaired at the order of Tang Xuanzong in 725, it was the site for a Golden Register Retreat (*jinlu zhai) in 735, performed by Princess Jade Perfected, daughter of Tang Ruizong (r. 684–90, 710–12), who is said to have studied here before her Taoist initiation in 711 (see Benn 1991).

Du Guangting's preface to the *Tiantan Wangwu shan shengji ji* 天壇王屋山聖迹記 (Records of Traces of the Saints on Mount Wangwu, the Celestial Altar; CT 969) provides a Taoist view of the history and geography of the mountain. The main peak, named Celestial Altar (Tiantan 天壇), is the locus for regular assemblies of transcendent officials of all the mountains and Grotto-Heavens who examine and judge the students of the Dao. This was also the site for the Yellow Emperor's (*Huangdi) encounter with the Queen Mother of the West (*Xiwang mu), whose envoys, the Mysterious Woman (*Xuannü) and the Azure Lad (*Qingtong), presented him with esoteric devices to repel the demon Chiyou 蚩尤. Du refers to an annual assembly on the mountain which was held on the fifteenth day of the eighth lunar month. The main text elaborates on these narratives, and includes a detailed description of the mythical topography of the mountain, a short biography of Sima Chengzhen, and several verses, among them two attributed to Tang Ruizong.

Gil RAZ

📖 Qing Xitai 1994, 4: 201–5

※ Wang Yuan; TAOIST SACRED SITES

wangye

王爺

Royal Lords

In premodern China, personages of authority with the Chinese character *wang* 王 (lit., "king") in their titles, ranging from imperial princes (*qinwang* 親王) to bandit leaders (*shanzhai dawang* 山寨大王), were frequently addressed using the respectful title of *wangye* (lit., "my lord" or "your lordship/high-ness"). Throughout much of Fujian and Taiwan, the term *wangye*, usually translated as Royal Lord, was and frequently still is used to refer to a wide variety of demons and deities, including plague spirits (*wenshen), vengeful ghosts (*ligui* 厲鬼), plague demons (*yigui* 疫鬼), and historical figures such as Koxinga (Zheng Chenggong 鄭成功, 1624–62; ECCP 108–9).

The origins of the *wangye* remain murky, but the term appears in Qing-dynasty gazetteers from Fujian, some of which claim that temples to these deities existed as early as the Song dynasty. While relatively little research on Fujian's *wangye* had been done until the 1990s, a significant body of scholarship exists on this cult in Taiwan (for bibliographic information see Kang Bao 1997, 248–57; Lin Meirong 1997). Government-compiled statistics on registered temples, while seriously underreporting actual numbers of temples, reveals the popularity the *wangye* enjoyed throughout Taiwan during the Japanese Occupation (1895–1945) and postwar periods. The data indicate that in 1918 the number of Royal Lords temples registered with the Japanese colonial government was 447 (12.86% of all temples), second only to Earth God (*Tudi gong) temples (669; 19.25%). The 1930 survey lists 534 Royal Lords temples (14.59%; again second to Earth God temples at 674 and 18.41%). Four temple surveys conducted after 1945 indicate that among registered temples those to Royal Lords had attained a position of supreme popularity, with 677 Royal Lords temples (17.63%) in 1960, 556 (13.26%) in 1966, 747 (13.99%) in 1975, and 753 (13.59%) in 1981 (Yu Guanghong 1983, 81–82). Most of these temples are located along the southwestern coast of Taiwan, but *wangye* are worshipped throughout the island. Numerous *wangye* temples may also be found in the Pescadores (Penghu 澎湖; Huang Youxing 1992; Wilkerson 1995), as well as Quemoy (Jinmen 金門).

Taiwan's most popular *wangye* has always been Lord Chi (Chi Wangye 池王爺), whose cult appears to have developed in Fujian and can be traced back to the cult of the plague-fighting martial deity *Wen Qiong. In Taiwan, Lord Chi is worshipped individually as the main deity (*zhushen* 主神) or a subsidiary deity (*peishen* 陪神) of numerous temples, and as one of a group of five very popular *wangye* known as the Lords of One Thousand Years of the Five Prince's Palaces (Wufu qiansui 五府千歲). Other popular *wangye* include plague spirits such as the Great Emperors of the Five Blessings (Wufu dadi 五福大帝), whose cult may be traced back to the Five Envoys of Epidemics (Wuwen shizhe 五瘟使者), as well as the Lords of One Thousand Years [Who Appear on Earth Every] Five Years (Wunian qiansui 五年千歲), whose cult may be traced back to the Twelve Year-Controlling Kings of Epidemics (Shi'er zhinian wenwang 十二值年瘟王).

Many different hagiographies of the *wangye* still circulate, but the most popular one is based on the hagiography of Wen Qiong and states that the *wangye* sacrificed their own lives to prevent plague spirits from poisoning local wells. Other stories describe the *wangye* as scholar-officials who died in battle or during a shipwreck, or who had been executed by China's first emperor Qin Shi huangdi (r. 221–210 BCE). One story, which appears to be based on an account preserved in *Dunhuang manuscripts (Waley 1960, 124–44), states

that Tang Xuanzong (r. 712–56) attempted to test the spiritual powers of the
*Tianshi dao patriarch by ordering these scholars to hide in a cellar at the
imperial palace and play music. The emperor then told this Taoist patriarch
that the palace was haunted, and asked him to perform an exorcism, which
he accomplished by locating the scholars in their hideout using a mirror. He
then put them to death, prompting the emperor to erect a shrine to appease
their spirits (Zheng Zhiming 1988a). What all these stories have in common is
the theme of untimely and wrongful death, and it appears that most *wangye*
are in fact demons who ended up being worshipped as divinities.

At present, Taiwan's most renowned *wangye* temples are the Daitian fu 代
天府 (Hall [of the Royal Lords] who Represent Heaven) of Madou 麻豆 and
Nankunshen 南鯤鯓 (Tainan), the Zhen'an gong 鎮安宮 (Palace of Securing
Tranquillity) at Mamingshan 馬鳴山 (Yunlin), and the Donglong gong 東隆宮
(Palace of Eastern Beneficence) in Donggang 東港 (Pingdong; Hiraki Kōhei
1987; Kang Bao 1991; Li Fengmao 1993b). The island's largest and most popular
plague expulsion festivals (commonly called *wenjiao*) are also staged at these
sites, as well as the Qing'an gong 慶安宮 (Palace of Felicitous Tranquillity),
a *Mazu temple in Xigang 西港 (Tainan; Jordan 1976).

Paul R. KATZ

📖 Cai Xianghui 1989; Harrell 1974; Katz P. R. 1987; Katz P. R. 1992; Katz P.
R. 1995a; Katz P. R. 1995b; Kang Bao 1997; Liu Zhiwan 1983b; Maejima Shinji
1938; Mio Yuko 2000; Schipper 1985b; Xu Xiaowang 1993; Yu Kuang-hung 1990;
Zheng Zhiming 1988a

※ Wen Qiong; *wenshen*; *wenjiao*; DEMONS AND SPIRITS; TAOISM AND POPULAR
RELIGION

Wangzi Qiao

王子喬

Wangzi Qiao (whose name is also transliterated as Wang Ziqiao) appears in
numerous early sources as an exemplary model for a successful adept. His hagiography in the *Liexian zhuan* (trans. Kaltenmark 1953, 109–14) identifies him
as Jin 晉, heir to King Ling of Zhou (Lingwang, r. 571–545 BCE). After studying
with Fu Qiu 浮丘 on Mount Song (*Songshan, Henan) for over thirty years,
he disappeared riding a white crane. Shrines were erected on Mount Goushi
(Goushi shan 緱氏山, Henan) and on Mount Song. A distinct, and probably
older, tradition is preserved in the *Tianwen* 天問 (Heavenly Questions) poem
of the *Chuci* 楚辭 (Songs of Chu; trans. Hawkes 1985, 122–51) and in Wang Yi's

王逸 (second century CE) commentary, which describe Wangzi Qiao manifesting himself as a rainbow before transforming into a great bird.

Wangzi Qiao's fame grew during the Han culminating in the *Wangzi Qiao bei* 王子喬碑 (Stele to Wangzi Qiao), erected in 165 at the prompting of Han Huandi (r. 146–168) at the shrine of the Wang family of Meng 蒙 (in Henan), to commemorate the transcendent's appearance in 137 CE during the *la* 臘 festival (the popular New Year's day; Bodde 1975, 49–74). Among the Perfected who appeared to *Yang Xi, Wangzi Qiao later was recognized in the *Shangqing scriptures as the official in charge of the Golden Court Cavern (Jinting dong 金庭洞) below Mount Tongbo (Tongbo shan 桐柏山, Zhejiang; *Zhengao*, 1.2b; *Zhenling weiye tu*, 5a). In 711, Tang Ruizong (r. 684–90, 710–12) sponsored the establishment of the *Tongbo guan (Abbey of the Paulownias and Cypresses). During his residency there, *Sima Chengzhen wrote a hagiography describing Wangzi Qiao's historical appearances, the *Shangqing shi dichen Tongbo zhenren zhentu zan* 上清侍帝晨桐柏真人真圖讚 (Appraisals to Authentic Pictures of the Perfected of Tongbo, Director Aide to Imperial Dawn of Highest Clarity; CT 612).

During the Five Dynasties, Wangzi Qiao was designated Perfected Lord and Primordial Aide (Yuanbi zhenjun 元弼真君). He was entitled Perfected Lord of Primordial Response (Yuanying zhenjun 元應真君) by Song Huizong in 1113, and Perfected of Benefic Munificence and Wide Deliverance (Shanli guangji zhenren 善利廣濟真人) by Song Gaozong during the Shaoxing reign period (1131–62).

Gil RAZ

📖 Campany 1996, 193–95; DeWoskin 1983, 52–53; Holzman 1991; Kaltenmark 1953, 109–14; Ngo 1976, 86–87

※ HAGIOGRAPHY

Wanli xu daozang

萬曆續道藏

Supplementary Taoist Canon of the Wanli Reign Period

The *Da Ming xu daozang jing* 大明續道藏經 (Scriptures in Supplement to the Taoist Canon of the Great Ming) is popularly known as the *Wanli xu daozang*. It dates to the thirty-fifth year of the Wanli reign period (1607) and serves as an addendum to the so-called *Zhengtong daozang (Taoist Canon of the Zheng-tong Reign Period) issued in 1445. Just how this supplement arose remains somewhat of mystery. What is clear is that, like the Zhengtong Canon itself, the compilation of this body of texts resulted from an imperial decree issued to the prevailing patriarch of the Celestial Master, or *Tianshi dao lineage.

The scant bibliographic data on this work to survive suggest that this supplement expanded over time, with components added one after the other. One clue comes from three different editions of the *Daozang mulu xiangzhu (Detailed Commentary on the Index of the Taoist Canon) compiled in 1626. Each edition of this index provides a variant form of the table of contents for the supplement. One lists titles encompassed in nine cases bearing labels from *du* 杜 to *fu* 府, according to the *Qianzi wen* 千字文 (Thousand-Word Text) classification sequence. Another provides the table of contents for a total of eleven cases, adding those labelled *luo* 羅 and *jiang* 將. The third form of the table of contents corresponds to the received version of the supplement, accounting for altogether thirty-two cases, the last of which is labelled *ying* 纓.

Variant forms of a colophon dating to the year Wanli 35 (1607) appear throughout the supplement itself, typically but not always recorded at the end of the last fascicle in a case. Eleven are dated to the fifteenth day of the first lunar month (*shangyuan jieri* 上元吉日) and one, the most concisely worded colophon, is dated to the fifteenth day of the second lunar month (*eryue shiwu ri* 二月十五日). Each colophon states that *Zhang Guoxiang (?–1611) undertook collation and publication by imperial command. All but the colophon with the variant date include a title conferred on Zhang by the Wanli Emperor (r. 1573–1620) in 1605. One also includes reference to his position as the fiftieth patriarch of the Celestial Master lineage. Another version of the colophon is also found at the close of the *Da Ming xu daozang jing mulu* 大明續道藏經目錄 (Index of the Scriptures in Supplement to the Taoist Canon of the Great Ming). An additional line here indicates that the blocks were entrusted to the Lingyou gong 靈佑宮 (Palace of Numinous Support). The construction of this hall in a temple complex outside Beijing can be dated to 1603.

The table of contents, appended to that of the *Da Ming daozang jing*, lists some fifty titles printed in 185 *juan*, or chapters. They were cut on 4,440 block surfaces, raising the total for the Ming Canon from 74,080 to approximately 78,520. The work on the supplement would appear to have been completed in a fairly short period of time. Prior to its compilation, the Wanli Emperor granted copies of a 1598 printing of the Zhengtong Canon to a number of temple compounds. A stele inscription marking his gift to the Chongxuan guan 冲玄觀 (Abbey of the Unfathomable Mystery) at Mount Wuyi (*Wuyi shan, Fujian) dates to 1605. Such bestowals are known to have been made on behalf of the emperor's mother, but the story behind his authorization of a supplement to the Canon remains to be discovered.

Judith M. BOLTZ

📖 Chen Guofu 1963, 179–81; Chen Yuan 1988, 1298–99; van der Loon 1984, 59–61; Qing Xitai 1988–95, 4: 15–17; Zhu Yueli 1992, 156–58

※ Zhang Guoxiang; *Zhengtong daozang*; DAOZANG AND SUBSIDIARY COMPILATIONS

Wei Huacun

魏華存

251–334; *zi*: Shen'an 賢安; *hao*: Nanyue furen 南嶽夫人
(Lady of the Southern Peak)

Wei Huacun is the main divine being who transmitted sacred scriptures to *Yang Xi between 364 and 370. Those scriptures formed the nucleus of the *Shangqing corpus, and Wei was later designated the first Shangqing Grand Master (*zongshi* 宗師)—the only woman to play a role of such eminence within Taoism.

Various sources contain fragmentary accounts of her life, the most detailed of which is in the *Taiping guangji* 太平廣記 (Extensive Records of the Taiping Xingguo Reign Period; 978; *j.* 58). Similar but shorter accounts are found in the *Taiping yulan* 太平御覽 (Imperial Readings of the Taiping Xingguo Reign Period; 983; *j.* 678) and the *Yunji qiqian (4.2a–b). Other relevant materials are in *juan* 3 of *Tao Hongjing's *Dengzhen yinjue. Finally, the *Xianquan ji* 峴泉集 (Anthology of Alpine Springs; CT 1311; 4.7b–9a), compiled by the forty-third Celestial Master *Zhang Yuchu, contains three hagiographies of Wei.

According to these sources, Wei Huacun was born in Rencheng 任城 (Shandong) as the daughter of Wei Shu 魏舒 (209–90), Minister of Education at the Jin court and a *Tianshi dao adept. From an early age, Huacun read widely from the Taoist classics and practiced longevity techniques. She wanted to pursue a secluded life devoted to Taoism, but at the age of twenty-four she was forced to marry Liu Wen 劉文, Grand Guardian (*taibao* 太保) in Nanyang 南陽 (southern Henan), with whom she had two sons, Pu 璞 and Xia 瑕. Later, Wei retired in Xiuwu 修武 (northern Henan) to practice Taoism, and there she was appointed Tianshi dao libationer (*jijiu). In 288, she received the visits of four immortals. One of them, Wang Bao 王褒, the Perfected of Clear Emptiness (Qingxu zhenren 清虛真人), became her spiritual patron and transmitted to her thirty-one scriptures, including the *Dadong zhenjing which later became the central Shangqing scripture. Some time later, Wei also received the *Huangting jing from the Perfected Jinglin (Jinglin zhenren 景林真

人). In 317, when the Eastern Jin dynasty took power, she fled to southeastern China with her two sons, and died there at the age of eighty-three.

Wei also became, by divine order of the Queen Mother of the West (*Xiwang mu), the holy spouse of Mao Ying 茅盈 (see *Maojun), forming a divine couple that was an ideal model for many generations of Shangqing adepts. She was later venerated as the Lady of the Southern Peak, an honorary title alluding to the first revelation she received on a mountain in the *Hengshan 衡山 range (Hunan). In the Tang period both Hengshan and Linchuan 臨川 (Jiangxi), another important site in her spiritual journey, became centers of intense worship of Wei. Yan Zhenqing 顏真卿 (709–85), the eminent district magistrate and scholar of the Linchuan area, restored the remains of an old shrine dedicated to her and wrote a commemorative stele (trans. Schafer 1977b), which is one of the main extant Tang hagiographic texts.

Elena VALUSSI

📖 Chen Guofu 1963, 31–32; Despeux 1990, 56–60; Qing Xitai 1988–95, 1: 336–39; Qing Xitai 1994, 1: 232–33; Robinet 1984, 2: 399–405; Strickmann 1981; Schafer 1977b; Schafer 1979

※ Shangqing; HAGIOGRAPHY

Wen Qiong

溫瓊

also known as Wen Yuanshuai 溫元帥 (Marshal Wen) and Zhongjing Wang 忠靖王 (Loyal and Defending King)

Wen Qiong was one of south China's most popular deities during the late imperial era. A number of different hagiographies about him survive, but most texts state that he resided in Wenzhou 溫州 (Zhejiang) during the Tang dynasty, and that after his death he joined the chthonic bureaucracy of the Great Emperor of the Eastern Peak (*Dongyue dadi). Vernacular novels and folktales about Wen describe him as sacrificing his own life to prevent plague spirits (*wenshen) from poisoning local wells, and he was frequently worshipped as a powerful martial figure who specialized in preventing or stopping outbreaks of epidemics.

Temples to Wen began to be built in southern Zhejiang during the twelfth century, including one in Yueqing 樂清 district allegedly supported by the renowned Neo-Confucian Zhu Xi 朱熹 (1130–1200). Wen also figured promi-nently in exorcistic rituals performed by *Shenxiao Taoists during the Song and Yuan dynasties (some of these texts are preserved in the *Daofa huiyuan*), and *daoshi* helped spread his cult throughout south China and founded some of his oldest temples (see *TAOISM AND LOCAL CULTS*). By the late Ming, large-scale plague expulsion festivals devoted to Wen had begun to appear throughout Zhejiang, the most famous being in Wenzhou and Hangzhou.

Wen's cult began to revive after the end of the Cultural Revolution (1966–76; see for example Lao Gewen and Lü Chuikuan 1993). He is also worshipped in Fujian and Taiwan as Lord Chi (Chi Wangye 池王爺), one of the most popular Royal Lords (*wangye*) in these regions.

Paul R. KATZ

📖 Boltz J. M. 1987a, 97–99; Katz P. R. 1990; Katz P. R. 1995a; Lagerwey 1987c, 241–52; Little 2000b, 264–65; Schipper 1985b

※ *wangye*; *wenshen*; DEMONS AND SPIRITS; TAOISM AND LOCAL CULTS; TAOISM AND POPULAR RELIGION

Wenchang

文昌

The Imperial Lord Wenchang was revered throughout late imperial China as the patron saint of literature, guardian of morality and giver of sons. Wenchang first occurs in the *Yuanyou* 遠遊 (Far Roaming) poem of the *Chuci* 楚辭 (Songs of Chu; trans. Kroll 1996b, 662) and Han astronomical works as a constellation, consisting of six stars in *Ursa Major*, arrayed in a crescent above the ladle of the Northern Dipper (*beidou*). Among these stars were the Director of Destinies (*siming* 司命; see *Siming) and Director of Emoluments (*silu* 司祿), which suggested a role in the administration of destiny. There is occasional mention of the constellation in Taoist scriptures of the Six Dynasties period, and an increasing association of the stars with literature at the popular level, no doubt linked to reinterpretation of the name as Literary Glory.

Worship of Wenchang grew rapidly after the association of the asterism with the god of a northern Sichuanese community named Zitong 梓潼. The god of Zitong began as the thunder-wielding snake deity of Mount Qiqiu (Qiqiu shan 七曲山, Sevenfold Mountain) just north of Zitong. The cult had a role in the early myth cycle of Sichuan and grew through the absorption of surrounding cults, such as the River-Flooding God (Xianhe shen 陷河神) of Qiongdu 邛都 and Transcendent Zhang (Zhang xian 張仙) of Chengdu. Positive, human traits of the god were promoted and the primitive, theriomorphic identity suppressed until by the Song the god was a heroic figure credited with suppressing rebellion and protecting the Sichuan region. The cult temple was situated on the main road from Sichuan to the capital and the god developed a reputation for predicting the results of supplicants on the civil service examinations, first through displays of meteorological phenomena, then through incubatory dreams, finally by spirit writing (see *fuji). A series of spirit-writing revelations in the late twelfth century established a new identity for the god as a high Taoist deity responsible for revealing a corrected version of the *Dadong zhenjing (Authentic Scripture of the Great Cavern) entitled Wenchang dadong xianjing 文昌大洞仙經 (Immortal Scripture of the Great Cavern by Wenchang; CT 5). The *Wenchang huashu (Book of Transformations of Wenchang) recounted a salvific mission encompassing numerous human avatars and divine appointments, culminating in the god's apotheosis and appointment as Wenchang, keeper of the Cinnamon Record (guiji 桂籍) that determines the fate of all literati.

The god's identity as Wenchang and role in the official canon of sacrifices was formally recognized by the Yuan in 1314 and maintained through most of late imperial China, despite occasional attacks by conservatives who sought to limit worship of the god to the Sichuan region. As the patron deity of the examinations, the god was worshipped by literati throughout China and a Wenchang Pavilion (Wenchang ge 文昌閣) became a common feature in the Confucian temple (Wenmiao 文廟). He is commonly portrayed as a seated official of stern visage flanked by the monstrous Kuixing 魁星, whose pictorial representational often forms the character kui 魁 or "top examinee," and Zhuyi 朱衣, a red-robed official carrying the record of fated examination results. Alternately, he may be flanked by two boys, Heavenly Deaf (Tianlong 天聾) and Earthly Dumb (Diya 地啞), whose physical disabilities encourage them to maintain the secrecy of the celestial records and the profane examination system. The god continues to manifest to spirit-writing groups in Taiwan and Hong Kong today and is a particular favorite of those studying for the college entrance examinations.

Terry KLEEMAN

📖 Kleeman 1993; Kleeman 1994a; Kleeman 1996; Maspero 1981, 129–31

※ *Wenchang huashu*; TAOISM AND LOCAL CULTS; TAOISM AND POPULAR RELIGION

Wenchang huashu

文昌化書

Book of Transformations of Wenchang

The *Book of Transformations of Wenchang*, also known as the *Book of Transformations of the Imperial Lord of Zitong* (*Zitong dijun huashu* 梓潼帝君化書), is a first-person chronicle of the lives and experiences of *Wenchang, patron deity of literature, literati, and the examination system. The text dates from the Southern Song, and was first revealed through spirit writing (see *fuji) to devotees of the god of Zitong in Northern Sichuan. In addition to serving as a charter for the worship of Wenchang, the *Book of Transformations* is also one of the earliest examples of the "morality book" (*shanshu) genre and was widely reprinted during the Ming and Qing dynasties.

The earliest hagiography of the god of Zitong was the *Qinghe neizhuan* 清河內傳 (Inner Biography of Qinghe), a short work detailing only one human incarnation of the god and his apotheosis. It was revealed through a Sichuanese spirit-writing medium named Liu Ansheng 劉安勝 around 1170. In 1181 Liu, his relatives, and supporters collaborated in producing the first seventy-three episodes of the *Book of Transformations*; this portion of the scripture is common to all editions. Anecdotes were assimilated from two other local Sichuanese deities, the River-flooding Dragon of Qiong Pool (Qiongchi Xianhe shen 邛池陷河神) and Transcendent Zhang (Zhang xian 張仙), a fertility god from Chengdu. It culminated with the god being appointed to supervise the Cinnamon Record (*guiji* 桂籍), that determines the fate of all literati, in the Wenchang Palace during the Jin 金 dynasty. The same medium also produced a new recension of the *Dadong zhenjing (Authentic Scripture of the Great Cavern), entitled *Wenchang dadong xianjing* 文昌大洞仙經 (Immortal Scripture of the Great Cavern by Wenchang; CT 5), and a *Precious Register* to this scripture that tied it into Zitong cult lore.

Episodes 74–94 of the *Book of Transformations* were added in 1194 by Feng Ruyi 馮如意 and Yang Xing 楊興. These chapters relate the further activities of the god, including the encounters with Tang Xuanzong (r. 712–56) and Tang Xizong (r. 873–88) that won the god his first official ennoblements and the god's activities on behalf of the Song. The final three episodes of the Song edition, added in 1267 by person or persons unknown, depict the god's role in the suppression of the rebellion of Wu Xi 吳曦 in 1206 and unsuccessful attempts to oppose the Mongol invaders in 1231 and 1255. In 1316, coinciding with the reinauguration of the civil service examinations, a new recension of the *Book of Transformations* was revealed. Presenting a new, authoritative collation of various printed and manuscript editions then in circulation, this new recension also excised all portions of the 1194 and 1267 additions that were unfavorable to non-Chinese peoples. It is this Yuan version that is preserved in the Ming Taoist Canon (*Zitong dijun huashu* 梓潼帝君化書; CT 170).

The *Book of Transformations* was reprinted widely in the Ming and Qing dynasties. The earliest surviving edition dates to 1645. The text was often included in collections of Wenchang scriptures and essays, such as the great compendium of Wenchang scriptures, *Wendi quanshu* 文帝全書 (Complete Writings of the Imperial Lord Wenchang), first published in 1743, and transmitted in this form to Japan and Korea. All these texts are based on the Song recension, which was reprinted in the *Daozang jiyao* of 1906 (vol. 23).

Terry KLEEMAN

📖 Kleeman 1994a (trans.)

※ Wenchang; *shanshu*

Weng Baoguang

翁葆光

fl. 1173; *zi*: Yuanming 淵明; *hao*: Wuming zi 無名子 (Master With No Name), Xiangchuan weng 象川翁 (Gentleman of Xiangchuan)

Weng Baoguang, a native of Xiangchuan 象川 (Sichuan), is mainly known for his commentary to *Zhang Boduan's *Wuzhen pian* (Folios on Awakening to Perfection) and the three essays collected in the *Wuzhen zhizhi xiangshuo sansheng biyao* 悟真直指詳說三乘祕要 (Straightforward Directions and Detailed Explanations on the *Wuzhen pian* and the Secret Essentials of the Three Vehicles; 1337; CT 143). Weng received the *Wuzhen pian* from Liu Yongnian 劉永年 (fl. 1138–68), a bibliophile who also published the *Zhouyi cantong qi in 1158.

Weng's commentary to the *Wuzhen pian* is available in two versions: the *Wuzhen pian zhushi* 悟真篇注釋 (Commentary and Exegesis to the *Wuzhen pian*; CT 145), with an undated preface, and the *Wuzhen pian zhushu* 悟真篇注疏 (Commentary and Subcommentary to the *Wuzhen pian*; CT 141), with a preface dated 1173. The *Xiuzhen shishu (CT 263, j. 26–30) also quotes from two versions, using the *hao* Wuming zi and Xiangchuan weng to distinguish them. Weng's commentary was soon falsely attributed to *Xue Daoguang, and appears under the latter's name in the *Wuzhen pian sanzhu* 悟真篇三注 (Three Commentaries to the *Wuzhen pian*; CT 142). This error was corrected by Dai Qizong 戴起宗 (fl. 1332–37), who edited the work in 1335 as the *Wuzhen pian zhushu* (CT 141).

Dai Qizong's edition also includes a preface dated 1174 by Chen Daling 陳達陵, a contemporary and admirer of Weng Baoguang (CT 141, preface, 4b–5a). Elsewhere, Dai says that he possessed an edition of Weng's commentary which included a short preface dated 1174 by Zixu zi 子虛子 (Master of Emptiness) that preceded Chen Daling's introduction (CT 143, 22b–23a). According to Dai, Zixu zi had condensed and distorted Weng's preface; moreover, he had divided the *Wuzhen zhizhi xiangshuo* into three sections, adding them at the beginning of each chapter of Weng's commentary (this indeed is the arrangement found in the *Wuzhen pian zhushi*). Dai also states that Zixu zi's interpretation of the *Wuzhen pian* was sexual and represented heterodox teachings (*xiezong* 邪宗); therefore he dared not divulge his name and used instead the appellation Zixu zi. Others, however, believed Zixu zi and Weng Baoguang to be the same person. Thus through the Chen edition Weng became associated with the sexual interpretations of *neidan.

In his works, Weng Baoguang combines the terminology of the *Zhong-Lü school with the language of the *Cantong qi* and the *Yinfu jing*. His *Wuzhen pian zhushi* presents the poems of the original text in a different order compared to other versions; moreover, Zhang Boduan's Buddhist poems are not reproduced. The commentary emphasizes the practice of acquiring the ingredients of the Golden Elixir, nurturing and refining them, and then using the elixir to transform one's viscera and bones into Yang. After a ten-month gestation period, the Embryo of Sainthood (*shengtai) is completed. Weng adds that only at this level should the adept withdraw from the world and practice *baoyi* 抱一 (embracing the One) for nine years.

Farzeen BALDRIAN-HUSSEIN

📖 Boltz J. M. 1987a, 174; Chen Bing 1985, 37–38

※ *neidan*; Nanzong

wenjiao

瘟醮

plague expulsion rituals

Wenjiao are plague expulsion Offering rituals (**jiao*) featuring the floating away or burning of a "plague boat" which have been performed by Taoist specialists throughout south China and Taiwan for at least a millennium. Strictly speaking, the term *wenjiao* refers only to those rites performed by Taoist priests, but sometimes local communities refer to the entire plague festival (which includes a large procession and communal feasting) as a *wenjiao*. In different parts of China, *wenjiao* are also referred to by other autonyms and exonyms, including Festival of the Eastern Peak (*dongyue hui* 東嶽會), *nuo* 儺, Sending off the Lords' Boat (*song wangchuan* 送王船), Sending off the Plague Spirits (*song wenshen* 送瘟神), Welcoming the Lords (*yingwang* 迎王), and so forth.

The exact origins of *wenjiao* are unknown, but they appear to derive from boat expulsion rites performed by Han and non-Han peoples in south China during the Dragon Boat Festival, which was held annually on the fifth day of the fifth lunar month to prevent outbreaks of epidemics during the summer months. In some areas, individuals burned or floated away miniature dragon boats, but in others one large dragon boat was built to represent the entire community (Eberhard 1968, 391–406; Huang Shi 1979; Katz P. R. 1995a; Kang Bao 1997).

The earliest surviving liturgical text for a *wenjiao* is a *Shenxiao exorcistic rite performed for individuals entitled *Shenxiao qianwen songchuan yi* 神霄遣瘟送船儀 (Divine Empyrean Liturgy for Expelling Epidemics and Sending off the Boats), which is preserved in the *Daofa huiyuan (Corpus of Taoist Ritual, *j.* 220). According to this text, the officiating Shenxiao priest first consecrated the altar by performing rites such as the Pace of Yu (*Yubu* 禹步; see *bugang). Then, thirteen different groups of spirits were invited to descend to the altar, including Shenxiao patriarchs and deities (groups 1–4), local and household deities, and deities capable of controlling plague spirits (groups 5–7), plague spirits (*wenshen) such as the Twelve Kings of Epidemics (groups 8–11), and other demonic forces seen as responsible for various social misfortunes (groups 12–13). A small boat used to expel the plague spirits and other demonic creatures was then carried to the sick person's room or the main room of the house. All the spirits invited to the ritual were offered a banquet, with the plague spirits and other demons receiving meat dishes and the Shenxiao and protective deities receiving purely vegetarian items and incense. The Shenxiao master proceeded to read a Statement (*shuwen* 疏文) which described the plague deities as carrying out Heaven's will by observing human behavior, rewarding the good and punishing the wicked. The text warns that those who follow the Dao shall flourish, while those who counter the Dao shall perish. After the Statement had been read, the Shenxiao master ordered the martial deities serving him, as well as stricken person's household deities, to capture the plague deities and force them onto the boat. Finally, the boat was taken out of the house and burned. Related texts may be found in *j.* 219, 221, and 256 of the *Daofa huiyuan*. Qing-dynasty liturgical texts from Sichuan include the *Hewen zhengchao ji* 和瘟正朝集 (Anthology of the Orthodox Audience of the Pacification of Plagues) and the *Hewen qianzhou quanji* 和瘟遣舟全集 (Complete Collection of the Pacification of Plagues Ritual for Expelling the Boats), both of which are reprinted in the *Zangwai daoshu* (see Katz P. R. 1995a; Katz P. R. 1995b).

As we are unable to determine the exact origins of the *wenjiao*, so do we encounter numerous difficulties attempting to trace its spread. We do not know exactly how it was transmitted throughout south China, although this was apparently done by *Zhengyi *daoshi* and their disciples. These rituals continued to follow the ritual structure presented above, but also began to be performed for entire communities. Local gazetteers and other sources from south China composed during the late imperial era reveal that boat expulsion festivals for entire communities had become increasingly common in these provinces' coastal regions, and that *daoshi* were usually summoned to perform *wenjiao* at these events. Some of the most famous *wenjiao* were held in urban centers such as Fuzhou (Fujian; Xu Xiaowang 1993) and Wenzhou 溫州 (Zhe-jiang; Katz P. R. 1995a; Xu Hongtu and Zhang Aiping 1997, 31–33, 45–47, and 136–46), although smaller scale rites are also held in other parts of south China (Xiao Bing 1992; Xu Hongtu 1995a, 85–86; Xu Hongtu 1995b, 32, 37, and 50). *Wenjiao* spread from Fujian to Taiwan during the seventeenth and eighteenth centuries and are still regularly performed at *wangye (Royal Lords) temples along the island's southwestern coast, the most famous being at Donggang 東港 (Pingdong district; Hiraki Kōhei 1987; Kang Bao 1991; Li Fengmao 1993b) and Xigang 西港 (Tainan district; Jordan 1976). Liturgical texts belonging to *daoshi* from Tainan district may be found in the collection edited by Ōfuchi Ninji (1983). Migrants from Fujian and Guangdong also transmitted *wenjiao* to parts of Southeast Asia (Cheu Hock Tong 1988; Tan Chee-Beng 1990a).

Paul R. KATZ

📖 Katz P. R. 1995a; Katz P. R. 1995b; Kang Bao 1997; Li Fengmao 1993b; Li Fengmao 1994; Liu Zhiwan 1983b; Schipper 1985b

※ *jiao*; *wangye*; *wenshen*

wenshen

瘟神

plague spirits

Plague spirits are generally conceived of as being deities belonging to the Ministry of Epidemics (Wenbu 瘟部) of the celestial bureaucracy who are charged with punishing wrong-doers by afflicting them with contagious diseases. As such they are often contrasted with vengeful ghosts (*ligui* 厲鬼) and plague demons (*yigui* 疫鬼), souls of the unruly dead who spread epidemics to extort offerings but do not belong to the celestial bureaucracy. However, some plague spirits (such as the *wangye or Royal Lords of Fujian and Taiwan) were originally conceived of as demons but ended up being worshipped as deities.

Plague spirits are mentioned in early Taoist texts such as the *Nüqing guilü (Demon Statutes of Nüqing) and the *Dongyuan shenzhou jing (see Li Fengmao 1993a), but cults to them do not seem to have become widespread until the Song dynasty. In late imperial China, the most widely worshipped plague spirits were the Five Envoys of Epidemics (Wuwen shizhe 五瘟使者) and the Twelve Year-Controlling Kings of Epidemics (Shi'er zhinian wenwang 十二值年瘟王). In terms of cosmology, the Five Envoys were linked to the *wuxing, while the Twelve Kings were worshipped as underlings of the stellar deity Taisui 太歲 (Jupiter). Temples and small shrines to these deities appear to have been founded by Taoist specialists and local worshippers as early as the Song dynasty (if not earlier), but their cults appear to have been most popular in Fujian (where the Five Envoys were worshipped as the Five Emperors or Wudi 五帝) and Taiwan (where they are worshipped among the island's numerous *wangye*). Migrants from Fujian and Guangdong also brought their cults into parts of Southeast Asia (Cheu Hock Tong 1988; Tan Chee-Beng 1990a). Plague spirits are often propitiated during large-scale Taoist Offering rituals commonly referred to as *wenjiao.

Paul R. KATZ

📖 Doolittle 1865–67, 157–67 and 276–87; Katz P. R. 1995a, 50–59; Li Fengmao 1993a; Li Fengmao 1994; Maejima Shinji 1938; Schipper 1985b; Szonyi 1997; Xu Xiaowang 1993

※ *wangye*; *wenjiao*; TAOISM AND POPULAR RELIGION

Wenzi

文子

Book of Master Wen

The *Wenzi* is a work with a complex and not yet entirely understood textual history. The bibliography in the *Hanshu* (History of the Former Han) states that its author was "a student of Laozi who lived at the same time as Confucius," but adds that "the work appears to be a forgery." Later, Li Xian 李暹 of the Northern Wei dynasty (386–534) wrote a commentary on it. He gave Wenzi's surname as Xin 辛 and his appellation as Jiran 計然. Wenzi reportedly had studied under Fan Li 范蠡 (sixth century BCE), but originally had received teachings from Laozi.

These early editions of the *Wenzi* are lost, but in 1973, bamboo strips of the text were excavated from a tomb in Dingxian 定縣 (Hebei). As this was the grave of Liu Xiu 劉修, who died in 55 BCE, and as the bamboo fragments are basically consistent with the received text, they are likely part of the original *Wenzi*. The received text, nevertheless, certainly represents a considerable revision of the original. The oldest fully extant version today is the twelve-chapter edition annotated by Xu Lingfu 徐靈府 (ca. 760–841), which is included in the Taoist Canon as the *Tongxuan zhenjing* 通玄真經 (Authentic Scripture of Pervading Mystery; CT 746). The Canon also contains a *Tongxuan zhenjing* (CT 749) by Zhu Bian 朱弁 (Song) and a *Tongxuan zhenjing zuanyi* 通玄真經纘義 (Successive Interpretations of the Authentic Scripture of Pervading Mystery; CT 748) by *Du Daojian (1237–1318). Five of twelve chapters of the former work have been lost. The twelve chapters of the latter work are divided into 188 sections; the commentary largely depends on the interpretations of Xu Lingfu and Zhu Bian, and the prose is clear. The titles of the versions in the Taoist Canon derive from the appellation Real Man of Pervading Mystery (Tongxuan zhenren 通玄真人) that Wenzi received in the mid-eighth century

As we know it today, the *Wenzi* takes the form of a record of Laozi's last words. In the course of its explanation of the *Daode jing*, it states that a ruler can bring about harmony in the world not through rewards and punishments, but by practicing non-action (*wuwei*). Most of the work, though, has no direct textual connection with the *Daode jing*. It includes quotations from the *Zhuangzi and the *Huainan zi, and shares many passages with early works such as the *Yijing, the *Mengzi* 孟子, the *Lüshi chunqiu* 呂氏春秋 (Springs and Autumns of Mr. Lü), the *Xiaojing* 孝經 (Book of Filiality), and the *Yi Zhoushu* 逸周書 (Surviving Documents of the Zhou).

While these references make the *Wenzi* appear as a source of ancient thought, in the form we know it today it is a forgery, with about eighty percent of the text quoted from the *Huainan zi*, and the rest consisting of an amplification of the *Daode jing* or quotations from other texts. The present version contains expressions similar to those found in the Taoist scriptures, such as *dao yue* 道曰 ("the Dao said . . .") and *dao zhiyan yue* 道之言曰 ("the words of the Dao say . . ."), as well as names that are clearly of a Taoist character, such as Zhonghuang zi 中黃子 (Master of the Central Yellow). These elements suffice to show that the extant *Wenzi* was written between the third and eighth centuries, before the time of Xu Lingfu.

SAKADE Yoshinobu

📖 Hebei sheng Wenwu yanjiusuo Dingzhou Han zhengli xiaozu 1995; Kandel 1974; Le Blanc 2000; Mukai Tetsuo 1989

wu

無

Non-being (Non-existence, Emptiness, Void)

See *wu and you 無 · 有.

wu and you

無 · 有

Non-being (Non-existence, Emptiness, Void) and Being (Existence)

The term *wu* (non-being) usually has the same meaning as *xu* 虛 or "void" and *kong* 空 or "emptiness" (the latter term has a Buddhist flavor). The notion has different levels of meaning, however, which imply some distinctions.

Metaphysical or ontological "void." The notion of a metaphysical or ontological "void" (or "emptiness") is found in the *Daode jing* and the *Zhuangzi, and later evolved under the influence of Buddhism. It negates the naive belief in a fundamental entity that lies behind existence, and in an ultimate beginning (*Zhuangzi*) or foundation for the world, and states that the Dao, the Ultimate Truth, is invisible and inconceivable, and has neither form nor name. Everything is fluctuant, and every being is caught in a net of relations and depends on others, so that no one can exist on its own. And the whole world is one; it is a continuum whose parts are only artificially separated (*Zhuangzi*), so that fundamentally and ontologically nothing exists. *Wu* is the absolute Emptiness that logically lies above and before the distinction between negation and affirmation.

Buddhism—particularly the Madhyamaka school—introduced a didactic type of dialectic that Taoism borrowed (especially in Tang times with the *Chongxuan, or Twofold Mystery, school of thought). This dialectic aims at preventing one from thinking that emptiness is *something*: emptiness is nothing, emptiness is empty; emptiness is only a medicine, a device to cure the belief in the substance of things, and must be rejected when one is cured. Real Emptiness (*zhenwu* 真無) is neither empty (*xu*) nor real or "full" (*shi* 實). It is a negation of a negation, and therefore an absolute affirmation. As *wu* is taken as a negation (non-existence of things by themselves) and *you* as an affirmation (existence of things), one has to integrate them and then go beyond them to grasp these "two truths" jointly, blended in a single unity. When one negates the existence of particular things and then affirms them again on the basis of their negation, one attains to the "real non-existence" (*zhenwu*) and the "wondrous existence" (*miaoyou* 妙有), each of which includes its opposite. This absolute vacuity is neutral: as is said of the Dao, it is "neither this nor that, and both this and that"; it is not different and yet different from this world. It does not annihilate the relative vacuity or plenitude that is its manifestation.

Cosmic "void." *Wu*, *xu*, and *kong* are also given a cosmic sense. In its absolute meaning, *wu* is "the non-existence that has not yet begun to begin" (*Zhuangzi* 2), the absolute and inconceivable absence and immobility, the grand and lone Unity where there is no thing, the primordial Chaos (*hundun) in its etymological meaning of "aperture," the desert and infinite space-time that is indeterminate, underived, and has "no form." Yet this original Void—beyond and before the manifestation of the Dao and the emergence of the world—is not nullity, as it is the source of everything and contains "a seed." Several Taoist texts have given names to primordial Chaos that indicate its emptiness, including *taixu* 太虛 (Great Emptiness), *kongdong* 空洞 (Void Cavern), and *taiwu* 太無 (Great Non-existence). Some state that there are three Voids—namely, *xu*, *wu*, and *dong* 洞 (lit., "cavern")—that preceded the Three Pneumas (*sanqi* 三氣; see *cosmogony) which in turn gave rise to the sacred scriptures and the world.

In their relative meaning, this is a second stage of the formation of the world. Emptiness is the space between the two cosmic polarities (Yin and Yang or Heaven and Earth) that gives place to their *qi (pneuma) so that they can combine and give life to all beings. It is a vacuity in the sense of a womb where everything can take place because it is empty. The necessary intermingling of relative *wu* (absence) and *you* (presence) is one and the same as that of Yin and Yang, which is necessary to give life.

Mythologically, this is the Great Peace (**taiping*, lit., Great Flatness), the Great Pervasiveness (*datong* 大通) without boundaries or obstacles, or the Great Equality (*datong* 大同) without discriminations that represents the Golden Age of the beginning of humanity.

"Void" as mental emptying. On the existential and functional plane, akin to the cosmic relative void, there is a relative emptiness, analogous to the absolute emptiness that is indispensable for life to happen, the intersticial void that makes movement possible, the hollow in a vessel that is receptiveness (*Daode jing* 11). As such it is Yin as relative to Yang. It is not "nothing" or else there would not be a void between things; but it is a relative void. It forms a couple with *you*, the existence of the things that delineate its frame. In the same way, it is quiescence (different from immobility, which is absolute absence of movement, which cannot occur in the world; see **dong* and *jing*) taking place between two moments of movement, or at the heart of movement.

On a psychical level, this vacuity is an act of emptying. It is the absence of thought (*wunian* 無念) and feelings, will, knowing, yearning, and concerns, which is the state "without heart-mind" (*wuxin* 無心), the absence of the "affairs" (*shi* 事) of the world, the state of purity and quiescence of meditation that is the ordinary way of being and living of the Saint (**shengren*): not knowing anything (even that one does not know) and not going in search of anything (even of emptiness). The *Zhuangzi* calls this the Fasting of the Mind (**xinzhai*). This emptiness, which is germane to purity and clarity, is receptivity and freedom. If one searches for the Dao or non-existence, which is not a thing, one gives it an existence and remains far away from it. As long as one has a goal there is no emptiness. It is the difference between the emptiness that is the functioning (**yong*) of the Dao (or the "small void") and the Real Emptiness (or the Great Void) that is the last step of the alchemical work, about which there is nothing to say. It is the state of mind, in some ways ecstatic, that *Zhuangzi* 7 depicts as Huzi's 壺子 (Gourd Master) emptiness when he has "not yet emerged from his source."

Emptying consists of forgetting all that we have learned, all our striving and aims, and in letting things unfold by themselves, in ourselves as well as in the world. Do not interfere, do not do anything (**wuwei*), say the Taoists; let the Celestial Mechanism (*tianji* 天機; see **ji*) operate naturally and freely. The Taoist spontaneous way of acting and living (**ziran*) is the positive face of emptiness and non-intervention. Emptiness is seeing in darkness and hearing silence within; it is not to be blind and deaf. It is not a disappearance of the visible, but a deliverance from it.

Emptiness is brought forth through analogy in paintings and poems inspired by Taoism and Buddhism—the blank spot left in a painting, or that which is left unsaid in a poem, allows the cosmic pneuma to circulate and make all things move and invisibly join to each other.

Isabelle ROBINET

📖 Boodberg 1957; Chen E. M. 1969; Chen E. M. 1974; Graham 1959; Graham 1965; Robinet 1977, 108–32; Sunayama Minoru 1990, 325–47; Yu Shiyi 2000, 93–121

※ Dao; COSMOGONY

Wu Quanjie

吳全節

1269–1346; *zi*: Chengji 成季; *hao*: Xianxian 閒閒 (Tranquil)

As a young Taoist of Mount Longhu (*Longhu shan, Jiangxi), Wu Quanjie was invited by the *Xuanjiao patriarch *Zhang Liusun to stay with him at court in 1287, and from then on ascended from honor to honor. He was made heir-patriarch in 1307, succeeded his master in 1322, and for the last twenty-four years of his life ruled over the administration of south China's Taoist clergy.

Wu, even more than his master, was well acquainted with the southern elite scholars. Like all leaders of the Xuanjiao organization, he came from a noted family that would educate at least one son each generation at one of the many colleges on Mount Longhu. These young men entered the Taoist ranks in their early teens; some would later marry, while others, aspiring to a career in the higher ranks of the Taoist administration, would remain celibate. While on the mountain, they would meet their own relatives and make acquaintance with other talented sons of good families. Wu later expanded these wealthy connections through poetic exchanges, family alliances, and favors he could extend as an influential figure at court. The friendships cultivated through these channels explain why several contemporary literati wrote inscriptions, poems, or letters to him that now form the main documentation of his life. Two cases in point are the poet Yu Ji 虞集 (1272–1348) and the philosopher Wu Cheng 吳澄 (1249–1333), who describe Wu as a paragon of Confucian virtues. Such praise may have been dictated by the circumstances, but Wu seems to have lived up to the ideal of detachment and benevolence expected from an accomplished Taoist.

Although Wu played an important role in the religious life of his time, both in his official capacity and as the master of disciples who later rose to

prominence, he did not write any works that have reached us. This is surely
due to the burden of his work as the court chaplain: every bad omen, un-
expected event, or special occasion saw him summoned to the inner palace.
Besides regular prayers, the court also often commissioned large rituals that
demanded most of the time and energy of those who, like Wu, took upon
themselves the task of maintaining the presence, good name, and aura of
Taoism at the highest level of the state.

Vincent GOOSSAERT

📖 Little 2000b, 220–23; Qing Xitai 1994, 1: 362–63; Sun Kekuan 1968, 156–211;
Sun K'o-k'uan 1981

※ Zhang Liusun; Xuanjiao

Wu Shouyang

伍守陽

1574–1644; *zi*: Duanyang 端陽; *hao*: Chongxu zi 冲虛子
(Master of the Unfathomable Emptiness)

Wu Shouyang, who came from Nanchang (Jiangxi; some write Ji'an 吉安), is
the putative founder of the *Wu-Liu school of *neidan, named after himself
and *Liu Huayang, that was popular in southeastern China during the Qing
dynasty. An eighth-generation disciple of the *Longmen movement, Wu traces
his immediate line of transmission to Zhang Jingxu 張靜虛 (fl. 1563–82), Li
Zhenyuan 利真元 (fl. 1579–87), and Cao Changhua 曹常化 (1563–1622) whom
Wu met in 1593. According to other sources, *Wang Changyue (?–1680) was
also among Wu's teachers.

Scholars have much debated Wu Shouyang's dates, variously indicating
them as 1563–1632, 1565–1644, or 1552–1641. According to details provided
by Wu himself in his *Tianxian zhengli zhilun zengzhu* 天仙正理直論增注
(Straightforward Essays on the Correct Principles of Celestial Immortality,
with Additional Commentaries), he was born in 1574. His father, Wu Xide 伍
希德, ranked first in the *huishi* 會試 examination in 1562 and was appointed
to various high posts. He was promoted prefect of Weimo 維摩 (Yunnan) in
1578 but died there the following year. Wu's mother was born in 1552 and died
in 1640.

In 1612, Wu Shouyang received teachings from Cao Changhua on the
common heritage of Buddhism and Taoism. Between 1613 and 1618, he was
appointed tutor of Prince Ji 吉王 in Changsha (Hunan), who granted him

the title of Instructor of the Country (*guoshi* 國師). Later, he returned to his native province and devoted himself to teaching and writing: the prefaces to his works date from between 1622 and 1640. In the latter year, Wu abandoned all religious activity to be with his mother, and waited for her passing away before becoming a total recluse and entering *samādhi* himself. According to *Min Yide, he died in 1644 (*Wu Chongxu lüshi zhuan* 伍冲虛律師傳; in *Daozang jinghua lu*, vol. 10).

Wu Shouyang describes his Taoist practice as a long, painstaking, and expensive process, and criticizes adepts who soon get discouraged. Wu himself selflessly served Cao Changhua, sometimes going without food to bring meals to his master. He also raised funds for Cao by selling some of his own ancestral land. The theme of financial support appears frequently in Wu's writings and is included among the requirements for the final stages of the practice in order to overcome the four difficulties (*sinan* 四難): time, financial resources, right companions, and choice of an auspicious site.

The following works are attributed to Wu Shouyang in the *Daozang jiyao* (vol. 17):

1. *Xian Fo hezong yulu* 仙佛合宗語錄 (Recorded Sayings on the Common Lineage of Immortals and Buddhas), collected by disciples with commentary by his brother, Wu Shouxu 伍守虛 (fl. 1630–40). Includes a supplement entitled *Wu zhenren xiuxian ge* 伍真人修仙歌 (Song of the Perfected Wu on the Cultivation of Immortality).

2. *Tianxian zhengli zhilun zengzhu*, written in 1622, completed with commentaries by Wu Shouyang himself and Wu Shouxu in 1639.

3. *Jindan yaojue* 金丹要訣 (Essential Instructions on the Golden Elixir), transmitted by spirit writing (see *fuji).

4. *Dandao jiupian* 丹道九篇 (Nine Essays on Elixir Techniques), bearing a preface by Wu Shouyang dated 1640.

The above works have been also included in vol. 8 of the Xinwenfeng reprint of the *Zhengtong daozang (1977), testifying to the importance of the Wu-Liu school in contemporary Taoism.

Farzeen BALDRIAN-HUSSEIN

📖 Boltz J. M. 1987a, 199–202; Chen Zhibin 1974; Liu Ts'un-yan 1984b; Qing Xitai 1988–95, 4: 37–59; Qing Xitai 1994, 1: 390–91; Sakade Yoshinobu 1987, 2–3

※ *neidan*; Wu-Liu pai

Wu Yun

吳筠

?–778; *zi*: Zhenjie 貞節; *hao*: Zongxuan xiansheng 宗玄先生文集
(Elder Who Takes Mystery as His Ancestor)

Wu Yun, posthumously called Zongxuan xiansheng by his disciples, is chiefly
known to history as the person responsible for bringing the poetic genius Li
Bai 李白 (Li Bo, 701–62) to the Tang court, where both served in the Hanlin
Academy, though experts on the biography of the poet have disproved this.
Wu was no mean poet himself, especially when describing ecstatic journeys
of the soul in the *Chuci* 楚辭 (Songs of Chu; trans. Hawkes 1985) tradition,
and in his final years was involved in the literary coterie of the poet-monk
Jiaoran 皎然 (730–99) in the lower Yangzi region. But he is equally significant
as the Taoist priest he became after quitting the court, even if he does not
fit the contemporary stereotype of vast erudition in occult lore favored for
Taoist hierarchs. Rather, his Taoist learning, derived from a fellow-disciple of
*Sima Chengzhen in the *Shangqing tradition, may have gone no further than
the mix of simple *Tianshi dao and Shangqing lore found in *Yunji qiqian 45,
which appears to mention him twice—though since it also mentions a work
of *Du Guangting, this particular compilation is clearly much later.

Certainly his surviving prose works, consisting of his "Collected Works,"
Zongxuan xiansheng wenji 宗玄先生文集 (Collected Works of the Elder Who
Takes Mystery as His Ancestor; CT 1051) in three chapters, and the *Zongxuan
xiansheng xuangang lun* 宗玄先生玄綱論 (Essay on the Outlines of Mystery,
by the Elder Who Takes Mystery as His Ancestor) in one chapter (CT 1052; an
attached biography, *Wu zunshi zhuan* 吳尊師傳, attributed to Quan Deyu 權
德輿 [759–818] is assigned CT 1053), are very restrained in their references to
Taoist texts, though well-known scriptures like the *Xisheng jing (Scripture of
Western Ascension) are occasionally cited, and lost passages from the *Baopu
zi and other works may also be found. Many of Wu's other writings, which
according to a preface to the "Collected Works" by Quan once amounted to
over four hundred items, have for their part also been lost, apparently including several highly critical of Buddhism.

This makes all the more intriguing his intellectual impact on young Buddhist
sympathizers like Quan and Liang Su 梁肅 (753–93; see under *Li Ao). But if we
examine the *Xuangang lun*, presented to the emperor in 754 during his stay at
court, and also the *Shenxian kexue lun (An Essay on How One May Become a

Divine Immortal Through Training), we find that although they do constitute an invitation to Taoist practice within the traditions of the religion, they also as a preliminary recommend mental self-cultivation, described in terms of "inner nature" and the "emotions" (*xing* 性 and *qing* 情) and other concepts which might be found in early Chinese texts. This appeal to a common language of self-cultivation was taken up by the Buddhists and later by Confucians, ultimately opening up the way for the construction of Neo-Confucianism as a path of personal development rather than a mere curriculum of basic education. Wu's impact may also be measured from the *Nantong dajun neidan jiuzhang jing* 南統大君內丹九章經 (Scripture in Nine Sections on the Inner Elixir by the Great Lord Encompassing the South; CT 1054), which claims to have been written by him for Li Bai's benefit in 818 after he (and presumably the poet) had achieved immortality, and which at the earliest must be taken as a product of continued late Tang admiration for him.

T. H. BARRETT

📖 Kamitsuka Yoshiko 1979; Kohn 1998c; de Meyer 1999; de Meyer 2000; Qing Xitai 1988–95, 2: 238–53; Schafer 1981–83; Schafer 1983

✻ *Shenxian kexue lun*

Wu-Liu pai

伍柳派

Branch of Wu Shouyang and Liu Huayang

The Ming and Qing periods witnessed an increasing number of new religious movements, especially in Jiangxi and the surrounding regions of southeastern China. One of these was the Wu-Liu branch of *neidan, named after *Wu Shouyang (1574–1644) and his putative disciple, *Liu Huayang (1735–99). The name "Wu-Liu" was first used in 1897 in the *Wu-Liu xianzong* 伍柳仙宗 (The Wu-Liu Lineage of Immortality), a compilation edited by Deng Huiji 鄧徽績 (fl. 1897) that includes two works by Wu Shouyang and two by Liu Huayang.

The Wu-Liu school is traditionally affiliated with the *Longmen movement, which some sources trace to the *Quanzhen patriarch *Qiu Chuji. Wu himself claimed to be a Longmen disciple of the eighth generation. Both Wu and Liu advocate Buddhist meditation to rediscover one's inner nature, and Taoist methods to replenish one's vital force (see *xing and ming). Accordingly, their texts bear such titles as *Huiming jing* (Scripture of Wisdom and Life) or *Xian Fo hezong* 仙佛合宗 (The Common Lineage of Immortals and Buddhas).

The aim of the Wu-Liu techniques is the joint cultivation (*shuangxiu*) of innate nature and vital force, corresponding to spirit (*shen*) and breath (*qi*) in human beings. As in Quanzhen, however, the alchemical œuvre begins with the cultivation of innate nature. This emphasis on spirit requires "reverting to Emptiness to purify the self" (*huanxu lianji* 還虛鍊己), i.e., emptying the mind of all thoughts, desires and emotions. The practice eventually allows one to see one's "original face" (*benlai mianmu* 本來面目) or original nature.

The school arranges the *neidan* practice into three stages (called *sancheng* 三成 or Three Accomplishments). In the first stage, mental concentration activates precosmic pneuma (*xiantian qi* 先天氣) within the lower Cinnabar Field (*dantian*), providing the basis for all alchemical action. The adept then continues on to "lay the foundations" (*zhuji* 築基) using physiological methods to strengthen the vital force and prevent its dissipation. This entails opening the inner channels and circulating the *qi* by the method known as the Lesser Celestial Circuit (*xiao zhoutian* 小周天; see *zhoutian*).

In the second stage, the union of spirit and breath engenders the seed of the inner elixir, which is fixed and nurtured within the middle Cinnabar Field. When the immortal embryo is complete, it is moved to the upper Cinnabar Field, crossing the Three Passes (*sanguan*) of the spinal column.

The third and last stage includes the method of the Greater Celestial Circuit (*da zhoutian* 大周天; see *zhoutian*) or intense concentration (*dading* 大定; see *ding*), the egress of the spirit (*chushen*), and the "suckling" (*rubu* 乳哺) of the infant. This leads one to the rank of "divine immortal" (*shenxian* 神仙). Three more transformations are needed to reach the rank of "celestial immortal" (*tianxian* 天仙). The final process transfiguration is described as "facing the wall for nine years" (*jiunian mianbi* 九年面壁) or "refining spirit and reverting to Emptiness" (*lianshen huanxu* 鍊神還虛). Like other authors, Liu Huayang illustrates this stage with an empty circle.

Despite the complexity of the methods, the basic tenets of the Wu-Liu school are easily comprehensible. The gradual approach to enlightenment held great appeal for adepts of advanced age, which has made this school one of the most popular of our times.

Farzeen BALDRIAN-HUSSEIN

📖 See the bibliographies for the entries *Wu Shouyang and *Liu Huayang

※ *neidan*; for other related entries see the Synoptic Table of Contents, sec. IV.3 ("Alchemy: Wu-liu pai")

Wuchu jing

五廚經

Scripture of the Five Cuisines

The twenty five-character verses that form the core of the *Laozi shuo wuchu jing zhu* 老子說五廚經注 (Commentary to the Scripture of the Five Cuisines Spoken by Laozi) concern a meditation technique for circulating the energies through the five viscera (*wuzang*) of the body. The goal is said to be reached through harmonizing and concentrating one's own Original Pneuma (*yuanqi*) with the Great Harmony (*taihe* 泰和). In this way, one obtains Unity, or the Dao. This method is also recommended by *Sima Chengzhen in his *Fuqi jingyi lun*.

In its independent edition in the Taoist Canon (CT 763), the *Wuchu jing zhu* contains a preface dated 735 and a commentary, both signed by Yin Yin 尹愔 (?–741), who was the head of the Suming guan 蕭明觀 (Abbey of Reviving Light) in Chang'an and a high official under Tang Xuanzong (r. 712–56). Another edition, entitled *Wuchu jing qifa* 五廚經氣法 (Method of Energy of the Scripture of the Five Cuisines; YJQQ 61.5b–10b), also includes Yin Yin's commentary, with slight variations. Although the presence of Yin Yin's preface might suggest a Tang date for the *Wuchu jing*, the origins of this text may be much earlier. *Ge Hong, in his *Baopu zi*, mentions a *Xingchu jing* 行廚經 (Scripture of the Movable Cuisines) and a *Riyue chushi jing* 日月廚食經 (Scripture of the Cuisine Meals of the Sun and the Moon), which could be the ancestors of the received text. *Du Guangting, in his *Daojiao lingyan ji*, also mentions the *Wuchu jing* with Yin Yin's commentary. Du claims a Taoist origin for the scripture and denounces a Buddhist forgery, saying that the text was fraudulently transformed into a *Fo shuo santing chujing* 佛說三停廚經 (Sūtra of the Three Cuisines Spoken by the Buddha). This counterfeit Buddhist *sūtra* can be no other than the identically-titled apocryphal text found among the Chinese *Dunhuang and Japanese Kōyasan 高野山 (Mount Kōya) manuscripts, and also in the Buddhist Canon (T. 2894).

Christine MOLLIER

📖 Makita Tairyō 1976, 345–68; Mollier 2000; Verellen 1992, 248–49

※ *chu*

Wudang shan

武當山

Mount Wudang (Hubei)

Mount Wudang is one of the holiest sites in Taoist geography, as it is present symbolically, along with Mount Longhu (*Longhu shan), on the altar prepared for all Offering (*jiao) rituals. Yet its preeminence is a rather late phenomenon in Chinese religious history. There are mentions of this beautiful mountain site (1600 m high, located in the northern part of Hubei province) in ancient geographical sources, and there were Taoist ascetics associated with it. But Mount Wudang only came to national fame during the late thirteenth century, when it was recognized as the place where the martial exorcist god *Zhenwu (Perfected Warrior, or Authentic Warrior) had practiced ascetic exercises leading to immortality. By that time, Zhenwu's cult had already been spreading throughout China for about two centuries, in close relation to the new Taoist exorcistic rituals that flourished during the Song. The mountain then came to be understood as the physical trace of Zhenwu's practice, and the pilgrimage trails lead to such spots—for instance, the well where an old lady ground a needle out of a rock (to teach Zhenwu endurance) or the cliff where Zhenwu meditated. This lore was transmitted in numerous books, beginning with Liu Daoming's 劉道明 *Wudang fudi zongzhen ji* 武當福地總真集 (Anthology of the Totality of Real Men from the Blissful Land of Wudang; CT 962; preface dated 1291 but present text later than 1293; see Qing Xitai 1994, 2: 209) and continued in hagiographic works, both written and painted, and a succession of gazetteers. At about the same time, the mountain was gradually becoming covered with monasteries and hermitages.

The early Ming was a period of exuberant imperial patronage of Zhenwu and Mount Wudang, beginning with the Hongwu Emperor (r. 1368–98) and reaching its apex with the Yongle Emperor (r. 1403–24). The latter took Zhenwu as the official protector of the dynasty and constructed a very arcane and elaborate lore around a saint from Mount Wudang, *Zhang Sanfeng. During the Yongle reign period, Mount Wudang was refashioned (1411–24) with splendid monasteries and temples, culminating with the Golden Pavilion (Jindian 金殿) on its peak. The mountain became an independent realm, with huge resources managed by eunuchs and military aristocrats who answered directly to the court and remained aloof from the civil bureaucracy. The Qing imperial patronage was incomparably more modest. The mountain suffered rather limited damage during the twentieth century compared with other sites, and thus has preserved valuable samples of Ming and Qing architecture, sculpture, and other works of art.

Mount Wudang was a very active pilgrimage center, and pilgrimage associations that came each year to pray to Zhenwu from faraway places, including the northern plain and the Suzhou area, are well attested by inscriptions and other sources throughout the Ming and Qing periods. The mountain has also been home to the largest Taoist clerical community in China in the modern period, with several hundred Taoists in residence in its five monasteries and dozens of smaller hermitages, most of them sojourning for several months or years for training. Mount Wudang has been, indeed, an important destination for all wandering Taoists. It housed both *Quanzhen and *Qingwei clerics, as was the case ever since the Yuan period, and in fact was one of the major points of close interaction between the two orders.

Last but not least, Mount Wudang emerged, apparently during the mid-Qing, at the center of a distinct school of martial arts associated with Zhang Sanfeng, known as *Taiji quan. Training in Taiji quan, with either Taoists or lay masters, is now one of the major attractions of the mountain.

Vincent GOOSSAERT

📖 Boltz J. M. 1987a, 119–21; de Bruyn 2004; Hachiya Kunio 1990, 1: 283–89 and 2: 269–82; Lagerwey 1992; Little 2000b, 301–5; Wang Guangde and Yang Lizhi 1993

※ Zhenwu; TAOIST SACRED SITES

Wudou jing

五斗經

Scriptures of the Five Dippers

The *Wudou jing* is a set of texts containing talismans of and invocations to the Dippers of the five directions. They are divided according to geographical direction into materials concerning the Northern, Southern, Eastern, Western, and Central Dippers, with two texts devoted to the Northern Dipper:

1. *Beidou benming yansheng zhenjing* 北斗本命延生真經 (Authentic Scripture of the Natal Destiny of the Northern Dipper for Extending Life; CT 622)

2. *Beidou benming changsheng miaojing* 北斗本命長生妙經 (Wondrous Scripture of the Natal Destiny of the Northern Dipper for Prolonging Life; CT 623)

3. *Nandou liusi yanshou duren miaojing* 南斗六司延壽度人妙經 (Wondrous Scripture of the Six Officers of the Southern Dipper for Extending Longevity and Salvation; CT 624)

4. *Dongdou zhusuan huming miaojing* 東斗主筭護命妙經 (Wondrous Scripture of the Governor of Life Spans of the Eastern Dipper for Protecting Life; CT 625)

5. *Xidou jiming hushen miaojing* 西斗記名護身妙經 (Wondrous Scripture of the Recording of Names of the Western Dipper for Protecting One's Person; CT 626)

6. *Zhongdou dakui baoming miaojing* 中斗大魁保命妙經 (Wondrous Scripture of the Great *Kui* [Stars] of the Central Dipper for Guarding Life; CT 627)

These texts purport to record a second major revelation by Laozi to *Zhang Daoling in 155 CE, granted after he received the Covenant with the Powers of Orthodox Unity (*zhengyi mengwei* 正一盟威) in 142. The preface to the *Scripture of the Southern Dipper*, in particular, details these circumstances and summarizes the standard biography of the first Celestial Master. Their actual date is post-Tang, probably Five Dynasties, and there is reason to locate them in Sichuan.

The *Wudou jing* presents sacred spells (*zhou* 咒) associated with the celestial constellation of *Ursa Major* and contains talismans (*FU) for summoning the gods of this constellation. Each of its texts outlines devotional measures for protection involving scriptural recitation (*songjing*) and formal rites for the Dippers, preferably undertaken on the devotees birthday, at a new moon, or on generally auspicious days. One says, for example:

> To recite this scripture, you must first develop utmost sincerity and purify your mind. Then, facing east, clench your teeth and pay reverence in your heart. Kneeling, close your eyes and visualize the gods [of the Eastern Dipper] as though you physically see the limitless realm of the east. Mysterious numinous forces, imperial lords, realized perfected, and great sages—a countless host lines up before you. Looking at them will help you overcome days of disaster. (CT 625, 2b)

In addition, the texts provide talismans to summon the six officers of the Dipper who protect life and help in difficulties, assuring the faithful that the perfected will respond immediately and grant a life "as long as the Dao itself" (CT 624, 5a). The talismans are used in the presentation of petitions and contain the power to make the gods respond. Today the *Scripture of the Northern Dipper* is among the central texts chanted during so-called Dipper Festivals (*lidou fahui* 禮斗法會) at popular shrines in Taipei, which last three to five days and serve to ensure good fortune.

In a separate development, the Taoist texts also inspired the creation of a Buddhist scripture of the Northern Dipper, the *Beidou qixing yanming jing* 北斗七星延命經 (Scripture of the Seven Stars of the Northern Dipper for Extending Destiny; T. 1307), which survives in Chinese, Uighur, Mongolian, and Tibetan versions. Several other *sūtras* on "rites and recitations for the Northern Dipper" that are associated with the eighth-century Tantric masters Vajrabodhi (Jingangzhi 金剛智, 671–741) and Amoghavajra (Bukong 不空, 705–74) do in fact date back to the Yuan dynasty.

Livia KOHN

📖 Franke H. 1990; Kohn 1998b, 97–100; Matsumoto Kōichi 1997

※ *beidou*

Wudoumi dao

五斗米道

Way of the Five Pecks of Rice

Way of the Five Pecks of Rice is an alternative appellation for the Way of the Celestial Masters (*Tianshi dao). Chang Qu's 常璩 *Huayang guozhi* 華陽國志 (Monograph of the Land South of Mount Hua) explains that, "Their contributions to the Way were limited to five pecks, therefore people of the day referred to them as the Way of Rice (*midao* 米道)." Thus, at least in the early days of the church, it was the obligation of each household of adherents to contribute five pecks of rice (approximately 9 liters) each year toward the maintenance of the organization and its clergy. Ōfuchi Ninji (1991, 389–96) has shown that if this was indeed the case and if this contribution was made in place of the normal annual taxes due the central government, then the practice constituted a significant decrease in the overall burden upon the average peasant.

It is nowhere specified exactly how this grain was used, but it seems likely that, in addition to providing food for certain full-time religious professionals (it is unclear whether the average *jijiu* or libationer was such a full-time professional), it provided food for the "charity lodges" (*yishe* 義舍), where it was made freely available to the needy, and for the "cuisines" (*chu, a type of communal meal) that each parish (*zhi) offered periodically, during the Three Assemblies (*sanhui). According to the *Xuandu lüwen* (Statutes of the Mysterious Metropolis, 11b), the preferred date for these contributions was the Middle Assembly on the seventh day of the seventh lunar month, and payments in the eighth and ninth lunar months won decreasing amounts of merit; grain contributed at the Lower Meeting in the tenth lunar month merely averted punishment. The *Taizhen ke* 太真科 (Code of the Great Perfected; quoted in *Yaoxiu keyi jielü chao* 要修科儀戒律鈔; CT 463, 10.2a), on the other hand, says, "We revere the five pecks of the rice of faith in order to establish Creation and the pneumas of the Five Virtues (*wuxing* 五行). The register of fates for the household members is tied to the rice. Every year at the appointed time, on the first day of the tenth lunar month, everyone assembles at the parish of the Celestial Master and pays it into the Celestial Treasury (*tianku* 天庫) and to the Lodges (*ting* 亭) within fifty *li*, lest the poor and destitute, in a time of famine, might while traveling lack food." Travelers did not pack food with them.

Although the term Wudoumi dao has become common in modern secondary scholarship on early Taoism, there is no evidence that it was ever used among believers; it seems rather to have been a derogatory term used by outsiders to make light of the more prosaic aspects of cult doctrine. A contemporary inscription refers to the group as "rice bandits" (*mizei* 米賊). It should probably be avoided by modern scholars in favor of terms like Celestial Master or *Zhengyi Taoists, which were used contemporaneously to refer to the movement.

Terry KLEEMAN

📖 Ōfuchi Ninji 1991, 309–406; Qing Xitai 1994, 1: 84–91; Robinet 1997b, 55; see also bibliographies for the entries *Tianshi dao and *Zhengyi

※ Tianshi dao; Zhengyi

wugong

午供

Noon Offering

The Noon Offering is a presentation of offerings to the deities that is performed around noon. In present-day Taiwan, it occurs as part of the *zhai (Retreat) and *jiao (Offering) rituals, but is not considered a formal part of the proceedings. The offering includes incense, flowers, candles, fruit, tea, wine, food (cooked rice and rice cakes stuffed with bean jam), water, and valuables such as gold, silver, and jewels. The priest holds each of these in his hands in turns and presents them while performing movements similar to a dance. During the ritual of Merit (*gongde) for the redemption of the deceased, after making the offerings at the altar, the priest moves to the Spirit Hall (*lingtang* 靈堂) where the deceased is enshrined and presents the offerings in the same way there.

Besides these practices, there is also a custom of offering "five animals" (*wusheng* 五牲, i.e., five kinds of meat, fish, and shellfish) and twelve bowls of cooked food at the outer altar, called the Table of the Three Realms (*sanjie zhuo* 三界卓).

ASANO Haruji

📖 Lagerwey 1987c, 54–55; Ōuchi Ninji 1983, 263–66 and 494–96

※ *gongde*; *jiao*

wuji

無極

Ultimateless

See *wuji* and *taiji* 無極 · 太極.

wuji and taiji

無極 · 太極

Ultimateless and Great Ultimate

The term *taiji*, or Great Ultimate (lit., "great ridgepole"), appears to have a Taoist origin. In the *Mawangdui manuscripts, the same notion appears as *daheng* 大恆 (Great Constancy). Taoist sources associate the Great Ultimate with the *Taiyi (Great One), the star divinity residing in the center of Heaven, and with *huangji* 皇極 (August Ultimate), another term that designates the center. The Great Ultimate is therefore the cosmic heart (*xin) as both the pole star (*jixing* 極星) and the human heart. In the *Xici* 繫辭 (Appended Statements, a portion of the *Yijing*), the Great Ultimate is the prime principle of the world, and in the *Xuanxue (Arcane Learning) milieu it is deemed to be cognate with Emptiness and the Taiyi.

Neo-Confucian thinkers used the term in the same sense as the *Xici*. Zhou Dunyi 周敦頤 (1017–73; SB 277–81), in particular, associated it with the Taoist term *wuji* (Ultimateless, Boundless, Infinite; lit., "without a ridgepole") in the famous phrase *wuji er taiji* 無極而太極. This phrase can mean either that *wuji* and *taji* are one and the same thing, or that *wuji* comes first followed by *taiji*. While Neo-Confucians tended to endorse the first meaning, most Taoists adopted the second: for them, the *taiji* is the beginning of the world, but the *wuji* is the unknowable Dao itself. This view derives from the Han "weft texts" (*weishu* 緯書; see *TAOISM AND THE APOCRYPHA), where *taiji* is the last of the five precosmic geneses called Five Greats (*wutai* 五太), representing the instant when pneuma (*qi*), form (*xing*), and matter (*zhi* 質) are still merged together but are ready to part from each other (see *COSMOGONY).

The *taiji* is the One that contains Yin and Yang, or the Three (as stated in *Hanshu* 21A). This Three is, in Taoist terms, the One (Yang) plus the Two (Yin), or the Three that gives life to all beings (*Daode jing* 42), the One that virtually contains the multiplicity. The *taiji* is said to be the function of the Dao, whose substance is Chaos (see *ti and yong*); the *wuji* is the Dao as the metaphysical One, a neutral "no-number" that is before movement and quiescence (*dong and jing*), unity and multiplicity. Thus, the *wuji* is a limitless void, whereas the *taiji* is a limit in the sense that it is the beginning and the end of the world, a turning point. The *wuji* is the mechanism of both movement and quiescence; it is situated before the differentiation between movement and quiescence, metaphorically located in the space-time between *kun* 坤 ䷁, or pure Yin, and *fu* 復 ䷗, the return of the Yang. In other terms, while the Taoists state that *taiji* is metaphysically preceded by *wuji*, which is the Dao, the Neo-Confucians say that the *taiji* is the Dao.

These two notions are variously represented in Taoism, as shown by the variants of the diagram usually known as *Taiji tu* (Diagram of the Great Ultimate; see fig. 70). In this diagram, the *wuji* is illustrated as a blank circle, and the *taiji* as a circle with a point in its center that stands for the embryo of the world, or as a circle that contains Yin and Yang (as two lines, one unbroken and one broken), or as two circles rolled up together, one black and the other white (or each of them half white and half black). In the diagram as it appears in Confucian works, which also has a Taoist origin, *wuji* is the blank circle above the black and white circles of the *taiji*.

The *taiji* is the limit and the juncture between the two worlds, the noumenal world that "antedates Heaven" and the phenomenal world that is "after Heaven and Earth" (see *xiantian and houtian*). It is the circle that represents the unity of beginning and end, and "turns without ending." It signifies the fecundity of the Dao, positive and dynamic. The *wuji* or the Infinite is its negative aspect, the invisible that can only be known by its effects but remains hidden even in its manifestations. In this sense *taiji* is synonymous with illumination, divine knowledge, the "real nature" of things, and the elixir. It is the light that lies within each human being, simultaneously the point of departure and the goal of the alchemical work. It is the Mysterious Pass (*xuanguan), the "sparkle of light," the pneuma anterior to Heaven and Earth that a child receives even before conception and that develops and gives life. The Taoists say that the *taiji* is the Center, the mediating central Agent (i.e., Soil; see *wuxing), or the pole star at the center of the sky. In meditation, it is the extreme of quiescence that turns into movement, life and thought, a hinge, an opening that gives way to the unity lying between the "transcendent Non-being" and the "transcendent Being," and their interpenetration (see *wu and *you*). The *taiji* is the positive way of cognition and the *wuji* the apophatic one, two aspects that are complementary in the divine knowledge, or knowing ignorance, both knowing and ignoring, neither knowing nor ignoring. In the body, the *taiji* is represented by the kidneys because the right one symbolizes the Great Yin (*taiyin* 太陰) and the left one the Minor Yang (or Young Yang, *shaoyang* 少陽), hence the passage from Yin to Yang (*Daoshu; 7.12a).

Isabelle ROBINET

& Chen Guying 1993; Li Yuanguo 1985c; Li Yuanguo 1990; Qing Xitai 1994, 2: 334–41; Rao Zongyi 1993a; Robinet 1990b; Wang Baoxuan 1993

※ *dong* and *jing*; *wu* and *you*; *xiantian* and *houtian*; *Taiji tu*; COSMOGONY

Wuneng zi

無能子

Book of the Master of No Abilities

The *Wuneng zi* is a short work of Taoist philosophy in three chapters from the latter part of the Tang dynasty. Wuneng zi's identity is not known. An anonymous preface to the work, ostensibly written by an acquaintance of Wuneng zi himself, claims that the text was written in March and April, 887 in the inn of a Mr. Jing 景 in Zuofu 左輔 in the vicinity of Chang'an. The preface says that Wuneng zi had been an official but had taken up a roving existence in the aftermath of the Huang Chao 黃巢 rebellion (874–84). The only reference within the text that may bear on its provenance occurs in the third chapter where a conversation with one Huayang zi 華陽子 is recorded. Huayang zi was the pseudonym of *Shi Jianwu (fl. 820–35), a Taoist author, poet, and *neidan practitioner.

The *Wuneng zi* advocates following the path of *wuwei (non-action), being spontaneous and without intention, doing what is fitting without consciously deciding. In doing so, self-preservation is most likely to be achieved. The problems of human life, the text argues, are due to the existence of social organization and the promulgation of the learning of the sages, a major target of Wuneng zi's attacks.

Part of the *Wuneng zi* is written in dialogue form where some well-known figures who lived from the Shang to the Jin—Taigong wang 太公王, Laozi, Confucius, Sun Deng 孫登, among others—endorse Wuneng zi's views.

The *Wuneng zi* appears in the *Daozang* (CT 1028) but the most convenient edition to use is that of Wang Ming (1981). There is a fine unpublished English translation by Nathan Woolley (1997).

Benjamin PENNY

📖 Naundorf 1972; Wang Ming 1981 (crit. ed.); Woolley 1997 (trans.); Zhu Yueli 1983a

Wupian zhenwen

五篇真文

Perfected (*or:* Authentic) Script in Five Tablets

The full title of this text in the Canon (CT 22) is *Yuanshi wulao chishu yu* [recte: *wu*] *pian zhenwen tianshu jing* 元始五老赤書玉 [五] 篇真文天書經 (The Perfected Script in Five Tablets Written in Red Celestial Writing on the [Celestial Worthy of] Original Commencement and the Five Ancient Lords). As the first text of the early fifth-century *Lingbao corpus, it narrates the origins of the scriptures in the ethers at creation and reveals the organizing rubrics of Lingbao cosmology and ritual.

The central revelation of the scripture is the Perfected Script, a series of 672 graphs resembling seal-script and divided into five groups, each under the control of one of the Five Ancient Lords of the four directions and center. The translation of this celestial writing is given, with some discrepancies, in the second scripture of the Lingbao canon, the *Lingbao yujue* 靈寶玉訣 (Jade Instructions of Lingbao; now found in *Chishu yujue miaojing* 赤書玉 訣妙經, CT 352). The *Wupian zhenwen* relates how this celestial writing appeared in the void at the beginning of time and was refined into permanent form by the Celestial Worthy (Tianzun 天尊) in the Halls of Flowing Fire (*liuhuo zhi ting* 流火之庭) for the salvation of all. The Perfected Script is thus the original form of the scriptures and is displayed on five altars in all Lingbao ritual. For the individual, the graphs serve as protective talismans, guarding the body against demons, flood, and stellar disorders and ensuring

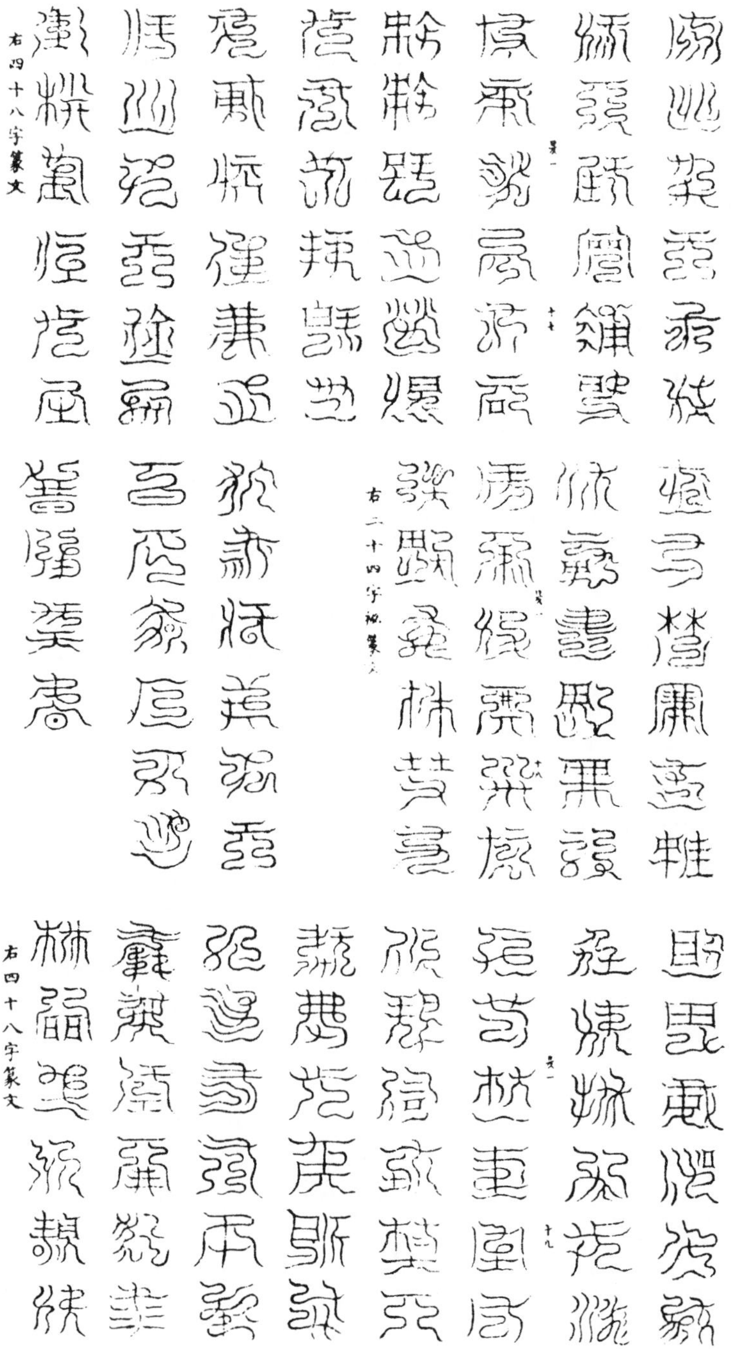

Fig. 76. A section of the *Wupian zhenwen*. *Yuanshi wulao chishu yu* [recte: *wu*] *pian zhenwen tian-shu jing* 元始五老赤書玉 [五] 篇真文天書經 (Perfected Script in Five Tablets Written in Red Celestial Writing on the [Celestial Worthy of] Original Commencement and the Five Ancient Lords; CT 22). See Benn 1991, 110.

the proper handling of one's name in the celestial registers of life (*shengji* 生籍).

After describing the origins of the Perfected Script, the scripture relates how the Most High Lord of the Dao (Taishang daojun 太上道君) prevailed upon the Celestial Worthy to release the text for the salvation of mortals. The Five Ancient Lords (Wulao 五老), known from imperial ritual and from Han "weft texts" (*weishu* 緯書; see *TAOISM AND THE APOCRYPHA), control each of the five sections and ensure the safe passage of the texts' recipients through the calamities of the end-times, which are graphically described. Talismans (*FU) associated with them are also given. Based on the information revealed here, the closely-related *Lingbao yujue* gives the script for a ritual to summon and feast the Five Ancient Lords. This is a version of the earliest extant description of the *jiao (Offering) ritual, drawn from the *Lingbao wufu xu* (Prolegomena to the Five Talismans of the Numinous Treasure).

Finally, the scripture gives several lists of dates important for ritual use. The "ten days of apposition" (*shi zhiri* 十直日, the first, eighth, fourteenth, fifteenth, eighteenth, twenty-third, twenty-fourth, twenty-eighth, twenty-ninth, and thirtieth days of each lunar month) are the days when the celestials of the Ten Heavens gather to check the records of those under their control. The eight nodal days of the year (*bajie* 八節, equinoxes, solstices, and the first day of each season) are likewise days when celestial records are checked and the good or bad deeds of all recorded. Each of these times are occasions for special rituals, detailed in the Lingbao scriptures.

Stephen R. BOKENKAMP

📖 Bell 1988; Benn 1991, 49–54; Bokenkamp 1983; Kobayashi Masayoshi 1990, 105–37; Ōfuchi Ninji 1978–79, 1: 17 (crit. notes on the Dunhuang mss.) and 2: 1 (reprod. of the Dunhuang mss.); Ōfuchi Ninji 1997, 89–128 passim; Qing Xitai 1988–95, 1: 382–88; Schipper 1991b

※ *jiao*; Lingbao

Wushang biyao

無上祕要

Supreme Secret Essentials

The *Wushang biyao*, compiled under imperial auspices between 577 and 588, is the oldest surviving compendium of Taoist literature. Ironically, Wudi (r. 560–78) of the Northern Zhou dynasty commissioned it. Earlier, in 574, he had proscribed both Taoism and Buddhism, abolishing their abbeys and monasteries. However, he apparently wanted to found a new church that would embrace all believers of whatever persuasion. Such a church would provide ideological support for his ambitious drive to reunite China after more than 250 years of division. One month after the proscription, he established the *Tongdao guan (Abbey of the Pervasive Way), a Taoist abbey, in his capital. The emperor had decided that Taoism was the proper religion to promote his political goals. It was undoubtedly that "think tank" that was responsible for the compilation of the *Wushang biyao*. Although its staff included Buddhist monks and secular scholars of Taoist thought, its aim was to produce a text derived entirely from the scriptures of Taoist religion.

The editors of the *Wushang biyao* established 292 rubrics to organize their materials. The complete internal structure of the work would have remained unclear had not a manuscript (P. 2861) containing its table of contents dating from the early eighth century been discovered at *Dunhuang. The manuscript shows that the 292 rubrics were divided into forty-nine sections (see table 24). Of the one-hundred chapters in the original edition of the text, thirty-three are now missing from the version in the *Daozang* (CT 1138), namely chapters 1, 2, 8, 10–14, 36, 58–64, 67–73, 75, 77, 79–82, 85, 86, 89, and 90. The bulk of the lost material vanished shortly after the text was completed since the bibliographic treatise of the *Jiu Tangshu* (Old History of the Tang) lists it as having only seventy-two chapters (van der Loon 1984, 143). The titles in the history's treatise were copied from a catalogue of the imperial library compiled early in the Kaiyuan reign period (713–41). The disappearance of those chapters means that a substantial number of rubrics in the Dunhuang table of contents have no citations whatsoever.

The *Wushang biyao* is not an encyclopedia in the modern sense of the word. The editors simply extracted passages from Taoist scriptures and pasted them together. There is no analysis, explication or even commentary that defines precisely the meaning of the terms, or rubrics, concerned. In most cases, however, the citations themselves provide the information. There are citations from nearly 120 texts, seventy-seven of which are still extant in the *Daozang*. Its contents were disproportionately derived from *Shangqing and *Lingbao works. The most blatant omissions are from the scriptures of the Celestial Master order (*Tianshi dao) for which there are only two quotations, but there are also few extracts from the *Dongshen* 洞神 canon. In 523 or shortly thereafter Ruan Xiaoxu 阮孝緒 (479–536) compiled the *Qilu* 七錄 (Seven Records), a bibliography now lost in which he listed the titles of 290 Taoist scriptures and precepts (see *Guang hongming ji* 廣弘明集; T. 2103, *j.* 3). One can only wonder what the other 170 texts overlooked by the compilers of the *Wushang biyao* were. To compound the problem the editors ignored,

Table 24

SEC.	RUBRIC	CHAPTER	CONTENT
1	1		Cosmogony: the creation of the universe by the Dao
2	2		Cosmogony: transformation of *qi
3	3–26	3–5	Cosmology: celestial realms of the gods; Sun, Moon, and stars; the Three Realms (sanjie 三界) of desire, form and formlessness; divine mountains, forests and fruits; mountain grottoes, grotto-heavens (*dongtian), and divine waters; humans
4	27	6.1a–5a	Cosmic cycles
5	28–29	6.5a–10a	Mythological monarchs; imaginary islands and lands
6	30–32	6.10a–12b	Thought and statecraft
7	33	7.1a–2b	Loss of perfection by pursuing worldly matters
8	34	7.2b–4b	Good and evil conduct
9	35	7.4b–6a	Difficulties
10	36	7.6a–8a	Problems
11	37	7.8a–12a	Disasters caused by the interaction of Yin and Yang
12	38–40		Bureaucracy of the unseen world
13	41	9.1a–2a	Promotions and demotions in the unseen world
14	42	9.2a–11a	Assemblies and deliberations in the unseen world
15	43		Life and death
16	44		Hell
17	45–46		Divine responses; "harmonizing with the lights" (heguang 和光)
18	47–66	15–16	Gods
19	67–110	17–23	Gods' regalia, corteges, music, palaces, and parishes
20	111–14	24	Three Treasures (sanbao 三寶), True Writs (zhenwen 真文), celestial omens, and terrestrial portents
21	115–20	25–29	Uses and powers of writs, talismans, petitions, and hymns
22	121–22	30	Scriptures: their origins and names
23	123–24	31.1a–7a	Scriptures: their powers and duration
24	125	31.7a–15a	Fate of those who obtain the scriptures
25	126–27	32	Transmission of scriptures, in heaven and on earth
26	128	33	Penalties for improper transmission
27	129–37	34–40	Transmission of scriptures: ordination rites
28	138–40	41	Liturgical instruments: staffs, boards, and tablets
29	141–42	42	Service to teachers and study
30	143–46	43.1a–4b	Liturgical vestments of the clergy
31	147–48	43.4b–15a	Lectures on and recitation of scripture
32	149–80	44–57	Precepts; *zhai (retreats)
33	181–82		Defenses for the scriptures
34	183–85		Immortals
35	186		Retribution (bao 報)
36	187–89		Averting catastrophes, confessing sins, and fortune/misfortune
37	190–93	65.1a–3b	Becoming a Taoist, eliminating impediments, taboos, and perseverance/accomplishments
38	194–97	65.3b–12b	The tender and frail (rouruo 柔弱), emptiness and quiescence (xujing 虛靖), retiring to the mountains, and rejecting the mores of the masses
39	198–207	66	Devotional practices: bathing, lighting lamps, burning incense, praying, visualization, etc.

Table 24 (*cont.*)

SEC.	RUBRIC	CHAPTER	CONTENT
40	208–11		Methods for controlling spirits of the body
41	212–13		Healing and eliminating the three corpses (*sanshi*; see **sanshi* and *jiuchong*)
42	214–16		Preservation of the body, treading the path of the three blessings (*sanfu* 三福), and dwelling in interior perfection (*neiquan* 內全)
43	217–20		Filiality, loyalty, merit, hidden virtue, and felicity
44	221–22	74	Desires and vows
45	223–33	76	Abstention from cereals (**bigu*), absorbing the Five Pneumas (*fu wuqi* 服五氣), etc.
46	234–49	78	Drugs and elixirs for acquiring immortality
47	250–51		Prudence and respect
48	252–88	83–100.2b	Taoists who obtained posts in the bureaucracy of the afterworld; methods of acquiring immortality; ascension to celestial realms
49	289–92	100.2b–9b	Responding to transformations, unification with double forgetfulness, "entering what is so by itself" (*ru ziran* 入自然), and "compenetrating obscure silence" (*dong mingji* 洞冥寂)

Contents of the *Wushang biyao*. Ch. 1, 2, 8, 10–14, 36, 58–64, 67–73, 75, 77, 79–82, 85, 86, 89, and 90 are lost.

for whatever reason, whole categories of texts; these include all works on the "arts of the bedchamber" (**fangzhong shu*; thirteen according to Ruan), alchemical works that were not part of the Shangqing or Lingbao corpora, and texts concerning talismans and charts (seventy according to Ruan).

Despite these deficiencies, the *Wushang biyao* is one of the main sources for the study of medieval Taoism. It citations make it possible to determine what scriptures and parts of scriptures composed in the Six Dynasties have survived in the *Daozang* today. Aside from the **Lingbao shoudu yi* (Ordination Ritual of the Numinous Treasure) by **Lu Xiujing, it contains the oldest liturgies for performing ordinations and Retreat rites (**zhai*) extant. Although edited at Emperor Wudi's insistence and abbreviated by the compilers, there are no other datable manuals for those rituals until the end of the Tang.

Finally, the table of contents to the *Wushang biyao* from the Dunhuang manuscripts supplies an excellent, if incomplete, overview of Taoist beliefs in the Six Dynasties. The editors of the collection systematized the tenets, rituals, and practices of the religion, providing a tool for exploring given topics. They also ordered the subjects in ascending or descending hierarchies of priority that reveals the values placed on them by Taoists (Lagerwey 1981b, 33 and 44). The compendium is an invaluable tool for guiding research in a number of areas.

Charles D. BENN

📖 Boltz J. M. 1987a, 228–29; Lagerwey 1981b; Ōfuchi Ninji 1978–79, 1: 337–44,

370–75 (crit. notes on the Dunhuang mss.) and 2: 747–75 (reprod. of the Dunhuang mss.); Ōfuchi Ninji 1997, 297–407; Ōfuchi Ninji and Ishii Masako 1988, 60–107 (list of texts cited); Ozaki Masaharu 1983c, 189–92; Sunayama Minoru 1990, 123–56

※ Tongdao guan

Wushang huanglu dazhai licheng yi

無上黃籙大齋立成儀

Standard Liturgies of the
Supreme Great Yellow Register Retreat

Assembled in the early thirteenth century, the *Wushang huanglu dazhai licheng yi* (CT 508) focuses on the Yellow Register Retreat (*huanglu zhai) rites to save the dead. It contains the teachings of the itinerant ritual master from Hubei, Liu Yongguang 留用光 (1134–1206), who studied *Zhengyi (Orthodox Unity), *Tongchu (Youthful Incipience), Thunder Rituals (*leifa), and probably the *Tianxin zhengfa (Correct Method of the Celestial Heart), before becoming head Taoist in Hangzhou in 1203. Liu's teachings were codified by his disciple, the official Jiang Shuyu 蔣叔輿 (1162–1223), who compiled a series of works on *Lingbao ritual during two decades of comparing ritual systems.

In giving a well-structured overview of the three-day Yellow Register Retreat, Jiang wanted to make sure that authentic rites (*zhengfa* 正法) of Lingbao programs—especially the texts and scriptures issued by *Lu Xiujing, but also those by *Zhang Wanfu and *Du Guangting—would remain central to ritual practice. Relying on Zhengyi forms of submitting petitions to heaven, Jiang condemns the ritual practices of the *Lingbao dafa (Great Rites of the Numinous Treasure). His praises for Tianxin, *Shenxiao (Divine Empyrean), and *Jingming dao (Pure and Bright Way), and *Lu Shizhong's (fl. 1120–30) Yutang 玉堂 (Jade Hall), are also noteworthy.

Lowell SKAR

📖 Asano Haruji 1999b; Boltz J. M. 1987a, 41–43; Davis E. 2001, 171–76; Lagerwey 1994

※ *huanglu zhai*

wuwei

無為

non-action; non-interference; non-intervention

Wuwei or "non-action" means to do things the natural way, by not interfering with the patterns, rhythms, and structures of nature, without imposing one's own intentions upon the organization of the world. The term appears first, and most prominently, in the *Daode jing*, where it is coupled several times with the phrase *wu buwei* 無不為, "and there will be nothing that is not done." In this early text, non-action means retaining an inner core of quietude and letting the world move along as it naturally proceeds. It is a quality of the sage (*shengren*), and thus also of the ideal ruler, that will ensure a general sense of harmony and well-being in the world.

In the *Zhuangzi*, non-action appears as a more psychological mode and is a characteristic of spontaneity (*ziran*), the main quality of the embodied Dao. It means to be free in mind and spirit and able to wander about the world with ease and pleasure (see *yuanyou*), to engage in an ecstatic oneness with all-there-is. Yet another dimension of non-action evolved with the rise of cosmological thought in the Han. In the thought of *Huang-Lao Taoism, non-action meant to be in perfect alignment with the movements of the seasons, the planets, and the times. Yin and Yang in their various alterations were the key pattern to follow and non-action meant less the not doing of something than the doing of the right thing at the right time. From this point onward, and in mainstream Chinese thought, non-action became a form of action, coinciding with the best possible action or *youwei* 有為 in both social and political practice.

A different slant on the topic was produced by the primitivists or anarchists whose texts have survived in parts of the *Zhuangzi*. Rejecting all forms of government and social or other organization, they proposed a radical vision of non-action as doing absolutely nothing. Any kind of interference, management, or organization could inevitably lead only to ruin. This radical position has been echoed in modern times, when Taoist revivalist thinkers have used the ancient thinkers to counter Communist policies.

Livia KOHN

📖 Duyvendak 1947; Fukunaga Mitsuji 1965; Liu Xiaogan 1991; Liu Xiaogan 1998; Qing Xitai 1994, 2: 269–72

※ Dao

wuxing

五行

Five Phases; Five Agents

The system of the *wuxing* forms an integral part of what A. C. Graham has called the "correlative cosmology" that had taken shape by the early imperial age under the Former Han. Various English translations have been attempted, but "five agents" and "five phases" are nowadays most commonly used by scholars.

In the case of Yin-Yang thinking, one draws up a list of entities under the two headings Yin and Yang, so that the cosmos is organized into sets of paired and parallel relationships (for some examples, see table 1). In the case of the *wuxing*, the list is organized into five columns, headed by the labels Wood (*mu* 木), Fire (*huo* 火), Soil (*tu* 土), Metal (*jin* 金), and Water (*shui* 水). With Yin-Yang the basic relation implied between the paired items is one of complementary alternation. With the fivefold scheme, however, the potential relationships are considerably more complex. The phases or agents are ordered in two ways (see fig. 77): the "production" or "generation" sequence (*xiangsheng* 相生) and the "conquest" sequence (*xiangke* 相克). It is easy to see the way the two sequences work, at least with reference to the natural entities after which the phases or agents are named. In the production order, Wood grows using Water; Fire can come from Wood; Soil (ashes) comes from Fire and (as all ancient peoples thought) Metals grow in the Soil; finally Water condenses on cold Metal. Turning to conquest, Water extinguishes Fire, Fire melts Metal, Metal cuts Wood, Wood (as in an ancient wooden spade) can dig up Soil, and Soil can dam up Water.

One major application of *wuxing* thinking was in the realm of medicine, in which we are concerned with a microcosm—the human body—that was seen as necessarily recapitulating the patterns of the macrocosm—Heaven and Earth. The partial listing given in table 25 serves to indicate how the correlative system functioned. Through the application of this scheme, the physician is enabled to make immediate sense of some symptoms. The patient who develops eye problems may have a malfunction of the liver; a bitter taste in the mouth may be indicative of heart trouble; a depressed patient may have overactivity of the phase or agent Metal associated with the lungs. But more subtle decisions can be guided by this system of thinking. Suppose for instance that the physician concludes that the patient is suffering from a liver disorder.

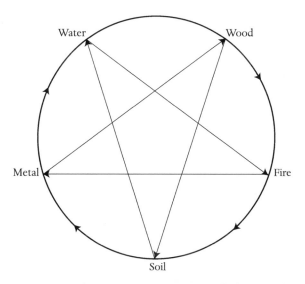

Fig. 77. "Production" sequence (*xiangsheng* 相生, along the
circumference) and "conquest" sequence (*xiangke* 相克, inside
the circle) of the Five Agents (or Five Phases, *wuxing*).

Noting that the liver is linked with the phase or agent Wood, a prescription
is chosen to strengthen the spleen (Soil) since the doctor knows that the liver
disease will be transmitted into the spleen (Wood conquers Soil). This is not
just a precaution—in fact the strengthening of the spleen acts round the cycle
to strengthen the liver as well.

Like the Yin-Yang scheme, the *wuxing* emerged from the intellectual ferment
of the late Warring States in ways that are not easy to trace in detail. There
were certainly alternative schemes stressing different numbers of categories.
The *Lüshi chunqiu* 呂氏春秋 (Springs and Autumns of Mr. Lü), which was
assembled in 239 BCE, gives the first full and clear evidence of the scheme in
action, and its application was developed further during the Former Han.
Traditional attributions to Zou Yan 騶衍 (third century BCE) as a major inno-
vator in *wuxing* thinking are probably baseless. At most he may have stressed
the application of the scheme to the revolutions of political power, with each
succeeding dynasty arising in connection with one of the phases or agents.

Christopher CULLEN

📖 Graham 1986c, 42–66 and 70–92; Graham 1989, 340–56; Ho Peng Yoke
1985, 11–17; Kalinowski 1991; Major 1984; Major 1987b; Major 1991; Major 1993,
29–30; Needham 1956, 273–78; Robinet 1997b, 10–11; Sivin 1987, 70–80

※ COSMOLOGY

Table 25

	WOOD	FIRE	SOIL	METAL	WATER
DIRECTIONS	east	south	center	west	north
SEASONS	spring	summer	(midsummer)	autumn	winter
COLORS	green (or blue)	red	yellow	white	black
EMBLEMATIC ANIMALS	green dragon	red bird	yellow dragon	white tiger	snake and turtle
NUMBERS	3, 8	2, 7	5, 10	4, 9	1, 6
YIN-YANG	minor Yang (shaoyang 少陽)	great Yang (taiyang 太陽)	balance	minor Yin (shaoyin 少陰)	great Yin (taiyin 太陰)
MUSICAL NOTES	jiao 角	zhi 徵	gong 宮	shang 商	yu 羽
STEMS	jia 甲, yi 乙	bing 丙, ding 丁	wu 戊, ji 己	geng 庚, xin 辛	ren 壬, gui 癸
BRANCHES	yin 寅, mao 卯	wu 午, si 巳	xu 戌, chou 丑, wei 未, chen 辰	you 酉, shen 申	hai 亥, zi 子
PLANETS	Jupiter	Mars	Saturn	Venus	Mercury
VISCERA	liver	heart	spleen	lungs	kidneys
RECEPTACLES	gallbladder	small intestine	stomach	large intestine	urinary bladder
BODY ORGAN	eyes	tongue	mouth	nose	ears
EMOTIONS	anger	joy	ratiocination	sorrow	apprehension
TASTES	sour	bitter	sweet	acrid	salty
CLIMATES	wind	hot	moist	dry	cold
FAMILY RELATIONS	father	daughter	ancestors	mother	son

The five agents (or five phases, *wuxing*) and their main correlations.

Wuyi shan

武夷山

Mount Wuyi (Fujian)

Mount Wuyi, in the Chong'an 崇安 district of Fujian, is part of a larger mountain range that demarcates the border between Fujian and Jiangxi. The highest peak has an elevation of about 700 m. Within Taoist sacred geography, Mount Wuyi was identified as the site of the sixteenth Grotto-Heaven (*dongtian). The mountain has a long history of being inhabited and served as an ancient burial ground, perhaps as early as the Shang dynasty. Ancient artifacts known as "coffin boats" (chuanguan 船棺; Chen Mingfang 1992), found in caves and niches tucked high up in the cliffs of the mountain, were integrated into Taoism as "boats of the immortals" after the establishment of the new religion within this sacred purlieu.

By the Tang dynasty, Taoist institutions were well established at Mount Wuyi, with the main center of activity being the Abbey of Unfathomable Protection (Chongyou guan 冲佑觀). The Song dynasty master *Bai Yuchan (1194–1229?) established a hermitage on this mountain in 1214. Due to its close proximity to Mount Longhu (*Longhu shan, Jiangxi), Mount Wuyi was also closely connected to the Taoist religious developments there.

James ROBSON

📖 Nara Yukihiro 1998, 140–41; Qing Xitai 1994, 4: 183–87; Ziegler 1996–97; Ziegler 1998

※ TAOIST SACRED SITES

wuying

五營

Five Camps

The Five Camps are the five encampments of "soldiers of the netherworld" (*yinbing* 陰兵), placed to the north, south, east, and west, as well as in the middle, of villages and ritual spaces for their protection. The term is also applied to the soldiers placed in those camps. In Taiwan, the Red-head (*hongtou* 紅頭)

ritual masters (see *hongtou* and *wutou*) use Five Camps banners (*wuying qi* 五營旗) and Five Camps heads (*wuying tou* 五營頭, i.e., sculpted heads of the commanders of the Five Camps on thick steel needles) in rituals to summon and dispatch spirit armies.

The commander of the Eastern Camp is Zhang Shengzhe 張聖者 (Fazhu gong 法主公), whose banner is green. The commander of the Southern Camp is Xiao Shengzhe 蕭聖者, whose banner is red. The commander of the Western Camp is Liu Shengzhe 劉聖者, whose banner is white. The commander of the Northern Camp is Lian Shengzhe 連聖者, whose banner is black. The commander of the Central Camp is Li Shengzhe 李聖者 (Nezha taizi 哪吒太子), whose banner is yellow. Each of them leads an army of spirit soldiers. The soldiers are those souls that have no one to venerate them, composing the lowest echelon of the spirit world.

ASANO Haruji

📖 Liu Zhiwan 1983b, 216–17; Liu Zhiwan 1983–84, 2: 37–38; Naoe Hiroji 1983, 1040–44, 1046, and 1051–52; Schipper 1985e, 28

wuyue

五嶽

Five Peaks; Five Marchmounts; Five Sacred Mountains

The *wuyue* began as sacred mountains for the imperial cult and later took on importance for both Taoists and Buddhists. While some scholars translate this term as "five peaks" or "five sacred mountains," others prefer "five marchmounts," as *wuyue* denoted a special set of mountains that were perceived to demarcate and protect the boundaries (or *marches*) of the Chinese imperium.

As commonly understood today, the set of five mountains includes:

1. Mount Tai (*Taishan, Shandong) in the East
2. Mount Heng (*Hengshan 衡山, Hunan) in the South
3. Mount Hua (*Huashan, Shaanxi) in the West
4. Mount Heng (*Hengshan 恆山, Shanxi) in the North
5. Mount Song (*Songshan, Henan) in the Center

The set of five, however, was not a static system, and its formation was the product of a long and involved history that paralleled the shifting political, cosmographic, and religious developments of the late Zhou and early Han dynasties. Originally, in fact, there were only four peaks (Gu Jiegang 1977, 34–45). Some of the mountains in this list, moreover, were sometimes replaced by others, with Mount Huo (*Huoshan, Anhui) often included as the Southern Peak.

Pinpointing the first extant use of the term *wuyue* is difficult and largely dependent on two sources with problematic dates. In the "Da zongbo" 大宗伯 (The Great Minister of Rites) chapter of the *Zhouli* 周禮 (Rites of the Zhou), which may date to about the mid-second century BCE or slightly earlier, the Five Peaks are mentioned in the category of "earthly deities," which fall in line behind the ancestral spirits of the nation and the heavenly deities in the Zhou hierarchy of spirits. The *Zhouli*, however, does not state which mountains were considered the Five Peaks at the time of its compilation. The second text that mentions the Five Peaks is the *Erya* 爾雅 (Literary Lexicon). This source presents two incompatible sets of five mountains, both of which include some of those that are later found in the set of Five Peaks. As the *Zhouli* and *Erya* sources reveal, prior to the Han dynasty there was no solidified group of Five Peaks. In fact, the set of Five Peaks that is known today did not coalesce until as late as the Sui dynasty.

The Five Peaks in Taoism. While the Five Peaks were initially part of the imperial cult, beliefs about them spread to a wider circle than those concerned with mapping out an imperial sacred geography. During the Han dynasty, for example, the *wuyue* appear in tomb ordinances (Seidel 1987e, 30) and in the "weft texts" (*weishu* 緯書; see *TAOISM AND THE APOCRYPHA). They are also included as a set at the beginning of *j.* 4 of *Ge Hong's (283–343) *Baopu zi* as sites for "attaining the medicines of the transcendents."

Within Taoism, the Five Peaks became important at different levels and in several contexts. Indeed, the Taoist influence on the Five Peaks has traditionally been understood to be so thorough that they are often referred to as "Taoist" mountains in opposition to the "Buddhist" Four Famous Mountains (*sida mingshan* 四大名山; Zheng Guoqian 1996). In the *Daozang*, however, there are texts for only three of the Five Peaks: the *Daishi* 岱史 (History of Mount Tai; CT 1472) by Zha Zhilong 查志隆 (fl. 1554–86) for the Eastern Peak; the *Xiyue Huashan zhi* 西嶽華山志 (Monograph of Mount Hua, the Western Peak; CT 307) by Wang Chuyi 王處一 (apparently not the same *Wang Chuyi as the twelfth-century Quanzhen master) for the Western Peak; and the *Nanyue xiaolu* (Short Record of the Southern Peak; CT 453) by Li Chongzhao 李沖昭 (ninth century; also known as Li Zhongzhao 李仲昭) and the *Nanyue zongsheng ji* (Anthology of Highlights of the Southern Peak; CT 606) by Chen Tianfu 陳田夫 (twelfth century) for the Southern Peak.

The Five Peaks were important sites where Taoist anchorites lived and Taoist institutions formed (see separate entries for each mountain). They were perceived to be potent sites of congealed pneumas (*qi) that were populated by transcendent beings, filled with the numinous herbs and minerals used to concoct elixirs, and capable of secreting sacred texts such as the *Lingbao *Wupian zhenwen (Perfected Script in Five Tablets). Correlations were further perceived to exist between the Five Peaks on earth, the five viscera (*wuzang) in the body, and the five planets (wuxing 五星) in the sky. In their more ethereal form, the Five Peaks became the objects of visualizations, and their deities were considered part of powerful spirit armies that adepts could summon. Moreover, the Five Peaks were often used symbolically in Taoist ritual contexts. The talismanic *Charts of the Real Forms of the Five Peaks* (*Wuyue zhenxing tu) were seen as powerful simulacra used for protection when entering the mountains, for defending one's home, and for garrisoning the alchemist's "elixir chamber." The *Charts* were also used in oath-taking rituals (Schipper 1967, and Doub 1979, 134). In these and other ways, the Five Peaks were perceived as important sites that came to pervade much of Taoist doctrine, myth, ritual, and history.

The Five Peaks attained particular importance within Taoism during the Tang dynasty. Their status was elevated with the rise of Taoist influence at the Tang court. This "imperial" Taoist role for the Five Peaks took off most dramatically under Tang Xuanzong (r. 712–56). After repeated rank increases for the Five Peaks, the Taoist control over them was finally formalized following the successful lobbying efforts of *Sima Chengzhen (647–735; Kroll 1983, 236–37; on the problematic dates of that shift see Barrett 1996, 55). But despite the imperial decree that placed them under the governance of *Shangqing Taoist deities, the Five Peaks have remained active sites—in varying degrees—for both Buddhist and Taoist institutions up to the present day.

James ROBSON

📖 Cui Xiuguo 1982; Geil 1926; Gu Jiegang 1977, 34–45; Gu Jiegang 1996, 551–85; Kleeman 1994c, 226–30; Landt 1994; Munakata Kiyohiko 1991; Tang Xiaofeng 1997b; Yokote Yutaka 1999; Yoshikawa Tadao 1991a

※ Hengshan [Hunan]; Hengshan [Shanxi]; Huashan; Songshan; Taishan; *Wuyue zhenxing tu;* TAOIST SACRED SITES

Wuyue zhenxing tu

五嶽真形圖

Charts of the Real Forms (*or*: True Forms) of the Five Peaks

Two distinct types of configurations bear the designation *Wuyue zhenxing tu*. The more familiar is the set of five insignia displayed on many stelae as well as bronze mirrors ostensibly dating to the Tang. These emblematic figures may very well have been devised in origin as representations of cosmic mountains. But as attested in stelae and texts dating to the fourteenth century, such figures have long been identified with the Five Peaks of Mount Tai (*Taishan, Shandong) in the east, Mount Heng (*Hengshan 恆山, Shanxi) in the north, Mount Song (*Songshan, Henan) in the center, Mount Heng (*Hengshan 衡山, Hunan) in the south, and Mount Hua (*Huashan, Shaanxi) in the west. Their innate apotropaic force is clearly denoted by the variant title "Wuyue zhenxing fu" 五嶽真形符 (Talismans of the Real Forms of the Five Peaks) given the insignia in the *Sanhuang neiwen yibi* 三皇內文遺祕 (Remaining Secrets of the Inner Script of the Three Sovereigns; CT 856). This set of figures stands in sharp contrast to the series of labyrinthine *Charts* featured in three major anthologies within the Taoist Canon, two of which appear to have been derived from Song printings. Cartographic as well as talismanic function seem to be accommodated by this alternative vision of the five sacred peaks.

A complex body of lore has evolved around the *Wuyue zhenxing tu*. Perhaps the best-known story is found in the sixth-century *Han Wudi neizhuan* (Inner Biography of Emperor Wu of the Han). The emergence of the *Charts* according to this account came with the demarcation of cosmic landmarks by Taishang daojun 太上道君 (Most High Lord of the Dao). This is how the deity *Xiwang mu (Queen Mother of the West) ostensibly answered the inquiries of Han Wudi (r. 141–87 BCE), to whom she reluctantly conveyed a copy of the *Wuyue zhenxing tu*. Alternative accounts bearing on the origins of the *Charts* are in two texts ascribed to the wonder-worker *Dongfang Shuo (ca. 160–ca. 93 BCE), both of which also apparently date no earlier than the sixth century. According to the *Shizhou ji* (Record of the Ten Continents), the legendary Yu 禹 is said to have had inscriptions carved into the Five Peaks after he brought flood waters under control. A *Wuyue tu xu* 五嶽圖序 (Preface to the Charts of the Five Peaks) fabricated in the name of Dongfang Shuo claims that *Huangdi created the *Five Charts* following his defeat of the monstrous Chiyou 蚩尤.

Fig. 78. "Real forms" of the Five Peaks (*wuyue*): (a) South; (b) West; (c) Center; (d) East; (e) North. *Wuyue guben zhenxing tu* 五嶽古本真形圖 (Ancient Version of the Charts of the Real Forms of the Five Peaks; CT 441), 8b–12a.

Close correspondences to the *Charts* may be found in the pentads of talismanic writ common to both the *Shangqing and *Lingbao codifications. Proponents of the latter laid claim to the *Charts*, apparently based on the accounts given by *Ge Hong (283–343) in the *Baopu zi* (Book of the Master Who Embraces Simplicity). Ge writes that his mentor *Zheng Yin (ca. 215–ca. 302) told him nothing surpassed the *Wuyue zhenxing tu* and *Sanhuang wen* (Script of the Three Sovereigns). Anyone possessing these sacred writs could reportedly count on divine guardianship at home and on the road. Ge states that they were to be passed down from master to disciple once every forty years, but adds that they could also be revealed by mountain deities to adepts like Bo He 帛和 (see under *Bojia dao). As told in the *Shenxian zhuan* (Biographies of Divine Transcendents) by Ge Hong, the *Wuyue zhenxing tu* came to be disclosed to Bo only after he had devoted three years to focusing on the cavern walls at Mount Xicheng (Xicheng shan 西城山, Shaanxi).

Keepers of the Shangqing legacy did not honor Bo He with possession of the *Wuyue zhenxing tu*, perhaps because of their critical views of sacrificial practices pursued by a so-called *Bojia dao (Way of the Bo Family) prevalent in the south. *Tao Hongjing (486–536) acknowledges that the family of his disciple Zhou Ziliang 周子良 (497–516) were adherents of the Bojia dao. After Tao bestowed the *Wuyue tu* and *Sanhuang wen* on Zhou in 512, family members who joined them at Mount Mao (*Maoshan, Jiangsu) presumably abandoned such ties.

The renowned protocols of *Zhang Wanfu (fl. 710–13) not only document the transmission of the *Wuyue zhenxing tu* to ordinands of the highest level, but also record accounts behind their association with Han Wudi. Supplementing this lore is a noteworthy set of instructions that Zheng Yin ostensibly conveyed to his disciple Ge Hong. Considerably amplified collections of texts accruing to the *Charts* appear in:

1. *Yunji qiqian (Seven Lots from the Bookbag of the Clouds; CT 1032, j. 79)

2. *Wuyue zhenxing xulun* 五嶽真形序論 (Preface and Essay on the Real Forms of the Five Peaks; CT 1281)

3. *Shangqing lingbao dafa (Great Rites of the Numinous Treasure of the Highest Clarity; CT 1221, j. 17)

4. *Lingbao wuliang duren shangjing dafa (Great Rites of the Superior Scripture of the Numinous Treasure on Limitless Salvation; CT 219, j. 21)

5. *Wuyue guben zhenxing tu* 五嶽古本真形圖 (Ancient Version of the Charts of the Real Forms of the Five Peaks; CT 441)

Diverse sets of labyrinthine illustrations are featured in the latter three anthologies. The earliest forms bear no commentary whereas later generations are credited with providing annotated versions identifying various natural features. Of special note in the last text listed above are copies of documents to be exchanged between master and disciple in a ceremony invoking the guardianship of spirits from each of the five peaks. Two fragments recovered from *Dunhuang provide additional background regarding an annual ritual of repentance by which communities in the sixth century paid homage to the guardian deities embodied in the *Wuyue zhenxing tu*. Renditions in vermilion and black on silk of high quality are to be carried in a pouch, according to a supporting account concerning Zheng Yin's transmission of the *Charts* to Ge Hong.

Judith M. BOLTZ

📖 Boltz J. M. 1994, 16–17 and 27; Chavannes 1910b, 415–24; Chen Guofu

1963, 77–78 and 276–77; Chen Yuan 1988, 1313–14; Little 2000b, 358–59; Schipper 1965, 26–33; Schipper 1967; Ware 1966, 282–83 and 312–16; Yamada Toshiaki 1987a

※ *wuyue*

wuzang

五臟

five viscera (lit., "five storehouses")

1. Medicine

In Chinese medicine, *wuzang* refers to a system of "orbs," "viscera," or "depositories," which have some features reminiscent of the organ system known from Western anatomy. The five viscera comprise the liver (*gan* 肝), heart (*xin* 心), spleen (*pi* 脾), lungs (*fei* 肺), and kidney system (*shen* 腎). Each has an inner and an outer aspect; thus the outer aspect of the liver is the gallbladder (*dan* 膽), that of the heart the small intestine (*xiaochang* 小腸), that of the spleen the stomach (*wei* 胃), that of the lungs the large intestine (*dachang* 大腸), and that of the kidneys the urinary bladder (*pangguang* 膀胱). The five organs mentioned as "outer aspects" of the *wuzang* are five of the "six receptacles" (*liufu* 六腑, lit., "six bureaus"), the sixth being the "triple burner" (*sanjiao* 三焦) that is sometimes identified with the Gate of the Vital Force (*mingmen*). Generally speaking, the inner aspect has functions of storage, and the outer of transformation, i.e., digestion, which comprises the absorption of refined *qi* (*jingqi* 精氣) and the evacuation of the dregs (*zaopo* 糟粕). The viscera resonate with the five seasons—spring, summer, late summer, autumn, and winter—and in the opening chapters of the *Suwen* 素問 (Plain Questions; see *Huangdi neijing*) they are frequently described as being responsible for illnesses that occur according to a seasonal pattern. In other words, seasonal *qi* and winds blowing from seasonally distinct directions were considered to stir the *qi* in the viscera in ways that gave rise to illness.

Reasoning in terms of *qi* and the visceral systems provided a means for expressing emotional distress in medical discourse; the *wuzang* refer to a system that makes no distinction between the psyche and the soma. Although it is possible that the recognition of different viscera was derived from dissection, which according to *Lingshu* 靈樞 12 (Numinous Pivot; see *Huangdi neijing*) was conducted on corpses, the *wuzang* are not primarily notions describing an

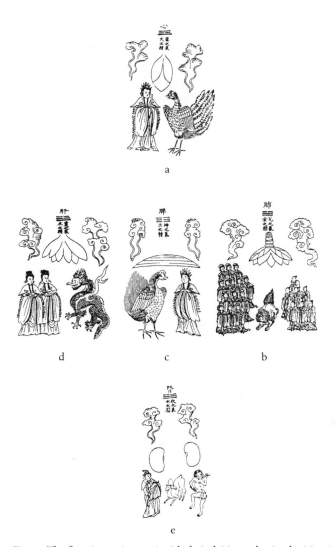

Fig. 79. The five viscera (*wuzang*) with their deities and animal spirits in a Korean medical text: (a) heart; (b) lungs; (c) spleen; (d) liver; (e) kidneys. *Uibang yuch'wi* 醫方類聚 (Classified Collection of Medical Methods; 1477). See also fig. 12(c).

anatomical body. In early medical writings, the heart and liver figure as repositories of strong emotions, grief (*you* 憂), and anger (*nu* 怒). In the *Huangdi neijing*, however, the attribution of specific emotions to the viscera is far from standardized; contemporary Chinese medicine generally attributes anger to the liver, joy (*xi* 喜) to the heart, worry (*si* 思) to the spleen, grief (*you* or *bei* 悲) to the lungs, and fear (*kong* 恐) to the kidneys.

The *wuzang* system went hand in hand with the integration of the Five Phases (*wuxing*) theory into medicine. From the fourth century BCE onward, the system of the Five Phases—Wood, Fire, Soil, Metal, and Water—developed in the context of divinatory calculations as a means for assessing cyclical change. In medicine it gained prominence not only as a schema for classifying many different aspects of the universe, from directions and seasons to colors and flavors, but also as a schema for accounting for physiological and pathological changes, and for changes to be attained through therapeutic intervention. This was so because the Five Phases were conceived cyclically to give birth to one another (*sheng* 生), or cyclically to "insult" (*wu* 侮) or "overcome" (*ke* 剋) or "multiply" (*cheng* 乘) one another, and their standard sequencing in such cycles of mutual production, insulting, overcoming, or multiplication was used for explaining and predicting the course of bodily processes.

Elisabeth HSU

📖 Farquhar 1994, 91–107; Hsu Elisabeth 1999, 198–217; Kohn 1993b, 164–68; Porkert 1974, 107–66; Sivin 1987, 213–36, 349–78; Yin Huihe 1984, 28–53

2. Meditation

The five viscera or energy storage centers of the body (liver, heart, spleen, lungs, and kidneys) are visualized variously in meditation—first with the help of different-colored lights, as described in the *Taiping jing shengjun bizhi* 太平經聖君祕旨 (Secret Directions of the Holy Lord on the Scripture of Great Peace; CT 1102; trans. Kohn 1993b, 193–97); then with specific sacred animals or bodily gods residing in them, as outlined in the *Huangting neijing wuzang liufu buxie tu* 黃庭內景五臟六腑補瀉圖 (Charts of the Strengthening and Weakening of the Five Viscera and the Six Receptacles, According to the Scripture of the Inner Effulgences of the Yellow Court; CT 432) by Hu Yin 胡愔 of the ninth century; and finally, within a Tantric Buddhist context, with sacred Sanskrit letters and holy numbers, as described in the *Wulun jiuzi bishi* 五輪九字祕釋 (Secret Exegesis of the Five Cakras and Nine Characters), a manuscript extant in Japan (Yoshioka Yoshitoyo 1964; Tanaka Fumio 1988).

In all cases, the basic system of association is the set of correspondences linked to the *wuxing*, which associates specific colors, physical energies, spiritual powers, numbers, and animals with each organ. The system also identifies specific gods and written symbols with each organ, allowing the meditator to reinvent the inner organs of her body as nodes in a larger cosmic network.

Livia KOHN

📖 Despeux 1994, 108–30 and passim; Ishida Hidemi 1989; Kamitsuka Yoshiko 1999, 348–53; Robinet 1993, 60–96

3. Neidan

In *neidan, in which the five viscera are energetic centers where transformation takes place, the term *wuqi* 五氣 (five pneumas) is often used as a synonym for *wuzang*. Besides the five viscera themselves, this term denotes the essence (*jing) situated in the kidneys, the spirit (*shen) in the heart, the *hun in the liver, the *po in the lungs, and the intention (*yi) in the spleen. Transformation occurs through refining these five components of the human being, and restores the original order of the Dao.

As stated in *Zhong-Lü texts, the Jade Liquor (*yuye* 玉液) or the Golden Elixir (*jindan) purify the pneuma (*qi) of the viscera and transform it into Yang spirit (*yangshen* 陽神). The purification of essence, spirit, *hun*, *po*, and intention is a process of harmonizing them in silence, as stated for instance in the *Jindan sibai zi (Four Hundred Words on the Golden Elixir), the *Zhonghe ji (Anthology of Central Harmony), and the *Xingming guizhi (Principles of Balanced Cultivation of Inner Nature and Vital Force). The next stage is to join these refined pneumas in the Origin, from which they were generated through the differentiation of the one *qi*. Their return to the Origin corresponds to an advanced stage of inner transformation, called "the five pneumas have audience at the Origin" (*wuqi chaoyuan* 五氣朝元).

Martina DARGA

📖 Baldrian-Hussein 1984, 147–48, 157, and 164–66; Darga 1999, 180–82 and 348–53; Despeux 1979, 75–79; Despeux 1994, 117–30 and 152–59

※ MEDITATION AND VISUALIZATION; TAOIST VIEWS OF THE HUMAN BODY

Wuzhen pian

悟真篇

Folios on Awakening to Perfection;
Folios on Awakening to Reality

The collection of poems by *Zhang Boduan (987?–1082) entitled *Wuzhen pian* is the main work of the Southern Lineage (*Nanzong) of *neidan. The text bears a preface dated 1075 and a postface dated 1078, both signed by Zhang Boduan. The preface reports that Zhang experienced a sudden realization of the Dao when he met a Perfected (*zhenren) in Chengdu (Sichuan) in 1069. After that, he wrote a set of eighty-one poems that form the nucleus of the *Wuzhen pian*.

Format and content. The title *Wuzhen pian* first designated only the original eighty-one poems (*Sandong qunxian lu*, 2.9b). According to the traditional account, the first sixteen heptasyllabic *lüshi* 律詩 (regulated poems) illustrate the principle of "two times eight" (*erba* 二八, symbolizing the balance of Yin and Yang); the next sixty-four heptasyllabic *jueju* 絕句 (stopped-short lines) are related to the *Yijing* hexagrams; and the final pentasyllabic poem expresses the magnificence of Great Unity (*taiyi*). Zhang Boduan later appended twelve alchemical *ci* 詞 (lyrics) to the melody of "Xijiang yue" 西江月 (West River Moon), which sum up the twelve stages of fire phasing (*huohou*). All of the above poems deal with the techniques of "nourishing life and stabilizing the form" (*yangming guxing* 養命固形). Finally, Zhang devoted himself to the study of Chan Buddhism and supplemented the *Wuzhen pian* with a miscellanea of thirty-two poems on the "nature of authentic awakening" (*zhenjue zhi xing* 真覺之性).

The verses of the *Wuzhen pian* are a work of literary craftsmanship and were probably intended to be sung or chanted. They teem with paradoxes, metaphors, and aphorisms, and their recondite style allows multiple interpretations. The verses are widely accepted as an elaboration of the *Zhouyi cantong qi*, but their philosophical basis is in the *Daode jing* and the *Yinfu jing*. Life, says Zhang Boduan, is like a bubble on floating water or a spark from a flint, and the search for wealth and fame results only in bodily degeneration; thus human beings should search for the Golden Elixir (*jindan*) to become celestial immortals (*tianxian* 天仙). Although the *Wuzhen pian* does not give practical instructions, it alludes to them in a symbolic way. The primary trigrams *qian* 乾 ☰ (pure Yang) and *kun* 坤 ☷ (pure Yin) are equated with the alchemical laboratory, while *kan* 坎 ☵ (Yang within Yin) and *li* 離 ☲ (Yin within Yang) are the two main ingredients. The sixty-four hexagrams are used to explain the modes of macrocosmic-microcosmic change. The text also outlines the fire phasing that one should apply in the process of transformation, and refers to the alchemical principle of "reversal" (*diandao* 顛倒).

Commentaries and interpretations. The *Wuzhen pian* was completed around 1075, but became widely known only from the mid-twelfth century onward. It is first mentioned in a compilation of 1154, and its earliest extant exegesis dates from 1161. The Taoist Canon includes the following commentaries and closely related texts:

    1. *Wuzhen pian*, in *Xiuzhen shishu* (CT 263), *j*. 26–30, with commentaries by Ye Shibiao 葉士表 (1161) and Yuan Gongfu 袁公輔 (1202).

2. *Wuzhen pian zhushu* 悟真篇注疏 (Commentary and Subcommentary to the *Wuzhen pian*; 1173; CT 141), by *Weng Baoguang, edited with a subcommentary by Dai Qizong 戴起宗 in 1335.

3. *Wuzhen zhizhi xiangshuo sansheng biyao* 悟真直指詳說三乘祕要 (Straightforward Directions and Detailed Explanations on the *Wuzhen pian* and the Secret Essentials of the Three Vehicles; CT 143), by Weng Baoguang, edited by Dai Qizong in 1337. Although this text is separately printed in the Taoist Canon, it is a continuation of CT 141 above.

4. *Wuzhen pian sanzhu* 悟真篇三注 (Three Commentaries to the *Wuzhen pian*; CT 142), with commentaries by *Xue Daoguang (1078?–1191, actually written by Weng Baoguang), Lu Shu 陸墅 (thirteenth century?), and *Chen Zhixu (1289-after 1335), edited by Zhang Shihong 張士弘 (fourteenth century).

5. *Wuzhen pian shiyi* 悟真篇拾遺 (Supplement to the *Wuzhen pian*; CT 144), by Weng Baoguang (see Wong Shiu Hon 1978b).

6. *Wuzhen pian zhushi* 悟真篇注釋 (Commentary and Exegesis to the *Wuzhen pian*; CT 145), with a commentary by Weng Baoguang different from no. 2 above.

7. *Wuzhen pian jiangyi* 悟真篇講義 (Explaining the Meaning of the *Wuzhen pian*; 1220 / 1226; CT 146), by Xia Yuanding 夏元鼎 (fl. 1225–27).

Among the main later commentaries are the following:

1. *Wuzhen pian xiaoxu* 悟真篇小序 (Short Introduction to the *Wuzhen pian*), by *Lu Xixing (1520–1601 or 1606).

2. *Wuzhen pian chanyou* 悟真篇闡幽 (Uncovering the Obscurities of the *Wuzhen pian*), by Zhu Yuanyu 朱元育 (fl. 1669).

3. *Wuzhen pian jizhu* 悟真篇集注 (Collected Commentaries to the *Wuzhen pian*; 1713), by *Qiu Zhao'ao (1638–1713), containing quotations from twenty-five earlier commentaries.

4. *Wuzhen pian zhengyi* 悟真篇正義 (The Correct Meaning of the *Wuzhen pian*; 1788), by *Dong Dening.

5. *Wuzhen zhizhi* 悟真直指 (Straightforward Directions on the *Wuzhen pian*; 1794), by *Liu Yiming (1734–1821; trans. Cleary 1987).

Most masters of the Nanzong lineage saw clear guidelines for practice in the poems of the *Wuzhen pian*. Different interpretations are apparent, however, within the two main Nanzong branches. The Pure Cultivation (Qingxiu 清修) branch of Zhang Boduan, *Shi Tai, Xue Daoguang, *Chen Nan, and *Bai Yuchan explained the text according to a Chan-Taoist trend of thought. The Joint Cultivation (*Shuangxiu) branch, whose main representatives are Liu

Yongnian 劉永年 (fl. 1138–68), Weng Baoguang, and Dai Qizong, interpreted it as a treatise on sexual practices. These two lines of transmission led to a multiplication of schools in later generations.

Farzeen BALDRIAN-HUSSEIN

📖 Azuma Jūji 1988; Boltz J. M. 1987a, 174; Cleary 1987 (trans.); Crowe 2000 (part. trans.); Davis and Chao 1939 (trans.); Imai Usaburō 1962; Kohn 1993b, 313–19 (part. trans.); Liu Ts'un-yan 1977; Miyazawa Masayori 1988a; Qing Xitai 1988–95, 2: 745–74; Robinet 1995a, 197–254 (part. trans.); Wang Mu 1990

✳ Zhang Boduan; *neidan*; Nanzong

Xi Kang

嵇康

223–62; *zi*: Shuye 叔夜

Xi Kang (or Ji Kang), a native of Qiao 譙 (Anhui), was one of the great literary figures of the Wei dynasty (220–65). His father died while he was still young, leaving him to be raised by an indulgent mother and older brother. Xi Kang would later trace his enduring love of independence and spontaneity back to his undisciplined childhood and his reading of the *Zhuangzi and the *Daode jing*. His unrestrained expression of feelings, a mode of conduct advocated in his *Shisi lun* 釋私論 (Essay on Dispelling Self-Interest; trans. Henricks 1983, 107–19), earned him many enemies and no doubt contributed to his premature death.

He married a princess of the ruling Cao 曹 clan sometime in the 240s, and remained loyal to the Wei for the rest of his life. He refused to hold office after the general Sima Yi 司馬懿 (178–251) seized effective control of the government in 249. When Guan Qiujian 毌丘儉 (?–255) rebelled against the Sima clan in 255, Xi Kang contemplated raising troops to assist him, but was dissuaded from doing so by Shan Tao 山濤 (205–83). In 261, he became entangled in a family conflict involving his friend Lü An 呂安 (?–262). Zhong Hui 鐘會 (225–64), a favorite of the Sima clan whom Xi Kang had slighted on a previous occasion, denounced him in court. Xi and Lü were both put to death in 262. In prison awaiting execution, Xi Kang wrote his famous *Youfen shi* 幽憤詩 (Poem on Anguish in Prison; trans. Holzman 1980, 354–56).

The danger and ultimate futility of Xi Kang's political entanglements no doubt reinforced his distaste for worldly affairs. This sentiment is eloquently expressed in a letter written to Shan Tao who had recommended him for an official post (*Yu Shan Juyuan juejiao shu* 與山巨源絕交書, or *Breaking Off Relations with Shan Juyuan*; trans. Hightower 1965).

Xi Kang's renunciation of a bureaucratic career left him free to pursue other interests. He was a master of Pure Conversation (*qingtan*), and became identified as one of the Seven Worthies of the Bamboo Grove (Zhulin qixian 竹林七賢), a group said to have met from time to time at his residence to drink, play the lute, and converse. (Besides Xi Kang and Shan Tao, the Seven Worthies include Ruan Ji 阮籍, 210–63; Xiang Xiu 向秀, 227–72; Ruan Xian 阮咸, third century; Wang Rong 王戎, third century; and Liu Ling 劉伶, third century.) Of his thirteen surviving treatises (*lun* 論), all but one follow the structure of the debates popular at the time.

Xi Kang had a strong interest in the practices of Nourishing Life (*yangsheng) and the pursuit of longevity, arguing in his Yangsheng lun 養生論 (Essay on Nourishing Life; trans. Henricks 1983, 21–30) that the human life span could be extended several hundred to a thousand years. He is said to have wandered in the mountains in search of herbal and mineral drugs, becoming so engrossed that he would forget to return.

He was also an accomplished poet and musician. His Qin fu 琴賦 (Rhapsody on the Lute; trans. van Gulik 1941) and Sheng wu aile lun 聲無哀樂論 (Essay on the Absence of Sorrow or Joy in Music; trans. Henricks 1983, 71–106) reveal the importance of music in his life and thought. He is said to have calmly strummed the lute in the final hours of his life.

Theodore A. COOK

   Dai Mingyang 1962 (crit. ed. of various works); van Gulik 1941; Henricks 1983 (trans. of various works); Henricks 1986a; Holzman 1957; Holzman 1980; Little 2000b, 185; Maspero 1981, 299–308

※ qingtan; yangsheng

xiang

象

image

The Dao is "the great image without form," says the Daode jing (sec. 41). "Heaven suspends its xiang . . . and the Sage imagines (xiang 像) them," says the Xici 繫辭 (Appended Statements, a portion of the *Yijing), which gives a special meaning to the term xiang by relating it to astral bodies and trigrams, and tying it with fa 法 (pattern). The alchemical art is said to be the art of the xiang, which refers to alchemical metaphors.

The term xiang may be rendered as "image," "figure," "symbol," or "configuration." The xiang are images that make things apparent; they are part of reality, and inherently contain and manifest the cosmic dimension of things and their structure. This is why the xiang are often considered to be the "real forms" (zhenxing 真形) of things, or the fundamental substance (*ti) of beings. They are visible but lie before and beyond the world of forms. They allow us to understand the world and to get along in the universe; hence they are guides and models of conduct.

On the subjective level, the xiang are the first idea, not yet conceptually formed and still intuitive; an intermediary mode between thought and its expression, as said by *Wang Bi; and a mediator between human intelligence and the world. On the objective level, the *xiang* are the way things are when they are about to appear and take form: they are their subtle and structural forms or outlines that pertain to Heaven, while the *fa* (patterns) pertain to Earth and are coarser. Related to numbers (*shu* 數), the *xiang* are tools that measure and order the world.

In *neidan*, besides these classical significations, the term *xiang* also takes on the wider sense of "metaphor." Alchemists say that theirs is an art of the *xiang*. In so doing they relate it to the *Yijing* and the diviner's endeavor to rationalize and organize the world. Alchemists criticize Buddhism (especially the Chan school) on the grounds that it operates without images, directly and without mediators; the alchemical language, on the other hand, is metaphorical and therefore can "speak without speaking" and go beyond ordinary language. Alchemists mean by this that their teaching is gradual as it is mediated; images are the mediators that stand midway between the formless Dao and the material world, between principles (*li* 理) and practice (*xing* 行). Even if the images must be forgotten once the sense they convey has been apprehended (as stated both in the *Zhuangzi* and by Wang Bi), they are necessary and one must go through them; they give the alchemical teaching its concrete dimension, which leads one to see in darkness instead of shutting one's eyes and remaining motionless and blind.

In their role as mediators, images also indicate structural relationships. For instance, the Sun as an image represents the Great Yang (*taiyang* 太陽, or Yang containing Yin); the Sun exists in the same relation to the Moon as the day to the night, Heaven to Earth, East to West, and the alchemical Dragon to the Tiger (see *longhu*). As images relate different things on various levels to each other, and are movable and interchangeable, they serve as instruments of the analogical mode of thought, which is the main mode of thought in alchemy. They can express a pattern as well as a process, they operate in diverse registers of sense, and they function as terms that indicate relations and functions rather than of particular things. This is why it is hardly possible to assign definitions to them: the sense of each of them is multiple and varies with the context.

Isabelle ROBINET

📖 Robinet 1989c, 159–62; Robinet 1993, 48–54; Robinet 1995a, 75–103; Wilhelm H. 1977, 190–222

※ Dao; *xing*

Xiang'er

想爾

See *Laozi Xiang'er zhu* 老子想爾注.

Xiang'er jie

想爾戒

The *Xiang'er* Precepts

The *Xiang'er jie* or *Xiang'er* precepts are a set of thirty-six rules (*jie*), nine expressed as positive imperatives and twenty-seven that are expressed as negative injunctions. Both the nine and the twenty-seven are themselves subdivided into three sets (of three and nine respectively) designated upper, middle, and lower. These divisions do not appear to rank the precepts in terms of importance or seriousness. The precepts, originally extracted from the *Xiang'er* commentary to the *Daode jing* and the *Daode jing* itself in the case of the nine imperatives, are translated by Stephen R. Bokenkamp (1993, 51 and revised in 1997, 49–50). His translations are used here. As the precepts were originally extracted from the commentary, their date of composition is clearly dependent on determining the date of composition of the commentary itself.

The *Xiang'er* precepts have been identified in three locations in the *Daozang*:

1. *Taishang Laojun jinglü* 太上老君經律 (Scriptural Regulations of the Most High Lord Lao; CT 786), 1a–2a, under the general title *Daode zun jingjie jiuxing ershiqi jie* 道德尊經戒九行二十七戒 (Nine Practices and Twenty-Seven Precepts of the Scriptural Injunctions of the Worthy of the Dao and Its Virtue), with the first group of nine called *Daode zun jing xiang'er jie* 道德尊經想爾戒 (Xiang'er Precepts of the Scripture of the Worthy of the Dao and Its Virtue) and the second group of twenty-seven called *Daode zun jingjie* 道德尊經戒 (Scriptural Injunctions of the Worthy of the Dao and Its Virtue)

2. *Taishang jingjie* 太上經戒 (Scriptural Injunctions of the Most High; CT 787), 17b–19a, under the title *Laojun ershiqi jie* 老君二十七戒 (Twenty-Seven Precepts of Lord Lao)

3. *Yaoxiu keyi jielü chao* 要修科儀戒律鈔 (Excerpts from the Essential Litur-

gies and Observances; CT 463), 5.4b–5b, under the title *Sanshiliu jie* 三十
六戒 (The Thirty-Six Precepts)

However, the most convenient way of consulting the Chinese text is in
Ōfuchi Ninji's edited version (1991, 254–57).

One of the main concerns of the precepts is with maintaining religious
orthodoxy. Thus, the recipient of the precepts is enjoined "not to delight in
deviance," "not to study deviant texts," or "not to pray or sacrifice to demons
and spirits." Similarly, their behavior should maintain discipline in "not acting
recklessly," "not pampering the body with good food and fine clothes," and
"not being obstinate." In several cases the precepts appear to repeat the same
message, or similar messages. Thus the fourth of the nine insists that the
recipient of the precepts practices "lacking fame," while the twelfth of the
twenty-seven prohibits the practitioner from "seeking fame"; the fifth prohibits
"envying the fame of others" and the fourteenth insists on "taking a humble
position." Similarly the first of the nine (in Bokenkamp's interpretation of the
wei 為 of *wuwei* being taken as "artificial, contrived, fabricated, false," 1997,
51) insists on lacking falseness, while the sixth of the twenty-seven prohibits
practicing false arts. This lends credence to the conjecture that the total number
of precepts, as well as their subdivisions, is numerologically significant.

Benjamin PENNY

📖 Bokenkamp 1993; Bokenkamp 1997, 48–58; Chen Shixiang 1957, 50–57;
Ōfuchi Ninji 1991, 247–308

※ *Laozi Xiang'er zhu*; *jie* [precepts]; Tianshi dao

xianglu

香爐

incense burner

Burning incense is an act of crucial importance in Taoist rites. Rituals can take
place without statues or scrolls representing the deities and without memorial
tablets, but not without an incense burner placed at the center of the sacred
space. Similarly, the offering of incense during the worship of the deities is
of far greater importance than the offering of tea or wine.

The offering of incense in Taoism has its origins in the "roasted offerings"
(*fanchai* 燔柴) of ancient China. Under Buddhist influence, both ideas about
incense and the variety of its types grew in complexity. During the Six Dynasties,

Fig. 80. Worshipper in the Wenchang gong 文昌宮 (Wenchang Palace), northern section of
Taichung, Taiwan (November 1977). Photograph by Julian Pas.

the Way of the Celestial Masters (*Tianshi dao) used "quiet chambers" or "oratories" (*jingshi) for their ritual practices, along the western wall of which an incense burner was always placed. According to the *Yaoxiu keyi jielü chao* 要修科儀戒律鈔 (Excerpts from the Essential Liturgies and Observances; CT 463), a large-scale "quiet chamber" had a two-storied Hall for the Veneration of Emptiness (*chongxu tang* 崇虛堂) in its center, and on the upper story stood a large incense burner measuring five feet in height. In Taoist rituals in modern Taiwan, a large incense burner is placed in front of the portraits of the Three Clarities (*sanqing) on the central table of the altar (the Cavern Bench, *dong'an* 洞案). During the rite of Lighting the Incense Burner (*falu), a hand-held burner (*shoulu* 手爐) is used by the high priest (*gaogong* 高功; see *daozhang), and incense burners are also placed before each deity.

In the logic of the ritual, incense performs a mediating function, enabling communication with the deities. Different names are given to it to describe its various functions. According to Wang Qizhen's 王契真 *Shangqing lingbao dafa* (Great Rites of the Numinous Treasure of Highest Clarity; CT 1221, 54.21b–22b), the "incense of the Way" (*daoxiang* 道香) represents the heart (*xin), the "incense of Virtue" (*dexiang* 德香) represents spirit (*shen), the "incense of non-action" (*wuwei xiang* 無為香) represents the intention (*yi), and the "incense of clarity and quiescence" (*qingjing xiang* 清靜香) represents the body (*shen* 身). Also, the "Wondrous Cavern incense" (*miaodong xiang* 妙洞香) transports the spirit of the Taoist priest to attend the morning audience in the Golden Portal of the Three Heavens (Santian jinque 三天金闕). The same work (56.10a–11a) gives spells for the offering of incense.

Burning incense is also important in Chinese folk beliefs. Incense is invariably offered when venerating ancestors and deities. Even if there is nothing else to represent a deity, an incense burner (the container) and the "incense fire" (*xianghuo* 香火, i.e., fire, smoke, ash) are necessary. The spiritual power of the deity dwells in the "incense fire," and by dividing the incense this power can be shared. When the "incense fire" for the burner at a shrine is to be renewed, the formal pilgrimage to transport it there is called "offering the incense" (*jinxiang) or "partitioning the incense" (*gexiang* 割香). In group worship, it is usual to have someone in charge of the incense (*luzhu* 爐主, "master of the burner") who is selected through divination.

MARUYAMA Hiroshi

📖 Feuchtwang 1992, 126–35 and passim; Huang Meiying 1994; Ōfuchi Ninji 1983, 225–27

※ *falu; jinxiang*

xianren

仙人

immortal; transcendent

A *xianren* is a person who has attained immortality and may possess supernormal powers such as the ability to fly. The word *xian*, now represented by the graph 仙, was originally attached to the graph 僊, which denotes the idea of "transfer" or "relocation," and refers specifically to ascending to Heaven by moving one's arms as wings.

Early descriptions of immortals can be found in the *Shiji* (Records of the Historian). For instance, the "Fengshan shu" 封禪書 (Book of the *Feng* and *Shan* Ceremonies; *j.* 28) describes how Qin Shi huangdi (r. 221–210 BCE) "toured the eastern seaboard, made sacrifices to illustrious mountains and great rivers, and sought out companions of the immortal Xianmen [Gao] 羨門 [高]." Elsewhere, the *Shiji* (*j.* 6) tells how *Xu Fu reported to Qin Shi huangdi that there were three mountains in the middle of the ocean called *Penglai, Fangzhang 方丈, and Yingzhou 瀛洲, inhabited by immortals, and asked that young men and women be sent to search them out, having first purified themselves and kept the precepts.

In early times, the paradise of the immortals was said to be located on islands that could not be easily approached (as in the above example) or on the peak of a steep mountain that would not permit easy access for ordinary mortals. Later, this paradise was thought to be in Heaven. The *Zhuangzi says: "After a thousand years of life, he grows weary of the world: he departs and rises up, and riding on a white cloud he reaches the realm of the [Celestial] Emperor" (chapter 12; see trans. Watson 1968, 130) This shows that the germ of the idea that the abode of the immortals was in Heaven had sprouted by the end of the Warring States.

In the *Shiji* accounts such as those referred to above, the immortals are entirely removed from the human realm. There was no thought that ordinary people could become immortals through cultivation or effort. Other than occasional stories in which a mortal either found his way to the abode of the immortals by some miraculous luck, or happened to meet an immortal who gave him the elixir of immortality, the way to eternal youth and life was closed. Even the elixir was something that could only be given; it could not be discovered or compounded by human beings. Later, however, the distance between ordinary people and immortals somehow narrowed,

Fig. 81. Early representation of immortals as winged beings walking on clouds and holding a *zhi ("numinous mushroom") in their hands. Source: Nanyang Wenwu yanjiusuo 1990, fig. 171.

and immortals were drawn closer within the reach of men. Now the immortal had come within human ken, since in principle anyone could gain immortality through his own effort (for an example of this view, see the entry *Shenxian kexue lun). Nonetheless, even *Ge Hong, who strongly asserted that "one's fate is in one's own hands, not in Heaven" (wo ming zai wo bu zai tian 我命在我不在天; *Baopu zi 16), could not escape saying that whether one's life is long or short depends on whether it falls under a good star (Baopu zi 7).

When Taoist religion emerged from the womb of conceptions such as those outlined above, changes were also wrought in the world of the immortals. An earthly bureaucratic system was projected into the celestial realm of the immortals, and differences in status were devised for them. In general, ranking descended from celestial immortals (tianxian 天仙) through earthly immortals (dixian 地仙) to immortals who had obtained "release from the corpse" (*shijie). They were associated with the celestial realm, the mountains (Grotto-Heavens, *dongtian), and the underworld, respectively. Becoming an immortal and gaining eternal youth and deathlessness was difficult beyond measure, yet Taoists in the Six Dynasties period developed a path for the majority of human beings who died without becoming immortal. They were able to achieve immortality from the status of *gui* (spirits). Such were the lowest ranked of all immortals, called *guixian* 鬼仙.

MIURA Kunio

📖 DeWoskin 1990; Girardot 1987b; Robinet 1984, 1: 163–66; Robinet 1986b; Robinet 1993, 42–48; Schipper 1993, 160–66; Sofukawa Hiroshi 1993; Yamada Toshiaki 1983b, 335–36

※ *shengren*; *shenren*; *zhenren*; TRANSCENDENCE AND IMMORTALITY

xiantian

先天

"before Heaven"; "prior to Heaven"; precelestial

See *xiantian* and *houtian* 先天 · 後天.

xiantian and houtian

先天 · 後天

"before Heaven" and "after Heaven"; "prior to Heaven" and "posterior to Heaven"; precelestial and postcelestial

Xiantian and *houtian* are two key notions in the Chinese view of the cosmos. The terms are sometimes translated "former Heaven" and "later Heaven," but occurrences of the phrase *xian tiandi sheng* 先天地生 ("generated before Heaven and Earth") in the *Daode jing*, the *Zhuangzi*, and other early texts show that *xiantian* and *houtian* designate the ontologic and cosmogonic stages before and after the generation of the cosmos.

In one of the Chinese accounts of cosmogony, Original Pneuma (*yuanqi*), or Pure Yang (*chunyang* 純陽), generates the cosmic pneuma (*qi*) through the union of Original Yin and Yang (*yuanyin* 元陰 and *yuanyang* 元陽), also known as Real Yin and Yang (*zhenyin* 真陰 and *zhenyang* 真陽). Cosmic pneuma then once more divides itself to form the cosmic Yin and Yang, or Heaven and Earth (this stage corresponds to the "opening of Heaven," *kaitian* 開天). Yin and Yang immediately join together again, leading to the final stage of creation, the "ten thousand things" (*wanwu* 萬物). "Before Heaven" refers to the stage before precosmic Yin and Yang join together, while "after Heaven" is the stage after they join and generate the cosmic pneuma. A notable aspect of this process is that the original, precosmic Yin and Yang are each enclosed within their opposites in the cosmos. This notion is referred to by the phrases "Yin within Yang" (*yang zhong zhi yin* 陽中之陰) and "Yang within Yin" (*yin zhong zhi yang* 陰中之陽).

A similar representation of cosmogony is seen in the *xiantian* and *houtian* arrangements of the eight trigrams (*bagua*), the first of which is traditionally attributed to the legendary emperor Fu Xi 伏羲 and the second to King Wen of the Zhou (Wenwang 文王, r. 1099–1050 BCE; see fig. 20). The *xiantian* diagram reproduces the stage after Original Yin and Yang (*kun* 坤 ☷ at due North and *qian* 乾 ☰ at due South) have joined their essences and have generated the trigrams *li* 離 ☲ and *kan* 坎 ☵ ("Yin within Yang" and "Yang within Yin") at due East and West; the other four trigrams are placed at the intermediate points. Here the cosmos is generated after *li* and *kan* attract each other and join their inner lines. In the *houtian* arrangement, the positions originally occupied by *qian* and *kun* are taken by *li* and *kan*, to show that the shift from the unconditioned to the conditioned state has occurred, and that Original Yin is now found within cosmic Yang (the trigram *li* or Fire), and Original Yang within cosmic Yin (the trigram *kan* or Water).

Fabrizio PREGADIO

📖 Lagerwey 1987c, 14–16

※ *jing, qi, shen*; *yuanqi*; COSMOGONY; COSMOLOGY

Xianyuan bianzhu

仙苑編珠

Paired Pearls from the Garden of Immortals

The *Xianyuan bianzhu* (CT 596) is a three-chapter anthology of selections from the lives of immortals by Wang Songnian 王松年, a Taoist monk from Mount Tiantai (*Tiantai shan*, Zhejiang). Judith M. Boltz (1987a, 59) dates the text to "sometime after 921." Some of these selections come from named preexisting collections of immortals biographies, such as the *Liexian zhuan* (Biographies of Exemplary Immortals); some come from named collections that have been lost such as the *Daoxue zhuan* (Biographies of Those who Studied the Dao); and some selections are not ascribed to any text.

The *Xianyuan bianzhu* has proved invaluable as a source for the reconstruction of texts that no longer survive and other bibliographical studies. The "paired pearls" of the title refers to the manner of citation where the extract from each of two biographies was listed under one heading ("Duzi changes shape, Guifu alters his appearance" or "Immortal Ge—Lingbao, Lord Wang—Shangqing"), or occasionally where two characters from the same original biography appear in the one extract. This method of citation was borrowed later by the *Sandong qunxian lu* (Accounts of the Gathered Immortals from the Three Caverns).

Benjamin PENNY

📖 Boltz J. M. 1987a, 59; Chen Guofu 1963, 240–41

※ HAGIOGRAPHY

Xiao Fudao

蕭 輔 道

fl. 1214–52; *zi*: Gongbi 公弼; *hao*: Dongying xiansheng 東瀛先生
(Elder of the Eastern Ying Island)

Xiao Fudao, the fourth patriarch of the *Taiyi jiao, seems to have been born in the family of Xiao Baozhen 蕭抱珍 (?–1166), the founder of this order. He became patriarch when the third patriarch, Xiao Zhichong 蕭志冲 (1151–1216, born in the Wang 王 family), chose him as his successor. Thus he did not have to change his name to be adopted and lead this very centralized, family-like order.

Xiao's official career had a difficult beginning. In 1232–34 the Mongol armies vanquished the remnants of the Jin empire in the Yellow River valley. The main Taiyi shrine, the Taiyi wanshou guan 太一萬壽觀 (Abbey of Ten-thousand-fold Longevity of the Great One; renamed Taiyi guangfu wanshou gong 太一廣福萬壽宮 or Palace of Vast Happiness and Ten-thousand-fold Longevity of the Great One in 1252) in Jixian 汲縣 (just north of the river in present-day Henan) was destroyed and Xiao was compelled to go southward into exile. He probably lived in the *Taiqing gong (Palace of Great Clarity), located at Laozi's supposed birthplace, which was managed by the Taiyi jiao before it shifted to *Quanzhen's control in the 1250s. Xiao returned to his ancestral seat some twenty years later, when the situation had calmed down, and rebuilt the temple, which seems to have then become a major ordination center. Xiao gained the attention of Khubilai, who was then only the brother of the Mongol Emperor and managed a fiefdom in present-day Hebei. Khubilai visited the Taiyi wanshou guan himself, and heaped honors on Xiao and the whole Taiyi order. Xiao Fudao died shortly thereafter, and was succeeded by

Xiao Jushou 蕭居壽 (1221–1280, born Li 李), who had been his disciple since the age of eleven. These two patriarchs witnessed the greatest development of the Taiyi order.

Vincent GOOSSAERT

※ Taiyi jiao

Xiao Yingsou

蕭應叟

fl. 1226; *hao*: Guanfu zi 觀復子 (Master Observing the Return)

Xiao Yingsou was an important Southern Song scholarly ritual master whose commentary to the *Duren jing (Scripture on Salvation), the Duren shangpin miaojing neiyi* 度人上品妙經內義 (Inner Meaning of the Wondrous Scripture of the Upper Chapters on Salvation; CT 90), stresses the importance of *neidan* for understanding this central *Lingbao scripture. Its memorial of presentation to the emperor bears the date 1226, and an essay on the scripture's cardinal meaning refers to the commentaries included in *Chen Jingyuan's (?–1094) *Duren shangpin miaojing sizhu* 度人上品妙經四注 (Four Commentaries to the Wondrous Scripture of the Upper Chapters on Salvation; CT 87), while stressing a mode of interpretation grounded in *neidan* theories and practices. The first chapter draws parallels between the Song ritual innovation known as the *Lingbao dafa (Great Rites of the Numinous Treasure) and the *neidan* tradition, and includes part of a preface to the scripture said to be composed by Song Zhenzong (r. 997–1022). Xiao's commentary, meanwhile, uses traditions of the *Yijing and microcosm-macrocosm analogies to link the *Duren jing* to *neidan*. The *neidan* diagrams found in Xiao's exegesis (preface, 6b–9b) are comparable with those in *Zhang Yuchu's (1361–1410) annotated *Duren jing (Duren shangpin miaojing tongyi* 度人上品妙經通義; CT 89, 1a and 4.26b–27a).

Lowell SKAR

📖 Boltz J. M. 1987a, 206 and 210

※ Lingbao dafa; *neidan*

Xiaodao lun

笑道論

Essays to Ridicule the Dao

Zhen Luan 甄鸞 (fl. 535–81), an official charged with investigating and impeaching officials in the capital, compiled the *Xiaodao lun* at the behest of Wudi (r. 560–78), ruler of the Northern Zhou dynasty. Between April 16 and May 2 of 569 the emperor convened three conferences of Buddhist monks, Taoist priests and Confucians as well as civil and military officials to discuss the merits of the three teachings: Taoism, Buddhism and Confucianism. The discussants tended to be defensive about the doctrines that they favored so they failed to produce the consensus that the emperor desired. It was his wish that they supply him with a synthesis of the tenets based on Taoism that he could employ to unify the empire ideologically. After the last meeting, Emperor Wu commissioned Zhen, who was a mathematician and astronomer, to carefully calculate the profundity and truth of Buddhism and Taoism. Ten months later, on March 7 of 570, Zhen submitted the *Xiaodao lun* in three fascicles to the throne. The work, a polemic against Taoism, did not please Emperor Wu so he summoned his ministerial corps on June 28 and ordered the officials to scrutinize the text. They concluded that it was deleterious to Taoism. The emperor agreed and ordered the work burned in the courtyard of a palace hall. Zhen made three mistakes in composing his work. First, he misjudged Emperor Wu's motives in commanding him to write the essays. Second, he violated the emperor's instructions by omitting virtually any consideration of Buddhism. Third, he adopted a provocative style of rhetoric that deliberately mocked Taoism. The latter, in particular, opened him to the charge that he was intent on maligning Taoism, and was no doubt the fundamental reason that the ministers condemned his treatise. Although the full text went up in flames, the author preserved an abbreviated version, about one-third of its original size, that still survives today in the *Guang hongming ji* 廣弘明集 (Expanded Collection Spreading the Light of Buddhism; T. 2103, 143c–152c; on this text see under *Hongming ji*).

The *Xiaodao lun* has thirty-six sections, corresponding to the sum total of the twelve subdivisions for the Three Caverns (*SANDONG) of the *Daozang* in the sixth century. Each section consists of two parts. The first is a citation or two from Taoist scriptures, hagiographies, codes, precepts, hymns, or catalogues. The second begins with the phrase, "I ridicule this saying . . . ," and contains

Zhen's attacks on the passages cited in the first. The topics covered include Taoist cosmogony, cosmology, chronology, theogony, demonology, mythology, scriptures, ritual, Laozi's conversion of the barbarians, the Buddha as an avatar of Laozi, immortality, clerical robes, Buddhism as a source of disorder in China, salvation, and sexual practices.

Zhen Luan was a polemicist intent on destroying Taoist pretensions. His focus, however, was narrower than that. He had no objections to the *Daode jing*, that is to Taoist thought, nor to the tenets of the *Shangqing order, the most esteemed in Taoism. His targets were the *Lingbao order that had been the most vigorous in adopting Buddhist doctrines, and the Celestial Master (*Tianshi dao) scriptures and texts related to the "conversion of the barbarians" theory (see *Huahu jing*). Zhen saw Taoist attempts to incorporate Buddhist doctrines as inept and ludicrous plagiarisms, which of course in some sense they were. Lingbao Taoists and others were attempting to capitalize on the immense popularity of Buddhism to further their own ends, but they had a poor understanding of what they imitated, and what they absorbed often contradicted their own native ideas. Zhen took issue with Celestial Master tenets because they favored magic in the form of talismans (*FU) and incantations and because they employed sexual rites of "merging pneumas" (*heqi*). However, Zhen's real object of scorn was the Taoist assertion that Laozi traveled west to "convert the barbarians" and became the Buddha. He was in reality a polemicist attacking a polemic since Taoists were attempting to assert their supremacy over Buddhism on the basis of the doctrine.

Zhen was apparently not a devout Buddhist, but he preferred its doctrines of *karma* and retribution over Taoist notions of immortality. For the most part he was a secularist who attacked Taoist doctrines on rational and textual grounds. He challenged Taoist assertions by exposing contradictions found in their scriptures, anachronisms that the texts contained, unbelievable exaggerations that they asserted, and mathematical and astronomical errors that they made in their cosmology.

In the main, the *Xiaodao lun* is a minor text in comparison with the large Buddhist polemics of the Tang. However, it is important because it contains some citations from Taoist scriptures now lost as well as variations in passages that have survived, and because it demonstrates that there was opposition to Emperor Wu's drive to construct an imperial ideology based on Taoism within his own bureaucracy.

Charles D. BENN

📖 Chen Guofu 1963, 235; Kohn 1995a (trans.); Lagerwey 1981b, 21–28

※ TAOISM AND CHINESE BUDDHISM

xin

心

heart; mind; heart-mind; spirit; center

The term *xin* traditionally designates the ruler of the entire person or, more specifically, the heart as the organ of mental and affective life (hence its translation as "heart-mind"). It is the "master" or "ruler" (*zhu* 主) of ideas, thought, will, and desire: many words expressing mental or affective activities (e.g., **yi* 意 "intention, idea," *si* 思 "thinking," *ai* 愛 "love," and *wu* 惡 "hate") have *xin* as their semantic indicator. Buddhism, especially the Chan school, gave *xin* the sense of spirit (**shen*), making it a synonym of the Buddha-nature (*foxing* 佛 性 or *buddhatā*) and the Ultimate Truth, which is both universal and empty. From the seventh century onward the term took on that definition also in Taoism, especially within **neidan*. Moreover, as Buddhists had before them, Taoists came to say that creation (**zaohua*) issues from *xin*.

Xin as a physiological organ and as heart-mind. As a physiological organ, the heart is depicted as a lotus flower with three petals. It is said that the heart of a worldly person has five openings, the heart of an average person has seven, and the heart of a sage has nine. The heart is the abode of the spirit, and its "gates" are the mouth and tongue. It is called Crimson Palace (*jianggong* 絳 宮), which relates it to what is above: fire, Yang, south (represented on top in traditional Chinese cartography), the planet Mars, and everything that corresponds to the agent Fire (see **wuxing*). As the center, the heart is also related to the Northern Dipper (**beidou*), whose deities reside in it.

As the heart-mind, *xin* is the center of the human being and the master of the whole body. The body and heart-mind cannot be apart from each other, just as a ruler cannot exist without subjects, and vice versa. As long as one's *xin* is quiescent, vacuous, and balanced, it guards the celestial and spiritual energies and ensures long life, and internal as well as external harmony. Hence one should "empty" one's *xin* (*xuxin* 虛心) or be "without" *xin* (*wuxin* 無心), i.e., without intentional desires or thoughts that stray from the natural course of things. This axiom, which had been expressed since early times in the history of Taoism, remained fundamental in later times. Sometimes, however, the heart is also compared to a horse or a monkey that one must tame.

Being the center, *xin* represents the center of the world and is located in the three Cinnabar Fields (**dantian*). Hence there are three *xin*: a celestial one above that generates the essence (**jing*), a terrestrial one below that generates pneuma (*qi), and a human one in the middle that generates blood. In this view, the center of the body is not the spleen but the heart. Moreover, as it is also located in the head, xin also denotes what is on high. Whether it is above or in the center, these two locations are equivalent, as they are those of the master and the central "palace" of the body. Therefore the dyad mind-spirit / body (xinshen 心身) is analogous to the dyads pneuma / essence (qijing 氣精) and fundamental nature / vital energy (*xing and ming). In the dyad heart / kidneys (xinshen 心腎), the heart is Mercury or Dragon and the kidneys are Lead or Tiger (see *longhu); they are also paralleled with Heaven and Earth.

"Human spirit" and "spirit of the Dao." In *neidan* texts, xin takes on a new meaning. As the spirit, it inherits the duality of the Buddhist xin, which can be pure or deluded. Taoists adopted the Neo-Confucian formulation, which alludes to a sentence of the *Shujing* 書經 (Book of Documents; trans. Legge 1879, 61) in distinguishing between a "human spirit," or *renxin* 人心 and a "spirit of the Dao," or *daoxin* 道心. The "spirit of the Dao" is the Ultimate Truth, absolute and subtle and present in every human being. The "human spirit," on the other hand, is both the heart-mind and the spirit; it is weak and frail. *Renxin* and *daoxin*, nevertheless, are one and the same, as they are only two aspects of the Ultimate Truth: *renxin* is the function (*yong) and the mechanism (*ji) of *daoxin*.

In fact, as Taoist texts often state, xin is the Dao and the Dao is xin. The human xin is the heart-mind that is always in motion (dongxin 動心); it oppresses the true nature (xing) with thoughts and concerns. The xin of the Dao is the "radiant xin" (zhaoxin 照心) and must be distinguished from the heart-mind. The latter should be pacified, stilled, and emptied; its "fire" should move downward, which means, according to certain texts, that one should repress one's anger. The radiant xin, however, should be nourished. It is equated with wisdom (hui 慧) and awakening, as distinguished from intention (yi); but the two cannot be separated. Xin is the parcel of precosmic light that lies in the trigram kan 坎 ☵. Some authors also distinguish between the radiant xin or daoxin and the precosmic light called Heart of Heaven (*tianxin), which is represented by the hexagram fu 復 ䷗ (Return, no. 24).

The daoxin is variously located, usually between two organs: it is below and between the kidneys, or above and between the eyebrows, or in the center of the body as the heart. Below, it is found within the trigram kan 坎 ☵ (Yang within Yin), which contains Real Metal, the alchemical Lead. Above, it is within the trigram li 離 ☲ (Yin within Yang), Mercury or the alchemical Water contained in Fire. Being above, it is associated with pneuma (qi) and contains the spirit (shen) and the celestial soul (*hun); it forms a triad with the body (shen) that is associated with the essence (jing) and contains the earthly soul (*po), and with the "intention" (yi) that is the central component of the triad. In terms of time, the *daoxin* is the "gathering" (*cai* 採), the inaugural moment of the alchemical work, when the precosmic light must be captured. As a mediator, *xin* is the "second pass" or the second stage of the alchemical process, the sublimation of pneuma into spirit, which follows the sublimation of essence in pneuma, and precedes the sublimation of spirit into emptiness (*xu* 虛; see **neidan*). But in reality *xin* cannot be located either in space or in time. It is the Real Emptiness *(zhenwu* 真無; see **wu* and *you*) to be found in everyday existence and in the phenomenal world. Finding it means rejoining *daoxin* and *renxin*.

In so far as it is situated at the junction between movement and quiescence (**dong* and *jing*), Non-being and Being, *xin* is the Ultimateless or Infinite (**wuji*) that is before the Great Ultimate (**taiji*), before the beginning of the differentiation between movement and quiescence.

Isabelle ROBINET

📖 Despeux 1990, 230–36; Fukunaga Mitsuji 1969; Kamitsuka Yoshiko 1999, 338–60; Nivison 1987a; Robinet 1995a, 191–95; Robinet 1997b, 207–9

※ yi [intention]

xing

形

form, shape

The term *xing* refers to that which has an outline and a structure, and is consequently sensible and intelligible. The term does not share the Platonic flavor of the Western notion of "form," and does not refer to a reality separated from the sensory world or composed of an invariable essence, as it generally does in Western philosophy.

The emergence of *xing* is a major stage in the formation of the cosmos. Taoist texts often quote the sentence in the *Xici* 繫辭 (Appended Statements, a portion of the **Yijing*) stating that "what is anterior to form (or: "above the form," *xing er shang* 形而上) is the Dao, and what is subsequent to form (or: "below the form," *xing er xia* 形而下) are the concrete objects (*qi* 器)." In this sentence, *xing* marks a boundary between the Dao and the phenomenal world, despite the claim often made by Taoists that "the Dao is the phenomena and the phenomena are the Dao." In cosmogony, form issues from the Formless (*wuxing* 無形), which is a synonym of the Dao; it appears with the One or the Great Ultimate (**taiji*), both of which are defined as "the beginning of form." In other instances, form originates with the third of the five states of Chaos in the precosmic geneses called the Five Greats (*wutai* 五太), and comes after pneuma (*qi) and before matter (*zhi* 質; see *COSMOGONY). It emerges through a process of condensation and definition that proceeds from Heaven, the most subtle realm, to Earth, the physical world. In this process, *xing* generally comes after images (*xiang) and before names (*ming* 名).

Taoists have often debated whether the One itself has a form. Some texts, including the *Zhuangzi, state that is has no form. According to the **Laozi Heshang gong zhangju*, the One has no form but fashions the forms. Other authors distinguish between a formless One and a One that has form. Others maintain that the Great One (*Taiyi) pertains to the level of forms and names (*xingming* 形名).

Beyond these distinctions, forms—as well as images and names—are indispensable to know the reality of things, and to make them return (*fan) to Ultimate Truth. Accordingly, one of the main roles of Taoist scriptures is to reveal the forms and names of deities, heavens, mountains, and so forth. Some scriptures contain charts that represent the "real form" (or "true form," *zhenxing* 真形) of sacred places, i.e., their divine and secret shapes, in order to give access to them. Others are devoted to revealing the "real forms" of deities, which can take various shapes. Important scriptures like the **Wuyue zhenxing tu* (Charts of the Real Forms of the Five Peaks) result from the "mysterious contemplation" of sacred peaks by Daojun 道君, the Lord of the Dao; they are talismans (*FU) that contain labyrinthine drawings revealing the forms and names of the grottoes or "stone chambers" (*shiwu* 石屋) to which hermits withdraw (see fig. 78). Those who possess these scriptures can travel back and forth between Heaven and Earth.

Isabelle ROBINET

📖 Lagerwey 1986; Pregadio 2004; Robinet 1993, 21 and 29

※ *bianhua*; Dao; *lianxing*; COSMOGONY

xing and *ming*

性 · 命

inner nature and vital force

Chinese philosophers debated about human nature in an effort to determine wether it was good, bad, or mitigated in its essence. Their conclusions were meant to determine conceptions about modes of government and basic principles of society. To them, Taoists replied by contending that those who consider human nature to be good, bad, or a mixture of both have simply lost sight of its authentic aspect. They are unaware of the "truthful and empty" nature of the human being, its immobile and quiet essence, which the texts refer to as "cavern" (*dong* 洞) or "gate of all wonders" (*zhongmiao zhi men* 眾妙之門). The deluded have no knowledge of the fundamental cosmic nature which itself forms the basis of human nature. This nature is found in the "middle." It is not the "middle-balance" of Confucians, that is to say, the state achieved by superior people through the discipline of cultivation in which passions are meticulously harmonized and balanced. It is rather the "middle-center," which is the state preceding the burgeoning of passions, a prime Middle, that of the Great Ultimate (**taiji*) that exists before Heaven and gives to humans, before Heaven and before their conception, the "parcel of divine light" that constitutes "nature," "veritable, one, and divine."

Taoist alchemy (**neidan*) contrasts this nature with the "material nature" of which Neo-Confucians speak. Such a "material nature" is composed of "the father's semen and the mother's blood." In other words, it comes about as a result of copulation and birth according to natural laws. This nature is the "spirit of desire" which, although originally weak, grows progressively stronger by the day. Conversely, the "precelestial breath" tends to weaken as a person's small-mindedness grows. One must thus aim to reverse this process that will inevitably lead to decline and death, and nourish the "precelestial breath" until it becomes perfectly ripe. *Xing* ("nature") is thus the celestial self, a trace of transcendence.

The principle that corresponds to *xing* is that of *ming*, the vital force (the term also means "destiny" and "order," "mandate," or "decree"). *Xing* and *ming* are the Breath (**qi*) and Spirit (**shen*), the former in relation to the Earth, the latter to Heaven. It is said that "*xing* is the name given to the divine parcel that is contained within the precelestial supreme Spirit; *ming* is the name given to the parcel of Breath that is contained within the precelestial supreme Essence" (**Zhonghe ji*, 4.1a). For others, *xing* represents the Dao, quietude, while *ming* embodies the dynamic aspect of life. One is the foundation for the other, while the other is its expression and operation (see under **ti* and *yong*). They are two aspects of the Dao, which is transcendent; yet the Dao contains life and dispenses it, hence it is also immanent. While certain texts present *xing* as an intrinsic salvation that exists fundamentally within each of us, they similarly emphasize the importance of *ming*. In this case, *ming* is corporeality, a nature incarnate that requires practice or necessary effort through which *xing* is actualized. One cannot, they say, access *xing* without passing through *ming*. Thus are resolved debates about grace and predestination, about intrinsic and acquired nature.

Xing is also the celestial Yin that is found in the *li* 離 ☲ trigram (Sun, Fire, two Yang lines encasing one Yin line), and *ming* is the Yang element found in the *kan* 坎 ☵ trigram (Moon, Water, two Yin lines encasing one Yang line).

Thus, the conjunction of *xing* and *ming* is the dynamic of the descending celestial influx and its subsequent reascension from the earth. *Xing* and *ming* are therefore the "true Yin" and "true Yang," the Lead and Mercury of the kidneys and heart, which constitute the essential elements of the alchemical process.

Xing and *ming* can be considered as two distinct entities, situated at two extreme poles, which must circulate and unite; but they can also be regarded as a unity that is immersed in original Chaos. This unity is lodged in the Mysterious Pass (*xuanguan*), the dark gate leading to the return to the Source. It contains all elements of the alchemical work and is situated neither inside the body nor outside of it (although "searching for it outside the body is as searching for a fish or dragon outside of water, searching for the Sun and Moon somewhere other than the sky"). It is a mysterious point often compared to the "original face" (*benlai mianmu* 本來面目) of Chan Buddhism or to the "middle" (*zhong* 中) of the *Liji* 禮記 (Records of Rites). This point is said to belong to no time or moment, yet it is a "Yang" time (of light), the immaculate and ungraspable instant when a thought is born (see under *zi*); the point of emergence that is "the root of life and death." It is this instant of immobility that is at the center of all things. It is this atemporal instant that precedes the arising of both the interior and exterior worlds. It is the instant of infinite possibility that precedes all creative action. It is the original base of the entire universe, the alchemist's *materia prima*. As a text relates, this "middle" (*zhong*) in which one must situate oneself is the "center of the compass." It is neither internal nor external, yet it is at the center of the body and at the very center of the core of thought. That is the space that one must constantly occupy.

Isabelle ROBINET

📖 Despeux 1990, 223–27; Qing Xitai 1994, 2: 294–99; Robinet 1995a, 165–95 and passim

※ *shuangxiu*

xingdao

行道

Walking (*or*: Practicing) the Way

The term *xingdao* is used in texts of the Six Dynasties as a generic term for practicing Taoist methods, but especially with reference to the performance of ritual. It occurs for instance in the *Wushang biyao* (j. 26–27), in connection with the description of the uses of the five *Lingbao talismans, which are worn on the body of the practitioner, as he "cultivates virtue and walks the Way" (*xiude xingdao* 修德行道), and which will eventually confer immortality on him.

In the context of the *Wushang biyao*, the term *xingdao* refers to the activity of the priests in all major rituals, including the central rituals of communication (corresponding to the Three Audiences, *sanchao), the Nocturnal Invocation (*suqi), and the *jiao (Offerings) that form part of the Retreat of the Three Sovereigns (*sanhuang zhai* 三皇齋; *Wushang biyao* 49; Lagerwey 1981b, 152–56). The term has the same use in present-day ritual (see for instance Ōfuchi Ninji 1983, 273, 288, 300, 358). It is equally true, however, that over time the term had come to be associated in particular with the Three Audiences. The special sanctity of the Audiences (and by implication, of the term *xingdao*) was explained with reference to the idea that they were modeled on the gatherings in the Jade Capitol (Yujing 玉京) of all the gods in heaven, who supposedly come together three times a day in order to have an audience with the Celestial Worthy of Original Commencement (Yuanshi tianzun 元始天尊; *Shangqing lingbao dafa*, CT 1221, 57.1a; see also under *daochang).

Poul ANDERSEN

📖 Lagerwey 1981b, 125 and 150–56; Lagerwey 1987c, 106–7 and 121–23; Matsumoto Kōichi 1983, 218–20; Ōfuchi Ninji 1983, 273 and passim

※ *sanchao*

Xingming guizhi

性命圭旨

Principles of Balanced Cultivation of Inner Nature and Vital Force

The *Xingming guizhi*, also known as *Xingming shuangxiu wanshen guizhi* 性命雙修萬神圭旨 (Principles of the Joint Cultivation of Inner Nature and Vital Force and of the Ten Thousand Spiritual Forces), is a comprehensive *neidan text dating from the Ming period. Its authorship is ascribed to an advanced student of Yin Zhenren 尹真人 (Perfected Yin), but the identities of both master and disciple are unclear. After its first edition in 1615, it was published several times during the Qing dynasty and again in a recent but undated edition of the *Baiyun guan (Abbey of the White Clouds) in Beijing. Another edition is in the *Daozang jinghua lu. The text includes four prefaces, written by She Yongning 佘永寧 (sixteenth/seventeenth century, dated 1615), Zou Yuanbiao 鄒元標 (1551–1624, undated; on Zou see DMB 1312–14), You Tong 尤侗 (1618–1704, dated 1669), and Li Pu 李樸 (?–1670, dated 1670).

The *Xingming guizhi* is usually considered to be a document of the Northern Lineage (Beizong 北宗; see under *neidan) or the Central Branch (Zhongpai 中派) of Ming and Qing *neidan*. Its ideas are mainly based on *Li Daochun's (fl. 1288–92) *Zhonghe ji* (Anthology of Central Harmony) and on *Zhang Boduan's (987?–1082) *Wuzhen pian* (Folios on Awakening to Perfection), and are also closely related to *neidan* texts associated with the *Quanzhen school. Although the *Xingming guizhi* promulgates the joint cultivation (*shuangxiu) of inner nature and vital force (*xing and *ming*), it does not attach much importance to physiological practices and emphasizes the spiritual aspects of inner transformation. The four books into which the work is divided give an overview of all basic principles of *neidan*. The foundations, dealt with in the first book, are explained in more detail in the following three books, whose chapters are organized to correspond to nine stages of transformation of the adept. Each book contains three main chapters, and each of the latter deals with one alchemical phase. Several chapters contain illustrations accompanied by short texts, frequently in the form of rhyming poems.

Compared to earlier *neidan* texts, the *Xingming guizhi* is characterized by lengthy and detailed explanations, many illustrations, the explicit representation of nine stages of transformation, and a pronounced syncretistic tendency. It integrates Taoist, Confucian, and Buddhist ideas—in particular those of the Yogācāra school—along with numerous quotations from sources related to these three teachings. One of the main concerns of the *Xingming guizhi* is to lead the adept through the multitude of alchemical methods and writings to the core of the true path of *neidan*. This core is to be sought at the basis of all phenomena and is proof of the undivided unity and the unchanging nature of the Dao. The author approaches this core from a variety of perspectives, employing a wealth of concepts but always returning to the central theme. He does not give any practical instructions for practicing inner alchemy, however; in fact, he dissociates himself from specific exercises, as these belong to the phenomenal domain from which he tries to lead away his readers.

Martina DARGA

📖 Darga 1999 (part. trans.); Despeux 1979, 21; Little 2000b, 348–49; Liu Ts'un-yan 1970, 306; Needham 1983, 229

※ *neidan*

xingqi

行氣

circulating breath

Methods for circulating breath are attested during the period of the Warring States, became well known during the Six Dynasties, and developed during the Tang and Song periods. Their most ancient source is an inscription dating from ca. 300 BCE that describes the circulation of breath throughout the body (see Harper 1998, 125–26). In the Han period, circulating breath is mentioned in several texts, including the *Huangdi neijing* (*Lingshu* 靈樞, sec. 11.73).

Circulating breath is often associated with gymnastics (*daoyin) and breath retention (*biqi). It is generally performed in a reclining position for 300 breaths, before one expires the breath slowly and inaudibly. One begins with retaining breath for twelve breaths (the so-called "small cycle," *xiaotong* 小通), and then progresses up to 120 breaths (the "great cycle," *datong* 大通). Tang documents add to this classical model a circulation of inner breath in which Intention (*yi) plays a major role. This technique is described in the *Songshan Taiwu xiansheng qijing* 嵩山太無先生氣經 (Scripture on Breath by the Elder of Great Non-Being from Mount Song; CT 824, 1.5b–6a; trans. Huang Jane 1987–90, 19–22) and the *Huanzhen xiansheng fu nei yuanqi jue* 幻真先生服內元氣訣 (Instructions on the Ingestion of the Inner Original Breath According to the Elder of Illusory Perfection; CT 828, 3b–5a, and YJQQ 60. 17a–18b; trans. Despeux 1988, 72–75, from the version in the *Chifeng sui*).

Catherine DESPEUX

📖 Despeux 1988, 34–38; Hu Fuchen 1989, 290–94; Li Ling 2000a, 341–81; Maspero 1981, 473–74 and 484–95

※ *yangsheng*

Xinyin jing

心印經

Scripture of the Mind Seal

The *Xinyin jing* is a short *neidan scripture associated with the *Quanzhen school, and routinely read by Taoist masters every morning and evening. Its complete title is *Gaoshang Yuhuang xinyin jing* 高上玉皇心印經 (Scripture of the Mind Seal, by the Most Exalted Jade Sovereign), and it is said to have been spoken by the Great Lord of the Dao of the Golden Portal of Supreme Mysterious Eminence (Wushang Xuanqiong zhu Jinque Da daojun 無上玄穹主金闕大道君; see *Jinque dijun). It probably dates from the late Tang period.

Besides the edition without commentary entitled *Xinyin miaojing* 心印妙經 (Wondrous Scripture of the Mind Seal; CT 13), the *Daozang* also includes the *Jiuyou bazui xinyin miaojing* 九幽拔罪心印妙經 (Wondrous Scripture of the Mind Seal for Removing Faults in the Nine Shades; CT 74) and the *Jiuyao xinyin miaojing* 九要心印妙經 (Wondrous Scripture of the Mind Seal and Its Nine Essentials; CT 225), which bears a *neidan* commentary attributed to *Zhang Guolao. Four other editions with annotations are found in the *Daozang jiyao* (vol. 7):

1. *Gaoshang Yuhuang xinyin miaojing* 高上玉皇心印妙經 (Wondrous Scripture of the Mind Seal, by the Most Exalted Jade Sovereign), which includes eight commentaries.

2. *Zhongnan Bazu shuo Xinyin miaojing jie* 終南八祖說心印妙經解 (Explication of the Wondrous Scripture of the Mind Seal, by the Eight Patriarchs of Zhongnan).

3. *Gaoshang Yuhuang xinyin jing* 高上玉皇心印經 (Scripture of the Mind Seal, by the Most Exalted Jade Sovereign) by Baozhen zi 抱真子 (Master Who Embraces the Real; Five Dynasties).

4. *Yuhuang xinyin jing* 玉皇心印經 (Scripture of the Mind Seal, by the Jade Sovereign), with a commentary attributed to the Imperial Lord of the Mysterious Valley (Xuangu dijun 玄谷帝君) edited by Gao Shiming 高時明 of the Ming period.

The text, consisting of only fifty sentences of four characters each, teaches that by merging essence (*jing*) with spirit (*shen*), spirit with pneuma (*qi*), and pneuma with reality (*zhen* 真), one will naturally be filled with Great Harmony (*taihe* 太和).

SAKADE Yoshinobu

📖 Balfour 1884, 66–67 (trans.); Olson 1993

※ Yuhuang; *neidan*; Quanzhen

xinzhai

心齋

"fasting of the mind" (*or*: "fasting of the heart")

Chapter 4 of the *Zhuangzi* reports an imaginary dialogue between Yan Hui 顏
回 and Confucius. Yan Hui, who had been urged by Confucius to fast, replies
that he has not drunk wine or eaten spicy foods for several months and asks
whether this means that he has fasted. Confucius replies:

> That is the fasting you do before a ceremony, not the Fasting of the Mind. . . .
> Make your will one. Don't listen with your ears, but with your mind. Indeed,
> don't even listen with your mind, but with your pneuma (*qi*). Your ears are
> limited to listening and your mind is limited to tallying, but pneuma is empty
> and awaits all things. Since the Dao only gathers in emptiness, emptiness is the
> Fasting of the Mind. (See also trans. Watson 1968, 57–58)

In other words, Fasting of the Mind means releasing the mind of all cognitive
thought and desire, and maintaining an empty mind, a condition of non-self.
This state of mind and its practice also underlie the ideas of "mourning the
self" (*sangwo* 喪我) mentioned in chapter 2, "sitting in oblivion" (*zuowang*)
in chapter 6, and "guarding the One" (*shouyi*) in chapter 11 of the *Zhuangzi*.

In later times, the idea of Fasting of the Mind in the *Zhuangzi* was developed
in two main directions, as the practice of "fasting and keeping the precepts"
(*zhaijie* 齋戒) and as the practice of "restraining the mind" (*shouxin* 收心). To
understand these shifts in meaning, one has to consider that *zhai*, in addition to
"fasting," also means "purification practices" or "purification rites," and is also
the general term that designates Taoist rituals (see the entry *zhai*). "Fasting and
keeping the precepts" represents the incorporation of *xinzhai* into the system
of ritual and ethical rules. The *Zhaijie lu* (Register of Retreats and Precepts)
divides the practice of "fasting" into three components: accumulating virtue
and dispelling sin (*shegong zhai* 設供齋), harmonizing the mind and extending
the length of life (*jieshi zhai* 節食齋), and releasing the mind from desire and
defilements and suppressing cognitive thought (*xinzhai*). The first two could
be practiced by middle-rank practitioners, but the third was for those of the
highest achievement. (The same text is contained in other works, including
the *Liuzhai shizhi shengji jing* 六齋十直聖紀經, CT 1200, and the *Zhiyan zong*
至言總, CT 1033.) In *Liu Yiming's (1734–1821) *Xiuzhen biannan* 修真辨難
(Discussions on the Cultivation of Authenticity), six forms of "fasting" (of
the body, intention, eyes, ears, nose, tongue) are established, plus a seventh,

called "complete fasting of the mind's domain" (*xinjing yizhai* 心境一齋), which doubtless is influenced by the *Zhuangzi*'s idea of Fasting of the Mind.

*Sima Chengzhen's (647–735) *Zuowang lun* (Essay on Sitting in Oblivion) signals a different development of Fasting of the Mind, toward the practice of "restraining the mind." In modern times, *Chen Yingning (1880–1969) called this "listening to the breath" (*tingxi* 聽息) and attempted to revive it as a *qigong* practice. According to Chen, the *Zhuangzi* passage about the Fasting of the Mind can be interpreted as a five-stage training method. The five stages are:

1. "Making your will one." Concentrating the mind and freeing it of all extraneous thoughts.

2. "Don't listen with your ears, but with your mind." Here "listening" means listening to the sound of one's own breathing; since there is no sound, it is said to be "listening with the mind."

3. "Don't listen with your mind, but with your pneuma." The state in which mind and *qi* are one; however, some degree of sensation persists.

4. "Your ears are limited to listening and your mind is limited to tallying." What tallies with or attaches (*fu* 符) to the mind is the spirit (*shen), so this is the state in which *shen* and *qi* are one, and the intellect vanishes.

5. "Emptiness is the Fasting of the Mind." The last stage, spontaneous entry into the realm of emptiness, without self-consciousness.

MIURA Kunio

📖 Schipper 1993, 195–208; Soymié 1977

※ *xin*; MEDITATION AND VISUALIZATION

Xishan

西山

Western Hills (Jiangxi)

Of the many highlands named Xishan in China, arguably the most renowned are those found south of Lake Poyang 鄱陽. These hills, also known as Xiaoyao shan 逍遙山 and located about 15 km northwest of Nanchang (Jiangxi), contained the twelfth of thirty-six minor Grotto-Heavens and were known as the thirty-eighth node in the web of seventy-two Blissful Lands in China's religious geography (see *dongtian* and *fudi*).

At the spiritual center of these highlands and sanctuaries, however, is the shrine to the official from Sichuan *Xu Xun (trad. 239–374), who served in the area. The early shrine, called the Abbey of the Flying Curtain (Youwei guan 游帷觀), marked the site of Xu Xun's ascension. This was also the site of his cult's renewal by 682, which became an important movement known as the Pure and Bright Way (*Jingming dao). For Song and later adepts, it was the haunt of alchemist-poet *Shi Jianwu (fl. 820–35) and his preceptors, *Zhongli Quan and *Lü Dongbin. Both remained subordinate, however, to Xu's cult center at the *Yulong wanshou gong (Palace of the Ten-thousand-fold Longevity of Jade Beneficence) and the later movement known as the Pure and Bright Way of Loyalty and Filiality (Jingming zhongxiao dao 淨明忠孝道). All these developments occurred as northern Jiangxi experienced an economic, cultural, and spiritual ascension in late imperial China.

Lowell SKAR

📖 Schipper 1985d

※ Xu Xun; TAOIST SACRED SITES

Xishan qunxian huizhen ji

西山群仙會真記

Records of the Gathered Immortals and
Assembled Perfected of the Western Hills

The *Xishan qunxian huizhen ji* is the third main text of the *Zhong-Lü corpus, after the *Lingbao bifa* (Complete Methods of the Numinous Treasure) and the *Zhong-Lü chuandao ji* (Anthology of Zhongli Quan's Transmission of the Dao to Lü Dongbin). Besides the independent edition in the Taoist Canon (CT 246), the mid-twelfth-century *Daoshu* (Pivot of the Dao, j. 38) includes an abbreviated and slightly variant version.

This *neidan text is attributed to *Shi Jianwu (fl. 820–35), a famous poet and recluse of the Western Hills (*Xishan, Jiangxi), but its authorship is highly doubtful. The bibliographic treatise of the *Xin Tangshu* (New History of the Tang; van der Loon 1984, 160) mentions a Shi Jianwu from Muzhou 睦州 (Zhejiang) as the author of the *Bianyi lun* 辯疑論 (Essay on Resolving Doubts), a short work found in the Taoist Canon as the *Yangsheng bianyi jue* 養生辯疑訣 (Instructions on Resolving Doubts in Nourishing Life; CT 853, and YJQQ 88). Muzhou is also mentioned in Shi Jianwu's biography in the *Lishi zhenxian tidao tongjian* (45.3a–3b). The *Daoshu* and other sources, however, state that Shi came from Jiujiang 九江 (Jiangxi). The attribution of the *Qunxian huizhen ji* was already challenged in the Song period, with the *Zhizhai shulu jieti* 直齋

書錄解題 (Annotated Register of Books in the Zhizhai Studio; van der Loon 1984, 108) suggesting that the poet Shi Jianwu and the author of the present text are two different people. Internal evidence, in fact, shows that the *Qunxian huizhen ji* dates from after the late tenth century, as it mentions Zhang Mengqian 張夢乾 (1.6a) who, according to other sources, died in 998.

The work is divided into five *juan* that represent the *wuxing*. Each chapter is further arranged into five sections, corresponding to the five "pneumas" (*qi*) of each phase. The subjects discussed in the five *juan* are:

1. Recognition (*shi* 識), i.e., the ability to recognize the right Way, method, master, season, and ingredients.

2. Nourishment (*yang* 養) of the vital principle, body, pneuma, mind, and life span.

3. "Repairing" (*bu* 補) the damage to the interior organs, pneuma, seminal essence, and diminished vitality, through techniques of visualization and breathing.

4. The true alchemical ingredients, i.e., the authentic Dragon and Tiger (*longhu*), Lead and Mercury, Fire and Water, Yin and Yang.

5. Transmutation (or refining, *lian* 鍊) using methods to enter the authentic Way; transformation of the body into pneuma, of pneuma into spirit (*shen*), and the union of spirit with the Dao, with a final section that underscores the importance of transmitting the doctrine only to the right disciples.

The theory and practices described in the *Qunxian huizhen ji* are similar to those of the *Zhong-Lü chuandao ji*, another work ascribed to Shi Jianwu. The author often compares the methods of the Xishan adepts to those of the Zhong-Lü tradition, stating for instance that the technique for transforming pneuma into spirit is similar to the one described in the *Lingbao bifa*.

Farzeen BALDRIAN-HUSSEIN

📖 Akizuki Kan'ei 1978, 45–46; Boltz J. M. 1987a, 139; Qing Xitai 1994, 1: 301–3; Sakauchi Shigeo 1985, 40–44

※ *neidan*; Zhong-Lü

Xisheng jing

西昇經

Scripture of Western Ascension

The *Xisheng jing* can be dated to the late fifth century. It survives in two Song editions, one by *Chen Jingyuan of the eleventh century entitled *Xisheng jing jizhu* 西昇經集注 (Collected Commentaries to the Scripture of Western Ascension; CT 726) and one by Song Huizong (r. 1100–1125) simply entitled *Xisheng jing* (CT 666). The former consists of six *juan* and contains five commentaries, which were edited independently during the Song.

The *Xisheng jing* is first mentioned in connection with the theory of the "conversion of the barbarians" (*huahu* 化胡; see *Huahu jing*), because it begins with Laozi's emigration to India and is connected with the transmission of the *Daode jing* to *Yin Xi. It seems, however, that the text was never primarily a conversion scripture but rather employed the motif of the emigration as a framework narrative for an essentially mystical doctrine, which was closely based on the *Daode jing* and couched in the form of oral instructions given by Laozi to Yin Xi.

The text has thirty-nine sections, which can be divided into five parts. First, it establishes the general setting, narrates the background story, outlines Yin Xi's practice, and discusses some fundamental problems of talking about the ineffable and transmitting the mysterious. Next, the inherence of the Dao in the world is described together with an outline of the way in which the adept can make this inherence practically useful to himself or herself. A more concrete explanation of the theory and practice, including meditation instruction, is given in the third part. The fourth part deals with the results of the practice and with the way of living a sagely life in the world. The fifth and last part is about "returning" (*fan); it describes the ultimate return of everything to its origin, and explains the death of the physical body as a recovery of a more subtle form of participation in the Dao.

The history of the text can be glimpsed through the five commentaries extant in Chen Jingyuan's edition. The oldest is by Wei Jie 韋節 who, according to his Yuan-dynasty biography (*Lishi zhenxian tidao tongjian*, 29.4a), lived in north China from 497 to 559 (Kohn 1991a, 167–87). He was originally a Confucian official who struck up a friendship with the Taoist master Zhao Jingtong 趙靜通 of Mount Song (*Songshan, Henan) while serving in a district close by. He spent many years writing commentaries to a large variety of texts, including the *Yijing, the *Lunyu* 論語 (Analects) of Confucius, the *Miaozhen jing* 妙真經 (Scripture of Wondrous Truth), and the *Xisheng jing*.

The second commentator is Xu Miao 徐邈 (or Daomiao 道邈) from Jurong 句容 near Nanjing (Jiangsu), the place of origin of the *Shangqing revelations in 364–70. He presumably was a descendant of the Xu brothers who transcribed the revelations granted to *Yang Xi by the immortal lady *Wei Huacun and other divine beings. He cites the *Zhengao of *Tao Hongjing in his commentary, which dates his life to at least the sixth century. Otherwise not much is known about him; *Du Guangting mentions him as a Taoist of the early Tang, and he was supposedly a disciple of *Wang Yuanzhi, one of the early Shangqing patriarchs. The third commentator is Chongxuan zi 冲玄子 (Master of the Unfathomable Mystery, fl. ca. 650), otherwise unknown. Fourth is *Li Rong, Daode jing commentator and *Chongxuan (Twofold Mystery) philosopher of the mid-seventh century. Fifth, finally, is Liu Renhui 劉仁會, a Taoist of the mid-to-late Tang, about whom information is scarce. In addition to the five commentaries, the Xisheng jing is cited frequently in mystical texts of the Tang.

Livia KOHN

📖 Kohn 1991a; Kohn 1992a, 130–38; Kusuyama Haruki 1979, 411–17; Maeda Shigeki 1989; Maeda Shigeki 1990a; Maeda Shigeki 1990b

※ Laozi and Laojun

xiu

宿

[lunar] lodges, [lunar] mansions

In the Western tradition of astronomy, one of the most familiar sets of celestial reference points are the signs of the zodiac, "[the circle of] the living creatures." These twelve equal divisions of the sun's annual cycle through the constellations along the great circle known as the ecliptic are each 30° in extent. They are named after the constellations (Aries the Ram, Taurus the Bull, Gemini the Twins, etc.) which more or less coincided with these divisions over two thousand years ago, but which have long since shifted out of position due to precession.

In China, however, the most ancient identifiable stellar reference system was quite different. This was the system of the ershiba xiu 二十八宿 or "twenty-eight lodges" (see table 26). The term xiu has often been translated into English as "lunar mansions" or "lunar lodges" but since in reality the xiu system has no closer links with the moon than with the sun or any other moving celestial body, it is best to use a translation close to the root meaning of xiu as "a place of [temporary] residence."

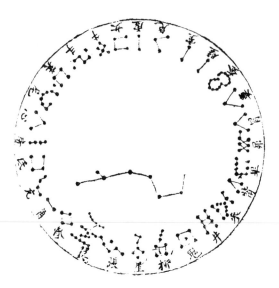

Fig. 82. The twenty-eight lunar lodges (*xiu*) arranged
around the Northern Dipper (**beidou*). *Wuliang duren
shangpin miaojing pangtong tu* 無量度人上品妙經旁通圖
(Supplementary Illustrations to the Wondrous Scripture of
the Upper Chapters on Limitless Salvation; CT 148), 2.1b.

Like the zodiac, the lodges were named after actual constellations—and
as is well known, the constellations of the traditional Chinese sky were quite
different from those of the West. Exactly when the whole system originated is
very unclear: it is obviously unsafe to base any conclusions on the occurrence
in early texts of just a few constellation names out of the whole twenty-eight.
The earliest evidence for the complete set of constellations comes from a
decorated box-lid found in the tomb of Zeng Hou Yi 曾侯乙 (Duke Yi of Zeng,
Hubei) dated from 433 BCE, in which they are shown as a rough circle centering
on the constellation of the Northern Dipper (*Ursa Major*, see **beidou*).

The earliest clear evidence for how the lodges were actually used in astronomy comes from the *Yueling* 月令 (Monthly Ordinances), a text preserved
in the *Lüshi chunqiu* 呂氏春秋 (Springs and Autumns of Mr. Lü), which was
assembled in 239 BCE. In this text we are told which of the lodges is "centered"
(*zhong* 中, i.e., seen in the sky directly due south) at dusk and at dawn for
each of the twelve months of the year. This provided an easy running check
of whether the lunar calendar was running in step with the seasons, with no
need for astronomical instruments (apart from a north-south sight line or
"meridian") or time-keeping devices. By around 100 BCE there is clear evidence
that astronomers were using water-clocks to time how long it took each lodge
to cross their meridians, and as a result it was possible to give each lodge a
"width" measured in Chinese degrees, *du* 度 (365¼ *du* = 360°). Any celestial

Table 26

East

1	jiao	角	Horn
2	kang	亢	Neck
3	di	氐	Root
4	fang	房	Room
5	xin	心	Heart
6	wei	尾	Tail
7	ji	箕	Winnowing-Basket

North

8	dou	斗	Dipper
9	niu (qianniu)	牛 (牽牛)	Ox [*or*: Ox-Leader]
10	nü (shunnü)	女 (須女)	Maid [*or*: Serving-Maid]
11	xu	虛	Emptiness
12	wei	危	Rooftop
13	shi (yingshi)	室 (營室)	Encampment
14	bi	壁	Wall

West

15	kui	奎	Stride
16	lou	婁	Bond
17	wei	胃	Stomach
18	mao	昴	Pleiades
19	bi	畢	Net
20	zi	觜	Turtle-Beak
21	can	參	Alignment

South

22	jing	井	Well
23	gui (yugui)	鬼 (輿鬼)	Spirit [*or*: Spirit-Bearer]
24	liu	柳	Willow
25	xing (qixing)	星 (七星)	[Seven] Stars
26	zhang	張	Extension
27	yi	翼	Wings
28	zhen	軫	Chariot-Platform

The twenty-eight lunar lodges (*xiu*). Translations based on Major 1993, 127.

body that crosses the meridian while a lodge is crossing it is said to be in that lodge. In modern terms it could be said that each lodge represented a slice of the celestial sphere in right ascension—although the concept of the celestial sphere is not required in order to use the lodge system. The lodges were highly unequal in extent, with widths varying from as little as 2 *du* to more than 30 *du*. The reasons for this are not clear, and the historical and geographical origin of the system is obscure. Modern scholars tend to discount any link with the Indian system of twenty-eight *nakṣatras*.

Unlike the case of the zodiac, the lodges always remained tied to their original constellations. As the effects of precession shifted the celestial pole, this meant that the widths of lodges shifted during the centuries, and from time to time it was necessary to change the choice of stars used to mark the beginning of each one.

Christopher CULLEN

📖 Cullen 1996, 35–66 passim; Kalinowski 1991, 71–73; Little 2000b, 128 and 249; Needham 1959, 229–62; Schafer 1977a, 79–84

※ COSMOLOGY

Xiuzhen shishu

修真十書

Ten Books on the Cultivation of Perfection

Consisting of ten "writings" (shu 書) assembled in the late thirteenth or early fourteenth centuries, this sixty-juan compendium (CT 263) includes many important texts associated with *Bai Yuchan (1194–1229?) and his circle. It is the largest collection of *neidan teachings, and most of its texts date from two generations before *Zhang Boduan (987?–1082) to two generations after Bai Yuchan. Although most of these practices involve inner cultivation and meditation, exercise and ritual also have an important place.

The collection includes the following works:

1. *Zazhu zhixuan pian* 雜著指玄篇 (Folios Pointing to the Mystery by Various Authors; j. 1–8), containing writings and diagrams related to Bai Yuchan and his teachings.

2. *Jindan dacheng ji* (Anthology on the Great Achievement of the Golden Elixir; j. 9–13), with writings by Xiao Tingzhi 蕭廷芝 (fl. 1260–64, Bai Yuchan's second-generation disciple).

3. *Zhong-Lü chuandao ji* 鍾呂傳道集 (Anthology of Zhongli Quan's Transmission of the Dao to Lü Dongbin; j. 14–16), ascribed to *Shi Jianwu 施肩吾 (fl. 820–35).

4. *Zazhu jiejing* 雜著捷徑 (Shortcuts [to Realization] by Various Authors; j. 17–25), containing writings by Zeng Zao 曾慥 (?–1155), *Yu Yan 俞琰 (1258–1314), and others.

5. *Wuzhen pian* (Folios on Awakening to Perfection; j. 26–30), by Zhang Boduan 張伯端 with commentaries by Ye Wenshu 葉文叔 and Yuan Shu 袁樞 (1131–1205).

6. *Yulong ji* 玉隆集 (Anthology of [the Abbey of] Jade Beneficence; *j.* 31–36), containing hagiographies related to the *Xu Xun cult on the Western Hills (*Xishan, Jiangxi). This and the following two texts are by Bai Yuchan and his disciples.

7. *Shangqing ji* 上清集 (Anthology of [the Abbey of] Highest Clarity; *j.* 37–44), with texts related to the *Zhengyi (Orthodox Unity) order of Mount Longhu (*Longhu shan, Jiangxi).

8. *Wuyi ji* 武夷集 (Anthology of [the Abbey of Mount] Wuyi; *j.* 45–52), with texts related to ritual activities in northern Fujian.

9. *Panshan yulu* 盤山語錄 (Conversation Records of [Wang] Panshan; *j.* 53), by *Wang Zhijin 王志謹 (1178–1263) and his disciples, especially Lun Zhihuan 論志煥 (fl. 1247). The text is a rearrangement of the *Panshan Qiyun Wang zhenren yulu* 盤山棲雲王真人語錄 (Recorded Sayings of the Perfected Wang Qiyun from Mount Pan; CT 1059).

10. *Huangting jing* 黃庭經 (Scripture of the Yellow Court; *j.* 54–60), with two Tang commentaries by Liangqiu zi 梁丘子 (fl. 729) on the "Inner" and "Outer" versions of the text, and a related work by Hu Yin 胡愔 dated 848.

Lowell SKAR

📖 Boltz J. M. 1987a, 234–37; Chen Guofu 1963, 285–86; Qing Xitai 1994, 2: 160–62

※ *neidan*

Xiwang mu

西王母

Queen Mother of the West

Even in modern times, Xiwang mu lives on in folk custom and popular religion with the Peach Festival (*pantao hui* 蟠桃會) of the third day of the third lunar month, and as Wang mu niangniang 王母娘娘 (Damsel Mother of the West), the wife of the Jade Emperor (Yudi 玉帝). She has an ancient pedigree, appearing in the *Shanhai jing* 山海經 (Scripture of Mountains and Seas; fourth/third century BCE?; trans. Mathieu 1983, 100, 481, and 587–88), where, however, there is no consistency about the place where she is supposed to live: on the Jade Mountain (Yushan 玉山), or north of Mount *Kunlun, or on Mount Kunlun itself. She appears as a fearsome deity, with a human face, tiger's teeth, a panther's tail, and hair flowing in cascades around her. She lives in a cave and brings pestilence to the world. By contrast, an episode in the *Zhushu jinian* 竹書紀年 (Bamboo Annals; originally ca. 300 BCE) describes how King Mu of Zhou (Muwang, r. 956–918 BCE) travelled west in the seventeenth year of his reign to meet her at the Kunlun mountain. The same year, Xiwang mu was entertained at his court. The *Mu tianzi zhuan* 穆天子傳 (Biography of Mu, Son of Heaven; ca. 350 BCE; trans. Mathieu 1978, 44–49) gives a vivid description of the banquet held by Xiwang mu for King Mu on the banks of the Turquoise Pond (Yaochi 瑤池), on which occasion the two exchanged poems. In hers, Xiwang mu identified herself as "the daughter of the Celestial Emperor (Tiandi 天帝)." Thus, unlike the *Shanhai jing*, the *Zhushu jinian* and the *Mu tianzi zhuan* portray her in a more human form, with a close connection to the rulers of this world.

During the Han period, the idea developed that Xiwang mu brought good omens to congratulate earthly rulers who had brought about to the realm. At the same time, her character as a savior was strengthened, and in 3 CE, a frenzied cult among people seeking world renewal grew up around her; it spread through twenty-six prefectures and provinces, extending even to the capital Chang'an (Loewe 1979, 98–101). It was during the Han dynasty also that her male counterpart, Dongwang gong 東王公 (King Lord of the East), made his appearance (Qing Xitai 1994, 3: 48–52). By the Six Dynasties period, as can be seen in works such as the *Bowu zhi* 博物志 (Monograph on Various Matters; third century), *Han Wu gushi* 漢武故事 (Ancient Stories of [Emperor] Wu of the Han; sixth century?) and *Han Wudi neizhuan (Inner Biography of Emperor Wu of the Han; sixth century), she had taken on the characteristics of a Taoist deity or immortal and occupied a position within the Taoist genealogy of divine beings. The episode of Xiwang mu bestowing the peaches of immortality on Han Wudi is famous in Chinese literature and folklore. In *Tao Hongjing's *Zhenling weiye tu (Chart of the Ranks and Functions of the Real Numinous Beings), she is classed as a Real Woman (*nüzhen* 女真) of second rank. In *Du Guangting's *Yongcheng jixian lu (Records of the Immortals Gathered in the Walled City), a collection of biographies of female immortals, she is given the role, as Yuanjun 元君 (Original Princess), of supervisor of all female immortals.

Xiwang mu and Dongwang gong are also known as Jinmu 金母 (Mother of Metal) and Mugong 木公 (Lord of Wood), respectively, from the names of the two agents associated with West and East (see *wuxing*).

YOSHIKAWA Tadao

📖 Cahill 1986a; Cahill 1986b; Cahill 1993; Despeux 1990, 43–49; Fracasso 1988; James 1995; Kohn 1993b, 55–63; Kominami Ichirō 1991; Little 2000b, 154–59 and 276–77; Loewe 1979, 86–126; Loewe 1987; Maspero 1981, 194–96; Schipper 1965; Seidel 1982, 99–106; Wu Hung 1987

※ *Han Wudi neizhuan*; DEITIES: THE PANTHEON; TAOISM AND CHINESE MYTHOLOGY; TAOISM AND POPULAR RELIGION

Xu Fu

徐福

fl. 219–210 BCE; *zi*: Junfang 君房; also known as Xu Shi 徐市

Xu Fu was a *fangshi* from Qi 齊 (Shandong). He submitted a memorial to Qin Shi huangdi (r. 221–210 BCE) in 219 BCE asking for children who could help him fetch herbs of immortality from *Penglai and other isles of the blessed in the eastern seas. The emperor presented him with several thousand (*Shiji*, 6.247). In the ensuing years, they went out to sea together, but to no avail. In 210 BCE, Xu Fu defended his efforts by claiming that a large fish prevented them from reaching the isles. The emperor gave him more equipment and even went out to sea himself to slay the fish (*Shiji*, 6.263).

Xu Fu's story captured people's imagination early on, as shown in the embellished account told to Liu An 劉安 (see *Huainan zi*) around 124 BCE, where Xu Fu sets himself up as a king in the east (*Shiji*, 118.3086). Perhaps the earliest textual source describing him as an immortal is the *Shizhou ji* (Record of the Ten Continents), a Six Dynasties text which relates that he was sent to find the life-restoring herb from Zuzhou 祖洲, one of the ten continents. He and 500 boys and girls sailed out, never to return. This tale is repeated in all subsequent accounts of Xu Fu in the Taoist Canon. Xu Fu also appears in the *Shenxian zhuan* (YJQQ 109.6b–7b; Campany 2002, 256–57).

Chinese sites associated with Xu Fu are found in Xuzhou 徐州 (Jiangsu) and especially the Laoshan 嶗山 district of Qingdao 青島 (Shandong). Legends about Xu Fu abound in Japan, where he is reputed to have landed in Kumano 熊野 (Kishū). There is also a tomb of Xu Fu in Shingū 新宮 (Wakayama), and another legend has him buried in Aomori Prefecture. The belief that Xu Fu transmitted Chinese culture to Japan has generated a large number of studies about him, both in Japanese and Chinese. Some, however, are wildly speculative, arguing for example that Xu Fu actually became the legendary first Japanese emperor, Jinmu (Wei Tingsheng 1953; Peng Shuangsong 1983; Peng Shuangsong 1984).

Thomas E. SMITH

📖 An Zhimin et al. 1990; Davis and Nakaseko 1937; Needham 1976, 17–19; Shandong Jiaonan Langya ji Xu Fu yanjiuhui 1995; Yamamoto Noritsuna 1979

※ HAGIOGRAPHY

Xu Jia

徐甲

Xu Jia is a fictional character who appears first in the *Shenxian zhuan* biography
of Laozi (trans. Campany 2002, 194–211) as the servant hired to accompany the
sage to the western lands. According to the story, by the time they reach *Yin
Xi's pass, Laozi owes Xu millions of cash, and the latter, seeing that Laozi is
indeed leaving China, decides he wants to stay home after all and demands his
money, which Laozi does not have. Instigated by a servant on the pass who
wants his daughter to marry Xu and get rich, Xu files a complaint against Laozi
before Yin Xi, who confronts the sage. Laozi, however, does not comply but
shouts at the servant that he should have been dead long ago and has only
remained alive with a talisman Laozi gave him. When Laozi takes back the
talisman, Xu Jia collapses in a heap of bones and is only revived and sent on
his way upon Yin Xi's pleas for mercy.

The story appears variously in the literature, adding a different twist to
Taoist myth each time. Its earliest version in the *Shenxian zhuan* shows Laozi as
a master of wondrous arts, controlling life and death with magic and talismans
(*FU). In sixth-century ordination materials, such as the *Wenshi neizhuan* 文
始內傳 (Inner Biography of Master Wenshi; Kohn 1997b, 109–13), it contrasts
the dedicated selfless Taoist (Yin Xi) with the greedy shaman (Xu Jia), emphasizing the priority of universal salvation over any material gain one could
achieve. In the seventh-century *Taishang hunyuan zhenlu* 太上混元真錄 (Real
Account of the Most High Chaotic Origin; CT 954), the episode appears as a
test for Yin Xi, to make sure of his sympathy for weaker beings and his ability
to stand up in a crisis as the representative of the Dao. *Du Guangting, in his
Daode zhenjing guangsheng yi 道德真經廣聖義 (Extended Interpretation of
the Emperor's Exegesis of the *Daode jing*; 901; CT 725), adds that Laozi had
raised Xu Jia from the dead even before he became his servant, having found
him as an exposed skeleton lying on the roadside.

In the Song hagiographies (*Youlong zhuan, *Hunyuan shengji), Laozi himself turns into the beautiful woman who seduces Jia in order to test both his
servant and Yin Xi. A modern story, collected by Kristofer Schipper in Tainan
in the 1970s, has Xu Jia start out as a dead skeleton who is then revived by
Laozi. The sage trains Xu in elementary Taoist methods but puts him to the
test by placing him into a seductive setting and the company of a beautiful
lady. Xu fails, succumbs to the woman's charms, and is punished by waking
up in a deserted graveyard. Despairing, he recites whatever spells come to

mind, without paying any attention to ritual purity and even while performing physical necessities. Laozi appears. He scolds Xu furiously and gives him two basic ritual implements, a buffalo horn and a bell, leaving him to practice the Dao in this primitive way—thus creating the Red-head (*hongtou* 紅頭) branch of Taoist priests (see *hongtou* and *wutou*) and giving legitimacy even to shamanic practice within the Taoist religion. In each variant, the story thus reflects the key concerns of Taoists at the time, while also documenting the continued aliveness of myths within the tradition.

Livia KOHN

📖 Kohn 1998b, 260–64; Schipper 1985e, 37–46

※ Laozi and Laojun; HAGIOGRAPHY

Xu xianzhuan

續仙傳

Sequel to Biographies of Immortals

The *Xu xianzhuan* (CT 295) was compiled by Shen Fen 沈汾 (or 沈玢) who lived under the Southern Tang dynasty (923–36). Internal evidence from the biography of *Nie Shidao in this collection implies that Shen lived in the state of Wu 吳 (Jiangsu and part of Zhejiang), one of the ten statelets (*shiguo* 十國) of the Five Dynasties, known at that time as Yangwu 楊吳. There is a short account of him in the *Jiang Huai yiren lu* 江淮異人錄 (Accounts of Extraordinary Men from Jiang and Huai; CT 595) that simply says he came from the end of the Tang.

The collection is divided into three chapters: the first contains sixteen biographies of those who have "ascended in flight" (*feisheng* 飛昇), the second has twelve biographies of those who "transformed in secret" (*yinhua* 隱化), with eight more secret transformers in the third.

The recipients of biographies in this collection are largely from the Tang period and are often important figures in non-religious history who receive notices in other secular and religious sources, including the Standard Histories. Indeed, the *Xu xianzhuan* is the first collection of immortals' biographies in which some of its sources are still extant. The biographies of Zhang Zhihe 張志和, Xie Ziran 謝自然, and Xu Xuanping 許宣平 derive from the hand of Yan Zhenqing 顏真卿 (709–85), Han Yu 韓愈 (768–824; IC 397–40), and Li Bai 李白 (Li Bo, 701–62) respectively, as the editors of *Siku quanshu* 四庫全書 (Complete Writings of the Four Repositories) noted. In addition, Liu Su's 劉

蕭 *Da Tang xinyu* 大唐新語 (New Sayings of the Great Tang) appears to be the source for the biography of *Sima Chengzhen, at least in part.

Benjamin PENNY

📖 Chen Guofu 1963, 240; Kirkland 1986a, 204–5, 247–50, and 274–75; Qing Xitai 1988–95, 2: 417–21

※ HAGIOGRAPHY

Xu Xun

許遜

trad. 239–374; *zi*: Jingzhi 敬之

Centuries of hagiographic lore surrounding Xu Xun convey a complex, often enigmatic, portrait of a divinely endowed healer, dragon-slayer, and exemplar of filiality active in the central Yangzi river basin area. The *Yulong wanshou gong (Palace of the Ten-thousand-fold Longevity of Jade Beneficence) dedicated to him at the Western Hills (*Xishan, Jiangxi) continues to be a popular site of pilgrimage. At this very location in 682, a Celestial Master named Hu Huichao 天師胡惠超 (?–703) succeeded in reviving a *Lingbao form of ritual practice known as Xiaodao 孝道 (Way of Filiality) that honored Xu as its founding father. Imperial patronage of the abbey escalated in 1112 when Song Huizong (r. 1100–1125) authorized the title Shengong miaoji zhenjun 神功妙濟真君 (Perfected Lord of Divine Merit and Wondrous Deliverance), endorsing Xu's role as a national guardian. By the late thirteenth century, Xu gained lasting recognition as the patriarch of an eclectic school of teachings known as Jingming zhongxiao dao 淨明忠孝道 (Pure and Bright Way of Loyalty and Filiality).

Accounts of Xu Xun's life vary according to changing perceptions of his divine destiny over time. Many reflect the assimilation of lore concerning the figures with whom he is said to have been associated. Xu's ancestry is commonly traced to the legendary recluse Xu You 許由 who, according to the story told in *Zhuangzi, declined ruler Yao's 堯 plea to take over the command of his kingdom. With the impending fall of the Han empire, Xu Xun's father Xu Su 許肅 is said to have fled from the family home in Xuchang 許昌 (Henan) south to Nanchang (Jiangxi). Xu's birth nearly twenty years later reportedly followed a prophetic dream of his mother Lady Fu 符氏. One hagiographic excerpt recorded in the *Yiwen leiju* 藝文類聚 (Categoric Collection of Literary Writings) of 624 claims that Xu lost his father at the age of seven and thereafter selflessly devoted himself to looking after his mother. The formative event of his youth is acknowledged overall to be the time he proved his skill in archery by bringing down a doe near parturition. Xu is said to have immediately cast aside his bow and arrow when he saw the dying animal licking its abruptly delivered offspring. He then turned to a broad course of study, ranging from the Classics and history to the art of cultivating refinement (*xiulian* 修鍊).

According to hagiographic convention, Xu went to Xi'an at the age of twenty to study with Wu Meng 吳猛 (?–374?), popularly recognized as one of the twenty-four paragons of filiality (*ershisi xiao* 二十四孝). Wu is said to have conveyed a set of prescriptions to Xu that he had earlier received from a physician named Ding Yi 丁義. This bestowal led Xu to concentrate on the contemplative pursuit of cultivating refinement at a retreat on Mount Xiaoyao (Xiaoyao shan 逍邀山) in the Western Hills range, allegedly established with Guo Pu 郭璞 (276–324). In the year 280 Xu was induced to leave his refuge to serve as Magistrate of Jingyang 旌陽 (identified as Zhijiang 枝江 in Hubei or, by the early fourteenth century, as Deyang 德陽 in Sichuan). There he reportedly gained widespread support for his compassionate form of government based on instruction in the fundamental values of filiality and honesty (*xiaolian* 孝廉). The story is also told of how countless residents in the Jingyang area and beyond also benefited from Xu's talismanic remedy for a deadly strain of pestilence.

Xu eventually left his post in anticipation of the collapse of the Western Jin empire (265–316). The journey back to Xishan provides the setting for many tales recounting his extraordinary ability to recognize and successfully combat malevolent forces, especially entrenched flood demons. Another remarkable episode concerns a female adept named Chen Mu 諶姆 to whom Xu and Wu paid homage at Danyang 丹陽. Their visit putatively gave her the opportunity to designate Xu as heir to the Xiaodao mingwang zhi fa 孝道明王之法 (Rituals from the Luminous Sovereign of the Way of Filiality), to fulfill the prophecy of her teacher Langong 蘭公. The story behind Xu's role as patriarch of Xiaodao thus elevates him to a position above his teacher Wu Meng.

Xu's devotions in the end were rewarded by a summons to join the ranks of transcendents on high. Operatic and artistic works have immortalized the vision of his ascent at Xishan, leading some forty-two members of his household, together with chickens and dogs. The earliest surviving intact hagiography dates the event to the second year of (Western) Jin Yuankang (292). Dominant hagiographic tradition claims that Xu Xun was one-hundred thirty-six years of age at the time, which corresponds to the second year of (Eastern) Jin Ningkang (374). The ascent allegedly occurred on the fifteenth day of the eighth lunar month, traditionally observed as the Mid-Autumn Festival (*zhongqiu jie* 中秋節), and is still commemorated at shrines honoring Xu Xun. Patrons of contemporary enshrinements include followers of the Lüshan 閭山 and Sannai 三奶 schools of ritual, both of which claim Xu Xun as their source of authority. Later generations of devotees also stand behind various ritual manuals and oracular verse (*qian* 籤) transmitted in the name of Xu Xun.

Two early hagiographic accounts about Xu and eleven disciples, lost texts attributed to Hu Huichao and Yu Bian 余卞 (fl. 1086–1125), presumably lie behind extant and largely derivative compilations. Aside from accounts in the *Jingming zhongxiao quanshu* (Complete Writings of the Pure and Bright [Way of] Loyalty and Filiality) and in assorted general hagiographic anthologies, the Taoist Canon contains the following individually printed biographies of Xu Xun:

1. *Xiaodao Wu Xu er zhenjun zhuan* 孝道吳許二真君傳 (Biography of Wu and Xu, the Two Perfected Lords of the Way of Filiality; CT 449), post 819;

2. *Jingyang Xu zhenjun zhuan* 旌陽許真君傳 (Biography of the Perfected Lord Xu of Jingyang) in the *Yulong ji* 玉隆集 (Anthology of [the Abbey of] Jade Beneficence) of *Bai Yuchan (1194–1229?), with supplements (*Xiuzhen shishu*, j. 33–36);

3. *Xishan Xu zhenjun bashiwu hua lu* 西山許真君八十五化錄 (Record of the Eighty-Five Metamorphoses of the Perfected Lord Xu of the Western Hills; CT 448), dated 1250;

4. *Xu zhenjun xianzhuan* 許真君仙傳 (Biography of Perfected Lord Xu; CT 447), post 1295;

5. *Xu Taishi zhenjun tuzhuan* 許太史真君圖傳 (Illustrated Biography of the Perfected Lord and Grand Scribe Xu; CT 440), post 1295.

Judith M. BOLTZ

📖 Akizuki Kan'ei 1978, 3–47; Boltz J. M. 1987a, 70–78; Little 2000b, 314–18; van der Loon 1984, 73, 127, 138, and 169; Schipper 1985d; Wang Ka 1996; Zhang Zehong 1990

※ Yulong wanshou gong; Xishan; Jingming dao; HAGIOGRAPHY

xuan

玄

mystery, mysterious; dark; arcane; remote

The primary connotation of *xuan* is the color of heaven or of the mountains seen from far away; hence the meaning of "dark" and "remote." Based on

Daode jing 1, where *xuan* refers to the mysterious origin and development of the world, Taoist authors have glossed this term as "profound and subtle," "obscure and silent," "absence of anything," "unspeakable," or "wondrous" (*miao* 妙) in the sense of unfathomable. *Ge Hong and others take *xuan* as a synonym of Dao, as the term also indicates the Primordial Unity before the distinction between Non-being and Being (*wu and *you*; *Daode zhenjing guangsheng yi* 道德真經廣聖義, CT 725, 4.9a). Some, including *Cheng Xuanying, equate *xuan* with the state of non-attachment and absence of obstructions. The term is also often paired with *xu* 虛 (void, emptiness), and as such it is defined as the mysterious conjunction of two complementary and opposite entities: Fire and Water, emptiness and existence, or inner nature and vital force (*xing and *ming*). As its meaning is close to *yuan* 元 (Origin), it has been substituted by the latter when the character *xuan* was tabooed, as in *Wang Bi's commentary to the *Daode jing* and in texts dating from almost the entire span of the Qing dynasty.

Xuan also appears in other compounds with related meanings. It is a synonym of Heaven in the compound *xuanhuang* 玄黃 or Mysterious and Yellow, which designates primordial Chaos (*hundun*), i.e., the state in which Heaven (*xuan*) and Earth (*huang*, yellow being the color of Soil in the *wuxing system) are still merged as a single entity. Similarly, in the expression *xuanpin or Mysterious Female (*Daode jing* 6), "mysterious" refers to Heaven and "female" to Earth according to the *Laozi Heshang gong zhangju* and other later commentaries. *Xuantong* 玄同 (Mysterious Equality) is often used to indicate the state of mystical oblivion and fusion with the Dao.

In other contexts, *xuan* denotes the Taoist teaching itself and appears in the name of some Taoist lineages and trends of thought. *Xuanxue (lit., Dark Learning or Mysterious Learning) is the name of a school of thought that flourished during the Six Dynasties; *Chongxuan (Twofold Mystery) is a school of commentaries on the *Daode jing*; and *Xuanjiao (Mysterious Teaching) is a Taoist institution created under the Mongols. The term *xuanmen* 玄門 (Gate of Mysteries) is also a name of Taoism itself.

Finally, in cosmogony, *xuan* is the name of the third of the three original pneumas (see under *sanyuan*).

Isabelle ROBINET

📖 Qing Xitai 1994, 2: 256–59; Yu Shiyi 2000, 59–91; Zhang Dainian 1994

※ Dao; *wu and *you*

Xuandu baozang

玄都寶藏

Precious Canon of the Mysterious Metropolis

To avoid confusion with the *Da Jin Xuandu baozang (Precious Canon of the Mysterious Metropolis of the Great Jin), the Xuandu baozang of 1244 has alternatively come to be known as the Da Yuan Xuandu baozang 大元玄都寶藏 (Precious Canon of the Mysterious Metropolis of the Great Yuan). The direct heir of its Jurchen namesake, this new Canon is the product of the *Quanzhen lineage that won a significant following in the Mongol empire. Variant accounts of how it evolved are found in biographical records of the Quanzhen patriarchy, many of which were composed as stele inscriptions.

The task of organizing this editorial venture was taken on by *Song Defang (1183–1247), disciple of the renowned Quanzhen patriarch *Qiu Chuji (1148–1227). It is unclear what may have led Song to initiate the compilation of a new Canon. He is said to have acted in response either to his late master Qiu's encouragement, to an imperial decree, or to a command issued in 1235 by Qiu's designated successor *Yin Zhiping (1169–1251). Work on the project reportedly began in 1237, with headquarters established in Pingyang 平陽 (Shanxi) at the Xuandu guan 玄都觀 (Abbey of the Mysterious Metropolis). Pingyang was at that time a well-established center of publication. Grand Councilor Hu Tianlu 胡天祿, provincial administrator, offered Song his support by granting a significant amount of cash to help fund the retrieval of lost scriptures.

Song put his disciple Qin Zhi'an 秦志安 (1188–1244) in charge of a network of local offices where several hundred people were employed as collators. The single Canon to which they are said to have had recourse was found in the former Jurchen outpost of Guanzhou 管州 (Shanxi). Among titles Qin himself contributed to the new Canon is a hagiography of the Quanzhen lineage, entitled *Jinlian zhengzong ji (Records of the Correct Lineage of the Golden Lotus). Others known to have served as members of the editorial staff include Mao Yangsu 毛養素 (1178–1259), He Zhiyuan 何志淵 (1189–1279), and Li Zhiquan 李志全 (1191–1256). When it was completed in 1244, the new Canon reportedly came to a total of 7,000 juan. Over one-hundred sets of the Xuandu baozang were printed for distribution. Following the death of Song Defang, the blocks of the Canon were transferred to the site of his burial, the Chunyang wanshou gong 純陽萬壽宮 (Palace of Ten-thousand-fold Longevity of Pure Yang), precursor of the *Yongle gong (Palace of Eternal Joy) in Ruicheng 芮城 (Shanxi).

By 1282, most texts as well as the printing blocks themselves were apparently destroyed upon the command of Khubilai khan (r. 1260–94). Fragments of the *Yunji qiqian (Seven Lots from the Bookbag of the Clouds) from the *Xuandu baozang* are in the National Library of Beijing and the National Palace Museum of Taipei. A copy of the *Taiqing fenglu jing* 太清風露經 (Scripture of Great Clarity on Wind and Dew) from the Canon, which came up missing in the Ming Canon, is also in the National Library of Beijing. These surviving texts from the *Xuandu baozang* are all printed on sheets of paper with thirty columns of seventeen characters each, matching the format of Song editions of the Buddhist Canon printed in the south. In similar fashion, the Yuan Canon also added a column in small print to each sheet providing: 1. serial identification according to the *Qianzi wen* 千字文 (Thousand-Word Text), 2. running title, 3. chapter and sheet numbers, and 4. the block-cutter's name. The names of more than twenty block-cutters have been found on the few fragments of the Canon thus far uncovered.

Judith M. BOLTZ

📖 Chen Guofu 1963, 160–74; Chen Yuan 1988, 486–87, 534–35, 546–49, 581–82, 613–14, and 652–53; Cleaves 1960; van der Loon 1984, 50–57; Zhu Yueli 1992, 152–54

※ Song Defang; DAOZANG AND SUBSIDIARY COMPILATIONS

Xuandu guan

玄都觀

Abbey of the Mysterious Metropolis (Chang'an)

The Xuandu guan was an important Taoist foundation of the late sixth century which still survived, less prominently, in the ninth. Wudi (r. 560–78), emperor of the Norther Zhou, used it as a base for the compilation of a definitive catalogue of the Taoist Canon, completed in 570 (Kohn 1995a, 218–19), and lectured there himself in 572; thereafter it seems to have formed the nucleus for his *Tongdao guan, which incorporated non-Taoist scholars also. With the restoration of Buddhism and the subsequent creation of the new capital of Chang'an by the Sui in 582, the Xuandu guan reappeared, a solely Taoist institution recreated out of the Tongdao guan, but balancing geographically a large Buddhist monastery, the recipient of much more significant imperial patronage. Now Wang Yan 王延 (520–604), a former Tongdao guan Taoist who had catalogued the earlier institution's vast library, was in charge, and it remained associated with bibliographical activities. Thus the only surviving manuscript of the *Laozi bianhua jing (Scripture of the Transformations of Laozi; *Dunhuang manuscript S. 2295), apparently composed in the late Han yet otherwise completely unknown, was collated by one of its Taoists in 612, according to the colophon. After the Sui, the abbey lost its importance.

T. H. BARRETT

📖 Chen Guofu 1963, 108–10; Lagerwey 1981b, 15–20; Yamazaki Hiroshi 1967a

※ Tongdao guan; TEMPLES AND SHRINES

Xuandu lüwen

玄都律文

Statutes of the Mysterious Metropolis

This sixth-century collection of Celestial Masters (*Tianshi dao) rules (CT 188) contains sets of statutes governing Taoist behavior: 1. Statutes on good and evil, emptiness and Non-being (1a–3a); 2. Statutes on precepts and recitations (3a–5a); 3. Statutes on the hundred remedies (5a–8a); 4. Statutes on the hundred diseases (8a–11a); 5. Statutes on organization and ritual (11a–18b); 6. Statutes on the presentation of petitions (18b–22a).

The first set consists of lists of the types of good and bad fortune one will experience if one commits good or evil deeds, numbering from one to one thousand. It introduces the list with a definition of thirteen desirable states (e.g., emptiness, Non-being, purity, tranquillity, subtlety, and simplicity) and thirteen beneficial attitudes or personal characteristics that will lead to immortal perfection, emphasizing that anybody who fails to comply with these will be punished by heaven.

The second set has twelve rules on concrete ritual practices, such as the visualization of gods, the chanting of scriptures, and the eating of sacrificial food, as well as the ritual schedule and attitudes toward teachers and family. It begins with a list of the undesirable attitudes of a deceiving nature, such as taking evil for good, crooked for straight, pure for turbid, and so on. Each statute, moreover, is associated with a particular punishment, usually the subtraction of 400 days from the life span.

The third and fourth sets each consist of one hundred entries focusing on the idea of sickness and healing. They begin by mentioning the celestial administration, specifying that the Director of Transgressions (Siguo 司過) reports all misdeeds while the Director of Destinies (*Siming) shortens the life span.

The fifth section has twenty-seven items of communal and ritual import, specifying subtractions of reckoning days (*suan* 算) and periods (*ji* 紀) from the life span for various improper actions, such as not following inheritance procedures when receiving transmission from one's father, squabbling over transmission after the death of a master, failure to attend assemblies or pay the right amount of dues, seeking fast promotion, making mistakes in setting out banquets, creating disturbances during the Three Assemblies (*sanhui), and so on. Punishments range from a subtraction of 200 days to three periods.

The last set of statutes consists of sixteen items focusing on the presentation of ritual petitions in the communal worship hall. They discuss entering the sacred space on the right day and at the right hour, properly purified and attired in ritual vestments, and performing the rite for the sake of the entire community and not for personal gain. In each case, failure to comply with a given statute results in a reduction in rank by one or two notches, a subtraction of days from the life span, or a visitation by sickness for a given number of days.

Livia KOHN

📖 Kobayashi 1990, 206–7; Sivin 1999a (part. trans.)

※ *jie* [precepts]; Tianshi dao

xuanguan

玄關

Mysterious Pass

In *neidan, the Mysterious Pass represents the time and place in which an alchemist joins the complementary antinomies on which he or she works, such as inner nature and vital force (*xing* and *ming*), Dragon and Tiger (*longhu*), lead and mercury, Fire and Water, heart and kidneys, or *kan* 坎 ☵ (Yang within Yin) and *li* 離 ☲ (Yin within Yang). The *neidan* texts often mention the One Opening of the Mysterious Pass (*xuanguan yiqiao* 玄關一竅) as a synonym of the Mysterious Female (*xuanpin), the Door of Life and Death (*shengsi hu* 生死戶), or the "border between divinity and humanity" (*tianren jie* 天人界), to designate the Center where Non-being and Being (*wu and *you) pervade each other (for a clear statement see *Liu Yiming's *Xiangyan poyi* 象言破疑 or *Smashing Doubts on Symbolic Language*; trans. Cleary 1986a, 80–81).

The Mysterious Pass, which opens beyond space and time, is inconceivable by means of discursive thought and has, by definition, no fixed position. Nevertheless, certain texts devoted to the description of the *neidan* practice place it in specific loci of the body defined as "dual" (*shuang* 雙), which allow the instantaneous manifestation of the One. These texts accordingly state that, at the beginning of the alchemical work, one can locate the Mysterious Pass between the two kidneys (the Gate of the Vital Force, *mingmen, or Gate of the Mysterious Female, *xuanpin zhi men* 玄牝之門, which are double gates, one Yin and one Yang; see *xuanpin), or between the heart and the vertebral column in the Dual Pass of the Spinal Handle (*jiaji shuangguan* 夾脊雙關; see *sanguan), or between the two eyes representing the sun (Yang) and the moon (Yin), and so forth.

These intermediary "double gates" are symbols both of duality and of its transcendence, and make the understanding—i.e., the opening of the Mysterious Pass—possible. In this way, one can find the Yin within the Yang and the Yang within the Yin; these are then joined again in the Center, which is the One Opening of the Mysterious Pass. Only here a new union can occur, as the Mysterious Pass is the ideal space and time to experience the interpenetrating fluctuations of Yin and Yang. The Mysterious Pass is therefore the primordial Chaos (*hundun) containing the germ of life—the precosmic sparkle of Original Yang and Original Yin—which is the prime mover and the *materia prima* of the alchemical work.

Monica ESPOSITO

📕 Cleary 1986a, 80–81; Esposito 1993, 52 and 58–59; Esposito and Robinet 1998; Robinet 1995a, 103–7

※ *mingmen; sanguan; xuanpin; neidan*

Xuanjiao

玄教

Mysterious Teaching

Xuanjiao is a peculiar creation of the Yuan period. When *Zhang Zongyan (1244–91), the thirty-sixth Celestial Master, gave his allegiance to the Mongol emperor in 1276, it was understood that he would move to Yanjing (Beijing) with his entourage. The Mongols based their control of the Chinese population largely on dialogue with delegates appointed by different quarters of the society, and granted unprecedented autonomy to various religious schools as long as their patriarchs agreed to reside in the capital and be readily available at court. Zhang Zongyan, however, found himself unable to live away from his headquarters on Mount Longhu (*Longhu shan, Jiangxi), and quickly returned there. His behavior surprised the court, but Khubilai khan (Shizu, r. 1260–1294) and his entourage took a strong liking to Zhang Zongyan's representative, *Zhang Liusun, who became the most eminent Taoist figure at court for the next forty years. As Liusun maintained his own allegiance to the Celestial Master, Khubilai formalized his position by making him the first patriarch of a new institution, the Xuanjiao, created in 1278, which had formal control over Taoism in southern China. The Xuanjiao patriarch also had a leading role at the Jixian yuan 集賢院 (Academy of Gathered Worthies), an institution that, among other things, managed the Taoist clergy throughout the empire. The management was actually collective—a typical feature of Yuan administration—since other orders, most notably *Quanzhen, also had permanent seats in the academy, and each enjoyed great autonomy until the end of Mongol rule in 1368.

Xuanjiao, therefore, is not a real religious order: it does not seem to have had any scriptures, liturgical registers, filiation lines, or indeed any feature of a Taoist school. It served as a means of communication, and some official documents carved on stone indicate that it mainly channeled paperwork between Mount Longhu and the imperial court. Xuanjiao did exert a strong influence, however, because of the high personal prestige of its first two patriarchs, Zhang Liusun and his disciple *Wu Quanjie. After Wu's death, his disciple Xia Wenyong 夏文泳 (1277–1349) was designated as the third patriarch, and three years later he was succeeded by Zhang Delong 張德隆, about whom not much is known. They all divided their time between personal service to the emperor and his relatives, performing official rituals throughout the country, and maintaining their headquarters at the Chongzhen gong 崇真宮 (Palace for the Veneration of Authenticity) in Yanjing.

This large institution disappeared at the end of the Yuan. At the beginning of the Ming, the *Zhengyi order took direct control of the Taoist administration, and there was no more place for a political structure without a basis in society such as the Xuanjiao.

Vincent GOOSSAERT

📖 Qing Xitai 1988–95, 3: 284–323; Qing Xitai 1994, 1: 187–92; Sun K'o-k'uan 1981; Takahashi Bunji 1997

Xuanmen dayi

玄門大義

Great Meaning of the School of Mysteries

The text commonly cited as the *Xuanmen dayi* is represented in the Taoist
Canon by a one-chapter work entitled *Dongxuan lingbao xuanmen dayi* 洞
玄靈寶玄門大義 (Great Meaning of the School of Mysteries of Lingbao,
Cavern of Mystery Section; CT 1124). This, however, ends in mid-sentence;
another source for the same material may be found in *Yunji qiqian* 6 and 7,
where the *Daomen dalun* 道門大論 (Great Essay on the School of the Dao) is
cited to cover the "twelve sections of scripture," the twelve subdivisions (still
marked) of each part of the threefold Taoist Canon into separate genres, e.g.
scripture, commentary, etc. The *Dunhuang manuscripts P. 2861.2, P. 2256
and P. 3001 show that this schema, ultimately of Buddhist inspiration (though
the Buddhist schema, rather different in its details, is not used in any Chinese
Buddhist canon known to us), derives from earlier materials, apparently of
Liang dynasty date.

But this by no means exhausts the materials ascribed to the *Xuanmen dayi*
(or texts with similar names) in quotation: substantial amounts on an entirely
different topic are quoted in *Yunji qiqian* 49 from a *Xuanmen dalun* 玄門大論
(Great Essay on the School of Mysteries); quotations may also be found in
chapter 21 (twice) from a *Xuanmen lun* 玄門論 (Essay on the School of Mysteries) and in 37 from both a *Daomen dalun* and a *Xuanmen dalun*. Initial caution
as to the identity of all these works (as seen in Malek 1985, 84–85) has given
way to the view that these quotations (and others in smaller encyclopedias
from the seventh century onward) must all be drawn—though perhaps at
different stages in its transmission—from the same work. That work would
seem to be mentioned in bibliographies of the Northern Song under the title
Changsheng zhengyi xuanmen dalun 長生正義玄門大論 (The Correct Meaning
of Long Life: A Great Discussion of the School of Mysteries) in twenty-eight
fascicles; the *Daozang quejing mulu (1.12a, 1.20a; an unsystematic collection of
titles mentioned in earlier works apparently put together in connection with
the compilation of the current Canon), lists both the title now in the Canon
and a twenty-fascicle *Xuanmen dalun* as lost.

Perhaps the best guide to the original *Xuanmen dayi* is the *Daojiao yishu
(Pivot of Meaning of the Taoist Teaching), which criticizes it at the end of its
preface for prolixity, but also cites it as *Xuanmen dalun* and *Xuanmen lun*, and
evidently took its organization as a template. On the basis of all the evidence,

then, it would seem that the *Xuanmen dayi* was a large Taoist encyclopedia of doctrine, probably of the Sui period, and certainly no earlier. Sunayama Minoru (1990, 193–196) has gone further than this bibliographical research in trying to integrate its teachings into his construction of a "School of Twofold Mystery" (*Chongxuan) which he takes to have flourished from the Six Dynasties into the Tang. His reconstruction has been subject to criticism from Robert Sharf (2002, 56–61) on the grounds that there is no proof of the existence of a self-conscious school united by adherence to a set of doctrines, but he has at least done much to document the influence of the *Xuanmen dayi* on later writers.

T. H. BARRETT

📖 Malek 1985, 84–85; Ōfuchi Ninji and Ishii Masako 1988, 115–17 (list of texts cited); Sunayama Minoru 1990, 193–96

Xuanmiao guan

玄妙觀

Abbey of Mysterious Wonder (Suzhou, Jiangsu)

The Abbey of Mysterious Wonder in Suzhou (Jiangsu) is one of the oldest and most important Taoist sacred sites in south China. Founded in 276, it was originally named Taoist Cloister of Perfection and Blessing (Zhenqing daoyuan 真慶道院), but later renamed Taoist Cloister of Supreme Perfection (Shang-zhen daoyuan 上真道院) after the emperor dreamed of the Three Clarities (*sanqing) informing him of their intention to visit Suzhou. This abbey was also patronized by emperors of the Tang and Song dynasties, who supported Taoism and sponsored temple construction projects. Accordingly, it was re-named Palace of Opening the Primordial (Kaiyuan gong 開元宮) in 714 and Abbey of Celestial Blessings (Tianqing guan 天慶觀) in 1012. The name Abbey of Mysterious Wonder was bestowed in 1295, after its reconstruction following a devastating fire. During the Ming, the imperial court recognized this site as a public monastery of the Orthodox Unity (*Zhengyi) movement.

During the Qing dynasty, the monastery's mammoth temple complex housed a total of thirty halls or pavilions (*dian* 殿), including halls to deities such as the Three Clarities, the Venerable Lord of Thunder (Leizun 雷尊), the Mother of the Dipper (*Doumu), the Three Offices (*sanguan), the Great Emperor of the Eastern Peak (*Dongyue dadi), Emperor Guan (Guandi 關帝; see *Guan Yu), *Wenchang, etc. Only the monastery's main gate (*shanmen* 山門) and the first three halls mentioned above survive intact, the rest having been partially or totally destroyed during the Taiping Rebellion (1851–64). The monastery has also played a role in the history of Taoist ritual music (Takimoto Yūzō and Liu Hong 2000, 755 and 762).

The main source on the history of the monastery is its Qing-dynasty temple gazetteer, entitled *Suzhou Yuanmiao guan zhi* 蘇州元妙觀志 (Monograph of Suzhou's Abbey of Mysterious Wonder; *xuan* was changed to *yuan* to avoid a taboo on the name of the Kangxi Emperor), compiled by Gu Yuan 顧沅 and reprinted in Gao Xiaojian 2000, vol. 11, from its 1927 edition. In addition, the *Suzhou Xuanmiao guan zhigao* 蘇州玄妙觀志稿 (Draft Monograph of Suzhou's Abbey of Mysterious Wonder; 1984) contains additional data on the monastery's development during the modern era.

Suzhou's Abbey of Mysterious Wonder was not only an important Taoist sacred site, but like other Taoist temples and monasteries throughout urban China also played a major role in the lives of the city's residents (Goossaert 2000b; Naquin 2000). In particular, the monastery was a site for the performance of judicial rites involving the making of an oath or the filing of an indictment, which were done in the presence of the Emperor of the Eastern Peak (Kang Bao 2000; Katz P. R. 2004; Wu Jenshu 2002).

Paul R. KATZ

    Kang Bao 2000; Katz P. R. 2004; Wu Jenshu 2002; Zhao Liang et al. 1994, 125–33

※ TEMPLES AND SHRINES

Xuannü

玄女

Mysterious Woman

Also known as Mysterious Woman of the Nine Heavens (Jiutian Xuannü 九天玄女) or Mysterious Woman, Damsel of the Nine Heavens (Jiutian Xuannü niangniang 九天玄女娘娘), the Mysterious Woman instructed the Yellow Emperor (*Huangdi) in military, sexual, alchemical, and divination techniques. Some scholars have traced her back to the ancient myth of the Mysterious Bird (Xuanniao 玄鳥) which had magically impregnated Jiandi 簡狄 who thereby gave birth to Xie 契, the ancestor of the Shang dynasty, as well as to Nü Ba 女魃, a drought deity who helped the Yellow Emperor defeat Chiyou 蚩尤 (*Shanhai jing* 山海經; trans. Mathieu 1983, 611–12). There is, however, no evidence for the existence of the Mysterious Woman prior to the Han.

The earliest extant references to the Mysterious Woman in relation to military techniques are in fragments of the *Longyu hetu* 龍魚河圖 (Chart of the [Yellow] River of the Dragon-Fish), a Han dynasty "weft" text (*weishu* 緯書; see *TAOISM AND THE APOCRYPHA), which interpolate the Mysterious Woman into the well-known narrative of the Yellow Emperor's battle with Chiyou. Sent by Heaven, the Mysterious Woman presents the Yellow Emperor with the Divine Talismans of Military Fealty (*bingxin shenfu* 兵信神符) which he employs to defeat Chiyou and secure the realm (Yasui Kōzan and Nakamura Shōhachi 1971–88, 6.89–90, 6.136). A later version of this narrative, found in the *Huangdi Xuannü zhanfa* 黃帝玄女戰法 (Military Techniques of the Yellow Emperor and the Mysterious Woman; *Taiping yulan*, j. 15) probably dating from the Six Dynasties, adds that the Mysterious Woman had a human head but a bird's body.

In relation to sexual practices (**fangzhong shu*), the Mysterious Woman is usually mentioned with the Pure Woman (Sunü 素女). While absent from the early manuals unearthed at *Mawangdui, their names are listed among the main sexual practitioners in post-Han sources, including the **Baopu zi* (8.150). *Ge Hong mentions a *Xuannü jing* 玄女經 (Scripture of the Mysterious Woman; 19.333), which is listed in the bibliography of the *Suishu* (History of the Sui) as part of the *Sunü bidao jing* 素女祕道經 (Scripture of the Secret Dao of the Pure Woman), with a *Sunü fang* 素女方 (Methods of the Pure Woman) listed separately (34.1050). No longer extant, sections of these works are preserved in *j*. 20 of the **Ishinpō* (Methods from the Heart of Medicine) on sexual practices.

Within numerological divination, the Mysterious Woman is particularly associated with the *liuren* 六壬 method (see Kalinowski 1983; Kalinowski 1989–90, 91) based on the *shi* 式 (cosmic board, cosmograph), which is also known as *Xuannü shi* 玄女式. Two related texts are preserved in the *Daozang*, the *Huangdi longshou jing* 黃帝龍首經 (Dragon's Head Scripture of the Yellow Emperor; CT 283) and the *Huangdi shou sanzi Xuannü jing* 黃帝授三子玄女經 (Scripture of the Mysterious Woman Transmitted by the Yellow Emperor to His Three Sons; CT 285).

Finally, within alchemical practices, the Mysterious Woman is related to the method of the Nine Elixirs (*jiudan* 九丹), as shown primarily by the **Jiudan jing* (Scripture of the Nine Elixirs).

Tang hagiographies describe the Mysterious Woman as a disciple and emissary of the Queen Mother of the West (**Xiwang mu) and elaborate on the methods she transmitted to the Yellow Emperor. Relevant texts include the **Yongcheng jixian lu* (6.2a6–4a3, and YJQQ 114.16a–18a); the *Guang Huangdi benxing ji* 廣黃帝本行紀 (Expanded Chronicle of the Deeds of the Yellow Emperor; CT 290, by Wang Guan 王瓘 of the Tang period); and the *Xuanyuan* *benji* 軒轅本紀 (Original Chronicle of Xuanyuan, the Yellow Emperor; YJQQ 100.2b–32a).

Gil RAZ

📖 Bokenkamp 1997, 43–44; Cahill 1992; Li Ling 2000b, 350–93; Xing Dongtian 1997

※ *fangzhong shu*; TAOISM AND CHINESE MYTHOLOGY; TAOISM AND THE MILITARY ARTS

xuanpin

玄牝

Mysterious Female

Xuanpin (see fig. 83) is a well-known but enigmatic term first found in *Daode jing* 6, which states that the Mysterious Female is "the Spirit of the Valley (*gushen*) [that] does not die," and that "its gate . . . [is] the root of Heaven and Earth." The first chapter of the *Liezi* (trans. Graham 1960, 18) equates the Mysterious Female with the transcendental origin that generates things without being generated, and changes them without being changed. *Neidan* alchemists take the Mysterious Female as the foundation of their art and give it the attributes of Ultimate Truth: like the Dao, they say, there is nothing inside nor outside of it. The Mysterious Female is also the Original Pneuma (*yuanqi*), the "full awakening" (*yuanjue* 圓覺), and the supreme Non-being that evolves into supreme Being (see *wu* and *you*). As a symbol of the Center, it is also called Mysterious Valley (*xuangu* 玄谷), Mysterious Pass (*xuanguan*), Heart of Heaven (*tianxin*), or Heart (*xin*), and is a synonym of the Yellow Dame (*huangpo* 黃婆) or the Yellow Court (*huangting* 黃庭). It is said to be an opening similar to those made in the body of Emperor Hundun 混沌 (Chaos) in the anecdote of the *Zhuangzi* (see under *hundun*).

As a "gate," the *xuanpin* is a passageway, an entrance situated at the junction of Non-being and Being; it allows Yin and Yang to communicate with each other, and is the place where Yang opens and Yin closes. Indeed, this gate is dual, just as the Center is in Taoism, and therefore suggests the dynamic bipolarity of the world: *xuan*, the Mystery, is equated with Heaven, and *pin*, the Female, with Earth. On the cosmic level, the Mysterious Female stands for what is above and what is below, and is represented by the trigrams *qian* 乾 ☰ (pure Yang) and *kun* 坤 ☷ (pure Yin). In alchemical language, it is the tripod and the furnace (*dinglu*), one above (*qian* or Yang) and the other below (*kun* or Yin).

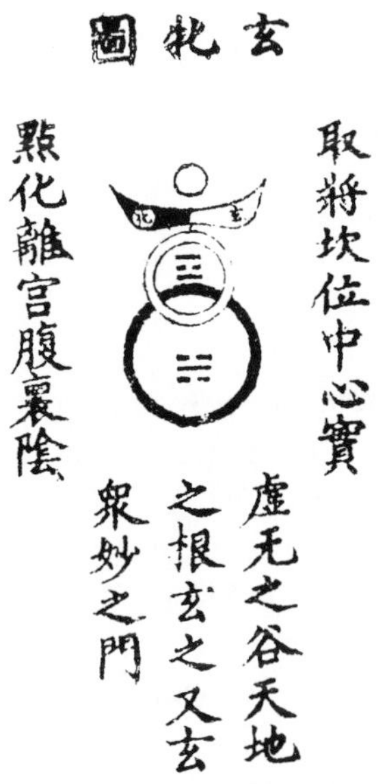

Fig. 83. The Mysterious Female (*xuanpin*, lit., "mysterious [= male] and female") as a symbol of the conjunction of Yin and Yang. The two trigrams are *li* 離 ☲ (Yin within Yang, or authentic Yin) and *kan* 坎 ☵ (Yang within Yin, or authentic Yang). The lower caption reads: "Valley of Emptiness and Non-being, Root of Heaven and Earth, Mystery within the Mystery, Gate of All Wonders." *Xiuzhen shishu (Ten Books on the Cultivation of Perfection; CT 263), 9.3a.

Some Taoist authors distinguish between an inner Mysterious Female, equated with the Real Pneuma (*zhenqi* 真氣), and an outer one, equated with the Real Spirit (*zhenshen* 真神) that "repairs" (*bu* 補) the Real Pneuma; these are also called the inner and outer Medicines (*neiyao* 內藥 and *waiyao* 外藥). In terms of psycho-physiological entities, the Mysterious Female represents the conjunction of spirit and body. On the bodily level, there have been several interpretations. Following the *Laozi Heshang gong zhangju, some authors say that *xuan* alludes to the nose, which corresponds to Heaven, and *pin* to the mouth, which corresponds to Earth. Other texts equate *xuan* with the upper Cinnabar Field (*dantian) or the sinciput, and *pin* with the lower one near the navel. Still others state that *xuanpin* designates the space between the two kidneys or the two openings of the heart, which respectively communicate with the *niwan above and the Ocean of Pneuma (*qihai* 氣海) below. *Neidan* writings, however, usually claim that the *xuanpin* cannot be exactly located in the body: like the Center itself, it has no shape, no direction, and no fixed position.

Isabelle ROBINET

📖 Chen Guofu 1963, 242–43; Despeux 1994, 87–89; Robinet 1998a

※ *gushen; tianxin; xin; xuanguan*

Xuanpin lu

玄品錄

Accounts of Varieties of the Mysterious

The *Xuanpin lu* (CT 781) is a collection of biographies in five chapters compiled by Zhang Yu 張雨. As Judith M. Boltz notes (1987a, 270, note 98), "there is much dispute over [Zhang Yu's] dates"; she suggests that Zhang was born in 1283 and died after 1356. This disputation has clearly created confusion in the minds of the compilers of the *Zhonghua daojiao da cidian* (Hu Fuchen 1995, 169 and 1628) who include two separate biographical entries for him, one with the dates 1277–1348, the other with 1283–1350. Zhang's own preface to *Xuanpin lu* is dated 1335.

The *Xuanpin lu* collects the biographies of 130 people from the Zhou to the Song. The entries are arranged chronologically, with helpful headings noting in which dynasty the figures lived. Further, the biographies are categorized under eleven headings describing the particular variety of Taoist sublimity they fell under: "Daode" 道德 (Virtue of the Dao), "Daoquan" 道權 (Power of the Dao), "Daohua" 道化 (Transformations of the Dao), "Daoru" 道儒 (Scholars of the Dao), "Daoshu" 道術 (Arts of the Dao), "Daoyin" 道隱 (Recluses of the Dao), "Daopin" 道品 (Ranks of the Dao), "Daomo" 道默 (Silence of the Dao), "Daoyan" 道言 (Words of the Dao), "Daozhi" 道質 (Substance of the Dao), and "Daohua" 道華 (Flourishing of the Dao). This collection does not include only figures who attained immortality or are usually considered notable in the history of the religion as such. The first section, for instance, gives the lives of Taoist philosophers (who fall under the category "Daode"). It also includes literary figures such as Li Bai 李白 (Li Bo, 701–62) and *Wu Yun (?–778, both in "Daohua"), and scholars such as Sima Tan 司馬談 (?–110 BCE) and Yang Xiong 揚雄 (53 BCE–18 CE, both in "Daoru"). Many of the biographies clearly derive from other collections but sources are not noted. Zhang Yu was himself associated with Mount Mao (*Maoshan, Jiangsu), and many of the figures in the *Xuanpin lu* have *Shangqing associations.

Yan Yiping published an annotated and edited version of the text, with introduction in vol. 1 of his *Daojiao yanjiu ziliao* (Yan Yiping 1974).

Benjamin PENNY

📖 Berkowitz 1996 (part. trans.); Boltz J. M. 1987a, 60–61

※ HAGIOGRAPHY

Xuanxue

玄學

Arcane Learning; Mysterious Learning; Profound Learning

Xuanxue refers to the main philosophical trend of the third century in northern China, after the downfall of the Han dynasty. This period saw a revival of Taoist and divination texts, such as the *Yijing*, over and above the Confucian classics, which had been dominant until then. Most thinkers of the period were either actively engaged in Xuanxue or strongly influenced by it, but two figures stand out among them: *Wang Bi (226–49) and *Guo Xiang (252?–312), editors of and most influential commentators on the *Daode jing* and the *Zhuangzi*, respectively.

The overall tendency of Xuanxue can be described as an intensification of philosophical discourse and a deepening and specification of philosophical concepts. In terms of the *Daode jing*, for example, the idea of the Dao in the original text is now reinterpreted with the help of the concept of *benwu* 本無 or "original Non-being," which in turn is defined as an underlying state or force of the universe, not only latent in its non-apparent phases but also permanently there as the base of all things. Similarly, the "free and easy wandering" (*xiaoyao* 逍遙; see *yuanyou) of the *Zhuangzi* is more specifically described as the complete harmony and alignment of the human being with one's inner nature and destiny (*xing and *ming), which in turn are defined as the share (*fen* 分) one has in the Dao and the universal Principle (*li* 理) that works everywhere and thus also in oneself.

In addition, both the Confucian dominance and the meditation practice of the preceding centuries left their imprint on Xuanxue. The Confucian influence is visible in the overall acceptance of a well-ordered and hierarchical society as one of the goals of philosophical speculation: Wang Bi accepts moral values as part of the Dao and Guo Xiang sees perfect alignment of the individual as the key to a perfect society, in which everyone plays the role predetermined for him or her by nature. Meditation practice enters the picture mainly in the *Zhuangzi* interpretation, where "sitting in oblivion" (*zuowang) and "fasting of the mind" (*xinzhai) are specific ways to attain the realization of one's inner nature and destiny, which will not only liberate one from the burden of personal consciousness but also make one a model citizen in the best of all worlds.

Livia KOHN

📖 Balázs 1948; Fung Yu-lan 1952–53, 2: 168–79; Yü Ying-shih 1985

※ Wang Bi; Guo Xiang

Xuanzhu lu

玄珠錄

Records of the Mysterious Pearl

The *Xuanzhu lu* (CT 1048) is a collection of the teachings of Wang Xuanlan 王玄覽 (626–97; Qing Xitai 1994, 1: 264–65), recorded by his disciple Wang Taixiao 王太霄 around the time of Empress Wu (r. 690–705). Wang came from Mianzhu 綿竹 (Sichuan). According to his disciple's preface, he began to study Buddhism in his thirties, but also wrote a commentary to the *Daode jing* based on *Yan Zun's interpretation. When Wang was around the age of forty-seven, Li Xiaoyi 李孝逸, a senior officer of Yizhou 益州 (Sichuan), invited him to debate with priests of Buddhist temples. He became a Taoist and was appointed head of the Zhizhen guan 至真觀 (Abbey of Ultimate Reality) in Chengdu. Empress Wu summoned him to court in 697 at the age of seventy-two, but Wang died on the way to the capital.

His work is divided into approximately 120 sections. Although it is not systematic, the unity of Taoism and Buddhism runs through it as one of the main underlying themes. An example of the combined use of Taoist and Buddhist notions is found in Wang's discussion of the Dao. Following section 1 of the *Daode jing*, he first describes the two aspects of the Dao, namely the "constant Dao" (*changdao* 常道) and the "Dao that can be told" (*kedao* 可道); the former gives rise to Heaven and Earth and the latter causes phenomena to arise and change. When he discusses Non-being and Being (*wu and *you), however, Wang does not develop the notion of section 2 of the *Daode jing* that "Being and Non-being generate each other" (*youwu xiangsheng* 有無相生) but instead, based on the Buddhist view of the Middle Way (*mādhyamaka*, *zhongdao* 中道), he explains the concept of "middle" as "neither Being nor Non-being."

The influence of Buddhism on Wang Xuanlan is both direct and indirect. Direct influence comes from such texts as Jizang's 吉藏 *Sanlun xuanyi* 三論玄義 (Mysterious Meaning of the Three Treatises), Nāgārjuna's *Madhyamakakārikā* (Verses on the Middle Way), and the *Vimalakīrti-nirdeśa-sūtra* (Teaching of Vimalakīrti). Indirect influence comes through Taoist works that had absorbed Yogācāra doctrines and the idea of *śūnyatā* (Emptiness), such as, respectively, the *Haikong zhizang jing* (Scripture of [the Perfected of] Sea-Like Emptiness, Storehouse of Wisdom) and the *Benji jing* (Scripture of the Original Bound).

SAKADE Yoshinobu

📖 Kamata Shigeo 1969; Qing Xitai 1988–95, 2: 205–25; Qing Xitai 1994, 2: 93–94; Zhu Senpu 1989 (crit. ed.)

※ TAOISM AND CHINESE BUDDHISM

Xuanzhu xinjing

玄珠心鏡

The Mysterious Pearl, Mirror of the Mind

The *Xuanzhu xinjing* is contained twice in the Taoist Canon, each time with a different commentary (CT 574 and 575). It consists of two sets of poems, the "Shouyi shi" 守一詩 (Verses on Guarding the One) and the "Dadao shouyi baozhang" 大道守一寶章 (Precious Stanzas of the Great Dao on Guarding the One). The first has fourteen lines of four characters each, the second ten lines of six characters each. The poems go back to Cui Shaoxuan 崔少玄, the wife of Lu Chui 盧陲 from Fujian, who was originally an immortal from the heaven of Highest Clarity (Shangqing 上清). She revealed the poems after her death, when she returned to the world after her husband implored to instruct him in the Dao. The poems were first published on Mount Wangwu (*Wangwu shan, Henan), the old residence of *Sima Chengzhen, in 817 by Qiao Juze 樵巨澤, a relative of the lady.

In content and diction, the verses are related to the *Zuowang lun and describe the late Tang Taoist understanding of salvation, the process of ascension into heaven, and the attainment of eternal life. The commentary found in the *Xuanzhu xinjing zhu* 玄珠心鏡注 (CT 574) is shorter and less speculative. It goes back to a certain Master Zhen (Zhenzi 真子) of Mount Heng (*Hengshan 衡山, Hunan) and shows a rather conventional understanding of basic Taoist concepts. The other work, also entitled *Xuanzhu xinjing zhu* (CT 575), contains a preface explaining the circumstances under which the poems were revealed, along with an extensive and more philosophical commentary by Qiao Juze.

Livia KOHN

📖 Kohn 1989a, 132–34; Kohn 1993b, 215–19; Robinet 1983a, 84–85 and 88–89

※ MEDITATION AND VISUALIZATION

Xue Daoguang

薛道光

1078?–1191; *zi*: Taiyuan 太源; *hao*: Zixian 紫賢 (Purple Worthy),
Piling chanshi 毗陵禪師 (Meditation Master of Piling); also known
as Xue Shi 薛式 and Xue Daoyuan 薛道源

A rather mysterious figure said to have lived 113 years, Xue Daoguang is the third patriarch of the Southern Lineage (*Nanzong) of *neidan. The main sources on his life are the "Xue Zixian shiji" 薛紫賢事蹟 (Traces of Xue Zixian; in *Wuzhen zhizhi xiangshuo sansheng biyao* 悟真直指詳說三乘祕要, CT 143, 16b–24b), the preface to his *Huandan fuming pian* 還丹復命篇 (Folios on Returning to Life through the Reverted Elixir; 1126; CT 1088), and his biography in the *Lishi zhenxian tidao tongjian* (49.13b–14b). According to these sources, Xue came from Mount Jizu (Jizu shan 雞足山, Yunnan). After he achieved enlightenment as a Chan Buddhist monk, he met *Shi Tai in 1106 (or, according to the preface to the *Huandan fuming pian*, in 1120) and received instructions on *neidan* from him. He renounced his Buddhist ties and lived among the ordinary people working as a tailor, which was also Shi Tai's profession. The *Lishi zhenxian tidao tongjian* adds that Xue wrote a commentary to the *Wuzhen pian* (Folios on Awakening to Perfection). The latter work is lost, and the commentary now attributed to Xue in the *Wuzhen pian sanzhu* 悟真篇三注 (Three Commentaries to the *Wuzhen pian*; CT 142) is actually by *Weng Baoguang.

The *Huandan fuming pian* follows the *neidan* tradition inaugurated by *Zhang Boduan and Shi Tai. It contains sixteen pentasyllabic poems that represent the principle of "two times eight" (*erba* 二八, symbolizing the balance of Yin and Yang), followed by thirty heptasyllabic poems corresponding to thirty days of alchemical practice, nine lyrics to the tune of "Xijiang yue" 西江月 (West River Moon) representing nine cycles of alchemical transmutation, and a short poem that summarizes the *neidan* process. The final part of the work is entitled "Dansui ge" 丹髓歌 (Song on the Marrow of the Elixir). According to the preface, the title *Huandan fuming pian* refers only to the poems in the first part of the text (1a–8a). The "Dansui ge" was appended later. Only the "Dansui ge" is included in the *Xiuzhen shishu* (7.4b–10b), with a postface attributed to Shi Tai.

Like the *Wuzhen pian*, the *Fuming pian* is replete with alchemical imagery. The text emphasizes the union of Yin and Yang, fire phasing (*huohou), and the final alchemical transmutation. Xue's main technique is the "coagulation of Spirit within the Cavity of Pneuma" (*ningshen ru qixue* 凝神入氣穴), i.e., concentration on the lower Cinnabar Field (**dantian*). In the "Dansui ge," Xue restates the teachings of Shi Tai, emphasizing that the alchemical work does not need to begin at any particular time because the Yang principle develops naturally within the body.

Farzeen BALDRIAN-HUSSEIN

📖 Boltz J. M. 1987a, 175; Chen Bing 1985, 36

※ *neidan*; Nanzong

Xue Jizhao

薛季昭

fl. 1304–16; *zi*: Xianweng 顯翁

This scholarly ritual master based on Mount Lu (**Lushan, northern Jiangxi) wrote a commentary to the **Duren jing* (Scripture on Salvation) in 1304 called *Duren shangpin miaojing zhujie* 度人上品妙經注解 (Commentary and Explication of the Wondrous Scripture of the Upper Chapters on Salvation; CT 92). Aiming for a wider audience with its simple annotations, this local printed edition was apparently also intended for the Mongol emperor Yuan Chengzong (r. 1295–1307). Xue's efforts gained further support in 1305 when a colleague from Mount Lu named Li Yueyang 李月陽 became convinced of the work's value after the mysterious Original Lady Wang (Wang yuanjun 王元君) claimed as much. The financial sponsorship of its publication by Cai Xiangfu 蔡翔夫 sought to make Xue's simple rendering of the scripture's basic meaning more widely available. In 1308, Xue had a divine encounter with the Thunder Rites (**leifa*) master **Lei Shizhong (1221–95). Lei instructed him to annotate the *Duren jing* with a complementary text entitled *Xuxuan pian* 虛玄篇 (Folios on the Mystery of the Void), which advocates an immersion in the Three Teachings (Confucianism, Taoism, and Buddhism). The text ends with a Precious Declaration (*baogao* 寶誥; 3.32a–33b) from the Celestial Worthy of Original Commencement (Yuanshi tianzun 元始天尊), who is the source of the scripture.

Lowell SKAR

📖 Boltz J. M. 1987a, 209

※ *leifa*

Y

Yan Zun

嚴遵 (or 嚴尊)

ca. 83 BCE–ca. 6 CE; zi: Xing 行, Junping 君平

Little is known about the life of Yan Zun, whose original surname, Zhuang 莊, was later changed to Yan because of a taboo on the personal name of Han Mingdi (r. 57–75). A retired literatus well versed in the *Yijing, he lived in Chengdu, earning his living by teaching the *Daode jing* and casting horoscopes. He is listed among a group of ten immortals, and the philosopher Yang Xiong 揚雄 (53 BCE–18 CE) reportedly was his disciple. Stelae were dedicated to his memory and he became the object of a cult at the beginning of the third century.

Yan Zun is ascribed with the *Daode zhigui* 道德指歸 (The Essential Meaning of the *Daode jing*), a text in thirteen or fourteen scrolls that was well known during the first centuries of the Common Era. The extant portion of this work consists of the last seven scrolls, which are included in the *Daozang* (CT 693) and in several anthologies with a subcommentary by a Gushen zi 谷神子 (Master of the Spirit of the Valley). Meng Wentong (1948b) and Yan Lingfeng (1964, vol. 1) have collected quotations of the missing portions, which were lost around the sixth century. While scholars in the past had deemed the text to be a Ming fabrication, most now agree there is no strong reason to doubt its attribution to Yan Zun. Stylistic and other internal evidence, in particular, suggest a Han date for its composition.

The commentary is concerned with both self-cultivation and the theory of government. From a philosophical point of view, Yan Zun emphasizes the reversibility of the opposites, which issue from a common origin and join in harmony: everything is changing and is constantly beginning anew. Action is born from non-action (*wuwei); knowledge must be rejected and quiescence is found in emptiness, which is fullness and spontaneity and is superior to all practices of longevity. Yan Zun's cosmogony is complex. First comes the Dao, the "Emptiness of Emptiness." The Dao is followed by its *de (virtue), which is equated with the One (*yi) and with Emptiness. In turn, *de* comes before Non-being and Being (*wu and *you). Then comes the Spirit (*shenming* 神明), which is related to the Two and is the "non-being of Non-being." The next stage, related to the Three, is Harmony (*he* 和), which corresponds to Non-being. From this state evolve Yin and Yang, Heaven and Earth, the saint (*shengren), pneuma (*qi), and forms (*xing). In

Yan Zun's view, this metaphysics is the basis of both social order and self-cultivation.

Isabelle ROBINET

📖 Chan A. K. L. 1988; Meng Wentong 1948b; Robinet 1977, 11–23, 209–14; Vervoorn 1988–89; Wang Deyou 1994; Yan Lingfeng 1964

Yang Xi

楊羲

330–86; *zi*: Xihe 羲和

Very little is known of the life of Yang Xi, a calligrapher and visionary who lived in Jurong 句容 (near Nanjing, Jiangsu). In 350, he received the *Lingbao wufu xu* (Prolegomena to the Five Talismans of the Numinous Treasure) from *Wei Huacun's eldest son, Liu Pu 劉璞. Between 364 and 370, he was appointed intercessor between heaven and humanity. In a series of nightly visions, several Perfected (*zhenren) from the Shangqing 上清 (Highest Clarity) heaven appeared to him and granted him the revelation of sacred scriptures. Among these Perfected was Wei Huacun herself, who became Yang's "subtle master" (*xuanshi* 玄師). Yang wrote the content of every vision in ecstatic verse, recording the date along with the name and description of each Perfected. The purpose of the revelations was to set up a new syncretic doctrine that claimed to be superior to all earlier traditions. The texts revealed to Yang Xi later formed the foundations of the *Shangqing school of Taoism, and are the main source of *Tao Hongjing's *Zhengao.

Yang Xi and the Xu family. The Perfected directed Yang to transmit their revelations to the Xu 許 family, of whom Yang was a client. The Xus, an aristocratic family also based in Jurong, traced their origins back to a minister of the legendary emperor Yao 堯 and counted many civil officials among their members. They were related to the Ge 葛 and the Tao 陶 families from which *Ge Hong and Tao Hongjing descended.

The head of the household, Xu Mai 許邁 (300–348), renounced his official career and turned to Taoism, pharmacopoeia, alchemy, meditation and physiological practices. He was a disciple of *Bao Jing and of a *Tianshi dao libationer (*jijiu), Li Dong 李東; some sources claim that he was also a follower of the *Bojia dao (Way of the Bo Family). His acquaintances included the scholar Guo Pu 郭璞 (276–324) and the eminent calligrapher Wang Xizhi 王羲之 (321?–379?). In 346, he changed his name to Xu Xuan 許玄, travelled to renowned mountains, and eventually disappeared as an immortal. Later he was among the Perfected who appeared to Yang Xi.

Xu Mai's younger brother, Xu Mi 許謐 (303–76), was informed by Yang Xi of the role that the Xu family would play in the revelations. Xu Mi took Yang under his protection and received his manuscripts, but completed his official career before retiring to Mount Mao (*Maoshan, Jiangsu). In the Shangqing texts, he is frequently called Zhangshi 長史 or Senior Officer.

Xu Mi's third son, Xu Hui 許翽 (341–ca. 370), on the other hand, left his official career, returned his wife to her family, and retired to Mount Mao in 362. An excellent calligrapher, he became a disciple of Yang Xi, who informed him that an office was set aside for him in the heavenly hierarchy. Xu Mi devoted himself to the study of the revealed scriptures but died an untimely death, possibly by committing an alchemical "ritual suicide" (Strickmann 1979, 137–38).

Grégoire ESPESSET

📖 Chen Guofu 1963, 32–37; Kamitsuka Yoshiko 1999, 18–32; Strickmann 1977; Strickmann 1981, 82–98

※ Shangqing

yangsheng

養生

Nourishing Life

The idea of "nourishing" (yang 養) is prominent in Chinese thought: one can nourish life (yangsheng), the inner nature (yangxing 養性), the body (yangxing 養形), the whole person (yangshen 養身), the will (yangzhi 養志), and the mind (yangxin 養心). The term yangsheng designates techniques based on the essence, the inner or outer breath, and the spiritual force (*jing, qi, shen); these techniques are grounded on physiological, psychological, and behavioral principles and include gymnastics (*daoyin), massage, breathing (*fuqi, *xingqi), sexual hygiene (*fangzhong shu), diets (*bigu), healing, *MEDITATION AND VISUALIZATION, and rules of daily behavior.

The term is first mentioned in *Zhuangzi 3, a chapter entitled "Mastery in Nourishing Life" ("Yangsheng zhu" 養生主). The Zhuangzi contrasts nourishing life (yangsheng) with nourishing the body (yangxing). It maintains that the best way of nourishing life consists of "depending on the Celestial Principle" (yi hu tianli 依乎天理) and that bodily techniques are minor practices. In chapter 19, it criticizes again the view that methods for nourishing the body are sufficient for attaining immortality. In the same vein, *Huainan zi 7* considers the *yangsheng* techniques to be inferior because they require external supports.

Han to Tang. The *yangsheng* practices flourished during the Han period. They are described in several *Mawangdui manuscripts dating to about 200 BCE, including the *He yinyang* 合陰陽 (Joining Yin and Yang), the *Tianxia zhidao tan* 天下至道談 (Discourse on the Ultimate Way Under Heaven), the *Yangsheng fang* 養生方 (Recipes for Nourishing Life), the *Shiwen* 十問 (Ten Questions), and the *Quegu shiqi* 卻穀食氣 (Refraining from Cereals and Ingesting Breath; see translations in Harper 1998). These manuscripts give importance to sexual hygiene and to the ingestion of breath (see *fuqi). Several Han literati mention *yangsheng* and some criticize it, like Wang Chong 王充 (27–ca. 100 CE), who wrote: "Some Taoists think that they can nourish inner nature (*yangxing*) through gymnastics and guiding breath (*daoqi* 導氣), and thus transcend the generations [of mortals] and become immortal" (*Lunheng* 論衡; see Forke 1907–11, 1: 348). In the *Shenjian* 申鑒 (Extended Reflections; trans. Ch'en Ch'i-yün 1980), Xun Yue 荀悅 (148–209, a thirteenth-generation descendant of the philosopher Xunzi 荀子) interpreted the cultivation of the vital principle in a Confucian way: one should seek moderation and harmony and avoid any excess, and breath should be circulated to avoid blocks and stagnation, just as the mythical emperor Yu 禹 did when he succeeded in quelling the flood waters.

During the Six Dynasties, *yangsheng* continued to develop in medical, Taoist, and *Xuanxue (Arcane Learning) circles. Both *Xi Kang (223–62) and Xiang Xiu 向秀 (227–72), the first prominent commentator on the *Zhuangzi*, wrote essays entitled *Yangsheng lun* 養生論 (Essay on Nourishing Life) and replied to each other's criticisms (see translations in Holzman 1957). The aim of *yangsheng* was essentially prophylactic and therapeutic, and *Ge Hong established a distinction between it and the achievement of immortality. According to him, in *yangsheng* there is complementarity and gradation among the different techniques: ingestion of drugs should be practiced together with circulation of breath; but to circulate breath one should also know the sexual techniques (*Baopu zi*, 5.114; trans. Ware 1966, 105). One of the most influential works of the time, preserved only in fragments, is the *Yangsheng yaoji (Essentials of Nourishing Life) of Zhang Zhan 張湛 (early fourth century). Later, an influence of Buddhist techniques (especially ānāpāna-smṛti or concentration on breathing) and Indian gymnastic movements, and the greater importance given to stillness of mind and meditation (*zuowang), is also apparent but difficult to evaluate.

In the Sui and Tang periods, gymnastics and breathing were at the heart of *yangsheng*. Taoist as well as medical circles transmitted these techniques. The *Zhubing yuanhou lun (Treatise on the Origin and Symptoms of Diseases), a medical work submitted to the Sui emperor in 610, is remarkable for its descriptions of *yangsheng* methods for clinical cases. *Sun Simiao (fl. 673) devoted to this subject two chapters of his *Qianjin fang* 千金方 (Prescriptions Worth a Thousand; *j.* 27 and 28), and some shorter texts are also attributed to him, including the **Yangxing yanming lu* (On Nourishing Inner Nature and Extending Life), the *Fushou lun* 福壽論 (Essay on Happiness and Longevity; CT 1426), and the *Baosheng ming* 保生銘 (Inscription on Protecting Life; CT 835). Also notable is *Sima Chengzhen (647–735), a Taoist of the *Shangqing school, who wrote the **Fuqi jingyi lun* (Essay on the Essential Meaning of the Ingestion of Breath).

Song to Qing. The *yangsheng* practices underwent significant changes from the Song period onward. On the one hand, they integrated elements drawn from **neidan* practices; on the other, they aroused the interest of learned people. For the Song dynasty alone, there are about twenty books on the subject. An important author of the time was Zhou Shouzhong 周守中, who wrote the *Yangsheng leizuan* 養生類纂 (Classified Compendium on Nourishing Life), the *Yangsheng yuelan* 養生月覽 (Monthly Readings on Nourishing Life), and other works. Literati living in retirement and away from official life also dealt with the subject, such as Su Shi 蘇軾 (Su Dongpo 蘇東坡, 1037–1101; SB 900–968) and some Neo-Confucians. With the development of Neo-Confucianism and the growth of syncretism among Taoism, Buddhism, and Confucianism in the Ming and Qing periods, a number of ethical elements appeared.

During the Ming period, Hu Wenhuan 胡文煥 wrote the main work on *yangsheng*: the *Shouyang congshu* 壽養叢書 (Collectanea on Longevity and Nourishment [of Life]; ca. 1596), which includes the *Yangsheng shiji* 養生食忌 (Prohibitions on Food for Nourishing Life) and the *Yangsheng daoyin fa* 養生導引法 (*Daoyin* Methods for Nourishing Life). Gao Lian's 高濂 (fl. 1573–81; IC 472–73) *Zunsheng bajian* 遵生八箋 (Eight Essays on Being in Accord with Life) deals with aspects of the life of literati, including the arrangement of the studio, diets, breathing methods, and ingestion of medicines. Unlike the Ming dynasty, the Qing dynasty produced no important work on *yangsheng*. In the twentieth century, *yangsheng* evolved into the modern science of *weisheng* 衛生 (hygiene) on the one hand, and into **qigong* on the other.

Catherine DESPEUX

📖 Despeux 1988; Engelhardt 1987; Engelhardt 1989; Engelhardt 2000; Harper 1998, 110–47 and passim; Huang Jane 1987–90; Kohn 1989c; Larre 1982, 217–19; Li Yuanguo 1988; Lo Vivienne 2001; Maspero 1981, 265–72, 324–46, and 445–554; Sakade Yoshinobu 1983a; Sakade Yoshinobu 1988a; Sakade Yoshinobu 1992a; Sakade Yoshinobu 1993b; Seidel 1989–90, 258–62; Stein S. 1999; Zhou Yimou 1994

※ *jing, qi, shen*; TAOIST VIEWS OF THE HUMAN BODY; for other related entries see the Synoptic Table of Contents, sec. IV.1 ("*Yangsheng*")

Yangsheng yaoji

養生要集

Essentials of Nourishing Life

As we learn from the *Shishuo xinyu* 世說新語 (New Account of Tales of the World; ca. 430; trans. Mather 1976, 387), the author of the *Yangsheng yaoji*, Zhang Zhan 張湛 (early fourth century), was a lower aristocrat under the late Eastern Jin whose family came from Shandong. His forefathers had served as officials under the Wei and Jin and had a strong interest in ancient texts, many of which they had brought south. As a result, he was educated in the philosophical classics and grew up with an awareness of longevity and immortality notions, and was also familiar with *Xi Kang's essays on the subject.

Zhang Zhan served as an official in the later part of his life, and is famous for two works. The first is a commentary to the *Liezi*, now found in the *Chongxu zhide zhenjing sijie* 沖虛至德真經四解 (Four Explications of the Authentic Scripture on the Ultimate Virtue of Unfathomable Emptiness; CT 732), which shows a familiarity with the thought of *Guo Xiang (252?–312) and Xiang Xiu 向秀 (227–72), but also a suspicious knowledge of the overlap between this and other ancient texts. He has been exonerated from forging the *Liezi* himself, but since it was unknown in its transmitted form before he introduced it to the world, it may have been forged by one of his forebears.

The second work is the *Yangsheng yaoji*, which played a role among health and immortality seekers that had been described as equal to that of the *Daode jing* and *Huangting jing*—in short, as a widely available source of information for the educated but not necessarily initiated reader—until the Tang-Song transition, when it was lost in China. It survives today in fragments and citations, notably in the *Yangxing yanming lu* (On Nourishing Inner Nature and Extending Life), ascribed to *Tao Hongjing, and in *Sun Simiao's *Qianjin fang* 千金方 (Prescriptions Worth a Thousand), as well as in Japanese medical texts such as the *Ishinpō (Methods from the Heart of Medicine) of 984, suggesting a somewhat longer circulation outside China.

From these fragments, it seems that the *Yangsheng yaoji* originally consisted of ten scrolls, which discussed such aspects of Nourishing Life (*yangsheng*) as endowment with spirit, love of energy, nourishing the body, practicing gymnastics (*daoyin*), use of language, eating and drinking, sexual techniques (*fangzhong shu*), going against the ordinary, and medicine and drugs, as well as taboos and prohibitions. This list of contents matches other longevity texts of the time, presenting coherent and largely standard information on the practice drawn from sources going back to the Han, mixed with later writings—including, it would seem, the *Baopu zi*—suggesting a willingness at the end of the Jin to combine southern and northern learning in this sphere.

To what extent Zhang exercised selectivity so as to conform to the expectations of a scholarly readership is now unclear, but his one appearance in the *Jinshu* (History of the Jin, 75.1988–89) emphasizes a philosophical approach to his topic, while his anthology perhaps prefigured the somewhat anodyne use of the *Baopu zi* by writers such as Sun Simiao. There are some indications that Zhang also wrote a commentary on the *Zhuangzi* which was soon lost.

T. H. BARRETT and Livia KOHN

📖 Barrett 1980a; Barrett 1982; Despeux 1989, 228–30; Sakade Yoshinobu 1986a; Stein S. 1999

※ *yangsheng*

Yangxing yanming lu

養性延命錄

On Nourishing Inner Nature and Extending Life

While the *Yunji qiqian* edition of this work (32.1a–24b) is anonymous, the independent edition in the *Daozang* (CT 838) is attributed to *Tao Hongjing (456–536) but its preface indicates that *Sun Simiao (fl. 673) may be the author. The text may actually date from the eighth century. It is written in the form of a small mnemonic encyclopedia, at least two-thirds of which consists of quotations from Zhang Zhan's 張湛 lost *Yangsheng yaoji* (Essentials of Nourishing Life). The *Yangxing yanming lu* does not cite the *Yangsheng yaoji* as such, but rather sources that were mentioned in it, including the *Zhuangzi, the *Liezi, the *Shennong jing* 神農經 (Scripture of the Divine Husbandman), the *Hunyuan daojing* 混元道經 (Scripture of the Dao of Chaotic Origin), the *Hunyuan miaojing* 混元妙經 (Wondrous Scripture of Chaotic Origin), the *Dayou jing* 大有經 (Scripture of Great Existence), the *Zhongjing* 中經 (Central Scripture), the *Yuanyang jing* 元陽經 (Scripture of Original Yang), the *Mingyi lun* 明醫論 (Essays of Illustrious Doctors), and the *Neijie* 內解 (Inner Explications).

The text is divided into six sections: 1. "Teachings and Precepts" ("Jiaojie" 教誡), on the general principles of cultivating the vital principle; 2. "Dietetic Precepts" ("Shijie" 食誡), containing advice and interdictions related to food; 3. "Miscellaneous Precepts" ("Zajie" 雜誡), on avoiding disturbances in everyday

life; 4. "Healing Diseases Through Ingestion of Breath" ("Fuqi liaobing" 服
氣療病), on methods for circulating breath (*xingqi*) and the "six sounds of
breathing" (see *liuzi jue*); 5. "Gymnastics and Massages" ("Daoyin anmo" 導
引按摩; see *daoyin*); 6. "Riding Women" ("Yunü" 御女), on sexual techniques
(*fangzhong shu*). The first and sixth sections are not included in the version
of the *Yunji qiqian*.

Catherine DESPEUX

📖 Despeux 1989, 233; Mugitani Kunio 1987; Ōfuchi Ninji and Ishii Masako
1988, 54–55 (list of texts cited); Zhu Yueli 1986

※ *yangsheng*

yaowang

藥王

Medicine Kings

The title *yaowang* was given to distinguished physicians, of whom the oldest
and best known was the legendary Bian Que 扁鵲, who is supposed to have
lived around 500 BCE. Evidence of shrines dedicated to him dates to the Song
period. Other famous Medicine Kings were Hua Tuo 華陀 (142–219), *Sun
Simiao (fl. 673), and Wei Shanjun 韋善君 (998–1023). They are generally accompanied by ten further famous and divinized physicians. Thus, to the left
of Bian Que are the statues of Zhang Zhongjing 張仲景 (ca. 150–220), the
author of the *Shanghan lun* 傷寒論 (Treatise on Cold Damage Disorders);
Huangfu Mi 皇甫謐 (215–82), the author of the *Zhenjiu jiayi jing* 針灸甲乙經
(Systematic Scripture of Acupuncture and Moxibustion); Qian Yi 錢乙 (ca.
1032–1113; SB 217–18), the well-known paediatric physician; Zhu Zhenheng
朱震亨 (1281–1358); and Tao Hua 陶華 (fifteenth century). To the right of
Bian Que are Wang Shuhe 王叔和 (late third century), the author of *Maijing*
脈經 (Scripture on the Pulse); Liu Wansu 劉完素 (1120–1200); Li Gao 李杲
(1180–1251); Wu Shu 吳恕 (Yuan?); and Xie Ji 薛己 (Ming?).

The Medicine Kings were honored particularly in popular belief, and shrines
devoted to them (called *Yaowang miao* 藥王廟 or Shrines of the Medicine Kings)
existed throughout China during the Ming and Qing periods. These shrines
were successors to the Shrines of the Three Sovereigns (*Sanhuang miao* 三皇
廟), popular in the Yuan period. For this reason, *yaowang* shrines to this day still
contain a hall with the statues of the three legendary emperors and patrons
of medicine, namely Fu Xi 伏羲, Shennong 神農 (the Divine Husbandman,

who is said to have tasted all plants and evaluated their toxicity), and *Huangdi (the Yellow Emperor, who is credited with the development of the theory of classical medicine).

Ute ENGELHARDT

📖 Despeux 1987, 31–33; Qing Xitai 1994, 3: 135–38; Zheng Jinsheng 1996

※ TAOISM AND POPULAR RELIGION

Ye Fashan

葉法善

631–720; *zi*: Daoyuan 道元, Taisu 太素

Ye Fashan, a celebrated figure both in his own day and throughout medieval times, is remarkable in that he fit few of the common patterns for Tang Taoists. He apparently wrote nothing, never held ecclesiastical office or associated with other historical Taoists, and may not even have been a *daoshi* at all. Yet, he was not only the subject of numerous later tales, but was honored in his own lifetime for his achievements as a thaumaturgical hero: he employed ritual powers and spirit-helpers to perform countless amazing rescues, saving ladies and gentlemen, emperors and courtiers, from death, disease, demons, coups, and unprincipled sorcerers. What will confound the modern mind is that his thaumaturgic exploits earned admiration and respect by centuries of emperors, officials, and historians.

Beginning with a panegyrical epitaph by Tang Xuanzong (r. 712–56), we have more than twenty substantial accounts of Ye's life, in the dynastic histories (*Jiu Tangshu*, 192.5107–8; *Xin Tangshu*, 204.5805) and other court documents, as well as in numerous Taoist collections (e.g., *Du Guangting's *Daojiao lingyan ji*, 14.8a–9a). Those accounts report that Ye was the scion of an ancient and noble house, whose father, grandfather, and great-grandfather had all been proficient in arcane arts. The father and grandfather received imperial honors in 713 and 717. Perhaps for that reason, Ye was always a figure of imperial significance, despite the fact that he had little connection with the cultural elite or with the Taoist leadership (e.g., *zongshi* 宗師 like *Sima Chengzhen). He was courted by five Tang rulers (from Gaozong to Xuanzong), and in the 739 epitaph he is already lauded as an immortal who had applied his subtle powers to protect ruler and nation from disloyal ministers and rebels alike. In a ninth-century text (Jiang Fang's 蔣防 *Huanxi zhi* 幻戲志, in *Tangdai congshu* 唐代叢書, 32.6a–9a), three deities revealed to him that he was a "banished immortal" (*zhexian* 謫仙), a heavenly official who had been lax in copying the sacred registers (*LU) and had consequently been banished to live as a mortal until he had built up sufficient merit (by good deeds toward others) to return to his heavenly station. That image guided most later accounts of Ye's life, especially the extensive *Tang Ye zhenren zhuan* 唐葉真人傳 (Biography of the Perfected Ye of the Tang Dynasty; CT 779), by the obscure thirteenth-century Taoist Zhang Daotong 張道統. Zhang essentially embroidered the already-substantial account of Ye that had appeared in the eleventh-century *Taiping guangji* 太平廣記 (Extensive Records of the Taiping Xingguo Reign Period; 978; *j*. 216). Each is replete with ahistorical elements, and qualify as historical fiction, but they do weave a complex and fascinating image of Ye as a moral and spiritual exemplar for all people: he benefitted "civilian and military, Han and foreign, male and female, children and youths," and his meritorious activities, in faithful service to grateful rulers, served to integrate the cosmos, uniting the world above, the world below, and every corner of the world of men, from imperial court to the most distant frontier.

Even the earliest texts report that Ye ascended as an immortal in broad daylight, 12 July 720. He quickly became a legendary figure, and accounts of his exploits expanded widely for centuries.

Russell KIRKLAND

📖 Barrett 1996, 33 and 52; Boltz J. M. 1987a, 96–97; Cadonna 1984; Giles L. 1948, 110–14; Kirkland 1986a, 126–46 and 366–443; Kirkland 1992a; Kirkland 1993; Schafer 1976

※ HAGIOGRAPHY

Yebao yinyuan jing

業報因緣經

Scripture on the Causes of Karmic Retribution

This scripture in ten chapter (CT 336) is first cited in the *Xuanmen dayi (Great Meaning of the School of Mysteries) and therefore dates from no later than the Sui dynasty. Its detailed picture of the workings of a Taoist version of the Buddhist system of *karma* caused the early incorporation of seven pages of its second chapter into the *Fengdao kejie (Codes and Precepts for Worshipping the Dao; trans. Reiter 1998, 57–67). An extended study by Livia Kohn (1998d) has now summarized the findings of Japanese scholars and supported a date of composition toward the end of the sixth century. Kohn further investigates fully the links between this text and three Buddhist works likewise giving full details of what consequences may be entailed by various transgressions or good actions.

Earlier work by Nakajima Ryūzō (1984), however, shows that this scripture synthesizes a wide range of Buddhist notions into a Taoist view of karmic process (which itself has much earlier roots). Also, while discussions of karmic consequences occur in many Indian Buddhist texts, none of those examined by Kohn are firmly identifiable as translations, but seem to be Chinese compositions of unknown date. All this suggests both Buddhists and Taoists working to a common agenda, rather than that the parallels reflect straightforward borrowing by the latter.

T. H. BARRETT

📖 Kohn 1998d; Nakajima Ryūzō 1984; Ōfuchi Ninji 1978–79, 1: 85–100 (crit. notes on the Dunhuang mss.) and 2: 147–72 (reprod. of the Dunhuang mss.)

※ ETHICS AND MORALS; TAOISM AND CHINESE BUDDHISM

Yellow Turbans

The Yellow Turban rebellion of 184, unsuccessful though it was, is considered a critical factor in the fall of the Han dynasty. Led by Zhang Jue 張角, the rebellion was organized by a religious movement based in the northeast of China called the Taiping dao 太平道 or Way of Great Peace. It is possible that the Taiping dao used the *Taiping jing (Scripture of Great Peace), or a precursor of that scripture, as its central text and inspiration. It was one of the movements that contributed to the milieu from which Taoist religion arose.

Zhang Jue came from Julu 鉅鹿 (Hebei). Little is known about him apart from his involvement in the religious movement he founded. This movement, in concert with standard Han cosmology, saw the cosmos as a tripartite structure of Heaven, Earth, and Humanity. Thus, while Zhang Jue took the title "General of Heaven" (*tiangong jiangjun* 天公將軍) for himself, his two brothers, also leaders in the movement, had the titles "General of Earth" (*digong jiangjun* 地公將軍) and "General of Humanity" (*rengong jiangjun* 人公將軍). The slogan used by the Yellow Turbans was, "The Blue Heaven (*qingtian* 青天) is already dead, the Yellow Heaven (*huangtian* 黃天) will replace it." This is often read in political terms as in the Han cosmological scheme dynastic rise and fall was viewed as conforming to the movement of the five elemental phases (*wuxing*). As each phase was accorded a color, the cycle of dynasties was seen to follow a cycle of colors. Since the Han ruled under the phase of

Fire, the subsequent dynasty had to rule under Soil, and the color attributed to Soil was yellow. Thus, the idea that the Yellow Heaven was about to be established signalled the movement's revolutionary intentions. However, for this reading to be consistent the Yellow Turbans should really have referred to the demise of the Red Heaven, the color adopted by the Han. Alternative readings that stress the religious use of the term "Blue Heaven," and therefore give their slogan a less political meaning, have also been proposed (Barrett 1986, 876). Nonetheless, the idea that the Yellow Heaven presaged the new society of Great Peace led to the adoption of the yellow headscarves (*huangjin* 黃巾; turbans is the traditional rendering) that gave rise to their name.

The Taiping dao followed practices that seem to have been reasonably common to religious movements at this time. Healing was a major part of their program—the period immediately prior to 184 saw terrible epidemics across the empire—with the confession of transgressions playing an important and novel role. More traditional methods such as drinking talismanic water (*fushui* 符水, i.e., water containing ashes of burned talismans, *FU) and the recitation of spells are also mentioned in the surviving sources. Also apparently novel was the use Zhang made of missionaries. Originally a localized movement, it is said that he sent out eight of his disciples to convert people throughout the empire, ultimately garnering several hundred thousand followers throughout eight provinces. These followers he organized into thirty-six administrative districts on the model of the great state of Daqin 大秦 to the west (imperial Rome in early Chinese sources).

The rebellion of the Yellow Turbans was set down for the year 184 which had the cyclical term *jiazi* 甲子, the first of a new sixty-year cycle, symbolizing a new beginning. Unfortunately for the rebels, one of their number leaked the news of their impending action to the emperor. As a result, Zhang had to launch the rebellion a few weeks early. Nonetheless, revolts spread across country and it took almost a year to quell the rebellion. Peace did not reign, however, as sporadic uprisings that were either spawned from the movement, or simply took its name continued to occur. The rebels must have remained a reasonably strong force for in 192, 300,000 Yellow Turbans joined Cao Cao's 曹操 army. The name "Yellow Turbans" disappears from the record in the early third century.

Benjamin PENNY

📖 Barrett 1986, 874–76; Eichhorn 1957; Fang Shiming 1995; Hendrischke 2000; Kandel 1979; Levy 1956; Mansvelt Beck 1980; Michaud 1958; Ōfuchi Ninji 1991, 79–136; Qing Xitai 1988–95, 1: 192–221; Robinet 1987a

※ *taiping*; MESSIANISM AND MILLENARIANISM

yi

intention

The *neidan notion of *yi* (intention) can only be understood in relation to the notion of *qi (vital breath or pneuma); together, they represent the inner link between body and mind. Through the *yi*, sensorial activities become the center of vision of a cosmic body (Merleau-Ponty 1945, 81–106) and a reflection of the macrocosm (Billeter 1985, 4). The *yi* is defined in the alchemical texts as the rider of *qi*, similar to a conductor who orchestrates the movement of *qi* within the body. When this attunement takes place in the center, it is called True Intention (*zhenyi* 真意) or True Soil (*zhentu* 真土). *Liu Yiming (trans. Cleary 1986a, 88–89) explains that the *yi* is also called Yellow Dame (*huangpo* 黃婆) as it represents the "communicative principle of the Yellow Center" (*huangzhong tongli zhe* 黃中通理者) that harmonizes Yin and Yang. In fact, the *yi* is also associated with the spleen and the heart (*xin), the two main central organs of the body.

Yi has two aspects, inner and outer, whose relation is the same as that between "substance and function" (*ti and *yong*). The first aspect is exemplified by its graph, consisting of *yin* 音 (sound) over *xin* 心 (heart). The *Shuowen jiezi* 說文解字 (Explanations of the Signs and Explications of the Graphs; 100 CE) defines the term *yi* as the "sound of the heart," the musical emission or creativity of the heart. Elsewhere, *yi* is defined as "what is emitted from the heart" (*xin zhi suo fa* 心之所發; see Despeux 1981b, 73). While the function (*yong) of *yi* is to conduct the *qi*, its essence (*ti) is originally associated with *xin* (heart-mind), the source of the animation of the *yi*. *Neidan* texts also state that *yi* is linked with *shen (Spirit) as the pure functionality of the *yi* (Li Yuanguo 1985a, 59). *Yi* is therefore related both to *xin*, which is its original source, and to *shen*, which is the expression of its dynamism—pure Thought, conducting Idea, function of the "theophanic imagination" (Corbin 1958, 13, 142). The relation between *yi* and *xin* does not contradict the relation between *yi* and *shen*. It only provides more definite indications on the organ, or sanctuary, of this "theophanic imagination": the Heart-Center and its pure creativity. This is helpful for understanding the expression "sound of the heart" that is linked to the graph *yi*.

With regard to the second aspect of *yi*, or its function, the meaning of "resonance of the heart" is emphasized during certain stages of the inner alchemical practice, when one discovers the unbreakable link between *yi* and *xin*. The two terms then become interchangeable: every movement starts from *xin* and is conducted by *yi*, and vice versa. The link is made more explicit in some martial arts, as shown by *taiji quan* texts (Despeux 1981b, 73 and 109–13) that mention the formula *yong yi buyong li* 用意不用力 ("use the resonance of the heart and not the strength"). One should not use *li* 力 (physical power) but *yi* (mental power), and should not make physical efforts but simply follow the movements of *qi* that lead to listening to one's heart. In this way, the heart becomes the center of every movement. Once the right harmony of *yi* as "resonance of the heart" is attained through the inner practices, *yi* becomes a mental power capable of spontaneously producing images, heat, and so forth; it can naturally anticipate one's own movements, and in martial arts also the movements of one's opponent (Vercammen 1990, Esposito 1992, Esposito 1997).

Monica ESPOSITO

📖 Cleary 1986a, 88–89; Despeux 1981b, 73; Esposito 1992, 434–35; Esposito 1997, 41–42; Li Yuanguo 1985a; Robinet 1995a, 191–95 and passim; Vercammen 1990, 1: 313–14 and 319

※ *xin*

yi

一

One; Oneness; Unity

The idea of Oneness or underlying unity is first expressed in the *Daode jing*, where the Dao is linked immediately with the One, which it brings forth directly. The One is "the Great Beginning" (*Zhuangzi* 12) and the unified state of creation. It contains everything, notably the two forces Yin and Yang, which interact to create and sustain all life. It is ultimate primordiality; it embraces the universe and represents the creative Principle at the root of all things: "Heaven, Earth and all beings are born from the One," as the *Xisheng jing* (Scripture of Western Ascension) says (trans. Kohn 1991a, 245). This state of non-differentiation is identified with the cosmic Chaos (*hundun*) in the *Huainan zi*.

In human beings the One is present as primordial *qi* or cosmic vital energy, the power that makes people come to life and be what they are. Conserving and guarding this cosmic power leads to immortality. As *Guangcheng zi* says in *Zhuangzi* 11: "I hold on to the One, abide in its harmony, and therefore I have

kept myself alive for 1200 years. And never has my body suffered any decay"
(see trans. Watson 1968, 120).

Livia KOHN

📖 Hu Fuchen 1989, 196–206; Kohn 1989a, 127–34; Qing Xitai 1994, 2: 260–63; Robinet 1995c; see also bibliographies for the entries *sanyi*, *shouyi*, and Taiyi

※ Taiyi; Dao; *sanyi*; *shouyi*; Yin and Yang; COSMOGONY

Yi Xinying

易心瑩

1896–1976; zi: Zongqian 綜乾

Yi Xinying was born on September 26, 1896, into a peasant family in Suining 遂寧 (Sichuan). Of a feeble constitution, he decided in 1913 to become a Taoist apprentice at the Changdao guan 常道觀 (Abbey of the Constant Dao) on Mount Qingcheng (*Qingcheng shan, Sichuan). His master was Wei Zhiling 魏至齡, twenty-first patriarch of the Dantai bidong 丹臺碧洞 (Jasper Cavern of the Cinnabar Terrace) branch of *Longmen. Yi Xinying later become its twenty-second patriarch. This branch originated with the tenth Longmen patriarch, Chen Qingjue 陳清覺 (1606–1705), and five other Taoists who established themselves in Sichuan. Chen left Mount Wudang (*Wudang shan, Hubei) and moved first in 1669 to Mount Qingcheng, then in 1686 to the *Qingyang gong (Palace of the Black Ram) in Chengdu. In 1700, the Kangxi Emperor conferred on this temple the name of Jasper Cavern of the Cinnabar Terrace (Dantai bidong), which also became the name of Chen's branch of Longmen.

In 1930, Yi Xinying became the chief abbot of the Changdao guan. He acquired erudition especially through his friendship with Yan Kai 顏楷 and corresponded with distinguished specialists in the history of Taoism, including *Chen Yingning (1880–1969), Chen Guofu 陳國符, and Meng Wentong 蒙文通. After the establishment of the People's Republic of China, he became active in the preservation of Taoism. In 1956 he went to Beijing for the founding of the Chinese Taoist Association (*Zhongguo daojiao xiehui), and in 1962 he gave lectures to young Taoist monks training at the *Baiyun guan (Abbey of the White Clouds) in Beijing. In the same year, he became president of the Sichuan Taoist Association.

Yi Xinying spent his life searching for Taoist writings. He edited, notably, a collection of texts devoted to women, *Nüzi daojiao congshu* 女子道教叢書

(Collectanea on Taoism for Women). Among other works, he wrote a *Dao-jiao sanzi jing* 道教三字經 (Scripture in Three-Character Lines on the Taoist Teaching), a *Daoxue keben* 道學課本 (Manual of Taoist Studies), a *Qingcheng zhinan* 青城指南 (Guide to Mount Qingcheng), and a commentary to the *Daode jing* entitled *Laozi tongyi* 老子通義 (Understanding the Meaning of the *Laozi*). Most of his works were destroyed during the Cultural Revolution.

Catherine DESPEUX

📖 Li Yangzheng 2000, 243–46 and passim; Qing Xitai 1988–95, 4: 415–26; Qing Xitai 1994, 1: 405–6

※ *neidan*; Zhongguo daojiao xiehui; TAOISM IN THE PEOPLE'S REPUBLIC OF CHINA

Yijing

易經

Book of Changes

Traditionally regarded as having been compiled at different times by the mythical emperor Fu Xi 伏羲, King Wen of the Zhou (Wenwang 文王, r. 1099–1050 BCE), the Duke of Zhou (Zhougong 周公, ?–1032 BCE), and Confucius (traditional dates 551–479 BCE), the *Yijing* was first used as a manual of divination but has been considered, at least from Confucius's time, as a source of wisdom and cosmological lore, and has also been submitted to a moralistic interpretation. Chinese tradition ranks it among the five main classics, with the *Shujing* 書經 (Book of Documents), the *Shijing* 詩經 (Book of Odes), the *Liji* 禮記 (Records of Rites), and the *Chunqiu* 春秋 (Spring and Autumn Annals).

Formation of the text. The very brief core text of the *Yijing* is based on sixty-four hexagrams (*gua* 卦), which are permutations of six broken or solid lines (*yao* 爻) probably derived from numerical symbols. Unlike the traditional interpretation, the arrangement of the lines into sixty-four hexagrams appears to antedate that of the eight trigrams (sets of three lines, see **bagua*). Each hexagram is given a name followed by a "hexagram statement" (*guaci* 卦辭) and by individual "line statements" (*yaoci* 爻辭), both of which usually contain oracular formulas. This part of the text, often referred to as the *Zhouyi* 周易 (Changes of the Zhou), was augmented by a group of seven commentaries, which are commonly called the Ten Wings (*shiyi* 十翼), as three of them are divided into two parts:

1–2. *Tuanzhuan* 彖傳 (Commentary to the Judgements)

3–4. *Xiangzhuan* 象傳 (Commentary to the Images)

5. *Wenyan zhuan* 文言傳 (Commentary to the Words of the Text) on the hexagrams *qian* 乾 ☰ and *kun* 坤 ☷

6–7. *Xici* 繫辭 (Appended Statements, also known as *Dazhuan* 大傳 and often translated as "Great Treatise")

8. *Shuogua* 說卦 (Explanation of the Trigrams)

9. *Xugua* 序卦 (Hexagrams in Sequence)

10. *Zagua* 雜卦 (Hexagrams in Irregular Order)

According to modern scholarship, the hexagrams and "statements" date from the late Western Zhou period, while the whole text took its present form in the early second century BCE, except for the *Xugua*, which seems to date from the late Han period. In the *Mawangdui manuscript, which probably dates from about 190 BCE and is the earliest known version of the text, the arrangement and names of the hexagrams are different and follow a more logical sequence than they do in the received text. Of the five commentaries included in this manuscript, only the *Xici* (which according to several scholars reflects a Taoist influence) is also found in the received text, but in the Mawangdui version contains important variants.

During the Han dynasty, the system of the *Yijing* played a major role in the cosmological theories of the New Text school (*jinwen jia* 今文家) and was the basis for the interpretations of the classics given in the "weft texts" (*weishu* 緯書; see *TAOISM AND THE APOCRYPHA). With the rise of the Old Text school (*guwen jia* 古文家) and later of the *Xuanxue (Arcane Learning) school of thought, whose members associated the exegesis of the *Yijing* with that of the *Daode jing* and the *Zhuangzi, the *Yijing* became one of the most influential texts in Chinese philosophy. Its study as a philosophical work was revived in the Song period with the Neo-Confucians, who referred to it as one of the main sources of their thought.

The Yijing in the history of Taoism. In pre-Han and Han times, there was often no clear-cut division between the study of the *Yijing*, the *Daode jing*, and the *Zhuangzi*. Diviners like Sima Jizhu 四馬季主 reportedly referred to both the *Yijing* and the *Daode jing*, and the *Huang-Lao school also combined studies of the two texts. References to the *Yijing* by Taoists can be traced back to one of the oldest extant Taoist scriptures, the Han-dynasty *Taiping jing (Scripture of Great Peace). Taoists of different backgrounds, such as *Yan Zun, Mao Ying 茅盈 (see *Maojun), and *Ziyang zhenren, who allegedly lived at that time, reportedly studied the *Yijing* along with the *Daode jing*. Even if the present text of the *Zhouyi cantong qi is not the same as the original one, its first version seems to have been closely related to the *Yijing*.

Texts dating from the fourth century onward—the *Laozi zhongjing* (Central Scripture of Laozi) and the *Shangqing text entitled *Yindi bashu jing* 隱地八術經 (Scripture of the Eight Arts to Conceal Oneself within the Earth; CT 1359)—employ the eight trigrams as deities or relate them to the corporeal spirits known as *bajing* (Eight Effulgences), and see them as detaining apotropaic power. An early *Lingbao text, the *Ziran zhenyi wucheng fu shangjing* 自然真一五稱符上經 (Superior Scripture of the Self-Generated Five Talismans of Correspondence of the Authentic One; CT 671), says that the eight trigrams developed from its five talismans (*FU). The *Shangqing huangshu guodu yi*, probably dating from the late Six Dynasties but representing an older *Tianshi dao tradition, connects the trigrams with the human body, as does the *Shuogua*. In Tang times, the *Kaitian jing* does the same. *Sima Chengzhen, *Li Quan, and other commentators on the *Yinfu jing*, as well as Liangqiu zi 梁丘子 (Bai Lüzhong 白履忠, fl. 722–29) in his commentary to the *Huangting jing*, also refer to the *Yijing*. During the Five Dynasties, *Chen Tuan was renowned for his exegesis of the *Yijing* and his *Wuji tu* 無極圖 (Diagram of the Ultimateless; see *Taiji tu*). Some centuries before its revival in Neo-Confucian thought, the *Yijing* acquired great importance within *neidan*, which depends heavily on its images and is imbued with speculations on hexagrams and trigrams.

Taoist uses of the Yijing. As Taoism was the main heir of Han cosmological and esoteric lore, most early Taoist interpretations of the *Yijing* are close to those of the New Text school and the "weft texts." Except for some divination techniques, however, the main concern of the Taoist use of the *Yijing* is with the spatio-temporal location of hexagrams and trigrams in relation to the ordering of the cosmos. This contrasts with the traditional exegesis of the text, which relies on the internal relationships of the hexagrams, their nuclear trigrams, and their lines.

Taoist texts refer to the *Yijing* mainly in three ways. One relates the eight trigrams to the body, connecting the trigrams with the body in the *houtian* or "posterior to Heaven" arrangement (see *xiantian and houtian), or locating them in the navel. Their spirits are the *Taiyi's envoys, and adepts meditate on them on the eight nodal days of the year (*bajie* 八節, namely, equinoxes, solstices, and the first day of each season) to achieve long life. These methods are mentioned in the *Laozi zhongjing* and the *Lingbao wufu xu. The *Yindi bashu jing* describes a method that consists of painting the trigrams on one's body for protection against cosmic catastrophes.

Another use of the text consists of taking the eight trigrams as cosmic reference points for the ordering of the universe. From medieval times to the present day, the trigrams are placed on the Taoist altar in the *houtian* sequence and the priest steps on them during the ritual; they are, moreover, painted on the priest's robe and are associated with various parts of his hand. In the

Thunder Rites (*leifa), the trigrams and the twelve "sovereign hexagrams" (bigua 辟卦; see *huohou) are used in dances for exorcistic and therapeutic purposes (see *bugang).

Third, the uses of the Yijing within neidan are manifold. In particular, trigrams and hexagrams are used to symbolize the alchemical ingredients and are related to the solar and lunar cycles. Sentences of the Yijing are often quoted in neidan texts to illustrate philosophical statements. Because of the Yijing's Neo-Confucian exegesis, neidan authors who claim that the Three Teachings (Confucianism, Taoism, and Buddhism) allude to the same ultimate truth often refer to the Yijing as the main Confucian scripture.

Isabelle ROBINET

📖   Chen Guying 1993; Csikszentmihalyi 2000; Graham 1989, 358–70; Ho Peng Yoke 1985, 34–51; Lynn 1994 (trans.); Needham 1956, 304–40; Peterson W. 1982; Ritsema and Kircher 1994 (trans.); Sakade Yoshinobu 2000; Shaughnessy 1993; Shaughnessy 1994; Shaughnessy 1996a (trans. of the Mawangdui ms.); Smith et al. 1990; Suzuki Yoshijirō 1974; Wilhelm H. 1960; Wilhelm H. 1975; Wilhelm H. 1977; Wilhelm R. 1950 (trans.)

※ bagua; COSMOGONY; COSMOLOGY; DIVINATION, OMENS, AND PROPHECY; TAOISM AND NEO-CONFUCIANISM; TAOISM AND THE APOCRYPHA

Yin and Yang

陰陽

In the Chinese worldview, the cosmos is generated from the undifferentiated Dao through the interaction of Yin and Yang, two principles or "pneumas" (*qi) that are aspects or functions of the Dao itself. Their continued hierogamy engenders everything within space and time, giving rise to the material and spiritual manifestation. The cosmos thus is not static but in constant change.

The term yin originally denoted the shady or northern side of a hill, while yang was its sunny or southern side. This early definition, found in sources of the Spring and Autumn period, was later expanded to include all that is shady, dark, and cool, and all that is sunny, bright, and warm, respectively. The notions of Yin and Yang were thus applied to various complementary entities and phenomena, such as female-male, dark-light, night-day, low-high, earth-heaven, passive-active, and so on (see table 1). This categorization, however, is relative: a minister, for instance, is Yin in relation to his ruler, but Yang in relation to his subordinates. Moreover, Yin and Yang are not absolute, since

Fig. 84. Yin (black) and Yang (white). The two inner dots represent Yin within Yang and Yang within Yin. Around the circumference are shown the eight trigrams (*bagua*), which in this case represent different stages in the cycles of increase and decrease of Yin and Yang (clockwise from the lower left corner: *zhen* 震 ☳, *li* 離 ☲, *dui* 兌 ☱, *qian* 乾 ☰, *sun* 巽 ☴, *kan* 坎 ☵, *gen* 艮 ☶, and *kun* 坤 ☷). Hu Wei 胡渭 (1633–1714), *Yitu mingbian* 易圖明辨 (Clarifications on Diagrams Related to the *Book of Changes*; 1706), *j. 3.*

each contains the seed of the other: the Yin of winter is transformed into the Yang of summer and the process is reversed in a ceaseless continuum. This cycle of coming and going is also expressed as contraction and expansion.

Around the third century BCE, the notion of Yin and Yang was merged with the theory of the *wuxing*. Water and Metal correspond to winter and autumn (Yin), Fire and Wood to summer and spring (Yang), and Soil is the neutral center. These associations gave rise to finer distinctions within the cycle of Yin and Yang, now defined by four terms (for further correlations with the *wuxing* see table 25):

1. Minor Yang (or Young Yang, *shaoyang* 少陽): East, spring

2. Great Yang (*taiyang* 太陽): South, summer

3. Minor Yin (or Young Yin, *shaoyin* 少陰): West, autumn

4. Great Yin (*taiyin* 太陰): North, winter

Another important development dating from around the same period was the combination of Yin and Yang with the eight trigrams (*bagua*) and the sixty-four hexagrams of the *Yijing*. From the Han period onward, these associations integrated all forms of classification and computation—Yin and Yang, the *wuxing*, the *ganzhi* (Celestial Stems and Earthly Branches), the trigrams and hexagrams of the *Yijing*, and other symbols of the endless cycle of phenomenal change—into a complex system of categorization, giving rise to the system of so-called correlative cosmology.

The workings of Yin and Yang affect everything within the universe, and humanity is no exception. When Yin and Yang alternate according to the natural order, the cycles of seasonal changes and those of growth and decay follow each other harmoniously. When humanity (especially represented by the emperor) acts in disagreement with the natural order, harmony of both society and the cosmos is disrupted, and calamities such as droughts, eclipses, and rebellions are the result.

While these notions are largely common to Chinese culture as a whole, they play a central role in Taoism. The early school of the Celestial Masters (*Tianshi dao) sought to ensure the proper functioning of Yin and Yang with their sexual rites for "merging pneumas" (*heqi). In other milieux, strict seasonal rules of diet and self-cultivation were followed since illnesses were deemed to be caused by a pathological and unseasonable excess of Yin or Yang in the bodily organs. On the other hand, the search for longevity required in some instances going against the laws of nature, in an attempt to invert (*ni* 逆) the sequence that leads to degeneration and death (*shun* 順, lit., "continuation"). *Neidan* alchemists obtained a pure Yang self through the elimination of Yin from the inner organs, this being the source of decay and death. Others practiced sexual techniques (*fangzhong shu) to retain the Yang essence. Rites and methods were also devised to keep the myriads of Yin and Yang spirits within the body from dispersing, thus avoiding illness and death.

Farzeen BALDRIAN-HUSSEIN

📖 Cheng Anne 1989; Fung Yu-lan 1952–53, 1: 383, 2: 19–30; Graham 1986c; Graham 1989, 330–40; Granet 1934, 115–48; Ho Peng Yoke 1985, 11–17; Major 1987b; Major 1993, 29–30; Needham 1956, 273–78; Robinet 1997b, 8–10; Sivin 1987, 59–70

※ Dao; *wuji* and *taiji*; *yi* [oneness]; COSMOGONY; COSMOLOGY

Yin Changsheng

陰長生

Yin Changsheng is one of the best-known immortals of the Taoist tradition. According to the *Shenxian zhuan (Biographies of Divine Immortals; trans. Campany 2002, 274–75), he came from Xinye 新野 (Henan) and lived during the Later Han period. Having become a disciple of *Maming sheng, he retired with his master to Mount Qingcheng (*Qingcheng shan, Sichuan) and received from him the *Taiqing (Great Clarity) scriptures of *waidan. Later he went to Mount Wudang (*Wudang shan, Hubei) to compound an elixir, and finally ascended to Heaven from Mount Pingdu (Pingdu shan 平都山, Sichuan). According to *Tao Hongjing's *Zhenling weiye tu (Chart of the Ranks and Functions of the Real Numinous Beings), he now dwells in the heaven of Great Clarity (Taiqing 太清).

In the fourth century, Yin Changsheng reappeared as the master of *Bao Jing (?–ca. 330), *Ge Hong's father-in-law, and in this capacity he is often mentioned in connection with a talisman for achieving "release from the corpse" (*shijie; see for instance *Zhengao, 12.3a). These accounts reinforced Yin Changsheng's connections to the traditions of the southeastern region of Jiangnan 江南. In the *Baopu zi, Ge Hong depicts him as one of the legendary founders of the Taiqing legacy, together with *Anqi Sheng and Maming sheng (trans. Ware 1966, 81 and 213).

Yin Changsheng is ascribed with several texts, most of which deal with alchemy. These include the second chapter of the Taiqing jinye shendan jing 太清金液神丹經 (Scripture of the Divine Elixir of the Golden Liquor of Great Clarity; CT 880), dating from the Six Dynasties, and the Jinbi wu xianglei cantong qi 金碧五相類參同契 (Gold and Jade and the Five Categories in the Cantong qi; CT 904), dating from the Tang period. The main work bearing Yin Changsheng's name is a commentary (CT 999) to the *Zhouyi cantong qi (Token for the Agreement of the Three According to the Book of Changes). Compiled around 700 CE, its content is distinguished by a cosmological interpretation of the scripture, but occasional references to actual practices show that it originated in a waidan context.

Fabrizio PREGADIO

📖 Campany 2002, 274–77; Giles L. 1948, 36

Yin Wencao

尹文操

622–88; *zi*: Jingxian 景先

According to a citation in his commentary on Laozi by *Du Guangting from the *Xuanzhong ji* 玄中記 (Record of the Mysterious Center; a lost text already cited before 527 in the *Shuijing zhu* 水經注), the Yin family provided the mother of Laozi, as well as *Yin Xi, the keeper of the pass who received Laozi's message in the form of the *Daode jing*. No wonder, then, that when the great sage's supposed descendants who ruled as the Tang dynasty wished to boost the cult of their ancestor they should have turned to Yin Wencao—whose dates have occasionally been extended to 695 through a misreading of his epitaph—as the most appropriate Taoist priest to create the necessary hagiography. In fact it was an apparition of Laozi riding a white horse in front of the whole court in Luoyang in 679 that prompted the emperor, Gaozong (r. 649–83), to commission a history of the divine ancestor Laozi and his interventions in this world in ten fascicles. This work, the *Xuanyuan huangdi shengji* 玄元皇帝聖紀 (Chronicle of the Holy August Emperor of Mysterious Origin), had a protracted and wide influence until the Southern Song, though it was subsequently lost. At one time it existed in Japan, and it is possible to tell from numerous citations from the *Zhenzheng lun* (Essays of Examination and Correction) onward that it must be an important source for several works of the same type dating to the Song period. According to Kusuyama Haruki (1979, 393–422), one work that still survives in the Taoist Canon, the *Taishang hunyuan zhenlu* 太上混元 真錄 (Real Account of the Most High Chaotic Origin; CT 954), appears to be yet more closely associated with Yin's original; it must be of Tang date, since it observes a taboo on the name of Gaozong's father.

Livia Kohn (1997b, 114–19) has shown that Yin's promotion of the Laozi legend must be placed within the history of the *Louguan (Tiered Abbey), the Taoist institution which commemorated Laozi's last gift to Yin Xi, which had already been renamed by Gaozong's father the Zongsheng guan 宗聖觀 (Abbey of the Ancestral Saint) in 626. Yin's other services to the Tang dynasty during over thirty years at court, which earned him a bureaucratic title, included the compilation of a new catalogue of the Taoist Canon and the abbacy of the Haotian guan 昊天觀 (Abbey of the Vast Heaven), an institution founded by Gaozong in memory of his father, allegedly at Yin's suggestion; according to one source this was combined with the abbacy of the Zongsheng guan from

677. Yin was also responsible for a number of other writings which are now lost, apart from a portion of the surviving hagiography of the masters of the Louguan, in which he appears to have had a hand. At least one of the lost works, quoted briefly in a later encyclopedia, appears from its title to have been polemical; it is probably the first work known to cite the *Fengdao kejie* (Codes and Precepts for Worshipping the Dao), suggesting that the organization of the Taoist Church during a period of intense ideological rivalry with Buddhism was one of Yin's concerns. Yin is also listed by Du Guangting as a commentator on the *Daode jing*. Although the involvement of the Tang dynasty in Taoism was to reach even greater heights in the eighth century, it is evident that Yin played an important part in helping Gaozong lay the foundations for this.

T. H. BARRETT

📖 Chen Guofu 1963, 112–14; Kohn 1997b, 114–19; Kusuyama Haruki 1979, 393–422

※ Louguan pai

Yin Xi

尹喜

hao: Wenshi xiansheng 文始先生
(Elder of the Beginning of the Scripture)

Yin Xi is first known as an ancient philosopher called Guanyin zi 關尹子 and as such is mentioned in the *Zhuangzi*, the *Lüshi chunqiu* 呂氏春秋 (Springs and Autumns of Mr. Lü), and the *Liezi*. He was then associated with a text of this title, mentioned in the bibliographic section of the *Hanshu* (History of the Former Han) but lost early on. A new version, with heavy *neidan* influence, was reconstituted in 1233 under the title *Wenshi zhenjing* 文始真經 (Authentic Scripture of Master Wenshi; CT 667).

His career as a Taoist immortal begins with the *Shiji* (Records of the Historian; 63.2139–43; trans. Lau 1982, x-xi), which names him as the border guard on the Hangu Pass (Hangu guan 函谷關) who requested Laozi's *Daode jing* and thus makes him the first recipient of the sage's teaching. Increasingly associated with Laozi and his expanded hagiographic accounts, Yin Xi becomes a sage in his own right with biographies in the *Liexian zhuan* (trans. Kaltenmark 1953, 65–67) and the *Shenxian zhuan* (trans. Campany 2002, 194–204), which characterize him as skilled in astrology and thus able to divine Laozi's approach.

Dedicating himself fully to the Dao, he then becomes the sage's partner on his western journey, "converting the barbarians" with him.

In the sixth century, Yin Xi is said to have attained his highest status as Taoist patriarch and Laozi's deputy among the barbarians, with the title of "buddha." This happened after a fifth-century descendant of the Yin family named Yin Tong 尹通 claimed that his family's home in the Zhongnan mountains (Zhongnan shan 終南山, Shaanxi) was not only Yin Xi's original estate but also the actual spot where the transmission of the *Daode jing* took place. Known as *Louguan (Tiered Abbey), it is located 70 km southwest of Xi'an and was, from the Tang through the Yuan, a major center of Taoist religion. The Taoists of this temple, rising to national prominence in the sixth century, compiled various new works that detailed Yin Xi's supernatural birth and divine faculties, his wondrous meeting with Laozi and attainment of the Dao, a second meeting of the two sages in Chengdu (Sichuan) with the help of a black ram (*qingyang* 青羊), their ecstatic journey through the heavens, and their joint conversion of the barbarians. They also equipped him with the title Wenshi xiansheng or Elder of the Beginning of the Scripture.

The main text recounting these events is the sixth-century *Wenshi neizhuan* 文始內傳 (Inner Biography of Master Wenshi), which survives in fragments (mainly in the *Sandong zhunang, j.* 9), supplemented by the *Huahu jing* (Scripture of the Conversion of Barbarians) also of the sixth century (*Sandong zhunang, j.* 9), and the *Taishang hunyuan zhenlu* 太上混元真錄 (Real Account of the Most High Chaotic Origin; CT 954) of the seventh century. Later Yin Xi is prominently mentioned in the inscription *Sansheng jibei* 三聖記碑 (Stele to the Three Saints; 826), in *Du Guangting's *Daode zhenjing guangsheng yi* 道德真經廣聖義 (Extended Interpretation of the Emperor's Exegesis of the *Daode jing*; 901; CT 725, *j.* 3), and in various collections of immortals' biographies. Under the Yuan, Yin Xi is formally named the first patriarch of the Louguan branch (*Louguan pai) and described in various inscriptions, some of which can still be seen at the Louguan.

Livia KOHN

📖 Boltz J. M. 1987a, 124–25; Decaux 1990 (trans. of the *Wenshi zhenjing*); Kaltenmark 1953, 65–67; Kohn 1997b; Kusuyama Haruki 1979, 393–422; Zhang Weiling 1990

※ Laozi and Laojun; HAGIOGRAPHY

Yin Zhiping

尹志平

1169–1251; *zi*: Dahe 大和; *hao*: Qinghe 清和
(Clear and Harmonious)

Yin Zhiping, the first *Quanzhen patriarch of the second generation, was a key figure in the institutionalization of his order. Until 1227, when Yin attained that powerful position, most of his life was spent under the aegis of his master *Qiu Chuji, and he may be seen as a successful continuer of Qiu's original project to turn Quanzhen into a nationwide independent organization. Born into a family from the Shandong peninsula (where *Wang Zhe had founded Quanzhen), Yin, when still a teenager, wanted to become a disciple of *Ma Yu. His parents prevented him from doing so, but when he was hardly an adult, he left to became a Quanzhen monk and a disciple of *Liu Chuxuan. He also studied divination with *Hao Datong and ritual with *Wang Chuyi. Later he was adopted by Qiu Chuji, who made him one of his most trusted assistants. Yin thus gathered the teachings of the Seven Real Men (*qizhen* 七真; see table 17) whom he later evoked in his collected sayings. After his formative period, Yin spent several years in seclusion, practicing according to the Quanzhen curriculum, and then founded new communities with the help of rich lay devotees, Chinese and Jurchen alike. While his new ventures grew, he never lost contact with Qiu Chuji, who then was busy coordinating and centralizing the network of many scattered Quanzhen monasteries. When Qiu was invited to court by the Mongol sovereign Chinggis khan (Taizu, r. 1206–27), he took Yin's advice to answer the summons, and Yin was one of the eighteen disciples who accompanied Qiu on his three-year journey (see *Changchun zhenren xiyou ji*).

After Qiu's death, his disciples and influential lay followers deliberated who would become the successor to the powerful position of patriarch (*zongshi* 宗師) that Qiu Chuji had created for himself and for which he had gained recognition from the Mongols. The main contenders were Yin and Li Zhichang 李志常 (1193–1256), who seems to have been less of an inspired preacher and more of a skillful organizer. Yin was elected and from then on devoted all his energy to relentlessly touring the various Quanzhen communities in the Mongol-dominated land, and to maintaining good relations with the Mongol generals and their Chinese allies. In 1232–34, the last vestiges of the Jin empire fell to the Mongol armies, and Yin immediately headed south, along with his fellow disciples such as *Song Defang and *Wang Zhijin. He spent several years in Shanxi and Shaanxi, where he secured the support of the local strongmen, integrated the local Quanzhen communities into his hierarchy, and engineered the conversion to Quanzhen of all major previously independent Taoist centers, like the *Louguan (Tiered Abbey) and the *Taiqing gong (Palace of Great Clarity) in Bozhou 亳州 (present-day Luyi 鹿邑, Henan). By that time old and tired after these years of incessant activity, Yin resigned from his position in 1241 and let his aide Li Zhichang become patriarch. He spent his final years in retirement.

Beside his institutional activity documented by numerous inscriptions—there are four extant memorial stelae for him and more information can be gathered from many other contemporary inscriptions—Yin also left an important legacy of teachings. His annals, entitled *Yingyuan lu* 應緣錄 (Accounts of Karmic Retribution), are lost, but his poems are anthologized in the *Baoguang ji* 葆光集 (Anthology of Concealed Radiance; 1239; CT 1146) and his oral teachings are collected in the *Qinghe zhenren beiyou yulu* 清和真人北游語錄 (Recorded Sayings from a Journey to the North, by the Real Man [Yin] Qinghe; 1240; CT 1310) and in the second *juan* of the *Zhenxian zhizhi yulu* 真仙直指語錄 (Straightforward Directions and Recorded Sayings of Real Men and Immortals; CT 1256), probably compiled in the fourteenth century. The two activities were actually linked: while on pastoral tours, Yin would gather the communities at night and hold lectures. The two final *juan* of the *Beiyou yulu* are devoted to elucidating the *Daode jing* in the style peculiar to the Quanzhen recorded sayings (*yulu*), i.e., with many anecdotes and parables and a rejection of esoteric interpretations. Yin was often willing to speak of his own ascetic training to encourage his audience, explaining for instance how he gradually managed to go without sleeping for weeks, or how, while in a state of trance, he experienced decapitation and resurrection at the hands of his first master. This combination of historical and autobiographical evidence makes Yin Zhiping an exceptionally familiar figure of early Quanzhen.

Vincent GOOSSAERT

📖 Boltz J. M. 1987a, 167–69; Eskildsen 2001; Kohn 1997b, 120–24; Qing Xitai 1994, 1: 335–37

※ Qiu Chuji; Quanzhen

Yinfu jing

陰符經

Scripture of the Hidden Accordance

The *Yinfu jing* exists in as almost many versions as its editions. The text first appears in the early seventh century. For this reason, it has been considered in the past to be a forgery by *Li Quan (fl. 713–60), an officer who wrote books on military strategy, and who claimed to have discovered it in a cave on Mount Song (*Songshan, Henan) where *Kou Qianzhi had supposedly hidden it. Modern scholars, however, have different opinions its date. Li Dahua (1995) deems it to date from the Six Dynasties, Wang Ming (1984d, first published in 1962) dates it to the early sixth century, Miyakawa Hisayuki (1984a, 1984b) suggests that it was written shortly before the Sui dynasty, and Christopher Rand (1979) considers it to be of a later date because of a lack of earlier evidence. The tradition that traces the text back to *Huangdi exists in two versions. According to the first one, the Mysterious Woman (*Xuannü) gave it to Huangdi to help him in his struggle against the demon Chiyou 蚩尤. According to the second, Huangdi discovered it on Mount Song and *Guangcheng zi explained its meaning to him.

Content and interpretations. The text comprises little more than three hundred words, to which one hundred more are often added, which supposedly consist of Huangdi's own explications. It is usually divided into three parts, said to deal with the art of "divine immortality and embracing the One (*baoyi* 抱一)," with "prosperity of the country and peace for humanity," and with "a strong army and victory in war," respectively. The title is interpreted in various ways, but most often as indicating a "tacit agreement" between the Way of Heaven and the Way of Humankind, or between self-cultivation and the management of one's family and the state. An alternative title is *Tianji jing* 天機經 (Scripture of the Celestial Mechanism); a text bearing this name immediately follows the version of the *Yinfu jing* in *Yunji qiqian 15.

Although the *Yinfu jing* has been linked to the military arts (Reiter 1984), Taoist commentaries generally understand it as advocating the harmony between nature and humanity. It is often mentioned together with the *Daode jing* and the *Zhouyi cantong qi, and is said to deal inwardly with the Celestial Mechanism (*tianji* 天機; see *ji) of the world and outwardly with human affairs. Most often, as in the *Yinfu jing jijie* 陰符經集解 (Collected Explications of the *Yinfu jing*; CT 111) and as quoted in many *neidan texts, it is interpreted in inner alchemical terms. In this case, the sections dealing with government and war are explained as symbolically representing the process of self-cultivation for achieving purity through expelling Yin and attaining to Pure Yang (*chunyang* 純陽, the state beyond the duality of Yin and Yang).

Commentaries. The *Daozang* contains no less than twenty commentaries on the *Yinfu jing* published as independent texts (CT 108 to CT 127), and another by *Li Daochun included in his *Santian yisui* 三天易髓 (The Mutable Marrow of the Three Heavens; CT 250, 10a–12b). Outside the *Daozang*, an important commentary by *Liu Yiming is found in his *Daoshu shi'er zhong* (Twelve Books on the Dao). The version containing Li Quan's own annotations (CT 109) appears to have suffered alterations, and its commentary was interpolated with the commentary ascribed to *Zhongli Quan (in CT 111). The commentary attributed to Zhang Guo 張果 (fl. mid-eight century; see *Zhang Guolao) is incomplete (CT 112, and YJQQ 15.1a–11a). Some quotations of the *Yinfu jing* that appear in Tang or even in Song sources cannot be found in its present text.

Isabelle ROBINET

📖 Balfour 1884, 49–62 (trans.); Legge 1891, 2: 255–264 (trans.); Li Dahua 1995; Miyakawa Hisayuki 1984a; Miyakawa Hisayuki 1984b; Qing Xitai 1988–95, 1: 416–25; Rand 1979 (trans.); Reiter 1984; Robinet 1997b, 210–11; Wang Ming 1962

※ Li Quan; *neidan*

Yinqueshan manuscripts

A large cache of texts written on slips of bamboo was discovered in April 1972 in tomb no. 1 in a Former Han cemetery at Yinqueshan 銀雀山, Linyi 臨沂 (Shandong), probably buried in the 130s BCE. The discovery led to the identification of 4,942 individual fragments together with five wooden boards containing the titles of some of the texts (Wu Jiulong 1985; Yinqueshan Hanmu zhujian zhengli xiaozu 1985). The more than one hundred titles belong to numerous genres, including the art of war, writings on government, literature, mathematics, divination, physiognomy, and other esoteric arts (Luo Fuyi 1974; Luo Fuyi 1985), and are affiliated with the Taoist, Confucian, Mohist, Military Writers (*bingjia* 兵家), Yin-Yang, and other Various Masters (*zajia* 雜家) traditions. Some of the fragments have been identified as early versions of texts, or sections of texts that have been continuously transmitted down from Warring States times. Others bear titles that appear in the bibliography of the Han imperial collection, found in the *Hanshu* (History of the Former Han), but were subsequently lost. Yet others are works whose titles were previously unknown.

Military texts. One of the boards contained the titles of the thirteen-section *Sunzi bingfa* 孫子兵法 (Master Sun's Art of War), although with some variation in the order and titles of the sections. This demonstrated that the organization of this military canon was already established by the early Han and was not a creation of a later commentator, such as Cao Cao 曹操 (155–220), founder of the Wei dynasty. Five other essays related to Sunzi or Sun Wu 孫武 were also found, one of them being a story about Sunzi's interview with the King of Wu, Helü (r. 514–496 BCE), another version of which the Han historian Sima Qian included as Sun Wu's biography in his *Shiji* (Records of the Historian; *j.* 65). One of the others, *Huangdi fa Chidi* 黃帝伐赤帝 (The Yellow Emperor Attacks the Red Emperor) shows the influence of Five Phase (**wuxing*) thinking on the Sunzi military tradition (Ames 1993; Li Ling 1995). Fragments of the long-lost *Bingfa* 兵法 (Art of War) of Sun Bin 孫臏, a descendant of Sun Wu, were also recovered (Lau and Ames 1996), as well as passages from two other of the Seven Military Canons, the *Liu Tao* 六韜 and the *Weiliao zi* 尉繚子, and texts on the defense of cities similar to those found in chapters 14 and 15 of the present *Mozi* 墨子 (Book of Master Mo).

Texts on administration and esoteric practices. A number of the essays on administration and esoteric practices might be related to works that were composed by Taoists at the Jixia 稷下 academy in the state of Qi 齊 (modern Shandong) in the Warring States period. One example is the *Dingxin guqi* 定心固氣 (Concentrating on the Heart-Mind and Stabilizing Energy). The divination texts, texts on seasonal orders, activities, prohibitions, and some military texts such as the *Di Dian* 地典 (Regulator of the Earth), derive from Yin-Yang and Five Phase specialists and reveal that in the early Former Han these two traditions had still not amalgamated and that there was a close intellectual relationship between them and composers of **Huang-Lao Taoist philosophy (Yates 1994b). The *Sanshi shi* 三十時 (Thirty Seasons) is similar to the calendar preserved in the *Guanzi* 管子 (Li Ling 2000b, 395–415) and the *Tiandi bafeng wuxing kezhu wuyin zhi ju* 天地八風五行客主五音之居 (Heaven and Earth, Eight Winds, Five Phases, Guests and Hosts, and Dwellings of the Five Notes), that is accompanied by a chart drawn in red ink, contains divination techniques on the Wind Angles (*fengjiao* 風角) and Matching Sounds (*nayin* 納音) that are similar to those found in later works, such as the **Huainan zi*, the *Wuxing dayi* 五行大義 (Great Meaning of the Five Agents), and **Li Chunfeng's *Yisi zhan* 乙巳占 (Prognostications for 645 CE; Rao Zongyi 1993b).

Robin D. S. YATES

📖 Luo Fuyi 1974; Luo Fuyi 1985; Wu Jiulong 1985; Yates 1994b; Yinqueshan Hanmu zhujian zhengli xiaozu 1985

yinsi

淫祀

licentious (*or*: excessive, illicit, heterodox) cult (*or*: sacrifice)

Yinsi is the most common Chinese term for heterodox religious behavior. *Yin* 淫, etymologically referring to a river overflowing its banks, denotes activities that transgress established norms, and can refer to sexual excess; *si* 祀 refers first to the cycle of sacrificial ritual that constituted the ritual year, and from this to worship involving sacrifice. Alternate translations include "excessive sacrifice," which focuses on the extravagance and expense of the elaborate sacrifices often associated with the term, and "lascivious sacrifice," which focuses on the sexual connotations of the character *yin*. "Licentious" may be preferred because the primary referent of the term involves religious activity that "takes license" with limitations of who may sacrifice what to whom. The term is also sometimes applied to the social group that engages in these practices, i.e., "licentious cults," and in this sense is sometimes found in the form *yinci* 淫祠 or "licentious shrine."

The term *yinsi* has both a formal definition and a practical application; failure to differentiate these two levels of meaning has led to much misunderstanding. The *Liji* 禮記 (Records of Rites; trans. Legge 1885, 1: 116) defines the term as "sacrifice to one to whom you should not sacrifice." Warring States texts record normative restrictions on sacrifice, limiting who may sacrifice what to whom and how often. These lists specify that the highest deities may only be worshipped by the ruler, with lower echelons addressing progressively less powerful gods. Commoners, when mentioned at all, may only worship their own ancestors. Moreover, the worship of the dead other than one's own agnatic ancestors was condemned already by Confucius (*Lunyu* 論語, trans. Legge 1893, 154; see also *Zuozhuan* 左傳, trans. Legge 1872, 157). During the imperial period, the term came to be defined as sacrifice offered to any deity not in the official Canon of Sacrifices (*sidian* 祀典), a list of deities that had been granted official recognition in the form of an ennoblement and the ceremonies appropriate to their worship. Local gazetteers sometimes include the portion of the Canon of Sacrifices appropriate to their regions, but no authoritative canon for the entire empire survives, if such a document truly ever existed. It is unclear if the gods listed in the Canon of Sacrifices where open to worship by commoners; surviving texts record only the ceremonies to be conducted by officials.

In practice, the term "licentious sacrifice" was applied to a variety of religious activities that the user viewed as inappropriate. This could include even the religious activities of the emperor (usually denounced only in retrospect, e.g. *Hou Hanshu*, *Zhi* 志, 9.3199 and 15.3311), but was most commonly applied to popular worship. All Buddhist and Taoist worship would seem to fit the formal definition but the term was not used in this connection, perhaps because they worshipped pantheons that did not overlap with that of the state and because they did not practice sacrifice. Instead the term is most often applied to cults served by ecstatic religious professionals often called *wu* 巫. The focus of much criticism is the extravagant wastefulness of the sacrifice and the ecstatic behavior of its celebrants. It is also claimed that such worship is ineffective, resulting in no blessings for the sacrificer. The personal predilections of the local official seem to have played a paramount role in the application of this criterion. The frequent accounts of a newly-appointed official who discovers his region to be infested with licentious cults, which he proceeds to uproot, reveal more about the intolerance of the new official than about the nature of the cults, most of which had no doubt existed undisturbed for generations, if not centuries.

Taoists also made use of the term *yinsi* to condemn expressions of popular religion. Rolf A. Stein (1979), noting that the same sort of cult that aroused the ire of officials is inveighed against in Taoist scriptures, assumed that the state and the Taoist Church shared a commonality of interest in this regard. But where the traditional critique focused on social aspects of the ritual, the usurpation of traditional religious roles and implications for societal order, the Taoists argued that such activity was heretical and evil. The Taoist stance was founded upon the original condemnation of all blood sacrifice enshrined in the Pure Bond (*qingyue* 清約): "The gods do not eat or drink." The fifth-century *Daomen kelüe (Abridged Codes for the Taoist Community; 1.1b) states that even the ancestors, the earth god, and the hearth may be worshipped only five times a year; more frequent worship is licentious. The *Wushang biyao (Supreme Secret Essentials, 22.23a) condemns those who, having received the true religion, perform licentious blood sacrifice, thus rebelling against the Dao and allying with demons. Thus for the Taoists, licentious sacrifice is efficacious, but immoral.

Terry KLEEMAN

📖 Kleeman 1994b; Stein R. A. 1979

※ TAOISM AND POPULAR RELIGION

Yiqie daojing yinyi

一切道經音義

Complete Taoist Scriptures, with Phonetic and Semantic Glosses

The *Yiqie daojing yinyi* was the greatest scholarly work on Taoism published in the medieval period before the year 1000. It was an imperial compilation begun and completed in the reign of Tang Ruizong (r. 684–90, 710–12). Shi Chongxuan 史崇玄 (or Shi Chong 史崇, ?–713), abbot of the Taiqing guan 太清觀 (Abbey of Great Clarity) in Chang'an, chaired the commission that researched and assembled the text. At the time a fierce struggle for power at court raged between Tang Xuanzong (r. 712–56) and his aunt Princess Taiping 太平 who was an ordained Taoist priestess. Abbot Shi was one of the princess's partisans and died when Xuanzong suppressed her clique in the summer of 713.

Forty-three members sat on the commission: nineteen priests (all except two from abbeys in Chang'an, the capital), twenty-two erudites from imperial academies in the capital (many of them among the most renowned scholars of their day), and two officials. According to Xuanzong's preface, the emperor charged this body with examining Taoist scriptures to correct errors and supply omissions that had crept into them through repeated transcriptions. He also directed it to compile a lexicon and pronunciation guide to arcane, obsolete and obscure terminology that appeared in the texts. Hence, he gave it the title "Complete Taoist Scriptures, with Phonetic and Semantic Glosses."

In the course of their endeavors the members of the commission examined texts of more than 2,000 scrolls from libraries in the capital and the palaces. Their final compilation in 253 scrolls included not only a glossary in 140 scrolls, but also a catalogue in 113 scrolls that encompassed both the works they had consulted and titles listed in older bibliographies.

In conjunction with his duties as head of the commission, Shi Chongxuan compiled a small treatise on basic Taoist tenets called the *Yiqie daojing yinyi miaomen youqi* 一切道經音義妙門由起 (The Sources of the School of Marvels, from the Complete Taoist Scriptures with Phonetic and Semantic Glosses; CT 1123). It has six sections:

1. "Elucidation of the Transformations of the Dao" ("Ming daohua" 明道化, 1a–2a).

2. "Elucidation of the Celestial Worthies" ("Ming Tianzun" 明天尊, 2a–10a).

3. "Elucidation of Dharma Realms" ("Ming fajie" 明法界, 10a–11a). The passages cited here concern various ethereal worlds, celestial and subterranean.

4. "Elucidation of Residences" ("Ming juchu" 明居處, 11a–15a). The citations in this part describe the palaces of the gods as well as abbeys, chapels and hermitages for mortals.

5. "Elucidation of Initiations and Ordinations" ("Ming kaidu" 明開度, 15b–20b). This section includes remarks on various classes of priests as well as their vestments.

6. "Elucidation of Scriptures and Rituals" ("Ming jingfa" 明經法, 20b–33b). This section consists entirely of excerpts from scriptures, protocols, manuals, and various other texts; it quotes from lost works and supplies passages from extant titles that can be used for collation.

Unfortunately all that remains of the *Yiqie daojing yinyi* are the *Miaomen youqi*, prefaces written by Xuanzong and Shi Chongxuan, *Zhang Wanfu's glosses to the *Duren jing*, and a small number of citations from the lexicon in an annotation of the *Dadong zhenjing (Shangqing dadong zhenjing yujue yinyi 上清大洞真經玉訣音義; CT 104) compiled by *Chen Jingyuan.

The *Yiqie daojing yinyi* was but the first of Xuanzong's projects to foster Taoism. He continued to collect texts and by 718 had amassed a collection in 3,744 scrolls. Then in 749 the emperor sent the entire corpus from the palace to the Chongxuan guan 崇玄館 (Institute for the Veneration of the Mystery) for transcription. His decree further stipulated that the duplicates were to be divided and forwarded to the provinces where they were to be recopied. The intent of that unprecedented act was to propagate Taoism throughout his realm.

Charles D. BENN

📖 Barrett 1996, 50–52; Benn 1977, 70–74 and 288–91; Chen Guofu 1963, 114–19; Ōfuchi Ninji 1978–79, 1: 316 (crit. notes on the Dunhuang ms.) and 2: 647 (reprod. of the Dunhuang ms.); Ōfuchi Ninji and Ishii Masako 1988, 170–73 (list of texts cited); Yoshioka Yoshitoyo 1955, 98–115

Yisheng baode zhuan

翊聖保德傳

Biography of [the Perfected Lord] Assisting Sanctity
and Protecting Virtue

The *Yisheng baode zhuan* is the comprehensive account of the revelations
bestowed in the period 960–94 by the divine protector of the Song dynasty,
Yisheng baode zhenjun 翊聖保德真君 (Perfected Lord Assisting Sanctity and
Protecting Virtue). The book was compiled by *Wang Qinruo (962–1025) on
the basis of earlier records. It was presented at court in 1016 (the memorial of
the author and the endorsement by the emperor are appended to the text) and
furnished with a preface by Song Zhenzong (r. 997–1022). The earliest edition
of the work is found in the *Yunji qiqian* (j. 103), but the text is also included
as a separate book in the *Daozang* (CT 1285). Unlike the *Yunji qiqian* version,
the latter attributes Zhenzong's preface to his successor, Song Renzong (r.
1022–63), and includes at the end the enfeoffment of the god by Song Huizong
(r. 1100–1125) in 1104.

The revelations had taken place in the Zhongnan mountains (Zhongnan
shan 終南山, Shaanxi), where the god spoke through Zhang Shouzhen 張守
真, a man from Zhouzhi 盩厔 district (north of the mountains and border-
ing on the prefecture of Chang'an). The great importance attached to the
revelations in the history of the Northern Song dynasty is due to the fact that
they include a passage allegedly received as a *fuming* 符命, an announcement
from heaven that the mandate was to be transferred to Taizong (r. 976–97), the
second emperor of the dynasty and the younger brother of the first emperor,
Song Taizu (r. 960–76). This revelation is said to have taken place on the night
before the death of Taizu (*Xu zizhi tongjian changbian*, j. 17). It is however
also said that Taizong had already taken an interest in the cult in the years
963–67 (CT 1285, 1.4a), and it seems likely that this played a role in securing
his position as the heir apparent. After the accession of Taizong, the god was
rewarded with the construction of a temple, Shangqing taiping gong 上清太
平宮 (Palace of Great Peace of the Highest Clarity, completed in 980), at the
site where Zhang Shouzhen received the revelations (1.6b–7b).

The main elements of the initial revelation are the "methods of the sword"
(*jianfa* 劍法; 1.2b–3a), and a new ritual code comprising a nomenclature for the
various kinds of Offerings (*jiao) and regulations for the numbers of places
for deities (*shenwei* 神位) on the altar (1.3a–4a). The code includes, at the

highest level, three Offerings, to be performed for the benefit of the dynasty and the whole country, named *putian dajiao* 普天大醮 (Great Offering of the Universal Heaven), *zhoutian dajiao* 周天大醮 (Great Offering of the Whole Heaven), and **luotian dajiao* (Great Offering of All Heaven). The system was later adopted as the imperial standard, and Wang Qinruo was ordered to edit a ritual compendium for the *luotian dajiao*, which he submitted in ten *juan* around the same time as the biography of the Perfected Lord.

Poul ANDERSEN

📖 Andersen 1991, 125–26; Boltz J. M. 1987a, 83–86; Davis E. 2001, 69–74; Yang Huarong 1986

※ Wang Qinruo; Heisha; Tianxin zhengfa

Yixia lun

夷夏論

Essay on the Barbarians and the Chinese

The *Yixia lun* of 467 by *Gu Huan (420/428–483/491) stands out as the first po-lemical critique of Buddhism to delineate Taoism (*DAOJIAO) as a fully-fledged religious alternative to it. An implicit contrast between Buddhism and *daojiao* is already made by the Buddhist Zhou Yong 周顒 in a slightly earlier debate over the essential unity and visible dissimilarity between the two religions; the fact that Gu opens his work with a restatement of the assumption of unity and continues with criticisms of a quotation made in the earlier debate assures us that he was already familiar with these polemics. Although the foreign origins of Buddhism had attracted adverse comment for well over a century before the composition of the *Yixia lun*, Gu's construction of the Taoist alternative allows him to deploy all kinds of invidious dichotomies to support his case that an Indian religion is not fit for Chinese to believe: now the lack of filiality of the Buddhists, the prolixity of their scriptures, and so forth, are set against the model behavior of the Taoists, the succinct simplicity of their texts, and other Chinese virtues.

One measure of the impact of the *Yixia lun* is the considerable number of Buddhist responses which it provoked, spilling from the sixth into the seventh chapter of the **Hongming ji* (Collection Spreading the Light of Buddhism). The content of these further shows the beginnings of a move away from the "clash of civilizations" mode of earlier debate in China over Buddhism toward specific critiques of the Taoist religion as a rival entity, adumbrating the fierce interreligious polemics of a century later. Xie Zhenzhi 謝鎮之, for example, makes for the first time the accusation of plagiarism from the Buddhist scriptures against the recent authors of Taoist texts. Ming Sengshao 明僧紹 (?–483), commenting on the alleged identity of *nirvāṇa* and immortality, questions the coherence of the Taoist tradition, not only contrasting the immortality cult and Laozi's ideas but also pointing to the newer notion of rewards within an otherworldly hierarchy, though that he sees as not deleterious to "worldly teachings." For him, moreover, the followers of the Zhangs 張 (i.e. the Celestial Masters or *Tianshi dao) and the Ges 葛 (i.e. the *Lingbao Taoists of *Ge Chaofu) have no legitimate standing at all. As yet, however, the underlying assumption of unity is not explicitly denied in favor of a clear assertion of the inferiority of all "worldly" religions and teachings over against the supramundane role of Buddhism. But that step, with its consequences for the polemical status of cosmology, was not far off.

The *Yixia lun* is copiously cited in the biographies of Gu Huan and in the *Hongming ji*, but this leaves open the possibility that a complete text has not been transmitted. The *Guang hongming ji* 廣弘明集 (T. 2103, 8.546b) speaks of a version in five chapters. Even if this was a text that circulated among Buddhists, incorporating also all their refutations, that figure seems too high to represent only the materials that we now possess.

T. H. BARRETT

📖 Kohn 1995a, 155–69; Robinet 1977, 77–89 and 215–19

※ Gu Huan; TAOISM AND CHINESE BUDDHISM

yong

用

function

See *ti and *yong* 體 · 用.

Yongcheng jixian lu

墉城集仙錄

Records of the Immortals Gathered in the Walled City

The *Yongcheng jixian lu* is a collection of biographies of female immortals compiled by *Du Guangting (850–933). In Du's preface, and in several book catalogues from the Song, this collection is recorded as having ten chapters; in addition, the *Tongzhi* 通志 (Comprehensive Monographs) notes that it contained 109 biographies (van der Loon 1984, 154–55). No current version of *Yongcheng jixian lu* approaches this size in either the number of chapters or biographies. There are two main sources of biographies that derive from this collection in the Taoist Canon: an independent text entitled *Yongcheng jixian lu* (CT 783), containing thirty-seven biographies, and three chapters in the *Yunji qiqian* (j. 114–16), containing twenty-eight biographies and Du's preface. Fortunately, very few of the biographies are duplicated in these two sets of selections. In addition, a significant number of biographies found in the "Nüxian" 女仙 (Female Immortals) chapters of the *Taiping guangji* 太平廣記 (Extensive Records of the Taiping Xingguo Reign Period) claim to have been excerpted from the *Yongcheng jixian lu*. Together, these three sources enable us to reconstruct between half and three quarters of the original collection. Although Du Guangting does not indicate the sources of his biographies, it is clear that many of them derive from earlier collections of immortals' lives.

The *Yongcheng jixian lu*, like another of Du's biographical collections, the *Wangshi shenxian zhuan* 王氏神仙傳 (Biographies of Immortals of the Family Name Wang; Yan Yiping 1974, vol. 1), is thematic and programmatic. The focal point of the collection is *Xiwang mu, the Queen Mother of the West, who rules over Yongcheng, the walled city and who, by Du's time, had become one of the supreme female deities of the *Shangqing school. In the Tang, she was regarded as the guardian deity of women. Not surprisingly, as far as can be discerned from the surviving biographies, the *Yongcheng jixian lu* stresses the Shangqing heritage over other streams of Taoism.

Benjamin PENNY

📖 Cahill 1986b; Cahill 1990; Cahill 1993, passim; Despeux 1990, passim; Verellen 1989, 208

※ Du Guangting; HAGIOGRAPHY; WOMEN IN TAOISM

Yongle gong

永樂宮

Palace of Eternal Joy (Ruicheng, Shanxi)

The Yongle gong is a mammoth Taoist temple in southern Shanxi dedicated to the immortal *Lü Dongbin. The original site, now submerged, was located near the town of Yongle along the northern bank of the Yellow River. During the late 1950s and early 1960s, the entire temple complex was moved about 15 km northeast to its present location in Ruicheng 芮城 to make way for a dam construction project.

Whether a historical Lü Dongbin ever lived in Yongle is unclear, but inscriptions carved on stone and preserved at the Yongle gong inform us that by the end of the tenth century local residents had built a shrine at the reputed site of Lü's former home. This shrine soon became an active cult site, with scholar-officials and commoners from throughout the area gathering there for annual rituals every spring on the date of Lü's birth, the fourteenth day of the fourth lunar month. The shrine to Lü Dongbin at Yongle appears to have thrived during the Song dynasty, and by the Jin dynasty was converted into a Taoist *guan* 觀 (abbey). This *guan* suffered greatly during the incessant warfare that raged in the area at the end of the Jin dynasty, so that by the time the *Quanzhen Taoist master *Song Defang (1183–1247) visited the site during the 1240s it had fallen into a state of disrepair.

At Song's urging, the Quanzhen patriarch *Yin Zhiping (1169–1251), along with Li Zhichang 李志常 (1193–1256), made plans for the *guan*'s reconstruction. The site's prestige was enhanced when the Mongol court decreed that the blocks used to print the *Xuandu baozang* be stored there. In 1246, the Quanzhen Taoist Pan Dechong 潘德冲 (1191–1256) was appointed to oversee the reconstruction of the *guan* at Yongle. When Li Zhichang visited the site during a pilgrimage in 1252, much of the construction had been completed, and the main halls of the complex were finished in 1262. The new temple complex was renamed the Chunyang wanshou gong 純陽萬壽宮 (Palace of Ten-thousand-fold Longevity of Pure Yang), and was also referred to as the Yongle gong.

Halls and murals. The spatial arrangement of the Yongle gong was essentially the same as it is today. The entire complex, covering an area of 8,600 square meters, was protected by an outer wall, which had fallen into a state of disrepair by the time Chinese archaeologists discovered the site during the 1950s.

Fig. 85. Pavilion of the Three Clarities (Sanqing dian 三清殿).
Yongle gong (Palace of Eternal Joy).

A second wall surrounded the main Taoist halls and the other temples to their west. The main gate, constructed during the early Qing dynasty, provided the only avenue of access to this sacred site. A path nearly eighty meters long led to the Gate of the Ultimateless (Wuji men 無極門), which was completed in the year 1294. The first murals pilgrims and visitors saw, which depicted divine soldiers and generals, were painted on this gate. The northern side of the Gate served as a stage for the performance of operas during festivals held at the Yongle gong.

Pilgrims and visitors then walked eighty meters past trees and two huge stelae dating from 1262 and 1689 to ascend a flight of stairs and enter a more exalted plane of sacred space, the Pavilion of the Three Clarities (Sanqing dian 三清殿; fig. 85), which was completed by 1262. This was and remains the largest hall of the entire complex, covering an area of over 430 square meters. Statues of the Taoist supreme deities, the Three Clarities (*sanqing), were enshrined inside the Pavilion, surrounded by murals depicting 286 members of the Taoist pantheon engaged in an audience ceremony with them. This massive work, known as the *Chaoyuan tu* 朝元圖 (Illustrations of the Audience with the [Three] Primes) was completed in 1325. It covers an area of over 402 square meters, the deities featured being as tall as two meters and the murals covering four meters from top to bottom.

After leaving the Pavilion of the Three Clarities, pilgrims and visitors proceeded another forty meters along the elevated walkway to the Pavilion of Pure Yang (Chunyang dian 純陽殿; Chunyang was Lü Dongbin's *daohao* 道號). This hall was also completed by 1262, but built on a much smaller scale, covering just over 300 square meters. A statue of Lü Dongbin was enshrined in this hall, surrounded by a pictorial hagiography depicting his life as a mortal and his deeds after becoming an immortal (see fig. 56). These murals, entitled *Chunyang dijun shenyou xianhua tu* 純陽帝君神游仙化圖 (The Divine Travels and Immortal Transformations of the Imperial Lord of Pure Yang), were completed in 1358. Most of the fifty-two scenes from Lü Dongbin's hagiography are accompanied by a cartouche (*tiji* 提記) describing the story portrayed. Nearly two-thirds of these cartouches (thirty-seven in all) are direct quotations from the *Chunyang dijun shenhua miaotong ji* 純陽帝君神化妙通紀 (Chronicle of the Divine Transformations and Wondrous Powers of the Imperial Lord of Pure Yang; CT 305; trans. Ang 1993), a work written by the southern Taoist master *Miao Shanshi (fl. 1288–1324).

From the Pavilion of Pure Yang, pilgrims and visitors then walked an additional twenty meters to the Pavilion of Double Yang (Chongyang dian 重陽殿). In this hall were enshrined statues of the Quanzhen founder *Wang Zhe (1113–70; Wang's *daohao* was Chongyang), as well as six of his seven disciples known as the *qizhen* 七真 (see table 17; *Sun Bu'er is excluded). A total of forty-nine murals adorn the walls of this hall, and appear to have been completed around 1368. Most of the scenes portray hagiographic works about Wang Zhe now preserved in the Taoist Canon. These murals are highly important sources for the study of Quanzhen beliefs and practices, portraying events such as Lü Dongbin's conversion of Wang Zhe, as well as Wang himself using a painting of a skeleton to instruct his disciples. Unfortunately, these artworks have yet to be systematically studied by either art historians or specialists in Taoist studies.

The main halls described above, while architecturally impressive, only occupied about half of the area of the Yongle gong. To the northwest of the main halls lay two Taoist cloisters (*daoyuan) built a few hundred meters south of the tombs of Song Defang and Pan Dechong. The area directly west of the main Taoist halls contained other temples in which both Taoist and popular deities were worshipped, as well as a local academy and a pilgrim's hostel. The most interesting site in the western portion of the Yongle gong is the Shrine to Ancestor Lü (Lüzu ci 呂祖祠), which may be a reconstruction of Lü Dongbin's shrine mentioned above. Almost all these buildings appear in a diagram of the Yongle gong published in the 1754 edition of the *Puzhou fuzhi* 蒲州府志 (Monograph of the Puzhou Prefecture). In addition, the reputed site of Lü Dongbin's tomb lay about 175 meters to the southeast of the Palace. This tomb was excavated by Chinese archaeologists before the Palace was moved to its new home in Ruicheng. Inside they found the skeletons of a man and a woman, which appear to date from the eleventh century.

In many ways, the Yongle gong is not as well documented as many sacred sites throughout China. However, we are fortunate that this site has been researched by archaeologists, historians, and specialists in art history. The Yongle gong also possesses large numbers of temple inscriptions and its world-famous murals. Su Bai (1962) has transcribed most of the Yongle gong's inscriptions, and some have been reprinted in modern punctuated form in *Daojia jinshi lüe* 道家金石略 (A Collection of Taoist Epigraphy; Chen Yuan 1988). The Yongle gong's murals have been described in detail by numerous scholars (including Idema 1993; Jing Anning 1993; Mori Yuria 1992a), while others have transcribed the cartouches accompanying them (Wang Chang'an 1963). Several catalogues of the Yongle gong murals are also available, including (at long last) a complete set of all the murals at this site (Jin Weinuo 1997). One brief description of an early twentieth-century festival at the Yongle gong has been published (Li Xianzhou 1983), while folklorists have recorded local stories about Lü Dongbin and the Yongle gong (Luo Shizheng et al. 1987).

Paul R. KATZ

📖 Idema 1993; Jin Weinuo 1997; Jing Anning 1993; Katz P. R. 1993; Katz P. R. 1994; Katz P. R. 1997; Katz P. R. 1999; Li Xianzhou 1983; Luo Shizheng et al. 1987; Mori Yuria 1992a; Su Bai 1962; Wang Chang'an 1963

※ Lü Dongbin; Quanzhen; TAOISM AND CHINESE ART; TEMPLES AND SHRINES

you

有

Being (Existence)

See *wu and *you* 無 · 有.

Youlong zhuan

猶龍專

Like unto a Dragon

The *Youlong zhuan* (CT 774) is a major Laozi hagiography of the Song dynasty. Its title picks up the description of Laozi given by Confucius, who was stunned into breathless admiration after a meeting with the sage, according to the *Shiji* (Records of the Historian; 63.2139–43; trans. Lau 1982, x-xi). Dated to 1086 and consisting of six *juan*, the hagiography was written by Jia Shanxiang 賈善翔, a Taoist serving at the *Taiqing gong (Palace of Great Clarity) in Laozi's birthplace of Bozhou 亳州 (present-day Luyi 鹿邑, Henan).

Originally from Pengzhou 蓬州 in Sichuan, Jia was a friend of the statesman and poet Su Shi 蘇軾 (Su Dongpo 蘇東坡, 1037–1101; SB 900–968). He wrote various Taoist works, including the *Chujia chuandu yi* 出家傳度儀 (Liturgies for Recluse Ordination; CT 1236), a technical manual detailing ordination procedures. The highlight of his Taoist career, as recorded in the *Lishi zhenxian tidao tongjian* (51.16a), was a miracle that happened during one of his lectures, when an old lady who had been blind for thirty-one years suddenly regained her eyesight. In addition, Jia anticipated his death in a dream that showed him endowed with celestial honors and as head of the celestial Taiqing gong.

The *Youlong zhuan* gives an account of the god Laozi in thirty sections, describing all his supernatural abilities and actions. It recounts how Laozi existed prior to all, created the world, descended as the teacher of dynasties, was born supernaturally to serve as an archivist under the Zhou, transmitted the *Daode jing* to *Yin Xi, emigrated to the west to "convert the barbarians" (*huahu* 化胡; see *Huahu jing*), and returned repeatedly to bestow revelations of the Dao and manifest himself in visions and miracles, all the way up to the Tang and Song dynasties.

The date of the *Youlong zhuan* coincides with that of Sima Guang's 司馬光 (1019–86) *Zizhi tongjian* 資治通鑑 (Comprehensive Mirror to Aid in Government), indicating that the text, within its own tradition, responds to the overarching historiographic concerns of the Song. Like the Buddhist *Fozu tongji* 佛祖統紀 (Comprehensive Chronicle of the Buddhas and Patriarchs; T. 2035) of the year 1250, the *Youlong zhuan* is thus not merely a devout account of Laozi's deeds but, more significantly, also a universal history of the Dao, proposing a Taoist view of how and why the world came into being and history took its course. Its account makes use of numerous earlier sources. In particular, it relies heavily on *Du Guangting's hagiographic works and especially on his description of the deity's life in the *Daode zhenjing guangsheng yi* 道德真經廣聖義 (Extended Interpretation of the Emperor's Exegesis of the *Daode jing*; 901; CT 725, *j.* 2). The *Youlong zhuan* in turn served as a key source and general model for the voluminous *Hunyuan shengji (Saintly Chronicle of Chaotic Origin) a century later.

Livia KOHN

📖 Boltz J. M. 1987a, 131–33; Kohn 1998b, passim; Qing Xitai 1994, 1: 314

※ Laozi and Laojun; HAGIOGRAPHY

Yu Daoxian

于道顯

1168–1232; *hao*: Lifeng zi 離峰子 (Master of the Solitary Peak)

Yu Daoxian is a good example of the third generation of *Quanzhen Taoists, whose impressive ascetic feats, predication, and temple-building ushered in the era of the order's institutionalization. His life is primarily known through a tomb inscription by the famous poet Yuan Haowen 元好問 (1190–1257; IC 952–55). As he does in eighteen other similar documents, Yuan expresses his admiration for the selflessness of Quanzhen masters and the efficiency of their organization, but also his misgivings at their transformation of the Confucian fabric of society. Other inscriptions, pertaining to Yu's many disciples, confirm his importance in the early thirteenth-century Quanzhen order. Besides being an eminently influential preacher, Yu was also one of the first Quanzhen masters to be appointed to an official post in the Taoist bureaucracy under the Jin in the 1220s, even before *Qiu Chuji's religious supremacy under the Mongols prompted the general conversion of Taoist institutions to Quanzhen.

When he had barely reached the age of twenty, Yu became a disciple of *Liu Chuxuan. After receiving his master's teaching, he devoted himself to a period of harsh asceticism, travelling long distances and begging alms for survival. Whereas most of his fellow adepts adopted enclosed meditation (*huandu) as their choice trial, Yu seems to have especially favored deprivation of sleep (*lian shuimo* 鍊睡魔). Until his death, he founded and animated communities in Shandong and Henan. The Taoist Canon contains an anthology of Yu's regulated poems (*shi* 詩) entitled *Lifeng laoren ji* 離峰老人集 (Anthology of the Old Man of the Solitary Peak; CT 1264). Many poems in this work are dedicated to community members, and document his predication among lay followers of the Quanzhen order.

Vincent GOOSSAERT

📖 Boltz J. M. 1987a, 169–70

※ Liu Chuxuan; Quanzhen

Yu Yan

俞琰

1258–1314; *zi*: Yuwu 玉吾; *hao*: Quanyang zi 全陽子 (Master of
Complete Yang), Linwu yiren 林屋逸人 (The Retired Man of the
Forest Cottage), Linwu shanren 林屋山人 (The Mountain Man
of the Forest Cottage)

Although Yu Yan, a native of present-day Suzhou, is sometimes said to have
developed an interest in *neidan late in life, his *magnum opus*, the *Zhouyi cantong
qi fahui* 周易參同契發揮 (Clarification of the *Zhouyi cantong qi*; CT 1005),
dates from his mid-twenties. By that time, according to his own statement,
the commentary had already undergone three or four drafts. Besides this
work, Yu Yan's extant texts in the Taoist Canon include the *Xuanpin zhi men
fu* 玄牝之門賦 (Rhapsody on the Gate of the Mysterious Female; CT 1010),
commentaries to the *Yinfu jing (Scripture of the Hidden Accordance; CT
125) and the *Qinyuan chun (Spring in the Garden by the Qin River; CT 136),
and a work on the system of the *Yijing entitled *Yiwai biezhuan* 易外別傳 (A
Separate Transmission Outside the *Changes*; CT 1009; a title alluding to the
Chan phrase, "a separate transmission outside the scriptural teaching," *jiaowai
biezhuan* 教外別傳). A full commentary to the *Yijing* entitled *Zhouyi jishuo*
周易集說 (Collected Explanations of the *Book of Changes*) is also among his
extant works (Qing Xitai 1994, 2: 115–16). While the *Jishuo* interprets the *Yijing*
based on Zhu Xi's 朱熹 (1130–1200) exegesis, Yu Yan points out in his preface
to the *Biezhuan* that this work deals with the application of the system of
the *Yijing* to alchemy. The texts consists of a series of diagrams illustrating
the relation between *xiantian and *houtian* (the states "prior to Heaven" and
"subsequent to Heaven"), followed by passages of the *Yijing* that are explicated
through quotations from the *Zhouyi cantong qi and other alchemical texts
(Zhan Shichuang 1989, 83–96).

The *Zhouyi cantong qi fahui* was completed in 1284, the same year Yu Yan
signed the preface of the *Biezhuan*. The first printed edition was honored with
a preface by the thirty-eighth Celestial Master, Zhang Yucai 張與材 (?–1316),
written in 1310. Most editions also include undated prefaces by Ruan Dengbing
阮登炳 and by the eminent commentator of the *Daode jing*, *Du Daojian
(1237–1318). The textual notes to the commentary were collected by Yu Yan in
a final section of his work, which is separately printed in the Taoist Canon as
the *Zhouyi cantong qi shiyi* 周易參同契釋疑 (Exegesis of Doubtful Points in
the *Zhouyi cantong qi*; CT 1006).

The *Shiyi* provides important details on the way Yu Yan established his recension. After remarks on mistakes found in the recensions by *Peng Xiao, *Chen Xianwei, and other authors, Yu Yan continues by saying that he based his text on a "Shu edition" (*Shu ben* 蜀本), a "Yue edition" (*Yue ben* 越本), a "Ji edition" (*Ji ben* 吉本), and on more than one Tang edition (CT 1006, preface, 3b). Despite the vagueness of these indications, the mention of Tang editions among Yu Yan's sources is especially worthy of note. Several variants noted in the *Shiyi* as coming from the "old text" (*jiuben* 舊本) of the *Cantong qi* correspond to the readings of one or both of the Tang recensions preserved in the Taoist Canon (see under *Zhouyi cantong qi*), and Yu Yan's references to them as the "old text" is further proof of the early date of those recensions. The other variants reported in the *Shiyi* are usually not attributed to specific authors or editions. Comparison of these notes and of Yu Yan's text to the other recensions in the Canon shows, nevertheless, that the *Fahui* is also based on Zhu Xi's 朱熹 recension (the *Zhouyi cantong qi kaoyi*).

The *Fahui*, which is one of the major commentaries to the *Cantong qi*, is firmly rooted in the textual legacy of the Southern and Northern lineages of Song Taoism (i.e., *Nanzong and *Quanzhen). The works quoted in it most often are those of the Southern lineage, including the *Wuzhen pian, *Xue Daoguang's *Huandan fuming pian* 還丹復命篇 (Folios on Returning to Life through the Reverted Elixir; CT 1088), *Chen Nan's *Cuixu pian* 翠虛篇 (Folios of the Master of Emerald Emptiness; CT 1090), and Xiao Tingzhi's 蕭廷芝 (fl. 1260–64) *Jindan dacheng ji (Anthology on the Great Achievement of the Golden Elixir). The Northern lineage is represented in works by its founder, *Wang Zhe, and its patriarchs, including *Ma Yu and *Qiu Chuji. Besides these, Yu Yan draws from such works as the *Yinfu jing*, the *Huangting jing (Scripture of the Yellow Court), the *Ruyao jing (Mirror for Compounding the Medicine), and more than one hundred other texts.

Fabrizio PREGADIO

📖 Xiao Hanming 1997; Zhan Shichuang 1989, 83–96; Zhao Liang 1993

※ *neidan*

yuanqi

元氣

Original Pneuma, Original Breath

Yuanqi is the pneuma of the *xiantian* ("prior to Heaven") ontologic and cosmogonic stage. Said to have spontaneously issued from the Dao or from Non-being (*wu*), it is described as earlier than or equivalent to Primordial Chaos (*hundun*), which is devoid of material or other properties but harbors an "essence" (*jing*) that is the seed of the generation of the cosmos by the Dao (*Daode jing* 21). Through the stages of the generation of the cosmos, Original Pneuma transforms itself into cosmic pneuma (*qi*), a process that is equivalent to the generation of Oneness (*yi*) from the Dao. Oneness then divides itself into Yin and Yang, with the lighter parts of pneuma ascending to become Heaven, and the grosser ones descending to become the Earth, thereby marking the shift to the state known as *houtian* ("subsequent to Heaven"). Yin and Yang, or Heaven and Earth, finally give birth to the "ten thousand things" (*wanwu* 萬物).

Since each stage is defined as an "alteration" or "transformation" (*bian* 變, *hua* 化) of the previous one, the cosmogonic sequence is primarily a representation of different states of Being and the relations that occur among them. For the same reason, the cosmogonic process also provides a model for "returning" (*fan*) to the Dao by tracing the individual stages in a reverse sequence. In alchemy, this attainment is represented by the elixir, which is equated with Original Pneuma.

Fabrizio PREGADIO

☐ Maspero 1981, 465–68

※ *dianhua*; *jing, qi, shen*; *xiantian* and *houtian*; COSMOGONY; COSMOLOGY

Yuanqi lun

元氣論

Treatise on Original Pneuma

The *Yuanqi lun* (YJQQ 56) is an important source for Taoist views of cosmogony and cosmology. The main topics discussed in its seven sections, which are not systematically organized, include the formation of the cosmos, the appearance of human beings and human culture, the establishment of the Way (*dao*), the movement of the heavens, human birth and the differentiation of the sexes, Original Pneuma (*yuanqi) in the human body, and self-cultivation methods. Based on some of the texts it quotes, this work appears to put forth views held by the *Shangqing school. Citations from the *Sancen ge* 三岑歌 (Song of the Three Summits), a work attributed to *Luo Gongyuan (fl. 712–13), show that it dates from the latter part of the Tang dynasty.

The discussion on the formation of the cosmos draws on the Han "weft texts" (*weishu* 緯書; see *TAOISM AND THE APOCRYPHA) and other early works. According to this description, the state before original Chaos (*hundun) is called Great Non-existence (*taiwu* 太無), and the state at the beginning of original Chaos is called Great Harmony (*taihe* 太和). This becomes the formless and obscure Great Simplicity (*taiyi* 太易), in which Original Pneuma has not yet come forth. Original Pneuma first sprouts at the stage of the Great Beginning (*taichu* 太初); then form (*xing* 形) appears at the stage of the Great Commencement (*taishi* 太始), and matter (*zhi* 質) at the stage of the Great Plainness (*taisu* 太素). Pneuma (*qi) is generated with the transformations of matter, at the stage called Great Ultimate (*taiji). At first, pneuma is not yet differentiated and exists in the shape of an egg; this is called Great Oneness (*taiyi). Then it begins to separate: the clearer pneuma rises to become Heaven and the grosser pneuma descends to become the Earth. The "central harmony" (*zhonghe* 中和) between them is humankind.

The first human being is Pan Gu 盤古. At his death, the various parts of his body become the Sun, the Moon, and the stars in heaven, and the mountains, the rivers, and the plants on earth. At the epoch of the Three Sovereigns (*sanhuang), regulations about food and clothing are established and eventually morality develops. The names of father and mother emerge, from which comes the Way (*dao*); from the Way come Yin and Yang, and from Original Pneuma come inner nature and vital force (*xing and *ming*). Next the text describes the size of heaven and earth and the movement of the heavens, based on the *Huainan zi and on Zhang Heng's 張衡 (78–139; IC 211–12) *Lingxian* 靈憲 (The Numinous Structure; see under *COSMOGONY).

A human being receives the Original Pneuma of heaven and earth and is born after ten months. It is also said that an infant is filled with the Original Pneuma; and, based on statements found in the *Huangdi bashiyi nanjing* 黃帝八十一難經 (Scripture of the Eighty-One Difficult Points [in the Inner Scripture] of the Yellow Emperor), that gender differences between men and women at birth derive from differences in how the pneuma has been received. Finally, the text states that the Original Pneuma in the human body is the "breath in movement between the kidneys," and emphasizes the role of the three Cinnabar Fields (*dantian).

These descriptions form the basis for specific discussions about Taoist practices. Methods described in detail in the *Yuanqi lun* include those of embryonic breathing (*taixi*) and meditation (*cunsi* 存思; see under *cun*).

SAKADE Yoshinobu

※ *yuanqi*; COSMOGONY; COSMOLOGY

Yuanyang zi

元陽子

Master of Original Yang

Yuanyang zi was a Taoist master of the Tang dynasty, but his exact dates are unknown. His name appears in bibliographic sources as the commentator on the *Jinbi qiantong jue* 金碧潛通訣 (Gold and Jasper Instructions for Pervading the Unseen), a work closely related to the *Zhouyi cantong qi*. Since Zheng Qiao's 鄭樵 (1104–62) *Tongzhi* 通志 (Comprehensive Monographs) names the compiler of the *Jinbi qiantong jue* as Yang Canwei 羊參微 (also known as Yang Sanwei 羊三微), Yuanyang zi may have been Yang Canwei of the Tang dynasty.

The Taoist Canon includes five works ascribed to Yuanyang zi, all of which focus on alchemy. The *Yuanyang zi wujia lun* 元陽子五假論 (Essay on the Five Borrowings, by the Master of Original Yang; CT 864) describes the technique of employing the Five Agents (*wuxing*) to conceal oneself in order to avoid accidents. The *Yuanyang zi jinye ji* 元陽子金液集 (Anthology on the Golden Liquor, by the Master of Original Yang; CT 238) contains a thirty-one-verse poem on the Golden Liquor (*jinye*), discussing alchemy based on the *Cantong qi* and the *Daode jing*. The *Huandan jinye gezhu* 還丹金液歌注 (Commentaries on Songs on the Reverted Elixir and the Golden Liquor; CT 239) consists of commentaries on poems about *waidan*. The *Huandan gejue* 還丹歌訣 (Songs and Instructions on the Reverted Elixir; CT 265) is a collection of poems about the Reverted Elixir (*huandan*). Finally, the *Yinfu jing song* 陰符經頌 (Lauds on the Scripture of the Hidden Accordance; CT 311) contains poems that interpret the *Yinfu jing* in alchemical terms.

SAKADE Yoshinobu

📖 Chen Guofu 1963, 287–89

※ *waidan*; *neidan*

yuanyou

遠遊

"far-off journeys"; ecstatic excursions

The tradition of far-off journeys goes back to the *Zhuangzi*, the *Yuanyou* poem of the *Chuci* 楚辭 (Songs of Chu; trans. Kroll 1996b), and Sima Xiangru's 司馬相如 (ca. 179–117 BCE) *Daren fu* 大人賦 (Rhapsody on the Great Man; trans. Watson 1961, 2: 332–35). These works, however, refer to the ecstatic excursions only in a poetic way, and do not elucidate the techniques that make them possible. Among Taoist texts, the *Shangqing scriptures not only describe celestial wanderings (sometimes in terms very close to those used by Sima Xiangru), but also introduce the relevant practices. Many invocations to gods, details of meditation techniques, and descriptions of places visited by the adept found in Shangqing texts were later adopted by other Taoist schools and incorporated into Taoist ritual.

Ecstatic excursions are both an instrument for and an expression of the process of cosmicization of the individual, which is one of the primary aims of Taoism. This process also involves purifications, prayers, use of talismans (*FU), and incantations to the gods encountered by the adept. It requires a knowledge of the esoteric forms and names of the places he visits, which are their "authentic" and original forms (*zhenxing* 真形) and their divine sounds, unveiled by the revelations given by the texts. It also demands the sharp and far-sighted vision characteristic of the saint (*shengren), which the adept must acquire.

The adept travels to the distant countries described as dangerous in the *Shanhai jing* 山海經 (Scripture of Mountains and Seas; fourth/third century BCE?; trans. Mathieu 1983) and the *Chuci*, but replete with blessings according to the Shangqing texts. Instead of monsters, he meets divinities who bestow the nourishments of immortality on him. This theme is related to the eremitic traditions of Taoist adepts, who "enter the mountain" (*rushan* 入山), a place full of dangerous forces, with the help of rites similar to those described in *Baopu zi 17 (Ware 1966, 279–300). It also implies the idea, underlying some exorcistic techniques, that the adept has the power to turn evil into good.

In his excursions, the adept visits the sacred mountains, rich in Yang power and the earthly counterparts of the planets, or the legendary isles of immortals (see *Penglai). He accompanies the Sun and Moon in their journey across the sky and along each of the stations located in the poles. These are blessed lands, whose trees bear the fruits of immortality and in whose waters the adept purifies himself. Ritually placed at the center of the world, the adept has the divinities of the poles enter his prayer room (*jingshi) and his own viscera. Thus the movement is double, both centrifugal and centripetal as it goes from the center to the periphery and back again. The adept's room and body contain the external world, which he crosses from end to end. He also ascends to the Sun and the Moon, where he meets deities who dwell there and bestow tokens of immortality on him. During these practices he feeds on light, so that he glows with light and the whole world becomes luminous "within and without." He also meditates on the alternating and parallel, opposed and complementary movements of the Moon and Sun, in a type of practice that anticipates those of *neidan.

These travels to or with the Moon and Sun relate to the dualism inherent in the universe. They are complementary to the adept's ascent to the Northern Dipper (*beidou), the central and celestial pole of the world, which signifies the attainment of the complex unity represented by the Dipper's nine stars.

Isabelle ROBINET

📖 Kohn 1993b, 249–79; Kroll 1996b; Robinet 1976; Robinet 1989c; Robinet 1993, 171–225; Robinet 1997b, 35–37 and 138–47; Schafer 1977a, 234–69

※ MEDITATION AND VISUALIZATION; Shangqing

Yue Zichang

樂子長

Yue Zichang is a transcendent figure named in the *Lingbao wufu xu* (Prolegomena to the Five Talismans of the Numinous Treasure) as having received portions of that text, written in "ancient tadpole script," from Han Zhong 韓終, the Transcendent of Huolin (Huolin xianren 霍林仙人). After having received this document, he is said to have copied it out and added passages detailing the text's history. This tradition places Yue Zichang in the area of Qi 齊 (Shandong), center of Prescription Masters (*fangshi) during the Han. His dates are unknown. Yue Zichang is particularly associated with the ingestion of sesame concoctions for prolonging life and gaining transcendence, although *Ge Hong, in his *Baopu zi, also credits him with an alchemical recipe.

Stephen R. BOKENKAMP

📖 Campany 2002, 316–18; Kobayashi Masayoshi 1990, 82–88; Yamada Toshiaki 1987b; Yamada Toshiaki 1989b, 103–7

※ HAGIOGRAPHY

Yuhuang

玉皇

Jade Sovereign; Jade Emperor

The title Yuhuang is conventionally rendered into English as "Jade Sovereign." More elaborate titles in common use for this deity are Yuhuang shangdi 玉皇上帝 (Jade Sovereign, Highest Emperor), Yuhuang dadi 玉皇大帝 (Jade Sovereign, Great Emperor), and Xuanqiong gaoshang Yuhuang dadi 玄穹高上玉皇大帝 (Jade Sovereign, Great Emperor, Most Exalted in Mysterious Eminence). Among the common people he is more intimately referred to as Tiangong 天公 (Lord of Heaven). The Jade Sovereign is the supreme deity of Chinese popular religion and also occupies a high position in the Taoist pantheon. His "birthday" is celebrated on the ninth day of the first lunar month as a major ritual occasion during the New Year holiday season.

Surprisingly, the Jade Sovereign's eminence is of comparatively recent date. His principal text, the *Yuhuang benxing jijing* 高上玉皇本行集經 (Collected Scripture on the Deeds of the Jade Sovereign; CT 10, variant version at CT 11) is likely a product of the late Tang or early Song. It is the earliest text devoted solely to the Jade Sovereign and attributes an importance to him not seen in earlier sources. There are some references in pre-Tang Taoist texts to a Jade Sovereign (Yuhuang) or Jade Emperor (Yudi 玉帝). In *Tao Hongjing's (456–536) *Zhenling weiye tu* (Chart of the Ranks and Functions of the Perfected Numinous Beings), an overview of the *Shangqing pantheon, we find a Yuhuang daojun 玉皇道君 (Jade Sovereign, Lord of the Dao) and a Gaoshang Yudi 高上玉帝 (Most Exalted Jade Emperor), both among the ranks of secondary deities resident in the Heaven of Jade Clarity (Yuqing 玉清). By the Tang dynasty, the title Yuhuang had been widely adopted for the popular god of Heaven, and the intensified attention Taoists gave to Yuhuang may perhaps be viewed as an attempt to capitalize on the name recognition of this popular deity by reintegrating it into the Taoist pantheon with a significantly higher rank than before. The nowadays standard Taoist view that crystallized out of conflicting interpretations of his position is that the Jade Sovereign is chief among the Four Sovereigns (*siyu* 四御, namely Yuhuang, Taihuang 太皇, Tianhuang 天皇, and Tuhuang 土皇; Qing Xitai 1994, 3: 18–21), i.e., the highest celestial functionary after the Three Clarities (*sanqing*). The preeminent position of Yuhuang within both Taoism and popular religion was reinforced when Emperors Zhenzong (r. 997–1022) and Huizong (r. 1100–1125) of the Northern Song dynasty in 1015 and 1116 respectively conferred

Fig. 86. The Jade Emperor (Yuhuang) surrounded by the deities of the mountains and the rivers. *Yongle gong (Palace of Eternal Joy), Pavilion of the Three Clarities (Sanqing dian 三清殿).

prestigious titles on the deity and added it to the roster of official sacrifices.

The Jade Sovereign's place close to the apex of the Taoist pantheon is reflected in his considerable importance in Taoist ritual practice. In addition to being venerated in every major ritual of the general liturgy, there has developed a corpus of liturgical texts specifically for his worship (e.g., *Yuhuang youzui xifu baochan* 玉皇宥罪錫福寶懺, CT 193; *Yuhuang manyuan baochan* 玉皇滿願寶懺, CT 194; and *Yuhuang shiqi ciguang dengyi* 玉皇十七慈光燈儀, CT 197). Many Taoist establishments contain shrines to Yuhuang, and the *Yuhuang benxing jijing* is a commonly recited scripture. A number of other scriptures are connected with the Jade Sovereign, most importantly the brief *Xinyin jing (Scripture of the Mind Seal), a *neidan text highly influential in the *Quanzhen tradition.

To this day, the Jade Sovereign remains an important shared symbol between Taoism and popular religion, even if his popular image, as shaped by oral tradition and vernacular literature, continues to diverge significantly from that of the Taoist orthodoxy.

Philip CLART

📖 Chen Jianxian 1994; Fêng 1936; Little 2000b, 170–71; Ma Shutian 1996, 36–46; Maspero 1981, 88–92; Seidel 1987f

※ *Xinyin jing*; DEITIES: THE PANTHEON; TAOISM AND POPULAR RELIGION

Yulong wanshou gong

玉隆萬壽宮

Palace of the Ten-thousand-fold Longevity of Jade Beneficence
(Western Hills)

The Yulong wanshou gong (a title granted in 1116) is the main temple in the Western Hills (*Xishan) near Nanchang (Jiangxi). Its name should be more literally translated as "Palace [where Sacrifices] for the Emperor's Ten-thousand-fold Longevity [are Performed]." It is dedicated to *Xu Xun, who is said to have risen to heaven there. Under the name Youwei guan 遊帷觀 (Abbey of the Flying Curtain), it was already active in 682 and possibly earlier. Other temples associated with Xu Xun's heroic deeds are found throughout the area, such as the Tiezhu gong 鐵柱宮 (Palace of the Iron Pillar, a pillar that Xu cast to crush local demons) in downtown Nanchang, or the Qingyun pu 青雲譜 (Abbey of Azure Clouds) just south of the city.

The Yulong gong has been known as a very active cult and pilgrimage center since the Tang period. The main pilgrimage season, now as then, is the day of mid-autumn, the date of Xu's flight to heaven. The temple represents one of the best-documented cases of the gradual merging between a local cult and Taoism. Indeed, already during the Tang, this local cult had a Taoist Offering (*jiao) as its focus, and Taoist priests helped the cult to gain national legitimacy and prestige by providing the god with a hagiography and scriptures—a process that occurred in similar ways for thousands of other local saints. With Taoists as intermediaries, the Yulong gong has since the Tang continually been host to a great many revelations (morality books or *shanshu, liturgical manuals, hagiographies) dispensed by Xu Xun and other saints, which were printed and stored there. A local Taoist order, the *Jingming dao (Pure and Bright Way), developed with Xu as its patriarch.

Yet the Yulong gong always remained a temple to a local saint before and above being a clerical institution. In modern times, it was a very impressive temple complex, drawing massive official support (Xu is the patron saint of all Jiangxi province), serviced by a community of *Quanzhen clerics, but above all the center of a thriving lay-dominated cult to Xu, healer, exorcist, and diviner.

Vincent GOOSSAERT

📖 Akizuki Kan'ei 1978, 63–86 and passim, Hachiya Kunio 1990, 1: 279–82, 2: 267; Qing Xitai 1994, 4: 253–54; Schipper 1985d

※ Xu Xun; Xishan; TEMPLES AND SHRINES

yulu

語錄

recorded sayings

Yulu, or "recorded sayings," are supposedly verbatim records of the oral teaching of a master to his community. The text provides each pronouncement with a context by noting whose and which question prompted it and under what circumstances it took place. Not all such texts are titled *yulu*, however, and not all works called *yulu* contain actual recorded sayings: many dialogic treatises are written in question-and-answer form but are not the proceedings of any actual lecture. Under discussion here are the real *yulu* which, as contextualized records, provide a unique view of the pedagogy of Taoist masters and their role in society.

Yulu is not a specifically Taoist genre. The Buddhist and Confucian *yulu* are more numerous and have a longer history (on the Buddhist *yulu*, see Yanagida Seizan 1983 and Berling 1987; for the Confucian *yulu*, see Gardner 1991). The widespread appearance of *yulu* in Taoist literature in the thirteenth century is closely related to the rise of new schools in the twelfth century, which spearheaded the great Taoist renewal of this period. Taoist masters of the traditional schools did not normally give teachings to assemblies, and this is still the case today among masters of the various *Zhengyi lineages in Taiwan and continental China. Their ritual activities do not include didactic explanations for lay participants. The new schools of the twelfth century, on the other hand, emphasized predication, and their recorded sayings are the most direct and precise evidence of these activities.

The school that produced the highest number of *yulu* is *Quanzhen; this is logical considering the importance given by this proselytising order to opening the Taoist tradition to society at large. The participation of lay believers in the discussions is attested to by questions raised by artisans in the recorded sayings of *Wang Zhijin, the *Panshan Qiyun Wang zhenren yulu* 盤山棲雲王真人語錄 (Recorded Sayings of the Real Man Wang Qiyun from Mount Pan; 1247; CT 1059). This work is the most lively of all Quanzhen *yulu* and its language is also the most vernacular, which points to its authenticity. Other Quanzhen *yulu* are those of *Ma Yu—the *Danyang zhenren zhiyan* 丹陽真人直言 (Straightforward Speeches of the Real Man [Ma] Danyang; ca. 1179; CT 1234) and the *Danyang zhenren yulu* 丹陽真人語錄 (Recorded Sayings of the Real Man [Ma] Danyang; CT 1057)—and of an unknown master Jin 晉, a contemporary of *Wang Zhe, the *Jin zhenren yulu* 晉真人語錄 (Recorded

Sayings of the Real Man Jin; CT 1056). The second generation of Quanzhen masters was even more prolific in this field, as their audiences grew to numbers undreamed of by the first patriarchs. The two most eminent masters in this regard are *Yin Zhiping, who left us the *Qinghe zhenren beiyou yulu* 清和真人 北游語錄 (Recorded Sayings from a Journey to the North, by the Real Man [Yin] Qinghe; 1240; CT 1310), and the above-mentioned Wang Zhijin. These masters gave open lectures (*pushuo* 普說) in various circumstances, and particularly at night in the monasteries, which allowed everyone to attend after the chores of the day.

The tradition of impromptu teachings and their verbatim recording continued beyond the glorious thirteenth century, as shown in the *Suiji yinghua lu* 隨 機應化錄 (Account of Induced Conversions According to Circumstances; 1401; CT 1076) of the early Ming Quanzhen master *He Daoquan. The popularity of such works is also evidenced by an anthology, the *Zhenxian zhizhi yulu* 真 仙直指語錄 (Straightforward Directions and Recorded Sayings of Real Men and Immortals; CT 1256), probably compiled in the fourteenth century, which quotes famous utterances by the Seven Real Men (*qizhen* 七真; see table 17) of the first generation of Quanzhen, along with a longer collection of Yin Zhiping's sayings.

While Quanzhen produced its recorded sayings in the north, the *Nanzong lineage also used this genre: most remarkable in this regard are *Bai Yuchan's *Haiqiong Bai zhenren yulu* 海瓊白真人語錄 (Recorded Sayings of the Real Man Bai of Haiqiong; 1251; CT 1307) and *Li Daochun's *Qing'an Yingchan zi yulu* 清庵瑩蟾子語錄 (Recorded Sayings of [Li] Qing'an, Master of the Shining Toad; CT 1060). Their teachings appear to be more technical, as they sometimes discuss *neidan concepts and quotations in a cryptic mode; such discussions may have been held for a restricted circle of disciples. However, they also exhibit the active participation one would expect from the adepts, and include riddles, non-verbal actions, and other pedagogical techniques developed by the Chan school of Buddhism and later adopted with caution and in moderation by most of the new Taoist schools.

Another new school that noted down and printed the oral teachings of its masters was the *Jingming dao (Pure and Bright Way). The best part of the *Jingming zhongxiao quanshu* (Complete Writings of the Pure and Bright [Way of] Loyalty and Filiality; 1327) is composed of the recorded sayings of the patriarch *Liu Yu (*juan* 3 to 5) and his disciple Huang Yuanji 黃元吉 (1271–1326; *juan* 6). Although they use language more distant from the vernacular, and are less prone to playing with the audience, the Jingming masters share with their Quanzhen and Nanzong colleagues a strong preference for explanations based on concrete parables developed at great length. Moreover, the way they elucidate basic concepts in purely spiritual terms is similar to Quanzhen pedagogy.

One feature common to these texts is their focus on actual practice, prompted by questions from the audience. Lay and ordained disciples alike ask for detailed instructions on meditation, ethical living and hygiene; they seem more concerned about the place of their own tradition within the landscape of Chinese religion than about doctrinal intricacies. Answering such practical questions, the masters often suggest modeling oneself on those with exemplary conduct. In these schools that flourished at the margins of the traditional ordination system, the role of the revealed scripture (*jing* 經) is not central; on the contrary, the deeds and words of the patriarchs—the immortal ones like *Lü Dongbin or *Xu Xun, as well as the human ones like *Qiu Chuji—are considered to be the clearest expression of the Dao in action. This accounts for the foremost importance of anecdotal narration in these teachings.

The Yuan period was the Golden Age of the Taoist *yulu*. Similar works were written during the Ming and Qing dynasties, but they are often dedicated only to the discussion of technical concepts of *neidan*. Moreover, the later *yulu* did not enjoy a distribution as wide as those of the thirteenth century.

Vincent GOOSSAERT

📖 Boltz J. M. 1986c, 161–70; Boltz J. M. 1987a, 137–202

yulu zhai

玉籙齋

Jade Register Retreat

The Jade Register Retreat is one of the Three Register Retreats (*sanlu zhai* 三籙齋), along with the Golden Register and Yellow Register Retreats (**jinlu zhai* and **huanglu zhai*). Unlike the other two, the Jade Register Retreat is not mentioned in the **Wushang biyao* (Supreme Secret Essentials) and is considered to have originated sometime between the Tang and Song dynasties.

According to the thirteenth-century **Lingbao yujian* (Jade Mirror of the Numinous Treasure; CT 547, *j.* 1), the Jade Register Retreat ranks second, between the Golden and Yellow Registers Retreats. It is said to "bring peace to the realms of the rulers, dukes, and officials who perform it. . . . It is not something that commoners should perform." The text of the Jade Register Retreat that is thought to have been used during the Song period is preserved in eight manuals in the Taoist Canon (CT 499 to CT 506).

Gradually, the Jade Register Retreat assumed the meaning of a ritual performed to bring salvation to deceased women. For instance, *j.* 17 of Zhou

Side's 周思得 (1359–1451) *Shangqing lingbao jidu dacheng jinshu* 上清靈寶濟度大成金書 (Golden Writings on the Great Achievement of Deliverance by the Numinous Treasure of Highest Clarity; in *Zangwai daoshu*) mentions three types of great Offering rites (*jiao*); the second, the Great Jade Register Retreat of the Middle Prime (*zhongyuan yulu dazhai* 中元玉籙大齋), is performed by the empress, the imperial consorts, and the nobility. Among the rites performed in present-day southern Taiwan, the Jade Register Retreat is only performed to rescue women who have died in childbirth from the hell known as Lake of Blood (*xuehu* 血湖).

MARUYAMA Hiroshi

📖 Ōfuchi Ninji 1983, 637–49

※ *huanglu zhai; jinlu zhai; zhai*

Yunji qiqian

雲笈七籤

Seven Lots from the Bookbag of the Clouds

Zhang Junfang 張君房 (961?–1042?) compiled the *Yunji qiqian* foremost as a tribute to Song Zhenzong (r. 997–1022), under whose mandate the first Taoist Canon of the Song was completed. In a preface dating to ca. 1028–29, Zhang explains how he came to undertake this anthology as a result of participating in the preparation of the *Da Song Tiangong baozang* (Precious Canon of the Celestial Palace of the Great Song). He may very well have exaggerated the degree to which he was involved in compiling the Canon but there is no question that the *Yunji qiqian* itself stands as an invaluable legacy of his assignment to the project. Although he submits the text to Zhenzong for "perusal during the second watch" (*yiye zhi lan* 乙夜之覽), internal evidence reveals that Zhang's prefatory statement of dedication could not have been completed until the reign of Song Renzong (r. 1022–63). The fact that he also offers the anthology to those engaged in the collation of texts suggests that the preface may have taken shape over a period of some twelve years.

Zhang writes that he created this anthology by drawing together exemplars from the "seven components of the bookbag of the clouds" (*yunji qibu zhi ying* 雲笈七部之英). The term *yunji* is a well-established poetic trope for a bagful of Taoist writings and *qibu* alludes to the Three Caverns (*SANDONG*) and Four Supplements (*sifu* 四輔) into which the Canon was organized. Precisely how much of the Canon of 1016 is reflected in this creatively devised and entitled anthology remains an open question. Its value as a resource of writings from diverse schools of Taoist teachings available in the early eleventh century is beyond dispute.

Editions and indices. According to his preface, Zhang completed an anthology comprising 120 *juan*. This is the size familiar to most Song bibliographers but all extant editions contain 122 *juan*. The earliest known complete copy is the *Yunji qiqian* in the Ming Canon of 1445 (CT 1032), the so-called **Zhengtong daozang* (Taoist Canon of the Zhengtong Reign Period). Its inconsistent use of alternative graphic forms in honor of Song taboos suggests that the editors of the Canon drew from a combination of editions in print or manuscript form. Such taboos are not observed in fragments of *j.* 95 and III–13 from the Yuan Canon of 1244, the **Xuandu baozang* (Precious Canon of the Mysterious Metropolis), held in library collections of Beijing and Taipei. Although these surviving pages generally correspond to the text in the Ming Canon, variant features of note in the latter chapters include the addition of a list of entries at the head of the chapter.

Zhang Xuan 張萱 (1558–1641; DMB 78–80) published a copy of the text in 1609, adding a table of contents. The Qingzhen guan 清真館 edition Zhang issued is reproduced in the *Siku quanshu* 四庫全書 and the first printing of the *Sibu congkan* 四部叢刊 in 1919–22. Apparently aware of the lacunae marring this edition, the compilers of the second printing of the *Sibu congkan* in 1929 chose to reproduce the superior copy in the Ming Canon. Reproductions of the text or portions of it are also found in a number of collectanea such as the **Daozang jiyao* (Essentials of the Taoist Canon; vols. 19–20) and **Daozang jinghua* (Essential Splendors of the Taoist Canon).

A remarkable modern edition of the *Yunji qiqian* published in 1988 by the Qilu shushe 齊魯書社 in Beijing is based on the copy of the text in the *Zhengtong daozang* issued by Hanfen lou 涵芬樓 in 1923–26. Instead of adopting the pagination introduced by Hanfen lou, with twenty columns per page, this edition reproduces the text as it appears in the Ming Canon, with twenty-five columns per sheet. It is also enhanced by the addition of an analytic table of contents compiled by members of the Linguistic Research Institute of the Chinese Academy of Social Sciences in Beijing.

Another outstanding modern reissue of the *Yunji qiqian* from the Ming Canon is the collated text edited by Jiang Lisheng 蔣力生. Huaxia chubanshe in Beijing published this punctuated, typeset edition in 1996. It provides invaluable documentation of variant readings from copies of the text contained in the *Siku quanshu*, *Sibu congkan*, collectanea of Taoist writings, and various other sources.

Early analytic studies of the contents of the *Yunji qiqian* by Yoshioka Yoshitoyo (1955) and Sun Kekuan (1965) have been superseded by two indices. The two-volume *Index du Yunji qiqian* compiled under the editorship of Kristofer Schipper as a contribution to the "Projet Tao-tsang" (1981) provides a concordance to not only titles but also terms and proper names appearing in the anthology. Following Schipper's "Introduction" is an account by John Lagerwey (1981a) describing the nature of the compilation and principles of organization, with a survey of its contents according to thirty-seven headings. The contents of the *Yunji qiqian* are also systematically analyzed in the index to Taoist texts compiled by Ōfuchi Ninji and Ishii Masako (1988).

Format and contents. Reference works disagree on the total number of subject headings in the *Yunji qiqian*. The discrepancies are largely due to the inconsistent form and occasional redundancy of headings. The suffix *bu* 部 (section) appearing in the first eight major headings is conspicuously absent from all but one of the succeeding headings. Many headings apply to a single chapter whereas a few encompass as many as a dozen or so chapters. In the latter case, subheadings are commonly recorded after the heading at the beginning of a chapter. The overall presentation of subject matter bears some resemblance to that of the sixth-century *Wushang biyao* (Supreme Secret Essentials).

Zhang Junfang does not rigorously identify the provenance of each text incorporated into the *Yunji qiqian*. Just how much can be considered his own writing remains to be determined. Some lengthy passages in the anthology seem to have been directly copied from its apparent exemplar, the *Wushang biyao*. Many scriptural and narrative texts are recorded in full and merit collation with their independently printed counterparts. A number of passages lacking any indication of title or authorship await identification. The vast majority of texts date before the Song. Among the latest to be included are three prefaces ascribed to Emperor Zhenzong (103.1a–2a, 117.1a–b, 122.16a–b). The contents of the 122 chapters are outlined below according to major headings in the anthology, primarily singling out titles and subjects taken up in related entries elsewhere in this volume.

1. *Daode jing*: prefaces of Tang Xuanzong (r. 712–56), *Wu Yun (?–778), and Lu Xisheng 陸希聲 (?–ca. 905).

2. Cosmogony: *Kaitian jing*.

3–5. Origin and Transmission of Scriptural Teachings: *Lingbao jingmu dated 437, Zhenxi [zhuan] 真系[傳] ([Biographies of the] True Lineage) with preface dated 805 by Li Bo 李渤.

6–20. Scriptural Teachings of the Three Caverns: *Basu jing, *Huangting jing, *Yinfu jing, *Shengshen jing, Neiguan jing 內觀經, *Dingguan jing, *Laozi zhongjing.

21–28. Cosmology, Astral Contemplative Procedures, Topography: *Shizhou ji, Ershiba zhi 二十八治, with corresponding text in j. 7 of *Sandong zhunang.

29–36. Gestation and Destiny, Hygiene, Diet, and Physical Therapy: *Yang-xing yanming lu, *Sheyang zhenzhong fang.

37–40. Retreat Regulations and Codes of Behavior, with corresponding text in *Zhaijie lu, *Laojun shuo yibai bashi jie.

41–55. Ritual Purification, Visualization and Actualization Procedures: *Taidan yinshu.

56–62. Embryonic Breathing: *Yuanqi lun, *Fuqi jingyi lun, *Wuchu jing.

63–78. Jindan 金丹 (Golden Elixir) Instructions and Pharmaceuticals: *Tai-qing danjing yaojue.

79–80. Talismans and Charts: *Wuyue zhenxing tu, *Ershisi sheng tu.

81–86. *Gengshen Purging of the Three Corpses (sanshi; see *sanshi and jiuchong) and Release from the Corpse (*shijie): with matching citations in Wushang biyao 87 as well as elsewhere in the Yunji qiqian.

87–95. Essential Teachings Conveyed by Perfected Beings and Transcendents: *Shenxian kexue lun, *Haikong zhizang jing, *Zuowang lun.

96–99. Verse and Song: with matching citations in the *Zhengao and other pre-Tang compilations in the Canon.

100–102. Chronicles: with matching citations in Wushang biyao 15, Xuanyuan benji 軒轅本紀 (Original Chronicle of Xuanyuan, the Yellow Emperor), or Xiantian ji 先天紀 (Chronicle of the Prior Heavenly Realm), by *Wang Qinruo (962–1025).

103–22. Biographies: *Yisheng baode zhuan, *Liexian zhuan, *Shenxian zhuan, *Dongxian zhuan, *Yongcheng jixian lu, *Daojiao lingyan ji.

Judith M. BOLTZ

📖 Boltz J. M. 1987a, 129–31; Lagerwey 1981a; Lin Fu-shih 1995, 97–100; van der Loon 1984, 31–34, 38, 53–54, and 145; Lu Renlong 1990; Nakajima Ryūzō 1986; Ōfuchi Ninji and Ishii Masako 1988, 209–81 (list of texts cited); Schipper 1981; Schipper 1986; Sun Kekuan 1965, 126–43; Yoshioka Yoshitoyo 1955, 422–81; Zhou Shengchun 2000, 90–92

※ DAOZANG AND SUBSIDIARY COMPILATIONS

yunü

玉女

jade woman; jade maiden

Although yunü is usually translated as "jade woman" or "jade maiden," this translation may be questionable since the term yu (jade) also means "precious" and "beautiful." Already at an early date, however, the term *yunü* also designated a female immortal, as it does for instance in Sima Xiangru's 司馬相如 (ca. 179–117 BCE) *Daren fu* 大人賦 (Rhapsody on the Great Man; trans. Watson 1961, 2: 332–35).

Taoist scriptures from the Han period onward offer more extensive information. Among the most valuable early sources is the *Laozi zhongjing (Central Scripture of Laozi). While in this work several deities are related to individual loci of the inner body, the Jade Woman of Mysterious Radiance of Great Yin, Taiyin Xuanguang Yunü 太陰玄光玉女), takes the place of the Queen Mother of the West (*Xiwang mu) as the spouse of the King Lord of the East (Dongwang gong 東王公), but at the same time is the companion of several other partners. Her most important function is that of Mother of the Dao (Daomu 道母) or of the immortal Red Infant (*chizi* 赤子) who dwells in the center of the human body.

Later Taoist lore, especially the *Shangqing scriptures, abounds with jade women of all sorts and descriptions, but they are invariably presented as splendid young creatures attired in glittering vestments. The iconography of the late Six Dynasties and Tang periods confirms the belief that the Jade Woman is the same as Lady Li (Li furen 李夫人), the mother of Laozi and therefore of the Dao. In mystical practices, the Jade Woman is also the celestial spouse of the practitioner. This is most extensively described in the *Mingtang yuanzhen jingjue* 明堂元真經訣 (Instructions on the Scripture of the Original Real Man of the Hall of Light; CT 424; see Schafer 1978a).

The term *yunü* is also applied as a generic appellation for young female deities in the popular pantheon, such as the Jade Woman of Mount Tai (Taishan yunü 泰山玉女), also known as *Bixia yuanjun.

Caroline GYSS

Yushi

雨師

Master of Rain

According to the *Liexian zhuan (Biographies of Exemplary Immortals; trans. Kaltenmark 1953, 35), *Chisong zi was the lord of rain during the age of Shennong 神農, the third of the legendary emperors. He may originally have been a shaman with rainmaking powers. Later he went to Mount *Kunlun and dwelt within the stone cavern of the Queen Mother of the West (*Xiwang mu). He ascended and descended the mountain accompanied by wind and rain, and attained immortality together with the daughter of Yandi 炎帝 (the Fiery Emperor). Pinghao 蓱號 in the *Tianwen* 天問 (Heavenly Questions) poem of the *Chuci* 楚辭 (Songs of Chu; trans. Hawkes 1985, 122–51) corresponds to the rain deity ("Pinghao causes rain"), as do Xuanming 玄冥, the water deity in the *Zuozhuan* 左傳 (Commentary of Zuo; trans. Legge 1872, 669–72), and Net (*bi* 畢, Hyades), one of the twenty-eight lunar lodges (see *xiu*). Several stories also connect the Master of Rain with the Count of the Wind (for some examples, see the entry *Fengbo). By the Ming period, images of Yushi were made in the form of a mature man with a black beard, carrying in his left hand a bowl decorated with a picture of a dragon, and sprinkling water with his right hand.

YOSHIKAWA Tadao

📖 Kaltenmark 1953, 35–36; Maspero 1981, 98–99

※ TAOISM AND CHINESE MYTHOLOGY

Yushu jing

玉樞經

Scripture of the Jade Pivot

This scripture's full title is *Jiutian yingyuan leisheng Puhua tianzun yushu jing* 九天應元雷聲普化天尊玉樞經 (Scripture of the Jade Pivot of the Celestial Worthy of Universal Transformation Whose Sound of Thunder Responds to the Primordials in the Nine Heavens). It seems to have evolved out of the key *Shenxiao (Divine Empyrean) movement scripture, the *Leiting yujing* 雷霆玉經 (Jade Scripture of the Thunderclap; CT 15). The present scripture (*Yushu baojing* 玉樞寶經, CT 16) was likely written several decades after its predecessor, perhaps in the late twelfth or early thirteenth centuries. Its early promoters, if not its first recipients, were tied to the Shenxiao master *Bai Yuchan (1194–1229?), who, in addition to *Lü Dongbin, Zhang Tianjun 張天君, and *Zhang Jixian, is ascribed with its earliest commentary (*Yushu baojing jizhu*, 玉樞寶經集注, CT 99). It is also associated with "precious penances" (*baochan* 寶懺; CT 195 and CT 196) revealed by the Celestial Worthy of Universal Transformation, and with ritual texts.

The scripture and its early commentaries inform us that its central deity, the Celestial Worthy of Universal Transformation (*Puhua tianzun), is at once the ninth son of the Celestial Worthy of Original Commencement (Yuanshi tianzun 元始天尊), a transformation of the Perfect King of Jade Clarity (Yuqing zhenwang 玉清真王, who revealed the Shenxiao tradition to Wang Huoshi 汪火師), and the exalted transformation of the Great Saint of the Nine Heavens Who is Upright and Luminous (Jiutian zhenming dasheng 九天貞明大聖). The deity's formal title likely emerged in the twelfth century. This central god divulged the scripture to his assistant, the Thunder Officer and Hoary Gentleman (Leishi haoweng 雷師皓翁), who uttered it for humanity.

The core of the scripture consists of two key parts, one dealing with the marvelous aspects of self-cultivation of the Utmost Way (*zhidao* 至道), and the other dealing with the regular patterns of the ebb and flow of vital energies in the cosmos (*qishu* 氣數). Practitioners believed that by reading the scripture or even calling out the name of its revealing deity, they could not only avoid misfortune, but also attain everlasting life. Such powers inherent in this scripture and its presiding divinity, and the self-cultivation practices built upon them, were later elaborated into a cult to commemorate the Thunder Deity's birthday on the twenty-fourth day of the sixth lunar month.

Lowell SKAR

📖 Legge 1891, 2: 265–68 (part. trans.)

※ Bai Yuchan; Puhua tianzun; *leifa*; Shenxiao

Z

Zangwai daoshu

藏外道書

Taoist Texts Outside the Canon

Photographic reproductions (some not easily legible) of 991 texts outside the Taoist Canon appear in this thirty-six-volume publication compiled under the editorship of Hu Daojing 胡道靜 (Chengdu: Bashu shushe, vols. 1–20 published in 1992, vols. 21–36 in 1994). Volume one opens with a preface dated 1990 by Ren Jiyu 任繼愈, outlining the history of Taoism and underscoring the need to make texts available for research. The succeeding preface of 1992 by Hu Daojing and coeditors Chen Yaoting 陳耀庭, Duan Wengui 段文桂, and Lin Wanqing 林萬清 traces the history of the Taoist Canon and names some of the outstanding titles selected for publication. The editors state that the intent behind this publication is to preserve textual resources of importance to Chinese culture and to encourage research in the field of Taoist studies, especially in regard to the Ming-Qing period. Indeed, only a small part of the texts predate the Ming, since most known pre-Ming Taoist texts are found in the *Daozang*.

The sources of the texts reproduced here are varied. Some are from other rather easily accessible Taoist or literary collections, such as the **Daozang jiyao* (Essentials of the Taoist Canon) and the *Wulin zhanggu congbian* 武林掌故叢編 (General Compilation of Historical Sources on Hangzhou). Others are rare editions or manuscripts held by Taoist or public libraries. In any case, this collection is a major resource for the history of Ming-Qing Taoism, as reflected in the compilation of vols. 3 and 4 of the *Zhongguo daojiao shi* (History of Chinese Taoism; Qing Xitai 1988–95). Several other collections of source material have been published since then, including the thirty-six-volume *Zhongguo daoguan zhi congkan* 中國道觀志叢刊 (Collectanea of Monographs of Taoist Temples in China; Nanjing: Jiangsu guangling shushe, 2000), which overlaps in part with vols. 19, 20, and 33 of the *Zangwai daoshu*.

Finding a text in *Zangwai daoshu* is made convenient by vol. 36, which is devoted to a comprehensive concordance to all characters in the 991 titles, modeled on Kristofer Schipper's concordance to *Daozang* titles (Schipper 1975b). A set of general guidelines (*fanli* 凡例) completing the prefatory material discloses plans to publish a *Zangwai daoshu tiyao* 藏外道書提要 (Conspectus of Taoist Texts Outside the Canon), which would be welcome considering the total absence of any literature on the large majority of the 991 texts. It also lists eleven organizational categories: 1. *Guyi daoshu* 古佚道書 (Ancient Lost Books on the Dao), 2. *Jingdian* 經典 (Scriptures), 3. *Jiaoli jiaoyi* 教理教義 (Pedagogy), 4. *Sheyang* 攝養 (Preserving and Nourishing Life), 5. *Jielü shanshu* 戒律善書 (Observances and Morality Books), 6. *Yifan* 儀範 (Ritual Codes), 7. *Zhuanji shenxian* 傳記神仙 (Hagiography), 8. *Gongguan dizhi* 宮觀地志 (Topographies and Temple Records), 9. *Wenyi* 文藝 (Literary Arts), 10. *Mulu* 目錄 (Bibliography), 11. *Qita* 其他 (Other Subjects). The publication itself adopts a modified version of this set of categories, omitting the last two altogether. The rarer or more remarkable components of each volume are listed below.

1. Published transcriptions of *Mawangdui manuscripts, a Beijing National Library copy of the *Taiqing fenglu jing* 太清風露經 (Scripture of Great Clarity on Wind and Dew) from the *Xuandu baozang (Precious Canon of the Mysterious Metropolis), and texts from the *Yongle dadian* 永樂大典 (Great Compendium of the Yongle Reign Period).

2. Four Ming-Qing commentaries to *Zhuangzi.

3. Duplicate of the third title in vol. 2, scriptural commentaries, a vernacular exegesis of the *Daode jing* dated 1920, and illustrated texts from Ming woodcut printings.

4. An 1845 exegesis of the *Yushu jing (Scripture of the Jade Pivot) and texts dedicated to *Guan Yu, *Wenchang, and *Zaoshen, including a manuscript dated 1845.

5. A 1915 printing of the *Fanghu waishi (The External Secretary of Mount Fanghu) by *Lu Xixing and anthologies from the legacies of *Bai Yuchan, the legendary *Zhang Sanfeng, *Wu Shouyang, and *Liu Huayang.

6. *Daoyan neiwai bijue quanshu* 道言內外祕訣全書 (Complete Writings of Secret Instruction on Inner and Outer Taoist Teachings) compiled by *Peng Haogu between 1597 and 1600, *Daotong dacheng* 道統大成 (Great Achievement of the Taoist Legacy) compiled by Wang Qihuo 王啟濩 in 1899, and the *Longmen xinfa* 龍門心法 (Core Teachings of Longmen) by *Wang Changyue (?–1680).

7. *Xuanzong neidian zhujing zhu* 玄宗內典諸經注 (Commentaries on All Scriptures of the Inner Canon of the Mysterious Lineage) compiled by *Shao Yizheng in 1460 and the *Lüzu quanshu (Complete Writings of Ancestor Lü) compiled by Liu Tishu 劉體恕 in 1741.

8. An 1880 printing of the *Daoshu shi'er zhong (Twelve Books on the Dao) compiled by *Liu Yiming (1734–1821).

9. Beijing library copy of a 1577 manuscript *Zhenxian shangsheng* 真仙上乘 (Higher Vehicle of Perfected Transcendence) and Ming-Qing publications on *neidan.

10. *Gu Shuyinlou cangshu* 古書隱樓藏書 (Collection of the Ancient Hidden Pavilion of Books; Qing Xitai 1994, 2: 184–86) compiled by *Min Yide (1748–1836) and *neidan* writings from the *Daozang jiyao* and the *Daoyan wuzhong* 道言五種 (Five Taoist Teachings) compiled during the Kangxi reign period (1662–1722) by Tao Susi 陶素耜 (fl. 1676).

11. *Daoshu shiqi zhong* 道書十七種 (Seventeen Books on the Dao) and *Jiyi zi dingpi daoshu sizhong* 濟一子頂批道書四種 (Four Books on the Dao with the Upper Marginal Critique of Jiyi zi) compiled in 1841 by *Fu Jinquan (1765–1844).

12. Variant forms of the ledgers of merit and demerit (*gongguo ge* 功過格; Brokaw 1991), commentaries on the *Taishang ganying pian* (Folios of the Most High on Retribution) and the *Yinzhi wen* 陰騭文 (Essay on Secret Virtue), and other types of morality books (*shanshu*) compiled from the Yuan to the Qing.

13–15. *Guangcheng yizhi* 廣成儀制 (Compendium of Guangcheng Liturgy) compiled by Chen Fuhui 陳復慧, a Qianlong (1735–95) Taoist master at Mount Qingcheng (*Qingcheng shan, Sichuan), with published and manuscript components dating from 1824 to 1914. Guangcheng is a Sichuan ritual tradition with strong *Quanzhen influence.

16–17. *Shangqing lingbao jidu dacheng jinshu* 上清靈寶濟度大成金書 (Golden Writings on the Great Achievement of Deliverance by the Numinous Treasure of Highest Clarity) compiled by Zhou Side 周思得 (1359–1451), codices on *liandu* rituals of 1552 and 1767 (the latter by *Lou Jinyuan) published by Yoshioka Yoshitoyo (1959–76, 1: 503–96), and an 1889 manuscript of a *fendeng* ritual formulary published by Kristofer Schipper (1975c).

18. Ming manuscript and published hagiographic texts including a chronicle of *Laojun by Xie Shouhao 謝守灝 (1134–1212), an illustrated *Qunxian ji* 群仙集 (Anthology of the Gathered Transcendents) dating to 1483, *Shenyin* 神隱 (Reclusion in Spirit) by *Zhu Quan (1378–1448), an account of the guardian of Mount Lu (*Lushan, Jiangxi) by Ye Yiwen 葉義問 (1098–1170), *Guang liexian zhuan* 廣列仙傳 (Expanded Biographies of Exemplary Immortals) compiled in 1583 by Zhang Wenjie 張文介, and the hagiographic anthology *Zhuding yuwen* 鑄鼎餘聞 (Residual Accounts of the Cast Tripod) compiled in 1899 by Yao Fujun 姚福均.

19. Five Ming and Qing topographies of the Luofu Mountains (*Luofu shan, Guangdong), Mount Longhu (*Longhu shan, Jiangxi), Mount Lao (*Laoshan, Shandong), and Mount Mao (*Maoshan, Jiangsu).

20. Topography of Mount Hua (*Huashan, Shaanxi) dated 1831, Ming and Qing monographs on sacred sites in the Hangzhou (Zhejiang) region from the *Wulin zhanggu congbian* of the late nineteenth century, a 1927 reprint of an 1832 monograph on the *Xuanmiao guan (Abbey of Mysterious Wonder) in Suzhou

(Jiangsu), the monograph on the Beijing *Baiyun guan (Abbey of the White Clouds) compiled in 1934 by Oyanagi Shigeta, and the *Xiaoyao shan Wanshou gong zhi* 逍遙山萬壽宮志 (Monograph of the Palace of Ten-thousand-fold Longevity at Mount Xiaoyao) dating to 1878.

21. Taoist manuscripts from *Dunhuang.

22. *Daode jing* and *Zhuangzi* editions, and various scriptures for ritual chanting revealed during the Qing through spirit writing (see *fuji*).

23. Late Qing manuals for spiritual practice, some revealed through spirit writing, and the works of the *neidan* master Liu Mingrui 劉名瑞 (1839–1931).

24. *Neidan* poetry and treatises of various late imperial spiritual masters, including the Baiyun guan abbot Chen Mingbin 陳明霦 (1854–1935) and the sectarian leader Yuan Zhiqian 袁志謙 (1761–1834); and documents pertaining to the Taoist Association (Daojiao hui 道教會) established in 1911, two Qing *Daozang* bibliographies, and works on cosmography.

25. Many short and rare Ming, Qing, and Republican *neidan* treatises, including texts revealed from *Lü Dongbin through spirit writing and published by groups of lay devotees, and two *nüdan* works.

26. More *neidan* and *nüdan* treatises by masters of the late Qing and Republican periods (including *Zhao Bichen and *Chen Yingning), and a manual on magical healing (*zhuyou ke* 祝由科).

27. Other commentaries to the *Ganying pian* and the *Yinzhi wen*, and morality books compiled by a Beijing spirit-writing group of the last decades of the Qing period (on which see Fan Chunwu and Wang Jianchuan 1996).

28. More Qing-period morality books, either compilations of classical tracts or anthologies of revelations obtained by spirit writing, including instructions for spiritual practice, and the remarkable semi-autobiographical essay on morality *Chuyu jiuben* 除欲究本 (Removing Desires and Searching for the Essential) by the Quanzhen monk Dong Qingqi 董清奇 (fl. 1806–13).

29. Various manuscript liturgical manuals, mostly consisting of exorcism rites, regulations for state ritual, and manuals for daily morning and evening services.

30. Printed Qing liturgical manuals: litanies (*chan* 懺) for merit-making, and *liandu* death rituals.

31. Hagiographic works, Quanzhen historiography (including the rare 1847 *Baiyun xianbiao* 白雲仙表 or *Charts of the Immortals of the White Clouds on the Baiyun guan*), lineage records of late Qing and twentieth-century lay Quanzhen groups, and descriptions of popular gods.

32. A Qing hagiographic compendium, and gazetteers on Mount Gezao (*Gezao shan, Jiangxi), the Luofu Mountains, and Mount Wudang (*Wudang shan, Hubei).

33. Mountain and temple gazetteers.

34. Poetic anthologies of various Yuan, Ming, and Qing Taoists.

35. A well-known Quanzhen novel, various tracts revealed by spirit writing and a sketchbook for Taoist iconography.

36. A concordance to the titles of texts included in the whole collection.

Judith M. BOLTZ and Vincent GOOSSAERT

📖 Tian Chengyang 1995; You Zi'an 1996

※ DAOZANG AND SUBSIDIARY COMPILATIONS

zaohua

造化

"creation"

The term *zaohua*, which means "to inform (*zao*) and transform (*hua*)," derives from the *Zhuangzi* and is generally used as a synonym for the cosmos. *Zaohua zhe* 造化者, lit., "what informs and transforms [the world]," is the Dao itself or its *qi* (pneuma), the energy of life that does not create anything, but, like a potter, gives a determinate and transient form to the indeterminate. The analogy ends here, because the *zaohua zhe* is neither a person nor an entity, and does everything naturally and spontaneously without working. In this sense, *zaohua* is a synonym of *ziran* (natural or spontaneous).

Zao is the coming of something out of nothing (*wu*), and *hua* is the return to emptiness. *Zao* is movement, and *hua* is quiescence (see *dong* and *jing*). In other instances, *zao* is said to be the foundation (*ti*) and the One, *hua* its operation (*yong*) and the Two, and *zaohua* their interaction or the Three. The "great *zaohua*" (*da zaohua* 大造化), however, neither forms and transforms, nor does it not form and not transform: it is the permanent Dao.

In *neidan*, the alchemical process aims to go out of or beyond *zaohua* to a different *zaohua*. This points to a dialectic between movement and quiescence, or between the generation of the world by the mind (*xin*) and the return (*fan*) to the emptiness of the Dao. The borderline that simultaneously joins and separates these two facets is the "secret of creation," the infinitesimal first movement of the beginning of life (*ji*) and of the mind (*xin*), which alchemists wish to "steal" (*dao* 盜) to go beyond *zaohua*.

Isabelle ROBINET

📖 Robinet 1997b, 8

❋ *bianhua*; Dao; *ji*; *ziran*

Zaoshen

竈神

Stove God

The Stove God, also known as King of the Stove (Zaowang 竈王), Lord of the Stove (Zaojun 竈君), or Royal Lord of the Stove (Zao wangye 竈王爺), is a household god popular throughout China. A paper image of the god, sometimes including depictions of his wife and children, is mounted on the wall near the stove. He is thought to observe the actions of family members, reporting their good or bad deeds to the Jade Sovereign (*Yuhuang) once a year. On the twenty-third or twenty-fourth day of the twelfth lunar month, the family offers food, incense, and prayers to the deity. Candy or sweet rice cakes are often smeared on the god's mouth, to make him speak sweetly in his report to heaven, or to seal his lips to prevent him from reporting at all. The image of the god is then burned, and he rises to heaven with the smoke. A new image is put up when he returns, usually on New Year's Day.

The cult to the Stove God is first referred to in the *Lunyu* 論語 (Analects) of Confucius (trans. Legge 1893, 159) and is recognized in the *Liji* 禮記 (Records of Rites; trans. Legge 1885, 1: 269, 272, 277) as a sacrificial cult (*si* 祀). The earliest surviving text dedicated to the Stove God is the *Anzao jing* 安竈經 (Scripture on Pacifying the Stove; CT 69), possibly dating to the Song dynasty (960–1279). This scripture lists prohibitions to be observed in the presence of the stove, and provides instructions for monthly observances.

Theodore A. COOK

📖 Chard 1990; Chard 1995; Maspero 1981, 112–15; Schafer 1975; Stein R. A. 1970; Yang Kun 1944

❋ Siming; TAOISM AND POPULAR RELIGION

zhai

齋

1. fast; purification; 2. Retreat

The *zhai* ritual is performed to obtain benefits through abstinence and purification. In the early tenth century, according to *Du Guangting (850–933), there were more than two dozen types of *zhai*. In 1201, Lü Yuansu 呂元素 (fl. 1188–1201) describes ten of them in his *Daomen dingzhi* 道門定制 (Regulations for the Taoist Community; CT 1224):

1. Retreat of the Great One (*Taiyi zhai* 太一齋), performed by the emperor himself
2. Retreat of the Nine Heavens (*jiutian zhai* 九天齋), for the welfare of the nation
3. Golden Register Retreat (**jinlu zhai*), for the protection of the emperor and the harmony and peace of the people
4. Jade Register Retreat (**yulu zhai*), for the court and the empress
5. Yellow Register Retreat (**huanglu zhai*), for the salvation of the dead
6. Retreat of the Luminous Perfected (*mingzhen zhai* 明真齋), for the ancestors
7. Retreat of the Cavernous Abyss (*dongyuan zhai* 洞淵齋), for relieving sickness
8. Retreat of the Nine Shades (*jiuyou zhai* 九幽齋), also for the salvation of the dead
9. Retreat of the Five Refinements (*wulian zhai* 五鍊齋), for removing sin and obtaining salvation
10. Retreat of Orthodox Unity (*zhengyi zhai* 正一齋), for bestowing scriptures and registers

The classification of the *zhai* into ten types actually dates from early times. In his **Bianzheng lun* (Essays of Disputation and Correction), the Buddhist priest Falin 法琳 (572–640) criticizes the contemporary Taoist rituals using the expression "Three Registers and Seven Grades" (*sanlu qipin* 三籙七品). The Three Registers were the Golden, Jade, and Yellow Registers, and the Seven Grades were the Retreats of Cavern of Perfection (*dongzhen zhai* 洞真齋), Spontaneity (*ziran zhai* 自然齋), Highest Clarity (*shangqing zhai* 上清齋), Mandating the Teachings (*zhijiao zhai* 指教齋), Mud and Soot (**tutan zhai*),

Luminous Perfected (*mingzhen zhai*), and Three Primes (*sanyuan zhai* 三元齋). Falin's list is based on pre-Tang sources and probably reflects the status of *zhai* rituals toward the end of the sixth century.

History. The term *zhai* originally referred to the purification of body and mind (see *xinzhai*). Clothes and food were changed, body and living quarters were cleansed, and the mind was purified through releasing negative thoughts. The "handwritten documents of the Three Offices" (*sanguan shoushu* 三官手書; see *sanguan*) of the early Way of the Celestial Masters (*Tianshi dao) were partly based on a similar idea: by reflecting on one's sins, offences resulting in misfortune would be extinguished. The Mud and Soot Retreat, in which penitents undid their hair, smeared mud on their faces, and then lay in the mud, expressed the idea of seeking forgiveness for sins through suffering, and was therefore a further extension of the same notion.

The most basic form of *zhai*, which stems from this concept of redemption, was first codified by *Lu Xiujing (406–77). In his *Wugan wen* 五感文 (Text on the Five Commemorations; CT 1278), Lu compiled liturgies for nine kinds of *zhai*: Golden Register, Yellow Register, Luminous Perfected, Three Primes, Eight Nodes (*bajie zhai* 八節齋), Spontaneity, Cavern of Perfection, Three Sovereigns (*sanhuang zhai* 三皇齋), Mandating the Teachings of the Great One (*taiyi zhijiao zhai* 太一指教齋), and Three Primes Mud and Soot (*sanyuan tutan zhai* 三元塗炭齋). In Lu's formulation, the *Lingbao zhai* focuses on repentance (*chanhui). Its features become clear when the Mud and Soot Retreat is compared to its later form, the Three Primes Mud and Soot Retreat. While the earlier *zhai* is a rite of repentance during which the faithful smear themselves with mud, in Lu's version the rite is performed by a priest with the faithful merely shouldering the financial burden of the ritual. Later Taoist *zhai* are, on the whole, successors of the liturgies compiled by Lu Xiujing. Their structure was continued by *Zhang Wanfu (fl. 710–13) and passed down to Du Guangting.

Structure. Today the *zhai* are not performed independently but rather during the first half of the *jiao (Offering) rituals. In most cases there is a recitation of a litany of repentance, followed by the Presentation of the Memorial (*jinbiao* 進表, see *baibiao) to notify the deities of the merits accrued from repentance. After the *zhai* rites have been performed, the *jiao* proper begins, during which the deities are thanked and given offerings.

YAMADA Toshiaki

📖 Bell 1988; Benn 2000; Chen Dacan 1987; Dean 2000; Kamitsuka Yoshiko 1999, 452–63; Lagerwey 1981b, 147–70; Lagerwey 1987c; Liu Zhiwan 1983b, 36–43; Matsumoto Kōichi 1983; Robinet 1997b, 166–83; Schipper 1993, 75–76;

Tian Chengyang 1990; Yamada Toshiaki 1995b; Yamada Toshiaki 1999; Zhang Zehong 1996; Zhang Zehong 1999a

※ *huanglu zhai; jiao; jinlu zhai; tutan zhai; xinzhai; yulu zhai*

Zhaijie lu

齋 戒 錄

Register of Retreats and Precepts

The *Zhaijie lu* is a short text in the Taoist Canon (CT 464) that describes the different types and times of *zhai in the middle ages. It dates from around the mid-eighth century, as it clearly cites materials from the *Yaoxiu keyi jielü chao* 要修科儀戒律鈔 (Excerpts from the Essential Liturgies and Observances; CT 463), a major ritual text of the early eighth century, and is itself cited in the *Zhiyan zong* 至言總 (Comprehensive Ultimate Words; CT 1033), a collection of Taoist methods of the ninth century. Besides the independent edition in CT 464, it is also included in *j. 37* of the *Yunji qiqian.*

The independent edition is divided into ten sections, which specify the *zhai* or periods of increased purification to be held within a given month or year, how these ceremonies can be classified, and how they are further used to celebrate the eight nodal days of the year (*bajie* 八節, namely, equinoxes, solstices, and the first day of each season). The last three sections describe food preparation for the ceremonies, specifics of moral prohibitions, as well as organizational guidelines. The text is comprehensive but does not go into much detail.

Livia KOHN

Malek 1985; Ōfuchi Ninji and Ishii Masako 1988, 181–82 (list of texts cited); Yoshioka Yoshitoyo 1967

※ *zhai*

zhan chilong

斬赤龍

"beheading the Red Dragon"

Menstrual blood is called Red Dragon (*chilong* 赤龍) in *neidan, by analogy with male semen, which is called White Tiger (*baihu* 白虎). As menstrual blood is the woman's energetic basis, it must be transformed, because the Original Pneuma (*yuanqi) is lost with menstruation as it is in men with ejaculation. In *nüdan (inner alchemy for women), the method consists of progressively reducing the menses so that the menstrual flow first becomes yellow and then disappears altogether. *Zhan chilong* and its synonym *duan chilong* 斷赤龍 refer to this process.

The term *chilong* to designate blood is found in the *Baopu zi (15.267; trans. Ware 1966, 245), but the earliest reference to the "beheading of the Red Dragon" dates from no earlier than 1310. It is found in the *Chunyang dijun shenhua miaotong ji* 純陽帝君神化妙通紀 (Chronicle of the Divine Transformations and Wondrous Powers of the Imperial Lord of Pure Yang; CT 305, 7.11b–12a; trans. Ang 1993), a work associated with *Lü Dongbin. The text recounts a story about the conversion of a woman called Perfected Guan (Guan zhenren 關真人) between 1241 and 1252: "The Perfected Guan from Siming 四明 (Zhejiang) came from a poor family. When her parents wanted her to marry at the age of seventeen, she fled and took refuge in the depth of the mountains. There she met an old man with blue eyes and thick eyebrows (i.e., Lü Dongbin). He drew a line on Guan's stomach and told her: 'I have beheaded the red dragon for you. Now you can join the Dao.'"

The method is also called "transmuting blood and returning it to whiteness" (*huaxue guibai* 化血歸白) or "refining the form of Great Yin" (*taiyin lianxing* 太陰鍊形). The return to the color white is explained by the link that exists, according to medical and alchemical conceptions, between maternal milk and menstrual blood. Two days before menstruation, the maternal juices descend to the abdomen, become red and flow out. According to the third precept in the *Xiwang mu nüxiu zhengtu shize* 西王母女修正途十則 (Ten Principles of the Queen Mother of the West on the Correct Path of Female Cultivation), "the supreme precelestial jewel (*xiantian zhibao* 先天至寶), similar to a star or a pearl, is placed in the uterus during puberty. . . . If at this time a girl knows how to maintain a pure nature and protect herself from licentious games, she can stop the flow at the Dark Enclosure (*youbi* 幽閉, the pubis). . . . This thing achieves Original Unity (*yuanyi* 元一) and neither transforms itself into Red

Pearls (*chizhu* 赤珠) nor into Celestial Waters (*tiangui* 天癸, the first menses). However, in a common woman . . . it becomes hot like fire, forces the gates and goes down, breaking the doors and flowing out" (see also Wile 1992, 194). The nineteenth-century *Taiyin lianxing fa* 太陰鍊形法 (Method of Refining the Form of Great Yin) says: "When Real Yang is blooming, the menses naturally end and the breasts retract like those of a man: this is called 'beheading of the Red Dragon.'"

"Beheading the Red Dragon" takes place during the first of the three stages in the Ming and Qing system of *neidan* practice. In men, this stage consists of refining essence to transmute it into pneuma. In women, it consists of "refining the form of Great Yin," which is achieved by developing inner concentration and by a controlled stimulation of sexual energy, especially through the massage of breasts.

Catherine DESPEUX

📖 Despeux 1990, 243–68; Furth 1999, 70–93

※ *nüdan*

Zhang Boduan

張伯端

987?–1082; *zi*: Pingshu 平叔; *hao*: Ziyang zhenren 紫陽真人 (Real Man of Purple Yang); also known as Zhang Yongcheng 張用成

A native of Tiantai 天臺 (Zhejiang), Zhang Boduan is considered the first patriarch of the Southern Lineage (*Nanzong) of *neidan. His work, the *Wuzhen pian* (Folios on Awakening to Perfection), is one of the foremost alchemical texts since the Northern Song period. The main documents on his life are his preface and postface to the *Wuzhen pian*, dated 1075 and 1078, respectively, and three other sources: Lu Sicheng's 陸思誠 "Wuzhen pian ji" 悟真篇記 (Note on the *Wuzhen pian*; 1161/1173), found at the beginning of the *Wuzhen pian sanzhu* 悟真篇三注 (Three Commentaries to the *Wuzhen pian*; CT 142); *Weng Baoguang's "Zhang zhenren benmo" 張真人本末 (The Story of the Perfected Zhang), in the *Wuzhen zhizhi xiangshuo sansheng biyao* 悟真直指詳說三乘祕要 (Straightforward Directions and Detailed Explanations on the *Wuzhen pian* and the Secret Essentials of the Three Vehicles; CT 143, 15a–16b); and the biography in the *Lishi zhenxian tidao tongjian* (49.7b–11a). The last work states that Zhang lived from 984 to 1082. Most scholars, however, accept the dates 987–1082 given in the *Sansheng biyao*.

According to these sources, Zhang Boduan, a scholar and *jinshi*, began his career as a civil servant. Shortly afterward, having committed an error while performing his duties, he was banished to Lingnan 嶺南 (the Guangdong/ Guangxi region) and placed in charge of the army register. During the Zhiping reign period (1064–67), Zhang served as advisor to Lu Shen 陸詵 (1022–70), an army commander in Guilin 桂林 (Guangxi), and followed Lu when he was transferred to Chengdu (Sichuan). There, in 1069, Zhang received alchemical teachings from a Perfected (or Real Man, *zhenren). After Lu's death in 1069, Zhang was sent to Qinlong 秦隴 (the Gansu/Shaanxi region) where he served Ma Mo 馬默 (fl. 1064–1100). When Ma was recalled to the capital, Zhang gave him the *Wuzhen pian* and asked him to circulate it. Zhang later accompanied Ma to Yunnan, and died there on April 15, 1082. After he was cremated, his disciples found an unusual amount of relics (*sheli* 舍利) in his ashes. In 1196, a bridge in Tiantai was renamed Wuzhen qiao 悟真橋 (Bridge of the Awakening to Perfection), and the following year Zhang's house was declared a monument, later becoming the site of a shrine in his honor.

Besides the *Wuzhen pian*, Zhang Boduan is credited with the authorship of three other works:

1. *Wuzhen pian shiyi* 悟真篇拾遺 (Supplement to the *Wuzhen pian*; CT 144; see Wong Shiu Hon 1978b).

2. *Yuqing jinsi Qinghua biwen jinbao neilian danjue* 玉清金笥青華祕文金寶內鍊丹訣 (Alchemical Instructions on the Inner Refinement of the Golden Treasure, a Secret Text from the Golden Box of the Jade Clarity Transmitted by the Immortal of Green Florescence; CT 240), actually written by a disciple in the Luofu Mountains (*Luofu shan, Guangdong; Chen Bing 1985, 36).

3. *Jindan sibai zi* (Four Hundred Words on the Golden Elixir), ascribed to Zhang but likely by *Bai Yuchan.

Zhang Boduan's basic premise was the unity of the Three Teachings, i.e., Confucianism, Taoism, and Buddhism. Although he advocated the joint cultivation (*shuangxiu) of one's inner nature and vital force (*xing and ming), his *neidan* practice begins with basic techniques to strengthen the vital force and ends with Chan methods of meditation and sudden enlightenment. In his later years, in fact, Zhang seems to have turned to Chan Buddhism, and his *Wuzhen pian shiyi* is a miscellanea dealing with Chan topics. The preface to the *Wuzhen pian zhushi* 悟真篇注釋 (Commentary and Exegesis to the *Wuzhen pian*; CT 145) even says that Zhang preached Buddhist doctrines before his death, with a disciple named Liu Fengzhen 劉奉真. In the postface to the *Wuzhen pian*, Zhang indeed presents himself as a follower of the Sixth Patriarch of Chan Buddhism, Huineng 慧能 (638–713).

The Perfected whom Zhang Boduan claims to have met in 1069 is never mentioned by name, but Weng Baoguang states that it was the deity Qingcheng zhangren 青城丈人 (Great Man of Mount Qingcheng; *Wuzhen pian zhushi* 悟真篇注釋, CT 145, preface, 1a). A later tradition followed by Bai Yuchan and his disciples identifies this deity as *Liu Haichan. Zhang's teachings were transmitted directly to *Shi Tai and indirectly to Liu Yongnian 劉永年 (fl. 1138–68), who was Weng Baoguang's master. Zhang himself did not found a school, but was acknowledged as the first patriarch of Nanzong in the thirteenth century.

Farzeen BALDRIAN-HUSSEIN

📖 Boltz J. M. 1987a, 173–74; Davis and Chao 1939; Hussein 1976; Qing Xitai 1994, 1: 304–6, 497

※ *Jindan sibai zi*; *Wuzhen pian*; *neidan*; Nanzong

Zhang Daoling

張道陵

second century; *zi*: Gongqi 公祺 *or* Fuhan 輔漢;
also known as Zhang Ling 張陵

Widely revered as the founder of Taoist religion, Zhang Daoling was a seminal figure closely linked to the origin of the Way of the Celestial Masters (*Tianshi dao). Traditional historical accounts say that he was born in Feng 豐, in the kingdom of Pei 沛 (Jiangsu) and journeyed to Sichuan, perhaps during Han Shundi's reign (125–144 CE), in search of the way of transcendence. *Ge Hong's fourth-century *Shenxian zhuan* portrays him as an alchemist and former student at the imperial academy, but there is no corroborating evidence for this within early Taoist history and it seems likely that this is yet another example of Ge transforming everyone into an advocate of his own practice.

The signal event in Zhang Daoling's life occurred according to tradition in 142, atop a mountain variously given as *Heming shan (Crane-call Mountain) or Huming shan 鵠鳴山 (Swan-call Mountain) and usually placed to the west of Chengdu. Although standard histories say merely that he fabricated Taoist (or talismanic) texts there, Taoist sources claim that he was visited by a divine figure, the Supreme Lord Lao (*Laojun), accompanied by a large retinue. This deity bestowed upon Zhang the aforementioned scriptures, the title of Celestial Master (*tianshi), and the Covenant with the Powers of Orthodox Unity (*zhengyi mengwei* 正一盟威). This marked the inception of the Way of the Celestial Masters or Way of Orthodox Unity (*Zhengyi), which was transmitted to his son *Zhang Heng, and through him to Daoling's grandson, *Zhang Lu. It is uncertain what elements of church organization and doctrine

Fig. 87. Painted scroll of Zhang Daoling. The scroll is owned by a Taoist master in Chingshui 清水, Taichung, Taiwan. Photograph by Julian Pas.

attested during Zhang Lu's life date to Zhang Daoling's period, but some sacred texts (Ge Hong records twenty-four scrolls and an inscription from 173 CE mentions twelve), the covenant, and the title of Celestial Master all seem to be part of the founding revelation.

Legends gathered quickly about the figure of Zhang Daoling. One of the earliest, known already to the painter Gu Kaizhi 顧愷之 (392–467), concerned two disciples, Wang Chang 王長 and Zhao Sheng 趙昇, whom Zhang Daoling tested on Mount Yuntai (Yuntai shan 雲臺山).

Zhang Daoling has a special place within the history of Taoism. He is frequently acknowledged in rituals as the patriarch of the liturgical tradition, and he is often represented among the set of paintings that constitute a priest's sacred arena or *tan* 壇. He is typically portrayed carrying a sword and riding a tiger, attributes associated with his exorcistic powers.

Terry KLEEMAN

📖 Bokenkamp 1997, 34 and passim; Campany 2002, 349–56; Giles L. 1948, 60–64; Liu Ts'un-yan 2005; Ōfuchi Ninji 1991, 39–46; Qing Xitai 1988–95, 1: 156–62; Robinet 1987c

※ Tianshi dao; Wudoumi dao; Zhengyi

Zhang Enpu

張恩溥

1904–69; *zi*: Heqin 鶴琴; *hao*: Ruiling 瑞齡
(Auspicious Longevity)

The first son of the sixty-second Celestial Master *Zhang Yuanxu (1862–1924) and Lady Wan 萬氏 (1874–1934), Zhang Enpu served as the Celestial Master of the sixty-third generation for a total of forty-five years, from 1924 until his demise. When Communist troops occupied the Celestial Master headquarters at Mount Longhu (*Longhu shan, Jiangxi) in 1931, Zhang took refuge in Shanghai where he continued his ritual practices until he was able to return home in 1936. Ten years later he went back to Shanghai and established the Shanghai Taoist Association (Shanghai daojiao hui 上海道教會) to serve as the center for an ambitious program of research and education.

In April 1949 Zhang vacated his home at Mount Longhu and settled in Taipei, Taiwan. Supported by a pension from the Ministry of the Interior, he took up residence at the Juexiu gong 覺修宮 (Palace of Awakened Cultivation), a *Quanzhen abbey in Taipei. Zhang sought and eventually gained permission in 1950 to set up the Taiwan Taoist Association (Taiwan sheng daojiao hui 臺灣省道教會) so as to revive Taoist practice in consonance with the *Zhengyi teachings of the newly relocated Celestial Master lineage. Seven years later a Taoist Devotees Association (Daojiao jushi hui 道教居士會) and Taoist Great Ritual Masters Association (Daojiao da fashi hui 道教大法師會) emerged to encourage teaching and publication, registration of temples, and proper training of all personnel. Chief among the publications that Zhang helped to achieve is the 1962 reprinting of the Ming Taoist Canon (see *Zhengtong daozang). He spoke of this goal during an interview with the American scholar Holmes Welch, whose published account records the date of Zhang's birth as 1894, the year of the horse, rather than the year of the dragon (1904) generally given in Chinese accounts of the patriarchy.

In 1964 Zhang carried his mission to the Malay Peninsula. Four years later he was elected to serve as director of the Taoist Association of the Republic of China (Zhonghua minguo daojiao hui 中華民國道教會), which superseded the Taiwan Taoist Association. Shortly after a visit to the Philippines Zhang perished at home in Taipei and the position of Celestial Master of the sixty-fourth generation fell to his nephew Zhang Yuanxian 張源先.

Judith M. BOLTZ

📖 Burkhardt 1953–58, 1: 132–35; Welch 1957–58; Zhang Jiyu 1990, 214–15; Zhang Yuanxian 1977, 103–5

※ Zhengyi

Zhang Guolao

張果老

Zhang Guolao, one of the Eight Immortals (*baxian), is actually Zhang Guo 張果, a Tang dynasty *fangshi (master of methods). Since his age was considered uncountable, he was given the appellation Lao 老 (Elder), and so was known as Zhang Guolao (Zhang Guo, the Elder). His biography appears in the *Jiu Tangshu* (Old History of the Tang) and the *Xin Tangshu* (New History of the Tang). According to it, Zhang Guo, while living as a hermit on Mount Zhongtiao (Zhongtiao shan 中條山) in Hengzhou 恆州 (Hebei), was invited to court by the Empress Wu (r. 690–705), but did not obey the summons, pretending to be dead. Later, in the time of Tang Xuanzong (r. 712–56), he was invited to court at the eastern capital of Luoyang. Xuanzong is said to have questioned him closely on everything from political issues to the drugs of immortality.

When Xuanzong had the *fangshi* Xing Hepu 邢和璞, skilled at calculating people's life spans, calculate Zhang Guo's, Zhang told him: "I was born in the *bingzi* 丙子 year of Emperor Yao 堯 and acted as a palace attendant to him." According to traditional chronology, this placed his birth around 2100 BCE. He was also asked to pit his skills against the *fangshi* Shi Yeguang 師夜光, who was famed for his clairvoyance, but Shi was not able even to see his form. Then Xuanzong told a eunuch, a famous strong man, that he had heard that a person who could drink an extract of *jin* 堇 (monkshood or wolfsbane, an herb containing a deadly poison) without writhing in agony was a true adept, and had Zhang Guo do so in the time of greatest cold. Zhang Guo drank down three cups of it, and only became gloriously drunk. "Bad wine, isn't it!" he exclaimed, and fell asleep. On waking, when he looked in a mirror, Zhang Guo found that his teeth had been completely burned. He ordered an attendant to fetch an iron staff, and proceeded to knock his teeth out. These he placed in his sash. Then he rubbed his gums with some ointment he had with him, and as he slept a little while later, new white teeth sprang forth. This persuaded Xuanzong that Zhang Guo truly was a divine person. He wanted to give his sister Yuzhen Gongzhu 玉真公主 to Zhang as a wife, but Zhang refused and returned to Hengzhou. At this time, the emperor bestowed on him the name of Tongxuan xiansheng 通玄先生 (Elder of Pervading Mystery). Nothing is known of his later whereabouts, but Xuanzong built a Taoist monastery at Puwu 蒲吾 (Hebei), where Zhang Guo had his hermitage, and called it Qixia guan 棲霞觀 (Abbey of Dwelling in Mist). It is said that Zhang Guo wrote a work called *Yinfu jing xuanjie* 陰符經玄解 (Arcane Explication of the *Yinfu jing*). This may perhaps be the "Yellow Emperor's *Yinfu jing* in one scroll" annotated by Zhang Guo and included in the Taoist Canon (CT 112, and YJQQ 15.1a–11a).

Both Standard Histories of the Tang dynasty contain much the same material as that given above, but in the story quoted in the "Divine Immortals" ("Shenxian" 神仙) section of the *Taiping guangji* 太平廣記 (Extensive Records of the Taiping Xingguo Reign Period; 978), Zhang Guo's mystical power is accentuated. For example, when the Taoist *Ye Fashan is asked by Xuanzong about Zhang Guo's real identity, he replies, "He is the essence of primordial Chaos, from the time when Heaven and Earth first split apart." Having revealed the secret, he is punished and falls dead, blood pouring from him. Later, when Zhang Guo's coffin is opened after his death, his body is found to have disappeared. The fact that there were no remains in the grave was believed to indicate that Zhang Guo had obtained "release from the corpse" (*shijie) and become immortal.

YOSHIKAWA Tadao

📖 Little 2000b, 328–29; see also bibliography for the entry *baxian

※ *baxian*; HAGIOGRAPHY

Zhang Guoxiang

張國祥

?–1611; *zi*: Wenzheng 文徵; *hao*: Xinzhan 心湛 (Mindful)

The loss of his son led the forty-ninth Celestial Master Zhang Yongxu 張永緒 (?–1566) to designate his nephew Zhang Guoxiang as his successor. The Longqing Emperor (r. 1567–72), however, did not look favorably on the *Zhengyi patriarchy and stripped Zhang of his title, demoting him to a Fifth Rank post as Supervisor of the *Shangqing gong (Palace of Highest Clarity) at Mount Longhu (*Longhu shan, Jiangxi). In 1577 the Wanli Emperor (r. 1573–1620) renewed imperial recognition of Zhang as Celestial Master of the fiftieth generation. When Zhang presented himself at the capital of Nanjing (Jiangsu), the emperor ordered a restoration of the Chaotian gong 朝天宮 (Palace in Homage to Heaven) to serve as Zhang's residence and personally inscribed a tablet identifying it as the Longhu shan zhenren fu 龍虎山真人府 (Bureau of the Perfected of Mount Longhu). He also arranged Zhang's betrothal to the daughter of his Commandant-escort Xie Gongzhao 謝公詔. Zhang remained in the capital for thirteen years.

In 1607 the emperor ordered Zhang to oversee the compilation and publication of a supplement to the Taoist Canon of the Zhengtong reign period, which came to be known as the *Wanli xu daozang (Supplementary Taoist Canon of the Wanli Reign Period). When a flood in 1609 left the Shangqing gong in ruins, Zhang appealed to the emperor for funds to repair the abbey but did not survive to see its full restoration. The emperor honored him with the construction of the Mingyang guan 明陽觀 (Abbey of Luminous Yang) at his burial site in Jinqi 金溪 (Jiangxi), southwest of Mount Longhu.

The 1607 supplement to the Taoist Canon includes a copy of the *Han tianshi shijia (Lineage of the Han Celestial Master) by *Zhang Zhengchang, with eight additional biographies supplied by Zhang Guoxiang. He is also credited with the compilation of a Longhu shanzhi 龍虎山志 (Monograph of Mount Longhu) in 3 juan.

Judith M. BOLTZ

📖 Oyanagi Shigeta 1934, 347–48; Zhang Jiyu 1990, 208–9; Zhang Yuanxian 1977, 90–91

※ *Han tianshi shijia; Wanli xu daozang; Zhengyi*

Zhang Heng

張衡

?–179; *zi*: Lingzhen 靈真

Zhang Heng is traditionally regarded as the second leader of the Way of the Celestial Masters (*Tianshi dao) and early church documents refer to him as the "inheriting master" (*sishi* 嗣師). Little else is known about him. Early historical sources merely state that he acceded to leadership of the movement on *Zhang Daoling's death and passed his position on to his son, *Zhang Lu. There are no dates for his birth, but a sixth-century source says that he became leader on the seventh day of the first lunar month of 178. He is said to have attained the Dao and ascended to Heaven the following year. Zhang Lu's mother, presumably Heng's wife, was famous for her magical powers and youthful appearance and was patronized by Liu Yan 劉焉, Governor of Yizhou 益州 (Sichuan). Commentators as early as Pei Songzhi 裴松之 (372–451) have speculated that the Zhang Xiu 張脩 mentioned as a local religious leader in Sichuan at this time might in fact be an error for Heng.

Terry KLEEMAN

📖 Ōfuchi Ninji 1991, 39–46

※ Tianshi dao; Wudoumi dao

Zhang Jixian

張繼先

1092–1126; *zi*: Jiawen 嘉聞, Daozheng 道正, Zunzheng 遵正; *hao*: Xiaoran zi 脩然子 (Master of Swiftness), Xujing xiansheng 虛靖 先生 (Elder of Empty Quiescence)

Zhang Jixian succeeded his uncle, the twenty-ninth Celestial Master Zhang Jingduan 張景端 (1049?–1100?), as *Zhengyi patriarch of the thirtieth genera-tion. His father Zhang Churen 張處仁 served as magistrate of Linchuan 臨 川 (Jiangxi). He is said to have remained mute until the age of five when the call of a rooster suddenly evoked from his lips a remarkably insightful quatrain. Four years later, at the age of nine, Zhang inherited the mantle of the Celestial Master patriarchy.

Accounts of Zhang's exploits as exorcist, rain-maker, and queller of flood demons are featured in a range of narrative texts, the best known of which is the opening episode of the *Shuihu zhuan* 水滸傳 (Water Margin). Two biographic resources in the Taoist Canon clearly drew on a comparable body of lore. A concise chronicle is recorded in the *Lishi zhenxian tidao tongjian* (19.11b–13a). Ostensibly verbatim transcriptions of Zhang's conversations with Song Huizong (r. 1100–1125) are included in the corresponding entry of the *Han tianshi shijia* (3.1a–6b).

Zhang Jixian reportedly answered the summons of Huizong four times. The emperor is said to have been so impressed with Zhang's success in ritual practice and his pedagogical approach that he honored him in 1105 with the title Xujing xiansheng (Elder of Empty Quiescence). Zhang resisted Huizong's effort to retain him in the capital. When he disclosed the need to restore the Celestial Master compound at Mount Longhu (*Longhu shan, Jiangxi), the emperor authorized a massive reconstruction and enlargement of the estate. Huizong's short-lived successor Song Qinzong (r. 1125–27) issued an urgent call for Zhang to return to Bianliang 汴梁 (Henan). Before he could comply, Zhang expired at the Tianqing guan 天慶觀 (Abbey of Celestial Blessings) in Sizhou 泗州 (Anhui) on the very day that the capital fell to the Jurchens. Numerous stories evolved around reputed sightings of Zhang throughout the countryside thereafter.

The Taoist Canon contains two collections of writings traced to Zhang Jixian. A sequence of heptasyllabic quatrains is printed without prefatory matter as the *Mingzhen powang zhangsong* 明真破妄章頌 (Exemplary Lauds on Illuminating Perfection and Smashing Falsity; CT 979). The late fourteenth-century *Daofa huiyuan* (Corpus of Taoist Ritual, j. 71) includes a variant form of this text under the title *Xujing tianshi powang zhang* 虛靖天師破妄章 (Stanzas by the Celestial Master of Empty Quiescence on Smashing Falsity). The *Sanshi dai tianshi Xujing zhenjun yulu* 三十代天師虛靖真君語錄 (Recorded Sayings of the Thirtieth Generation Celestial Master, Perfected Lord of Empty Quiescence; CT 1249), compiled by *Zhang Yuchu, brings together a diverse body of both verse and prose. According to his preface of 1395, the forty-third Celestial Master prepared this text for publication after searching through temple libraries for the lost works of his ancestor. High-ranking officials are named as the recipients of a number of Zhang Jixian's communications. Among the best known compositions is the "Dadao ge" 大道歌 (Song of the Great Dao) that, according to Zhang Yuchu's hagiographic account, the thirtieth Celestial Master submitted to Song Huizong. Closing the anthology is Zhang Jixian's farewell address, also recorded in the Celestial Master hagiography. The authenticity of writings ascribed to Zhang in these two anthologies remains in some cases open to question. Additional texts in his name appear in various other compilations within the Taoist Canon.

Judith M. BOLTZ

📖 Boltz J. M. 1987a, 63, 116, 189, and 194–95; Kubo Noritada 1987a; Sun Kekuan 1968, 33–40; Zhang Yuanxian 1977, 71–73

※ Zhengyi

Zhang Keda

張可大

1218–63; *zi*: Zixian 子賢; *hao*: Guanmiao xiansheng 觀妙先生
(Elder Who Observes the Marvelous)

Named the thirty-fifth Celestial Master in 1230 after more than two decades of unclear leadership in the *Zhengyi (Orthodox Unity) headquarters on Mount Longhu (*Longhu shan, Jiangxi), Zhang Keda held tenure at a time of both great confusion and vitality in the centers of Taoist authority. After Zhang Jingyuan 張景淵, the heir apparent of the thirty-fourth Celestial Master Zhang Qingxian 張慶先 (?–1209?, Keda's uncle), passed away prematurely, Zhang Boyu 張伯瑀 (Keda's grandfather) took over the affairs of Celestial Master, but his early death without a ready heir apparent put the instructional and ritual duties of Celestial Master in the hands of Zhang Tianlin 張天麟 (?–1230, Keda's father). When Tianlin passed away in 1230 under the reign of Song Lizong (r. 1224–64), Zhang Keda, just twelve years old, became the thirty-fifth Celestial Master.

During Keda's tenure, many ritual masters reportedly came to his mountain to receive their official Taoist registers (*LU). His spiritual pedigree was helpful in getting him summoned to Lizong's court in 1236, 1238, and 1239 to deal with various disruptions in the natural order. In 1239 he received the title Elder Who Observes the Marvelous (Guanmiao xiansheng). In 1254 the Mongol court summoned him again, giving him control over the three main Taoist initiation centers (Longhu shan, *Maoshan, and *Gezao shan) and Taoist abbacies in the Southern Song, and put him in charge of the Palace of the Dragon's Soaring (Longxiang gong 龍翔宮). He oversaw the rebuilding of the Abbey of Perfect Virtuousness (Zhenyi guan 真懿觀) on Mount Longhu, and extended its land holdings, while also succeeding in removing them from the tax rolls. In the fourth lunar month of 1262 he handed over his ceremonial sword and seal to his second son, *Zhang Zongyan (1244–91), who became the thirty-sixth Celestial Master, before passing away.

Lowell SKAR

📖 Boltz J. M. 1987a, 58

※ Zhengyi

Zhang Liang

張良

?–187 BCE; *zi*: Zifang 子房

Zhang Liang was the chief military strategist and political adviser to Liu Bang 劉邦 (?–195 BCE), the first emperor of the Han, in the campaigns that established that dynasty. Zhang's extraordinary ability to predict the right course of action seems to have derived from the teachings of the *Taigong bingfa* 太公兵法 (The Grand Duke's Art of War), a book bestowed on him by an old man in plain clothes who turned out to be Sir Yellow Stone (Huangshi gong 黃石公) after their celebrated encounter. Zhang's success in advising Liu Bang is detailed in his biography in *Shiji* 55 (trans. Watson 1961, 134–51). For services rendered he was enfeoffed as the Marquis of Liu (Liu hou 留侯). In this otherwise standard narrative of diplomacy and war, Zhang is credited with practices and attitudes that appear unmistakably Taoist. When ill, he is said to have practiced *daoyin* exercises and to have given up eating grain. Later, he retired from public life, expressing the desire to "roam with *Chisong zi." In retirement he studied abstaining from grains (*bigu*), *daoyin*, and lightening the body (*qingshen* 輕 身). In later Taoist tradition, he is said to have been the eighth (or sometimes sixth or ninth) generation ancestor of *Zhang Daoling.

Benjamin PENNY

📖 Bauer 1956

※ HAGIOGRAPHY

Zhang Liusun

張留孫

1248–1322; *zi*: Shihan 師漢

Zhang Liusun is one of the few court Taoists who managed to influence the religious policy of the Chinese empire while keeping his reputation untarnished. Born into a family remotely related to the Celestial Masters, Zhang was educated on Mount Longhu (*Longhu shan, Jiangxi), a hereditary calling for his clan. He was only twenty-eight when, in 1276, he accompanied the thirty-sixth Celestial Master, *Zhang Zongyan (1244–91), to an audience with the Mongol emperor Khubilai khan (Shizu, r. 1260–1294). At that time Khubilai had entered Jiangnan 江南 in a campaign to annihilate the Song empire, which would take three more years to complete. Zhang Zongyan was invited to stay at court, like the patriarchs of other religious orders recognized and granted autonomy by the Mongols. However, Zhang Zongyan disliked the climate of Yanjing (Beijing) and returned to Mount Longhu, leaving Liusun as his delegate. The imperial family took a strong liking to the young Taoist, and after the latter cured Khubilai's mother, he rose to a position of prestige that he was never to abandon. Several miracles performed for Khubilai and the next four emperors augmented his aura and helped to maintain his political advisory role. He was proposed as a candidate to become Celestial Master, but declined firmly; he was then made the first patriarch of a newly created institution, the *Xuanjiao.

Zhang's influence at court enabled him to further the cause of southern intellectuals willing to assume high political positions, but he did so carefully and never found himself too involved with the losing side in the volatile world of mid-Yuan politics. His support and stable position endeared him so much to southern scholars that they unanimously heaped praise on him, especially in several funerary inscriptions. He also successfully pushed for institutional independence for the Taoist administration. Many of his disciples filled the higher positions within the Taoist administration in southern China. His influence, privileges, and titles (but not his nobility rank, which no other Taoist attained under the Yuan) passed on to his disciple *Wu Quanjie (1269–1346) when the latter became his successor.

While Zhang Liusun is widely documented as a political figure, his private life and attitudes are little known, and none of his writings survive. Nevertheless, Zhang left an important legacy independent of his imperial connections: just before his death, he initiated the building of Beijing's *Dongyue miao (Shrine of the Eastern Peak) with his own private funds, to repay the favors that fate had granted him. The Dongyue miao was to become one of China's most important temples.

Vincent GOOSSAERT

📖 Qing Xitai 1994, 1: 357–59; Takahashi Bunji 1997; Rinaker Ten Broeck and Yiu 1950–51

※ Xuanjiao

Zhang Lu

張魯

?–215 or 216; *zi*: Gongqi 公祺

Zhang Lu was the grandson of *Zhang Daoling and the third hereditary leader of the Way of the Celestial Masters (*Tianshi dao). While alive he was called simply "master" (*shijun* 師君) and early church documents refer to him as the "continuing master" (*xishi* 系師). Zhang Lu's mother was said to possess demonic arts (*guidao* 鬼道) and maintained a "youthful appearance" (*shaorong* 少容); through these arts she drew close to Liu Yan 劉焉, Governor of Yizhou 益州 (Sichuan), and no doubt facilitated Lu's rise to power.

Standard histories record that in 191, Zhang Lu, having taken a commission as Commander of Volunteers (*duyi sima* 督義司馬) under Liu Yan, attacked and killed the Governor of Hanzhong 漢中, then established a theocratic state in Hanzhong and Ba 巴 commanderies (modern Sichuan / Shaanxi), uniting the indigenous population of Zong 賨 tribesmen and the local Han Chinese inhabitants. One account says that at this time he also killed Zhang Xiu 張脩 and assimilated his followers. In 200, a rift developed between Lu and Liu Yan's son and successor, Liu Zhang 劉璋, whom Lu thought "stupid and cowardly"; when Lu rebelled, Liu Zhang killed his mother and younger brother. Zhang Lu came to an accommodation with the Han state and accepted from them the titles Leader of Palace Attendants Quelling the People (Zhengmin zhonglang jiang 鎮民中郎將) and Governor of Hanning 漢寧 (Hunan). The Hanzhong state survived until 215, when, after initially retreating into Ba commandery, Zhang Lu surrendered to Cao Cao 曹操. Cao enfeoffed him as Marquis in Lang 閬 (Sichuan) and General Quelling the South (Zhennan jiangjun 鎮南將軍), and married daughters to some of his sons, but Lu died soon thereafter, in 215 or 216, and was buried in Ye 鄴 (Henan). The Hanzhong community was divided, with one portion being transferred to the northwest and another being settled near the capital of Ye, in central China.

In fact, Zhang Lu's role in the founding of the Celestial Master sect was of great significance. All of the social features of the sect, including the system of parishes (*zhi), the "charity lodges" (yishe 義舍), the public works, the Three Assemblies (*sanhui), etc., are clearly attested only within the context of Lu's millennial Hanzhong state, though all are sometimes traced back to Zhang Daoling. Moreover, Lu is the likely author of the *Xiang'er commentary to the Laozi (Bokenkamp 1997, 58–59). As such, he can be seen as a significant theorist within the Taoist Church. His grandfather usually gets the credit, but Lu can legitimately be called the father of Taoist religion, much as Paul is the father of Christianity.

Terry KLEEMAN

📖 Bokenkamp 1997, 34–35 and passim; Goodman 1994; Kleeman 1998, 76–79; Ōfuchi Ninji 1991, 46–55; Qing Xitai 1988–95, 1: 178–81; Robinet 1987b

※ Tianshi dao; Wudoumi dao

Zhang Sanfeng

張三丰 (*or*: 張三峰)

ming: Quanyi 全一; *zi*: Junbao 君寶

Zhang Sanfeng ("Zhang Triple Abundance" or "Zhang Three Peaks") is a famous Taoist said to have lived between the end of the Yuan and beginning of the Ming periods. His historical existence, however, is unproved. In early biographies—including the one in the *Mingshi* (History of the Ming, 299.7641–43)—he is usually said to be a native of Yizhou 懿州 (Liaoning), but other sources give different birthplaces. According to these works he was seven feet high and had enormously big ears and eyes, his appearance suggested the longevity of a turtle and the immortality of a crane, and his beard and whiskers bristled like the blades of a halberd. He tied his hair into a knot and, regardless of the season, wore only a garment made of leaves. In his youth, Zhang is supposed to have studied Buddhism under the Chan master Haiyun 海雲 (1201–56), but then mastered *neidan and reached immortality. He was known for his extraordinary magical powers as well as his ability to prophesy.

In the first years of the Ming period, Zhang reportedly established himself on Mount Wudang (*Wudang shan, Hubei), where he lived in a thatched hut. With his pupils he rebuilt the mountain monasteries destroyed during the wars at the end of the Mongol dynasty. From Mount Wudang, Zhang went to the Jintai guan 金臺觀 (Abbey of the Golden Terrace) in Baoji 寶雞 (Shaanxi), where he announced his departure, composed a hymn, and passed away. Later he came back to life, travelled to Sichuan, and visited Mount Wudang again.

Zhang Sanfeng as a patron saint and god. The belief in the real existence of Zhang Sanfeng during the early Ming dynasty is reflected in the emperors' continued efforts to locate him. The search for Zhang started in 1391 by order of the Hongwu Emperor (r. 1368–98) and was extended from 1407 to 1419 by the Yongle Emperor (r. 1403–24). Both sent out delegates several times, but they all returned without success. Promoted by the Ming emperors' interest, a cult developed around Zhang that spread widely and lasted until the later years of the Qing dynasty.

As time went on, the legends multiplied and became increasingly exaggerated. Zhang is known as the founder of *taiji quan (a claim without historical evidence) and the patron saint of practitioners of this technique. During the sixteenth and seventeenth centuries, a connection to the sexual techniques (*fangzhong shu) was also established and texts dealing with these practices were ascribed to him. The belief that Zhang was the master of Shen Wansan 沈萬三, a popular deity of wealth, led to his own identity as a god of wealth in the seventeenth century. The Western Branch (Xipai 西派) of *neidan* and various Qing sects also regarded Zhang Sanfeng as their first patriarch.

Works of Zhang Sanfeng. The *Zhang Sanfeng quanji* 張三丰全集 (Complete Collection of Zhang Sanfeng) contains writings both ascribed to and about Zhang Sanfeng (Qing Xitai 1994, 2: 222–23). This work consists of eight *juan* whose content is as follows:

1. Prefaces, Edicts, Biographies, Taoist Schools, Correcting Errors, Manifestations

2. Prose Writings, Concealed Mirrors (*Yinjian* 隱鑑)

3. Essays on the Great Dao (*Dadao lun* 大道論), Straightforward Explanation of the Mysterious Moving Power (*Xuanji zhijiang* 玄機直講), Speaking Simply about the Dao (*Daoyan qianjin* 道言淺近)

4. Mysterious Essentials (*Xuanyao* 玄要, in two parts, with a supplement)

5. Clouds and Waters (*Yunshui* 雲水, in three parts)

6. Folios of Celestial Words (*Tiankou pian* 天口篇), Admonitions to the World (*Xunshi wen* 訓世文)

7. Scriptures of the Nine Sovereigns (*Jiuhuang jing* 九皇經), Scripture of the Three Teachings (*Sanjiao jing* 三教經), Scripture on Salvation (*Duren jing* 度人經), Scripture on Enlightenment (*Puti jing* 菩提經), Buddhist Hymns

8. Leisurely Talks among Water and Rocks (*Shuishi xiantan* 水石閒談), Past and Contemporary Poems, Concealed Mirrors (*Yinjing* 隱鏡), Collected Records

An edition of the *Zhang Sanfeng quanji* is found in the *Daozang jiyao (vols. 17–18).

Martina DARGA

📖 Qing Xitai 1988–95, 3: 391–94 and 515–6; Seidel 1970; Wong Shiu Hon 1979; Wong Shiu Hon 1982

※ HAGIOGRAPHY

Zhang Sicheng

張嗣成

?–1344?; *zi*: Ciwang 次望; *hao*: Taixuan zi 太玄子
(Master of Great Mystery)

Zhang Sicheng became the thirty-ninth Celestial Master after the death of his father, Zhang Yucai 張與材 (?–1316), the thirty-eighth Celestial Master. Like his predecessors under Mongol rule, Sicheng maintained control over the three major Taoist ordination centers (*Longhu shan, *Maoshan, and *Gezao shan) and all Taoist affairs south of the Yangzi River, and continued to issue ordination certificates and ritual registers (*LU) to Taoist priests.

Receiving an imperial title from Yuan Renzong (r. 1312–20) in 1318, he was summoned in 1325 by Yuan Taiding (r. 1324–28) and presided over a major Offering (*jiao) ritual in the Palace of Perpetual Spring (Changchun gong 長春宮, the present *Baiyun guan) in Beijing, assisted by Sun Lüdao 孫履道 and *Wu

Quanjie (1269–1346). He became head of the Academy of Gathered Worthies (Jixian yuan 集賢院) in 1326. After traveling to various sacred mountains, he passed away and was succeeded by his younger brother Zhang Side 張嗣德 (?–1353), who became the fortieth Celestial Master.

Zhang Sicheng is credited with the *Daode zhenjing zhangju xunsong* 道德真經章句訓頌 (Instructional Lauds on the Sections and Sentences of the Authentic Scripture of the Dao and Its Virtue; CT 698), and had a hand in compiling the annotated *Yushu jing* (Scripture of the Jade Pivot; CT 99).

Lowell SKAR

📖 Boltz J. M. 1987a, 243–44

※ Zhengyi

Zhang Wanfu

張萬福

fl. 710–13; *hao*: Dade 大德 (Great Virtue)

Except for remarks that he made in his own works, we know virtually nothing of Zhang Wanfu's life. He was a priest residing at the Taiqing guan 太清觀 (Abbey of Great Clarity) in Chang'an during the reign of Tang Ruizong (r. 684–90, 710–12) and participated in the compilation of the *Yiqie daojing yinyi* (Complete Taoist Scriptures, with Phonetic and Semantic Glosses). He also witnessed and perhaps participated in the *Lingbao and *Shangqing ordinations of Princesses Jinxian 金仙 (Gold Immortal) and Yuzhen 玉真 (Jade Perfected), Ruizong's daughters, on February 11 of 711 and December 1 of 712. Eight of his works, most written in this period, have survived in the *Daozang*:

1. *Duren jingjue yinyi* 度人經訣音義 (Instructions on the Scripture on Salvation, with Phonetic and Semantic Glosses; 710/713; CT 95). This annotation of the *Duren jing* is undoubtedly a rare fragment from the *Yiqie daojing yinyi*.

2. *Sandong zhongjie wen* 三洞眾戒文 (All Precepts of the Three Caverns; 710/713; CT 178). Here Zhang supplies eleven sets of precepts that officiants administered to aspirants during initiations and ordinations. His enumeration is incomplete.

3. *Sanshi minghui xingzhuang juguan fangsuo wen* 三師名諱形狀居觀方所文 (Taboo Names, Vitae, and Locations of Home Abbeys of the Three Masters; 710/713; CT 445). This is a collection of blank forms that priests

filled in with information about the officiants who presided at their ordination: the Ordination Master (*dushi* 度師), the Registration Master (*jishi* 籍師), and the Scripture Master (*jingshi* 經師). These documents were used whenever a priest performed his offices.

4. *Juan* 16 of the **Wushang huanglu dazhai licheng yi* 無上黃籙大齋立成儀 (Standard Liturgies of the Supreme Great Yellow Register Retreat; CT 508). Here Zhang revised and enlarged *Lu Xiujing's liturgy for the performance of the Nocturnal Invocation (**suqi*). In the signatures to this text and CT 1240 below, Zhang's title is given as priest of the Qingdu guan 清都觀 (Abbey of the Clear Metropolis) so they were probably written after 713.

5. *Sandong fafu kejie wen* 三洞法服科戒文 (Codes and Precepts for the Liturgical Vestments of the Three Caverns; 710/713; CT 788). This is a work devoted to describing the vestments of priests and raiments of the gods.

6. *Jiao sandong zhenwen wufa Zhengyi mengwei lu licheng yi* 醮三洞真文五法正一盟威籙立成儀 (Liturgy for Establishing an Offering with the Authentic Scripts and the Five Methods of the Three Caverns, and the Registers of the Covenant with the Powers of Orthodox Unity; date unknown; CT 1212; part. trans. Lagerwey 1994). Here Zhang constructed a liturgy in thirteen parts for petitioning the gods to bestow blessings on the souls of the dead by manipulating various sacred writs.

7. *Daoshi shou sandong jingjie falu zhairi li* 道士受三洞經誡法籙擇日曆 (Calendar for Selecting the Days on which Taoist Priests should Receive Scriptures, Precepts, and Liturgical Registers of the Three Caverns; CT 1240). This work supplies the proper dates for transmitting various registers (**LU*) and scriptures (Kalinowski 1989–90, 95–96).

8. *Chuanshou sandong jingjie falu lüeshuo* 傳授三洞經戒法籙略說 (Synopsis of Transmissions for Scriptures, Precepts, and Liturgical Registers of the Three Caverns; dated January 1 of 713; CT 1241). This is a survey of Taoist initiations and ordinations that describes admonitions, texts, oaths, pledges, and various other aspects of the rite. Zhang's account of the princesses' investitures appears at the end of the text. Next to the **Fengdao kejie*, this is the main source for materials on medieval ordinations (Schipper 1985c).

Charles D. BENN

📖 Benn 1991, 137–51; Qing Xitai 1988–95, 2: 282–95

※ *Yiqie daojing yinyi*; *Wushang huanglu dazhai licheng yi*

Zhang Yuanxu

張元旭

1862–1924; *zi*: Xiaochu 曉初

The son of the sixty-first Celestial Master Zhang Renzheng 張仁晸 (1841–1903), Zhang Yuanxu held the position of Celestial Master of the sixty-second generation for twenty-one years, from 1904 until his demise. In 1910 the American Methodist missionary Carl Kupfer called upon Zhang and published an account of his visit, together with photographs. Upon the establishment of the Republic of China in 1912, the Chief Military Commission of Jiangxi terminated the authority of the Celestial Master patriarchy, confiscating their estate at Mount Longhu (*Longhu shan, Jiangxi) and revoking their entitlement.

Two years later President Yuan Shikai 袁世凱 (1859–1916) restored both land and title to Zhang Yuanxu. He travelled widely thereafter, extending the influence of his legacy from Beijing and Tianjin to Shanghai and Hankou. At a meeting in Shanghai of the Taoist Association of the Republic of China (Zhonghua minguo daojiao zonghui 中華民國道教總會) attended by representatives of *Zhengyi temples throughout Jiangsu and Zhejiang, Zhang proposed building schools, hospitals, and various industries to revitalize the Taoist heritage of China. He perished in Shanghai without seeing the fruition of these plans and was succeeded by his eldest son *Zhang Enpu. His grave at Mount Longhu was completely restored in 1994, under the initiative of a devotee from Malaysia.

Zhang's writings include the *Bu Han tianshi shijia* 補漢天師世家 (Supplementary Lineage of the Han Celestial Master), with a colophon dating to 1918. This continuation of the *Han tianshi shijia*, published by Oyanagi Shigeta, includes biographies for patriarchs from the fiftieth to the sixty-first generation.

Judith M. BOLTZ

📖 Boltz J. M. 1987a, 63; Kupfer 1911, 91–106; Oyanagi Shigeta 1934, 347–56; Shanren 1994; Zhang Jiyu 1990, 213–14; Zhang Yuanxian 1977, 102

※ Zhengyi

Zhang Yuchu

張宇初

1361–1410; *zi*: Zixuan 子璿, Xinfu 信甫; *hao*: Jishan 耆山
(Venerable Mound), Wuwei zi 無為子 (Master of Non-action)

Zhang Yuchu was the eldest son of the forty-second Celestial Master *Zhang Zhengchang (1335–78) and Lady Bao 包氏, a fifth-generation descendant of Bao Hui 包恢 (1182–1268; SB 832–34) of Nancheng 南城 (Jiangxi). Succeeding his father as the forty-third Celestial Master, Zhang is remembered not only for his role as an influential leader of the *Zhengyi school but also as a renowned scholar with a substantial literary legacy to his name.

The Hongwu Emperor (r. 1368–98) put Zhang in charge of all Taoist affairs of state in 1380 and authorized an honorary title for his mother. Over the years Zhang obliged the emperor by presiding over ritual services held in and around the capital of Nanjing (Jiangsu). In 1390 Hongwu ordered the restoration of the central abbey of the Celestial Master headquarters at Mount Longhu (*Longhu shan, Jiangxi), the *Shangqing gong (Palace of Highest Clarity). The next year covertly issued talismanic registers were banned by imperial decree. Zhang was then given possession of a new seal in the name of the Zhengyi patriarchy, to be used in producing talismanic registers as safeguards for sacred mountain sites.

Hongwu's successor, the Jianwen Emperor (r. 1399–1402), dismissed Zhang and so he went into retirement at a new retreat built outside Mount Longhu, which he called Xianquan 峴泉 (Alpine Spring). By the Yongle reign period (1403–24), Zhang was back in favor at court. In 1406 the Yongle Emperor assigned him the task of collecting and classifying Taoist writings, an endeavor that ultimately led to the compilation of the *Da Ming daozang jing* 大明道藏經 (Scriptures of the Taoist Canon of the Great Ming), popularly known as the *Zhengtong daozang (Taoist Canon of the Zhengtong Reign Period). In addition to serving in a ritual capacity on behalf of the emperor, Zhang went twice by imperial decree to Mount Wudang (*Wudang shan, Hubei) in search of the legendary *Zhang Sanfeng. Not long after this quest Zhang conveyed his sword and seal of office to his brother Zhang Yuqing 張宇清 (1364–1427) and took his last breath.

Zhang compiled a *Longhu shanzhi* 龍虎山志 (Monograph of Mount Longhu) in ten *juan*, a fragmentary copy of which served as the foundation for a reedition of the text in 1740. In addition to prefaces and colophons attached to various texts, the Ming Taoist Canon contains four titles in Zhang Yuchu's name:

Daomen shigui (Ten Guidelines for the Taoist Community), *Duren shangpin miaojing tongyi* 元始無量度人上品妙經通義 (Comprehensive Meaning of the Wondrous Scripture of the Upper Chapters on Salvation; CT 89), *Sanshi dai tianshi Xujing zhenjun yulu* 三十代天師虛靖真君語錄 (Recorded Sayings of the Thirtieth Generation Celestial Master, Perfected Lord of Empty Quiescence; CT 1249), and *Xianquan ji* 峴泉集 (Anthology of Alpine Spring; CT 1311). A variant edition of the last title is included in the *Siku quanshu* 四庫全書 (Complete Writings of the Four Repositories) of 1782. Zhang's vast writings display the many ways he sought to locate the unifying features behind an increasing diversity of religious expression during the Ming.

Judith M. BOLTZ

📖 Boltz J. M. 1987a, 193–95, 210–11, and 241–42; Ding Changyun 2002; Sun Kekuan 1977, 313–47; Tu Fang 1976b; Zhang Jiyu 1990, 203–4

※ *Daomen shigui*; *Zhengtong daozang*; *Zhengyi*

Zhang Zhengchang

張正常

1335–78; *zi*: Zhongji 仲紀; *hao*: Chongxu zi 沖虛子
(Master of the Unfathomable Emptiness)

When Zhang Zhengchang's father, the thirty-ninth Celestial Master *Zhang Sicheng (?–1344?) drowned on a pilgrimage to the Five Peaks (*wuyue*), his uncle Zhang Side 張嗣德 (?–1353) became Celestial Master of the fortieth generation. Upon his uncle's demise, Zhang supported the succession of Zhang Side's son Zhang Zhengyan 張正言 (?–1359) as the forty-first Celestial Master. With the death of his cousin, Zhang Zhengchang became the forty-second Celestial Master in the very year his father had prophesied.

Zhang offered a pledge of support in 1361 to the troops occupying Jiangxi under Zhu Yuanzhang 朱元璋 (1328–98), as the Mongol empire began to collapse, and gained protection of the patriarchal estate at Mount Longhu (*Longhu shan, Jiangxi). Twice, in 1365 and 1366, Zhu warmly received Zhang as an honored guest at his headquarters in Nanjing (Jiangsu). Following Zhu's enthronement in 1368 as the Hongwu Emperor (r. 1368–98), Zhang again paid homage and was given the title of Da zhenren 大真人 (Great Man of Perfection), which, according to the official historical record, was devised to replace the title *tianshi that the emperor found offensive. Authorized by Hongwu to be in charge of all Taoist affairs of state, Zhang oversaw appointments to and restorations of temple compounds throughout the country. The emperor often summoned him to the capital for consultation, once notably in 1370 to inquire into the nature of ghosts and spirits. Zhang's mother Lady Hu 胡氏 (1291-after 1371) celebrated her eightieth birthday the same year, leading the emperor to bestow honorary titles on both her and Zhang's father.

In 1377, at the emperor's behest, Zhang joined the imperial entourage paying homage to the Five Peaks. Like his father, he did not live to complete the journey. After a visit to Mount Song (*Songshan, Henan), Zhang returned to Mount Longhu where he perished on the fifth day of the twelfth lunar month (4 January 1378). His eldest son *Zhang Yuchu succeeded him as the forty-third Celestial Master.

The Ming Taoist Canon includes an amplified version of one compilation produced under Zhang's direction, the *Han tianshi shijia (Lineage of the Han Celestial Master). Song Lian 宋濂 (1310–81), author of a preface to this work, also composed the stele inscription mounted at Zhang's grave. The emperor himself submitted a eulogy for the memorial service held at Mount Longhu.

Judith M. BOLTZ

📖 Boltz J. M. 1987a, 62; Chen Yuan 1988, 1233–42; Shiga Takayoshi 1963; Tu Fang 1976a; Zhang Jiyu 1990, 202–3

※ *Han tianshi shijia*; Zhengyi

Zhang Zixiang

張子祥

fl. ca. 600 (?); *zi*: Linbo 麟伯

Zhang Zixiang is now listed as *tianshi (Celestial Master) during the Sui (581–618) period, tenth in line of succession from *Zhang Daoling. Yet there are no contemporary sources on him, and no texts that mention him by name for well over half a millennium after his supposed existence. The first textual evidence for any line of masters claiming Zhang Daoling's spiritual authority dates only to the ninth century: at best, references of that period can be used to grant some historicity to figures in this line going back to the start of the eighth century or a little earlier.

This is not to deny the existence during the Sui of Taoists who claimed descent from Zhang Daoling. Even earlier, several such persons are mentioned by generation (twelve and thirteen) in contemporary sources of the early and middle sixth century, and Daoxuan 道宣 (596–667) speaks of both Laozi and Zhang Daoling having descendants living everywhere in the empire in his day (see *Guang hongming ji* 廣弘明集, T. 2103, 7.134a). But in the same fashion that a tendency began to emerge soon after this to treat the Tang imperial house as the descendants of Laozi *par excellence*, so one particular family of Zhangs based at *Longhu shan (Dragon and Tiger Mountain) in Jiangxi gradually turned into the sole representatives of all the descendants of Zhang Daoling. The pace of this second development, however, was certainly much slower, since in the mid-eighth century, long after the assertion of right to rule by divine descent by the Tang dynasty, we still find Zhangs unconnected with Longhu shan claiming descent from Daoling without assuming any position of privilege within Taoism.

A shift in this situation may however have been stimulated by the spread of the cult of Zhang Daoling's image beyond the narrow circles of the Taoist priesthood to become, as it is today, the common property (particularly through calendars and other mass printed materials) of anyone without special Taoist affiliations throughout China. Again, the firmest textual evidence for the start of this process comes from the ninth century, though there is a source of that period which ascribes to a painter of the mid-eighth century an icon of a *"tianshi"* (perhaps not the great Taoist) in a Buddhist temple (see *Lidai minghua ji* 歷代名畫記, Huashi congshu ed., 3.45). As for the family base of the Zhangs at Longhu shan, this connection can only be verified too from sources of the late ninth, though there is some evidence that the line of *tianshi* were already in residence there in the early ninth century. Other materials both earlier (eighth century) and indeed contemporary suggest that Longhu shan was among a number of sites that claimed Zhang Daoling's legacy.

In short, there is no absolute proof that Zhang Zixiang and his immediate successors never existed, but the conception of his role would seem to be the ninth-century outcome of eighth-century developments.

T. H. BARRETT

📖 Barrett 1994b; Boltz J. M. 1987a, 63

※ Tianshi dao

Zhang Zongyan

張宗演

1244–91; *zi*: Shichuan 世傳; *hao*: Jianqi 簡齊 (Simple and Even)

Zhang Zongyan, the second son of the thirty-fifth Celestial Master *Zhang Keda (1218–63), became the thirty-sixth Celestial Master after his father's passing. His tenure was marked by an expansion of the *Zhengyi (Orthodox Unity) religious authority at a time when the reins of political authority over China passed into Mongol hands. After Khubilai khan captured the Southern Song capital in 1276, he summoned Zongyan to his court and put him in charge of all Taoist affairs south of the Yangzi River. Zhang presided over an Offering (*jiao) in the court that year and another Offering in the Palace of Perpetual Spring (Changchun gong 長春宮, the present *Baiyun guan) in 1277 before returning home to Mount Longhu (*Longhu shan, Jiangxi). Zongyan left his disciple *Zhang Liusun (1248–1322) behind as his proxy at court, thus beginning the remarkable (and short-lived) history of an ad hoc Taoist religious institution known as the Mysterious Teaching (*Xuanjiao). Zongyan returned to the capital again in 1281 to preside over another Offering and to extend the practice to the Taoist ordination centers on Mount Longhu, Mount Mao (*Maoshan, Jiangsu), and Mount Gezao (*Gezao shan, Jiangxi). The thirty-sixth Celestial Master was succeeded by his eldest son, Zhang Yudi 張與棣 (?–1294).

Lowell SKAR

📖 Boltz J. M. 1987a, 58

※ Xuanjiao; Zhengyi

Zhao Bichen

趙避塵

1860-after 1933; *hao*: Qianfeng laoren 千峰老人
(Old Man of the Thousand Peaks), Shunyi zi 順一子
(Master Who Follows the One)

Zhao Bichen was born in Yangfang 陽坊 (Hebei). His appellation Qianfeng laoren was inspired by the name of Mount Qianfeng (Hebei), one of the centers of the *Longmen school in northern China. He was the eleventh master in the lineage of the *Wu-Liu school, and the founder of its branch known as Thousand Peaks (Qianfeng 千峰).

Zhao received teachings from several Taoist and Buddhist masters. The first was Liu Mingrui 劉名瑞 (1839–1931), a *neidan master of Mount Qianfeng who prophesied his own death in 1901. His second teacher was Wuchan 悟 蟾, whom Zhao met in 1893 in a temple in Jiangsu. Although Wuchan usually taught Buddhism, he reserved his teachings on *xing and *ming* for a select few. In 1895, Zhao met the Venerable Master Liaokong (Liaokong shizun 了空師

尊), who claimed to have received the methods of *xing* and *ming* directly from
*Liu Huayang in 1799. Liaokong instructed Zhao to found the branch of the
Thousand Peaks in 1921. Zhao's last teacher was Tan Zhiming 譚至明, the
second patriarch of the Gold Mountain (Jinshan 金山) branch founded by
the fourth-generation disciple of Longmen, Sun Xuanqing 孫玄清 (1517–69).
Tan not only had a profound influence on Zhao, but also appointed him third
patriarch of the Gold Mountain.

Zhao Bichen is the author of three popular books on Nourishing Life
(*yangsheng): the *Weisheng shenglixue mingzhi* 衛生生理學明指 (Clear Directions on Hygiene and Physiology; after 1921; trans. Despeux 1979); the
Weisheng sanzi fajue jing 衛生三字法訣經 (Scripture of Methods of Hygiene
in Three-Character Verses; after 1921); and the *Xingming fajue mingzhi* 性命法
訣明指 (Clear Directions on Methods for Inner Nature and Vital Force; 1933;
part. trans. Lu K'uan Yü 1970).

Farzeen BALDRIAN-HUSSEIN

📖 Despeux 1979; Lu K'uan Yü 1970

※ *yangsheng*; *neidan*

Zhao Guizhen

趙歸真

?–846

Zhao Guizhen was probably the most controversial Taoist master in Chinese
history, if only because he was responsible for unleashing the only fullscale,
empire-wide persecution of Buddhism that China ever witnessed, but even
among those sympathetic to Taoism his reputation appears to have been decid-
edly mixed. He seems to have been summoned to court in the 820s, a period
when a succession of emperors were shortening their lives with alchemical
experiments, and rose rapidly in imperial favor: by 826 he had been given a
title so grandiloquent as to be rivalled only by those bestowed by Tibetans on
contemporary Chinese Buddhist hierarchs in *Dunhuang. But the following
year, after another imperial alchemical fatality, he was exiled to the far south,
in response to the criticisms of ministers like Li Deyu 李德裕 (787–850) who
opposed the influence of holy men at court. Since Li was a patron of the
current leader of the *Maoshan Taoist community, we must suppose that
he was in his own eyes distinguishing between respectable holy men acceptable to aristocrats like himself and opportunists. The two men were to meet

again when Zhao was recalled to court by a new and enthusiastically Taoist emperor, Wuzong, in 840.

Zhao's exploitation of this opportunity to egg his monarch on against the Buddhists was probably not offensive to Li: he patronized Buddhism too in a small but affluent way, but having risen by this point to a chief ministership could doubtless see good fiscal and other political reasons for a purge of that religion. On the other hand Zhao's promotion of further experiments in imperial alchemy, which according to the diary of the visiting Japanese monk Ennin 圓仁 ("not a neutral observer," especially since he was expelled from the country at this point) drove the emperor to grossly violent acts of insanity, must have filled Li with foreboding. After he had wasted prodigious amounts of labor on constructing a sort of landing strip for flying immortals, Wuzong died from the effects of the alchemical materials he had been ingesting in 846, and his successor exiled Li to the deep south, where he did not long survive.

Zhao's punishment, however, was more immediate, since reliable sources suggest that he was beaten to death in the market as a public spectacle. Yet some late Tang writers preferred to believe that he had only been exiled once again, and recount stories of his days at Wuzong's court reminiscent of the glorious high noon of imperial patronage for Taoist wonder workers one hundred years earlier. No doubt these anecdotes simply reflect bias of another type, or wishful thinking in an era of palpable decline, or at least confusion, since one of Zhao's colleagues, a man of some standing in the Taoist priesthood, was indeed exiled rather than (as some sources have it) put to death. But the fact remains that most of what we know of Zhao Guizhen as an actor in history stems from the writings of those who had no reason to like him. His real level of attainment as a Taoist priest remains unknowable.

T. H. BARRETT

📖 Barrett 1996, 84–90; Qing Xitai 1994, 1: 282–83; Sunayama Minoru 1990, 389–415

Zhao Yizhen

趙宜真

?–1382; *hao*: Yuanyang zi 原陽子 (Master of Primary Yang)

An initiate and major codifier of the *Qingwei (Pure Tenuity) tradition, Zhao Yizhen also exemplified the broad learning of Yuan and early Ming dynasty Taoist priests. He was born in Anfu 安福 district, Jizhou 吉州 (Jiangxi), where his father had been an official. His main biography, by the forty-third Celestial Master, *Zhang Yuchu (1361–1410), claims Zhao was a thirteenth-generation descendant of Zhao Dezhao 趙德昭 (951–78; SB 70–71), the second son of Song Taizong (r. 976–97), who had lived in Junyi 浚儀 near the Northern Song capital, Kaifeng (Henan). Although Zhao wanted to be an official, an illness reportedly kept him from taking the exams to become a Presented Scholar (*jinshi*), and a dream, bolstered by his father's assent, prompted him to turn to Taoism.

Zhao first studied with the Qingwei master Zeng Guikuan 曾貴寬, who dwelt at the Abbey of the Cavernous Abyss (Dongyuan guan 洞淵觀) in Anfu. He also later studied with Zhang Tianquan 張天全, a disciple of the renowned *neidan* specialist and self-proclaimed *Quanzhen master Jin Zhiyang 金志陽 (1276–1336), at the Abbey of the Great Space (Taiyu guan 泰宇觀) in Ji'an 吉安 (Jiangxi). Zhao then went north to learn from Li Xuanyi 李玄一 at Nanchang (Jiangxi), and he also learned more about alchemy from a Feng Waishi 馮外 史. Afterward, Zhao concentrated on the Thunder Rites (*leifa*) and attracted many disciples in the process.

Before the Red Turbans passed through northern Jiangxi, Zhao and his disciples moved west to Sichuan, after which he returned to Mount Longhu (*Longhu shan, Jiangxi) during the term of the forty-second Celestial Master *Zhang Zhengchang (1335–78) and most likely when the great painter and Jin Zhiyang's disciple, Fang Congyi 方從義 (1301?–1391) was there, too. From Mount Longhu, Zhao passed south to Yudu 雩都 in Ganzhou 贛州 (Jiangxi), and while at the Abbey of Purple Yang (Ziyang guan 紫陽觀) he instructed disciples such as the Ganzhou native *Liu Yuanran (1351–1432). Two months after announcing his imminent death to his disciples in 1382, Zhao passed away. The hagiography states that a Liu Ruoyuan 劉若淵 (i.e., Liu Yuanran?) and Cao Ximing 曹希鳴 (?–1397) were his main disciples.

Works. Several texts survive that Zhao may have had a hand in compiling. The most renowned is likely the *Xianchuan waike bifang* 仙傳外科祕方 (Secret Methods Transmitted by Transcendents for External Ailments; CT 1165). Its 1378 preface by Zhao states that the original text had been compiled by a Yang Qing 楊清. It was only after Zhao's death, however, that a disciple named Wu Youren 吳有壬 saw to the work's publication. The brief *Lingbao guikong jue* 靈寶歸空訣 (Instructions of the Numinous Treasure for Returning to the Void; CT 568) is an annotated poem on meditation, followed by a long afterword by Zhao. A liturgical text, the *Bao fumu en zhongjing* 報父母恩重經 (Important Scripture on Repaying One's Parents' Blessings; CT 663), contains an undated colophon signed by Zhao and shows his interest in the Perfected Warrior (*Zhenwu) cult in Yuan and Ming times. Zhao (or his disciples) may also have edited the opening eight or so chapters of the *Daofa huiyuan* (Corpus of Taoist Ritual), and several others as well among the first fifty-five, which focus on Qingwei ritual. Finally, the *Yuanyang zi fayu* 原陽子法語 (Exemplary Sayings of the Master of Primary Yang; CT 1071) contains materials purported to have be written by Zhao, even though they were edited by his disciple Liu Yuanran, who taught *Shao Yizheng (?–1462), the final editor of the Taoist Canon of the Zhengtong reign period.

Lowell SKAR

📖 Boltz J. M. 1987a, 190–92; Qing Xitai 1994, 1: 372–73; Schipper 1987

※ Qingwei

Zhen dadao

真大道

Authentic Great Way

When *Liu Deren (1122–80) founded the Taoist teaching called Dadao 大道, later known as Zhen dadao, the northern plain along the Yellow River was witnessing a large religious revival, with many movements proselytizing and building new shrines. The Zhen dadao shares several features with these movements, and especially with *Quanzhen, into which it seems to have been partly assimilated after its decline. The Zhen dadao, however, stands out for its emphasis on austerity and autarchy. Its communities were encouraged to live from tilling the land and to refrain from eating meat, drinking alcohol, and committing other worldly sins. Its somewhat apocalyptic overtones, communal values, and rejection of medicine in favor of faith healing make it appear as an agrarian egalitarian movement not unlike the early *Tianshi dao.

Despite their ideology of self-sufficiency, however, the Zhen dadao patriarchs travelled all around northern China to convert new adepts and initiate the founding of new communities. Their predication was supported by miracles in healing or exorcism. In one instance, these are described as pertaining to the method of "accusation and summons" (*hezhao* 劾召), apparently in relation to the *Tianxin zhengfa rites. Under the fifth patriarch, Li Xicheng 酈 希成 (fl. 1246), the Zhen dadao was recognized by the Mongol regime as an independent entity and the patriarchy was moved to Beijing. The order then began its most glorious period, as shown by the extant epigraphic evidence, which dates from 1278 to 1343. During this period, the order sent missionaries into the newly-conquered territory of southern China, but no traces of its presence there have been found.

The Zhen dadao communities were organized around monasteries often called Tianbao gong 天寶宮 (Palace of the Celestial Treasure). The little remaining epigraphic evidence suggests, at least in core areas like Henan, the existence of a dense network of one or more convents and assembly halls per district, subordinated to the larger monasteries, which housed ordained predicators. Adepts were divided into celibate (*chujia* 出家) and married (*zaijia* 在家) groups. The hierarchy of the Zhen dadao and its rank titles are very specific and will probably never be fully understood because of the lack of sources. None of its scriptures, neither the liturgical texts used by the order nor the literary anthologies published by its masters, seems to have survived.

Vincent GOOSSAERT

📖 Chen Yuan 1962, 81–109; Qing Xitai 1988–95, 3: 20–31 and 243–66; Qing Xitai 1994, 1: 164–69; Yao Tao-chung 1980, 34–40

※ Liu Deren

Zhengao

真誥

Declarations of the Perfected; Authentic Declarations

The *Zhengao* is a collection of *Shangqing materials based on notes taken by *Yang Xi and his patrons Xu Mai 許邁 (300–348) and Xu Mi 許謐 (303–76). Although it is a minor work compared to the Shangqing revealed writings, it has enjoyed greater fame due to the renown of its compiler, *Tao Hongjing, who completed it probably in 499. A similar compilation by *Gu Huan (420/428–483/491), now lost, was of great help to Tao, whose main contribution was to judge the authenticity of the fragmentary manuscripts he possessed on the basis of his remarkable acquaintance with the calligraphy of both Yang and the Xus. The present text (CT 1016) has a preface by Gao Sisun 高似孫 dated 1223, and underwent interpolations including the addition of some commentaries.

Content. The edition of the *Zhengao* in the Taoist Canon is divided into seven *pian* (sections) and twenty *juan* (scrolls), but this was not the original format. The work was initially arranged into ten *juan*, although some later quotations refer to ten *pian*. In the present text, in fact, *pian* 1, 2, and 4 are each split in two parts, making ten *pian* altogether; the arrangement into twenty *juan* results from the further subdivision of each *pian* into two parts.

The division into seven *pian* resulted from an effort, sometimes clumsy, made by Tao Hongjing to give coherence to the whole. The first *pian* (corresponding to *juan* 1–4) contains texts that relate Yang Xi's visions and hymns sung by the divinities on those occasions. The second and third *pian* (*juan* 5–8 and 9–10) are devoted to minor recipes and methods, with information on the afterlife of the Xus' relatives and acquaintances in *juan* 7 and 8. The fourth *pian* (*juan* 11–14) contains a semimythical description and history of Mount Mao (*Maoshan, Jiangsu), the early center of the Shangqing school. The fifth *pian* (*juan* 15–16) is devoted to a description of the netherworld. The sixth *pian* (*juan* 17–18) consists of writings from Yang Xi and the Xus. The seventh and last *pian* (*juan* 19–20) contains Tao's own writings about his editorial method, the history of the Shangqing corpus of writings—especially how they were plagiarized and scattered—and the genealogy of the Xu family. This ideal sequence, however, is often disturbed by interpolations, repetitions, and insertion of fragments in wrong places.

The Zhengao and the Shangqing revelations. Unlike the *Dengzhen yinjue (Concealed Instructions for the Ascent to Reality), which was also compiled by Tao Hongjing, the *Zhengao* was intended to reach a wider audience; Gao Sisun's preface states that it contains the "weft" (*wei* 緯), i.e., the background of the Shangqing revelations. The collected fragments relate the circumstances of the revelations and describe Yang Xi's visions of spiritual beings. They contain instructions given by the divinities on the meaning of the scriptures, on the history of the methods, and on those who transmitted them. Other fragments respond to questions asked by Yang Xi or the Xus, or specify rules for daily life. Tao also includes passages of texts pertaining to the revelations or external to them. He often comments on the authenticity of purported Shangqing scriptures circulating in his time, stating whether he considers a text to be original and specifying the sources of the quoted passages. His notes are an important resource to identify texts whose titles changed over the time.

Some textual fragments quoted in the *Zhengao* belong to scriptures that had not yet been revealed to the world by Yang Xi's time, and therefore complement the original sources. This is the case with the revelations granted by Peijun 裴君 (Lord Pei), a Shangqing immortal who, according to Tao Hongjing, was a Buddhist adept before he took *Chisong zi as his master and converted to Taoism (Robinet 1984, 2: 375–84). Peijun plays an important role in the *Zhengao*. A large part of *juan* 5 contains materials attributed to him (5.4b–17a); similarly, most of *juan* 9 is devoted to the *Baoshen jing* 寶神經 (Scripture for Treasuring the Spirit), revealed by Peijun and also contained in the *Baoshen qiju jing* 寶神起居經 (Scripture on the Behavior for Treasuring the Spirit; CT 1319; Robinet 1984, 2: 359–62). The *Baoshen jing* attests to a tradition different from early Shangqing, that emphasizes faith and effort in the practice.

Another set of textual fragments is related to the Mao 茅 brothers and their biography, now partly lost (see *Maojun, and Robinet 1984, 2: 389–98). They include a visionary description of Mount Mao, a method to absorb the efflorescences of the Sun and Moon, and the story of Guo Sichao 郭四朝, an early inhabitant of Mount Mao. These fragments seem to derive from earlier texts and orally transmitted local traditions, and belong to a larger corpus that also contained the recipes for drugs now found in the *Jiuzhuan huandan jing yaojue* 九轉還丹經要訣 (Essential Instructions on the Scripture of the Reverted Elixir in Nine Cycles; CT 889; Robinet 1984, 2: 395–96), and the method of the *Mingtang xuanzhen* 明堂玄真 (Mysterious Real Man of the Hall of Light) which is now found in the *Yupei jindang shangjing* 玉佩金璫上經 (Superior Scripture of the Jade Pendant and the Golden Ring; CT 56; Robinet 1984, 2: 213–18, 396–97).

Finally, *juan* 4 and 14 contain parts of the lost *Jianjing* 劍經 (Scripture of the Sword), a work devoted to a method revealed to *Ziyang zhenren for making a magic sword used to obtain *shijie* (release from the corpse). The "Prolegomena on the Ingestion of Atractyl" ("Fuzhu xu" 服朮敘), ascribed to the Lady of Purple Tenuity (Ziwei furen 紫微夫人), one of the divinities who appeared to Yang Xi, is scattered in *juan* 6 and 10. Parts of *juan* 15 and 16 may have constituted the *Fengdu ji* 酆都記 (Records of Fengdu), so entitled after the name of the subterranean town that hosts the headquarters of the underworld administration (see *Fengdu).

Isabelle ROBINET

📖 Bokenkamp 1996b (part. trans. of *j.* 1); Chen Guofu 1963, 19–27 and 233–35; Ishii Masako 1980, 121–372; Ishii Masako 1991 (part. trans.); Kamitsuka Yoshiko 1999, 17–122; Kroll 1996c; Mugitani Kunio 1991 (concordance); Ōfuchi Ninji and Ishii Masako 1988, 36–49 (list of texts cited); Robinet 1984, 1: 35–57, 2: 313–45; Strickmann 1977; Strickmann 1981; Yoshikawa Tadao and Mugitani Kunio 2000 (trans.); Zhong Laiyin 1992

※ Tao Hongjing; Shangqing

Zheng Yin

鄭隱

ca. 215–ca. 302; *zi*: Siyuan 思遠

Although Zheng Yin is frequently mentioned in *Lingbao texts, very little is known of his life. He devoted himself to classical Confucian learning but turned late in life to the Dao, physiological and dietary practices, medicine, prognostication, and related disciplines. *Ge Hong (283–343), who was one of his disciples, draws in the *Baopu zi* a picture of his master as a strong and young-looking eighty-year-old man who could easily go without food for fifty days and had succeeded twice in compounding elixirs (trans. Ware 1966, 309–17). Zheng reportedly travelled to various mountains, including Mount Maji (Maji shan 馬迹山, Jiangsu) where he lived among wild beasts, and finally became an immortal.

Beyond the hagiographic elements, information on Zheng Yin focuses on his role as recipient of local textual and doctrinal corpora. As one of the major figures of the southern *fangshi* milieu during the early Six Dynasties, he inherited the oral and written legacy of *Zuo Ci and *Ge Xuan. Ge Hong reports that Zheng had collected about 1,200 scrolls (*juan*) of texts. Most notably, these included major talismanic writings such as the *Sanhuang wen* (Script of the Three Sovereigns) and the *Wuyue zhenxing tu* (Charts of the Real Forms of the Five Peaks), texts that later became part of the Lingbao corpus, as well as alchemical treatises of the early *Taiqing tradition.

Grégoire ESPESSET

📖 Chen Guofu 1963, 93–95

※ Ge Xuan; Ge Hong

Zhenghe Wanshou daozang

政和萬壽道藏

Taoist Canon of the Ten-Thousand-Fold Longevity of the
Zhenghe Reign Period

Compiled during the Zhenghe reign period (1111–17) of Song Huizong (r. 1100–1125), the *Zhenghe Wanshou daozang* superseded the *Da Song Tiangong baozang* (Precious Canon of the Celestial Palace of the Great Song) completed a century earlier under Song Zhenzong (r. 997–1022). This second Taoist Canon of the Song is the first to have been produced as a woodcut printing. The history of its compilation reflects the pervasive imperial effort to define the limits of acceptable religious practice according to the authority of a state-sanctioned Canon.

The origins of this Canon, like its predecessor, may be traced to imperial directives regarding liturgical practice. In 1108 Huizong ordered the distribution of a vast ritual code to Taoist abbeys throughout the empire. He also commanded prefectural and district officials to call on Taoist masters (*daoshi*) willing to uphold this very code of ritual. Enactment of this decree was apparently deferred for at least two years due to conflicting opinions of those compiling the new code. To overcome these problems, Huizong wrote to Councillor of State Zhang Shangying 張商英 (1043–1121) in 1110, asking him to prepare a definitive edition of the liturgical code he had commissioned.

By the turn of 1114, the emperor ordered circuit intendants and prefects to have the residents of their respective domains submit all Taoist writings in their possession. The texts retrieved from this nationwide search were initially gathered at the Shuyi ju 書藝局 (Office of Calligraphy) of the Hanlin Academy in the capital Kaifeng (Henan). In his 1116 preface to a corpus of *Tianxin zhengfa ritual, Yuan Miaozong 元妙宗 speaks of being summoned in mid-1115 to collate these texts in the preparation of a printed Canon (*Taishang zhuguo jiumin zongzhen biyao*; preface, 1b). Among other clergymen known to have been assigned to the same task are Liu Yuandao 劉元道 of Kaifeng and Wang Daojian 王道堅 of Mount Longhu (*Longhu shan, Jiangxi). A Taoist official (*daoguan* 道官) named Cheng Ruoqing 程若清 may well have served as editor-in-chief since he is the collator to whom Manichaean texts printed in Fujian were falsely ascribed. The prefect of Fuzhou, Huang Shang 黃裳 (1043–1129), was also named in these fake attributions, as overseer of the block cutting.

It was in fact Prefect Huang who was instrumental in providing the site and means for the printing of the Canon. By 1114, he had already petitioned the emperor to approve construction of a library to accommodate the collected Taoist writings at the Tianning wanshou guan 天寧萬壽觀 (Abbey of the Ten-thousand-fold Longevity of Celestial Tranquillity) on Mount Jiuxian (Jiuxian shan 九仙山, Fujian). In a decree issued the same year, Huizong announced the establishment of the new facility, giving it the name by which the new Canon itself came to be known, Zhenghe Wanshou daozang. Nearly five years passed before Huang was able to assemble a team of block-cutters, financed by a special levy. Fuzhou was at that time known for its skilled block-cutters, whose accomplishments included a reprint of the Buddhist Canon entitled *Chongning Wanshou dazang* 崇寧萬壽大藏 (Great Canon of the Ten-Thousand-Fold Longevity of the Chongning Reign Period). The blocks of the new Taoist Canon completed by 1119 at Mount Jiuxian were eventually dispatched to the capital where prints appear to have been issued periodically according to demand.

It is estimated that a total of about 70,000 blocks were cut to produce the *Zhenghe Wanshou daozang*. This new Canon was notably larger than its immediate predecessor, with altogether 5,381 *juan* filling 540 *han* 函 (cases). The table of contents as well as a catalogue in ten *juan* are both lost. Among indisputable contributions are commentaries authorized for inclusion by Huizong in late 1118. Just how many copies of the Canon were printed from the blocks cut in Fuzhou remains a mystery. Records of the holdings of numerous abbeys, as well as personal accounts and anecdotal evidence, seem to indicate that it was widely copied, often by hand.

Judith M. BOLTZ

📖 Chen Guofu 1963, 135–56; van der Loon 1984, 39–47; Zhu Yueli 1992, 148–49

※ DAOZANG AND SUBSIDIARY COMPILATIONS

zhengjiao

正醮

Orthodox Offering

The Orthodox Offering is a rite performed as part of the *jiao* (Offering). Its purpose is to request that the deities descend, and to offer food and drink to them. In present-day southern Taiwan, it is included in large-scale *jiao* lasting more than two days, and is performed on the evening or night of the last day (usually the second or third day, depending on the length of the *jiao*). Thus it is the last rite performed at the *jiao* altar.

In this ritual, a black banner hangs above the main altar, stretching from the Altar of the Three Clarities (*sanqing tan* 三清壇) to the Altar of the Three Realms (*sanjie tan* 三界壇). The banner is called Celestial Bridge (*tianqiao* 天橋) and is used by the deities to descend to this world. The rite begins with Pacing the Void (*buxu* 步虛; see *bugang) and the Purification of the Altar (*jingtan* 淨壇; Lagerwey 1987c, 73–77), followed by the Lighting of the Incense Burner (*falu). Next, during the first half of the rite, the priest faces each table of the altar and in turn offers incense and veneration. Then he invites the deities, in order from the lowest to the highest. During the second half of the rite, the priest and community representatives kneel before the Altar of the Three Realms and invite eighteen supreme deities (including the Three Clarities, *sanqing) in six groups (6 x 3), again from the lowest to the highest. After each invitation, firecrackers are set off to announce that the deities have descended, and two of the priests, the leader of the troupe (*yinban* 引班) and the keeper of the incense (*shixiang* 侍香), wave purificatory pennants over the heads of the community representatives. When the deities have been welcomed, the whole audience turns to face the Three Clarities. The deities are venerated again and wine is presented three times to each. Their names are called in inverse order to the rite of Petitioning the Deities (*qingshen* 請神), which thus exists in a corresponding relationship with the Orthodox Offering.

After the offering of wine and the Extinction of the Incense Burner (*fulu* 復爐; Lagerwey 1987c, 146–47), the rite continues with the removal of the Authentic Scripts (*zhenwen* 真文). This corresponds to the act of placing the Scripts in the five directions around the altar during the Nocturnal Invocation (*suqi). After the Scripts have been removed, the altar is dismantled. Finally, the audience stands facing the altar of the Three Realms, and the deities are dismissed.

ASANO Haruji

📖 Lagerwey 1987c, 56–58; Ōfuchi Ninji 1983, 356–68

※ *jiao*

Zhengtong daozang

正統道藏

Taoist Canon of the Zhengtong Reign Period

The *Da Ming daozang jing* 大明道藏經 (Scriptures of the Taoist Canon of the Great Ming) completed during the reign of the Zhengtong Emperor (r. 1436–49) has come to be known in modern printings as the *Zhengtong daozang*. It is the successor to the *Xuandu baozang (Precious Canon of the Mysterious Metropolis) produced in 1244. The precise chronology of the Ming compilation is difficult to reconstruct, but its origins may be traced to the Yongle Emperor (r. 1403–24). Like earlier canonical collections of Taoist writings, the story of how the *Zhengtong daozang* took shape is closely tied to the story of a ruling house determined to regulate religious affairs.

History of the compilation. In a decree issued at the close of 1406, the Yongle Emperor enjoins the forty-third Celestial Master *Zhang Yuchu (1361–1410) to submit the body of Taoist texts he had been charged with collecting so that blocks could be cut for printing. Variant compositions by Zhang himself speak of receiving an imperial mandate to compile a Taoist Canon in the summer of either 1406 or 1407. How much he actually accomplished before his demise in 1410 is not known. The extent to which his younger brother and successor Zhang Yuqing 張宇清 (1364–1427) may have pursued this venture also remains to be determined. One person known to have been summoned to serve on the editorial team during the Yongle reign period is Tu Xinggong 涂省躬, a disciple of Taoist Master Luo Suxing 羅素行 at the Yuxu guan 玉虛觀 (Abbey of the Jade Void) in Nanchang (Jiangxi).

Further imperial support of the project came when the Zhengtong Emperor finally took up where his great-grandfather, the Yongle Emperor, had left off. In 1444 he authorized *Shao Yizheng 邵以正 (?–1462) to supervise the collation of texts and overcome what lacunae remained so that publication of the Canon could proceed. The task appears to have been completed in short order. The date recorded on the frontispiece of each case (han 函) of the *Zhengtong daozang* reads "eleventh day of the eleventh month of Zhengtong 10 (1445)." Yu Daochun 喻道純 of Changsha 長沙 (Hunan) and Tang Xiwen 湯希文 (?–1461) of Liyang 溧陽 (Jiangsu) have been identified as members of the editorial staff under Shao Yizheng.

Imperial presentations of the Canon. Copies of the Canon were presented to several major temples throughout the empire. A stele inscription marks the imperial bestowal of the new Canon to the *Baiyun guan (Abbey of the White Clouds) in Beijing. It opens with the statement of presentation composed by the Zhengtong Emperor on the tenth day of the eighth month of 1447. He entrusts the Canon to the clergy, charging them in their reading and incantations to pray for order in the country and the well-being of its people (上為 國家祝釐，下與生民祈福). Only authorized personnel were to be allowed access to the Canon, ensuring not only proper veneration but also its safekeeping within the abbey.

The stele inscription of 1447 also includes a dedication composed by Senior Compiler in the Hanlin Academy Xu Bin 許彬 (*jinshi* 1415). In addition to reiterating the force of the imperial commendation, Xu traces the publication of the *Daozang jing* 道藏經 from the Yongle Emperor's decree to the fulfillment of his intent by the reigning Emperor. Once supplemental texts had been prepared, according to Xu, the resulting Canon came to a total of 5,305 *juan* 卷 in 480 cases. The ambiguous term *juan* is understood here to refer to chapters. Altogether 4,551 volumes or fascicles (*ce* 冊) were accommodated within the 480 cases.

Additional accounts attest to the imperial gift of a Canon in 1447 to temples in the south, including the *Shangqing gong (Palace of Highest Clarity) on Mount Longhu (*Longhu shan, Jiangxi) and the Yuanfu gong 元符宮 (Palace of the Original Tally) on Mount Mao (*Maoshan, Jiangsu). A copy of the Canon is also known to have been presented in 1476 by the Chenghua Emperor (r. 1465–87) to the Chaotian gong 朝天宮 (Palace in Homage to Heaven) in Nanjing (Jiangsu). At least seven temples, moreover, received a print of the Canon made in 1598 on behalf of the Empress Dowager Li 李氏, mother of the Wanli Emperor (r. 1573–1620).

Format, size, and sources. The Ming Canon was produced in a format corresponding to that of the Buddhist Canon printed in 1440 by imperial mandate. In both cases, the sheets were folded accordion-style, just as editions of the Buddhist Canon issued in the south had been produced. But instead of 30 columns of text folded in five units of six columns, each sheet of the Ming Canon was printed with 25 columns of text folded in five units of five columns. Each column accommodated seventeen characters. Data recorded within the folds include the case label according to the first 480 words (*tian* 天 to *ying* 英) of the *Qianzi wen* 千字文 (Thousand-Word Text), followed by the number of the fascicle and of the printed sheet. Unlike the *Xuandu baozang* of 1244, these small-print annotations lack running title and the names of block-cutters.

It is estimated that approximately 74,080 blocks were used to cut the 1445 Canon, whereas nearly 10,000 more would have been required to match the size of the larger-format Song Canon produced in 1119. In overall quantity of print, the Ming Canon is thus about 12% smaller than the size documented for the *Zhenghe Wanshou daozang* (Taoist Canon of the Ten-Thousand-Fold Longevity of the Zhenghe Reign Period). Just how many texts in the *Zhengtong daozang* can be traced back to the Song Canon remains unclear, but certainly among likely candidates are those honoring Song taboos. About half of the titles in the Ming Canon are post-Song compilations. It is thought unlikely that any texts from the Jurchen Canon of 1192 would have been available to the fifteenth-century editors, but nearly forty titles in the Ming Canon may have come from the Yuan Canon of 1244. Very few titles bear Ming period dates but a number of texts in the *Zhengtong daozang* include reference to "Da Ming guo" 大明國 (Great Ming state).

Table of contents and classification of texts. The final component of the Canon includes a *Daozang jing mulu* 道藏經目錄 (Index of the Scriptures in the Taoist Canon of the Great Ming; CT 1431), listing some 1,400 titles by case labels. It is prefaced by an introduction entitled "Daojiao zongyuan" 道教宗源 (Lineal Origins of the Taoist Teaching) and "Fanli" 凡例 (General Guidelines), outlining the organization of the Canon. The first half of the introduction corresponds to the opening passage in the *Daomen jingfa xiangcheng cixu* 道門經法相承次序 (The Scriptures and Methods of Taoism in Orderly Sequence; CT 1128, 1.1a–2a), compiled no earlier than the latter half of the seventh century. A slightly variant version of the same text appears in the eleventh-century *Yunji qiqian* (Seven Lots from the Bookbag of the Clouds, 3.4b–5b), under the title "Daojiao sandong zongyuan" 道教三洞宗元 (Lineal Origins of the Three Caverns of the Taoist Teaching).

As the introduction explains, the contents of the Canon are presented within seven units known as the Three Caverns (*SANDONG) and Four Supplements (*sifu* 四輔). The supplements Taixuan 太玄 (Great Mystery), Taiping 太平

Table 27

1	Basic Texts (*benwen* 本文)
2	Divine Talismans (*shenfu* 神符)
3	Jade Instructions (*yujue* 玉訣)
4	Numinous Charts (*lingtu* 靈圖)
5	Catalogues and Registers (*pulu* 譜錄)
6	Precepts and Observances (*jielü* 戒律)
7	Ceremonial Protocols (*weiyi* 威儀)
8	Methods (*fangfa* 方法)
9	Techniques (*zhongshu* 眾術)
10	Records and Biographies (*jizhuan* 記傳)
11	Encomia and Lauds (*zansong* 讚頌)
12	Memorials and Announcements (*biaozou* 表奏)

The twelve divisions (*shi'er bu* 十二部) of the Taoist Canon.

(Great Peace), and Taiqing 太清 (Great Clarity) are regarded as appendices to the initial three units, Dongzhen 洞真 (Cavern of Perfection), Dongxuan 洞玄 (Cavern of Mystery), and Dongshen 洞神 (Cavern of Spirit), respectively. The last unit, Zhengyi 正一 (Orthodox Unity), is said to serve as a common thread to the caverns and supplements (正一通貫洞輔). This sequence of units is thought to mirror seven levels of ordination, from the highest rank of Dongzhen to Zhengyi. Each of the Three Caverns is subdivided into twelve components (see table 27).

The actual distribution of texts within the Ming Canon is not necessarily in keeping with these categorical headings. Nevertheless, the fact that the editors of this Canon chose to honor a pre-Song classification of texts into three "caverns" of thirty-six components seems to underscore their commitment to sustaining a continuity in canonic organization. No subdivisions are found in either the four supplements following the Three Caverns or the *Wanli xu daozang* (Supplementary Taoist Canon of the Wanli Reign Period) compiled in 1607.

Judith M. BOLTZ

📖 Bokenkamp 1986c; Boltz J. M. 1986b; Boltz J. M. 1986c; Boltz J. M. 1987c; Boltz J. M. 1994; Chen Guofu 1963, 174–204; Chen Yuan 1988, 1257–60, 1265–66, and 1298–99; Liu Ts'un-yan 1973; van der Loon 1984, 58–63; Ozaki Masaharu 1983b; Ozaki Masaharu 1986a; Ren Jiyu and Zhong Zhaopeng 1991; Schipper 1975b; Schipper and Verellen 2004; Weng Dujian 1935; Zhong Zhaopeng 1993; Zhong Zhaopeng 1999; Zhu Yueli 1992, 155–62; Zhu Yueli 1996

※ Shao Yizheng; Zhang Yuchu; *Daozang mulu xiangzhu*; *Daozang quejing mulu*; *Wanli xu daozang*; DAOZANG AND SUBSIDIARY COMPILATIONS

Zhengyi

正一

Orthodox Unity; Correct Unity

Together with *Quanzhen, the Zhengyi school is one of the two main branches of Taoist religion. It is also known as Way of the Orthodox Unity (Zhengyi dao 正一道), Teaching of the Orthodox Unity (Zhengyi jiao 正一教), and Branch of the Orthodox Unity (Zhengyi pai 正一派).

The term Orthodox Unity, or Correct Unity, has been used since the formative period of Taoist religion. According to tradition, in 142 CE *Laojun bestowed the Covenant with the Powers of Orthodox Unity (*zhengyi mengwei* 正一盟威) on *Zhang Daoling. This is deemed to be the founding act of Taoism as an organized religion. According to the *Xiang'er* commentary to the *Daode jing*, dating from ca. 200 CE, "the One is the Dao" (*yi zhe dao ye* 一者道也; Bokenkamp 1997, 89). The teaching was called "orthodox" to distinguish it from the many "false skills" (*weiji* 偽伎) or unorthodox practices prevalent in the waning years of the Later Han dynasty. Zhang's contemporaries referred to his teaching as the Way of the Five Pecks of Rice (*Wudoumi dao), while during the Six Dynasties the southern Taoists called it the Way of the Celestial Masters (*Tianshi dao). Thus, the designations of Way of the Five Peck of Rice, Way of the Celestial Masters, and Covenant of Orthodox Unity all refer to the Zhengyi teaching; but "Way of the Five Peck of Rice" usually refers to the earliest period, while some scholars tend to use "Way of the Celestial Masters" with reference to the Six Dynasties and Tang periods and "Teaching of Orthodox Unity" for the later periods. This entry is mainly concerned with Zhang Daoling's school from the Song period onward; on its history and features through the Tang period, see the entries *Wudoumi dao and *Tianshi dao.

History in the Song-Yuan period. The Celestial Masters (*tianshi; see table 23) resided on Mount Longhu (*Longhu shan, Jiangxi). After the mid-Tang period, they frequently received imperial appointments, and Taoist priests traveled to the mountain to obtain transmissions of methods and registers (*LU). In 1239, the Southern Song emperor Lizong (r. 1224–64) ordered the thirty-fifth Celestial Master, *Zhang Keda, to bring together the Talismans and Registers of the Three Mountains (*sanshan fulu* 三山符籙). This expression denoted the three Taoist schools—Zhengyi, *Shangqing, and *Lingbao—formally based on Mount Longhu, Mount Mao (*Maoshan, Jiangsu) and Mount Gezao (*Gezao shan, Jiangxi), respectively. These schools were united under the leadership of Mount Longhu, but only Zhang Keda was bestowed the honorary name "Elder" (*xiansheng* 先生). After the Yuan dynasty had vanquished the Southern Song, Khubilai khan (r. 1260–94) acknowledged the claim of Zhang Daoling's descendants to the title Celestial Master, and from the thirty-sixth generation onward they were granted the right to act as the leaders of Taoism in Jiangnan. Any important affair relating to Taoism in that area was managed by or brought to the attention of the Celestial Master at Mount Longhu.

In 1304, the thirty-eighth Celestial Master, Zhang Yucai 張與材 (?–1316), was appointed Head of the Teaching of Orthodox Unity, Guarding the Talismans and Registers of the Three Mountains (*Zhengyi jiaozhu zhuling sanshan fulu* 正一教主注領三山符籙). Reaffirming its position of supremacy, Mount Longhu was put in charge of the other two ranges by imperial decree. This led to the formation of the Zhengyi school with a structure similar to that of Quanzhen. All schools of Taoist religion, with the exception of Quanzhen, were in fact reunited at Mount Longhu and together came to be called the Teaching of Orthodox Unity.

Main features. Throughout its history, the Zhengyi school has been distinguished by four main characteristics. First, the school regards the Celestial Master as its religious leader. The title of Celestial Master is said to have been passed on from generation to generation, beginning with Zhang Daoling. After Zhang Yucai was declared Head of the Teaching of Orthodox Unity, successive Celestial Masters also inherited this title. Although the court later suppressed the designation Celestial Master, and Mount Longhu lost its power to actually control the other mountains and oversee regional Taoist offices, the Celestial Master continued to be commonly regarded as the Zhengyi spiritual leader, and he is still revered as such today.

The second main feature is the institution of conferring registers (*lu*) when entering Taoism. Registers serve as proof of the continued transmission of Taoist schools, and people studying the Dao were considered as ordained priests only after they were conferred registers. These were divided into grades; different grades expressed different degrees of familiarity with the Taoist practices and rites. Therefore, conferring registers was an important Zhengyi institution to guarantee the completeness and purity of its organizational structure. (For more details on this institution, see the entry *LU.)

Third, Zhengyi regards Laozi as the ancestor of its teaching, but developed its own corpus of scriptures and writings. The extant Ming edition of the Taoist Canon records altogether thirty-one works under the heading Orthodox Unity (*zhengyi*). These works are traditionally said to interconnect the three major sections of the Canon (*SANDONG or Three Caverns).

Fourth, the main religious practices of the Teaching of Orthodox Unity are the *zhai (Retreat) and *jiao (Offering) rituals, as well as the use of talismans

(*FU) and registers. The liturgy also integrates popular customs and culture, and can be performed in the local dialects. Zhengyi priests can leave their families and live in temples, or they may also stay with their families. They are usually allowed to eat meat and abstain from it only when they perform rituals.

Later history. In the Hongwu reign period (1368–98) of the Ming dynasty, the emperor suppressed the use of the title of Celestial Master within Zhengyi, but this only increased veneration for him. From the end of the Ming, the Teaching of Orthodox Unity gradually declined. In the Daoguang period (1821–50) of the Qing dynasty, the Celestial Master was no longer invited to the capital to see the emperor and relations between the court and Zhengyi came to an end. Thus, the teaching could only be handed down among the populace, and its traditional institutions and activities were kept alive only within the school itself.

In the last twenty years, after an interruption of more than half a century, the Teaching of Orthodox Unity in the People's Republic of China has re-instated its statutes for conferring registers (Lai Chi-tim 2003). The residence of the Celestial Master at Mount Longhu was renovated, the scriptures rites were rearranged, and a great number of young Taoist priests were educated and are now filling all echelons of the school's organizations. The Zhengyi teaching is displaying new vitality, and its future development deserves the close attention of everyone concerned with Taoism.

CHEN Yaoting

📖 Barrett 1994b; Chen Bing 1986; Guo Shusen 1990; Ishida Kenji 1992; Matsu-moto Kōichi 1982; Qing Xitai 1988–95, vols. 3 and 4, passim; Qing Xitai 1994, 1: 193–99; Ren Jiyu 1990, 547–60, 628–46; Schipper 1982–83; Welch 1957–58; Zhang Jintao 1994; Zhang Jiyu 1990; Zhuang Hongyi 1986

※ Tianshi dao; Wudoumi dao; for other related entries see the Synoptic Table of Contents, sec. III.7 ("Song, Jin, and Yuan: Zhengyi") and sec. III.9 ("Ming and Qing: Zhengyi")

Zhengyi fawen jing

正一法文經

Scripture of the Code of Orthodox Unity

The *Zhengyi fawen* 正一法文 (Code of Orthodox Unity) was an extensive collection of the rules and rites of the Way of the Celestial Masters (*Tianshi dao) that first arose in the fifth century. Over the years it grew to sixty scrolls, then was divided into separate sections and, for the most part, lost. The Harvard-Yenching index of the Taoist Canon lists twenty-five texts with the title "Zhengyi fawen," nine of which are still extant (Weng Dujian 1935, 67). No traces of the compendium were recovered from *Dunhuang, but citations of its contents begin with the *Wushang biyao and continue into the early Song (*Yunji qiqian, Taiping yulan).

One of the most frequently cited among these sources is the *Zhengyi fawen jing* (CT 1204), set as a dialogue of the Most High (Taishang 太上) with the first Celestial Master, *Zhang Daoling. Asked about the causes for people's misfortunes (1a), the Most High explains that they are due to lack of faith in the laws of retribution, contempt for the Dao, breaking of the precepts (*jie), and indulgence in sensual pleasures. People should rather pursue devotional activities, such as performing rites of repentance, burning incense, giving charity, sponsoring monasteries, and making sacred images (1b–2a). These lists, as well as the Buddhist tenor of the text, suggest a sixth-century date.

The work then specifies nine states of danger that cause people to be restless and unable to sleep. They are: sickness, imprisonment, war, floods, fires, poisonous creatures, earthquakes, inner terror, and hunger and cold. These nine are brought as punishments for human sins by a group of nine major demons who each have nine billion lesser entities at their disposal (2a–3b). In addition, there are five evil Emperors, associated with the five directions and the five colors, who each spread sicknesses, poisons, and disasters that match their colors (3b–4b). And there are five punishing swords that are distributed by celestial officers and bring diseases and disasters in a pattern corresponding to the Five Phases (*wuxing), e.g., the sword of Wood brings hunger and cold, that of Fire, headaches and fevers, and so forth (4b–5a).

The last section of the text focuses on countermeasures, especially centering around the worship of the Celestial Worthies (tianzun 天尊) of the ten directions. Their names as listed here (7a–b) are identical with those found in the *Fengdao kejie (Codes and Precepts for Worshipping the Dao), but the order is different: instead of bowing first to the cardinal, then to the intermediate directions, here the practitioner is to follow a consecutive circle, moving clockwise and beginning with the east. For each deity, on the other hand, worship procedures, production of statues, and copying and recitation of scriptures (*songjing) closely match similar instructions given in the *Fengdao kejie*.

Livia KOHN

※ *jie* [precepts]; Tianshi dao

Zhengyi weiyi jing

正一威儀經

Scripture of Dignified Liturgies of Orthodox Unity

The *Zhengyi weiyi jing* (CT 791), probably dating from the late sixth century, contains 132 entries under a total of thirty headings, formulating concrete instructions for priests and renunciants of the Way of the Celestial Masters (*Tianshi dao). In a concluding note (19b–20a), the text claims that it originated with the Celestial Worthy of Original Commencement (Yuanshi tianzun 元始天尊) and was transmitted to the Most High (Taishang 太上), who in turn passed it on to the first Celestial Master *Zhang Daoling.

In content, the *Zhengyi weiyi jing* deals with ordination procedures and daily religious behavior, including sections on receiving the Dao, ritual vestments and shoes, reciting and explaining scriptures, serving the teacher, performing obeisances, sounding bells and lighting lamps, residences and furniture, eating and drinking, travels, and the ceremonies surrounding death.

Many of the text's instructions are compatible and even identical with instructions given in other texts on monastic and ritual organization of the early Tang, such as the *Fengdao kejie (Codes and Precepts for Worshipping the Dao). The rules here are less well organized, however, and do not appear in a structured setting of systematic explanation. Also, they are limited in a sectarian context by their close link to the first Celestial Master Zhang Daoling, who was particularly venerated among the southern Celestial Masters. The work is thus a precursor of the monastic codes proper. It provides an idea of how much of the monastic organization was directly inherited from the lay priesthood of the Celestial Masters.

Livia KOHN

※ *jie*[precepts]; Tianshi dao; MONASTIC CODE; ORDINATION AND PRIESTHOOD

Zhenling weiye tu

真靈位業圖

Chart of the Ranks and Functions of the Real
(*or*: Perfected) Numinous Beings

The *Zhenling weiye tu*, compiled by *Tao Hongjing (456–536), was originally part of the *Dengzhen yinjue* (Concealed Instructions for the Ascent to Reality). It is not found in the current version of this work (CT 421) but survives in a reedition (CT 167) by *Lüqiu Fangyuan (?–902). The text ranks the *zhenling* in seven degrees according to their ranks and functions. Each rank is further divided into middle, left and right, and in some cases female *zhenren and miscellaneous groups are added. Many of the *zhenling* are also mentioned in such texts as the *Zhengao, the *Yuanshi shangzhen zhongxian ji* 元始上真眾仙記 (Records of the Supreme Perfected and All the Immortals of Original Commencement; CT 166), and the *Zhoushi mingtong ji* 周氏冥通記 (Records of Mr. Zhou's Communications with the Unseen; CT 302; trans. Mugitani Kunio and Yoshikawa Tadao 2003). Most of the lower-ranking ones, however, do not appear to be recorded elsewhere.

While the classification of the *Zhenling weiye tu* is similar to the one found in the "Gujin ren biao" 古今人表 (Charts of People of Antiquity and the Present Day) chapter of the *Hanshu* (History of the Former Han), the division into seven ranks is also closely related to Tao's view of numerology, which ascribes a special meaning to the number 7. In the *Zhengao*, for instance, Tao refers to the highest *Shangqing scriptures, the *Lotus Sūtra* (*Saddharmapuṇḍarīka-sūtra*), and the "Inner Chapters" of the *Zhuangzi as each incorporating the truth; all these works were composed of seven scrolls. Both the *Zhengao* and the *Dengzhen yinjue* were also divided into seven sections.

The main deities and immortals mentioned in the descriptions of the seven ranks are the following:

1. Deities of the Jade Clarity (Yuqing 玉清) heaven, with the Lord of the Dao, Sovereign of Emptiness (Xuhuang daojun 虛皇道君, i.e., the Celestial Worthy of Original Commencement or Yuanshi tianzun 元始天尊) in the center, the Most Exalted Lord of the Dao (Gaoshang daojun 高上道君) leading the deities on the left side, and the Lord of the Dao, Original Sovereign (Yuanhuang daojun 元皇道君) leading those on the right.

2. Deities and *zhenling* of the Highest Clarity (Shangqing 上清) heaven, with the Most High Great Lord of the Dao, Mysterious Sovereign of

the Jade Dawn (Taishang yuchen xuanhuang da daojun 太上玉晨玄皇大道君) in the middle, the Lord of the Dao, Celestial Emperor of the Great Tenuity of the Purple Dawn (Zichen taiwei tiandi daojun 紫晨太微天帝道君) leading the deities on the left, and the Lord of the Dao of Mysterious Origin, Saint of the Latter Age of the Imperial Dawn of the Golden Portal (Jinque dichen housheng xuanyuan daojun 金闕帝晨後聖玄元道君) leading those on the right, while the Great Authentic Original Princess of the Nine Numina (Jiuling taizhen yuanjun 九靈太真元君) leads the female *zhenren*.

3. Deities of the Taiji 太極 (Great Ultimate) heaven, with the Imperial Lord of the Golden Portal (*Jinque dijun) in the center, the Yellow Old Lord (Huanglao jun 黃老君) leading the deities on the left, and Xiliang Ziwen 西梁子文 leading those on the right.

4. Deities of the Great Clarity (Taiqing 太清) heaven, with the Most High Lord Lao (*Laojun) in the center, *Zhang Daoling leading the deities on the left, and Zhao Chezi 趙車子 leading those on the right.

5. Miscellaneous immortals of the Nine Palaces (*Jiugong 九宮) who have not yet been assigned to one of the higher heavens. In the center is the Secretary of the Nine Palaces (*jiugong shangshu* 九宮尚書), namely Zhang Feng 張奉, leading the immortals on the left is the Minister of the Left (*zuoxiang* 左相), and leading those on the right is the Minister of the Right (*youxiang* 右相).

6. Earthbound male and female immortals in the Huayang 華陽 Grotto-Heaven (*dongtian), with the Middle Lord Mao (Zhong Maojun 中茅君, i.e., Mao Gu 茅固, on whom see under *Maojun) in the middle, the Minor Lord Mao (Xiao Maojun 小茅君, i.e., Mao Zhong 茅衷) leading the immortals on the left, and Liu Yi 劉翊 leading the immortals on the right.

7. Various deities who control the bureaus of the underworld (*Fengdu); at the center is the Great Emperor of Northern Yin (Beiyin dadi 北陰大帝), leading the deities on the left is Qin Shihuang 秦始皇, and leading those on the right is Dai Yuan 戴淵.

MUGITANI Kunio

📖 Ishii Masako 1983a, 130–39; Ma Xiaohong 1998; Ren Jiyu 1990, 183–89; Strickmann 1979, 179–81

※ Tao Hongjing; Shangqing; DEITIES: THE PANTHEON

zhenren

真人

Real Man or Woman; Authentic Man or Woman;
True Man or Woman; Perfected

The term *zhenren* denotes one of the highest states in the Taoist spiritual hierarchy. While the word *zhen* does not appear in the five Confucian classics, it
is found in both the *Daode jing* and the **Zhuangzi*. *Daode jing* 21 says, "Within
[the Dao] is an essence (**jing*); this essence is the highest reality (*zhen*)," and
Zhuangzi 31 defines the term saying: "Reality (*zhen*) is what is received from
Heaven; it is so of itself (**ziran*) and cannot be altered (*yi* 易)." In *Zhuangzi* 2,
the ruler of the universe is called *zhenzai* 真宰 (Real Ruler) and *zhenjun* 真君
(Real Lord), and one who has attained the Dao is called *zhenren*.

Elsewhere in the *Zhuangzi*, the *zhenren* is described as follows:

> What is the meaning of *zhenren*? The *zhenren* of ancient times did not struggle
> against adversity, was not proud of success, did not plan his actions. . . . One
> who was like this could climb high places and not be afraid, go into water and
> not get wet, enter fire and not be burned. This is because his knowledge was
> able to rise to the Dao. The *zhenren* of ancient times slept without dreaming,
> and woke without any worry. He ate without caring about taste, and his breath
> was very deep. A *zhenren* breathes through his heels whereas the ordinary man
> breathes through his throat. . . . The *zhenren* of ancient times knew nothing
> about delighting in life, nor did he hate the world of death. He was not glad
> of coming forth, nor reluctant to go in. He merely went with composure and
> came with composure. (Chapter 6; see also trans. Watson 1968, 77–78)

While the *Zhuangzi* does not describe a person with supernormal powers as
a *zhenren*, it is easy to see how the idea could be adopted into the search for
eternal youth and immortality. The words quoted above no doubt influenced
the speech of the **fangshi* Lu Sheng 盧生 when he was trying to influence
Qin Shi huangdi (r. 221–210 BCE), who was fascinated by the idea of immortality: "The *zhenren* enters water but does not get wet, enters fire but does not
get burned, flies among the clouds, and has a length of life equal to that of
Heaven and Earth" (*Shiji* 6).

Thus the *zhenren* entered Taoist religion colored by the idea of immortality. The Taoist *zhenren* was ranked higher than the immortal (**xianren*) in the
celestial hierarchy. For instance, the *Ziyang zhenren neizhuan* 紫陽真人內傳
(Inner Biography of the Real Man of Purple Yang; see **Ziyang zhenren*) says

that "there are various degrees of *xian*," upper, middle and lower. "Those whose names appear in the Golden Script (*jinshu* 金書, i.e., the list of the upper ranks of the celestial bureaucracy) are *zhenren*." The Grotto-Heavens and Blissful Lands (*dongtian* and *fudi*) that Taoists conceived as being scattered all over China were inhabited by middle-ranking immortals (the earthly immortals, *dixian* 地仙) and were ruled by *zhenren* who had been appointed by Heaven.

Sometimes the *zhenren* would descend from Heaven into the body of the practitioner. The Six Dynasties *Laozi zhongjing* (Central Scripture of Laozi) explains a technique for nourishing the Real Man Child-Cinnabar (Zidan zhenren 子丹真人) within one's own body. Zidan is a lord (*jun* 君), an infant (*chizi* 赤子), and the embryo of immortality.

From around the end of the Former Han dynasty the idea spread that a *zhenren* who had received the Heavenly Mandate (*tianming* 天命) would appear to renew the world. Liu Xiu 劉秀, who founded the Later Han dynasty, was called Baishui zhenren 白水真人 (Real Man of the White Water), and Cao Cao 曹操 (155–220) of Wei was also sometimes called *zhenren*. These examples show a correspondence with the thought of the *Taiping jing* (j. 71), which considers the *zhenren* to be a ruler on earth in contrast to the "divine man" (*shenren*) who rules in heaven.

MIURA Kunio

📖 Chen Guofu 1963, 279; Kamitsuka Yoshiko 1999, 52–101; Izutsu Toshihiko 1983, 444–56; Lagerwey 1987a; Larre 1982, 239–46; Robinet 1993, 42–48; Yamada Toshiaki 1983b, 336–38; Yearley 1983

※ *shenren*; *xianren*; TRANSCENDENCE AND IMMORTALITY

Zhenwu

真武

Perfected Warrior

Zhenwu, also known as the Dark Warrior (Xuanwu 玄武) or Highest Emperor of the Dark Heaven (Xuantian shangdi 玄天上帝), is a divinity known for his powers of healing and exorcism. In Han dynasty cosmology, the Dark Warrior was one of the four animals corresponding to the cardinal directions (see under *siling*). Usually depicted as a serpent coiled around a tortoise, the Dark Warrior was correlated with winter, water, the color black, and the constellations of the northern quadrant of the sky.

Fig. 88. Zhenwu (Perfected Warrior). Chen Yan-qing 陳彥清 (fl. early fifteenth century). Photograph by Robert Hashimoto. The Art Institute of Chicago. See Little 2000b, 294.

The Perfected Warrior was later worshipped as an individual deity, perhaps as early as the seventh century. In 1018, during the reign of Song Zhenzong, he received the title Perfected Warrior, Numinous Response Perfected Lord (Zhenwu lingying zhenjun 真武靈應真君). In 1304, under the Yuan dynasty, he was granted the title Primordial Sage of the Dark Heaven, Benevolent and Majestic Highest Emperor (Xuantian yuansheng renwei shangdi 玄天元聖仁威上帝). The peak of the Perfected Warrior's importance, however, came during the Ming dynasty. In 1412, the Yongle Emperor sponsored a major reconstruction project on Mount Wudang (*Wudang shan, Hubei), the Perfected Warrior's center of worship. By the Ming, depictions of the Perfected Warrior had acquired a number of distinctive iconographic features, including the loose hair and bare feet characteristic of spirit mediums. Also in Ming times, the vernacular novel *Beiyou ji* 北遊記 (Journey to the North; trans. Seaman 1987), attributed to Yu Xiangdou 余象斗 (fl. 1596; DMB 1612–14), recounts the Perfected Warrior's adventures over the course of seven incarnations.

Theodore A. COOK

📖 Boltz J. M. 1987a, 86–91; de Bruyn 2004; Despeux 1994, 138–40; Grootaers 1952; Lagerwey 1992; Little 2000b, 291–311; Major 1985–86

※ Wudang shan; *siling*; DEITIES: THE PANTHEON

Zhenxian beiji

真仙碑記

Epigraphic Records of Real Men and Immortals

The *Zhongnan shan Shuojing tai lidai zhenxian beiji* 終南山說經臺歷代真仙
碑記 (Epigraphic Records of the Successive Generations of Real Men and
Immortals Who Lived at the Platform for Explaining the Scriptures on the
Zhongnan Mountains; CT 956) is a collection of thirty-five biographies written by Zhu Xiangxian 朱象先 (fl. 1279–1308). The stele, still standing today at
the *Louguan (Tiered Abbey), is one of the most impressive monuments of
Taoist *EPIGRAPHY of the Yuan dynasty. Its format and size are rather unusual
for a stele inscription. Zhu Xiangxian abbreviated a Six Dynasties hagiographic
work, now lost, adding the biographies of the *Quanzhen masters *Yin Zhiping
and Li Zhirou 李志柔 (1189–1266). Yin Zhiping was considered to be a novel
*Yin Xi who restored the primal age of Taoism, and his biography echoes the
first and longest one in the collection, devoted to Yin Xi himself. The other
biographies are very short and focus on Taoists from the late Warring States
to the late Six Dynasties, most of whom we only know through quotations
of this same work.

Zhu Xiangxian, who hailed from Mount Mao (*Maoshan, Jiangsu), moved
early to the Louguan and became a Quanzhen monk there, spending his life
in the various shrines of this major center. He took upon himself the task of
commemorating the legacy of the holy place, from the time of Laozi to the
spectacular revival after Quanzhen took control of it in 1236. Zhu also compiled the *Gu Louguan ziyun yanqing ji* 古樓觀紫雲衍慶集 (Anthology from
the Continued Celebration [of the Appearance] of the Purple Clouds at the
Tiered Abbey of Antiquity; CT 957; Boltz J. M. 1987a, 126), a collection of inscriptions, prose texts, and poetry pertaining to the history of the Louguan.

Vincent GOOSSAERT

📖 Chen Guofu 1963, 235–39; Wang Shiwei 1993; Wang Zhongxin 1995

※ Louguan; Quanzhen; EPIGRAPHY

Zhenyuan

真元

[Lineage of the] True Origin

The Taoist Canon contains nine works belonging to Zhenyuan textual lineage. Some of them are incomplete, while others derive from the division of one text into two parts. They all approximately date from the twelfth century, but internal evidence supports their claim to represent a tradition that goes back to Tang times (eighth-ninth centuries). The nine texts—the last two of which are addressed to beginners—are the following:

1. *Zhenyuan tongxian daojing* 真元通仙道經 (Zhenyuan Scripture of the Dao on Entering Immortality; CT 57), incomplete.

2. *Xiuzhen liyan chaotu* 修真歷驗鈔圖 (Excerpts and Diagrams on Successive Experiences of Cultivating Authenticity; CT 152, and YJQQ 72.16b–38b).

3. *Zhenyuan miaojing pin* 真元妙經品 (Wondrous Scripture in Sections of Zhenyuan; CT 436), with a preface spuriously attributed to Tang Xuanzong (r. 712–56).

4. *Zhenyuan miaojing tu* 真元妙經圖 (Wondrous Scripture and Diagrams of Zhenyuan; CT 437).

5. *Zhenyuan yinyang zhijiang tushu houjie* 真元陰陽陟降圖書後解 (Later Explications of the Zhenyuan Diagrams and Writings on the Ascent and Descent of Yin and Yang; CT 438). This and the previous text were probably a single work later divided into two parts. Altogether, they contain a set of twelve diagrams.

6. *Zhenyuan tushu jishuo zhongpian* 真元圖書繼說終篇 (Final Folios with Additional Explanations on the Diagrams and Writings of Zhenyuan; CT 439).

7. *Zhenyuan miaodao yaolüe* 真元妙道要略 (Abridged Essentials of the Wondrous Way of Zhenyuan; CT 924). This text, which is incomplete, appears to be the second part of no. 2 above.

8. *Kaihua zhenjing* 開化真經 (Authentic Scripture on the Opening of Transformation; CT 1133).

9. *Juntian yanfan zhenjing* 鈞天演範真經 (Authentic Scripture Explaining the Rules for Harmonizing with Heaven; CT 1134).

The main doctrinal feature of these texts is a synthesis of Confucian ethics, Taoist philosophy, medical traditions, numerology, *neiguan* (inner observation), *neidan, and Buddhism. In its ideal of universal salvation (*pudu), the lineage also reveals a *Lingbao influence. The term zhenyuan itself is a synonym for Dao borrowed from *Shangqing, a school to which the texts claim to be affiliated.

The Zhenyuan pantheon consists of ten major gods who are appellations (hao 號) of the supreme divinity (tian chenzun 天宸尊). Among them are Laozi, Lingbao tianzun 靈寶天尊 (Celestial Worthy of the Numinous Treasure; see *sanqing), and a Buddhist-like god of universal compassion. The supreme divinity takes on different forms in relation to diverse human characteristics and social functions, each of which requires specific virtues. The man of superior rank aims to achieve universal salvation by practicing non-interference (*wuwei).

The Great Ultimate (*taiji) plays the same major role of primordial Unity as does the Great One (*Taiyi) in Han times: it connects the trigrams and hexagrams of the *Yijing and Han cosmology with the void of the Daode jing, the Original Pneuma (*yuanqi), and the circulation of pneuma in the cosmos and in the human body. The neidan language and spirit are noticeable: practices are performed on double levels, body and spirit, cosmos and human. This remarkably syncretic lineage represents a link between Shangqing and neidan.

Isabelle ROBINET

📖   Robinet 1989–90; Wang Ka 1993b

※   neidan

Zhenzheng lun

甄正論

Essays of Examination and Correction

The Zhenzheng lun (T. 2112) is Buddhist polemical work in three chapters. The author, Xuanyi 玄嶷 (fl. 684–704), formerly a metropolitan Taoist priest named Du You 杜乂, had renounced his original religious career some time toward 695, and after being granted thirty years of seniority as a Buddhist monk so as to assure him an equivalent position in the Buddhist hierarchy, produced this attack on his former colleagues some time before the end of the reign of the Empress Wu in 705. No doubt the official dominance of the Buddhistic ideology espoused by the Empress from 690 onward inspired his conversion, though discreet imperial support for Taoism continued throughout this period. Xuanyi's revelations are somewhat disappointing, sounding polemical themes already well developed by predecessors. Even his allegations concerning the forgery of Taoist texts such as the *Benji jing (Scripture of the Original Bound) by Taoist priests (in this case, Liu Jinxi 劉進喜 and Li Zhongqing 李仲卿) through the plagiarization of Buddhist works, though more detailed than most, can be found in earlier sources.

His analysis of Taoism is, however, unique. For though he follows the tactic of attempting to deny Taoism "cultural space" by distinguishing the otherworldly goals of Buddhism from the legitimate but worldly concerns of both Laozi and his like (considered as Chinese political thinkers), and also of practitioners of the macrobiotic arts (considered purely as hygienic regimes), he adds a surprising third category. Opposed as he is to the pretensions of those Taoists who have confected through plagiarism a false religion to rival Buddhism, the Taoism of "talismans and registers" (*fulu* 符籙) associated with the Celestial Masters (*Tianshi dao) he condones, by contrast, as mere folk belief. There was probably a political motive at work here, too. The Empress Wu showed a remarkably tolerant attitude toward popular religious cults, including Taoist ones, since she needed their support for her legitimation as the only female emperor in Chinese history. It was the readiness of the erudite Taoist priests of the metropolis to see their religion become during the reign of her husband the state sponsored family cult of the dynasty which she eventually supplanted that was her real target. Taoists of this type, the monastic, celibate rivals of the Buddhists, Xuanyi denounced in a most obliging fashion. After the Empress Wu we hear no more of the Buddhist acceptance of the married priesthood of Taoism among the people; indeed, even the Chinese state seems to have relaxed only when it was assigned to the hereditary oversight of the Zhang family many centuries later. On this point the *Zhenzheng lun* provides a unique insight into a highly unusual phase in Chinese religious history; for the rest it tends to supplement information available elsewhere.

T. H. BARRETT

📖 Barrett 1998, 424; Forte 1976, 119, 123

※ TAOISM AND CHINESE BUDDHISM

zhi

芝

"numinous mushrooms"; "excrescences"

The term *zhi*, which has no equivalent in Western languages, refers to a variety of supermundane substances often described as plants, fungi, or "excrescences." Also known as *lingzhi* 靈芝 (numinous *zhi*), *yinzhi* 隱芝 (concealed

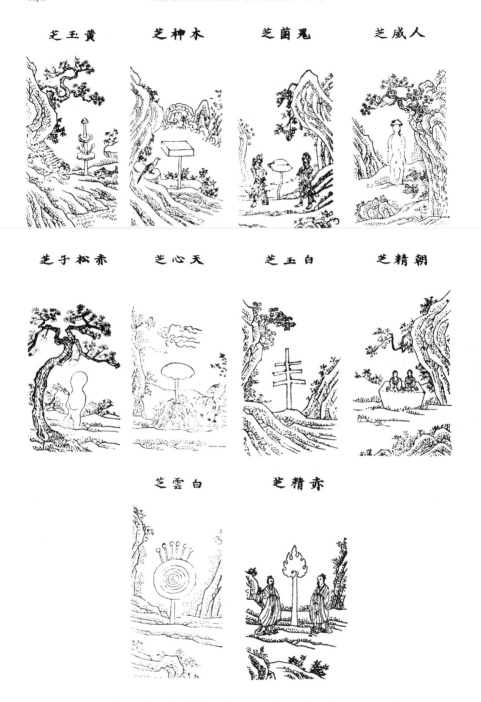

Fig. 89. Illustrations of *zhi* ("numinous mushrooms," or "excrescences").
Zhicao pin 芝草品 (Classified *Zhi* Plants; CT 1406).

zhi), or zhicao 芝草 (zhi plants), and often associated with jade (for instance in the expression yuzhi 玉芝, "jade and zhi"), they are said to grow spontaneously in mythical places like *Penglai or on mountains that also produce precious minerals. While there may be no better term than "mushrooms" or "excrescences" to refer to them, and even though *Ge Hong states that they "are not different from natural mushrooms (ziran zhi 自然芝)" (*Baopu zi, 16.287), the zhi pertain to an intermediate dimension between mundane and transcendent reality. Early sources associate them with some female divine beings, and consider them to be auspicious portents sent by Heaven. Ingesting them confers longevity and immortality to a degree equivalent to that of the alchemical elixirs.

The first classical discussion of the zhi is found in chapter 11 of the Baopu zi (trans. Ware 1966, 179–85). Drawing from texts now lost that described them with illustrations, Ge Hong distinguishes five sorts of zhi—each of which is said to include more than one hundred varieties—based on their shapes: stone zhi (shizhi 石芝), wood zhi (muzhi 木芝), plant zhi (caozhi 草芝), flesh zhi (rouzhi 肉芝), and mushroom zhi (junzhi 菌芝). Ge Hong also adds a significant detail, saying that unless the deities and spirits of a mountain agree to disclose the zhi, "one could even step right over them without seeing them." Accordingly, ascending a mountain to collect the zhi requires preliminary purification rites and the performance of breathing practices and the Pace of Yu (Yubu 禹步; see *bugang). Another meaningful aspect that emerges from Ge Hong's discussion is that some zhi continuously radiate light. The Stone Elephant (shixiang 石象), for instance, yields a light "visible by night at one hundred feet." The zhi of the Seven Brilliancies and the Nine Radiances (qiming jiuguang 七明九光) issues a brightness that "resembles that of the stars; by night these lights are visible at one hundred feet, and each beam can clearly be distinguished from the others, spreading out without merging with the others."

Two of Ge Hong's descriptions correspond to those given in the Jiuzhuan huandan jing yaojue 九轉還丹經要訣 (Essential Instructions on the Scripture of the Reverted Elixir in Nine Cycles; CT 889), a *Shangqing text that originally was part of *Maojun's revealed biography (Robinet 1984, 2: 389–98), and that describes Maojun as planting five zhi on Mount Mao (*Maoshan, Jiangsu), the early seat of the Shangqing school. This is also the topic of the Zhong zhicao fa 種芝草法 (Methods for Planting the Zhi Plants; CT 933), a work probably dating from the late Six Dynasties that in turn shares passages with another Shangqing text, the Mingjian yaojing 明鑑要經 (Essential Scripture of the Bright Mirror; CT 1206; 8b–13a). It contains instructions attributed to Laozi and states that the best zhi are those growing above deposits of cinnabar, gold, malachite, and realgar. Accordingly, the text teaches how to plant these minerals in the four directions of a mountain at the solstices and equinoxes so that they generate the zhi.

At least in some contexts, the imagery originally attached to the *zhi* was progressively lost, resulting in more "secular" views. Incorporation of the *zhi* in some pharmacopoeias may have played a role in this process, as the *zhi* sometimes became associated with common mushrooms, resulting in an emphasis on their healing properties. A different trend is the aesthetic appeal exerted by the *zhi* for some writers. An example is found in the Taoist Canon with the *Zhicao pin* 芝草品 (Classified *Zhi* Plants; CT 1406; see fig. 89). Although a *Zhipin* 芝品 (Classified *Zhi*) is listed in *Lu Xiujing's catalogue of *Lingbao scriptures (Ōfuchi Ninji 1974, 39; see table 16), this work, containing illustrations and descriptions of 127 *zhi* and probably dating from the early Song period, may be reckoned among the catalogues (*pu* 譜) of uncommon objects compiled by Song and later literati.

Fabrizio PREGADIO

📖 Campany 2002, 27–29; Little 2000b, 340–41; Needham 1974, 121–23; Strickmann 1966

zhi

治

parish

Accounts in secular historical sources of the founding of Celestial Master Taoism (*Tianshi dao) relate that a series of twenty-four administrative centers or *zhi* were established throughout the area of Sichuan and southern Shaanxi province that they controlled. Later sectarian sources record their establishment by *Zhang Daoling in 143, one year after the revelation, but it is unlikely that the faith could have spread so widely in one year. As the name indicates, these centers combined governmental functions with their religious role, and during the period of de facto independence, they came to be both the administrative nexus for the surrounding district and a gathering place and place of worship for the faithful. For this reason, the term is often translated "parish" or even "diocese."

The original twenty-four parishes (see table 28) were divided into three ranked groups of eight. The superior group consisted of the Yangping 陽平 parish, the parish associated with the Celestial Master, Lutang 鹿堂 parish, Heming 鶴鳴 parish, Liyuan 漓沅 parish, Gegui 葛璝 parish, Gengchu 更除 parish, Qinzhong 秦中 parish, and Zhenduo 真多 parish. These are also referred to as "great parishes" and "orthodox parishes," and first three of this group—Yangping, Lutang and Heming—had special significance, each

Table 28

1	Yangping 陽平	13	Beiping 北平
2	Lutang shan 鹿堂山	14	Benzhu 本竹
3	Heming shan 鶴鳴山	15	Mengqin 蒙秦
4	Liyuan shan 漓沅山	16	Pinggai 平蓋
5	Gegui shan 葛瓆山	17	Yuntai shan 雲臺山
6	Gengchu 更除	18	Jinkou 瀘口
7	Qinzhong 秦中	19	Houcheng 後城
8	Zhenduo 真多	20	Gongmu 公慕
9	Changli 昌利	21	Pinggang 平剛
10	Lishang 隸上	22	Zhubu shan 主簿山
11	Yongquan 湧泉	23	Yuju 玉局
12	Chougeng 稠粳	24	Beimang 北邙

The twenty-four parishes (*ershisi zhi* 二十四治) of early Tianshi dao.
Source: *Wushang biyao (CT 1138), 23.4a–9a (see Lagerwey 1981b, 103–4).

representing one of the founding pneumas of the group. The leaders of these three parishes were the highest ranking priests in the movement. The second tier of parishes consisted of the Changli 昌利, Lishang 隸上, Yongquan 湧泉, Chougeng 稠粳, Beiping 北平, Benzhu 本竹, Mengqin 蒙秦, and Pinggai 平蓋 parishes. The lowest tier of parishes encompassed Yuntai 雲臺, Jinkou 瀘口, Houcheng 後城, Gongmu 公慕, Pinggang 平剛, Zhubu 主簿, Yuju 玉局, and Beimang 北邙 parishes.

When plotted on a map, the parishes cover most of Sichuan province and parts of southern Shaanxi, but do not group into meaningful regional units. Eventually, when the Taoist community spread across North China in 215, then on to South China following the fall of the Western Jin, these parishes ceased to have meaning to the faithful. They were replaced by a system linking each parish to a constellation in the Chinese zodiac (see under *xiu), with membership determined by birth. The *Taizhen ke* 太真科 (Code of the Great Perfected) says that in 196 Zhang Lu added four additional parishes (Jushan 具山, Zhongmao 鍾茂, Baishi 白石, and Ganghu 剛互 parishes), called "supplementary parishes" (*beizhi* 配治) or "separate parishes" (*biezhi* 別治), so that the twenty-eight parishes would correspond directly with the twenty-eight constellations. Wang Chunwu (1996) points out that these four parishes are all on the northern edge of Celestial Master territory and suggests that they were originally established following the expansion to Hanzhong 漢中. There is also a list of eight "roaming parishes" (*youzhi* 遊治), including Jiyang 吉陽, Pingdu 平都, Afeng 阿逢, Cimu 慈母, Huangjin 黃金, Taihua 太華, Qingcheng 青城, and Emei 峨嵋 parishes.

There is a description of a parish, perhaps the central parish of the Celestial Master, in a Tang collection of codes, in the *Yaoxiu keyi jielü chao* 要修科儀戒律鈔 (Excerpts from the Essential Liturgies and Observances; CT 463, j. 10), which cites the lost Celestial Master scripture *Taizhen ke*. It describes a compound 150 meters to a side, with a large central hall called the Hall for the Veneration of Emptiness (Chongxu tang 崇虛堂), topped by a terrace with a huge incense burner called the Terrace for the Veneration of Mystery (Chongxuan tai 崇玄臺). A more average parish is described in the *Xuandu lüwen* (Statutes of the Mysterious Metropolis) as being parallel in function to but somewhat larger than the oratory (*jingshi*) found in the home of all practicing Taoists, hence a single, freestanding building on the west side of the main dwelling, facing east. It should thus be furnished in the same spare fashion, containing only "an incense burner, a lamp, a petition table and a small knife." It is uncertain when the parish disappeared in Taoist communities, or if it in some sense evolved into later Taoist temples and monasteries. *Lu Xiujing (406–77), in his abbreviated version of the Taoist code (see *Daomen kelüe*), complains that people in his day were often attending the wrong parish, but it seems to have still been a functioning institution.

Terry KLEEMAN

📖 Verellen 2003; Wang Chunwu 1996

※ Tianshi dao

zhiqian

紙錢

paper money

In Chinese folk religion, paper money is burned and sent to ancestors, deities, or spirits of the dead. This custom can be traced back to the inclusion of real or imitation daily items in tombs. Real money was used during the Han and the Six Dynasties, but paper money made its appearance around the sixth century in southern China; its use proliferated during the Tang and the Five Dynasties and became common by the Song period. As shown by Tang and Song records, it was thought that paper money was demanded by officers of hell in the underworld after death.

In present-day Taiwan, the various types of paper money are generally divided into "gold" and "silver." Gold paper money is gold foil and is sent to the deities. Within this category, *dingji jin* 頂極金 (also called *tiangong jin* 天公金

and *da taiji* 大太極) is sent to the Jade Sovereign (*Yuhuang); *zhongtai ji* 中太極 to the Three Offices (*sanguan, of Heaven, Earth, and Water); *caizi shoujin* 財子壽金 to the deities of the Northern and Southern Dippers; *shoujin* 壽金, *fujin* 福金, and *zhongjin* 中金 to deities and Buddhas in general; and *yijin* 刈金 to minor deities. Silver paper money is silver foil and is sent to denizens of the underworld, such as ancestors and spirits of the dead; *dayin* 大銀 is used for ancestral festivals and *xiaoyin* 小銀 for other spirit festivals. Another type of paper money is called "treasury money" (*kuqian* 庫錢), consisting of wads of yellow paper wrapped in white paper, for the use of the newly-ordained dead person in the underworld. It is employed in the ritual of Merit (*gongde) for the dead. Other kinds include "rebirth money" (*wangsheng qian* 往生錢), stamped with a lotus flower, and "natal-destiny money" (*benming qian* 本命錢), used to "refill the treasury" (see *tianku). In Hong Kong and Sichuan, paper money in the shape of modern bank bills, called *mingbi* 冥幣, is also used.

Paper money is indispensable as an offering during birth, marriage, or death rites, and also at annual events. It is used as a fee to cross bridges and pass barrier gates on the journey to the underworld, as a deposit to reimburse the loan that the dead person has received from the Celestial Treasury at birth, and also as funds to cover the daily needs of the dead person in the underworld, where one has to meet the same kinds of expenses as in this world.

Paper money does not appear to be used in Confucian rituals, such as national rites and Confucian temple festivals. It is also noteworthy that it is rarely used in Buddhist and Taoist formal rites.

MARUYAMA Hiroshi

📖 Hou Ching-lang 1975; Seidel 1978a; Su Suqing 1999

※ *tianku*; *gongde*; HELL

Zhong-Lü

鍾呂

[Lineage of] Zhongli Quan and Lü Dongbin

The texts attributed to the semilegendary immortals *Zhongli Quan and *Lü Dongbin, and their putative disciple *Shi Jianwu, represent one of the highest achievements in the history of *neidan. These texts, dating from the Song period, are commonly referred to as the Zhong-Lü corpus and the tradition to which they belong as the Zhong-Lü school. Although their exact date, origin, and authorship cannot be ascertained with any accuracy, they predate the mid-twelfth century since the *Daoshu (Pivot of the Dao) includes several of them.

Both Zhongli Quan and Lü Dongbin were renowned in the mid-eleventh century for their poems and calligraphy. The earliest work attributed to Zhongli is the Zhixuan pian 指玄篇 (Folios Pointing to the Mystery), a work in verse now lost but often quoted in neidan texts of the Song period. Another famous work of the mid-eleventh century, the *Qinyuan chun (Spring in the Garden by the Qin River), is ascribed to Lü Dongbin. It is also around this time that the names of the two immortals began to be linked to each other: a poem by Lü Dongbin for his master is included in a work of 1052 (Huandan zhongxian lun 還丹眾仙論, CT 233, 14b), and the poet Chen Shidao 陳師道 (1052–1102; IC 233–35) mentions their master-disciple relationship. By the end of the Northern Song in 1127, several prose texts attributed to Zhong and Lü were in circulation.

The Zhong-Lü corpus. The main sources of the Zhong-Lü school are the *Lingbao bifa (Complete Methods of the Numinous Treasure), attributed to Zhongli Quan, and the *Zhong-Lü chuandao ji (Anthology of Zhongli Quan's Transmission of the Dao to Lü Dongbin), attributed to Lü Dongbin and transcribed by Shi Jianwu. Both works were popular among *Quanzhen Taoists in northern China and were included in the *Xuandu baozang, the Taoist Canon of the Jin dynasty (*Jinlian zhengzong ji; 5a). They were, however, frowned upon by *Nanzong adepts (*Xiuzhen shishu, 52.3b; Chunyang dijun shenhua miaotong ji 純陽帝君神化妙通紀, CT 305, 6.12a; trans. Ang 1993). Another important work belonging to this group is the *Xishan qunxian huizhen ji (Records of the Gathered Immortals and Assembled Perfected of the Western Hills), which associates the Zhong-Lü tradition with the Western Hills (*Xishan) of Nanchang (Jiangxi), the center of the cult of *Xu Xun and the *Shenxiao movements.

The Daoshu contains other Zhong-Lü texts, such as the Baiwen pian 百問篇 (Folios of the Hundred Questions; 5.7a–22a; trans. Homann 1976), the Huayang pian 華陽篇 (Folios of the Flourishing Yang; 10.1a–7b), the Zhixuan pian (Folios Pointing to the Mystery; 13.1a–4b), and the Xiuzhen zhixuan pian 修真指玄篇 (Folios Pointing to the Mystery for the Cultivation of Perfection; 19.9a–22a). The last two texts, which are different from the original Zhixuan pian in verse, were the object of several works illustrated with diagrams, notably the Xiuzhen taiji hunyuan tu 修真太極混元圖 (Diagrams of the Chaotic Origin of the Great Ultimate for the Cultivation of Perfection; CT 149; trans. Baryosher-Chemouny 1996) and the Xiuzhen taiji hunyuan zhixuan tu 修真太極混元指玄圖 (Diagrams Pointing to the Mystery of the Chaotic Origin of the Great Ultimate for the Cultivation of Perfection; CT 150). The Dadan zhizhi 大丹直指 (Straightforward Directions on the Great Elixir; CT 244), attributed to the Quanzhen patriarch *Qiu Chuji (1148–1227), was also inspired by them. Another popular work was the *Zhouhou sancheng pian* 肘後三成篇 (Folios of the Three Accomplishments to Keep at Hand; *Daoshu, j.* 25), which was printed and distributed to the people of Yueyang 嶽陽 (Hunan) during the Shunxi reign period (1174–89; see *Chunyang dijun miaotong ji*, 6.10b).

Teachings and practices. While the Zhong-Lü texts are quite disparate as to content and provenance, they share a common theoretical basis and are consistent in the use of certain technical terms. The genesis of the world in five stages—*taishi* 太始 (Great Commencement), *taiwu* 太無 (Great Non-being), *taixu* 太虛 (Great Void), *taikong* 太空 (Great Emptiness), and *taizhi* 太質 (Great Matter)—the distance between heaven and earth (calculated as 84,000 *li*), the interaction of Yin and Yang, the sequence of the seasons, the annual and diurnal cycles of increase and decay, the trigrams and hexagrams of the *Yijing, and so forth, are correlated with patterns in the human body. Malfunctioning of the five viscera (*wuzang) is explained in terms drawn from medical texts, while psycho-physiological techniques are couched in alchemical language and imagery. The texts are also strongly imbued with Neo-Confucian speculations on *qi (especially those of Cheng Yi 程頤, 1033–1107; see Fung Yu-lan 1952–53, 2: 512–14). All accept the division of the practice into three main stages (*sancheng* 三成 or Three Accomplishments), but the *Lingbao bifa* indicates four methods for the lower stage, and the *Zhouhou sancheng pian* seven stages.

The Zhong-Lü methods include massage and gymnastics in the early stages of practice, as well as breathing exercises that vary according to the adept's level of advancement. Other techniques involve the opening of the Three Passes (*sanguan), refining and returning the essence (*jing), inner observation (*neiguan), and the egress of the Spirit (*chushen).

Farzeen BALDRIAN-HUSSEIN

📖 Baldrian-Hussein 1984, 13–57; Boltz J. M. 1987a, 139–43

※ *neidan*; for other related entries see the Synoptic Table of Contents, sec. IV.3 ("Alchemy: Zhong-Lü")

Zhong-Lü chuandao ji

鍾呂傳道集

Anthology of Zhongli Quan's Transmission of the Dao to
Lü Dongbin

The *Zhong-Lü chuandao ji* is one of the main works in the *Zhong-Lü corpus of *neidan texts. It is conceived as providing the theoretical foundation to the

Lingbao bifa (Complete Methods of the Numinous Treasure), a practical text that explains techniques to attain immortality. It is attributed to *Zhongli Quan and *Lü Dongbin, but was transmitted by *Shi Jianwu (fl. 820–35), the author of the *Xishan qunxian huizhen ji* (Records of the Gathered Immortals and Assembled Perfected of the Western Hills). *Yu Yan (1258–1314) states that it was actually written by Shi Jianwu himself (*Zhouyi cantong qi fahui* 周易參同契發揮; CT 1005, 8.3a).

The text is included in two collections found in the Taoist Canon. The earlier version is in the *Daoshu* (Pivot of the Dao; ca. 1151; *j.* 39–41). This version is mentioned in the thirteenth-century *Zhizhai shulu jieti* 直齋書錄解題 (Annotated Register of Books in the Zhizhai Studio; van der Loon 1984, 164). The other version is in the *Xiuzhen shishu* (Ten Books on the Cultivation of Perfection; late thirteenth or early fourteenth century, *j.* 14–16). The latter cites honorary titles bestowed on Zhongli Quan and Lü Dongbin in 1126, hence this edition seems to have appeared after this date.

Like the *Baiwen pian* 百問篇 (Folios of the Hundred Questions; trans. Homann 1976), another text belonging to the Zhong-Lü group, the *Chuandao ji* is cast in dialogue form, with Lü Dongbin asking questions on various technical terms and Zhongli Quan explaining them. The text is divided into eighteen essays (*lun* 論) dealing with the Zhong-Lü system of *neidan*. The first six essays are concerned with the cosmos, the middle six with the alchemical practice, and the final six with its purposes. These three divisions correspond to the Three Accomplishments (*sancheng* 三成) or Three Vehicles (*sansheng* 三乘). The last section states that the eighteen essays are related to the techniques described in the *Lingbao bifa*.

Besides the two editions in the Taoist Canon, the *Chuandao ji* is also found in the *Daozang jiyao* (vol. 12), the *Daoshu quanji* 道書全集 (Complete Collection of Books on the Dao; 1591), and the *Daozang jinghua lu*. The popularity of the text was so great during the Song and Yuan dynasties that murals depicting the transmission of the Dao were painted in temples. One of them is found in the hall dedicated to Lü Dongbin in the *Yongle gong.

Farzeen BALDRIAN-HUSSEIN

📖 Boltz J. M. 1987a, 139–41; Sakauchi Shigeo 1985

※ Lü Dongbin; Zhongli Quan; *neidan*; Zhong-Lü

Fig. 90. Monks in front of the head-
quarters of the Zhongguo daojiao
xiehui (Chinese Taoist Association).
*Baiyun guan (Abbey of the White
Clouds), Beijing. Reproduced from
Zhongguo daojiao xiehui 1983.

Zhongguo daojiao xiehui

中國道教協會

Chinese Taoist Association

This organization of Chinese Taoists was founded in April 1957, with its
headquarters at the *Baiyun guan (Abbey of the White Clouds) in Beijing.
The founding charter was drafted at an initial meeting in November 1956 in
Beijing, and the first assembly was held the following year; it was attended by
ninety-one representatives including Taoist scholars and priests from Taoist
lineages, mountains, and temples located throughout China. Sixty-one members were elected as officers and Yue Chongdai 嶽崇岱 (1888–1958), the abbot
of the Baiyun guan, was chosen as its president. The stated purposes of the
Association were to unite Taoists from all over the country, promote patrio-
tism and love of Taoism, and have Taoists contribute to the construction of
a socialist society. At the second assembly, held in 1961, *Chen Yingning was
elected president. It was decided at that time to expand the area of Taoist

studies, and a research seminar was subsequently established. A group was formed to train Taoist priests and a journal, *Daoxiehui kan* 道協會刊 (Journal of the Taoist Association), was inaugurated.

The Association suspended its activities between 1967 and 1979 during the Cultural Revolution. At the third assembly, held in May 1980, Li Yuhang 黎遇航 was elected president. Religious activities were reinaugurated, and repairs to temples (including the Baiyun guan) were carried out throughout the country. In 1987 the Association's journal was renamed *Zhongguo daojiao* 中國道教 (Chinese Taoism), and since then has been published officially and distributed both in China and overseas. A Taoist cultural center was also established, for both religious training of Taoist priests and academic research purposes. Regional branches of the Association have been organized at the district and city levels. The largest of these is the Shanghai Taoist Association, which publishes its own journal, *Shanghai daojiao* 上海道教 (Taoism in Shanghai). In 2004, the president of the Chinese Taoist Association was Min Zhiting 閔智亭.

SAKADE Yoshinobu

📖 Kandel 1980; Kurihara Akira 1987

※ TAOISM IN THE PEOPLE'S REPUBLIC OF CHINA

Zhonghe ji

中和集

Anthology of Central Harmony

The *Zhonghe ji* (CT 249) consists of a set of *Li Daochun's (fl. 1288–92) treatises, dialogues, songs, and poems collected by his disciple Cai Zhiyi 蔡志頤 (fl. 1288–1306), with a preface by *Du Daojian dated 1306. Some portions of the text (4.6b, 4.9a) are dated to 1292. Li associates the title of his work with a passage of the *Zhongyong* 中庸 (Centrality and Commonality; trans. Legge 1893, 384–85): the Center lies in the state of mind not yet manifested, which is the hidden and unfathomable spirit, while Harmony is its manifested state, which is in accord with the activating force of the world (1.2a–b, 1.9a).

In *j*. 1 and part of *j*. 4, Li deals at length with the basic unity and dialectical relation of pairs of complementary notions such as movement and quiescence (*dong* and *jing*), substance and function (*ti* and *yong*), change and permanence, human and celestial mind (*xin*), inner nature and vital force (*xing* and *ming*), body and spirit, knowledge and action, contraction and expansion, and so forth. He stresses their fundamental unity and underscores the *coincidentia oppositorum* operated by a *tertium quid*. This third element is the central one, the Mysterious Pass (*xuanguan), represented for instance by the intention (*yi) in the pair body and spirit.

The second *juan* is largely devoted to *neidan. It contains several diagrams and an exposition of the degrees of practice (three for the gradual teaching, followed by a final superior degree) and the three main stages of the alchemical work. The latter three stages are the Three Passes (*sanguan) or Three Primes (*sanyuan), which are related to essence, pneuma, and spirit (*jing, qi, shen). Li rejects many old practices as erroneous (including the sexual techniques or *fangzhong shu) or inferior (for example, *waidan, diets, and visionary meditation).

The third *juan*, which is also partly found in *j*. 6 of the *Qing'an Yingchan zi yulu* 清庵瑩蟾子語錄 (Recorded Sayings of [Li] Qing'an, Master of the Shining Toad; CT 1060), is cast in the form of answers to his disciples. Here Li defines several alchemical terms and explains basic sentences used by *neidan* or Neo-Confucian authors, taken from the *Xici* 繫辭 (Appended Statements, a portion of the *Yijing), the *Shujing* 書經 (Book of Documents), and the *Lunyu* 論語 (Analects) of Confucius. He dwells at length on the importance of the precosmic particle of light that is the *materia prima* of *neidan* as well as its final goal (see *dianhua).

Part of *j*. 4, and *j*. 5 and 6, contain songs and poems.

Li Daochun's syncretism is closely related to his inclination toward a subitist (*dun* 頓) method of teaching and learning. He repeatedly states that the only necessary thing is the Mysterious Pass, equated with the precosmic and transcendent particle of light and more important than the practices themselves. The highest degree of alchemy does not use the *Yijing* system as do many *neidan* texts (4.2b). In Li's view, the Buddhist "full awakening" (*yuanjue* 圓覺) and the Confucian Great Ultimate (*taiji) are synonyms of the Golden Elixir (*jindan).

Isabelle ROBINET

📖 Boltz J. M. 1987a, 181–82; Qing Xitai 1994, 2: 166–68; Robinet 1995a, 22–24, 45–46, 75–77, 147–64, and passim

※ Li Daochun; *neidan*

Zhongli Quan

鍾離權

Zhongli Quan, also called Han Zhongli 漢鍾離, is one of the Eight Immortals (*baxian). He is venerated in the *Quanzhen school as the second patriarch, having received the teachings from the first, Donghua dijun 東華帝君 (Imperial

Lord of Eastern Florescence; see *Wang Xuanfu). According to the *Jinlian zhengzong ji (Records of the Correct Lineage of the Golden Lotus) compiled by Qin Zhi'an 秦志安 (1188–1244), he was a man of Xianyang 咸陽 (Shaanxi) who lived during the Han dynasty. His style was Yunfang 雲房 and his appellation was Zhengyang zi 正陽子 (Master of Correct Yang). At the end of the Han dynasty he received the title of Grand Master of Remonstrance (jianyi dafu 諫議大夫), but his opinions were not well received and he was demoted. Later he served Wudi (r. 265–90) of the Western Jin and engaged in conquest as a general. Having lost a battle he fled to the mountains, and, following the directions of an old man, arrived at the palace of Donghua dijun, from whom he received talismans, texts, methods for compounding elixirs, and other techniques. Having instructed Zhongli Quan in all of them, Donghua dijun departed.

The biography goes on to recount that during the Kaicheng reign period of the Tang (836–40), Zhongli Quan taught *Lü Dongbin the fencing technique called tiandun 天遁 ("hiding in Heaven") when he met him on Mount Lu (*Lushan, Jiangxi). He then made his retreat at Mount Yangjiao (Yangjiao shan 羊角山) in Shanxi. He compiled the Zhenxian chuandao ji 真仙傳道集 (Anthology of the Authentic Immortals' Transmission of the Dao) and the *Lingbao bifa (Complete Methods of the Numinous Treasure), and transmitted them also to Lü Dongbin. Eventually he went again to Lushan, and gained immortality. At the end of the biography, Qin Zhi'an added in praise, "Five hundred years from the Han to the Tang: in all that time the only person whom Zhongli Quan liberated was Lü Dongbin. How difficult it is to bring people to liberation!" Included in the Taoist Canon is a work in the form of a dialogue between Zhongli Quan and Lü Dongbin entitled *Zhong-Lü chuandao ji (Anthology of Zhongli Quan's Transmission of the Dao to Lü Dongbin), ascribed to *Shi Jianwu (fl. 820–35). Both this work and the Lingbao bifa are concerned with *neidan.

The image of Zhongli Quan as an immortal became fixed during the Song dynasty and his popularity increased after that. For example, in the biography of Wang Laozhi 王老志 in the Songshi (History of the Song), a strange man called Zhongli xiansheng 鍾離先生 (Elder Zhongli) makes an appearance and gives an elixir to Wang. Moreover, the Xuanhe huapu 宣和畫譜 (Catalogue of Paintings of the Xuanhe Reign Period) records the existence of a picture of the "Real Man Zhongli Quan," and according to the Xuanhe shupu 宣和書譜 (Catalogue of Calligraphic Works of the Xuanhe Reign Period), there even existed an autograph copy of a verse in cursive script that Zhongli Quan presented to Wang Dingguo 王定國 in 1092. Perhaps as a result of this popularity, his name was added to those of the patriarchs of the Quanzhen school, and he also came to be counted among the Eight Immortals.

YOSHIKAWA Tadao

📖 See the bibliography for the entry *baxian

※ *baxian*; *neidan*; Nanzong; Quanzhen; Zhong-Lü; HAGIOGRAPHY

zhongmin

種民

"seed-people", chosen people, elected people

The notion of *zhongmin* or "seed-people" originated in the early *Tianshi dao movement. The Celestial Masters adepts believed in the possibility of generating perfect human beings, the "seed-children" (*zhongzi* 種子) ritually conceived during the ceremonies of "merging pneumas" (*heqi*). These sexual rites were performed by initiated adepts. Boys and girls, starting at seven years of age, were given religious instruction that enabled them to receive various registers (*LU). At intervals of a few years, they received the Registers of One, Ten, and Seventy-five Generals. The bestowal of the latter register usually marked the transition to adult age. After the age of twenty, adepts could get married by "combining their registers" (*helu* 合錄). Through the union of their respective registers, forming the One Hundred and Fifty Generals Register, they were allowed to practice the ritual of *guodu* 過度 (Passage, or Crossing), that is, the sexual rites. In this way, they gained access to the diocesan ordination.

These rites, severely criticized by Buddhist polemicists of the sixth and seventh centuries, are known to us through liturgical manuals preserved in the Taoist Canon. Two complementary works, the *Shangqing huangshu guodu yi (Liturgy of Passage of the Yellow Writ of Highest Clarity; CT 1294) and the *Dongzhen huangshu* 洞真黄書 (Yellow Writ of the Cavern of Perfection; CT 1343), in particular, give a precise description of the unfolding of the *guodu* ceremonies. These scriptures, ascribed to the first Celestial Master, *Zhang Daoling, actually date to no later than the fifth century. The first presents the whole sequence of the ritual of Passage performed in the sacred enclave, the "oratory" (*jing* 靜; see *jingshi*), where the adept couple acts under the supervision of their parish Master. The rite consists of a symbolic, choreographic sexual performance, two or three hours long, entirely codified and punctuated with recitations of incantations and prayers. The aim of these exacting mating rituals was the creation of an "embryo of immortality": adepts expected to obtain immortal bodies, and to beget a seed-child. The second text consists of a series of recipes, prescriptions, and interdictions dealing with private sexual techniques (*fangzhong shu*).

The various Taoist schools have displayed ambiguous attitudes to these early Tianshi dao techniques, sometimes called the Way of Yellow and Red (*huangchi zhi dao* 黃赤之道; yellow represents the female energies, and red the male ones). Sexual rituals underwent a rather nuanced censure by *Shangqing Taoists, who simply warned their adepts against the danger of such practices (*Zhengao* 2). During the fifth century, *Kou Qianzhi, the court Taoist reformer who was himself a Celestial Master, also expressed his worries about the popularity and vulgarization of sexual techniques, and suggested a "reform of the Yellow and the Red" aimed at "reducing the 120 methods of the arts of the bedchamber to a single and pure orthodox method" (*Laojun yinsong jiejing*, 18a–19b). However, the art of the seed-children is said to have been still performed as late as the tenth century (Yang Liansheng 1956).

The term "seed-people" was later disjoined from its sexual connotations and became a synonym of "good people" (*liangmin* 良民) or "perfect people" (*zhenmin* 真民). In this sense it appears throughout medieval Taoist scriptures, especially in the literature of apocalyptic eschatology. It generally designates virtuous people, the initiates who are promised salvation or immortality, and more specifically the chosen people who will survive the cataclysms at the end of the world. The notion of "seed" nevertheless continues to prevail: in the apocalyptic literature, the "seed-people" are obviously considered to be the basic stock who are somehow predestined to salvation and from which a new, unblemished humanity will grow. The "genetic" quality of the initiates is conferred both by their genealogical lineage and their *karma*. They have naturally inherited the virtues of their forbearers and ancestors, and, thanks to the merits gained in their own former lives, are born with "immortal bones" (*xiangu* 仙骨).

Christine MOLLIER

📖 Mollier 1990, passim; Strickmann 1981, passim; Yoshioka Yoshitoyo 1976b

※ APOCALYPTIC ESCHATOLOGY; MESSIANISM AND MILLENARIANISM

zhongxi

踵息

"breathing through the heels"

"Breathing through the heels" is first mentioned in *Zhuangzi* 6, which states that "the Real Man (*zhenren*) breathes through his heels whereas the ordinary man breathes through his throat" (see also trans. Watson 1968, 78). A study by Ishida Hidemi (1988) shows that *zhongxi* designated in antiquity one of four kinds of breathing: through the skin, through the nose and mouth, through the throat (to absorb the celestial breath), and through the heels (to absorb the earthly breath).

This original meaning evolved through the centuries. Wang Shuzhi's 王叔之 fifth-century commentary to the *Zhuangzi* mentions that "one should practice inner breathing as deeply as possible." In this context, *zhongxi* denotes the movement of Original Breath (**yuanqi*) within the body. The term also refers to the methods for regulating the breath (**tiaoqi*) found in several Tang sources. From the Song period, under the influence of **neidan*, *zhongxi* also refers to the circulation of the inner energies that descend to the heels and then rise from the *yongquan* 涌泉 point, located in the middle of the sole of the foot, to the top of the head.

Catherine DESPEUX

📖 Ishida Hidemi 1988

※ *yangsheng*

zhoutian

周天

Celestial Circuit

The term *zhoutian* denotes the continuously circular movement of the universe. In **neidan* and also in **qigong*, this term is related to a method of purification and transformation. Two main types of *zhoutian* are distinguished, namely, the Lesser Celestial Circuit (*xiao zhoutian* 小周天) and the Greater Celestial Circuit (*da zhoutian* 大周天). The main notion underlying both is that the human being is a microcosm that embodies all natural laws inherent in the macrocosm. The universe is in continuous motion, fundamentally consisting of the operation of the two complementary forces, Yin and Yang. Summer alternates with winter and day with night, but together the two forces constitute a unity, such as a year or a day. The motions of Yin and Yang taking place in definite time spans represent the order of the universe. Human beings can experience these movements within themselves. According to *neidan* texts, their ultimate aim should be restoring the universal order within to regain unity with the Dao.

The Lesser Celestial Circuit. The main purpose of the Lesser Celestial Circuit is to preserve the essence (**jing*) and transform it into energy (**qi*). This method, also known as "returning the essence to replenish the brain" (**huanjing bunao*), is performed in the first stage of the *neidan* process, the second and third being the transformation of energy into spirit (*shen*) and the transformation of spirit into emptiness (*xu* 虛).

The Control and Function Channels (*dumai* and *renmai*) and the lower Cinnabar Field (*dantian*) are the main energetic centers involved in this practice. The Control Channel is Yang, and the Function Channel is Yin. Each channel is divided into six sections, and a cyclical sign, a "double hour" (*shi* 時), and a hexagram are assigned to each section (see table 13). The hexagrams related to the Control Channel are Yang, whereas those related to the Function Channel are Yin. The time from midnight to noon is associated with the Control Channel, the time from noon to midnight with the Function Channel.

The essence is preserved and transformed into energy by making it ascend through the Control Channel along the back of the body to the top of the head and then descend through the Function Channel along the front of the body. As the essence flows through the twelve points of the two channels, it is increasingly refined. The transformed substance is collected in the lower Cinnabar Field and is then refined again. It is important to establish a closed linking of the two channels to allow the energy to flow without hindrances. Thus the unity of Yin and Yang is created within the body.

Active imagination (see *yi*) is an important aspect of this practice, which should also be performed according to a certain rhythm. This rhythm, consisting of the Martial Fire (*wuhuo* 武火) and the Civil Fire (*wenhuo* 文火), is called fire phasing (*huohou*) and in this context is also related to breathing.

The Greater Celestial Circuit. The practice of the Greater Celestial Circuit is meant to transform energy into spirit and is therefore related to the second stage of the inner alchemical work. The lower Cinnabar Field is likened to a furnace, while the middle Cinnabar Field is a crucible. The energy should circulate through the twelve channels (*jingluo*). There is no division of the channels into sections in this practice: the whole body is involved. Energy should circulate without stopping, while heart and mind dwell in absolute quiescence.

The Celestial *maoyou* Circuit (*maoyou zhoutian* 卯酉周天) is complementary to the Lesser and Greater Celestial Circuits. As its name suggests—*mao* and *you* are the two cyclical signs related to the east and west—the motion here is horizontal, while the other two circuits are characterized by the vertical motion of ascent and descent.

Neidan texts of the Ming period equate the Celestial Circuit with the Wheel of the Law (*falun* 法輪), the Buddha-truth that crushes all opposition, and stress the importance of a transition from the phenomenal world to the noumenal world.

Martina DARGA

📖 Darga 1999, 203–4 and 232–33; Despeux 1979, 57–63; Despeux 1994, 168–69; Wilhelm R. 1929, 135–37

※ *huohou*; *dumai* and *renmai*; *neidan*

Zhouyi cantong qi

周易參同契

Token for the Agreement of the Three According to the *Book of Changes*

According to the traditional account, the legendary Han immortal from Guiji 會稽 (Zhejiang), Wei Boyang 魏伯陽, wrote the *Zhouyi cantong qi* after reading the *Longhu jing (Scripture of the Dragon and Tiger). Later he transmitted it to Xu Congshi 徐從事, who appended a commentary, and to Chunyu Shutong 淳于叔通, who first circulated it in the world. While some features of this account provide significant details—especially about the reputed Han date of the text, and about its formation having taken place in stages—the received *Cantong qi* actually is not the product of a single generation of authors, but the result of several centuries of textual accretions. At the end of this process, the text rose to the status of main scripture within both the *waidan and *neidan traditions. Its primary received version, on which about two thirds of the extant commentaries are based, consists of four parts:

1. The main text, in four- or five-character sentences (mostly in rhymes)

2. A section usually entitled "The Five Categories" ("Wu xianglei" 五相類) or "Filling Lacunae" ("Busai yituo" 補塞遺脫), deemed to address matters not accounted for in the main text

3. The "Song of the Tripod" ("Dingqi ge" 鼎器歌), a poem in three-character lines

4. A "Eulogium" ("Zanxu" 讚序), not found in all recensions, which some commentators regard as a synopsis of the *Cantong qi* and others as the postface to an early commentary

More than thirty recensions of the *Cantong qi*, each with a different commentary, are extant in at least 120 editions, not including reprints. This testifies to the prestige that the work enjoyed not only within the alchemical traditions, but also among Neo-Confucian thinkers and Qing scholars.

Early history. Chunyu Shutong's relation to divination, as well as some passages in the received text, suggest that the original Han version of the *Cantong qi*

was closely related to the "weft" texts (*weishu* 緯書; see *TAOISM AND THE APOCRYPHA*). According to some scholars, the received text faithfully reproduces the original version; according to others, the original version was lost after the Han, and the received text was entirely fabricated in the early Tang period. There are reasons, however, to assume that the text was expanded during the Six Dynasties, and that no major break in transmission took place at that time. Quotations or mentions of the *Cantong qi* in works by Jiang Yan 江淹 (444–505; IC 267–68), *Tao Hongjing (456–536), and Yan Zhitui 顏之推 (531–91; IC 923–25), all of whom came from or lived in Jiangnan, show that the *Cantong qi* circulated in southeastern China after the end of the Han. It appears likely that the text was transmitted there by the lineage of the Later Han cosmologist Yu Fan 虞翻 (164–233), who also came from Guiji and whose cosmological doctrines are reflected in the *Cantong qi* (Yu Fan is attributed with a lost commentary to the text, mentioned in *Zhouyi cantong qi*, CT 999, 3.11a).

Further evidence for the circulation of the *Cantong qi* in Jiangnan during the Six Dynasties, and for the existence of a textual layer dating from that time, is provided by several dozens of terms and expressions shared with the *Huangting jing* (Scripture of the Yellow Court) and the *Laozi zhongjing* (Central Scripture of Laozi), two texts whose meditation and visualization methods are nonetheless criticized in the *Cantong qi* together with physiological practices. A poem by Jiang Yan (trans. Waley 1930–32, 8) attests, on the other hand, that the *Cantong qi* was used in association with the compounding of elixirs by 500 CE. We know nothing about the lineages that created or transmitted the alchemical version of the scripture, but one of two extant Tang *waidan* commentaries on it, the anonymous *Zhouyi cantong qi zhu* 周易參同契注 (CT 1004), appears to be related to the legacy of *Hugang zi. Dating from ca. 700 CE, this commentary—the latter half of which is lost—is contemporary with another extant Tang exegesis, entitled *Zhouyi cantong qi* (CT 999) and attributed to the immortal *Yin Changsheng. From around that time, mentions and quotations of the *Cantong qi* in other texts begin to multiply. In the mid-eighth century, moreover, *Liu Zhigu wrote his *Riyue xuanshu lun* 日月玄樞論 (Essay on the Mysterious Pivot, the Sun and Moon), which is the first of a series of short essays on the *Cantong qi* as well as the earliest firmly datable *neidan* text.

Commentaries. The exegetical tradition expanded in later times. Besides the two mentioned above, the Taoist Canon includes the following six commentaries, all related to *neidan*:

1. *Zhouyi cantong qi fenzhang tong zhenyi* 周易參同契分章通真義 (Real Meaning of the *Zhouyi cantong qi*, with a Division into Sections; CT 1002) by *Peng Xiao (?–955), dated 947. The final part of the text is separately printed in the Taoist Canon as *Zhouyi cantong qi dingqi ge mingjing tu* 周

易參同契鼎器歌明鏡圖 (The "Song of the Tripod" and the "Diagram of the Bright Mirror" of the *Zhouyi cantong qi*; CT 1003).

2. **Zhouyi cantong qi kaoyi* 周易參同契考異 (Critical Investigation of the *Zhouyi cantong qi*; CT 1001) by Zhu Xi 朱熹 (1130–1200; SB 282–90), written between the end of 1197 and the beginning of 1198.

3. *Zhouyi cantong qi* 周易參同契注 (Commentary to the *Zhouyi cantong qi*; CT 1008) by Chu Yong 儲泳 (fl. ca. 1230), whose text is based on Zhu Xi's recension.

4. *Zhouyi cantong qi zhu* (Commentary to the *Zhouyi cantong qi*; CT 1000), with an anonymous commentary written after 1208.

5. *Zhouyi cantong qi jie* 周易參同契解 (Explication of the *Zhouyi cantong qi*; CT 1007) by *Chen Xianwei (fl. 1223–54), dated 1234.

6. *Zhouyi cantong qi fahui* 周易參同契發揮 (Clarification of the *Zhouyi cantong qi*; CT 1005) by *Yu Yan (1258–1314), dated 1284. The notes, mainly philological, attached to this commentary are separately printed in the Taoist Canon as the *Zhouyi cantong qi shiyi* 周易參同契釋疑 (Exegesis of Doubtful Points in the *Zhouyi cantong qi*; CT 1006).

Other major commentaries outside the Taoist Canon include those by *Chen Zhixu (ca. 1330), *Lu Xixing (1569), and Zhu Yuanyu 朱元育 (1669). In the early sixteenth century, moreover, a new version of the scripture appeared, entitled *Guwen Zhouyi cantong qi (Ancient Text of the *Zhouyi cantong qi*), and became prominent in some *neidan* milieux. *Peng Haogu (fl. 1597–1600), *Qiu Zhao'ao (1638–1713), and *Liu Yiming (1734–1821) are among those who wrote commentaries to this version.

Role in the history of alchemy. Written in a poetical style and in a densely metaphoric and allusive language, the *Cantong qi* does not fully describe any *waidan* or *neidan* method, and only occasionally refers to actual practices related to *waidan* or *neidan*. Nevertheless, the *Cantong qi* has been the only scripture cherished within both traditions, and the influence it has exerted on their history from the Tang period onward is not matched by any other work.

The main focus of the text is the Dao and its relation to the cosmos, explicated by means of a wide array of alchemical, cosmological and other emblems. Among the main recurrent themes are the distribution of Original Pneuma (*yuanqi) from the center (the Norther Dipper, *beidou, or Heart of Heaven, *tianxin); the view of time as caused by the continuous upward and downward movement of Original Pneuma; and the joining of the essences of the Sun and Moon, or Yin and Yang, which occurs at the end of each time cycle and generates the next one. Both space and time are thus seen as essential vehicles for the circulation of the "essence" (*jing) originally issued by the Dao in the cosmos.

Borrowing from a passage in *Laozi* 38, the *Cantong qi* states that "superior virtue (*shangde* 上德) takes no action, and does not employ examining or seeking; inferior virtue (*xiade* 下德) takes action, and its operation is unceasing." Some commentators explain these sentences as referring to two ways of realization that are reflected in this work. The first, also known as "entering from Non-being into Being" (*cong wu ru you* 從無入有), is based on the immediate realization of the non-distinction of Dao and existence, Non-being and Being. In the second, also known as "using Being to enter Non-being" (*yi you ru wu* 以有入無), one attains to the Dao through the alchemical practice. While the doctrines of the *Cantong qi* apply to both approaches, the text does not focus on either *waidan* or *neidan*. The task of presenting alchemical methods based on those doctrines is left to the commentaries and to a large number of associated texts.

Fabrizio PREGADIO

📖 Bertschinger 1994 (trans. of *guwen* version); Chen Guofu 1983, 352–55; Fukui Kōjun 1974; Ho Peng Yoke 1972; Imai Usaburō 1960; Meng Naichang 1993b; Meng Naichang and Meng Qingxuan 1993; Needham 1976, 50–75; Pan Qiming 1990; Pregadio 1995; Pregadio 2002; Pregadio 2006a; Suzuki Yoshijirō 1974, 595–656; Suzuki Yoshijirō 1977 (trans.); Wang Ming 1984g; Wu and Davis 1932 (trans.); Xiao Hanming and Guo Dongsheng 2000; Zhou Shiyi 1988 (trans.)

※ *Cantong qi*; *Guwen Zhouyi cantong qi*; *jindan*; *neidan*; *waidan*

Zhouyi cantong qi kaoyi

周易參同契考異

Critical Investigation of the *Zhouyi cantong qi*

The best-known commentary to the *Zhouyi cantong qi* outside the Taoist tradition is that of Zhu Xi 朱熹 (1130–1200; SB 282–90), whose *Zhouyi cantong qi kaoyi* is the first of several works, written through the Qing period, testifying to the attention that Neo-Confucians thinkers and scholars paid to this text. Quotations in Zhu Xi's *Yixue qimeng* 易學啟蒙 (Instructing the Young in the Studies on the *Changes*; 1186) suggest that his interest in the *Cantong qi* arose in the last decades of his life. His commentary, which was almost certainly completed between the end of 1197 and the beginning of 1198, offers an interpretation that is primarily cosmological, with detailed remarks on passages related to the system of the *Yijing* and scarcely any interest in an alchemical reading of the text. However, the junctures at which Zhu Xi inserted his comments are more accurate than the divisions into *zhang* made by *Peng Xiao.

Like Peng Xiao before him, Zhu Xi does not state which recension of the *Cantong qi* served as the basis of his work. Textual comparison suggests that he relied on Peng Xiao but often accepted readings of the recension ascribed to *Yin Changsheng, which dates from around 700 CE (*Zhouyi cantong qi*; CT 999). Other sources likely to have been used by Zhu Xi include the lost commentary by Yuan Shu 袁樞 (1131–1205) to which he wrote a colophon in 1197, and two recensions that he refers to as the "Ji edition" (*Ji ben* 濟本) and the "Qiu edition" (*Qiu ben* 丘本) without further details. The *Kaoyi* was edited in the first half of the fourteenth century by Huang Ruijie 黃瑞節 (fl. 1335), who included it in his *Zhuzi chengshu* 朱子成書 (Complete Writings of Master Zhu). Huang added an undated preface and notes consisting of his own comments as well as quotations from other works by Zhu Xi. Apparently all editions of the *Kaoyi*, including the one in the Taoist Canon (CT 1001), contain Huang Ruijie's additions, and therefore ultimately derive from the *Zhuzi chengshu*.

As Zhu Xi states in a postface (3.8a), his recension was inspired by the disappointing textual state of the *Cantong qi*, resulting from alterations that had been introduced into it by earlier editors and commentators. In principle, this would make the *Kaoyi* the earliest extant exegesis based on a critical examination of different recensions of the text. In contrast with its title and with Zhu Xi's own statements, however, the commentary contains only a handful of critical notes. In other works, though, Zhu Xi points out variants and suggests emendations that are altogether ignored in the *Kaoyi*. This discrepancy suggests that an indefinite number of critical notes were expunged either by Huang Ruijie or by someone before him. An indirect confirmation of this supposition is provided by *Yu Yan, who, writing fifty years before Huang Ruijie, states that he has found it superfluous to duplicate variants already pointed out by Zhu Xi (*Zhouyi cantong qi shiyi* 周易參同契釋疑; CT 1006, preface, 3b). This remark would hardly have been necessary if the critical apparatus in the *Kaoyi* had been as exiguous as it is in the received version.

Based on quotations in later works, the *Zhouyi cantong qi kaoyi* does not seem to have enjoyed any particular prestige within the Taoist tradition, but its recension served as the basis for the commentary by Chu Yong 儲泳 (early thirteenth century), entitled *Zhouyi cantong qi* 周易參同契 (CT 1008) and preserved only in the Taoist Canon. This *neidan* work, which bears no preface or postface, is distinguished by short, straightforward annotations, and by a sentence placed at the end of almost every section to summarize its meaning. The text of the *Cantong qi* is clearly based on the *Kaoyi*. Chu Yong introduces some variants not found elsewhere, while most of the others are shared with the Yin Changsheng edition, which Chu may have consulted independently from Zhu Xi's work.

Fabrizio PREGADIO

📖 Azuma Jūji 1984; Wong Shiu Hon 1978a

※ *Zhouyi cantong qi*; TAOISM AND NEO-CONFUCIANISM

Zhu Quan

朱權

1378–1448; *hao*: Da Ming qishi 大明奇士 (Strange Gentleman of the Great Ming), Quxian 臞仙 (Gaunt Transcendent), Hanxu zi 涵虛子 (Master Who Encompasses Emptiness), Danqiu xiansheng 丹邱先生 (Elder of the Cinnabar Mound), Nanji xialing laoren 南極遐齡老人 (Long-lived Old Man of the Southern Pole)

Zhu Quan was the seventeenth son of the Hongwu Emperor Zhu Yuanzhang 朱元璋 (1328–98, r. 1368–98), born of his consort Lady Yang 楊氏. He was granted the title Prince of Ning 寧王 in 1391 and two years later was put in charge of the strategic garrison of Daning 大寧 (Liaoning). After his brother Zhu Di 朱棣 (1360–1424; DMB 355–65) succeeded in deposing their nephew, the Jianwen Emperor Zhu Yunwen 朱允炆 (r. 1399–1402), Zhu Quan was transferred to the remote post of Nanchang (Jiangxi), contrary to his preference for a coastal seat of authority. He found himself the target of slander and, to avoid further harassment, took refuge in a cabin where he could read and play his zither in peace. With fellow literati as his companions, Zhu produced several compilations ranging from treatises on agriculture, geography, and geomancy to literary criticism, history, drama, and a primer on the zither. A prolific playwright, he is known to have composed twelve *zaju* 雜劇 (variety plays), only two of which survive. Zhu established himself as an expert in this dramatic form with the authorship of the *Taihe zhengyin pu* 太和正音譜 (Formulary for Correct Tunes in Great Harmony). Among his latest works is an important encyclopedic anthology on Taoist lore entitled *★Tianhuang zhidao Taiqing yuce* (Jade Fascicles of Great Clarity on the Ultimate Way of the Celestial Sovereign).

Historical sources date Zhu's interest in Taoist studies to the last years of his life. A biography in the *Xiaoyao shan Wanshou gong zhi* 逍遙山萬壽宮志 (Monograph of the Palace of Ten-Thousand-Fold Longevity at Mount Xiaoyao; Du Jiexiang 1983, 6: 331–33) alternatively claims that he abandoned official duties for a life of reclusion spanning more than thirty years. According to this account, Zhu viewed himself as an incarnation of a transcendent named Nanji chongxu zhenjun 南極冲虛真君 (Perfected Lord of the Unfathomable Emptiness of the Southern Pole). At some undisclosed time he is said to have told his staff at Nanchang that he found noble rank to be utterly hollow and had his mind set on taking up Xiandao 仙道, or the Way of Transcendence. He further informed them that he intended to go in search of a master whom an oracle revealed had emerged in Yuzhang 豫章 (Jiangxi). Advised not to take on a long journey because of the gravity of his responsibilities, Zhu nonetheless abruptly took leave of his palatial headquarters and headed southwest down the Gan 贛 River to Yuzhang. There he lived in austerity at a retreat he constructed in the Tianbao dong 天寶洞 (Cavern of the Celestial Treasure). An unidentified old man reportedly instructed Zhu in the sublime teachings of Jingming zhongxiao dao 淨明忠孝道 (Pure and Bright Way of Loyalty and Filiality; see *Jingming dao).

Zhu repeatedly refused summons from his brother, the Yongle Emperor (r. 1403–24), in favor of pursuing a state of perfection. Among those whose company he allegedly enjoyed is the legendary *Zhang Sanfeng. The story is told that Zhu witnessed Zhang's ascent and established a Wangxian lou 望仙樓 (Pavilion for Viewing Transcendents) at the site. There he remained until the end, refusing contact with his peers the entire time. The heading "Jingming Zhu zhenren zhuan" 淨明朱真人傳 (Biography of the Perfected Zhu of the Pure and Bright [Way]) given the account of his life in the monograph on Mount Xiaoyao (Xiaoyao shan 逍遙山) indicates that late Jingming hagiographers deemed Zhu successful in his quest to join the ranks of the perfected.

Judith M. BOLTZ

📖 Idema 1986; Jonker 1976

※ *Tianhuang zhidao Taiqing yuce*; Jingming dao; TAOISM AND CHINESE THEATRE

Zhu Ziying

朱自英

976–1029; *zi*: Yingzhi 隱芝; *hao*: Guanmiao xiansheng 觀妙先生
(Elder Who Observes the Marvelous)

This Jurong 句容 (*Maoshan, Jiangsu) native was one of the most renowned court Taoists of the early Northern Song, becoming the twenty-third patriarch

in the *Shangqing tradition and claiming both Zhenzong (r. 997–1022) and
Renzong (r. 1022–63) as patrons.

After becoming a Taoist priest under Zhu Wenji 朱文吉, Zhu practiced
intensive self-cultivation with Zhang Shaoying 張紹應. As an itinerant priest,
Zhu worshipped the August Emperor of Chaotic Origin (Hunyuan huangdi 混
元皇帝) at Haozhou 亳州 (Henan), paid respects to the first Celestial Master
at Mount Qingcheng (*Qingcheng shan, Sichuan), and received instructions
in *neidan from Chen Tiejiao 陳鐵腳, all the while seeking old manuscripts
in the *Taiqing tradition to help him correct error-ridden and incomplete
Shangqing scriptures. Upon his return to Maoshan, his was given the Seal of
the Nine Ancient Lords of the Immortal Metropolis (Jiulao xiandu jun yin 九
老仙都君印), which bolstered his ritual credentials.

In 1004 Zhu was named the twenty-third patriarch in the Shangqing tradition
and summoned to Zhenzong's court. In 1023 Renzong called on him to reside
in the Palace of Brilliant Resonance (Zhaoying gong 昭應宮) and initiate his
mother, Dowager Liu (Liu taihou 劉太后). The *Zhangxian Mingsu huanghou
shou Shangqing bifa luji* 章獻明肅皇后受上清畢法錄記 (CT 777), dated to
1024, recorded the event, and prompted Renzong to give Zhu the title Elder
Who Observes the Marvelous (Guanmiao xiansheng). Zhu's preface to the
Shangqing dadong zhenjing 上清大洞真經 (Authentic Scripture of the Great
Cavern of the Highest Clarity; CT 6; see *Dadong zhenjing) is also extant. Little
is known of his remaining years at Maoshan.

Lowell SKAR

📖 Boltz J. M. 1987a, 205

※ Shangqing

Zhuang-Lin xu daozang

莊林續道藏

Supplementary Taoist Canon of
Zhuang[-Chen Dengyun] and Lin [Rumei]

The *Zhuang-Lin xu daozang* is a 25-volume anthology of photographically reproduced texts of Taoist ritual collected by Michael R. Saso (Taipei: Chengwen,
1975). The table of contents follows a 33-page English-language introduction
by Saso, outlining the history and content of this diverse body of texts. After
completing a Master's degree at Yale University in 1964, Saso made a pilgrimage
to Taiwan where he became a disciple of Zhuang-Chen Dengyun 莊陳登雲

(1911–76) in the northern city of Xinzhu 新竹. Master Zhuang was heir to the so-called Black-head (*wutou* 烏頭; see **hongtou* and *wutou*) fraternity of the Zhengyi sitan 正一嗣壇 (Hereditary Altar of Orthodox Unity) established in 1888 by Lin Rumei 林汝梅 (?–1894), following his ordination at the **Zhengyi* headquarters on Mount Longhu (**Longhu shan*, Jiangxi). Chen Jiesan 陳捷三 (1861–1901), many of whose manuscripts are published here, succeeded Lin as head of the fraternity. The title of the collection reflects the ultimate transmission of the fraternity's leadership from Lin to Zhuang.

A total of 104 titles are arranged under four headings. Fifty texts categorized as *Jinlu* 金籙 (Golden Register; see **jinlu zhai*) are used for Offering rituals (**jiao*). Nineteen texts categorized as *Huanglu* 黃籙 (Yellow Register; see **huanglu zhai*) are applied in mourning services. Ten texts categorized as *Wenjian fuzhou mijue* 文檢符咒祕訣 (Secret Instructions on Writing Models, Talismans, and Spells) include exemplars of ritual communiqués and privately transmitted manuals of incantation, as well as a volume with *gongche* 工尺 musical notation. Twenty-five texts categorized as *Lüshan Shenxiao xiaofa* 閭山神霄小法 (Minor Rites of the Divine Empyrean at Mount Lü) are largely devised for various exorcistic rituals. The first three categories are considered the primary resources of the Black-head fraternity. All but the last six titles in the fourth category of texts also fall within their repertoire. Adherents to branches of the **Shenxiao* school, popularly known as Red-head (*hongtou* 紅頭) Taoists, are said to use only those texts in the fourth category.

Judith M. BOLTZ

📖 Saso 1978b; Saso 1979; Saso 1989

※ DAOZANG AND SUBSIDIARY COMPILATIONS

Zhuangzi

莊 子

Book of Master Zhuang

The *Zhuangzi*, also known as *Nanhua zhenjing* 南華真經 or *Authentic Scripture of Southern Florescence*, goes back to Zhuang Zhou 莊周 (Zhuangzi), a Taoistic thinker of the fourth century BCE (?–290) who lived in the southern part of China and had various contacts but little official relation with the aristocracy of his time. As we have it today, the text consists of thirty-three chapters divided into three groups: Inner Chapters (*neipian* 內篇; chapters 1–7), Outer Chapters (*waipian* 外篇; 8–22), and Miscellaneous Chapters (*zapian* 雜篇; 23–33). While the final chapter is considered a sort of postface appended by later (probably Han-dynasty) editors, the Inner Chapters are those associated primarily with Zhuangzi himself. In addition, a good portion of the later chapters (16–27) can also be associated with his ideas and was probably compiled by his direct followers. Beyond that, the text contains materials of three other early Taoist schools, identified by A. C. Graham (1980) as follows: the primitivists (chapters 8–10, some of 11), the syncretists (11–15), and the hedonists or followers of Yang Zhu 楊朱 (28–31).

Most of the text was compiled after the death of Zhuang Zhou, and scholars today debate how much of it existed around 250 BCE, some saying all (Liu Xiaogan 1994), others saying hardly any (Graham 1980, Roth 1991b). Whichever the case, there is little doubt that the *Zhuangzi* under the Han was about one third longer than it is today, consisting of fifty-two chapters that were only edited down by *Guo Xiang, the text's main commentator of the third century CE. In a postface lost in China but recovered from the Kōzan-ji 高山寺 monastery in Kyoto (Japan), he describes his editorial efforts, mentioning that he eliminated large portions of the text mainly dealing with popular superstitions, dream interpretations, shamanic practices, and the like (Knaul 1982).

Taoist thought in the Zhuangzi. The ideas of Master Zhuang himself can be described as a continuation of the thought of the *Daode jing* with certain major developments. In contrast to the *Daode jing*, Zhuangzi is not concerned with society but finds the individual mind of central importance. He thoroughly rejects involvement with government and reinterprets non-action (*wuwei) as a mental state to be realized by the individual instead of as a political doctrine. In this his view is similar to the later Chan Buddhist idea of no-mind (*wuxin* 無心) and anticipates the notion of oblivion (see *zuowang). Moreover, Zhuangzi does not see history and moral development as key factors but insists that the Golden Age of the past is gone once and for all, the sages of old being only dust and bones. Instead of trying to recover what is gone, one should rather look forward, enjoy life as long as it lasts in "free and easy wandering" (*xiaoyao* 逍遙; see *yuanyou), by going along with the changes and transformations of the world in as much of a realization of spontaneity (*ziran) as one can manage.

The primitivists, in contrast, continue the notions of the *Daode jing* directly. They want to abolish all government and official morality; return to small, independent, and isolated communities; do away with all distant trade, luxury goods, elaborate clothes, fancy music, and so forth; and embrace a reclusive idea of tranquil isolation. Next, the syncretists combine Laozi's ideas with the *Yijing philosophy of change and with the doctrine of Yin and Yang and the *wuxing. They propose a concept of organic, cyclical harmony of the universe, which is valid not only for the rhythmical changes of nature but can also be realized in social structures and interactions. They are the forerunners of *Huang-Lao, the dominant Taoist school of the Han.

The hedonists, finally, believe "what is good for me is good for the universe." For them, universal harmony is best attained when everybody is satisfying all of his or her wishes and desires, because all these wishes and desires are an organic part of nature and the Dao to begin with. Any form of denial, rejection, or suppression of emotional or physical wishes thus constitutes a breach of natural harmony and has to be avoided. The hedonists can be described as the forerunners of some immortals (*xianren) of later ages.

Many commentaries to the *Zhuangzi* are contained in the Taoist Canon, the most important of which are the following:

1. Guo Xiang's interpretation and edition, *Nanhua zhenjing zhushu* 南華真經注疏 (Commentary and Subcommentary to the *Nanhua zhenjing*; CT 745), which formed the image of the text not only in Taoist circles but in China as a whole.

2. *Cheng Xuanying's (fl. 631–50) reading (found in the above text together with Guo Xiang's commentary) under strong Buddhist influence and within the school of Twofold Mystery (*Chongxuan).

3. Lin Xiyi's 林希逸 (fl. 1235) textual glosses on terms and expressions, *Nanhua zhenjing kouyi* 南華真經口義 (Glosses to the *Nanhua zhenjing*; CT 735).

4. The "chapter and verse" commentary by *Chen Jingyuan (?–1094), *Nanhua zhenjing zhangju yinyi* 南華真經章句音義 (Phonetic and Semantic Glosses to the Sections and Sentences of the *Nanhua zhenjing*; CT 736) and *Nanhua zhenjing zhangju yushi* 南華真經章句餘事 (Supplement to the Phonetic and Semantic Glosses to the Sections and Sentences of the *Nanhua zhenjing*; CT 737).

5. The integrated collection of numerous interpretations by Jiao Hong 焦竑 (1541–1620) in his *Zhuangzi yi* 莊子翼 (Wings to the *Zhuangzi*; CT 1487).

In style, narrative content, and technical terminology, the *Zhuangzi* is not only a key document of early Taoism but also the first collection of Chinese prose fiction. Its many fables, parables, and dialogues form an important part of the Chinese literary repertory. In the middle ages, moreover, the text had a great impact not only on poets and writers, such as the Seven Sages of the Bamboo Grove (see *Xi Kang), but also on both the diction and visions of *Shangqing Taoism.

Livia KOHN

📖 Allinson 1989; Fung Yu-lan 1952–53, 1: 221–45; Graham 1969–70; Graham 1980; Graham 1981 (part. trans.); Kohn 1992a, 52–58, 69–80; Liu Xiaogan 1994; Mair 1983a; Mair 1983b; Mair 1994 (trans.); Mair 2000; Pastor 1990 (part. trans.);

Robinet 1983a; Robinet 1996b; Robinet 1997b, 30–35; Roth 1991b; Roth 1993; Watson 1968 (trans.); Watson 1987; Wilhelm H. 1983

※ TAOISM AND EARLY CHINESE THOUGHT

Zhubing yuanhou lun

諸病源候論

Treatise on the Origin and Symptoms of Diseases

The *Zhubing yuanhou lun*, presented in 610 to Sui Yangdi (r. 604–17), was compiled on imperial decree by a committee of physicians and literati under the auspices of Chao Yuanfang 巢元方 (or, according to some sources, Wu Jingxian 吳景賢). It is the first compilation on Chinese nosology and contains a detailed description of over 1,700 different syndromes (*hou* 候) in fifty *juan*. Even today, clinicians consider it to contain up-to-date information for medical practice, though it records in parts rather fabulous accounts of illness events. In Chinese medical history, it only gained significance during the Song period, where it belonged among the canons of secondary importance. It is however frequently cited in the *Shengji zonglu* 聖濟宗錄 (General Record of Sagely Benefaction; 1117), the Japanese **Ishinpō* (Methods from the Heart of Medicine; 984), and the Korean *Ŭibang yuch'wi* 醫方類聚 (Classified Collection of Medical Methods; 1477). Its Northern Song recension is now lost and the oldest extant ones date to the Yuan period.

The book is remarkable for its extensive reference to the art of Nourishing Inner Nature (*yangxing* 養性), which is the most frequently recommended therapeutic prescription. It contains over one hundred citations from a work now lost, the *Yangsheng lun* 養生論 (Essay on Nourishing Life), forty-one of which can be traced to the **Yangsheng yaoji* (Essentials of Nourishing Life), which may have been the main textbook on **daoyin* (gymnastics) during the Six Dynasties. About seventy of the cited techniques are already given in the *Daoyin jing* 導引經 (Scripture of *daoyin*; fourth century?). Further citations are from the *Daolin lun* 道林論 (An Essay by Daolin; i.e., Zhi Dun 支盾, 314–66) and the **Yangxing yanming lu* (On Nourishing Inner Nature and Extending Life). The book indicates as its sources, furthermore, the *Shennong bencao jing* 神農本草經 (Canonical Pharmacopoeia of the Divine Husbandman), the *Xiaopin fang* 小品方 (Lesser Medical Recipes) by Chen Yanzhi 陳延之 of the Jin, a work by Zhang Zhongjing 張仲景 (ca. 150–220) with recipes now recorded in the *Jingui yaolüe* 金匱要略 (Abridged Essentials from the Golden Casket), and Huangfu Mi 皇甫謐 (215–82), the author of the *Zhenjiu jiayi jing*

針灸甲乙經 (Systematic Scripture of Acupuncture and Moxibustion). Finally, it contains many more unacknowledged citations taken from the *Huangdi neijing, the Maijing 脈經 (Scripture on the Pulse), and the Shanghan lun 傷寒論 (Treatise on Cold Damage Disorders).

Elisabeth HSU

📖 Despeux 1989; Despeux and Obringer 1997, 61–104; Ma Jixing 1990, 142–44; Unschuld 1985, 176 and 296–302

※ *daoyin*

zi

子

Zi is the first of the twelve Earthly Branches (*dizhi* 地支; see *ganzhi). Among the directions, it indicates due north, in contrast to *wu* 午 which stands for due south. As a division of time, within the day it indicates the "double hour" (*shi* 時) between 11 p.m. and 1 a.m., and within the yearly cycle it indicates the winter solstice, in contrast to *wu* which stands for the summer solstice. Thus *zi* is the point where the sun, representing the Yang principle, begins to rise. After the sun reaches its zenith in midsummer at *wu*, it begins its declining phase and gives rise to Yin. In the *Yijing, the winter solstice (*zi*) corresponds to the hexagram *fu* 復 ䷗ (Return, no. 24) and the summer solstice (*wu*) corresponds to the hexagram *gou* 姤 ䷫ (Encounter, no. 44).

In *neidan, the rise of Yang at the winter solstice is replicated in the microcosm of the human body, and *zi* represents the time when the elixir germinates. The use of *zi* to denote time, however, is not limited to the season of the winter solstice or the hours of the day: *neidan* also refers to the "time of the living *zi*" (*huozi shi* 活子時), which is the timeless moment when Yang arises and the elixir is generated.

MIURA Kunio

📖 Robinet 1995a, 107–11

※ *ganzhi*; COSMOLOGY

ziran

自然

"so of its own"; spontaneous, spontaneity

As an adjective, the term *ziran* means "spontaneous," "natural," "so of its own," "so of itself." As a noun, it denotes spontaneity, naturalness, the things as they are. It is a synonym of *zizai* 自在 (self-existent) and *ziyou* 自有 (self-produced), and is very close in meaning to *zide* 自得 (self-attaining) and *ziwei* 自為 (working by itself, doing spontaneously).

Ziran implies a free working; it is the positive side of the Dao, whose negative side is **wu* (no-thing). On the one hand, *wu* is the indeterminate and unknowable Dao, which is lost if it is given a name or an attribute: it is the Origin of life as it cannot be grasped and has no beginning. On the other hand, *ziran* is the Dao as producing life, its **de* (virtue), and is sometimes equated with the Original Pneuma (**yuanqi*). In this sense, *ziran* is like the water of a spring that never ceases to flow anew, and is a synonym of Origin (*yuan* 元) and Chaos (**hundun*). It is the permanence of the Dao and its *de*, the rule of Heaven and Earth that has no beginning and penetrates to the utmost of existence beyond the Void (*Zongxuan xiansheng xuangang lun* 宗玄先生玄網論; CT 1052, 1a–b). Hence *ziran*, as a quality ascribed to something, means "true" and "primal," and denotes transcendence.

On the cosmological level, *ziran* defines the way the world goes on by itself without anyone "doing" it, and expresses the faith in a world well-ordered and self-regulated in a natural way. Epistemologically, it means that we do not know what is producing life or how life is achieved. *Ziran* is then the ultimate word, not in the sense of an explication but as an expression of human ignorance and respect of the secret of life. As *Daode jing* 25 says, "The Dao models itself on *ziran*," which means that it "models itself on what is so of its own," which is a tautology. *Ziran* can therefore also be an expression of agnosticism, as in **Guo Xiang's* commentary to the **Zhuangzi*. Under Buddhist influence, *ziran* also took on the meaning of "non-substantial," "fundamentally having no nature of its own," as opposed to what has cause and effect. In this sense, it is a synonym of "real emptiness" (*zhenkong* 真空; see for instance **Daojiao yishu*, 8.4a, and **Zhonghe ji*, 3.14a).

In human beings, *ziran* means being free from dependence on some other thing or substance (*wudai* 無待, as the *Zhuangzi* says), being natural (*tian* 天, the contrary of "made by man" or *wei* 偽, which is the artificial in *Zhuangzi's* terms), and being creative. It means that each being has its own spring of life within itself. So to be *ziran* is to be natural in the highest sense, to nourish within oneself one's own nature that is one's own profound and true sprout of life.

To respect *ziran* one should not interfere (*wuwei*), and gently let life act and speak through oneself rather than acting and speaking individually. In that sense, *ziran* is the principle of handling affairs that guides the saint (*shengren*) or the sage king who respects the workings of the Dao in the world and in human affairs. To act spontaneously is to have no intention of one's own, to let the natural force that is within everything work freely. This is not the same as giving free rein to one's own fantasy (as the term has been misunderstood by some *Xuanxue thinkers), because this fantasy is a only superficial desire to satisfy one's immediate wishes, and not the profound naturalness without desires that is *ziran*.

Isabelle ROBINET

📖 Liu Xiaogan 1998; Murakami Yoshimi 1965; Muroya Kuniyuki 1988, 16–31; Qing Xitai 1994, 2: 264–68; Wang Deyou 1995; Wang Zhongjiang 1995

※ *bianhua*; Dao; *zaohua*

Ziyang zhenren

紫陽真人

Real Man of Purple Yang

The Real Man of Purple Yang is Zhou Yishan 周義山, who bestowed the *Shangqing revelations on *Yang Xi with other spiritual beings. His biography, entitled *Ziyang zhenren neizhuan* 紫陽真人內傳 (Inner Biography of the Real Man of Purple Yang), was allegedly dictated by Zhou himself to Hua Qiao 華僑, who had received a visit from both this immortal and Peijun 裴君 (Lord Pei). Two versions of the biography survive in the Taoist Canon, but both differ from the original one: the version in the *Yunji qiqian* (106.8a–15b) may be an abridgement of the original one, or vice versa, the independent version in the Taoist Canon (CT 303), dated 399, may be an enlargement.

According to the biography, Zhou was born in 80 BCE. As a young man he was very virtuous and liked to climb mountains and absorb the Sun's light. Then he became a disciple of *Su Lin, who gave him alchemical and dietetic recipes to expel the Three Corpses (*sanshi*; see *sanshi and *jiuchong*). After this, he spent several years searching for the method of the Three Ones (*sanyi*), going to sacred mountains, and visiting their grottoes and immortals to receive teachings and texts. He finally discovered the method he was looking for within himself and devoted himself to its practice.

The *Ziyang zhenren neizhuan* is closely related to Su Lin's hagiography, the *Suling jing*, and the methods of the Three Ones and the *dongfang* 洞房 (the Cavern Chamber located in the brain). Like other Shangqing "esoteric" (*nei* 內) hagiographies, which are addressed to adepts, it has two main purposes: recounting the initiatory quest of the saint, and tracing his lineage. Accordingly, it contains a list of texts and methods received and practiced by Zhou, and establishes a hierarchy among various immortals and secret scriptures. The list of texts is similar to the one found in *Wei Huacun's biography. The independent version (CT 303) contains poems dating from no later than the sixth century that apparently correspond to part of the *Basu yinyang ge* 八素陰陽歌 (Song on Yin and Yang of the Eight Pure Ladies) of the Shangqing revelation. The details on Hua Qiao found in the preface are close to those given in the *Zhengao (20.13b–14a), and the appended commentary is reminiscent of Su Lin's biography. Some features, like the connection with the *Suling jing*, seem to indicate that the biography pertains to a group of texts slightly later than the original Shangqing revelation, which attempt to arrange Taoists texts in three hierarchical classes.

Isabelle ROBINET

📖 Chen Guofu 1963, 8–9; Ōfuchi Ninji and Ishii Masako 1988, 30–33 (list of texts cited); Porkert 1979; Robinet 1981; Robinet 1984, 2: 385–88

※ Shangqing; HAGIOGRAPHY

Zuo Ci

左慈

zi: Yuanfang 元放

Several sources mention Zuo Ci as a *fangshi (master of methods) who lived between the end of the Han and the beginning of the Six Dynasties. The details of his historical existence, however, are far from reliable, and he is an example of the process by which different early traditions ascribe their origins and teachings to a supposed beginner, turning him into a divine or semidivine being. The increment of these legendary traits runs parallel to the development of the traditions that devise them, and is often visible in the physical expansion of the relevant hagiographic accounts.

The main early accounts of Zuo Ci are in found the *Hou Hanshu* (History of the Later Han, 82B.2747–48; trans. Ngo 1976, 138–39) and in the *Shenxian zhuan (Biographies of Divine Immortals; trans. Campany 2002, 279–86). According to both sources, Zuo Ci was born in Lujiang 廬江 (Anhui). The story in the *Hou Hanshu* tells of his feats of magic and his ability to appear in several places at once, undergo metamorphosis (in particular, into a sheep), and disappear altogether. The *Shenxian zhuan* adds to this the knowledge of the *liujia* system of divination (see *liujia and *liuding*), the power of summoning the "movable cuisines" (*xingchu* 行廚; see *chu), and the practice of alchemy. Other early references to Zuo Ci are in *Ge Hong's *Baopu zi*, which associates Zuo Ci with abstention from cereals (*bigu*), enchantments by breath (*jinjia* 禁架; see Ngo 1976, 200–201), and the practice of guarding the One (*shouyi).

Ge Hong, moreover, places Zuo Ci at the beginning of the *Taiqing tradition of *waidan*, stating that at the end of the Han, Zuo had received the main scriptures of that tradition from a "divine person" (*shenren) on Mount Tianzhu (Tianzhu shan 天柱山, Anhui; Ware 1966, 69–70). Zuo brought those scriptures to Jiangnan 江南 and transmitted them to Ge Hong's granduncle, *Ge Xuan, who then gave them to Ge Hong's master, *Zheng Yin. Several other sources mention or allude to this story, sometimes adding new elements. Those mentioned in *Tao Hongjing's *Zhengao (11.10a and 12.3b) reflect the development of the religious history of Jiangnan. According to Tao Hongjing, Zuo Ci had ingested the Elixir of the Nine Efflorescences (*jiuhua dan* 九華 丹, a synonym of the Elixir of Great Clarity or *taiqing dan* 太清丹), had lived on Mount Mao (*Maoshan, the early seat of the *Shangqing school), and had received teachings from Li Zhongfu 李仲甫, a disciple of one of the main Shangqing saints, *Wang Yuan.

Despite these credentials, Tao ranks Zuo Ci at a low level in the hierarchy of the immortals in both the *Zhengao* and the *Zhenling weiye tu (Chart of the Ranks and Functions of the Real Numinous Beings; 19a). Similarly, the *Wushang biyao (Supreme Secret Essentials; 84.13a), states that Zuo Ci now dwells in the Taiqing heaven, the lowest of the *sanqing or Three Clarities. Thus Zuo Ci typifies the integration of different elements and trends: the early local traditions of Jiangnan, the alchemical Taiqing tradition, and the absorption of those traditions into the new religious scene created by the founding of new Taoist lineages in the same area from the latter half of the fourth century.

Fabrizio PREGADIO

📖 Campany 2002, 279–86; Chen Guofu 1963, 90–95; DeWoskin 1983, 83–86; Kohn 1993b, 296–99; Ngo 1976, 138–39 and passim; Robinet 1984, 1: 9–24 passim

※ *fangshi*; *waidan*; Taiqing; HAGIOGRAPHY

zuobo

坐鉢

"sitting around the bowl"

Zuobo, "sitting (in meditation) around the (clepsydra-)bowl," is a collective meditation practice that originated in *Quanzhen communities at the very end of the thirteenth century and was practiced in Taoist monasteries until the Qing dynasty. Although few texts are devoted to this exercise, its continued presence can be traced in gazetteers and epigraphic sources through the mention of *botang* 鉢堂, the meditation hall, and *bozhu* 鉢主, the Taoist master who conducts the retreats "around the bowl."

A text in the *Daozang*, the *Quanzhen zuobo jiefa* 全真坐鉢捷法 (Short Method for the Bowl-Meditation of Quanzhen; CT 1229), describes the construction of the object, actually made of two bowls: a large one filled with water, and a smaller one with a hole in its center, which floats on the surface of the water. The pierced bowl slowly sinks, and the system is contrived so that it takes one *shi* 時 (double hour) to reach the bottom. Another description adds bells that ring when the smaller bowl is filled with water. This ingenious system, which actually had already been described in a Tang text, is hailed as more reliable than the incense or the outflow clepsydra commonly used for time measurement in Buddhist and Taoist communities. The technical aspect, however, is but a small part of the story. Several texts on the *zuobo* meditation stress the symbolic importance of the bowl in *neidan terms; the character *bo* itself is made of the "metal" and "wood" elements, and their meeting allows the water to spring upward. The bowl therefore provides for a precise appreciation of time—a crucial element in *neidan*—but also allows the adepts to see a representation of the processes taking place within their own bodies. In this regard, the *zuobo* appears very Taoist and rather different from the Buddhist *zuochan* 坐禪 ("sitting in meditation"; Jap.: *zazen*), with which it has obvious formal links.

The originality of the *zuobo* practice is as the first communal procedure for *neidan* meditation, which had been until then mainly conducted on an individual basis. At least during the golden age of Quanzhen communities in the fourteenth century, meditation around the bowl took place during the hundred-days retreats, the most important of which lasted from the first day of the tenth lunar month to the tenth day of the first lunar month. This specific period seems to have evolved from the retreat in the *huandu, which was often conducted on the same dates. The most precise description of the procedure is found in the early Ming encyclopedia *Tianhuang zhidao Taiqing yuce (Jade

Fascicles of Great Clarity on the Ultimate Way of the Celestial Sovereign), and the ritualized setting and sounds used to discipline the group of adepts are similar to those used in *zuochan*.

Botang were built in many larger monasteries, usually to accommodate the travelling monks who would typically spend the winter in a *zuobo* retreat, and then depart for other destinations. These occasions were an important element in the education of Taoist adepts (especially but not only those belonging to the Quanzhen order), and their role in fashioning a common identity is stressed in monastic codes such as the *Quanzhen qinggui* 全真清規 (Rules of Purity of Quanzhen; fourteenth century; CT 1235).

Vincent GOOSSAERT

📖 Boltz J. M. 1987a, 239; Goossaert 1997, 220–58

※ *huandu*; Quanzhen; MEDITATION AND VISUALIZATION

zuodao

左道

"left ways"

Also called *xiejiao* 邪教 (perverse teachings) and *yiduan* 異端 (heresy, heterodoxy), the so-called "left ways" include several types of magical practices that were regarded as dangerous by the central or provincial governments, or from the standpoint of orthodox teachings. A common criticism of the authorities against individuals and organizations that used such practices was that "the people are being led astray by the 'left ways.'"

The term first appears in the *Liji* 禮記 (Records of Rites): "The death penalty will be exacted for those who throw rule into disorder by employing the 'left ways'" (see trans. Legge 1885, 1: 237). Here, according to a commentary by Zheng Xuan 鄭玄 (127–200), *zuodao* refers specifically to *wugu* 巫蠱 (using magic to inflict injury) and *sujin* 俗禁 (lit., "secular enchantments"). In answer to why the character for "left" was used, Kong Yingda's 孔穎達 (574–648) subcommentary to Zheng's commentary says: "The 'left ways' refer to heretical teachings. The Way of the Earth (*didao* 地道) reveres the right and ranks it high. Therefore correct teachings are termed 'right' and incorrect teachings are termed 'left.'"

Some early Taoist movements were regarded as *zuodao*. Zhang Jue 張角, who promoted the Way of Great Peace (Taiping dao 太平道) in the second century, was described as a practitioner of "sorcery" (*yaoshu* 妖術) and as a "wizard bandit" (*yaozei* 妖賊), like the leaders of other religious rebellions that broke out around his time. Once Taoism became accepted by the state and its teachings were more systematized, attacks on it as *zuodao* by the authorities ceased and attention shifted to doctrinal conflicts in which Taoists sought to assert the superiority of their tradition over Confucianism and Buddhism, in the fight for hegemony among the Three Teachings. In early modern times, the authorities often branded new religious movements and popular cults that were felt to be dangerous as *zuodao*. In the Ming and Qing legal codes, in particular, severe punishment was prescribed for "the arts of the left ways that corrupt the right ways," such as summoning evil deities, writing talismans, and practicing planchette writing (*fuji*).

MIURA Kunio

※ MAGIC

zuowang

坐忘

"sitting in oblivion"

The term *zuowang* designates a state of deep trance or intense absorption, during which no trace of ego-identity is felt and only the underlying cosmic current of the Dao is perceived as real. The classical passage describing the state occurs in *Zhuangzi* 6: "I smash up my limbs and body, drive out perception and intellect, cast off form, do away with understanding, and make myself identical with the Great Thoroughfare (*datong* 大通)" (trans. Watson 1968, 90). This passage presents a mental state of complete unknowing, of loss of personal identity and self, and a kind of total immersion in the Non-being of the universe.

The passage was interpreted in the late third century by the commentator *Guo Xiang, who says:

> In a state of sitting in oblivion, what could there be unforgotten? First one forgets all outer manifestations (*ji* 迹), then one also forgets that which causes the manifestations. On the inside, one is unaware that there is a self (*shen* 身), on the outside one never knows that there is heaven and earth. Thus one becomes utterly empty and can unite with the changes, leaving nothing unpervaded. (*Nanhua zhenjing zhushu* 南華真經注疏; CT 745, 8.39b)

This adds the philosophical distinction, first made by *Xuanxue (Arcane Learning) thinkers, between the "traces" or "outer manifestations" (reality as it appears to the senses) and that which causes them (the underlying ground of Being). In addition, Guo Xiang interprets the attained state of oneness as one of going along with the changes, adding an ecstatic element of transformation to the basically enstatic notion of oblivion.

At the beginning of the Tang, the notion of oblivion was adopted by the *Chongxuan (Twofold Mystery) thinkers. Here *Cheng Xuanying, another commentator on the *Zhuangzi*, links it with Jizang's 吉藏 (549–623) theory of two truths and develops a Madhyamaka-like pattern of twofold forgetfulness (*jianwang* 兼忘). First one forgets the outer reality (Being), then one forgets its underlying ground (Non-being). Once beyond these two, one reaches a state of both Being and Non-being, which, once again obliterated, becomes one of neither Being nor Non-being, a state of perception that neither accepts nor negates, and is sensorially aware yet utterly pure.

In the eighth century, finally, *zuowang* is the key expression in a work by *Sima Chengzhen, the *Zuowang lun* (Essay on Sitting in Oblivion), which not only takes up all previous interpretations of the term but adds to them a series of seven steps of attainment. These go from basic faith in the Dao and renunciation of the world to full attainment of mystical union. In this way, "sitting in oblivion" comes to mean both the ultimate purified state of no-mind and the process of meditative and mystical attainment as a whole.

Livia KOHN

📖 Kohn 1987a; Qing Xitai 1994, 2: 309–11

※ *Zuowang lun*; MEDITATION AND VISUALIZATION

Zuowang lun

坐忘論

Essay on Sitting in Oblivion

The *Zuowang lun* is a work by the twelfth *Shangqing patriarch, *Sima Chengzhen (647–735). The text has survived in two editions, of which the one in the *Yunji qiqian* (j. 94), also found in the *Quan Tang wen* 全唐文 (Complete Prose of the Tang, j. 924), appears to be later than the one found independently in the Taoist Canon (CT 1036). In addition, an inscription entitled *Zuowang lun* was engraved in 829 and erected in Jiyuan 濟源 on Mount Wangwu (*Wangwu shan, Henan), where Sima spent the latter part of his life.

The inscription suggests that the text was put together by disciples of Sima on the basis of Sima's lectures to aspiring students. Written by the Taoists Liu Ningran 柳凝然 and Zhao Jingyuan 趙景元, it was displayed on the mountain, where it was still seen by Gu Xieguang 顧燮光 during the Ming period. Its contents, however, apparently go back to the earlier part of Sima's life, when he taught on Mount Tongbo (Tongbo shan 桐柏山, Zhejiang). His teachings seem to have been orally transmitted to his disciples, and a certain Mr. Xu 徐, of whom nothing else is known, then brought the materials to Mount Wangwu. The text of the inscription contains many phrases and quotations also found in the *Zuowang lun* proper, and matches its basic outline of Taoist progress and essential practice. In addition, it bears a close relationship to the *Cunshen lianqi ming* and the *Dingguan jing*, which appear as appendixes to the *Zuowang lun* in the Taoist Canon.

The text in either of its versions outlines the practitioner's gradual progress toward the Dao in seven steps: 1. "Respect and Faith" ("Jingxin" 敬信); 2. "Interception of *karma*" ("Duanyuan" 斷緣); 3. "Restraining the Mind" ("Shouxin" 收心); 4. "Detachment from Affairs" ("Jianshi" 簡事); 5. "True Observation" ("Zhenguan" 真觀); 6. "Intense Concentration" ("Taiding" 泰定); 7. "Realizing the Dao" ("Dedao" 得道). Sima Chengzhen encourages aspiring Taoists first to develop a firm trust and strong faith in the Dao, never doubting that it is possible to leave the shackles of this world behind and become immortal. Next the training necessitates the physical departure from the ordinary world, giving up worldly involvements and affairs and thus avoiding the creation of new *karma* (*yuan* 緣) that would keep one away from the Dao. Third, the first steps of meditation are undertaken in a secluded mountain setting, in an effort of mental concentration, gathering one's thoughts, and achieving an emptiness and one-pointedness of mind. With the mind thus under full control, disciples can become detached from the world even in their thinking, no longer worrying about affairs and seeing their lives and destinies as part of a larger pattern of the Dao rather than the center of their particular universe.

The last three steps bring about the complete transformation of personality and eventually also body into those of a being of the Dao. First, through "true observation" one's life is viewed as a manifestation of the energy of the Dao; attachments to self, life, and body are loosened, and all critical evaluations of the world and its objects are eliminated. Next, in "intense concentration" the mind is completely submerged in the deep, dark streams of the Dao, absorbed in an engulfing trance that eliminates any remaining traces of ego-identity. Finally, the Dao is realized in an ecstatic going-beyond of all, and physical longevity and spiritual immortality are reached in the free and easy ascent to heaven and the pure realm of the Dao. The realization of the final state is a form of mystical union with the Dao, its ultimate culmination in the ascent to heaven representing a particularly Taoist vision of eternal life in paradise among the gods.

Livia KOHN

📖 Kamitsuka Yoshiko 1982; Kohn 1987a, 119–24 (trans.); Kohn 1993b, 235–41 (part. trans); Qing Xitai 1994, 2: 141–43; Wu Shouqu 1981 (crit. ed.)

※ Sima Chengzhen; *zuowang*; MEDITATION AND VISUALIZATION

Appendix
Reference Works for Taoist Studies

Fabrizio Pregadio

This appendix contains a brief bibliographic survey of the main reference works for Taoist studies. With few exceptions, it does not list studies on specific topics, which may be found in the bibliographies appended to the entries of this book. Asterisks mark items that have an independent entry in the book. For ease of reference, full bibliographic data are provided for all studies mentioned below, even when they are also cited in the general bibliography at the end of the volume.

1. General Bibliography

1A. GENERAL STUDIES OF TAOISM

The modern study of Taoism began after the mid-1920s, when a publisher in Shanghai reprinted the entire Ming-dynasty Taoist Canon (*Zhengtong daozang*; see below, sec. 2b). Until then, scholarly knowledge of Taoism outside China—and, to a large extent, within China as well—was virtually limited to the major texts on Taoist thought. In 1949, Chen Guofu published his survey of the Canon (reprinted with several appendixes in 1963), which may be considered as the first extensive scholarly study of Taoism in Chinese. At approximately the same time, the French scholar Henri Maspero worked on the Canon in Paris and produced several ground-breaking studies until his death in 1945 (republished in Maspero 1971). Maspero's legacy was expanded by Max Kaltenmark and other scholars based in France during the 1960s and 1970s, including Kristofer Schipper, Anna Seidel, and Isabelle Robinet. In Japan, Yoshioka Yoshitoyo, Fukui Kōjun, and Ōfuchi Ninji were among the scholars who produced major studies on Taoism during the 1950s and 1960s (for their works see below, sec. 2a).

Compared to other fields—in particular, Buddhist studies—the study of Taoism is therefore a relatively young area of research. The field has grown rapidly, however, and the scholarly understanding of Taoism has improved substantially in recent decades. Several general presentations of Taoism in Western languages that cover wide segments of the tradition include Kaltenmark 1969, Lagerwey 1991, Robinet 1997, and Schipper 1993b. Shorter outlines are found in Baldrian 1987; Barrett 2000; Kaltenmark 1970; Lagerwey 1987a, 1987b, and 1987c; Schipper 1968, 1993a, and 2000; Seidel 1974 and 1997; and Strickmann 1974.

Baldrian, Farzeen. 1987. "Taoism: An Overview." In Mircea Eliade, ed., *Encyclopedia of Religion*, 14: 288–306. New York: Macmillan.

Barrett, T. H. 2000. "Daoism: A Historical Narrative." In Livia Kohn, ed., *Daoism Handbook*, xviii–xxvii. Leiden: E. J. Brill.

Chen Guofu 陳國符. 1963. *Daozang yuanliu kao* 道藏源流考 [Studies on the origins and development of the Taoist Canon]. 2 vols. Beijing: Zhonghua shuju.

Kaltenmark, Max. 1969. *Lao Tzu and Taoism*. Translated by Roger Greaves. Stanford: Stanford University Press. Originally published as *Lao tseu et le taoïsme* (Paris: Editions du Seuil, 1965).

———. 1970. "Le taoïsme religieux." In Henri-Charles Puech, ed., *Histoire des religions*, 1: *Les religions antiques*, 1216–48. Paris: Gallimard.

Lagerwey, John. 1987a. "Taoist Cultic Life." In Mircea Eliade, ed., *Encyclopedia of Religion*, 15: 482–86. New York: Macmillan.

———. 1987b. "Taoist Priesthood." In Mircea Eliade, ed., *Encyclopedia of Religion*, 11: 547–50. New York: Macmillan.

———. 1987c. "The Taoist Religious Community." In Mircea Eliade, ed., *Encyclopedia of Religion*, 14: 306–17. New York: Macmillan.

———. 1991. *Le continent des esprits: La Chine dans le miroir du taoïsme*. Bruxelles: La Renaissance du Livre.

Maspero, Henri. 1971. *Le Taoïsme et les religions chinoises*. Paris: Gallimard. Translated into English by Frank A. Kierman, Jr., as *Taoism and Chinese Religion* (Amherst: University of Massachusetts Press, 1981)

Robinet, Isabelle. 1997. *Taoism: Growth of a Religion*. Translated by Phyllis Brooks. Stanford: Stanford University Press.

Schipper, Kristofer M. 1968. "Taoïsme." In *Encyclopaedia Universalis*, 15: 738–44. Paris: Encyclopaedia Universalis France. Reprint, 1973, 1980.

———. 1993a. "Le taoïsme." In Jean Delumeau, ed., *Le fait religieux*, 513–77. Paris: Fayard.

———. 1993b. *The Taoist Body*. Translated by Karen C. Duval. Berkeley: University of California Press. Originally published as *Le corps taoïste: Corps physique, corps social* (Paris: Librairie Arthème Fayard, 1979).

———. 2000. "The Story of the Way." In Stephen Little, *Taoism and the Arts of China*, 33–55. Chicago: The Art Institute of Chicago.

Seidel, Anna K. 1974. "Taoism." In *Encyclopaedia Britannica*, fifteenth edition, *Macropaedia*, 17: 1034–44.

———. 1997. "Taoism: The Unofficial High Religion of China." *Taoist Resources* 7.2: 39–72.

Strickmann, Michel. 1974. "Taoism, History of," and "Taoist Literature." *Encyclopaedia Britannica*, fifteenth edition, *Macropaedia*, 17: 1044–50, 1051–55.

1B. INTRODUCTIONS TO THE FIELD AND SURVEYS OF STUDIES

The main survey of Taoist studies is Seidel 1989–90. This masterly overview presents and critically evaluates the major works on Taoism published in Western languages between 1950 and 1990. It also includes some pre-1950 publications not yet outdated, some unpublished dissertations, important background studies, and major works in Chinese and Japanese. The discussion is divided into sections on the sources of Taoism, the history of Taoism, the "Taoist universe" (immortals, sacred geography, supernatural bureaucracy, human body and longevity practices, alchemy, ritual, and iconography), Taoism in Chinese culture, Taoism and Buddhism, and Taoism outside China. The bibliography includes more than 500 titles.

Other Western-language surveys of Taoist studies include Barrett 1981, Barrett 1987, Kohn 2000, Schipper 1995, and Verellen 1995 (the latter is part of a multi-author state-of-the-field survey of Chinese religions published in *Journal of Asian Studies* 54.1 and 54.2). For overviews of Taoist studies in China see Hendrischke 1984, Jan Yün-hua 1984, Matsumoto Kōichi 1986, and Ding Huang 2000. The main contributions of Japanese scholarship are discussed in Barrett 1981 and Barrett 1987. Japanese studies are also surveyed in Sakai Tadao and Noguchi Tetsurō 1979, Fukui Fumimasa 1986, Sakade Yoshinobu 1989, and Fukui Fumimasa 1995.

Barrett, T. H. 1981. "Introduction." In Henri Maspero, *Taoism and Chinese Religion*, vii–xxiii. Amherst: University of Massachusetts Press.

———. 1987. "Taoism: History of Study." In Mircea Eliade, ed., *Encyclopedia of Religion*, 14: 329–32. New York: Macmillan.

Ding Huang. 2000. "The Study of Daoism in China Today." In Livia Kohn, ed., *Daoism Handbook*, 765–91. Leiden: E. J. Brill.

Fukui Fumimasa 福井文雅. 1986. "Dōkyō shisō no kenkyū to mondaiten" 道教思想の研究と問題点 [Studies and issues of Taoist thought]. In Akizuki Kan'ei 秋月観暎, ed., *Dōkyō kenkyū no susume: Sono genjō to mondaiten o kangaeru* 道教研究のすすめ—その現状と問題点を考える [An invitation to Taoist studies: Reflections on its state and issues], 39–78. Tokyo: Hirakawa shuppansha.

———. 1995. "The History of Taoist Studies in Japan and Some Related Issues." *Acta Asiatica* 68: 1–18.

Hendrischke, Barbara. 1984. "Chinese Research into Daoism after the Cultural Revolution." *Asiatische Studien / Études Asiatiques* 38: 25–42.

Jan Yün-hua. 1984. "The Religious Situation and the Studies of Buddhism and Taoism in China: An Incomplete and Imbalanced Picture." *Journal of Chinese Religions* 12: 37–64.

Kohn, Livia. 2000. "Research on Daoism." In Livia Kohn, ed., *Daoism Handbook*, xxvii-xxxiii. Leiden: E. J. Brill.

Matsumoto Kōichi 松本浩一. 1986. "Chūgoku, Taiwan ni okeru Dōkyō kenkyū no genjō" 中国・台湾における道教研究の現状 [The present state of Taoist studies in the People's Republic of China and Taiwan]. In Akizuki Kan'ei 秋月観暎, ed., *Dōkyō kenkyū no susume: Sono genjō to mondaiten o kangaeru* 道教研究のすすめ—その現状と問題点を考える [An invitation to Taoist studies: Reflections on its state and issues], 235–55. Tokyo: Hirakawa shuppansha.

Sakade Yoshinobu. 1989. "Longevity Techniques in Japan: Ancient Sources and Contemporary Studies." In Livia Kohn, ed. in cooperation with Yoshinobu Sakade, *Taoist Meditation and Longevity Techniques*, 1–40. Ann Arbor: Center for Chinese Studies, University of Michigan.

Sakai Tadao and Noguchi Tetsurō. 1979. "Taoist Studies in Japan." In Holmes Welch and Anna K. Seidel, eds., *Facets of Taoism: Essays in Chinese Religion*, 269–87. New Haven and London: Yale University Press.

Schipper, Kristofer M. 1995. "The History of Taoist Studies in Europe." In Wing Milson and John Cayley, eds., *Europe Studies China*, 467–91. London: Han-Shan Tang Books.

Seidel, Anna K. 1989–90. "Chronicle of Taoist Studies in the West 1950–1990." *Cahiers d'Extrême-Asie* 5: 223–347.

Verellen, Franciscus. 1995. "Chinese Religions—The State of the Field: Taoism." *Journal of Asian Studies* 54: 322–46.

1C. BIBLIOGRAPHIES

The main general bibliography of Western-language studies of Taoism is Pas 1997. The bibliography in Walf 2003 deals primarily with Taoist thought. Other useful bibliographies include Cohen 1989, Kardos 1998, and (especially for the earlier stage of research) Soymié and Litsch 1967–71. The main Western-language bibliographies are reviewed in Dragan 1989. For studies of alchemy see Pregadio 1996.

The bibliography of Western-language studies of Chinese religion edited by Laurence G. Thompson includes several sections on Taoism. The four volumes published to date respectively cover the years through 1980, 1981 to 1990, 1991 to 1995, and 1996 to 2000.

Bibliographies of Japanese studies are found in Ishii Masako et al. 1983, Noguchi Tetsurō and Ishida Hidemi 1983, Sakai Tadao 1972, and Ishida Kenji 2001. For bibliographies of Chinese studies see He Guang 1984, Leung Man Kam 1989, and Yang Guangwen 1985.

Cohen, Alvin P. 1989. "Western Language Publications on Chinese Religions, 1981–1987." In Julian F. Pas, ed., *The Turning of the Tide: Religion in China Today*, 313–45. Hong Kong: Royal Asiatic Society, Hong Kong Branch, and Oxford University Press.

Dragan, Raymond A. 1989. "Ways to the Way: A Review of Bibliographies on Taoism." *Taoist Resources* 1.2: 21–27.

He Guang 和光. 1984. "Jiefang hou guanyu Daojia, Daojiao, Xuanxue bufen lunwen suoyin 1949–1984" 解方後關於道家道教玄學部分論文所引 [Bibliography of studies on Taoist thought, Taoist religion, and the "Mysterious Learning," 1949–1984]. *Zhongguo zhexue* 中國哲學 1984: 505–25.

Ishii Masako 石井昌子, et al. 1983. "Chūgoku Dōkyō kenkyū bunken mokuroku" 参考文献目録—中国道教研究文献目録 [Bibliography of studies on Chinese Taoism]. In Kanaoka Shōkō 金岡照光, Ikeda On 池田温, and Fukui Fumimasa 福井文雅, eds., *Tonkō to Chūgoku dōkyō* 敦煌と中國道教 [Dunhuang and Chinese Taoism], 347–411. Tokyo: Daitō shuppansha.

Ishida Kenji 石田憲司, ed. 2001. *Dōkyō kankei bunken sōran* 道教関係文献総覧. [A comprehensive bibliography of studies on Taoism]. Tokyo: Fūkyōsha.

Kardos, Michael A. 1998. "Western Language Publications on Religions in China, 1990–1994." *Journal of Chinese Religions* 26: 67–134.

Leung Man Kam 梁文金. 1989. "1977–1987 nian Zhongguo chuban youguan Zhongguo zongjiao zhi shuji ji lunwen suoyin" 1977–1987 年中國出版有關中國宗教之書籍及論文所引 [A bibliography of books and articles on Chinese religion published in China from 1977 to 1987]. In Julian F. Pas, ed., *The Turning of the Tide. Religion in China Today*, 346–73. Hong Kong: Royal Asiatic Society, Hong Kong Branch, and Oxford University Press.

Noguchi Tetsurō 野口鉄郎 and Ishida Hidemi 石田秀実. 1983. "Dōkyō kenkyū bunken mokuroku" 道教研究文献目録 [A bibliography of studies on Taoism]. In Fukui Kōjun 福井文雅 et al., eds., *Dōkyō* 道教 [Taoism], 3: 387–486. Tokyo: Hirakawa shuppansha.

Pas, Julian F. 1997. *A Select Bibliography on Taoism*. Second enlarged edition. Saskatoon: China Pavilion.

Pregadio, Fabrizio. 1996. "Chinese Alchemy: An Annotated Bibliography of Works in Western Languages." *Monumenta Serica* 44: 439–76.()

Sakai Tadao 酒井忠夫. 1972. *Dōkyō kenkyū bunken mokuroku (Nihon)* 道教研究文献目録（日本）[A bibliography of Japanese studies on Taoism]. Tokyo: N.p.

Soymié, Michel, and F. Litsch. 1967–71. "Bibliographie du taoïsme: Études dans les langues occidentales." *Dōkyō kenkyū* 3 (1967): 247–313; 4 (1971): 225–87.

Thompson, Laurence G. 1985, 1993, 1998, 2002. *Chinese Religion in Western Languages*. 4 vols. Ann Arbor: Association for Asian Studies.

Walf, Knut. 2003. *Westliche Taoismus-Bibliographie / Western Bibliography of Taoism*. Fifth edition. Essen: Verlag Die Blaue Eule.

Yang Guangwen 楊光文. 1985. "Quanguo bufen baokan Daojiao lunwen mulu suoyin (1905–1983)" 全國部分報刊道教論文目錄所引]1905–1983） [A bibliography of studies on Taoism in Chinese periodicals, 1905–1983]. *Zongjiaoxue yanjiu lunji* 宗教學研究論集, 132–44.

Updates on recent studies are available from several sources. The journal *Tōhō shūkyō* 東方宗教 publishes an annual bibliography of books and articles in Japanese, Chinese, and Western languages mainly focused on Taoism. For publications in Western languages see especially the annual *Revue bibliographique de sinologie*, published by the École des Hautes Sciences Sociales, and the annual *Bibliography of Asian Studies*, published by the Association for Asian Studies. For Chinese studies, one of several available sources is the annual bibliography published in the journal *Shijie zongjiao yanjiu* 世界宗教研究.

2. Taoist Canon

2A. HISTORY

The present Taoist Canon—the *Zhengtong daozang* 正統道藏, or *Taoist Canon of the Zhengtong Reign Period*—was printed in 1445, with a supplement known as *Wanli xu daozang* 萬曆續道藏 (Supplementary Taoist Canon of the Wanli Reign Period) added in 1607. It is the last in a series of compilations of Taoist texts known to have existed from the fifth century, when *Lu Xiujing 陸修靜 (406–77) wrote his now lost *Sandong *jingshu mulu* 三洞經書目錄 (Index of Scriptures and Writings of the Three Caverns). The main compilations prior to the *Zhengtong daozang* are:

(a) *Sandong qionggang 三洞瓊綱 (Exquisite Compendium of the Three Caverns), or *Kaiyuan daozang* 開元道藏 (Taoist Canon of the Kaiyuan Reign Period; 713/741)

(b) *Da Song Tiangong baozang 大宋天宮寶藏 (Precious Canon of the Celestial Palace of the Great Song Dynasty; 1016)

(c) *Zhenghe Wanshou daozang 正和萬壽道藏 (Taoist Canon of the Ten-Thousand-Fold Longevity of the Zhenghe Reign Period; 1111/1117)

(d) *Da Jin Xuandu baozang 大金玄都寶藏 (Precious Canon of the Mysterious Metropolis of the Great Jin Dynasty; 1192)

(e) *Xuandu baozang 玄都寶藏 (Precious Canon of the Mysterious Metropolis; 1244)

With the exception of fragments of the *Xuandu baozang*, none of the compilations listed above has survived.

General studies on the history of the Canon, its organization, and the formation of the main Taoist corpora through the Tang period are found in Chen Guofu 1963, 105–231, Fukui Kōjun 1958, 133–213, Ōfuchi Ninji 1964, 215–547, and Yoshioka Yoshitoyo 1955, 1–180. Shorter accounts in Western languages are found in Liu Ts'un-yen 1973, Needham 1976, 113–17, and Boltz 1987, 4–7.

Boltz, Judith M. 1987. *A Survey of Taoist Literature: Tenth to Seventeenth Centuries.* Berkeley: Institute of East Asian Studies, University of California. Reprinted with corrigenda, 1995.

Chen Guofu 陳國符. 1963. *Daozang yuanliu kao* 道藏源流考 [Studies on the origins and development of the Taoist Canon]. 2 vols. Beijing: Zhonghua shuju.

Fukui Kōjun 福井康順. 1958. *Dōkyō no kisoteki kenkyū* 道教の基礎的研究 [Introductory studies on Taoism]. Tokyo: Shoseki bunbutsu ryūtsūkai.

Liu Ts'un-yan. 1973. "The Compilation and Historical Value of the Tao-tsang." In Donald D. Leslie, Colin Mackerras, and Wang Gungwu, eds., *Essays on the Sources for Chinese History*, 104–19. Canberra: Australian National University Press.

Needham, Joseph. 1976. *Science and Civilisation in China.* Vol. V: *Chemistry and Chemical Technology.* Part 3: *Spagyrical Discovery and Invention: Historical Survey, from Cinnabar Elixirs to Synthetic Insulin.* With the collaboration of Ho Ping-Yü and Lu Gwei-Djen. Cambridge: Cambridge University Press.

Ōfuchi Ninji 大淵忍爾. 1964. *Dōkyōshi no kenkyū* 道教史の研究 [Studies on the history of Taoism]. Okayama: Okayama daigaku kyōsaikai shosekibu.

Yoshioka Yoshitoyo 吉岡義豊. 1955. *Dōkyō kyōten shiron* 道教經典史論 [Historical studies on Taoist scriptures]. Tokyo: Dōkyō kankōkai.

In addition to those mentioned above, other studies are especially concerned with individual periods or compilations. On the origins of the *Daozang* see Ōfuchi Ninji 1979. The Six Dynasties Canon is partially reconstructed in Lagerwey 1981b, 222–73, based on the texts quoted in the *Wushang biyao 無上祕要 (Supreme Secret Essentials; CT 1138). On the Song dynasty Canons see Schipper 1981–82. For the history of the Taoist Canon from the Song period onward the most detailed study in a Western language is found in van der Loon 1984, 29–63; this work is also useful for tracing the history of individual Taoist texts mentioned in catalogues of the Standard Histories and of private libraries, and in other Taoist texts. On the *Yunji qiqian 雲笈七籤 (Seven Lots from the Bookbag of the Clouds; CT 1032), an encyclopedia compiled in ca. 1028 for inclusion in the Da Song Tiangong baozang, see (in addition to the reference works mentioned in sec. 6 below) Schipper 1981, 1: i–xvii, and Lagerwey 1981a. An imperial edict concerned with the publication of the thirteenth-century Xuandu baozang has been translated and studied in Cleaves 1960. On the compilation of the Zhengtong daozang see especially Schipper 1983 and Boltz 1986.

The present-day Daozang also includes a *Daozang quejing mulu 道藏闕經目錄 (Index of Scriptures Missing from the Taoist Canon; CT 1430), which lists canonical texts found in earlier versions of the Daozang but not included in the present Canon either because they were lost or because they were unavailable to its editors. For an index to this catalogue, see sec. 4b below.

Boltz, Judith M. 1986. "Tao-tsang." In William H. Nienhauser, Jr., ed., The Indiana Companion to Traditional Chinese Literature, 763–66. Second revised edition. Bloomington: Indiana University Press.

Cleaves, Francis Woodman. 1960. "The Sino-Mongolian inscription of 1240." Harvard Journal of Asiatic Studies 23: 62–75.

Lagerwey, John. 1981a. "Le Yun-ji qi-qian: Structure et sources." In Schipper 1981, xix–lxxi.

————. 1981b. Wu-shang pi-yao: Somme taoïste du VIe siècle. Paris: École Française d'Extrême-Orient.

Ōfuchi Ninji. 1979. "The Formation of the Taoist Canon." In Holmes Welch and Anna K. Seidel, eds., Facets of Taoism: Essays in Chinese Religion, 253–67. New Haven and London: Yale University Press.

Schipper, Kristofer M. 1981. Projet Tao-tsang: Index du Yunji qiqian. 2 vols. Paris: École Française d'Extrême-Orient.

————. 1981–82. "Les canons taoïstes des Song." Annuaire de l'École Pratique des Hautes Études, Ve Section, 90: 115–19.

————. 1983. "The Compilation of the Taoist Canon of the Ming Dynasty (With Special Reference to the 'Tao-men shih-kuei' 道門十規 by Chang Yü-ch'u 張宇初 [1361–1410])." Unpublished ms.

van der Loon, Piet. 1984. Taoist Books in the Libraries of the Sung Period: A Critical Study and Index. London: Ithaca Press.

2B. MODERN REPRINTS

The exemplar of the Zhengtong daozang originally kept at the *Baiyun guan 白雲觀 (Abbey of the White Clouds) in Beijing serves as the basis for all the modern reprints listed below.

(1) Shangwu yinshuguan reprint (Shanghai, 1923–26); 1120 fascicles (ce 冊)

Each folio contains 20 columns of text, compared to the 25 columns of the original; five folios correspond therefore to four folios in the original edition, an arrangement that has resulted in the cutting of many illustrations. This reprint, which is often referred to as the "Hanfenlou 涵芬樓 reprint," was published in only 350 copies.

(2) Yiwen chubanshe reprint (Taipei, 1963); 120 fascicles

Reprint of reprint no. (1).

(3) Xinwenfeng chubanshe reprint (Taipei, 1977); 1+60 volumes

Each page reproduces, on two horizontal registers, *recto* and *verso* of two folios of reprint no. (1). In addition to various prefaces, the introductory volume includes:

(a) an index of the texts reproduced in each volume;

(b) the *Baiyun guan chongxiu Daozang ji* 白雲館重修道藏記 (Note on the Restoration of the Taoist Canon of the Abbey of the White Clouds), on integrations made in 1845 to the copy kept at the Baiyun guan;

(c) a short text entitled "Daojiao zongyuan" 道教宗源 (Origins of Taoism), which is part of the *Da Ming daozang jing mulu* 大明道藏經目錄 (Index of the Scriptures in the Taoist Canon of the Great Ming; CT 1431);

(d) the **Daozang mulu xiangzhu* 道藏目錄詳注 (Detailed Commentary on the Index of the Taoist Canon) by Bai Yunji 白雲霽 (see sec. 4a below), reproduced from a copy of the *Siku quanshu* 四庫全書 edition kept at the Tuigeng Tang 退耕堂 (the private library of Xu Shichang 徐世昌, president of the Republic of China between 1918 and 1922).

Because of the relatively large size of the reproduction and the presence of the Chinese-style pagination, this is the best reprint of the Taoist Canon among those bound in Western-style volumes.

(4) Yiwen chubanshe reprint (Taipei, 1977); 1+60 volumes

Reprint in volumes smaller than those of reprint no. (3).

(5) Chūbun shuppansha reprint (Kyoto, 1986); 30 volumes

Vol. 1 includes an index of the texts reproduced in each volume, and a concordance to the titles of texts with references to the volumes and page numbers in this reprint. Except for these references, the concordance is the same as the one published by Kristofer Schipper in 1975 (see below, sec. 4b).

(6) Wenwu chubanshe reprint (Beijing, 1988); 36 volumes

Each page reproduces, on three horizontal registers, *recto* and *verso* of three folios of reprint no. (1). This reprint, as well as reprint no. (5) above, omits the Chinese-style pagination of individual texts, and provides only a Western-style pagination for the entire collection.

For a list of missing and misplaced folios in the Taipei reprints of the Canon, and of corrected or newly introduced defects in the Beijing reprint, see Boltz 1994.

Boltz, Judith M. 1994. "Notes on the *Daozang tiyao.*" *China Review International* 1.2: 1–33.

The *Zhonghua daozang* 中華道藏 or *Taoist Canon of China*, published by Huaxia chubanshe in 2003, is the first new complete edition of the Taoist Canon since the *Zhengtong daozang*. In the *Zhonghua daozang*, texts are punctuated and printed in mobile type, and are arranged into broad categories such as lineages (e.g., *Shangqing, *Lingbao, *Taiqing, *Quanzhen), genres (e.g., literary collections, ritual compendia, hagiography, descriptions of practices, encyclopedias), and commentaries on major texts (e.g., *Daode jing* and *Zhuangzi*).

3. Surveys of Texts

3A. SURVEYS OF THE ENTIRE CANON

The classical study on the scriptural corpora found in the present Taoist Canon is Chen Guofu 1963 (first edition published in 1949). The chapter entitled "Origin and Transmission of the Three Caverns and the Four Supplements" (pp. 1–104) traces the formation of these sections of the Canon through the Tang period. Yoshioka Yoshitoyo 1955 offers another broad overview that supplements the one provided by Chen Guofu. In Boltz 1987a, texts dating from the Song, Yuan and Ming periods are introduced in chapters concerned not with scriptural corpora, but with literary genres (revelation, ritual, hagiography, topography, epigraphy, historiography, literary anthologies, dialogic treatises, exegesis, and encyclopedic compilations).

A shorter survey of texts found in the Canon was published in two parts by Stephen R. Bokenkamp and Judith M. Boltz, respectively, in 1986 as one of the introductory essays in William H. Nienhauser's *Indiana Companion to Traditional Chinese Literature*. See also another survey of Taoist texts by Boltz (1987b) in Mircea Eliade's *Encyclopedia of Religion*. Two surveys in Japanese were published by Ozaki Masaharu in 1983 and 1986.

Bokenkamp, Stephen R. 1986. "Taoist Literature. Part 1: Through the T'ang Dynasty." In William H. Nienhauser, Jr., ed., *The Indiana Companion to Traditional Chinese Literature*, 138–52. Second revised edition. Bloomington: Indiana University Press.

Boltz, Judith M. 1986. "Taoist Literature. Part 2: Five Dynasties to the Ming." In William H. Nienhauser, Jr., ed., *The Indiana Companion to Traditional Chinese Literature*, 152–74. Second revised edition. Bloomington: Indiana University Press.

———. 1987a. *A Survey of Taoist Literature: Tenth to Seventeenth Centuries*. Berkeley: Institute of East Asian Studies, University of California. Reprinted with corrigenda, 1995.

———. 1987b. "Taoism: Taoist Literature." In Mircea Eliade, ed., *Encyclopedia of Religion*, 14: 317–29. New York: Macmillan.

Chen Guofu 陳國符. 1963. *Daozang yuanliu kao* 道藏源流考 [Studies on the origins and development of the Taoist Canon]. 2 vols. Beijing: Zhonghua shuju.

Ozaki Masaharu 尾崎正治. 1983. "Dōkyō kyōten" 道教経典 [Taoist texts]. In Fukui Kōjun 福井文雅 et al., eds., *Dōkyō* 道教 [Taoism], 1: 73–120. Tokyo: Hirakawa shuppansha.

———. 1986. "Dōzō no seiritsu to sono shūhen" 道藏の成立とその周辺 [The formation of the Taoist Canon and its circumstances]. In Akizuki Kan'ei 秋月観暎, ed., *Dōkyō kenkyū no susume: Sono genjō to mondaiten o kangaeru* 道教研究のすす

め—その現状と問題点を考える [An invitation to Taoist studies: Reflections on its state and issues], 79–109. Tokyo: Hirakawa shuppansha.

Yoshioka Yoshitoyo 吉岡義豊. 1955. *Dōkyō kyōten shiron* 道教經典史論 [Historical studies on Taoist scriptures]. Tokyo: Dōkyō kankōkai.

3B. SURVEYS OF INDIVIDUAL CORPORA

The only extensive systematic study of a major Taoist textual corpus in a Western language is found in Robinet 1984; vol. 2 of this work analyzes several dozen texts belonging or closely related to the Shangqing corpus. Shorter Western-language surveys of major Taoist textual corpora include Ōfuchi Ninji 1974 and Bokenkamp 1993 on Lingbao, and Strickmann 1981, 58–81, on Shangqing. Brief presentations of the main sources belonging or related to individual traditions are also found in *Daoism Handbook*, edited by Livia Kohn in 2000.

Bokenkamp, Stephen R. 1983. "Sources of the Ling-pao Scriptures." In Michel Strickmann, ed., *Tantric and Taoist Studies in Honour of Rolf A. Stein*, 2: 434–86. Bruxelles: Institut Belge des Hautes Études Chinoises.

Kohn, Livia, ed. 2000. *Daoism Handbook*. Leiden: E. J. Brill.

Ōfuchi, Ninji. 1974. "On *Ku Ling-pao-ching* 古靈寶經." *Acta Asiatica* 27: 33–56.

Robinet, Isabelle. 1984. *La révélation du Shangqing dans l'histoire du taoïsme*. 2 vols. Paris: École Française d'Extrême-Orient.

Strickmann, Michel. 1981. *Le Taoïsme du Mao Chan: Chronique d'une révélation*. Paris: Collège de France, Institut des Hautes Études Chinoises.

4. Catalogues

4A. PRE-MODERN CATALOGUES

The Taoist Canon contains an index to its own texts entitled *Da Ming daozang jing mulu* 大明道藏經目錄 (Index of Scriptures in the Taoist Canon of the Great Ming; CT 1431). Two annotated indexes of the texts in the Canon were compiled in the Qing period by Bai Yunji 白雲霽 and Li Jie 李杰, respectively. Their contents are similar, and both are entitled *Daozang mulu xiangzhu* 道藏目錄詳注 (Detailed Commentary on the Index of the Taoist Canon). On these catalogues see Ozaki Masaharu 1987.

Ozaki Masaharu 尾崎正治. 1987. "*Dōzō mokuroku shōchū* kanken"「道藏目錄詳注」管見 [A review of the *Daozang mulu xiangzhu*]. In Akizuki Kan'ei 秋月観暎, ed., *Dōkyō kenkyū no susume: Sono genjō to mondaiten o kangaeru* 道教研究のすすめ—その現状と問題点を考える [An invitation to Taoist studies: Reflections on its state and issues], 529–53. Tokyo: Hirakawa shuppansha.

The Chinese bibliography on the Taoist Canon found an epigone in P. Léon Wieger's *Taoïsme: Bibliographie générale* (1911). Although this was the first catalogue compiled by a Western scholar, it may also be considered the last traditional catalogue of the Canon. According to his introduction, Wieger compiled his work on the basis of two sets of the *Daozang* that he personally examined, namely those kept at the

Baiyun guan in Beijing and at the Imperial Library in Tokyo, and with the help of five Chinese catalogues, including Li Jie's *Daozang mulu xiangzhu*. Wieger's catalogue lists 1464 titles. It also includes a classification of the texts into fifty sections, an alphabetical title index, an author index, and (a useful addition) the relevant portions of several pre-modern bibliographies found in the Standard Histories or in catalogues of private libraries. The notes on each entry are usually very short and often generic (if not inexact or even "fantaisistes," as Kristofer Schipper calls them in his own catalogue, to be mentioned in sec. 4b below). On some occasions, moreover, Wieger does not hesitate to evaluate a text as "insignifiant" or as a "traité inepte."

This is not the only reason that the *Bibliographie générale* is nowadays inadequate as a tool to orient oneself in the Taoist Canon. Its major shortcomings are high-lighted by Weng Dujian, the author of one of the two best catalogues of the Canon (see sec. 4b). Weng remarks that since Wieger's work was published before the first modern reprint of the Canon (1923–26), it does not provide references to the number of fascicles in that reprint, but only to the *Qianzi wen* 千字文 characters with which the Ming editors labeled each fascicle. Weng also points out that Wieger's title index does not contain frequently-used abbreviated or alternative forms, that his author index omits many names, and that his catalogue neglects to mention some titles. As Weng notes, the missing titles are the same as those also omitted in Li Jie's *Daozang mulu xiangzhu*. Finally, again due to its substantial dependency on Li Jie's catalogue, Wieger's catalogue contains some erroneous transcriptions and annotations.

Wieger, Leon. 1911. *Taoïsme*. Vol. I: *Bibliographie générale: I. Le canon (Patrologie), II. Les index officiels et privés*. Hien-hien (Ho-kien-fou): [Imprimerie de la Mission catholique].

4B. MODERN CATALOGUES

The first modern reference work on the Taoist Canon is *Daozang zimu yinde* 道藏子目引得 (*Combined Indices to the Authors and Titles of Books in Two Collections of Taoist Literature*), published by Weng Dujian in 1935 in the Harvard-Yenching Index Series. This work is divided into four parts:

(a) an analytic catalogue of the Canon

(b) a title index

(c) an author index

(d) an index to biographies found in 77 texts

The introductory section includes, among other materials, a transcription of the "Daojiao zongyuan" 道教宗源 (Lineal Origins of the Taoist Teaching) and the "Dao-zang mulu fanli" 道藏目錄凡例 (Index of the Taoist Canon: General Guidelines), both of which are part of the *Da Ming daozang jing mulu* 大明道藏經目錄 (Index of the Scriptures in the Taoist Canon of the Great Ming; CT 1431), as well as a revised version of Wieger's classification of the texts.

According to Weng's preface, his catalogue is based on the *Daozang jing mulu*. It includes 1476 titles, twelve of which are not listed in Wieger's catalogue. For each text, the catalogue provides references to both the *Qianzi wen* character and the number of fascicle(s) in the 1923–26 reprint. An appendix lists 114 texts that are not included in the *Daozang* but are found in the **Daozang jiyao* 道藏輯要 (Essentials of the Taoist Canon), a collection of Taoist texts compiled in the Qing period (see sec. 5a below; this appendix is not entirely reliable). The title index, which includes many alternative or abbreviated forms, lists all works found in the *Daozang* and the *Daozang jiyao*, together with the titles of the lost works cited in the **Daozang quejing mulu* 道藏闕 經目錄 (Index of Scriptures Missing from the Taoist Canon; CT 1430; see above, sec. 2a). In addition, the index of biographies makes Weng's catalogue especially useful.

Weng Dujian 翁獨健. 1935. *Daozang zimu yinde* 道藏子目引得 (*Combined Indices to the Authors and Titles of Books in Two Collections of Taoist Literature*). Harvard-Yenching Institute Sinological Index Series, no. 25. Beiping [Beijing]: Yenching University Library. Reprint, Taipei: Chengwen Publishing Company, 1966.

Although Weng Dujian's catalogue remains a key reference work, many recent works—including the present *Encyclopedia of Taoism*—refer to the *Daozang* texts according to the numbering in Kristofer Schipper's *Concordance du Tao-tsang: Titres des ouvrages* (1975). The catalogue found at the beginning of this work lists 1487 texts, i.e. eleven more than those found in Weng Dujian's catalogue (more precisely, fourteen texts that Weng deems to be parts of other works are listed by Schipper as independent works, while three texts that Weng lists as independent works are deemed by Schipper to be parts of other works). The catalogue is followed by a concordance to the individual characters that form the titles of the 1487 texts.

Schipper's catalogue is also entirely reproduced in the Yiwen chubanshe reprint of the Canon published in 1977, and the concordance alone in the Chūbun shuppansha reprint published in 1986. It has also been republished as Shi Zhouren and Chen Yaoting 1996, together with an index to the titles in the above-mentioned *Daozang quejing mulu*.

Schipper, Kristofer M. 1975. *Concordance du Tao-tsang: Titres des ouvrages*. Paris: École Française d'Extrême-Orient.

Shi Zhouren 施舟人 [Kristofer Schipper] and Chen Yaoting 陳耀庭, eds. 1996. *Daozang suoyin* 道藏索引 [Index to the Taoist Canon]. Shanghai: Shanghai shudian chubanshe.

A comparison of the numbering of texts in the catalogues by Weng Dujian and Schipper, with details on titles added or omitted in each of them, is found in Boltz 1987a, 247–50 (listed in sec. 3a above). Some issues in both catalogues are discussed in Fukui Fumimasa 1988. Fukui also suggests in an earlier study (1985) that neither catalogue actually lists all works contained in the Canon. The present confusion arising due to the use of two different numbering systems was first criticized more than a quarter century ago by Strickmann (1977, 15–17).

Fukui Fumimasa 福井文雅. 1985. "Saikin (1) no Dōkyō kankei ōbun bunken (1)" 最近 の道教関係欧文文献 (1) [Recent publications on Taoism in Western languages; part 1]. *Tōyō no shisō to shūkyō* 東洋の思想と宗教 1: 118–25.

———. 1988. "Dōzō shiryō no hyōji-hō ni tsuite. Haabaado Dōzō bunrui intoku to Shipeeru Dōzō sō mokuroku to no mondaiten" 道藏資料の表示法について―ハーヴァード道藏分類引得とシペール道藏総目録との問題点 [The numbering of texts of the Taoist Canon: Problems in the Harvard-Yenching index and in K. Schipper's catalogue]. *Tōhō shūkyō* 東方宗教 71: 70–81.

Strickmann, Michel. 1977. "Bibliographic Notes on Chinese Religious Studies." *Newsletter of the Society for the Study of Chinese Religions* 3: 11–17.

Another major catalogue of the Canon is *Daozang tiyao* 道藏提要, edited by Ren Jiyu and Zhong Zhaopeng in 1991 with a revised edition published in 1999. This catalogue, the result of a project based at the Research Institute on World Religions, Chinese Academy of Social Sciences (Zhongguo shehui kexueyuan Shijie zongjiao yanjiusuo), lists 1473 titles, i.e., three less then those in Weng's catalogue and fourteen less than those in Schipper's catalogue. In addition to abstracts—of a somewhat unequal value—of each text, this volume contains several appendixes, the most useful of which are one containing short biographical notes on about 500 authors, and one containing a classification of the texts into nine main categories and several sub-categories. On this catalogue see Boltz 1994. Some entries preliminarily published by the Shijie zongjiao yanjiusuo Daojiao yanjiushi in 1984 are still worthy of being consulted, as they are more detailed compared to the corresponding entries in the final publication.

Boltz, Judith M. 1994. "Notes on the Daozang tiyao." *China Review International* 1.2: 1–33.

Ren Jiyu 任繼愈 and Zhong Zhaopeng 鍾肇鵬, eds. 1991. *Daozang tiyao* 道藏提要 [A conspectus of the Taoist Canon]. Beijing: Zhongguo shehui kexue chubanshe.

Shijie zongjiao yanjiusuo Daojiao yanjiushi 世界宗教研究所道教研究室 [Research Group on Taoism of the Research Institute on World Religions], ed. 1984. "Daozang tiyao xuankan" 道藏提要選刊 [Selections from *Daozang tiyao*]. *Shijie zongjiao yanjiu* 世界宗教研究 1984.2: 1–29; 1984.3: 84–101.

Two relatively recent catalogues (Zhu Yueli 1996; Zhong Zhaopeng 1999) list the *Daozang* texts according to "modern" classification systems. While these revised arrangements offer valuable alternatives to the traditional classification system, they sometimes produce questionable results, such as the listing of ritual texts under "Literature" ("Wenxue" 文學) or the listing of texts on meditation under "Other Healing Methods" ("Qita liaofa" 其它療法).

Zhong Zhaopeng 锺肇鵬. 1999. *Xinbian Daozang mulu* 新编道藏目录 [A newly compiled index to the Taoist Canon]. 2 vols. Beijing: Beijing tushuguan chubanshe.

Zhu Yueli 朱越利. 1996. *Daozang fenlei jieti* 道经分类解题 [Classified descriptive notes on the Taoist Canon]. Beijing: Huaxia chubanshe.

Two other catalogues of the Canon, of lesser importance compared to those mentioned above, are found in Kyōto joshi daigaku toshokan 1965 and in Chen 1989.

Chen, William Y. 1989. *A Guide to Cheng-t'ung Tao-tsang*. Taipei: Chinese Materials Center.

Kyōto joshi daigaku toshokan 京都女子大學圖書館 [Library of the Kyoto University for Women], ed. 1965. *Min Seitō bon Dōzō shomei jikaku sakuin* 明正統本道藏書名字畫索引 [A stroke-number index to texts found in the *Zhengtong daozang* of the Ming period]. Kyoto: Kyōto joshi daigaku.

For the sake of completeness, it should be added that the *Daozang* texts are also listed in *Zhongguo congshu zonglu* 中國叢書總録 (Union catalogue of Chinese collectanea), edited by the Shanghai tushuguan (1959–62; 1: 791–808), and in *Kyōto daigaku Jinbun kagaku kenkyūjo kanseki mokuroku* 京都大学人文科学研究所漢籍目録 (Catalogue of Chinese texts at the Institute for Research in Humanities, Kyoto University), edited by the Kyōto daigaku Jinbun kagaku kenkyūjo (1964–65; 1: 446–70). The first of these is defined as "the best analytical list" of the Taoist Canon by van der Loon (1984, 65).

4C. ANNOTATED CATALOGUES

As mentioned above, the catalogue edited by Ren Jiyu and Zhong Zhaopeng (1991) contains abstracts of the individual texts in the *Daozang*. A better overview of the entire collection is now possible with the publication of *The Taoist Canon: A Historical Companion to the Daozang* (dated 2004, published June 2005), the fruit of a project promoted by the European Science Foundation and directed by Kristofer Schipper at the École Pratique des Hautes Études in Paris during the years 1979 to 1984. The catalogue, edited by Kristofer Schipper and Franciscus Verellen, contains entries for each text, arranged by tradition and chronologically, with details on date, authorship, transmission, relation to other sources, and contents of each text.

Schipper, Kristofer M., and Franciscus Verellen, eds. 2004. *The Taoist Canon: A Historical Companion to the Daozang*. 3 vols. Chicago: Chicago University Press.

5. Other Collections of Taoist Texts

In addition to the **Zhengtong daozang*, a large number of Taoist sources are found in several other collections. This section lists the main reference works on the most important collections; for more details on the works cited here, see the relevant entries in the present book.

5A. 'DAOZANG JIYAO'

The **Daozang jiyao* 道藏輯要 (Essentials of the Taoist Canon), first published in the Qing period and expanded in the early twentieth century, contains, according to one count, 287 texts. An index has been published by W. Y. Chen (1987); it contains 309 titles, due to the compiler's choice of considering several texts as independent works rather than as parts of other texts. Weng Dujian's index to the *Daozang* mentioned in sec. 4a above contains a not entirely dependable list of *Daozang jiyao* texts that are not also found in the *Daozang*.

Chen, William Y. 1978. *A Guide to Tao-tsang chi yao*. Stony Brook, N. Y.: Institute for Advanced Studies of World Religions.

5B. 'DAOZANG XUBIAN'

The *Daozang xubian 道藏續編 (Sequel to the Taoist Canon) is a collection of twenty-three *neidan 內丹 texts, none of which is found in the *Daozang*. On this collection, published by *Min Yide 閔一得 (1758–1836, eleventh patriarch of the *Longmen 龍門 tradition) and reprinted in 900 copies in 1989 (Beijing: Haiyang chubanshe), see Despeux 1990, 163–72, and Esposito 1988.

Despeux, Catherine. 1990. *Immortelles de la Chine ancienne: Taoïsme et alchimie féminine*. Puiseaux: Pardès.

Esposito, Monica. 1988. "Présentation d'une partie des texts du 'Daozang xubian.'" Mémoire de D.E.A., Université de Paris VII.

5C. 'DAOZANG JINGHUA LU,' 'DAOZANG JINGHUA,' AND 'DAOJIA WENXIAN'

Taoist works not included in the *Zhengtong daozang* are also found among the 100 texts of the *Daozang jinghua lu 道藏精化綠 (Record of the Essential Splendors of the Taoist Canon), compiled by Ding Fubao 丁福保 (1874–1952) and published by the Yixue shuju (Shanghai, 1922; repr. Hangzhou: Zhejiang Gushi chubanshe, 1989), and among the more than 600 texts of the *Daozang jinghua* 道藏精化 (Essential Splendors of the Taoist Canon), compiled by Xiao Tianshi 蕭天石 (1908–86) and published by the Ziyou chubanshe in Taipei at various dates. (The index to the *Daozang jinghua* found in Chen 1984 does not always match the contents of the individual volumes, some of which have been republished with different works compared to those included in the first edition). Nine more texts are collected in *Daojia wenxian* 道教文獻 (Taoist Texts), published by Du Jiexiang 杜潔祥 (Taipei: Danqing tushu, 1983; 20 vols.).

Chen, William Y. 1984. *A Guide to the Tao tsang ching hua*. N.p.: Chinese Materials Center.

5D. 'ZANGWAI DAOSHU'

The main recently published collection of Taoist texts is the *Zangwai daoshu 藏外道書 (Taoist Texts Outside the Canon). This collection, published by the Ba-Shu Shushe in 1992 with a sequel published in 1995, includes several hundred texts, some of which are not easily available elsewhere. On the works found in the *Zangwai daoshu* see Tian Chengyang 1995.

Tian Chengyang 田誠陽. 1995. "*Zangwai daoshu* shumu lüexi" 「藏外道书」书目略析 [A brief analysis of the contents of the *Zangwai daoshu*]. Parts 1 and 2. *Zhongguo daojiao* 中國道教 1995.1: 37–42; 1995.2: 42–45.

5E. RITUAL MANUSCRIPTS

Fieldwork done in Taiwan and the People's Republic of China has enabled several scholars to collect manuscripts especially concerned with Taoist ritual. The mss. collected by Schipper are housed at the Collège de France; on this collection see Shi Bo'er 1966. Two sets of mss. collected by Michael Saso are published in Saso 1975 and in Saso 1978; on the former set see Saso 1979 and Ōfuchi Ninji 1976. The mss. collected by Ōfuchi Ninji are published in Ōfuchi Ninji 1983. The mss. collected by Kenneth Dean in the People's Republic of China are catalogued in Dean 1988.

Dean, Kenneth. 1988. "Manuscripts from Fujian." *Cahiers d'Extrême-Asie* 4: 217–26.

Ōfuchi Ninji 大淵忍爾. 1976. "Sasō-shi hen *Sō-Rin zoku dōzō* no shuppan ni yosete" サソー氏編「莊林續道藏」の出版によせて [The *Zhuang-Lin xu daozang* compiled by Michael Saso]. *Tōhō shūkyō* 東方宗教 47: 65–70.

———. 1983. *Chūgokujin no shūkyō girei: Bukkyō, dōkyō, minkan shinkō* 中國人の宗教儀礼—佛教・道教・民間信仰 [Liturgies of the Chinese people: Buddhism, Taoism, and popular cults]. Tokyo: Fukutake shoten.

Saso, Michael R., ed. 1975. *Zhuang-Lin xu daozang* 莊林續道藏 [The Zhuang-Lin Supplement to the Taoist Canon]. 25 vols. Taipei: Chengwen chubanshe.

———. 1978. *Dōkyō hiketsu shūsei* 道教祕訣集成 [A collection of Taoist esoterica]. Tokyo: Ryūkei shosha.

———. 1979. "A Guide to the *Chuang Lin Hsü Tao-tsang.*" *Journal of the China Society* 16–17: 9–28.

Shi Bo'er 施博爾 [Kristofer Schipper]. 1966. "Taiwan zhi daojiao wenxian" 臺灣之道教文獻 [Taoist texts in Taiwan]. *Taiwan wenxian* 臺灣文獻 17.3: 173–92.

5F. EPIGRAPHY

A large collection of epigraphic sources was posthumously published in Chen Yuan 1988.

Chen Yuan 陈垣. 1988. *Daojia jinshi lüe* 道家金石略 [A collection of Taoist epigraphy]. Edited by Chen Zhichao 陈智超 and Zeng Qingying 曾庆瑛. Beijing: Wenwu chubanshe.

6. Concordances and Indexes

Among the main results of the Tao-tsang Project was the compilation of indexes to several hundred texts in the Canon, distributed in a limited number of copies to contributors and libraries in microfiche format. The indexes contain names of persons, authors, subjects of biographies, emperors, deities, places, temples, religious and administrative titles, dates, lineages, and iconographic representations. The full collection includes about thirty-five microfiches, most of which contain the equivalent of 270 pages of fifteen lines each, corresponding to more than 100,000 references altogether. On these indexes see Schipper 1983.

Schipper, Kristofer M. 1983. "Une banque de données informatisée sur l'histoire du taoïsme." *Études chinoises* 1: 48–54.

In addition to the indexes and concordances of individual texts listed below, Ōfuchi Ninji and Ishii Masako 1988 contains indexes to texts quoted in forty-five works (mainly Taoist but also including some Buddhist works, as well as encyclopedias and Dunhuang manuscripts), together with tables of contents of each indexed work. The indexes of texts quoted in fifteen Taoist works, found in Yoshioka Yoshitoyo 1955, 341–481, are also useful.

Ōfuchi Ninji 大淵忍爾 and Ishii Masako 石井昌子, eds. 1988. *Rikuchō Tō Sō no kobunken shōin Dōzō tenseki mokuroku, sakuin* 六朝唐宋の古文献所引道藏典籍目録・索引 [A catalogue with index to Taoist texts cited in ancient sources of the Six Dynasties, Tang, and Song]. Tokyo: Kokusho kankōkai.

Yoshioka Yoshitoyo 吉岡義豊. 1955. *Dōkyō kyōten shiron* 道教經典史論 [Historical studies on Taoist scriptures]. Tokyo: Dōkyō kankōkai.

6A. 'DAODE JING,' XIANG'ER COMMENTARY, 'HESHANG GONG' COMMENTARY, AND WANG BI'S COMMENTARY

A concordance to the *Daode jing* is included in the ICS Ancient Chinese Text Concordance Series (Lau 1996). It is based on the *Wang Bi 王弼 (226–49) text of the *Daode jing* and the *Sibu congkan* 四部叢刊 edition of both the text and the commentary in the *Laozi Heshang gong zhangju* 老子河上公章句. A concordance to Wang Bi's commentary is separately available in Kitahara Mineki 1987. A concordance to the *Xiang'er 想爾 commentary (ca. 200 CE) was published by Mugitani Kunio in 1985. Another concordance to the *Daode jing* is mentioned below in section 6b, and more are listed in D. L. McMullen, *Concordances and Indexes to Chinese Texts* (San Francisco: Chinese Materials Center, 1975).

Kitahara Mineki 北原峰樹. 1987. *Rōshi Ō Hitsu chū sakuin* 「老子王弼注」索引 [Concordance to Wang Bi's commentary to the *Laozi*]. Kita-Kyushu: Chūgoku shoten.

Lau, D. C., ed. 1996. *Laozi zhuzi suoyin* 老子逐字索引 (*A Concordance to the Laozi*). The ICS Ancient Chinese Text Concordance Series; Philosophical Works, 24. Hong Kong: Shangwu yinshuguan.

Mugitani Kunio 麦谷邦夫. 1985. *Rōshi Sōji chū sakuin* 「老子想爾注」索引 [Concordance to the *Xiang'er* commentary to the *Laozi*]. Kyoto: Hōyū shoten.

6B. 'ZHUANGZI' AND GUO XIANG'S COMMENTARY

The text of the *Zhuangzi 莊子 established by Guo Qingfan 郭慶藩 (1844–97), *Zhuangzi jishi* 莊子集釋 (first published in 1895), is the basis for the concordance published by the Harvard-Yenching Institute in 1947. (A 1986 reprint of this book also includes a concordance to the *Daode jing*.) The Song text of the *Zhuangzi* found in the *Xu guyi congshu* 續故逸叢書 is the basis for the concordance published in the ICS Ancient Chinese Text Concordance (Lau 2000). There is a concordance to *Guo Xiang's 郭象 (?–312) commentary in Kitahara Mineki 1989.

Harvard-Yenching Institute, ed. 1947. *Zhuangzi yinde* 莊子引得. *A Concordance to Chuang Tzu*. Harvard-Yenching Institute Sinological Index Series, Supplement 20. Beijing: Harvard-Yenching Institute. Reprint, Cambridge, Mass.: Harvard University Press, 1956. Reprint, Taipei: Zongqing guo tushu, 1986, in the series *Zhuzi yinde* 諸子引得 [Concordances of philosophical texts], with a concordance to the *Laozi* 老子.

Kitahara Mineki 北原峰樹. 1989. *Sōshi Kaku Shō chū sakuin*「莊子郭象注」索引 [Concordance to Guo Xiang's commentary to the *Zhuangzi*]. Kita-Kyushu: Chūgoku shoten.

Lau, D. C., ed. 2000. *Zhuangzi zhuzi suoyin* 莊子逐字索引 (*A Concordance to the Zhuangzi*). The ICS Ancient Chinese Text Concordance Series; Philosophical Works, 43. Hong Kong: Shangwu yinshuguan.

6C. 'LIEZI' AND ZHANG ZHAN'S COMMENTARY

For the *Liezi* 列子 there is a concordance in Yamaguchi Yoshio 1960. A concordance to Zhang Zhan's 張湛 early-fourth-century commentary was published in 1988 by Kitahara Mineki.

Kitahara Mineki 北原峰樹. 1988. *Resshi Chō Tan chū sakuin*「列子張湛注」索引 [Concordance to Zhang Zhan's commentary to the *Liezi*]. Kita-Kyushu: Chūgoku shoten.

Yamaguchi Yoshio 山口義男. 1960. *Resshi sakuin*「列子」索引 [Concordance to *Liezi*]. Nishinomiya: Mukogawa joshi daigaku Chūgoku bungaku kenkyūshitsu.

6D. 'BAOPU ZI NEIPIAN' AND
'BAOPU ZI WAIPIAN'

For *Ge Hong's 葛洪 (283–343) *Baopu zi neipian* 抱朴子內篇 and *Baopu zi waipian* 抱朴子外篇 (see under *Baopu zi*) there are two concordances edited by Schipper in 1965 and 1970, respectively. Both are based on the text established by Sun Xingyan 孫星衍 (1753–1818; preface dated 1813) and give references to the editions in the *Zhuzi jicheng* 諸子集成, with a table of conversion to the editions in the *Sibu congkan*.

Schipper, Kristofer M., ed. 1965. *Baopu zi neipian tongjian* 抱朴子內篇通檢. *Concordance du Baopu zi neipian*. Paris: Institut des Hautes Études Chinoises.

———. 1970. *Baopu zi waipian tongjian* 抱朴子外篇通檢. *Concordance du Baopu zi waipian*. Paris: Institut des Hautes Études Chinoises.

6E. 'HUANGTING JING' AND
LIANGQIU ZI'S COMMENTARY

The concordance to the *Huangting jing* 黃庭經 edited by Schipper (1975) is based on the versions of the *Neijing* 內經 and the *Waijing* 外經 with Liangqiu zi's 梁丘子 (fl. 722) commentaries, both of which are found in the *Xiuzhen shishu* 修真十書 (CT 263).

Schipper, Kristofer M., ed. 1975. *Concordance du Houang-t'ing king: Nei-king et Wai-king*. Paris: École Française d'Extrême-Orient.

6F. 'DONGYUAN SHENZHOU JING'

The concordance to the *Dongyuan shenzhou jing* 太上洞淵神咒經 published by Yamada Toshiaki and Yusa Noboru (1984) is based on the text included in the Taoist Canon (CT 335).

Yamada Toshiaki 山田利明 and Yusa Noboru 遊佐昇. 1984. *Tajō dōen shinju-kyō goi sakuin*「太上洞淵神呪経」語彙索引 [Index to terms in the *Taishang dongyuan shenzhou jing*]. Tokyo: Shōun-dō shoten.

6G. 'ZHENGAO'

A concordance to *Tao Hongjing's 陶弘景 (454–536) *Zhengao* 真誥 was published by Mugitani Kunio in 1991. The concordance is based on the edition in the Taoist Canon (CT 1016). An index published by Ishii Masako in 1987 is concerned with names of persons, names of places, titles of texts, and selected terms found in the text. This publication, in turn, replaced an index published by Ishii Masako in the three parts (names of persons; names of places and titles of texts; terms) in 1971–72.

Ishii Masako 石井昌子. 1971–72. "*Shinkō* jinmei sakuin"「真誥」人名索引 [Index to names of persons in the *Zhengao*]; "*Shinkō* shomei, chimei sakuin"「真誥」書名・地名索引 [Index to titles of texts and names of places in the *Zhengao*]; "*Shinkō* goi sakuin"「真誥」語彙索引 [Index to terms in the *Zhengao*]. *Tōyō gakujutsu kenkyū* 東洋学術研究 10.3 (1971): 141–72; 11.1 (1972): 157–74; 11.3 (1972): 143–71.

———. 1987. "*Shinkō* sakuin"「真誥索引」 [Index to the *Zhengao*]. Tokyo: Sōka daigaku Ippan kyōikubu. (Supplement to vol. 11 of *Ippan Kyōikubu Ronshū* 一般教育部論集.)

Mugitani Kunio 麥谷邦夫. 1991. *Shinkō sakuin*「真誥」索引 [Concordance to the *Zhengao*]. Kyoto: Kyōto daigaku Jinbun kagaku kenkyūjo.

6H. 'ZHOUSHI MINGTONG JI'

A concordance to another work by Tao Hongjing, the *Zhoushi mingtong ji* 周氏冥通記, was published by Mugitani Kunio in 2003. The concordance is based on the edition in the Taoist Canon (CT 302).

Mugitani Kunio 麥谷邦夫. 2003. *Shūshi meitsūki sakuin*「周氏冥通記」索引 [Concordance to the *Zhoushi mingtong ji*]. Kyoto: Kyōto daigaku Jinbun kagaku kenkyūjo Fuzoku kanji jōhō sentaa.

6I. 'ZHOUYI CANTONG QI' AND 'HUANGDI YINFU JING'

A work by Kitahara Mineki and Sugita Shigeo (1987) includes concordances of both the *Zhouyi cantong qi* 周易參同契 and the *Huangdi yinfu jing* 黃帝陰符經. The concordance to the *Zhouyi cantong qi* is based on Zhu Xi's 朱熹 (1130–1200) *Zhouyi cantong qi kaoyi* 周易參同契考異 (CT 1001). The concordance to the *Huangdi yinfu jing* is based on the text found in the Taoist Canon with Xiao Zhenzai's 蕭真宰 commentary (CT 118).

Kitahara Mineki 北原峰樹 and Sugita Shigeo 杉田茂夫. 1987. *Shūeki sandōkei sakuin, Kōtei yinbu kyō sakuin*「周易参道契」索引・「黄帝陰符経」索引 [Concordances to the *Zhouyi cantong qi* and the *Huangdi yinfu jing*]. Kita-Kyushu: Chūgoku shoten.

6J. 'DAOSHU'

A concordance to Zeng Zao's 曾慥 (?–1155) *Daoshu 道樞 (CT 1017) was published by Miyazawa Masayori, Mugitani Kunio, and Jin Zhengyao in 2002.

Miyazawa Masayori 宮澤正順, Mugitani Kunio 麦谷邦夫, and Jin Zhengyao 金正耀. 2002. *Dōsu ichiji sakuin*「道樞」一字索引 [Concordance to the *Daoshu*]. Kyoto: Shōkadō.

6K. 'SHIYAO ERYA'

An index to the synonyms and secret names of substances mentioned in the *Shiyao erya 石藥爾雅, a work compiled by Mei Biao 梅彪 (fl. 806) and found in the Taoist Canon (CT 901), is available in Wong 1989. The index also includes names found in several other *waidan 外丹 texts.

Wong Shiu Hon 黃兆漢. 1989. *Daozang danyao yiming suoyin* 道藏丹藥異名索引. *Chinese Alchemical Terms: Guide Book to the Daozang Pseudonyms*. Taipei: Taiwan xuesheng shuju.

6L. 'DAOJIAO YISHU'

The index to the *Daojiao yishu 道教義樞 published by Nakajima Ryūzō (1980) is based on the only extant edition of this encyclopedia, compiled by Meng Anpai 孟安排 (fl. 699) and found in the Taoist Canon (CT 1129).

Nakajima Ryūzō 中島隆蔵, ed. 1980. *Dōkyō gisū sakuin kō*「道教義樞」索引稿 [A draft index to the *Daojiao yishu*]. Kyoto: private publication.

6M. 'YUNJI QIQIAN'

The index to the *Yunji qiqian 雲笈七籤 edited by Schipper (1981) as part of the Tao-tsang Project is based on the edition in the Taoist Canon (CT 1032) of this encyclopedia, compiled by Zhang Junfang 張君房 et al. in ca. 1028. A comparison of the individual chapters and sections in the three extant editions (*Daozang*; Qingzhen guan 清真館, reproduced in the *Sibu congkan*; and *Daozang jiyao*) is found in Nakajima Ryūzō 1987. The three editions are also the object of a separate study by Nakajima Ryūzō (1986).

Nakajima Ryūzō 中島隆蔵. 1986. "Unkyū shichisen no shohon ni tsuite"「雲笈七籤」の諸本について [On the editions of the *Yunji qiqian*]. *Shūkan tōyōgaku* 週間東洋学 56: 66–76.

———. 1987. "Sanbon taishō *Unkyū shichisen* mokuroku" 三本対照「雲笈七籤」目録 [Comparative tables of contents of three editions of the *Yunji qiqian*]. Chūgoku kodai yōsei shisō no sōgōteki kenkyū: Kenkyū seika hōkokusho no yon 中国古代養生思想の総合的研究—研究成果報告書の四. Kyoto: n.p.

Schipper, Kristofer M. 1981. *Projet Tao-tsang: Index du Yunji qiqian*. 2 vols. Paris: École Française d'Extrême-Orient.

7. Encyclopedias and Dictionaries

Encyclopedic works on Taoism published in English include Pas 1998 and Kohn 2000. In Chinese, among several other similar works, see especially Li Yuanguo 1991, Qing Xitai 1994, Zhongguo daojiao xiehui and Suzhou daojiao xiehui 1994, and Hu Fuchen 1995. The main encyclopedic works in Japanese are Fukui Kōjun et al. 1983, Noguchi Tetsurō et al. 1994, and Sakade Yoshinobu 1994.

Fukui Kōjun 福井康順 et al., eds. 1983. *Dōkyō* 道教 [Taoism]. 3 vols. Tokyo: Hirakawa shuppansha.

Hu Fuchen 胡孚琛, ed. 1995. *Zhonghua daojiao da cidian* 中华道教大辞典 [Great dictionary of Chinese Taoism]. Beijing: Zhongguo shehui kexue chubanshe.

Kohn, Livia, ed. 2000. *Daoism Handbook*. Leiden: E. J. Brill.

Li Yuanguo 李远国, ed. 1991. *Zhongguo daojiao qigong yangsheng daquan* 中國道教氣功養生大全 [Compendium of Chinese Taoism, *qigong*, and Nourishing Life]. Chengdu: Sichuan cishu chubanshe.

Noguchi Tetsurō 野口鐵郎 et al., eds. 1994. *Dōkyō jiten* 道教事典 [Encyclopedia of Taoism]. Tokyo: Hirakawa shuppansha.

Pas, Julian, in cooperation with Man Kam Leung. 1998. *Historical Dictionary of Taoism*. Lanham, Md., and London: The Scarecrow Press.

Qing Xitai 卿希泰, ed. 1994. *Zhongguo daojiao* 中国道教 [Chinese Taoism]. 4 vols. Shanghai: Dongfang chuban zhongxin.

Sakade Yoshinobu 坂出祥伸, ed. 1994. *Dōkyō no daijiten* 道教の大事典 [Great encyclopedia of Taoism]. Tokyo: Shin jinbutsu ōrai sha.

Zhongguo daojiao xiehui 中国道教协会 [Chinese Taoist Association] and Suzhou daojiao xiehui 苏州道教协会 [Suzhou Taoist Association], eds. 1994. *Daojiao dacidian* 道教大辭典 [Great dictionary of Taoism]. Beijing: Huaxia chubanshe.

Most of the works listed above contain short entries on various subjects related to Taoism, but some (in particular, Kohn 2000, Qing Xitai 1994, and Sakade Yoshinobu 1994) contain longer articles.

Entries relevant to Taoism are also found in general encyclopedias and dictionaries of religion and thought. Those containing reliable articles include the *Encyclopedia of Religion* edited by Mircea Eliade (New York: Macmillan, 1987) and the *Encyclopédie philosophique universelle* edited by André Jacob (Paris, Presses Universitaires de France, 1989–).

BIBLIOGRAPHIES

SOURCES IN THE *DAOZANG*
(TAOIST CANON)

This bibliography lists titles of *Daozang* texts cited in the entries of the present book. It provides:

(a) Full titles of texts cited in abbreviated form.

(b) References to three catalogues of the *Daozang*:

    (1) *Concordance du Tao-tsang: Titres des ouvrages* (Schipper 1975b, abbreviated as CT)

    (2) the Harvard-Yenching *Daozang zimu yinde* 道藏子目引得 (Weng Dujian 1935, abbreviated as HY)

    (3) *Daozang tiyao* 道藏提要 (Ren Jiyu and Zhong Zhaopeng 1991, abbreviated as TY)

(c) References to *Daozang* texts that are also entirely or partially included in the *Yunji qiqian (abbreviated as YJQQ); these references are based on Lagerwey 1981a, which should be consulted for further details.

(d) References to texts also published in the *Daozang jiyao (abbreviated as DZJY; numbers of volumes and pages are those of the Xinwenfeng reprint, Taipei 1977).

Asterisks (*) indicate texts with independent entries in the present book. Translations of almost all titles are found in the entries.

CT	HY	TY	
1	1	1	*Lingbao wuliang duren shangpin miaojing* 靈寶無量度人上品妙經. DZJY 1–3: 411–946. See *Duren jing.
5	5	5	*Wenchang dadong xianjing* 文昌大洞仙經. Full title: *Taishang wuji zongzhen Wenchang dadong xianjing* 太上無極總真文昌大洞仙經. See *Dadong zhenjing.
6	6	6	*Shangqing dadong zhenjing* 上清大洞真經. Part. in YJQQ 30 and 42. See *Dadong zhenjing.
7	7	7	*Dadong yujing* 大洞玉經. DZJY 3: 1127–74, with a section entitled "Dadong xianjing guanxiang yaojue" 大洞仙經觀想要訣 (3: 1130–38) not found in the *Daozang* text. See *Dadong zhenjing.
9	9	9	*Haikong zhizang jing* 海空智藏經. Full title: *Taishang yisheng Haikong zhizang jing* 太上一乘海空智藏經. Part. in YJQQ 39, 93, and 95.
10	10	10	*Yuhuang benxing jijing* 玉皇本行集經. Full title: *Gaoshang Yuhuang benxing jijing* 高上玉皇本行集經.
11	11	11	*Yuhuang benxing jijing* 玉皇本行集經. Full title: *Gaoshang Yuhuang benxing jijing* 高上玉皇本行集經. DZJY 7: 2587–2632.

CT	HY	TY	
13	13	13	*Xinyin miaojing* 心印妙經. Full title: *Gaoshang Yuhuang xinyin miaojing* 高上玉皇心印妙經. See *Xinyin jing.
14	14	14	*Yuhuang taixi jing* 高上玉皇胎息經 胎息經. Full title: *Gaoshang Yuhuang taixi jing* 高上玉皇胎息經. See *Taixi jing.
15	15	15	*Leiting yujing* 雷霆玉經. Full title: *Wushang jiuxiao Yuqing dafan ziwei Xuandu leiting yujing* 無上九霄玉清大梵紫微玄都雷霆玉經.
16	16	16	*Yushu baojing* 玉樞寶經. Full title: *Jiutian yingyuan leisheng Puhua tianzun yushu baojing* 九天應元雷聲普化天尊玉樞寶經. See *Yushu jing.
17	17	17	*Chaotian xielei zhenjing* 朝天謝雷真經. Full title: *Taishang shuo chaotian xielei zhenjing* 太上說朝天謝雷真經.
19	19	19	*Xiaozai huming miaojing* 消災護命妙經. Full title: *Taishang shengxuan xiaozai huming miaojing* 太上昇玄消災護命妙經.
22	22	22	*Wupian zhenwen 五篇真文. Full title: *Yuanshi wulao chishu yu* [recte: *wu*] *pian zhenwen tianshu jing* 元始五老赤書 (玉) [五] 篇真文天書經.
45	45	45	*Beidou bensheng zhenjing* 北斗本生真經. Full title: *Yuqing wushang Lingbao ziran beidou bensheng zhenjing* 玉清無上靈寶自然北斗本生真經.
55	55	55	*Taixiao langshu qiongwen dizhang jing* 太霄琅書瓊文帝章經. Full title: *Gaoshang taixiao langshu qiongwen dizhang jing* 高上太霄琅書瓊文帝章經. See *Taixiao langshu.
56	56	56	*Yupei jindang shangjing* 玉佩金璫上經. Full title: *Taishang yupei jindang taiji jinshu shangjing* 太上玉佩金璫太極金書上經. Part. in YJQQ 51 and 54.
57	57	57	*Zhenyuan tongxian daojing* 真元通仙道經. Full title: *Shangfang tianzun shuo zhenyuan tongxian daojing* 上方天尊說真元通仙道經.
59	59	59	*Jueyi jing* 決疑經. Full title: *Yuanshi dongzhen jueyi jing* 元始洞真決疑經. See *Benji jing.
69	69	69	*Anzao jing* 安灶經. Full title: *Taishang dongzhen anzao jing* 太上洞真安灶經.
74	74	74	*Jiuyou bazui xinyin miaojing* 九幽拔罪心印妙經. Full title: *Taishang shuo jiuyou bazui xinyin miaojing* 太上說九幽拔罪心印妙經. See *Xinyin jing.
78	78	78	*Taishang sandong shenzhou* 太上三洞神咒.
87	87	87	*Duren shangpin miaojing sizhu* 度人上品妙經四注. Full title: *Yuanshi wuliang duren shangpin miaojing sizhu* 元始無量度人上品妙經四注. See *Duren jing.
88	88	88	*Duren shangpin miaojing zhu* 度人上品妙經注. Full title: *Yuanshi wuliang duren shangpin miaojing zhu* 元始無量度人上品妙經注.

CT	HY	TY	
89	89	89	*Duren shangpin miaojing tongyi* 度人上品妙經通義. Full title: *Yuanshi wuliang duren shangpin miaojing tongyi* 元始無量度人上品妙經通義.
90	90	90	*Duren shangpin miaojing neiyi* 度人上品妙經內義. Full title: *Yuanshi wuliang duren shangpin miaojing neiyi* 元始無量度人上品妙經內義.
91	91	91	*Duren shangpin miaojing zhu* 度人上品妙經注. Full title: *Taishang dongxuan Lingbao wuliang duren shangpin miaojing zhu* 太上洞玄靈寶無量度人上品妙經注. DZJY 3: 947–998.
92	92	92	*Duren shangpin miaojing zhujie* 度人上品妙經注解. Full title: *Yuanshi wuliang duren shangpin miaojing zhujie* 元始無量度人上品妙經注解.
95	95	95	*Duren jingjue yinyi* 度人經訣音義. Full title: *Dongxuan Lingbao wuliang duren jingjue yinyi* 洞玄靈寶無量度人經訣音義.
97	97	97	*Zhutian neiyin ziran yuzi* 諸天內音自然玉字. Full title: *Taishang Lingbao zhutian neiyin ziran yuzi* 太上靈寶諸天內音自然玉字.
99	99	99	*Yushu baojing jizhu* 玉樞寶經集注. Full title: *Jiutian yingyuan leisheng Puhua tianzun yushu baojing jizhu* 九天應元雷聲普化天尊玉樞寶經集注. See *Yushu jing.
100	100	100	*Xiaozai huming miaojing zhu* 消災護命妙經注. Full title: *Taishang shengxuan shuo xiaozai huming miaojing zhu* 太上昇玄說消災護命妙經注. DZJY 4: 1294–98.
101	101	101	*Xiaozai huming miaojing zhu* 消災護命妙經注. Full title: *Taishang shengxuan xiaozai huming miaojing zhu* 太上昇玄消災護命妙經注.
103	103	103	*Wenchang dadong xianjing* 文昌大洞仙經. Full title: *Yuqing wuji zongzhen Wenchang dadong xianjing* 玉清無極總真文昌大洞仙經. See *Dadong zhenjing.
104	104	104	*Shangqing dadong zhenjing yujue yinyi* 上清大洞真經玉訣音義.
105	105	105	*Datong jingzhu* 大通經注. Full title: *Taishang datong jingzhu* 太上大通經注. DZJY 5: 2136–37.
107	107	107	*Donggu zhenjing zhu* 洞古真經注. Full title: *Wushang chiwen donggu zhenjing zhu* 無上赤文洞古真經注.
108	108	108	*Yinfu jing jizhu* 陰符經集注. Full title: *Huangdi yinfu jing jizhu* 黃帝陰符經集注.
109	109	109	*Yinfu jing jiangyi* 陰符經講義. Full title: *Huangdi yinfu jing jiangyi* 黃帝陰符經講義.
110	110	110	*Yinfu jing shu* 陰符經疏. Full title: *Huangdi yinfu jing shu* 黃帝陰符經疏.

CT	HY	TY	
111	111	111	*Yinfu jing jijie* 陰符經集解. Full title: *Huangdi yinfu jing jijie* 黃帝陰符經集解. DZJY 8: 3148–59.
112	112	112	*Yinfu jing zhu* 陰符經注. Full title: *Huangdi yinfu jing zhu* 黃帝陰符經注. YJQQ 15.
113	113	113	*Yinfu jing jie* 陰符經解. Full title: *Huangdi yinfu jing jie* 黃帝陰符經解.
114	114	114	*Yinfu jing zhujie* 陰符經注解. Full title: *Huangdi yinfu jing zhujie* 黃帝陰符經注解.
115	115	115	*Yinfu jing zhu* 陰符經注. Full title: *Huangdi yinfu jing zhu* 黃帝陰符經注.
116	116	116	*Yinfu jing zhu* 陰符經注. Full title: *Huangdi yinfu jing zhu* 黃帝陰符經注. DZJY 8: 3175–77.
117	117	117	*Yinfu jing zhu* 陰符經注. Full title: *Huangdi yinfu jing zhu* 黃帝陰符經注.
118	118	118	*Yinfu jing jieyi* 陰符經解義. Full title: *Huangdi yinfu jing jieyi* 黃帝陰符經解義.
119	119	119	*Yinfu jing sanhuang yujue* 陰符經三皇玉訣.
120	120	120	*Yinfu jing xinfa* 陰符經心法. Full title: *Huangdi yinfu jing xinfa* 黃帝陰符經心法.
121	121	121	*Yinfu jing zhu* 陰符經注. Full title: *Huangdi yinfu jing zhu* 黃帝陰符經注.
122	122	122	*Yinfu jing zhu* 陰符經注. Full title: *Huangdi yinfu jing zhu* 黃帝陰符經注.
123	123	123	*Yinfu jing zhu* 陰符經注. Full title: *Huangdi yinfu jing zhu* 黃帝陰符經注.
124	124	124	*Yinfu jing zhujie* 陰符經注解. Full title: *Huangdi yinfu jing zhujie* 黃帝陰符經注解.
125	125	125	*Yinfu jing zhu* 陰符經注. Full title: *Huangdi yinfu jing zhu* 黃帝陰符經注.
126	126	126	*Yinfu jing jiasong jiezhu* 陰符經夾頌解注. Full title: *Huangdi yinfu jing jiasong jiezhu* 黃帝陰符經夾頌解注.
127	127	127	*Yinfu jing jijie* 陰符經集解. Full title: *Huangdi yinfu jing jijie* 黃帝陰符經集解.
129	129	129	*Taixiao langshu qiongwen dizhang jue* 太霄琅書瓊文帝章訣. See *Taixiao langshu.
130	130	130	*Taixi jing zhu* 胎息經注. YJQQ 60. DZJY 7: 2848–49. See *Taixi jing.
131	131	131	*Taixi biyao gejue* 胎息祕要歌訣.
133	133	133	*Dongfang neijing zhu* 洞房內經注. Full title: *Taishang dongfang neijing zhu* 太上洞房內經注.

CT	HY	TY	
135	135	135	*Cui gong ruyao jing zhujie* 崔公入藥鏡注解. See *Ruyao jing*.
136	136	136	*Qinyuan chun danci zhujie* 沁園春丹詞注解. Full title: *Lü Chunyang zhenren qinyuan chun danci zhujie* 呂純陽真人沁園春丹詞注解. See *Qinyuan chun*.
140	140	140	*Shangqing wozhong jue* 上清握中訣.
141	141	141	*Wuzhen pian zhushu* 悟真篇注疏. Full title: *Ziyang zhenren wuzhen pian zhushu* 紫陽真人悟真篇注疏. See *Wuzhen pian*.
142	142	142	*Wuzhen pian sanzhu* 悟真篇三注. Full title: *Ziyang zhenren wuzhen pian sanzhu* 紫陽真人悟真篇三注. DZJY 14: 6045–99. See *Wuzhen pian*.
143	143	143	*Wuzhen zhizhi xiangshuo sansheng biyao* 悟真直指詳說三乘祕要. Full title: *Ziyang zhenren wuzhen zhizhi xiangshuo sansheng biyao* 紫陽真人悟真直指詳說三乘祕要. DZJY 14: 6108–12. See *Wuzhen pian*.
144	144	144	*Wuzhen pian shiyi* 悟真篇拾遺. Full title: *Ziyang zhenren wuzhen pian shiyi* 紫陽真人悟真篇拾遺. DZJY 14: 6100–6108. See *Wuzhen pian*.
145	145	145	*Wuzhen pian zhushi* 悟真篇注釋. See *Wuzhen pian*.
146	146	146	*Wuzhen pian jiangyi* 悟真篇講義. Full title: *Ziyang zhenren wuzhen pian jiangyi* 紫陽真人悟真篇講義. See *Wuzhen pian*.
147	147	147	*Duren shangpin miaojing futu* 度人上品妙經符圖. Full title: *Lingbao wuliang duren shangpin miaojing futu* 靈寶無量度人上品妙經符圖.
148	148	148	*Wuliang duren shangpin miaojing pangtong tu* 無量度人上品妙經旁通圖.
149	149	149	*Xiuzhen taiji hunyuan tu* 修真太極混元圖.
150	150	150	*Xiuzhen taiji hunyuan zhixuan tu* 修真太極混元指玄圖.
152	152	152	*Xiuzhen liyan chaotu* 修真歷驗鈔圖. YJQQ 72.
156	156	156	*Jiugong zifang tu* 九宮紫房圖. Full title: *Shangqing dongzhen jiugong zifang tu* 上清洞真九宮紫房圖.
166	166	165	*Yuanshi shangzhen zhongxian ji* 元始上真眾仙記.
167	167	166	*Zhenling weiye tu* 真靈位業圖. Full title: *Dongxuan Lingbao zhenling weiye tu* 洞玄靈寶真靈位業圖. DZJY 19: 8293-7.
171	171	170	*Qingwei xianpu* 清微仙譜.
173	173	172	*Jinlian zhengzong ji* 金蓮正宗記. DZJY 25: 10937–59.
174	174	173	*Jinlian zhengzong xianyuan xiangzhuan* 金蓮正宗仙源像傳. DZJY 25: 10960–80.
175	175	174	*Qizhen nianpu* 七真年譜. DZJY 25: 10981–88.
176	176	175	*Xuanfeng qinghui lu* 玄風慶會錄.

CT	HY	TY	
177	177	176	*Zhihui shangpin dajie* 智慧上品大誡. Full title: *Taishang dongzhen zhihui shangpin dajie* 太上洞真智慧上品大誡. DZJY 23: 10271–76.
178	178	177	*Sandong zhongjie wen* 三洞眾戒文. DZJY 23: 10277–83.
179	179	178	*Taiwei lingshu ziwen xianji zhenji shangjing* 太微靈書紫文仙忌真記上經. DZJY 23: 10283–84. See *Lingshu ziwen*.
180	180	179	*Xuhuang tianzun chuzhen shijie wen* 虛皇天尊初真十戒文. DZJY 23: 10285–87.
184	184	183	*Siji mingke jing* 四極明科經. Full title: *Taizhen Yudi siji mingke jing* 太真玉帝四極明科經.
185	185	184	*Chisong zi zhong jiejing* 赤松子中誡經.
186	186	185	*Taiwei xianjun gongguo ge* 太微仙君功過格.
188	188	187	*Xuandu lüwen* 玄都律文.
189	189	188	*Chaotian xiezui dachan* 朝天謝罪大懺. Full title: *Taishang Lingbao chaotian xiezui dachan* 太上靈寶朝天謝罪大懺. DZJY 22: 9873–9916.
193	193	192	*Yuhuang youzui xifu baochan* 玉皇宥罪錫福寶懺. DZJY 7: 2850–58.
194	194	193	*Yuhuang manyuan baochan* 玉皇滿願寶懺. Full title: *Gaoshang Yuhuang manyuan baochan* 高上玉皇滿願寶懺.
195	195	194	*Jiutian yingyuan leisheng Puhua tianzun yushu baochan* 九天應元雷聲普化天尊玉樞寶懺.
196	196	195	*Leiting yushu youzui fachan* 雷霆玉樞宥罪法懺.
197	197	196	*Yuhuang shiqi ciguang dengyi* 玉皇十七慈光燈儀. DZJY 7: 2859–66.
208	208	207	*Dongchu siming dengyi* 東廚司命燈儀.
215	215	214	*Difu shiwang badu yi* 地府十王拔度儀.
218	218	217	*Qingwei xuanshu zougao yi* 清微玄樞奏告儀.
219	219	218	*Lingbao wuliang duren shangjing dafa* 靈寶無量度人上經大法.
220	220	219	*Wushang xuanyuan santian Yutang dafa* 無上玄元三天玉堂大法.
221	221	220	*Wushang santian Yutang zhengzong gaoben neijing yushu* 無上三天玉堂正宗高奔內景玉書.
222	222	221	*Qingwei shenlie bifa* 清微神烈祕法.
223	223	222	*Qingwei yuanjiang dafa* 清微元降大法.
224	224	223	*Qingwei zhaifa* 清微齋法.
225	225	224	*Jiuyao xinyin miaojing* 九要心印妙經. Full title: *Taishang jiuyao xinyin miaojing* 太上九要心印妙經. See *Xinyin jing*.
233	233	232	*Huandan zhongxian lun* 還丹眾仙論.
238	238	237	*Yuanyang zi jinye ji* 元陽子金液集.

CT	HY	TY	
239	239	238	*Huandan jinye gezhu* 還丹金液歌注.
243	243	242	*Guizhong zhinan* 規中指南. Full title: *Chen Xubai guizhong zhinan* 陳虛白規中指南. DZJY 16: 7109–16.
244	244	243	*Dadan zhizhi* 大丹直指.
245	245	244	*Yuqi zi danjing zhiyao* 玉谿子丹經指要.
246	246	245	*Xishan qunxian huizhen ji* 西山群仙會真記. DZJY 25: 11015–35.
247	247	246	*Huizhen ji* 會真集.
248	248	247	*Qizhen ji* 啟真集.
249	249	248	*Zhonghe ji* 中和集. DZJY 17: 7287–7335.
250	250	249	*Santian yisui* 三天易髓.
251	251	250	*Quanzhen jixuan biyao* 全真集玄祕要.
254	254	253	*Jinhua yujing* 金華玉經. Full title: *Dadong jinhua yujing* 大洞金華玉經.
255	255	254	*Taiwei lingshu ziwen langgan huadan shenzhen shangjing* 太微靈書紫文琅玕華丹神真上經. See *Lingshu ziwen*.
263	263	262	*Xiuzhen shishu* 修真十書. Part. DZJY 16: 7087–7108 (slightly abbreviated version of *j.* 9–13) and 12: 5113–42 (*j.* 14–16).
265	265	264	*Huandan gejue* 還丹歌訣.
267	267	266	*Shangsheng xiuzhen sanyao* 上乘修真三要.
273	273	272	*Mingdao pian* 明道篇.
276	276	275	*Xiyi zhimi lun* 析疑指迷論. DZJY 14: 6188–94 (includes a postface dated 1917).
277	277	276	*Xiuzhen jingyi zalun* 修真精義雜論. Part. in YJQQ 57.
278	278	277	*Qingwei danjue* 清微丹訣.
283	283	282	*Huangdi longshou jing* 黃帝龍首經.
285	285	284	*Huangdi shou sanzi Xuannü jing* 黃帝授三子玄女經.
290	290	289	*Guang Huangdi benxing ji* 廣黃帝本行記.
292	292	291	*Han Wudi neizhuan* 漢武帝內傳. Part. in YJQQ 79.
294	294	293	*Liexian zhuan* 列仙傳. Part. in YJQQ 85 and 108.
295	295	294	*Xu xianzhuan* 續仙傳. Part. in YJQQ 113 下.
296	296	295	*Lishi zhenxian tidao tongjian* 歷世真仙體道通鑑.
297	297	296	*Lishi zhenxian tidao tongjian xubian* 歷世真仙體道通鑑續編
298	298	297	*Lishi zhenxian tidao tongjian houji* 歷世真仙體道通鑑後集.
302	302	301	*Zhoushi mingtong ji* 周氏冥通記.
303	303	302	*Ziyang zhenren neizhuan* 紫陽真人內傳.
304	304	303	*Maoshan zhi* 茅山志.
305	305	304	*Chunyang dijun shenhua miaotong ji* 純陽帝君神化妙通紀.
306	306	305	*Taihua Xiyi zhi* 太華希夷志.

CT	HY	TY	
307	307	306	*Xiyue Huashan zhi* 西嶽華山誌.
308	308	307	*Ningyang Dong zhenren yuxian ji* 凝陽董真人遇仙記.
311	311	310	*Yinfu jing song* 陰符經頌. Full title: *Huangdi yinfu jing song* 黃帝陰符經頌. DZJY 8: 3181–84.
317	317	316	*Hong'en lingji zhenjun miaojing* 洪恩靈濟真君妙經. Full title: *Lingbao tianzun shuo Hong'en lingji zhenjun miaojing* 靈寶天尊說洪恩靈濟真君妙經.
318	318	317	*Ziran jiutian shengshen zhangjing* 自然九天生神章經. Full title: *Dongxuan Lingbao ziran jiutian shengshen zhangjing* 洞玄靈寶自然九天生神章經. YJQQ 16. See *Shengshen jing.
325	325	324	*Zhihui dingzhi tongwei jing* 智慧定志通微經. Full title: *Taishang dongxuan Lingbao zhihui dingzhi tongwei jing* 太上洞玄靈寶智慧定志通微經.
326	326	325	*Guanmiao jing* 觀妙經. Full title: *Taishang dongxuan Lingbao guanmiao jing* 太上洞玄靈寶觀妙經.
329	329	328	*Kaiyan bimi zang jing* 開演祕密藏經. Full title: *Taishang dongxuan Lingbao kaiyan bimi zang jing* 太上洞玄靈寶開演祕密藏經. DZJY 4: 1632–37.
335	335	334	*Dongyuan shenzhou jing 洞淵神咒經. Full title: *Taishang dongyuan shenzhou jing* 太上洞淵神咒經.
336	336	335	*Yebao yinyuan jing 業報因緣經. Full title: *Taishang dongxuan Lingbao yebao yinyuan jing* 太上洞玄靈寶業報因緣經. Part. DZJY 4: 1653–58 (j. 4 of the *Daozang* text).
339	339	338	*Chujia yinyuan jing* 出家因緣經. Full title: *Taishang dongxuan Lingbao chujia yinyuan jing* 太上洞玄靈寶出家因緣經. DZJY 4: 1658–65.
346	346	345	*Zhenyi quanjie falun miaojing* 真一勸誡法輪妙經. Full title: *Taishang dongxuan Lingbao zhenyi quanjie falun miaojing* 太上洞玄靈寶真一勸誡法輪妙經.
352	352	351	*Chishu yujue miaojing* 赤書玉訣妙經. Full title: *Taishang dongxuan Lingbao chishu yujue miaojing* 太上洞玄靈寶赤書玉訣妙經.
358	358	357	*Shenzhou yanshou miaojing* 神咒延壽妙經. Full title: *Taishang shenzhou yanshou miaojing* 太上神咒延壽妙經. DZJY 4: 1595.
364	364	363	*Buxie Zaowang jing* 補謝灶王經. Full title: *Taishang Lingbao buxie Zaowang jing* 太上靈寶補謝灶王經.
369	369	368	*Miedu wulian shengshi miaojing* 滅度五鍊生尸妙經. Full title: *Taishang dongxuan Lingbao miedu wulian shengshi miaojing* 太上洞玄靈寶滅度五鍊生尸妙經.
388	388	387	*Lingbao wufu xu 靈寶五符序. Full title: *Taishang Lingbao wufu xu* 太上靈寶五符序.
393	393	392	*Lingbao dagang chao* 靈寶大綱鈔. Full title: *Taishang dongxuan Lingbao dagang chao* 太上洞玄靈寶大綱鈔.

CT	HY	TY	
396	396	395	*Ziran jiutian shengshen zhangjing jieyi* 自然九天生神章經解義. Full title: *dongxuan Lingbao ziran jiutian shengshen zhangjing jieyi* 洞玄靈寶自然九天生神章經解義. DZJY 4: 1451–89. See *Shengshen jing.
397	397	396	*Ziran jiutian shengshen yuzhang jingjie* 自然九天生神玉章經解. Full title: *Dongxuan Lingbao ziran jiutian shengshen yuzhang jingjie* 洞玄靈寶自然九天生神玉章經解. DZJY 4: 1491–1533. See *Shengshen jing.
398	398	397	*Ziran jiutian shengshen zhangjing zhu* 自然九天生神章經注. Full title: *Dongxuan Lingbao ziran jiutian shengshen zhangjing zhu* 洞玄靈寶自然九天生神章經注. DZJY 4: 1535–62. See *Shengshen jing.
400	400	399	*Dingguan jing* 定觀經. Full title: *Dongxuan Lingbao dingguan jingzhu* 洞玄靈寶定觀經注. YJQQ 17. DZJY 4: 1629–32.
401	401	400	*Huangting neijing yujing zhu* 黃庭內景玉經注.
403	403	402	*Huangting neiwai yujing jingjie* 黃庭內外玉景經解.
405	405	404	*Dongfang shangjing* 洞房上經. Full title: *Shangqing zijing junhuang chuzi ling daojun dongfang shangjing* 上清紫精君皇初紫靈道君洞房上經. Part. in YJQQ 25, 31, and 52.
407	407	406	*Lingbao dalian neizhi xingchi jiyao* 靈寶大鍊內旨行持機要.
410	410	409	*Lingbao zhongjian wen* 靈寶眾簡文. Full title: *Taishang dongxuan Lingbao zhongjian wen* 太上洞玄靈寶眾簡文.
411	411	410	*Lingbao wudi jiaoji zhaozhen yujue* 靈寶五帝醮祭招真玉訣. Full title: *Taishang dongxuan Lingbao wudi jiaoji zhaozhen yujue* 太上洞玄靈寶五帝醮祭招真玉訣.
421	421	420	*Dengzhen yinjue* 登真隱訣. Part. in YJQQ 45 and 48.
424	424	423	*Mingtang yuanzhen jingjue* 明堂元真經訣. Full title: *Shangqing mingtang yuanzhen jingjue* 上清明堂元真經訣.
426	426	425	*Basu zhenjing* 八素真經. Full title: *Shangqing taishang basu zhenjing* 上清太上八素真經. Part. in YJQQ 25. See *Basu jing.
428	428	427	*Feixing jiuchen yujing* 飛行九晨玉經. Full title: *Taishang feixing jiuchen yujing* 太上飛行九晨玉經. YJQQ 20.
429	429	428	*Shangqing changsheng baojian tu* 上清長生寶鑑圖.
431	431	430	*Hanxiang jianjian tu* 含象劍鑑圖. Full title: *Shangqing hanxiang jianjian tu* 上清含象劍鑑圖.
432	432	431	*Huangting neijing wuzang liufu buxie tu* 黃庭內景五臟六腑補瀉圖.
434	434	433	*Xuanlan renniao shan jingtu* 玄覽人鳥山經圖.
436	436	435	*Zhenyuan miaojing pin* 真元妙經品. Full title: *Shangfang dadong zhenyuan miaojing pin* 上方大洞真元妙經品.
437	437	436	*Zhenyuan miaojing tu* 真元妙經圖. Full title: *Shangfang dadong zhenyuan miaojing tu* 上方大洞真元妙經圖.

CT	HY	TY	
438	438	437	*Zhenyuan yinyang zhijiang tushu houjie* 真元陰陽陟降圖書後解. Full title: *Shangfang dadong zhenyuan yinyang zhijiang tushu houjie* 上方大洞真元陰陽陟降圖書後解.
439	439	438	*Zhenyuan tushu jishuo zhongpian* 真元圖書繼說終篇. Full title: *Shangfang dadong zhenyuan tushu jishuo zhongpian* 上方大洞真元圖書繼說終篇.
440	440	439	*Xu Taishi zhenjun tuzhuan* 許太史真君圖傳.
441	441	440	*Wuyue guben zhenxing tu* 五嶽古本真形圖. Full title: *Dongxuan Lingbao wuyue guben zhenxing tu* 洞玄靈寶五嶽古本真形圖.
442	442	441	**Housheng daojun lieji* 後聖道君列紀. Full title: *Shangqing Housheng daojun lieji* 上清後聖道君列紀. See **Lingshu ziwen*.
445	445	444	*Sanshi minghui xingzhuang juguan fangsuo wen* 三師名諱形狀居觀方所文. Full title: *Dongxuan Lingbao sanshi minghui xingzhuang juguan fangsuo wen* 洞玄靈寶三師名諱形狀居觀方所文.
447	447	446	*Xu zhenjun xianzhuan* 許真君仙傳.
448	448	447	*Xishan Xu zhenjun bashiwu hua lu* 西山許真君八十五化錄.
449	449	448	*Xiaodao Wu Xu er zhenjun zhuan* 孝道吳許二真君傳.
450	450	449	*Taiji Ge Xiangong zhuan* 太極葛仙公傳. DZJY 10: 4435–45.
452	452	451	**Nanyue jiu zhenren zhuan* 南嶽九真人傳.
453	453	452	*Nanyue xiaolu* 南嶽小錄.
455	455	454	*Santu wuku quanjie jing* 三途五苦勸戒經. Full title: *Taishang Xuanyi zhenren shuo santu wuku quanjie jing* 太上玄一真人說三途五苦勸戒經.
456	456	455	*Lingbao sanyuan pinjie gongde qingzhong jing* 靈寶三元品戒功德輕重經. Full title: *Taishang dongxuan Lingbao sanyuan pinjie gongde qingzhong jing* 太上洞玄靈寶三元品戒功德輕重經.
461	461	460	*Shangqing gusui lingwen guilü* 上清骨髓靈文鬼律.
463	463	462	*Yaoxiu keyi jielü chao* 要修科儀戒律鈔. DZJY 23: 10355–74 (includes only the first four *juan* of the 16-*juan* text in the *Daozang*).
464	464	463	**Zhaijie lu* 齋戒錄. YJQQ 37.
465	465		*Lingbao lingjiao jidu jinshu mulu* 靈寶領教濟度金書目錄. [*Daozang tiyao* considers this text to be part of the next one (CT 466, TY 464).]
466	466	464	**Lingbao lingjiao jidu jinshu* 靈寶領教濟度金書.
468	468	466	*Hong'en lingji zhenjun ziran xingdao yi* 洪恩靈濟真君自然行道儀.
469	469	467	*Hong'en lingji zhenjun jifu suqi yi* 洪恩靈濟真君集福宿啟儀.
470	470	468	*Hong'en lingji zhenjun jifu zaochao yi* 洪恩靈濟真君集福早朝儀.
471	471	469	*Hong'en lingji zhenjun jifu wuchao yi* 洪恩靈濟真君集福午朝儀.
472	472	470	*Hong'en lingji zhenjun jifu wanchao yi* 洪恩靈濟真君集福晚朝儀.

CT	HY	TY	
473	473	471	*Hong'en lingji zhenjun qixie shejiao ke* 洪恩靈濟真君祈謝設醮科.
474	474	472	*Hong'en lingji zhenjun liyuan wen* 洪恩靈濟真君禮願文.
475	475	473	*Hong'en lingji zhenjun qizheng xingdeng yi* 洪恩靈濟真君七政星燈儀.
476	476	474	*Hong'en lingji zhenjun shishi* 洪恩靈濟真君事實.
483	483	479	*Jinlu zhai qitan yi* 金籙齋啟壇儀.
488	488	484	*Jinlu zhai chanfang yi* 金籙齋懺方儀.
499	499	495	*Yulu zidu suqi yi* 玉籙資度宿啟儀.
500	500	496	*Yulu zidu jietan yi* 玉籙資度解壇儀.
501	501	497	*Yulu zidu shejiao yi* 玉籙資度設醮儀.
502	502	498	*Yulu zidu zao wu wan chao yi* 玉籙資度早午晚朝儀.
503	503	499	*Yulu shengshen zidu zhuanjing yi* 玉籙生神資度轉經儀.
504	504	500	*Yulu shengshen zidu kaishou yi* 玉籙生神資度開收儀.
505	505	501	*Yulu sanri jiuchao yi* 玉籙三日九朝儀.
506	506	502	*Yulu jiyou panhu yi* 玉籙濟幽判斛儀
507	507	503	*Huanglu zhaiyi* 黃籙齋儀. Full title: *Taishang huanglu zhaiyi* 太上黃籙齋儀.
508	508	504	**Wushang huanglu dazhai licheng yi* 無上黃籙大齋立成儀. Part. DZJY 23: 10401–39 (includes only the section entitled "Fuming men" 符命門, corresponding to *j.* 41–43 in the *Daozang* text).
514	514	510	*Huanglu jiuyou jiao wu'ai yezhai cidi yi* 黃籙九幽醮無礙夜齋次第儀.
519	519	515	*Yukui mingzhen zhai chanfang yi* 玉匱明真齋懺方儀. Full title: *Taishang Lingbao yukui mingzhen zhai chanfang yi* 太上靈寶玉匱明真齋懺方儀.
520	520	516	*Yukui mingzhen dazhai chanfang yi* 玉匱明真大齋懺方儀. Full title: *Taishang Lingbao yukui mingzhen dazhai chanfang yi* 太上靈寶玉匱明真大齋懺方儀.
521	521	517	*Yukui mingzhen dazhai yangong yi* 玉匱明真大齋言功儀. Full title: *Taishang Lingbao yukui mingzhen dazhai yan gong yi* 太上靈寶玉匱明真大齋言功儀.
524	524	520	*Lingbao zhai shuo guangzhu jiefa dengzhu yuanyi* 靈寶齋說光燭戒罰燈祝願儀. Full title: *Dongxuan Lingbao zhai shuo guangzhu jiefa dengzhu yuanyi* 洞玄靈寶齋說光燭戒罰燈祝願儀.
525	525	521	*Dongyuan sanmei shenzhou zhai chan xieyi* 洞淵三昧神咒齋懺謝儀. Full title: *Taishang dongyuan sanmei shenzhou zhai chan xieyi* 太上洞淵三昧神咒齋懺謝儀.
526	526	522	*Dongyuan sanmei shenzhou zhai qingdan xingdao yi* 洞淵三昧神咒齋清旦行道儀. Full title: *Taishang dongyuan sanmei shenzhou zhai qingdan xingdao yi* 太上洞淵三昧神咒齋清旦行道儀.

CT	HY	TY	
527	527	523	*Dongyuan sanmei shenzhou zhai shifang chanyi* 洞淵三昧神咒齋十方懺儀. Full title: *Taishang dongyuan sanmei shenzhou zhai shifang chanyi* 太上洞淵三昧神咒齋十方懺儀.
528	528	524	*Lingbao shoudu yi* 靈寶授度儀. Full title: *Taishang dongxuan Lingbao shoudu yi* 太上洞玄靈寶授度儀.
532	532	528	*Lingbao zhaijie weiyi zhujing yaojue* 靈寶齋戒威儀諸經要訣. Full title: *Taiji zhenren fu Lingbao zhaijie weiyi zhujing yaojue* 太極真人敷靈寶齋戒威儀諸經要訣.
541	541	537	*Dongyue dasheng baochan* 東嶽大生寶懺.
543	543	539	*Jiuyou chan* 九幽懺. Full title: *Taishang cibei daochang xiaozai jiuyou chan* 太上慈悲道場消災九幽懺.
546	546		*Lingbao yujian mulu* 靈寶玉鑑目錄. [*Daozang tiyao* considers this text to be part of the next one (CT 547, TY 542).]
547	547	542	*Lingbao yujian* 靈寶玉鑑.
562	562	558	*Lingbao jingming xinxiu jiulao shenyin fumo bifa* 靈寶淨明新修九老神印伏魔祕法.
566	566	561	*Shangqing tianxin zhengfa* 上清天心正法.
568	568	563	*Lingbao guikong jue* 靈寶歸空訣.
574	574	569	*Xuanzhu xinjing zhu* 玄珠心鏡注. DZJY 15: 6829. See *Xuanzhu xinjing.*
575	575	570	*Xuanzhu xinjing zhu* 玄珠心鏡注. DZJY 15: 6829. See *Xuanzhu xinjing.*
576	576	571	*Baoyi hansan bijue* 抱一函三祕訣.
577	577	572	*Cunshen guqi lun* 存神固氣論.
578	578	573	*Shesheng zuanlu* 攝生纂錄.
584	584	579	*Shangqing liujia qidao bifa* 上清六甲祈禱祕法.
589	589	584	*Taishang chiwen dongshen sanlu* 太上赤文洞神三籙.
590	590	585	*Daojiao lingyan ji* 道教靈驗記.
591	591	586	*Luyi ji* 錄異記.
592	592	587	*Shenxian ganyu zhuan* 神仙感遇傳. Part. in YJQQ 112.
593	593	588	*Lidai chongdao ji* 歷代崇道記.
594	594	589	*Tixuan zhenren xianyi lu* 體玄真人顯異錄.
595	595	590	*Jiang Huai yiren lu* 江淮異人錄.
596	596	591	*Xianyuan bianzhu* 仙苑編珠.
597	597	592	*Daoji lingxian ji* 道跡靈仙記.
598	598	593	*Shizhou ji* 十洲記. YJQQ 26.
599	599	594	*Dongtian fudi yuedu mingshan ji* 洞天福地嶽瀆名山記. DZJY 25: 10989–94.
601	601	596	*Jinhua Chisong shanzhi* 金華赤松山志.
603	603	598	*Tiantai shanzhi* 天臺山志.

CT	HY	TY	
606	606	601	*Nanyue zongsheng ji* 南嶽總勝集. DZJY 25: 10995–11004.
607	607	602	*Yuyin fashi* 玉音法事.
612	612	607	*Shangqing shi dichen Tongbo zhenren zhentu zan* 上清侍帝晨桐柏真人真圖讚.
615	615	610	**Chisong zi zhangli* 赤松子章曆.
616	616	611	*Guangcheng ji* 廣成集.
620	620	615	*Qingjing miaojing* 清靜妙經. Full title: *Taishang Laojun shuo chang qingjing miaojing* 太上老君說常清靜妙經. See **Qingjing jing*.
621	621	616	*Doumu dasheng yuanjun benming yansheng xinjing* 斗姆大聖元君本命延生心經. Full title: *Taishang xuanling Doumu dasheng yuanjun benming yansheng xinjing* 太上玄靈斗姆大聖元君本命延生心經.
622	622	617	*Beidou benming yansheng zhenjing* 北斗本命延生真經. Full title: *Taishang xuanling beidou benming yansheng zhenjing* 太上玄靈北斗本命延生真經. DZJY 7: 2913–16. See **Wudou jing*.
623	623	618	*Beidou benming changsheng miaojing* 北斗本命長生妙經. Full title: *Taishang xuanling beidou benming changsheng miaojing* 太上玄靈北斗本命長生妙經. See **Wudou jing*.
624	624	619	*Nandou liusi yanshou duren miaojing* 南斗六司延壽度人妙經. Full title: *Taishang shuo nandou liusi yanshou duren miaojing* 太上說南斗六司延壽度人妙經. DZJY 7: 2917–18. See **Wudou jing*.
625	625	620	*Dongdou zhusuan huming miaojing* 東斗主筭護命妙經. Full title: *Taishang shuo dongdou zhusuan huming miaojing* 太上說東斗主筭護命妙經. DZJY 7: 2919. See **Wudou jing*.
626	626	621	*Xidou jiming hushen miaojing* 西斗記名護身妙經. Full title: *Taishang shuo xidou jiming hushen miaojing* 太上說西斗記名護身妙經. DZJY 7: 2920–21. See **Wudou jing*.
627	627	622	*Zhongdou dakui baoming miaojing* 中斗大魁保命妙經. Full title: *Taishang shuo zhongdou dakui baoming miaojing* 太上說中斗大魁保命妙經. DZJY 7: 2921–22. See **Wudou jing*.
633	633	628	*Tiantong yinfan xianjing* 天童隱梵仙經. Full title: *Taishang Taiqing Huanglao dijun Yunlei tiantong yinfan xianjing* 太上泰清皇老帝君運雷天童隱梵仙經.
639	639	634	*Huangtian Shangqing Jinque dijun lingshu ziwen shangjing* 皇天上清金闕帝君靈書紫文上經. Part. in YJQQ 54. See **Lingshu ziwen*.
641	641	636	*Neiguan jing* 內觀經. Full title: *Taishang Laojun neiguan jing* 太上老君內觀經. YJQQ 17. DZJY 5: 2141–43.
647	647	642	*Zhuanlun wudao suming yinyuan jing* 轉輪五道宿命因緣經. Full title: *Taishang shuo zhuanlun wudao suming yinyuan jing* 太上說轉輪五道宿命因緣經. DZJY 5: 2145–47.
649	649	644	*Taishang Laojun shuo Tianfei jiuku lingyan jing* 太上老君說天妃救苦靈驗經.

CT	HY	TY	
651	651	646	*Sanyuan miaoben fushou zhenjing* 三元妙本福壽真經. Full title: *Taishang dongshen sanyuan miaoben fushou zhenjing* 太上洞神三元妙本福壽真經.
663	662	658	*Bao fumu en zhongjing* 報父母恩重經. Full title: *Xuantian shangdi shuo bao fumu en zhongjing* 玄天上帝說報父母恩重經.
665	665	660	*Daode jing guben pian* 道德經古本篇.
666	666	661	**Xisheng jing* 西昇經.
667	667	662	*Wenshi zhenjing* 文始真經. Full title: *Wushang miaodao Wenshi zhenjing* 無上妙道文始真經.
668	668	663	*Chongxu zhide zhenjing* 沖虛至德真經. See **Liezi*.
669	669	664	*Dongling zhenjing* 洞靈真經.
671	671	666	*Ziran zhenyi wucheng fu shangjing* 自然真一五稱符上經. Full title: *Taishang wuji dadao ziran zhenyi wucheng fu shangjing* 太上無極大道自然真一五稱符上經. DZJY 5: 2152–62.
677	677	672	*Tang Xuanzong yuzhu daode zhenjing* 唐玄宗御注道德真經.
678	678	673	*Tang Xuanzong yuzhi daode zhenjing shu* 唐玄宗御製道德真經疏.
682	682	677	*Daode zhenjing zhu* 道德真經注. See **Laozi Heshang gong zhangju*.
693	693	688	*Daode zhenjing zhigui* 道德真經指歸.
698	698	693	*Daode zhenjing zhangju xunsong* 道德真經章句訓頌. DZJY 5: 1827–44.
699	699	694	*Daode huiyuan* 道德會元.
702	702	697	*Daode xuanjing yuanzhi* 道德玄經原旨.
703	703	698	*Xuanjing yuanzhi fahui* 玄經原旨發揮.
705	705	700	*Daode zhenjing jijie* 道德真經集解.
707	707	702	*Daode zhenjing jizhu* 道德真經集注. DZJY 5: 1845–1999.
708	708	703	*Daode zhenjing jijie shiwen* 道德真經集注釋文. DZJY 5: 2000–2008.
709	709	704	*Daode zhenjing jijie zashuo* 道德真經集注雜說. DZJY 5: 2008–28.
710	710	705	*Daode zhenjing zhushu* 道德真經注疏.
711	711	706	*Daode zhenjing xuande zuanshu* 道德真經玄德纂疏.
714	714	709	*Daode zhenjing zangshi zuanwei pian* 道德真經藏室纂微篇.
722	722	717	*Daode zhenjing zhu* 道德真經注.
725	725	719	*Daode zhenjing guangsheng yi* 道德真經廣聖義.
726	726	720	*Xisheng jing jizhu* 西昇經集注.
728	728	722	*Wenshi zhenjing yanwai zhi* 文始真經言外旨. DZJY 10: 4189–4239.
729	729	723	*Chongxu zhide zhenjing Juanzhai kouyi* 沖虛至德真經鬳齋口義. See **Liezi*.
730	730	724	*Chongxu zhide zhenjing jie* 沖虛至德真經解. DZJY 10: 4241–4344. See **Liezi*.
731	731	725	*Chongxu zhide zhenjing yijie* 沖虛至德真經義解. See **Liezi*.

CT	HY	TY	
732	732	726	*Chongxu zhide zhenjing sijie* 沖虛至德真經四解. See *Liezi.
733	733	727	*Chongxu zhide zhenjing shiwen* 沖虛至德真經釋文. Full title: *Liezi chongxu zhide zhenjing shiwen* 列子沖虛至德真經釋文. See *Liezi.
735	735	729	*Nanhua zhenjing kouyi* 南華真經口義.
736	736	730	*Nanhua zhenjing zhangju yinyi* 南華真經章句音義.
737	737	731	*Nanhua zhenjing zhangju yushi* 南華真經章句餘事.
745	745	739	*Nanhua zhenjing zhushu* 南華真經注疏. DZJY 9: 3515–3989.
746	746	740	*Tongxuan zhenjing* 通玄真經. DZJY 10: 4345–4408.
748	748	742	*Tongxuan zhenjing zuanyi* 通玄真經纘義.
749	749	743	*Tongxuan zhenjing* 通玄真經.
755	754	749	*Qingjing jingzhu* 清靜經注. Full title: *Taishang Laojun shuo chang qingjing jingzhu* 太上老君說常清靜經注. DZJY 5: 2117–20. See *Qingjing jing.
756	755	750	*Qingjing jingzhu* 清靜經注. Full title: *Taishang Laojun shuo chang qingjing jingzhu* 太上老君說常清靜經注. See *Qingjing jing.
757	756	751–52	*Qingjing jingzhu* 清靜經注. Full title: *Taishang Laojun shuo chang qingjing jingzhu* 太上老君說常清靜經注. See *Qingjing jing.
758	757	753	*Qingjing jingzhu* 清靜經注. Full title: *Taishang Laojun shuo chang qingjing jingzhu* 太上老君說常清靜經注. See *Qingjing jing.
759	758	754	*Qingjing jingzhu* 清靜經注. Full title: *Taishang Laojun shuo chang qingjing jingzhu* 太上老君說常清靜經注. See *Qingjing jing.
760	759	755	*Qingjing miaojing zuantu jiezhu* 清靜妙經纂圖解注. Full title: *Taishang Laojun shuo chang qingjing miaojing zuantu jiezhu* 太上老君說常清靜妙經纂圖解注. See *Qingjing jing.
763	762	758	*Wuchu jing zhu* 五廚經注. Full title: *Laozi shuo wuchu jingzhu* 老子說五廚經注. YJQQ 61. DZJY 5: 2138–41. See *Wuchu jing.
770	769	764	*Hunyuan shengji* 混元聖紀. DZJY 6: 2407–2523.
771	770	765	*Laojun nianpu yaolüe* 老君年譜要略. Full title: *Taishang Laojun nianpu yaolüe* 太上老君年譜要略. DZJY 6: 2401–5.
773	772	767	*Laozi shilüe* 老子史略. Full title: *Taishang Hunyuan Laozi shilüe* 太上混元老子史略.
774	773	768	*Youlong zhuan* 猶龍傳. DZJY 6: 2335–74.
777	776	771	*Zhangxian Mingsu huanghou shou Shangqing bifa luji* 章獻明肅皇后受上清畢法籙記.
779	778	773	*Tang Ye zhenren zhuan* 唐葉真人傳.
780	779	774	*Diqi shangjiang Wen taibao zhuan* 地祇上將溫太保傳.
781	780	775	*Xuanpin lu* 玄品錄.
782	781	776	*Dadi dongtian ji* 大滌洞天記.
783	782	777	*Yongcheng jixian lu* 墉城集仙錄. Part. in YJQQ 114–16.

CT	HY	TY	
784	783	778	*Taishang Laojun jiejing* 太上老君戒經. Part. in YJQQ 39. DZJY 23: 10259–70.
785	784	779	*Laojun yinsong jiejing* 老君音誦誡經.
786	785	780	*Taishang Laojun jinglü* 太上老君經律. Part. in YJQQ 39.
787	786	781	*Taishang jingjie* 太上經戒. YJQQ 38.
788	787	782	*Sandong fafu kejie wen* 三洞法服科戒文.
789	788	783	*Zhengyi fawen Tianshi jiaojie kejing* 正一法文天師教戒科經.
790	789	784	*Nüqing guilü* 女青鬼律.
791	790	785	*Zhengyi weiyi jing* 正一威儀經.
792	791	786	*Xuanmen shishi weiyi* 玄門十事威儀.
796	795	790	*Sanwu zhengyi mengwei yuelu jiaoyi* 三五正一盟威閱籙醮儀. Full title: *Taishang sanwu zhengyi mengwei yuelu jiaoyi* 太上三五正一盟威閱籙醮儀.
800	799	794	*Zhengyi chitan yi* 正一敕壇儀.
803	802	797	*Taishang dongshen sanhuang yi* 太上洞神三皇儀.
804	803	798	*Dongshen sanhuang qishi'er jun zhaifang chanyi* 洞神三皇七十二君齋方懺儀.
805	804	799	*Taiyuan hetu sanyuan yangxie yi* 太元河圖三元仰謝儀. Full title: *Taishang dongshen taiyuan hetu sanyuan yangxie yi* 太上洞神太元河圖三元仰謝儀.
808	807	802	*Sandong chuanshou Daode jing zixu lu baibiao yi* 三洞傳授道德經紫虛籙拜表儀. Full title: *Taishang sandong chuanshou daode jing zi xu lu baibiao yi* 太上三洞傳授道德經紫虛籙拜表儀.
814	813	808	*Zhenwu lingying hushi xiaozai miezui baochan* 真武靈應護世消災滅罪寶懺.
815	814	809	*Beiji Zhenwu puci dushi fachan* 北極真武普慈度世法懺.
818	817	812	*Daoyin yangsheng jing* 導引養生經. Full title: *Taiqing daoyin yangsheng jing* 太清導引養生經. Part. in YJQQ 34.
819	818	813	*Yangsheng taixi qijing* 養生胎息氣經. Full title: *Taishang yangsheng taixi qijing* 太上養生胎息氣經.
820	819	814	*Tiaoqi jing* 調氣經. Full title: *Taiqing tiaoqi jing* 太清調氣經.
821	820	815	*Taishang Laojun yangsheng jue* 太上老君養生訣.
822	821	816	*Fuqi koujue* 服氣口訣. Full title: *Taiqing fuqi koujue* 太清服氣口訣.
824	823	818	*Songshan Taiwu xiansheng qijing* 嵩山太無先生氣經.
825	824	819	*Yanling xiansheng ji xinjiu fuqi jing* 延陵先生集新舊服氣經. Part. in YJQQ 58, 59, and 61.
826	825	820	*Zhuzhen shengtai shenyong jue* 諸真聖胎神用訣.
827	826	821	*Taixi baoyi ge* 胎息抱一歌.
828	827	822	*Huanzhen xiansheng fu nei yuanqi jue* 幻真先生服內元氣訣. YJQQ 60.

CT	HY	TY	
829	828	823	*Taixi jingwei lun* 胎息精微論.
830	829	824	*Fuqi jingyi lun* 服氣精義論. YJQQ 57.
831	830	825	*Qifa yao miaozhi jue* 氣法要妙至訣.
834	833	828	*Cunshen lianqi ming* 存神鍊氣銘. Part. in YJQQ 33.
835	834	829	*Baosheng ming* 保生銘.
837	836	831	*Zhenzhong ji* 枕中記.
838	837	832	*Yangxing yanming lu* 養性延命錄. YJQQ 32.
841	840	835	*Sheyang lun* 攝養論. Full title: *Sun zhenren sheyang lun* 孫真人攝養論.
853	852	847	*Yangsheng bianyi jue* 養生辯疑訣.
856	855	850	*Sanhuang neiwen yibi* 三皇內文遺祕.
864	863	858	*Yuanyang zi wujia lun* 元陽子五假論.
871	870	865	*Chu sanshi jiuchong baosheng jing* 除三尸九蟲保生經. Full title: *Taishang chu sanshi jiuchong baosheng jing* 太上除三尸九蟲保生經.
875	874	869	*Taishang Laojun da cunsi tuzhu jue* 太上老君大存思圖注訣. Part. in YJQQ 43.
880	879	874	*Taiqing jinye shendan jing* 太清金液神丹經.
881	880	875	*Taiqing shibi ji* 太清石壁記.
883	882	877	*Taiqing jing tianshi koujue* 太清經天師口訣. See *Taiqing jing*.
885	884	879	*Huangdi jiuding shendan jingjue* 黃帝九鼎神丹經訣. See *Jiudan jing*.
889	888	883	*Jiuzhuan huandan jing yaojue* 九轉還丹經要訣. Full title: *Taiji zhenren jiuzhuan huandan jing yaojue* 太極真人九轉還丹經要訣.
890	889	884	*Xiufu lingsha miaojue* 修伏靈砂妙訣. Full title: *Dadong lian zhenbao jing xiufu lingsha miaojue* 大洞鍊真寶經修伏靈砂妙訣. YJQQ 69.
891	890	885	*Jiuhuan jindan miaojue* 九還金丹妙訣. Full title: *Dadong lian zhenbao jing jiuhuan jindan miaojue* 大洞鍊真寶經九還金丹妙訣. YJQQ 68.
896	895	890	*Dashen dansha zhenyao jue* 大神丹砂真要訣. Full title: *Yudong dashen dansha zhenyao jue* 玉洞大神丹砂真要訣.
900	899	894	*Danfang xuzhi* 丹房須知.
901	900	895	*Shiyao erya* 石藥爾雅.
902	901	896	*Zhichuan zhenren jiaozheng shu* 稚川真人校證術.
904	903	898	*Jinbi wu xianglei cantong qi* 金碧五相類參同契.
907	906	901	*Jinshi bu wujiu shu jue* 金石簿五九數訣.
914	913	908	*Chongbi danjing* 冲碧丹經. Full title: *Jinhua chongbi danjing bizhi* 金華冲碧丹經祕旨.
917	916	911	*Baopu zi shenxian jinzhuo jing* 抱朴子神仙金汋經.

CT	HY	TY	
919	918	913	*Qianhong jiageng zhibao jicheng* 鉛汞甲庚至寶集成.
921	920	915	*Zhigui ji* 指歸集.
924	923	918	*Zhenyuan miaodao yaolüe* 真元妙道要略.
925	924	919	**Danfang jianyuan* 丹方鑑源.
930	929	924	**Sanshiliu shuifa* 三十六水法.
933	932	927	*Zhong zhicao fa* 種芝草法.
934	933	928	*Taibai jing* 太白經.
935	934	929	*Danlun jue zhixin jian* 丹論訣旨心鑑. YJQQ 66.
948	947	942	*Shenxian yangsheng bishu* 神仙養生祕術.
950	949	944	*Shangdong xindan jingjue* 上洞心丹經訣.
952	951	946	*Jiuzhuan liuzhu shenxian jiudan jing* 九轉流珠神仙九丹經.
954	953	948	*Taishang Hunyuan zhenlu* 太上混元真錄.
955	954	949	*Zhongnan shan zuting xianzhen neizhuan* 終南山祖庭仙真內傳. DZJY 24: 10501–28.
956	955	950	**Zhenxian beiji* 真仙碑記. Full title: *Zhongnan shan Shuojing tai lidai zhenxian beiji* 終南山說經臺歷代真仙碑記.
957	956	951	*Gu Louguan ziyun yanqing ji* 古樓觀紫雲衍慶集.
962	960	956	*Wudang fudi zongzhen ji* 武當福地總真集.
969	967	963	*Tiantan Wangwu shan shengji ji* 天壇王屋山聖跡記.
972	970	966	*Gongguan beizhi* 宮觀碑誌.
973	971	967	**Ganshui xianyuan lu* 甘水仙源錄. DZJY 24: 10573–10674.
974	972	968	*Qingjing jing songzhu* 清靜經頌注. Full title: *Taishang Laojun shuo chang qingjing jing songzhu* 太上老君說常清靜經頌注. See **Qingjing jing.*
979	977	973	*Mingzhen powang zhangsong* 明真破妄章頌. DZJY 16: 7148–51.
981	979	975	*Da Ming yuzhi xuanjiao yuezhang* 大明御製玄教樂章.
996	994	990	*Guwen longhu jing zhushu* 古文龍虎經注疏. YJQQ 73. DZJY 8: 3064–92. See **Longhu jing.*
997	995	991	*Guwen longhu shangjing zhu* 古文龍虎上經注. See **Longhu jing.*
999	996	993	*Zhouyi cantong qi* 周易參同契. See **Zhouyi cantong qi.*
1000	997	994	*Zhouyi cantong qi zhu* 周易參同契注. See **Zhouyi cantong qi.*
1001	998	995	*Zhouyi cantong qi* 周易參同契 (i.e., *Zhouyi cantong qi kaoyi* 周易參同契考異). See **Zhouyi cantong qi.*
1002	999	996	*Zhouyi cantong qi fenzhang tong zhenyi* 周易參同契分章通真義. See **Zhouyi cantong qi.*
1003	1000		*Zhouyi cantong qi dingqi ge mingjing tu* 周易參同契鼎器歌明鏡圖. See **Zhouyi cantong qi.* [*Daozang tiyao* considers this text to be part of the previous one (CT 1002, TY 996).]
1004	1001	997	*Zhouyi cantong qi zhu* 周易參同契注. See **Zhouyi cantong qi.*

CT	HY	TY	
1005	1002	998	*Zhouyi cantong qi fahui* 周易參同契發揮. See *Zhouyi cantong qi.
1006	1003	999	*Zhouyi cantong qi shiyi* 周易參同契釋疑. See *Zhouyi cantong qi.
1007	1004	1000	*Zhouyi cantong qi jie* 周易參同契解. DZJY 11: 4583–4612. See *Zhouyi cantong qi.
1008	1005	1001	*Zhouyi cantong qi* 周易參同契. See *Zhouyi cantong qi.
1009	1006	1002	*Yiwai biezhuan* 易外別傳.
1010		1003	*Xuanpin zhi men fu* 玄牝之門賦. [The Harvard-Yenching catalogue considers this text to be part of the previous one (CT 1009, HY 1006).]
1011	1007	1004	*Yishi tongbian* 易筮通變.
1012	1008	1005	*Kongshan xiansheng yitu tongbian* 空山先生易圖通變.
1013			*Hetu* 河圖. [The Harvard-Yenching catalogue and *Daozang tiyao* consider this text to be part of CT 1012 (HY 1008, TY 1005).]
1014			*Yitu tongbian* 易圖通變. [The Harvard-Yenching catalogue and *Daozang tiyao* consider this text to be part of CT 1012 (HY 1008, TY 1005).]
1015	1009	1006	**Jinsuo liuzhu yin* 金鎖流珠引.
1016	1010	1007	*Zhengao 真誥. Part. in YJQQ 45, 84, 86, and 96–98. DZJY 18: 7907–8042.
1017	1011	1008	*Daoshu 道樞. DZJY 18–19: 8043–8292.
1024	1018	1015	*Huangdi bashiyi nanjing zuantu jujie* 黃帝八十一難經纂圖句解.
1025	1019	1016	*Guigu zi* 鬼谷子.
1026	1020	1017	*Tianyin zi 天隱子. DZJY 12: 5291–92.
1028	1022	1019	*Wuneng zi 無能子.
1032	1026	1023	*Yunji qiqian 雲笈七籤. DZJY 19–20: 8403–8970.
1033	1027	1024	*Zhiyan zong* 至言總. Part. in YJQQ 35, 40, and 41.
1035	1029	1026	*Daoti lun* 道體論.
1036	1030	1027	*Zuowang lun 坐忘論. YJQQ 94.
1040	1034	1031	*Huangji jingshi* 皇極經世.
1042	1036	1033	*Yichuan jirang ji* 伊川擊壤集.
1044	1038	1035	*Huashu 化書.
1048	1042	1039	*Xuanzhu lu 玄珠錄.
1050	1044	1041	*Huayang Tao Yinju ji* 華陽陶隱居集.
1051	1045	1042	*Zongxuan xiansheng wenji* 宗玄先生文集.
1052	1046	1043	*Zongxuan xiansheng xuangang lun* 宗玄先生玄綱論.
1053			*Wu zunshi zhuan* 吳尊師傳. [The Harvard-Yenching catalogue and *Daozang tiyao* consider this text to be part of the previous one (CT 1052, HY 1046, TY 1043).]
1054	1047	1044	*Nantong dajun neidan jiuzhang jing* 南統大君內丹九章經.

CT	HY	TY	
1055	1048	1045	*Chunyang zhenren huncheng ji* 純陽真人渾成集.
1056	1049	1046	*Jin zhenren yulu* 晉真人語錄. DZJY 17: 7337–42.
1057	1050	1047	*Danyang zhenren yulu* 丹陽真人語錄. DZJY 15: 6820–26.
1058	1051	1048	*Wuwei Qingjing Changsheng zhenren zhizhen yulu* 無為清靜長生真人至真語錄. DZJY 15: 6656–68.
1059	1052	1049	*Panshan Qiyun Wang zhenren yulu* 盤山棲雲王真人語錄. DZJY 17: 7360–76.
1060	1053	1050	*Qing'an Yingchan zi yulu* 清庵瑩蟾子語錄.
1061	1054	1051	*Taixuan ji* 太玄集. Full title: *Shangqing taixuan ji* 上清太玄集.
1064	1056	1053	*Dongyuan ji* 洞淵集.
1065	1057	1054	*Xuanjiao da gong'an* 玄教大公案.
1067	1059	1056	**Jindan dayao* 金丹大要. Full title: *Shangyang zi jindan dayao* 上陽子金丹大要. DZJY 16: 6975–7086 (includes CT 1067–70).
1068	1060	1057	*Jindan dayao tu* 金丹大要圖. Full title: *Shangyang zi jindan dayao tu* 上陽子金丹大要圖. DZJY 16: 6975–7086 (includes CT 1067–70). YJQQ 18–19. See **Jindan dayao*.
1069	1061	1058	*Jindan dayao liexian zhi* 金丹大要列仙誌. Full title: *Shangyang zi jindan dayao liexian zhi* 上陽子金丹大要列仙誌. DZJY 16: 6975–7086 (includes CT 1067–70). See **Jindan dayao*.
1070	1062	1059	*Jindan dayao xianpai* 金丹大要仙派. Full title: *Shangyang zi jindan dayao xianpai* 上陽子金丹大要仙派. DZJY 16: 6975–7086 (includes CT 1067–70). See **Jindan dayao*.
1071	1063	1060	*Yuanyang zi fayu* 原陽子法語.
1074	1066	1063	*Huanzhen ji* 還真集.
1076	1068	1065	*Suiji yinghua lu* 隨機應化錄.
1077	1069	1066	*Xiulian xuzhi* 修鍊須知.
1081	1073	1070	**Jindan sibai zi* 金丹四百字.
1083	1075	1072	*Longhu yuanzhi* 龍虎元旨.
1084	1076	1073	*Longhu huandan jue* 龍虎還丹訣.
1088	1080	1077	*Huandan fuming pian* 還丹復命篇. DZJY 14: 6168–75.
1090	1082	1079	*Cuixu pian* 翠虛篇. DZJY 14: 6175–88 (title: *Nihuan ji* 泥洹集).
1091	1083	1080	*Huanyuan pian* 還源篇. DZJY 14: 6165–67.
1096	1088	1085	*Chen xiansheng neidan jue* 陳先生內丹訣.
1100	1092	1089	**Minghe yuyin* 鳴鶴餘音. DZJY 19: 8309–72.
1101	1093	1090–92	**Taiping jing* 太平經.
1102	1094	1093	*Taiping jing shengjun bizhi* 太平經聖君祕旨.
1110	1102	1101	**Jingming zhongxiao quanshu* 淨明忠孝全書.
1111	1103	1102	*Taixuan zhenyi benji miaojing* 太玄真一本際妙經. See **Benji jing*.

CT	HY	TY	
1123	1115	1114	*Yiqie daojing yinyi miaomen youqi* 一切道經音義妙門由起. See **Yiqie daojing yinyi*.
1124	1116	1115	**Xuanmen dayi* 玄門大義. Full title: *Dongxuan Lingbao xuanmen dayi* 洞玄靈寶玄門大義.
1125	1117	1116	**Fengdao kejie* 奉道科戒. Full title: *Dongxuan Lingbao sandong fengdao kejie yingshi* 洞玄靈寶三洞奉道科戒營始.
1127	1119	1118	**Daomen kelüe* 道門科略. Full title: *Lu xiansheng daomen kelüe* 陸先生道門科略.
1128	1120	1119	*Daomen jingfa xiangcheng cixu* 道門經法相承次序.
1129	1121	1120	**Daojiao yishu* 道教義樞.
1130	1122	1121	**Daodian lun* 道典論.
1132	1124	1123	**Shangqing dao leishi xiang* 上清道類事相.
1133	1125	1124	*Kaihua zhenjing* 開化真經. Full title: *Shangfang Lingbao wuji zhidao kaihua zhenjing* 上方靈寶無極至道開化真經.
1134	1126	1125	*Juntian yanfan zhenjing* 鈞天演範真經. Full title: *Shangfang juntian yanfan zhenjing* 上方鈞天演範真經.
1138	1130	1129	**Wushang biyao* 無上祕要. Part. in YJQQ 8, 9, 74, 84–86, 91, 101, 102.
1139	1131	1130	**Sandong zhunang* 三洞珠囊. Part. in YJQQ 28, 40.
1140	1132	1131	*Yunshan ji* 雲山集. DZJY 16: 7173–7242.
1141	1133	1132	*Xianle ji* 仙樂集. DZJY 15: 6625–55.
1142	1134	1133	*Jianwu ji* 漸悟集. DZJY 15: 6773–6804.
1146	1138	1137	*Baoguang ji* 葆光集. DZJY 16: 6911–49.
1149	1141	1140	*Jinyu ji* 金玉集. Full title: *Dongxuan jinyu ji* 洞玄金玉集. DZJY 15: 6695–6772.
1150	1142	1141	*Shenguang can* 神光燦. Full title: *Danyang shenguang can* 丹陽神光燦. DZJY 15: 6804–20.
1152	1144	1143	*Yunguang ji* 雲光集. DZJY 16: 6859–6909.
1153	1145	1144	**Chongyang quanzhen ji* 重陽全真集. DZJY 15: 6393–6485.
1154	1146	1145	*Jiaohua ji* 教化集. Full title: *Chongyang jiaohua ji* 重陽教化集. DZJY 15: 6487–6514.
1155	1147	1146	*Fenli shihua ji* 分梨十化集. Full title: *Chongyang fenli shihua ji* 重陽分梨十化集. DZJY 15: 6514–24.
1156	1148	1147	*Jinguan yusuo jue* 金關玉鎖訣. Full title: *Chongyang zhenren jinguan yusuo jue* 重陽真人金關玉鎖訣.
1158	1149	1149	*Chongyang zhenren shou Danyang ershisi jue* 重陽真人授丹陽二十四訣.
1159	1151	1150	*Panxi ji* 磻溪集. DZJY 15: 6582–6624.
1160	1152	1151	*Shuiyun ji* 水雲集. DZJY 15: 6669–93.

CT	HY	TY	
1161	1153	1152	*Taigu ji* 太古集. DZJY 16: 6835–57.
1165	1157	1155	*Xianchuan waike bifang* 仙傳外科祕方.
1166	1158	1156	*Fahai yizhu* 法海遺珠.
1167	1159	1157	**Taishang ganying pian* 太上感應篇.
1168	1160	1158	*Laojun zhongjing* 老君中經. Full title: *Taishang Laojun zhongjing* 太上老君中經. See **Laozi zhongjing*.
1169	1161	1159	*Qingjing xinjing* 清靜心經. Full title: *Taishang Laojun qingjing xinjing* 太上老君清靜心經. YJQQ 17. See **Qingjing jing*.
1184	1176	1174	*Huainan honglie jie* 淮南鴻烈解. See **Huainan zi*.
1185	1177	1175	*Baopu zi neipian* 抱朴子內篇. Part. in YJQQ 67. DZJY 11: 4813–96. See **Baopu zi*.
1187	1179	1177	*Baopu zi waipian* 抱朴子外篇. DZJY 11: 4897–4905. See **Baopu zi*.
1191	1182	1181	**Lingbao bifa* 靈寶畢法. Full title: *Bichuan Zhengyang zhenren lingbao bifa* 祕傳正陽真人靈寶畢法. DZJY 12: 5097–5112.
1195	1186	1185	*Laojun bianhua wuji jing* 老君變化無極經.
1200	1191	1190	*Liuzhai shizhi shengji jing* 六齋十直聖紀經. Full title: *Dongxuan Lingbao taishang liuzhai shizhi shengji jing* 洞玄靈寶太上六齋十直聖紀經.
1203	1194	1193	*Santian zhengfa jing* 三天正法經. Full title: *Taishang santian zhengfa jing* 太上三天正法經.
1204	1195	1194	*Zhengyi fawen jing* 正一法文經. Full title: *Taishang zhengyi fawen jing* 太上正一法文經.
1205	1196	1195	**Santian neijie jing* 三天內解經.
1206	1197	1196	*Mingjian yaojing* 明鑑要經. Full title: *Shangqing mingjian yaojing* 上清明鑑要經. Part. in YJQQ 48.
1208	1199	1198	*Sanwu zhengyi mengwei lu* 三五正一盟威籙. Full title: *Taishang sanwu zhengyi mengwei lu* 太上三五正一盟威籙.
1212	1202	1201	*Jiao sandong zhenwen wufa zhengyi mengwei lu licheng yi* 醮三洞真文五法正一盟威籙立成儀.
1220	1210	1209	**Daofa huiyuan* 道法會元.
1221	1211	1210	**Shangqing lingbao dafa* 上清靈寶大法.
1222	1212		*Shangqing lingbao dafa mulu* 上清靈寶大法目錄. See **Shangqing lingbao dafa*. [Daozang tiyao considers this text to be part of the next one (CT 1223, TY 1211).]
1223	1213	1211	**Shangqing lingbao dafa* 上清靈寶大法.
1224	1214	1212	*Daomen dingzhi* 道門定制.
1225	1215	1213	**Daomen kefan da quanji* 道門科範大全集.
1227	1217	1215	*Taishang zhuguo jiumin zongzhen biyao* 太上助國救民總真祕要.
1229	1219	1217	*Quanzhen zuobo jiefa* 全真坐缽捷法.
1232	1222	1220	**Daomen shigui* 道門十規.

CT	HY	TY

1233 1223 1221 *Chongyang lijiao shiwu lun* 重陽立教十五論. DZJY 15: 6524–26.

1234 1224 1222 *Danyang zhenren zhiyan* 丹陽真人直言. DZJY 15: 6527.

1235 1225 1223 *Quanzhen qinggui* 全真清規. DZJY 23: 10299–10304.

1236 1226 1224 *Chujia chuandu yi* 出家傳度儀. Full title: *Taishang chujia chuandu yi* 太上出家傳度儀.

1240 1230 1228 *Daoshi shou sandong jingjie falu zhairi li* 道士受三洞經誡法籙擇日曆. Full title: *Dongxuan Lingbao daoshi shou sandong jingjie falu zhairi li* 洞玄靈寶道士受三洞經誡法籙擇日曆.

1241 1231 1229 *Chuanshou sandong jingjie falu lüeshuo* 傳授三洞經戒法籙略說.

1248 1238 1236 *Sandong qunxian lu* 三洞群仙錄. DZJY 24: 10675–10819.

1249 1239 1237 *Sanshi dai Tianshi Xujing zhenjun yulu* 三十代天師虛靖真君語錄. DZJY 25: 10913–36.

1250 1240 1238 *Chongxu tongmiao shichen Wang xiansheng jiahua* 冲虛通妙侍宸王先生家話.

1252 1242 1240 *Jingyu xuanwen* 靜餘玄問.

1253 1243 1241 *Daofa xinzhuan* 道法心傳. DZJY 16: 7152–67.

1254 1244 1242 *Leifa yixuan pian* 雷法議玄篇.

1256 1246 1244 *Zhenxian zhizhi yulu* 真仙直指語錄.

1264 1254 1252 *Lifeng laoren ji* 離峰老人集.

1271 1261 1259 *Yannian yisuan fa* 延年益算法. Full title: *Dongxuan Lingbao zhenren xiuxing yannian yisuan fa* 洞玄靈寶真人修行延年益算法.

1273 1263 1261 *Zhengyi Tianshi gao Zhao Sheng koujue* 正一天師告趙昇口訣.

1275 1265 1263 *Yuyang qihou qinji* 雨暘氣候親機.

1277 1267 1265 *Daofa zongzhi tu yanyi* 道法宗旨圖衍義.

1278 1268 1266 *Wugan wen* 五感文. Full title: *Dongxuan Lingbao wugan wen* 洞玄靈寶五感文.

1281 1271 1269 *Wuyue zhenxing xulun* 五嶽真形序論. Part. in YJQQ 79.

1282 1272 1270 *Gaoshang Shenxiao zongshi shoujing shi* 高上神霄宗師受經式.

1285 1275 1273 *Yisheng baode zhuan* 翊聖保德傳. YJQQ 103.

1286 1276 1274 *Lushan Taiping xingguo gong Caifang zhenjun shishi* 盧山太平興國宮採訪真君事實.

1294 1284 1282 *Shangqing huangshu guodu yi* 上清黃書過度儀.

1306 1295 1294 *Zhouhou beiji fang* 肘後備急方. Full title: *Ge Xianweng zhouhou beiji fang* 葛仙翁肘後備急方. DZJY 11: 4907–5034.

1307 1296 1295 *Haiqiong Bai zhenren yulu* 海瓊白真人語錄. DZJY 14: 6367–89 (lacks the last *juan* of the *Daozang* text).

1308 1297 1296 *Haiqiong wendao ji* 海瓊問道集.

1309 1298 1297 *Haiqiong chuandao ji* 海瓊傳道集.

1310 1299 1298 *Qinghe zhenren beiyou yulu* 清和真人北遊語錄. DZJY 17: 7377–7402.

CT	HY	TY	
1311	1300	1299	*Xianquan ji* 峴泉集.
1313	1302	1301	*Ciyi yujian wulao baojing* 雌一玉檢五老寶經. Full title: *Dongzhen Gaoshang Yudi dadong ciyi yujian wulao baojing* 洞真高上玉帝大洞雌一玉檢五老寶經. Part. in YJQQ 41 and 77. See **Ciyi jing*.
1314	1303	1302	*Suling Dayou miaojing* 素靈大有妙經. Full title: *Dongzhen taishang Suling dongyuan Dayou miaojing* 洞真太上素靈洞元大有妙經. YJQQ 43, 47, and 50. See **Suling jing*.
1316	1305	1304	*Bu tiangang fei diji jing* 步天綱飛地紀經. Full title: *Dongzhen Shangqing Taiwei dijun bu tiangang fei diji jinjian yuzi shangjing* 洞真上清太微帝君步天綱飛地紀金簡玉字上經.
1319	1308	1307	*Baoshen qiju jing* 寶神起居經. Full title: *Dongzhen Xiwang mu baoshen qiju jing* 洞真西王母寶神起居經. Part. in YJQQ 54 and 83. DZJY 8: 3461–68. See **Suling jing*.
1323	1312	1311	*Basu zhenjing fushi riyue huanghua jue* 八素真經服食日月皇華訣. Full title: *Dongzhen taishang basu zhenjing fushi riyue huanghua jue* 洞真太上八素真經服食日月皇華訣. See **Basu jing*.
1328	1317	1316	*Badao mingji jing* 八道命籍經. Full title: *Dongzhen taishang badao mingji jing* 洞真太上八道命籍經. Part. in YJQQ 51 and 91.
1330	1319	1318	*Taiyi dijun Taidan yinshu xuanjing* 太一帝君太丹隱書玄經. Full title: *Dongzhen Taiyi dijun Taidan yinshu dongzhen xuanjing* 洞真太一帝君太丹隱書洞真玄經. YJQQ 23, 30, 43, and 44. See **Taidan yinshu*.
1331	1320	1319	*Shenzhou qizhuan qibian wutian jing* 神州七轉七變舞天經. Full title: *Dongzhen Shangqing shenzhou qizhuan qibian wutian jing* 洞真上清神州七轉七變舞天經.
1343	1332	1331	*Dongzhen huangshu* 洞真黃書.
1344	1333	1332	*Xiaomo jing* 消魔經. Full title: *Dongzhen Taishang shuo zhihui xiaomo zhenjing* 洞真太上說智慧消魔真經.
1352	1341	1340	*Taishang taixiao langshu* 太上太霄琅書. Full title: *Dongzhen taishang taixiao langshu* 洞真太上太霄琅書. DZJY 8: 3193–3252. See **Taixiao langshu*.
1355	1344	1343	*Miemo shenhui gaoxuan zhenjing* 滅魔神慧高玄真經. Full title: *Shangqing taishang Yuqing yinshu miemo shenhui gaoxuan zhenjing* 上清太上玉清隱書滅魔神慧高玄真經.
1359	1348	1347	*Yindi bashu jing* 隱地八術經. Full title: *Shangqing danjing daojing yindi bashu jing* 上清丹景道精隱地八術經. YJQQ 53.
1360	1349	1348	*Shangqing jiutian Shangdi zhu baishen neiming jing* 上清九天上帝祝百神內名經.
1364	1353	1352	*Shangqing dongzhen zhihui guanshen dajie wen* 上清洞真智慧觀身大戒文.
1366	1355	1354	*Tianguan santu jing* 天關三圖經. Full title: *Shangqing tianguan santu jing* 上清天關三圖經.

CT	HY	TY	
1373	1362	1361	*Waiguo fangpin Qingtong neiwen* 外國放品青童內文. Full title: *Shangqing waiguo fangpin Qingtong neiwen* 上清外國放品青童內文. YJQQ 22.
1376	1365	1364	*Dijun jiuzhen zhongjing* 帝君九真中經. Full title: *Shangqing Taishang dijun jiuzhen zhongjing* 上清太上帝君九真中經. YJQQ 23, 30, 51, 52, 68, 74, 77, and 101. See *Jiuzhen zhongjing*.
1377	1366	1365	*Jiuzhen zhongjing jiangsheng shendan jue* 九真中經降生神丹訣. Full title: *Shangqing taishang jiuzhen zhongjing jiangsheng shendan jue* 上清太上九真中經降生神丹訣. See *Jiuzhen zhongjing*.
1382	1371	1370	*Taijing zhongji jing* 胎精中記經. Full title: *Shangqing jiudan shanghua taijing zhongji jing* 上清九丹上化胎精中記經. YJQQ 29.
1384	1373	1372	*Taidan yinshu jie bao shi'er jiejie tujue* 太丹隱書解胞十二結節圖訣. Full title: *Shangqing Taiyi dijun Taidan yinshu jie bao shi'er jiejie tujue* 上清太一帝君太丹隱書解胞十二結節圖訣. See *Taidan yinshu*.
1398	1387	1386	*Dasheng miaolin jing* 大乘妙林經. YJQQ 92, 93, and 95. DZJY 4: 1273–94.
1405	1394	1393	*Changsheng taiyuan shenyong jing* 長生胎元神用經. DZJY 8: 3454–61.
1406	1395	1394	*Zhicao pin* 芝草品. Full title: *Taishang Lingbao zhicao pin* 太上靈寶芝草品.
1407	1396	1395	*Ershisi sheng tu* 二十四生圖. Full title: *Dongxuan Lingbao ershisi sheng tu jing* 洞玄靈寶二十四生圖經. YJQQ 80.
1410	1399	1398	*Qianzhen ke* 千真科. Full title: *Dongxuan Lingbao qianzhen ke* 洞玄靈寶千真科.
1411	1400	1399	*Mingzhen ke* 明真科. Full title: *Dongxuan Lingbao changye zhi fu jiuyou yukui mingzhen ke* 洞玄靈寶長夜之府九幽玉匱明真科.
1412	1401	1400	*Taishang Yuanshi tianzun shuo Beidi fumo shenzhou miaojing* 太上元始天尊說北帝伏魔神咒妙經.
1426	1415	1414	*Fushou lun* 福壽論. Full title: *Tang taigu miaoying Sun zhenren fushou lun* 唐太古妙應孫真人福壽論.
1427	1416	1415	*Daolin shesheng lun* 道林攝生論. Full title: *Taiqing Daolin shesheng lun* 太清道林攝生論.
1429	1418	1417	*Changchun zhenren xiyou ji* 長春真人西遊記. DZJY 15: 6559–82.
1430	1419	1418	*Daozang quejing mulu* 道藏闕經目錄.
1431	1420–21	1419–20	*Daozang jing mulu* 道藏經目錄. [The Harvard-Yenching catalogue and *Daozang tiyao* consider this text to be made of two texts: *Da Ming daozang jing mulu* 大明道藏經目錄 (HY 1420, TY 1419) and *Xu da Ming daozang jing mulu* 續大明道藏經目錄 (HY 1421, TY 1420).]
1437	1425	1424	*Kaitian jing* 開天經. Full title: *Taishang Laojun kaitian jing* 太上老君開天經. YJQQ 2.

CT	HY	TY	
1439	1427	1426	*Yujing shan buxu jing* 玉京山步虛經. Full title: *Dongxuan Lingbao Yujing shan buxu jing* 洞玄靈寶玉京山步虛經.
1442	1430	1429	*Taishang sanyuan cifu shezui jie'e xiaozai yansheng baoming miaojing* 太上三元賜福赦罪解厄消災延生保命妙經.
1447	1435	1434	*Chenghuang ganying xiaozai jifu miaojing* 城隍感應消災集福妙經. Full title: *Taishang Laojun shuo Chenghuang ganying xiaozai jifu miaojing* 太上老君說城隍感應消災集福妙經.
1452	1440	1439	*Xiantian Doumu zougao xuanke* 先天斗母奏告玄科.
1463	1451	1450	*Han Tianshi shijia* 漢天師世家. DZJY 25: 10873–10912.
1468	1456	1455	*Xuxian hanzao* 徐仙翰藻.
1472	1460	1459	*Daishi* 岱史.
1476	1466	1464	★*Soushen ji* 搜神記.
1477	1467	1464	*Taichu yuanqi jieyao baosheng zhi lun* 太初元氣接要保生之論.
1478	1468	1465	★*Huashu* 化書.
1480	1470	1467	*Xu zhenjun yuxia ji* 許真君玉匣記. [The Harvard-Yenching catalogue and *Daozang tiyao* consider this text to also include the *Fashi xuanzhai ji* 法師選擇記, separately listed in *Concordance du Tao-tsang* (CT 1481).]
1483	1472	1469	★*Tianhuang zhidao Taiqing yuce* 天皇至道太清玉冊.
1484	1473	1470	*Lüzu zhi* 呂祖志.
1487	1476	1473	*Zhuangzi yi* 莊子翼.

ABBREVIATIONS OF SERIALS

AM	*Asia Major*
ASEA	*Asiatische Studien / Études asiatiques*
BEFEO	*Bulletin de l'École Française d'Extrême-Orient*
CEA	*Cahiers d'Extrême-Asie*
DT	*Daojiaoxue tansuo* 道教學探索
DWY	*Daojia wenhua yanjiu* 道家文化研究
EC	*Early China*
HJAS	*Harvard Journal of Asiatic Studies*
HR	*History of Religions*
HXYJ	*Hanxue yanjiu* 漢學研究
JAOS	*Journal of the American Oriental Society*
JCP	*Journal of Chinese Philosophy*
JCR	*Journal of Chinese Religions*
JRAS	*Journal of the Royal Asiatic Society of Great Britain and Ireland*
KDKK	*Kagawa daigaku kyōiku gakubu kenkyū hōkōku* 香川大學教育學部研究報告
MQC	*Minsu quyi congshu* 民俗曲藝叢書
MS	*Monumenta Serica*
NCG	*Nippon Chūgoku gakkaihō* 日本中國學會報
SZY	*Shijie zongjiao yanjiu* 世界宗教研究
TBKK	*Tōyō bunka kenkyūjo kiyō* 東洋文化研究所紀要
TG	*Tōhō gakuhō* 東方學報
TP	*T'oung Pao*
TR	*Taoist Resources*
TS	*Tōhō shūkyō* 東方宗教
ZGDJ	*Zhongguo daojiao* 中国道教
ZLJ	*Zhongyang yanjiuyuan Lishi yuyan yanjiusuo jikan* 中央研究院歷史語言研究所集刊 (Bulletin of the Institute of History and Philology, Academia Sinica)
ZMJ	*Zhongyang yanjiuyuan Minzuxue yanjiusuo jikan* 中央研究院民族學研究所集刊 (Bulletin of the Institute of Ethnology, Academia Sinica)
ZY	*Zongjiaoxue yanjiu* 宗教学研究
ZZJ	*Zhongyang yanjiuyuan Zhongguo wenzhe yanjiu jikan* 中央研究院中國文哲研究集刊 (Bulletin of the Institute of Chinese Literature and Philosophy, Academia Sinica)

STUDIES

Akahori Akira 赤堀昭. 1988. "Kanshokusan to yōsei" 寒食散と養生 [The Cold Food Powder and Nourishing Life]. In Sakade Yoshinobu 1988a, 116–43.

Akima Toshio. 1993. "The Myth of the Goddess of the Undersea World and the Tale of Empress Jingū's Subjugation of Silla." *Japanese Journal of Religious Studies* 20.2–3: 95–185.

Akizuki Kan'ei 秋月観暎. 1961. "Dōkyō no sangen shisō ni tsuite" 道教の三元思想について [On Taoist notions of the Three Primes]. *Shūkyō kenkyū* 宗教研究 166: 1–15.

———. 1965. "Sairon sangen shisō no keisei" 再論三元思想の形成 [A new discussion of the formation of the Taoist notions of the Three Primes]. *Hirosaki daigaku bunkyō ronsō* 弘前大學文教論叢 1: 437–56.

———. 1978. *Chūgoku kinsei dōkyō no keisei: Jōmyōdō no kisoteki kenkyū* 中國近世道教の形成—浄明道の基礎的研究 [The formation of modern Taoism in China: An introductory study of Jingming dao]. Tokyo: Sōbunsha.

———, ed. 1986. *Dōkyō kenkyū no susume: Sono genjō to mondaiten o kangaeru* 道教研究のすすめ—その現状と問題点を考える [An invitation to Taoist studies: Reflections on its state and issues]. Edited in cooperation with Noguchi Tetsurō 野口鐵郎 and Fukui Fumimasa 福井文雅. Tokyo: Hirakawa shuppansha.

———, ed. 1987. *Dōkyō to shūkyō bunka* 道教と宗教文化 [Taoism and religious culture]. Tokyo: Hirakawa shuppansha.

———. 1991. "Jōmyōdō keisei ronkō: Chūgoku ni okeru saikin no kenkyū seika o yonde" 浄明道形成論考—中國における最近の研究成果を讀んで [Studies on the formation of the Jingming dao: Reflections on the results of resent research in China]. *TS* 78: 23–44.

Alexéiev, Basil M. 1928. *The Chinese Gods of Wealth*. London: School of Oriental Studies in conjunction with The China Society.

Allan, Sarah. 1991. *The Shape of the Turtle: Myth, Art, and Cosmos in Early China*. Albany: State University of New York Press.

Allan, Sarah, and Crispin Williams, eds. 2000. *The Guodian Laozi: Proceedings of the International Conference, Dartmouth College, May 1998*. Berkeley: Society for the Study of Early China and Institute of East Asian Studies, University of California.

Allinson, Robert E. 1989. *Chuang-tzu for Spiritual Transformation: An Analysis of the Inner Chapters*. Albany: State University of New York Press.

———. 1994. "Moral Values and the Taoist Sage in the *Tao te ching*." *Asian Philosophy* 4: 127–36.

Ames, Roger T. 1983. *The Art of Rulership: A Study in Ancient Chinese Political Thought*. Honolulu: University of Hawaii Press. Reprinted as *The Art of Rulership: A Study of Ancient Chinese Political Thought*, New York: State University of New York Press, 1994.

———. 1989. "Putting the *Te* Back into Taoism." In Callicott and Ames 1989, 113–44.

———. 1993. *Sun-tzu: The Art of Warfare. The First English Translation Incorporating the Recently Discovered Yin-ch'üeh-shan Texts*. New York: Ballantine Books.

An Zhimin 安志敏 et al. 1990. *Ni Chū gōdō shinpojiumu: Jo Fuku densetsu o saguru* 日中合同シンポジウム—徐福傳説を探る [A Japanese-Chinese joint symposium: Exploring the legend of Xu Fu]. Tokyo: Shogakkan.

Andersen, Poul. 1979. *The Method of Holding the Three Ones: A Taoist Manual of Meditation of the Fourth Century A.D.* London and Malmö: Curzon Press.

———. 1989–90a. "A Visit to Hua-shan." *CEA* 5: 349–54.

———. 1989–90b. "The Practice of *Bugang.*" *CEA* 5: 15–53.

———. 1990. "Guideline of the Eight Trigrams." In Arendrup, Heilesen, and Petersen 1990, 13–30.

———. 1991. "Taoist Ritual Texts and Traditions, With Special Reference to *Bugang,* the Cosmic Dance." Ph.D. diss., University of Copenhagen.

———. 1994. "Talking to the Gods: Visionary Divination in Early Taoism (The Sanhuang Tradition)." *TR* 5.1: 1–24.

———. 1995. "The Transformation of the Body in Taoist Ritual." In Law 1995, 186–208.

———. 1996. "Taoist Talismans and the History of the Tianxin Tradition." *Acta Orientalia* 57: 141–52. [Review of Drexler 1994.]

———. 2001. *The Demon Chained under Turtle Mountain: The History and Mythology of the Chinese River Spirit Wuzhiqi.* Berlin: GH Verlag.

———. 2002. "Taoist Ritual in the Shanghai Area." In Overmyer 2002, 263–83.

Ang, Isabelle. 1993. "Le culte de Lü Dongbin des origines jusqu'au début du XIVème siècle: Caractéristiques et transformations d'un Saint Immortel dans la Chine prémoderne." Ph.D. diss., Université de Paris VII.

———. 1997. "Le culte de Lü Dongbin sous les Song du Sud." *Journal Asiatique* 285: 473–507.

Aoki Takashi 青木隆. 1993. "Goshinmei shisō to dōkyō" 護身命思想と道教 [Conceptions about protecting the vital force and Taoism]. *Indogaku bukkyōgaku kenkyū* 印度學佛教學研究 41.1: 252–55.

App, Urs. 1994. *Master Yunmen: From the Record of the Chan Master "Gate of the Clouds."* New York: Kodansha.

Araki kyōju taikyū kinenkai 荒木教授退休記念会 [Committee for the Commemoration of the Retirement of Professor Araki Kengo], ed. 1981. *Chūgoku tetsugakushi kenkyū ronshū: Araki kyōju taikyū kinen* 中國哲學史研究論集—荒木教授退休記念 [Collected studies on the history of Chinese philosophy in commemoration of the retirement of Professor Araki Kengo]. Fukuoka: Ishobō.

Arendrup, Birthe. 1974. "The First Chapter of Guo Xiang's Commentary to *Zhuang zi*: A Translation and Grammatical Analysis." *Acta Orientalia* 36: 311–415.

Arendrup, Birthe, Simon B. Heilesen, and Jens Østergård Petersen, eds. 1990. *The Master Said: To Study and . . . To Søren Egerod on the Occasion of his Sixty-Seventh Birthday.* Copenhagen: East Asian Institute, University of Copenhagen.

Asano Haruji 浅野春二. 1994. "Dōshi to dōshidan: Gendai Taiwan nanbu no jirei kara" 道士と道士団—現代臺湾南部の事例から [Taoist priests and Taoist priests' groups, based on the example of modern southern Taiwan]. In Dōkyō bunka kenkyūkai 1994, 5–49.

———. 1999a. "Dōkyō girei no kumotsu: Kesshoku hitei to kajitsu, bunbō shihō" 道教儀礼の供物—血食否定と果実文房四宝 [Offerings in Taoist ritual: Taboos

against "bloody sacrifices," and the "four treasures of the scholar's studio"].
Kokugakuin daigaku Nihon bunka kenkyūjo kiyō 國學院大學日本文化研究所紀
要 83: 289–311.

———. 1999b. *"Mujō kōroku taisai ritsusei gi ni okeru yūkon, seisen bōi e no kumotsu"*
「無上黄籙大斎立成儀」における幽魂・正薦亡位への供物 [Offerings to the
lost souls of the deceased in the *Wushang huanglu dazhai licheng yi*]. *Kokugakuin
Chūgoku gakkaihō* 國學院中國學会報 45: 36–52.

Asano Yūichi 浅野裕一. 1988. *"Resshi to shinsen, yōsei shisō"* 「列子」と神仙・養生
思想 [Conceptions of "divine immortality" and Nourishing Life in the *Liezi*]. In
Sakade Yoshinobu 1988a, 198–243.

Azuma Jūji 吾妻重二. 1984. *"Shu Ki Shūeki sandōkei kōi ni tsuite"* 朱熹「周易三同契
考異」について [On Zhu Xi's Zhouyi cantong qi kaoyi]. *NCG* 36: 175–90.

———. 1988. *"Goshinhen no naitan shisō"* 「悟真篇」の内丹思想 [The *neidan* thought
of the *Wuzhen pian*]. In Sakade Yoshinobu 1988a, 600–627.

Balázs, Étienne. 1948. "Entre révolte nihiliste et évasion mystique: Les courants intel-
lectuels en Chine au IIIe siècle de notre ère." *ASEA* 2: 27–55.

Balázs, Etienne, and Yves Hervouet, eds. 1978. *A Sung Bibliography (Bibliographie des
Sung)*. Hong Kong: Chinese University Press.

Baldrian-Hussein, Farzeen. 1984. *Procédés secrets du joyau magique: Traité d'alchimie
taoïste du XIe siècle*. Paris: Les Deux Océans.

———. 1985. "Yüeh-yang and Lü Tung-pin's *Ch'in-yüan ch'un*: A Sung Alchemical
Poem." In Naundorf, Pohl, and Schmidt 1985, 19–31.

———. 1986. "Lü Tung-pin in Northern Sung Literature." *CEA* 2: 133–69.

———. 1989–90. "Inner Alchemy: Notes on the Origin and Use of the Term *Neidan*."
CEA 5: 163–90.

———. 1996–97. "Alchemy and Self-Cultivation in Literary Circles of the Northern
Song Dynasty: Su Shi (1037–1101) and his Techniques of Survival." *CEA* 9: 15–53.

Balfour, Frederic Henri. 1884. *Taoist Texts, Ethical, Political, and Speculative*. London:
Trubner and Company; Shanghai: Kelley and Walsh.

Banks, David J., ed. 1976. *Changing Identities in Modern Southeast Asia*. The Hague:
Mouton.

Baptandier, Brigitte. 1996. "The Lady Linshui: How a Woman Became a Goddess."
In Shahar and Weller 1996, 105–49.

Baptandier-Berthier, Brigitte [Brigitte Baptandier]. 1994. "The Kaiguan 開關 Ritual and the
Construction of the Child's Identity." In Hanxue yanjiu zhongxin 1994, 1: 523–86.

Barnhart, Michael, ed. 2002. *Varieties of Ethical Reflection: New Directions for Ethics in a
Global Context*. New York: Lexington Books.

Barrett, T. H. 1980a. "On the Transmission of the *Shen tzu* and of the *Yang-sheng yaochi*." *JRAS* 1980: 168–76.

———. 1980b. "Taoist Ritual and the Development of Chinese Magic." *Modern Asian
Studies* 14: 164–69. [Review of Saso 1978b.]

———. 1982. "Taoist and Buddhist Mysteries in the Interpretation of the *Tao-te ching*."
JRAS 1982: 35–43.

———. 1986. "Postscript to Chapter 16." In Twitchett and Fairbank 1986, 873–78. [Ad-
denda to Paul Demiéville, "Philosophy and Religion from Han to Sui," 808–72.]

———. 1987a. "Ko Hung." In Eliade 1987, 8: 359–60.

———. 1987b. "Li Shao-chün." In Eliade 1987, 8: 558.

———. 1990. "Religious Traditions in Chinese Civilization: Buddhism and Taoism." In Ropp 1990, 138–63.

———. 1991a. "Buddhism, Taoism and the Rise of the City Gods." In Skorupski 1991, 13–25.

———. 1991b. "Devil's Valley to Omega Point: Reflections on the Emergence of a Theme from the Nō." In Skorupski 1991, 1–12.

———. 1992. *Li Ao: Buddhist, Taoist, or Neo-Confucian?* Oxford: Oxford University Press.

———. 1993. "*Lieh tzu.*" In Loewe 1993, 298–308.

———. 1994a. "The Taoist Canon in Japan: Some Implications of the Research of Ho Peng Yoke." *TR* 5.2: 71–77.

———. 1994b. "The Emergence of the Taoist Papacy in the T'ang Dynasty." *AM*, third series, 7: 89–106.

———. 1996. *Taoism under the T'ang: Religion and Empire during the Golden Age of Chinese History*. London: Wellsweep Press.

———. 1997. "The *Feng-tao k'o* and Printing on Paper in Seventh-Century China." *Bulletin of the School of Oriental and African Studies* 60: 538–40.

———. 1998. "Science and Religion in Medieval China." *JRAS*, third series, 8: 423–30.

———. 2000. "Shinto and Taoism in Early Japan." In Breen and Teeuwen 2000, 13–31.

Baryosher-Chemouny, Nuriel. 1996. *La quête de l'immortalité en Chine: Alchimie et paysage intérieur sous les Song*. Paris: Éditions Dervy.

Bauer, Wolfgang. 1956. "Der Herr vom Gelben Stein." *Oriens Extremus* 3: 137–52.

———, ed. 1979. *Studia Sino-Mongolica: Festschrift für Herbert Franke*. Wiesbaden: Franz Steiner Verlag.

Baxter, William H. 1998. "Situating the Language of the Lao-tzu: The Probable Date of the *Tao-te-ching.*" In Kohn and LaFargue 1998, 231–53.

Bedini, Silvio A. 1994. *The Trail of Time: Time Measurement with Incense in East Asia*. Cambridge: Cambridge University Press.

Bell, Catherine M. 1987a. "Lu Hsiu-ching." In Eliade 1987, 9: 50–51.

———. 1987b. "T'ao Hung-ching." In Eliade 1987, 14: 287–88.

———. 1987c. "Tu Kuang-t'ing." In Eliade 1987, 15: 80–81.

———. 1988. "Ritualization of Texts and Textualization of Ritual in the Codification of Taoist Liturgy." *HR* 27: 366–92.

———. 1996a. "'A Precious Raft to Save the World': The Interaction of Scriptural Traditions and Printing in a Chinese Morality Book." *Late Imperial China* 17.1: 158–200.

———. 1996b. "Stories from an Illustrated Explanation of the Tract of the Most Exalted on Action and Response." In Lopez 1996, 437–45.

Benn, Charles D. 1977. "Taoism as Ideology in the Reign of Emperor Hsüan-tsung (712–755)." Ph.D. diss., University of Michigan.

———. 1991. *The Cavern-Mystery Transmission: A Taoist Ordination Rite of A.D. 711*. Honolulu: University of Hawaii Press.

————. 2000. "Daoist Ordination and *Zhai* Rituals in Medieval China." In Kohn 2000b, 309–39.

————. 2002. *Daily Life in Traditional China: The Tang Dynasty*. Westport, CT: Greenwood Press.

Bennett, Tony. 1986. "The Politics of 'the Popular' and Popular Culture." In Bennett, Mercer, and Woollacott 1986, 6–21.

Bennett, Tony, Colin Mercer, and Janet Woollacott, eds. 1986. *Popular Culture and Social Relations*. Milton Keynes and Philadelphia: Open University Press.

Benoist, Jean, ed. 1996. *Soigner au pluriel: Essais sur le pluralisme médical*. Paris: Karthala.

Berkowitz, Alan J. 1996. "Record of Occultists." In Lopez 1996, 446–70.

Berling, Judith A. 1979. "Paths of Convergence: Interactions of Inner Alchemy Taoism and Neo-Confucianism." *JCP* 6: 123–47.

————. 1980. *The Syncretic Religion of Lin Chao-en*. New York: Columbia University Press.

————. 1993. "Channels of Connection in Sung Religion: The Case of Pai Yü-ch'an 白玉蟾." In Ebrey and Gregory 1993, 307–33.

————. 1998. "Taoism in Ming Culture." In Twitchett and Fairbank 1998, 953–86.

Bernos, Marcel, ed. 1988. *Sexualité et religion*. Paris: Éditions du Cerf.

Berthier, Brigitte [Brigitte Baptandier]. 1987. "Enfant de divination, voyageur du destin." *L'Homme* 101: 86–100.

————. 1988. *La Dame-du-bord-de-l'eau*. Nanterre: Société d'éthnologie.

Bertschinger, Richard. 1994. *The Secret of Everlasting Life: The First Translation of the Ancient Chinese Text of Immortality*. Shaftesbury, Dorset: Element.

Bertuccioli, Giuliano. 1974. "Reminiscences of the Mao-shan." *East and West* 24: 403–15.

Bielenstein, Hans. 1980. *The Bureaucracy of Han Times*. Cambridge: Cambridge University Press.

Billeter, Jean François. 1985. "Essai d'interprétation du chapitre 15 du *Laozi*." *ASEA* 39: 7–44.

Biot, Édouard. 1861. *Le Tcheou-li ou Rites des Tcheou*. 3 vols. Paris: Imprimerie Nationale.

Birch, Cyril, ed. 1965–72. *Anthology of Chinese Literature*. 2 vols. Vol. 1: *From Early Times to the Fourteenth Century*. Vol. 2: *From the Fourteenth Century to the Present Day*. New York: Grove Press.

Birdwhistell, Anne D. 1989. *Transition to Neo-Confucianism: Shao Yung on Knowledge and Symbols of Reality*. Stanford: Stanford University Press.

Birrell, Anne. 1993. *Chinese Mythology: An Introduction*. Baltimore and London: Johns Hopkins University Press.

Blanchon, Flora, ed. 1993. *Asies*. Vol. 2: *Aménager l'espace*. Paris: Presses de l'Université de Paris-Sorbonne.

Blondeau, Anne-Marie, and Kristofer Schipper. 1988–95. *Essais sur le rituel: Colloque du centenaire de la Section des sciences religieuses de l'École Pratique des Hautes Études*. 3 vols. Louvain and Paris: Peeters.

Blussé, Leonard, and Harriet T. Zurndorfer, eds. 1993. *Conflict and Accommodation in Early Modern East Asia: Essays in Honour of Erik Zürcher*. Leiden: E. J. Brill.

Bock, Felicia G. 1985. *Classical Learning and Taoist Practices in Early Japan: With a Translation of Books XVI and XX of the Engi-shiki. Tempe, AZ: Center for Asian Studies, Arizona State University.

Bodde, Derk. 1975. *Festivals in Classical China: New Year and Other Annual Observances During the Han Dynasty*. Princeton: Princeton University Press and The Chinese University of Hong Kong.

————. 1991. *Chinese Thought, Society, and Science: The Intellectual and Social Background of Science and Technology in Pre-Modern China*. Honolulu: University of Hawaii Press.

Bokenkamp, Stephen R. 1981. "The 'Pacing the Void Stanzas' of the Ling-pao Scriptures." Master's thesis, University of California, Berkeley.

————. 1983. "Sources of the Ling-pao Scriptures." In Strickmann 1981–85, 2: 434–86.

————. 1986a. "Ko Ch'ao-fu." In Nienhauser 1986, 479–81.

————. 1986b. "Ko Hung." In Nienhauser 1986, 481–82.

————. 1986c. "Taoist Literature. Part 1: Through the T'ang Dynasty." In Nienhauser 1986, 138–52.

————. 1986d. "The Peach Flower Font and the Grotto Passage." *JAOS* 106: 65–77.

————. 1989. "Death and Ascent in Ling-pao Taoism." *TR* 1.2: 1–20.

————. 1990. "Stages of Transcendence: The *Bhūmi* Concept of Taoist Scripture." In Buswell 1990, 119–47.

————. 1991. "Taoism and Literature: The *Pi-lo* Question." *TR* 3.1: 57–72.

————. 1993. "Traces of Early Celestial Master Physiological Practice in the *Xiang'er* Commentary." *TR* 4.2: 37–51.

————. 1994. "Time After Time: Taoist Apocalyptic History and the Founding of the Tang Dynasty." *AM*, third series, 7: 59–88.

————. 1996a. "Answering a Summons." In Lopez 1996, 188–202.

————. 1996b. *"Declarations of the Perfected."* In Lopez 1996, 166–79.

————. 1996c. "The Purification Ritual of the Luminous Perfected." In Lopez 1996, 268–77.

————. 1996–97. "The Yao Boduo Stele as Evidence for the 'Dao-Buddhism' of the Early Lingbao Scriptures." *CEA* 9: 54–67.

————. 1997. *Early Daoist Scriptures*. With a contribution by Peter Nickerson. Berkeley: University of California Press.

————. 2001. "Lu Xiujing, Buddhism, and the First Daoist Canon." In Pearce, Spiro, and Ebrey 2001, 181–99.

————. 2004. "The Prehistory of Laozi: His Prior Career as a Woman in the Lingbao Scriptures." *CEA* 14: 403–21.

Boltz, Judith M. 1983. "Opening the Gates of Purgatory: A Twelfth-Century Taoist Meditation Technique for the Salvation of Lost Souls." In Strickmann 1981–85, 2: 487–511.

————. 1985. "Taoist Rites of Exorcism." Ph.D. diss., University of California, Berkeley.

————. 1986a. "In Homage to T'ien-fei." *JAOS* 106: 211–32.

————. 1986b. "Tao-tsang." In Nienhauser 1986, 763–66.

————. 1986c. "Taoist Literature. Part 2: Five Dynasties to the Ming." In Nienhauser 1986, 152–74.

————. 1987a. *A Survey of Taoist Literature: Tenth to Seventeenth Centuries*. Berkeley: Institute of East Asian Studies, University of California. Reprinted with corrigenda, 1995.

————. 1987b. "Lao-tzu." In Eliade 1987, 8: 454–59.

————. 1987c. "Taoism: Taoist Literature." In Eliade 1987, 14: 317–29.

————. 1993a. "Not by the Seal of Office Alone: New Weapons in Battles with the Supernatural." In Ebrey and Gregory 1993, 241–305.

————. 1993b. "Notes on Modern Editions of the Taoist Canon." *Bulletin of the School of Oriental and African Studies* 56: 86–95.

————. 1994. "Notes on the *Daozang tiyao*." *China Review International* 1.2: 1–33.

————. 1996. "Singing to the Spirits of the Dead: A Daoist Ritual of Salvation." In Yung, Rawski, and Watson 1996, 177–225.

Boltz, William G. 1984. "Textual Criticism and the Ma wang tui *Lao-tzu*." *HJAS* 44: 185–224. [Review article on Lau 1982.]

————. 1993. "*Lao tzu Tao te ching*." In Loewe 1993, 269–92.

————. 1996. "Notes on the Authenticity of the So Tan Manuscript of the *Lao-tzu*." *Bulletin of the School of Oriental and African Studies* 59: 508–15.

————. 1999. "The Fourth-Century B.C. Guodiann Manuscripts from Chuu and the Composition of the *Laotzyy*." *JAOS* 119: 590–608.

Boodberg, Peter A. 1957. "Philological Notes on Chapter One of the *Lao Tzu*." *HJAS* 20: 598–618.

Bourdieu, Pierre. 1984. *Distinction: A Social Critique of the Judgement of Taste*. Translated by Richard Nice. Cambridge, MA: Harvard University Press. Originally published as *La Distinction: Critique sociale du jujement* (Paris: Les Éditions de Minuit, 1979).

Brandon, James R. 1987. "Drama: East Asian Dance and Theatre." In Eliade 1987, 4: 459–62.

Brashier, K. E. 1996. "Han Thanatology and the Division of 'Souls.'" *EC* 21: 125–58.

Breen, John, and Mark Teeuwen, eds. 2000. *Shinto in History: Ways of the Kami*. Honolulu: University of Hawaii Press.

Brokaw, Cynthia J. 1991. *The Ledgers of Merit and Demerit: Social Change and Moral Order in Late Imperial China*. Princeton: Princeton University Press.

Brown, Peter. 1981. *The Cult of the Saints: Its Rise and Function in Latin Christianity*. Chicago: University of Chicago Press.

————. 1982. *Society and the Holy in Late Antiquity*. Berkeley and Los Angeles: University of California Press.

Bumbacher, Stephan Peter. 1998. "The Earliest Manuscripts of the *Laozi* Discovered to Date." *ASEA* 52: 1175–84.

————. 2000a. "On Pre-Tang Daoist Monastic Establishments at Mao Shan, according to *Daoxue zhuan*." *JCR* 28: 145–60.

————. 2000b. "On the *Shenxian zhuan*." *ASEA* 54: 729–814.

————. 2000c. *The Fragments of the Daoxue zhuan: Critical Edition, Translation and Analysis of a Medieval Collection of Daoist Biographies*. Frankfurt: Peter Lang.

Burkhardt, Valentine Rudolphe. 1953–58. *Chinese Creeds and Custom*. 3 vols. Hong Kong: South China Morning Post.

Bush, Susan. 1983. "Tsung Ping's Essay on Painting Landscape and the 'Landscape Buddhism' of Mount Lu." In Bush and Murck 1983, 132–64.

Bush, Susan, and Christian Murck, eds. 1983. *Theories of the Arts in China*. Princeton: Princeton University Press.

Buswell, Robert E., Jr., ed. 1990. *Chinese Buddhist Apocrypha*. Honolulu: University of Hawaii Press.

Butler, Anthony R., et al. 1987. "The Solubilization of Metallic Gold and Silver: Explanations of Two Sixth-Century Chinese Protochemical Recipes." *Polyedron* 6: 483–88.

Cabezon, José Ignacio. 1998. *Scholasticism: Cross-Cultural and Comparative Perspectives*. Albany: State University of New York Press.

Cadonna, Alfredo. 1984. *Il Taoista di sua Maestà*. Venezia: Cafoscarina.

Cahill, Suzanne E. 1980. "Taoism at the Sung Court: The Heavenly Text Affair of 1008." *Bulletin of Sung-Yüan Studies* 16: 23–44.

———. 1985. "Sex and Supernatural in Medieval China: Cantos on the Transcendent who Presides over the River." *JAOS* 105: 197–220.

———. 1986a. "Performers and Female Taoist Adepts: Hsi Wang Mu as the Patron Deity of Women in Medieval China." *JAOS* 106: 155–68.

———. 1986b. "Reflections of a Metal Mother: Tu Kuang-t'ing's Biography of Hsi Wang Mu." *JCR* 13–14: 127–42.

———. 1990. "Practice Makes Perfect: Paths to Transcendence for Women in Medieval China." *TR* 2.2: 23–42.

———. 1992. "Sublimation in Medieval China: The Case of the Mysterious Woman of the Nine Heavens." *JCR* 20: 91–102.

———. 1993. *Transcendence and Divine Passion: The Queen Mother of the West in Medieval China*. Stanford: Stanford University Press.

Cahill, Suzanne E., and Julia K. Murray. 1987. "Recent Advances in Understanding the Mystery of Ancient Chinese 'Magic Mirrors': A Brief Summary of Chinese Analytical and Experimental Studies." *Chinese Science* 8: 1–8.

Cai Maotang 蔡懋棠. 1974–76. "Taiwan xianxing de shanshu" 臺彎現行的善書 [Morality books currently circulating in Taiwan]. Parts 1 and 2. *Taiwan fengwu* 臺彎風物 24.4 (1974): 86–116; 26.4 (1976): 84–123.

Cai Xianghui 蔡相輝. 1989. *Taiwan de wangye yu Mazu* 臺灣的王爺與媽祖 [Royal Lords and Mazu in Taiwan]. Taipei: Taiyuan chubanshe.

Callicott, J. Baird, and Roger T. Ames, eds. 1989. *Nature in Asian Traditions of Thought: Essays in Environmental Philosophy*. Albany: State University of New York Press.

Cammann, Schuyler. 1961. "The Magic Square of Three in Old Chinese Philosophy and Religion." *HR* 1: 37–80.

———. 1962. "Old Chinese Magic Squares." *Sinologica* 7: 14–53.

———. 1990. "The Eight Trigrams: Variants and their Uses." *HR* 29: 301–17.

Campany, Robert F. 1990. "Return-from-Death Narratives in Early Medieval China." *JCR* 18: 91–125.

———. 1993. "Buddhist Revelation and Taoist Translation in Early Medieval China." *TR* 4.1: 1–29.

———. 1996. *Strange Writing: Anomaly Accounts in Early Medieval China*. Albany: State University of New York Press.

———. 2002. *To Live as Long as Heaven and Earth: A Translation and Study of Ge Hong's Traditions of Divine Transcendents*. Berkeley: University of California Press.

Cao Benye 曹本冶, ed. 1991. *Yijiujiuyi nian Xianggang di'er jie Daojiao keyi yinyue yantao hui lunwen ji* 一九九一年香港第二屆道教科儀音樂研討會論文集 [Proceedings of the Second Conference on Taoist Ritual Music, Hong Kong, 1991]. Beijing: Renmin yinyue chubanshe.

Cao Benye 曹本冶 and Liu Hong 劉紅. 1996. *Longhu shan Tianshi dao yinyue yanjiu* 龍虎山天師道音樂研究 [Studies on the music of the Way of the Celestial Masters on Mount Longhu]. Taipei: Xinwenfeng chuban gongsi.

Carman, John, and Mark Juergensmeyer, eds. 1991. *A Bibliographic Guide to the Comparative Study of Ethics*. Cambridge: Cambridge University Press.

Carré, Patrik. 1999. *Le Livre de la Cour Jaune: Classique taoïste des IVe-Ve siècles*. Paris: Éditions du Seuil.

Carrozza, Paola. 1999. "A Comparative Study of the Mawangdui Manuscripts *Jingfa* and *Jing*: Rhetorical Strategies and Philosophical Terms." Master's thesis, McGill University.

Cazenave, Michel, ed. 1998. *La face féminine de Dieu*. Paris: Noésis.

Cedzich, Ursula-Angelika. 1985. "Wu-t'ung: Zur bewegten Geschichte eines Kultes." In Naundorf, Pohl, and Schmidt 1985, 33–60.

———. 1987. "Das Ritual der Himmelsmeister im Spiegel früher Quellen: Übersetzung und Untersuchung des liturgischen Materials im dritten chüan des *Teng-chen yin-chüeh*." Ph.D. diss., Julius-Maximilians-Universität, Würzburg.

———. 1993. "Ghosts and Demons, Law and Order: Grave Quelling Texts and Early Taoist Liturgy." *TR* 4.2: 23–35.

———. 1995. "The Cult of the Wu-t'ung/Wu-hsien in History and Fiction: The Religious Roots of the *Journey to the South*." In Johnson 1995b, 137–218.

Ch'a Chuhwan 車柱環. 1984. *Han'guk ŭi togyo sasang* 韓國의道教思想 [Taoist thought in Korea]. Seoul: Donghwa chulpan kongsa. Translated into Japanese by Miura Kunio 三浦國雄 and Nozaki Mitsuhiko 野崎充彦 as *Chōsen no dōkyō* 朝鮮の道教 (Kyoto: Jinbun shoin, 1990).

Chamberlayne, John H. 1966. "The Chinese Earth-Shrine." *Numen* 13: 164–82.

Chambliss, J. J., ed. 1996. *Philosophy of Education: An Encyclopedia*. New York: Garland.

Chan Hok-lam and Wm. Theodore de Bary, eds. 1982. *Yüan Thought: Chinese Thought and Religion Under the Mongols*. New York: Columbia University Press.

Chan, Alan K. L. 1988. "The Essential Meaning of the Way and Virtue: Yan Zun and 'Laozi Learning' in Early Han China." *MS* 46: 105–27.

———. 1990. "Goddesses in Chinese Religion." In Hurtado 1990, 9–81.

———. 1991a. "The Formation of the Heshang Gong Legend." In Ching and Guisso 1991, 101–34.

———. 1991b. *Two Visions of the Way: A Study of the Wang Pi and Ho-shang Kung Commentaries on the Lao-tzu*. Albany: State University of New York Press.

———. 1998. "A Tale of Two Commentaries: Ho-shang-kung and Wang Pi on the *Lao-tzu*." In Kohn and LaFargue 1998, 89–117.

———. 2000. "The *Daode jing* and its Tradition." In Kohn 2000b, 1–29.

Chan Wing-tsit. 1963. *The Way of Lao Tzu (Tao-te ching)*. Indianapolis, New York: Bobbs-Merrill.

———. 1986. *Neo-Confucian Terms Explained: Pei-hsi tzu-i by Ch'en Ch'un*. New York: Columbia University Press.

———. 1989. *Chu Hsi: New Studies*. Honolulu: University of Hawaii Press.

Chang Fu-jui. 1968. "Le *Yi kien tche* et la société des Song." *Journal asiatique* 256: 55–93.

Chang, Leo S., and Yu Feng. 1998. *The Four Political Treatises of the Yellow Emperor*. Honolulu: University of Hawaii Press.

Chao Wei-pang. 1942. "The Origin and Growth of the Fu Chi." *Folklore Studies* 1: 9–27.

Chappell, David W., ed. 1987. *Buddhist and Taoist Practice in Medieval Chinese Society*. Honolulu: University of Hawaii Press.

Chard, Robert L. 1990. "Folktales on the God of the Stove." *HXYJ* 8: 149–82.

———. 1995. "Rituals and Scriptures of the Stove Cult." In Johnson 1995b, 3–54.

Chavannes, Édouard. 1895–1905. *Les Mémoires historiques de Se-ma Ts'ien*. 5 vols. Paris: Leroux. Reprint, with an additional sixth volume edited and completed by Paul Demiéville, Max Kaltenmark, and Timoteus Pokora, Paris: Adrien Maisonneuve, 1969.

———. 1910a. "Le dieu du sol dans la Chine antique." In Chavannes 1910b, 437–525.

———. 1910b. *Le T'ai chan: Essai de monographie d'un culte chinois*. Paris: Ernest Leroux.

———. 1919. "Le jet des dragons." *Mémoires concernant l'Asie Orientale* 3: 53–220.

Chavannes, Édouard, and Paul Pelliot. 1911–13. "Un traité manichéen retrouvé en Chine." Parts 1 and 2. *Journal Asiatique*, tenth series, 18 (1911): 499–617; eleventh series, 1 (1913): 99–394.

Che, Philippe. 1999. *La Voie des Divins Immortels: Les chapitres discursifs du Baopu zi neipian*. Paris: Gallimard.

Chen Bali 陈巴黎. 2002. *Beijing Dongyue miao* 北京东岳庙 [The Dongyue miao in Beijing]. Beijing: Zhongguo shudian chubanshe.

Ch'en Ch'i-yün. 1980. *Hsün Yüeh and the Mind of Late Han China*. Princeton: Princeton University Press.

Chen Bing 陈兵. 1985. "Jindan pai Nanzong qiantan" 金丹派南宗浅探 [A brief exploration of the Southern Lineage of the Golden Elixir Branch]. *SZY* 1985.4: 35–49.

———. 1986. "Yuandai Jiangnan daojiao" 元代江南道教 [Taoism in Jiangnan during the Yuan dynasty]. *SZY* 1986.2: 65–80.

———. 1988. "Qingdai Quanzhen dao Longmen pai de zhongxing" 清代全真道龙门派的中兴 [The renewal of the Longmen branch of Quanzhen during the Qing period]. *SZY* 1988.2: 84–96.

———. 1989. "Zhonghua qigong zai daojiao zhong de fazhan" 中华气功在道教中的发展 [Chinese *qigong* in the development of Taoism]. *SZY* 1989.4: 8–20.

Chen Dacan 陈大灿, ed. 1987. *Zhongguo daojiao zhaijiao* 中国道教斋醮 [Chinese Taoist *zhai* and *jiao* rituals]. 8 videotapes. Shanghai: Zhongguo changpian gongsi.

———. 1988. "Notes sur un voyage à Gezaoshan." *CEA* 4: 167–73.

Chen Feilong 陳飛龍. 1980. *Ge Hong zhi wenlun ji qi shengping* 葛洪之文論及其生平 [Life and work of Ge Hong]. Taipei: Wenshizhe chubanshe.

Chen Guofu 陳國符. 1963. *Daozang yuanliu kao* 道藏源流考 [Studies on the origins and development of the Taoist Canon]. 2 vols. Beijing: Zhonghua shuju.

———. 1981. "Ming Qing daojiao yinyue kaogao" 明清道教音乐考稿 [Research notes on Taoist music of the Ming and Qing periods]. *Zhonghua wenshi luncong* 中华文史论丛 1981.2: 1–28.

———. 1983. *Daozang yuanliu xukao* 道藏源流續考 [Further studies on the origins and development of the Taoist Canon]. Taipei: Mingwen shuju.

Chen Guying 陳鼓應. 1987. *Laozi zhuyi ji pingjie* 老子注譯及評介 [The *Laozi* with notes and comments]. Beijing: Zhonghua shuju.

———. 1993. "*Xici zhuan* de daojialun ji *taiji, daheng* shuo" 「繫辭傳」的道家論及太極大恆說 [Taoist views of the *Xici zhuan*, and the notions of Great Ultimate and Great Constancy]. *DWY* 3: 64–72.

———. 1995. *Huangdi sijing jinzhu jinyi: Mawangdui Hanmu chutu boshu* 黃帝四經今注今譯—馬王堆漢墓出土帛書 [The "Four Scriptures of the Yellow Emperor" with a modern commentary and translation: Silk manuscripts from the Han tombs at Mawangdui]. Taipei: Taiwan shangwu yinshuguan.

Chen Hsiang-ch'un. 1942. "Examples of Charms against Epidemics with Short Explanations." *Folklore Studies* 1: 37–54.

Chen Jianxian 陈建宪. 1994. *Yuhuang dadi xinyang* 玉皇大帝信仰 [The belief in the Jade Emperor]. Beijing: Xueyuan chubanshe.

Chen Jinhong 陈津洪. 1992. "Tangdai *Daozang* de bianzuan yu chuanxie" 唐代道藏的编纂与传写 [The compilation and transmission of the Taoist Canon in the Tang period]. *ZGDJ* 1992.4: 39–44.

Ch'en, Kenneth K. S. 1945–47. "Buddhist-Taoist Mixtures in the *Pa-shi-i-hua t'u*." *HJAS* 9: 1–12.

Ch'en Ku-ying [Chen Guying]. 1977. *Lao Tzu: Text, Notes, and Comments*. Translated by Rhett Y. W. Young and Roger T. Ames. San Francisco: Chinese Materials Center. Originally published as *Laozi jinzhu jinyi ji pingjie* 老子今注今譯及評介 [The *Laozi* with explications, notes, and comments] (Taipei: Shangwu yinshuguan 1970).

Chen Mingfang 陈明芳. 1992. *Zhongguo xuanguan zang* 中国悬棺葬 [Cliff burial in China]. Chongqing: Chongqing chubanshe.

Chen Minhui 陳敏慧. 1988. "Lai zi minjian koutou chuantong de xinsheng: Yi yichang Chen Jinggu gushi zhi zhuanshu wei li" 來自民間口頭傳統的心聲—以一場陳靖姑故事之轉述為例 [Voices from popular oral traditions: A case study of an account of Defending Maiden Chen]. *HXYJ* 6: 309–26.

Chen Pan 陳槃. 1948. "Zhanguo Qin Han jian fangshi kaolun" 戰國秦漢間方士考論 [A study of the "masters of methods" in the Warring States, Qin, and Han periods]. *ZLJ* 17: 7–57. Reprinted in Chen Pan 1993, 179–256.

———. 1993. *Gu chenwei yantao ji qi shulu jieti* 古讖緯研討及其書錄解題 [Studies and bibliographic notes on the ancient apocryphal texts]. Taipei: Guoli bianyiguan.

Chen Shixiang 陳世驤. 1957. "Xiang'er *Laozi* daojing Dunhuang canjuan lunzheng" 「想爾」老子道經敦煌殘卷論證. English title: "On the Historical and Religious Significance of the Tun-huang Ms. of Lao-tzu, Book 1, with Commentaries by 'Hsiang Erh.'" *Qinghua xuebao* 清華學報 (*The Tsing Hua Journal of Chinese Studies*) 1.2: 41–62.

Chen Songchang 陳松長. 2001. *Mawangdui boshu Xingde yanjiu lungao* 馬王堆帛書「刑德」研究論稿 [Studies on the Mawangdui silk manuscript of the *Xingde*]. Taipei: Taiwan guji chuban youxian gongsi.

Chen Xia 陈霞. 1999. *Daojiao quanshan shu yanjiu* 道教劝善书研究 [A study of Taoist books of moral exhortation]. Chengdu: Ba Shu shushe.

Chen Yuan 陳垣 (陈垣). 1962. *Nan Song chu Hebei xin daojiao kao* 南宋初河北新道教考 [A study of the new Taoism north of the Yellow River in the early Southern Song period]. Beijing: Zhonghua shuju.

———. 1988. *Daojia jinshi lüe* 道家金石略 [A collection of Taoist epigraphy]. Edited by Chen Zhichao 陈智超 and Zeng Qingying 曾庆瑛. Beijing: Wenwu chubanshe.

Chen Zhentao 陈振涛. 1991. "Laoshan daojiao yinyue kaocha ji" 崂山道教音乐考查记 [Notes on the Taoist music of Mount Lao]. *ZGDJ* 1991.4: 22–29.

Chen Zhibin 陳志濱. 1974. *Quanzhen xianpai yuanliu* 全真仙派源流 [Origins and development of the Lineage of the Immortals within Quanzhen]. Taipei: Taiwan xuesheng shuju.

Chen, Ellen Marie. 1969. "Nothingness and the Mother Principle in Early Chinese Taoism." *International Philosophical Quarterly* 9: 391–405.

———. 1973a. "Is there a Doctrine of Physical Immortality in the Tao Te Ching?" *HR* 12: 231–49.

———. 1973b. "The Meaning of *Te* in the *Tao Te Ching*: An Examination of the Concept of Nature in Chinese Taoism." *Philosophy East and West* 23: 457–70.

———. 1974. "The Origin and Development of Being (*Yu*) and Non-Being (*Wu*) in the *Tao Te Ching*." *International Philosophical Quarterly* 13: 403–17.

———. 1989. *The Tao Te Ching: A New Translation with Commentary*. New York: Paragon House.

Chen, William Y. 1978. *A Guide to Tao-tsang chi yao*. Stony Brook, N. Y.: Institute for Advanced Studies of World Religions.

———. 1984. *A Guide to the Tao tsang ching hua*. N.p.: Chinese Materials Center.

Chen Yaoting. 1988. "Des systèmes religieux." *CEA* 4: 189–98.

Cheng, Anne. 1989. "'Un Yin, un Yang, telle est la Voie': Les origines cosmologiques du parallélisme dans la pensée chinoise." *Extrême-Orient, Extrême-Occident* 11: 35–43.

Chenivesse, Sandrine. 1997a. "A Journey to the Depths of a Labyrinth-Landscape: The Mount Fengdu, Taoist Holy Site and Infernal Abyss." In MacDonald 1997, 41–74.

———. 1997b. "Le mont Fengdu: Lieu saint taoïste émergé de la géographie de l'au-delà." *Sanjiao wenxian: Matériaux pour l'étude de la religion chinoise* 1: 79–86.

———. 1998. "Fengdu: Cité de l'abondance, cité de la male mort." *CEA* 10: 287–339.

Cheu Hock Tong. 1988. *The Nine Emperor Gods: A Study of Chinese Spirit-Medium Cults*. Singapore: Times Books International.

Ching, Julia, and Robert W. L. Guisso, eds. 1991. *Sages and Filial Sons: Mythology and Archaeology in Ancient China*. Hong Kong: Chinese University Press.

Ch'iu K'un-liang. 1989. "Mu-lien 'Operas' in Taiwanese Funeral Rituals." In Johnson 1989, 105–25.

Ch'oe Chinsŏk 崔真哲. 1995. "Cheng Xuanying 'Dao' gainian fenxi" 成玄英「道」概念分析 [An analysis of Cheng Xuanying's notion of Dao]. *DWY* 7: 175–98.

Choi Chi-Cheung. 1995. "Reinforcing Ethnicity: The Jiao Festival in Cheung Chau." In Faure and Siu 1995, 104–22.

Chu Kun-liang. 1991. *Les aspects rituels du théâtre chinois*. Paris: Collège de France.

Clart, Philip. 1994–95. "The Birth of a New Scripture: Revelation and Merit Accumulation in a Taiwanese Spirit-Writing Cult." *British Columbia Asian Review* 8: 174–203.

————. 1997. "The Phoenix and the Mother: The Interaction of Spirit Writing Cults and Popular Sects in Taiwan." *JCR* 25: 1–32.

Cleary, Thomas. 1986a. *The Inner Teachings of Taoism*. Boston and London: Shambhala.

————. 1986b. *The Taoist I Ching*. Boston and London: Shambhala.

————. 1987. *Understanding Reality: A Taoist Alchemical Classic*. Honolulu: University of Hawaii Press.

————. 1988. *Awakening to the Tao*. Boston and Shaftesbury: Shambhala.

————. 1991a. *Energy, Vitality, Spirit: A Taoist Sourcebook*. Boston and London: Shambhala.

————. 1991b. *The Secret of the Golden Flower: The Classic Chinese Book of Life*. San Francisco: HarperCollins.

Cleaves, Francis Woodman. 1960. "The Sino-Mongolian inscription of 1240." *HJAS* 23: 62–75.

Coakley, Sarah, ed. 1997. *Religion and the Body*. Cambridge: Cambridge University Press.

Cohen, Alvin P. 1987. "Chinese Religion: Popular Religion." In Eliade 1987, 3: 289–96.

————. 1992. "Biographical Notes on a Taiwanese Red-Head Taoist." *JCR* 20: 187–201.

Corbin, Henry. 1977. *L'Imagination créatrice dans le Soufisme d'Ibn 'Arabî*. Paris: Flammarion.

Corless, Roger J. 1987. "T'an-luan: Taoist Sage and Buddhist Bodhisattva." In Chappell 1987, 36–45.

Corradini, Piero, ed. 1996. *Conoscenza e interpretazione della civiltà cinese*. Venezia: Libreria Editrice Cafoscarina.

Creel, Heerlee G. 1970. *What is Taoism? And Other Studies in Chinese Cultural History*. Chicago and London: University of Chicago Press.

————. 1974. *Shen Pu-hai: A Chinese Political Philosopher of the Fourth Century B.C.* Chicago and London: University of Chicago Press.

Crowe, Paul. 2000. "Chapters on Awakening to the Real: A Song Dynasty Classic of Inner Alchemy Attributed to Zhang Boduan (ca. 983–1081)." *British Columbia Asian Review* 12: 1–40.

Csikszentmihalyi, Mark. 1994. "Emulating the Yellow Emperor: The Theory and Practice of HuangLao, 180–141 B.C.E." Ph.D. Diss., Stanford University.

————. 1997. "Jia Yi's 'Techniques of the Dao' and the Han Confucian Appropriation of Technical Discourse." *AM*, third series, 10: 49–67.

————. 1998. "Fivefold Virtue: Reformulating Mencian Moral Psychology in Han Dynasty China." *Religion* 28: 77–89.

————. 2000. "Han Cosmology and Mantic Practices." In Kohn 2000b, 53–73.

————. 2002. "Traditional Taxonomies and Revealed Texts in the Han." In Kohn and Roth 2002, 81–101.

Csikszentmihalyi, Mark, and Philip J. Ivanhoe, eds. 1999. *Religious and Philosophical Aspects of the Laozi*. Albany: State University of New York Press.

Cui Xiuguo 崔秀国. 1982. *Wuyue shihua* 五岳史话 [Historical talks on the Five Peaks]. Beijing: Zhonghua shuju.

Cullen, Christopher. 1996. *Astronomy and Mathematics in Ancient China: The Zhou bi suan jing*. Cambridge: Cambridge University Press.

Dai Mingyang 戴明扬, ed. 1962. *Xi Kang ji jiaozhu* 嵇康集校注 [Annotated edition of Xi Kang's works]. Beijing: Renmin wenxue chubanshe.

Daojia wenhua yanjiu 道家文化研究 [Studies on Taoist culture] 13. [Special issue on Dunhuang studies.]

Darga, Martina. 1999. *Das alchemistische Buch von innerem Wesen und Lebensenergie: Xingming guizhi*. München: Eugen Diederichs Verlag.

Davis, Edward L. 2001. *Society and the Supernatural in Song China*. Honolulu: University of Hawaii Press.

Davis, Tenney L. 1934. "Ko Hung (Pao P'u Tzu), Chinese Alchemist of the Fourth Century." *Journal of Chemical Education* 11: 517–20.

Davis, Tenney L., and Ch'en Kuo-fu. 1941. "The Inner Chapters of Pao-p'u-tzu." *Proceedings of the American Academy of Arts and Sciences* 74: 297–325.

———. 1942. "Shang-yang Tzu, Taoist Writer and Commentator on Alchemy." *HJAS* 7: 126–29.

Davis, Tenney L., and Chao Yün-ts'ung. 1939. "Chang Po-tuan of T'ien-t'ai, his Wu Chên P'ien, Essay on the Understanding of the Truth: A Contribution to the Study of Chinese Alchemy." *Proceedings of the American Academy of Arts and Sciences* 73: 97–117.

———. 1940a. "A Fifteenth Century Chinese Encyclopedia of Alchemy." *Proceedings of the American Academy of Arts and Sciences* 73: 391–99.

———. 1940b. "Four Hundred Word Chin Tan of Chang Po-tuan." *Proceedings of the American Academy of Arts and Sciences* 73: 371–76.

Davis, Tenney L., and Rokuro Nakaseko. 1937. "The Tomb of Jofuku or Joshi, the Earliest Alchemist of Historical Record." *Ambix* 1: 109–15.

Day, Clarence B. 1928. "Shanghai Invites the God of Wealth." *The China Journal* 8: 289–94. Reprinted in Day 1975, 39–46.

———. 1975. *Popular Religion in Pre-Communist China*. San Francisco: Chinese Materials Center.

de Bary, Wm. Theodore, and Irene Bloom, eds. 1999. *Sources of Chinese Tradition*. Second edition. 2 vols. New York: Columbia University Press.

de Bary, Wm. Theodore, and the Conference on Ming Thought. 1970. *Self and Society in Ming Thought*. New York and London: Columbia University Press.

de Bruyn, Pierre-Henri. 1999. "Vie, mort et immortalité dans la tradition taoïste." In Servais 1999, 21–50.

———. 2004. "Wudang Shan: The Origins of a Major Center of Modern Taoism." In Lagerwey 2004b, 2: 553–90.

de Groot, J. J. M. 1886. *Les fêtes annuellement célébrées à Émoui (Amoy); Étude concernant la religion populaire des Chinois*. Translated by C. G. Chavannes. 2 vols. Paris: Ernest Leroux. Reprint, with a new introduction by Inez de Beauclair and Harvey Molé, San Francisco: Chinese Materials Center, 1977.

———. 1892–1910. *The Religious System of China*. 6 vols. Leiden: E. J. Brill. Reprint, Taipei: Ch'eng Wen Publishing Company, 1972.

de Mallmann, Marie-Thérèse. 1975. *Introduction à l'iconographie du Tantrisme bouddhique*. Paris: Adrien Maisonneuve.

de Meyer, Jan A. M. 1999. "Mountain Hopping: The Life of Wu Yun." *T'ang Studies* 17: 171–211.

———. 2000. "Linked Verse and Linked Faiths: An Inquiry into the Social Circle of an Eminent Tang Dynasty Taoist Master." In de Meyer and Engelfriet 2000, 148–83.

de Meyer, Jan A. M., and Peter M. Engelfriet, eds. 2000. *Linked Faiths: Essays on Chinese Religions and Traditional Culture in Honour of Kristofer Schipper*. Leiden: E. J. Brill.

de Rachewiltz, Igor. 1962a. "The *Hsi-yu lu* by Yeh-lü Ch'u-ts'ai." *MS* 21: 1–121.

———. 1962b. "Yeh-lü Ch'u-ts'ai (1189–1243): Buddhist Idealist and Confucian States-man." In Wright and Twitchett 1962, 189–216.

de Rachewiltz, Igor, and Terry Russell. 1984. "Ch'iu Ch'u-chi (1148–1227)." *Papers on Far Eastern History* 29: 1–26. Reprinted in de Rachewiltz et al. 1993, 208–23.

de Rachewiltz, Igor, et al., eds. 1993. *In the Service of the Khan: Eminent Personalities of the Early Mongol-Yüan Period (1200–1300)*. Wiesbaden: Harrassowitz.

de Santillana, Giorgio, and Hertha von Dechend. 1969. *Hamlet's Mill: An Essay on Myth and the Frame of Time*. Boston: Gambit.

de Vos, George A., and Takao Sofue, eds. 1986. *Religion and the Family in East Asia*. Berkeley: University of California Press.

Dean, Kenneth. 1986. "Field Notes on Two Taoist *Jiao* Observed in Zhangzhou in December 1985." *CEA* 2: 191–209.

———. 1989a. "Lei Yu-sheng ("Thunder is Noisy") and Mu-lien in the Theatrical and Funerary Traditions of Fukien." In Johnson 1989, 46–104.

———. 1989b. "Revival of Religious Practices in Fujian: A Case Study." In Pas 1989b, 51–78.

———. 1993. *Taoist Ritual and Popular Cults of Southeast China*. Princeton: Princeton University Press.

———. 1996. "Daoist Ritual in Contemporary Southeast China." In Lopez 1996, 306–26.

———. 1998. *Lord of the Three in One: The Spread of a Cult in Southeast China*. Princeton: Princeton University Press.

———. 2000. "Daoist Ritual Today." In Kohn 2000b, 659–82.

Decaux, Jacques. 1989. *Les Quatre Livres de l'Empereur Jaune: Le Canon Taoïque retrouvé*. Taipei: European Languages Publications.

———. 1990. "True Classic of the Original Word of Laozi by Master Guanyin." Parts 1 and 2. *Chinese Culture* 31.1: 1–43; 31.2: 1–46.

Defoort, Carine. 1997. *The Pheasant Cap Master (He guan zi): A Rhetorical Reading*. Albany: State University of New York Press.

Delahaye, Hubert. 1981. *Les premières peintures de paysage en Chine: Aspects religieux*. Paris: École Française d'Extrême-Orient.

Demiéville, Paul. 1948. "Le miroir spirituel." *Sinologica* 1: 112–37. Reprinted in Demiéville 1973, 131–56.

———. 1973. *Choix d'études bouddhiques*. Leiden: E. J. Brill.

Deng Qiubo 鄧球柏. 1996. *Boshu Zhouyi jiaoshi* 帛書「周易」校釋 [Annotated critical edition of the silk manuscript of the *Book of Changes*]. Enlarged edition. Changsha: Hunan chubanshe.

Denny, Frederick M., and Rodney L. Taylor, eds. 1985. *The Holy Book in Comparative Perspective*. Columbia, SC: University of South Carolina Press.

des Rotours, Robert. 1952. "Les insignes en deux parties (*fou*) sous la dynastie des T'ang." *TP* 41: 1–148.

Despeux, Catherine. 1979. *Zhao Bichen: Traité d'Alchimie et de Physiologie taoïste (Weisheng shenglixue mingzhi)*. Paris: Les Deux Océans.

———. 1981a. *Le chemin de l'éveil illustré par le dressage du buffle dans le bouddhisme Chan, le dressage du cheval dans le taoïsme, le dressage de l'éléphant dans le bouddhisme tibétain.* Paris: L'Asiathèque.

———. 1981b. *Taiji quan: Art martial, technique de longue vie*. Paris: Guy Trédaniel. Revised edition of *T'ai-ki k'iuan, technique de longue vie, technique de combat* (Paris: Guy Trédaniel, 1975).

———. 1985. "Les lectures alchimiques du *Hsi-yu-chi*." In Naundorf, Pohl, and Schmidt 1985, 61–75.

———. 1986. "L'ordination des femmes taoïstes sous les Tang." *Études chinoises* 5: 53–100.

———. 1987. *Prescriptions d'acuponcture valant mille onces d'or: Traité d'acuponcture de Sun Simiao du VIIe siècle*. Paris: Guy Trédaniel.

———. 1988. *La Moelle du phénix rouge: Santé et longue vie dans la Chine du XVIe siècle*. Paris: Guy Trédaniel, Éditions de la Maisnie.

———. 1989. "Gymnastics: The Ancient Tradition." In Kohn 1989c, 225–61.

———. 1990. *Immortelles de la Chine ancienne: Taoïsme et alchimie féminine*. Puiseaux: Pardès.

———. 1994. *Taoïsme et corps humain: Le Xiuzhen tu*. Paris: Guy Trédaniel.

———. 1995. "L'expiration des six souffles d'après les sources du Canon taoïque: Un procédé classique du *qigong*." In Diény 1995, 129–63.

———. 1996. "Le corps, champ spatio-temporel, souche d'identité." *L'Homme* 137: 87–118.

———. 1997. "Le *qigong*, une expression de la modernité en Chine." In Gernet and Kalinowski 1997, 267–81.

———. 2000a. "Talismans and Sacred Diagrams." In Kohn 2000b, 498–540.

———. 2000b. "Women in Daoism." In Kohn 2000b, 384–412.

———. 2001. "The System of the Five Circulatory Phases and the Six Seasonal Influences (*Wuyun liuqi*), a Source of Innovation in Medicine under the Song (960–1279)." Translated by Janet Lloyd. In Hsu Elisabeth 2001, 121–65.

Despeux, Catherine, and Livia Kohn. 2003. *Women in Daoism*. Cambridge, Mass.: Three Pines Press.

Despeux, Catherine, and Frederic Obringer, eds. 1997. *La maladie dans la Chine médiévale: La toux*. Paris: L'Harmattan.

DeWoskin, Kenneth J. 1981. "A Source Guide to the Lives and Techniques of Han and Six Dynasties *Fang-shih*." *Society for the Study of Chinese Religions Bulletin* 9: 79–105.

———. 1983. *Doctors, Diviners, and Magicians of Ancient China*. New York: Columbia University Press.

———. 1986. "Fang-shih." In Nienhauser 1986, 378–80.

———. 1990. "*Xian* Descended: Narrating *Xian* Among Mortals." *TR* 2.2: 70–86.

DeWoskin, Kenneth J., and J. I. Crump, Jr. 1996. *In Search of the Supernatural: The Written Record*. Stanford: Stanford University Press.

Didier, John. 1998. "Messrs. T'an, Chancellor Sung, and the *Book of Transformation* (*Hua shu*): Texts and the Transformations of Traditions." *AM*, third series, 11: 99–151.

Diény, Jean-Pierre, ed. 1995. *Hommage à Kwong Hing Foon: Études d'histoire culturelle de la Chine*. Paris: Collège de France, Institut des Hautes Études Chinoises.

Diesinger, Gunther. 1984. *Vom General zum Gott: Kuan Yü (gest. 220 n. Chr.) und seine "posthume Karriere."* Frankfurt: Haag und Herchen.

Ding Changyun 丁常雲 (丁常云). 1997. "Daojiao de siling chongbai ji qi shehui sixiang neirong" 道教的四靈崇拜及其社會思想內容 [Taoist worship of the Four Luminaries and its social aspects]. *DT* 10: 113–31.

———. 1999. "Daojiao zhaijiao jinji" 臺谅斋醮禁忌 [Interdictions in Taoist *zhai* and *jiao* rituals]. *Shanghai daojiao* 上海道教 1999.3: 23–27.

———. 2002. "Ji lingxiu yu xuezhe yu yishen de tianshi Zhang Yuchu" 集领袖与学者于一身的天师张宇初 [Celestial Master Zhang Yuchu, a Taoist leader and scholar]. *SZY* 2002.1: 17–29.

Ding Huang 丁煌. 1979–80. "Tangdai daojiao Taiqing gong zhidu kao" 唐代道教太清宮制度考 [A study of the institution of the Taoist Palace of Great Clarity in the Tang period]. Parts 1 and 2. *Chengong daxue Lishixue xi lishi xuebao* 成功大學歷史學系歷史學報 6 (1979): 275–314; 7 (1980): 177–220.

Ding Peiren 丁培仁. 1984. "Taiyi xinyang yu Zhang Jue de Zhonghuang Taiyi dao" 太一信仰与张角的中黄太一道 [The cult of the Great One, and the Way of the Central Yellow Great One of Zhang Jue]. *ZY* 1984.5: 48–58.

Ding Zhenyan 丁禎彥 and Li Sizhen 李似珍, eds. 1996. *Huashu* 化書 [Book of Transformation]. Beijing: Zhonghua shuju.

Dōkyō bunka kenkyūkai 道教文化研究会 [Research Group on Taoist Culture], ed. 1994. *Dōkyō bunka e no tenbō* 道教文化への展望 [Perspectives on Taoist Culture]. Tokyo: Hirakawa shuppansha.

Doolittle, Justus. 1865–67. *Social Life of the Chinese*. 2 Vols. New York: Harper. Reprint, Singapore: Graham Brash, 1986.

Doub, William Coligny. 1979. "Mountains in Early Taoism." In Tobias and Drasdo 1979, 129–35.

Drexler, Monica. 1994. *Daoistische Schriftmagie: Interpretationen zu den Schriftamuletten Fu im Daozang*. Stuttgart: Franz Steiner Verlag.

Du Jiexiang 杜潔祥, ed. 1983. *Daojiao wenxian* 道教文獻 [Literary sources on Taoism]. 20 vols. Taipei: Danqing tushu youxian gongsi.

Duara, Prasenjit. 1988. "Superscribing Symbols: The Myth of Guandi, Chinese God of War." *Journal of Asian Studies* 47: 778–95.

Dubs, Homer H. 1941. "The Date and Circumstances of the Philosopher Lao-dz." *JAOS* 61: 215–21.

———. 1942. "An Ancient Chinese Mystery Cult." *Harvard Theological Review* 35: 221–40.

Dufresne, T., and J. Nguyen. 1994. *Taiji quan: Art martial de la famille Chen*. Paris: Budostore.

Dull, Jack. 1966. "A Historical Introduction to the Apocryphal (*Ch'an-wei*) Texts of the Han Dynasty." Ph.D. diss., University of Washington, Seattle.

Durrant, Stephen. 1986. "Shen-hsien chuan." In Nienhauser 1986, 677–78.

Duyvendak, J. J. L. 1947. "The Philosophy of Wu Wei." *ASEA*, 1: 81–102.

Eberhard, Wolfram. 1942. *Lokalkulturen im alten China*. Vol. 1: *Die Lokalkulturen des Nordens und Westens*. Leiden: E. J. Brill.

———. 1949. *Das Toba-Reich Nordchinas: Eine soziologische Untersuchung*. Leiden: E. J. Brill.

———. 1967. *Guilt and Sin in Traditional China*. Berkeley and Los Angeles: University of California Press.

———. 1968. *The Local Cultures of South and East China*. Translated by Alide Eberhard. Leiden: E. J. Brill. Revised translation of *Lokalkulturen im alten China*, vol. 2: *Die Lokalkulturen des Südens und Ostens* (Leiden: E. J. Brill, 1942).

Ebrey, Patricia Buckley, and Peter N. Gregory, eds. 1993. *Religion and Society in T'ang and Sung China*. Honolulu: University of Hawaii Press.

Eichhorn, Werner. 1954a. "Description of the Rebellion of Sun Ên (孫恩) and Earlier Taoist Rebellions." *Mitteilungen des Instituts für Orientforschung* 2: 325–52.

———. 1954b. "Nachträgliche Bemerkungen zum Aufstande des Sun Ên." *Mitteilungen des Instituts für Orientforschung* 2: 463–76.

———. 1957. "T'ai-p'ing and T'ai-p'ing Religion." *Mitteilungen des Instituts für Orientforschung* 5: 113–40.

———. 1964. "Die Wiedereinrichtung der Staatsreligion im Anfang der Sung-Zeit." *MS* 23: 205–63.

———. 1985. "Das *Tung-ming chi* des Kuo Hsien." In Naundorf, Pohl, and Schmidt 1985, 291–300.

Eliade, Mircea. 1978. *The Forge and the Crucible*. Second edition. Chicago and London: University of Chicago Press. Originally published as *Forgerons et alchimistes* (second edition, Paris: Flammarion, 1977).

———, ed. 1987. *The Encyclopedia of Religion*. New York: Macmillan.

Elliott, Alan J. A. 1955. *Chinese Spirit-Medium Cults in Singapore*. London: Department of Anthropology, London School of Economics and Political Science.

Emerson, John. 1992. "The Highest Virtue Is Like the Valley." *TR* 3.2: 47–61.

Emmerich, Reinhard. 1995. "Bemerkungen zu Huang und Lao in der frühen Han-Zeit: Erkenntnisse aus *Shiji* and *Hanshu*." *MS* 43: 53–140.

Endres, Günther. 1985. *Die sieben Meister der vollkommenen Verwirklichung: Der taoistische Lehrroman Ch'i-chen chuan in Übersetzung und im Spiegel seiner Quellen*. Frankfurt: Peter Lang.

Engelhardt, Ute. 1981. *Theorie und Technik des Taiji quan*. Schondorf: WBV Biologisch-medizinische Verlags.

———. 1987. *Die klassische Tradition der Qi-Übungen (Qigong): Eine Darstellung anhand des Tang-zeitlichen Textes Fuqi jingyi lun von Sima Chengzhen*. Wiesbaden: Franz Steiner Verlag.

———. 1989. "Qi for Life: Longevity in the Tang." In Kohn 1989c, 263–96.

———. 2000. "Longevity Techniques and Chinese Medicine." In Kohn 2000b, 74–108.

———. 2001. "Dietetics in Tang China and the First Extant Works of *Materia Medica*." In Hsu Elisabeth 2001, 173–91.

Eno, Robert. 1990. *The Confucian Creation of Heaven: Philosophy and the Defense of Ritual Mastery*. Albany: State University of New York Press.

Erkes, Eduard. 1916–17. "Das Weltbild des Huai-nan-tze." *Ostasiatische Zeitschrift* 5: 27–80.

———. 1950. *Ho-shang-kung's Commentary on Lao-tse*. Ascona: Artibus Asiae.

Eskildsen, Stephen E. 1990. "Asceticism in Ch'üan-chen Taoism." *British Columbia Asian Review* 3–4: 153–91.

———. 1998. *Asceticism in Early Chinese Religion*. Albany: State University of New York Press.

———. 2001. "Seeking Signs of Proof: Visions and Other Trance Phenomena in Early Quanzhen Taoism." *JCR* 29: 139–60.

Espesset, Grégoire. 2002. "Cosmologie et trifonctionnalité dans l'idéologie du *Livre de la Grande paix* (*Taiping jing*)." Ph.D. diss., Université de Paris VII.

Esposito, Monica. 1992. "Il *Daozang xubian*, raccolta di testi alchemici della scuola Longmen." *Annali dell'Istituto Universitario Orientale* 4: 429–49.

———. 1993. "La Porte du Dragon: L'école Longmen du Mont Jin'gai et ses pratiques alchimiques d'après le *Daozang xubian* (Suite au canon taoïste)." Ph.D. diss., Université de Paris VII.

———. 1995. *Il qigong: La nuova scuola taoista delle cinque respirazioni*. Padova: Meb.

———. 1996. "Il Segreto del Fiore d'Oro e la tradizione Longmen del Monte Jin'gai." In Corradini 1996, 151–69.

———. 1997. *L'alchimia del soffio: La pratica della visione interiore nell'alchimia taoista*. Roma: Ubaldini Editore.

———. 1998a. "Alchimie féminine." In Servier 1998, 51–52.

———. 1998b. "Souffle et respiration embryonnaire." In Servier 1998, 1216–18.

———. 1998c. "The Different Versions of the *Secret of the Golden Flower* and their Relationship to the Longmen School." *Transactions of the International Conference of Eastern Studies* 43: 90–109.

———. 2000. "Daoism in the Qing (1644–1911)." In Kohn 2000b, 623–58.

———. 2001. "Longmen Taoism in Qing China: Doctrinal Ideal and Local Reality." *JCR* 29: 191–231.

——— [エスポジト・モニカ]. 2004a. "Gyakuten shita zō: Jotan no shintai kan" 逆轉した像—女丹の身體観 [The Inverted Mirror: The Vision of Body in Feminine Inner Alchemy]. Translated by Umegawa Sumiyo 梅川純代. In Sakade Yoshinobu sensei taikyū kinen ronshū kankōkai 2004, 113–29.

———. 2004b. "Sun-Worship in China: The Roots of Shangqing Taoist Practices of Light." *CEA* 14: 345–84.

———. 2004c. "The Longmen School and its Controversial History during the Qing Dynasty." In Lagerwey 2004b, 2: 621–98.

Esposito, Monica, and Isabelle Robinet. 1998. "Alchimie intérieure." In Servier 1998, 55–58.

Fan Chunwu 范純武 and Wang Jianchuan 王見川. 1996. "Qingmo Minchu Beijing luantang de ge'an yanjiu: Qingyun tan ji qi lishi" 清末民初北京鸞堂的個案研究—青雲壇及其歷史 [A case study of the spirit-writing halls in late Qing and early Republican Peking: The Qingyun Altar and its history]. *Minjian zongjiao* 民間宗教 2: 261–80.

Fang Shiming. 1995. "The Forerunner of the Yellow Turban Uprising and its Relationship with Shamanism and Primitive Daoism." *Social Sciences in China*, Spring 1995, 142–52.

Farquhar, Judith. 1994. *Knowing Practice. The Clinical Encounter of Chinese Medicine*. Boulder, CO: Westview Press.

Faure, David, and Helen F. Siu, eds. 1995. *Down to Earth: The Territorial Bond in South China*. Stanford: Stanford University Press.

Feher, Michel, ed. 1989. *Fragments for a History of the Human Body*. New York: Zone.

Feifel, Eugene. 1941–46. "Pao-p'u tzu nei-p'ien." Parts 1–3. *MS* 6 (1941): 113–211; 9 (1944): 1–33; 11 (1946): 1–32.

Fêng, H. Y. 1936. "The Origin of Yü Huang." *HJAS* 1: 242–50.

Feuchtwang, Stephan. 1977. "School-Temple and City God." In Skinner 1977, 581–608.

———. 1992. *The Imperial Metaphor: Popular Religion in China*. London and New York: Routledge.

Fisher, Carney T. 1990. *The Chosen One: Succession and Adoption in the Court of Ming Shizong*. Sydney: George Allen and Unwin.

Fong, Mary H. 1989. "Wu Daozi's Legacy in the Popular Door Gods (Menshen) Qin Shubao and Yuchi Gong." *Archives of Asian Art* 42: 6–24.

Forest, Alain, Yoshiaki Ishizawa, and Léon Vandermeersch, eds. 1991. *Cultes populaires et sociétés asiatiques: Appareils cultuels et appareils de pouvoir*. Paris: L'Harmattan.

Forke, Alfred. 1907–11. Lun-heng. Part 1: *Philosophical Essays of Wang Ch'ung*. Part 2: *Miscellaneous Essays of Wang Ch'ung*. 2 vols. London, Leipzig, and Shanghai: Harrassowitz, 1907; Berlin: Georg Remier, 1911.

Forte, Antonino. 1976. *Political Propaganda and Ideology in China at the End of the Seventh Century*. Napoli: Istituto Universitario Orientale.

Foster, Lawrence C. 1974. "The *Shih-i-chi* and its Relationship to the Genre Known as *chih-kuai hsiao-shuo*." Ph.D. diss., University of Washington.

Fracasso, Riccardo. 1988. "Holy Mothers of Ancient China: A New Approach to the Hsi-wang-mu Problem." *TP* 74: 1–46.

Franke, Herbert, ed. 1976. *Sung Biographies*. 3 vols. Wiesbaden: Franz Steiner Verlag.

———. 1990. "The Taoist Elements in the Buddhist *Great Bear Sūtra* (Pei-tou ching)." *AM*, third series, 3: 75–111.

Franke, Wolfgang. 1973. "Some Remarks on Lin Chao-en (1517–1598)." *Oriens Extremus* 20: 161–74.

Fraser, J. T., N. Lawrence, and F. C. Haber, eds. 1986. *Time, Science, and Society in China and the West*. The Study of Time, 5. Amherst: University of Massachusetts Press.

Frédéric, Louis. 1992. *Les dieux du Bouddhisme: Guide iconographique*. Paris: Flammarion.

Fu Juyou 傅舉有 and Chen Songchang 陳松長. 1992. *Mawangdui Hanmu wenwu* 馬王堆漢墓文物 [Cultural relics from the Han tombs at Mawangdui]. Changsha: Hunan chubanshe.

Fu Lo-shu. 1965. "Teng Mu: A Forgotten Chinese Philosopher." *TP* 52: 35–96.

Fujiwara Takao 藤原高男. 1961a. "*Rōshi* kai jūgenha kō" 「老子」解重玄派考 [A study of the explication of the *Laozi* by the Chongxuan school]. *Kangi bunka* 漢魏文化 2: 32–49.

————. 1961b. "Son Tō *Rōshi chū kō*" 孫登「老子注」考 [A study of Sun Deng's commentary to the *Laozi*]. *Kanbun gakkai kaihō* 漢文學會會報 20: 1–40.

————. 1979. "Dōshi Ri Ei no *Dōtoku kyō* chū ni tsuite" 道士李榮の「道德經」注について [On the commentary to the *Daode jing* by the Taoist master Li Rong]. *KDKK* 47: 1–30.

————. 1980a. "*Genshi muryō dojin jōhin myōkyō* Sei Gen'ei chū"「元始無量度人上品妙經」成玄英注 [Cheng Xuanying's commentary to the *Yuanshi wuliang duren shangpin miaojing*]. *KDKK* 49: 37–60.

————. 1980b. "Sei Gen'ei hon *Dōtoku kyō* ni tsuite" 成玄英本「道德經」について [On Cheng Xuanying's edition of the *Daode jing*]. *KDKK* 50: 137–72.

————. 1983. "*Saishō kyō* Ri Ei chū"「西昇經」李榮注 [Li Rong's commentary to the *Xisheng jing*]. *Kagawa daigaku ippan kyōiku kenkyū* 香川大學一般教育研究 23: 117–50.

————. 1985. "Dōshi Ri Ei no *Saishōkyō* chū ni tsuite" 道士李榮の「西昇經」注について [On the commentary to the *Xisheng jing* by the Taoist master Li Rong]. *Kagawa daigaku kokubun kenkyū* 香川大學國文研究 10: 6–16.

————. 1986–88. "Ri Ei *Dōtoku kyō* chū" 李榮「道德經」注 [Li Rong's commentary to the *Daode jing*]. Parts 1–3. *Tokushima bunri daigaku bungaku ronsō* 德島文理大學文學論叢 3 (1986): 97–132; 4 (1987): 139–77; 5 (1988): 103–39.

Fukui Fumimasa 福井文雅. 1973. "Tokō no kigen to shokunō: Chūgoku, Indo kōshō no issetten" 都講の起源と職能—中國・インド交渉の一接点 [The origin and function of the *dujiang* (chief cantor): A point of contact in the relations between India and China]. In Kushida Ryōkō hakushi shōju kinenkai 1973, 795–822.

————. 1983. "Dōkyō to bukkyō" 道教と佛教 [Taoism and Buddhism]. In Fukui Kōjun et al. 1983, 2: 95–134.

————. 1987. *Hannya shingyō no rekishiteki kenkyū*「般若心經」の歴史的研究 [Historical studies on the *Heart Sūtra*]. Tokyo: Shunjūsha.

————. 1995. "The History of Taoist Studies in Japan and Some Related Issues." *Acta Asiatica* 68: 1–18.

Fukui Hakase shōju kinen ronbunshū kankōkai 福井博士頌壽記念論文集刊行会 [Editorial Committee for the Collected Essays Presented to Dr. Fukui Kōjun on his Seventieth Birthday], ed. 1969. *Fukui Hakase shōju kinen Tōyō bunka ronshū* 福井博士頌壽記念東洋文化論集 [Collected studies on Eastern culture presented to Dr. Fukui Kōjun on his seventieth birthday]. Tokyo: Waseda daigaku shuppanbu.

Fukui Kōjun 福井康順. 1951. "*Shinsenden kō*"「神仙傳」考 [A study of the *Shenxian zhuan*]. *TS* 1: 1–20.

————. 1958. *Dōkyō no kisoteki kenkyū* 道教の基礎的研究 [Introductory studies on Taoism]. Tokyo: Shoseki bunbutsu ryūtsūkai.

————. 1974. "A Study of *Chou-i Ts'an-t'ung-ch'i*." *Acta Asiatica* 27: 19–32.

————. 1983. *Shinsenden* 神仙傳 [*Shenxian zhuan*]. Tokyo: Meitoku shuppansha.

Fukui Kōjun 福井康順 et al., eds. 1983. *Dōkyō* 道教 [Taoism]. 3 vols. Tokyo: Hirakawa shuppansha.

Fukunaga Mitsuji 福永光司. 1954. "Kaku Zō no *Sōshi* kaishaku" 郭象の「莊子」解釈 [Guo Xiang's interpretation of the *Zhuangzi*]. *Tetsugaku kenkyū* 哲學研究 37: 46–62, 167–77.

———. 1965. "Mui o toku hitobito" 無為を説く人々 [The masters of Non-action]. *Shisō no rekishi* 思想の歴史 2: 209–57.

———. 1969. "'No-Mind' in Chuang-tzu and in Ch'an Buddhism." *Zinbun* 12: 9–45.

———. 1982. *Dōkyō to Nihon bunka* 道教と日本文化 [Taoism and Japanese culture]. Kyoto: Jinbun shoin.

———. 1986. *Dōkyō to kodai Nihon* 道教と古代日本 [Taoism and ancient Japan]. Kyoto: Jinbun shoin.

———. 1987. *Dōkyō shisōshi kenkyū* 道教思想史研究 [Studies on the history of Taoist thought]. Tokyo: Iwanami shoten.

———, ed. 1989. *Dōkyō to higashi Ajia: Chūgoku, Chōsen, Nihon* 道教と東アジア—中國・朝鮮・日本 [Taoism and East Asia: China, Korea, Japan]. Kyoto: Jinbun shoin.

Fung Chia-Loh and H. Bruce Collier. 1937. "A Sung Dynasty Alchemical Treatise: 'Outline of Alchemical Prescriptions' by Tu-ku T'ao." *Journal of the West China Border Research Society* 9: 199–209.

Fung Yu-lan. 1933. *Chuang Tzu: A New Selected Translation with an Exposition of the Philosophy of Kuo Hsiang*. Shanghai: Commercial Press. Reprint, New York: Paragon, 1964.

———. 1952–53. *A History of Chinese Philosophy*. Translated by Derk Bodde. 2 vols. Princeton: Princeton University Press. Originally published as *Zhongguo zhexue shi* 中國哲學史 (Shanghai: Shenzhou chubanshe, 1931, 1934).

Furth, Charlotte. 1995. "From Birth to Birth: The Growing Body in Chinese Medicine." In Kinney 1995, 157–91.

———. 1999. *A Flourishing Yin: Gender in China's Medical History, 960–1665*. Berkeley, Los Angeles, and London: University of California Press.

Furuie Shinpei 古家信平. 1999. *Taiwan kanjin shakai ni okeru minkan shinkō no kenkyū* 臺湾漢人社会における民間信仰の研究 [A study of Chinese popular cults in Taiwanese society]. Tokyo: Tōkyōdō shuppan.

Gan Shaocheng 甘紹成. 1996. "Zhengyi dao yinyue yu Quanzhen dao yinyue de bijiao yanjiu" 正一道音樂與全真道音樂的比較研究 [A comparative study of the music of the Zhengyi school and the music of the Quanzhen school]. *DWY* 9: 402–23.

Gao Ming 高明. 1996. *Boshu Laozi jiaozhu* 帛書「老子」校注 [Annotated edition of the silk manuscripts of the *Laozi*]. Beijing: Zhonghua shuju.

Gao Xiaojian 高小健, ed. 2000. *Zhongguo daoguan zhi congkan* 中國道觀志叢刊 [Collectanea of monographs of Taoist temples in China]. Suzhou: Jiangsu guji chubanshe.

Ge Zhaoguang 葛兆光. 1999. "Huangshu, heqi yu qi ta: Daojiao guodu yi de sixiangshi yanjiu" 黄书合气与其它—道教过度仪的思想史研究 ["Yellow Writs" and "Union of Breaths": A study of the intellectual history of the Taoist Liturgy of Passage]. *Gujin lunheng* 古今论衡 2: 62–76.

Geil, William E. 1926. *The Sacred 5 of China*. Boston: Houghton Mifflin.

Gernet, Jacques. 1981. "Techniques de recueillement, religion et philosophie: À propos du *jingzuo* néo-confucéen." *BEFEO* 69: 289–305.

Gernet, Jacques, and Marc Kalinowski, eds. 1997. *En suivant la Voie Royale: Mélanges en hommage à Léon Vandermeersch*. Paris: École Française d'Extrême-Orient.

Gernet, Jacques, et al., eds. 1970-. *Catalogue des manuscrits chinois de Touen-houang, Fonds Pelliot chinois de la Bibliothèque Nationale*. Vols. 1, 3, 4, and 5 published to date. Paris: École Française d'Extrême-Orient.

Giles, Herbert A. 1906. "Lao-tzu and the Tao-te-ching." In Giles H. A. 1914, 8–78. Originally published as an independent essay in 1906.

———. 1914. *Adversaria Sinica*. Shanghai: Kelly and Walsh.

Giles, Lionel. 1948. *A Gallery of Chinese Immortals: Selected Biographies Translated from Chinese Sources*. London: John Murray.

———. 1957. *Descriptive Catalogue of the Chinese Manuscripts from Tunhuang in the British Museum*. London: Trustees of the British Museum.

Girardot, Norman J. 1976. "The Problem of Creation Mythology in the Study of Chinese Religion." *HR* 15: 289–318.

———. 1977. "Myth and Meaning in the *Tao te ching*: Chapters 25 and 42." *HR* 16: 294–328.

———. 1978a. "Chaotic 'Order' (*Hun-tun*) and Benevolent 'Disorder' (*Luan*) in the *Chuang Tzu*." *Philosophy East and West* 28: 299–321.

———. 1978b. "'Returning to the Beginning' and the Arts of Mr. Hun-tun in the *Chuang-tzu*." *JCP* 5: 21–69.

———. 1983. *Myth and Meaning in Early Taoism: The Theme of Chaos (Hun-tun)*. Berkeley: University of California Press.

———. 1987a. "Chinese Religion: Mythic Themes." In Eliade 1987, 3: 296–305.

———. 1987b. "Hsien." In Eliade 1987, 6: 475–77.

Girardot, Norman J., James Miller, and Liu Xiaogan, eds. 2001. *Daoism and Ecology: Ways within a Cosmic Landscape*. Cambridge, MA: Harvard University Press.

Glidewell, Christopher. 1989. "Ancient and Medieval Chinese Protochemistry: The Earliest Examples of Applied Inorganic Chemistry." *Journal of Chemical Education* 66: 631–33.

Gong Qun 龔群. 1995. "Xiao Tianshi xiansheng jianlüe" 蕭天石先生簡略 [A brief presentation of Xiao Tianshi]. *Daojiao wenhua* 道教文化 5.1: 2–44.

Goodman, Howard L. 1985. "Exegetes and Exegeses of the *Book of Changes* in the Third Century AD: Historical and Scholastic Contexts for Wang Pi." Ph.D. diss., Princeton University.

———. 1994. "Celestial-Master Taoism and the Founding of the Ts'ao-Wei Dynasty: The Li Fu Document." *AM*, third series, 7: 5–33.

Goodrich, Anne S. 1964. *The Peking Temple of the Eastern Peak: The Tung-yüeh Miao of Peking and its Lore*. Nagoya: Monumenta Serica.

———. 1991. *Peking Paper Gods: A Look at Home Worship*. Nettetal: Steyler Verlag.

Goodrich, L. Carrington, and Chaoying Fang, eds. 1976. *Dictionary of Ming Biography, 1368–1644*. 2 vols. New York and London: Columbia University Press.

Goossaert, Vincent. 1997. "La création du taoïsme moderne: L'ordre Quanzhen." Ph.D. diss., École Pratique des Hautes Études, Section des Sciences Religieuses, Paris.

———. 1998. "Portrait épigraphique d'un culte: Les inscriptions des dynasties Jin et Yuan de temples du Pic de l'Est." *Sanjiao wenxian: Matériaux pour l'étude de la religion chinoise* 2: 41–83.

———. 1999. "Entre quatre murs: Un ermite taoïste du XXe siècle et la question de la modernité." *TP* 85: 391–421.

———. 2000a. "Counting the Monks: The 1736–1739 Census of the Chinese Clergy." *Late Imperial China* 21.2: 40–85.

———. 2000b. *Dans les temples de la Chine: Histoire des cultes, vie des communautés.* Paris: Albin Michel.

———. 2001. "The Invention of an Order: Collective Identity in Thirteenth-Century Quanzhen Taoism." *JCR* 29: 111–38.

———. 2004. "The Quanzhen Clergy, 1700–1950." In Lagerwey 2004b, 699–771.

———. 2005. "Liu Yuan, taoïste et sculpteur dans le Pékin mongol." *Sanjiao wenxuan: Matériaux pour l'étude de la religion chinoise* 4: 164–81.

Graham, A. C. 1959. "Being in Western Philosophy Compared with *shih/fei* and *yu/wu* in Chinese Philosophy." *AM* 7: 79–112. Reprinted in Graham 1986a, 322–59.

———. 1960. *The Book of Lieh-tzu.* London: John Murray.

———. 1961. "The Date and Composition of *Liehtzyy*." *AM*, second series, 8: 139–98. Reprinted in Graham 1986a, 216–82.

———. 1965. "'Being' in Linguistics and Philosophy: A Preliminary Inquiry." *Foundations of Language* 1: 223–31.

———. 1969–70. "Chuang-tzu's Essay on Seeing Things as Equal." *HR* 9: 137–59. Reprinted in Roth 2003, 104–29.

———. 1978. "Death and the Tao." *Montemora* 4: 216–21. [Selections from the *Zhuangzi.*]

———. 1980. "How much of *Chuang-tzu* did Chuang-tzu Write?" *Journal of the American Academy of Religion* 47: 459–501. Reprinted in Graham 1986a, 283–321, and in Roth 2003, 58–103.

———. 1981. *Chuang-tzu: The Seven Inner Chapters and Other Writings.* London: George Allen and Unwin. [See also the related monograph, *Chuang-tzu: Textual Notes to a Partial Translation*, London: School of Oriental and African Studies, University of London, 1982.]

———. 1986a. *Studies in Chinese Philosophy and Philosophical Literature.* Singapore: Institute of East Asian Philosophies, National University of Singapore. Reprint, Albany: State University of New York Press, 1990.

———. 1986b. "The Origins of the Legend of Lao Tan 老聃." In Graham 1986a, 111–24.

———. 1986c. *Yin-Yang and the Nature of Correlative Thinking.* Singapore: Institute of East Asian Philosophies, National University of Singapore.

———. 1989. *Disputers of the Tao: Philosophical Argument in Ancient China.* La Salle, IL: Open Court.

Granet, Marcel. 1934. *La pensée chinoise.* Paris: La Renaissance du Livre.

Granoff, Phyllis, and Koichi Shinohara, eds. 2003. *Pilgrims, Patrons, and Place: Localizing Sanctity in Asian Religions.* Vancouver: University of British Columbia Press.

Greenblatt, Sidney L., Richard W. Wilson, and Amy Auerbacher Wilson. 1982. *Social Interaction in Chinese Society.* [New York]: Praeger.

Grootaers, Willem A. 1951. "Une séance de spiritisme dans une religion secrète à Pékin en 1948." *Mélanges chinois et bouddhiques* 9: 92–98. Bruxelles: Institut Belge des Hautes Études Chinoises.

———. 1952. "The Hagiography of the Chinese God Chen-wu." *Folklore Studies* 11: 139–81.

Gu Jiegang 顾颉刚. 1977. *Shilin zashi* 史林杂识 [Historical knowledge]. Beijing: Zhonghua shuju.

———. 1996. *Gu Jiegang juan* 顾颉刚卷 [Works by Gu Jiegang], edited by Gu Chao 顾潮 and Gu Hong 顾洪. *Zhongguo xiandai xueshu jingdian* 中国现代学术经典 [The learning of contemporary China]. Shijiazhuang: Hebei jiaoyu chubanshe.

Güntsch, Gertrud. 1988. *Das Shen-hsien chuan und das Erscheinungsbild eines Hsien*. Bern and Frankfurt: Peter Lang.

Guo Fan 郭藩, ed. 1982. *Zhongguo gudian xiaoshuo yanjiu zhuanji* 中國古典小說研究專集 [Anthology for the study of classical Chinese fiction]. Taipei: Lianjing chuban shiye gongsi.

Guo Shusen 郭树森. 1990. *Tianshi dao* 天师道 [The Way of the Celestial Masters]. Shanghai: Shanghai shehui kexueyuan chubanshe.

Guojia wenwuju Guwenxian yanjiushi 國家文物局古文獻研究室 [Research Group on Ancient Literature of the National Administration for Cultural Heritage]. 1980–85. *Mawangdui Hanmu boshu* 馬王堆漢墓帛書 [The silk manuscripts from the Han tombs at Mawangdui]. Vols. 1, 3, and 4 published to date. Beijing: Wenwu chubanshe.

Hachiya Kunio 蜂屋邦夫. 1983. "*Taihei kyō* ni okeru genji bunsho" 「太平經」における言辞文書 [Speech and texts in the *Taiping jing*]. *TBKK* 92: 35–82.

———. 1987. "Ba Tanyō no shukke o megutte" 馬丹陽の出家をめぐって [On Ma Danyang's entering into priesthood]. In Akizuki Kan'ei 1987, 387–402.

———. 1989. "Tan Chōshin no shōgai to shisō" 譚長真の生涯と思想 [Tan Chuduan's life and thought]. *TBKK* 108: 41–122.

———, ed. 1990. *Chūgoku dōkyō no genjō: Dōshi, dōkyō, dōkan* 中國道教の現状—道士・道協・道観 [The state of Taoism in China: Masters, associations, temples]. Tokyo: Tōkyō daigaku Tōyō bunka kenkyūjo.

———. 1992a. *Kindai dōkyō no kenkyū: Ō Chōyō to Ba Tanyō* 金代道教の研究—王重陽と馬丹陽 [Studies on Taoism in the Jin dynasty: Wang Chongyang and Ma Danyang]. Tokyo: Kyūko shoin.

———. 1992b. "Ryū Chōsei no shōgai to kyōsetsu" 劉長生の生涯と教説 [Liu Changsheng's life and teaching]. *TBKK* 117: 273–331.

———, ed. 1995. *Chūgoku no dōkyō: Sono katsudō to dōkan no genjō* 中國の道教—その活動と道観の現状 [Chinese Taoism: Current activities and the state of Taoist temples]. Tokyo: Kyūko shoin.

———. 1998. *Kin-Gen jidai no dōkyō: Nanashin kenkyū* 金元時代の道教—七真研究 [Taoism during the Jin-Yuan period: A study of the Seven Perfected]. Kyoto: Kyūko shoin.

Hackmann, Heinrich. 1919–20. "Die Mönchsregeln des Klostertaoismus." *Ostasiatische Zeitschrift* 8: 142–70.

———. 1931. *Die dreihundert Mönchsgebote des chinesischen Taoismus*. Amsterdam: Koninklijke Academie van Wetenschappen.

Hahn, Thomas H. 1986. "On Doing Fieldwork in Daoist Studies in the People's Republic: Conditions and Results." *CEA* 2: 211–17.

———. 1988. "The Standard Taoist Mountain and Related Features of Religious Geography." *CEA* 4: 145–56.

———. 1989. "New Developments Concerning Buddhist and Taoist Monasteries." In Pas 1989b, 79–101.

———. 2000. "Daoist Sacred Sites." In Kohn 2000b, 683–708.

Hall, David A. 1990. "Marishiten: Buddhism and the Warrior Goddess." Ph.D. diss., University of California, Berkeley.

Hamashima Atsutoshi. 1992. "The City-God Temples of Chiangnan in the Ming and Ch'ing Dynasties." *Memoirs of the Research Department of Toyo Bunko* 50: 1–28.

Han Bingfang 韩秉方. 1986. "Luojiao *Wubu liuce* baojuan de sixiang yanjiu 罗教「五部六册」宝卷的思想研究 [A study of the thought of the Luo Teaching "Precious Scrolls" entitled *Five Books in Six Volumes*]." *SZY* 1986.4: 34–48.

Hansen, Valerie. 1990. *Changing Gods in Medieval China, 1127–1276*. Princeton: Princeton University Press.

———. 1993. "Gods on Walls: A Case of Indian Influence on Chinese Lay Religion?" In Ebrey and Gregory 1993, 75–113.

Hanxue yanjiu zhongxin 漢學研究中心 [Center for Chinese Studies], ed. 1994. *Minjian xinyang yu Zhongguo wenhua guoji yantaohui lunwen ji* 民間信仰與中國文化國際研討會論文集 [Proceedings of the International Conference on Popular Belief and Chinese Culture]. 2 vols. Taipei: Hanxue yanjiu zhongxin.

———. 1995. *Simiao yu minjian wenhua yantao hui lunwen ji* 寺廟與民間文化研討會論文集 [Proceedings of the Conference on Temples and Popular Culture]. 2 vols. Taipei: Hanxue yanjiu zhongxin.

Happold, F. Crossfield. 1970. *Mysticism: A Study and an Anthology*. Revised edition. Harmondsworth: Penguin Books.

Harada Jirō 原田二郎. 1984. "*Taihei kyō* no seimei kan, chōsei setsu ni tsuite"「太平經」の生命観・長生説について [On the view of life and death and the theory of long life in the *Taiping jing*]. *NCG* 36: 71–83.

———. 1988. "Yōseisetsu ni okeru 'sei' no gainen no tenkai" 養生説における「精」の概念の展開 [The notion of "essence" in the theory of Nourishing Life and its development]. In Sakade Yoshinobu 1988a, 342–78.

Harada Masami 原田正巳. 1955. "Kan U shinkō no ni san no yōsu ni tsuite" 關羽信仰の二三の要素について [On some aspects of the belief in Guan Yu]. *TS* 8–9: 29–40.

Harper, Donald J. 1978–79. "The Han Cosmic Board (*shih* 式)." *EC* 4: 1–10.

———. 1985. "A Chinese Demonography of the Third Century B.C." *HJAS* 45: 439–98.

———. 1987a. "Magic in East Asia." In Eliade 1987, 9: 112–15.

———. 1987b. "The Sexual Arts of Ancient China as Described in Manuscript of the Second Century B.C." *HJAS* 47: 539–93.

———. 1994. "Resurrection in Warring States Popular Religion." *TR* 5.2: 13–28.

———. 1995. "The Bellows Analogy in *Laozi* V and Warring States Macrobiotic Hygiene." *EC* 20: 381–91.

———. 1996. "Spellbinding." In Lopez 1996, 241–50.

———. 1998. *Early Chinese Medical Literature: The Mawangdui Medical Manuscripts*. London and New York: Kegan Paul International.

———. 1999. "Warring States Natural Philosophy and Occult Thought." In Loewe and Shaughnessy 1999, 813–84.

Harrell, C. Stevan. 1974. "When a Ghost Becomes a God." In Wolf 1974, 193–206.

Hartman, Charles. 1986. "Li Ao." In Nienhauser 1986, 529–30.

Hashimoto Keizō, Catherine Jami, and Lowell Skar, eds. 1995. *East Asian Science: Tradition and Beyond. Papers from the Seventh International Conference on the History of Science in East Asia, Kyoto, 2–7 August 1993*. Osaka: Kansai University Press.

Haussig, Hans Wilhelm. 1994. *Wörterbuch der Mythologie*. Vol. 6: *Götter und Mythen Ostasiens*, edited by Egidius Schmalzriedt and Hans Wilhelm Haussig. Stuttgart: Klett-Cotta.

Hawkes, David. 1981. "Quanzhen Plays and Quanzhen Masters." *BEFEO* 69: 153–70. Reprinted in Hawkes 1989, 181–204.

———. 1985. *The Songs of the South: An Anthology of Ancient Chinese Poems by Qu Yuan and Other Poets*. Harmondsworth: Penguin Books.

———. 1989. *Classical, Modern and Humane: Essays in Chinese Literature*. Edited by John Minford and Siu-kit Wong. Hong Kong: Chinese University Press.

Hay, John, ed. 1994. *Boundaries in China*. London: Reaktion Books.

He Zhiguo and Vivienne Lo. 1996. "The Channels: A Preliminary Examination of a Lacquered Figurine from the Western Han Period." *EC* 21: 81–123.

Hearn, Maxwell K., and Judith K. Smith, eds. 1996. *Arts of the Sung and Yüan*. New York: The Metropolitan Museum of Art.

Hebei sheng Wenwu yanjiusuo Dingzhou Hanjian zhengli xiaozu 河北省文物研究所定洲汉简整理小组 [Editorial Group of the Institute for Cultural Heritage of the Hebei Province for the Han Bamboo Slips from Dinzhou]. 1995. "Dingzhou Xi Han Zhongshan Huai Wang mu zhujian *Wenzi* shiwen" 定洲西汉中山怀王墓竹简「文子」释文 [Transcription of the Han bamboo slips of the *Wenzi* from the Western Han tomb of King Huai at Zhongshan, Dingzhou]. *Wenwu* 文物 1995.12: 27–34.

Henderson, John B. 1984. *The Development and Decline of Chinese Cosmology*. New York: Columbia University Press.

———. 1991. *Scripture, Canon, and Commentary: A Comparison of Confucian and Western Exegesis*. Princeton: Princeton University Press.

Hendrischke, Barbara. 1985. "How the Celestial Master Proves Heaven Reliable." In Naundorf, Pohl, and Schmidt 1985, 77–86.

———. 1991. "The Concept of Inherited Evil in the *Taiping jing*." *East Asian History* 2: 1–30.

———. 1992. "The Taoist Utopia of Great Peace." *Oriens Extremus* 35: 61–91.

———. 2000. "Early Daoist Movements." In Kohn 2000b, 134–64.

Hendrischke, Barbara, and Benjamin Penny. 1996. "*The 180 Precepts Spoken by Lord Lao*: A Translation and Textual Study." *TR* 6.2: 17–29.

Henricks, Robert G. 1983. *Philosophy and Argumentation in Third-Century China: The Essays of Hsi K'ang*. Princeton: Princeton University Press.

———. 1986a. "Hsi K'ang." In Nienhauser 1986, 410–12.

———. 1986b. "Ma-wang-tui." In Nienhauser 1986, 614–17.

———. 1989. *Lao-tzu: Te-tao ching. A New Translation Based on the Recently Discovered Ma-wang-tui Texts*. New York: Ballantine Books.

———. 2000. *Lao Tzu's Tao-te ching. A Translation of the Startling New Documents Found at Guodian*. New York: Columbia University Press.

Hertz, Robert. 1983. "St. Besse: A Study of an Alpine Cult." In Wilson 1983, 55–100.

Hervouet, Yves. 1972. *Le chapitre 117 du Che-ki (Biographie de Sseu-ma Siang-jou)*. Paris: Presses Universitaires de France.

Hightower, J. R. 1965. "Hsi K'ang: Letter to Shan T'ao." In Birch 1965–72, 1: 162–66.

Hillery, George A., Jr. 1992. *The Monastery: A Study in Love, Freedom, and Community*. Westport, CT: Praeger.

Hirano Minoru 平野実. 1969. *Kōshin shinkō* 庚申信仰 [The *kōshin* (*gengshen*) cult]. Tokyo: Kadokawa shoten.

Hirayama Shū 平山周. 1911. *Shina Kakumeitō oyobi himitsu kessha* 支那革命党及秘密結社 [The Chinese Revolutionary Party and secret societies]. Published as a supplement to the journal *Nihon oyobi Nihonjin* 日本及日本人 (Japan and the Japanese people).

Ho Kwok Man and Joanne O'Brien. 1990. *The Eight Immortals of Taoism: Legends and Fables of Popular Taoism*. London: Rider.

Ho Peng Yoke [何丙郁]. 1972. "The System of the *Book of Changes* and Chinese Science." *Japanese Studies in the History of Science* 11: 23–39.

——. 1979. *On the Dating of Taoist Alchemical Texts*. Brisbane: Griffith University.

——. 1980. *Tuku Tao's Tan-fang chien-yüan: A Tenth-Century Alchemical Sourcebook*. Hong Kong: Center of Asian Studies, University of Hong Kong. [In Chinese, with an introduction in English.]

——. 1985. *Li, Qi and Shu: An Introduction to Science and Civilization in China*. Hong Kong: Hong Kong University Press.

Holm, David L. 1994. "The Labyrinth of Lanterns: Taoism and Popular Religion in Northwest China." In Hanxue yanjiu zhongxin 1994, 2: 797–852.

Holzman, Donald J. 1957. *La vie et la pensée de Hi K'ang (223–262 ap. J.-C.)*. Leiden: E. J. Brill.

——. 1976. *Poetry and Politics: The Life and Works of Juan Chi, A.D. 210–263*. Cambridge: Cambridge University Press.

——. 1980. "La poésie de Ji Kang." *Journal Asiatique* 268: 107–77, 323–78.

——. 1991. "The Wang Ziqiao Stele." *Rocznik Orientalistyczny* 47.2: 77–83. Reprinted in Holzman 1998, essay II.

——. 1998. *Immortals, Festivals and Poetry in Medieval China*. Aldershot: Ashgate.

Homann, Rolf. 1971. *Die wichtigsten Körpergottheiten im Huang-t'ing ching*. Göppingen: Alfred Kümmerle.

——. 1976. *Pai Wen P'ien or the Hundred Questions: A Dialogue between Two Taoists on the Macrocosmic and Microcosmic System of Correspondences*. Leiden: E. J. Brill.

Hosokawa Kazutoshi 細川一敏. 1987. "'Seijō' to iu go ni tsuite no ikkōsatsu" 清浄という語についての一考察 [A note on the term *qingjing* ("clarity and purity")]. In Akizuki Kan'ei 1987, 154–69.

Hosoya Yoshio 細谷良夫. 1986. "Yōshō chō no Shōitsukyō" 雍正朝の正一教 [Zhengyi during the Yongzheng reign period]. *Tōhōgaku* 東方學 72: 97–110.

Hou Ching-lang. 1975. *Monnaies d'offrande et la notion de Trésorerie dans la religion chinoise*. Paris: Collège de France, Institut des Hautes Études Chinoises.

——. 1979. "The Chinese Belief in Baleful Stars." In Welch and Seidel 1979, 193–228.

Hsia, Emil C. H., Ilza Veith, and Robert H. Geertsma, eds. 1986. *The Essentials of Medicine in Ancient China and Japan: Yasuyori Tamba's Ishimpō*. 2 vols. Leiden: E. J. Brill.

Hsiao Kung-chuan. 1979. *A History of Chinese Political Thought*. Vol. 1: *From the Beginnings to the Sixth Century A.D.* Translated by F. W. Mote. Princeton: Princeton University Press. Originally published as *Zhongguo zhengzhi sixiang shi* 中國政治思想史 [A History of Chinese Political Thought] (Taipei: Zhonghua wenhua chubanshe, 1968).

Hsü Cho-yun. 1975. "The Concept of Predetermination and Fate in the Han." *EC* 1: 51–56.

Hsu, Elisabeth. 1999. *The Transmission of Chinese Medicine*. Cambridge: Cambridge University Press.

———, ed. 2001. *Innovation in Chinese Medicine*. Cambridge: Cambridge University Press.

Hsu, Francis L. K. 1952. *Religion, Science and Human Crises: A Study of China in Transition and its Implications for the West*. London: Routledge and Kegan Paul.

Hu Fuchen 胡孚琛. 1989. *Wei-Jin shenxian daojiao: Baopu zi neipian yanjiu* 魏晋神仙道教—「抱朴子内篇」研究 [Immortality Taoism in the Wei-Jin period: A study of the *Baopu zi neipian*]. Beijing: Renmin chubanshe.

———, ed. 1995. *Zhonghua daojiao da cidian* 中华道教大辞典 [Great dictionary of Chinese Taoism]. Beijing: Zhongguo shehui kexue chubanshe.

Hu Tiancheng 胡天成, ed. 1999. *Minjian jili yu yishi xiju* 民间祭礼与仪式戏剧 [Popular ceremonies and liturgical drama]. Guiyang: Guizhou minzu chubanshe.

Hu Tiancheng 胡天成, He Dejun 何德君, and Duan Ming 段明. 1999. *Juegang mipu huibian: Sichuan sheng Chongqing shi Baxian Jielong qu* 訣罡密譜彙編—四川省重慶市巴縣接龍區 [Compendium of secret manuals of hand gestures and ritual steps: Sichuan province, Chongqing city, Ba county, Jielong district]. Taipei: Nantian shuju.

Huang Chun-chieh and Erik Zürcher, eds. 1995. *Time and Space in Chinese Culture*. Leiden: E. J. Brill.

Huang Meiying 黃美英. 1994. *Taiwan Mazu de xianghuo yu yishi* 臺灣媽祖的香火與儀式 [Incense sticks and liturgies for Mazu in Taiwan]. Taipei: Zili wanbao wenhua chubanbu.

Huang Shi 黃石. 1979. *Duanwu lisu shi* 端午禮俗史 [The history of the Dragon Boat Festival]. Taipei: Dingwen shuju.

Huang Xiaoshi 黄小石. 1999. *Jingming dao yanjiu* 净明道研究 [A study of the Pure and Bright Way]. Chengdu: Ba Shu shushe.

Huang Youxing 黃有興. 1992. *Penghu de minjian xinyang* 澎湖的民間信仰 [Popular cults in the Pescadores]. Taipei: Taiyuan chubanshe.

Huang, Jane. 1987–90. *The Primordial Breath: An Ancient Chinese Way of Prolonging Life through Breath Control*. 2 vols. (vol. 1 in collaboration with Michael Wurmbrand). Torrance, CA: Original Books.

Huang, Paolos. 1996. *Lao Zi: The Book and the Man*. Helsinki: Finnish Oriental Society.

Hucker, Charles O. 1985. *A Dictionary of Official Titles in Imperial China*. Stanford University Press.

Hummell, Arthur, ed. 1943–44. *Eminent Chinese of the Ch'ing Period*. Washington, DC: U.S. Government Printing Office.

Hurtado, Larry W., ed. 1990. *Goddesses in Religions and Modern Debate*. Atlanta: Scholars Press.

Hurvitz, Leon. 1962. *Chih-i (538–597): An Introduction to the Life and Ideas of a Chinese Buddhist Monk*. Bruxelles: Institut Belge des Hautes Études Chinoises.

Hussein, Farzeen [Farzeen Baldrian-Hussein]. 1976. "Chang Po-tuan." In Franke H. 1976, 1: 26–29.

Huters, Theodore, R. Bin Wong, and Pauline Yu, eds. 1997. *Culture and State in Chinese History: Conventions, Accommodations, and Critiques*. Stanford: Stanford University Press.

Hymes, Robert P. 1996. "Personal Relations and Bureaucratic Hierarchy in Chinese Religion: Evidence from the Song Dynasty." In Shahar and Weller 1996, 37–69.

———. 1997. "A Jiao Is a Jiao Is a? Thoughts on the Meaning of a Ritual." In Huters, Wong, and Yu 1997, 129–60.

———. 2002. *Way and Byway. Taoism, Local Religion, and Models of Divinity in Sung and Modern China*. Berkeley and Los Angeles: University of California Press.

Idema, Wilt L. 1985. *The Dramatic Oeuvre of Chu Yu-tun (1379–1439)*. Leiden: E. J. Brill.

———. 1986. "Chu Ch'üan." In Nienhauser 1986, 329–30.

———. 1993. "Skulls and Skeletons in Art and on Stage." In Blussé and Zurndorfer 1993, 191–215.

———. 1997. "The Pilgrimage to Taishan in the Dramatic Literature of the Thirteenth and Fourteenth Centuries." *Chinese Literature: Essays, Articles, Reviews* 19: 23–57.

Idema, Wilt L., and Erik Zürcher, eds. 1990. *Thought and Law in Qin and Han China: Studies Dedicated to Anthony Hulsewé on the Occasion of his Eightieth Birthday*. Leiden: E. J. Brill.

Idema, Wilt L., and Stephen H. West. 1982. *Chinese Theater 1100–1450: A Source Book*. Wiesbaden: Franz Steiner Verlag.

Igarashi Kenryū 五十嵐賢隆. 1938. *Taiseikyū shi* 太清宮志 [A monograph of the Palace of Great Clarity]. Tokyo: Kokusho kankōkai.

Ikeda Suetoshi hakase koki kinen jigyōkai 池田末利博士古稀記念事業會 [Committee for the Commemoration of the Seventieth Birthday of Dr. Ikeda Suetoshi], ed. 1980. *Ikeda Suetoshi hakase koki kinen Tōyōgaku ronshū* 池田末利博士古稀記念東洋學論集 [Studies on East Asia presented to Dr. Ikeda Suetoshi on his seventieth birthday]. Hiroshima: Ikeda Suetoshi hakase koki kinen jigyōkai.

Ikeda Tomohisa 池田知久. 1995. "Zhongguo gudai zhexue zhong de hundun" 中國古代哲學中之混沌 [The notion of Chaos in ancient Chinese philosophy]. *DWY* 8: 122–36.

Imai Usaburō 今井宇三郎. 1960. "*Shūeki sandōkei* to Sōgaku"「周易三同契」と宋學 [The *Zhouyi cantong qi* and Song Learning]. *Tōkyō kyōiku daigaku Bungakubu kiyō* 東京教育大學文學部紀要 27 (= *Kokubugaku kanbungaku ronsō* 國文學漢文學論叢 4): 1–47.

———. 1962. "*Goshinhen* no seisho to shisō"「悟真篇」の成書と思想 [The compilation and thought of the *Wuzhen pian*]. *TS* 19: 1–19.

Inagaki Hisao. 1998. *Ōjōronchū: T'an-luan's Commentary on Vasubhandhu's Discourse on the Pure Land*. Kyoto: Nagata Bunshodo.

Inahata Kōichirō 稲畑耕一郎. 1979. "Shimei shinzō no tenkai" 司命神像の展開 [The development of the image of the Director of Destinies]. *Chūgoku bungaku kenkyū* 中國文學研究 5: 1–17.

Inoue Ichii 井上以智為. 1931. "Tendaisan ni okeru dōkyō to bukkyō" 天臺山に於ける道教と佛教 [Taoism and Buddhism at Mount Tiantai]. In Kuwabara hakushi kanreki kinen shukugakai 1931, 595–649.

———. 1933. "Rosan bunka no reimei" 廬山文化の黎明 [The dawn of the Mount Lu culture]. Shi'en 史淵 8: 53–95.

———. 1934. "Rosan bunka to Ei'en" 廬山文化と慧遠 [The Mount Lu culture and Huiyuan]. Shi'en 史淵 9: 1–33.

———. 1941. "Kan U shibyō no yūrai narabi ni hensen" 關羽祠廟の由来並に変遷 [The origins and transformations of the shrines and temples to Guan Yu]. Shirin 史林 26: 41–51, 242–83.

Iriya kyōju Ogawa kyōju taikyū kinenkai 入矢教授小川教授退休記念会 [Committee for the Commemoration of the Retirement of Professor Iriya Yoshitaka and Professor Ogawa Tamaki], ed. 1974. Iriya kyōju Ogawa kyōju taikyū kinen Chūgoku bungaku gogaku ronshū 入矢教授小川教授退休記念中國文學語學論集 [Collected studies on Chinese literature and language in commemoration of the retirement of Professor Iriya Yoshitaka and Professor Ogawa Tamaki]. Kyoto: Iriya kyōju Ogawa kyōju taikyū kinenkai.

Ishida Hidemi 石田秀美 1987a. Ki: Nagareru shintai 気—流れる身体 [Qi (pneuma): The flowing body]. Tokyo: Hirakawa shuppansha.

———. 1987b. "Taijō Rōkun setsu Jō seijō kyō honbun kōtei narabi ni nihongo yakuchū" 「太上老君説常清浄經」本文校訂並びに日本語訳注 [A critical edition and Japanese annotated translation of the Taishang Laojun shuo chang qingjing jing]. Yahata daigaku ronshu 八幡大學論集 38: 86–114.

———. 1988. "Shōsoku kō" 踵息考 [A study of "breathing through the heels"]. In Sakade Yoshinobu 1988a, 80–115.

———. 1989. "Body and Mind: The Chinese Perspective." In Kohn 1989c, 41–71.

———. 1991. "Shoki no hōchū yōsei shisō to sensetsu" 初期の房中養生思想と仙説 [The early notions of Nourishing Life through sexual practices and the theory of immortality]. TS 77: 1–21.

Ishida Kenji 石田憲司. 1992. "Mindai dōkyō shijō no Zenshin to Shōitsu" 明代道教史上の全真と正一 [Quanzhen and Zhengyi in Ming-dynasty Taoism]. In Sakai Tadao 1992, 145–85.

Ishii Masako 石井昌子. 1971. "Tō Kōkei denki kō" 陶弘景傳記考 [A study of the biographical records of Tao Hongjing]. Études taoïstes / Dōkyō kenkyū 道教研究 4: 29–113. Reprinted in Ishii Masako 1980, 25–119.

———. 1980. Dōkyō gaku no kenkyū 道教學の研究 [Studies on Taoism]. Tokyo: Kokusho kankōkai.

———. 1981. "Reihō gofu kyō no ikkōsatsu" 「霊宝五符經」の一考察 [A note on the Lingbao wufu jing]. Sōka daigaku ippan kyōikubu ronshū 創価大學一般教育部論集 5: 1–20.

———. 1983a. "Dōkyō no kamigami" 道教の神々 [The gods of Taoism]. In Fukui Kōjun et al. 1983, 1: 121–87.

———. 1983b. "Reihō kyō rui" 霊宝經類 [Texts related to Lingbao (among the Dunhuang manuscripts)]. In Kanaoka Shōkō, Ikeda On, and Fukui Fumimasa 1983, 143–76.

———. 1984. *"Taijō reihō gofu jo no ikkōsatsu"*「太上霊宝五符序」の一考察 [A note on the *Taishang lingbao wufu xu*]. In Makio Ryōkai hakushi shōju kinen ronshū kankōkai 1984, 13–31.

———. 1987. *"Shinkō ni toku 'seishitsu' ni tsuite"*「真誥」に説く「静室」について [On the "quiet chamber" in the *Zhengao*]. In Akizuki Kan'ei 1987, 136–53.

———. 1991. *Shinkō* 真誥 [*Zhengao*]. Tokyo: Meitoku shuppansha.

Ivanhoe, Philip J. 1999. "The Concept of *De* ('Virtue') in the *Laozi*." In Csikszentmihalyi and Ivanhoe 1999, 239–55.

Izutsu Toshihiko. 1983. *Sufism and Taoism: A Comparative Study of Key Philosophical Concepts*. Tokyo: Iwanami shoten.

James, Jean M. 1995. "An Iconographic Study of Xiwangmu During the Han Dynasty." *Artibus Asiae* 55: 17–41.

Jan Yün-hua. 1977. "The Silk Manuscripts on Taoism." *TP* 63: 65–84.

———. 1980. *"Tao Yuan or Tao: The Origin."* *JCP* 7: 195–204.

———. 1983. "Political Philosophy of the *Shih-liu ching* Attributed to the Yellow Emperor Taoism." *JCP* 10: 205–28.

———. 1984. "The Religious Situation and the Studies of Buddhism and Taoism in China: An Incomplete and Imbalanced Picture." *JCR* 12: 37–64.

———. 1986. "Cultural Borrowing and Religious Identity: A Case Study of the Taoist Religious Codes." *HXYJ* 4: 281–94.

Jiang Guozhu 姜国柱. 1998. *Daojia yu bingjia* 道家与兵家 [Taoism and the Military School]. Beijing: Xiyuan chubanshe.

Jin Weinuo 金維諾, ed. 1977. *Yongle gong bihua quanji* 永樂宮壁畫全集 [Complete collection of Yongle gong murals]. Tianjin: Tianjin meishu chubanshe.

Jing Anning. 1993. "Yongle Palace: The Transformation of the Daoist Pantheon during the Yuan Dynasty (1260–1368)." Ph.D. diss., Princeton University.

———. 1996. "The Eight Immortals: The Transformation of T'ang and Sung Taoist Eccentrics During the Yüan Dynasty." In Hearn and Smith 1996, 213–29.

Jingmen shi Bowuguan 荊門市博物館. 1998. *Guodian Chumu zhujian* 郭店楚墓竹簡 [The bamboo slips manuscripts from the Chu tombs in Guodian]. Beijing: Wenwu chubanshe.

Johnson, David. 1985a. "Communication, Class, and Consciousness in Late Imperial China." In Johnson, Nathan, and Rawski 1985, 34–72.

———. 1985b. "The City-God Cults of T'ang and Sung China." *HJAS* 45: 363–457.

———, ed. 1989. *Ritual Opera, Operatic Ritual: "Mu-lien Rescues His Mother" in Chinese Popular Culture*. Berkeley: University of California Press.

———. 1995a. "Mu-lien in *Pao-chüan*: The Performance Context and Religious Meaning of the *Yu-ming Pao-chüan*." In Johnson 1995b, 55–103.

———, ed. 1995b. *Ritual and Scripture in Chinese Popular Religion: Five Studies*. Berkeley: Publications of the Chinese Popular Culture Project.

Johnson, David, Andrew J. Nathan, and Evelyn S. Rawski, eds. 1985. *Popular Culture in Late Imperial China*. Berkeley: University of California Press.

Jones, Stephen. 1995. *Folk Music of China: Living Instrumental Traditions*. Oxford: Clarendon Press.

Jonker, D. R. 1976. "Chu Ch'üan." In Goodrich and Fang 1976, 305–7.

Jordan, David K. 1972. *Gods, Ghosts, and Ancestors: The Folk Religion of a Taiwanese Village*. Berkeley: University of California Press.

———. 1976. "The Jiaw of Shigaang (Taiwan): An Essay in Folk Interpretation." *Asian Folklore Studies* 35.2: 81–107.

Jordan, David K., and Daniel L. Overmyer. 1986. *The Flying Phoenix: Aspects of Chinese Sectarianism in Taiwan*. Princeton: Princeton University Press.

Julien, Stanislas. 1835. *Le livre des récompenses et des peines*. Paris: Oriental Translation Fund.

Jung Jae-seo. 2000. "Daoism in Korea." In Kohn 2000b, 792–820.

Kaelber, Walter O. 1987. "Asceticism." In Eliade 1987, 1: 441–45.

Kagan, Richard C., and Anna Wasescha. 1982. "The Taiwanese Tang-ki: The Shaman as Community Healer and Protector." In Greenblatt, Wilson, and Wilson 1982, 112–41.

Kaguraoka Masatoshi 神楽岡昌俊. 1988. "*Hōbokushi* no yōsei shisō" 「抱朴子」の養生思想 [Conceptions of Nourishing Life in the *Baopu zi*]. In Sakade Yoshinobu 1988a, 431–51.

Kakiuchi Tomoyuki 垣内智之. 1998. "Tōbu kukū no zaishi to Tai'itsu" 頭部九宮の存思と太一 [The visualization of the Nine Palaces in the head and the Great One]. *TS* 91: 22–40.

Kalinowski, Marc. 1983. "Les instruments astro-calendériques des Han et la méthode *liu ren*." *BEFEO* 72: 309–419.

———. 1985. "La transmission du dispositif des Neuf Palais sous les Six-Dynasties." In Strickmann 1981–85, 3: 773–811.

———. 1989–90. "La littérature divinatoire dans le *Daozang*." *CEA* 5: 85–114.

———. 1991. *Cosmologie et divination dans la Chine ancienne: Le Compendium des Cinq Agents (Wuxing dayi, VIe siècle)*. Paris: École Française d'Extrême-Orient.

———. 1996. "Mythe, cosmogénèse et théogonie dans la Chine ancienne." *L'Homme* 137: 41–60.

———. 1998–99. "The *Xingde* Texts from Mawangdui." Translated by Phyllis Brooks. *EC* 23–24: 125–202.

———. 2004. "Technical Traditions in Ancient China and *Shushu* Culture in Chinese Religion." In Lagerwey 2004b, 1: 223–48.

Kaltenmark, Max. 1947. "Les Tch'an-wei." *Han hiue* 2: 363–73.

———. 1953. *Le Lie-sien tchouan* 列仙傳 (*Biographies légendaires des Immortels taoïstes de l'antiquité*). Pékin: Université de Paris, Publications du Centre d'Études Sinologiques de Pékin.

———. 1959. "La naissance du monde en Chine." In *La naissance du monde*, 453–68. Sources orientales, 1. Paris: Éditions du Seuil.

———. 1960. "*Ling-pao* 靈寶: Note sur un terme du taoïsme religieux." *Mélanges publiés par l'Institut des Hautes Études Chinoises, Collège de France* 2: 559–88. Paris: Institut des Hautes Études Chinoises, Collège de France.

———. 1961. "Religion et politique dans la Chine des Ts'in et des Han." *Diogène* 34: 18–46.

———. 1967–68. "Au sujet du *Houang-t'ing king*." *Annuaire de l'École Pratique des Hautes Études, Ve Section*, 75: 117–18.

————. 1969a. "*Jing* yu *bajing*" 景與八景 [The *jing* and the eight *jing*]. In Fukui Hakase Shōju Kinen Ronbunshū Kankōkai 1969, 1147–54.

————. 1969b. *Lao Tzu and Taoism*. Translated by Roger Greaves. Stanford: Stanford University Press. Originally published as *Lao tseu et le taoïsme* (Paris: Editions du Seuil, 1965).

————. 1974. "Miroirs magiques." In *Mélanges de sinologie offerts à Paul Demiéville*, 2: 151–66. Paris: Institut des Hautes Études Chinoises.

————. 1979a. "Notes sur le *Pen-tsi king* (Personnages figurant dans le sutra)." In Soymié 1979, 91–98.

————. 1979b. "The Ideology of the *T'ai-p'ing ching*." In Welch and Seidel 1979, 19–52.

————. 1982. "Quelques remarques sur le '*T'ai-chang ling-pao wou-fou siu*.'" *Zinbun: Memoirs of the Research Institute for Humanistic Studies* 18: 1–10.

Kamata Shigeo 鎌田茂雄. 1966. "Dōsei shisō no keisei katei" 道性思想の形成過程 [The formation of the notion of "Nature of the Dao"]. *TBKK* 42: 61–154.

————. 1968. *Chūgoku bukkyō shisōshi kenkyū* 中國佛教思想史研究 [Studies on the history of Chinese Buddhist thought]. Tokyo: Shunjūsha.

————. 1969. "*Genju roku* ni arawareta bukkyō shisō" 「玄珠録」にあらわれた佛教思想 [Buddhist thought in the *Xuanzhu lu*]. *Chūgoku gakushi* 中國學誌 5: 119–43.

Kamitsuka Yoshiko 神塚淑子. 1979. "Go In no shōgai to shisō" 呉筠の生涯と思想 [Wu Yun's life and thought]. *TS* 54: 33–51.

————. 1982. "Shiba Shōtei *Zabōron* ni tsuite" 司馬承禎「座忘論」について [On Sima Chengzhen's *Zuowang lun*]. *Tōyō bunka* 東洋文化 62: 213–42.

————. 1990. "Hōsho Seidōkun o megutte: Rikucho Jōseiha dōkyō no ikkōsatsu" 方諸青童君をめぐって－六朝上清派道教の一考察 [On the Azure Lad, Lord of Fangzhu: A note on the Shangqing school in the Six Dynasties period]. *TS* 76: 1–23. Reprinted in Kamitsuka Yoshiko 1999, 123–48.

————. 1993. "Nanbokuchō jidai no dōkyō zōzō: Shūkyō shisōshiteki kōsatsu o chūshin ni" 南北朝時代の道教造像—宗教思想史的考察を中心に [Taoist statues in the Northern and Southern Dynasties, with special reference to the history of religious thought]. In Tonami Mamoru 1993, 225–89. Reprinted in Kamitsuka Yoshiko 1999, 464–545. Partially translated into English in Kamitsuka Yoshiko 1998.

————. 1996. "The Concept of Māra and the Idea of Expelling Demons." Translated by Amy Lynn Miller and Thomas H. Peterson. *TR* 6.2: 30–50. Partial translation of "Ma no kannen to shōma no shisō" 魔の観念と消魔の思想, in Yoshikawa Tadao 1992a, 80–144; reprinted in Kamitsuka Yoshiko 1999, 211–71.

————. 1998. "Lao-tzu in Six Dynasties Taoist Sculpture." In Kohn and LaFargue 1998, 63–85.

————. 1999. *Rikuchō dōkyō shisō no kenkyū* 六朝道教思想の研究 [Studies on Taoist thought in the Six Dynasties]. Tokyo: Sōbunsha.

Kanai Noriyuki 金井徳幸. 1983. "Shashin to dōkyō" 社神と道教 [Local gods and Taoism]. In Fukui Kōjun et al. 1983, 2: 169–208.

Kanaoka Shōkō 金岡照光. 1983. "Tonkō to dōkyō" 敦煌と道教 [Dunhuang and Taoism]. In Fukui Kōjun et al. 1983, 3: 173–218.

Kanaoka Shōkō 金岡照光, Ikeda On 池田温, and Fukui Fumimasa 福井文雅, eds.

1983. *Tonkō to Chūgoku dōkyō* 敦煌と中國道教 [Dunhuang and Chinese Taoism]. Tokyo: Daitō shuppansha.

Kanaya Osamu 金谷治. 1959. *Rō-Sōteki sekai: Enanji no shisō* 老荘的世界—淮南子の思想 [The world of Lao-Zhuang Taoism: The thought of the *Huainan zi*]. Kyoto: Heirakuji shoten.

Kandel, Barbara [Barbara Hendrischke]. 1974. *Wen Tzu: Ein Beitrag zur Problematik und zum Verständnis eines taoistischen Textes*. Bern and Frankfurt: Peter Lang.

———. 1979. *Taiping jing: The Origin and Transmission of the 'Scripture on General Welfare': The History of an Unofficial Text*. Hamburg: Gesellschaft für Natur- und Völkerkunde Ostasiens.

———. 1980. "A Visit to the China Taoist Association." *Society for the Study of Chinese Religions Bulletin* 8: 1–4.

Kandre, Peter K. 1976. "Yao (Iu Mien) Supernaturalism, Language, and Ethnicity." In Banks 1976, 171–97.

Kang Bao 康豹 [Paul R. Katz]. 1991. "Pingdong xian Donggang zhen de yingwang jidian: Taiwan wenshen yu wangye xinyang zhi fenxi" 屏東縣東港鎮的迎王祭典—臺灣瘟神與王爺信仰之分析 [The Welcoming the Lords Festival of East Haven, Pingdong District: An analysis of the cults of the Plague Gods and Royal Lords in Taiwan]. *ZMJ* 70: 95–211.

———. 1997. *Taiwan de wangye xinyang* 臺灣的王爺信仰 [The cult of the Royal Lords in Taiwan]. Taipei: Shangding wenhua chubanshe.

———. 2000. "Hanren shehui de shenpan yishi chutan: Cong zhanjitou shuoqi" 漢人社會的神判儀式初探—從斬雞頭說起 [A preliminary exploration of Han Chinese judicial rituals, beginning with a discussion of chicken-beheading rites]. *ZMJ* 88: 173–202.

Katō Chie 加藤千恵. 1996. "*Rōshi chūkyō* to naitan shisō no genryū" 「老子中經」と内丹思想の源流 [The *Laozi zhongjing* and the origins of *neidan*]. *TS* 87: 21–38.

———. 2000. "Tai no shisō" 胎の思想 [The notion of "embryo"]. In Miura Kunio, Horiike Nobuo, and Ōgata Tōru 2000, 100–119.

———. 2002. *Furō fushi no shintai: Dōkyō to "tai" no shisō* 不老不死の身体—道教と「胎」の思想 [The ageless and deathless body: Taoism and the notion of "embryo"]. Tokyo: Taishūkan shoten.

Katz, Paul R. 1987. "Demons or Deities? The *Wangye* of Taiwan." *Asian Folklore Studies* 46.2: 197–215.

———. 1990. "Wen Ch'iung: The God of Many Faces." *HXYJ* 8: 183–219.

———. 1992. "Changes in Wang-yeh Beliefs in Postwar Taiwan: A Case Study of Two Wang-yeh Temples." *JCR* 20: 203–14.

———. 1993. "The Function of Temple Murals in Imperial China: The Case of the Yung-lo Kung." *JCR* 21: 45–68.

———. 1994. "The Interaction between Ch'üan-chen Taoism and Local Cults: A Case Study of the Yung-lo Kung." In Hanxue yanjiu zhongxin 1994, 1: 201–50.

———. 1995a. *Demon Hordes and Burning Boats: The Cult of Marshal Wen in Late Imperial Chekiang*. Albany: State University of New York Press.

———. 1995b. "The Pacification of Plagues: A Chinese Rite of Affliction." *Journal of Ritual Studies* 9: 55–100.

———. 1996. "Enlightened Alchemist or Immoral Immortal? The Growth of Lü Dongbin's Cult in Late Imperial China." In Shahar and Weller 1996, 70–104.

———. 1997. "Temple Inscriptions and the Study of Taoist Cults: A Case Study of Inscriptions at the Palace of Eternal Joy." *TR* 7.1: 1–22.

———. 1999. *Images of the Immortal: The Cult of Lü Dongbin at the Palace of Eternal Joy*. Honolulu: University of Hawaii Press.

———. 2001. "Writing History, Creating Identity: A Case Study of *Xuanfeng qinghui tu*." *JCR* 29: 161–78.

———. 2004. "Divine Justice in Late Imperial China: A Preliminary Study of Indictments, Oaths, and Ordeals." In Lagerwey 2004b, 869–902.

Katz, Steven T., ed. 1983. *Mysticism and Religious Traditions*. Oxford and New York: Oxford University Press.

Kawakita Yoshio, Sakai Shizu, and Otsuka Yasuo, eds. 1991. *History of Hygiene: Proceedings of the 12th International Symposium on the Comparative History of Medicine—East and West*. Tokyo: Ishiyaku EuroAmerica.

Keegan, David J. 1988. "The 'Huang-ti Nei-ching': The Structure of the Compilation; The Significance of the Structure." Ph.D. diss., University of California, Berkeley.

Keightley, David N. 1978a. *Sources of Shang History: The Oracle-Bone Inscriptions of Bronze Age China*. Berkeley: University of California Press.

———. 1978b. "The Religious Commitment: Shang Theology and the Genesis of Chinese Political Culture." *HR* 17: 211–25.

———. 1984. "Late Shang Divination: The Magico-Religious Legacy." In Rosemont 1984, 11–34.

———. 1990. "Early Civilization in China: Reflections on How it Became Chinese." In Ropp 1990, 15–54.

Kiang Chao-yuan [Jiang Shaoyuan 江紹原]. 1937. *Le voyage dans la Chine ancienne, considéré principalement sous son aspect magique et religieux*. Translated by Fan Jen. Shanghai: Commission mixte des œuvres franco chinoises. Reprint, Ventiane: Éditions Vithagna, 1975. Originally published as *Zhongguo gudai lüxing zhi yanjiu* 中國古代旅行之研究 (Shanghai: Shangwu yinshuguan, 1935).

Kim Daeyeol. 2000. "Le symbolisme de la force vitale en Chine ancienne: Modèles et significations dans l'alchimie taoïste opératoire (Études des pratiques alchimiques du *Baopuzi neipian*)." Ph.D. diss., Université de Paris-Sorbonne.

Kinney, Anne Behnke, ed. 1995. *Chinese Views of Childhood*. Honolulu: University of Hawaii Press.

Kirkland, Russell. 1984. "Chang Kao: Noteworthy T'ang Taoist?" *T'ang Studies* 2: 31–36.

———. 1986a. "Taoists of the High T'ang: An Inquiry into the Perceived Significance of Eminent Taoists in Medieval Chinese Society." Ph.D. diss., Indiana University.

———. 1986b. "The Last Taoist Grand Master at the T'ang Imperial Court: Li Han-kuang and T'ang Hsüan-tsung." *T'ang Studies* 4: 43–67.

———. 1989. "From Imperial Tutor to Taoist Priest: Ho Chih-chang at the T'ang Court." *Journal of Asian History* 23: 101–33.

———. 1991. "Huang Ling-wei: A Taoist Priestess in T'ang China." *JCR* 19: 47–73.

————. 1992a. "Tales of Thaumaturgy: T'ang Accounts of the Wonder-Worker Yeh Fa-shan." *MS* 40: 47–86.

————. 1992b. "The Making of an Immortal: The Exaltation of Ho Chih-chang." *Numen* 38: 214–39.

————. 1992–93. "Three Entries for a T'ang Biographical Dictionary: Wang Hsi-i, Huang Ling-wei, Ho Chih-chang." *T'ang Studies* 10–11: 153–65.

————. 1993. "A World in Balance: Holistic Synthesis in the *T'ai-p'ing kuang-chi*." *Journal of Sung-Yuan Studies* 23: 43–70.

————. 1994. Review of Wile 1992. *Chinese Literature: Essays, Articles, Reviews* 16: 161–66.

————. 1995a. "Dong Zhongshu (Tung Chung-shu)." In McGreal 1995, 67–70.

————. 1995b. "Taoism." In Reich 1995, 5: 2463–69.

————. 1996a. "Taoism." In Chambliss 1996, 633–36.

————. 1996b. "The *Book of the Way*." In McGreal 1996, 24–29.

————. 1997a. "Ssu-ma Ch'eng-chen and the Role of Taoism in the Medieval Chinese Polity." *Journal of Asian History* 31: 105–38.

————. 1997b. "Varieties of Taoism in Ancient China: A Preliminary Comparison of Themes in the *Nei Yeh* and Other Taoist Classics." *TR* 7.2: 73–86.

————. 1997–98. "Dimensions of Tang Taoism: The State of the Field at the End of the Millennium." *T'ang Studies* 15–16: 79–123.

————. 2001. "'Responsible Non-Action' in a Natural World: Perspectives from the *Neiye*, *Zhuangzi*, and *Daode jing*." In Girardot, Miller, and Liu 2001, 283–304.

————. 2002. "Self-Fulfillment through Selflessness: The Moral Teachings of the *Daode jing*." In Barnhart 2002, 21–48.

————. 2004. *Taoism: The Enduring Tradition*. London and New York: Routledge.

Kleeman, Terry F. 1991. "Taoist Ethics." In Carman and Juergensmeyer 1991, 162–94.

————. 1993. "The Expansion of the Wen-ch'ang Cult." In Ebrey and Gregory 1993, 45–73.

————. 1994a. *A God's Own Tale: The Book of Transformations of Wenchang, the Divine Lord of Zitong*. Albany: State University of New York Press.

————. 1994b. "Licentious Cults and Bloody Victuals: Sacrifice, Reciprocity and Violence in Traditional China." *AM*, third series, 7: 185–211.

————. 1994c. "Mountain Deities in China: The Domestication of the Mountain God and the Subjugation of the Margins." *JAOS* 114: 226–38.

————. 1996. "The Lives and Teachings of the Divine Lord of Zitong." In Lopez 1996, 64–71.

————. 1998. *Great Perfection: Religion and Ethnicity in a Chinese Millennial Kingdom*. Honolulu: University of Hawaii Press.

————. 2002. "Ethnic Identity and Daoist Identity in Traditional China." In Kohn and Roth 2002, 23–38.

Kleine, Christoph, and Livia Kohn. 1999. "Daoist Immortality and Buddhist Holiness: A Study and Translation of the *Honchō shinsen-den*." *Japanese Religions* 24: 119–96.

Kleinman, Arthur, and Tsung-yi Lin, eds. 1980. *Normal and Abnormal Behavior in Chinese Culture*. Dordrecht and Boston: D. Reidel.

Knaul, Livia [Livia Kohn]. 1981. *Leben und Legende des Ch'en T'uan*. Frankfurt: Peter Lang.

———. 1982. "Lost *Chuang-tzu* Passages." *JCR* 10: 53–79.

———. 1985a. "Kuo Hsiang and the *Chuang tzu*." *JCP* 12: 429–47.

———. 1985b. "The Winged Life: Kuo Hsiang's Mystical Philosophy." *Journal of Chinese Studies* 2: 17–41.

Knechtges, David R. 1982–96. *Wen Xuan, or, Selections of Refined Literature*. 3 vols. Princeton: Princeton University Press.

Knoblock, John, and Jeffrey Riegel. 2000. *The Annals of Lü Buwei: A Complete Translation and Study*. Stanford: Stanford University Press.

Kobayashi Masayoshi 小林正美. 1990. *Rikuchō dōkyōshi kenkyū* 六朝道教史研究 [Studies on the history of Taoism in the Six Dynasties]. Tokyo: Sōbunsha.

———. 1992. "The Celestial Masters under the Eastern Jin and Liu-Song Dynasties." *TR* 3.2: 17–45.

———. 1995. "The Establishment of the Taoist Religion (*Tao-chiao*) and its Structure." *Acta Asiatica* 68: 19–36.

Kohn, Livia. 1987a. *Seven Steps to the Tao: Sima Chengzhen's Zuowanglun*. Nettelal: Steyler Verlag.

———. 1987b. "The Teaching of T'ien-yin-tzu." *JCR* 15: 1–28.

———. 1988. "*Mirror of Auras*: Chen Tuan on Physiognomy." *Asian Folklore Studies* 47: 215–56.

———. 1989a. "Guarding the One: Concentrative Meditation in Taoism." In Kohn 1989c, 125–58.

———. 1989b. "Taoist Insight Meditation: The Tang Practice of *Neiguan*." In Kohn 1989c, 193–224.

———, ed. 1989c. *Taoist Meditation and Longevity Techniques*. Edited in cooperation with Yoshinobu Sakade. Ann Arbor: Center for Chinese Studies, University of Michigan.

———. 1990a. "Chen Tuan in History and Legend." *TR* 2.1: 8–31.

———. 1990b. "Eternal Life in Taoist Mysticism." *JAOS* 110: 622–40.

———. 1990c. "The Life of Chen Tuan after the History of the Song (chap. 457)." *TR* 2.1: 1–7.

———. 1991a. *Taoist Mystical Philosophy: The Scripture of Western Ascension*. Albany: State University of New York Press.

———. 1991b. "Taoist Visions of the Body." *JCP* 18: 227–52.

———. 1992a. *Early Chinese Mysticism: Philosophy and Soteriology in the Taoist Tradition*. Princeton: Princeton University Press.

———. 1992b. "Philosophy as Scripture in the Taoist Canon." *JCR* 20: 61–76.

———. 1993a. "Quiet Sitting with Master Yinshi: Religion and Medicine in China Today." *Zen Buddhism Today* 10: 79–95.

———. 1993b. *The Taoist Experience: An Anthology*. Albany: State University of New York Press.

———. 1993–95. "Kōshin: A Taoist Cult in Japan." Parts 1–3. *Japanese Religions* 18 (1993): 113–39; 20 (1995): 34–55; 20 (1995): 123–42.

———. 1994. "Cosmology, Myth, and Philosophy in Ancient China: New Studies on the *Huainan zi*." *Asian Folklore Studies* 53.2: 319–36.

————. 1995a. *Laughing at the Tao: Debates among Buddhists and Taoists in Medieval China*. Princeton: Princeton University Press.

————. 1995b. "Taoism in Japan: Positions and Evaluations." *CEA* 8: 389–412.

————. 1996a. "Laozi: Ancient Philosopher, Master of Longevity, and Taoist God." In Lopez 1996, 52–63.

————. 1996b. "The Taoist Adoption of the City God." *Ming Qing yanjiu* 1996: 69–106.

————. 1997a. "The Date and Compilation of the *Fengdao kejie*, the First Handbook of Monastic Daoism." *East Asian History* 13–14: 91–118.

————. 1997b. "Yin Xi: The Master at the Beginning of the Scripture." *JCR* 25: 83–139.

————. 1998a. "Counting Good Deeds and Days of Life: The Quantification of Fate in Medieval China." *ASEA* 52: 833–70.

————. 1998b. *God of the Dao: Lord Lao in History and Myth*. Ann Arbor: Center for Chinese Studies, University of Michigan.

————. 1998c. "Mind and Eyes: Sensory and Spiritual Experience in Taoist Mysticism." *MS* 46: 129–56.

————. 1998d. "Steal Holy Food and Come Back as a Viper: Conceptions of *Karma* and Rebirth in Medieval Daoism." *Early Medieval China* 4: 1–48.

————. 1998e. "Taoist Scholasticism: A Preliminary Inquiry." In Cabezon 1998, 115–40.

————. 1998f. "The Beginnings and Cultural Characteristics of East Asian Millenarianism." *Japanese Religions* 23: 29–51.

————. 1998g. "The Lao-tzu Myth." In Kohn and LaFargue 1998, 41–62.

————. 1998h. "The *Tao-te-ching* in Ritual." In Kohn and LaFargue 1998, 143–61.

————. 2000a. "A Home for the Immortals: The Layout and Development of Medieval Daoist Monasteries." *Acta Orientalia Academiae Scientiarum Hungaricae* 53: 79–106.

————, ed. 2000b. *Daoism Handbook*. Leiden: E. J. Brill.

————. 2000c. "The Northern Celestial Masters." In Kohn 2000b, 283–308.

————. 2001. "Daoist Monastic Discipline: Hygiene, Meals, and Etiquette." *TP* 87: 153–93.

————. 2003a. "Medieval Daoist Ordination: Origins, Structure, and Practices." *Acta Orientalia* 56: 379–98.

————. 2003b. *Monastic Life in Medieval Daoism: A Cross-Cultural Perspective*. Honolulu: University of Hawaii Press.

————. 2003c. "Monastic Rules in Quanzhen Daoism: As Collected by Heinrich Hackmann." *MS* 51: 367–97.

————. 2004a. *Cosmos and Community: The Ethical Dimension of Daoism*. Cambridge, Mass.: Three Pines Press.

————. 2004b. *The Daoist Monastic Manual: A Translation of the Fengdao kejie*. New York: Oxford University Press.

Kohn, Livia, and Michael LaFargue, eds. 1998. *Lao-tzu and the Tao-te-ching*. Albany: State University of New York Press.

Kohn, Livia, and Harold D. Roth, eds. 2002. *Daoist Identity: History, Lineage, and Ritual*. Honolulu: University of Hawaii Press.

Kominami Ichirō 小南一郎. 1974. *"Shinsenden no fukugen"*「神仙傳」の復元 [The reconstruction of the *Shenxian zhuan*]. In Iriya kyōju Ogawa kyōju taikyū kinenkai 1974, 301–13.

———. 1975–81. *"Kan Butei naiden no seiritsu"*「漢武帝内傳」の成立 [The compilation of the *Han Wudi neizhuan*]. Parts 1 and 2. *TG* 48 (1975): 183–227; 53 (1981): 423–546.

———. 1978. "Gishin jidai no shinsen shisō: *Shinsenden* o chūshin to shite" 魏晉時代の神仙思想—「神仙傳」を中心として [The notion of "divine immortality" in the Wei-Jin period, with special reference to the *Shenxian zhuan*]. In Yamada Keiji 1978, 573–626.

———. 1989. *"Tsubogata no uchū"* 壺型の宇宙 [The cosmos shaped as a jar]. *TG* 61: 165–221.

———. 1991. *Saiōbo to Tanabata denshō* 西王母と七夕傳承 [The Queen Mother of the West and the traditions of the Weaver Festival]. Tokyo: Heibonsha.

———. 1992. "Jinyaku kara sonshi e: Shinsen shisō to dōkyō shinkō to no aida" 尋藥から存思へ—神仙思想と道教信仰との間 [From seeking drugs to visualizations: Between ideas of immortality and Taoist cults]. In Yoshikawa Tadao 1992a, 1–54.

Kraft, Eva. 1957–58. "Zum Huai-nan-tzu: Einführung, Übersetzung (Kapitel I und II) und Interpretation." Parts 1–2. *MS* 16: (1957): 191–286; 17 (1958): 128–207.

Kroll, Paul W. 1978. "Szu-ma Ch'eng-chen in T'ang Verse." *Society for the Study of Chinese Religions Bulletin* 6: 16–30.

———. 1981. "Notes on Three Taoist Figures of the T'ang Dynasty." *Society for the Study of Chinese Religions Bulletin* 9: 19–41.

———. 1983. "Verses From on High: The Ascent of T'ai Shan." *TP* 69: 223–60.

———. 1985. "In the Halls of the Azure Lad." *JAOS* 105: 75–94.

———. 1986a. "Li Po's Transcendent Diction." *JAOS* 106: 99–117.

———. 1986b. "Spreading Open the Barrier of Heaven." *ASEA* 40: 22–39.

———. 1996a. "Body Gods and Inner Vision: *The Scripture of the Yellow Court*." In Lopez 1996, 149–55.

———. 1996b. "On 'Far-Roaming.'" *JAOS*, 116: 653–69.

———. 1996c. "Seduction Songs of One of the Perfected." In Lopez 1996, 180–87.

Kubo Noritada 窪德忠. 1956. *Kōshin shinkō no kenkyū* 庚申信仰の研究 [A study of the *kōshin* (*gengshen*) cult]. Tokyo: Tōkyō daigaku Tōyō bunka kenkyūjo.

———. 1967. *Chūgoku no shūkyō kaikaku: Zenshinkyō no seiritsu* 中國の宗教改革—全真教の成立 [Religious reform in China: The formation of Quanzhen]. Kyoto: Hōzōkan.

———. 1968. "Prolegomena on the Study of the Controversies between Buddhists and Taoists in the Yuan Period." *Memoirs of the Research Department of the Toyo Bunko* 26: 39–61.

———. 1977. *Dōkyōshi* 道教史 [History of Taoism]. Tokyo: Yamagawa shuppansha.

———. 1980. "Futatsu no Tsūdōkan" 二つの通道観 [The two Tongdao guan]. *TS* 55: 1–25.

———. 1986. *Dōkyō no kamigami* 道教の神々 [The gods of Taoism]. Tokyo: Hirakawa shuppansha.

———. 1987a. "Chang Chi-hsien." In Eliade 1987, 3: 196–97.

———. 1987b. "Wang Che." In Eliade 1987, 15: 331.

———. 1997. "*Rōshi shū kōshin kyū chōsei kyō* ni tsuite"「老子守庚申求長生經」につ
いて [On the *Rōshi shū kōshin kyū chōsei kyō*]. In Noguchi Tetsurō et al. 1996–97,
2: 215–30.

Kupfer, Carl F. 1911. *Sacred Places in China*. Cincinnati: Press of the Western Methodist
Book Concern.

Kurihara Akira 栗原啓. 1987. "Chūgoku dōkyō kyōkai to sono kikanshi *Dōkyōkai
kan*" 中國道教協会とその機関誌「道協会刊」[The Chinese Taoist Association
and its journal *Daoxuehui kan*]. In Akizuki Kan'ei 1987, 635–59.

Kushida Ryōkō hakushi shōju kinenkai 櫛田良洪博士頌壽記念会 [Committee for
the Commemoration of the Seventieth Birthday of Dr. Kushida Ryōkō], ed. 1973.
Kōsōden no kenkyū: Kushida Ryōkō hakushi shōju kinen 高僧傳の研究—櫛田良洪
博士頌壽記念 [Studies on the *Biographies of Eminent Monks*: In commemoration
of the seventieth birthday of Dr. Kushida Ryōkō]. Tokyo: Sankibō busshorin.

Kusuyama Haruki 楠山春樹. 1978. "Seiyoshi densetsu kō" 青洋肆傳説考 [A study
of the traditions concerning the Qingyang si]. *TS* 52: 1–14. Reprinted in Kusuyama
Haruki 1979, 423–35.

———. 1979. *Rōshi densetsu no kenkyū* 老子傳説の研究 [A study of the traditions
concerning Laozi]. Tokyo: Sōbunsha.

———. 1983a. "Dōkyō to jukyō" 道教と儒教 [Taoism and Confucianism]. In Fukui
Kōjun et al. 1983, 2: 49–93.

———. 1983b. "Dōtoku kyō rui" 道徳經類 [Texts related to the *Daode jing* (among
the Dunhuang manuscripts)]. In Kanaoka Shōkō, Ikeda On, and Fukui Fumimasa
1983, 3–58.

———. 1983c. "Taihei kyō rui" 太平經類 [Texts related to the *Taiping jing* (among
the Dunhuang manuscripts)]. In Kanaoka Shōkō, Ikeda On, and Fukui Fumimasa
1983, 119–35.

———. 1987. "Enan chūhen to Enan banpitsu"「淮南中篇」と「淮南万畢」[The *Huainan
zhongpian* and the *Huainan wanbi*]. In Akizuki Kan'ei 1987, 27–44.

———. 1992. *Dōka shisō to dōkyō* 道家思想と道教 [Taoist thought and Taoist religion].
Tokyo: Hirakawa shuppansha.

Kuwabara hakushi kanreki kinen shukugakai 桑原博士還暦記念祝賀會 [Committee
for the Commemoration of the Sixtieth Birthday of Dr. Kuwabara Jitsuzō], ed.
1931. *Tōyōshi ronsō: Kuwabara hakushi kanreki kinen* 東洋史論叢: 桑原博士還暦
記念 [Collected studies on East Asian history in commemoration of the Sixtieth
Birthday of Dr. Kuwabara Jitsuzō]. Kyoto: Kōbundō shobō.

LaFargue, Michael. 1992. *The Tao of the Tao Te Ching: A Translation and Commentary*.
Albany: State University of New York Press.

———. 1994. *Tao and Method: A Reasoned Approach to the Tao Te Ching*. Albany: State
University of New York Press.

LaFargue, Michael, and Julian Pas. 1998. "On Translating the *Tao-te-ching*." In Kohn
and LaFargue 1998, 277–301.

Lagerwey, John. 1981a. "Le *Yun-ji qi-qian*: Structure et sources." In Schipper 1981,
xix–lxxi.

———. 1981b. *Wu-shang pi-yao: Somme taoïste du VIe siècle*. Paris: École Française
d'Extrême-Orient.

———. 1986. "Écriture et corps divin en Chine." In Malamoud and Vernant 1986, 275–85.

———. 1987a. "Chen-jen." In Eliade 1987, 3: 231–33. New York: Macmillan.

———. 1987b. "Taoist Priesthood." In Eliade 1987, 11: 547–50.

———. 1987c. *Taoist Ritual in Chinese Society and History*. New York: Macmillan.

———. 1987d. "The Taoist Religious Community." In Eliade 1987, 14: 306–17.

———. 1991. *Le continent des esprits: La Chine dans le miroir du taoïsme*. Bruxelles: La Renaissance du Livre.

———. 1992. "The Pilgrimage to Wu-tang Shan." In Naquin and Yü 1992, 293–332.

———. 1993a. "L'espace sacré taoïste." In Blanchon 1993, 323–31. Also published in English as "Taoist Ritual Space and Dynastic Legitimacy," *CEA* 8 (1993): 87–94.

———. 1993b. "*Wu Yüeh ch'un ch'iu*." In Loewe 1993, 473–76.

———. 1994. "Le sacrifice taoïste." In Neusch 1994, 249–73.

———. 1996. "Entre taoïsme et cultes populaires." *BEFEO* 83: 438–58.

———. 2004a. "Deux écrits taoïstes anciens." *CEA* 14: 139–71.

———, ed. 2004b. *Religion and Chinese Society*. 2 vols. Hong Kong: Chinese University Press and École Française d'Extrême-Orient.

Lai Chi-tim. 1998a. "Ko Hung's Discourse of Hsien Immortality: A Taoist Configuration of an Alternate Ideal Self-Identity." *Numen* 45: 1–38.

———. 1998b. "The Opposition of Celestial-Master Taoism to Popular Cults during the Six Dynasties." *AM*, third series, 11: 1–20.

———. 2002. "The *Demon Statutes of Nüqing* and the Problem of the Bureaucratization of the Netherworld in Early Heavenly Master Daoism." *TP* 88: 251–81.

———. 2003. "Daoism in China Today, 1980–2002." In Overmyer 2003, 107–121.

Lai T'ien-ch'ang. 1972. *The Eight Immortals*. Kowloon, Hong Kong: Swindon.

Lai, Whalen, and Lewis R. Lancaster, eds. 1983. *Early Chan in China and Tibet*. Berkeley: Berkeley Buddhist Studies Series.

Lanciotti, Lionello, ed. 1984. *Incontro di religioni in Asia tra il III e il X secolo d. C.* Firenze: Leo S. Olschki.

Lanciotti, Lionello, and Piero Corradini, eds. 1979. *Understanding Modern China: Problems and Methods*. Roma: Centro Ricerche Sinologiche, Istituto Italiano per il Medio ed Estremo Oriente.

Landt, Frank A. 1994. *Die fünf heiligen Berge Chinas: Ihre Bedeutung und Bewertung in der Ch'ing Dynastie*. Berlin: Köster.

Langlois, John D., Jr., ed. 1981. *China under Mongol Rule*. Princeton: Princeton University Press.

Lao Gewen 勞格文 [John Lagerwey] and Lü Chuikuan 呂錘寬. 1993. "Zhejiang sheng Cangnan diqu de daojiao wenhua" 浙江省倉南地區的道教文化 [Taoist culture in the Cangnan region of Zhejiang]. *Dongfang zongjiao yanjiu* 東方宗教研究 3: 171–98.

Larre, Claude. 1977. *Tao Te King: Le Livre de la Voie et de la Vertu*. Paris: Desclée de Brouwer.

———. 1982. *Le Traité VII du Houai nan tseu: Les esprits légers et subtils animateurs de l'essence*. Taipei, Paris, and Hong Kong: Institut Ricci.

Larre, Claude, Isabelle Robinet, and Elisabeth Rochat de la Vallée. 1993. *Les grands traités du Huainan zi*. Paris: Institut Ricci, Éditions du Cerf.

Lau, D. C. 1982. *Tao Te Ching*. Hong Kong: Hong Kong University Press.

Lau, D. C., and Roger T. Ames. 1996. *Sun Pin: The Art of Warfare*. New York: Ballantine Books.

———. 1998. *Yuan Dao: Tracing Dao to its Source*. New York: Ballantine Books.

Law, Jane Marie, ed. 1995. *Religious Reflections on the Human Body*. Bloomington and Indianapolis: Indiana University Press.

Le Blanc, Charles. 1985. *Huai-nan tzu: Philosophical Synthesis in Early Han Thought. The Idea of Resonance (Kan-ying), With a Translation and Analysis of Chapter Six*. Hong Kong: Hong Kong University Press.

———. 1989. "From Ontology to Cosmogony: Notes on *Chuang Tzu* and *Huai-nan Tzu*." In Le Blanc and Blader 1989, 117–29.

———. 1993. "*Huai nan tzu*." In Loewe 1993, 189–95.

———. 2000. *Le Wen zi à la lumière de l'histoire et de l'archéologie*. Montréal: Presses de l'Université de Montréal.

Le Blanc, Charles, and Rémi Mathieu, eds. 1992. *Mythe et philosophie à l'aube de la Chine impériale: Études sur le Huainan zi*. Montréal: Presses de l'Université de Montréal.

Le Blanc, Charles, and Rémi Mathieu. 2003. *Philosophes taoïstes*. Vol. 2: *Huainan zi*. Paris: Gallimard.

Le Blanc, Charles, and Susan Blader, eds. 1989. *Chinese Ideas about Nature and Society: Studies in Honour of Derk Bodde*. Hong Kong: Hong Kong University Press.

Lee Cheuk Yin 李焯然 and Chan Man Sing 陳萬成, eds. 2002. *Daoyuan binfen lu* 道苑 繽紛錄 [A Taoist florilegium]. Hong Kong: Shangwu yinshuguan.

Lee, Mabel, and A. D. Syrokomla-Stefanowska. 1993. *Modernization of the Chinese Past*. Broadway, Australia: Wild Peony.

Legeza, László. 1975. *Tao Magic: The Secret Language of Diagrams and Calligraphy*. London: Thames and Hudson.

Legge, James. 1872. *The Ch'un Ts'ew, with The Tso Chuen*. The Chinese Classics, 5. Oxford: Clarendon Press.

———. 1879. *The Shoo king*. The Texts of Confucianism, 1; The Sacred Books of the East, edited by F. Max Müller, 3. Oxford: Clarendon Press.

———. 1885. *The Lî kî: Book of Rites*. The Texts of Confucianism, 3–4; The Sacred Books of the East, edited by F. Max Müller, 27–28. 2 vols. Oxford: Clarendon Press.

———. 1891. *The Texts of Taoism*. The Sacred Books of the East, edited by F. Max Müller, 39–40. 2 vols. Oxford: Clarendon Press.

———. 1893. *Confucian Analects, The Great Learning, and The Doctrine of the Mean*. The Chinese Classics, 1. Second revised edition. Oxford: Clarendon Press.

———. 1895. *The Works of Mencius*. The Chinese Classics, 2. Second revised edition. Oxford: Clarendon Press.

Lei Hongan 雷宏安. 1989–90. "Lijiang Dongjing hui diaocha" 丽江洞经会调查 [An inquiry into the *Dongjing* associations of Lijiang]. Parts 1 and 2. *ZY* 1989.3–4: 47–54; 1990.1–2: 29–34.

Lemoine, Jacques. 1982. *Yao Ceremonial Paintings*. With the assistance of Donald Gibson. Bangkok: White Lotus.

———. 1983. "Yao Religion and Society." In McKinnon and Bhruksasri 1983, 194–211.

Lemoine, Jacques, and Chiao Chien, eds. 1991. *The Yao of South China: Recent International Studies*. Paris: Pangu.

Leslie, Donald D., Colin Mackerras, and Wang Gungwu, eds. 1973. *Essays on the Sources of Chinese History*. Canberra: Australian National University Press.

Lévi, Jean. 1983. "L'abstinence des céréales chez les taoïstes." *Études chinoises* 1: 3–47.

———. 1989a. *Les fonctionnaires divins: Politique, despotisme et mystique en Chine ancienne*. Paris: Éditions du Seuil.

———. 1989b. "The Body: The Taoists' Coat of Arms." In Feher 1989, 1: 105–26.

Levy, Howard S. 1956. "Yellow Turban Religion and Rebellion at the End of the Han." *JAOS* 76: 214–27.

———. 1965. *The Dwelling of Playful Goddesses: China's First Novelette*. Tokyo: Dai Nippon Insatsu.

Lewis, Mark E. 1990. *Sanctioned Violence in Early China*. Albany: State University of New York Press.

Li Dahua 李大華. 1995. "Lun *Yinfu jng* chansheng de lishi guocheng ji qi Tangdai quanshi de sixiang tedian" 論「陰符經」產生的歷史過程及其唐代詮釋的思想特點 [The historical process of formation of the *Yinfu jing*, and the distinctive traits of the thought of its Tang-dynasty commentaries]. *DWY* 7: 259–74.

———. 1996. "Lun Peng Xiao de 'huandan' shuo ji qi 'shu' lun" 論彭曉的「还丹」说及其「数」论 [Peng Xiao's notion of the Reverted Elixir and its numerology]. *SZY* 1996.2: 52–58.

Li Daoping 李道平. 1994. *Zhouyi jijie zuanshu* 「周易」集解纂疏 [Collected commentaries to the *Book of Changes*]. Beijing: Zhonghua shuju.

Li Defan 李德范, ed. 1999. *Dunhuang daozang* 敦煌道藏 [Taoist Canon of Dunhuang]. 5 vols. Beijing: Quanguo tushuguan wenxian suowei fuzhi zhongxin.

Li Ding 李鼎, ed. 1984. *Jingluo xue* 经络学 [The acumoxa conduits]. Shanghai: Shanghai kexue jishu chubanshe.

Li Fengmao 李豐楙. 1986. *Liuchao, Sui, Tang xiandaolei xiaoshuo yanjiu* 六朝隋唐仙道類小說研究 [Studies on Taoist fiction from the Six Dynasties, Sui, and Tang periods]. Taipei: Taiwan xuesheng shuju.

———. 1993a. "*Daozang* suo shou zaoqi daoshu de wenyi guan" 道藏所收早期道書的瘟疫觀 [Concepts of epidemics as seen in early Taoist texts preserved in the Taoist Canon]. *ZZJ* 3: 1–38.

———. 1993b. *Donggang wangchuan ji* 東港王船祭 [The Plague Boat ceremony at East Haven]. Pingdong: Pingdong xian zhengfu.

———. 1994. "Xingwen yu songwen: Wenshen xinyang yu zhuyi yishi de yiyi" 行瘟與送瘟—瘟神信仰與逐疫儀式的意義 [Spreading and sending off epidemics: The significance of Plague God cults and Plague Expulsion liturgies]. In Hanxue yanjiu zhongxin 1994, 1: 373–422.

———. 1996. *Wuru yu zhexiang: Liuchao, Sui, Tang daojiao wenxue lunji* 誤入與謫降—六朝隋唐道教文學論集 [Mistaken ascent and banishment: Studies on the Taoist literature of the Six Dynasties, Sui, and Tang periods]. Taipei: Taiwan xuesheng shuju.

Li Guohao 李国豪, Zhang Mengwen 张孟闻, and Cao Tianqin 曹天钦, eds. 1982. *Explorations in the History of Science and Technology in China*. Shanghai: Shanghai

Chinese Classics Publishing House. Also published in Chinese as *Zhongguo keijishi tansuo* 中国科技史探索 [Explorations in the history of Chinese science and technology] (Shanghai: Shanghai guji chubanshe, 1982).

Li Guorong 李国荣. 1994. *Diwang yu liandan* 帝王与炼丹 [Emperors and alchemy]. Beijing: Zhongyang minzu daxue chubanshe.

Li Huilin. 1979. *Nan-fang ts'ao-mu chuang: A Fourth Century Flora of Southeast Asia*. Hong Kong: Chinese University Press.

Li Jianguo 李剑国. 1984. *Tang qian zhiguai xiaoshuo shi* 唐前志怪小说史 [A history of pre-Tang "Records of the Strange"]. Tianjin: Nankai daxue chubanshe.

Li Ling 李零. 1991. "Mawangdui Hanmu 'Shenqi tu' yingshu bibing tu" 马王堆汉墓「神祇图」应属辟兵图 [The "Divinity Chart" of the Han tombs in Mawangdui as a chart for avoiding harm from weapons]. *Kaogu* 考古 1991.10: 940–42.

———. 1994. "Kaogu faxian yu shenhua chuanshuo" 考古發現與神話傳說 [Archaeological discoveries and mythological traditions]. *Xueren* 學人 5: 115–47.

———. 1995. *Sunzi guben yanjiu* 「孙子」古本研究 [A study of the ancient editions of the *Sunzi*]. Beijing: Beijing daxue chubanshe.

———. 1995–96. "An Archaeological Study of Taiyi (Grand One) Worship." Translated by Donald Harper. *Early Medieval China* 2: 1–39. Also published in Chinese as "Taiyi chongbai de kaogu yanjiu" 太一崇拜的考古研究, in Li Ling 2000b, 207–38.

———. 2000a. *Zhongguo fangshu kao* 中国方术考 [Studies on the Chinese "Methods and Arts"]. Revised edition. Beijing: Zhongguo renmin chubanshe.

———. 2000b. *Zhongguo fangshu xukao* 中国方术续考 [Further studies on the Chinese "Methods and Arts"]. Beijing: Zhongguo renmin chubanshe.

Li Lulu 李露露. 1994. *Mazu xinyang* 妈祖信仰 [The cult of Mazu]. Beijing: Xueyuan chubanshe.

Li Mingyou 李明友. 1992. "*Guang hongming ji* yu Sui Tang chuqi de fo dao ru lunzheng" 「广弘明集」与隋唐初期的佛道儒论争 [The *Guang hongming ji* and the polemics among Buddhism, Taoism, and Confucianism in the Sui and early Tang periods]. *SZY* 1992.2: 78–88.

Li Shen 李申. 1991. "*Taiji tu* yuanyuan bian" 「太极图」渊源辨 [An inquiry into the origins of the *Taiji tu*]. *Zhouyi yanjiu* 周易研究 1991.1: 24–35.

———. 1995. "Cong daojia dao daojiao" 從道家到道教 [From *daojia* to *daojiao*]. *DWY* 7: 59–69.

Li Shiyu 李世瑜. 1957. "Baojuan xinyan" 寶卷新研 [A new study of the "Precious Scrolls"]. *Wenxue yichan zengkan* 文學遺產增刊 4: 165–81.

———. 1961. *Baojuan zonglu* 寶卷綜錄 [A catalogue of "Precious Scrolls"]. Shanghai: Zhonghua shuju.

Li Xianzhang 李獻璋. 1968. "Daojiao jiaoyi de kaizhan yu xiandai de jiao: Yi Taiwan Zhanghua Nanyao gong de Qingcheng qingjiao wei xiandai jiaoli" 道教醮儀的開展與現代的醮—以臺灣彰化南瑤宮的慶成清醮為現代醮例 [The development of Taoist *jiao* liturgy and the present-day *jiao*: The Pure Offering for celebrating the completion of the Nanyao gong in Zhanghua, Taiwan, as a present-day example of a *jiao*]. *Chūgoku gakushi* 中國學誌 5: 201–62.

———. 1979. *Maso shinkō no kenkyū* 媽祖信仰の研究 [Studies on the cult of Mazu]. Tokyo: Taizan bunbutsusha.

Li Xianzhou 里仙舟. 1983. "Yongji gumiao: Yongle gong" 永濟古廟—永樂宮 [The ancient shrine of Yongji: The Yongle gong]. *Shanxi wenxian* 山西文獻 22: 101–5.

Li Xueqin 李学勤. 1990. "Fan Li sixiang yu boshu Huangdi shu" 范蠡思想与帛书黄帝书 [The thought of Fan Li and the silk manuscript of the "Books of the Yellow Emperor"]. *Zhejiang xuekan* 浙江学刊 1990.1: 97–99.

Li Yangzheng 李养正, ed. 2000. *Dangdai daojiao* 当代道教 [Contemporary Taoism]. Beijing: Dongfang chubanshe.

Li Yuanguo 李远国. 1985a. "Daojiao qigong yu neidan shu yanjiu" 道教气功与内丹术研究 [A study of Taoist *qigong* and inner alchemy]. In Li Yuanguo 1985b, 44–63.

———. 1985b. *Daojiao yanjiu wenji* 道教研究文集 [Studies on Taoism]. Chengdu: Sichuan sheng Shehui kexueyuan Zhexue yanjiusuo.

———. 1985c. "Shilun Chen Tuan de yuzhou shengcheng lun" 试论陈抟的宇宙生成论 [A preliminary study of Chen Tuan's theories on the generation of the cosmos]. *SZY* 1985.2: 48–61.

———. 1987. "Chen Tuan *Wuji tu* sixiang tansuo, jianji qi yuanyuan yu yingxiang de kaocha" 陈抟「无极图」思想探索—兼及其渊源与影响的考察 [An exploration of the thought of Chen Tuan's *Wuji tu*, with notes on its origins and influence]. *SZY* 1987.2: 95–105.

———. 1988. *Daojiao qigong yangshengxue* 道教气功养生学 [Taoist *qigong* and the Nourishment of Life]. Chengdu: Sichuan sheng shehui kexueyuan chubanshe.

———. 1990. "Chen Tuan's Concepts of the Great Ultimate." *TR* 2.1: 32–53.

———. 1991. "Shilun Chen Zhixu de *Jindan dayao*" 试论陈致虚的金丹大要 [A preliminary study of Chen Zhixu's *Jindan dadao*]. *ZGDJ* 1991.1: 44–48.

———. 2002. "Daojiao leifa yange kao" 道教雷法沿革考 [A study of the evolution of the Taoist Thunder Rites]. *SZY* 2002.3: 88–96.

Liao, W. K. 1939–59. *The Complete Works of Han Fei Tzu: A Classic of Chinese Legalism*. 2 vols. London: Arthur Probsthain.

Libbrecht, Ulrich. 1990. "Prāna = Pneuma = Ch'i?" In Idema and Zürcher 1990, 42–62.

Liebenthal, Walter. 1952. "The Immortality of the Soul in Chinese Thought." *Monumenta Nipponica* 8: 327–97.

Lin Congshun 林聰舜. 1991. *Xi Han qianqi sixiang yu Fajia de guanxi* 西漢前期思想與法家的關係 [The thought of the early Han period and its relation to Legalism]. Taipei: Da'an chubamshe.

Lin Fushi 林富士. 1988. *Handai de wuzhe* 漢代的巫者 [Han dynasty shamans]. Taipei: Daoxiang chubanshe.

Lin Fu-shih. 1995. "Religious Taoism and Dreams: An Analysis of the Dream-Data Collected in the *Yün-chi ch'i-ch'ien*." *CEA* 8: 95–112.

Lin Guoping 林国平 and Peng Wenyu 彭文宇. 1993. *Fujian minjian xinyang* 福建民间信仰 [Popular cults in Fujian]. Fuzhou: Fujian renmin chubanshe.

Lin Meirong 林美容, ed. 1997. *Taiwan minjian xinyang yanjiu shumu (zengding ban)* 臺灣民間信仰研究書目（增訂版）[A bibliography of studies on Taiwanese popular cults (enlarged edition)]. Taipei: Zhongyang yanjiuyuan Minzuxue yanjiusuo.

Lin Shengli 林胜利. 1989. "Zixiao zhenren Tan Qiao kaolüe" 紫霄真人谭峭考略 [A brief study of Tan Qiao, the Perfected of the Purple Empyrean]. *ZGDJ* 1989.3: 33–34.

Lin Wanchuan 林萬傳. 1986. *Xiantian dao yanjiu* 先天道研究 [A study of the Way of the Prior Heavenly Realm]. Tainan: Tianju shuju.

Lin Yuping 林玉萍. 1995. "Liang Han shiqi Han yi yu fangshi yi de bijiao yanjiu" 兩漢時期漢醫與方士醫的比較研究 [A comparative study of classical Chinese medicine and the medicine of the *fangshi*]. *DT* 9: 42–57.

Lin Yutang. 1938. *The Wisdom of Confucius*. New York: The Modern Library.

Little, Stephen. 2000a. "Daoist Art." In Kohn 2000b, 709–46.

———. 2000b. *Taoism and the Arts of China*. With Shawn Eichman. Chicago: The Art Institute of Chicago.

Liu Hui 劉慧. 1994. *Taishan zongjiao yanjiu* 泰山宗教研究 [History of religion on Mount Tai]. Beijing: Wenwu chubanshe.

Liu Ts'un-yan [柳存仁]. 1965. "Lu Hsi-hsing: A Confucian Scholar, Taoist Priest and Buddhist Devotee of the Sixteenth Century." *ASEA* 18–19: 115–42. Reprinted in Liu Ts'un-yan 1976b, 175–202.

———. 1967. "Lin Chao-ên (1517–1598): The Master of the Three Teachings." *TP* 53: 252–78. Reprinted in Liu Ts'un-yan 1976b, 149–74.

———. 1968. "Lu Hsi-hsing and his Commentaries on the *Ts'an-t'ung-ch'i*." *Qinghua xuebao* 清華學報 (*The Tsing Hua Journal of Chinese Studies*), n.s., 7: 71–98. Reprinted in Liu Ts'un-yan 1976b, 203–31.

———. 1970. "Taoist Self-Cultivation in Ming Thought." In de Bary and the Conference on Ming Thought 1970, 291–330.

———. 1971. "The Penetration of Taoism into the Ming Neo-Confucianist Elite." *TP* 57: 31–102.

———. 1973. "The Compilation and Historical Value of the Tao-tsang." In Leslie, Mackerras, and Wang 1973, 104–19.

———. 1976a. "Lu Hsi-hsing." In Goodrich and Fang 1976, 991–94.

———. 1976b. *Selected Papers from the Hall of the Harmonious Wind*. Leiden: E. J. Brill.

———. 1976c. "Shao Yüan-chieh." In Goodrich and Fang 1976, 1169–70.

———. 1976d. "T'ao Chung-wen." In Goodrich and Fang 1976, 1266–68.

———. 1977. "Zhang Boduan yu *Wuzhen pian*" 張伯端與「悟真篇」 [Zhang Boduan and the *Wuzhen pian*]. In Yoshioka Yoshitoyo hakase kanreki kinen kenkyū ronshū kankōkai 1977, 791–803.

———. 1982. "*Daozang* keben zhi sige riqi" 道藏刻本之四個日期 [The four dates of the printing of the Taoist Canon]. In Sakai Tadao sensei koki shukuga kinen no kai 1982, 1049–67.

———. 1984a. *New Excursions from the Hall of Harmonious Wind*. Leiden: E. J. Brill.

———. 1984b. "Wu Shou-yang: The Return to the Pure Essence." In Liu Ts'un-yan 1984a, 184–208.

———. 1997. *Hefeng tang xinwen ji* 和風堂新文集 [New essays from the Hall of Harmonious Wind]. Taipei: Xinwenfeng chuban gongsi.

———. 2006. "Was Celestial Master Zhang a Historical Figure?" In Penny 2006, 189–263.

Liu Ts'un-yan and Judith Berling. 1982. "The 'Three Teachings' in the Mongol-Yüan Period." In Chan and de Bary 1982, 479–512.

Liu Yang. 2001a. "Images for the Temple: Imperial Patronage in the Development of Tang Daoist Art." *Artibus Asiae* 61: 189–261.

———. 2001b. "Origins of Daoist Iconography." *Ars Orientalis* 31: 31–64.

Liu Zhiwan 劉枝萬. 1983a. "Taiwan dōkyō no hōki" 臺湾道教の法器 [Ritual tools of Taoism in Taiwan]. In Fukui Kōjun et al. 1983, 3: 2–9 (front matter).

———. 1983b. *Taiwan minjian xinyang lunji* 臺灣民間信仰論集 [Studies on popular cults in Taiwan]. Taipei: Lianjing chuban shiye gongsi.

———. 1983c. "Taiwan no dōkyō" 臺湾の道教 [Taoism in Taiwan]. In Fukui Kōjun et al. 1983, 3: 129–71.

———. 1983–84. *Chūgoku dōkyō no matsuri to shinkō* 中國道教の祭りと信仰 [Festivals and cults of Chinese Taoism]. 2 vols. Tokyo: Eifusha.

———. 1986. "Raishin shinkō to raihō no tenkai" 雷神信仰と雷法の展開 [The cult of the Thunder deity and the development of the Thunder Rites]. *TS* 67: 1–21.

———. 1987. "Tenhōshin to tenhōju ni tsuite" 天蓬神と天蓬呪について [The Tianpeng deity and the *tianpeng* spell]. In Akizuki Kan'ei 1987, 403–24.

———. 1994. *Taiwan no dōkyō to minkan shinkō* 臺湾の道教と民間信仰 [Taoism and popular cults in Taiwan]. Tokyo: Fūkyōsha.

Liu Zhongyu 刘仲宇. 1993. "*Sanhuang wen* xintan" 「三皇文」新探 [A new exploration of the *Sanhuang wen*]. *ZGDJ* 1993.3: 27–31.

———. 2002. "Jianlun daojiao fashu keyi de biaoyan tezheng" 简论道教法术科仪的表演特征 [A brief discussion of the performative aspects of Taoist ritual practice]. *SZY* 2002.2: 111–19.

Liu, James J. Y. 1987. "Poetry: Chinese Religious Poetry." In Eliade 1987, 11: 378–80.

Liu Xiaogan. 1991. "*Wuwei* (Non-Action): From *Laozi* to *Huainanzi*." *TR* 3.1: 41–56.

———. 1994. *Classifying the Zhuangzi Chapters*. Ann Arbor: Center for Chinese Studies, University of Michigan.

———. 1998. "Naturalness (*Tzu-jan*), the Core Value in Taoism: Its Ancient Meaning and its Significance Today." In Kohn and LaFargue 1998, 211–28.

Lo, Vivienne. 1993. "The Legend of the Lady of Linshui." *JCR* 21: 69–96.

———. 2001. "The Influence of Nurturing Life Culture on the Development of Western Han Acumoxa Therapy." In Hsu Elisabeth 2001, 19–50.

Loewe, Michael. 1974. *Crisis and Conflict in Han China, 104 BC to AD 9*. London: George Allen and Unwin.

———. 1977. "Manuscripts Found Recently in China: A Preliminary Survey." *TP* 63: 99–136.

———. 1979. *Ways to Paradise: The Chinese Quest for Immortality*. London: George Allen and Unwin.

———. 1982. *Chinese Ideas of Life and Death: Faith, Myth, and Reason in the Han Period (202 BC-AD 220)*. London: George Allen and Unwin.

———. 1987. "Hsi Wang Mu." In Eliade 1987, 6: 479–80.

———. 1993. *Early Chinese Texts: A Bibliographical Guide*. Berkeley: Society for the Study of Early China and Institute of East Asian Studies, University of California.

———. 1994a. *Divination, Mythology and Monarchy in Han China*. Cambridge: Cambridge University Press.

———. 1994b. "Huang Lao Thought and the *Huainanzi*." *JRAS*, third series, 4: 377–95.

Loewe, Michael, and Edward L. Shaughnessy, eds. 1999. *The Cambridge History of Ancient China: From the Origins to 221 B.C.* Cambridge: Cambridge University Press.

Long Bide 龍彼得 [Piet van der Loon]. 1993. "Fashi xi chutan" 法事戲初探 [A preliminary exploration of liturgical drama]. *Minsu quyi* 民俗曲藝 84: 9–30.

Lopez, Donald S., Jr., ed. 1996. *Religions of China in Practice*. Princeton: Princeton University Press.

Lou Yulie 樓宇烈. 1980. *Wang Bi ji jiaoshi* 王弼集校釋 [Annotated critical edition of Wang Bi's works]. Beijing: Zhonghua shuju.

Lü Ch'ui-k'uan [Lü Chuikuan] 呂錘寬. 1988. "Taiwan de daojiao yinyue yuanliu lüegao" 臺灣的道教音樂源流略稿 [An outline of the origins and development of Taoist music in Taiwan]. *CEA* 4: 79–126. Includes a French summary by John Lagerwey, "Sur la musique taoïste de Taiwan" (pp. 113–26).

Lü Chuikuan 呂錘寬, ed. 1994. *Taiwan de daojiao yishi yu yinyue* 臺灣的道教儀式與音樂 [Taoist liturgy and music in Taiwan]. Taipei: Xueyi chubanshe.

Lü Chui-kuan [Lü Chuikuan] 呂錘寬 and John Lagerwey. 1992. "Le taoïsme du district de Cangnan, Zhejiang." *BEFEO* 79: 19–55.

Lu Gong 路工. 1982. "Daojiao yishu de zhenpin: Ming Liaoning kanben *Taishang Laojun bashiyi hua tushuo*" 道教艺术的珍品—明辽宁刊本「太上老君八十一化图说」 [A gem of Taoist art: The Ming-dynasty Liaoning edition of the *Taishang Laojun bashiyi hua tushuo*]. *SZY* 1982.2: 51–55.

Lu Guolong 廬國龍. 1993. *Zhongguo chongxuanxue* 中国重玄学 [The doctrine of the Twofold Mystery in China]. Beijing: Renmin Zhongguo chubanshe.

———. 1994. "Sun Deng 'tuo chongxuan yi jizong' de sixiang genyuan" 孫登 "托重玄以寄宗" 的思想根源 [The origins of the thought of Sun Deng and its foundations in the Twofold Mystery]. *DWY* 4: 300–317.

Lu Gwei-Djien and Joseph Needham. 1980. *Celestial Lancets: A History and Rationale of Acupuncture and Moxa*. Cambridge: Cambridge University Press.

Lu Renlong 卢仁龙. 1990. "Zhang Junfang shiji kaoshu" 张君房事迹考述 [An investigation into the life of Zhang Junfang]. *SZY* 1990.1: 55–64.

Lü Xichen 呂錫琛. 1991. *Daojia, fangshi yu wangchao zhengzhi* 道家、方士与王朝政治 [Taoism, the "masters of methods," and the imperial government]. Changsha: Hunan chubanshe.

Lu Yusan 卢育三. 1987. "'Fan zhe dao zhi dong' zhuyi" 「反者道之动」刍议 [An opinion on "Return is the movement of the Dao"]. *Zhongguo zhexueshi yanjiu* 中国哲学史研究 1: 26–31.

Lü Zongli 呂宗力 and Luan Baoqun 欒保群. 1991. *Zhongguo minjian zhushen* 中國民間諸神 [Chinese popular gods]. Taipei: Taiwan xuesheng shuju.

Lu K'uan Yü (Charles Luk). 1964. *The Secrets of Chinese Meditation: Self-Cultivation by Mind Control as Taught in the Ch'an Mahayana and Taoist schools in China*. London: Rider.

———. 1970. *Taoist Yoga: Alchemy and Immortality. A Translation, with Introduction and Notes, of The Secrets of Cultivating Essential Nature and Eternal Life (Hsing Ming Fa Chueh Ming Chih) by the Taoist Master Chao Pi Ch'en, born 1860*. London: Rider. Reprint, New York: Samuel Weiser, 1973.

Luo Fuyi 罗福颐. 1974. "Linyi Hanjian gaishu" 临沂汉简概述 [Summary report on the Han bamboo slips from Linyi]. *Wenwu* 文物 19742: 32–35.

———. 1985. "Linyi Hanjian suojian guji gailüe" 临沂汉简所见古籍概略 [Summary

of the ancient texts in the Han bamboo slips from Linyi]. *Guwenzi yanjiu* 古文字
研究 11: 10–51.

Luo Shizheng 骆士正 et. al., eds. 1987. *Yongle gong de chuanshuo* 永乐宫的传说 [Traditions on the Yongle gong]. Ruicheng: Zhongguo luyou chubanshe.

Lynn, Richard John. 1994. *The Classic of Changes: A New Translation of the I Ching as Interpreted by Wang Bi*. New York: Columbia University Press.

———. 1999. *The Classic of the Way and Virtue: A New Translation of the Tao-te Ching of Laozi as Interpreted by Wang Bi*. New York: Columbia University Press.

Ma Jixing 马继兴. 1990. *Zhongyi wenxianxue* 中医文献学 [A study of Chinese medical literature]. Shanghai: Shanghai kexue jishu chubanshe.

Ma Shutian 马书田. 1996. *Zhongguo daojiao zhushen* 中国道教诸神 [The gods of Chinese Taoism]. Beijing: Tuanjie chubanshe.

———. 1997. *Zhongguo minjian zhushen* 中国民间诸神 [Chinese popular gods]. Beijing: Tuanjie chubanshe.

Ma Xiaohong 马晓宏. 1986. "Lü Dongbin shenxian xinyang suyuan" 吕洞宾神仙信仰溯源 [Origins of the cult of the immortal Lü Dongbin]. *SZY* 1986.3: 79–95.

———. 1988a. "*Daozang* deng zhuben suoshou Lü Dongbin shumu jianzhu" 道藏等诸本所收吕洞宾书目简注 [A catalogue with brief annotations of Lü Dongbin's works in the *Daozang* and other collections]. *ZGDJ* 1988.3: 34–37.

———. 1988b. "Lü Dongbin wenji kao" 吕洞宾文集考 [A study of Lü Dongbin's collected works]. *ZGDJ* 1988.4: 37–40.

———. 1989b. "Lü Dongbin shici kao" 吕洞宾诗词考 [A study of Lü Dongbin's poems]. *ZGDJ* 1989.1: 30–32.

———. 1989a. "Lü Dongbin jinggao kao" 吕洞宾经诰考 [A study of Lü Dongbin's scriptures and pronouncements]. *ZGDJ* 1989.2: 39–42.

———. 1998. "The First Taoist Pantheon: T'ao Hung-ching (456–536 CE) and his 'Chen-ling-wei-yeh-t'u.'" Ph.D. diss., Temple University.

Ma Xisha 马西沙. 1986. "Zuizao yibu baojuan de yanjiu" 最早一部宝卷的研究 [A study of the earliest "Precious Scroll"]. *SZY* 1986.1: 56–72.

———. 1994. "Baojuan yu daojiao de lianyang sixiang" 宝卷与道教的炼养思想 [The "Precious Scrolls" and Taoist conceptions of refining and nourishing]." *SZY* 1994.3: 63–73.

Ma Xisha 马西沙 and Han Bingfang 韩秉芳. 1992. *Zhongguo minjian zongjiao shi* 中国民间宗教史 [History of Chinese popular religion]. Shanghai: Shanghai renmin chubanshe.

MacDonald, A. W., ed. 1997. *Mandala and Landscape*. New Delhi: D. K. Printworld.

Maeda Ryōichi 前田良一. 1989. "'Kyū kyū nyo ritsurei' o sagaru" 「急急如律令」を探る [On "Promptly, promptly, in accordance with the statutes and ordinances!"]. In Fukunaga Mitsuji 1989, 121–25.

Maeda Shigeki 前田繁樹. 1985a. "Rikuchō jidai ni okeru Kan Kichi den no hensen" 六朝時代に於ける干吉傳の變遷 [Changes in the biography of Gan Ji during the Six Dynasties]. *TS* 65: 44–62.

———. 1985b. "*Rōkun setsu ippyaku hachijū kai jo* no seiritsu ni tsuite" 「老君説一百八十戒序」の成立について [On the compilation of the *Preface to the Hundred and Eighty Precepts Spoken by Lord Lao*]. *Tōyō no shisō to shūkyō* 東洋の思想と宗教 2: 81–94.

———. 1988. "*Rōshi chūkyō* oboegaki"「老子中經」覚書 [Notes on the *Laozi zhongjing*]. In Sakade Yoshinobu 1988a, 474–502.

———. 1989. "*Rōshi saishōkyō* no tekisuto ni tsuite"「老子西昇經」のテキストについて [On the text of the *Laozi xisheng jing*]. *Yamamura joshi tanki daigaku kiyō* 山村女子短期大學紀要 1: 1–30.

———. 1990a. "Butsu-dō ronsō ni okeru *Rōshi saishōkyō*" 佛道論爭における「老子西昇經」 [The *Laozi xisheng jing* in the debates between Buddhists and Taoists]. *TS* 75: 61–77.

———. 1990b. "*Rōshi saishō kyō kō*"「老子西昇經」考 [A study of the *Laozi xisheng jing*]. *NCG* 42: 77–90.

———. 1995. "The Evolution of the Way of the Celestial Masters: Its Early View of Divinities." *Acta Asiatica* 68: 54–68.

Maejima Shinji 前島信次. 1938. "Taiwan no onyakugami, ōya, to sōō no fūshū ni tsuite" 臺湾の瘟疫神、大爺、と送王の風習について [On the Plague Gods, the Royal Lords, and the custom of "sending off the plague boat" in Taiwan]. *Minzokugaku kenkyū* 民族學研究 4.4: 25–66.

Mair, Victor H., ed. 1983a. *Chuang-tzu: Composition and Interpretation.* Symposium issue. *JCR* 11.

———, ed. 1983b. *Experimental Essays on Chuang-tzu.* Honolulu: University of Hawaii Press.

——— 1990. *Tao Te Ching: The Classic Book of Integrity and the Way.* New York: Bantam Books.

——— 1994. *Wandering on the Way: Early Taoist Tales and Parables of Chuang Tzu.* New York: Bantam Books.

——— 2000. "The *Zhuangzi* and its Impact." In Kohn 2000b, 30–52.

Major, John S. 1978. "Myth, Cosmology, and the Origins of Chinese Science." *JCP* 5: 1–20.

———. 1984. "The Five Phases, Magic Squares, and Schematic Cosmography." In Rosemont 1984, 133–66.

———. 1985–86. "New Light on the Dark Warrior." *JCR* 13–14: 65–86.

———. 1987a. "Ch'i." In Eliade 1987, 3: 238–39.

———. 1987b. "Yin-Yang Wu-hsing." In Eliade 1987, 15: 515–16.

———. 1990. "Numerology in the *Huai-nan-tzu*." In Smith K. 1990, 3–10.

———. 1991. "Substance, Process, Phase: *Wuxing* in the *Huainanzi*." In Rosemont 1991, 67–78.

———. 1993. *Heaven and Earth in Early Han Thought: Chapters Three, Four and Five of the Huainanzi.* With an appendix by Christopher Cullen. Albany: State University of New York Press.

Makio Ryōkai hakushi shōju kinen ronshū kankōkai 牧尾良海博士頌壽記念論集刊行会 [Editorial Committee for the Collected Essays Presented to Dr. Makio Ryōkai on his Seventieth Birthday], ed. 1984. *Makio Ryōkai hakushi shōju kinen ronshū: Chūgoku no shūkyō, shisō to kagaku* 牧尾良海博士頌壽記念論集—中國の宗教・思想と科學 [Religion, thought and science in China: Collected essays presented to Dr. Makio Ryōkai on his seventieth birthday]. Tokyo: Kokusho kankōkai.

Makita Tairyō 牧田諦亮, ed. 1973–75. *Gumyōshū kenkyū* 弘明集研究 [Studies on the *Hongming ji*]. 3 vols. Kyoto: Kyōto daigaku Jinbun kagaku kenkyūjo.

———. 1976. *Gikyō kenkyū* 疑經研究 [Studies on apocryphal *sūtras*]. Kyoto: Kyōto daigaku Jinbun kagaku kenkyūjo.

Malamoud, Charles, and Jean-Pierre Vernant, eds. 1986. *Corps des dieux*. Le temps de la réflexion, 7. Paris: Gallimard.

Malek, Roman. 1985. *Das Chai-chieh-lu: Materialen zur Liturgie im Taoismus*. Frankfurt: Peter Lang.

Mansvelt Beck, Burchard. 1980. "The Date of the *Taiping jing*." *TP* 66: 149–82.

Marsone, Pierre. 1999. "Le Baiyun guan de Pékin." *Sanjiao wenxian: Matériaux pour l'étude de la religion chinoise* 3: 73–136.

———. 2001a. "Accounts of the Foundation of the Quanzhen Movement: A Hagiographic Treatment of History." *JCR* 29: 95–110.

———. 2001b. "Wang Chongyang (1113–1170) et la fondation du mouvement Quanzhen." Ph.D. diss., École Pratique des Hautes Études, Section des Sciences Religieuses.

Maruyama Hiroshi 丸山宏. 1986a. "Shōitsu dōkyō no jōshō girei ni tsuite: Chōshōshō o chūshin to shite" 正一道教の上章儀禮について―「冢訟章」を中心として [On the Zhengyi Taoist rite of submitting petitions, with special reference to the *Zhongsong zhang*]. *TS* 68: 44–64.

———. 1986b. "Yao zoku to dōkyō: Chūgoku ni okeru shūhen shōsū minzoku no dōkyō jūyō o megutte" ヤオ族と道教―中國における周邊少數民族の道教受容をめぐって [The Yao and Taoism: On the Taoism of a minority nationality in China]. *Shikyō* 史境 12: 10–18. With a comment by Oguma Makoto 小熊誠, 19–21.

———. 1992. "Tainan no dōkyō to *Dōzō hiyō*" 臺南の道教と「道藏祕要」 [Taoism in Tainan and the *Daozang miyao*]. In Sakai Tadao 1992, 43–90.

———. 1994a. "Kin Inchū no dōkyō gireigaku ni tsuite" 金允中の道教儀禮學について [On the study of Taoist ritual by Jin Yunzhong]. In Dōkyō bunka kenkyūkai 1994, 50–79.

———. 1994b. "Taiwan nanbu no kudoku ni tsuite: Dōkyō girei shi kara no kōsatsu" 臺湾南部の功徳について―道教儀礼史からの考察 [On the ritual of Merit in southern Taiwan: Notes based on the history of Taoist liturgy]. In Noguchi Tetsurō 1994, 15–47.

———. 1995. "The Historical Traditions of Contemporary Taoist Ritual." *Acta Asiatica* 68: 84–104.

Maspero, Henri. 1914. "Rapport sommaire sur une mission archéologique au Tchökiang." *BEFEO* 14.8: 1–75.

———. 1924. "Légendes mythologiques dans le Chou King." *Journal Asiatique* 204: 1–100.

———. 1933. "Le mot *ming* 明." *Journal Asiatique* 223: 249–96.

———. 1951. "Le Ming-t'ang et la crise religieuse avant les Han." *Mélanges chinois et bouddhiques* 9: 1–71. Bruxelles: Institut Belge des Hautes Études Chinoises.

———. 1981. *Taoism and Chinese Religion*. Translated by Frank A. Kierman, Jr. Amherst: University of Massachusetts Press. Originally published as *Le Taoïsme et les religions chinoises* (Paris: Gallimard, 1971).

Masuo Shin'ichirō 増尾伸一郎. 1988. "'Chōsei kyūshi' no hōhō to sono keifu: Nihon kodai no chishiki kaisō ni okeru yōsei to yakubutsu" 「長生久視」の方法とその系譜－日本古代の知識階層における養生と薬物－ [The methods of "long life and lasting presence" and their genealogy: Drugs and Nourishing Life among the intellectuals of ancient Japan]. In Sakade Yoshinobu 1988a, 725–50.

———. 1991. "Nihon kodai no chishikisō to Rōshi" 日本古代の知識層と「老子」 [Intellectuals in ancient Japan and the Laozi]. Toyoda tanki daigaku kenkyū kiyō 豊田短期大學研究紀要 1: 80–88.

———. 2000. "Daoism in Japan." In Kohn 2000b, 821–42.

Mather, Richard B. 1961. "The Mystical Ascent of the T'ien t'ai Mountains: Sun Ch'o's Yu T'ien-t'ai-shan fu." MS 20: 226–45.

———. 1976. Shih-shuo hsin-yu: A New Account of Tales of the World. Minneapolis: University of Minnesota Press.

———. 1979. "K'ou Ch'ien-chih and the Taoist Theocracy at the Northern Wei Court, 425–451." In Welch and Seidel 1979, 103–22.

———. 1987. "K'ou Ch'ien-chih." In Eliade 1987, 8: 377–79.

Mathieu, Rémi. 1978. Le Mu tianzi zhuan: Traduction annotée, étude critique. Paris: Collège de France, Institut des Hautes Études Chinoises.

——— 1983. Étude sur la mythologie et l'ethnologie de la Chine ancienne. 2 vols. Paris: Collège de France, Institut des Hautes Études Chinoises.

——— 1992. "Une création du monde." In Le Blanc and Mathieu 1992, 69–87.

——— 2000. Démons et merveilles dans la littérature chinoise des Six Dynasties: Le fantastique et l'anecdotique dans le Soushen ji de Gan Bao. Paris: Éditions You-Feng.

Matsumoto Kōichi 松本浩一. 1979. "Sōdai no raihō" 宋代の雷法 [The Thunder Rites of the Song dynasty]. Shakai bunkashi gaku 社会文化史學 17: 45–65.

———. 1982. "Chō Tenshi to Nan Sō no dōkyō" 張天師と南宋の道教 [The Zhang Celestial Masters and Taoism in the Southern Song period]. In Sakai Tadao sensei koki shukuga kinen no kai 1982, 337–50.

———. 1983. "Dōkyō to shūkyō girei" 道教と宗教儀礼 [Taoism and religious liturgies]. In Fukui Kōjun et al. 1983, 1: 189–237.

———. 1997. "Taihoku-shi no shibyō to reito hōkai" 太北市の祠廟と禮斗法會 [The Festival of Worshipping the Dippers and shrines in Taipei]. TS 90: 22–44.

Matsumura Takumi 松村巧. 1992. "Tenmon chito kō" 天文地戸考 [The Gate of Heaven and the Doorway of Earth]. In Yoshikawa Tadao 1992a, 145–74.

McGreal, Ian P., ed. 1995. Great Thinkers of the Eastern World. New York: Harper-Collins.

———, ed. 1996. Great Literature of the Eastern World. New York: HarperCollins.

McKinnon, John, and Wanat Bhruksasri, eds. 1983. Highlanders of Thailand. Kuala Lumpur: Oxford University Press.

Mei, Y. P. 1987. "Lieh-tzu." In Eliade 1987, 8: 540–41.

Meng Naichang 孟乃昌. 1989. "Shuo Zhongguo liandan shu nei-wai dan zhi lianxi" 说中国炼丹术内外丹之联系 [The relation between waidan and neidan in Chinese alchemy]. Parts 1 and 2. Shanghai daojiao 上海道教 1989.1–2: 32–38; 1989.3–4: 19–23.

———. 1993a. Daojiao yu Zhongguo liandan shu 道教与中国炼丹术 [Taoism and Chinese alchemy]. Beijing: Beijing Yanshan chubanshe.

———. 1993b. *Zhouyi cantong qi kaobian* 「周易参同契」考辯 [An inquiry into the *Zhouyi cantong qi*]. Shanghai: Shanghai guji chubanshe.

Meng Naichang 孟乃昌 and Meng Qingxuan 孟庆轩. 1993. *Wan gu danjing wang: "Zhouyi cantong qi" sanshisi jia zhushi jicui* 万古丹经王—「周易参同契」三十四家注释集萃 ["The King of Ancient Alchemical Scriptures": Selections from thirty-four commentaries to the *Zhouyi cantong qi*]. Beijing: Huaxia chubanshe.

Meng Wentong 蒙文通. 1945. "Jiaoli *Laozi Cheng Xuanying shu* xulu" 校理「老子成玄英疏」敘錄 [Introductory remarks to a critical edition of Cheng Xuanying's commentary to the *Laozi*]. *Tushu jikan* 圖書集刊 7: 1–24.

———. 1948a. "Jijiao *Laozi Li Rong zhu* ba" 輯校「老子李榮注」跋 [Postface to a critical edition of Li Rong's commentary to the *Laozi*]. *Tushu jikan* 圖書集刊 8: 1–8.

———. 1948b. "Yan Junping *Daode zhigui lun* yiwen" 嚴君平「道德指歸論」譯文 [An explanation of Yan Junping's *Daode zhigui lun*]. *Tushu jikan* 圖書集刊 6: 23–38.

Merleau-Ponty, Maurice. 1945. *Phénoménologie de la perception*. Paris: Gallimard.

Meslin, Michel. 1990. *Maître et disciples dans les traditions religieuses*. Paris: Éditions du Cerf.

Michaud, Paul. 1958. "The Yellow Turbans." *MS* 17: 47–127.

Michihata Ryōshū 道端良秀. 1961. "Donran no chōjuhō ni tsuite" 曇鸞の長寿法について [On Tanluan's methods for longevity]. *TS* 18: 1–18.

———. 1969. "Donran to dōkyō to no kankei" 曇鸞と道教との関係 [Tanluan and his relation to Taoism]. In Fukui Hakase shōju kinen ronbunshū kankōkai 1969, 1001–20.

Micollier, Évelyne. 1996. "Entre science et religion, tradition et modernité: Le discours pluriel des pratiquants de *qigong*." In Benoist 1996, 205–23.

Miller, Amy Lynn. 1995. "Doing Time in Taoist Hell: Annotated Translations, Dating and Analysis of Punishments in Two Six Dynasties *Ling-pao* Texts on Hell." Master's thesis, Indiana University.

Miller, Naomi. 1982. *Heavenly Caves: Reflections on the Garden Grotto*. New York: G. Braziller.

Miller, Tracy G. 2000. "Constructing Religion: Song Dynasty Architecture and the Jinci Temple Complex." Ph.D. diss., University of Pennsylvania.

Min Zhiting 閔智亭. 1995. *Daojiao yifan* 道教儀範 [Taoist liturgy]. Taipei: Xinwenfeng chuban gongsi.

Mio Yūko 三尾裕子. 2000. "Taiwan wangye xinyang de fazhan: Taiwan yu dalu lishi he shikuang de bijiao" 臺灣王爺信仰的發展—臺灣與大陸歷史和實況的比較 [The development of the cult of the Royal Lords in Taiwan: A comparison of the history and current state of the cult in Taiwan and continental China]. In Xu Zhengguang and Lin Meirong 2000, 31–67.

Mitamura Keiko 三田村圭子. 1994. "*Taijō Rokun setsu Jō seijō kyōchū* ni tsuite: Dō Kōtei bon no shiryōteki kentō" 「太上老君説常清浄経注」について—杜光庭本の資料的檢討 [On the *Taishang Laojun shuo chang qingjing jing zhu*: An examination of the sources of Du Guangting's edition]. In Dōkyō bunka kenkyūkai 1994, 80–98.

———. 1998. "Kagisho ni mieru shuketsu no henyō" 科儀書に見える手訣の変容 [Changes in the mudrās seen in Taoist liturgical texts]. *TS* 92: 15–30.

———. 2002. "Daoist Hand Signs and Buddhist Mudras." In Kohn and Roth 2002, 235–56.

Miura Kunio 三浦國雄. 1983. "Dōten fukuchi shōkō"「洞天福地」小考 [A short study of the Grotto-Heavens and Blissful Lands]. *TS* 61: 1–23. Translated into Chinese by Wang Xiande 王賢德 as "Dongtian fudi xiaolun"「洞天福地」小論, *DT* 6 (1993): 233–78.

———. 1989. "The Revival of *Qi*: Qigong in Contemporary China." In Kohn 1989c, 331–62.

Miura Kunio 三浦國雄, Horiike Nobuo 堀池信夫, and Ōgata Tōru 大形徹, eds. 2000. *Dōkyō no seimeikan to shintairon* 道教の生命観と身体論 [Views of life and theories of the body in Taoism]. Dōkyō kōza 道教講座, edited by Noguchi Tetsurō 野口鐵郎, 3. Yūzankaku shuppansha.

Miura Shūichi 三浦秀一. 1992. "Gendai shisō kenkyū josetsu: Zenshin dōshi Ri Dōken no dōkō o shujiku ni" 元代思想研究序説—全真道士李道謙の動向を主軸に [A preliminary study of Yuan thought, based on the stance of the Quanzhen master Li Daoqian]. *Shūkan tōyōgaku* 集刊東洋學 67: 66–84.

Miyakawa Hisayuki 宮川尚志. 1954. "Ryū Ichimei no *Goshin chokushi* ni tsuite" 劉一明の「悟真直指」について [On Liu Yiming's *Wuzhen zhizhi*]. *Okayama daigaku Hōbungakubu gakujutsu ki* 岡山大學法文學部學術紀要 3: 49–59.

———. 1964. *Rikuchōshi kenkyū: Shūkyō hen* 六朝史研究—宗教篇 [Studies on the history of the Six Dynasties: Religion]. Kyoto: Heirakuji shoten.

———. 1971. "Son On Ro Jun no ran ni tsuite" 孫恩盧循の亂について [On the rebellion of Sun En and Lu Xun]. *Tōyōshi kenkyū* 東洋史研究 30.2–3: 1–30.

———. 1972. "Son On Ro Jun no ran hokō" 孫恩盧循の亂補考 [A supplementary study of the rebellion of Sun En and Lu Xun]. In Suzuki hakushi koki kinen shukugakai 1972, 533–48. Tokyo: Meitoku shuppansha.

———. 1975. "Rin Reiso to Sō no Kisō" 林霊素と宋の徽宗 [Lin Lingsu and Song Huizong]. *Tōkai daigaku kiyō: Bungaku bu* 東海大學紀要—文學部, 24: 1–8.

———. 1978. "Nan-Sō no dōshi Haku Gyokusen no jiseki" 南宋の道士白玉蟾の事蹟 [The life of the Southern Song Taoist Bai Yuchan]. In Uchida Ginpū hakushi shōju kinenkai 1978, 499–517.

———. 1979. "Local Cults around Mount Lu at the Time of Sun En's Rebellion." In Welch and Seidel 1979, 83–101.

———. 1984a. "*Inbu kyō* kenkyū josetsu"「陰符經」研究序説 [Preliminary remarks on the study of the *Yinfu jing*]. In Makio Ryōkai hakushi shōju kinen ronshū kankōkai 1984, 425–43.

———. 1984b. "*Inbu kyō* no ikkōsatsu"「陰符經」の一考察 [A note on the *Yinfu jing*]. *TS* 63: 1–21.

Miyazawa Masayori 宮澤正順. 1984a. "Dōkyō no jinshinron: Nyūtai kara shuttai made o chūshin to shite" 道教の人身論ｂ入胎から出胎までを中心として [The view of the human body in Taoism, with special reference to the period from conception to birth]. In Takenaka Shinjō hakase shōju kinen ronbunshū kankōkai 1984, 1209–29.

———. 1984b. "*Dōsū* no ikkōsatsu"「道枢」の一考察 [A note on the *Daoshu*]. *TS* 63: 22–35.

———. 1984c. "Kyū kyū nyo ritsurei ni tsuite: Chū-Nichi girei no kōshō" 急急如律令について—中日儀礼の交渉 [On "Promptly, promptly, in accordance with the statutes and ordinances!": Connections between Chinese and Japanese rites]. *Girei bunka* 儀礼文化 20: 14–35.

———. 1988a. *"Dōsū 'Goshinhen' to Chō Heishuku no Goshinhen ni tsuite"* 「道枢」悟真篇と張平叔の「悟真篇」について [On the "Wuzhen pian" in the *Daoshu* and the *Wuzhen pian* by Zhang Pingshu]. *Chūgokugaku kenkyū* 中國學研究 7: 2–21.

———. 1988b. *"Dōsū no kōsei ni tsuite: Zabōhen o chūshin to shite"* 「道枢」の構成について—座忘篇を中心として [On the composition of the *Daoshu*: With special reference to the "Zuowang pian"]. *Taishō daigaku kenkyū kiyō* 大正大學研究紀要 73: 31–62.

———. 1990. *"Dōsū Kōtei mon hen ni tsuite"* 「道枢」黄帝問篇について [On the "Huangdi wen pian" chapter of the *Daoshu*]. In Saitō Akitoshi kyōju kanreki kinen ronbunshū kankōkai 1990, 383–402.

Miyazawa Masayori 宮澤正順, Mugitani Kunio 麥谷邦夫, and Jin Zhengyao 金正耀. 2002. *Dōsu ichiji sakuin* 「道樞」一字索引 [Concordance to the *Daoshu*]. Kyoto: Shōkadō.

Miyuki Mokusen. 1967. "The 'Secret of the Golden Flower': Studies and Translation." Inaugural Dissertation, Jung Institute (Zürich).

Mollier, Christine. 1990. *Une apocalypse taoïste du Ve siècle: Le Livre des Incantations Divines des Grottes Abyssales*. Paris: Collège de France, Institut des Hautes Études Chinoises.

———. 1991. "La tradition liturgique du *Dongyuan shenzhou jing*." In Sakai Tadao, Yamada Toshiaki, and Fukui Fumimasa 1991, 157–67.

———. 1997. "La méthode de l'Empereur du Nord du Mont Fengdu: Une tradition exorciste du taoïsme médiéval." *TP* 83: 329–85.

———. 2000. "Les cuisines de Laozi et du Buddha." *CEA* 11: 45–90.

Monastra, Giovanni. 1998. "Le symbole du 'yin-yang' sur les enseignes de l'empire romain?" *Nouvelle école* 50: 112–18.

Morgan, Evan. 1933. *Tao, The Great Luminant: Essays from Huai nan tzu*. Shanghai: Kelly and Walsh.

Mori Yuria 森由利亜. 1990. "Sōdai ni okeru Ro Dōhin setsuwa ni kan suru ichi shiron" 宋代における呂洞賓説話に関する一試論 [A preliminary study of the legends on Lü Dongbin in the Song period]. *Bungaku kenkyūka kiyō bessatsu* 文學研究科紀要別冊 17: 55–65.

———. 1992a. *"Junyō teikun shinka myōtsū ki ni mieru Zenshinkyōteki na tokuchō ni tsuite"* 「純陽帝君神化妙通紀」に見える全真教的な特徴について [On the features of Quanzhen Taoism as seen in the *Chunyang dijun shenhua miaotong ji*]. *Tōyō no shisō to shūkyō* 東洋の思想と宗教 9: 31–47.

———. 1992b. *"Taigen shinjin ken'i roku ni mieru Ō Gyokuyō no shin'i tan"* 「體玄真人顯異録」に見える王玉陽の神異譚 [Wang Yuyang's miraculous stories as seen in the *Tixuan zhenren xianyi lu*]. *Tōyō tetsugaku ronsō* 東洋哲學論叢 1: 186–203.

———. 1994. *"Zenshinkyō Ryūmonha keifu kō* 全真教龍門派系譜考" [A study of the lineage of the Longmen branch of Quanzhen]. In Dōkyō bunka kenkyūkai 1994, 180–211.

———. 1998. *"Taiitsu kinka shūshi no seiritsu to hensen"* 「太乙金華宗旨」の成立と変遷 [The compilation of the *Taiyi jinhua zongzhi* and its transformations]. *Tōyō no shisō to shūkyō* 東洋の思想と宗教 15: 43–64.

———. 2001. "*Dōzo shūyō* to Shō Yobu no Roso fukei sinkō"「道蔵輯要」と蒋予蒲の呂祖扶乩信仰 [The *Daozang jiao* and Jiang Yupu's plachette-writing cult to Ancerstor Lü]. *TS* 98: 33–52.

———. 2002. "Identity and Lineage: The *Taiyi jinhua zongzhi* and the Spirit-Writing Cult to Patriarch Lü in Qing China." In Kohn and Roth 2002, 165–84.

Morrison, Hedda, and Wolfram Eberhard. 1973. *Hua Shan. The Sacred Mountain in West China: Its Scenery, Monasteries, and Monks*. Hong Kong: Vetch and Lee.

Mou Zongsan 牟宗三. 1974. *Caixing yu xuanli* 才性與玄理 [Natural endowment and the Mysterious Principle]. Taipei: Taiwan xuesheng shuju.

Mueller, Herbert. 1911. "Über das taoistische Pantheon der Chinesen, seine Grundlagen und seine historische Entwicklung." *Zeitschrift für Ethnologie* 43: 393–428.

Mugitani Kunio 麥谷邦夫. 1976. "Tō Kōkei nenpu kōryaku" 陶弘景年譜考略 [A brief study of Tao Hongjing's chronology]. *TS* 47: 30–61; 48: 56–83.

———. 1979. "Dōkyōteki seiseiron no keisei to tenkai: *Ki no shisō* horon" 道教的生成論の形成と展開—「氣の思想」補論 [The formation and development of Taoist cosmogony: A supplement to *Ki no shisō*]. *Chūtetsubun gakkaihō* 中哲文學會報 4: 87–99.

———. 1981. "*Kōtei naikei kyō* shiron"「黄庭内景經」試論 [A preliminary study of the *Huangting neijing jing*]. *Tōyō bunka* 東洋文化 62: 29–59.

———. 1985. *Rōshi Sōji chū sakuin*「老子想爾注」索引 [Concordance to the *Xiang'er* commentary to the *Laozi*]. Kyoto: Hōyū shoten.

———. 1987. *Yōsei enmeiroku kunchū* 養生延命録訓注 [A Japanese translation of the *Yangxing yanming lu*, with annotations]. Tokyo: N.p.

———. 1991. *Shinkō sakuin*「真誥」索引 [Concordance to the *Zhengao*]. Kyoto: Kyōto daigaku Jinbun kagaku kenkyūjo.

———. 1992. "*Daidō shinkyō sanjūkyū shō* o megutte"「大洞真經三十九章」をめぐって [On the *Dadong zhenjing* in thirty-nine stanzas]. In Yoshikawa Tadao 1992a, 55–87.

———, ed. 2002. *Chūgoku chūsei shakai to shūkyō* 中國中世社會と宗教 [Society and religion in medieval China]. Kyoto: Dōkisha.

Mugitani Kunio 麥谷邦夫 and Yoshikawa Tadao 吉川忠夫, eds. 2003. *Shūshi meitsūki kenkyū (yakuchū hen)*「周氏冥通記」研究（譯注篇）[A study of the *Zhoushi mingtong ji*: Japanese annotated translation]. Kyoto: Kyōto daigaku Jinbun kagaku kenkyūjo.

Mukai Tetsuo 向井哲生. 1989. "Konpon *Bunshi* no shin to gi" 今本「文子」の真と偽 [On the authenticity of the extant *Wenzi*]. *TS* 73: 1–18.

Müller, Claudius C. 1980. *Untersuchungen zum "Erdaltar" she im China der Chou- und Han-Zeit*. München: Minerva.

Munakata Kiyohiko. 1991. *Sacred Mountains in Chinese Art: An Exhibition Organized by the Krannert Art Museum at the University of Illinois*. Urbana: University of Illinois Press.

Munro, Donald J. 1969. *The Concept of Man in Early China*. Stanford: Stanford University Press.

———, ed. 1985. *Individualism and Holism: Studies in Confucian and Taoist Values*. Ann Arbor: Center for Chinese Studies, University of Michigan.

Murakami Yoshimi 村上嘉美. 1965. "'Nature' in Lao-Chuang Thought and 'No-Mind' in Ch'an Buddhism." *Kwansei Gakuin University Annual Studies* 14: 15–31.

———. 1981. "Kanbo shin hatsugen no isho to *Hōbokushi*" 漢墓新發現の醫書と 「抱朴子」 [The medical texts recently discovered in Han tombs and the *Baopu zi*]. *TG* 53: 387–421.

———. 1983. "Renkin jutsu" 錬金術 [Alchemy]. In Fukui Kōjun et al. 1983, 1: 285–328.

Muroya Kuniyuki 室谷邦行. 1988. "'Shizen gainen no seiritsu ni tsuite" 「自然」概念の成立について [On the formation of the notion of *ziran* ("so of its own"; naturalness)]. *NCG* 40: 16–31.

Murray, Dian H. 1994. *The Origins of the Tiandihui: The Chinese Triads in Legend and History*. In collaboration with Qin Baoqi. Stanford: Stanford University Press.

Nakajima Ryūzō 中島隆蔵, ed. 1980. *Dōkyō gisū sakuin kō* 「道教義樞」索引稿 [A draft index to the *Daojiao yishu*]. Kyoto: private publication.

———. 1981. "Dōkyō ni okeru innen setsu juyō no ichi sokumen" 道教における因縁説受容の一側面 [One aspect of the reception of the doctrines of *karma* in Taoism]. In Araki kyōju taikyū kinenkai 1981, 225–41.

———. 1984. "*Taijō gōhō innen kyō* ni okeru ōhō ron" 「太上業報因縁經」における応報論 [Karmic retribution in the *Taishang yebao yinyuan jing*]. In Makio Ryōkai hakushi shōju kinen ronshū kankōkai 1984, 335–53.

———. 1986. "*Unkyū shichisen* no shohon ni tsuite" 「雲笈七籤」の諸本について [On the editions of the *Yunji qiqian*]. *Shūkan tōyōgaku* 集刊東洋學 56: 66–76.

Nakamura Hiroichi 中村裕一. 1983. "Dōkyō to nenchū gyōji" 道教と年中行事 [Taoism and annual observances]. In Fukui Kōjun et al. 1983, 2: 371–411.

Nakamura Shōhachi 中村璋八. 1983. "Nihon no dōkyō" 日本の道教 [Taoism in Japan]. In Fukui Kōjun et al. 1983, 3: 3–47.

Nanyang Wenwu yanjiusuo 南陽文物研究所 [Nanyang Institute for Cultural Heritage], ed. 1990. *Nanyang Handai huaxiangbei* 南陽漢代畫像磚 [Han-dynasty stone reliefs from Nanyang, Hunan]. Beijing: Wenwu chubanshe.

Naoe Hiroji 直江廣治. 1983. "Taiwan kajin shakai no minkan shinkō no shosō" 臺灣華人社會の民間信仰の諸相 [Aspects of Chinese popular cults in Taiwan]. In Ōfuchi Ninji 1983, 1059–83.

Naquin, Susan. 1976. *Millenarian Rebellion in China: The Eight Trigrams Uprising of 1813*. New Haven: Yale University Press.

———. 1992. "The Peking Pilgrimage to Miao-feng Shan: Religious Organizations and Sacred Site." In Naquin and Yü 1992, 333–77.

———. 2000. *Peking: Temples and City Life, 1400–1900*. Berkeley: University of California Press.

Naquin, Susan, and Chün-fang Yü, eds. 1992. *Pilgrims and Sacred Sites in China*. Berkeley: University of California Press.

Nara Yukihiro 奈良行博. 1998. *Dōkyō seichi: Chūgoku tairitsu tōsa kiroku* 道教聖地—中國大陸踏査記録 [Taoist sacred sites: Notes from a survey in continental China]. Tokyo: Hirakawa shuppansha.

Nattier, Jan. 1991. *Once Upon a Future Time: Studies in a Buddhist Prophecy of Decline*. Berkeley: Asian Humanities Press.

Naundorf, Gert. 1972. *Aspekte des anarchischen Gedankens in China: Darstellung der Lehre und Übersetzung des Textes Wu Neng Tzu*. Würzburg: Schmitt und Meyer.

Naundorf, Gert, Karl-Heinz Pohl, and Hans-Hermann Schmidt, eds. 1985. *Religion und Philosophie in Ostasien: Festschrift für Hans Steininger zum 65. Geburtstag.* Würzburg: Königshausen und Neumann.

Needham, Joseph. 1956. *Science and Civilisation in China.* Vol. II: *History of Scientific Thought.* With the research assistance of Wang Ling. Cambridge: Cambridge University Press.

———. 1959. *Science and Civilisation in China.* Vol. III: *Mathematics and the Sciences of the Heavens and the Earth.* With the collaboration of Wang Ling. Cambridge: Cambridge University Press.

———. 1962. *Science and Civilisation in China.* Vol. IV: *Physics and Physical Technology.* Part 1: *Physics.* With the collaboration of Wang Ling and the special co-operation of Kenneth G. Robinson. Cambridge: Cambridge University Press.

———. 1974. *Science and Civilisation in China.* Vol. V: *Chemistry and Chemical Technology.* Part 2: *Spagyrical Discovery and Invention: Magisteries of Gold and Immortality.* With the collaboration of Lu Gwei-Djen. Cambridge: Cambridge University Press.

———. 1976. *Science and Civilisation in China.* Vol. V: *Chemistry and Chemical Technology.* Part 3: *Spagyrical Discovery and Invention: Historical Survey, from Cinnabar Elixirs to Synthetic Insulin.* With the collaboration of Ho Ping-Yü and Lu Gwei-Djen. Cambridge: Cambridge University Press.

———. 1980. *Science and Civilisation in China.* Vol. V: *Chemistry and Chemical Technology.* Part 4: *Spagyrical Discovery and Invention: Apparatus, Theories and Gifts.* With the collaboration of Ho Ping-Yü and Lu Gwei-Djen, and a contribution by Nathan Sivin. Cambridge: Cambridge University Press.

———. 1983. *Science and Civilisation in China.* Vol. V: *Chemistry and Chemical Technology.* Part 5: *Spagyrical Discovery and Invention: Physiological Alchemy.* With the collaboration of Lu Gwei-Djen. Cambridge: Cambridge University Press.

———. 1986. *Science and Civilisation in China.* Vol. V: *Chemistry and Chemical Technology.* Part 7: *Military Technology: The Gunpowder Epic.* With the collaboration of Ho Ping-yü, Lu Gwei-Djen, and Wang Ling. Cambridge: Cambridge University Press.

Neusch, Marcel. 1994. *Le sacrifice dans les religions.* Paris: Beauchesne.

Ngo Van Xuyet. 1976. *Divination, magie et politique dans la Chine ancienne. Essai suivi de la traduction des "Biographies des Magiciens" tirées de l'"Histoire des Han postérieurs."* Paris: Presses Universitaires de France.

Ni Run'an 倪润安. 1999. "Lun Liang Han siling de yuanliu" 论两汉四灵的源流 [A discussion of the origins and development of the Four Numina in the Han period]. *Zhongyuan wenwu* 中原文物 1999.1: 83–91.

Nickerson, Peter S. 1994. "Shamans, Demons, Diviners, and Taoists: Conflict and Assimilation in Medieval Chinese Ritual Practice (c. A.D. 100–1000)." *TR* 5.1: 41–66.

———. 1996a. "Abridged Codes of Master Lu for the Daoist Community." In Lopez 1996, 347–59.

———. 1996b. "Taoism, Death, and Bureaucracy in Early Medieval China." Ph.D. diss., University of California, Berkeley.

———. 1997. "The Great Petition for Sepulchral Plaints." In Bokenkamp 1997, 230–60.

———. 2000. "The Southern Celestial Masters." In Kohn 2000b, 256–82.

Nielsen, Bent. 1990. "Notes on the Origins of the Hexagrams of the *Book of Changes*." *Studies in Central and East Asian Religions* 3: 42–59.

Nienhauser, William H., Jr., ed. 1986. *The Indiana Companion to Traditional Chinese Literature*. Second revised edition. Bloomington: Indiana University Press.

Nishitani Keiji 西谷啓治 and Yanagida Seizan 柳田聖山, eds. 1974. *Zenke goroku* 禅家語録 [Recorded sayings of the Chan School]. Tokyo: Chikuma shobō.

Nivison, David S. 1987a. "Hsin." In Eliade 1987, 6: 477–78.

———. 1987b. "Tao and Te." In Eliade 1987, 14: 283–86.

———. 1994a. *The Ways of Confucianism: Investigations in Chinese Philosophy*. Edited by Bryan W. van Norden. La Salle, IL: Open Court.

———. 1994b. "'Virtue' in Bone and Bronze." In Nivison 1994a, 17–30.

Noguchi Tetsurō 野口鐵郎. 1983. "Dōkyō to minshū shūkyō kessha" 道教と民衆宗教結社 [Taoism and popular religious associations]. In Fukui Kōjun et al. 1983, 2: 209–53.

———, ed. 1994. *Chūgokushi ni okeru shūkyō to kokka* 中國史における宗教と國家 [Religion and the state in Chinese history]. Tokyo: Yūzankaku shuppansha.

Noguchi Tetsurō 野口鐵郎 et al., eds. 1994. *Dōkyō jiten* 道教事典 [Encyclopedia of Taoism]. Tokyo: Hirakawa shuppansha.

———, eds. 1996–97. *Senshū: Dōkyō to Nihon* 選集・道教と日本 [Collected studies on Taoism and Japan]. 3 vols. Tokyo: Yūzankaku shuppansha.

Nose Makoto 野瀬真, ed. 1994. *Ishinpō no kenkyū* 「醫心方」の研究 [Studies on the *Ishinpō*]. Osaka: Oriento shuppansha.

Obringer, Frédéric. 1995. "Poisoning and Toxicomany in Medieval China: Physiological Reality or Political Accusation?" In Hashimoto, Jami, and Skar 1995, 215–21.

———. 1997. *L'aconit et l'orpiment: Drogues et poisons en Chine ancienne et médiévale*. Paris: Fayard.

Ōfuchi Ninji 大淵忍爾. 1964. *Dōkyōshi no kenkyū* 道教史の研究 [Studies on the history of Taoism]. Okayama: Okayama daigaku kyōsaikai shosekibu.

———. 1974. "On *Ku Ling-pao-ching* 古靈寶經." *Acta Asiatica* 27: 33–56.

———. 1978. *Tonkō dōkyō* 敦煌道經 [Taoist scriptures from Dunhuang]. 2 vols. Vol. 1: *Mokuroku hen* 目録篇 [Index]. Vol. 2: *Zuroku hen* 圖録篇 [Reproductions]. Tokyo: Fukutake shoten.

———. 1979. "The Formation of the Taoist Canon." In Welch and Seidel 1979, 253–67.

———. 1983. *Chūgokujin no shūkyō girei: Bukkyō, dōkyō, minkan shinkō* 中國人の宗教儀礼—佛教・道教・民間信仰 [Liturgies of the Chinese people: Buddhism, Taoism, and popular cults]. Tokyo: Fukutake shoten.

———. 1991. *Shoki no dōkyō* 初期の道教 [Early Taoism]. Tokyo: Sōbunsha.

———. 1997. *Dōkyō to sono kyōten* 道教とその經典 [Taoism and its scriptures]. Tokyo: Sōbunsha.

Ōfuchi Ninji 大淵忍爾 and Ishii Masako 石井昌子, eds. 1988. *Rikuchō Tō Sō no kobunken shōin Dōkyō tenseki mokuroku, sakuin* 六朝唐宋の古文献所引道教典籍目録・索引 [A catalogue with index to Taoist texts cited in ancient sources of the Six Dynasties, Tang, and Song]. Tokyo: Kokusho kankōkai.

Ogawa Yōichi 小川陽一. 1983. "Dōkyō setsuwa" 道教説話 [Taoist narrative]. In Kanaoka Shōkō, Ikeda On, and Fukui Fumimasa 1983, 291–304.

Okuzaki Hiroshi 奥崎裕司. 1983. "Minshū no dōkyō" 民衆の道教 [Popular Taoism]. In Fukui Kōjun et al. 1983, 2: 135–68.

Olson, Stuart A. 1993. *The Jade Emperor's Mind Seal Classic: A Taoist Guide to Health, Longevity and Immortality*. St. Paul, MN: Dragon Door Publications.

Ono Shihei 小野四平. 1964. "Dōjō ni tsuite" 道情について [On the *daoqing* (poems of Taoist inspiration)]. *Shūkan tōyōgaku* 集刊東洋學 12: 25–39.

———. 1982. "Tō Shibo no dōkyō shōsetsu ni tsuite" 鄧志謨の道教小説について [On the Taoist novel of Deng Zhimo]. In Guo Fan 1982, 4: 151–75.

Onozawa Seiichi 小野沢精一, Fukunaga Mitsuji 福永光司, and Yamanoi Yū 山井湧, eds. 1978. *Ki no shisō* 氣の思想 [Conceptions of *qi* (pneuma)]. Tokyo: Tōkyo daigaku shuppankai.

Orzech, Charles D. 2002. "*Fang Yankou* and *Pudu*: Translation, Metaphor, and Religious Identity." In Kohn and Roth 2002, 213–34.

Overmyer, Daniel L. 1976. *Folk Buddhist Religion: Dissenting Sects in Late Traditional China*. Cambridge, MA: Harvard University Press.

———. 1985. "Values in Chinese Sectarian Literature: Ming and Ch'ing Pao-chüan." In Johnson, Nathan, and Rawski 1985, 219–54.

———. 1991. "Women in Chinese Religion: Submission, Struggle, Transcendence." In Shinohara and Schopen 1991, 91–120.

———. 1999. *Precious Volumes: An Introduction to Chinese Sectarian Scriptures from the Sixteenth and Seventeenth Centuries*. Cambridge, MA, and London: Harvard University Press.

———, ed. 2002. *Ethnography in China Today: A Critical Assessment of Methods and Results*. Edited with the assistance of Shin-Yi Chao. Taipei: Yuan-Liou Publishing Company.

———, ed. 2003. *Religion in China Today*. Cambridge: Cambridge University Press.

Overmyer, Daniel L., and Thomas Li Shiyu. 1992. "The Oldest Chinese Sectarian Scripture." *JCR* 20: 17–31.

Ownby, David. 1996. *Brotherhoods and Secret Societies in Early and Mid-Qing China: The Formation of a Tradition*. Stanford: Stanford University Press.

Oyanagi Shigeta 小柳司気太. 1934. *Hakuunkan shi* 白雲觀志 [Monograph of the Abbey of the White Clouds]. Tokyo: Tōhō bunka gakuin Tōkyō kenkyūjo. Reprinted in *Zangwai daoshu* 藏外道書 (Taoist Texts Outside the Canon), vol. 20.

Ozaki Masaharu 尾崎正治. 1974. "*Taijō santen seihō kyō* seiritsu kō" 「太上三天正法經」成立考 [A study of the compilation of the *Taishang santian zhengfa jing*]. *TS* 43: 13–29.

———. 1977. "*Shikyoku meika* shomondai" 四極明科諸問題 [Issues concerning the *Siji mingke*]. In Yoshioka Yoshitoyo hakase kanreki kinen kenkyū ronshū kankōkai 1977, 341–63.

———. 1979. "Ko Kenshi no shinsen shisō" 寇謙之の神仙思想 [Kou Qianzhi's conceptions of immortality]. *TS* 54: 52–69.

———. 1983a. "*Dōen shinju kyō*" 洞淵神呪經 [The *Dongyuan shenzhou jing*]. In Kanaoka Shōkō, Ikeda On, and Fukui Fumimasa 1983, 177–82.

———. 1983b. "Dōkyō kyōten" 道教經典 [Taoist scriptures]. In Fukui Kōjun et al. 1983, 1: 73–120.

———. 1983c. "Dōkyō no ruisho" 道教の類書 [Taoist encyclopedias (among the Dunhuang manuscripts)]. In Kanaoka Shōkō, Ikeda On, and Fukui Fumimasa 1983, 189–206.

———. 1983d. "Jōsei kyō rui" 上清經類 [Texts related to Shangqing (among the Dunhuang manuscripts)]. In Kanaoka Shōkō, Ikeda On, and Fukui Fumimasa 1983, 137–42.

———. 1983e. "Sono ta dōten rui" 其他道典類 [Other texts (among the Dunhuang manuscripts)]. In Kanaoka Shōkō, Ikeda On, and Fukui Fumimasa 1983, 183–88.

———. 1986a. "Dōzō no seiritsu to sono shūhen" 道藏の成立とその周辺 [The compilation of the Taoist Canon and its circumstances]. In Akizuki Kan'ei 1986, 79–109.

———. 1986b. "The Taoist Priesthood: From Tsai-chia to Ch'u-chia." In de Vos and Sofue 1986, 97–109.

———. 1987. "Dōzō mokuroku shōchū kanken" 「道藏目録詳注」管見 [A review of the Daozang mulu xiangzhu]. In Akizuki Kan'ei 1987, 529–53.

———. 1996. "Rekisei shinsen taidō tsūkan no tekisuto ni tsuite" 「歷世真仙体道通鑑」 のテキストについて [On the texts of Lishi zhenxian tidao tongjian]. TS 88: 37–54.

Pan Qiming 潘启明. 1990. Zhouyi cantong qi tongxi 「周易参同契」通析 [An analysis of the Zhouyi cantong qi]. Shanghai: Fanyi chubanshe.

Pang Pu 庞朴. 1980. Boshu Wuxing pian yanjiu 帛书五行篇研究 [Studies on the silk manuscript of the Wuxing pian]. Jinan: Qi Lu shushe.

Pang, Duane. 1977. "The P'u-tu Ritual: A Celebration of the Chinese Community of Honolulu." In Saso and Chappell 1977, 95–122.

Pas, Julian F. 1989a. "Revival of Temple Worship and Popular Religious Traditions." In Pas 1989b, 158–209.

———, ed. 1989b. The Turning of the Tide: Religion in China Today. Hong Kong: Royal Asiatic Society, Hong Kong Branch, and Oxford University Press.

Pastor, Jean-Claude. 1990. Zhuangzi (Tchouang-tseu): Les chapitres intérieurs. Paris: Éditions du Cerf.

Pearce, Scott, Audrey Spiro, and Patricia Ebrey, eds. 2001. Culture and Power in the Reconstitution of the Chinese Realm, 200–600. Cambridge, MA: Harvard University Press.

Peerenboom, Randall P. 1990. "Cosmogony, the Taoist Way." JCP 17: 157–74.

———. 1993. Law and Morality in Ancient China: The Silk Manuscripts of Huang-Lao. Albany: State University of New York Press.

Pelliot, Paul. 1912. "Autour d'une traduction sanscrite du Tao Tö King." TP 13: 351–430.

———. 1920. "Meou-tseu ou Les doutes levés." TP 19: 255–433.

Peng Shuangsong 彭双松. 1983. Xu Fu ji shi Shenwu tianhuang 徐福即是神武天皇 [Xu Fu was Emperor Jinmu]. Miaoli: Fuhui tushu chubanshe.

———. 1984. Xu Fu yanjiu 徐福研究 [A study of Xu Fu]. Miaoli: Fuhui tushu chubanshe.

Penny, Benjamin. 1990. "A System of Fate Calculation in Taiping jing." Papers in Far Eastern History 41: 1–8.

———. 1993. "Qigong, Daoism and Science: Some Contexts for the Qigong Boom." In Lee and Syrokomla-Stefanowska 1993, 166–79.

———. 1996a. "Buddhism and Daoism in *The 180 Precepts Spoken by Lord Lao*." *TR* 6.2: 1–16.

———. 1996b. "The Text and Authorship of *Shenxian zhuan*." *Journal of Oriental Studies* 34: 165–209.

———. 1998. "Meeting the Celestial Master." *East Asian History* 15–16: 53–66.

———. 2000. "Immortality and Transcendence." In Kohn 2000b, 109–33.

———, ed. 2006. *Daoism in History: Essays in Honour of Liu Ts'un-yan*. London: Routledge.

Peterson, J. O. 1989–90. "The Early Traditions Relating to the Han Dynasty Transmission of the *Taiping jing*." Parts 1 and 2. *Acta Orientalia* 50: 133–71, 51: 173–216.

Peterson, Thomas H. 1995. "Recorded for the Ritual of Merit and Virtue for Repairing the Various Observatories of Ch'ing-ch'eng Mountain." *TR* 6.1: 41–55.

Peterson, Willard. 1982. "Making Connections: 'Commentary on the Attached Verbalizations' of the *Book of Change*." *HJAS* 42: 67–116.

Pokora, Timotheus. 1961. "On the Origin of the Notions *T'ai-p'ing* and *Ta-t'ung* in Chinese Philosophy." *Archiv Orientální* 29: 448–54.

Pontynen, Arthur. 1980. "The Deification of Laozi in Chinese History and Art." *Oriental Art* 26: 192–200.

Poo, Mu-chou. 2004. "The Concept of Ghost in Chinese Religion." In Lagerwey 2004b, 1: 173–91.

Porkert, Manfred. 1974. *The Theoretical Foundations of Chinese Medicine. Systems of Correspondence*. Cambridge, MA: MIT Press.

———. 1979. *Biographie d'un taoïste légendaire: Tcheou Tseu-yang*. Paris: Collège de France, Institut des Hautes Études Chinoises.

Porter, Bill. 1993. *Road to Heaven: Encounters with Chinese Hermits*. San Francisco: Mercury House.

Pouillon, J. and P. Maranda, eds. 1970. *Échanges et communications: Mélanges offerts à Claude Lévi-Strauss à l'occasion de son 60ème anniversaire*. The Hague: Mouton.

Pourret, Jess G. 2002. *The Yao: The Mien and Mun Yao in China, Vietnam, Laos and Thailand*. London: Thames and Hudson.

Pregadio, Fabrizio. 1986. "Un lessico alchemico cinese: Nota *sullo Shih yao erh ya di Mei Piao*." *Cina* 20: 7–38.

———. 1987. *Ko Hung: Le Medicine della Grande Purezza, dal "Pao-p'u tzu nei-p'ien."* Roma: Edizioni Mediterranee.

———. 1991. "The *Book of the Nine Elixirs* and its Tradition." In Yamada Keiji and Tanaka Tan 1989–91, 2: 543–639.

———. 1995. "The Representation of Time in the *Zhouyi cantong qi*." *CEA* 8: 155–73.

———. 1996. "Chinese Alchemy: An Annotated Bibliography of Works in Western Languages." *MS* 44: 439–76.

———. 1997. "A Work on the Materia Medica in the Taoist Canon: *Instructions on an Inventory of Forty-Five Metals and Minerals*." *Asiatica Venetiana* 2: 139–60.

———. 2000. "Elixirs and Alchemy." In Kohn 2000b, 165–95.

———. 2002. "The Early History of the *Zhouyi cantong qi*." *JCR* 30: 149–76.

———. 2004. "The Notion of 'Form' and the Ways of Liberation in Daoism." *CEA* 14: 95–130.

———. 2006a. "Early Daoist Meditation and the Origins of Inner Alchemy." In Penny 2006, 121–58.

———. 2006b. *Great Clarity: Daoism and Alchemy in Early Medieval China*. Stanford: Stanford University Press.

Pregadio, Fabrizio, and Lowell Skar. 2000. "Inner Alchemy (*Neidan*)." In Kohn 2000b, 464–97.

Qiang Yu 強昱. 1995. "Cheng Xuanying *Daode jing yishu* zhong de Chongxuan sixiang" 成玄英「道德經義疏」中的重玄思想 [Chongxuan thought in Cheng Xuanying's *Commentary on the Signification of the Daode jing*]. *DWY* 7: 199–210.

Qing Xitai 卿希泰, ed. 1988–95. *Zhongguo daojiao shi* 中国道教史 [History of Chinese Taoism]. 4 vols. Chengdu: Sichuan renmin chubanshe.

———, ed. 1994. *Zhongguo daojiao* 中国道教 [Chinese Taoism]. 4 vols. Shanghai: Dongfang chuban zhongxin.

———. 1999. "Tianxin zhengfa pai chutan" 天心正法派初探 [A preliminary exploration of the Correct Method of the Celestial Heart]. *SZY* 1999.3: 19–24.

Qing Xitai 卿希泰 and Li Gang 李刚. 1985. "Shilun daojiao quanshan shu" 试论道教劝善书 [A preliminary study of Taoist books of moral exhortation]. *SZY* 1985.4: 50–57.

Qiu Maoliang 邱茂良. 1985. *Zhenjiuxue* 针灸学 [Acumoxa]. Shanghai: Shanghai kexue jishu chubanshe.

Queen, Sarah. 1996. *From Chronicle to Canon: The Hermeneutics of the Spring and Autumn, According to Tung Chung-shu*. Cambridge and New York: Cambridge University Press.

Rand, Christopher C. 1979–80. "Chinese Military Thought and Philosophical Taoism." *MS* 34: 171–218.

———. 1979. "Li Ch'üan and Chinese Military Thought." *HJAS* 39: 107–37.

Rao Zongyi 饒宗頤. 1956. *Laozi Xiang'er zhu jiaojian* 「老子想爾注」校箋 [Annotated critical edition of the *Xiang'er* commentary to the *Laozi*]. Hong Kong: Tong Nam.

———. 1993a. "Boshu *Xici zhuan daheng* shuo" 帛書「繫辭傳」大恆說 [The notion of Great Constancy in the silk manuscript of the *Xici*]. *DWY* 3: 6–19.

———. 1993b. "Tan Yinqueshan jian *Tiandi bafeng wuxing kezhu wuyin zhi ju*" 談銀雀山簡「天地八風五行客主五音之居」 [A discussion of the Yinqueshan bamboo slips of the *Tiandi bafeng wuxing kezhu wuyin zhi ju*]. *Jianbo yanjiu* 簡帛研究 1: 113–19.

———. 1998. "(Chuan Laozi shi) Rong Cheng yishuo gouchen" （传老子师）容成遗说钩沉 [Seeking the lost teachings of Rong Cheng (Laozi's teacher)]. *Beijing daxue xuebao (Zhexue shehui kexue ban)* 北京大学学报（哲学社会科学版） 1998.3: 63–68.

Rao Zongyi 饒宗頤 and Zeng Xiantong 曾憲通. 1982. *Yunmeng Qinjian rishu yanjiu* 雲夢秦簡日書研究 [Studies on the Qin hemerological manuscripts from Yunmeng]. Hong Kong: Zhongwen daxue chubanshe.

Raz, Gil. 2003. "Creation of Tradition: The Five Talismans of the Numinous Treasure and the Formation of Early Daoism." Ph.D. diss., Indiana University.

Reich, Warren Thomas, ed. 1995. *The Encyclopedia of Bioethics*. Revised edition. New York: Macmillan.

Rees, Helen. 2000. *Echoes of History: Naxi Music in Modern China*. Oxford: Oxford University Press.

Reischauer, Edwin O. 1955. *Ennin's Diary: The Record of a Pilgrimage to China in Search of the Law*. New York: Ronald Press.

Reiter, Florian. 1981. "The Soothsayer Hao Ta-t'ung (1140–1212) and his Encounter with Ch'üan-chen Taoism." *Oriens Extremus* 28: 198–205.

———. 1983. "Some Observations Concerning Taoist Foundations in Traditional China." *Zeitschrift der Deutschen Morgenländischen Gesellschaft* 133: 363–76.

———. 1984. "The 'Scripture of the Hidden Contracts' (Yin-fu ching), a Short Survey on Facts and Findings." *Nachrichten der Gesellschaft für Natur- und Völkerkunde Ostasiens* 136: 75–83.

———. 1984–85. "'Ch'ung-yang Sets Forth his Teachings in Fifteen Discourses': A Concise Introduction to the Taoist Way of Life of Wang Che." *MS* 36: 33–54.

———. 1985. "Der Name Tung-hua ti-chün und sein Umfeld in der taoistischen Tradition." In Naundorf, Pohl, and Schmidt 1985, 87–101.

———. 1986. "Die 'Einundachtzig Bildtexte zu den Inkarnationen und Wirkungen Lao-chün's.' Dokumente einer tausendjährigen Polemik in China." *Zeitschrift der Deutschen Morgenländischen Gesellschaft* 136: 450–91.

———. 1988a. *Grundelemente und Tendenzen des religiösen Taoismus: Das Spannungsverhältnis von Integration und Individualität in seiner Geschichte zur Chin-, Yüan- und frühen Ming-Zeit*. Stuttgart: Franz Steiner Verlag.

———. 1988b. "The Visible Divinity: The Sacred Icon in Religious Taoism." *Nachrichten der Gesellschaft für Natur- und Völkerkunde Ostasiens* 144: 51–70.

———. 1990a. *Der Perlenbeutel aus den Drei Höhlen (San-tung chu-nang): Arbeitsmaterialien zum Taoismus der frühen T'ang Zeit*. Wiesbaden: Harrassowitz.

———. 1990b. *Leben und Wirken Lao Tzu's in Schrift und Bild: Lao-chün pa-shih-i-hua t'u-shuo*. Würzburg: Königshausen und Neumann.

———. 1992. *Kategorien und Realien im Shang-ch'ing Taoismus: Arbeitsmaterialien zum Taoismus der frühen T'ang Zeit*. Wiesbaden: Harrassowitz.

———. 1994. "How Wang Ch'ung-yang (1112–1170), the Founder of Ch'üan-chen Taoism, Achieved Enlightenment." *Oriens* 34: 497–508.

———. 1996. "The Ch'üan-chen Patriarch T'an Ch'u-tuan (1123–1185) and the Chinese Talismanic Tradition." *Zeitschrift der Deutschen Morgenländischen Gesellschaft* 146: 139–55.

———. 1998. *The Aspirations and Standards of Taoist Priests in the Early T'ang Period*. Wiesbaden: Harrassowitz.

———. 2001. "An Introduction to the Book 'Explanations and Pictures Concerning the Responses and Incarnations of Lao-chün During All Generations' (*Lao-chün li-shi ying-hua t'u-shuo*, Chengdu 1936)." *Zeitschrift der Deutschen Morgenländischen Gesellschaft* 151: 163–205.

Ren Jiyu 任继愈, ed. 1990. *Zhongguo daojiao shi* 中国道教史 [History of Chinese Taoism]. Shanghai: Shanghai renmin chubanshe.

Ren Jiyu 任繼愈 and Zhong Zhaopeng 鍾肇鵬, eds. 1991. *Daozang tiyao* 道藏提要 [A conspectus of the Taoist Canon]. Beijing: Zhongguo shehui kexue chubanshe.

Ren Zongquan 任宗权. 2000. "Daojiao *Quanzhen zhengyun* de yuanyuan ji yanbian"

道教「全真正韵」的渊源及演变 [On the origins and evolution of the Taoist text *Quanzhen zhengyun*]. *ZGDJ* 2000.1: 14–18.

Rickett, W. Allyn. 1985–98. *Guanzi: Political, Economic, and Philosophical Essays from Early China*. 2 vols. Princeton: Princeton University Press.

———. 1993. "Kuan tzu." In Loewe 1993, 244–51.

Ricoeur, Paul. 1967. *The Symbolism of Evil*. Translated by Emerson Buchanan. New York: Harper and Row. Originally published as *La symbolique du mal* (Paris: Aubier, 1960).

Riegel, Jeffrey K. 1975. "A Summary of Some Recent *Wenwu* and *Kaogu* Articles on Mawangtui Tombs Two and Three." *EC* 1: 10–15.

———. 1993. "Ta Tai Li chi." In Loewe 1993, 460–66.

Rinaker Ten Broeck, Janet, and Yiu Tong. 1950–51. "A Taoist Inscription of the Yüan Dynasty: The *Tao-chiao pei*." *TP* 40: 60–122. Also published as an appendix to Goodrich 1964.

Ritsema, Rudolf, and Stephen Kircher. 1994. *I ching: The Classic Chinese Oracle of Change*. Shaftesbury, Dorset: Element.

Robinet, Isabelle. 1976. "Randonnées extatiques des taoïstes dans les astres." *MS* 32: 159–273.

———. 1977. *Les commentaires du Tao tö king jusqu'au VIIe siècle*. Paris: Collège de France, Institut des Hautes Études Chinoises.

———. 1979a. "Introduction au *Kieou-tchen tchong-king*." *Society for the Study of Chinese Religions Bulletin* 7: 24–45.

———. 1979b. "Metamorphosis and Deliverance from the Corpse in Taoism." *HR* 19: 37–70.

———. 1981. Review of Porkert 1979. *TP* 67: 123–36.

———. 1983a. "*Chuang-tzu* et le taoïsme 'religieux.'" *JCR* 11: 59–109.

———. 1983b. "Kouo Siang ou le monde comme absolu." *TP* 69: 73–107.

———. 1983c. "Le *Ta-tung chen-ching*: Son authenticité et sa place dans les textes du *Shang-ch'ing ching*." In Strickmann 1981–85, 2: 394–433.

———. 1984. *La révélation du Shangqing dans l'histoire du taoïsme*. 2 vols. Paris: École Française d'Extrême-Orient.

———. 1985a. "Jing, qi et shen." *Revue française d'acupuncture* 43: 27–36.

———. 1985b. "L'unité transcendante des trois enseignements selon les taoïstes des Sung et des Yüan." In Naundorf, Pohl, and Schmidt 1985, 103–26.

———. 1986a. "La notion du *hsing* dans le taoïsme et son rapport avec celle du confucianisme." *JAOS* 106: 183–96.

———. 1986b. "The Taoist Immortal: Jesters of Light and Shadow, Heaven and Earth." *JCR* 13–14: 87–105.

———. 1987a. "Chang Chüeh." In Eliade 1987, 3: 197.

———. 1987b. "Chang Lu." In Eliade 1987, 3: 198–99.

———. 1987c. "Chang Tao-ling." In Eliade 1987, 3: 199–200.

———. 1987d. "Kuo Hsiang." In Eliade 1987, 8: 404–5.

———. 1987e. "Ssu-ma Ch'eng-chen." In Eliade 1987, 14: 40–41.

———. 1987f. "Wang Pi." In Eliade 1987, 15: 334–35.

———. 1988. "Sexualité et taoïsme." In Bernos 1988, 51–71.

———. 1989a. "Original Contributions of *Neidan* to Taoism and Chinese Thought." In Kohn 1989c, 297–330.

———. 1989b. "Taoïsme et mystique." *Cahiers d'Études Chinoises* 8: 65–103.

———. 1989c. "Visualization and Ecstatic Flight in Shangqing Taoism." In Kohn 1989c, 159–91.

———. 1989–90. "Recherche sur l'alchimie intérieure (*neidan*): L'école Zhenyuan." *CEA* 5: 141–62.

———. 1990a. "Nature et rôle du maître spirituel dans le taoïsme non liturgique." In Meslin 1990, 37–51.

———. 1990b. "The Place and Meaning of the Notion of Taiji in Taoist Sources prior to the Ming Dynasty." *HR* 29: 373–411.

———. 1991. "Sur le sens des termes *waidan* et *neidan*." *TR* 3.1: 3–40.

———. 1992. "Le monde à l'envers dans l'alchimie intérieure taoïste." *Revue de l'Histoire des Religions* 209: 239–57.

———. 1993. *Taoist Meditation: The Mao-shan Tradition of Great Purity.* Translated by Julian F. Pas and Norman J. Girardot. Albany: State University of New York Press. Originally published as *Méditation taoïste* (Paris: Dervy Livres, 1979).

———. 1994a. "Le rôle et le sens des nombres dans la cosmologie et l'alchimie taoïstes." *Extrême-Orient, Extrême-Occident* 16: 93–120.

———. 1994b. "Primus movens et création récurrente." *TR* 5.2: 29–70.

———. 1995a. *Introduction à l'alchimie intérieure taoïste: De l'unité et de la multiplicité. Avec une traduction commentée des Versets de l'éveil à la Vérité.* Paris: Éditions du Cerf.

———. 1995b. "Les marches cosmiques et les carrés magiques dans le taoïsme." *JCR* 23: 81–94.

———. 1995c. "Un, deux, trois: Les différentes modalités de l'Un et sa dynamique." *CEA* 8: 175–220.

———. 1996a. *Lao zi et le Tao.* Paris: Bayard Éditions.

———. 1996b. "Une lecture du *Zhuangzi*." *Études chinoises* 15: 109–58.

———. 1997a. "Genèses: Au début, il n'y a pas d'avant." In Gernet and Kalinowski 1997, 121–40.

———. 1997b. *Taoism: Growth of a Religion.* Translated by Phyllis Brooks. Stanford: Stanford University Press. Originally published as *Histoire du Taoïsme des origines au XIVe siècle* (Paris: Éditions du Cerf, 1991).

———. 1998a. "La 'Mère' et la 'Femelle obscure' de Laozi." In Cazenave 1998, 137–67.

———. 1998b. "Later Commentaries: Textual Polysemy and Syncretistic Interpretations." In Kohn and LaFargue 1998, 119–42.

———. 1999a. "Lun *Taiyi sheng shui*" 論「太一生水」 [On the *Taiyi sheng shui*]. Translated by Edmund Ryden. *DWY* 17: 332–39.

———. 1999b. "The Diverse Interpretations of the *Laozi*." In Csikszentmihalyi and Ivanhoe 1999, 127–59.

———. 2000. "Shangqing: Highest Clarity." In Kohn 2000b: 196–224.

———. 2002. "Genesis and Pre-Cosmic Eras in Daoism." Translated by Phillis Brooks. In Lee Cheuk Yin and Chan Man Sing 2002, 144–84.

———. 2004. "De quelques effects du Bouddhisme sur la problématique taoïste: Aspects de la confrontation du Taoïsme au Bouddhisme." In Lagerwey 2004b, 1: 411–516.

————. Forthcoming. *La cosmologie chinoise speculative et mystique, et ses fondements.* Paris: Éditions du Cerf.

Robson, James. 1995. "The Polymorphous Space of the Southern Marchmount [Nanyue 南嶽]." *CEA* 8: 221–64.

Rochat de la Vallée, Elisabeth. N.d. *Symphonie corporelle: La notion de corps dans le Shiming.* Paris: Institut Ricci.

Rochat de la Vallée, Elisabeth, and Claude Larre. 1993. *Su Wen: Les 11 premiers traités.* Paris: Institut Ricci.

Rolston, David L., ed. 1991. *How to Read the Chinese Novel.* Princeton: Princeton University Press.

Rong Zhaozu 容肇祖. 1994. "Zhou Dunyi yu daojiao" 周敦頤與道教 [Zhou Dunyi and Taoism]. *DWY* 5: 262–70.

Ropp, Paul S., ed. 1990. *Heritage of China: Contemporary Perspectives on Chinese Civilization.* Berkeley: University of California Press.

Rosemont, Henry, Jr., ed. 1984. *Explorations in Early Chinese Cosmology.* Chico, CA: Scholars Press.

————, ed. 1991. *Chinese Texts and Philosophical Contexts: Essays Dedicated to Angus C. Graham.* La Salle, IL: Open Court.

Roth, Harold D. 1985. "The Concept of Human Nature in the *Huai-nan Tzu.*" *JCP* 12: 1–22.

————. 1987a. "Fang-shih." In Eliade 1987, 5: 282–84.

————. 1987b. "Huang-lao Chün." In Eliade 1987, 6: 483–84.

————. 1987c. "Liu An." In Eliade 1987, 9: 1–2.

————. 1990. "The Early Taoist Concept of *Shen*: A Ghost in the Machine?" In Smith K. 1990, 11–32.

————. 1991a. "Psychology and Self-Cultivation in Early Taoistic Thought." *HJAS* 51: 599–650.

————. 1991b. "Who Compiled the *Chuang Tzu*?" In Rosemont 1991, 79–128.

————. 1992. *The Textual History of the Huai-nan tzu.* Ann Arbor: Association for Asian Studies.

————. 1993. "*Chuang tzu.*" In Loewe 1993, 56–66.

————. 1995. "Some Issues in the Study of Chinese Mysticism: A Review Essay." *China Review International* 2.1: 154–73.

————. 1996. "The Inner Cultivation Tradition of Early Daoism." In Lopez 1996, 123–48.

————. 1999a. *Original Tao: Inward Training (Nei-yeh) and the Foundations of Taoist Mysticism.* New York: Columbia University Press.

————. 1999b. "The *Laozi* in the Context of Early Daoist Mystical Praxis." In Csikszentmihalyi and Ivanhoe 1999, 59–96.

————. 2003. *A Companion to Angus C. Graham's Chuang Tzu.* Honolulu: University of Hawaii Press.

Rouget, Gilbert. 1985. *Music and Trance: A Theory of the Relations between Music and Possession.* Translated by Derek Coltman and Brunhilde Biebuyck in collaboration with the author. Chicago: Chicago University Press. Originally published as *La musique et la transe* (Paris: Gallimard, 1980).

Rousselle, Edwin. 1933. "Ne Ging Tu, 'Die Tafel des inneren Gewebes': Ein Taoistisches Meditationsbild mit Beschriftung." *Sinica* 8: 207–16.

Ruan Renze 阮仁泽 and Gao Zhennong 高振农, eds. 1992. *Shanghai zongjiao shi* 上海宗教史 [History of religion in Shanghai]. Shanghai: Shanghai renmin chubanshe.

Ruitenbeek, Klaas. 1999. "Mazu, the Patroness of Sailors, in Chinese Pictorial Art." *Artibus Asiae* 58: 281–329.

Ruizendaal, Robin. 2000. "Ritual Text and Performance in the Marionette Theatre of Southern Fujian and Taiwan." In de Meyer and Engelfriet 2000, 336–60.

Rump, Ariane. 1979. *Commentary on the Lao Tzu by Wang Pi*. In collaboration with Wing-tsit Chan. Honolulu: University of Hawaii Press.

Russell, Terence C. 1990a. "Chen Tuan at Mount Huangbo: A Spirit-Writing Cult in Late Ming China." *ASEA* 44: 107–40.

———. 1990b. "Chen Tuan's Veneration of the Dharma: A Study in Hagiographic Modification." *TR* 2.1: 54–72.

Ryden, Edmund. 1997. *The Yellow Emperor's Four Canons: A Literary Study and Edition of the Text from Mawangdui*. Taipei: Ricci Institute and Kuangchi Press.

———. 1998. *Philosophy of Peace in Han China: A Study of the "Huainanzi" Ch. 15, "On Military Strategy."* Taipei: Taipei Ricci Institute.

Sailey, Jay. 1978. *The Master Who Embraces Simplicity: A Study of the Philosopher Ko Hung, A.D. 282–343*. San Francisco: Chinese Materials Center.

Saitō Akitoshi kyōju kanreki kinen ronbunshū kankōkai 斎藤昭俊教授還暦記念論文集刊行会 [Editorial Committee for the Collected Studies Presented to Professor Saitō Akitoshi on his Sixtieth Birthday], ed. 1990. *Shūkyō to bunka* 宗教と文化 [Religion and culture]. Tokyo: Kobian shobō.

Sakade Yoshinobu 坂出祥伸. 1980. "Dōin kō: Kodai no yōseijutsu to igaku to no kakawari" 導引考－古代の養生術と医學とのかかわり [A study of *daoyin*: The relation between the ancient arts of Nourishing Life and medicine]. In Ikeda Suetoshi hakase koki kinen jigyōkai 1980, 225–40. Reprinted in Sakade Yoshinobu 1999, 17–31.

———. 1983a. "Chōseijutsu" 長生術 [The arts of long life]. In Fukui Kōjun et al. 1983, 1: 239–84. Reprinted as "Chōseijutsu no shosō: Dōinjutsu, kokyūhō, hōchūjutsu" 長生術の諸相—導引術・呼吸法・房中術 [Aspects of the arts of long life: *Daoyin*, breathing, and sexual arts] in Sakade Yoshinobu 1999, 32–72.

———. 1983b. "Shinsen shisō no shintaikan: Yōkei to naikan o chūshin ni" 神仙思想の身体観－養形と内観を中心に [The view of the body in the conceptions of "divine immortality," with special reference to "nourishing the form" and inner contemplation]. *Risō* 理想 604 (1983): 63–75. Reprinted in Sakade Yoshinobu 1993b, 53–72.

———. 1985. "Hōso densetsu to *Hōso kyō*" 彭祖傳説と「彭祖經」 [The traditions concerning Pengzu and the *Pengzu jing*]. In Yamada Keiji 1985, 2: 405–62. Revised version in Sakade Yoshinobu 1992a, 23–105.

———. 1986a. "Chō Tan *Yōsei yōshū* itsubun to sono shisō" 張湛「養生要集」佚文とその思想 [On the *Yangsheng yaoji*, a lost work by Zhang Zhan, and its conceptions]. *TS* 68: 1–24. Reprinted in Sakade Yoshinobu 1992a, 107–41.

———. 1986b. "Dōin no enkaku" 導引の沿革 [The evolution of *daoyin*]. Published as an appendix to a reprint of Kitamura Toshikatsu 喜多村利且, *Dōin taiyō* 導引体要 [The essentials of *daoyin*] (Taniguchi: Taniguchi shoten, 1986). Reprinted in Sakade Yoshinobu 1992a, 223–54.

————. 1986c. "The Taoist Character of the 'Chapter on Nourishing Life' of the *Ishinpō*." *Kansai daigaku bungaku ronshū* 関西大學文學論集 36.2: 775–98. Also published in Japanese as "*Ishinpō* Yōseihen no dōkyōteki seikaku" 「醫心方」養生篇の道教的性格 [The Taoist nature of the chapters on Nourishing Life in the *Ishinpō*], in Akizuki Kan'ei 1987, 315–31.

————, ed. 1987. *Rentan shuyōhō* 錬丹修養法 [Methods of refining the elixir and nourishing life]. Tokyo: Taniguchi shoten. [A reedition of the 1927 work by Itō Kōen 伊藤光遠, with additional notes by Sakade Yoshinobu.]

————, ed. 1988a. *Chūgoku kodai yōsei shisō no sōgōteki kenkyū* 中國古代養生思想の総合的研究 [Collected studies on the conceptions of Nourishing Life in ancient China]. Tokyo: Hirakawa shuppansha.

————. 1988b. "Zui-Tō jidai ni okeru fukutan to naikan to naitan" 隋唐時代における服丹と内観と内丹 [Ingestion of elixirs, inner contemplation, and inner alchemy in the Sui and Tang periods]. In Sakade Yoshinobu 1988a, 566–99. Shorter English version: "Methods and Ideas on Increasing Vitality in Ancient China: The Transition from *Neiguan* to *Neidan* in the Sui and Tang Dynasties," in Kawakita Yoshio, Sakai Shizu, and Otsuka Yasuo 1991, 99–115.

————. 1989a. "Longevity Techniques in Japan: Ancient Sources and Contemporary Studies." In Kohn 1989c, 1–40.

————. 1989b. "Son Shibaku ni okeru iryō to dōkyō" 孫思邈における医療と道教 [Medical treatment and Taoism in Sun Simiao]. In Sakade Yoshinobu 1999, 246–67.

————. 1991. "*Naikeizu* to sono enkaku" 「内景圖」とその沿革 [The *Neijing tu* and its evolution]. In Yamada Keiji and Tanaka Tan 1989–91, 2: 45–85. Reprinted in Sakade Yoshinobu 1999, 73–112.

————. 1992a. *Dōkyō to yōsei shisō* 道教と養生思想 [Taoism and the conceptions of Nourishing Life]. Tokyo: Perikan sha.

————. 1992b. "Sun Simiao et le Bouddhisme." *Kansai daigaku bungaku ronshū* 関西大學文學論集 42.1: 81–98. Also published in Japanese as "Son Shibaku to bukkyō" 孫思邈と佛教 [Sun Simiao and Buddhism], *Chūgoku koten kenkyū* 中國古典研究 37 (1992), 1–19; reprinted in Sakade Yoshinobu 1999, 268–82.

————. 1993a. "Bōchū jutsu to yōsei: Furō kaishun no jutsu" 房中術と養生－不老回春の術 ["Arts of the bedchamber" and Nourishing Life: The arts of perennial youth]. In Sakade Yoshinobu 1993b, 95–100.

————. 1993b. "*Ki*" to yōsei: Dōkyō no yōsei jutsu to jujutsu" 「気」と養生－道教の養生術と呪術 [*Qi* (pneuma) and Nourishing Life: The Taoist arts of Nourishing Life and spells]. Kyoto: Jinbun shoin.

————. 1993c. "Wazawai o sakeru hokō jutsu = Uho" 災いを避ける歩行術＝禹歩 [The art of walking to avert calamities, or "Pace of Yu"]. In Sakade Yoshinobu 1993b, 247–52.

————, ed. 1994a. *Dōkyō no daijiten* 道教の大事典 [Great encyclopedia of Taoism]. Tokyo: Shin jinbutsu ōrai sha.

———. 1994b. *"Ishinpō ni okeru iryō to dōkyō"* 「醫心方」における醫療と道教 [Medical treatment in the *Ishinpō* and Taoism]. In Nose Makoto 1994, 89–98.

———. 1994c. *"Ki to dōkyō shinzō no keisei"* 気と道教神像の形成 [*Qi* (pneuma) and the development of Taoist sculpture]. *Bungei ronsō* 文藝論叢 42: 256–93.

———. 1999. *Chūgoku shisō kenkyū: Iyaku yōsei, kagaku shisō hen* 中國思想研究—醫藥養生・科學思想篇 [Studies on Chinese thought: Drugs, Nourishing Life, and scientific thought]. Osaka: Kansai daigaku shuppanbu.

———. 2000. "Divination as Daoist Practice." In Kohn 2000b, 541–66.

Sakade Yoshinobu sensei taikyū kinen ronshū kankōkai 坂出祥伸先生退休記念論集刊行會 [Editorial Committee for the Essays in Commemoration of the Retirement of Professor Sakade Yoshinobu], ed. 2004. *Sakade Yoshinobu sensei taikyū kinen ronshū: Chūgoku shisō ni okeru shintai, shizen, shinkō* 坂出祥伸先生退休記念論集—中國思想における身體・自然・信仰 [Essays in Commemoration of the Retirement of Professor Sakade Yoshinobu: Body, Nature, and Religious Beliefs in Chinese Thought]. Tokyo: Tōhō shoten.

Sakai Tadao 酒井忠夫. 1960. *Chūgoku zensho no kenkyū* 中國善書の研究 [Studies on Chinese morality books]. Tokyo: Kōbundō.

———, ed. 1977. *Dōkyō no sōgōteki kenkyū* 道教の総合的研究 [Collected studies on Taoism]. Tokyo: Kokusho kankōkai.

———, ed. 1992. *Taiwan no shūkyō to Chūgoku bunka* 臺湾の宗教と中國文化 [Taiwanese religion and Chinese culture]. Tokyo: Fūkyōsha.

Sakai Tadao 酒井忠夫 and Fukui Fumimasa 福井文雅. 1983. *"Dōkyō to wa nanika"* 道教とは何か [What is Taoism?]. In Fukui Kōjun et al. 1983, 1: 3–29.

Sakai Tadao 酒井忠夫, Yamada Toshiaki 山田利明, and Fukui Fumimasa 福井文雅, eds. 1991. *Nihon, Chūgoku no shūkyō bunka no kenkyū* 日本・中國の宗教文化の研究 [Studies on the religious culture of Japan and China]. Tokyo: Hirakawa shuppansha.

Sakai Tadao sensei koki shukuga kinen no kai 酒井忠夫先生古稀祝賀記念の会 [Committee for the Commemoration of the Seventieth Birthday of Professor Sakai Tadao], ed. 1982. *Rekishi ni okeru minshū to bunka* 歴史における民衆と文化 [Peoples and cultures in history]. Tokyo: Kokusho kankōkai.

Sakamoto Kaname 坂本要, ed. 1990. *Jigoku no sekai* 地獄の世界 [The world of hell]. Tokyo: Hokushindō.

Sakauchi Shigeo 坂内榮夫. 1985. *"Shō-Ro dendō shū to naitan shisō"* 「鍾呂傳道集」と内丹思想 [The *Zhong-Lü chuandao ji* and *neidan* thought]. *Chūgoku shisōshi kenkyū* 中國思想史研究 7: 39–76.

———. 1988. *"Ō Seika to sono jidai: Godai dōkyō shotan"* 王棲霞とその時代—五代道教初探 [Wang Qixia and his time: A preliminary exploration of Taoism in the Five Dynasties]. *TS* 72: 1–19.

Samuels, Mike, and Nancy Samuels. 1975. *Seeing with the Mind's Eye: The History, Techniques, and Uses of Visualization*. New York: Random House.

Saso, Michael R. 1970. "The Taoist Tradition in Taiwan." *The China Quarterly* 41: 83–103.

———, ed. 1975. *Zhuang-Lin xu daozang* 莊林續道藏 [The Zhuang-Lin Supplement to the Taoist Canon]. 25 vols. Taipei: Chengwen chubanshe.

————, ed. 1978a. *Dōkyō hiketsu shūsei* 道教祕訣集成 [A collection of Taoist esoterica]. Tokyo: Ryūkei shosha.

————. 1978b. *The Teachings of Taoist Master Chuang.* New Haven and London: Yale University Press. Revised edition: *Taoist Master Chuang* (Eldorado Springs, CO: Sacred Mountain Press, 2000).

————. 1978c. "What is the *Ho-t'u?*" *HR* 17: 399–416.

————. 1979. "A Guide to the *Chuang Lin Hsü Tao-tsang.*" *Journal of the China Society* 16–17: 9–28.

————. 1989. *Taoism and the Rite of Cosmic Renewal.* Second edition. Pullman, WA: Washington State University Press.

————. 1995. *The Gold Pavilion: Taoist Ways to Peace, Healing, and Long Life.* Boston: Charles E. Tuttle.

————. 1997. "The Taoist Body and Cosmic Prayer." In Coakley 1997, 231–47.

Saso, Michael R, and David W. Chappell, eds. 1977. *Buddhist and Taoist Studies I.* Honolulu: University of Hawaii Press.

Satō Hitoshi 佐藤仁. 1958. "*Kikokushi* ni tsuite" 「鬼谷子」について [On the *Guigu zi*]. *Kyūshū daigaku tetsugaku nenpō* 九州大學哲學年報 18: 276–95.

Sattler, Gabriele. 1976. "Shao Yung." In Goodrich and Fang 1976, 849–57.

Sawada Mizuho 澤田瑞穗. 1968. *Jigoku hen: Chūgoku no meikai setsu* 地獄変—中國の冥界説 [The transformation of hell: Chinese views on the realm of darkness]. Kyoto: Hōzōkan.

————. 1975. *Zōho Hōkan no kenkyū* 増補宝巻の研究 [Studies on the "Precious Scrolls" (enlarged edition)]. Tokyo: Kokusho kankōkai.

————. 1988. *Retsusenden, Shinsenden* 列仙傳・神仙傳 [*Liexian zhuan* and *Shenxian zhuan*]. Tokyo: Hirakawa shuppansha.

Schafer, Edward H. 1954. *The Empire of Min.* Rutland, VT, and Tokyo: Charles E. Tuttle.

————. 1975. "The Stove God and the Alchemists." In Thompson 1975, 261–66.

————. 1976. "A Trip to the Moon." *JAOS* 96: 27–37.

————. 1977a. *Pacing the Void: T'ang Approaches to the Stars.* Berkeley, Los Angeles, and London: University of California Press.

————. 1977b. "The Restoration of the Shrine of Wei Hua-ts'un at Lin-ch'uan in the Eighth Century." *Journal of Oriental Studies* 15: 124–37.

————. 1978a. "The Jade Woman of Greatest Mystery." *HR* 17: 387–98.

————. 1978b. "The Transcendent Vitamin: Efflorescence of Lang-kan." *Chinese Science* 3: 27–38.

————. 1978–79. "A T'ang Taoist Mirror." *EC* 4: 48–49.

————. 1979. "Three Divine Women of South China." *Chinese Literature: Essays, Articles, Reviews* 1: 31–42.

————. 1981. "Wu Yün's 'Cantos on Pacing the Void.'" *HJAS* 41: 377–415.

————. 1981–83. "Wu Yün's Stanzas on 'Saunters in Sylphdom.'" *MS* 35: 1–37.

————. 1985. *Mirages on the Sea of Time: The Taoist Poetry of Ts'ao T'ang.* Berkeley: University of California Press.

————. 1987. "The Dance of the Purple Culmen." *T'ang Studies* 5. 45–68.

————. 1989. *Mao-shan in T'ang Times.* Second edition. Boulder, CO: Society for the Study of Chinese Religions.

———. 1997. "The Scripture of the Opening of Heaven by the Most High Lord Lao." *TR* 7.2: 1–20.

Schafer, Edward H., and Cordell Yee. 1986. "Tu Kuang-t'ing." In Nienhauser 1986, 821–24.

Schipper, Kristofer M. 1960. "Les pèlerinages en Chine: Montagnes et pistes." In *Les pèlerinages*. Sources orientales, 3. Paris: Éditions du Seuil.

———. 1965. *L'Empereur Wou des Han dans la légende taoïste: Han Wou-ti nei-tchouan*. Paris: École Française d'Extrême-Orient.

———. 1966. "The Divine Jester, Some Remarks on the Gods of the Chinese Marionette Theater." *ZMJ* 21: 81–94.

———. 1967. *"Gogaku shingyō zu no shinkō"*「五岳真形圖」の信仰 [The belief in the *Wuyue zhenxing tu*]. *Études taoïstes / Dōkyō kenkyū* 道教研究 2: 114–62.

———. 1971. "Démonologie chinoise." In *Génies, Anges, et Démons*, 403–29. Sources orientales, 8. Paris: Éditions du Seuil

———. 1974. "The Written Memorial in Taoist Ceremonies." In Wolf 1974, 309–24.

———, ed. 1975a. *Concordance du Houang-t'ing king: Nei-king et Wai-king*. Paris: École Française d'Extrême-Orient.

———. 1975b. *Concordance du Tao-tsang: Titres des ouvrages*. Paris: École Française d'Extrême-Orient.

———. 1975c. *Le Fen-teng: Rituel taoïste*. Paris: École Française d'Extrême-Orient.

———. 1977a. "Neighborhood Cult Associations in Traditional Tainan." In Skinner 1977, 651–76.

———. 1977b. *"'Tokō' no shokinō ni kansuru ni, san no kōsatsu"*「都功」の職能に関する二、三の考察 [Notes on the function of the Inspector of Merit]. In Sakai Tadao 1977, 252–90.

———. 1978. "The Taoist Body." *HR* 17: 355–81.

———. 1979a. "Le Calendrier de Jade: Note sur le *Laozi zhongjing*." *Nachrichten der Gesellschaft für Natur- und Völkerkunde Ostasiens* 125: 75–80.

———. 1979b. "Millénarismes et messianismes dans la Chine ancienne." In Lanciotti and Corradini 1979, 31–49.

———. 1981. *Projet Tao-tsang: Index du Yunji qiqian*. 2 vols. Paris: École Française d'Extrême-Orient.

———. 1982–83. "Les Maîtres Célestes à l'époque Song." *Annuaire de l'École Pratique des Hautes Études, Ve Section*, 91: 133–37.

———. 1984. "Le monachisme taoïste." In Lanciotti 1984, 199–215.

———. 1985a. "Comment on crée un lieu-saint: À propos de *Danses et légendes de la Chine ancienne*." *Études chinoises* 4.2: 41–61.

———. 1985b. "Seigneurs royaux, dieux des épidémies." *Archives de Sciences Sociales des Religions* 59: 31–40.

———. 1985c. "Taoist Ordination Ranks in the Tunhuang Manuscripts." In Naundorf, Pohl, and Schmidt 1985, 127–48.

———. 1985d. "Taoist Ritual and Local Cults of the T'ang Dynasty." In Strickmann 1981–85, 3: 812–34.

———. 1985e. "Vernacular and Classical Ritual in Taoism." *Journal of Asian Studies* 45: 21–57.

————. 1986. "Yün-chi ch'i-ch'ien." In Nienhauser 1986, 966–68.

————. 1987. "Master Chao I-chen 趙宜真 (?–1382) and the Ch'ing-wei 清微 School of Taoism." In Akizuki Kan'ei 1987, 715–34. [Page citations are to the parallel Western-style pagination, from p. 1 to p. 20.]

————. 1989a. "A Study of Buxu: Taoist Liturgical Hymn and Dance." In Tsao and Law 1989, 110–20. Translated into Chinese by Liao Wenying 寥文英 and Zeng Yuzhen 曾于真 as "Buxu de yanjiu" 步虛的研究 [A study of buxu], DT 2 (1989): 437–50.

————. 1989b. "Mu-lien Plays in Taoist Liturgical Context." In Johnson 1989, 126–54.

————. 1990. "The Cult of Pao-sheng ta-ti and its Spreading to Taiwan: A Case Study of Fen-hsiang." In Vermeer 1990, 397–416.

————. 1991a. "Le culte de l'immortel Tang Gongfang." In Forest, Ishizawa, and Vandermeersch 1991, 59–72.

————. 1991b. "Reihō kagi no tenkai" 霊宝科儀の展開 [The development of Ling-bao liturgy]. Translated by Yamada Toshiaki 山田利明. In Sakai Tadao, Yamada Toshiaki, and Fukui Fumimasa 1991, 219–31.

————. 1993. The Taoist Body. Translated by Karen C. Duval. Berkeley: University of California Press. Originally published as Le corps taoïste: Corps physique, corps social (Paris: Librairie Arthème Fayard, 1979).

————. 1995a. "An Outline of Taoist Ritual." In Blondeau and Schipper 1988–95, 97–126.

————. 1995b. "Note sur l'histoire du Dongyue miao de Pékin." In Diény 1995, 255–69.

————. 1995c. "The Inner World of the Laozi zhongjing." In Huang and Zürcher 1995, 114–31.

————. 1997a. "Structures liturgiques et société civile à Pékin." Sanjiao wenxian: Matériaux pour l'étude de la religion chinoise 1: 9–23.

————. 1997b. "Une stèle taoïste des Han orientaux récemment découverte." In Gernet and Kalinowski 1997, 239–47.

————. 1999a. "Commandments of Lord Lao." In de Bary and Bloom 1999, 1: 395–96.

————. 1999b. "The Doctrine of the Three Heavens." In de Bary and Bloom 1999, 1: 400–402.

————. 2001. "Daoist Ecology: The Inner Transformation. A Study of the Precepts of the Early Daoist Ecclesia." In Girardot, Miller, and Liu 2001, 79–93.

————. 2005. "The True Form: Reflections on the Liturgical Basis of Taoist Art." Sanjiao wenxian: Matériaux pour l'étude de la religion chinoise 4: 91–113.

Schipper, Kristofer M., and Franciscus Verellen, eds. 2004. The Taoist Canon: A Historical Companion to the Daozang. Chicago: Chicago University Press.

Schipper, Kristofer M., and Wang Hsiu-huei. 1986. "Progressive and Regressive Time Cycles in Taoist Ritual." In Fraser, Lawrence, and Haber 1986, 185–205.

Schlegel, Gustave. 1866. Thian ti hwui: The Hung-League, or Heaven-Earth-League, a Secret Society with the Chinese in China and India. Batavia: Lange. Reprint, New York: AMS Press, 1974.

Schmidt, Hans-Hermann. 1985. "Die Hundertachtzig Vorschriften von Lao-chün." In Naundorf, Pohl, and Schmidt 1985, 149–59.

Schmidt-Glintzer, Helwig. 1976. *Das Hung-ming chi und die Aufnahme des Buddhismus in China*. Wiesbaden: Franz Steiner Verlag.

———. 1981. "Die Manipulation von Omina und ihre Beurteilung bei Hofe: Das Beispiel der Himmelsbriefe Wang Ch'ing-jos unter Chen-tsung (regierte 998–1023)." *ASEA* 35: 1–14.

Schwartz, Benjamin. 1985. *The World of Thought in Ancient China*. Cambridge, MA: Harvard University Press.

Seaman, Gary. 1980. "In the Presence of Authority: Hierarchical Roles in Chinese Spirit Medium Cults." In Kleinman and Lin 1980) 61–74.

———. 1987. *Journey to the North: An Ethnohistorical Analysis and Annotated Translation of the Chinese Folk Novel Pei-yu chi*. Berkeley: University of California Press.

Seidel, Anna K. 1969. *La divinisation de Lao tseu dans le Taoïsme des Han*. Paris: École Française d'Extrême-Orient.

———. 1969–70. "The Image of the Perfect Ruler in Early Taoist Messianism: Lao-tzu and Li Hung." *HR* 9: 216–47.

———. 1970. "A Taoist Immortal of the Ming Dynasty: Chang San-feng." In de Bary and the Conference on Ming Thought 1970, 483–531.

———. 1978a. "Buying One's Way to Heaven: The Celestial Treasury in Chinese Religions." *HR* 17: 419–31.

———. 1978b. "Das Neue Testament des Tao: Lao-tzu und die Enstehung der Taoistischen Religion am Ende der Han-Zeit." *Saeculum* 29: 147–72.

———. 1979. "Le Fils du Ciel et le Maître Céleste: Note à propos des 'Registres' taoïques." *Transactions of the International Conference of Orientalists in Japan* 24: 119–27.

———. 1981. "Kokuhō 國寶: Note à propos du terme 'Trésor National' en Chine et au Japon." *BEFEO* 69: 229–61.

———. 1982. "Tokens of Immortality in Han Graves." With an appendix by Marc Kalinowski. *Numen* 29: 79–122.

———. 1983a. "Imperial Treasures and Taoist Sacraments: Taoist Roots in the Apocrypha." In Strickmann 1981–85, 2: 291–371.

———. 1983b. "Taoist Messianism." *Numen* 31: 161–74.

———. 1984. "Le sūtra merveilleux du Ling-pao suprême, traitant de Lao tseu qui convertit les barbares (le manuscrit S. 2081): Contribution à l'étude du Bouddho-taoïsme des Six Dynasties." In Soymié 1984, 305–52.

———. 1987a. "Afterlife: Chinese Concepts." In Eliade 1987, 1: 124–27.

———. 1987b. "Huang-ti." In Eliade 1987, 484–85.

———. 1987c. "*Post-Mortem* Immortality, or: The Taoist Resurrection of the Body." In Shaked, Shulman, and Stroumsa 1987, 223–37.

———. 1987d. "T'ai-p'ing." In Eliade 1987, 14: 251–52.

———. 1987e. "Traces of Han Religion in Funeral Texts Found in Tombs." In Akizuki Kan'ei 1987, 678–714. [Page citations are to the parallel Western-style pagination, from p. 21 to p. 57.]

———. 1987f. "Yü-huang." In Eliade 1987, 15: 541.

———. 1988. "Early Taoist Ritual." *CEA* 4: 199–204.

———. 1989–90. "Chronicle of Taoist Studies in the West 1950–1990." *CEA* 5: 223–347.

———. 1997. "Taoism: The Unofficial High Religion of China." *TR* 7.2: 39–72.

Servais, Paul, ed. 1999. *La mort et l'au-delà: Une rencontre de l'Orient et de l'Occident*. Louvain-la-Neuve: Academia-Bruylant.

Servier, Jean, ed. 1998. *Dictionnaire critique de l'ésotérisme*. Paris: Presses Universitaires de France.

Shahar, Meir, and Robert P. Weller. 1996. *Unruly Gods: Divinity and Society in China*. Honolulu: University of Hawaii Press.

Shaked, S., D. Shulman, and G. G. Stroumsa, eds. 1987. *Gilgul: Essays on Transformation, Revolution and Permanence in the History of Religions, dedicated to R. J. Zwi Werblowsky*. Leiden: E. J. Brill.

Shandong Jiaonan Langya ji Xu Fu Yanjiuhui 山東膠南琅琊暨徐福研究會 [Jiaonan (Shandong) Society for the Study of Langya and Xu Fu], ed. 1995. *Langya yu Xu Fu yanjiu lunwen ji* 琅琊與徐福研究論文集 [Studies on Langya and Xu Fu]. Beijing: Huaxia chubanshe.

Shanren 山人 [pseud.]. 1994. "Longhu shan liushi'er dai Tianshi Zhang Yuanxu mu chongxiu yixin" 龙虎山62代天师张元旭墓重修一新 [On the complete restoration of the grave of the sixty-second Celestial Master Zhang Yuanxu at Mount Longhu]. *ZGDJ* 1994.2: 40.

Shao Wenshi 邵文实. 1996. "Dunhuang daojiao shishu" 敦煌道教试述 [A preliminary study of Taoism in Dunhuang]. *SZY* 1996.2: 68–79.

Shapiro, Deane N., Jr., and Roger N. Walsh, eds. 1984. *Meditation: Classic and Contemporary Perspectives*. New York: Aldine.

Sharf, Robert H. 2002. *Coming to Terms with Chinese Buddhism. A Reading of the Treasure Store Treatise*. Honolulu: University of Hawaii Press.

Shaughnessy, Edward L. 1993. "*I ching* (*Chou i*)." In Loewe 1993, 216–28.

———. 1994. "A First Reading of the Mawangdui *Yijing* Manuscript." *EC* 19: 47–73.

———. 1996a. *I Ching: The Classic of Changes*. New York: Ballantine Books.

———. 1996b. "The Key and the Flow: Drying out the Wet Women of the *Yijing's Xici zhuan*." Paper presented at the Annual Meeting of the Association for Asian Studies, 11 April 1996, Honolulu, Hawaii.

———. 1997. *Before Confucius: Studies in the Creation of the Chinese Classics*. Albany: State University of New York Press.

Shek, Richard. 1987. "Millenarianism: Chinese Millenarian Movements." In Eliade 1987, 9: 532–35.

Shi Bo'er 施博爾 [Kristofer Schipper] and Li Diankui 李殿魁, eds. 1977. *Zhengtong daozang mulu suoyin* 正統道藏目錄索引 [Index to the Taoist Canon of the Zhengtong reign period]. Taipei: Yiwen yinshuguan.

Shi Huaci 史華慈 [Benjamin I. Schwartz]. 1994. "Huang-Lao xueshuo: Song Xing he Shen Dao lunping" 黄老學說—宋鈃和慎到論評 [The Huang-Lao views: On Song Xing and Shen Dao]. *DWY* 4: 128–46.

Shi Mingfei. 1993. "Li Po's Ascent of Mount O-mei: A Taoist Vision of the Mythology of a Sacred Mountain." *TR* 4.1: 31–45.

Shi Xinmin 史新民. 1987. *Zhongguo Wudang shan daojiao yinyue* 中国武当山道教音乐 [Taoist music at Mount Wudang in China]. Beijing: Zhongguo wenlian chuban gongsi.

Shi Yanfeng 石衍丰. 1992. "Ming Shizong chongxin de daoshi Shao Yuanjie yu Tao Zhongwen" 明世宗宠信的道士邵元节与陶仲文 [Shao Yuanjie and Tao Zhongwen, the favorite Taoist masters of Ming Shizong]. *SZY* 1992.2: 89–94.

Shi Zhouren 施舟人 [Kristofer Schipper] and Chen Yaoting 陳耀庭, eds. 1996. *Daozang suoyin* 道藏索引 [Index to the Taoist Canon]. Shanghai: Shanghai shudian chubanshe.

Shiga Takayoshi 滋賀高義. 1963. "Min no Taiso to Tenshidō ni tsuite: Toku ni Chō Seijō o chūshin to shite" 明の太祖と天師道について—特に張正常を中心として [On Ming Taizu and the Way of the Celestial Masters: With special reference to Zhang Zhengchang]. *TS* 22: 45–58.

Shiina Kōyū 椎名宏雄. 1981. "*Sandōkai* no seikaku to genbun" 「參同契」の性格と原文 [The nature and original text of the *Cantong qi*]. (*Komazawa daigaku*) *Shūgaku kenkyū* (駒澤大學) 宗學研究 23: 189–201.

Shimode Sekiyo 下出積與. 1968. *Shinsen shisō* 神仙思想 [The notion of "divine immortality"]. Tokyo: Yoshikawa kōbunkan.

———. 1972. *Nihon kodai no shingi to dōkyō* 日本古代の神祇と道教 [Ancient Japanese deities and Taoism]. Tokyo: Yoshikawa kōbunkan.

———. 1975. *Dōkyō to Nihonjin* 道教と日本人 [Taoism and the Japanese people]. Tokyo: Kōdansha.

———. 1997. *Nihon kodai no dōkyō, Onmyōdō to shingi* 日本古代の道教・陰陽道と神祇 [Taoism, the Way of Yin and Yang, and the deities of ancient Japan]. Tokyo: Yoshikawa kōbunkan.

Shinkawa Tokio 新川登亀男. 1997. "Nihon kodai ni okeru bukkyō to dōkyō" 日本古代における佛教と道教 [Buddhism and Taoism in ancient Japan]. In Noguchi Tetsurō et al. 1996–97, 2: 51–83.

Shinohara Koichi and Gregory Schopen, eds. 1991. *From Benares to Beijing: Essays on Buddhism and Chinese Religion*. Oakville, Ontario: Mosaic Press.

Shiratori Yoshirō 白鳥芳朗. 1975. *Yōjin monjo* 傜人文書 [Writings of the Yao]. Tokyo: Kōdansha.

Si Xiuwu 司修武. 1992. *Huang-Lao xueshuo yu Han chu zhengzhi pingyi* 黃老學說與漢初政治評議 [The Huang-Lao views and the early Han debates on government]. Taipei: Taiwan xuesheng shuju.

Sieffert, René. 1993. *Le Livre des contes*. Paris: POF.

Sivin, Nathan. 1968. *Chinese Alchemy: Preliminary Studies*. Cambridge, MA: Harvard University Press.

———. 1976. "Chinese Alchemy and the Manipulation of Time." *Isis* 67: 513–27. Reprinted in Sivin 1977, 109–22.

———, ed. 1977. *Science and Technology in East Asia: Articles from Isis, 1913–1975*. New York: Science History Publications.

———. 1980. "The Theoretical Background of Elixir Alchemy." In Needham 1980, 210–305.

———. 1987. *Traditional Medicine in Contemporary China: A Partial Translation of Revised Outline of Chinese Medicine (1972) with an Introductory Study on Change in Present-Day and Early Medicine*. Ann Arbor: Center for Chinese Studies, University of Michigan.

———. 1991. "Change and Continuity in Early Cosmology: *The Great Commentary to the Book of Changes.*" In Yamada Keiji and Tanaka Tan 1989–91, 2: 3–43.

———. 1993. "*Huang ti nei ching.*" In Loewe 1993, 196–215.

———. 1995. "State, Cosmos, and Body in the Last Three Centuries B.C." *HJAS* 55: 5–37.

———. 1998. "On the Dates of Yang Shang-shan and the *Huang-ti nei ching t'ai su.*" *Chinese Science* 15: 29–36.

———. 1999a. "Regulations for Petitioning." In de Bary and Bloom 1999, 1: 396–99.

———. 1999b. "The Divine Incantations Scripture." In de Bary and Bloom 1999, 1: 406–10.

Skar, Lowell. 1996–97. "Administering Thunder: A Thirteenth-Century Memorial Deliberating the Thunder Rites." *CEA* 9: 159–202.

———. 2000. "Ritual Movements, Deity Cults, and the Transformation of Daoism in Song and Yuan Times." In Kohn 2000b, 413–63.

Skinner, G. William, ed. 1977. *The City in Late Imperial China.* Stanford: Stanford University Press.

Skorupski, Tadeusz, ed. 1991. *The Buddhist Forum.* Vol. 2: *Seminar Papers 1988–1990.* London: School of Oriental and African Studies.

Smith, Kidder, Jr., ed. 1990. *Sagehood and Systematizing Thought in Warring States and Han China.* Brunswick, ME: Asian Studies Program, Bowdoin College.

Smith, Kidder, Jr., Peter K. Bol, Joseph A. Adler, and Don J. Wyatt. 1990. *Sung Dynasty Uses of the I Ching.* Princeton: Princeton University Press.

Smith, Thomas E. 1990. "Record of the Ten Continents." *TR* 2.2: 87–119.

———. 1992. "Ritual and the Shaping of Narrative: The Legend of the Han Emperor Wu." Ph.D. diss., University of Michigan.

———. 1998. "Rikuchō ni okeru butsu-dō ronsō to *Retsusenden* no denshō" 六朝における佛道論争と「列仙傳」の傳承 [Debates between Buddhists and Taoists in the Six Dynasties and the transmission of the *Liexian zhuan*]. Translated by Yamada Takashi 山田俊. In Yamada Toshiaki and Tanaka Fumio 1998, 145–66.

Smith, Wilfred Cantwell. 1993. *What Is Scripture? A Comparative Approach.* Minneapolis: Fortress Press.

Sofukawa Hiroshi 曽布川寛. 1993. "Kandai gazō-seki ni okeru shōsen-zu no keifu 漢代畫像石における昇仙圖の系譜 [Images of the ascent to immortality in Han-dynasty stone reliefs and their lineage]. *TG* 65: 23–221.

Soymié, Michel. 1956. "Le Lo-feou chan: Étude de géographie religieuse." *BEFEO* 48: 1–137.

———. 1977. "Les dix jours du jeûne taoiste." In Yoshioka Yoshitoyo hakase kanreki kinen kenkyū ronshū kankōkai 1977, 1–21.

———, ed. 1979. *Contributions aux études sur Touen-houang.* [Vol. 1.] Genève and Paris: Librairie Droz.

———, ed. 1984. *Contributions aux études de Touen-houang.* Vol. 3. Paris: École Française d'Extrême-Orient.

Spiro, Audrey. 1990. "How Light and Airy: Upward Mobility in the Realm of the Immortals." *TR* 2.2: 43–69.

Stanton, William. 1900. *The Triad Society; or, Heaven and Earth Association.* Hong Kong: Kelly and Walsh.

Stein, Rolf A. 1963. "Remarques sur les mouvements du taoïsme politico-religieux au IIe siècle ap. J.-C." *TP* 50: 1–78.

———. 1968. "Aspects de la foi jurée en Chine." *Annuaire du Collège de France* 67: 411–15.

———. 1969a. "Textes taoïstes relatifs à la transmission des livres révélés." *Annuaire du Collège de France* 68: 453–57.

———. 1969b. "Un example de relations entre taoïsme et religion populaire." In Fukui Hakase shōju kinen ronbunshū kankōkai 1969, 79–90.

———. 1970. "La légende du foyer dans le monde chinois." In Pouillon and Maranda 1970, 2: 1280–1305.

———. 1971. "Les fêtes de cuisine du taoïsme religieux." *Annuaire du Collège de France* 71: 431–40.

———. 1972. "Spéculations mystiques et thèmes relatifs aux 'cuisines' du taoïsme." *Annuaire du Collège de France* 72: 489–99.

———. 1973. "Conceptions relatives à la nourriture en Chine." *Annuaire du Collège de France* 73: 547–63.

———. 1979. "Religious Taoism and Popular Religion from the Second to Seventh Centuries." In Welch and Seidel 1979, 53–81.

———. 1990. *The World in Miniature: Container Gardens and Dwellings in Far Eastern Religious Thought*. Translated by Phyllis Brooks. Stanford: Stanford University Press. Originally published as *Le monde en petit: Jardins en miniature et habitations dans la pensée religieuse d'Extrême-Orient* (Paris: Flammarion, 1987).

Stein, Stephan. 1999. *Zwischen Heil und Heilung: Zur frühen Tradition des Yangsheng in China*. Helzen: Medizinisch Literarische Verlagsgesellschaft.

Steinhardt, Nancy S. 1987. "Taoist Temple Compounds." In Eliade 1987, 14: 380–81.

———. 1998. "The Temple to the Northern Peak in Quyang." *Artibus Asiae* 58: 69–90.

———. 2000. "Taoist Architecture." In Little 2000b, 57–75.

Stevens, Keith G. 1997. *Chinese Gods: The Unseen World of Spirits and Demons*. London: Collins and Brown.

———. 2001. *Chinese Mythological Gods*. Oxford and New York: Oxford University Press.

Strickmann, Michel. 1966. "Notes on Mushroom Cults in Ancient China." Paper presented at the 4e Journée des Orientalistes Belges, June 1966, Bruxelles.

———. 1974. "Taoism, History of." *Encyclopaedia Britannica*, fifteenth edition, *Macropedia*, 17: 1044–50.

———. 1975. "Sōdai no raigi: Shinshō undō to dōka Nansō ni tsuite no ryakusetu" 宋代の雷儀—神霄運動と道家南宗についての略説 [On the Thunder Rites during the Song Dynasty: A brief discussion of the Shenxiao movement and the Taoist Southern Lineage]. *TS* 46: 15–28.

———. 1977. "The Mao shan Revelations: Taoism and the Aristocracy." *TP* 63: 1–64.

———. 1978a. "A Taoist Confirmation of Liang Wu Ti's Suppression of Taoism." *JAOS* 98: 467–74.

———. 1978b. "The Longest Taoist Scripture." *HR* 17: 331–54.

———. 1979. "On the Alchemy of T'ao Hung-ching." In Welch and Seidel 1979, 123–92.

————. 1981. *Le Taoïsme du Mao Chan: Chronique d'une révélation*. Paris: Collège de France, Institut des Hautes Études Chinoises.

————, ed. 1981–85. *Tantric and Taoist Studies in Honour of Rolf A. Stein*. 3 vols. Bruxelles: Institut Belge des Hautes Études Chinoises.

————. 1982. "The Tao among the Yao: Taoism and the Sinification of South China." In Sakai Tadao sensei koki shukuga kinen no kai 1982, 23–30.

————. 1985. "Therapeutische Rituale und das Problem des Bösen im frühen Taoismus." In Naundorf, Pohl, and Schmidt 1985, 185–200.

————. 1990. "The *Consecration Sūtra*: A Buddhist Book of Spells." In Buswell 1990, 75–118.

————. 1994. "Saintly Fools and Chinese Masters (Holy Fools)." *AM*, third series, 7: 35–57.

————. 1996. *Mantras et mandarins: Le bouddhisme tantrique en Chine*. Paris: Gallimard.

————. 2002. *Chinese Magical Medicine*. Edited by Bernard Faure. Stanford: Stanford University Press.

Su Bai 宿白. 1962. "Yongle gong chuangjian shiliao nianbian" 永乐宫创建史料年编 [A chronicle of historical materials on the construction of the Yongle gong]. *Wenwu* 文物 1962:4–5: 80–87.

Su Jinren 蘇晉仁. 1998. "Dunhuang yishu *Laozi bianhua jing* shuzheng" 敦煌逸書「老子變化經」疏證 [Notes on the Dunhuang manuscript of the *Laozi bianhua jing*]. *DWY* 13: 130–55.

Su Suqing 蘇素卿. 1999. "Taiwan kanzoku ni okeru saishi katsudō to kami seihin no kenkyū: Omo ni kinginshi o chūshin ni shite" 臺湾漢族における祭祀活動と紙製品の研究—主に金銀紙を中心にして [Rituals and paper objects among the Chinese in Taiwan, with special reference to "gold" and "silver" paper money]. *Hikaku minzoku kenkyū* 比較民俗研究 16: 47–104.

Sun K'o-k'uan [Sun Kekuan]. 1981. "Yü Chi and Southern Taoism during the Yüan Period." In Langlois 1981, 212–53.

Sun Kekuan 孫克寬. 1965. *Song Yuan daojiao zhi fazhan* 宋元道教之發展 [The development of Taoism in the Sung and Yuan periods]. Taizhong: Donghai daxue chubanshe.

————. 1968. *Yuandai daojiao zhi fazhan* 元代道教之發展 [The development of Taoism during the Yuan dynasty]. Taizhong: Donghai daxue chubanshe.

————. 1977. *Hanyuan daolun* 寒原道論 [Essays on Taoism from Hanyuan]. Taipei: Lianjing chuban shiye gongsi.

Sunayama Minoru 砂山稔. 1975. "Kōsa yōsō kō: Nanchō ni okeru bukkyō to no hanran ni tsuite" 江左妖僧考—南朝における佛教徒の反乱について [A study of a priest-magician in southeastern China: On a Buddhist rebellion in the Southern Dynasties period]. *TS* 46: 26–62.

————. 1983. "Dōkyō to Rōshi" 道教と老子 [Taoism and Laozi]. In Fukui Kōjun et al. 1983, 2: 3–47. Reprinted in Sunayama Minoru 1990, 27–68.

————. 1984. "*Lingbao duren jing sizhu* zhaji" 「灵宝度人经」四注札记 [Notes on the *Lingbao duren jing sizhu*]. *SZY* 1984.2: 30–48. Also published in Japanese in Sunayama Minoru 1990, 272–304.

————. 1990. *Zui-Tō dōkyō shisōshi kenkyū* 隋唐道教思想史研究 [Studies on the history of Taoist thought in the Sui and Tang dynasties]. Tokyo: Hirakawa shuppansha.

————. 1993. "*Ōyō Shū no seishi ni tsuite: Ōyō Shū to dokyō shisō*" 歐陽脩の青詞について—歐陽脩と道教思想 [On the Green Declaration (*qingci*) by Ouyang Xiu: Ouyang Xiu and Taoist thought]. *TS* 81: 1–21.

Suter, Rufus O. 1943–44. "P'eng Ting-ch'iu." In Hummell 1943–44, 616–17.

Suzuki hakushi koki kinen shukugakai 鈴木博士古稀記念祝賀会編 [Committee for the celebration of the seventieth birthday of Dr. Suzuki Yoshijirō], ed. 1972. *Tōyōgaku ronsō: Suzuki hakushi koki kinen* 東洋學論叢—鈴木博士古稀記念 [Collected essays in Oriental Asian studies: In honor of Dr. Suzuki Yoshijirō on his seventieth birthday]. Tokyo: Meitoku shuppansha.

Suzuki Yoshijirō 鈴木由次郎. 1974. *Kan Eki kenkyū* 漢易研究 [Studies on the *Book of Changes* in the Han period]. Revised edition. Tokyo: Meitoku shuppansha.

————. 1977. *Shūeki sandōkei* 周易参同契 [*Zhouyi cantong qi*]. Tokyo: Meitoku shuppansha.

Suzuki, D. T., and Paul Carus. 1906a. *T'ai-shang kan-ying p'ien: Treatise on Response and Retribution*. Chicago: Open Court.

————. 1906b. See Suzuki Teitaro and Paul Carus 1906b.

Suzuki Shunryū. 1999. *Branching Streams Flow in the Darkness: Zen Talks on the Sandokai*. Edited by Mel Weitsman and Michael Wenger. Berkeley: University of California Press.

Suzuki Teitaro [Suzuki, D. T.] and Paul Carus. 1906b. *Yin chih wen: The Tract of the Quiet Way, with Extracts from the Chinese Commentary*. La Salle, IL: Open Court.

Szonyi, Mike. 1997. "The Illusion of Standardizing the Gods: The Cult of the Five Emperors in Late Imperial China." *Journal of Asian Studies* 56: 113–35.

Takahashi Bunji 高橋文治. 1997. "Chō Ryūson no tōjō zengo" 張留孫の登場前後 [The advent of Zhang Liusun and its circumstances]. *Tōyōshi kenkyū* 東洋史研究 56.1: 66–96.

Takahashi Tadahiko 高橋忠彦. 1984. "*Taihei kyō no shisō no kōzō*" 「太平經」の思想の構造 [The structure of thought in the *Taiping jing*]. *TBKK* 95: 295–336.

————. 1986. "*Taihei kyō no shisō no shakaiteki sokumen*" 「太平經」の思想の社会的側面 [The social aspects of the thought of the *Taiping jing*]. *TBKK* 100: 249–84.

————. 1988. "*Taihei kyō no kaiwatai no seikaku ni tsuite*" 「太平經」の会話体の性格について [On the nature of the dialogical chapters of the *Taiping jing*]. *TBKK* 105: 243–81.

Takahashi Yōichirō 高橋庸一郎. 1988. "Kodai Chūgoku ni okeru yōseijutsuteki 'nioi' no hottan" 古代中國における養生術的「匂い」の発端 [The origins of the use of 'smell' as a means of Nourishing Life in ancient China]. In Sakade Yoshinobu 1988a, 144–72.

Takenaka Shinjō hakase shōju kinen ronbunshū kankōkai 竹中信常博士頌壽記念論文集刊行会 [Editorial Committee for the Collected Essays Presented to Dr. Takenaka Shinjō on his Seventieth Birthday], ed. 1984. *Shūkyō bunka no shosō* 宗教文化の諸相 [Aspects of religious culture]. Tokyo: Takenaka Shinjō hakase shōju kinen ronbunshū kankōkai.

Takeuchi Yoshio 武内義雄. 1929. *"Kikokushi o yomu"*「鬼谷子」を読む [A reading of the *Guigu zi*]. *Shinagaku* 支那學 5.4, 47–62.

———. 1930. *Takeuchi Yoshio zenshū* 武内義雄全集 [Collected works of Takeuchi Yoshio]. 10 vols. Tokyo: Kadokawa shoten.

Takimoto Yūzō 瀧本祐造. 1992. "Chūgoku no dōkyō ongaku ni tsuite" 中國の道教音楽について [On Taoist music in continental China]. *TS* 79: 1–22.

Takimoto Yūzō and Liu Hong. 2000. "Daoist Ritual Music." In Kohn 2000b, 747–64.

Tan Chee-Beng. 1990a. "Chinese Religion and Local Chinese Communities in Malaysia." In Tan Chee-Beng 1990b, 5–27.

———, ed. 1990b. *The Preservation and Adaptation of Tradition: Studies of Chinese Religious Expression in Southeast Asia*. Columbus: Ohio State University, Department of Anthropology.

Tanaka Fumio 田中文雄. 1988. *"Gorin kuji hishaku* to yōsei shisō"「五輪九字秘釈」と養生思想 [The *Wulun jiuzi bishi* and the conceptions of Nourishing Life]. In Sakade Yoshinobu 1988a, 674–98.

Tanaka Issei 田仲一成. 1981. *Chūgoku saishi engeki kenkyū* 中國祭祀演劇研究 [Studies on ritual theatre in China]. Tokyo: Tōkyō daigaku Tōyō bunka kenkyūjo.

———. 1985. *Chūgoku no sōzoku to engeki* 中國の宗族と演劇 [Kinship and theatre in China]. Tokyo: Tōkyō daigaku Tōyō bunka kenkyūjo. Also published in Chinese as *Zhongguo de zongzu yu xiju* 中國的宗族與戲劇 (Shanghai: Shanghai guji chubanshe, 1992).

———. 1989a. "Daojiao yili yu sishen xiju zhi jian de guanxi" 道教儀禮與祀神戲劇之間的關係 [The relationship between Taoist liturgy and religious plays]. In Tsao and Law 1989, 155–65.

———. 1989b. "The Jiao Festival in Hong Kong and the New Territories." In Pas 1989b, 271–98.

———. 1993. *Chūgoku fukei engeki kenkyū* 中國巫系演劇研究 [Studies on shamanic theatre in China]. Tokyo: Tōkyō daigaku Tōyō bunka kenkyūjo.

Tang Changru 唐長孺. 1955. *Wei Jin Nanbei chao shi luncong* 魏晉南北朝史論叢 [Studies on the history of the Wei, Jin, and Northern and Southern Dynasties]. Beijing: Sanlian shudian.

Tang Junyi 唐君毅. 1986. *Zhongguo zhexue yuanlun: Yuandao pian* 中國哲學原論—原道篇 [Foundational studies in Chinese philosophy: The Original Dao]. 3. vols. Taipei: Taiwan xuesheng shuju.

Tang Lan 唐兰. 1974. "Huangdi sijing chutan" 黄帝四经初探 [A preliminary exploration of the "Four Scriptures of the Yellow Emperor"]. *Wenwu* 文物 1974.10: 48–52.

Tang Xiaofeng 唐晓峰, ed. 1997a. *Jiuzhou* 九州 [The Nine Provinces]. Beijing: Zhongguo huanjing kexue chubanshe.

———. 1997b. "Wuyue dili shuo" 五岳地理说 [A geographical approach to the Five Peaks]. In Tang Xiaofeng 1997a, 60–70.

Tang Yongtong 湯用彤 and Tang Yijie 湯一介. 1961. "Kou Qianzhi de zhuzuo yu sixiang" 寇謙之的著作與思想 [The work and thought of Kou Qianzhi]. *Lishi yanjiu* 歷史研究 1961.5: 64–77.

Taylor, Rodney L. 1988. *The Confucian Way of Contemplation: Okada Takehiko and the Tradition of Quiet-Sitting*. Columbia, SC: University of South Carolina Press.

Taylor, Romeyn. 1977. "Ming T'ai-tsu and the Gods of the Walls and Moats." *Ming Studies* 4: 31–49.

Teiser, Stephen F. 1993. "The Growth of Purgatory." In Ebrey and Gregory 1993, 115–45.

———. 1994. *The Scripture of the Ten Kings and the Making of Purgatory in Medieval Chinese Buddhism*. Honolulu: University of Hawaii Press.

ter Haar, Barend J. 1991. *The White Lotus Teachings in Chinese Religious History*. Leiden: E. J. Brill.

———. 1993. "The Gathering of Brothers and Elders (*Ko-lao hui*): A New View." In Blussé and Zurndorfer 1993, 259–83.

———. 1998a. "A New Interpretation of the Yao Charters." In van der Velde and McKay 1998, 3–19.

———. 1998b. *The Ritual and Mythology of the Chinese Triads: Creating an Identity*. Leiden: E. J. Brill.

———. 2000a. "Teaching with Incense." *Studies in Central and East Asian Religions* 11: 1–15.

———. 2000b. "The rise of the Guan Yu Cult: The Daoist Connection." In de Meyer and Engelfriet 2000, 184–204.

Teri Takehiro. 1990. "The Twelve Sleep-Exercises of Mount Hua, from the *Chifengsui* of Zhou Lüjing." *TR* 2.1: 73–94.

Tetsui Yoshinori 鐵井慶紀. 1970. "Kōtei densetsu ni tsuite" 黄帝傳説について [On the traditions concerning the Yellow Emperor]. *Shinagaku kenkyū* 支那學研究 34: 78–89.

———. 1972. "Kōtei to Shiyū no tōsō setsuwa ni tsuite" 黄帝と蚩尤の闘争説話について [On the legends of the fight between the Yellow Emperor and Chiyou]. *TS* 39: 50–63.

Thompson, Laurence G., ed. 1975. *Studia Asiatica: Essays in Asian Studies in Felicitation of the Seventy-Fifth Birthday of Professor Ch'en Shou-yi*. San Francisco: Chinese Materials Center.

———. 1985. "Taoism: Classic and Canon." In Denny and Taylor 1985, 204–23.

———. 1987a. "Chiao." In Eliade 1987, 239–40.

———. 1987b. "Chinese Religious Year." In Eliade 1987, 3: 323–28.

———. 1987c. "Iconography: Taoist Iconography." In Eliade 1987, 7: 51–54.

———. 1989. "On the Prehistory of Hell in China." *JCR* 17: 27–41.

———. 1993. "What is Taoism? (With Apologies to H. G. Creel)." *TR* 4.2: 9–22.

Thompson, Paul M. 1979. *The Shen Tzu Fragments*. Oxford: Oxford University Press.

Tian Chengyang 田诚阳. 1990. "Daojiao zhaijiao keyi" 道教斋醮科仪 [Taoist *zhai* and *jiao* rituals]. *SZY* 1990.3: 93–104.

———. 1995. "*Zangwai daoshu* shumu lüexi" 「藏外道书」书目略析 [A brief analysis of the contents of the *Zangwai daoshu*]. Parts 1 and 2. *ZGDJ* 1995.1: 37–42; 1995.2: 42–45.

Tian Qing 田青. 1997. *Zhongguo zongjiao yinyue* 中国宗教音乐 [Religious music in China]. Beijing: Zongjiao wenhua chubanshe.

To Kwangsun 都珖淳. 1983. "Kankoku no dōkyō" 韓国の道教 [Taoism in Korea]. In Fukui Kōjun et al. 1983, 3: 49–127.

Tobias, Michael Charles, and Harold Drasdo, eds. 1979. *The Mountain Spirit*. Woodstock, NY: The Overlook Press.

Tonami Mamoru 礪波護, ed. 1993. *Chūgoku chūsei no bunbutsu* 中國中世の文物 [Cultural treasures of medieval China]. Kyoto: Kyōto daigaku Jinbun kagaku kenkyūjo.

———. 1999. *Zui-Tō bukkyō to kokka* 隋唐佛教と國家 [Buddhism and the state during the Sui and Tang dynasties]. Tokyo: Chūō kōronsha.

Topley, Marjorie. 1963. "The Great Way of Former Heaven: A Group of Chinese Secret Religious Sects." *Bulletin of the School of Oriental and African Studies* 26: 362–92.

Tsao Benyeh [Cao Benye] and Shi Xinmin. 1992. "Current Research of Taoist Ritual Music in Mainland China and Hong Kong." *Yearbook for Traditional Music* 24: 118–25.

Tsao Pen-Yeh [Cao Benye 曹本冶] and Daniel P. L. Law [Luo Bingliang 羅炳良], eds. 1989. *Studies of Taoist Rituals and Music of Today*. Hong Kong: The Society for Ethnomusicological Research. (Chinese title: *Guoji daojiao keyi ji yinyue yantaohui lunwen ji* 國際道教科儀及音樂研討會論文集.)

Ts'ao T'ien-ch'in, Ho Ping-Yü, and Joseph Needham. 1959. "An Early Mediaeval Chinese Alchemical Text on Aqueous Solutions." *Ambix* 7: 122–58.

Tsuchiya Masaaki 土屋昌明. 1996. *"Rekisei shinsen taidō tsūkan to Shinsenden"* 「歷世真仙体道通鑑」と「神仙傳」 [The *Lishi zhenxian tidao tongjian* and the *Shenxian zhuan*]. *Kokugakuin zashi* 國學院雜誌 97.11: 155–69.

———. 2002. "Confession of Sins and Awareness of Self in the *Taiping jing*." In Kohn and Roth 2002, 39–57.

Tsuda Sōkichi 津田左右吉. 1996. *"Tennō kō"* 天皇考 [A study of the term *tennō* ("august sovereign")]. In Noguchi Tetsurō et al. 1996–97, 1: 25–38.

Tsui, Bartholomew. 1991. *Taoist Tradition and Change: The Story of the Complete Perfection Sect in Hong Kong*. Hong Kong: Hong Kong Christian Study Center on Chinese Religion and Culture.

Tsukamoto Zenryū 塚本善隆. 1975. *Shina bukkyōshi kenkyū* 支那佛教史研究 [Studies on the history of Buddhism]. Tokyo: Kōbundō shobō.

Tsuzuki Akiko 都築晶子. 2002. *"Dōkan ni okeru kairitsu no seiritsu"* 道観における戒律のせいりつ [The formation of Taoist monastic discipline]. In Mugitani Kunio 2002, 59–81.

Tu Ching-i, ed. 2000. *Classics and Interpretations: The Hermeneutic Traditions in Chinese Culture*. New Brunswick, NJ: Transaction Publishers.

Tu Fang Lienche. 1976a. "Chang Cheng-ch'ang." In Goodrich and Fang 1976, 44–45.

———. 1976b. "Chang Yü-ch'u." In Goodrich and Fang 1976, 107–8.

———. 1976c. "Lin Chao-en." In Goodrich and Fang 1976, 912–15.

Tu Wei-ming. 1979. "The 'Thought of Huang-Lao': A Reflection on the Lao tzu and Huang ti Texts in the Silk Manuscripts of Ma-wang-tui." *Journal of Asian Studies* 39: 95–110.

———. 1985. *Confucian Thought: Selfhood as Creative Transformation*. Albany: State University of New York Press.

———. 1987a. "Soul: Chinese Concepts." In Eliade 1987, 13: 447–50.

———. 1987b. "Tai-chi." In Eliade 1987, 14: 247–49.

Turner, Karen. 1989. "The Theory of Law in the *Ching-fa*." *EC* 14: 55–76.

Twitchett, Denis, and John K. Fairbank, eds. 1986. *The Cambridge History of China.* Vol. 1: *The Ch'in and Han Empires, 221 B.C.-A.D. 220,* edited by Denis Twitchett and Michael Loewe. Cambridge: Cambridge University Press.

———, eds. 1998. *The Cambridge History of China.* Vol. 8: *The Ming Dynasty, 1368–1644,* Part 2, edited by Denis Twitchett and Frederick W. Mote. Cambridge: Cambridge University Press.

Uchida Ginpū hakushi shōju kinenkai 内田吟風博士頌壽記念会 [Committee for the Commemoration of the Seventieth Birthday of Dr. Ginpū Uchida], ed. 1978. *Uchida Ginpū hakushi shōju kinen Tōyōshi ronshū* 内田吟風博士頌壽記念東洋史論集. English title: *Asiatic Studies in Honour of Dr. Ginpū Uchida on the Occasion of his Seventieth Birthday.* Kyoto: Dōhōsha.

Ueda Masaaki 上田正昭. 1989. *Kodai no dōkyō to Chōsen bunka* 古代の道教と朝鮮文化 [Ancient Taoism and Korean culture]. Kyoto: Jinbun shoin.

Unschuld, Paul U. 1985. *Medicine in China: A History of Ideas.* Berkeley, Los Angeles, and London: University of California Press.

———. 1986. *Medicine in China: A History of Pharmaceutics.* Berkeley, Los Angeles, and London: University of California Press.

———. 1994. "Der chinesische 'Arzneikönig' Sun Simiao: Geschichte — Legende — Ikonographie." *MS* 42: 217–57.

Valussi, Elena. 2003. "Beheading the Red Dragon: A History of Female Inner Alchemy in China." Ph.D. diss., University of London.

van der Loon, Piet. 1977. "Les origines rituelles du théâtre chinois." *Journal Asiatique* 265: 141–68.

———. 1979. "A Taoist Collection of the Fourteenth Century." In Bauer 1979, 401–5.

———. 1984. *Taoist Books in the Libraries of the Sung Period: A Critical Study and Index.* London: Ithaca Press.

van der Velde, Paul, and Alex McKay, eds. 1998. *New Developments in Asian Studies: An Introduction.* London: Kegan Paul International.

van Ess, Hans. 1993a. "Die geheimen Worte des Ssu-ma Ch'ien." *Oriens Extremus* 36: 5–28.

———. 1993b. "The meaning of Huang-Lao in *Shiji* and *Hanshu*." *Études chinoises* 12.2: 161–77.

van Gulik, Robert H. 1940. *The Lore of the Chinese Lute: An Essay in Ch'in Ideology.* Tokyo: Sophia University.

———. 1941. *Hsi K'ang and his Poetical Essay on the Lute.* Tokyo: Sophia University.

———. 1954. "The Mango 'Trick' in China: An Essay on Taoist Magic." *Transactions of the Asiatic Society of Japan,* third series, 3: 117–75.

———. 1961. *Sexual Life in Ancient China: A Preliminary Survey of Chinese Sex and Society from ca. 1500 B.C. till 1644 A.D.* Leiden: E. J. Brill.

Vercammen, Dan. 1990. "Neijia Wushu, de inwendige school der Chinese vechtkunsten: De teksten met historische een filosofische achtergronden en de relatie met qigong." 2 vols. Ph.D. diss., Universität Gent.

———. 1991. *The History of Taijiquan.* Antwerp: Belgian Taoist Association.

Verellen, Franciscus. 1987. "Luo Gongyuan: Légende et culte d'un saint taoïste." *Journal Asiatique* 275: 283–332.

———. 1989. *Du Guangting (850–933): Taoïste de cour à la fin de la Chine médiévale*. Paris: Collège de France, Institut des Hautes Études Chinoises.

———. 1992. "'Evidential Miracles in Support of Taoism': The Inversion of a Buddhist Apologetic Tradition in Late Tang China." *TP* 78: 217–63.

———. 1994. "Die Mythologie des Taoismus." In cooperation with Caroline Gyss-Vermande. In Haussig 1994, 737–863.

———. 1995. "The Beyond Within: Grotto-Heavens (*Dongtian* 洞天) in Taoist Ritual and Cosmology." *CEA* 8: 265–90.

———. 1999. "The Five Sentiments of Gratitude." In de Bary and Bloom 1999, 1: 404–6.

———. 2003. "The Twenty-Four Dioceses and Zhang Daoling: Spatio-Liturgical Organization in Early Heavenly Master Taoism." In Granoff and Shinohara 2003, 15–67.

———. 2004. "The Heavenly Master Liturgical Agenda According to Chisong zi's Petition Almanac." *CEA* 14: 291–343.

Vermeer, E. B., ed. 1990. *Development and Decline of Fukien Province in the 17th and 18th Centuries*. Leiden and New York: E. J. Brill.

Vervoorn, Aat. 1988–89. "Zhuang Zun: Daoist Philosopher of the Late First Century B.C." *MS* 38: 69–94.

———. 1990. *Men of the Cliffs and Caves: The Development of the Chinese Eremitic Tradition to the End of the Han Dynasty*. Hong Kong: Chinese University Press.

———. 1990–91, "Cultural Strata of Hua Shan, The Holy Peak of the West." *MS* 39: 1–30.

von Falkenhausen, Lothar. 1994. "Sources of Taoism: Reflections on Archaeological Indicators of Religious Change in Eastern Zhou China." *TR* 5.2: 1–12.

von Glahn, Richard. 1991. "The Enchantment of Wealth: The God Wutong in the Social History of Jiangnan." *HJAS* 51: 651–714.

Wädow, Gerd. 1992. *T'ien-fei hsien-sheng lu: "Die Aufzeichnungen von der manifestierten Heiligkeit der Himmelsprinzessin." Einleitung, Übersetzung, Kommentar*. Nettetal: Steyler Verlag.

Wagner, Rudolf G. 1973. "Lebensstil und Drogen im chinesischen Mittelalter." *TP* 59: 79–178.

———. 1986. "Wang Bi: 'The Structure of the Laozi's Pointers' (*Laozi weizhi lilüe*)." *TP* 72: 92–129.

———. 1989. "Wang Bi's Recension of the *Laozi*." *EC* 14: 27–54.

———. 2000. *The Craft of a Chinese Commentator: Wang Bi on the Laozi*. Albany: State University of New York Press.

Waley, Arthur. 1922. *The Nō Plays of Japan*. New York: Alfred A. Knopf.

———. 1926–33. *The Tale of Genji*. 2 vols. Boston: Houghton Mifflin.

———. 1930–32. "Notes on Chinese Alchemy (Supplementary to Johnson's *A Study of Chinese Alchemy*)." *Bulletin of the School of Oriental Studies* 6: 1–24.

———. 1931. *The Travels of an Alchemist*. London: Headley.

———. 1934. *The Way and its Power: A Study of the Tao Te Ching and its Place in Chinese Thought*. London: George Allen and Unwin.

———. 1960. *Ballads and Stories from Tun-huang*. London: George Allen and Unwin.

Wallacker, Benjamin. 1962. *The Huai-nan-tzu, Book Eleven: Behavior, Culture and the Cosmos*. New Haven: American Oriental Society.

———. 1972. "Liu An, Second King of Huai-nan (180–122 B.C.)." *JAOS* 92: 36–51.

Wan Yi 萬毅. 1998. "Dunhuang daojiao wenxian *Benji jing* luwen ji jieshuo" 敦煌道教文獻「本際經」錄文及解說 [Transcription of the *Benji jing*, a Taoist text from Dunhuang, with an explanatory note]. *DWY* 13: 367–484.

Wang Baoxuan 王葆玹. 1993. "Boshu *Xici* yu Zhanguo Qin Han daojia yixue" 帛書「繫辭」與戰國秦漢道家易學 [The silk manuscript of the *Xici* and the Taoist *Yijing* learning of the Warring States, Qin, and Han periods]. *DWY* 3: 73–88.

Wang Buxiong 王卜雄 and Zhou Shirong 周世榮. 1989. *Zhongguo qigong xueshu fazhan shi* 中国气功学术发展史 [The historical development of the Chinese art of *qigong*]. Changsha: Hunan kexue jishu chubanshe.

Wang Chang'an 王畅安. 1963. "Yongle gong bihua tiji luwen" 永乐宫壁画题记录文 [Transcriptions of the cartouches on the Yongle gong murals]. *Wenwu* 文物 1963.8: 65–78.

Wang Chunwu 王春五. 1994. *Qingcheng shanzhi* 青城山志 [Monograph of Mount Qingcheng]. Chengdu: Sichuan renmin chubanshe.

———. 1996. *Tianshi dao ershisi zhi kao* 天师道二十四治考 [A study of the twenty-four parishes of the Way of the Celestial Masters]. Chengdu: Sichuan daxue chubanshe.

Wang Deyou 王德有. 1994. "Yan Zun yu Wang Chong, Wang Bi, Guo Xiang zhi xue yuanliu" 嚴遵與王充王弼郭象之學源流 [Origins and development of the thought of Yan Zun, Wang Chong, Wang Bi, and Guo Xiang]. *DWY* 4: 222–32.

———. 1995. "Jianlun "Dao fa ziran" zai Zhongguo zhexueshi shang de yingxiang" 簡論「道法自然」在中國哲學史上的影響 [""The Dao models itself on being so of its own": A brief discussion of the influence of this notion in the history of Chinese thought]. *DWY* 6: 47–59.

Wang Fang 王仿 and Jin Chongliu 金崇柳. 1994. "Yongjia longdeng yu Chen Shisi niangniang: Chen Jinggu xinyang zhiyi" 永嘉龙灯与陈十四娘娘—陈靖姑信仰之一 [Dragon lanterns and Fourteenth Damsel Chen in Yongjia (Zhejiang): A cult of Defending Maiden Chen]. *Zhongguo minjian wenhua* 中国民间文化 16: 139–50.

Wang Guangde 王光德 and Yang Lizhi 杨立志. 1993. *Wudang daojiao shilüe* 武当道教史略 [Historical summary of Taoism at Mount Wudang]. Beijing: Huawen chubanshe.

Wang Guoliang 王國良. 1984. *Wei Jin nanbei chao zhiguai xiaoshuo yanjiu* 魏晉南北朝志怪小說研究 [A study of "Records of the Strange" in the Wei, Jin, Northern and Southern Dynasties]. Taipei: Wenshizhe chubanshe.

———. 1989. *Han Wu Dongming ji yanjiu* 「漢武洞冥記」研究 [A study of the *Han Wu Dongming ji*]. Taipei: Wenshizhe chubanshe.

———. 1993. *Hainei shizhou ji yanjiu* 「海內十洲記」研究 [A study of the *Hainei zhizhou ji*]. Taipei: Wenshizhe chubanshe.

Wang Guowei 王國維. 1926. *Changchun zhenren xiyou ji zhu* 「長春真人西遊記」注 [Commentary to the *Changchun zhenren xiyou ji*]. In Yan Yiping 1974, vol. 2.

Wang Jiqin 王集钦, ed. 1999. *Laoshan beijie yu shike* 崂山碑碣与石刻 [Stelae and stone inscription of Mount Lao]. Qingdao: Qingdao chubanshe.

Wang Ka 王卡, ed. 1993a. *Laozi Daode jing Heshang gong zhangju* 老子道德經河上公章句 [The *Daode jing* by Laozi, Divided into Sections and Sentences by Heshang gong]. Beijing: Zhonghua shuju.

———1993b. Zhenyuan miaodao yu *Zhenyuan miaojing tu*. Jian lun Zhouzi *Taiji tu* zhi yuanyuan" 真元妙道与「真元妙经图」—兼论周子太极图之渊源 [The Wondrous Way of the True Origin and the *Zhenyuan miaojing tu*, with a discussion of the origins of Zhou Dunyi's *Taiji tu*]. *SZY* 1993.2: 49–60.

———. 1996. "Sui Tang xiaodao zongyuan" 隋唐孝道宗源 [The origins of the Way of Filiality in the Sui and Tang periods]. *DWY* 9: 100–121.

Wang Kuike 王奎克. 1964. "Zhongguo liandan shu zhong de 'jinye' he huachi" 中国炼丹术中的「金液」和华池 [The "Golden Liquor" and the Flowery Pond in Chinese alchemy]. *Kexue shi jikan* 科学史集刊 7: 53–62.

Wang Ming 王明. 1960. *Taiping jing hejiao* 「太平經」合校 [Collated edition of the *Taiping jing*]. Second revised edition. Beijing: Zhonghua shuju.

———. 1981. *Wuneng zi jiaozhu* 「無能子」校注 [Annotated edition of the *Wuneng zi*]. Beijing: Zhonghua shuju.

———. 1984a. *Daojia he daojiao sixiang yanjiu* 道家和道教思想研究 [Studies on Taoist thought]. Beijing: Zhongguo shehui kexue chubanshe.

———. 1984b. "*Huangting jing* kao" 「黄庭经」考 [A study of the *Huangting jing*]. In Wang Ming 1984a, 324–71. First published in *ZLJ* 20 (1948): 539–76.

———. 1984c. "Lun *Taiping jing* de shucheng shidai he zuozhe" 论「太平经」的书成时代和作者 [The date of composition and authorship of the *Taiping jing*]. In Wang Ming 1984a, 183–200. First published in *SZY* 1982.1: 17–26.

———. 1984d. "Lun *Taiping jing* jiabu zhi wei" 论「太平经」甲部之伪 [The *jia* section of the *Taiping jing* as a non-authentic text]. In Wang Ming 1984a, 201–14. First published in *ZLJ* 18 (1948): 375–84.

———. 1984e. "Lun Tao Hongjing" 论陶弘景 [About Tao Hongjing]. In Wang Ming 1984a, 80–98. First published in *SZY* 1981.1: 10–21.

———. 1984f. "Shilun *Yinfu jing* ji qi weiwu zhuyi sixiang" 试论「阴符经」及其唯物主义思想 [A preliminary study of the *Yinfu jing* and its materialistic thought]. In Wang Ming 1984a, 139–58. First published in *Zhexue yanjiu* 哲学研究 5 (1962): 59–68.

———. 1984g. "*Zhouyi cantong qi* kaozheng" 「周易参同契」考证 [An examination of the *Cantong qi*]. In Wang Ming 1984a, 241–92. First published in *ZLJ* 19 (1948): 325–66.

———. 1985. *Baopu zi neipian jiaoshi* 「抱朴子内篇」校釋 [Annotated critical edition of the *Baopu zi neipian*]. Second revised edition. Beijing: Zhonghua shuju.

Wang Mu 王沐. 1990. *Wuzhen pian qianjie (wai san zhong)* 「悟真篇」淺解（外三種） [A simple explanation of the *Wuzhen pian* and three other works]. Beijing: Zhonghua shuju.

Wang Qing 王青. 1998. *Hanchao de bentu zongjiao yu shenhua* 漢朝的本土宗教與神話 [Indigenous religion and mythology of the Han dynasty]. Taipei: Hongye wenhua.

Wang Shiren 王世仁. 1987. "Mingtang xingzhi chutan" 明堂形制初探 [A preliminary exploration of the form of the Hall of Light]. *Zhongguo wenhua yanjiu jikan* 中国文化研究集刊 4: 1–43.

Wang Shiwei 王士伟. 1993. *Louguan dao yuanliu kao* 楼观道源流考 [A study of the origins and development of Taoism at the Louguan]. Xi'an: Shaanxi renmin chubanshe.

Wang Shumin 王叔岷. 1950. *Guo Xiang Zhuangzi zhu jiaoji* 「郭象莊子注」校記 [Critical edition of Guo Xiang's commentary to the *Zhuangzi*]. Shanghai: Shangwu yinshuguan.

Wang Yucheng 王育成. 1996. "Wenwu suojian Zhongguo gudai daofu shulun" 文物所見中國古代道符述論 [A discussion of the ancient Taoist talismans archeologically recovered in China]. *DWY* 9: 267–301.

———. 1999. "Dong Han tiandi shizhe lei daoren yu daojiao qiyuan" 東漢天帝使者類道人與道教起源 [Men of the Way represented by the Eastern Han term "Envoys of the Celestial Emperor" and the origins of Taoism]. *DWY* 16: 181–203.

Wang Zhizhong 王志忠. 1995. "Quanzhen jiao Longmen pai qiyuan lunkao" 全真教龙门派起源论考 [A study of the origins of the Longmen branch of the Quanzhen School]. *ZY* 1995.4: 9–13.

Wang Zhongjiang 王中江. 1995. "Cunzai ziran lun" 存在自然論 [On Naturalness and existence]. *DWY* 6: 10–23.

Wang Zhongxin 王忠信, ed. 1995. *Louguan tai daojiao beishi* 楼观台道教碑石 [Taoist stelae at the Louguan tai]. Xi'an: Sanqin chubanshe.

Wang Zongyu 王宗昱. 1999. "Daojiao de 'liutian' shuo" 道教的「六天」說 [The views of the Six Heavens in Taoism]. *DWY* 16: 22–49.

———. 2001. *Daojiao yishu yanjiu* 「道教义枢」研究 [A study of the *Daojiao yishu*]. Shanghai: Shanghai wenhua chubanshe.

Wang, David Teh-Yu. 1991–92. "*Nei Jing Tu*, a Daoist Diagram of the Internal Circulation of Man." *The Journal of the Walters Art Gallery* 49–50: 141–58.

Wang Jing. 2001. Guest Editor's introduction to special issue on "Chinese Popular Culture and the State." *Positions: East Asia Cultures Critique* 9.1: 1–27.

Ward, Julian. 1995. *Cave Paradises and Talismans: Voyages through China's Sacred Mountains*. Leeds: University of Leeds.

Ware, James R. 1933. "The *Wei shu* and the *Sui shu* on Taoism." *JAOS* 53: 215–50. [See also "Corrigenda and Addenda," *JAOS* 54 (1934): 290–94.]

———. 1966. *Alchemy, Medicine and Religion in the China of A.D. 320: The Nei P'ien of Ko Hung (Pao-p'u tzu)*. Cambridge, MA: MIT Press.

Watson, Burton. 1961. *Records of the Grand Historian of China*. 2 vols. New York and London: Columbia University Press.

———. 1968. *The Complete Works of Chuang Tzu*. New York: Columbia University Press.

———. 1987. "Chuang-tzu." In Eliade 1987, 3: 467–69.

Wechsler, Howard J. 1985. *Offerings of Jade and Silk: Ritual and Symbol in the Legitimation of the T'ang Dynasty*. New Haven and London: Yale University Press.

Wei Qipeng 魏啟鵬. 1991. *Mawangdui boshu Dexing jiaoshi* 馬王堆帛書「德行」校釋 [Annotated critical edition of the silk manuscript of the *Dexing* from Mawangdui]. Chengdu: Ba Shu shushe.

Wei Tingsheng 衛挺生. 1953. *Xu Fu yu Riben* 徐福與日本 [Xu Fu and Japan]. Hong Kong: Xin shiji.

Weinstein, Stanley. 1987. *Buddhism under the T'ang*. Cambridge: Cambridge University Press.

Welch, Holmes. 1957–58. "The Chang T'ien Shih and Taoism in China." *Journal of Oriental Studies* 4: 188–212.

———. 1967. *The Practice of Chinese Buddhism 1900–1950*. Cambridge, MA: Harvard University Press.

Welch, Holmes, and Anna K. Seidel, eds. 1979. *Facets of Taoism: Essays in Chinese Religion*. New Haven and London: Yale University Press.

Weng Dujian 翁獨健. 1935. *Daozang zimu yinde* 道藏子目引得 (*Combined Indices to the Authors and Titles of Books in Two Collections of Taoist Literature*). Harvard-Yenching Institute Sinological Index Series, no. 25. Beiping [Beijing]: Yenching University Library. Reprint, Taipei: Chengwen Publishing Company, 1966.

Weng, T. H. 1976. "Leng Ch'ien." In Goodrich and Fang 1976, 802–4.

Whitaker, K. P. K. 1957. "Tsaur Jyr and the Introduction of *Fannbay* 梵唄 into China." *Bulletin of the School of Oriental and African Studies* 20: 585–97.

White, William Charles. 1945. "The Lord of the Northern Dipper." *Bulletin of the Royal Ontario Museum of Archaeology* 13: 4–30.

Wieger, Leon. 1911. *Taoïsme*. Vol. I: *Bibliographie générale: I. Le canon (Patrologie), II. Les index officiels et privés*. Hien-hien (Ho-kien-fou): [Imprimerie de la Mission catholique.]

Wile, Douglas. 1983. *T'ai Chi Touchstones: Yang Family Secret Transmission*. Brooklyn, NY: Sweet Chi Press.

———. 1992. *Art of the Bedchamber: The Chinese Sexual Yoga Classics Including Women's Solo Meditation Texts*. Albany: State University of New York Press.

———. 1996. *Lost T'ai-chi Classics from the Late Ch'ing Dynasty*. Albany: State University of New York Press.

Wilhelm, Hellmut. 1960. *Change: Eight Lectures on the I Ching*. Translated by Cary F. Baynes. New York: Pantheon Books.

———. 1975. *The Book of Changes in the Western Tradition: A Selective Bibliography*. Seattle: Institute for Comparative and Foreign Area Studies, University of Washington.

——— 1977. *Heaven, Earth, and Man in the Book of Changes: Seven Eranos Lectures*. Seattle: University of Washington Press.

———. 1983. "Chuang-tzu Translations: A Bibliographical Appendix." In Mair 1983b, 158–61.

Wilhelm, Richard. 1929. *Das Geheimnis der Goldenen Blüte: Ein chinesisches Lebensbuch*. Zürich and Stuttgart: Rascher Verlag. Translated into English by Cary F. Baynes, with Carl G. Jung's "Commentary," as *The Secret of the Golden Flower: A Chinese Book of Life* (London: Routledge and Kegan Paul, 1962; New York: Harcourt, Brace and World, 1962).

———. 1950. *The I-ching or Book of Changes*. Translated by Cary F. Baynes. New York: Bollingen.

Wilkerson, James R. 1995. "Rural Village Temples in the P'enghu Islands and their Late Imperial Corporate Organization." In Hanxue yanjiu zhongxin 1995, 1: 67–95.

Wilson, Stephen, ed. 1983. *Saints and their Cults: Studies in Religious Sociology, Folklore and History*. Cambridge: Cambridge University Press.

Witzleben, J. Lawrence. 1995. *"Silk and Bamboo" Music in Shanghai: The Jiangnan Sizhu Instrumental Ensemble Tradition*. Kent and London: Kent State University Press.

Wolf, Arthur P., ed. 1974. *Religion and Ritual in Chinese Society*. Stanford: Stanford University Press.

Wong Shiu Hon 黃兆漢. 1978a. "Chou-i ts'an-t'ung ch'i chu." In Balázs and Hervouet 1978, 369–70.

———. 1978b. "Tzu-yang chen-jen wu-chen p'ien shih-i." In Balázs and Hervouet 1978, 371–72.

———. 1979. "The Cult of Chang San-feng." *Journal of Oriental Studies* 17: 10–53.

———. 1982. *Investigations into the Authenticity of the Chang San-Feng Ch'uan-Chi: The Complete Works of Chang San-feng*. Canberra: Australian National University Press.

———. 1988a. *Daojiao yanjiu lunwen ji* 道教研究論文集 [Studies on Taoism]. Hong Kong: The Chinese University Press.

———. 1988b. "Qiu Chuji de *Panxi ji*" 丘處機的「磻溪集」 [*The Panxi ji* by Qiu Chuji]. In Wong Shiu Hon 1988a, 183–210.

———. 1989. *Daozang danyao yiming suoyin* 道藏丹藥異名索引. English title: *Chinese Alchemical Terms: Guide Book to the Daozang Pseudonyms*. Taipei: Taiwan xuesheng shuju.

Wong Shiu-hon [Wong Shiu Hon] 黃兆漢. 1981. "Quanzhen jiaozhu Wang Chongyang de ci" 全真教主王重陽的詞 [The lyrics of the Quanzhen master Wang Chongyang]. *Journal of Oriental Studies* 19: 19–43.

Wong, Eva. 1992. *Cultivating Stillness: A Taoist Manual for Transforming Body and Mind*. Boston and London: Shambhala.

———. 1994. *Lao-Tzu's Treatise on the Response of the Tao: T'ai-shang kan-ying p'ien*. San Francisco: HarperCollins.

———. 1997. *Harmonizing Yin and Yang: The Dragon-Tiger Classic*. Boston and London: Shambhala.

———. 1998. *Cultivating the Energy of Life*. Boston and London: Shambhala.

Wong, Isabel. 1987. "Music and Religion in China, Korea, and Tibet." In Eliade 1987, 10: 195–203.

Woolley, Nathan. 1997. "*Wunengzi* and the Early *Zhuangzi* Commentaries." BA Hons. thesis. Canberra: Faculty of Asian Studies, Australian National University.

Wright, Arthur F. 1951. "Fu I and the Rejection of Buddhism." *Journal of the History of Ideas* 12: 33–47. Reprinted in Wright 1990, 112–23.

———. 1990. *Studies in Chinese Buddhism*. Edited by Robert M. Somers. New Haven: Yale University Press.

Wright, Arthur F., and Denis Twitchett, eds. 1962. *Confucian Personalities*. Stanford: Stanford University Press.

Wu Chi-yu. 1960. *Pen-tsi king (Livre du terme originel): Ouvrage taoïste inédit du VIIe siècle. Manuscrits retrouvés à Touen-houang reproduits en fac-similé*. Paris: Centre National de la Recherche Scientifique.

Wu Gangji 吴刚戟. 1994. "Lishui Chen Shisi furen chongbai fengsu" 丽水陈十四夫人崇拜风俗 [Customs of the worship of Fourteenth Lady Chen in Lishui (Zhejiang)]. *Zhongguo minjian wenhua* 中国民间文化 16: 151–77.

Wu Hung. 1987. "Xiwang mu, the Queen Mother of the West." *Orientations* 18.4: 24–33.

———. 1989. *The Wu Liang Shrine: The Ideology of Early Chinese Pictorial Art*. Stanford: Stanford University Press.

———. 1992. "Art in a Ritual Context: Rethinking Mawangdui." *EC* 17: 111–44.

Wu Jenshu 巫仁恕. 2002. "Ming Qing Jiangnan Dongyue shen xinyang yu chengshi minbian" 明清江南東嶽神信仰與城市民變 [The cult of the God of the Eastern Peak and urban riots in Jiangnan, during the Ming and Qing periods]. Paper presented at the International Conference on Chinese Urban History from the Fourteenth to the Seventeenth Centuries, 19–21 December 2002., Chi Nan University, Nantou, Taiwan.

Wu Jiulong 吳九龍. 1985. *Yinqueshan Hanjian shiwen* 銀雀山漢簡釋文 [Transcription of the Han bamboo slips from Yinqueshan]. Beijing: Wenwu chubanshe.

Wu Kuang-ming. 2000. "Textual Hermeneutics and Beyond: With the *Tao te ching* and the *Chuang tzu* as Examples." In Tu Ching-i 2000, 291–313.

Wu Lu-ch'iang, and Tenney L. Davis. 1932. "An Ancient Chinese Treatise on Alchemy Entitled *Ts'an T'ung Ch'i*." *Isis* 18: 210–89.

Wyatt, Don J. 1996. *The Recluse of Loyang: Shao Yung and the Moral Evolution of Early Sung Thought*. Honolulu: University of Hawaii Press.

Xiao Bing 蕭兵. 1992. *Nuo zha zhi feng: Changjiang liuyu zongjiao xiju wenhua* 儺蜡之风—长江流域宗教戏剧文化 [The *nuo* and *zha* customs: The culture of religious dramas in the Yangzi River delta]. Nanjing: Jiangsu renmin chubanshe.

Xiao Dengfu 蕭登福. 1984. *Guigu zi yanjiu* 鬼谷子研究 [Studies on Guigu zi]. Taipei: Wenlü chubanshe.

———. 1988. *Zhou Qin Liang Han zaoqi daojiao* 周秦两汉早期道教 [Early Taoism in the Zhou, Qin, and Han periods]. Tianjin: Wenjin chubanshe.

———. 1989. *Han Wei Liuchao fo-dao liangjiao zhi tiantang diyu shuo* 漢魏六朝佛道兩教之天堂地獄說 [Buddhist and Taoist views on the Heavenly Halls and Earth Prisons in the Han, Wei, and Six Dynasties]. Taipei: Taiwan xuesheng shuju.

———. 1993. *Daojiao yu mizong* 道教與密宗 [Taoism and Tantric Buddhism]. Taipei: Xinwenfeng chuban gongsi.

Xiao Hanming 蕭漢明. 1997. "Lun Yu Yan yixue zhong de daojiao yi" 論俞琰易學中的道教易 [The Taoist notion of "change" in Yu Yan's learning in the *Yijing*]. *DWY* 11: 265–91.

Xiao Hanming 蕭汉明 and Guo Dongsheng 郭东升. 2000. *Zhouyi cantong qi yanjiu* 「周易参同契」研究 [A study of the *Zhouyi cantong qi*]. Shanghai: Shanghai wenhua chubanshe.

Xiao Tianshi 蕭天石. 1983. "Xinbian *Daozang jinghua* yaozhi liyan" 新編「道藏精華」要旨例言 [Introductory remarks to the new edition of the *Daozang jinghua*]. In *Daozang jinghua* 道藏精華 [Essential Splendors of the Taoist Canon], 1: 1–12. Taipei: Ziyou chubanshe.

Xing Dongtian 邢东田. 1997. "Xuannü de qiyuan, zhineng ji yanbian" 玄女的起源、职能及演变 [Origins, functions, and evolution of the Mysterious Woman]. *SZY* 1997.3: 92–103.

Xing Wen 邢文. 1997. *Boshu Zhouyi yanjiu* 「帛书周易」研究 [Studies on the silk manuscript of the *Book of Changes*]. Beijing: Renmin chubanshe.

Xing Yitian 邢義田. 1997. "Dong Han de fangshi yu qiuxian fengqi: Fei Zhi bei duji" 東漢的方士與求仙風氣—肥致碑讀記 [The "masters of methods" and the trend of seeking immortality in the Eastern Han period: Notes on reading the *Stele to Fei Zhi*]. *Dalu zazhi* 大陸雜誌 94.2: 49–61.

Xu Boying 徐伯英 and Yuan Jiegui 袁介圭, eds. 1976. *Zhonghua xianxue* 中華仙學 [The doctrine of immortality in China]. Taipei: Zhenshanmei chubanshe.

Xu Dishan 許地山. 1966. *Fuji mixin di yanjiu* 扶乩迷信底研究 [A study of the superstition of spirit writing]. Taipei: Taiwan shangwu yinshuguan.

Xu Hongtu 徐宏圖. 1995a. *Zhejiang sheng Pan'an xian Shenze cun de lianhuo yishi* 浙江省磐安縣深澤村的煉火儀式 [The bonfire liturgy of Shenze Village, Pan'an District, Zhejiang]. *MQC* 25. Taipei: Shi Hezheng minsu wenhua jijinhui.

———. 1995b. *Zhejiang sheng Pan'an xian Yangtou cun de Xifangle* 浙江省磐安縣仰頭村的「西方樂」 ["Delights of the Western Region": A Buddhist play from Yangtou Village, Pan'an District, Zhejiang]. *MQC* 24. Taipei: Shi Hezheng minsu wenhua jijinhui.

Xu Hongtu 徐宏圖 and Zhang Aiping 張愛萍, eds. 1997. *Zhejiang Nuoxi ziliao huibian* 浙江儺戲資料匯編 [The Nuo dramas of Zhejiang: A collection of materials]. *MQC* 55. Taipei: Shi Hezheng minsu wenhua jijinhui.

Xu Xiaowang 徐曉望. 1993. *Fujian minjian xinyang yuanliu* 福建民间信仰源流 [Origins and development of popular cults in Fujian]. Fuzhou: Fujian jiaoyu chubanshe.

Xu Xihua 徐西华. 1983. "Jingming jiao yu lixue" 净明教与理学 [Jingming teachings and Neo-Confucianism]. *Sixiang zhanxian* 思想战线 1983.3: 35–40, 34.

Xu Zhengguang 徐正光 and Lin Meirong 林美容, eds. 2000. *Renleixue zai Taiwan de fazhan: Jingyan yanjiu pian* 人類學在臺灣的發展—經驗研究篇 [The development of anthropology on Taiwan: Research experiences]. Taipei: Zhongyang yanjiuyuan Minzuxue yanjiusuo.

Xu Jian. 1999. "Body, Discourse, and the Cultural Politics of Contemporary Chinese Qigong." *Journal of Asian Studies* 58: 961–91.

Yamada Keiji 山田慶児, ed. 1978. *Chūgoku no kagaku to kagakusha* 中國の科學と科學者 [Science and scientists in China]. Kyoto: Kyōto daigaku Jinbun kagaku kenkyūjo.

———. 1979. "The Formation of the *Huang-ti nei-ching*." *Acta Asiatica* 36: 67–89.

———, ed. 1985. *Shin hatsugen Chūgoku kagakushi shiryō no kenkyū* 新発現中國科學史資料の研究 [Studies on newly discovered materials for the history of Chinese science]. 2 vols. Vol. 1: *Yakuchū hen* 訳注篇 [Annotated translations]. Vol. 2: *Ronkō hen* 論考篇 [Essays]. Kyoto: Kyōto daigaku Jinbun kagaku kenkyūjo.

Yamada Keiji 山田慶児 and Tanaka Tan 田中淡, eds. 1989–91. *Chūgoku kodai kagakushi ron* 中國古代科學史論 [Studies on the history of ancient Chinese science]. 2 vols. Kyoto: Kyōto daigaku Jinbun kagaku kenkyūjo.

Yamada Takashi 山田俊. 1999. *Tōsho dōkyō shisōshi kenkyū: Taigen shin'itsu honsai kyō no seiritsu to shisō* 唐初道教思想史研究—「太玄真一本際經」の成立と思想 [Studies on the history of Taoist thought in the early Tang period: The compilation and thought of the *Taixuan zhenyi benji jing*]. Kyoto: Heirakuji shoten.

Yamada Toshiaki 山田利明. 1977. "Shinsen Ri Happyaku den kō" 神仙李八百傳考 [A study of the biography of the immortal Li Babai]. In Yoshioka Yoshitoyo hakase kanreki kinen kenkyū ronshū kankōkai 1977, 145–63.

———. 1983a. "*Rōshi kako kyō rui*" 老子化胡經類 [Texts related to the *Laozi huahu jing* (among the Dunhuang manuscripts)]. In Kanaoka Shōkō, Ikeda On, and Fukui Fumimasa 1983, 97–118.

———. 1983b. "Shinsen dō" 神仙道 [The Way of "divine immortality"]. In Fukui Kōjun et al. 1983, 1: 329–76.

———. 1984. "*Reihō gofu* no seiritsu to sono fuzuiteki seikaku" 「靈宝五符」の成立とその符瑞的性格 [The compilation of the *Taishang lingbao wufu* and its talismanic nature]. In Yasui Kōzan 1984, 165–96.

———. 1987a. "Futatsu no shinpu: *Gogaku shingyōzu* to *Reihō gofu*" 二つの神符—「五岳真形圖」と「靈寶五符」 [Two divine talismans: The *Wuyue zhenxing tu* and the *Lingbao wufu*]. *Tōyōgaku ronsō* 東洋學論叢 40: 147–65.

———. 1987b. "*Gofu jo* keisei kō: Gaku Shichō o megutte" 「五符序」形成考—樂子長をめぐって [A study of the formation of the *Wufu xu*: On Yue Zichang]. In Akizuki Kan'ei 1987, 122–35.

———. 1988a. "Deigan kyūkyū setsu kō" 泥丸九宮説考 [A study of the Muddy Pellet and the Nine Palaces]. *Tōyōgaku ronsō* 東洋學論叢 41: 103–18.

———. 1988b. "Tankai fukyō no seishi: *Gokanjo Hōjutsuden* no tetsugaku" 誕怪不經の正史—「後漢書」方術傳の哲學 [Extending the strange and unorthodox in the Standard Histories: The philosophy of the "Methods and Arts" chapter of the *History of the Later Han*]. *Chūgoku kenkyū shūkan* 中國研究集刊 21: 1965–79.

———. 1989a. "Dōbō shin sonshi kō" 洞房神存思考 [A study of the visualization of the gods in the Cavern Chamber]. *TS* 74: 20–38.

———. 1989b. "Longevity Techniques and the Compilation of the *Lingbao wufuxu*." In Kohn 1989c, 99–124.

———. 1995a. "Dōkyō shizō no sūhai" 道教神像の崇拝 [The worship of images of Taoist deities]. *Chūgoku tetsugakubun gakkai kiyo* 中國哲學文學科紀要 3: 17–33.

———. 1995b. "The Evolution of Taoist Ritual: K'ou Ch'ien-chih and Lu Hsiu-ching." *Acta Asiatica* 68: 69–83.

———. 1999. *Rikuchō dōkyō girei no kenkyū* 六朝道教儀禮の研究 [Studies on Taoist ritual in the Six Dynasties]. Tokyo: Tōhō shoten.

———. 2000. "The Lingbao School." In Kohn 2000b, 225–55.

Yamada Toshiaki 山田利明 and Tanaka Fumio 田中文雄, eds. 1998. *Dōkyō no rekishi to bunka* 道教の歴史と文化 [Taoist history and culture]. Tokyo: Yūzankaku shuppansha.

Yamamoto Noritsuna 山本紀綱. 1979. *Nihon ni ikiru Jo Fuku no denshō* 日本に生きる徐福の傳承 [Traditions on Xu Fu's life in Japan]. Tokyo: Kenkōsha.

Yamanaka Yutaka 山中裕. 1972. *Heianchō no nenchū gyōji* 平安朝の年中行事 [The calendar of annual observances at the Heian Court]. Tokyo: Hanawa shobō.

Yamauchi, M. 1976. "Wang Ch'in-jo." In Franke H. 1976, 2: 1105–9.

Yamazaki Hiroshi 山崎宏. 1967a. "Zui no Gentokan to sono keifu" 隋の玄都観とその系譜 [The Xuandu guan of the Sui period and its genealogy]. In Yamazaki Hiroshi 1967b, 65–84.

———. 1967b. *Zui Tō bukkyōshi no kenkyū* 隋唐佛教史の研究 [Studies on the history of Buddhism in the Sui and Tang Dynasties]. Kyoto: Hōzōkan.

———. 1974. "Tōsho no dōshi Son Shibaku ni tsuite" 唐初の道士孫思邈について [Sun Simiao, a Taoist master of the early Tang period]. *Risshō daigaku bungakubu ronsō* 立証大學文學部論叢 50: 19–40.

———. 1979. "Hokushū no Tsūdōkan ni tsuite" 北周の通道観について [On the Tongdao guan of the Northern Zhou]. *TS* 54: 1–13.

Yan Lingfeng 嚴靈峰. 1964. "Bian Yan Zun *Daode zhigui lun* fei weishu" 辯嚴遵「道德指歸論」非偽書 [The authenticity of Yan Zun's *Daode zhigui*]. *Dalu zazhi* 大陸雜誌 29.4: 107–13. Reprinted in Yan Lingfeng 1965, vol. 1.

———, ed. 1965. *Wuqiu beizhai Laozi jicheng chubian* 無求備齋「老子」集成初編 [Complete collection of editions of the *Laozi*, from the Wuqiu beizhai Studio; First series]. Taipei: Yiwen yinshuguan.

Yan Shanzhao 嚴善炤. 2001. "Shoki dōkyō to kōshaku konki hōchūjutsu" 初期道教と黄赤混氣房中術 [The sexual arts of mixing red and yellow pneumas in early Taoism]. *TS* 97: 1–19.

Yan Yiping 嚴一萍, ed. 1974. *Daojiao yanjiu ziliao* 道教研究資料 [Materials for the study of Taoism]. 2 vols. Banqiao, Taiwan: Yiwen yinshuguan.

Yanagida Seizan 柳田聖山. 1974. "*Sandōkai*" 参同契 [*Cantong qi*]. In Nishitani Keiji and Yanagida Seizan 1974, 128–31.

———. 1983. "The 'Recorded Sayings' Texts of Chinese Ch'an Buddhism." Translated by John R. McRae. In Lai and Lancaster 1983, 185–205.

Yang Huarong 羊华荣. 1986. "*Yisheng baode zhenjun zhuan* jieshao" 「翊圣保德真君传」介绍 [An introduction to the *Yisheng baode zhenjun zhuan*]. *SZY* 1986.3: 96–101.

Yang Guanghui 姜廣輝 and Chen Hanming 陳寒鳴. 1995. "Zhou Dunyi *Taiji tu shuo* yuanyuan shensi" 周敦頤「太極圖說」淵源慎思 [Reflections on the sources of Zhou Dunyi's *Taiji tu shuo*]. *DWY* 7: 211–20.

Yang Kun 楊堃. 1944. "Zaoshen kao" 電神考 [A study of the Stove God]. *Hanxue* 漢學 1: 108–68.

Yang Liansheng 楊聯陞. 1956. "*Laojun yinsong jiejing* jiaoshi" 「老君音誦誡經」校釋 [Annotated critical edition of the *Laojun yinsong jiejing*]. *ZZJ* 28: 17–54.

Yang Ming 杨铭. 1995. *Daojiao yangshengjia Lu Xixing he ta de Fanghu waishi* 道教养生家陆西星和他的「方壶外史」 [Lu Xixing, the Taoist adept of Nourishing Life, and his *Fanghu waishi*]. Chengdu: Sichuan daxue chubanshe.

Yang Shizhe 杨仕哲 et al. 1998. "Wang Bing shengping zhi mi" 王冰生平之谜 [The riddle of Wang Bing's life story]. *Zhonghua yishi zazhi* 中华医史杂志 28.3: 174–76.

Yang, C. K. 1961. *Religion in Chinese Society: A Study of Contemporary Social Functions of Religion and Some of their Historical Factors*. Berkeley, Los Angeles, and London: University of California Press.

Yang, Richard F. S. 1958. "A Study of the Origin of the Legends of the Eight Immortals." *Oriens Extremus* 5: 1–22.

Yao Tao-chung. 1980. "Ch'üan-chen: A New Taoist Sect in North China During the Twelfth and Thirteenth Centuries." Ph.D. diss., University of Arizona.

———. 1986. "Ch'iu Ch'u-chi and Chinggis Khan." *HJAS* 46: 201–19.

Yao, Tad [Yao Tao-chung]. 2000. "Quanzhen: Complete Perfection." In Kohn 2000b, 565–93.

Yasui Kōzan 安居香山. 1979. *Isho no seiritsu to sono tenkai* 緯書の成立とその展開 [The formation and development of the apocryphal texts]. Tokyo: Kokusho kankōkai.

———, ed. 1984. *Shin'i shisō no sōgōteki kenkyū* 讖緯思想の総合的研究 [Collected studies on the thought of the apocryphal texts]. Tokyo: Kokusho kankōkai.

———. 1987. "Dōkyō no seiritsu to shin'i shisō" 道教の成立と讖緯思想 [The formation of Taoism and the influence of the thought of the apocryphal texts]." In Akizuki Kan'ei 1987, 45–60.

Yasui Kōzan 安居香山 and Nakamura Shōhachi 中村璋八. 1966. *Isho no kisoteki kenkyū* 緯書の基礎的研究 [Introductory studies on the apocryphal texts]. Kyoto: Kan Gi bunka kenkyūkai. Reprint, Tokyo: Kokusho kankōkai, 1976 and 1986.

———, eds. 1971–88. *Isho shūsei* 緯書集成 [Complete collection of apocryphal texts]. 6 vols. projected. Tokyo: Meitoku shuppansha.

Yates, Robin D. S. 1994a. "Body, Space, Time and Bureaucracy: Boundary Creation and Control Mechanisms in Early China." In Hay 1994, 56–80.

———. 1994b. "The Yin-Yang Texts from Yinqueshan: An Introduction and a Partial Reconstruction, with Notes on their Significance in Relation to Huang-Lao Daoism." *EC* 19: 75–144.

———. 1997. *Five Lost Classics: Tao, Huanglao, and Yin-Yang in Han China*. New York: Ballantine Books.

Ye Mingsheng 葉明生 and Yuan Hongliang 袁洪亮, eds. 1996. *Fujian Shanghang Luantan kuileixi Furen zhuan* 福建上杭亂彈傀儡戲夫人傳 [The Story of the Goddess: A Luantan marionette play of Shanghang, Fujian]. *MQC* 44. Taipei: Shi Hezheng minsu wenhua jijinhui.

Yearley, Lee. 1983. "The Perfected Person in the Radical Chuang-tzu." In Mair 1983b, 125–39.

Yetts, W. Perceval. 1916. "The Eight Immortals." *JRAS* 1916: 773–807.

———. 1922. "More Notes on the Eight Immortals." *JRAS* 1922, 397–426.

Yi Nŭnghwa 李能和. 1959. *Chosŏn togyosa* 朝鮮道教史 [History of Taoism in Korea]. Seoul: Bosŏng munhwasa.

Yin Huihe 印会河, ed. 1984. *Zhongyi jichu lilun* 中医基础理论 [Fundamental theories of traditional Chinese medicine]. Shanghai: Shanghai kexue jishu chubanshe.

Yinqueshan Hanmu zhujian zhengli xiaozu 銀雀山漢墓竹簡整理小組 [Editorial Group for the Bamboo Slips from the Han Tomb at Yinqueshan]. 1985. *Yinqueshan Hanmu zhujian* 銀雀山漢墓竹簡 [The bamboo slips from the Han tomb at Yinqueshan]. Volume 1. Beijing: Wenwu chubanshe.

Yokote Yutaka 横手裕. 1996a. "Haku Gyokusen to Nansō Kōnan dōkyō" 白玉蟾と南宋江南道教 [Bai Yuchan and Southern Song Taoism in Jiangnan]. *TG* 68: 77–182.

———. 1996b. "Zhenshinkyō no henyō" 全真教の変容 [Metamorphoses of Quanzhen]. *Chūgoku tetsugaku kenkyū* 中國哲學研究 2: 23–93.

———. 1999. "Sameisan sanjō shisan kō" 佐命山三上司山考 [A study of the Three Superior Mountains among the assistants of the Five Peaks]. *TS* 94: 20–39.

Yoshikawa Tadao 吉川忠夫. 1980. "Shiju kō" 師授考 [A study of transmission from master to disciple]. *TG* 52: 285–315. Reprinted in Yoshikawa Tadao 1984, 425–61.

———. 1984. *Rikuchō seishinshi kenkyū* 六朝精神史研究 [Studies on the spiritual history of the Six Dynasties]. Kyoto: Dōhōsha.

———. 1987. "'Seishitsu' kō" 「静室」考 [A study of the "pure chamber"]. *TG* 59: 125–62.

———. 1990. "Ō Enchi kō" 王遠知考 [A study of Wang Yuanzhi]. *TG* 62: 69–98.

———. 1991a. "Gogaku to saishi" 五岳と祭祀 [The Five Peaks and ritual]. In Yoshikawa Tadao 1991b.

———. 1991b. *Zero bitto no sekai* ゼロ・ビットの世界 [The world of 'zero bits']. Tokyo: Iwanami shoten.

———, ed. 1992a. *Chūgoku ko dōkyōshi kenkyū* 中國古道教史研究 [Studies on the ancient history of Chinese Taoism]. Kyoto: Dōhōsha.

———. 1992b. "Nicchū mu'ei: Shikai sen kō" 日中無影—尸解仙考 [Throwing no shadow at noon: Immortals delivered from the corpse]. In Yoshikawa Tadao 1992a, 175–216.

———. 1995a. "Chōju kara fushi e: Hōso zō no hensen" 長寿から不死へ—彭祖像の変遷 [From long life to immortality: Changes in the image of Pengzu]. In Yoshikawa Tadao 1995b, 15–41.

———. 1995b. *Kodai Chūgokujin no fushi gensō* 古代中國人の不死幻想 [Visions of immortality among the ancient Chinese]. Tokyo: Tōhō shoten.

Yoshikawa Tadao 吉川忠夫 and Mugitani Kunio 麥谷邦夫, eds. 2000. *Shinkō kenkyū: Yakuchū hen* 「真誥」研究—譯注篇 [Studies on the *Zhengao*: Japanese annotated translation]. Kyoto: Kyōto daigaku Jinbun kagaku kenkyūjo.

Yoshioka Yoshitoyo 吉岡義豊. 1952. *Dōkyō no kenkyū* 道教の研究 [Studies on Taoism]. Kyoto: Hōzōkan.

———. 1955. *Dōkyō kyōten shiron* 道教經典史論 [Historical studies on Taoist scriptures]. Tokyo: Dōkyō kankōkai.

———. 1959a. "Tōsho ni okeru dō-butsu ronsō no ichi shiryō *Dōkyō gisū* no kenkyū" 唐初における道佛論争の一資料「道教義樞」の研究 [A study of the *Daojiao yishu*, a source on the debates between Taoists and Buddhists in the early Tang period]. In Yoshioka Yoshitoyo 1959–76, 1: 309–68.

———. 1959b. "Zenshinkyō no Taijō hachijūichi ka zu" 全真教の「太上八十一化圖」 [The *Illustrations of the Eighty-one Transformations of the Most High* of Quanzhen]. In Yoshioka Yoshitoyo 1959–76, 1: 172–246.

———. 1959–76. *Dōkyō to bukkyō* 道教と佛教 [Taoism and Buddhism]. 3 vols. Vol. 1, Tokyo: Nihon gakujutsu shinkōkai, 1959; vol. 2, Tokyo: Toyoshima shobō, 1970; vol. 3, Tokyo: Kokusho kankōkai, 1976.

———. 1964. "Gorin kuji hishaku to dōkyō gozōkan" 「五輪九字秘釈」と道教五蔵観 [The *Wulun jiuzi bishi* and the Taoist view of the five viscera]. *Mikkyō bunka* 密教文化 69–70: 77–97.

———. 1967. "*Saikai roku to Shigonsō*" 「斎戒録」と「至言総」[The *Zhaijie lu* and the *Zhiyan zong*]. *Taishō daigaku kenkyū kiyō* 大正大學研究紀要 52: 283–301.

———. 1969. *Tonkō bunken bunrui mokuroku: Dōkyō no bu* 敦煌文献分類目録—道教の部 [A classified catalogue of Dunhuang literature: Taoism]. Tokyo: Tōyō bunko Tonkō bunken kenkyū i'yinkai.

———. 1970a. "*Dōkyō kōka (rinri) shisō to chūgen urabon*" 道教功過〈倫理〉思想と中元盂蘭盆 [Taoist conceptions of merit and demerit (or ethics) and the day of Middle Prime / *avalambana*]. In Yoshioka Yoshitoyo 1959–76, 2: 163–367.

———. 1970b. "*Tonkō bon Taiheikyō to bukkyō*" 敦煌本「太平教」と佛教 [The Tunhuang version of the *Taiping jing* and Buddhism]. In Yoshioka Yoshitoyo 1959–76, 2: 9–161.

———. 1976a. "*Dōkyō no shuitsu shisō*" 道教の守一思想 [The notion of Guarding the One in Taoism]. In Yoshioka Yoshitoyo 1959–76, 3: 285–380.

———. 1976b. "*Rikuchō dōkyō no shumin shisō*" 六朝道教の種民思想 [The notion of "seed-people" in Six Dynasties Taoism]. In Yoshioka Yoshitoyo 1959–76, 3: 221–83.

———. 1976c. "*Sandō hōdō kakai gihan no kenkyū*" 「三洞奉道科誡儀範」の研究 [A study of the *Sandong fengdao kejie yihan*]. In Yoshioka Yoshitoyo 1959–76, 3: 75–129.

———. 1976d. "*Yonjūni shō kyō to Rōshi kako kyō*" 「四十二章經」と「老子化胡經」 [The *Sūtra in Forty-two Sections* and the *Laozi huahu jing*]. In Yoshioka Yoshitoyo 1959–76, 3: 1–73.

———. 1979. "Taoist Monastic Life." In Welch and Seidel 1979, 229–52.

Yoshioka Yoshitoyo hakase kanreki kinen kenkyū ronshū kankōkai 吉岡義豊博士還暦記念論集刊行会 [Editorial Committee for the Collected Essays Presented to Dr. Yoshioka Yoshitoyo on his Sixtieth Birthday], ed. 1977. *Yoshioka Yoshitoyo hakase kanreki kinen dōkyō kenkyū ronshū* 吉岡義豊博士還暦記念道教研究論集 [Collected studies on Taoism presented to Dr. Yoshioka Yoshitoyo on his sixtieth birthday]. Tokyo: Kokusho kankōkai.

You Zi'an [Yau Chi-on] 游子安. 1996. "*Zōgai dōsho shoshū no kanzensho: Kaku hanbon no kaishaku to ryūtsū o chūshin to shite*" 「藏外道書」所收の勸善書—各版本の解釈と流通を中心として [Morality books in the *Zangwai daoshu*: With explicatory notes on the individual texts and their circulation]. Translated by Mitamura Keiko 三田村圭子. *TS* 87: 56–71.

———. 1999. *Quandai jinzhen: Qingdai shanshu yanjiu* 劝代金箴—清代善书研究 [Maxims for admonishing the age: A study of the morality books in the Qing period]. Tianjin: Renmin chubanshe.

Yu Dunkang 余敦康. 1997. "*Lun Shao Yong de xiantian zhi xue yu houtian zhi xue*" 論邵雍的先天之學與後天之學 [Shao Yong's views on the noumenal and the phenomenal world]. *DWY* 11: 402–23.

Yu Guanghong 余光弘. 1983. "*Taiwan diqu minjian zongjiao de fazhan*" 臺灣地區民間宗教的發展 [The development of popular religion in Taiwan]. *ZMJ* 53: 67–103.

Yu Kuang-hung [Yu Guanghong]. 1990. "Making a Malefactor a Benefactor: Ghost Worship in Taiwan." *ZMJ* 70: 39–66.

Yu Mingguang 余明光. 1989. *Huangdi sijing yu Huang-Lao sixiang* 黄帝四经与黄老思想 [The "Four Scriptures of the Yellow Emperor" and Huang-Lao thought]. Harbin: Heilongjiang renmin chubanshe.

Yu Mingguang et al. 余明光. 1993. *Huangdi sijing jinzhu jinyi* 黄帝四经今注今译 [A modern commentary on and translation of the "Four Scriptures of the Yellow Emperor"]. Changsha: Yuelu shuju.

Yu, Anthony C. 1991. "How to Read *The Original Intent of the Journey to the West*." In Rolston 1991, 299–315.

Yu Shiyi. 2000. *Reading the Chuang-tzu in the T'ang Dynasty: The Commentary of Ch'eng Hsüan-ying (fl. 631–652)*. New York: Peter Lang.

Yü Ying-shih. 1964. "Life and Immortality in the Mind of Han China." *HJAS* 25: 80–122.

———. 1981. "New Evidence on the Early Chinese Conception of Afterlife: A Review Article." *Journal of Asian Studies* 41: 81–85.

———. 1985. "Individualism and the Neo-Taoist Movement in Wei-Chin China." In Munro 1985, 121–55.

———. 1987. "'O Soul, Come Back!': A Study in the Changing Conceptions of the Soul and Afterlife in Pre-Buddhist China." *HJAS* 47: 363–95.

Yuan Ke 袁珂. 1980. *Shanhai jing jiaozhu* 「山海經」校注 [Annotated edition of the *Shanhai jing*]. Shanghai: Shanghai guji chubanshe.

Yuan Zhihong 袁志鸿. 1990. "Daojiao jieri" 道教节日 [Taoist festivals]. *SZY* 1990.4: 101–12.

Yung, Bell, Evelyn S. Rawski, and Rubie S. Watson, eds. 1996. *Harmony and Counterpoint: Ritual Music in Chinese Context*. Stanford: Stanford University Press.

Yūsa Noboru 遊佐昇. 1983. "Dōkyō to bungaku" 道教と文學 [Taoism and literature]. In Fukui Kōjun et al. 1983, 2: 311–69.

———. 1986. "Seito Seiyōkyū, Seijōsan oyobi Shisen ni okeru dōkyō kenkyū no genjō" 成都青羊宮・青城山及び四川における道教研究の現状 [The Qingyang gong in Chengdu, Mount Qingcheng, and the present state of Taoist studies in Sichuan]. *TS* 68: 86–98.

———. 1987. "Ra Kō'en to minkan shinkō" 羅公遠と民間信仰 [Luo Gongyuan and popular cults]. In Akizuki Kan'ei 1987, 245–63.

———. 1989. "Tōdai ni mirareru Kyūku tenson shinkō ni tsuite" 唐代に見られる救苦天尊信仰について [On the cult of the Celestial Worthy Who Saves from Suffering in the Tang period]. *TS* 73: 19–40.

Zeng Zhaonan 曾召南. 1996. "Daoshi Fu Jinquan sixiang shulüe" 道士傅金銓思想述略 [A short account of the thought of the Taoist master Fu Jinquan]. *DWY* 9: 177–200.

Zhanran Huizhen zi 湛然慧真子, ed. 1921. *Changsheng shu Xuming fang hekan* 長生術續命方合刊 (Joint Publication of *The Art of Long Life* and *Methods for Increasing the Vital Force*). Beijing: N.p.

Zhan Renzhong 詹仁中. 1998. *Laoshan yun ji Jiaodong Quanzhen dao qiyuequ yanjiu* 「嶗山韻」及膠東全真道器樂曲研究 [Studies on the "Hymns of Mount Lao" and the scores of instrumental music of Quanzhen in Jiaodong]. Taipei: Xinwenfeng chuban gongsi.

Zhan Shichuang 詹石窗. 1989. *Nan Song Jin Yuan de daojiao* 南宋金元的道教 [Taoism in the Southern Song, Jin and Yuan periods]. Shanghai: Guji chubanshe.

———. 1990. *Daojiao yu nüxing* 道教与女性 [Taoism and women]. Shanghai: Guji chubanshe.

———. 1997a. "Jianlun daojiao dui chuantong xiju de yingxiang" 简论道教对传统戏剧的影响 [A brief discussion of the influence of Taoism on traditional Chinese opera]. *SZY* 1997.4: 107–16.

———. 1997b. "Li Daochun Yixue sixiang kaolun" 李道純易學思想考論 [A study of Li Daochun's learning in the *Yijing*]. *DWY* 11: 292–308.

Zhang Dainian 張岱年. 1994. "Daojia xuan zhi lun" 道家「玄」旨論 [The purport of the term *xuan* in Taoism]. *DWY* 4: 1–8.

Zhang Enpu 張恩溥, ed. 1954. *Zhengyi baibiao keshu* 正一拜表科書 [Ritual manual for the Presentation of the Memorial of Orthodox Unity]. Taipei: Si Han Tianshi fu.

Zhang Guangbao 張廣保. 1997. "Lei siqi de *He Luo* xinshuo" 雷思齊的「河」「洛」新說 [Lei Siqi's new views on the *Hetu* and the *Luoshu*]. *DWY* 11: 309–37.

Zhang Jintao 张金涛. 1994. *Zhongguo Longhu shan tianshi dao* 中国龙虎山天师道 [The Way of the Celestial Masters on Mount Longhu in China]. Nanchang: Jiangxi renmin chubanshe.

Zhang Jiyu 张继禹. 1990. *Tianshi dao shilüe* 天师道史略 [Historical summary of the Way of the Celestial Masters]. Beijing: Huawen chubanshe.

Zhang Liwen 张李文, ed. 1990. *Qi* 气 [*Qi*]. Beijing: Zhongguo renmin daxue chubanshe.

Zhang Mengwen 张孟闻. 1982. "Siling kao" 四灵考 [A study of the Four Numina]. In Li Guohao, Zhang Mengwen, and Cao Tianqin 1982, 524–52.

Zhang Weiling 張煒玲. 1990. "Guanling Yin Xi shenhua yanjiu" 關令尹喜神話研究 [A study of the legends on Yin Xi, the Guardian of the Pass]. *DT* 3: 21–74.

———. 1991. "Beichao zhi qian Louguan daojiao xiuxingfa de lishi kaocha" 北朝之前樓觀道教修行法的歷史考察 [An exploration of the methods of self-cultivation in Louguan Taoism before the Northern Dynasties]. *DT* 4: 67–117.

Zhang Zehong 张泽洪. 1990. "Xu Xun yu Wu Meng" 许逊与吴猛 [Xu Xun and Wu Meng]. *SZY* 1990.1: 65–73.

———. 1994. *Bugang tadou: Daojiao jili yidian* 步罡踏斗—道教祭礼仪典 ["Walking along the Guideline and Treading on the Dipper": Liturgical texts for Taoist ritual]. Chengdu: Sichuan renmin chubanshe.

———. 1996. "Songdai daojiao zhaijiao" 宋代道教斋醮 [Taoist *zhai* and *jiao* rituals in the Song period]. *ZY* 1996.1: 34–40.

———. 1999a. *Daojiao zhaijiao keyi yanjiu* 道教斋醮科仪研究 [A study of the Taoist *zhai* and *jiao* rituals]. Chengdu: Ba Shu shushe.

———. 1999b. "Daojiao zhaijiao keyi yu minsu xinyang" 道教斋醮科仪与民俗信仰 [Taoist *zhai* and *jiao* rituals, and popular cults]. *ZY* 1999.2: 38–46.

———. 1999c. "Daojiao zhaijiao keyi zhong de cunxiang" 道教斋醮科仪中的存想 [Visualization in the Taoist *zhai* and *jiao* rituals]. *ZGDJ* 1999.4: 21–26.

Zhang Zhaoyu 張兆裕, ed. 1995. *Taishang ganying pian* 太上感應篇 [Folios of the Most High on Retribution]. Beijing: Beijing Yanshan chubanshe. [Abridged edition of Huang Zhengyuan's 黃正元 *Taishang ganying pian tushuo* 太上感應篇圖說 (Illustrated Explanations on the Folios of the Most High on Retribution; 1755).]

Zhao Kuanghua 赵匡华. 1985a. "Hugang zi ji qi dui Zhongguo gudai huaxue de zhuo-yue gongxian" 狐刚子及其对中国古代化学的卓越贡献 [Hugang zi and his great contribution to ancient Chinese chemistry]. In Zhao Kuanghua 1985b: 184–210.

———. ed. 1985b. *Zhongguo gudai huaxue shi yanjiu* 中国古代化学史研究 [Studies on the history of ancient Chinese chemistry]. Beijing: Beijing daxue chubanshe.

———. 1989. *Zhongguo liandan shu* 中国炼丹术 [Chinese alchemy]. Hong Kong: Zhonghua shuju.

Zhao Kuanghua 赵匡华 and Zhou Xihua 周喜华. 1998. *Huaxue juan* 化学卷 [Chemistry]. Zhongguo kexue jishu shi 中国科学技术史 [History of Chinese science and technology]. Beijing: Kexue chubanshe.

Zhao Liang 赵亮. 1993. "Yu Yan daojiao sixiang qianxi" 俞琰的道教思想浅析 [A simple analysis of Yu Yan's Taoist thought]. *ZGDJ* 1993.1: 21–27.

Zhao Liang 赵亮 et al., eds. 1994. *Suzhou daojiao shilüe* 苏州道教史略 [A brief history of Taoism in Suzhou]. Beijing: Huawen chubanshe.

Zhao Yi 赵益. *Qiu Chuji* 丘处机 [Qiu Chuji]. Nanjing: Jiangsu renmin chubanshe.

Zhao Zhongming 赵仲明. 1993. *Wushi, wushu, mijing* 巫师巫术秘竟 [Inquiry into the secrets of the shamans and their techniques]. Kunming: Yunnan daxue chubanshe.

Zheng Chenghai 鄭成海. 1971. *Laozi Heshang gong zhu jiaoli* 「老子河上公注」斠理 [Critical edition of the Heshang gong commentary to the *Laozi*]. Taipei: Taiwan zhonghua shuju.

Zheng Guoqian 郑国铨. 1996. *Shan wenhua* 山文化 [Mountain culture]. Beijing: Zhongguo renmin daxue chubanshe.

Zheng Jinsheng 郑金生. 1996. "Zhongguo lidai Yaowang ji Yaowang miao tanyuan" 中国历代药王及药王庙探源 [An exploration of the origins of the Medicine Kings and the Shrines of the Medicine Kings in Chinese history]. *Zhonghua yishi zazhi* 中华医史杂志 1996.2: 65–72.

Zheng Zhenduo 鄭振鐸. 1938. *Zhongguo suwenxue shi* 中國俗文學史 [History of Chinese popular literature]. 2 vols. Taipei: Taiwan shangwu yinshuguan.

Zheng Zhiming 鄭志明. 1988a. "Wangye chuanshuo" 王爺傳說 [Traditions on the Royal Lords]. Parts 1 and 2. *Minsu quyi* 民俗曲藝 52: 17–37; 53: 101–18.

———. 1988b. *Zhongguo shanshu yu zongjiao* 中國善書與宗教 [Chinese morality books and religion]. Taipei: Taiwan xuesheng shuju.

Zhong Laiyin 钟来因. 1992. *Changsheng busi de tanqiu: Daojing Zhengao zhi mi* 长生不死的探求—道经「真诰」之谜 [Searching for longevity and immortality: The riddle of the Taoist scripture *Zhengao*]. Shanghai: Wenhui chubanshe.

Zhong Zhaopeng 锺肇鹏. 1986. "Daozang mulu xiangzhu jiaobu" 「道藏目录详注」校补 [Emendations and additions to the *Daozang mulu xiangzhu*]. *Wenshi* 文史 27: 338–43.

———. 1988. "Fuji yu daojing" 扶乩与道经 [Planchette writing and Taoist scriptures]. *SZY* 1988.4: 9–16.

———. 1993. "Daozang tiyao dingbu" 「道藏提要」订补 [Corrections and additions to *Daozang tiyao*]. *SZY* 1993.1: 30–37. [See Ren Jiyu and Zhong Zhaopeng 1991.]

———. 1999. *Xinbian Daozang mulu* 新编道藏目录 [A newly-compiled index to the Taoist Canon]. 2 vols. Beijing: Beijing tushuguan chubanshe.

Zhongguo daojiao xiehui 中国道教协会 [Chinese Taoist Association], ed. 1983. *Beijing Baiyun guan* 北京白云观 [The Abbey of the White Clouds in Beijing]. Beijing: Zhongguo daojiao xiehui.

Zhongguo daojiao xiehui 中国道教协会 [Chinese Taoist Association] and Suzhou daojjiao xiehui 苏州道教协会 [Suzhou Taoist Association], eds. 1994. *Daojiao dacidian* 道教大辭典 [Great dictionary of Taoism]. Beijing: Huaxia chubanshe.

Zhou Shaoxian 周紹賢. 1966. *Wei Jin qingtan shulun* 魏晉清談述論 [A study of Pure Conversation in the Wei and Jin periods]. Taipei: Shangwu yinshuguan.

———. 1982. *Daojiao Quanzhen dashi Qiu Changchun* 道教全真大師丘長春 [The great master Qiu Changchun of Quanzhen Taoism]. Taipei: Shangwu yinshuguan.

Zhou Shengchun 周生春. 2000. "*Siku quanshu zongmu* zibu Shijia lei, Daojia lei tiyao buzheng" 「四库全书总目」子部释家类、道家类提要补正 [A supplement to the descriptive notes in the Buddhist and Taoist categories of the Philosophy section in the *General Catalogue of the Complete Writings of the Four Repositories*]. *SZY* 2000.1: 86–92.

Zhou Shirong 周世荣. 1990. "*Mawangdui Hanmu de 'Shenqi tu' bohua*" 马王堆汉墓的「神祇图」帛画 [The "Divinity Chart" silk painting of the Han tombs in Mawangdui]. *Kaogu* 考古 1990.10: 925–28.

Zhou Shiyi. 1988. *The Kinship of the Three*. Changsha: Hunan jiaoyu chubanshe.

Zhou Yimou 周一謀. 1994. "Cong zhujian *Shiwen* deng kan Dao yu yangsheng" 從竹簡「十問」等看道與養生 [The Dao and Nourishing Life in the *Shiwen* and other manuscripts]. *DWY* 5: 239–46.

Zhou Yixin 周益新 and Zhang Furong 张芙蓉. 1999. "Wushi san zhi zhiliao zuoyong ji dufu zuoyong chuyi" 五石散之治疗作用及毒副作用刍议 [An opinion on the therapeutic and toxic effects of the Five Minerals Powder]. *Zhonghua yishi zazhi* 中华医史杂志 1999.10: 230–32.

Zhou Zhenxi 周振锡 and Shi Xinmin 史新民, eds. 1994. *Daojiao yinyue* 道教音乐 [Taoist music]. Beijing: Beijing yanshan chubanshe.

Zhou Zhiyuan 周至元. 1993. *Laoshan zhi* 崂山志 [A monograph of Mount Lao]. Jinan: Qi Lu shuju.

Zhu Haoxi 朱浩熙, ed. 1995. *Pengzu* 彭祖 [Pengzu]. Beijing: Zuojia chubanshe.

Zhu Senpu 朱森溥. 1989. *Xuanzhu lu jiaoshi* 「玄珠錄」校釋 [Annotated critical edition of the *Xuanzhu lu*]. Chengdu: Ba Shu shushe.

Zhu Yueli 朱越利. 1982. "Qi qi erzi yitong bian" 「炁」、「气」二字异同辨 [On the difference between the two graphs for *qi* ("breath, pneuma")]. *SZY* 1982.1: 50–59.

———. 1983a. "Shilun Wuneng zi" 试论「无能子」 [A preliminary study of the *Wuneng zi*]. *SZY* 1983.1: 107–22.

———. 1983b. "*Taishang ganying pian* yu Bei Song mo Nan Song chu de daojiao gaige" 「太上感应篇」与北宋末南宋初的道教改革 [The *Taishang ganying pian* and the Taoist reformation of the late Northern Song and early Southern Song]. *SZY* 1983.4: 81–94.

———. 1986. "*Yangxing yanming lu* kao" 「养性延命录」考 [A study of the *Yangxing yanming lu*]. *SZY* 1986.1: 101–15.

———. 1992. *Daojing zonglun* 道经总论 [A general study of Taoist scriptures]. Shenyang: Liaoning jiaoyu chubanshe.

———. 1996. *Daozang fenlei jieti* 道经分类解题 [Classified descriptive notes on the Taoist Canon]. Beijing: Huaxia chubanshe.

Zhuang Hongyi 莊宏誼. 1986. *Mingdai daojiao zhengyi pai* 明代道教正一派 [The Zhengyi branch of Ming Taoism]. Taipei: Taiwan xuesheng shuju.

Ziegler, Delphine. 1996–97. "Entre ciel et terre: Le culte des 'bateaux-cercueils' du Mont Wuyi." *CEA* 9: 203–31.

———. 1998. "The Cult of the Wuyi Mountains and its Cultivation of the Past: A Topo-Cultural Perspective." *CEA* 10: 255–86.

Zimmerman, James. 1975. "Chinese Historiography and Sung Hui-tsung." Ph.D. diss., Yale University.

Zito, Angela R. 1987. "City Gods, Filiality, and Hegemony in Late Imperial China." *Modern China* 13: 333–71.

———. 1996. "City Gods and their Magistrates." In Lopez 1996, 71–81.

Zong Li 宗力 and Liu Qun 刘群. 1987. *Zhongguo minjian zhushen* 中国民间诸神 [Chinese popular gods]. Shijiazhuang: Hebei renmin chubanshe.

Zürcher, Erik. 1972. *The Buddhist Conquest of China: The Spread and Adaptation of Buddhism in Early Medieval China*. 2 vols. Leiden: E. J. Brill.

———. 1980. "Buddhist Influence on Early Taoism: A Survey of Scriptural Evidence." *TP* 66: 84–147.

———. 1982. "'Prince Moonlight': Messianism and Eschatology in Early Medieval Chinese Buddhism." *TP* 68: 1–75.

Periodization of Chinese History

DYNASTIES OR PERIODS			DATES
Shang 商			ca. 1600–1045
Zhou 周			1045–256
Western Zhou 西周		1045–771	
Eastern Zhou 東周		770–256	
Springs and Autumns 春秋	770–476		
Warring States 戰國	403–221		
Qin 秦			221–206
Han 漢			202 BCE–220 CE
Former Han (*or* Western Han) 前漢 (西漢)		202 BCE–23 CE	
Xin 新 (Wang Mang 王莽)	9–23		
Later Han (*or* Eastern Han) 後漢 (東漢)		25–220	
Six Dynasties 六朝(*)			220–589
Three Kingdoms 三國		220–80	
Wei 魏	220–65		
Han 漢	221–63		
Wu 吳	222–80		
Jin 晉		265–420	
Western Jin 西晉	265–316		
Eastern Jin 東晉	317–420		
Southern and Northern Dynasties 南北朝		420–589	

(*) The Six Dynasties proper are Wu (222–80), Eastern Jin (317–420), Liu Song (420–79), Qi (479–502), Liang (502–57), and Chen (557–89), but the term is sometimes applied to the whole period from 220 to 589.

DYNASTIES OR PERIODS	DATES

Six Dynasties 六朝 (*cont.*)

Southern Dynasties 南朝		420–589
Liu Song 劉宋	420–79	
Southern Qi 南齊	479–502	
Liang 梁	502–57	
Chen 陳	557–89	
Northern Dynasties 北朝		386–581
Northern Wei 北魏	386–534	
Eastern Wei 東魏	534–50	
Western Wei 西魏	535–56	
Northern Qi 北齊	550–77	
Northern Zhou 北周	557–81	

Sui 隋	581–618
Tang 唐	618–907

Five Dynasties and Ten Kingdoms		902–79
Five Dynasties 五代 (Northern China)		907–60
Later Liang 後梁	907–23	
Later Tang (*or* Southern Tang) 後唐 (南唐)	923–36	
Later Jin 後晉	936–46	
Later Han 後漢	947–50	
Later Zhou 後周	951–60	
Ten Kingdoms 十國 (Southern China)		902–79

Song 宋		960–1279
Northern Song 北宋	960–1127	
Southern Song 南宋	1127–1279	

Liao 遼 (Qidan 契丹, Khitan)	916–1125
Jin 金 (Nüzhen 女真, Jurchen)	1115–1234
Yuan 元	1260–1368
Ming 明	1368–1644
Qing 清	1644–1911
Republic of China 中華民國	1911–
People's Republic of China 中華人民共和國	1949–

RULERS AND REIGN PERIODS

This list includes only rulers and reign periods (*nianhao* 年號) mentioned in the present book. For the pre-imperial period, the dates indicated are those given in the *Cambridge History of Ancient China* (Loewe and Shaughnessy 1999). Reign periods are shown under the name of the relevant emperor. Ming and Qing emperors are commonly referred to with the name of their reign period.

PRE-IMPERIAL PERIOD

Muwang 穆王 (King of Zhou, r. 956–918 BCE)

Lingwang 靈王 (King of Zhou, r. 571–545 BCE)

Helü 闔閭 (King of Wu, r. 514–496 BCE)

Weiwang 威王 (King of Qi, r. 334–320 BCE)

Xuanwang 宣王 (King of Qi, r. 319–301 BCE)

Nanwang 赧王 (King of Zhou, 314–256 BCE)

Zhaowang 昭王 (King of Yan, r. 311–279 BCE)

QIN (221–206)

Qin Shi huangdi (r. 221–210 BCE) (ascended to the throne in 246 BCE as King of Qin)

FORMER HAN (202 BCE–23 CE)

Gaozu 高祖 (r. 202–195 BCE)

Wendi 文帝 (r. 180–157 BCE)

Jingdi 景帝 (r. 157–141 BCE)

Wudi 武帝 (r. 141–87 BCE)

Yuandi 元帝 (r. 49–33 BCE)

Chengdi 成帝 (r. 33–7 BCE)

LATER HAN (25–220)

Guangwu di 光武帝 (r. 25–57 CE)

Mingdi 明帝 (r. 57–75 CE)

LATER HAN (25–220, *cont.*)

    Zhangdi 章帝 (r. 75–88 CE)

    Hedi 和帝 (r. 88–106 CE)

    Shundi 順帝 (r. 125–144 CE)

    Huandi 桓帝 (r. 146–168 CE)

WU (222–80)

    Dadi 大帝 (Sun Quan 孫權, r. 222–52)

    Wucheng gong 烏程公 (Sun Hao 孫皓, r. 264–80)

WEI (220–65)

    Qiwang 齊王 (r. 240–254)
    Zhengshi 正始 (240–48)

WESTERN JIN (265–316)
    Wudi 武帝 (r. 265–90)

EASTERN JIN (317–420)

    Xiaowu di 孝武帝 (r. 372–96)

    Andi 安帝 (r. 396–418)

LIU SONG (420–79)

    Mingdi 明帝 (r. 465–72)

SOUTHERN QI (479–502)

    Gaodi 高帝 (r. 479–82)

    Wudi 武帝 (r. 482–93)

LIANG (502–57)

    Wudi 武帝 (r. 502–49)

NORTHERN WEI (386–534)

Taiwu di 太武帝 (r. 424–52)

NORTHERN ZHOU (557–81)

Wudi 武帝 (r. 560–78)

SUI (581–618)

Wendi 文帝 (r. 581–604)
Kaiguang 開皇 (581–600)

Yangdi 煬帝 (r. 604–17)

TANG (618–907)

Gaozu 高祖 (r. 618–26)

Taizong 太宗 (r. 626–49)
Zhenguan 貞觀 (627–49)

Gaozong 高宗 (r. 649–83)
Yonghui 永徽 (650–55)
Yongchun 永淳 (682–83)

Zhongzong 中宗 (r. 684, 705–10)

Ruizong 睿宗 (r. 684–90, 710–12)

Empress Wu 武后 (r. 690–705)

Xuanzong 玄宗 (r. 712–56)
Xiantian 先天 (712–13)
Kaiyuan 開元 (713–41)
Tianbao 天寶 (742–56)

Suzong 肅宗 (r. 756–62)

Daizong 代宗 (r. 762–79)

Dezong 德宗 (r. 779–805)

Xianzong 憲宗 (r. 805–20)

Wendi 文帝 (r. 826–40)
Kaicheng 開成 (836–40)

Wuzong 武宗 (r. 840–46)

TANG (618–907, *cont.*)

Xuanzong 宣帝 (r. 846–59)

Xizong 僖宗 (r. 873–88)

Zhaozong 昭宗 (r. 888–904)

LATER ZHOU (951–60)

Shizong 世宗 (r. 954–59)

NORTHERN SONG (960–1127)

Taizu 太祖 (r. 960–76)

Taizong 太宗 (r. 976–97)
  Taipingxingguo 太平興國 (976–83)

Zhenzong 真宗 (r. 997–1022)
  Tianxi 元禧 (1017–21)

Renzong 仁宗 (r. 1022–63)
  Jiayou 嘉祐 (1056–63)

Yingzong 英宗 (r. 1064–67)
  Zhiping 治平 (1064–67)

Shenzong 神宗 (r. 1067–85)

Zhezong 哲宗 (r. 1085–1100)

Huizong 徽宗 (r. 1100–1125)
  Chongning 崇寧 (1102–06)
  Zhenghe 政和 (1111–17)
  Xuanhe 宣和 (1119–25)

Qinzong 欽宗 (r. 1125–27)

SOUTHERN SONG (1127–1279)

Gaozong 高宗 (r. 1127–62)
  Shaoxing 紹興 (1131–62)

Xiaozong 孝宗 (1162–1189)
  Shunxi 淳熙 (1174–89)

Guangzong 光宗 (1190–1194)
  Shaoxi 紹熙 (1190–94)

SOUTHERN SONG (1127–1279, *cont.*)

Ningzong 寧宗 (1195–1224)
  Qingyuan 慶元 (1195–1200)
  Jiatai 嘉泰 (1201–4)

Lizong 理宗 (r. 1224–64)
  Baoyou 寶祐 (1253–58)

JIN (1115–1234)

Shizong 世宗 (r. 1161–90)

Zhangzong 章宗 (r. 1190–1208)

YUAN (1279–1368)

Taizu 太祖 (Chinggis khan, r. 1206–27)

Shizu 世祖 (Khubilai khan, r. 1260–1294)

Chengzong 成宗 (r. 1295–1307)

Renzong 仁宗 (r. 1312–20)

Taiding 泰定 (r. 1324–28)

MING (1368–1644)

Hongwu 洪武 (Taizu 太祖, r. 1368–98)

Jianwen 建文 (Huidi 惠帝, r. 1399–1402)

Yongle 永樂 (Chengzu 成祖, r. 1403–24)

Hongxi 洪熙 (Renzong 仁宗, r. 1425)

Xuande 宣德 (Xuanzong 宣宗, r. 1426–35)

Zhengtong 正統 (Yingzong 英宗, r. 1436–49)

Chenghua 成化 (Xianzong 憲宗, r. 1465–87)

Jiajing 嘉靖 (Shizong 世宗, r. 1522–66)

Longqing 隆慶 (Muzong 穆宗, r. 1567–72)

Wanli 萬曆 (Shenzong 神宗, r. 1573–1620)

QING (1644–1911)

Kangxi 康熙 (Shengzu 聖祖, r. 1662–1722)

Yongzheng 雍正 (Shizong 世宗, r. 1723–35)

Qianlong 乾隆 (Gaozong 高宗, r. 1735–95)

Pinyin to Wade-Giles
Conversion Table

PY	W-G	PY	W-G	PY	W-G
a	a	che	ch'e	dong	tung
ai	ai	chen	ch'en	dou	tou
an	an	cheng	ch'eng	du	tu
ang	ang	chi	ch'ih	duan	tuan
ao	ao	chong	ch'ung	dui	tui
ba	pa	chou	ch'ou	dun	tun
bai	pai	chu	ch'u	duo	to
ban	pan	chuai	ch'uai	e	o
bang	pang	chuan	ch'uan	en	en
bao	pao	chuang	ch'uang	er	erh
bei	pei	chui	ch'ui	fa	fa
ben	pen	chun	ch'un	fan	fan
beng	peng	chuo	ch'o	fang	fang
bi	pi	ci	tz'u	fei	fei
bian	pien	cong	ts'ung	fen	fen
biao	piao	cou	ts'ou	feng	feng
bie	pieh	cu	ts'u	fo	fo
bin	pin	cuan	ts'uan	fou	fou
bing	ping	cui	ts'ui	fu	fu
bo	po	cun	ts'un	ga	ka
bu	pu	cuo	ts'o	gai	kai
ca	ts'a	da	ta	gan	kan
cai	ts'ai	dai	tai	gang	kang
can	ts'an	dan	tan	gao	kao
cang	ts'ang	dang	tang	ge	ko
cao	ts'ao	dao	tao	gen	ken
ce	ts'e	de	te	geng	keng
cen	ts'en	deng	teng	gong	kung
ceng	ts'eng	di	ti	gou	kou
cha	ch'a	dian	tien	gu	ku
chai	ch'ai	diao	tiao	gua	kua
chan	ch'an	die	tieh	guai	kuai
chang	ch'ang	ding	ting	guan	kuan
chao	ch'ao	diu	tiu	guang	kuang

PY	W-G	PY	W-G	PY	W-G
gui	kuei	kong	k'ung	mian	mien
gun	kun	kou	k'ou	miao	miao
guo	kuo	ku	k'u	mie	mieh
ha	ha	kua	k'ua	min	min
hai	hai	kuai	k'uai	ming	ming
han	han	kuan	k'uan	miu	miu
hang	hang	kuang	k'uang	mo	mo
hao	hao	kui	k'uei	mou	mou
he	ho	kun	k'un	mu	mu
hei	hei	kuo	k'uo	na	na
hen	hen	la	la	nai	nai
heng	heng	lai	lai	nan	nan
hong	hung	lan	lan	nang	nang
hou	hou	lang	lang	nao	nao
hu	hu	lao	lao	nei	nei
hua	hua	le	le	nen	nen
huai	huai	lei	lei	neng	neng
huan	huan	leng	leng	ni	ni
huang	huang	li	li	nian	nien
hui	hui	lian	lien	niang	niang
hun	hun	liang	liang	niao	niao
huo	huo	liao	liao	nie	nieh
ji	chi	lie	lieh	nin	nin
jia	chia	lin	lin	ning	ning
jian	chien	ling	ling	niu	niu
jiang	chiang	liu	liu	nong	nung
jiao	chiao	long	lung	nou	nou
jie	chieh	lou	lou	nu	nu
jin	chin	lu	lu	nuan	nuan
jing	ching	luan	luan	nüe	nüeh
jiong	chiung	luan	lüan	nuo	no
jiu	chiu	lüe	lüeh	nü	nü
ju	chü	lun	lun	ou	ou
juan	chüan	luo	lo	pa	p'a
jue	chüeh	lü	lü	pai	p'ai
jun	chün	ma	ma	pan	p'an
ka	k'a	mai	mai	pang	p'ang
kai	k'ai	man	man	pao	p'ao
kan	k'an	mang	mang	pei	p'ei
kang	k'ang	mao	mao	pen	p'en
kao	k'ao	mei	mei	peng	p'eng
ke	k'o	men	men	pi	p'i
ken	k'en	meng	meng	pian	p'ien
keng	k'eng	mi	mi	piao	p'iao

PY	W-G	PY	W-G	PY	W-G
pie	p'ieh	shan	shan	wai	wai
pin	p'in	shang	shang	wan	wan
ping	p'ing	shao	shao	wang	wang
po	p'o	she	she	wei	wei
pou	p'ou	shen	shen	wen	wen
pu	p'u	sheng	sheng	weng	weng
qi	ch'i	shi	shih	wo	wo
qia	ch'ia	shou	shou	wu	wu
qian	ch'ien	shu	shu	xi	hsi
qiang	ch'iang	shua	shua	xia	hsia
qiao	ch'iao	shuai	shuai	xian	hsien
qie	ch'ieh	shuan	shuan	xiang	hsiang
qin	ch'in	shuang	shuang	xiao	hsiao
qing	ch'ing	shui	shui	xie	hsieh
qiong	ch'iung	shun	shun	xin	hsin
qiu	ch'iu	shuo	shuo	xing	hsing
qu	ch'ü	si	ssu	xiong	hsiung
quan	ch'üan	song	sung	xiu	hsiu
que	ch'üeh	sou	sou	xu	hsü
qun	ch'ün	su	su	xuan	hsüan
ran	jan	suan	suan	xue	hsüeh
rang	jang	sui	sui	xun	hsün
rao	jao	sun	sun	ya	ya
re	je	suo	so	yai	yai
ren	jen	ta	t'a	yan	yen
reng	jeng	tai	t'ai	yang	yang
ri	jih	tan	t'an	yao	yao
rong	jung	tang	t'ang	ye	yeh
rou	jou	tao	t'ao	yi	i
ru	ju	te	t'e	yin	yin
ruan	juan	teng	t'eng	ying	ying
rui	jui	ti	t'i	yo	yo
run	jun	tian	t'ien	you	yu
ruo	jo	tiao	t'iao	yu	yü
sa	sa	tie	t'ieh	yuan	yüan
sai	sai	ting	t'ing	yue	yüeh
san	san	tong	t'ung	yun	yün
sang	sang	tou	t'ou	yung	yong
sao	sao	tu	t'u	za	tsa
se	se	tuan	t'uan	zai	tsai
sen	sen	tui	t'ui	zan	tsan
seng	seng	tun	t'un	zang	tsang
sha	sha	tuo	t'o	zao	tsao
shai	shai	wa	wa	ze	tse

PY	W-G	PY	W-G	PY	W-G
zei	tsei	zheng	cheng	zhun	chun
zen	tsen	zhi	chih	zhuo	cho
zeng	tseng	zhong	chung	zi	tzu
zha	cha	zhou	chou	zong	tsung
zhai	chai	zhu	chu	zou	tsou
zhan	chan	zhua	chua	zu	tsu
zhang	chang	zhuai	chuai	zuan	tsuan
zhao	chao	zhuan	chuan	zui	tsui
zhe	che	zhuang	chuang	zun	tsun
zhen	chen	zhui	chui	zuo	tso

Wade-Giles to *Pinyin* Conversion Table

W-G	PY	W-G	PY	W-G	PY
a	a	ch'ih	chi	chung	zhong
ai	ai	chin	jin	ch'ung	chong
an	an	ch'in	qin	en	en
ang	ang	ching	jing	erh	er
ao	ao	ch'ing	qing	fa	fa
cha	zha	chiu	jiu	fan	fan
ch'a	cha	ch'iu	qiu	fang	fang
chai	zhai	chiung	jiong	fei	fei
ch'ai	chai	ch'iung	qiong	fen	fen
chan	zhan	cho	zhuo	feng	feng
ch'an	chan	ch'o	chuo	fo	fo
chang	zhang	chou	zhou	fou	fou
ch'ang	chang	ch'ou	chou	fu	fu
chao	zhao	chu	zhu	ha	ha
ch'ao	chao	ch'u	chu	hai	hai
che	zhe	chü	ju	han	han
ch'e	che	ch'ü	qu	hang	hang
chen	zhen	chua	zhua	hao	hao
ch'en	chen	chuai	zhuai	hei	hei
cheng	zheng	ch'uai	chuai	hen	hen
ch'eng	cheng	chuan	zhuan	heng	heng
chi	ji	ch'uan	chuan	ho	he
ch'i	qi	chüan	juan	hou	hou
chia	jia	ch'üan	quan	hsi	xi
ch'ia	qia	chuang	zhuang	hsia	xia
chiang	jiang	ch'uang	chuang	hsiang	xiang
ch'iang	qiang	chüeh	jue	hsiao	xiao
chiao	jiao	ch'üeh	que	hsieh	xie
ch'iao	qiao	chui	zhui	hsien	xian
chieh	jie	ch'ui	chui	hsin	xin
ch'ieh	qie	chun	zhun	hsing	xing
chien	jian	ch'un	chun	hsiu	xiu
ch'ien	qian	chün	jun	hsiung	xiong
chih	zhi	ch'ün	qun	hsü	xu

W-G	PY	W-G	PY	W-G	PY
hsüan	xuan	k'ou	kou	ma	ma
hsüeh	xue	ku	gu	mai	mai
hsün	xun	k'u	ku	man	man
hu	hu	kua	gua	mang	mang
hua	hua	k'ua	kua	mao	mao
huai	huai	kuai	guai	mei	mei
huan	huan	k'uai	kuai	men	men
huang	huang	kuan	guan	meng	meng
hui	hui	k'uan	kuan	mi	mi
hun	hun	kuang	guang	miao	miao
hung	hong	k'uang	kuang	mieh	mie
huo	huo	kuei	gui	mien	mian
i	yi	k'uei	kui	min	min
jan	ran	kun	gun	ming	ming
jang	rang	k'un	kun	miu	miu
jao	rao	kung	gong	mo	mo
je	re	k'ung	kong	mou	mou
jen	ren	kuo	guo	mu	mu
jeng	reng	k'uo	kuo	na	na
jih	ri	la	la	nai	nai
jo	ruo	lai	lai	nan	nan
jou	rou	lan	lan	nang	nang
ju	ru	lang	lang	nao	nao
juan	ruan	lao	lao	nei	nei
jui	rui	le	le	nen	nen
jun	run	lei	lei	neng	neng
jung	rong	leng	leng	ni	ni
ka	ga	li	li	niang	niang
k'a	ka	liang	liang	niao	niao
kai	gai	liao	liao	nieh	nie
k'ai	kai	lieh	lie	nien	nian
kan	gan	lien	lian	nin	nin
k'an	kan	lin	lin	ning	ning
kang	gang	ling	ling	niu	niu
k'ang	kang	liu	liu	no	nuo
kao	gao	lo	luo	nou	nou
k'ao	kao	lou	lou	nu	nu
ken	gen	lu	lu	nü	nü
k'en	ken	lü	lü	nuan	nuan
keng	geng	luan	luan	nüeh	nüe
k'eng	keng	lüan	luan	nung	nong
ko	ge	lüeh	lüe	o	e
k'o	ke	lun	lun	ou	ou
kou	gou	lung	long	pa	ba

W-G	PY	W-G	PY	W-G	PY
p'a	pa	shao	shao	ting	ding
pai	bai	she	she	t'ing	ting
p'ai	pai	shen	shen	tiu	diu
pan	ban	sheng	sheng	to	duo
p'an	pan	shih	shi	t'o	tuo
pang	bang	shou	shou	tou	dou
p'ang	pang	shu	shu	t'ou	tou
pao	bao	shua	shua	tu	du
p'ao	pao	shuai	shuai	t'u	tu
pei	bei	shuan	shuan	tuan	duan
p'ei	pei	shuang	shuang	t'uan	tuan
pen	ben	shui	shui	tui	dui
p'en	pen	shun	shun	t'ui	tui
peng	beng	shuo	shuo	tun	dun
p'eng	peng	so	suo	t'un	tun
pi	bi	sou	sou	tung	dong
p'i	pi	ssu	si	t'ung	tong
piao	biao	su	su	tsa	za
p'iao	piao	suan	suan	ts'a	ca
pieh	bie	sui	sui	tsai	zai
p'ieh	pie	sun	sun	ts'ai	cai
pien	bian	sung	song	tsan	zan
p'ien	pian	ta	da	ts'an	can
pin	bin	t'a	ta	tsang	zang
p'in	pin	tai	dai	ts'ang	cang
ping	bing	t'ai	tai	tsao	zao
p'ing	ping	tan	dan	ts'ao	cao
po	bo	t'an	tan	tse	ze
p'o	po	tang	dang	ts'e	ce
p'ou	pou	t'ang	tang	tsei	zei
pu	bu	tao	dao	tsen	zen
p'u	pu	t'ao	tao	ts'en	cen
sa	sa	te	de	tseng	zeng
sai	sai	t'e	te	ts'eng	ceng
san	san	teng	deng	tso	zuo
sang	sang	t'eng	teng	ts'o	cuo
sao	sao	ti	di	tsou	zou
se	se	t'i	ti	ts'ou	cou
sen	sen	tiao	diao	tsu	zu
seng	seng	t'iao	tiao	ts'u	cu
sha	sha	tieh	die	tsuan	zuan
shai	shai	t'ieh	tie	ts'uan	cuan
shan	shan	tien	dian	tsui	zui
shang	shang	t'ien	tian	ts'ui	cui

W-G	PY	W-G	PY	W-G	PY
tsun	zun	wei	wei	yen	yan
ts'un	cun	wen	wen	yin	yin
tsung	zong	weng	weng	ying	ying
ts'ung	cong	wo	wo	yo	yo
tzu	zi	wu	wu	yu	you
tz'u	ci	ya	ya	yü	yu
wa	wa	yai	yai	yüan	yuan
wai	wai	yang	yang	yüeh	yue
wan	wan	yao	yao	yün	yun
wang	wang	yeh	ye	yung	yong

Index